# GENERAL HISTORY OF AFRICA · II

## Ancient Civilizations of Africa

Unesco General History of Africa

UNESCO International Scientific Committee for the Drafting of a General History of Africa

# GENERAL HISTORY OF AFRICA · II

## Ancient Civilizations of Africa

### EDITOR G.MOKHTAR

HEINEMANN · CALIFORNIA · UNESCO

First published 1981 by the
United Nations Educational, Scientific
and Cultural Organization,
7 Place de Fontenoy, 75700 Paris

and

Heinemann Educational Books Ltd
22 Bedford Square, London WCIB 3HH
P.M.B. 5205, Ibadan   PO. Box 45314, Nairobi
EDINBURGH   MELBOURNE   AUCKLAND
HONG KONG   SINGAPORE   KUALA LUMPUR   NEW DELHI
KINGSTON   PORT OF SPAIN

First published 1981
in the United States of America by the
University of California Press
2223 Fulton Street, Berkeley
California 94720, United States of America

Heinemann Educational Books   ISBN 0 435 94805 9 (cased)
                              ISBN 0 435 94806 7 (paper)
Unesco                        ISBN 92–3–101–708–X
University of California Press ISBN 0–520–03913–0
                              LCN 78–57321

Filmset in 11pt Monophoto Ehrhardt by
Northumberland Press Ltd, Gateshead, Tyne and Wear
Printed and bound in Great Britain by
Richard Clay (The Chaucer Press) Ltd, Bungay, Suffolk

# Contents

# List of figures

x

# List of plates

* *Plates 19.7 to 19.15 appear between pages 512 and 513.*

# Acknowledgements for plates

Art and Archaeology Museum of Madagascar, 28.1, 28.2
Ashmolean Museum, Oxford, 11.4, 11.5 (bottom right)
Atomic Energy Commission, Paris, 5.13
Badawy, A., *A History of Egyptian Architecture*, Los Angeles, 1966, 3.2
Balout, L., *Les hommes préhistoriques du Maghreb et du Sahara*, 17.1, 17.2, 17.3
Bardo Museum, Algiers, 17.1, 17.2, 17.3, 19.1, 19.2
Bichart, L., *Das GraldenKnal des Königs Sahu – Ré*, Vol. 2, Leipzig, 1973, 4.1
Bovis, M., 17.1, 17.2
Brack, A., 4.5
Breccia, E., *Terracotta* II (1934), Nos 317–18, 7.3, 7.4
British Museum, 11.5 (top right)
Brugsch, H., Intro. 3
Cairo Museum, Intro. 4, 6.2, 7.2, 7.6, 7.7, 10.3
Capart, J., 5.6
Chicago University, 4.2, 11.1, 11.2
Correa-Buchet-Chastel, 4.5
Delorme, 17.3
Diop, C. A., *Anteriorité des civilisations nègres. Mythe ou réalité historique*, Présence
    Africaine, 1967, 1.1, 1.2, 1.3, 1.5, 1.6, 1.7, 1.8, 1.9, 1.10, 1.11, 1.12, 1.13, 1.14, 1.15,
    1.16, 1.17, 1.18
Editions Alinari (Rome) (no. 29773), 6.5
Editions de la Baconnière, Intro. 3, 2.1
Editions Leipzig, 11.6, 11.7, 11.8
Ethiopian Institute of Archaeology, 13.1, 13.2, 13.3, 13.4, 13.5, 14.1, 14.2, 14.3, 14.4, 14.5,
    14.6, 14.7, 14.8
French Archaeological Mission to the Sudan, 3.9, 5.3
Gardiner, A. H., *Egypt of the Pharaohs*, Oxford University Press, 1961, Intro. 2
Gast, M., 20.1
Graeco-Roman Museum, Alexandria, 6.3, 6.8, 6.9, 7.3, 7.4
Griffith Institute, Oxford, 1954, Intro. 5, 2.9
Hintze, F. 1971a (see Bibliography)
Kenet, F. L., 2.5, 2.6, 2.7, 2.8
Khartoum Museum, 10.4
Louvre Museum, 1.19
Mastaba du Louvre, Archives Photographiques, Paris, 3.6, 3.7, 3.8
Menil Foundation, Paris, 6.7, 6.9, 7.3, 7.4
Menil Hickey Robertson–Allard Pierson Museum, Inv., 1991, 7.5
Metropolitan Museum of Art, New York, 2.2, 3.4, 4.3, 4.4, 5.8, 5.9, 5.10, 5.11, 5.12
Ministry of Culture and Information of the Democratic Republic of Sudan, 9.1, 9.2, 9.3,
    9.4, 9.5, 9.6, 9.7, 9.8, 9.9, 9.10, 9.11
Mokhtar, G. 2.3, 5.14, 5.15, 12.7, 12.8
Museum of Antiquity, Algiers, 17.4
Museum of Fine Arts, Boston, Intro. 4, 3.1, 10.1
Oriental Institute, University of Chicago, 4.2, 11.1, 11.2
Otonoz, 5.14
Pirenne, J., *Histoire de la civilisation de l'Egypte Ancienne*, Vol. 1, Neuchâtel, Paris, 1961,
    2.1, 3.1, 3.5, 3.6a, b, 3.7, 5.4, 5.5, 5.6, 5.7

Polish excavations, 7.1a, b, c

Salama, P., 19.9, 19.11, 19.12, 19.13, 19.14, 19.15, 20.1, 20.2, 20.3, 20.4, 20.5

School of Oriental and African Studies, London

Shinnie, Professor W. S., *Meroe: A Civilisation of the Sudan*, London, 1967, 11.3, 11.4, 11.5 (top left, centre, bottom left)

Staatliche Museum, Berlin, 3.4, 11.8

Tripoli Museum, 20.4

Unesco/Alexis Vorontzoff, 8.1

*Unesco Courier* (July 1977), Intro. 1

University Museum, Philadelphia, 1.4

Warsaw National Museum, 12.1, 12.2, 12.3, 12.4, 12.5, 12.6

Wessel, K., *Koptische Kunst*, Rechlinghausen, 1963, 7.7

Worcester Art Museum, Massachusetts, 11.3

Yale University Press, 1965, 4.1

# Note on chronology

It has been agreed to adopt the following method for writing dates. With regard to prehistory, dates may be written in two different ways.

One way is by reference to the present era, that is, dates BP (before present), the reference year being + 1950; all dates are negative in relation to + 1950.

The other way is by reference to the beginning of the Christian era. Dates are represented in relation to the Christian era by a simple + or − sign before the date. When referring to centuries, the terms BC and AD are replaced by 'before our era' and 'of our era'.

Some examples are as follows:

(i) 2300 BP = − 350
(ii) 2900 BC = − 2900
 AD 1800 = + 1800
(iii) 5th century BC = 5th century before our era
 3rd century AD = 3rd century of our era

# Introduction

G. MOKHTAR
*with the collaboration of* J. VERCOUTTER

The present volume of *A General History of Africa* deals with that long period of the continent's history extending from the end of the Neolithic era, that is, from around the eighth millennium before our era, to the beginning of the seventh century of our era.

That period, which covers some nine thousand years of Africa's history, has been, not without some hesitation, subdivided into four major geographical zones:

(1) the corridor of the Nile, Egypt and Nubia (Chapters 1 to 12);
(2) the Ethiopian highlands (Chapters 13 to 16);
(3) that part of Africa often later called the Maghrib, and its Saharan hinterland (Chapters 17 to 20);
(4) the rest of Africa as well as the African islands in the Indian Ocean (Chapters 21 to 29).

This division is governed by the present compartmental nature of research into African history. It might have seemed more logical to arrange the volume according to the continent's chief ecological divisions, which offer the same living conditions to the human groups inhabiting them without any true physical barriers which serve to block cultural and other exchanges within the region.

In that case we would have obtained an entirely different picture, which, running from north to south, would have comprised what has been called since the eighth century of our era the Maghrib island, largely Mediterranean in its geology, climate and general ecology; and the wide subtropical band of the Sahara and its tectonic accident, the Nile valley. Next would have come the zone of the great subtropical and equatorial river basins, with their Atlantic coast. Then, to the east, we would have had the Ethiopian highlands and the Horn of Africa that looks towards Arabia and the Indian Ocean. Lastly, the region of the great equatorial lakes would have linked the Nile, Nigerian and Congo basins with southern Africa and its annexes of Madagascar and the other ocean islands near Africa.

Such a division, more satisfying to the mind than the one that has had to be used, was unfortunately impossible. The researcher wishing to study the history of Africa in antiquity is, in fact, considerably impeded by the weight of the past. The separation into sections imposed on him, which is reflected in the plan adopted here, derives very largely from the colonization of the nineteenth and twentieth centuries: the historian, whether he was a colonist interested in the country in which he was living or one of the colonized reflecting on his people's past, was, in spite of himself, confined within arbitrarily fixed territorial limits. It was difficult, if not impossible, for him to study relations with neighbouring countries, although these more often than not formed a whole, historically speaking, with the country with which he was concerned.

This heavy weight of the past has not altogether ceased to exist, partly because of inertia – once in a rut, one is, in spite of oneself, inclined to remain in it – but also because the archives of the history of Africa, which consist of reports of excavations or of texts and iconography, are for some regions assembled, classified and published according to an order which is irrelevant and arbitrary to the present situation in Africa but which is very difficult to call in question.

This volume of *A General History of Africa*, perhaps even more than the volume that preceded it, must depend on suppositions. The period it covers is obscure, owing to the scarcity of sources in general, and of solidly dated sources in particular. This applies both to the very uneven collections of archaeological sources and to the written or pictorial sources, except in respect of certain relatively privileged regions such as the Nile valley and the Maghrib. It is this lack of firm documentary bases that makes it necessary to resort to suppositions, since facts established with certainty are always the exception.

Another point should be stressed: the archaeological sources available to the historian are extremely inadequate. Excavations are not uniformly spread over the continent as a whole. There is not everywhere the density of excavations that is found notably along the coast, in the hinterland of the northern fringe and, above all, in the Nile valley from the sea to the Second Cataract.

This lack of archaeological information cannot, unfortunately, be supplemented by the reports of foreign travellers, contemporaries of the events or facts that concern this volume. The continent's rugged nature, and its very size, discouraged, in antiquity as later, deep penetration by those from outside. It will be noted that, in the present state of our knowledge, Africa is the only continent where voyages around the coastline have thrown an important light on history (cf. Chapters 18 and 22).

These considerations explain why the history of Africa, from −7000 to +700, still consists largely of suppositions. However, these suppositions are never unfounded; they are based on information, rare and inadequate certainly, but which exists none the less. The task of the contributors to this work has been to collect, weigh and assess those sources. As specialists in the regions whose history – no matter how fragmentary – they trace, they present here the synthesis of what may legitimately be deduced from the documents at their disposal. The suppositions which they present, although subject to re-examination when further sources are available, will, we are sure, provide encouragement and research guidelines to future historians.

Among the many cloudy zones which still conceal the path of Africa's history from us, that overspreading the continent's ancient inhabitants is among the darkest. Even now extremely little is known about those inhabitants. The various opposing ideas, which too often rest on an inadequate number of scientifically valid observations, are difficult to test at a period when physical anthropology is in the process of rapid change. 'Monogenism' itself, for example (cf. Chapter 1), is still only a working hypothesis. In addition, the enormous lapse of time between the appearance of pre- or proto-humans discovered in the Omo valley or at Olduvai (cf. Volume I) and that of beings of well-defined human type, notably in southern Africa, must lead us to regard the view that there was unbroken continuity and evolution *in situ* as unfortunately only a point of view, until consolidated by proof or the discovery of intermediate links.

Some evaluation of the density of Africa's population during the crucial period between −8000 and −5000 is very necessary, because this is in fact the birth period of the cultures that were later to become differentiated. And a high or low population density would encourage or make unnecessary the development of writing. The originality of ancient Egypt, in contrast with the rest of Africa at the same period, perhaps resides mainly in the fact that the high population density found in ancient times along the banks of the Nile between the First Cataract and the southern portion of the Delta gradually compelled the use of writing, simply in order to co-ordinate the irrigation system vital to these peoples' survival. In contrast, the use of writing was not essential south of the Aswan Cataract, which was a region of low population density where the small somatic groups which occupied the country remained independent of each other. As can be seen, it is thus very regrettable that population density during that period remains a matter of supposition.

Lastly ecology, which altered considerably both in space and in time, plays an important part. The last wet phase of the Neolithic age ended around −2400, within the historic period, when the Pharaohs of the fifth dynasty were reigning in Egypt. The climatic, and hence agricultural, conditions that obtained at the dawn of the first great civilizations of Africa were not the same as those which prevailed later and this must be taken into account when studying the relationship of those civilizations with the peoples around them. The environment of −7000 to −2400, a period of 4600 years, which is much more than half the period studied in this volume, was very different from that which pertained after the second half of the third millennium. This latter environment, which seems to have been very similar to the present, strongly marked the human societies living in it. Community life is not and cannot be the same in the great subtropical

3

desert zones, southern as well as northern, as in the great equatorial forest; or in the mountain ranges as in the great river basins; or in the swamps as in the great lakes. The influence of these major ecological zones is of capital importance for the growth of the routes which permitted movement from one sphere to another, for example, from the Maghrib or mountainous Ethiopia or the Nile valley towards the central basins of the Congo, Niger and Senegal rivers; or again, from the Atlantic coast towards the Red Sea and the Indian Ocean. Yet those routes are still very little explored. They are guessed at, or rather they are 'presumed', much more than actually known. A systematic archaeological study of them should teach us a great deal about the history of Africa. In fact, it is only when they have been discovered and fully investigated that we shall be able to undertake a fruitful study of the migrations between −8000 and −2500 which followed the last great climatic changes and which profoundly altered the distribution of human groups in Africa.

As yet we possess all too few landmarks for some of those routes. It is even conceivable that there may be some completely unknown to us. A study of satellite photographs should throw completely new light on the major ancient axes of trans-African communication, as well as on the no less important secondary routes. But no systematic study of these photographs has yet been carried out. It would also enable us to direct and facilitate archaeological verification in the field, essential for evaluation, among other things, of the reciprocal influences that major culture areas exerted on one another in antiquity. It is perhaps in this domain that we may expect the most from the research to be undertaken.

As may be seen, the chapters of Volume II of *A General History of Africa* constitute points of departure for future research much more than a rehearsal of well-established facts. Unfortunately, facts of this kind are extremely rare except in the case of some regions that are very small in comparison with the immense size of the continent of Africa.

The Nile valley from Bahr el Ghazal in the south to the Mediterranean in the north holds a special place in the history of ancient Africa. It owes that special place to several facts: first, to its geographical position, then to the particular nature of its ecology in relation to the rest of the continent, lastly, and above all, to the abundance – relative, of course, but unique for Africa – of well-dated original sources, which enable us to follow its history from the end of the Neolithic period around −3000 to the seventh century of our era.

# Egypt: geographical position

In large part parallel to the shores of the Red Sea and the Indian Ocean, to which depressions perpendicular to its course give it access, the Nile valley, south of the eighth parallel north and as far as the Mediterranean, is also wide open to the west, thanks to valleys starting in the Chad region, the Tibesti and the Ennedi and ending in its course. Lastly, the broad span of the Delta, the Libyan oases and the Suez isthmus give it wide access to the Mediterranean. Thus open to east and west, to south and north, the Nile Corridor is a zone of privileged contacts, not only between the African regions bordering it, but also with the more distant centres of ancient civilization of the Arabian peninsula, the Indian Ocean and the Mediterranean world, western as well as eastern.

However, the importance of this geographical position varied with time. In Africa the end of the Neolithic age was characterized by a final wet phase that lasted till around −2300 in the northern hemisphere. During that period, which extended from the seventh to the third millennium before our era, the regions east and west of the Nile enjoyed climatic conditions favourable to human settlement and, consequently, contacts and relations between the east and the west of the continent were as important as those established between the north and the south.

In contrast, after −2400, the very drying-up of that part of Africa lying between the thirtieth and fifteenth parallels north made the Nile valley the major route of communication between the continent's Mediterranean coast and what is now called Africa south of the Sahara. It was via the Nile valley that raw materials, manufactured objects and, no doubt, ideas moved from north to south and vice versa.

It is clear that, because of climatic variations, the geographical position of the middle Nile valley, as of Egypt, did not have the same importance, or more exactly the same impact, during the period from −7000 to −2400 as it did after that date. Between those years, human groups and cultures could move freely in the northern hemisphere between east and west as well as between south and north. This was the primordial period for the formation and individualization of African cultures. It was also the period when free relations between east and west, between the Nile valley and the civilizations of the Middle East, on the one hand, and between West Africa and East, on the other, were easiest.

From −2400 to the seventh century of our era, however, the Nile valley became the privileged route between the continent's north and south. It was via that valley that exchanges of various kinds took place between black Africa and the Mediterranean.

## Sources for the history of the Nile valley in antiquity

The Nile valley derived its importance and advantages from its geographical position in the north-eastern corner of the continent. It might have remained merely a mentally stimulating theme, at best serving as an introduction to historical research, if that valley had not also been the region of Africa richest in ancient historical sources. Those sources enable us to test and evaluate, from about − 5000, the role of geographical factors in the history of Africa as a whole. They also allow us to gain not only a fairly accurate knowledge of the history of events in Egypt proper, but, more especially, a precise idea of the material, intellectual and religious culture of the lower and middle Nile valley as far as the marshes of Bahr el Ghazal.

The sources at our disposal are of an archaeological nature and thus silent – at least apparently – and literary. The former, especially for the earliest periods, have only recently been sought out and collected together. They are still not only incomplete and uneven but also little or poorly used. The literary sources, on the other hand, have a long tradition.

Well before Champollion, in fact, mysterious Egypt had aroused curiosity. As early as the archaic period of the sixth century before our era successors of pre-Hellenes had already called attention to the difference between their customs and beliefs and those of the Nile valley. Thanks to Herodotus, their observations have come down to us. To gain a better understanding of their new subjects, the Ptolemaic kings, surprised by the originality of Egyptian civilization, had a history of Pharaonic Egypt, dealing with the political, religious and social aspects, compiled on their own behalf in the third century before our era. Manetho, an Egyptian by birth, was put in charge of writing this general history of Egypt. He had access to the ancient archives and was able to read them. If his work had come down to us in its entirety, we would have been spared many uncertainties. Unfortunately it disappeared when the Library of Alexandria was burned. The excerpts preserved in various compilations, which were too often assembled for apologetic purposes, none the less provide us with a solid framework of Egyptian history. In fact, the thirty-one Manethonian dynasties remain today the firm foundation of the relative chronology of Egypt.

The closing of the last Egyptian temples under Justinian I in the sixth century of our era led to the abandonment of Pharaonic forms of writing, whether hieroglyphic, hieratic or demotic. Only the spoken language survived, in Coptic; the written sources gradually fell into disuse. It was not until 1822, when Jean-Francois Champollion (1790–1852) deciphered the script, that we once again had access to ancient documents drawn up by the Egyptians themselves.

These ancient Egyptian literary sources have to be used with caution, for they are of a particular nature. Most often they were prepared with a specific purpose: to enumerate a Pharaoh's achievements to show that he had fully carried out his terrestrial mission to maintain the universal order willed by the gods (Ma'at) and to resist the forces of chaos that increasingly threatened that order. Or to ensure eternal worship and remembrance of Pharaohs who had earned the gratitude of the generations to come. Into these two categories of documents fall the lengthy texts and historical images that adorn some parts of Egyptian temples, and also the venerable ancestor lists such as those carved in the Karnak temples during the eighteenth dynasty and at Abydos during the nineteenth.

For compiling royal lists like those referred to above, the scribes used documents drawn up either by priests or by royal officials, which pre-supposes the existence of properly maintained official archives. Un-fortunately, only two of these documents have come down to us and even they are incomplete. They are:

*The Palermo Stone* (so called because the largest fragment of the text is preserved in the museum of that Sicilian city) is a diorite slab carved on both faces, which preserves for us the names of all the Pharaohs who reigned in Egypt from the beginning to the fifth dynasty, around −2450. Starting with the third dynasty, the Palermo Stone lists not only the names of the sovereigns in the order of their succession but also, year by year, the most important events of each reign. These lists constitute veritable annals and it is all the more regrettable that this incomparable document is broken and has thus come to us incomplete.

*The Turin Papyrus*, preserved in that city's museum, is no less impor-tant, although it consists only of a list of rulers, with their complete protocol and the number of years, months and days of their reigns, arranged in chronological order. It provides a complete list of all the Pharaohs from the earliest times to around −1200. Unfortunately, though discovered intact in the nineteenth century, it was so badly mishandled in shipment that it fell into pieces, and years of work were required to restore it. Even so, a great many gaps still exist today. One of the peculiari-ties of the Turin Papyrus is that it groups the Pharaohs in series. At the end of each series the scribe added up the total number of years reigned by the Pharaohs of each group. Undoubtedly we have here the source of Manetho's dynasties.

# Egyptian chronology

The Palermo Stone, the Turin Papyrus and the royal lists on monuments are all the more important for the history of Egypt in that the Egyptians did not use any continuous or cyclical eras similar to our systems: such as, for example, before or after Christ, the years of the Hegira, or the Olympiads. Their computation is based on the person of the Pharaoh himself and each date is given by reference to the sovereign ruling at the time the document was drawn up. For example, a stele will be dated 'Year 10 of Pharaoh *N*, second month of *Akhet* [season], 8th day', but the computation starts again at 1 when the next ruler mounts the throne. This practice explains the importance, for establishing chronology, of knowing both the *names* of all the Pharaohs who reigned and the *duration* of each one's reign. If they had come down to us intact, the Turin Papyrus and Palermo Stone would have given us that essential knowledge. Unfortunately this did not happen, and other documents that usefully fill some of the gaps in these two major sources still leave us without a complete and certain list of all the Pharaohs of Egypt. Not only does the order of succession itself remain controversial for certain periods, when the Turin Papyrus and Palermo Stone have no references, but even the exact length of reign of some sovereigns remains unknown. At best, we have only the earliest known date of a given Pharaoh, but his reign may have lasted long after the erection of the monument carrying that date.

Even with these gaps, all the dates provided by the sources at our disposal added together give a total of over 4000 years. This is the *long* chronology accepted by the first Egyptologists until about 1900. It was then realized that such time span was impossible, for further study of the texts and monuments showed, first, that at certain periods several Pharaohs reigned simultaneously and that there were thus parallel dynasties, and, secondly, that occasionally a Pharaoh took one of his sons as co-regent. Since each of the rulers dated his monuments according to his own reign, there was thus some overlapping, and by adding together the reigns of parallel dynasties and those of co-regents, with the reigns of the official sovereigns, one necessarily arrived at a total figure which was much too high.

It would probably have been impossible to solve this problem, if one peculiarity of the ancient Pharaonic calendar had not provided a sure chronological framework, by linking that calendar to a permanent astronomical phenomenon the tables for which were easy to establish. We are here referring to the rising of the star Sothis – our Sirius – co-ordinated with the rising of the sun, at a latitude of Heliopolis-Memphis. This is what is called the 'heliacal rising of Sothis', which was observed and noted in antiquity by the Egyptians. These observations supplied the 'Sothic' dates on which Egyptian chronology rests today.

At the outset the Egyptians, like most of the peoples of antiquity, seem to have used a lunar calendar, notably to set the dates of religious festivals. But alongside that astronomical calendar they used another. A peasant people, their daily round was strongly marked by the rhythm of agricultural life: sowing, reaping, harvest home, preparation of the new seed. Now in Egypt the agricultural rhythm of the valley is set by the Nile, its changes determining the dates of the various operations. Hence there is nothing surprising in the fact that, parallel to a religious lunar calendar, the ancient inhabitants of the valley should also have

8

used a natural calendar based on the periodic repetition of an event that was all-important for their existence – the flood of the Nile.

In that calendar the first season of the year, called 'Akhet' in Egyptian, saw the beginning of the flood. The river's waters rose little by little and covered the land dried up by the torrid summer. For about four months the fields would become saturated with water. In the next season the land gradually emerging from the flood waters became ready for sowing. This was the season of Peret, literally 'coming out', a term that no doubt alludes both to the 'coming out' of the land from the water and the 'coming out' of the vegetation. Once sowing was over the peasant awaited germination, then the ripening of the grain. In the third and final season the Egyptians harvested and then stored the harvest. After that they had only to await the new flood and to prepare the fields for its arrival. This was the season of Shemou.

It is possible, and even highly probable, that for a very long time the Egyptians were satisfied with this calendar. The year then began with the actual rise of the waters. The season of Akhet so initiated lasted to the actual retirement of the waters, which marked the commencement of the season of Peret. This in turn ended when the ripened grain was ready for the sickle, marking the beginning of the season of Shemou, which ended only with the new rise. It mattered little to the peasant that one season might be longer than another; what mattered to him was the organization of his work, which varied according to the three seasons.

At what moment and for what reasons did the Egyptians link the flood of the Nile with the simultaneous appearance on the horizon of the sun and the star Sothis? This will surely be difficult to determine. No doubt that linking was the result both of repeated observations and of profound religious beliefs. The star Sothis (Sirius), in Egyptian Sepedet, the Pointed One, was later to be identified with Isis, whose tears were thought to determine the flood of the Nile. Perhaps we have here the reflection of a very ancient belief associating the appearance of the deified star with the rise of the waters. Whatever their reasons, by linking the beginning of the flood, and consequently the first day of the new year, with an astronomical phenomenon, the Egyptians have provided us with a means of setting positive reference points for their long history.

At the latitude of Memphis the very gentle beginning of the flood took place about the middle of July. Observation over a few years appears to have sufficed to show the Egyptians that the beginning of the flood recurred on average every 365 days. They thereupon divided their year of three empirical seasons into a year of twelve months of thirty days each. They then assigned four months to each of the seasons. By adding five additional days (in Egyptian the '5 heryou renepet', the five over – in addition to – the year), which the Greeks called the 'epagomenes', the scribes obtained a year of 365 days, which was by far the best of all those adopted in antiquity. However, although very good, that year was not perfect. In fact, the earth completes its revolution around the sun, not in 365 days, but in $365\frac{1}{4}$ days. Every four years the Egyptians' official year lagged one day behind the astronomical year, and it was only after 1460 years – what is called a *Sothic period* – that the three phenomena, sunrise, rise of Sothis and beginning of the flood occurred simultaneously on the first day of the official year.

This gradual lag between the two years had two important consequences: first, it enabled modern astronomers to determine when the Egyptians adopted their calendar, that date necessarily having to coincide with the beginning of a Sothic period. The coincidence of the phenomena – beginning of the flood rise and heliacal rising of Sothis – occurred three times in the five millennia before our era: in −1325–1322, in −2785–2782 and in −4245–4242. It was long believed that it was between −4245 and −4242 that the Egyptians adopted their calendar. It is now accepted that it was only at the beginning of the following Sothic period, that is, between −2785 and −2782.

The second consequence of the adoption by the Egyptians of the fixed solar calendar was gradually to bring about a lag between the natural *seasons* determined by the very rhythm of the river itself and the *official* seasons used by the government which were based on a year of 365 days. This lag, at first barely perceptible, being one day every four years, increased little by little from one week to one month, and then to two months until the official calendar fell during the height of the natural season of Peret. This shift could not fail to strike the Egyptian scribes, and we possess texts noting, very officially, the difference between the real heliacal rising of Sothis and the beginning of the official year. Those observations have enabled us to establish, within an approximation of four years, the following dates:

(1) The reign of Senusret III must include the years − 1882–1879.
(2) Year 9 of Amenhotep I fell between the years −1550 and −1547.
(3) The reign of Thutmose III includes the years −1474–1471.

By combining these dates with the relative dates provided by the sources at our disposal – the Turin Papyrus, the Palermo Stone, the dated monuments of various epochs – we have been able to reach a basic chronology, the most certain of all those of the ancient Orient. It sets the beginning of the history of Egypt at −3000. Manetho's great divisions may be dated as follows:

third to sixth dynasty (Old Kingdom): around −2750–2200
seventh to tenth dynasty (First Intermediate Period): −2200–2150
eleventh to twelfth dynasty (Middle Kingdom): −2150–1780
thirteenth to seventeenth dynasty (Second Intermediate Period): −1780–1580

eighteenth to twentieth dynasty (New Empire): −1580–1080
twenty-first to twenty-third dynasty (Third Intermediate Period): −1080–730
twenty-fourth to thirtieth dynasty (New Era): −730–330.

The conquest by Alexander of Macedonia in −332 marks the end of the history of Pharaonic Egypt and the beginning of the hellenistic period (cf. Chapter 6).

## The Nilotic environment

It is perhaps useful to quote here a sentence written by Herodotus (II, 35) at the end of his description of Egypt: 'Not only is the Egyptian climate peculiar to that country, and the Nile different in its behaviour from other rivers elsewhere, but the Egyptians themselves in their manners and customs seem to have reversed the ordinary practices of mankind' (transl. A. de Sélincourt). Of course, when he wrote that sentence Herodotus was thinking only of the countries bordering on the Mediterranean. It is none the less true that, of all the countries of Africa, Egypt is the one with the most distinctive environment. It owes this to the regime of the Nile. Without the river, Egypt would not exist. This has been said over and over again since Herodotus: it is a basic truth.

In fact, the severe requirements imposed by the river to which they owed their subsistence on the human societies living on its banks were only gradually recognized. They became inescapable only when Egyptian civilization was already over 700 years old. The human groups that built that civilization thus had time to accustom themselves little by little to the demands slowly imposed on them by the ecology of the Nile.

From the end of the Neolithic age, around −3300 to −2400, north-western Africa, the Sahara included, enjoyed a relatively moist climatic system. At that period Egypt was not dependent solely on the Nile for its subsistence. The steppe still extended both east and west of the valley, providing cover for abundant game and favouring considerable cattle-raising. Agriculture was then still only one of the components of daily life, and cattle-raising – even hunting – played at least as important a role, as is attested by the Palermo Stone, which leads us to infer that the tax owed to the central authority by the regime's notables was based, not on income from the land they might own, but on the number of head of cattle entrusted to their herdsmen. A census of this basic wealth was made every two years. The scenes decorating the mastabas of the Old Kingdom from the end of the fourth dynasty to the sixth dynasty (−2500 to −2200) clearly show that cattle-raising occupied an essential place in Egyptian life at that time.

We may thus suspect that man's search for control of the river – the fundamental achievement of Egyptian civilization, which enabled it to flourish – was probably stimulated in the beginning not by the desire to make better use of the flood for agriculture, but more especially to prevent damage by the rising waters. It is sometimes forgotten that the over-flowing of the Nile is not solely beneficial: it can bring disaster, and it was no doubt for themselves that the valley's inhabitants learned to build dikes and dams to shield their villages and to dig canals to dry out their fields. So they slowly acquired experience that became vital for them when the climate of Africa between the thirtieth and fifteenth parallels north gradually became as dry as it is today, transforming into absolute desert the immediate neighbourhood of the Nile valley, both in Egypt and in Nubia. Thereafter, all life in the valley was strictly conditioned by the river's rise.

Using the dike-building and canal-digging techniques which they had perfected over the centuries, the Egyptians little by little developed the system of irrigation by basins (hods), thus securing not only their survival in a climate increasingly desert-like, but even the possibility of expansion (cf. Chapters 4 and 8 below). The system was simple in principle, complex in operation, and demanded synchronization. It made use of two natural higher ridges created by the Nile along its banks in the course of thousands of yearly floods. These natural defences, gradually reinforced by the shore-dwellers to protect themselves from too sudden a flood, were supplemented by retaining embankments, veritable artificial dams, which undoubtedly owed their origin to those built by the earliest inhabitants to protect their settlements during the river's rise.

At the same time embankments were constructed parallel to the river and the result was to divide Egypt into a series of basins which gave their name to the system. The soil in these basins was levelled, so that when the river rose the entire basin would be submerged when the flood arrived; drains were cut in the embankments parallel to the river to let the basins fill up. After standing for a time, in order to saturate the fields, the water was returned to the Nile. In addition, a system of canals using the valley's natural slope led water taken upstream towards areas that were lower because located downstream to irrigate lands that even a high flood could not have reached.

The advantages of the system which the Egyptians gradually learned by experience were to ensure an even distribution of the water and mud over all the cultivable land; to irrigate those parts of the valley that would otherwise have remained sterile; lastly and above all, to control the river and its flooding. By filling the basins and deflecting upstream water through canals to areas downstream the current was slowed down, which presented the disastrous consequences of a sudden release of millions of cubic metres of water which uprooted everything in its passage. In turn, the slowing of the current running over the fields increased the precipitation of mud, with which the water was loaded.

It is no exaggeration to say that this unique system of irrigation is at the very root of the development of Egyptian civilization. It explains how human ingenuity slowly managed to overcome great difficulties and succeeded in changing the valley's natural ecology.

The new ecology resulting from human intervention entailed a considerable amount of work. After each flood it was necessary to repair the embankments, strengthen the cross-dams and clear the canals. It was a continual collective task, which in primitive times was probably carried out at the level of the village. In the historic period it was conducted and supervised by the central government. If the latter failed to ensure in due time the detailed maintenance of the entire system, the next flood might carry it all away, returning the valley to its original state. In Egypt, the political order conditioned to a very large extent the natural order. To ensure the subsistence of all, it was not enough that the system of basins should function regularly. One of the characteristics of the Nile flood is that its volume varies enormously from one year to another. Floods may be either too great – destroying everything in their passage – or too slight – failing to provide adequate irrigation. In the thirty years from 1871 to 1900, for example, barely half the floods were sufficient for Egypt's needs.

Experience quickly taught the Egyptians to distrust the river's fickleness. To compensate for periodical shortages it was necessary to stockpile grain to feed the population, and – more important for the future – to ensure sufficient seed-corn for the next sowing no matter what the circumstances. These reserve stocks were provided by the central government thanks to the double royal granary, which stored grain in warehouses set up throughout the country. By limiting the consumption in periods of plenty and by stockpiling the maximum possible amount to provide against inadequate or excessive floods, the government took over, so to speak, from the natural order and came to play an extremely important role.

By profoundly changing the conditions imposed upon him by nature, man played an essential part in the emergence and expansion of civilization in the Nile valley. Egypt is not only a *gift of the Nile*; it is, above all, a creation of man. Hence the importance of the anthropological problems in the valley.

## The settlement of the Nile valley

As early as the Palaeolithic era man occupied, if not the actual valley, at least its immediate neighbourhood and notably the terraces overlooking it. Successions of wet and dry periods during the Palaeolithic and Neolithic ages (cf. Volume I) inevitably changed the population density, first one way then the other, but the fact remains that, as far back in time as we can go, *homo sapiens* has always been living in Egypt.

To what race did he belong? Few anthropological problems have given rise to so much impassioned discussion. Yet this problem is not new.

Already in 1874 there was argument about whether the ancient Egyptians were 'white' or 'black'. A century later a Unesco-sponsored symposium in Cairo proved that the discussion was not, nor was likely soon to be, closed. It is not easy to find a physical definition of 'black' acceptable to all. Recently an anthropologist cast doubt upon the very possibility of finding positive means of determining the race to which a given skeleton belongs – at least as regards very ancient human remains, such as those from the Palaeolithic era, for instance. The traditional criteria applied by physical anthropologists – facial index, length of limbs, etc. – are no longer accepted by everyone today, and, like the Ancients, we come back to determining 'black' by the nature of the hair and the colour of the skin, measured scientifically, it is true, by the proportion of *melanin*. However, the value of these indices is, in its turn, challenged by some. At this rate, after having lost over the years the very notion of a 'red' race, we run a serious risk of soon having to abandon the notion of 'white' or 'black' races. Nevertheless, it is highly doubtful whether the inhabitants that introduced civilization into the Nile valley ever belonged to one single, pure race. The very history of the peopling of the valley refutes such a possibility.

Man did not penetrate all at once into a valley that was empty or inhabited only by wild animals. He settled there gradually in the course of thousands of years, as the very density of the human groups or the variations in climate forced him to seek additional resources or greater security. Owing to its position at the north-eastern corner of the African continent, it was inevitable that the Nile valley as a whole, and Egypt in particular, should become the terminal point for movements of people coming not only from Africa but also from the Middle East, not to mention more distant Europe. It is therefore not surprising that anthropologists should have believed they could discern, among the several very ancient Nilotic skeletons at their disposal, representatives of the Cro-Magnon race, Armenoids, negroids, leucoderms, etc., although these terms should only be accepted with caution. If an Egyptian race ever existed – and this is open to doubt – it was the result of mixtures whose basic elements varied in time as well as in space. This could be verified if it were possible – which is far from being the case – to obtain a sufficient number of human remains for each of the historical periods and the various parts of the valley.

One fact remains, however, and that is the continued existence in Egypt, as in Nubia, of a certain physical type which it would be vain to call a race, since it varies slightly according to whether we are concerned with Lower or Upper Egypt. Darker in the south than in the north, it is in general darker than in the rest of the Mediterranean basin, including North Africa. The hair is black and curly and the face, rather round and hairless, is in the Old Kingdom sometimes adorned with a moustache. Relatively slim as a rule, it is the human type that frescoes, bas-reliefs and statues of the Pharaohs have made familiar to us; and we must not forget that these were *portraits*, as Egyptian funerary beliefs demanded, since it was the individual himself, not an abstract notion, that survived beyond the tomb.

It would of course be easy, by selecting certain portraits and not taking account of the total of those that have come to us, to assign the Egyptian type to a particular race, but it would be equally easy to choose other examples that would nullify such conclusions. In fact, for those with eyes to see, the individuals that Egyptian art has made familiar to us are variety itself, with their 'straight profiles, prognathous profiles, sometimes high cheekbones as in the case of Sesostris III, fleshy, often curling lips; sometimes a slightly arched nose (Hemeoumou, Pepi I, Gamal Abd el Nasser), most often a large straight nose like Chephren's, and in the south, in particular, flattish noses and thicker lips' (Jean Yoyotte).

This very variety shows that in the Nile valley we have to do with a human type, not a race, a type gradually brought into being as much by the habits and conditions of life peculiar to the valley as by the mixtures of which it is the product. A striking example of this is provided by the statue of 'Sheik el Beled', a vivid portrait of the mayor of the village of Saqqara at the time when the statue, more than 4000 years old, was discovered. It is more than probable that the African strain, black or light, is preponderant in the ancient Egyptian, but in the present state of our knowledge it is impossible to say more.

## Writing and environment

Egypt was the first African country to make use of writing, if we judge from the employment in the hieroglyphic system of pictograms representing objects that had long ago ceased to be used. It is possible to set its invention at the Amratian period, called also the Nagada I (cf. Volume I), that is, around −4000, if we follow the dates suggested by Carbon 14 dating, at the beginning of the historic period. Thus it is one of the oldest known systems of writing. It developed very rapidly, since it appears already established on the Narmer palette, the first historic Egyptian monument, which can be dated at −3000. Moreover, the fauna and flora used in the signs are essentially African.

Egyptian writing is fundamentally pictographic, like many ancient types of writing, but whereas in China and Mesopotamia, for example, the originally pictographic signs rapidly evolved towards abstract forms, Egypt remained faithful to its system till the end of its history.

Every object or living thing that could be drawn was used as a sign or character in Egyptian writing: to write the word 'harpoon' or 'fish' the scribe had merely to draw a harpoon or fish. These are what are called word-signs, because a single sign suffices for the writing of a whole word. This principle remained in use throughout the Pharaonic civilization, which enabled the scribes to create as many new word-signs as were needed to denote beings or objects unknown at the time when the writing system was first created; such, for instance, as the horse or the chariot. In the pure pictographic system *actions* can also be represented by drawings. To write the verbs 'to run' or 'to swim', the scribe had merely to draw an individual running or swimming.

However, in spite of all its ingenuity, the pictographic system was incapable of writing abstract terms like 'to love', 'to remember', 'to become'. To overcome this difficulty the Egyptians had to go beyond the stage of pure pictography. They did so by the use of two other principles: *homophony*, on the one hand, and *ideography*, on the other. And it is the *simultaneous* use of the three principles – pure pictography, homophony and ideography – that has made the decipherment of the hieroglyphics so difficult in modern times. In Egyptian writing, some signs are read phonetically and others are not: they serve only to specify how to read the sound, or the meaning of the word.

The principle of homophony is simple: for example, in the spoken language the written word for 'chess-board' was pronounced *men*. Thanks to this principle the pictographic sign representing a chess-board could at will be used either to signify the object itself or to write *phonetically* all the 'homophones', that is, all the words also pronounced *men*, among them the abstract term 'to be stable'. In the same way the sign for 'hoe' was pronounced *mer*; it could thus be used to write the verb 'to love', which was pronounced *mer*. In these cases the original word-signs became phonetic signs. Since the number of simple homophones, word for word, of the type *men*–chess-board for *men*–to be stable, or *mer*–hoe for *mer*–to love, is relatively small, the innovation would have offered only limited advantages if the scribes had not extended it to complex words. For example, to write the abstract verb 'to establish' which was pronounced *semen* and which had no simple homophone, they employed two word-signs, using their phonetic values: a piece of pleated fabric, pronounced (*e*), and *men*, chess-board. Placed side by side these two signs were then read phonetically s(*e*) + *men* = *semen* and the combination meant 'to establish', 'to found'. Having reached this stage, the Egyptian scribe had at his disposal an instrument capable of expressing phonetically, through images, any word in the language, no matter how complex. All he had to do was to break the word down into as many sounds as he could transcribe by means of a word-sign with approximately the same pronunciation. Hieroglyphic writing had already reached this stage at the 'Thinite' period, around −3000, which presupposes a fairly long period of prior development.

However, the system thus completed had flaws. It necessarily utilized a greater number of signs – more than 400 ordinary ones are known – which could leave the reader perplexed as to how to read them. Let us take the simple example of a drawing of a boat. Should it read as: barque, boat, ship, dinghy, vessel, etc.? In addition, it was impossible at first sight to know whether a given sign was employed as a word-sign designating the object represented, or whether it was being used as a phonetic sign.

The first difficulty was easily overcome: the scribes adopted the habit of adding a vertical line after the word-sign designating the object itself. For the second difficulty a complex system was gradually set up: what Egyptologists call phonetic complements. These consist of twenty-four word-signs that each have only one consonant. The scribes gradually came to use them to indicate phonetic reading of the signs. To take an example: the sign representing a mat on which bread is placed is read as *hetep*. Gradually it became customary to follow the word-sign employed phonetically with two other signs: 'bread', which was pronounced *t* and 'seat', pronounced *p*. These two signs immediately told the reader to read *hetep*.

It is evident that these twenty-four simple signs in fact play the part of our letters, and that we have here in embryo the invention of the alphabet, since these signs express all the consonants of the Egyptian language and since Egyptian, like Arabic and Hebrew, does not write the vowels. Hence there was no word in the language that could not have been written simply by means of signs. However, the Egyptians never took the final step in this direction, and, far from employing only the simple, almost alphabetic signs alone, they further complicated their writing system, at least in appearance, by bringing into it, in addition to the signs used phonetically and their phonetic complements, new purely ideographic signs. These signs were placed at the end of the words. They made it possible to classify those words into a given category at first sight. Verbs designating a physical action, such as 'to strike', 'to kill', were followed by the sign of a human arm holding a weapon. Those designating an abstract concept, such as 'to think', 'to love', were followed by the sign representing a roll of papyrus. Similarly, for nouns, the word 'basin' would be followed by the ideogram for 'water', three wavy horizontal lines; the names of foreign countries would be followed by the sign for mountain – in contrast to Egypt, which is flat – and so on.

If the Egyptians never used a simplified form of writing – we possess only one text in alphabetic writing, and it is very late and may have been influenced by the examples of the alphabetic writings used by Egypt's neighbours – that conservatism can doubtless be explained by the importance to them of the image, and therefore of the sign that is an image. The image possessed a latent magic power. Even around −1700, scribes in some cases mutilated the signs representing dangerous beings, at least those dangerous in their eyes: snakes had their tails cut off, certain birds were deprived of feet. That magic power possessed by the sign extended to the whole world; it was such that when one wished to harm a person, his *name* would be carefully chiselled out or erased wherever it was written. The name was, in fact, part of the individual and in one sense it *was* the person himself: to destroy it was to destroy him.

With its intricate system of word-signs, plurisyllabic phonetic signs, phonetic complements and ideographic determinatives – a medley of signs, some to be pronounced and others not to be pronounced – hieroglyphic writing is complex, certainly, but it is also very evocative. The determinatives cut the words up well, the strict word order of the sentences – verb, subject, object – facilitates interpretation, and the difficulties that the modern translator may encounter stem from the fact that we sometimes do not know the exact meaning of many words. Even so, thanks to the determinatives, we can know into what categories they should be classified.

It has often been implied that Egyptian hieroglyphic writing had been either brought to the valley by invaders from the East or borrowed from Mesopotamia by the Egyptians. The least we can say is that no material trace of such borrowing is visible in the writing of Pharaonic Egypt as we find it at the dawn of history around − 3000. On the contrary, we are able to follow its slow formation stage by stage: from pure pictography, to the stage of complex phonograms, to that of phonetic complements, and finally to that of determinatives. Some signs employed phonetically represent objects that were no longer in use when the first texts appear, which proves that the writing was formed in the *pre*-historic era, when those objects were still in current use. Lastly, and perhaps most important of all, the ancient hieroglyphic symbols were *all* taken from Nilotic fauna and flora, thus proving that the writing is of purely African origin. If we accept external influence on the advent of Egyptian writing, it can only be at most the influence of the *idea* of writing, which is none the less unlikely, taking into account how very early writing took form in Egypt, in the fourth millennium before our era.

One of the forces presiding over the invention and development of hieroglyphic writing in the Nile valley is undoubtedly to be found in the need for its inhabitants to act together in a concerted manner to combat the disasters periodically threatening them, among others the flooding of the Nile. Although a family, a group of families, or even a small village might be powerless to build up sufficient protection against an unexpected rise of the waters, the same did not apply in the case of large human groups acting together. The very configuration of Egypt favours the creation of such groups. The valley is not regular in width, being sometimes limited to the very course of the river itself and then widening out and forming small basins of sometimes considerable breadth. Each of these natural basins is a geographical unit with a definite agricultural potential. They seem rapidly to have tended to develop into small political units under the authority of the largest settlement of the basin area, whose tutelary deity became that of the entire community. This was probably the origin of the *nomes* that emerge already formed at the dawn of the historic period.

There is certainly a very great geographical contrast between Upper Egypt, the Saïd, segmented into a succession of very well-defined natural basins, and Lower Egypt, the Delta, where, as it splits into its many arms, the river itself cuts the soil into units of an entirely different and less distinct character than those of the Saïd.

It should be recalled here that the traditional terms 'Upper' and 'Lower' Egypt are fallacious when employed for the period of the Pharaonic state's formation. In the present state of our knowledge of the predynastic cultures, what we call Upper Egypt did not extend south of the El Kab region and ended in the north in the neighbourhood of Fayyum. Its political centre was located at Naqada in the Theban basin but was to descend northward to the Abydos region, another natural basin that was to play a great part in Egypt's history. Lower Egypt, in turn, began at Fayyum but ended to the north at the point of the Delta. Although we have very little information about its extent at so ancient an era, it seems certain that it did not reach the sea. Its centre was located in the region of modern Cairo-Heliopolis.

In this cradle of Pharaonic Egypt the southern basins constituted a force at least equal to that of the north. And that force was better structured, thanks to the individuality of the basins composing it. We can thus readily understand that it should be the Confederation of the southern provinces that finally imposed cultural unity on the valley, by subjugating the Confederation of the northern provinces, whose originality was less marked.

The small political units of the south, which corresponded to the area of the basins they occupied, had enough available manpower to undertake the collective work indispensable for the province's survival, such as reinforcement of the river banks, which they gradually transformed into veritable embankments (see above), and then construction of dams to protect the settlements. To be effective, that work required organization. In its turn the latter must have facilitated, if not the invention of writing, at least its rapid development. For it was necessary to transmit orders to a large number of men spread out over fairly great distances, for the accomplishment of a task that had perforce to be carried out within a limited time: *after* the harvest, *before* the new rise of the waters. Apportionment of the work, order of priority, provision of tools (even rudimentary ones), victualling of the workers on the spot, all this demanded an administration, however simple. That administration could only be effective if it could foresee, plan and direct the various stages of the operations from a centre that was sometimes inevitably far from the site where the work was to be done. This is difficult to imagine without the incomparable instrument of writing for the recording of the essential data – number of men, rations, height of the embankment to be built – and, above all, for the rapid transmission of orders to the various points of the territory.

The political unification of Egypt by Menes around −3000 was bound to strengthen further the development of administration and, therefore, of writing. In fact, the chief was no longer concerned with the organizing of works of community interest solely within a limited area, but for the entire country, one of the characteristics of which is extreme length, and where, consequently, the capital giving the orders is always very distant from a large portion of the territory. Moreover, because of the very fickleness of the blood (cf. Pl. Intro. 4), one of the central government's responsibilities was to stock as much food as possible in times of plenty, to palliate the shortages which might always occur at short notice. Consequently the leaders, in this case the Pharaoh, must know exactly what the country had available, so as to be able, in case of need, either to ration or to distribute the existing resources to the regions most seriously affected by the famine. This was the basis of Egypt's economic organization and, in fact, of its very existence. It required on the material level a complex accounting system for incomings and outgoings, as regards both commodities and personnel, which explains the essential role devolving on the *scribe* in the civilization of ancient Egypt.

The scribe was thus the veritable linchpin of the Pharaonic system. From the third dynasty, around −2800, the highest state officials had themselves depicted with the writing-case over their shoulder, and the princes of the Old Kingdom ordered statues of themselves as crouching scribes (cf. Pl. Intro. 4). In one famous tale the king himself took up the pen, so to speak, to record what a prophet was about to tell him. The magic power always associated with writing added to the scribe's importance in society. To know the name of things was to have power over them. It is no exaggeration to say that the whole Egyptian civilization rested on the scribe and that it was writing that permitted its development.

The contrast between Egypt and the Nubian Nile valley gives us a better understanding of the role of writing and the reasons for its existence in the emergence and development of the Egyptian civilization. South of the First Cataract, we are in the presence of a population having the same composition as that of Upper Egypt. However, Nubia was always unwilling to accept the use of writing, although the permanent contacts which it maintained with the Egyptian valley could not have left it in ignorance of that use. The reason for this state of affairs seems to reside in the difference in the way of life. On the one hand, we have a dense population that the requirements of irrigation and control of the river on which its very existence depends have closely bound into a hierarchical society where each individual plays a specific role in the country's development.

On the other hand, in Nubia we have a population that at the dawn of history possessed a material culture equal, if not superior, to that of Upper Egypt, but the population was divided into smaller groups spaced farther apart. Those groups were more independent and more mobile, because stock-raising required frequent moves and played at least as important a part in the economy as did agriculture, which was very limited in a valley narrower than in Egypt. The Nubian peoples did not feel the need for writing. They were always to remain in the domain of oral tradition, only very occasionally using writing and then solely, it seems, for religious purposes or when they were subject to a central monarchical type of government (cf. below, Chapters 10 and 11).

The difference in behaviour between two populations of similar ethnic composition throws significant light on an apparently abnormal fact: one of them adopted and perhaps even invented, a system of writing, while the other, which was aware of that writing, disdained it. The life-style imposed on the group inhabiting the lower valley by the exigencies of control of the Nile was to favour the emergence and then the development of writing. This, in its turn, was to make of that group one of the world's first great civilizations.

## African Egypt – receptacle of influence

Around −3700 a unification is to be noted of the material culture in the two centres of civilization in the Nile valley or, to be more precise, the southern centre, while still maintaining its distinctive characteristics, partially adopted the culture of the northern centre. This penetration southward of the northern civilization is often associated, on the one hand, with the invention of writing and, on the other, with the appearance in Egypt of invaders more advanced than the autochthonous inhabitants.

As regards writing, we have seen earlier that a purely Nilotic hence African origin is not only not excluded, but probably reflects the reality. Moreover, an invasion of civilizing elements from outside, notably from Mesopotamia, rests only on the flimsiest evidence. However, the originality and the antiquity of the Egyptian civilization should not hide the fact that it was also a receptacle for many influences. Moreover, its geographical position predisposed it in this direction.

The relatively moist climate at the end of the Neolithic era and throughout the predynastic period, which saw the formation of civilization in Egypt, made the Arabian desert between the Red Sea and the Nile valley permeable, so to speak. It was undoubtedly by that route that Mesopotamian influences, whose importance, incidentally, may have been exaggerated, penetrated into Egypt. In contrast, for lack of sufficient investigation, we know little about Egypt's contacts with the cultures of the eastern Sahara at the end of the Neolithic era. Certain symbols inscribed on protodynastic palettes, however, allow us to suppose that common features existed between the populations of the Libyan desert and those of the Nile valley.

To the north, it seems that in very early times the links, by way of the isthmus of Suez between Egypt and the Syro-Palestinian corridor, were not as close as they were to become after the establishment of the Old Kingdom; although, there again, very ancient traces of contacts with Palestine are to be noted, and the Osiris myth may have risen out of relationships between the Deltaic centre of civilization and the wooded coast of Lebanon – relationships which would thus date back to extremely ancient times.

At first glance the ties with the south seem much clearer, but their importance is difficult to assess. From the fourth century before our era peoples south of the First Cataract (cf. Chapter 10 below) were in close contact with the lower Nile valley. In the pre- and protodynastic eras exchanges between the two groups of peoples were numerous in pottery techniques and the manufacture of enamelled clay (Egyptian faience), use of the same figments, use of similar weapons, same belief in a life after death, related funerary rites. During these contacts the Egyptians must have had relations, direct or through intermediaries, with the peoples of more distant Africa, as may be deduced from the number of ivory and ebony objects that have been collected from the oldest Egyptian tombs. Even if we accept that the ecological boundary line of ebony was farther north than it is today, it was still very far from Lower Nubia, and this provides us with a precious piece of evidence of contacts between Africa south of the Sahara and Egypt. Apart from ivory and ebony, incense – which appears very early – and obsidian, both items foreign to the Nile valley, could have been imported by the Egyptians. Through this trade, techniques and ideas would have passed the more easily from one area to the other in that, as we have seen, there was in the Egyptians a considerable African strain.

Thus, whichever way we turn, whether west or east, north or south, we see that Egypt received outside influences. However, these never profoundly affected the originality of the civilization that was gradually taking shape on the banks of the Nile, before in its turn influencing adjoining regions.

## Obscure points in our knowledge

To allow of an estimation of the part that outside influences may have played at the beginning of civilization in the Nile valley, a good knowledge would be needed of the archaeology of the whole country in ancient times.

A very comprehensive knowledge is required for a profitable comparison of the archaeological material collected in Egypt with that provided by the neighbouring cultures, designed to bring to light importations or imitations, the sole tangible proofs of large-scale contacts.

But, while the archaeology of the fourth millennium before our era is fairly well known, both in Upper Egypt and in Lower Nubia (between the First and Second Cataracts), the same does not apply to the other parts of the Nile valley. The Delta, in particular, is virtually unknown to us in respect of the pre- and protodynastic periods except for some very rare localities on its desert fringe. All references to possible influences coming from Asia during those periods, by way of the Suez isthmus or the Mediterranean coast, thus belong to the realm of supposition.

We encounter the same difficulties in the case of the upper Nile valley, between the Second and Sixth Cataracts. Our ignorance of the earliest archaeology of the vast region is all the more regrettable in that it must have been there that contacts and trade between the Egyptian part of the Nile valley and Africa south of the Sahara took place. That ignorance prevents us from comparing the achievements of the nascent Pharaonic civilization with those of the cultures then obtaining, not only in the upper valley, but also in the regions east, west and south of the Nile. Recent discoveries between the Fifth and Sixth Cataracts suggest the existence, if not of direct contacts, at least of a disconcerting similarity in the forms and decoration of funerary and everyday furniture between the predynastic Upper Egypt and the Sudan south of the seventeenth parallel.

The deficiency of our knowledge in space, so to speak, is matched by that of our knowledge in time. The Pharaonic civilization proper was to last more than 3000 years; for about one-third of that enormous stretch of time we do not know, or we know very little about, what happened in Egypt. The history of the Pharaohs is divided into strong periods and weak periods (cf. Chapter 2). During the periods of marked centralization of the royal power, we possess many documents and monuments enabling us to reconstitute with certainty the important events. These are the periods that are usually called the *Old Kingdom*, from − 2700 to − 2200, the *Middle Kingdom*, from − 2000 to − 1800, and the *New Empire*, from − 1600 to − 1100. During the periods when the central power was weak, on the other hand, the sources of our knowledge dwindle and even vanish, so that Pharaonic history presents gaps, which the Egyptologists call Intermediate Periods. There are three of these: the first extending from − 2200 to − 2000, the second from − 1800 to − 1600, and the third from − 1100 to − 750. If we add to these the beginnings of the Pharaonic monarchy, from − 3000 to − 2700, which are still very inadequately known, we see that over ten centuries of the history of Egypt remain for us, if not totally unknown, at least very hazy.

## Conclusions

Despite the flaws in our knowledge of the Pharaonic civilization to which we have just drawn attention, that civilization nevertheless occupies a primordial place in the history of ancient Africa. Through its monuments, its texts and the interest it aroused in the travellers of bygone days, it provides us with a large amount of information on African ways of thought, feeling and living in periods that we could not possibly approach otherwise than through it.

Although primordial, that place is probably insignificant by comparison with the role that knowledge of ancient Egypt and Nubia could play in the history of the continent. When the archaeology of the countries bordering on the Nile valley is better explored and therefore better known, Egypt and the Nilotic Sudan will provide the historian and the archaeologist with means of comparison and dating indispensable for the resurrection of the past and for the study of those currents of influence which, from south to north and from east to west, constitute the very fabric of the history of Africa.

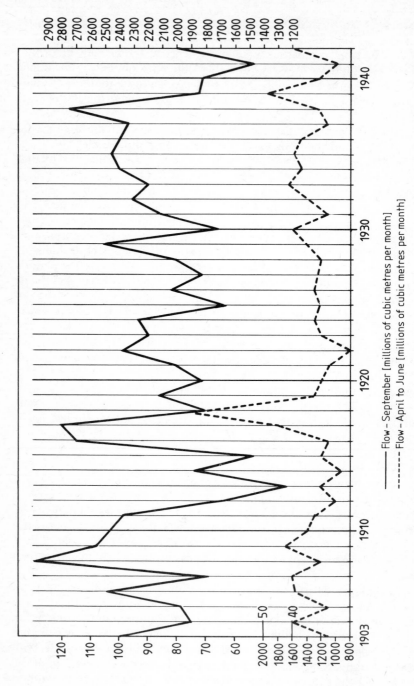

FIG. INTRO. Seasonal flooding of the Nile (after Jacques Besançon, *L'Homme et le Nil*, Paris, Gallimard NRF, 1957, p. 79)

Flow – September [millions of cubic metres per month]

Flow – April to June [millions of cubic metres per month]

PLATE INTRO.1 *Onslaught on the Nile*

PLATE INTRO.2 *The Palermo Stone*

PLATE INTRO.3 *Palette of Narmer*

PLATE INTRO.4 *Statue of squatting scribe, Knoumbaf*

PLATE INTRO.5 *Papyrus of Turin*

26

# Origin of the ancient Egyptians

## 1

### CHEIKH ANTA DIOP

The general acceptance, as a sequel to the work of Professor Leakey, of the hypothesis of mankind's monogenetic and African origin, makes it possible to pose the question of the peopling of Egypt and even of the world in completely new terms. More than 150 000 years ago, beings morphologically identical with the man of today were living in the region of the great lakes at the sources of the Nile and nowhere else. This notion, and others which it would take too long to recapitulate here, form the substance of the last report presented by the late Dr Leakey at the Seventh Pan-African Congress of Pre-History in Addis Ababa in 1971.[1] It means that the whole human race had its origin, just as the ancients had guessed, at the foot of the Mountains of the Moon. Against all expectations and in defiance of recent hypotheses it was from *this place* that men moved out to people the rest of the world. From this two facts of capital importance result:

(*a*) of necessity the earliest men were ethnically homogeneous and negroid. Gloger's law, which would also appear to be applicable to human beings, lays it down that warm-blooded animals evolving in a warm humid climate will secrete a black pigment (eumelanin).[2] Hence if mankind originated in the tropics around the latitude of the great lakes, he was bound to have brown pigmentation from the start and it was by differentiation in other climates that the original stock later split into different races;

(*b*) there were only two routes available by which these early men could move out to people the other continents, namely, the Sahara and the Nile valley. It is the latter region which will be discussed here.

From the Upper Palaeolithic to the dynastic epoch, the whole of the river's basin was taken over progressively by these negroid peoples.

1. *Proceedings of the Seventh Pan-African Congress of Pre-History and Quaternary Studies*, December 1971.
2. M. F. A. Montagu, 1960, p. 390.

## Evidence of physical anthropology on the race of the ancient Egyptians

It might have been thought that, working on physiological evidence, the findings of the anthropologists would dissipate all doubts by providing reliable and definitive truths. This is by no means so: the arbitrary nature of the criteria used, to go no farther, as well as abolishing any notion of a conclusion acceptable without qualification, introduces so much scientific hair-splitting that there are times when one wonders whether the solution of the problem would not have been nearer if we had not had the ill luck to approach it from this angle.

Nevertheless, although the conclusions of these anthropological studies stop short of the full truth, they still speak unanimously of the existence of a negro race from the most distant ages of prehistory down to the dynastic period. It is not possible in this paper to cite all these conclusions: they will be found summarized in Chapter X of Dr Emile Massoulard's *Histoire et protohistoire d'Egypte* (Institut d'Ethnologie, Paris, 1949). We shall quote selected items only.

> Miss Fawcett considers that the Negadah skulls form a sufficiently homogeneous collection to warrant the assumption of a Negadah race. In the total height of the skull, the auricular height, the length and breadth of the face, nasal length, cephalic index and facial index this race would seem to approximate to the negro; in nasal breadth, height of orbit, length of palate and nasal index it would seem closer to the Germanic peoples; accordingly the Pre-Dynastic Negadians are likely to have resembled the negroes in certain of their characteristics and the white races in others. (pp. 402–3)

It is worth noting that the nasal indices of Ethiopians and Dravidians would seem to approximate them to the Germanic peoples, though both are black races.

These measurements, which would leave an open choice between the two extremes represented by the negro and the Germanic races, give an idea of the elasticity of the criteria employed. A sample follows:

> An attempt was made by Thomson and Randall MacIver to determine more precisely the importance of the negroid element in the series of skulls from El 'Amrah, Abydos and Hou. They divided them into three groups: (1) negroid skulls (those with a facial index below 54 and a nasal index above 50, i.e. short broad face and broad nose); (2) non-negroid skulls (facial index above 54 and nasal index below 50, long narrow face and narrow nose); (3) intermediate skulls (assignable to one of the two previous groups on the basis of either

the facial index or on the evidence of the nasal index, plus individuals marginal to either group). The proportion of negroids would seem to have been 24% of men and 19% of women in the early Pre-Dynastic and 25% and 28% respectively in the late Pre-Dynastic.

Kieth has disputed the value of the criterion selected by Thomson and Randall MacIver to distinguish the negroid from the non-negroid skulls. His opinion is that if the same criteria were applied to the study of any series of contemporary English skulls, the sample would be found to contain approximately 30% of negroid types. (pp. 420–1)

The converse of Kieth's proposition could also be asserted, namely, that if the criterion were applied to the 140 million negroes now alive in black Africa a minimum of 100 million negroes would emerge white-washed.

It may also be remarked that the distinction between negroid, non-negroid and intermediary is unclear: the fact is that 'non-negroid' does not mean of white race and 'intermediary' still less so.

'Falkenburger reopened the anthropological study of the Egyptian population in a recent work in which he discusses 1,787 male skulls varying in date from the old Pre-Dynastic to our own day. He distinguishes four main groups' (p. 421). The sorting of the predynastic skulls into these four groups gives the following results for the whole predynastic period: '36% negroid, 33% Mediterranean, 11% Cro-Magnoid and 20% of individuals not falling in any of these groups but approximating either to the Cro-Magnoid or to the negroid'. The proportion of negroids is definitely higher than that suggested by Thomson and Randall MacIver, though Kieth considers the latter too high.

'Do Falkenburger's figures reflect the reality? It is not our task to decide this. If they are accurate, the Pre-Dynastic population far from representing a pure bred race, as Elliot-Smith has said, comprised at least three distinct racial elements – over a third of negroids, a third of Mediterraneans, a tenth of Cro-Magnoids and a fifth of individuals cross-bred – to varying degrees' (p. 422).

The point about all these conclusions is that despite their discrepancies the degree to which they converge proves that the basis of the Egyptian population was negro in the Pre-Dynastic epoch. Thus they are all incompatible with the theories that the negro element only infiltrated into Egypt at a late stage. Far otherwise, the facts prove that it was preponderant from the beginning to the end of Egyptian history, particularly when we note once more that 'Mediterranean' is not a synonym for 'white', Elliot-Smith's 'brown or Mediterranean race being nearer the mark'. 'Elliot-Smith classes these Proto-Egyptians as a branch of what he calls the brown race, which is the same as Sergi's "Mediterranean or Eurafrican race".' The term 'brown' in this context refers to skin colour and is simply a euphemism for negro.[3] It is thus clear that it was the whole of the Egyptian population which was negro, barring an infiltration of white nomads in the proto-dynastic epoch.

In Petrie's study of the Egyptian race we are introduced to a possible classification element in great abundance which cannot fail to surprise the reader.

> Petrie ... published a study of the races of Egypt in the Pre-Dynastic and Proto-Dynastic periods working only on portrayals of them. Apart from the steatopygian race, he distinguishes six separate types: an aquiline type representative of a white-skinned libyan race; a 'plaited-beard' type belonging to an invading race coming perhaps from the shores of the Red Sea; a 'sharp-nosed' type almost certainly from the Arabian Desert; a 'tilted nose' type from Middle Egypt; a 'jutting beard' type from Lower Egypt; and a 'narrow-nosed' type from Upper Egypt. Going on the images, there would thus have been seven different racial types in Egypt during the epochs we are considering. In the pages which follow we shall see that study of the skeletons seems to provide little authority for these conclusions. (p. 391)

The above mode of classification gives an idea of the arbitrary nature of the criteria used to define the Egyptian races. Be that as it may, it is clear that anthropology is far from having established the existence of a white Egyptian race and would indeed tend rather to suggest the opposite.

Nevertheless, in current textbooks the question is suppressed: in most cases it is simply and flatly asserted that the Egyptians were white and the honest layman is left with the impression that any such assertion must necessarily have a prior basis of solid research. But there is no such basis, as this chapter has shown. And so generation after generation has been misled. Many authorities skate around the difficulty today by speaking of red-skinned and black-skinned whites without their sense of common logic being in the least upset. 'The Greeks call Africa "Libya", a misnomer ab initio since Africa contains many other peoples besides the so-called Libyans, who belong among the whites of the northern or Mediterranean periphery and hence are many steps removed from the brown (or red) skinned whites (Egyptians).'[4]

In a textbook intended for the middle secondary school we find the following sentence: 'A Black is distinguished less by the colour of his skin (for there are black-skinned "whites") than by his features: thick lips, flattened nose ...'[5] It is only through these twistings of the basic definitions that it has been possible to bleach the Egyptian race.

3. The study of this race's pigmentation can be carried farther by the method described; actually Elliot-Smith often found patches of skin on the bodies and the mummification methods which cause skin deterioration were not yet in use.

4. D. P. de Pedrals, p. 6.

5. *Géographie*, classe de 5⁰, 1950.

It is worthwhile calling to mind the exaggerations of the theorists of anthropo-sociology in the last century and the beginnings of the present one whose minute physiognomical analyses discovered racial stratifications even in Europe, and particularly in France, when in fact there was really a single and by now practically homogeneous people.[6] Today Occidentals who value their national cohesion are careful to avoid examining their own societies on so divisive a hypothesis, but continue unthinkingly to apply the old methods to the non-European societies.

## Human images of the protohistoric period: their anthropological value

The study of human images made by Flinders Petrie on another plane shows that the ethnic type was black: according to Petrie these people were the Anu whose name, known to us since the protohistoric epoch, is always 'written' with three pillars on the few inscriptions extant from the end of the fourth millennium before our era. The natives of the country are always represented with unmistakable chiefly emblems for which one looks in vain among the infrequent portrayals of other races, who are all shown as servile foreign elements having reached the valley by infiltration (cf. Tera Neter[7] and the Scorpion king whom Petrie groups together: 'The Scorpion King ... belonged to the preceding race of Anu, moreover he worshipped Min and Set.').[8]

As we shall see later Min, like the chief gods of Egypt, was called by the tradition of Egypt itself 'the great negro'.

After a glance at the various foreign types of humanity who disputed the

6. In his 'Lutte des races' (1883) L. Gumplovicz asserts that the diverse classes making up a people always represent different races, of which one has established its domination over the others by conquest. G. de Lapouge in an article published in 1897 postulated no less than a dozen 'fundamental laws of anthropo-sociology' of which the following are typical: his 'law of distribution of wealth' posits that, in countries of mixed European–Alpine populations, wealth is greater in inverse proportion to the cephalic index; the 'law of urban indices' given prominence by Ammon in connexion with his research on Badener conscripts asserted that town dwellers exhibit greater dolichocephaly than the people in the adjacent countryside; the 'law of stratification' was formulated in the following terms: 'the cephalic index decreases and the proportion of dolichocephalics rises the higher the social class, in each locality'. In his 'Sélections sociales' the same writer has no hesitation in asserting that 'the dominant class in the feudal epoch belongs almost exclusively to the variety "Homo Europaeus" so that it is not pure chance which has kept the poor at the foot of the social ladder but their congenital inferiority'.

'We thus see that German racism was inventing nothing new, when Alfred Rosenberg asserted that the French Revolution must be deemed a revolt of the brachycephalics of the Alpine stock against the dolichocephalics of the Nordic race.' (A. Cuvillier, p. 155).

7. W. M. F. Petrie, 1939, Fig. 1.

8. ibid., p. 69.

valley with the indigenous blacks, Petrie describes the latter, the Anu, in the
following terms:

> Besides these types, belonging to the North and East, there is the
> aboriginal race of the Anu, or Annu, people (written with three pillars)
> who became a part of the historic inhabitants. The subject ramifies
> too doubtfully if we include all single pillar names, but looking for
> the Annu written, with the three pillars, we find that they occupied
> southern Egypt and Nubia, and the name is also applied in Sinai and
> Libya. As to the southern Egyptians, we have the most essential
> document, one portrait of a chief, Tera Neter, roughly modelled in
> relief in green glazed faïence, found in the early temple at Abydos.
> Preceding his name, his address is given on this earliest of visiting
> cards, 'Palace of the Anu in Hemen city, Tera Neter'. Hemen was
> the name of the god of Tuphium. Erment, opposite to it, was the
> palace of Annu of the south, Annu Menti. The next place in the south
> is Aunti (Gefeleyn), and beyond that Aunyt-Seni (Esneh).[9]

Amélineau lists in geographical order the fortified towns built along
the length of the Nile valley by the Annu blacks.

= Ant = (Esneh)

= An = the southern 'On' (now Hermonthis)

= Denderah, the traditional birthplace of Isis

= A town also called 'On' in the nome of Tinis

= The town called the northern 'On', the renowned city of Heliopolis

9. ibid., p. 68.

The common ancestor of the Annu settled along the Nile was Ani or An, a name determined by the word ⌕ (khet) and which, dating from the earliest versions of the 'Book of the Dead' onwards, is given to the god Osiris.

The wife of 𓇋𓈖𓈖𓀭 the god Ani is the goddess Anet 𓇋𓈖𓈖𓁗 who is also his sister, just as Isis is the sister of Osiris.

The identity of the god An with Osiris has been demonstrated by Pleyte;[10] we should, indeed, recall that Osiris is also surnamed by (?) the Anou: 'Osiris Ani'. The god Anu is represented alternatively by the symbol 𓊽 and the symbol 𓊾 . Are the Aunak tribes now inhabiting the upper Nile related to the ancient Annu? Future research will provide the answer to this question.

Petrie thinks it possible to make a distinction between the predynastic people represented by Tera Neter and the Scorpion King (who is himself a Pharaoh even at that date as his head-dress shows) and a dynastic people worshipping the falcon and probably represented by the Pharaohs Narmer,[11] Khasekhem, Sanekhei and Zoser.[12] By reference to the faces reproduced in the figure it is easily perceived that there is no ethnic difference between the two lots, and both belong to the black race.

The mural in tomb SD 63 (Sequence Date 63) of Hierakonpolis shows the native-born blacks subjugating the foreign intruders into the valley if we accept Petrie's interpretation: 'Below is the black ship at Hierakonpolis belonging to the black men who are shown as conquering the red men.'[13]

The Gebel-el-Arak knife haft shows similar battle scenes: 'There are also combats of black men overcoming red men.'[13] However, the archaeological value of this object, which was not found *in situ* but in the possession of a merchant, is less than that of the preceding items.

What the above shows is that the images of men of the protohistoric and even of the dynastic period in no way square with the idea of the Egyptian race popular with Western anthropologists. Wherever the autochthonous racial type is represented with any degree of clearness, it is evidently negroid. Nowhere are the Indo-European and Semitic elements shown even as ordinary freemen serving a local chief, but invariably as conquered foreigners. The rare portrayals found are always shown with the distinctive marks of captivity, hands tied behind the back or strained

10. E. Amélineau, 1908, p. 174.
11. Pl. 1.2
12. Pl. 1.3
13. W. M. F. Petrie, 1939, p. 67.

over the shoulders.[14] A protodynastic figurine represents an Indo-European prisoner with a long plait on his knees, with his hands bound tight to his body. The characteristics of the object itself show that it was intended as the foot of a piece of furniture and represented a conquered race.[15] Often the portrayal is deliberately grotesque as with other proto-dynastic figures showing individuals with their hair plaited in what Petrie calls pigtails.[16]

In the tomb of king Ka (first dynasty) at Abydos, Petrie found a plaque showing an Indo-European captive in chains with his hands behind his back.[17] Elliot-Smith considers that the individual represented is a Semite. The dynastic epoch has also yielded the documents illustrated in Pls 1.9 and 1.14 showing Indo-European and Semitic prisoners. In contrast, the typically negroid features of the Pharaohs (Narmer, first dynasty, the actual founder of the Pharaonic line; Zoser, third dynasty, by whose time all the technological elements of the Egyptian civilization were already in evidence; Cheops, the builder of the Great Pyramid, a Cameroon type;[18] Menthuhotep, founder of the eleventh dynasty, very black;[19] Sesostris I; Queen Ahmosis Nefertari; and Amenhophis I) show that all classes of Egyptian society belong to the same black race.

Pls 1.15 and 1.16, showing the Indo-European and Semitic types, have been included deliberately to contrast them with the quite dissimilar physiognomies of the black Pharaohs and to demonstrate clearly that there is no trace of either of the first two types in the whole line of Pharaohs if we exclude the foreign Libyan and Ptolemaic dynasties.

It is usual to contrast the negresses on the tomb of Horemheb with the Egyptian type also shown. This contrast is surely a false one: it is social and not ethnic and there is as much difference between an aristocratic Senegalese lady from Dakar and those antique African peasant women with their horny hands and splay feet as between the latter and an Egyptian lady of the cities of antiquity.

There are two variants of the black race:

(*a*) straight-haired, represented in Asia by the Dravidians and in Africa by the Nubians and the Tubbou or Tedda, all three with jet-black skins;

(*b*) the kinky-haired blacks of the Equatorial regions.

Both types entered into the composition of the Egyptian population.

14. Pl. 1.11.

15. Pl. 1.5.

16. Pl. 1.8.

17. Pl. 1.7 I know that 'Indo-European' is usually said to be a language, not a race, but I prefer this term to 'Aryan' wherever its use causes no confusion.

18. Pl. 1.12.

19. Pl. 1.13.

## Melanin dosage test

In practice it is possible to determine directly the skin colour and hence the ethnic affiliations of the ancient Egyptians by microscopic analysis in the laboratory; I doubt if the sagacity of the researchers who have studied the question has overlooked the possibility.

Melanin (eumelanin), the chemical body responsible for skin pigmentation, is, broadly speaking, insoluble and is preserved for millions of years in the skins of fossil animals.[20] There is thus all the more reason for it to be readily recoverable in the skins of Egyptian mummies, despite a tenacious legend that the skin of mummies, tainted by the embalming material, is no longer susceptible of any analysis.[21] Although the epidermis is the main site of the melanin, the melanocytes penetrating the derm at the boundary between it and the epidermus, even where the latter has mostly been destroyed by the embalming materials, show a melanin level which is non-existent in the white-skinned races. The samples I myself analysed were taken in the physical anthropology laboratory of the Musée de l'Homme in Paris off the mummies from the Marietta excavations in Egypt.[22] The same method is perfectly suitable for use on the royal mummies of Thutmoses III, Seti I and Ramses II in the Cairo Museum, which are in an excellent state of preservation. For two years past I have been vainly begging the curator of the Cairo Museum for similar samples to analyse. No more than a few square millimetres of skin would be required to mount a specimen, the preparations being a few $\mu$m in thickness and lightened with ethyl benzoate. They can be studied by natural light or with ultra-violet lighting which renders the melanin grains fluorescent.

Either way let us simply say that the evaluation of melanin level by microscopic examination is a laboratory method which enables us to classify the ancient Egyptians unquestionably among the black races.

## Osteological measurements

Among the criteria accepted in physical anthropology for classifying races, the osteological measurements are perhaps the least misleading (in contrast to craniometry) for distinguishing a black man from a white man. By this criterion, also, the Egyptians belong among the black races. This study was made by the distinguished German savant Lepsius at the end of the nineteenth century and his conclusions remain valid: subsequent methodological progress in the domain of physical anthropology in no

20. R. A. Nicolaus, p. 11.
21. T. J. Pettigrew, 1834, pp. 70–71.
22. C. A. Diop, 1977.

way undermines what is called the 'Lepsius canon' which, in round figures, gives the bodily proportions of the ideal Egyptian, short-armed and of negroid or negrito physical type.[23]

## Blood-groups

It is a notable fact that even today Egyptians, particularly in Upper Egypt, belong to the same Group B as the populations of western Africa on the Atlantic seaboard and not to the A2 Group characteristic of the white race prior to any crossbreeding.[24] It would be interesting to study the extent of Group A2 distribution in Egyptian mummies, which present-day techniques make possible.

## The Egyptian race according to the classical authors of antiquity

To the Greek and Latin writers contemporary with the ancient Egyptians the latter's physical classification posed no problems: the Egyptians were negroes, thick-lipped, kinky-haired and thin-legged; the unanimity of the authors' evidence on a physical fact as salient as a people's race will be difficult to minimize or pass over. Some of the following evidence drives home the point.

(a) Herodotus, 'the father of history', −480(?) to −425.

With regard to the origins of the Colchians[25] he writes:

> It is in fact manifest that the Colchidians are Egyptian by race ... several Egyptians told me that in their opinion the Colchidians were descended from soldiers of Sesostris. I had conjectured as much myself from two pointers, firstly because they have black skins and kinky hair (to tell the truth this proves nothing for other peoples have them too) and secondly and more reliably for the reason that alone among mankind the Egyptians and the Ethiopians have practised circumcision since time immemorial. The Phoenicians and Syrians of Palestine themselves admit that they learnt the practice from the Egyptians while the Syrians in the river Thermodon and Pathenios

23. M. E. Fontane, pp. 44–5 (see reproduction: T).
24. M. F. A. Montagu, p. 337.
25. In the fifth century before our era, at the time when Herodotus visited Egypt, a black-skinned people, the Colchians, were still living in Colchis on the Armenian shore of the Black Sea, east of the ancient port of Trebizond, surrounded by white-skinned nations.
   The scholars of antiquity wondered about this people's origins and Herodotus in 'Euterpe', the second book of his history on Egypt, tries to prove that the Colchians were Egyptians, whence the arguments we quote. Herodotus, on the strength of commemorative stelae, erected by Sesostris in conquered countries, asserts that this monarch had got as far as Thrace and Scythia, where stelae would seem to have been still standing in his day (Book II, 103).

region and their neighbours the Macrons say they learnt it recently from the Colchidians. These are the only races which practise circumcision and it is observable that they do it in the same way as the Egyptians. As between the Egyptians themselves and the Ethiopians I could not say which taught the other the practice, for among them it is quite clearly a custom of great antiquity. As to the custom having been learnt through their Egyptian connections, a further strong proof to my mind is that all those Phoenicians trading to Greece cease to treat the pudenda after the Egyptian manner and do not subject their offspring to circumcision.[26]

Herodotus reverts several times to the negroid character of the Egyptians and each time uses it as a fact of observation to argue more or less complex theses. Thus to prove that the Greek oracle at Dodona in Epirus was of Egyptian origin, one of his arguments is the following: '. . . and when they add that the dove was black they give us to understand that the woman was Egyptian'.[27] The doves in question – actually there were two according to the text – symbolize two Egyptian women who are said to have been carried off from the Egyptian Thebes to found the oracles in Greece at Dodona and in Libya (Oasis of Jupiter Amon) respectively. Herodotus did not share the opinion of Anaxagoras that the melting of the snows on the mountains of Ethiopia was the source of the Nile floods.[28] He relied on the fact that it neither rains nor snows in Ethiopia 'and the heat there turns men black'.[29]

(*b*) Aristotle, −389 to −332, scientist, philosopher and tutor of Alexander the Great.

In one of his minor works, Aristotle attempts, with unexpected *naïveté*, to establish a correlation between the physical and moral natures of living beings and leaves us evidence on the Egyptian–Ethiopian race which confirms what Herodotus says. According to him, 'Those who are too black are cowards, like for instance, the Egyptians and Ethiopians. But those who are excessively white are also cowards as we can see from the example of women, the complexion of courage is between the two.'[30]

(*c*) Lucian, Greek writer, +125(?) to +190.

The evidence of Lucian is as explicit as that of the two previous writers. He introduces two Greeks, Lycinus and Timolaus, who start a conversation.

Lycinus (describing a young Egyptian): 'This boy is not merely black;

---

26. Herodotus, Book II, 104. As with many peoples in black Africa, Egyptian women underwent excision of the clitoris: cf. Strabo, *Geography*, Book XVII, Ch. I.

27. Herodotus, Book II, 57.

28. Seneca, *Questions of Nature*, Book IV, 17.

29. Herodotus, Book II, 22.

30. Aristotle, *Physiognomy*, 6.

he has thick lips and his legs are too thin ... his hair worn in a plait behind shows that he is not a freeman.'

Timolaus: 'But that is a sign of really distinguished birth in Egypt, Lycinus. All freeborn children plait their hair until they reach manhood. It is the exact opposite of the custom of our ancestors who thought it seemly for old men to secure their hair with a gold brooch to keep it in place.'[31]

(*d*) Apollodorus, first century before our era, Greek philosopher.

'Aegyptos conquered the country of the black-footed ones and called it Egypt after himself.'[32]

(*e*) Aeschylus, −525(?) to −456, tragic poet and creator of Greek tragedy.

In *The Suppliants*, Danaos, fleeing with his daughters, the Danaïds, and pursued by his brother Aegyptos with his sons, the Aegyptiads, who seek to wed their cousins by force, climbs a hillock, looks out to sea and describes the Aegyptiads at the oars afar off in these terms: 'I can see the crew with their black limbs and white tunics.'[33]

A similar description of the Egyptian type of man recurs a few lines later in verse 745.

(*f*) Achilles Tatius of Alexandria.

He compares the herdsmen of the Delta to the Ethiopians and explains that they are blackish, like half-castes.

(*g*) Strabo, −58 to about +25.

Strabo visited Egypt and almost all the countries of the Roman empire. He concurs in the theory that the Egyptians and the Colchoi are of the same race but holds that the migrations to Ethiopia and Colchoi had been from Egypt only.

'Egyptians settled in Ethiopia and in Colchoi.'[34] There is no doubt whatever as to Strabo's notion of the Egyptians' race for he seeks elsewhere to explain why the Egyptians are darker than the Hindus, a circumstance which would permit the refutation, if needed, of any attempt at confusing 'the Hindu and Egyptian races'.

(*h*) Diodorus of Sicily, about −63 to +14, Greek historian and contemporary of Caesar Augustus.

According to Diodorus it was probably Ethiopia which colonized Egypt (in the Athenian sense of the term, signifying that, with overpopulation, a proportion of the people emigrate to new territory).

> *The Ethiopians say that the Egyptians are one of their colonies,* [35] which was led into Egypt by Osiris. They claim that at the beginning

31. Lucian, *Navigations*, paras 2–3.
32. Apollodorus, Book II, 'The family of Inachus', paras 3 and 4.
33. Aeschylus, *The Suppliants*, vv. 719–20. See also v. 745.
34. Strabo, *Geography*, Book I, ch. 3, para. 10.
35. My italics.

of the world Egypt was simply a sea but that the Nile, carrying down vast quantities of loam from Ethiopia in its flood waters, finally filled it in and made it part of the continent ... They add that the Egyptians have received from them, as from authors and their ancestors, the greater part of their laws.[36]

(*i*) Diogenes Laertius.

He wrote the following about Zeno, founder of the Stoic School (−333 to −261): 'Zeno son of Mnaseas or Demeas was a native of Citium in Cyprus, a Greek city which has taken in some Phoenician colonists.' In his *Lives*, Timotheus of Athens describes Zeno as having a twisted neck. Apollonius of Tyre says of him that he was gaunt, very tall and black, hence the fact that, according to Chrysippus in the First Book of his Proverbs, certain people called him an Egyptian vine-shoot.[37]

(*j*) Ammianus Marcellinus, about +33 to +100, Latin historian and friend of the Emperor Julian.

With him we reach the sunset of the Roman empire and the end of classical antiquity. There are about nine centuries between the birth of Aeschylus and Herodotus and the death of Ammianus Marcellinus, nine centuries during which the Egyptians, amid a sea of white races, steadily crossbred. It can be said without exaggeration that in Egypt one household in ten included a white Asiatic or Indo-European slave.[38]

It is remarkable that, despite its intensity, all this crossbreeding should not have succeeded in upsetting the racial constants. Indeed Ammianus Marcellinus writes: '... the men of Egypt are mostly brown or black with a skinny and desiccated look'.[39] He also confirms the evidence already cited about the Colchoi: 'Beyond these lands are the heartlands of the Camaritae[40] and the Phasis with its swifter stream borders the country of the Colchoi, an ancient race of Egyptian origin.'[41]

This cursory review of the evidence of the ancient Graeco-Latin writers on the Egyptians' race shows that the extent of agreement between them is impressive and is an objective fact difficult to minimize or conceal, the two alternatives between which present-day Egyptology constantly oscillates.

An exception is the evidence of an honest savant, Volney, who travelled

---

36. Diodorus, *Universal History*, Book III. The antiquity of the Ethiopian civilization is attested by the most ancient and most venerable Greek writer, Homer, in both the *Iliad* and the *Odyssey*:
    'Jupiter followed today by all the gods receives the sacrifices of the Ethiopians' (*Iliad*, I, 422).
    'Yesterday to visit holy Ethiopia Jupiter betook himself to the ocean shore' (*Iliad*, I, 423).
37. Diogenes Laertius, Book VII, 1.
38. The Egyptian notables liked to have a Syrian or Cretan female slave in their harems.
39. Ammianus Marcellinus, Book XXII, para. 16 (23).
40. Pirate gangs who worked from small ships called *Ćamare*.
41. Ammianus Marcellinus, Book XXII, para. 8 (24).

in Egypt between +1783 and +1785, i.e. at the peak period of negro slavery, and made the following observations on the true Egyptian race, the same which produced the Pharaohs, namely, the Copts:

> All of them are puffy-faced, heavy-eyed and thick-lipped, in a word, real mulatto faces. I was tempted to attribute this to the climate until, on visiting the Sphinx, the look of it gave me the clue to the enigma. Beholding that head characteristically Negro in all its features, I recalled the well-known passage of Herodotus which reads: 'For my part I consider the Colchoi are a colony of the Egyptians because, like them, they are black-skinned and kinky-haired'. In other words the ancient Egyptians were true negroes of the same stock as all the autochthonous peoples of Africa and from that datum one sees how their race, after some centuries of mixing with the blood of Romans and Greeks, must have lost the full blackness of its original colour but retained the impress of its original mould. It is even possible to apply this observation very widely and posit in principle that physiognomy is a kind of record usable in many cases for disputing or elucidating the evidence of history on the origins of the peoples ...

After illustrating this proposition citing the case of the Normans, who 900 years after the conquest of Normandy still look like Danes, Volney adds:

> but reverting to Egypt, its contributions to history afford many subjects for philosophic reflection. What a subject for meditation is the present-day barbarity and ignorance of the Copts who were considered, born of the alliance of the deep genius of the Egyptians and the brilliance of the Greeks, that this race of blacks who nowadays are slaves and the objects of our scorn is the very one to which we owe our arts, our sciences and even the use of spoken word; and finally recollect that it is in the midst of the peoples claiming to be the greatest friends of liberty and humanity that the most barbarous of enslavements has been sanctioned and the question raised whether black men have brains of the same quality as those of white men![42]

To this testimony of Volney, Champollion-Figeac, brother of Champollion the Younger, was to reply in the following terms: 'The two physical traits of black skin and kinky hair are not enough to stamp a race as negro and Volney's conclusion as to the negro origin of the ancient population of Egypt is glaringly forced and inadmissible.'[43]

Being black from head to foot and having kinky hair is not enough to make a man a negro! This shows us the kind of specious argumentation to which Egyptology has had to resort since its birth as a science. Some

42. M. C. F. Volney, *Voyages en Syrie et en Egypte*, Paris, 1787, Vol. I, pp. 74–7.
43. J. J. Champollion-Figeac, 1839, pp. 26–7.

scholars maintain that Volney was seeking to shift the discussion to a philosophic plane. But we have only to re-read Volney: he is simply drawing the inferences from crude material facts forcing themselves on his eyes and his conscience as proofs.

## The Egyptians as they saw themselves

It is no waste of time to get the views of those principally concerned. How did the ancient Egyptians see themselves? Into which ethnic category did they put themselves? What did they call themselves? The language and literature left to us by the Egyptians of the Pharaonic epoch supply explicit answers to these questions which the scholars cannot refrain from minimizing, twisting or 'interpreting'.

The Egyptians had only one term to designate themselves: = kmt = the negroes (literally).[44] This is the strongest term existing in the Pharaonic tongue to indicate blackness; it is accordingly written with a hieroglyph representing a length of wood charred at the end and not crocodile scales.[45] This word is the etymological origin of the well-known root *kamit* which has proliferated in modern anthropological literature. The biblical root *kam* is probably derived from it and it has therefore been necessary to distort the facts to enable this root today to mean 'white' in Egyptological terms whereas, in the Pharaonic mother tongue which gave it birth, it meant 'coal black'.

In the Egyptian language, a word of assembly is formed from an adjective or a noun by putting it in the feminine singular. 'Kmt' from the adjective = km = black; it therefore means strictly negroes or at the very least black men. The term is a collective noun which thus described the whole people of Pharaonic Egypt as a black people.

In other words, on the purely grammatical plane, if one wishes to indicate negroes in the Pharaonic tongue, one cannot use any other word than the very one which the Egyptians used of themselves. Furthermore, the language offers us another term, kmtjw = the negroes, the black men (literally) = the Egyptians, as opposed to 'foreigners' which comes from the same root km and which the Egyptians also used to describe themselves as *a people as distinguished from all foreign peoples*.[46] These are

44. This important discovery was made, on the African side, by Sossou Nsougan, who was to compile this part of the present chapter. For the sense of the word see *Wörterbuch der Aegyptischen Sprache*, Vol. 5, 1971, pp. 122 and 127.

45. ibid., p. 122.

46. ibid., p. 128.

the only adjectives of nationality used by the Egyptians to designate themselves and both mean 'negro' or 'black' in the Pharaonic language. Scholars hardly ever mention them or when they do it is to translate them by euphemisms such as the 'Egyptians' while remaining completely silent about their etymological sense.[47] They prefer the expression $\overset{\frown}{\underset{\bigcirc}{}}$ 𓂝𓏏𓏥 𓄿𓏤 ⊗ Rmt kmt = the men of the country of the black men or the men of the black country.

In Egyptian, words are normally followed by a determinative which indicates their exact sense, and for this particular expression Egyptologists suggest that ⊿𓅓 km = black and that the colour qualifies the determinative which follows it and which signifies 'country'. Accordingly, they claim, the translation should be 'the black earth' from the colour of the loam, or the 'black country', and not 'the country of the black men' as we should be inclined to render it today with black Africa and white Africa in mind. Perhaps so, but if we apply this rule rigorously to 𓏏𓂝𓏏𓏥 = kmit, we are forced to 'concede that here the adjective "black" qualifies the determinative which signifies the whole people of Egypt shown by the two symbols for "man" and "woman" and the three strokes below them which indicate the plural'. Thus, if it is possible to voice a doubt as regards the expression 𓂝 ⊗ = kme, it is not possible to do so in the case of the two adjectives of nationality 𓂝𓏏 𓀀𓁐 = kmt and kmtjw unless one is picking one's arguments completely at random.

It is a remarkable circumstance that the ancient Egyptians should never have had the idea of applying these qualificatives to the Nubians and other populations of Africa to distinguish them from themselves; any more than a Roman at the apogee of the empire could use a 'colour' adjective to distinguish himself from the Germani on the other bank of the Danube, of the same stock but still in the prehistoric age of development.

In either case both sides were of the same world in terms of physical anthropology, and accordingly the distinguishing terms used related to level of civilization or moral sense. For the civilized Romans, the Germans, of the same stock, were barbarians. The Egyptians used the expression 𓃛𓂝𓏤 = nahas to designate the Nubians; and nahas[48] is the name of a people, with no colour connotation in Egyptian. It is a deliberate mistranslation to render it as negro as is done in almost all present-day publications.

---

47. R. O. Faulkner, 1962, p. 286.
48. Wörter buch der ägyptischen Sprache, p. 128.

## The divine epithets

Finally, black or negro is the divine epithet invariably used for the chief beneficent gods of Egypt, whereas all the malevolent spirits are qualified as desrêt = red; we also know that to Africans this form applies to the white nations; it is practically certain that this held good for Egypt too but I want in this chapter to keep to the least debatable facts.

The surnames of the gods are these:

⌂🐂 = Kmwr = the 'Great Negro' for Osiris[49]

= km = the black + the name of the god[50]

= kmt = the black + the name of the goddess[51]

The km (black) qualificative is applied to Hathor, Apis, Min, Thoth, etc.[52] set kmt = the black woman = Isis.[53] On the other hand 'seth', the sterile desert, is qualified by the term desrêt = red.[54] The wild animals which Horus fought to create civilization are qualified as dešrêt = red, especially the hippopotamus.[55] Similarly the maleficent

beings wiped out by Thoth are Des = = dèsrtjw = the red ones;

this term is the grammatical converse of Kmtjw and its construction follows the same rule for the formation of 'nisbés'.

## Witness of the Bible

The Bible tells us: '... the sons of Ham [were] Cush, and Mizraim [i.e. Egypt], and Phut, and Canaan. And the sons of Cush; Seba, and Havilah, and Sabtah, and Raamah, and Sabtechah.'[56]

Generally speaking all Semitic tradition (Jewish and Arab) classes ancient Egypt with the countries of the blacks.

The importance of these depositions cannot be ignored, for these are peoples (the Jews) which lived side by side with the ancient Egyptians and sometimes in symbiosis with them and have nothing to gain by presenting a false ethnic picture of them. Nor is the notion of an erroneous interpretation of the facts any more tenable.[57]

49. ibid., p. 124.
50. ibid., p. 125.
51. ibid., p. 123.
52. It should be noted that set = kem = black wife in Walaf.
53. Wörter buch der ägyptischen Sprache, p. 492.
54. ibid., p. 493.
55. Dešrêt = blood in Egyptian; deret = blood in Walaf: ibid., p. 494.
56. Genesis, 10: 6–7.
57. C. A. Diop, 1955, pp. 33ff.

## Cultural data

Among the innumerable identical cultural traits recorded in Egypt and in present-day black Africa, it is proposed to refer only to circumcision and totemism.

According to the extract from Herodotus quoted earlier, circumcision is of African origin. Archaeology has confirmed the judgement of the Father of History for Elliot-Smith was able to determine from the examination of well-preserved mummies that circumcision was the rule among the Egyptians as long ago as the protohistoric era,[58] i.e. earlier than −4000.

Egyptian totemism retained its vitality down to the Roman period[59] and Plutarch also mentions it. The researches of Amélineau,[60] Loret, Moret and Adolphe Reinach have clearly demonstrated the existence of an Egyptian totemic system, in refutation of the champions of the zoolatric thesis.

> If we reduce the notion of the totem to that of a fetish, usually representing an animal of a species with which the tribe believes it has special ties formally renewed at fixed intervals, and which is carried into battle like a standard; if we accept this minimal but adequate definition of a totem, it can be said that there was no country where totemism had a more brilliant reign than in Egypt and certainly nowhere where it could better be studied.[61]

## Linguistic affinity

Walaf,[62] a Senegalese language spoken in the extreme west of Africa on the Atlantic Ocean, is perhaps as close to ancient Egyptian as Coptic. An exhaustive study of this question has recently been carried out.[63] In this chapter enough is presented to show that the kinship between ancient Egyptian and the languages of Africa is not hypothetical but a demonstrable fact which it is impossible for modern scholarship to thrust aside.

As we shall see, the kinship is genealogical in nature.

| | EGYPTIAN | COPTIC | WALAF |
|---|---|---|---|
| | = kef = to grasp, to take a strip (of something)[64] | (Saïdique dialect) keh = to tame[65] | kef = seize a prey |

58. E. Massoulard, 1949, p. 386.
59. Juvénal, *Satire* XV, vv. 1–14.
60. E. Amélineau, *op. cit.*
61. A. Recnach, 1913, p. 17.
62. Often spelt Wolof.
63. C. A. Diop, 1977(a).
64. R. Lambert, 1925, p. 129.
65. A. Mallon, pp. 207–34.

| PRESENT | PRESENT | PRESENT |
|---|---|---|
| kef i | keh | kef na |
| kef ek | keh ek | kef nga |
| kef et | keh ere | kef na |
| kef ef | kef ef | |
| kef es | keh es | kef ef ⎱ na |
| | | kef es ⎰ |
| kef n | keh en | kef nanu |
| kef ton | keh etetû | kef ngen |
| kef sen[66] | keh ey | kef nañu |
| PAST | PAST | PAST |
| kef ni | keh nei | kef (on) na |
| kef (o) nek | keh nek | kef (on) nga |
| kef (o) net | keh nere | kef (on) na |
| kef (o) nef | keh nef | kef (on) ef ⎱ na |
| kef (o) nes | keh nes | kef (on) es ⎰ |
| kef (o) nen | keh nen | kef (on) nanu |
| kef (o) n ten | keh netsten | kef (on) ngen |
| kef (o) n sen[67] | keh ney[68] | kef (on) nañu |

| EGYPTIAN | WALAF |
|---|---|
| = feh = go away | feh = rush off |

We have the following correspondences between the verb forms, with identity or similarity of meaning: all the Egyptian verb forms, except for two, are also recorded in Walaf.

| EGYPTIAN | WALAF |
|---|---|
| feh-ef | feh-ef |
| feh-es | feh-es |
| feh-n-ef | feh-ôn-ef |
| feh-n-es | feh-ôn-es |
| feh-w | feh-w |
| feh-wef | feh-w-ef |
| feh-w-es | feh-w-es |
| feh-w-n-ef | feh-w-ôn-ef |
| feh-w-n-es | feh-w-ôn-es |
| feh-in-ef | feh-il-ef |
| feh-in-es | feh-il-es |

66. A. de Buck, 1952.
67. ibid.
68. A. Mallon, pp. 207–34.

feh-t-ef  feh-t-ef
feh-t-es  feh-t-es

feh-tyfy  feh-ati-fy
feh-tysy  feh-at-ef
          feh-at-es

feh-tw-ef  mar-tw-ef
feh-tw-es  mar-tw-es

feh-kw(i)  fahi-kw

feh-n-tw-ef  feh-an-tw-ef
feh-n-tw-es  feh-an-tw-es

feh-y-ef  feh-y-ef
feh-y-es  fey-y-es

| EGYPTIAN | WALAF |
|---|---|
| = mer = love | mar = lick[69] |
| mer-ef | mar-ef |
| mer-es | mar-es |
| mer-n-ef | mar-ôn-ef |
| mer-n-es | mar-ôn-es |
| mer-w | mar-w |
| mer-w-ef | mar-w-ef |
| mer-w-es | mar-w-es |
| mer-w-n-f | mar-w-ôn-ef |
| mer-w-n-es | mar-w-ôn-es |
| mer-in-ef | mar-il-ef |
| mer-in-es | mar-il-es |
| mer-t-ef | mar-t-ef |
| mer-t-es | mar-t-es |
| mer-tw-ef | mar-tw-ef |
| mer-tw-es | mar-tw-es |
| mer-tyfy | mar-at-ef |
| mer-t̲-tysy | mar-at-es |
|  | mar-aty-sy |
|  | mar-aty-sy |
| mer-kwi | mari-kw |
| mer-y-ef | mar-y-ef |
| mer-y-es | mar-y-es |
| mer-n-tw-ef | mar-an-tw-ef |
| mer-n-tw-es | mar-antw-es |
|  | mar-tw-ôn-ef |
|  | mar-tw-ôn-es |

69. By extension = love intensely (hence the verb mar-maral) after the fashion of a female animal licking the cub which she has just borne. This sense does not conflict with the other notion which the determinative may convey of a man raising hand to mouth.

## Egyptian and Walaf demonstratives

There are the following phonetic correspondences between Egyptian and Walaf demonstratives.

| EGYPTIAN | | WALAF | |
|---|---|---|---|
| | | | ep ⟶ w |
| ⌑🦅 | = pw | | ⎧ p ⟶ b |
| | (ipw) ⟶ bw | | ⎨ w ⟶ w |
| | | | |
| ⌑🦅 ⸌⸌ | = pwy | | ⎧ p ⟶ ƀ |
| | (ipw) ⟶ bwy | | ⎨ w ⟶ w |
| | | | ⎩ y ⟶ y |
| ⌑ 〰 | = pn | ⎧ bané | ⎧ p ⟶ ƀ |
| | (ipn) ⟶ | ⎨ | ⎨ n ⟶ n |
| | | ⎩ balé | ⎧ p ⟶ ƀ |
| | | | ⎩ n ⟶ l [70] |
| ⌑ 〰 | = pf | bafe | p ⟶ b |
| | (ipf) ⟶ | | f ⟶ f |
| ⌑ 🦅 | = pf3 ⟶ bafa | | p ⟶ ƀ |
| | | | f ⟶ f |
| | | | 3 ⟶ a |
| ⌑ ⸌⸌ | = pfy | | p ⟶ ƀ |
| | (ipfy) ⟶ bafy | | f ⟶ f |
| | | | y ⟶ y |
| 𓆈🦅 | = p3 ⟶ bâ | | p ⟶ b |
| | | | 3 ⟶ â |
| 𓏲⌑🦅 | = iptw ⟶ baṯw | | p ⟶ b |
| | | | ṯ ⟶ t |
| | | | w ⟶ w |
| 𓏲⌑〰 | = iptn ⟶ | ⎧ batné | ⎧ p ⟶ b |
| | | ⎨ | ⎧ ṯ ⟶ t |
| | | ⎩ Batalé | ⎨ n ⟶ n |
| | | | ⎩ n ⟶ l |
| 𓏲⌑ | = iptf | | p ⟶ ƀ |
| | = iptf ⟶ batafé | | t ⟶ t |
| | | | f ⟶ f |

These phonetic correspondences are not ascribable either to elementary affinity or to the general laws of the human mind for they are regular correspondences on outstanding points extending through an entire system,

70. See below for the explanation of this important law.

that of the demonstratives in the two languages and that of the verbal languages. It is through the application of such laws that it was possible to demonstrate the existence of the Indo-European linguistic family.

The comparison could be carried further to show that the majority of the phonemes remain unchanged between the two languages. The few changes which are of great interest are the following.

(*a*) The correspondence n (E) ⟶ l (W)

| EGYPTIAN | | WALAF |
|---|---|---|
| n | | l |
| 〓〓〓 | = nad̲ = ask | lad̲ = ask |
| 〓〓〓 | = nah = protect | lah = protect |
| 〓〓〓 | = ben ben = well up | bel bel = well up |
| 〓〓〓 | = teni = grow old | talé = important |
| 〓〓〓 | = tefnwt = the goddess born of Ra's spittle | tefnit = 'spit out' a human being<br>teflit = spittle<br>tefli = spitter |
| 〓〓〓 | = nebt = plait | let = plait<br>nâb = to plait hair temporarily |

(*b*) The correspondence h (E) ⟶ g (W)

| EGYPTIAN | | WALAF |
|---|---|---|
| h | | g |
| 〓〓〓 | = hen = phallus | gen = phallus |
| 〓〓〓 | = hwn = adolescent | gwné<br>goné } = adolescent |
| 〓〓〓 | = hor = Horus | gor = vir (? male ?) |
| 〓〓〓 | = hor gwn = the youth Horus | gor gwné = young man (m.ǎ.m) |

It is still early to talk with precision of the vocalic accompaniment of the Egyptian phonemes. But the way is open for the rediscovery of the vocalics of ancient Egyptian from comparative studies with the languages of Africa.

# Conclusion

The structure of African royalty, with the king put to death, either really or symbolically, after a reign which varied in length but was in the region of eight years, recalls the ceremony of the Pharaoh's regeneration through the Sed feast. Also reminiscent of Egypt are the circumcision rites mentioned earlier and the totemism, cosmogonies, architecture, musical instruments, etc., of black Africa.[71] Egyptian antiquity is to African culture what Graeco-Roman antiquity is to Western culture. The building up of a corpus of African humanities should be based on this fact.

It will be understood how difficult it is to write such a chapter in a work of this kind, where euphemism and compromise are the rule. In an attempt to avoid sacrificing scientific truth, therefore, we made a point of suggesting three preliminaries to the preparation of this volume, all of which were agreed to at the plenary session held in 1971.[72] The first two led to the holding of the Cairo Symposium from 28 January to 3 February 1974.[73] In this connection I should like to refer to certain passages in the report of that symposium. Professor Vercoutter, who had been commissioned by Unesco to write the introductory report, acknowledged after a thorough discussion that the conventional idea that the Egyptian population was equally divided between blacks, whites and half-castes could not be upheld. 'Professor Vercoutter agreed that no attempt should be made to estimate percentages, which meant nothing, as it was impossible to establish them without reliable statistical data'. On the subject of Egyptian culture: 'Professor Vercoutter remarked that, in his view, Egypt was African in its way of writing, in its culture and in its way of thinking'.

Professor Leclant, for his part, 'recognized the same African character in the Egyptian temperament and way of thinking'.

In regard to linguistics, it is stated in the report that 'this item, in contrast to those previously discussed, revealed a large measure of agreement among the participants. The outline report by Professor Diop and the report by Professor Obenga were regarded as being very constructive'.

Similarly, the symposium rejected the idea that Pharaonic Egyptian was a Semitic language. 'Turning to wider issues, Professor Sauneron drew attention to the interest of the method suggested by Professor Obenga following Professor Diop. Egyptian remained a stable language for a period of at least 4500 years. Egypt was situated at the point of convergence of outside influences and it was to be expected that borrowing had been made from foreign languages, but the Semitic roots numbered only a few

71. See C. A. Diop, 1967.
72. See *Final Report of the First Plenary Session of the International Scientific Committee for the Drafting of a general History of Africa*, UNESCO, 30 March–8 April 1974.
73. Symposium on 'The peopling of ancient Egypt and the deciphering of the Meroitic script'. Cf. Studies and Documents No. 1, UNESCO, 1978.

hundred as compared with a total of several thousand words. The Egyptian language could not be isolated from its African context and its origin could not be fully explained in terms of Semitic, it was thus quite normal to expect to find related languages in Africa'.

The genetic, that is, non-accidental relationship between Egyptian and the African languages was recognized: 'Professor Sauneron noted that the method which had been used was of considerable interest, since it could not be purely fortuitous that there was a similarity between the third person singular suffixed pronouns in Ancient Egyptian and in Wolof, he hoped that an attempt would be made to reconstitute a palaeo-African language, using present-day languages as a starting point'.

In the general conclusion to the report it was stated that: 'Although the preparatory working paper sent out by Unesco gave particulars of what was desired, not all participants had prepared communications comparable with the painstakingly researched contributions of Professors Cheikh Anta Diop and Obenga. There was consequently a real lack of balance in the discussions'.

A new page of African historiography was accordingly written in Cairo. The symposium recommended that further studies be made on the concept of race. Such studies have since been carried out, but they have not contributed anything new to the historical discussion. They tell us that molecular biology and genetics recognize the existence of populations alone, the concept of race being no longer meaningful. Yet whenever there is any question of the transmission of a hereditary taint, the concept of race in the most classic sense of the term comes into its own again, for genetics tells us that 'sickle-cell anaemia occurs only in negroes'. The truth is that all these 'anthropologists' have already in their own minds drawn the conclusions deriving from the triumph of the monogenetic theory of mankind without venturing to put them into explicit terms, for if mankind originated in Africa, it was necessarily negroid before becoming white through mutation and adaptation at the end of the last glaciation in Europe in the Upper Palaeolithic; and it is now more understandable why the Grimaldian negroids first occupied Europe for 10 000 years before Cro-Magnon Man – the prototype of the white race – appeared (around −2000).

The ideological standpoint is also evident in apparently objective studies. In history and in social relations, it is the phenotype, that is, the individual or the people as that individual or people is perceived, which is the dominant factor, as opposed to the genotype. For present-day genetics, a Zulu with the 'same' genotype as Vorster is not impossible. Does this mean that the history we are witnessing will put the two phenotypes, that is, the two individuals, on the same footing in all their national and social activities? Certainly not – the opposition will remain not social but ethnic.

This study makes it necessary to rewrite world history from a more scientific standpoint, taking into account the Negro-African component which was for a long time preponderant. It means that it is now possible to build up a corpus of Negro-African humanities resting on a sound historical basis instead of being suspended in mid-air. Finally, if it is true that only truth is revolutionary, it may be added that only *rapprochement* brought about on a basis of truth can endure. The cause of human progress is not well served by casting a veil over the facts.

The rediscovery of the true past of the African peoples should not be a divisive factor but should contribute to uniting them, each and all, binding them together from the north to the south of the continent so as to enable them to carry out together a new historical mission for the greater good of mankind; and that is in keeping with the ideal of Unesco.[74]

[74] NOTE BY THE EDITOR OF THE VOLUME
The opinions expressed by Professor Cheikh Anta Diop in this chapter are those which he presented and developed at the Unesco symposium on 'The peopling of ancient Egypt' which was held in Cairo in 1974. A summary of the proceedings of this symposium will be found at the end of this chapter. The arguments put forward in this chapter have not been accepted by all the experts interested in the problem (cf. Introduction, above).
Gamal Mokhtar

PLATE 1.2 *A pharaoh of the First Egyptian Dynasty, said to be Narmer.*

PLATE 1.4 (*below*) *Door socket from Hierakonpolis, First Egyptian Dynasty*

PLATE 1.1 *Protohistoric figure of Tera-Neter, a negro nobleman of the Anous race who were the first inhabitants of Egypt*

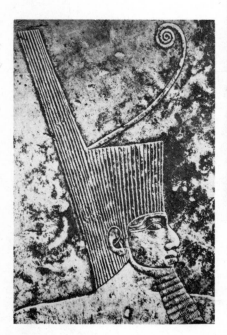

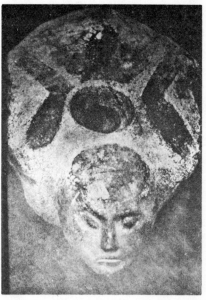

PLATE 1.3 (*left*) *Djeser, typical negro, pharaoh of the Third Dynasty; this ushered in the great age of dressed-stone architecture: the step pyramid and burial complex at Sakkara. By his reign, all the technological features of Egyptian civilization were already developed*

PLATE 1.5 *Libyan prisoner*

PLATE 1.6 *Foreigner*

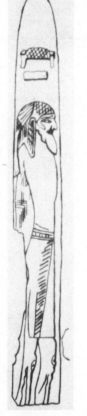

PLATE 1.8 *Predynastic figurines*

PLATE 1.7 *Semitic captive*

PLATE 1.9 *Indo-European captives*

PLATE 1.10 *Indo-European captive*

PLATE 1.11 *Indo-European captive*

PLATE 1.12 *Cheops, Pharaoh of the Fourth Egyptian Dynasty, builder of the Great Pyramid*

PLATE 1.14 *Pharaoh Mentouhotep I*

PLATE 1.13 *Semitic captives at the time of the pharaohs; Sinai rock*

PLATE 1.15 *Four Indo-European types (Zeus, Ptolemy, Sarapis, Trajan). Compare with Egyptian groups II and III.*

PLATE 1.16 *Two Semites. Like the Indo-European type, the Semitic type was totally absent from the Egyptian ruling class, entering Egypt only as war captives*

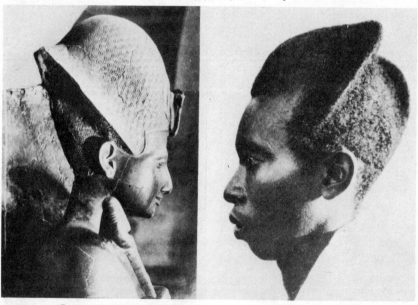

PLATE 1.17 *Ramses II, and a modern Batutsi*

PLATE 1.18 *Statue of the Sphinx as found by the first French scientific mission in the nineteenth century. The typically Negro profile is thought to be that of the pharaoh Khafre or Khefren (ca. − 2600, IV Dynasty), the builder of the second pyramid of Giza.*

PLATE 1.19 *The Gebel-el-Arak knife haft, back and front views*

# Annex to Chapter 1: Report of the symposium on 'The Peopling of Ancient Egypt and the Deciphering of the Meroitic Script'[1]

Cairo, 28 January–3 February 1974

## Summary report[2]

The symposium was held in two stages: the first took place from 28 to 31 January 1974 and concerned 'The peopling of ancient Egypt', the second dealt with 'The deciphering of the Meroitic script' and took place from 1 to 3 February 1974.

The participants were as follows:

Professor Abdelgadir M. Abdalla (Sudan)
Professor Abu Bakr (Arab Republic of Egypt)
Mrs N. Blanc (France)
Professor F. Debono (Malta)
Professor J. Devisse (France)
Professor Cheikh Anta Diop (Senegal)
Professor Ghallab (Arab Republic of Egypt)
Professor L. Habachi (Arab Republic of Egypt)
Professor R. Holthoer (Finland)
Mrs J. Gordon-Jaquet (United States of America)
Professor S. Husein (Arab Republic of Egypt)
Professor Kaiser (Federal Republic of Germany)
Professor J. Leclant (France)
Professor G. Mokhtar (Arab Republic of Egypt)
Professor R. El Nadury (Arab Republic of Egypt)
Professor Th. Obenga (People's Republic of the Congo)
Professor S. Sauneron (France)
Professor T. Säve-Söderbergh (Sweden)
Professor P. L. Shinnie (Canada)
Professor J. Vercoutter (France)

Professor Hintze (German Democratic Republic), Professor Knorossov, Professor Piotrovski (Union of Soviet Socialist Republics) and Professor Ki-Zerbo (Upper Volta) were invited to the symposium but were unable to attend and sent their apologies.

In accordance with the decisions of the International Scientific Committee, Professor J. Devisse, the Committee's Rapporteur, was present and prepared the final report of the symposium.

Unesco was represented by Mr Maurice Glélé, programme specialist, Division of Cultural Studies, representing the Director-General, and Mrs Monique Melcer, Division of Cultural Studies.

1. This annex should have been inserted as an Annex to the whole volume and placed after the Conclusion.

2. The present report is an abridged version of the final report of the symposium. It was prepared by the International Scientific Committee's Rapporteur at the request of the Committee, for insertion in this volume. The Proceedings of the Symposium have been published in the series *The General History of Africa – Studies and Documents* No. 1, Unesco, Paris, 1978.

# I  Symposium on the peopling of ancient Egypt

Two papers previously commissioned by Unesco from Professor J. Vercoutter and Mrs N. Blanc² provided a basis for discussion.

Three important stages may be distinguished in the discussion.

A  Summary of the introductory papers.

B  Preliminary statements made by most of the participants.

C  General discussion.

## A  Summary of the introductory papers

(1) Professor Vercoutter drew attention to a number of points dealt with in greater detail in his written report, and made a number of further observations.

(a) In spite of recent progress, physical anthropology had so far provided relatively little reliable data except in Nubia. The information available was insufficient to enable provisional conclusions to be drawn with regard to the peopling of ancient Egypt and the successive phases through which it may have passed. Furthermore, this information was not homogeneous as regarded either time or space and historians often disagreed as to how it should be interpreted. The methods themselves were being called in question; but it was now generally agreed that craniometry did not meet the requirements of such research.

A number of regions had still not been studied in any depth. This applied to the entire Delta during the predynastic and protodynastic periods, and to Upper Egypt prior to Neolithic times. Little was known of the area between the Second and Sixth Cataracts in Neolithic and protodynastic times. Similarly, the links existing in ancient times between the Sahara, Darfur and the Nile had as yet been very little studied.

In that respect, the work that had been done lagged behind what had been achieved in North Africa and in the Syria–Palestine zone.

Evidence at present available did not warrant the assertion that the populations of northern Egypt had been different from those in the south. Similarly, the gap between Palaeolithic and Neolithic was probably due to the fact that insufficient research had yet been done in that field.

(b) Insufficient and unsatisfactory use had been made of iconography; the studies which had been carried out were based mainly on cultural criteria. The iconographic material available, however, has extremely significant characteristics from the the eighteenth dynasty onwards.

(c) Outline of the two opposing theories in their most extreme form:

(i) The people who lived in ancient Egypt were 'white', even though their pigmentation was dark, or even black, as early as the predynastic period. Negroes made their appearance only from the eighteenth dynasty onwards.

From the protodynastic period onwards, according to some, the population remained the same; others believed that foreign penetration into Africa profoundly altered the conditions of cultural life.

(ii) Ancient Egypt was peopled, 'from its Neolithic infancy to the end of the native dynasties', by black Africans.

(2) Mrs Blanc reported on her research findings.

(a) Mindful of the fact that, for reasons which were themselves historical, the historiography of the valleys of the Nile had been based on the assumption

2. These documents are attached to the Final Report, 1974.

that there was a civilized Egyptian valley providing a wealth of historical evidence, and another valley farther south, which was black and primitive, and of interest only to anthropologists, Mrs Blanc hoped that historical research in the valley as a whole would in future be more balanced. This would mean abandoning traditional historical methods and broadening the field of inquiry to embrace a new methodology. Mrs Blanc saw the work which had been going on in Nubia for the last twenty years or so as a first step towards the re-examination of the question which faced the symposium.

(b) In order to escape from the traditional view of the Nile valley which traced its historical development in a north–south direction, from the 'more civilized' to the 'less civilized', Mrs Blanc drew attention to the Nile regions situated between the twenty-third parallel and the sources of the river in Uganda. Her analysis took into account the dividing line, which she regarded as being of fundamental ecological importance, along the tenth parallel, where the advance of Islam stopped.

Between the twenty-third and the tenth parallels, the Nile, being a navigable waterway, could apparently have played a role comparable to that which it played farther north, in Egypt. This did not occur, and the ecological conditions in this reach of the river no doubt provided the principal explanation.

Mrs Blanc went on to make an overall examination, in the light of this fact, of the respective contributions of settled and nomadic populations throughout the area considered.

But after tracing the history of the population changes since the coming of the Muslim Arabs, she concentrated particularly on reviewing hypotheses concerning the peopling of this zone prior to their arrival. She emphasized that the Nile valley facilitated communication with West Africa and sub-Saharan Africa and that it was reasonable to put forward the hypothesis that the civilizations which emerged there might be authentically African rather than civilizations intermediate between the Mediterranean world and black Africa.

Darfur, to the west, about the social and political organization of which, prior to the seventeenth century, little is known, nevertheless played an important part as a regional centre of economic development.

To the east, the region of Sennar, inhabited by the Funj, was the centre of a 'black sultanate' which was originally neither Arab nor Muslim.

The zone between the Nile and the Red Sea occupied by the Beja was barely able to support settled populations, on account of the harsh ecological conditions.

South of the tenth parallel, the ecological conditions were totally different. In this area, there were isolated populations about which little was known either from archaeological research or from oral traditions. Hypotheses on the peopling and history of this zone today have little evidence to support them, and it is only in more southerly regions, in the interlacustrine zone in East Africa, that fairly thorough historical studies have been carried out.

# B   Preliminary statements by participants

(1) Professor Säve-Söderbergh gave information about the Scandinavian excavations in the Sudan between 1960 and 1964. These excavations established that there were contacts between the Nile valley and North Africa and the Sahara. The subjects covered by the publications[3] included 7000 rock drawings and the analysis of the remains of 1546 human

---

3. See Scandinavian Joint Expedition to Sudanese Nubia, publications (especially Vol. 1, *Rock Pictures*; Vol. 2, *Pre-Ceramic Sites*; Vol. 3, *Neolithic and A-Group Sites*; and Vol. 9, *Human Remains*).

individuals. Van Nielson (Vol. 9) had defined the relations between the A Group, C Group, New Kingdom Group, etc. Comparative studies yielded different results, depending on whether craniometry only was used or anthropological and technological factors as a whole. Inconographical and physical anthropology studies lent support to the idea that there had been a migration of Saharan peoples and of groups coming from the south, and that they also had had considerable contacts with the ancient Egyptians. For the Mesolithic period, comparisons had to be made on the basis of fewer than 100 skeletons. Valid conclusions were impossible in the case of Nubia, but more accurate data could be obtained on the Neolithic period.

In any event, Professor Säve-Söderbergh thought that it was impossible to base a study of the peopling of Egypt in ancient times, or any other similar study, on racial distinctions. In future, other lines of inquiry should be followed. Different cultures, contemporary with one another but isolated, might nevertheless belong to the same techno-complex. This new method confirmed that Egypt was African. But, if one looked beyond this finding, it was apparent that there were many other problems. Nagada I and II did not belong to the same techno-complex as Nubia or the contemporary Sudan. In the Sudan, the zone extending from Kassala to Chad and from Wadi Halfa to Khartoum was a single, large techno-complex unit. The A Group constituted another and more recent techno-complex between the First and Third Cataracts and possibly beyond.

(2) Professor Cheikh Anta Diop gave an extensive account of his ideas. He summarized a written paper, picking out the main points.

(a) From the anthropological point of view, research carried out since the discoveries of Professor Leakey led to the conclusion that the human race first came into existence in Africa in the region of the sources of the Nile. Gloger's law, which presumably applied just as much to the human race as the other species, stated that warm-blooded animals which evolved in a warm, humid climate had a dark (eumelanin) pigmentation. The earliest human beings on earth were therefore ethnically homogeneous and negroid. The population spread out from this original area, reaching other regions of the earth by only two routes: the Nile valley and the Sahara.

In the Nile valley, this spread took place from the south in a northerly direction, in a progressive movement, between the Upper Palaeolithic and the protohistoric periods.

Even Professor Massoulard had reached the conclusion that the population of ancient Egypt perhaps comprised at least three different racial elements: negroids, amounting to over one-third of the total, 'Mediterranean' people and people of the Cro-Magnon type. Professor Diop inferred from this that the population of Egypt was basically negro during the predynastic period, a conclusion contradicting the theory that the negro element spread to Egypt in later times.

Skeletons with fragments of skin attached, dating from very ancient times, before the practice of mummification was introduced, had been discovered by Elliot Smith. These fragments, stated Professor Diop, contain melanin in sufficient quantity to establish them as negro skin.

In the quest for positive proof, Professor Diop had studied a number of preparations being subjected to laboratory examination in Dakar. These consisted of samples of skin taken from mummies found in Mariette's excavations. They all reaveled – and Professor Diop invited the specialists present to examine the samples – the presence of a considerable quantity of melanin between the epidermis and the dermis. Melanin, which was not present in white skin, persisted for millions of years (notwithstanding frequent affirmations to the contrary) as could be seen from an examination of the skins of fossil animals. Professor Diop hoped to be given the opportunity of carrying out similar research on the skins of the Pharaohs whose mummies were in the Cairo Museum collection.

He went on to state that a conclusive anthropological study would also include

61

osteological measurements and the study of blood-groups. It was remarkable, for example, that present-day Egyptians, particularly in Upper Egypt, belonged to the same blood-group, B, as the population of West Africa, and not to Group A2, which was characteristic of the white race.

(b) *Iconography:* On the basis of an important iconographical drawing and the definitions given in this work, Professor Diop contended that it was unnecessary to dwell on details which, for example, distinguished negroes from other personages – the latter being aristocratic – in the same tomb: this difference of representation was of social origin. The common people were iconographically distinguished from members of the ruling class.

(c) Professor Diop went on to speak of the evidence provided by *ancient written sources*, pointing out that Greek and Latin authors described the Egyptians as negroes. He referred to the testimony of Herodotus, Aristotle, Lucian, Apollodorus, Aeschylus, Achilles Tatius, Strabo, Diodorus Siculus, Diogenes Laertius and Ammianus Marcellinus. Modern scholars, he said, refused to take account of those texts. By contrast, an eighteenth-century author, Volney, did speak of the inhabitants of ancient Egypt as negroes. Furthermore, the biblical tradition also considered Egypt as belonging to the descendants of Ham. Professor Diop considered that the science of Egyptology, a product of imperialism, had much to answer for in denying all the facts to which he had just referred.

(d) Professor Diop then turned his attention to the way in which the Egyptians described themselves. They used only one word for this purpose: KMT,[4] 'the strongest term existing in the language of the Pharaohs to indicate blackness', which was translated by Professor Diop as 'the negroes'. Consequently, this hieroglyph was not written with crocodile scales but with a piece of charcoal.

(3) Professor Debono contributed an extensive review of the information given in Volume I.

(4) Professor Leclant began by stressing the African character of Egyptian civilization. But it was necessary to distinguish clearly, as Professor Vercoutter had done, between 'race' and culture.

Physical anthropology in Egypt was in its infancy. Nevertheless, there was no justification for relying on the totally outmoded studies of Chantre, Elliot Smith, Sergi, or Dr Derry. Furthermore, there had already been important restatements of current knowledge such as that by Wierczinski.[5] Groups working in Nubia had also shown considerable interest in physical anthropology, with the result that Nubia, reputedly 'poor' in archaeological remains, paradoxically seemed likely to become far better known than Egypt in this respect.[6] Archaeological expeditions now gave great prominence to osteological studies, an innovation which was greatly to be welcomed.[7]

In cultural studies, rock engravings, which showed an enormous degree of uniformity from the Red Sea to the Atlantic, were worthy of careful study. These traces had been left by successive cultural groups, hunters, herdsmen, or others.

The peopling of ancient Egypt was a considerable problem and it would be very premature, at this stage, to adopt a synoptic approach as a means of solving it. The problem should be approached through separate, precise studies. For this purpose, the

4. This word gave rise to the term 'Hamite' which has been much used subsequently. It is also found in the Bible in the form 'Ham'.

5. *Bulletin of the Egyptian Geographical Society*, 31, 1958, pp. 73–83.

6. Professor Leclant referred to the work of Nielsen, Strouhal, Armelagos, Rogalsky, Prominska, Chemla and Billy.

7. cf. An important recent article, D. P. van Gerven, D. S. Carlson and G. J. Armelagos, (Racial History and Bio-cultural Adaptation of Nubian Archaeological Populations), *JAH*, vol. XIV, no. 4, 1973, pp. 555–64.

collaboration of specialists in disciplines not represented at this symposium was indispensable. All the participants were 'general historians', qualified to compile and synthesize data supplied by specialists; such data were, for the moment, very inadequate.

In any case, it was retrograde to have recourse to authorities who were today completely outdated, such as Lepsius or Petrie. They might be recognized as having 'historical' importance but Egyptology had made great progress since their day.

As for iconographical evidence, the only problem was to know how the Egyptians considered themselves in relation to other men. They called themselves RMT (Rame), that is to say 'men'; other people they regarded as an amorphous mass extending in all directions, designated by the cardinal points. For example, the statues of prisoners at Sakkara (Sixth dynasty, 2300 before our era) were partly northerners (Asians, Libyans) and partly southerners (Nubians, negroes). Stereotypes of northerners (whites) and southerners (negroes) under the sandals of Pharaoh confirmed that representation.

(5) Professor Ghallab spoke of the successive elements which could be identified in the peopling of Africa between the Palaeolithic period and the third millennium before our era.

In north-east Africa, a large quantity of stone objects dating from the second pluvial period had been found in the Nile valley and the oases. Professor Ghallab distinguished at least six ethnic groups in Egyptian population during the Mesolithic period, which, however, were united by a homogeneous culture. He considered that the human race during the Palaeolithic period was more or less homogeneous and 'Caucasian'; the first negro types in Africa were Asselar man and Omdurman man. In the late Palaeolithic period, the black race appeared from the Atlantic to the Red Sea. Among the earliest Egyptians, however, traces had been found of 'Bushmen', some of whose characteristics were modified as a result of their becoming acclimatized to Mediterranean ecological conditions. Even today, there were vestiges of this 'Bushman' type in the population of Egypt. A negro culture did not really appear prior to the Neolithic period.

(6) Professor Abdelgadir M. Abdalla did not think it important to establish whether the ancient Egyptians were black or negroid: what was most remarkable was the degree of civilization they had achieved.

Iconographic evidence made it clear that the creators of the Napata culture had nothing in common with the Egyptians: their anatomical characteristics were completely different. If the Egyptians were black, what colour were the men of the Napata culture?

Turning to the subject of linguistics, Professor Abdalla stated that KM (Kem) did not mean 'black' and its derivatives did not refer to the colour of individuals. He gave a linguistic demonstration in his turn to illustrate his theory, which differed from that of Professor Diop. He concluded that the Egyptian language was not a purely African language; it belonged to a proto-Semitic group, as could be abundantly demonstrated by supporting examples. Professor Abdalla considered that the linguistic examples given by Professor Diop were neither convincing nor conclusive and that it was hazardous to make too uncompromising a correlation between a language and an ethnic structure or an individual. A comparison drawn between a dead language and living languages was bound to be inconclusive; the similarities which had been pointed out were fortuitous and nothing was so far known of the evolution of ancient African languages. The evidence which had been given to support the theory of kinship was in fact far more consistent with the theory of the spread of ancient Egyptian throughout Africa than of its kinship with present-day African languages. Why should it be assumed that ancient Egyptian and Wolof were related, but not ancient Egyptian and Meroitic, for example? The language of Napata and Meroitic were at opposite poles from one another.

Professor Abdalla hoped that the inquiry would be pursued in the strictest fashion.

(a) He considered it impossible to establish any automatic correlation between an ethnic group, a socioeconomic system and a language.

63

(*b*) It was impossible to reach scientifically valid conclusions by working 'on a large scale'. There were almost no unambiguous examples in history of major migrations accompanying major cultural transformations.

(*c*) 'Negro' was not a clearly defined concept today as far as physical anthropologists were concerned. A skeleton did not provide evidence of skin colour. Only the tissues and the skin itself were important in that respect.

(*d*) It was imperative to broach the study of palaeopathology and of funerary practices without delay.

(7) Professor Sauneron intervened in the course of a lively exchange of views on linguistic matters between Professors Abdalla and Diop. Professor Sauneron stated that in Egyptian *KM* (feminine *KMT*) meant 'black'; the masculine plural was *KMU* (Kemou), and the feminine plural *KMNT*.

The form *KMTYW* could mean only two things: 'those of Kmt', 'the inhabitants of Kmt' ('the black country'). It was a derived adjective (*nisba*) formed from a geographical term which had become a proper name; it was not necessarily 'felt' with its original meaning (cf. Frank, France, French).

To designate 'black people', the Egyptians would have said *Kmt* or *Kmu*, not *Kmtyw*. In any case, they never used this adjective to indicate the black people of the African hinterland whom they knew about from the time of the New Kingdom onwards; nor, in general, did they use names of colours to distinguish different peoples.

(8) Professor Obenga in his turn reverted to the linguistic demonstration which had been begun by Professor Diop.[8]

(*a*) After criticizing Professor Greenberg's method, on the basis of the recent work by Professor Istvan Fodor[9] and remarking that, since the work of Ferdinand de Saussure, it was an accepted fact that linguistic evidence was the most obvious means of establishing whether two or more than two peoples were culturally related, Professor Obenga endeavoured to prove that there was a genetic linguistic relationship between Egyptian (ancient Egyptian and Coptic) and modern negro-African languages.

Before making any comparison, one must be on one's guard against confusing typological linguistic relationship, which gave no clue as to the predialectal ancestor common to the languages being compared, and genetic relationship. For example, modern English, considered from the typological point of view, had affinities with Chinese; but, from the genetic point of view, the two languages belonged to distinct language families. Similarly, Professor Obenga rejected the notion of a mixed language as linguistic nonsense.

Genetic relationship depended on establishing phonetic laws discovered by comparison between morphemes and phonemes of similar languages. On the basis of such morphological, lexicological and phonetic correspondences, one could arrive at common earlier forms. In this way, a theoretical 'Indo-European' language had been reconstructed in the abstract and had been used as an operational model. It was indicative of a common cultural macrostructure shared by languages which subsequently evolved along separate lines.

(*b*) Professor Obenga drew attention to important typological similarities in grammar: the feminine gender formed by the use of the suffix -*t*, the plural of nouns by the suffix -*w* (*ou*, *u*). He next analysed complete word-forms and noted similarities between those of ancient Egyptian and a considerable number of African languages; between Egyptian and Wolof the correspondence was total. This series of demonstrations led Professor Obenga to the conclusion that morphological,

8. The full text, as transmitted to the Rapporteur by Professor Obenga, is attached as Annex II in the Final Report of the symposium.

9. I. Fodor, *The Problems in the Classification of the African Languages* (Centre for Afro-Asian Research of the Hungarian Academy of Sciences, Budapest, 1966), p. 158.

lexicological and syntactic similarities amounted to convincing proof of the close relationship between ancient Egyptian and negro-African languages of today. This kind of parallelism was impossible between Semitic, Berber and Egyptian.

He then dealt with comparisons of ways of expressing 'to be' in verb – noun combinations: the common archaic form in the Bantu language was the same in this respect as that of the most archaic form of ancient Egyptian. The analysis of negative morphemes, of the emphatic future and of linking particles led to the same conclusions as the previous examples. Professor Obenga considered, therefore, that it would prove possible to discover a common genetic structure.

(*c*) Lastly, Professor Obenga spoke of what he considered to be the most interesting aspect of the comparison.

He drew parallels between the forms taken in different languages by certain words: palm, spirit, tree, place; and also between certain small phonemes: for example, *KM* (*Kem*), black in ancient Egyptian, becomes *Kame, kemi, kem* in Coptic; *ikama* in Bantu (with the meaning of charred by exposure to excessive heat), *kame* in Azer (cinder). *Romé*, 'man' in ancient Egyptian, becomes *lomi* in Bantu. The same phonemes have the same functions in the different languages compared.

Professor Obenga inferred from these comparisons that it would be possible in the future to identify a 'negro-Egyptian' language, analogous to 'Indo-European'. In this context, and in view of the undeniable common cultural background of all these languages, there was a sound basis for the development of future studies.

(9) Professor Gordon-Jaquet stated that the study of Egyptian toponomy could perhaps be brought to bear in support of the assertion that no massive immigrations or invasions of foreign populations had arrived in Egypt at least since Neolithic times. It was a well known phenomenon that topographical names were extremely long-lived and that each successive language group inhabiting the same area would leave its mark on that area in the form of place names, more or less numerous, depending on the size of the population and the length of time of its predominance in that area. Any important permanent addition to the Egyptian population from the exterior would certainly have left its mark on the toponomy of the country. This was not the case. The toponomy of Egypt was very homogeneous, displaying names whose etymology could almost without exception be explained by the Egyptian language itself. It was only at the Ptolemaic period and still later, after the Arab conquest, that names of respectively Greek and Arabic origin were added to the basic fund of Egyptian names. It was only in the peripheral regions, Nubia, the Western Oases and the Eastern Delta – regions in immediate contact with neighbouring peoples speaking other languages – where names whose etymology could be traced to these foreign languages were to be found.

(10) Professor Devisse briefly abandoned his role as Rapporteur to inform the symposium of the unexpected results of an iconographic study.[10]

Three manuscripts[11] included representations of black Egyptians which merited consideration. After eliminating what could be attributed to biblical tradition (the descendants of Ham), and allegorical representations in a consciously archaic manner (Hades, Night), there remained a variable proportion of Egyptians represented with negro features and colouring. Admittedly, some of these were servants, but – and on this point the scenes

10. This very wide-ranging international study will be the subject of a publication in three volumes two of which have already been published. The study has been carried out by the Menil Foundation (Houston, United States of America), a unit of which in Paris has co-ordinated the collection of a vast quantity of iconographic material.

11. Paris, Bibliothèque Nationale, New Acquisitions: latin 2334 (VI–VIIe?), Vatican grec 747 (XIe), Vatican grec 746 (XIIe).

selected were extremely interesting – others were free Egyptians. Some of them – about a third of the participants – were around the table of Joseph, who was giving a banquet for his Israelite brothers seated at another table; others were taking part in the sale of Joseph to Potiphar, who was himself represented as white. Probably the most remarkable aspect of these representations, which were consistently realistic in their details, lay in the characteristic costume worn by these black Egyptians (particularly in the eleventh-century octateuch). The negroes, who were clearly differentiated from Egyptians wearing beards and turbans, were in many cases carrying spears and wore a 'panther skin' leaving the right shoulder bare. Professor Devisse considered these observations all the more interesting because there were considerable contacts between Byzantium and Egypt during the Fatimid period, and because the representations which dated from this period were far more realistic than in the older manuscript.

It was very difficult to interpret these documents: they pointed both to the Byzantine cultural background and to the biblical tradition. Nevertheless, they reflected a 'northerner's view' of the Egyptians which was not consistent with the standard 'white-skinned' theory.

# C   General discussion

The general discussion made it clear that a number of participants, in varying degrees, thought it desirable, in the present state of knowledge, to undertake macro-analyses embracing the history of ancient Egypt as a whole, or, in some cases, the entire continent of Africa; certain other participants, on the other hand, thought that it would be wiser to take geographical micro-analyses very much further on a disciplinary or interdisciplinary basis.

## (1) Chronological analysis of the results achieved

The discussion on this point was opened by Professor Cheikh Anta Diop. Since the Upper Palaeolithic period, the initial homogeneity of the human race had gradually declined; the population of Egypt was neither more nor less homogeneous than the population of other parts of the world. The first appearance of the human race was currently believed to have occurred in Africa 5 300 000 years ago B.P. The origins were African.

*Homo sapiens* appeared about −150 000 and progressively spread to all the then habitable parts of the Nile basin. Men living in Egypt at that time were black.

Rejecting the opposing theory, referred to by Professor Vercoutter in his report concerning the peopling of Egypt during the predynastic period, Professor Diop stated that the 33 per cent of 'white' Egyptians with a fairly dark, or even black, pigmentation were in fact, black, as were the 33 per cent of half-castes; adding the last 33 per cent of the population mentioned by Dr Massoulard and admitted to be black, Professor Diop expressed the opinion that the population of Egypt as a whole was black throughout the protodynastic period.

He went on to reassert the general theory which he had previously outlined concerning the black population of Egypt which gradually became hybridized.

At another point in the discussion, Professor Diop explicitly stated that the black population of Upper Egypt began to retreat only at the time of the Persian occupation.

He ended by making two general observations: one concerned the use of the word *negroid*, a term which he considered unnecessary and pejorative; the other concerned the arguments which were being put forward to contest his ideas, and which he considered to be negative, lacking in critical rigour and not based on the facts.

Professor Diop's theory was rejected in its entirety by one participant.

None of the participants explicitly voiced support for the earlier theory concerning a population which was 'white' with a dark, even black, pigmentation. There was no more than tacit agreement to abandon this old theory.

Numerous objections were made to the ideas propounded by Professor Diop. These objections revealed the extent of a disagreement which remained profound even though it was not voiced explicitly. In respect of certain sequences, the criticisms arose out of the line of argument put forward.

In so far as very ancient times were concerned – those earlier than what the French still called the 'Neolithic' period – participants agreed that it was very difficult to find satisfactory answers.

Professor Debono noted the considerable similarity between pebble cultures in the different regions where they had been discovered (Kenya, Ethiopia, Uganda, Egypt). The same was true of the Acheulean period, during which biface core tools were similar in a number of regions of Africa.

On the other hand, the homogeneity of the Sangoan industry, found in East Africa, progressively diminished as one moved farther north. At Khor Abu Anga (Sai Island in the Sudan), there was a more or less complete range of tools. From Wadi Halfa onwards, a number of elements were apparently lost. In Egypt, only one of the industry's typological characteristics was retained, between Thebes and Dahshur near Cairo.

In the Middle Palaeolithic period, the striking of Levallois flakes with Mousterian variants differed greatly between Egypt and areas situated farther south or west.

In the Palaeolithic period, for reasons which remain obscure but which were probably due to changed climatic and ecological conditions, Egypt became isolated from the rest of Africa with regard to the stone tool-making industry, and original industries were created (Sebilian, Epi-Levalloisian or Hawarian, Khargian).

Furthermore, at the same period there was an attempt at foreign penetration by the Aterians from north-east Africa. Traces of them were found as far as the southern Sahara. Having reached the Siwah oasis and also, in large numbers, the Khargah oasis, they spread out in the Nile valley and their traces had been found at Thebes. Other evidence dating from the same period had been noted at Wadi Hamamat (Eastern Desert), at Esna (mingled with Khargian remains), at Dara, at Jebel Ahmar near Cairo, and as far as Wadi Tumilat in the Eastern Delta (mingled with Epi-Levalloisian remains). It was probable that at the same time there was a small-scale admixture of other races, rapidly absorbed by the native population.

An equally interesting intrusion of foreign peoples into Egypt was that of the Natoufians of Palestine, whose presence at Halwan near Cairo had long been an established fact. Recent excavations had shown that these people inhabited a larger area. Stone implements, attributable to these Natoufians, had been found at Fayum and in the Eastern Desert along a belt extending in an east–west direction across the Nile valley at this point.

Professor Sauneron considered that, in view of the existence of chipped pebbles in the old Pleistocene strata of the Theban hills, it could be inferred that human beings had inhabited the Nile valley since very ancient times.

Professor Ghallab stated that the inhabitants of Egypt in Palaeolithic times were Caucasoids. He went on to say the recent excavations had provided evidence of the existence of men of the 'San' type in the population during the predynastic period.

Professor Shinnie was in agreement regarding the settlement of *Homo sapiens*, but without mentioning the colour of his skin, and dated the first settled population of the Nile valley at about 20 000 years ago. Subsequently, various human groups came from different regions, increasing this population and altering its composition.

The discussion was no less lively concerning the Neolithic and predynastic periods. Professor Abu Bakr emphasized that the Egyptians had never been isolated from other peoples. They had never constituted a pure race and it was impossible to accept the

67

idea that in the Neolithic period the population of Egypt was entirely black. The population of Egypt in Neolithic times was a mingling of men from the west and east, who had been incorrectly called Hamitic.

This was also the theory of Professor El Nadury. In Neolithic times migrants from all parts of the Sahara had infiltrated the sedentary population settled in the north-western part of the Delta, resulting in an intermingling of many ethnic groups. From that period onwards there was no break in continuity as regards the population until dynastic times. The site of Merimdé with its wealth of clearly stratified archaeological material showed that the peopling of this area had been a gradual process.

Professor Vercoutter firmly stated his conviction, with regard to the peopling of Egypt in ancient times, that the inhabitants of the Nile valley had always been mixed; outside elements coming from west and east had been numerous, particularly in predynastic times.

During the predynastic period and the beginning of the dynastic period, a further element, coming from the north-east and described as Semitic, was added to the population. Like Professor Abu Bakr, Professor El Nadury thought it a striking fact that, during the first dynasty, fortifications had been built at Abydos, in all probability for the purpose of preventing immigration from the south towards the north.

Professor Abu Bakr referred to the case of the yellow-haired, blue-eyed wife of Cheops as an example of the existence of 'non-black' people in Egypt. Professor Diop regarded this isolated instance as an exception which proved the rule.

In the course of the discussion, Professor Obenga added some important points and emphasized the interest of ancient written sources concerning the population of Egypt. Herodotus, in a passage concerning the Colchians which was neither disputed by modern scholarship nor invalidated by the comparative critical study of manuscripts, endeavoured to show, through a series of critical arguments, that the Colchians were similar to the Egyptians: 'They speak in the same way as they do, they and the Egyptians are the only peoples to practise circumcision, they weave linen like the Egyptians'; these similarities were in addition to two other features which they had in common, their black pigmentation and their crinkly hair.

Professor Leclant maintained that ancient writers used the expression 'burnt face' (Ethiopians) to refer to Nubians and negroes but not to Egyptians. Professor Obenga replied that the Greeks applied the word 'black' (*melas*) to the Egyptians. Professor Vercoutter, in particular, asked in what precise context Herodotus had defined the Egyptians as negroes. Professor Diop replied that Herodotus referred to them on three occasions: in speaking of the origin of the Colchians, in speaking of the origin of the Nile floods, and in discussing the oracle of Zeus-Amon.

In Professor Leclant's opinion, the unity of the Egyptian people was not racial but cultural. Egyptian civilization had remained stable for three millennia; the Egyptians described themselves as REMET (*Rome* in Coptic) and, particularly in their iconographic representations, drew a distinction between themselves and the peoples of the north and those of the south who differed from them. Professor Obenga denied that Egyptians, in using the word REMET, drew a racial distinction between themselves and their neighbours; he considered the distinction made to be similar to that which led the Greeks to differentiate between themselves and other peoples, whom they termed Barbarians.

Professor Leclant noted that important palaeo-African features in the cultural life of Egypt were worthy of study. As an example, he mentioned the baboon, which was an attribute of the God Thoth, and the frequent appearance in iconography of 'panther' skins as a ritual garment during the worship of Osiris by Horus. In his opinion, however, the Egyptians, whose civilization was culturally stable for three millennia, were neither white nor negro.

Professor Sauneron then questioned the very idea of a homogeneous population, particularly if it was alleged to have existed from the earliest appearance of man in Egypt up to the predynastic period. He considered that none of the evidence currently available gave grounds for doubting that the population of Egypt was mixed.

The conclusion of the experts who did not accept the theory, put forward by Professors Cheikh Anta Diop and Obenga, that the Nile valley population had been homogeneous from the earliest times until the Persian invasion, was that the basic population of Egypt settled there in neolithic times, that it originated largely in the Sahara and that it comprised people from the north and from the south of the Sahara who were differentiated by their colour. In opposition to this theory, Professors Diop and Obenga submitted their own theory to the effect that the valley was peopled uniformly by black people and that the movement had been from south to north.

## (2) Existence or non-existence of migrations of consequence towards the Nile valley

As regards this item, the proceedings of the symposium remained very confused. More than one discussion was inconclusive.

Generally speaking, participants considered that the 'large-scale migrations' theory was no longer tenable as an explanation of the peopling of the Nile valley, at least up to the Hyksos period, when linguistic exchanges with the Near East began to take place (Holthoer). On the other hand, several experts thought that population exchanges had evidently occurred with immediately adjacent regions in the valley, although very divergent opinions were expressed concerning the role played by geographical or ecological factors in creating natural or artificial obstacles to such population movements.

At all events, it was generally agreed that Egypt had absorbed these migrants of various ethnic origins. It followed that the participants in the symposium implicitly recognized that the substratum of the Nile valley population remained generally stable and was affected only to a limited extent by migrations during three millennia.

When the later periods came to be examined, however, it proved impossible to reach this very broad measure of theoretical agreement.

As regards the Palaeolithic period, Professor Cheikh Anta Diop put forward the hypothesis that *Homo sapiens* settled progressively in the valley as far as the latitude of Memphis. Professor Abu Bakr said that too little information was available concerning this period and that the northern part of the Nile valley might not have been inhabited at all. Professor Obenga, on the other hand, considered that between the Upper Palaeolithic and the Neolithic periods there had been continuous settlement by a uniform population; the Egyptians themselves had laid emphasis on this in their oral traditions, mentioning the Great Lakes as their original homeland and Nubia as a country identical with theirs.

Where the Mesolithic merged with the Neolithic (Professor Vercoutter) or during the Neolithic period (Professors Habachi and Ghallab), it seemed likely that fairly large movements of population took place from the Sahara towards the Nile valley. Professor Vercoutter hoped that these movements, about which very little was at present known, would be dated accurately and that the relevant archaeological material would be collected and studied.

Professor Cheikh Anta Diop submitted certain details by way of reply: Radio-carbon dating for the Western Sahara showed that a period of damp climate had extended from about 30 000 B.P. to 8 000 B.P., with intermittent periods of drought; similarly, the dating of the ensuing dry period was becoming clearer. Similar datings should be obtained for the Eastern Sahara; by combining the results obtained with palaeo-climatic research and with studies of tombs and carvings, the information which Professor Vercoutter wanted would be obtained.

Professor Habachi unreservedly supported the theory of migrations from the Sahara on the basis of known studies. Professor Säve-Söderbergh considered that the majority of

Neolithic cultures in the Nile valley belonged to a techno-complex of Saharan and Sudanese cultures; nevertheless, migratory movements were probably intense, especially prior to and at the end of the neolithic subpluvial period.

As an alternative to the hypothesis postulating a migration from the Sahara largely during Neolithic times, Professor Diop put forward the hypothesis that the population had spread northwards from the south. He restated the idea, to which reference had been made several times during the discussion, that, during the Capsian period, this culture covered a vast area extending from Kenya to Palestine.

On the subject of the protodynastic and predynastic periods, Professors Diop and Vercoutter agreed that the population of the Egyptian reaches of the Nile valley was homogeneous as far as the southern extremity of the Delta. These two experts were in partial agreement on the hypothesis of migration southwards from the north, Professor Vercoutter finding this theory difficult to accept and Professor Diop rejecting it. Disagreement emerged on the subject of defining the nature of these people more precisely. Professor Diop regarded them as being the Anu and identified them in the picture noted by Petrie in the temple of Abydos.

During the dynastic period, the stability of the population of the Egyptian reaches of the Nile valley was attested by the stability of its culture; Professor Diop showed that the Egyptian calendar had been in use as early as $-4236$ and, from the beginning, had a cyclic pattern of 1461 years. He considered that, until the Persian invasion, that stability had been threatened only by a very powerful earthquake which occurred in about $-1450$. This had given rise to a series of migrations which affected the equilibrium of all countries bordering the eastern Mediterranean basin. Seafaring peoples then attacked the Egyptian Delta at a period contemporaneous with the disappearance of the Hittites and the appearance of the proto-Berbers in North Africa. Apart from this major upheaval, the only important episode in the life of the Egyptian people, even if it were not associated with a migration, was the conquest of Egypt in a south–north direction by the unifying Pharaoh Narmer in about $-3300$.

There was no discussion of this analysis, but other analyses were put forward: Professor Säve-Söderbergh sought to establish, on the basis of the Nubian excavations, at what periods and in what conditions the Egypt of the Pharaohs had become cut off from the south. In Nubia, the most ancient culture gradually disappeared at the end of the first dynasty or perhaps at the beginning of the second. The C Group which succeeded it did not appear before the sixth dynasty. This meant that there was a 'chronological gap' of about 500 years, between $-2800$ and $-2300$, on which no information was available today. It was clear that, as a result of this situation, active contacts between Pharaonic Egypt and the south were destroyed or discontinued.

There was another instance of the same situation: no archaelogical remains dating from the period between $-1000$ and the beginning of the Christian era were to be found in Lower Nubia. The earliest Meroitic remains which had been discovered there dated from the first century of our era; exchanges between Egypt and the south had therefore varied considerably between $-2800$ and the Meroitic period.

Professors Vercoutter and Leclant noted the appearance, from the eighteenth dynasty onwards, of a type of negro representation which was totally different from anything that had existed earlier (the tomb of *Houy* or the tomb of *Rekhmire*, for example). How did these new populations make their appearance in Egyptian iconography? Was it the result of contacts between Egyptians and the south or because of migrations northwards into Nubia of populations living farther south? Professor Shinnie objected that this information gave no grounds for inferring that there had been a northward migration from the south which had affected the population of Egypt.

Professor Leclant considered that, with the exception of the eighteenth-dynasty example already mentioned, no important change had occurred prior to the twenty-fifth dynasty, when the Kushites from the Dongola region appeared in Egypt. He was inclined, incidentally, to regard this as attributable rather to the transitory increase of a particular influence in the life of the Egyptian population than to migrations of peoples.

Two main facts became very plain during the discussion and were not seriously contested:

(*a*) There is a twofold problem in connection with the Nile Delta[12] in prehistoric times.

Firstly, as Professor Debono pointed out, this region, unlike Upper Egypt, is very little known, as the excavations being carried out at Merimde, El Omari and Meadi-Heliopolis have not yet been completed.

The human remains so far discovered dating from prehistoric times and from the archaic period are different from those found in Upper Egypt.

Secondly, it appears certain that human factors which affected life in Lower Egypt or the Delta, in so far as they can be discerned prior to the dynastic period, differ from those which were operative in the valley south of this region.

(*b*) The study of the ancient substratum of the population has been made possible in northern Nubia by the intensive archaeological research organized under Unesco's auspices. For a great variety of reasons, this has not been the case in the remainder of the Egyptian part of the Nile valley, where research concerning predynastic times and ancient material cultures had produced far fewer results than in northern Nubia. The reservations and the unwillingness of some of the experts to draw final conclusions are probably due in part to this fact.

There is no doubt that one other factor at least added to the complexity of a discussion which often took the form of successive and mutually contradictory monologues. This factor emerged clearly from a phrase uttered by Professor Obenga, although it was not commented upon. Professor Obenga considers it self-evident that a homogeneous cultural substratum necessarily implies a homogeneous ethnic substratum.

Whether or not these two ideas lend themselves to simultaneous consideration, it seems likely that they were not kept sufficiently apart during the discussions and that, as a result, the conclusions reached were less clear-cut than they might otherwise have been. The possibility of finding points of agreement was probably affected by this fact.

Nevertheless, if they are considered without reference to racial issues, two major themes did ultimately meet with almost unanimous agreement, at least as working hypotheses.

It was probably in Neolithic times that the population of the Egyptian Nile valley was most affected by large-scale migrations. Two theories are current in this connection: according to one, the migrants came, in the main, in a north–south direction from the entire area of the Eastern Sahara; according to the other, these movements of population came along the Nile from the south; from protodynastic times onwards, the population of Egypt was very stable. The nature of the peopling was not radically altered by the various population movements which affected the political life and the military situation of Egypt, by the consequences of Egypt's commercial relations, by the internal efforts towards agricultural settlement or by infiltrations from nearby regions. This ethnic stability was accompanied by a high degree of cultural stability.

However, during the discussion of the hypothesis of a homogeneous population, which was favoured by Professor Diop, and the hypothesis of a mixed population, which was supported by several other experts, it became clear that there was total disagreement.

12. Professor Holthoer drew attention to the following work: D. G. Réder, 'The Economic Development of Lower Egypt (Delta) during the Archaic Period (V–IV [centuries] before our era)', a collection of articles which appeared in the *Journal of Ancient Egypt*, 1960 (translation of the Russian title).

## (3) Results of the physical anthropology inquiry

At various points in the discussion, it became apparent that the terms used hitherto for the purposes of racial description required to be more clearly defined.

Mr Glélé, the representative of the Director-General of Unesco, intervened to reassure those experts who advocated outlawing the terms 'negro', 'black' and 'negroid' on the grounds that the concept of race was outmoded and efforts should be made to bring men closer together by repudiating any reference to race. Mr Glélé reminded the participants that Unesco was committed to the cause of promoting international understanding and co-operation in the cultural sphere and that it had not been the intention of the Organization, when deciding to hold the symposium, to give rise to tensions between peoples or races but rather, as far as the present state of knowledge permitted, to elucidate and clarify one of several subjects which were matters of doubt, namely, the question of the peopling of ancient Egypt from the point of view of its ethnic origin and of its anthropological relationships. What was needed, therefore, was to compare the alternative theories, to assess the scientific arguments on which they were based, and to take stock of the situation, drawing attention, where appropriate, to any gaps. He emphasized that the terms negro, negroid, black, had, in any case, been used hitherto; that they appeared in all scientific studies, as also did the word 'Hamitic' or 'Chamitic', even though doubts had been expressed on their validity in the course of the current symposium; he also stated that the authors of the *General History of Africa* would make use of those words, to which readers were already accustomed. Whatever general opinion one might have, it remained true that these words, as used in both scholarly and popular works, were not devoid of meaning and were inseparable from value judgements, whether implicit or otherwise. He corroborated a statement made by one expert with reference to Unesco's publications on racial problems. Unesco had not repudiated the idea of race; the Organization had drawn up a special programme to study race relations and had stepped up its efforts to combat racial discrimination. There had been several publications on this important problem. It was therefore out of the question for the symposium, in studying problems bearing on the peopling of ancient Egypt, to reject out of hand, and without proposing any new system, the generally accepted classification of peoples as white, yellow and black — a typology which had traditionally been used by Egyptologists to classify the people of Egypt. Furthermore, if the traditional vocabulary currently used by historians needed revision, it should not be revised merely for the history of Africa but for the entire world; if the symposium considered the matter important, it could be submitted for consideration at the international level to the historians' association. Pending the introduction of new terms, the terms black, negro, negroid and Hamitic, which were currently used, should be more clearly defined.

The debate on this point was opened by Professor Vercoutter. He recalled that the problem had been raised by the work of Junker, when he used the word 'negro' to denote the type of representations which appeared under the eighteenth dynasty, and was subsequently caricatured by the Egyptians. Junker used the word negro primarily in reference to West Africa, emphasizing both the pigmentation and certain facial characteristics.

Professor Vercoutter was inclined to think that, in place of this old point of view, more specific criteria were essential in order to provide a scientific definition of the black race; in particular, he mentioned a blood criterion, the question of the precise significance of the degree of skin pigmentation and whether, for example, the Nubians should be considered as negroes.

Various attitudes emerged with regard to these questions. Several participants hoped that the word 'race', which on a number of recent occasions had aroused strong feelings, would be used with circumspection. Professor Obenga replied that the notion of race was recognized as valid by scientific research and that the study of races did not necessarily involve racialism.

The discussion brought out the difficulty of giving a scientific content to the terms under review. Even more, perhaps, it brought out the fact that more than one expert was reluctant, for highly respectable reasons, to use those terms, which could rightly be regarded as having dangerous or pejorative implications. Some experts pointed out, moreover, that the basic answers on this issue could not be expected to come from historians and archaeologists, but only from specialists in physical anthropology.

Professor Säve-Söderbergh was supported by a considerable number of the participants when he expressed the hope that racial terminology would be studied by specialists on modern physical anthropology. A strict scientific definition would be of use with regard not only to Africa but also, and perhaps more so, to Asia; similarly, the concepts of mixed population, composite population and groups of populations needed sharper definition. Unesco already had before it a request to this effect in connection with research being carried out in Nubia.

Mr Glélé said that if the criteria for classifying a person as black, white or yellow were so debatable, and if the concepts which had been discussed were so ill-defined and perhaps so subjective or inseparable from habitual patterns of thought, this should be frankly stated and a revision should be made of the entire terminology of world history in the light of new scientific criteria, so that the vocabulary should be the same for every one and that words should have the same connotations, thus avoiding misconceptions and being conducive to understanding and agreement.

Professors Diop and Obenga were ill-advised, however, to refer to the series of criteria established by anthropologists to characterize the negro: black skin, facial prognathism, crinkly hair, flat nose (the facial and nasal indicators being very arbitrarily selected by different anthropologists) negritic bone structure (ratio between upper and lower limbs). According to Montel, the negro had a flat and 'horizontal' face. Professor Abu Bakr observed that, if that were the case, the Egyptians could certainly not be considered as negroes.

Professor Diop went on to specify that cranial measurements had never provided any statistical basis for specifying that a particular brain size was characteristic of one race or another.

He considered that there were two black races, one with smooth hair and the other with crinkly hair and, if the skin colour was black, it was unlikely that the other fundamental characteristics which he had previously enumerated would not be found. Lastly, whereas the blood-group $A_2$ was characteristic of white people, black people tended to have Group B, or, in a more limited number of cases, Group C.

Professor Shinnie replied that the American specialists whom he had consulted while preparing for the symposium had told him that skeletal studies had some importance but that they did not in themselves provide a basis for determining race, and that the criteria regarded as adequate by Professor Diop were, rightly or wrongly, no longer considered to be so by American specialists.

Professor Obenga considered that there were two groups within a single black race, one with smooth hair and the other crinkly hair. Professor Obenga reverted to the general question which was before the symposium: if the notion of race was accepted as valid and if the notion of a black race was not rejected, what was to be said of the relationship between this race and the ancient Egyptians?

Professor Diop considered that the findings of the anthropological inquiry already provided an adequate basis on which to draw conclusions. Negroid Grimaldian man appeared about − 32 000, Crô-Magnon man, the prototype of the white race, about − 20 000, Chancelade man, the prototype of the yellow race, in the Magdalenian period, about −15 000. The Semitic races were a social phenomenon characteristic of an urban environment and were a cross between black and white races.

He was, therefore, in no doubt: the first inhabitants of the Nile valley belonged to the black race, as defined by the research findings currently accepted by specialists in anthropology and prehistory. Professor Diop considered that only psychological and educational factors prevented the truth of this from being accepted.

As the assumption behind the research being carried out in Nubia was favourable to a universalistic view, the research findings were of little use in the current discussion. Professor Diop was not in favour of setting up commissions to verify patent facts which, at the present time, simply needed formal recognition: in his view, all the information currently available, even that which derived from the superficial studies made in the nineteenth century, supported the theory that, in the most ancient times, the Egyptians were black-skinned and that they remained so until Egypt ultimately lost its independence. In response to the various questions put to him, Professor Diop stated that the samples already provided by archaeology were adequate to support his argument. He was unable to accept Professor Vercoutter's proposal that anthropological documentation antedating about 1939 should be regarded as of dubious reliability owing to its lack of scientific rigour.

Professor Diop's forceful affirmation was criticized by many participants.

The main criticism was voiced by Professor Sauneron, who observed that the total number of people who had occupied the Nile valley between the beginning of historical times and the present day could reasonably be estimated at several hundred million individuals. A few hundred sites had been excavated and some 2000 bodies studied; in view of the sparseness of the data thus obtained, it was totally unrealistic to infer from them such ambitious general conclusions. As the available samples gave nothing like a complete picture, it was advisable to wait until a rigorous and sufficiently comprehensive inquiry into general features had provided universally acceptable evidence.

## (4) The validity of the iconographic inquiry

In this field also there were two opposing theories. Professor Diop considered that, as the Egyptians were black, their painted iconography, which, incidentally, he had not cited in support of his argument, could represent only black people. Professor Vercoutter, who was supported by Professors Ghallab and Leclant, considered that Egyptian iconography, from the eighteenth dynasty onwards, showed characteristic representations of black people who had not previously been depicted; these representations meant, therefore, that at least from that dynasty onwards the Egyptians had been in contact with peoples who were considered ethnically distinct from them.

Professor Diop remarked that, in the course of his introductory statement, he had submitted a series of representations drawn exclusively from sculpture. He regarded all these as representing black people or as showing features characteristic of black societies. He asked for specific criticisms of these records and invited participants to produce comparable representations of whites in dignified or commanding postures dating from early Pharaonic times. Various participants replied that there had never been any question of discovering in Egypt representations comparable to those of Greek statuary, for example. Professor Vercoutter said that numerous representations could be produced in which human beings were painted red rather than black, but that Professor Diop would refuse to recognize these as non-black. Professor El Nadury did not deny that there were black elements in the population of Egypt during the Old Kingdom but said that it seemed hardly likely that the entire population was black.

Professor Vercoutter stated that the photographic reproduction of Pharaoh Narmer was considerably enlarged, that the features were probably distorted, and that to regard the person represented as black involved a subjective assessment. This was also the opinion of Professor Säve-Söderbergh, who said that the photograph could just as well be interpreted as a picture of a Laplander.

Professor Vercoutter did not dispute that there might have been black elements in Egypt throughout history, and he himself adduced a number of further examples of their being represented graphically. He took issue with the facts as presented, however, on two counts: they had been drawn indiscriminately from the whole Pharaonic period, without clear references; and the selection had been made to support a theory. On this score, Professor Diop replied that he had made a point of submitting only carved objects or scenes in order to avoid the likelihood of discussion on the significance of colours, but that he had been obliged to use the material available to him at Dakar. The list was comprehensive; it extended from the Old Kingdom to the end of the Pharaonic period. The evidence did, indeed, support a theory and any contrary theory must of necessity be supported by iconographic representations of 'non-black' Egyptians.

During the lengthy discussion on colours, Professors Vercoutter, Sauneron and Säve-Söderbergh, on the one hand, and Professor Diop on the other, were again in disagreement. During the discussion, nothing was conceded by either side. The only apparent point of agreement was that the matter warranted further study, in particular with the help of specialized laboratories.

Professor Vercoutter conceded that there were representations of black people in Egyptian sculpture during the Old Kingdom, and he gave supporting examples. But he did not consider that they were representative of the Egyptian population as a whole, which was, in any case, also represented by contemporary sculptures showing quite different features.

Professor Vercoutter wondered why the Egyptians, if they did regard themselves as black, rarely, if ever, used carbon black in their representations of themselves but used a red colour instead. Professor Diop considered that this red colour was indicative of the black Egyptian race and that the yellow colouring of the womenfolk illustrated the fact, to which attention had been drawn by American anthropologists, that women, in a number of racial groups studied, were, as a rule, of a paler hue than the men.

## (5) Linguistic analyses

This item, in contrast to those previously discussed, revealed a large measure of agreement among the participants. The outline report by Professor Diop and the report by Professor Obenga were regarded as being very constructive.

Discussion took place on two levels.

In response to Professor Diop's statement that Egyptian was not a Semitic language, Professor Abdalla observed that the opposite opinion had often been expressed.

A grammatical and semantic debate took place between Professor Diop on the radical which he reads *KMT*, derives from *KM* 'black' and considers to be a collective noun meaning 'blacks, i.e. negroes' and Professor Abdelgadir M. Abdallah who adopts the accepted reading of it as *KMTYW* and translation as 'Egyptians', the plural of *KMTY* 'Egyptian', the *nisba*-form from *KMT* 'black land, i.e. Egypt'. The latter reading and translation were affirmed by Professor Sauneron.

Turning to wider issues, Professor Sauneron drew attention to the interest of the method suggested by Professor Obenga following Professor Diop. Egyptian remained a stable language for a period of at least 4500 years. Egypt was situated at the point of convergence of outside influence and it was to be expected that borrowings had been made from foreign languages; but the Semitic roots numbered only a few hundred as compared with a total of several thousand words. The Egyptian language could not be isolated from its

African context and its origin could not be fully explained in terms of Semitic; it was thus quite normal to expect to find related languages in Africa.

However, a rigorous methodical approach required the difficult problem of the 5000-year gap to be faced: this was the period separating ancient Egyptian from present-day African languages.

Professor Obenga drew attention to the fact that a language which was not fixed by a written form and which developed normally might retain certain ancient forms; he had cited examples of this in the communication he had given on the first day of the symposium.

Professor Sauneron noted that the method which had been used was of considerable interest, since it could not be purely fortuitous that there was a similarity between the third person singular suffixed pronouns in ancient Egyptian and in Wolof; he hoped that an attempt would be made to reconstitute a palaeo-African language, using present-day languages as a starting point. This would facilitate comparison with ancient Egyptian. Professor Obenga considered this method to be acceptable. Professor Diop thought it essential to derive a research method from linguistic comparisons, and he provided a specific example of what he had in mind. He regarded the Dinka, Nuer and Shilluk groups and their respective languages, on the one hand, and Wolof, on the other, as being ethnically and, to a lesser extent, linguistically related. Senegalese proper names occurred in the groups in question at clan level. More specifically, Professor Diop believed that he had found among the Kaw-Kaw, in the Nubian hills, the clearest link between ancient Egyptian and Wolof.

Professor Vercoutter pointed out, as a matter of interest, that in the tomb of Sebek-Hotep there were representations of three Nilotes who were indubitably ancestors of the Dinka or the Nuer.

## (6) Development of an interdisciplinary and pluridisciplinary methodology

There was complete agreement on this point as to the necessity of studying in as much detail as possible all the zones bordering on the Nile valley which were likely to provide fresh information on the question submitted to the symposium.

Professor Vercoutter considered it necessary to give due weight to the palaeo-ecology of the Delta and to the vast region which Professor Balout had termed the African Fertile Crescent.

Professor Cheikh Anta Diop advocated tracing the paths taken by peoples who migrated westwards from Darfur, reaching the Atlantic seaboard by separate routes, to the south along the Zaïre valley and to the north towards Senegal, on either side of the Yoruba. He also pointed out how worthwhile it might be to study Egypt's relations with the rest of Africa in greater detail than hitherto, and he mentioned the discovery, in the province of Shaba, of a statuette of Osiris dating from the seventh century before our era.

Similarly, a general study might be made of the working hypothesis that the major events which affected the Nile valley, such as the sacking of Thebes by the Syrians; or the Persian invasion of −525, had far-reaching repercussions on the African continent as a whole.

# D   General conclusion

It is to be expected that the overall results of the symposium will be very differently assessed by the various participants.

Although the preparatory working paper sent out by Unesco gave particulars of what was desired, not all participants had prepared communications comparable with the painstakingly researched contributions of Professors Cheikh Anta Diop and Obenga. There was consequently a real lack of balance in the discussions.

Nevertheless, for a number of reasons, the discussions were very constructive.

1 In many cases, they clearly showed the importance of exchanging new scientific information.

2 They brought home to almost all the participants the shortcomings of the methodological criteria which had hitherto been used in research.

3 They drew attention to examples of new methodological approaches on the basis of which the question before the symposium could be studied in a more scientific manner.

4 This first meeting should, in any case, be regarded as providing a basis for further international and interdisciplinary discussions, and as a starting point for further researches which were clearly shown to be necessary. The large number of recommendations is a reflection of the desire of the symposium to suggest a future programme of research.

5 Lastly, the symposium enabled specialists who had never previously had the opportunity of comparing and contrasting their points of view to discover other approaches to problems, other sources of information and other lines of research than those to which they were accustomed. From this point of view also, the symposium undeniably proved constructive.

# E    Recommendations

The symposium draws the attention of Unesco and of other competent bodies to the following recommendations.

## (1) Physical anthropology

It is desirable:

(i) that an international inquiry be organized by Unesco, either by consulting universities in a sufficient number of countries, or by consulting individual experts of international repute, or alternatively by convening a symposium, with a view to establishing very precise standards on the strictest possible scientific principles for defining races and for identifying the racial type of exhumed skeletons;

(ii) that the collaboration of the medical services of several Unesco member states be sought for the purpose of carrying out statistical observations during post-mortem examinations on the osteological characteristics of skeletons;

(iii) that a re-examination be made of human remains which are already in the possession of museums throughout the world, and that a rapid study be made of remains discovered during recent excavations in Egypt, in particular in the Delta, with a view to adding to the available information;

(iv) that the Egyptian authorities do everything in their power to facilitate the necessary study of examinable vestiges of skin, and that these authorities agree to set up a department specializing in physical anthropology.

## (2) Study of migrations

It is desirable that the following studies be undertaken:

(i) a systematic archaeological study of the earliest periods during which the Delta was inhabited. This operation might be preceded by the analysis of a core sample taken from the soil of the Delta. The study and the dating of this geological core sample could be carried out simultaneously in Cairo and in Dakar;

(ii) a comparable inquiry in the regions of the Sahara near to Egypt and in the oases. This inquiry should comprise the simultaneous study of rock drawings and paintings and of all available archaeological material. Here again, geological samples might be analysed and dated at the same time;

(iii) a survey in the valley itself, comparable to that which has been carried out in northern Nubia, which would be concerned with non-Pharaonic tombs, with the study of ancient material cultures and, in general, with the prehistory of the valley as a whole;

(iv) an inquiry on palaeo-African vestiges in Egyptian iconography and their historical significance. The cases of the baboon and of the leopard ('panther') skin have already been cited by the symposium. It would undoubtedly be possible to discover others.

## (3) Linguistics

The symposium recommends that a linguistic study be made without delay on the African languages which are in imminent danger of disappearing: Kaw-Kaw has been suggested as a very significant case in point.

At the same time, the co-operation of specialists in comparative linguistics should be enlisted at international level in order to establish all possible correlations between African languages and ancient Egyptian.

## (4) Interdisciplinary and pluridisciplinary methodology

The symposium earnestly hopes that:

(i) interdisciplinary regional studies may be undertaken in several regions, with the following priorities:

Darfur

the region between the Nile and the Red Sea

the eastern fringe of the Sahara

the Nile region south of the tenth parallel

the Nile valley between the Second and Sixth Cataracts.

(ii) an interdisciplinary inquiry be made as a matter of urgency on the Kaw-Kaw who are in imminent danger of extinction.

# II   Deciphering of the Meroitic script

(1) A preliminary report had been prepared by Professor J. Leclant at the request of Unesco.[13]

(*a*) The Meroitic language, which was used by the cultures of Napata and Meroe, was still not understood, although the script had already been deciphered.

The historical account of the studies made on Meroitic showed how systematic research on the inscriptions, which had gradually been collected in a haphazard way in the course of excavations, had been started only in recent years. Archaeological research was likely to bring to light more inscriptions in the future; none had so far been discovered in the region between the Second and Fourth Cataracts: the same was true of the travel routes in the direction of the Red Sea, the great valleys of the West, Kordofan and Darfur.

It was particularly important to persevere with archaeological work as it could reasonably be hoped that a bilingual inscription might one day be discovered.

(*b*) The results were published in full in the *Meroitic Newsletters*, thirteen issues of which had so far appeared, which made it possible rapidly to publicize findings when they were sometimes still only tentative. Regular meetings of specialists had taken place – at Khartoum in December 1970, in East Berlin in September 1971, and in Paris in June

13. See this preliminary report in Annex IV of the Final Report of the symposium (1974).

1972 and again in July 1973; the results of the last-mentioned meeting were set out in Information Note No. 34 issued by the International Scientific Committee for the Drafting of a General History of Africa, Unesco.

Computer processes had also been used for analysing the Meroitic language for a number of years. As a result, there had been considerable and rapid progress in this field.

By compiling lists of *stichs*, it had been possible to make a start on analysing the structure of the language. The index of words recorded now comprised 13 405 units and a means had been found of putting questions to the machine.

On this basis, an effort had been made, by using words of which the meaning was known or could be inferred, to compare the language with Egyptian or Nubian.

(*c*) Professor Leclant ended his presentation with an account of the lines of research now being followed:

Professor Hintze was working on structures;
Professor Schaenkel was working on improving the data to be recorded by the computer;
Professor Abdelgadir M. Abdalla was going forward with an inquiry about which he was to speak briefly; it had achieved results which corroborated the findings of the international team.

Future efforts would include making a comparison between Meroitic and other African languages and discovering its place among a group of African languages, in particular in relation to Nubian; other comparisons would be made with the languages spoken in areas bordering on the Ethiopian region. Lastly, it would be desirable to compare Meroitic with African languages as a whole.

# Discussion

(2) Professor Abdalla confirmed that he endorsed the system adopted for transcribing Meroitic and the method which had been devised for recording the texts. He drew attention to the gaps in our knowledge: almost complete ignorance of the system of pronouns, of the use of demonstrative pronouns, of the nature of prefixes and suffixes. It was essential to know with what other languages Meroitic was linked.

Professor Abdalla was in favour of carrying out a kind of dissection of the language, so as to study its components. He drew attention to the mobility of the elements forming personal names in which these elements had social implications: the same mobile elements recurred in the names of several members of a given family; the names of certain children comprised elements taken from the names of their mother and father; certain names were titles; others contained place-names.

(3) Professor Shinnie said that there were three possible methods of approach: the discovery of a bilingual text; the internal analysis of the structure of the language; and comparison with other African languages.

Direct comparison between the two principal non-Arabic languages of northern Sudan and of the M Group had proved fruitless: Meroitic might prove to be a help in making this comparison.

(4) Professor Kakosy, who was present as an observer, laid stress on the necessity of studying documentary sources. He stated that there were in Budapest fragments of offering tables which came from a site close to Abu Simbel; he proposed to include these fragments forthwith in the Repertory of Meroitic Epigraphy.

(5) Professor Cheikh Anta Diop was very pleased with the progress achieved. Pending the possible future discovery of a bilingual text, he suggested that use should be made of the computer-based methods which had made possible the partial deciphering of the Maya

hieroglyphs by the Leningrad team headed by Professor Knorossov. Most scripts had been deciphered with the help of bilingual or multilingual texts. The correct procedure in the case of Meroitic would be to combine multilingualism and the potentialities of the computer in the following manner:

- (*a*) Purely as a methodological procedure, a relationship should be postulated between Meroitic and negro-African languages, thus creating a multilingual situation.
- (*b*) As, at the present time, 22 000 Meroitic words could be read with some degree of certainty, a 500-word basic vocabulary should be drawn up on punched cards for each of 100 African languages carefully selected by a suitable group of linguists. The words selected might be those indicating, for example, the parts of the body, terms of kingship, religious terminology, terms relating to material culture, and so on.
- (*c*) The computer should be programmed to recognize, for example, three identical consonants, two identical consonants, etc.
- (*d*) On the basis of the results obtained, a comparison should be made of the structures of the languages thus juxtaposed.

This method was more rational than the haphazard comparison of linguistic structures, because too little was as yet known about the grammar of Meroitic. The method was more efficient than awaiting the result of a non-comparative study of the internal structure of Meroitic.

Professor Leclant endorsed this investigatory and operational procedure as being likely to provide very valuable information. He thought that it would be useful not only to make a concordance of features actually present but also of features not present (the absence of certain structures or certain sequences).

Mr Glélé asked to what extent the methods used for deciphering other languages could also serve to clear up the mystery surrounding the Meroitic language. He stated that Professor Knorossov and Professor Piotrovski had been invited to the meeting on the same basis as Professor Holthoer and Professor Hintze in order to provide the required information.

Professor Leclant said that a very wide-ranging study of this matter had been made at meetings held in Paris and London during the summer of 1973. The work both on the Mohenjodaro script and on Maya had not yet got beyond the stage of working hypotheses.

Professor Diop hoped, however, that the idea of using comparative methods side by side with the study of structures would not be abandoned. His proposal was approved by Professor Sauneron, who took the opportunity of emphasizing the importance of the work which had already been done by the Meroitic Studies Group.

Subsequent discussion bore more especially on the languages of the Sudan; Professor Säve-Söderbergh emphasized that, in any case, it was important that they be studied, since quite apart from the comparison with Meroitic, a knowledge of these languages would assist in advancing African linguistics. Professor Säve-Söderbergh at this stage submitted the outline of a recommendation to this effect. He also emphasized that it was possible, even with quite small funds, to set up an efficient secretariat and to accelerate the collection of material, its processing by computer and the redistribution of information.

Lastly, there was discussion of the content of the recommendation. Professor Diop hoped that the excellent work done by the Meroitic Studies Group would be continued with full international collaboration, that a systematic compilation of the vocabulary would be made in the Sudan and that an identical compilation would be carried out in other regions of Africa with the collaboration of Professor Obenga. Professor Sauneron accepted these proposals in their entirety. As it was uncertain what bearing this work would ultimately prove to have on the deciphering of Meroitic, he hoped that the study of African languages would be developed independently, for its own sake, even if it were partly incorporated in the overall project. It was likely to be very protracted and it was essential that a thoroughly sound method should be established from the outset, after strict critical appraisal. Professor Obenga endorsed this idea and suggested that an inventory should be made of the grammatical features of Meroitic which were currently known. Professor Leclant considered that this proposal could be put into effect immediately. Professor Habachi hoped that the need for an archaeological inquiry would not be neglected.

In response to a methodological proposal made by Professor Obenga, Mr Glélé stated that the methods to be adopted would be decided when the membership of the international team responsible was finalized. He explained that Unesco was supporting the studies being carried out in Khartoum with regard to Sudanese languages and was in a position to provide study grants in accordance with its normal procedures. Unesco was financing and directing a programme on African linguistics and had just adopted a ten-year plan for this purpose.

# Recommendations

(1) (a) The meeting expresses its satisfaction for the work accomplished by the Meroitic Study Group in Paris in collaboration with scholars of many other countries, and wishes to express its opinion that the work is well grounded and promises good results.

(b) The meeting has unanimously decided to suggest the following measures to further the project:

    (i) the speeding up of the computer processes by making available additional funds, and circulating the information, in revised and improved form, to the main centres of Meroitic studies;

    (ii) to produce lists and where possible, of Meroitic personal names, place names and titles, and to classify linguistic structures, and to pursue collaboration with specialists in African linguistics;

    (iii) to establish and publish a complete corpus of all Meroitic texts with bibliography, photographs, facsimiles and transcriptions on the basis of the existing files (Répertoire d'Epigraphie Méroitique);

    (iv) to produce a complete Meroitic vocabulary.

(c) Since the results of the project so far obtained are scientifically sound and promise a successful development, and since the greater expense of the project as a whole has already been met with funds from various sources, this meeting now considers it to be imperative to assure the continuation and completion of the project by providing funds for the following purposes:

    (i) costs of secretariat and personnel for the documentation and scientific publication of the material;

    (ii) costs of inquiries in collections and museums;

    (iii) travel expenses of specialists;

    (iv) costs of card punching and computer time.

(2) The next step of research would be comparative structural and lexicographical studies of African languages, in the first place the languages of the Sudan and the border regions of Ethiopia, some of which are now dying out. This would best be done by giving Sudanese students at the University of Khartoum a linguistic training, preferably such students who have these languages as their mother tongue.

Such training would also be of value for many other purposes. Such a project, which would complement the valuable work already under way in the Sudan, would require to be negotiated with the University of Khartoum, and funds would be required for the necessary scholarships.

(3) In addition a wider linguistic survey of all African languages with the purpose of collecting key words was desirable. Such a survey should be made in collaboration with the Meroitic Study Group and be directed by specialists chosen by Unesco in collaboration with the International Scientific Committee for the General History of Africa. The choice should be limited to about 500 words of selected categories from some 100 languages.

This collection, when computerized, would be a valuable tool not only for the deciphering of the Meroitic language but for many other linguistic problems of modern Africa.

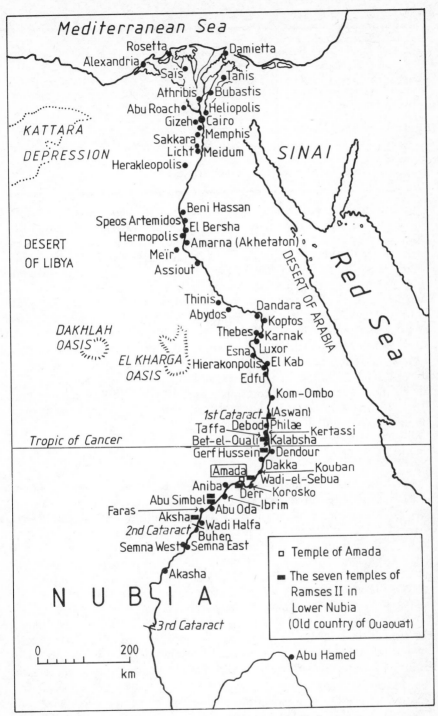

FIG. 2.1 *The Nile from the Third Cataract to the Mediterranean*

83

# Pharaonic Egypt

## A. ABU BAKR

The end of the glacial period in Europe brought major climatic changes to the lands south of the Mediterranean. The decrease in rain caused the nomadic peoples of Saharan Africa to immigrate to the Nile valley in search of a permanent water supply. The first actual settlement of the Nile valley may thus have begun in early Neolithic times (about −7000). The Egyptians then entered on a pastoral and agricultural life. While perfecting their stone tools and weapons, they also invented or adopted pottery which has greatly helped us to reconstruct a complete schedule of the different cultures of Egypt during the Neolithic period.[1]

Shortly before the dawn of history, the Egyptians learned the use of metals[2] in what is called the Chalcolithic (or Cuprolithic) period, in which metal gradually supplanted flint. Gold and copper also made their first appearance, though bronze was not used until the Middle Kingdom and the use of iron apparently did not become widespread until the closing period of Pharaonic history.

## Prehistory

Egypt, situated in the north-eastern corner of Africa, is a small country compared to the huge continent of which it forms a part. Yet it has produced one of the world's greatest civilizations. Nature herself divided the country into two different parts: the narrow stretches of fertile land adjoining the river from Aswan to the region of modern Cairo, which we call Upper Egypt, and the broad triangle formed in the course of millennia from the silt deposits of the river flowing north into the Mediterranean, which we call Lower Egypt or the Delta.

The first settlers did not find life easy and there must have been fierce competition among the different human groups to secure the land along the edge of the Nile and in the relatively restricted area of the Delta. Only the strongest and most able could have survived. These people, coming from the west and east as well as from the south, were doubtless of

1. See Unesco, *A General History of Africa*, Vol. I, ch. 25, 'Prehistory of the Nile valley'.
2. ibid., ch. 28, 'The invention and spreading use of metals and the development of social systems up to the fifth century before our era'.

different somatic groups. It is not surprising that the different natural obstacles, together with the diversity of origin, should at first have separated from one another the groups which settled in different areas along the valley. In these groups, we can see the origin of the nomes, or territorial divisions, which formed the basis of the political structure of Egypt in historical times. However, the Nile provided an easy means of communication between the different localities along its banks and facilitated the growth of the unity of language and culture which ultimately overshadowed the particular characteristics of each group.

The great achievement of the prehistoric period was control of the land (see Introduction). Settling at first on stony outcrops above the alluvial plain, or on the higher ground along the edge of the desert, the early Egyptians managed to clear the ground in their immediate neighbourhood for cultivation, drain the swamps and build dykes against the incursions of flood water. Gradually the benefit of using canals for irrigation was learned. Such work required organized effort on a large scale and this led to the growth of a local political structure within each district.

Some memory of the growth of political unity in Egypt may perhaps be deduced from some of the fragments of early literary evidence.[3] This suggests that in the dim and distant past, the nomes of the Delta had apparently formed themselves into coalitions. The western nomes of this region were traditionally united under the god Horus, while those of the eastern part of the Delta were joined under the god Andjty, Lord of Djedu, who was later assimilated by Osiris. The western nomes, it has been suggested, conquered those of the east and formed a united kingdom in northern Egypt, so that the worship of Horus as the chief god prevailed throughout the Delta, spreading gradually to Upper Egypt to overwhelm Seth, the chief god of an Upper Egyptian coalition.[4]

## Archaic period (−3200 to −2900)

The first event of historical importance known to us is the union of these two prehistoric kingdoms, or rather the subjugation of Lower Egypt by the Upper Egyptian ruler whom tradition designated as Menes while archaeological sources seem to call him Narmer. He begins the first of the thirty dynasties or ruling families into which the Egyptian historian Manetho (−280) divided the long line of rulers down to the time of Alexander the Great. The family of Menes resided at Thinis in Upper Egypt, the foremost city of the district which embraced the sacred town of Abydos. It was near Abydos, with its sanctuary of the god Osiris, that Petrie excavated the huge tombs of the kings of the first two dynasties. Certainly it was the southern kingdom which gained dominance over the

3. On the Pyramid Texts, see the English translation by R. O. Faulkner, 1969.
4. The basic reference for this now disputed theory is K. Sethe.

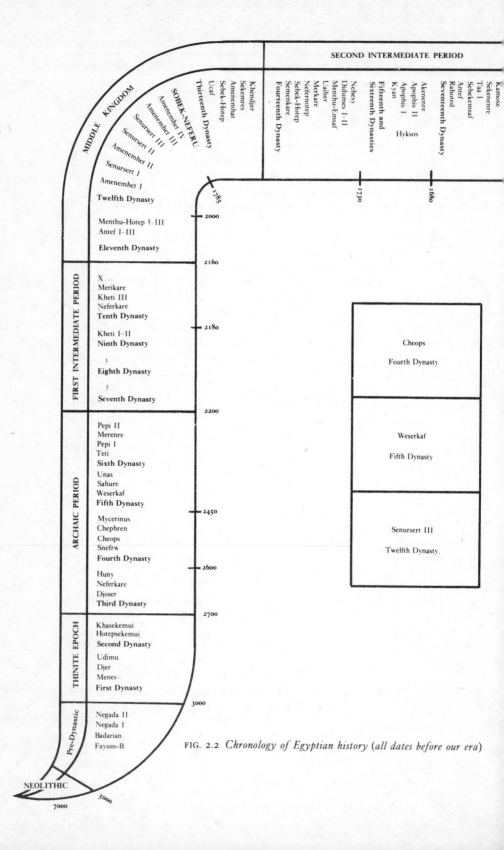

**SECOND INTERMEDIATE PERIOD**

Kamose
Sekenenre
Taa I
Sebekemsaf
Antef
Rahotel
Seventeenth Dynasty

Akenenre
Apophis II
Apophis I
K'an
    Hyksos

Nehesy
Didumes I–II
Menthu-Emsaf
Uaiber
Merkare
Nefernotep
Neferhotep
Sebek-Hotep
Semenkare
Fourteenth Dynasty

1730

1680

Khendjer
Sekemres
Amenemhat
Sebek-Hotep
Thirteenth Dynasty

Uaf

1785

**SOBEK-NEFERU**
Amenemhet IV
Amenemhet III
Senursert III
Senursert II
Amenemhet II
Senursert I
Amenemhet I
**Twelfth Dynasty**

**MIDDLE KINGDOM**

2000
Menthu-Hotep I–III
Antef I–III
**Eleventh Dynasty**

2160

**FIRST INTERMEDIATE PERIOD**

X...
Merikare
Kheti III
Neferkare
**Tenth Dynasty**

2180
Kheti I–II
**Ninth Dynasty**

?

**Eighth Dynasty**

?

**Seventh Dynasty**

2200

**ARCHAIC PERIOD**

Pepi II
Merenre
Pepi I
Teti
**Sixth Dynasty**
Unas
Sahure
Weserkaf
**Fifth Dynasty**

Mycerinus
Chephren
Cheops
Snefrw
**Fourth Dynasty**

2450

2600
Huny
Neferkare
Djoser
**Third Dynasty**

2700

**THINITE EPOCH**

Khasekemui
Hotepsekemui
**Second Dynasty**
Udimu
Djer
Menes
**First Dynasty**

3000

**Pre-Dynastic**
Negada II
Negada I
Badarian
Fayum-B

**NEOLITHIC**

7000       5000

Cheops

Fourth Dynasty

Weserkaf

Fifth Dynasty

Senursert III

Twelfth Dynasty

FIG. 2.2 *Chronology of Egyptian history (all dates before our era)*

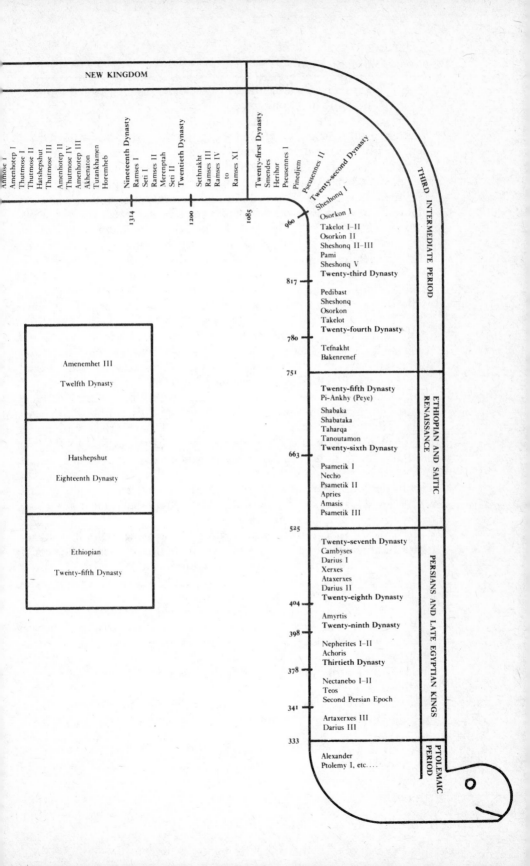

NEW KINGDOM

Ahmose I
Amenhotep I
Thutmose I
Thutmose II
Hatshepshut
Thutmose III
Amenhotep II
Thutmose IV
Amenhotep III
Akhenaton
Tutankhamen
Horemheb

Nineteenth Dynasty
Ramses I
Seti I
Ramses II
Merenptah
Seti II
Twentieth Dynasty

Sethnakht
Ramses III
Ramses IV
to
Ramses XI

Twenty-first Dynasty
Smendes
Herihor
Pseusennes I
Pinedjem
Pseusennes II
Twenty-second Dynasty

1314

1200

1085

THIRD INTERMEDIATE PERIOD

960
Sheshonq I
Osorkon I
Takelot I–II
Osorkon II
Sheshonq II–III
Pami
Sheshonq V
Twenty-third Dynasty

817
Pedibast
Sheshonq
Osorkon
Takelot
Twenty-fourth Dynasty

780
Tefnakht
Bakenrenef

751
Twenty-fifth Dynasty
Pi-Ankhy (Peye)
Shabaka
Shabataka
Taharqa
Tanoutamon
Twenty-sixth Dynasty

663
Psametik I
Necho
Psametik II
Apries
Amasis
Psametik III

ETHIOPIAN AND SAITIC RENAISSANCE

525
Twenty-seventh Dynasty
Cambyses
Darius I
Xerxes
Ataxerxes
Darius II
Twenty-eighth Dynasty

404
Amyrtis
Twenty-ninth Dynasty

398
Nepherites I–II
Achoris
Thirtieth Dynasty

378
Nectanebo I–II
Teos
Second Persian Epoch

341
Artaxerxes III
Darius III

PERSIANS AND LATE EGYPTIAN KINGS

333
Alexander
Ptolemy I, etc. . . .

PTOLEMAIC PERIOD

Amenemhet III

Twelfth Dynasty

Hatshepshut

Eighteenth Dynasty

Ethiopian

Twenty-fifth Dynasty

whole country and soon after their first victory Narmer set up a capital at Memphis, near the junction of the two lands.[5]

The kings of the first two dynasties of the archaic period (see Chapter 1) still remain rather nebulous figures to us, nor can we learn much more concerning the events of their individual reigns. Yet without doubt this period was one of hard work for consolidation. During the 300 years after the first dynasty the culture of the later years of the predynastic period continued, but during the third and fourth dynasties political unity was achieved and the new state was stable enough to express itself in a distinctively Egyptian way. This took the form of a new dogma by which the Egyptian king was regarded as other than human, as a god, in fact, reigning over humans. The dogma of the divinity of the Pharaoh[6] may have been a concept worked out during the early dynasties to consolidate a single rule over the two lands. From the third dynasty onwards one would be justified in saying that the head of the state was not an Upper Egyptian nor a Lower Egyptian, but a god.

In the full theory of kingship, the Pharaoh was the state and was responsible for every activity carried out in the country (see Chapter 3). Moreover, he was high priest of all the gods and served them in every temple every day. Obviously it was not possible for him to do, in practice, all that he was supposed to do. It was necessary for him to have deputies to carry out his divine word: cabinet ministers, officials in the provinces, generals in the army and priests in the temples. True, his theoretical power was absolute. Yet, in effect, he was not free to carry out his will. He was the embodiment of beliefs and practices which had long been in existence and which were progressively elaborated with the passage of years. The lives of the kings were actually so codified that they could not even take a walk or a bath except according to a pattern laid down for them, regulated by ceremonies and obligations.

Yet beneath their elaborate crowns the Pharaohs naturally had human hearts and human minds reacting to love and hate, ambition and mistrust, anger and desire. Art and literature set up an ideal standard to depict a stylized god king of Egypt from the beginning of the history of ancient Egypt to the end, and it is remarkable that we nevertheless come to know individual kings as distinct personalities in their own right.

We all know the great interest that ancient nations took in Egyptian beliefs, and how those that had lost faith in the credence of their forefathers turned to the wise men of Egypt. A certain reverence for the wisdom of Egypt survived until the disappearance of polytheistic religions.

Like other contemporary peoples, the Egyptians of the Neolithic age saw their gods in their natural surroundings, believing that the earth and heaven

5. See W. C. Hayes, 1965; J. L. de Cénival.
6. On the actual conception of the divinity of the Pharaoh, consult G. Posener, 1960.

were filled by countless spirits. These spirits, they believed, made their earthly abode in animals or plants, or in any object remarkable for its size or form. Subsequently, however, they no longer considered the animals or objects themselves as gods, for they progressively came to believe rather that these were the visible manifestation or seat of an abstract divine force. The animal or object selected as the manifestation of a god could be either a friendly and useful beast such as the cow, the ram, the dog or the cat, or a savage and awe-inspiring creature such as the hippopotamus, the crocodile or the cobra. In each case the Egyptian would pay homage and make sacrifices to one single specimen on earth. He worshipped the cow, yet he slaughtered it to supply himself with meat. He also worshipped the crocodile yet he would kill it to defend himself.

These were local gods and each in his own district was the supreme god and the undisputed master of the territory, with one exception. The local god of a town in which the chief of a group rose to power took precedence. If the chief ascended the throne and succeeded in uniting the southern and the northern kingdoms, this local god would be promoted to be the state god of the whole land.

Moreover, the first Egyptians saw divine forces present in the sun, the moon, the stars, the sky and the Nile floods. They must have feared these phenomena and felt their influence, for they worshipped them and made powerful gods out of them, namely, the cosmic gods such as Re the sun, Nut the sky, Nun the ocean, Shu the atmosphere, Geb the earth and Hapi the flood.[7]

They were represented in human or in animal form and their worship was not confined to any specific locality. Goddesses, too, played a decisive role in religion and enjoyed widespread reverence. The number, however, could not have exceeded a dozen though some, such as Hathor, Isis, Neith and Bastet, played important roles throughout the whole country. Hathor was usually connected with Horus, Isis with Osiris, Neith was the protective goddess of the prehistoric capital of the Delta, and Bastet (the Cat-goddess) enjoyed great popularity after the second dynasty in the eighteenth nome of Lower Egypt.

Among no other peoples, ancient or modern, has the idea of a life beyond the grave played such a prominent part and so influenced the lives of the believers as among the ancient Egyptians.[8] The belief in the hereafter was no doubt both favoured and influenced by the natural conditions of Egypt where the dryness of the soil and the hot climate resulted in a remarkable preservation of dead bodies. This must have greatly stimulated the conviction in a continuation of life after death.

During the course of history, the Egyptians came to believe that their

7. A detailed systematic account of Egyptian beliefs is to be found in H. Kees, 1941.
8. The amplified basic work on the funerary beliefs of the Egyptians is by H. Kees, 1926; 2nd edn., 1956.

bodies comprised different immortal elements. These were the Ba, represented in the form of a human-headed bird, having the same features as the deceased and possessing human arms. This Ba took over at the death of the individual, and the prayers and food offered by the priest presiding over the funerary ceremonies aided in transforming the dead man into a Ba or soul. The second element was known as the Ka which was a guardian spirit which inhabited each person when he was born. When the god Khnum, the Ram-god of Aswan, the creator of humans, moulded them from the slime, he created two models for each individual, one for his body and the second for his Ka. The Ka exactly resembled the man and remained with him throughout his life, yet it passed before him to the afterworld. It was for the service of the Ka that the Egyptians provided their tombs with that abundance of what we call funerary furniture (a complete duplicate of all the owner possessed in his earthly house). Though the Ka was believed to spend most of the time inside the tomb, he could also leave it. Thus the necropolis was the city of Kas, just as the town was the place of the living. The third important element was the Ib, the heart. This was considered the centre of the emotions and the conscience of the individual. It was the guide of his deeds during his life on earth. The fourth element was the Akh which the Egyptians believed to be a divine or supernatural power only attained after death. They believed that the shining stars in the sky were the Akhs of the deceased. Finally, there was the body itself, the Khat or outer shell, which perished but which could be embalmed to enable it to endure in a suitable form to share with the Ka and the Ba eternal life in the hereafter.

Apart from these ideas of a future life in the tomb and the necropolis, the Egyptians gradually developed a number of other conceptions regarding the hereafter and the destiny which awaited the Ba. Two of these, the Solar and the Osirian theories, became widespread. The deceased Pharaoh, since he was himself divine, was at first believed to reside with the gods and he was identified with both the Sun-god (Horus or Re) and with Osiris. In time, however, the concept was adopted by influential noblemen in the Middle Kingdom, and later on by all Egyptians, regardless of social rank.

This is apparent from the mortuary texts, the earliest preserved versions of which are the so-called Pyramid Texts, written in hieroglyphics on the walls of the burial chambers in the pyramid of King Unias, the last Pharaoh of the fifth dynasty, and in the pyramid of a king of the sixth dynasty. When the Pyramid Texts were appropriated by the local chiefs and petty kings of the First Intermediate Period, and then by the nobles of the Middle Kingdom, many of the spells and rituals were eliminated, altered or interpreted to make them appropriate for individuals without rank. These texts, usually known as the Sarcophagus Texts,[9] were mostly

9. For the 'Sarcophagus Texts', the basic edition of the text alone is by A. de Buck, 1935–61. An English translation of the texts is to be found in R. O. Faulkner, 1974, 1978.

written in cursive hieroglyphic script on the interior surfaces of the rectangular coffins typical of the Middle Kingdom; the body of the spells in black ink, the titles in red. In the New Kingdom most of the spells of the Sarcophagus Texts, in addition to a host of new ones, were written on rolls of papyrus and placed on the mummified bodies of the deceased. These texts, comprising some 200 strophes, are somewhat misleadingly called the Book of the Dead.[10] Actually no such book ever existed; the selection of the strophes written on each papyrus varied according to the size of the roll, the taste of its purchaser, and the judgement of the priestly scribe who wrote it. Between forty and fifty strophes were an average-sized Book of the Dead. In addition to it, the priests of the New Kingdom developed and popularized a number of other, more or less related funerary books written on papyrus, or inscribed on the walls of the tombs. These included what is known as the Book of He-who-is-in-the-Underworld (Imj-Dwat) and the Book of the Gates, magical guide-books describing the journey of the sun through the subterranean regions during the hours of the night.

# The Old Kingdom (−2900 to −2280)[11]

## Third dynasty

It has already been noted that the kings of the first two dynasties (archaic period) appear to have been primarily concerned with conquest and consolidation. We believe that the new dogma of divine kingship actually began with the third dynasty and that it was not until then that Egypt became a single, united nation. The dynasty was founded by King Zoser who was evidently a strong and able ruler. Yet his fame has been overshadowed, to a great extent, by that of his subject I-em-htp, a man renowned from his own day until now as an architect, physician, priest, magician, writer and maker of proverbs. Two thousand three hundred years after his death he became a god of medicine in whom the Greeks (who called him Imeuthes) recognized their own Askelepios. His outstanding accomplishment as an architect was the step pyramid, an extensive funerary complex built for his Pharaoh at Sakkara, on an area of 15 hectares in a rectangle 544 by 277 metres. He endowed the construction with a fortress-like enclosure wall but introduced a striking innovation in substituting stone for brick.

The other kings of the third dynasty are as shadowy as those of the first two dynasties, although the huge unfinished step pyramid of

10. A French translation is given in P. Barguet. The Oriental Institute of Chicago, for its part, has published an annotated English translation, a complete 'Book of the Dead'. See T. G. Allen.

11. In English, see W. S. Smith; in French, J. Vandier, 'L'Ancien Empire' and 'La Fin de l'Ancien Empire et la Première Période Intermédiaire', in E. Drioton and J. Vandier, pp. 205–38 and 239–49.

King Sekhem-Khet (who was perhaps Zoser's son and successor) at Sakkara, and the immense excavation of an unfinished tomb at Zawijet-el-Aryan, in the desert south of Giza, are sufficient indication that Zoser's pyramid complex was not unique. King Huny, who closes the third dynasty, is the immediate predecessor of Snefru, the founder of the fourth dynasty. A pyramid at Meidum, some 70 kilometres to the south of Cairo, was built for him. This structure, originally constructed in steps, underwent several enlargements and changes of design before it was finished (perhaps by Snefru) as a true pyramid.

## Fourth dynasty

The fourth dynasty, one of the high points in Egyptian history, opens with the long and active reign of Snefru, whose annals, as preserved in part on the Palermo Stone,[12] tell us of successful military campaigns against the Nubians to the south and the Libyan tribesmen to the west, the maintenance of traffic (particularly in timber) with the Syrian coast, and extensive building operations carried out year after year and involving the erection of temples, fortresses and palaces throughout Egypt. Snefru reigned for twenty-four years and probably belonged to a minor branch of the royal family. To legitimize his position he married Hetep-Heres,[13] the eldest daughter of Huny, thus carrying the royal blood over to the new dynasty. He had two pyramids constructed at Dahshur, the southern being rhomboidal in shape, the northern of true pyramidal form and of a size which begins to approach that of the Great Pyramid of Khufu at Giza.

Snefru's successors Khufu (Cheops), Khafre (Chephren) and Mankaure (Mycerinus) are remembered chiefly by the three pyramids which they erected on the high promontory at Giza, 10 kilometres south-west of modern Cairo. The pyramid of Khufu has the distinction of being the largest single building ever constructed by man,[14] and for the excellence of its workmanship, accuracy of its planning and beauty of its proportions remains the chief of the seven wonders of the world. The pyramids of Khufu's son and grandson, though smaller, are similar both in construction and in the arrangement of their subsidiary buildings.

12. See Introduction.

13. The tomb of Queen Hetep-Heres was discovered at Giza. It yielded furniture of excellent quality showing the skill of Egyptian craftsmen during the Old Kingdom. See G. A. Reisner, 1955.

14. We know that the pyramid proper, a sun symbol, which contains or surmounts the burial vault where the royal mummy lay, is but one element of the complex constituting the complete royal burial place. The latter comprises, in addition to the pyramid, a low temple on the plain, often referred to as the 'Temple of the Valley', and an open alley or roadway running up from the temple to the high part of the complex, on the desert plateau, consisting of the pyramid proper and the funerary temple built on to its eastern face, the whole precinct being surrounded by a wall. See I. E. S. Edwards.

There were several interruptions in the royal succession of the fourth dynasty, owing to fraternal strife between the children of the various queens of Khufu. His son Dedefre ruled Egypt for eight years before Khafre, and another son seized the throne for a short time at the end of Khafre's reign. A third may possibly have followed the last effective king of the dynasty, Shepseskaf.

## Fifth dynasty

This dynasty stemmed from the growing strength of the priesthood of Heliopolis. A legend in the Westcar Papyrus[15] relates that the first three kings of the fifth dynasty were the offspring of the god Re and a lady named Radjeded, wife of a priest at Heliopolis. These three brothers were Weserkaf, Sahure and Neferirkare. Sahure is known chiefly for the splendid bas-reliefs which decorated his funerary temple at Abusir, north of Saqqara. It is well known that though the royal pyramids of the fifth dynasty were far smaller than the great tombs of the fourth dynasty and of inferior construction the funerary temples adjoining the pyramids were elaborate structures extensively decorated with painted bas-reliefs, some of a semi-historical nature. Near the pyramid complex most of the kings of this dynasty built great temples to the Sun-god, each dominated by a towering solar obelisk.

In addition to the erection and endowments of many temples listed in the Palermo Stone the Pharaohs of the fifth dynasty were active in safeguarding the frontiers of Egypt and in expanding the existing trade relations with neighbouring countries. Punitive expeditions against the Libyans of the western desert, the Bedouins of Sinai and the Semitic peoples of southern Palestine were recorded on the walls of their funerary temples. Great sea-going ships visited the coast of Palestine during the reigns of Sahure and Issessi. Egyptian ships also reached the shores of the land of Punt on the Somali coast to procure highly valued cargoes of myrrh, ebony and animals, among other goods. The traffic with Syria in cedar wood continued to thrive, and the ancient port of Byblos on the coast below the wooded slopes of Lebanon saw more and more of the Egyptian timber fleet. Trade relations with Byblos are known to have existed from the earliest dynasties (see Chapter 8). An Egyptian temple was erected there during the fourth dynasty and objects inscribed with the names of several Pharaohs of the Old Kingdom have been found in the town and in the old harbour area.

15. Written during the Middle Kingdom: see G. Lefebvre, 1949, p. 79. The Westcar Papyrus account is fictional. The first kings of the fifth dynasty were descended from the kings of the fourth dynasty. See L. Borchardt, 1938, pp. 209–15. However, the priesthood of Heliopolis seems definitely to have played an important part at the time of the transition from the fourth to the fifth dynasty.

## Sixth dynasty

There is no evidence that political disturbances in the country accompanied the transition from the fifth to the sixth dynasty. With the long and vigorous reign of Pepi I (the third king) the dynasty showed its strength. For the first time an Egyptian king abandoned purely defensive military tactics and carried the might of his army into the heart of the enemy country. With the large army under Uni, the Egyptian general, the enemies were driven back to their homelands as far north as Carmel and trapped, in the last five campaigns, by landing troops from an Egyptian fleet far up the Palestine coast.

There are some indications that Pepi I may have taken his son Merenre as co-regent, for it is apparent that he did not reign alone for more than five years. During this time, however, he did much to expand and consolidate Egyptian power in Nubia, and shortly before he died he appeared in person at the First Cataract to receive the homage of the Nubian provincial chiefs.

On the death of his brother Merenre, Pepi II, a child of 6, ascended the throne and ruled the country for ninety-four years, dying in his hundredth year after one of the longest reigns in history. During the king's minority the government of the country was in the hands of his mother and her brother. The second year of Pepi's reign was marked by the return of Herkhuf, the nomarch of Elephantine, who had been travelling in Nubia and had reached the province of Yam, whence he had brought back a rich cargo of treasures and a dancing Pygmy as a gift for the king. With great enthusiasm, the 8-year-old king sent a letter of thanks to Herkhuf, requesting him to take every precaution that the Pygmy should arrive at Memphis in good condition.[16]

The very long reign of Pepi II came to an end in political confusion which can be traced back to the beginning of the sixth dynasty when the growing power of the nomarchs of Upper Egypt enabled them to build their tombs in their own districts and not near the king's pyramid on the necropolis. A rapidly increasing process of decentralization took place. As the king lost control of the districts, more and more power passed into the hands of the powerful provincial rulers. The impoverishment of the royal house is plain from the absence of monuments after those built by Pepi II. As disintegration rapidly set in, this poverty spread throughout all classes of society. It is not clear whether the forces of disintegration were already too strong for any Pharaoh to combat, or whether the very long and feebly defensive reign of Pepi II hastened the collapse. What is clear is that the

---

16. Herkhuf, the nomarch, had the actual text of the royal letter engraved on the walls of his tomb at Aswan. A translation of the text is given in J. H. Breasted, 1906, pp. 159-61. The anthropological aspect of the problem of 'the dancing dwarf of the god' has been studied by W. R. Dawson, 1938, pp. 185-9.

Old Kingdom ended almost immediately after his death and then began a period of anarchy which we call the First Intermediate Period.

## The First Intermediate Period

On the death of Pepi II, Egypt disintegrated in an explosion of feudal disorder. A period of anarchy, social chaos and civil war began. Along the length of the Nile valley local princelings battled with each other amid such confusion that Manetho mentioned in his history of Egypt that the seventh dynasty included seventy kings who reigned for seventy days. This probably represents an emergency regime set up at Memphis to replace temporarily the kingship which disappeared with the collapse of the sixth dynasty.[17]

Little is known of the seventh dynasty and even when we have a record of the names of the kings the order of their reigns is disputed. Soon, however, a new royal house emerged at Heracleopolis (in Middle Egypt) and some attempt was made to continue the Memphis culture. These kings of the ninth and tenth dynasties evidently controlled the Delta, which had become a prey to marauding desert nomads. Upper Egypt, however, had split up into its old units, each nome under the control of a local ruler. The subsequent history of Egypt is characterized by the growth of a Theban power which, in the eleventh dynasty, was destined to gain control, first of Upper Egypt and, not very long afterwards, of the whole country.

The condition of Egypt following the collapse of the Old Kingdom, which had realized the highest material and intellectual achievements of the country and had called forth the highest abilities of the individual, is best described by the sage Ipu-wer. His writings, which seemingly go back to the First Intermediate Period,[18] have been preserved in a papyrus of the New Kingdom which is now in the Leiden Museum. This passage indicates the social revolution which took place in the early part of the First Intermediate Period and the absence of any sort of centralized authority:

> All is ruin. A man smites his brother, [the son] of his mother; plague is throughout the land. Blood is everywhere. A few lawless men have ventured to despoil the land of the Kingship. A foreign tribe from abroad has come to Egypt. The nomads of the deserts have become Egyptians everywhere. Elephantine and Thinis [are the domination] of Upper Egypt, without paying taxes owing to civil strife . . . The plunderer is everywhere . . . gates, columns and walls are

17. The First Intermediate Period (abbreviated FIP) still presents a great many problems. General accounts will be found in J. Spiegel and H. Stock. Very good summaries of the problems are given in E. Drioton and J. Vandier, pp. 235–7 and 643–5.

18. The date of the text is controversial. It is tentatively ascribed to the Second Intermediate Period in J. Van Seters, 1964, pp. 13–23. However, this new date has not gained acceptance.

consumed by fire. No longer do men sail northwards to [Byblos]. What shall we do for cedars? Gold is lacking. Corn has perished on every side ... The laws of the judgement hall are cast forth ... He who never possessed property is now a man of wealth. The poor of the land have become rich, and the possessor of property has become one who has nothing ...[19]

Yet out of the turmoil certain positive values were born; an inspiring new emphasis on individualism, for example, social equality and the dignity of the common man. Thus, amidst the chaos, the Egyptians evolved a set of moral standards upholding the individual. This is apparent from the well-known papyrus known as the Protests of the Eloquent Peasant[20] dating from the tenth dynasty. It is the story of a poor peasant who, having been robbed of his belongings by a wealthy landowner, insists upon his rights:

Do not plunder of his property a poor man, a weakling as thou knowest him. His property is the [very breath] of a suffering man, and he who takes it away is one who stops up his nose. Thou wert appointed to conduct hearings, to judge between two men and to punish the brigand [but] behold, it is the upholder of the thief which thou wouldst be. One trusts in thee, whereas thou art become a transgressor. Thou wert appointed to be a dam for the sufferer, guarding lest he drown [but] behold thou art his flowing lake.[21]

It is clear that the Egyptians thought of democracy as the equality of all men before the gods on the one hand and the rulers on the other. The most striking change, however, may be observed in the democratization of the funerary religion. During the Old Kingdom only personnages of royal rank or who had been distinguished by the Pharaoh could be sure of joining the gods in the after-life. With the weakening of the king's authority, however, the powerful of this world appropriated the royal funerary texts and inscribed them on their own coffins. Wealthy commoners were interred with proper ceremony and memorial stelae. Class barriers were thus dissolved at death and it was actually thanks to the god Osiris that this took place.

Osiris was one of the gods of the Delta, known from very early times, whose cult soon spread throughout the country. His success was due less to the political importance achieved by his worshippers than to the funerary character of his attributes, and by the eleventh dynasty his cult was firmly established in Abydos, the great city which remained, throughout Egyptian history, the centre of the cult of dead kingship. The fact that the priests of Abydos did not nourish political ambitions spared Osiris the fate of

19. According to A. H. Gardiner, 1909.
20. A French translation of the text is to be found in G. Lefebvre, 1949, pp. 47–69. A recent English translation is given in W. K. Simpson, 1972, pp. 31–49.
21. According to J. A. Wilson, in J. B. Pritchard, p. 409.

certain other gods whose cults survived no longer than the kings whose accession had prompted them. Late in Egyptian history the cult of Osiris and Isis became more widespread than ever, extending to the Greek islands, Rome and even the forests of Germany.[22] In Egypt itself there was no temple to any deity which did not reserve some shrine to the cult of the great God of the Dead, and some rites at feast days to his resurrection.

## The Middle Kingdom (−2060 to −1785)[23]

Although the Egyptian glimpsed democratic values, the vision did not endure. It seemed clear in times of trouble, yet dimmed with the return of prosperity and discipline in the Middle Kingdom, which was the second great period of national development. Egypt was once more reunited by force of arms. Thebes, previously an unknown and unimportant name, put an end to the rule of Heracleopolis and laid claim to the entire state of Egypt and in winning the war reunited the Two Lands under a single rule.

King Menthuhotep stands out as the dominant personality of the eleventh dynasty. His great task was the reorganization of the country's administration. All resistance to the royal house had been crushed but there may have been occasional minor uprisings. However, the political atmosphere of the Middle Kingdom differed from that of earlier times in that the peaceful security of the Old Kingdom was a thing of the past. Menthuhotep II, who had a long reign, built the funerary temple at Deir el Bahari which is the greatest monument of the period at Thebes. His architect there created a new and effective architectural form. This was a terraced structure with colonnades, surmounted by a pyramid set in the midst of a columned hall on the upper level.[24]

Following Menthuhotep II's rule, the family began to decline. Under the last king of the eleventh dynasty, a certain Amenemhet, vizier to the king who also bore other titles, is probably identical with the founder of the twelfth dynasty, King Amenemhet, and the first of a succession of powerful rulers.

Amenemhet I adopted three important measures which were strictly adhered to by his successors. He established a new capital called Ithet-Tawi (Holder-of-the-Two Lands) not far south of Memphis, from which he could better control Lower Egypt; he initiated the custom of placing his son beside him on the throne as co-regent, probably considered expedient

22. The fullest account we have of the legend of Osiris is that gathered together and published by Plutarch in his *De Iside et Osiride*. See in English J. G. Griffith, and in French J. Hani.

23. See E. Drioton and J. Vandier, 1962, ch. 7, pp. 239–81; W. C. Hayes, 1971; H. E. Winlock, 1947.

24. E. Naville.

following a palace conspiracy which seriously endangered his life (and to which he referred bitterly in the admonitions he left for the guidance of his son Senusret I);[25] and he planned the subjugation of Nubia and established a trading station farther south than had ever been attempted before. He was perhaps the founder of the fortified trading post at Kerma (near the Third Cataract) which was seemingly a centre of Egyptian influence from the reign of Senusret I.

Senusret I followed in the steps of his father and through his own energy, ability and breadth of vision was able to implement plans for the enrichment and expansion of Egypt. A series of expeditions led by the king himself, or by his able officers, tightened Egyptian control over Lower Nubia. It was at this time that the fortress of Buhen[26] was built, below the Second Cataract. The king's activities to the west seem to have been confined to punitive expeditions against the Temenw Libyans and to the maintenance of communications with the oases. His policy with the countries of the north-west was to defend his boundaries and to continue trading with the countries of western Asia.

The two subsequent kings, Amenemhet II and Senusret II, were apparently not interested in the consolidation and expansion of Egypt's foreign conquests.[27] Senusret III, however, is remembered for the reconquest and subjugation of Lower Nubia, which he reduced to the status of a province of Egypt. The long and prosperous reign of his successor Amenemhet III was characterized by an ambitious programme of irrigation, leading to vast agricultural and economic expansion in the Fayyum, an oasis with a large lake fed by a channel from the Nile. This channel passed through a narrow break in the desert hills bordering the valley about 80 kilometres south of Cairo. By damming it, the flow of water into the lake when the Nile was high was controlled, and the cutting of irrigation canals and the building of dykes resulted in massive land reclamation.

With Amenemhet IV the royal family was evidently beginning to lose its vigour. His brief and undistinguished reign, followed by an even briefer reign of Queen Sobek Neferu, marks the end of the dynasty.

## The Second Intermediate Period[28]

The names borne by some of the Pharaohs of the thirteenth dynasty

25. On the accession of this dynasty consult G. Posener, 1956.

26. See accounts of recent excavations and work at Buhen, following the campaign launched by Unesco to save the monuments of Nubia; see R. A. Caminos, 1975, and H. S. Smith, 1976.

27. It will be noted that the fortress of Mirgissa south of the Second Cataract, the largest fortification in the Nubian Batn-el-Haggar region, was built by Senusret II (see J. Vercoutter, 1964, pp. 20–2) and that consequently Nubia was still under Egyptian control during his reign.

28. The whole of this very obscure period of Egyptian history is covered in a publication, J. von Beckerath, 1965.

reflect the existence in Lower Egypt of a large Asiatic population. This element was no doubt increased by the immigration of large groups from the lands north-east of Egypt, forced southwards as a result of widespread population movements in western Asia. The leaders of these groups were called Hka-Hasut by the Egyptians, meaning Rulers of Foreign Countries, from which was derived the Manethonian term Hyksos which is now generally applied to the people as a whole.

The Hyksos only began seriously to challenge the political authority of the thirteenth dynasty about the year −1729. By −1700, however, they had emerged as a well-organized, well-equipped and warlike people, and they conquered the eastern part of the Delta, including the town of Hat-Wcrt (Avaris) which they refortified and used as their capital. It is generally admitted that the Hyksos domination of Egypt was not the outcome of a sudden invasion of the country by the armies of a single Asiatic nation. As we have said, it was the result of an infiltration during the declining years of the thirteenth dynasty, of groups of several western Asiatic chiefly Semitic peoples. Indeed, most of their kings had Semitic names, such as Anat-Hr, Semken, Amu or Jakub-Hr.

There is no doubt that the Hyksos occupation had a profound effect on the nation.[29] They introduced the horse, the chariot and body armour into Egypt. The Egyptians, who had never before had need of such equipment, eventually turned them successfully against the Hyksos and expelled them from the land. This was the first time in their history that the Egyptians found themselves under foreign domination. The humiliation shook their ancient sense of supremacy and of security in the protection of their gods. They began a war of liberation, conducted by the rulers of the Theban nome. The few surviving records of this period mostly concern the war fought by the kings of the late seventeenth dynasty against the Asiatic oppressors after nearly 150 years of occupation. Ahmose finally succeeded in driving the invaders out of the Delta, capturing their capital, Avaris, and following them into Palestine where he laid siege to the stronghold of Sharuhen. After that he proceeded northwards and raided the land of Zahi (the Phoenician coast). Thus Hyksos power was finally broken.

# The New Kingdom (−1580 to −1085)

## Eighteenth dynasty[30]

King Ahmose I, hailed by posterity as the father of the New Kingdom and the founder of the eighteenth dynasty, was evidently a man of

29. On the Hyksos and the various problems raised by their occupation of Egypt and its consequences, see J. Van Seters, 1966.

30. See E. Drioton and J. Vandier, 1962, ch. 9, pp. 335–42 and ch. 10, pp. 390–414; T. G. H. James; W. C. Hayes, 1973.

exceptional vigour and ability. He was followed by his son Amenhotep I, a worthy successor of his father, whose internal and foreign policy he vigorously carried forward. Though probably more concerned with the organization of the kingdom than with foreign conquest, he nevertheless found time to consolidate and expand the conquest of Nubia as far as the Third Cataract. Palestine and Syria remained quiet during his reign of nine years.

Amenhotep I appears to have merited his reputation for greatness which culminated in his being made, as was his mother Ahmes-Nefertari, a titulary divinity of the Theban necropolis.[31] He was followed by Thutmose I and II and then by Queen Hatshepsut, who married each of her half-brothers in turn, Thutmose II and III. In the fifth year of her reign, however, Hatshepsut was powerful enough to declare herself supreme ruler of the country. In order to legitimize her claims,[32] she announced that her father was the state god Amon-Re, who came to her mother in the guise of her father Thutmose I. The two peaceful decades of her reign were prosperous ones for Egypt. She concentrated her attention upon the country's internal affairs and upon great building enterprises. The two achievements of which she was most proud were the expedition to Punt and the raising of two great obelisks at Karnak temple. Both were intended to celebrate her devotion to her 'father' Amon-Re.

Following the death of Hatshepsut, Thutmose III at last came into his own. A mature man in his early thirties, he himself tells us that, while serving as a youthful priest in a ceremony at Karnak at which his father was officiating, the statue of Amon singled him out and by an oracle chose him as king. His first act as king was to overthrow the statues of Hatshepsut and erase her name and image wherever they appeared. His revenge appeased, he swiftly formed an army and marched against a coalition of the city states of the Palestine–Syria–Lebanon region, which had joined forces at the city of Megiddo and which were preparing to revolt against Egypt's domination. Marching with astonishing speed, Thutmose surprised the enemy and drove them to cover within the city walls. With the surrender of Megiddo the whole country as far as the southern Lebanon came under Egyptian control. In all, Thutmose III undertook seventeen campaigns abroad and Egyptian arms commanded respect in Syria and northern Mesopotamia for many years thereafter. Egypt was firmly established as a world power with a far-reaching empire. No other reign supplies us with such complete records as the annals of Thutmose III, carved on the walls of Karnak temple. Other details were recorded by his generals, and events were even woven into popular tales like that of the surprise of

31. J. Černý, 1927, pp. 159–203.
32. Much has been written about the 'Hatshepsut problem' and the 'persecution' of the queen by Thutmosis III. A good account of the problem and of the solutions proposed will be found in E. Drioton and J. Vandier, 1962, pp. 381–3.

Joppa by General Djehuty who concealed his men in sacks and smuggled them into the beleaguered city, much as in the tale of Ali Baba and the forty thieves.

Thutmose III was followed by two able and energetic Pharaohs, Amenhotep II and Thutmose IV, the latter being closely connected with the kingdom of Mittani for he married the daughter of the royal house. It was this lady, under her Egyptian name of Mut-em-Wa, who appears on the monuments as the Pharaoh's chief queen and the mother of Amenhotep III.

When Amenhotep III succeeded his father he was probably already married to his principal queen, Teye. The young king's accession to the throne came at a time when, thanks to some two centuries of unparalleled achievement both at home and abroad, the country was at the peak of its political power, and was economically prosperous and culturally developed. Moreover, the world was at peace and both the Pharaoh and his people could enjoy the many pleasures and luxuries which life now had to offer them. It seems that Amenhotep III was little interested in maintaining his power abroad, though he did endeavour to retain his northern vassal states and allies by means of liberal gifts of Nubian gold. Towards the end of his reign, as is evident from the Tell-el-Amarna letters,[33] the absence of a show of military force encouraged energetic men to scheme for independent power and to revolt against Egyptian authority. Amenhotep III, however, seems not to have been unduly concerned. It was as a builder and patron of the arts that he earned his reputation for magnificence. To him we owe the Luxor temple, which is considered the most beautiful of all the constructions of the New Kingdom, other large buildings at Karnak, and many others both in Egypt and elsewhere such as at Soleb in Nubia.

Though the cult of Aton began under Amenhotep III, its growth seems to have had little effect on the worship of the other gods until later in his reign, possibly not until the thirtieth year of the reign, the probable date when his son Amenhotep IV (later known as Akhenaton) became co-regent. Physically weak, with a frail, effeminate body, the new king had in him the makings of neither soldier nor statesman. He was mostly concerned with matters of the mind and spirit or, rather, his own mind and spirit. Exulting in the epithet He-who-lives-on-Truth, he sought an ever closer and more harmonious relationship with nature and in religion a more direct and rational relationship with his deity.[34]

In his youthful fanaticism, Amenhotep IV instituted a radical change of

33. Three hundred and seventy-seven cuneiform tablets found in the ruins of the Record Offices at the capital and consisting chiefly of correspondence between Amenhotep III and Akhenaton, and the kings of Hatti, Arzawam, Mittania, Assyria, Babylonia, Cyprus and the city rulers of Palestine and Syria. On these texts, see W. F. Albright, 1973.

34. Amenhotep IV – Akhenaton – and his period have recently been covered in numerous publications, including C. Aldred, 1968.

policy which led to a direct attack on the priesthood of Amon. The reasons were possibly as much political as religious for the high priests of the state god Amon-Re at Thebes had gained such wealth and power as to be a distinct menace to the throne. Amenhotep IV at first continued to live at Thebes, where he had a great temple to Aton erected east of Amon's temple of Karnak. Then, obviously embittered by the reaction to his reforms in Thebes, he decided to withdraw from the city. He founded a new residence at Tell-el-Amarna in Middle Egypt. By the sixth year of his reign he and his family, together with a considerable retinue of officials, priests, soldiers and craftsmen, moved to the new residence which he called Akhet Aton (the Horizon of Aton) where he lived until his death some fourteen years later. He changed his name to Akh-en-Aton or He-who-is-serviceable-to-Aton, and conferred upon his queen the throne name of Nefer-Neferu-Aton, meaning Beauty-of-Beauty-is-Aton.

Not content with proclaiming Aton as the sole true god, Akhenaton assailed the older deities. He ordered that the name Amon in particular should be erased from all inscriptions, even in personal names such as that of his father. He further decreed the dissolution of the priesthood and temple estates. It was here that Akhenaton aroused the most violent opposition for the temples were sustained by government grants bestowed in return for formal blessings on the undertakings of the state.

While tumult raged about him, Akhenaton lived in his capital worshipping his sole god. It was the worship of the creative power of the sun in the name of Aton which required no images of the god and which was carried out in the open air of the temple court, when flowers and fruit were placed on the altar. The Aton religion was far simpler than the traditional one. It laid emphasis on truth and on individual liberty. This was bound up with a love of nature, for the life-giving powers of the sun were universally expressed in all living things. The hymn composed by the king[35] expresses, above all, a spontaneous joy in living and love for all things created, in which the spirit of Aton found embodiment.

Akhenaton deprecated the stylized forms of traditional portraiture and insisted on a free naturalism in which the artist sought to represent immediate instead of eternal space and time. He thus allowed himself and his family to be depicted in informal attitudes: embracing, eating, playing with their children. He made no attempt to conceal his domestic life from the public eye, and so shocked the contemporary Egyptian, who found this informality belittling to the status of the god king.

The Atonist revolution did not survive the death of Akhenaton. His co-regent and successor Semenekh-Ka-Re almost immediately initiated a reconciliation with the priesthood of Amon. A compromise was reached in which Amon was again recognized. Semenekh-Ka-Re did not reign for more than three years and was followed by Tut-Ankh-Aton, who

35. A translation by J. A. Wilson is to be found in J. B. Pritchard, pp. 369–71.

eventually changed his name to Tutankhamun.[36] Since we know that this young Pharaoh died at about 18 years of age and that he reigned for at least nine years, he was probably about eight years old at his accession. The origin of these two kings is disputed, yet both based their claims to the throne upon marriages to the daughters of Akhenaton. During the reign of Tut-Ankh-Amon, and even after his death, there was some hesitation in repudiating Aton who, in spite of the restoration of Amon, maintained a place among the gods which continued during the short reign of King Ay who followed Tut-Ankh-Amon. It was only with Horemheb that the persecution of Aton began with the same persistence that had formerly applied to Amon.

## Nineteenth dynasty[37]

Horemheb came from a line of provincial noblemen in a small town of Middle Egypt. His long career as commander of the Egyptian army and as an administrator gave him an opportunity of assessing the political corruption which had increased dangerously since the beginning of Akhenaton's reign. On accession he promptly initiated a widespread series of reforms which were beneficial to the country. He also issued a decree to expedite the collection of national revenue and abolish corruption among military and civil officials.

Horemheb showed great favour to an army officer called Pa-Ramesses whom he made vizier and chose to succeed him on the throne. However, Pa-Ramesses was already an old man and reigned for only two years, to be followed by his son and co-regent Seti I, the first of a line of warriors who turned all their efforts towards recovering Egypt's prestige abroad. As soon as Seti I came to the throne, he faced serious danger from a coalition of Syrian city states encouraged, and even sustained, by the Hittites. He was able to defeat the coalition and enable Egypt to regain control over Palestine. After repulsing a Libyan attack, we find Seti once again in northern Syria where Egyptian troops came into contact with the Hittites for the first time. He captured Kadeshm but though the Hittites were forced to retire temporarily they retained their influence in northern Syria. The war was continued by his successor Ramses II.

Under Ramses II the royal residence and administrative centre was moved to a city in the north-east part of the Delta, called Per-Ramesse, where a military base was established, suitable for marshalling large bodies of infantry and chariotry. In the fifth year of his reign Ramses II set out at the head of four armies against a powerful coalition of Asiatic

36. The sensational discovery, in 1926, of the practically inviolate tomb of the young Pharaoh gave rise to a great many articles, including more particularly, H. Carter and A. C. Mace; C. Desroches-Noblecourt.

37. See E. Drioton and J. Vandier, 1962, ch. 9, pp. 349–56, and ch. 10, pp. 418–22; R. O. Faulkner, 1975.

people assembled by the Hittite King Mutawallis, and continued his father's attempts to regain Egypt's holdings in northern Syria. Though, in the famous battle near Kadesh on the River Orontes, Ramses led the vanguard of his forces into an enemy trap, saw one of his armies routed by the Hittite chariotry, and had to fight his way out of a desperate situation, he nevertheless managed to gather his forces and convert what might have been a defeat into a somewhat questionable victory. Detailed representations and accounts of this battle, and of some of the more successful campaigns in Palestine and Syria which preceded and followed it, were carved on the walls of Ramses II's rock-cut temples at Abu-Simbel and at El-Derr in Lower Nubia, in his temples at Abydos and Karnak, on the pylon which he added to Luxor temple as well as in his funerary temple called the Ramesseum. Hostilities between the two countries continued for a number of years. It was not, in fact, until the twenty-first year of his reign that Ramses II finally signed a remarkable peace treaty with the Hittite King Hattusilis. Thereafter cordial relations were maintained between the two powers and Ramses married the eldest daughter of Hattusilis in a ceremony widely announced as a symbol of peace and brotherhood. As a result of this arrangement, Egyptian influence extended along the coast to the north Syrian town of Ras Shamra (Ugarit). Though the Hittites still retained their power in the interior, in the valley of the Orontes their power was nearing its close. With the death of Hattusilis a new danger from the movement of the Sea Peoples began. This mass migration radiated from the Balkans and the Black Sea region throughout the eastern Mediterranean world, and soon overwhelmed the Hittite kingdom. The ageing Ramses, who reigned for sixty-seven years after signing the treaty, neglected the ominous signs from abroad and his vigorous successor, Merneptah, found himself faced with a serious situation when he came to the throne.

Great numbers of warlike Sea Peoples[38] had moved into the coastal region to the west of the Delta and, entering into an alliance with the Libyans, threatened Egypt. Merneptah met them and, in a great battle in the western Delta in the fifth year of his reign, he inflicted an overwhelming defeat upon the invaders. On the Merneptah stelae he also records his military activities in the Syro-Palestine region and lists a number of conquered cities and states including Canaan, Askalon, Gezer, Yenoam and Israel – the last mentioned for the first time in Egyptian records.

## Twentieth dynasty[39]

Merneptah's death was followed by a dynastic struggle and the throne was successively occupied by five rulers whose order and relationship one to

38. On the 'Sea Peoples', see the bold theory of A. Nibbi.
39. See E. Drioton and J. Vandier, 1962, ch. 9, pp. 356–66 and ch. 10, pp. 432–9.

another has not yet been clearly established. Order was restored by Seth-nakht, who reigned for two years as the first king of the twentieth dynasty. He was succeeded by his son Ramses III who, in a reign of thirty-one years, did as much as could be done to revive the glories of the New Kingdom. In his fifth and eleventh years of rule he decisively defeated invading hordes of western Libyans and, in the eighth year, beat back a systematic invasion by land and sea of the Sea Peoples. It is significant that these three wars were defensive and were fought, apart from a single land operation against the Sea Peoples, on or within Egyptian borders. Defeat in any one of them would have meant the end of Egypt's history as a nation, for these invasions were designed not merely for plunder or political domination, but for the occupation of the rich Delta and the valley by whole nations of land-hungry peoples who brought with them their families, herds and chattels as well as fighting men.

In dealing with the internal ills which also beset the country, Ramses III was less successful than in defending it against foreign armies. The country was harassed by labour troubles, turbulence among government workers, an inflationary rise in wheat prices and a fall in the value of bronze and copper. Decadence grew in the reigns of subsequent kings from Ramses IV to Ramses XI. The feeble hold of the royal house became still more precarious as the power of the priests of Amon increased, till finally they chose a high priest, Heri-Hor, to ascend the throne and begin a new dynasty.

## Period of decline[40]

### Twenty-first to twenty-fourth dynasties

In the twenty-first dynasty rule was divided by common consent between the princes of Tanis in the Delta[41] and the Heri-Hor dynasty at Thebes. On the death of the latter, Smendes (ruler of the Delta) seems to have taken control of the whole country. This period saw the flowering of a new power, a family of Libyan descent from the Fayyum. Perhaps they had originally been mercenary soldiers who settled there when Egypt with-drew.[42] However, one of the members of this family, named Sheshonq, seized the throne of Egypt and started a dynasty which lasted for about 200 years.

Towards the end of the twenty-second dynasty, Egypt was divided into squabbling petty kingdoms and was menaced both by Assyria and by a powerful independent Sudan. Then a man named Pedibast set up a rival dynasty. Although Manetho calls this twenty-third dynasty the Tanite,

40. See K. A. Kitchen. The genealogy and chronology of this confused period are studied by M. Bierbrier.

41. See J. Yoyotte, 1961, pp. 122–51.

42. See W. Hölscher.

the kings continued nevertheless to bear the names of the twenty-second dynasty Pharaohs, namely Sheshonq, Osorkon and Takelot. During these two dynasties Egypt maintained peaceful relations with Solomon in Jerusalem, who even took an Egyptian princess to wife. In the fifth year of the reign of Solomon's successor, however, Sheshonq attacked Palestine. Though Egypt did not endeavour to hold Palestine, she regained something of her former influence and profited by a greatly increased foreign trade.

The twenty-fourth dynasty had one king only, namely Bakenrenef, whom the Greeks called Bocchoris, son of Tefnakht. It was probably Tefnakht who made a treaty with Hosea of Samaria against the Assyrians. Bocchoris endeavoured to give support to the King of Israel against the Assyrian King Sargon II, but his army was beaten at Raphia in −720. His reign ended when the Sudanese King Shabaka invaded Egypt.

## The Sudanese twenty-fifth dynasty[43]

There was another invasion of Egypt in about −720 but this time from the south. From a capital at the Fourth Cataract, Piankhi, a Sudanese who ruled the Sudan between the First and Sixth Cataracts, found himself powerful enough to challenge the throne of the Pharaohs. A certain Tefnakht of Sais had succeeded in uniting the Delta, had occupied Memphis and was laying siege to Heracleopolis. Piankhi seized upon the report that the ruler of Hermopolis in Middle Egypt had joined forces with Tefnakht to send an army into Egypt. He was no doubt a gallant ruler. His chivalry in battle, his austere avoidance of captured princesses, his love of horses, his scrupulous performance of religious ritual and his refusal to deal with conquered princes, who were ceremonially unclean (they were uncircumcised and eaters of fish), are indicative of his character. This dynasty lasted for sixty years before the Assyrians, after many campaigns, succeeded in putting an end to it.

## Saitic kingdom[44]

Egypt was freed from Assyrian domination by an Egyptian named Psammetik. In −658 he managed, with the help of Gyges of Lydia and Greek mercenaries, to throw off all vestiges of Assyrian overlordship and start a new dynasty, the twenty-sixth. The kings of this dynasty tried valiantly to restore Egypt's position by promoting commercial expansion. Upper Egypt became a rich agricultural region growing produce which Lower Egypt sold.

43. See also Chapter 11. An overall view is to be found in H. von Zeissl. For further details on this period, see Chapter 10 below.

44. See E. Drioton and J. Vandier, 1962, ch. 13, pp. 574–600. On the Saitic intervention in Nubia, which is of great importance for the history of Africa, see S. Sauneron and J. Yoyotte, 1952, pp. 157–207.

## Persian period[45]

In the reign of Psammetik III, Egypt had to endure conquest by the Persians under Cambyses and with this occupation the history of the country as an independent power was in effect ended. The twenty-seventh dynasty was headed by Persian kings. The twenty-eighth was a local dynasty known as the Amyrtaios, who organized a revolt during the troubled reign of Darius II. By means of alliances with Athens and Sparta the kings of the twenty-ninth and thirtieth dynasties contrived to maintain the independence thus gained for about sixty years.

The second Persian domination of Egypt began under Artaxerxes III in −341. This was soon brought to an end by Alexander the Great, who invaded Egypt in −332 after defeating Persia at the battle of Issus.

45. The basic work on this period remains G. Posener, 1936.

PLATE 2.1a *Kephren*

PLATE 2.1b *Detail of Plate 2.1a, enlarged*

PLATE 2.2 *Queen Hatshepsut seated*

PLATE 2.3 *Akhenaton before the sun*

PLATE 2.4 *Howard Carter, the archaeologist who discovered Tutankhamun's tomb, had to open a stone sarcophagus and three coffins, one within the other, before reaching the inner one containing the mummy*

PLATE 2.5 *Tutankhamun's solid gold funeral mask*

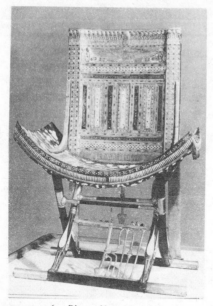

PLATE 2.6a *Pharaoh's ecclesiastical throne: the remains of the openwork decoration between the feet refer to 'The Union of Two Countries'*

PLATE 2.6b *Back of the gold-plated throne: Queen Ankhesenamun is putting the final touches to the King's toilet*

PLATE 2.7 *Back of a chair decorated with royal names and symbols of the wish that the Pharaoh may live 'a million years'*

PLATE 2.8 *Unguent box, in the shape of a double cartouche, probably used for ritual purposes*

PLATE 2.9 *Anubis at the entry to the treasury*

PLATE 2.10 *Interior of the antechamber, west side – the Hathor Couch*

# 3

# Pharaonic Egypt: society, economy and culture

## Economy and society

### Fields and marshes

The establishment of the Pharaonic state around the year −3000 and the little-known period that followed undoubtedly corresponded with great economic development. We can see some evidence of this in the royal and private tombs of the Thinite era: the buildings become larger and the many *objects d'art* suggest increased luxury and the consummate skill of the craftsmen. There is no means of knowing whether the need to co-ordinate irrigation was the principal cause of the formation of a unified state or whether the unification of the country under the Thinite kings, together with the development of writing, made it possible to co-ordinate the regional economies by rationalizing basic construction work and ensuring the organized distribution of food resources. The fact remains that, until the nineteenth century of our era, Egypt's prosperity and vitality were to be tied to the cultivation of cereals (wheat, barley). A system of flood basins, which controlled and distributed the flood water and silt inside earth embankments, endured until the modern triumph of year-round irrigation: there is evidence that it existed as early as the Middle Kingdom and we may assume that it had taken shape even earlier.[1] Obviously, this system only permitted one crop a year; on the other hand, the shortness of the agricultural cycle made plenty of manpower available for the major operations on the construction of the religious and royal buildings. The Ancients also practised year-round irrigation by raising water from the canals or from pits dug down to the water table, but for a long time human legs and human shoulders bearing yokes were the only 'machines' for raising water known, and watering by means of ditches was used only for vegetables, fruit trees and vineyards. (It is possible, however, that the invention of the *shaduf* during the New Kingdom made

---

1. Texts relating to irrigation techniques are very rare. The oldest positive reference to irrigation by basins (*hod*) is found in the Middle Kingdom coffin texts: A. de Buck, 1935–61, p. 138, b–c.

two crops of grain a year possible in places.)[2] Lacking the knowledge of how to store water, they did not yet know how to mitigate the consequences of unusually low floods, which were the cause of infertility in many basins, and unusually high floods, which devastated land and homes. However, the development of granaries and river transport enabled them to ensure food supplies from one province to another or from one year to the next. Average yields were good: the surpluses fed the large numbers of government officials and the workers in medium-sized places of employment (shipyards and weapon factories, spinning mills attached to certain temples, etc.). Through their control over food resources, which varied according to the period, the temple authorities and high officials exercised powers of patronage.

Bread and beer made from grain were the staple diets, but the ancient Egyptians' food was astonishingly varied. One is struck by the number of types of cakes and bread listed in the texts. As today, gardens provided broad beans, chick peas and other pulses, onions, leeks, lettuces and cucumbers. Orchards furnished dates, figs, sycamore nuts and eating-grapes. Skilful cultivation of the vine, practised mainly in the Delta and in the oases, produced a great variety of wines. Bee-keeping provided honey. Oil was extracted from sesame and nabk, the olive tree introduced during the New Kingdom remaining rare and not very successful.

Pharaonic Egypt did not transform the entire valley into productive land and gardens. It exploited also the vast marshes and lakes along the northern edges of the Delta and the shores of Lake Moeris, and the low-lying land on the edge of the desert and in the meanders of the Nile. In these *pehu*, abundant and varied wildfowl were hunted or trapped. There was fishing with seine-net, eel-pot, line or basket for the Nile offered a wide variety of fish and, in spite of the prohibition of their consumption in certain provinces or by certain categories, they had a definite place in the people's diet, which was also supplemented by the gathering of the roots of the edible cyperus (earth almond), papyrus hearts and, after the Persian era, the seeds of the Indian lotus. Finally, the marshland gave pasturage for cows and oxen.

Although the climate was not particularly favourable to cattle-raising because it was so wet, and herds depleted by these conditions had regularly to be supplemented from Nubia and Asia, it was of considerable importance in the country's life and religious conceptions. The tables of the gods and the great had to be well furnished with beef. The cutting-up of the carcass was a fine art, the animal fats being widely used to make perfumed unguents. We know that the Old Kingdom Egyptians tried to raise a number of species – oryx, antelope, gazelle, etc., and even cranes and hyenas – but this proved labour-consuming and the results disappointing,

2. See the ingenious interpretation proposed for the Wilbur Papyrus data by W. Helck and E. Otto, 1973.

and it was abandoned, the desert ruminants later becoming, in proverbs and in rites of sorcery, the symbol of untameable creatures.[3] In contrast, they were very successful in raising poultry, notably the Nile goose. The meat of goats, so harmful to the valley's few trees, and sheep raised on fallow land and the fringes of the desert, as well as pigs (in spite of some prohibitions), acquired a considerable place in the people's diet. Well into historic times, we see a change take place in the type of sheep reared: an earlier type of ram with horizontal, twisted horns, which was the incarnation of Khnum, Bes, Hershef and other ancient gods, was gradually replaced round about −2000 by the ram with curved horns, dedicated to the god Amon. There is debate over whether it is of African or Asian origin. Two African species domesticated by the Egyptians were particularly successful and are closely linked, in our minds, with the Pharaonic past: the ass, used as early as the archaic period, not for riding but as a beast of burden (and paradoxically dedicated to the evil god Seth), and the domestic cat, which does not appear until the end of the Old and the beginning of the Middle Kingdom (and which was worshipped as a more peaceable form of the dangerous goddesses).

## Mining and industry

The nobility and guards hunted hare and big game in the desert for sport and as a means of varying the ordinary fare, but this could not have had much economic importance. What the desert did offer was a wide range of mineral resources: the green and black dyes of the Arabian desert used to treat and embellish the eyes even in prehistoric times; the beautiful hard stone used by the builders and sculptors (fine limestone from Toura, Silsila sandstone, Aswan granite, Hatnoub alabaster, Jebel el Ahmar quartzite, Hammamet 'grauwacke'),[4] and semi-precious stones like the Sinai turquoise or Nubian cornelians and amethysts. The manufacture of glazes (glazed steatite and 'Egyptian faïence' with a quartz core) developed very early, prompting the manufacture of objects with the look of turquoise or lapis lazuli. New Kingdom Egypt improved its glass-making techniques, thanks to contacts with Asia, and became a pastmaster in these processes.

One of the riches derived by the country from the arid wastes surrounding it was gold, which came from the Arabian desert and Nubia. The symbol of perfect immortality, it did not yet play the essential economic role it was to have in later civilizations but was considered a basic sign of wealth and was more highly prized than silver, although the latter, an imported metal, was always rarer and, in the Old Kingdom, more

3. Zanzing Papyrus, 3, 8–9; R. A. Caminos, 1954, p. 382. On the religious significance of the oryx, see Ph. J. Derchain.

4. Grauwacke or greywacke (incorrectly called 'schist' in many works) is a 'fine-grained, compact, hard, crystalline, quartz ore rock, very like slate in appearance and generally of various shades of grey': A. Lucas, pp. 419–20.

precious than gold. The deserts contained a number of copper deposits, of a rather low grade, except in Sinai, and Egypt soon became dependent on copper from Asia. It should be noted that changes in Pharaonic metal-working techniques always lagged behind those of the Near East. The bronze age and then the iron age developed later here than elsewhere. Metal was relatively rare and precious; wood and flint successfully took their place in agricultural implements and hard stone in sculpting instruments; metal tools and arms were stored and distributed by the government services.[5]

If Ancient Egypt had to import metals and timber from its Asian neighbours, its industrial capacity was unsurpassed in two domains. The Pharaohs exported textiles, Egyptian linen being then of an unequalled fineness, and paper. Papyrus, useful in so many ways – for sails, ropes, clothing, footwear – above all made possible the manufacture of a very flexible writing-surface, which was the source of the scribe's power and which was in heavy demand abroad from the moment alphabetic writing spread around the eastern Mediterranean. Intensive cultivation of this plant probably contributed greatly to the disappearance of the marshes, the haunt of the birds, crocodiles and hippopotamuses that, as the Ancients themselves felt, brightened the Egyptian landscape.

The development of transport was one determining factor in the progress of the Pharaonic regime. Oxen were hardly ever harnessed to anything but the plough or the funeral sledge; the ass, hardier and less demanding, was the ideal beast of burden in the fields as on the desert trails (we know that the horse, introduced during the second millennium, remained a luxury for the warriors, and that the rich economic potential of the wheel, the principle of which was known as early as the Old Kingdom,[6] was not exploited). Less efficient, certainly, although the technique of using them in teams was known, the ass preceded and supplemented the camel, which only came very slowly into use in the countryside after the Persian era. For bulk transport over long distances Egypt used its river and its canals: small craft and large boats were rapid and reliable. Egypt's precocious navigational skill made possible both the centralization of the economy and the prodigious architectural achievements (pyramids, enormous temples, colossi, obelisks). In addition, even at a very early date, sailing boats plied the Red Sea and the Mediterranean (there is nothing to prove the theory that the Phoenicians originally taught the Egyptians how to sail). For moving the heavy stone blocks needed for sacred buildings in particular, Pharaonic engineering had invented ingenious methods of an astonishing simplicity, using, for instance, the lubricating properties of

5. During the thirteenth dynasty, flint arrows and javelin heads were made in imitation of metal models, but by archaic traditional techniques, as shown by the weapons found in the fortress of Mirgissa: A. Vila, pp. 171–99.

6. A siege ladder mounted on wheels is shown in a sixth-dynasty tomb: W. S. Smith, 1949, p. 212, Fig. 85.

wet mud to move simple sledges (without wheels or rollers), profiting from the rise of the Nile to float barges loaded with enormous blocks, or using reed matting for drogues.[7] By reconstructing methods like these, which a modern would never think of, bemused as he is by sophisticated technologies and other notions of efficiency, research is on the way to providing the key to the mysteries of Pharaonic science.[8]

Most agricultural and industrial processes had been invented by the third millennium and it seems that Egypt was slow and timid, indeed hidebound, when it came to introducing technical innovations from abroad. In the present state of documentation and studies, it would seem that the remarkable achievements of the early days had provided solutions for the vital problems facing the valley's inhabitants and led to the establishment of an effective social and political system, 'Pharaonic despotism', whose shortcomings were pushed into the background by a religious outlook so coherent that it still survived in the temples several centuries after conquest by foreign powers had demonstrated the inability of tradition and social praxis to meet the challenge from newer powers.

## The economic and social system

It is best to refrain from abstract terms when describing the Pharaonic methods of production, which we shall never be able to do more than glimpse, for lack of sufficient records.[9]

Some general data emerge from the available documents. Foreign trade, mining and quarrying were state activities. The majority of the commercial transactions we know about from the records involve small amounts of commodities and are private contracts between individuals; the intervention of professional middlemen is rare and they usually seem to be the commercial agents of the king or a temple. There is no reason to believe in the existence of a 'bourgeoisie' of entrepreneurs and private traders, and although the expression sometimes used, 'state socialism', is ambiguous and anachronistic, it does seem that, in general, production and distribution were in the hands of the state.

A survey of the available material, in fact, gives the impression that everything stemmed from the king. In principle, certainly, all powers of decision and all material resources belonged to him. He had a religious duty to ensure the cosmic order, the security of Egypt and the happiness of its people in this world and the next, not only by exercising his authority as king, but by maintaining the worship of the gods, with the result that he shared his economic prerogative with the temples. On the other hand, both in officiating in those temples and in managing the

7. G. Goyon, 1970, pp. 11–41.
8. Most recently, H. Chevrier, 1964, pp. 11–17; 1970, pp. 15–39; 1971, pp. 67–111.
9. Critical notes and bibliography in J. J. Janssen, pp. 127–85.

nation's affairs, Pharaoh, theoretically the sole priest, sole warrior, sole judge and sole producer, delegated his power to a whole hierarchy: one way of paying these officials was to assign them land, the revenue of which became theirs. In fact, at all periods the royal monopoly of the means of production was more theoretical than real.

Certainly, the expeditions to Punt, Byblos, Nubia and the deserts to seek out exotic commodities and stones were normally sent out by the king and led by government officials. The building of the temples was likewise a government function, whilst, during the imperial era, the annexed territory of Kush and the Palestinian and Syrian protectorates were, for instance, directly exploited by the crown. In contrast, the development of the land in Egypt itself did not depend exclusively on the crown. Alongside the royal domain there were the lands owned by the gods, who possessed fields, flocks, workshops, etc. (in the heyday of the cult of Amon, the god himself could own mines), and had their own bureaucratic hierarchy. The fact that the gods were sometimes granted royal charters exempting them from certain taxes and levies is, ultimately, a sign that the temples were the 'owners' of their lands, personnel and tools. Moreover, at least from the eighteenth dynasty on, warriors were given hereditary tenure of land. High officials received gifts of land that they managed themselves. Scenes of domestic life carved in Old Kingdom mastabas show that their households included their own flocks and craftsmen and their own flotilla of boats. We do not know how inheritable private fortunes were made, but it is obvious that there were some and that apart from the official position that one could only hope to be able to hand on to one's children, there were 'household effects' that could be bequeathed freely. However, virtually at every period, land tenure covered limited and scattered areas, so that the great fortunes did not take the form – of which the authorities were apprehensive – of large landed estates. Smallholdings are known to have existed, notably in the New Kingdom, when the term 'fields of poor men' in fact designated the lands of small independent farmers quite distinct from tenants working the fields of the king or the gods. Relatively few in number, the foreigners deported to Egypt in the era of the great conquests were specialists (Palestinian viticulturists, Libyan drovers) or military settlers; the slaves acquired by private individuals were often only household servants and, although there is evidence that it existed, slave labour (sometimes penal labour) is believed to have provided only a limited amount of manpower for agriculture (even though the likening in later times of the magic 'respondents' placed at the disposal of the dead to a troop of bought slaves[10] would lead one to believe that under the Ramses it was slavery that made possible the major works of irrigation and land improvement). It remains true that the mass of the working population seems to have

10. J. Černý, 1942, pp. 105–33.

been tied *de facto* to the land, land that it had no occasion to flee except in the event of inability to pay the taxes.

We may assume that housekeeping was the predominant activity in the villages, the bulk of the fieldwork being done by the men. In the market towns, royal domains and temples, specialization was carried to a high degree. Guilds, sometimes with an elaborate hierarchy, of bakers, potters, flower-arrangers, founders, sculptors, draughtsmen, goldsmiths, water-carriers, watchmen of all kinds, dog-keepers, shepherds, goat-herds, goose-herds, etc., worked for the king or the temples, skills being handed down from father to son. We know comparatively well how the community of workers quartered in a village adjoining the Valley of the Kings (present site of Deir el Medina) lived while digging and decorating the tombs of the Pharaohs and their queens. The artists and excavators were public employees under the direction of a royal scribe and two overseers appointed by the sovereign.[11] They received a regular allowance of grain, which was sometimes directly levied from the revenues of a temple, and rations of fish, vegetables or other food. They exchanged small services and goods among themselves and administered their own justice (except for appeal to the oracular verdict of a local god), and their status was high enough and their moral position strong enough for the community to be able to go on strike in the event of delays in the distribution of their rations.

## The civil service

The organization and distribution of production, the management of public order and the supervision of all activities were the responsibility of civil servants under the authority of either the prince – the Pharaoh or, in periods of schism, the local chiefs – or the temples. These officials were recruited from the scribes, the knowledge of writing being the gateway to all learning and all higher technical skills and thus, as those concerned enjoyed pointing out in their *Satires of the Professions* and epistolary essays, an arrogated source of power and comfort. Those scribes, trustees of both the religious and lay cultures, reigned over all professional activities (in the New Kingdom the highest army officers themselves were scribes). They might be engineers, agronomists, accountants or ritualists, and many combined several capacities. Taught with a certain brutal strictness, they professed a moral code that was often lofty, full of benevolent intentions and a certain scorn for the commonalty and of respect for the social order as being the perfect expression of the harmony of the universe. Even if they avoided the malpractices against which they were constantly warned by the principles governing their service, they enjoyed rewards in proportion to their rank in the hierarchy (the range of those rewards being wide, at least in the twelfth dynasty):[12] land grants, salaries in the form of food

11. In D. Valbelle.
12. For a typical text, see G. Goyon, 1957.

rations, priestly profits taken from regular temple revenue and royal gifts, honorific gifts or funeral presents received directly from the sovereign. The greatest of them lived in fine style in this world and the one to come and their wealth, not to speak of their influence, gave them powers of patronage.

Title lists and genealogies clearly show that there was not a caste of scribes separate from that of warriors or of priests. The ruling class was all one and merged with officialdom. Every good student could normally find a post and climb in his career if his competence and zeal singled him out for the attention of the king, theoretically the sole arbiter in matters of social advancement.

It was, however, normal to pass on to one's children at least part of one's functions, and we should not lend too much credence to a rhetoric that hastens to represent every official as someone whom the king had raised from nothing. We know of dynasties of high officials, and in the Thebes of the first millennium we see several families sharing out the posts and priesthoods of the 'House of Amon' at a time, it must be said, when the right of inheritance assumed considerable importance.

Pharaonic history seems to have been acted out to the rhythm of the struggle between high officialdom, which tended to set itself up as a hereditary and autonomous power, and the monarchy, clinging to the right to control appointments. Thus the Old Kingdom disappeared when, in the southern provinces, the dynasties of hereditary 'great chiefs' or prefects became strong. In the Second Intermediate Period, high office became a personal property that could be bought and sold. The end of the New Kingdom came when the Theban priesthood and the southern military command were joined and became the appanage of a dynasty of high priests of Amon, and the Libyan period saw repeated in the Delta the fissiparous process that Upper Egypt had gone through in the First Intermediate Period. The economic implications and the causes and consequences of these changes cannot be identified with any certainty, but it may be said that in each period of weakened central power and territorial fragmentation of the system of administration, internal struggles disturbed the peace of the countryside and international influence and the security of the frontiers were compromised; temples were built less frequently and on a more modest scale and the quality of the works of art declined.

## Political organization

The avowed ideal of Egyptian society was thus a strong monarchy, regarded as the sole means of giving the country the driving force necessary for its well-being. The sovereign was the embodiment of the public service: the term 'Pharaoh' comes from *per-ao*, which in the Old Kingdom designated the 'Great House' of the prince, including his residence and his ministers, and which in the New Kingdom finally came to designate the person of the king. He was of a different nature from the rest of mankind: the legends about his predestination, the four canonic names and the epithets that he added to his personal name, the protocol surrounding him, the pomp and circumstance accompanying his appearances and decisions, his endlessly repeated likenesses, cartouches and title lists in the sacred buildings, his jubilee celebrations, the style of his tomb (Memphis pyramid, Theban rock-cut tomb) – all stress this difference. One of the most obvious demonstrations of the periodic attrition of authority and of certain social pressures is the adoption by a growing number of private individuals of tomb styles,[13] iconographic themes and funerary texts formerly reserved for the king alone. In addition, whereas monogamy seems to have been the rule among ordinary mortals, the god-king commonly took several wives, sometimes marrying his sister and even his daughters.

There is some mystery about royal succession. It was certainly customary for son to succeed father on the throne, in conformity with the mythical model of Osiris and Horus, the prototype of the son who buries his father and avenges his death, and the hereditary principle sometimes, as in the twelfth dynasty, resulted in the premature coronation of the successor. However, it should not be thought that the right of kingship lay simply in mere hereditary transmission from male to male by primogeniture. The few sovereigns who tell us of their forebears stress their fathers' free choice of them as lieutenant-general and heir presumptive (Seti I, Ramses II, Ramses III, Ramses IV). However, the words of the formulae by which the 'legitimacy' of the king is recalled are identical, whether he be the eldest son of his predecessor or a parvenu. Each ruler inherits 'the royalty of Ra, the function of Shu, the throne of Geb', so being the direct successor of the gods who created and ordered the world; each was 'chosen' by the god of his native town. Predestined to his position, the king was begotten from the very acts of the Sun-god (figurative myth of theogamy)[14] and in the New Kingdom designation or recognition of the new king by the oracle of Amon was the guarantee of the new monarch's legitimacy. Thus direct 'divine right' outweighed dynastic legitimacy. In fact, each reign was a new beginning. It was ritual that made and maintained the sovereign and each time he acted as priest or law-giver, the same purifications, the same anointings, the same ornaments renewed his 'appearance as the king'. Thus likened to a god, sometimes worshipped during his lifetime as a veritable god – Amenhotep III or Ramses II, for example, through their stupendous colossi – the Pharaoh assumed a supernatural role without, however,

13. The phenomenon of differentiation in the posthumous treatment of the kings and then gradual usurpation of the sovereign's funerary privileges by private individuals occurs several times. The first cycle began during the Old Kingdom and was accelerated by the weakening of royal power during the First Intermediate Period; but it can no longer be argued that at that period there was an abrupt democratization of funerary privileges.

14. H. Brunner, 1964.

seriously claiming to possess supernatural gifts and, on the contrary, remaining above all the exemplar of man dependent on the gods and owing them service.[15] Four women became Pharaohs: Strangely enough, the first two (Nitokris and Sebeknefru) mark the end of a dynasty and the other two (Hatshepsut and Tauosre) were treated as usurpers by posterity. Honours were showered on the mothers, wives and daughters of the king. Some princesses of the Middle Kingdom, and more especially later, Teye, first wife of Amenhotep III, and Nefertari, first wife of Ramses II, received exceptional honours. Ahhotep, under Amasis, or Ahmosis-Nefertari, under Amenhotep I, seem to have wielded a determining influence in political or religious matters. The attribution of the ritual function of 'divine wife of Amon' to princesses or queens shows the key role of femininity and the female in the worship of the cosmic god. However, there is no positive evidence of a matriarchal regime in the Egyptian concept of royalty[16] and in particular, the theory according to which, in the Amosid era, dynastic right was normally transmitted through the female is far from being proved.

A study of the title lists of high and low officials and the few legislative and administrative texts that have come down to us gives a more or less accurate notion of government organization: the government of the nomes, the hierarchy of the priesthood and distribution of the religious obligations of the priests, royal or priestly administration of the arable land, flocks, mines, granaries, treasuries, river transport, justice, and so on. Scholarly if not strict organization charts – which obviously varied depending on the period – give evidence of sophisticated management skills and remarkable techniques of secretarial work and accountancy (headings, brackets, cross-tabulation, etc.). This paperwork was none the less effective. Egypt probably owed its power abroad more to its advanced organization than to its aggressiveness, and its monuments, which have withstood time, certainly owe their existence to the scribes' skill in manipulating labour and heavy materials on a grand scale.

At the top of the system sat the *tjaty* or 'vizier', to use a traditional Egyptological term. This prime minister, responsible for public order, was likened to the god Thoth, 'the heart and tongue of the Sun Ra'; he was before all else the supreme legal authority in the land after Pharaoh and the Minister of Justice. Some viziers serving during several consecutive reigns must have dominated the country's political life. None the less, the *tjaty* (of whom there were two in the New Kingdom) was not the king's sole counsellor, nor even necessarily the principal one. Many dignitaries boast of having been consulted by their sovereign behind closed doors or having been selected for special missions and, in the imperial era, the governor of Nubia, an honorary 'royal son', was answerable directly to

15. G. Posener, 1960.
16. Useful data in B. Gross-Mertz.

Pharaoh and was almost sovereign in his own territory. In fact, it does not seem that the hierarchy of government gave an exact image of ministers' political power. Some personalities, Amenhotep, the scribe of recruits and the son of Hapi, an architect gradually elevated to the ranks of the gods for his wisdom, or Khamois, the high priest of Ptah and one of Ramses II's many sons,[17] were no doubt as influential as the viziers of their time. The fundamental despotism of the Pharaonic monarchy resulted in the residency being responsible for resolving major political conflicts: the 'unpersoning' of various high officials, not only Senmut and the other intimates of Hatshepsut, but individuals having served less controversial sovereigns (two royal princes and Usersatet, viceroy of Nubia under Amenhotep II), is the mute witness of government crises.

## Military organization

The king was responsible for national security. In theory, all credit for victories and conquests was his. Ramses II made great propaganda capital, in words and images, from having stood alone with his bodyguard at Kadesh, reaffirming the primacy of the king, sole saviour by divine grace, over an army from which his dynasty had in fact emerged. Naturally, as early as the time of the pyramids, the country had had a specialized high command, simultaneously military and naval, commanding troops already accustomed to manoeuvring and parading in disciplined ranks. In the third millennium, however, the peoples of the neighbouring countries posed no very great threat. Raiding parties easily thinned out the population of Nubia to Egypt's advantage; triumphal campaigns for which the rural population was levied *en masse* were enough to intimidate and plunder the sedentary peoples on the Libyan and Asian borders, while 'desert scouts' supervised the movements of the hungry Bedouins. What we know best about the Memphis troops relates to their participation in operations of economic interest and in the great building operations. The 'teams of elite young recruits' serving as the king's bodyguard supervised the transport of stone for the pyramids and some major expeditions to the Sinai mines or the eastern quarries. A specialized paramilitary corps, the *sementi*,[18] prospected and exploited the gold mines of Nubia and the desert, while 'interpreters' travelled far afield to negotiate for – or to grab – Asian or African goods. With the First Intermediate Period, the division of the kingdom into rival principalities modified military organization: the prince's personal retinue and the contingents from the nomes were joined by auxiliary shock troops recruited from the Nubians or Asian Amus. Two features already apparent in the third millennium were always to characterize Pharaonic armies: participation by the troops in major economic or construction projects, as supervisors or as labour force; and

17. Concerning this personality, see the recent thesis of F. Gomaa.
18. On this little-known corps of gold-hunters, see J. Yoyotte, 1975, pp. 44–55.

the use of fresh and fierce troops recruited abroad. Naturally military-minded through its sense of order and a taste for prestige, Egypt was not of warlike temperament.

Of course, the New Kingdom, a time of great international conflicts, was to see an unprecedented expansion of the professional army, divided into two arms of service, chariots and infantry, and subdivided into large army corps commanded by a complex hierarchy and served by a large bureaucracy, a vast structure that resisted the empires and principalities of Asia and seems to have successfully settled the crisis arising from the Aton heresy. The soldiers received small grants of land, and under the Ramses many captives – Nubians, Syrians, Libyans, the pirate Sea Peoples – were enlisted and also given such grants. In spite of their relatively rapid assimilation, the Libyans (perhaps reinforced by invaders of the same stock) set themselves up as an autonomous force and ended by making their chieftain Pharaoh. Nevertheless, this Egypt of Libyan Meshwesh warriors could not adjust to new military techniques, whereas Assyria was organizing itself into a formidable war machine. In the new clash of empires, the Saite kings, rather than depending on these warriors, were to rely on new military settlers recruited from the Ionians, Carians, Phoenicians and Judaeans, whilst in the final wars against the Persian empire, the last native Pharaohs, like their opponents, hired Greek mercenaries recruited by cosmopolitan adventurers. The breakdown of the nation's defensive apparatus, which failed to dispel either the ancient myth of Pharaoh as sole victor, the nostalgia for past conquests (epic of Sesostris) or complacent recollections of the civil wars (Petubastis cycle), was the weak point of a renascent Egypt, neither the economy nor the culture of which had fallen into decline.

## Religious and moral conceptions

### Myths

Certainly one of the great achievements of Pharaonic civilization, and perhaps one of its weaknesses, was its splendid image of the world and the forces ruling it, a coherent image manifesting itself in its myths, rituals, art, language and works of wisdom. One trait of this Egyptian mentality should be recalled to explain why the brief and incomplete summary of Pharaonic mythology below will provide neither a clear hierarchy or genealogy of the pantheon, nor a systematic cosmogony and cosmography. To apprehend the forces of nature and natural phenomena, mythology accepted all the images and legends handed down by tradition. There may be several 'sole' deities; the sky is a liquid ceiling, the belly of a cow, the body of a woman, a sow, etc. Thus there existed several conceptions of the origins of the universe, which were combined in various ways into the great syntheses elaborated on a local basis through the ages, each of which could be re-enacted in all its purity through performance of a given ritual act, on which it conferred a cosmic dimension. There are major features common to all these systems. The present world was organized and is maintained by the sun, after the goddess (Methyer, Neith), who was swimming in the Nun, the primeval flood, or else a college of earlier gods (the Ogdoad or the 'dead gods' at Edfu and Isna), or else the first dry land (Ptah-Tenen), had prepared the way for the appearance of that demiurge, who existed as an 'inert' potentiality in the heart of chaos and who then unleashed the generative process with the help of His Hand, the first goddess, and hived himself off into successive pairs: Shu (the atmosphere) and Tefnut (force of fire), both leonine beings, Geb (the earth) and Nut (the sky), and thereafter all the members of the Enneads, more precisely the many manifestations of the divine, proceeded from him. The present structure of the cosmos, willed by the demiurge, was established and completed by his divine word, by the giving of form to sounds, so that, for example, man (*rome*) emerged from his tears (*rame*), as did fish (*remu*).

The power of the solar divinity, a vital radiation that may also be destructive, is the 'Eye of Ra', a female entity occasionally blending with the goddess via whom procreation of the animal world occurred when the god split into two and who, at once consort and daughter, is manifested in the royal hair-style and crowns and may take the aspect of a cobra, a lion, a torch and the incense consumed by the fire. Genesis, which only threw back the primary darkness, is repeated practically every day at sunrise. Each day, as in the beginning, the creator must face hostile forces: the dragon Apopis, who threatens to dry up the heavenly river or halt the progress of the sun with his evil eye,[19] the mysterious tortoise and the unnameable 'enemies' who rage in the east. Before each dawn appearance the sun must also wash itself in the pools at the world's edge and purify itself from night and death. It ages in the course of its daily voyage and it mysteriously regenerates itself while, throughout the night, on another river it travels across another world. In the New Kingdom, works of fantasy like the *Book of Am Duat* or the *Book of Gates* were to symbolize the phases of that physical regeneration of Ra's 'flesh', describing the shores haunted by subordinate gods, enigmatic forms and forces, the blessed and the damned.

Our world is very precarious. At night the moon, a second divine Eye, takes the place of the other, but it continually declines, attacked by the knife of a terrible god, Thoth or Khons, later to be tentatively identified with the sun itself,[20] or by Seth, a pig, an oryx ... Various

19. This mythological theme has recently been spotlighted by J. F. Borghouts, pp. 114–50.
20. Selection of texts in S. Sauneron and J. Yoyotte, 1952. On the archaic aspect of the lunar gods, G. Posener, 1960.

legends, as well, recount that the Right Eye, the burning goddess, flies far from the sun and must be brought back. One such legend explicitly links this escapade to an attempt to annihilate mankind, which was conspiring against the ageing Ra: one fine day 'revolt' was born here below and men lost their primal equality.[21] Periodically, also, the wrath of the Eye of Ra is aroused, the 'powerful' Sekhmet afflicts men with disease, and the Nile flood is low, adding to the 'calamities of the year'.

Ra forgave man his rebellion and gave him magic to ensure his survival, but withdrew himself from man. A divine dynasty ruled this world. In those days Seth killed Osiris; revived by the attentions of Isis and Anubis, the embalmer, Osiris became the paragon of all dead kings and, by extension, of all the dead. He is also the image of the sun that dies every evening, and the lymph that flowed from his body is taken to be the water that rises each year (one image among many others of the Nile flood). Seker-Osiris is also the seed that is buried and that germinates. Banned from the Osirian tombs and sanctuaries, Seth was long worshipped as a god, the brutal life force, a turbulent being, Ra's helper against Apopis, the disorder necessary to order.[22] It was only around the eighth century before our era that a new fervour drew Osiris and Isis from the funerary cult, where their myth was the basis for the notion of an after-life, degraded Seth to the rank of Apopis and treated him as the personification of evil and the patron of the invaders.

Harmony presupposes unity; unity, always precarious, calls for re-unification. Seth, rival of Horus, son of Osiris, is his indispensable counterpart. According to the original tradition, each king embodies in his own person the reconciliation of Horus and Seth, just as the two plains of the north and south, or the black soil of the valley and the red soil of the desert, must be reunited. The myth according to which the eye of Horus was torn out by Seth and treated by Thoth was to become the subject of many ritual glosses that likened every offering, every further addition of nourishing grain and the moon itself, symbol of everything that must be complete to ensure fertility and fullness, to the recovery of the healed Eye (*oudjat*).

Corresponding to the divine order there is not only the structure and rhythms of the physical world, but a moral order – Ma'at – the norm of truth and justice which declares itself when Ra triumphs over his enemy and which, for the happiness of mankind, should reign in the functioning of institutions and in individual behaviour. 'Ra lives by Ma'at.' Thoth, the god of scholars, Ra's accountant, the judge of the gods, is 'happy by Ma'at'.[23]

21. A. de Buck, 1935–61, pp. 462–4.
22. H. TeVelde.
23. Texts associate natural disorders with disturbances in the political and social order. However, Ma'at is a moral and judicial concept and, in spite of a fairly common theory, it is not obvious that this concept includes the physical order of the world.

## The gods

All the doctrines and images we have just seen are accepted in all temples. The hymns singing the cosmic attributes and the wondrous providence of the god-creator take up the same themes, whether it be a primordial goddess like Neith, an earth-god like Ptah, or even Amon-Ra, Khnum-Ra, Sebek-Ra. The great myths – the Eye of Ra, the Eye of Horus, the passion of Osiris – as well as the basic ritual practices are common to all centres of population; but different gods, each with his own name, traditional image, animal manifestation and associated gods, are the 'masters' of the various towns: Khnum at Elephantine, Isna and elsewhere, Min at Coptos and Akhmim, Mont at Hermonthis, Amon at Thebes, Sebek at Sumenu, the Fayyum and elsewhere, Ptah-Seker at Memphis, Ra-Harakhte-Atum at Heliopolis, Neith at Sais, Bast at Bubastis, Uadjit at Buto, Nekhbet at El Kab, etc., and there were many local gods called by the name of Horus, many goddesses who are fearsome Sekhmets or kindly Hathors. Had figures associated in more or less forgotten myths been in ancient times scattered across the country? It is possible, and in any event the existence of different local religions in prehistoric times might explain much of the polytheism that proliferates in a religion whose unity is obvious. It seems that this religion tended, through the identification of certain gods with others, to reduce that plurality to a few types: a supreme deity, generally a sun-god and often explicitly identified with Ra (Amon-Ra, Mont-Ra, Haroeris-Ra, etc.); a consort goddess who is the Eye of Ra (Mut = Bast = Sekhmet = Hathor, etc.); the warrior god-son of the Horus–Anhur type; a dead god of the Osiris type (Seker, Seph, etc.). The New Kingdom theologians represented each 'initial' town as a stopping-place of the demiurge in the course of his wandering genesis and considered that the state's three principal gods, Amon of the air, Ra of the sun, and Ptah of the underworld, were three cosmographic and political manifestations of one and the same divinity. The maze of theoretical problems presented by a multiform pantheon gave rise to much theological and even philosophical speculation: Ptah conceiving in 'his heart which is Horus' and creating via 'his tongue which is Thoth'; Sia, 'knowledge', and Hu, 'order', major attributes of the sun; the four Souls which are Ra (fire), Shu (air), Geb (earth) and Osiris (water); the unknowable and infinite God who is 'the sky, the earth, the Nun, and everything that lies between them'; and so on. A feeling of the unity of the godhead predominated among the educated, at least from the New Kingdom on, that feeling going with a faith that worshipped, as so many approximations to the ineffable, the myths, names and idols of all the country's gods. The attitude of the celebrated Akhenaton, who would recognize only the visible disc of the sun as the sole true god, still lay in the mainstream of Egyptian thought, but was heretical in the manner in which it upset tradition, which, allowing for the mysterious, accepted and reconciled all forms of piety and thought.

## The temple

Each god created his town, each looked after his own domain and, beyond that domain, all Egypt. The king concerned himself with all the gods simultaneously. Heir to the sun and successor of Horus, it was his responsibility to maintain the order created by divine providence and, in order to do so, to support divine beings themselves threatened by possible relapse into chaos, to turn aside the wrath of the goddess, to resort to perpetual collaboration with the divine in order to ensure the cycle of the year, the rise of the Nile, the normal growth of vegetation, the increase of the flocks, the frustration of rebellion, the security of the frontiers, and happiness and the rule of Ma'at among his subjects. To achieve this, sacred science employed the magic of word and gesture, of writing and images and of architectural forms, all processes also used to ensure the after-life of the dead. The ceremonies conducted by the initiate priests accompanied the ritual acts by verbal formulas reinforcing their power of compulsion by means of spells recalling mythical precedents. The depiction of these rites and the writing of these texts on the walls of the temples perpetuated their action. Likewise, the many statues of the king and images of private individuals in the sacred precincts enabled those portrayed to serve the god for ever, to dwell with him and to receive additional life force from him. The architect made the temple a scale model of the universe, thus giving it permanence: the pylon is the mountain of the rising sun, the dark sanctuary is the place where the sun sleeps, the columns represent the primordial swamp out of which creation arose and the base of its walls are the soil of Egypt. A high brick perimeter wall isolates it and its gardens and service buildings from the impurities that might pollute the divine; the officiating priests and those privileged persons admitted to the temenos are required to perform ritual purifications and observe prohibitions relating to food, clothing and sexual activity. In order to show that it is actually Pharaoh performing the ritual, scenes carved into the walls depict him carrying out the various rites and presenting in long processions the nomes of Egypt, the phases of the flood and the minor gods that preside over the various economic activities of life. Throughout the day the idol, in other words the shape through which one may communicate with the god, is purified, censed, clothed, fed and invoked at length in hymns which exhort the god to awake, reaffirm his divine power and entreat his benevolent activity. During the great festivals, the god emerges in procession to recharge himself with divine energy from the rays of the sun, to visit the tombs of dead kings and past gods, and to re-enact the mythical events through which the world took shape.[24]

24. Our understanding of temple symbolism and decor, as well as the rituals, is based on the great monuments built and decorated in the Greek and Roman eras (Edfu, Ombos, Dandarah, Philae, etc.). For general information, see S. Sauneron and H. Stierlin.

Above all, the temple is a work-place where the king, supported by priestly initiates, makes high state magic to ensure the orderly course of events (primarily to ensure that his people are fed). Distant though they be, the gods, those prime movers of the world, are none the less felt as personal beings, near to each mortal. In the New Kingdom, the common people come to pray to them before the side gates of the temples, in village chapels or in the ruins of ancient monuments, where their presence can be felt (the Great Sphinx of Giza, notably, was considered an idol of both the sun and Hurun, the healing god borrowed from the Canaanites). Hymns are carved on small stelae witnessing to the faith of mere mortals in the god of their town, and the favours of great Amon himself, 'impartial judge, who turns to him who calls upon him, who hears entreaties', are besought for one's health or business affairs. Throughout history, proper names show us that all classes of the population claimed the direct patronage of the greatest gods. Moreover, in spite of its strong specificity and a priesthood which jealously guarded the secrets that ruled the life of the nation, Egyptian religion was singularly hospitable. In the New Empire it annexed the Syro-Palestinian deities, made Bes, the tutelary genius of women and babies, an inhabitant of eastern Sudan, accepted and Egyptianized Dedun, the lord of Nubia, recognized Amon in the Nubians' Ram-god and firmly implanted the worship of the Theban god in the land of Kush, later identified its gods with the Greek pantheon and, in the rural areas, won the hearts of the Greek settlers in the Ptolemaic era.

None the less, the identification of the land of Egypt with the organized world throws a singular light on the ideas of the Pharaoh's subjects about the world outside. The African and Semitic peoples and foreign cities and monarchies were equated with the forces of chaos, always ready to subvert creation (hieroglyphic writing depicts every foreign country as a mountainous desert!). On either side of the temple gates are facing tablets showing, on the south, the king vanquishing the Nubians and, on the north, the king conquering the Asians.[25] These images at the entrance-ways to the microcosm annihilate by the power of magic the 'rebels' who endanger order; in the New Kingdom the vast sequences of carvings on the outside walls showing victorious campaigns and the booty brought back to the god simply illustrate by historical anecdotes the constant co-operation between sovereign and deity in maintaining the equilibrium of the universe. An interesting manifestation of this outlook and one which somewhat qualified the 'chauvinism' of dogma is that the magic rites directed against the princes and peoples of Asia, Nubia and Libya are not aimed so much at destroying them as at ridding them of hostile intentions.

## Ethics

Perfect harmony was created and the king exists to maintain it. Thus the

25. C. Desroches-Noblecourt and C. Kuentz, pp. 49–57 and notes 178–9 (pp. 167–8).

ideal era was 'the days of Ra' and the priests of the Late Period even conceived of a lost golden age when serpents did not bite, thorns did not prick, walls did not crumble and Ma'at reigned on earth.[26] The perfect system is not a utopia that one tries to achieve by inventing new rules; it existed in the beginning and it becomes real again from the moment one conforms to Ma'at. This means that the morality professed in the *Teachings* written by high Memphis officials (Djedefhor, Ptahhotep) and by various scribes in later periods (Ani, Amenemope), as well as the instructions to priests carved in the later temples, are fundamentally conformist and that teaching was scarcely propitious to the development of originality. Texts where someone describes his new findings are very few in number by comparison with the conventional autobiographies and standard formulas. The talent of the many sculptors who managed to put their own personal stamp on their works while unaffectedly complying with the traditional constraints is thus all the more remarkable.

Everyday ethics equated the virtues proper with the intellectual qualities, rectitude with decorum, physical impurity with baseness of character. Based on a psychology without illusions, it extolled submission to superiors and benevolence to inferiors. It was accepted that worldly success is the customary consequence of virtue, and although the idea of posthumous retribution for one's deeds developed very early, the magical expedients provided in the funerary formulas in order to escape divine judgement set limits thereto. Great care was taken in teaching correct behaviour: not to talk too much, to remain calm in one's gestures and moderate in one's reactions, an ideal that Egyptian statuary expresses to perfection. All excess is harmful: he who is carried away by emotion disturbs others and courts perdition himself. Some sages, however, introduced into their reflections a strong personal religious feeling and expressed aspirations to individual excellence. Better an upright heart than formal compliance with ritual. In God one finds the 'path of life'. The debt of biblical wisdom to Egyptian culture should not be underestimated. Even though it usually relates more to social necessities than to charitable understanding, the concern for others is great. Kings and scribes have left us good lessons in social ethics: wholeheartedly to attend to the interests of the king and his people, not to benefit the strong at the expense of the weak, not to let oneself become corrupt, not to cheat over weight or measure. Egypt also developed the concept of human dignity: 'do not use violence to men ... they were born from the eyes of Ra, they are his issue'; in one of the celebrated tales in the Westcar Papyrus, a magician refuses to carry out a dangerous experiment on a prisoner 'for it is forbidden so to behave towards God's flock'.

The picture of the ideal order presented by the official ideology corresponded, all things considered, to that presented by the country when,

26. E. Otto, pp. 93–108.

the Two Lands having been duly reunited, a strong monarchy and conscientious government ensured general prosperity and peace. With the First Intermediate Period, civil wars, the infiltrations of the barbarians and the sudden changes in circumstances awakened anxiety. 'Changes are taking place, things are no longer as they were last year.' 'New words' had to be found, said the writer Khakhêperre-sonb, called Ankhu, in his *Discourses*, to apprehend unprecedented happenings. And so a pessimistic literature emerged, from which proceeds, notably, the *Prophecy of Neferti*, which evokes the crisis that put an end to the eleventh dynasty, and the *Admonitions* of the choirmaster Ipu-ur on the eve of the Hyksos era.[27] The *Neferti* and later the *Potter's Oracle* and the various tales relating to the expulsion of the *Impure* stigmatize the subversion of Ma'at only in order to bring out to greater effect the final victory of the saviour-king and of order. In contrast, the *Dialogue of the Desperate Man with his Soul* casts doubt on the utility of the funerary rites, while the *Songs of the Harpist* are an invitation to 'carpe diem'. Sometimes hedonistic asides slip into conventional works. If it had been better preserved, secular literature would reveal a more diversified world of thought than do the royal and priestly inscriptions on stone. Some tales, the Songs of Love, comic details enlivening domestic scenes in the funerary chapels and the lighthearted sketches drawn on potsherds reveal, beyond Pharaonic conformism, a people fundamentally happy, skilful, humorous and friendly, such as it remains today.

## Law

As we have seen, religion and ethics stress the maintenance of strict discipline, which benefits the whole community of subjects, and the exclusive activity of the royal person in government and ritual. Art itself is more interested in the general than in the individual, in the typical example rather than individual spontaneity. It is thus all the more striking that Pharaonic law remained resolutely individualistic. In relation to royal decisions and to legal procedure and penalties, men and women of all classes seem to have been equals before the law. The family was limited to father, mother and their young children, and women enjoyed equal rights of property ownership and judicial relief. In general, responsibility was strictly personal. The extended family had no legal substance and the status of a man was not defined in relation to his lineage. In the domain of law, Pharaonic Egypt was distinctly different from traditional Africa and curiously anticipates the modern societies of Europe.

27. cf. J. Van Seters, 1964, pp. 13–23.

## Funerary beliefs and practices

The same individualism reigned in regard to beliefs and practices concerning life after death. Each, according to his means, provided for his own after-life, that of his spouse and that of his children, in the event of their premature death. The son should participate in his father's funeral rites and, if the need should arise, ensure his burial. The human (or divine) being includes, in addition to the mortal flesh, several ingredients – the *Ka*, the *Ba*, and other lesser-known entities – whose nature remains difficult to define and whose inter-relationships are obscure. Funerary practices are intended to ensure the survival of these 'souls', but a well-known feature of Egyptian religion is to have tied that survival to preservation of the body itself by means of mummification, and to have made elaborate arrangements for the dead to be able to enjoy an after-life at least as active and happy as life in this world. A tomb is composed of a superstructure open to the surviving relatives and a vault where the deceased lies accompanied by magical or domestic objects. Persons of wealth paid a regular stipend under contract to processional priests, who from father to son would be responsible for bringing offerings of food; and, as a final precaution, the compelling power of the spoken and written word and the magic of carved and painted images were employed. In the chapel – mastaba or hypogeum – the effective rituals of internment and offering are made eternal; other scenes re-create the work and pleasures of an ideal world; statues and statuettes create a multitude of substitute bodies. On the planks of the coffin, on the stones of the vault, on a 'Book of the Dead' given into the mummy's keeping, are copied the formulae recited at the time of burial and spells enabling the deceased to enjoy all his faculties, escape the dangers of the Other World and fulfil his divine destiny. As in theology, Egyptian beliefs regarding life after death juxtaposed various conceptions: survival as a companion of the sun, residence within the tomb with daily awakening at dawn, emergence of the *Ba* into the open air and enjoyment of familiar objects, life in a wonderful elysium with Osiris. In any case, he who was given a fine burial would change status: he is an equal of the gods, of Osiris, and of all the kings, each of whom is an Osiris.

PLATE 3.1 *Harvesting corn*

PLATE 3.2 *Making a hayrick*

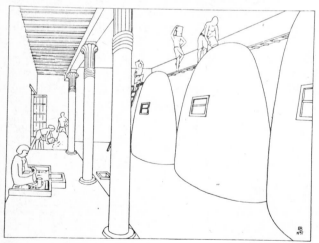

PLATE 3.3 *Filling the granaries*

PLATE 3.4 *Rendering the accounts*

PLATE 3.5 *Grape harvest and press*

PLATE 3.6 *Tame pelicans*

PLATE 3.7a *Fishing*

PLATE 3.7b *Hunting hippopotamuses*

PLATE 3.8 *Naval operations*

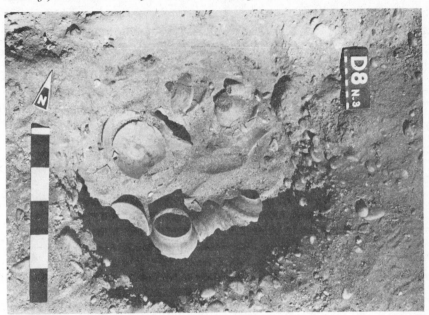

# Egypt's relations with the rest of Africa

A. HAMID ZAYED

*with the collaboration of* J. DEVISSE

It is now commonly acknowledged that archaeological research has revealed no decisive evidence of contacts between Egypt and Africa south of Meroe. This does not, of course, rule out theories based on hypotheses, but they must be considered as such until evidence has lent them the necessary weight.

A few years ago, there was talk of the discovery of Egyptian objects far away in the heart of the continent. A statuette of Osiris, dating from the seventh century before our era, was found in Zaïre on the banks of the River Lualaba, near the confluence of the Kalmengongo; a statue inscribed with the cartouche of Thutmose III ($-1490$ to $-1468$) was found south of the Zambezi. However, a critical study of the circumstances in which these objects were discovered makes it impossible at the present time to conclude that they indicate the existence of relations in the seventh or fifteenth centuries before our era between Egypt and the regions mentioned above.[1] A. Arkell reached the conclusion, on the strength of not very convincing evidence, that there were contacts between Byzantine Egypt and modern Ghana.

However, this by no means signifies that we should conclude on the basis of *a silentio* reasoning that no links existed in ancient times between Egypt and the rest of the African continent. Given the paucity of information in this field and the conclusions sometimes drawn from inadequate evidence, we should proceed with even stricter regard than usual for scientific accuracy and rely solely on facts which we are confident have been scientifically established.

For instance, the influence, in certain respects, of Egyptian civilization on other African civilizations may be regarded by some as established. Even if this were proved, *this influence* would not be a proof of ancient *contacts*. Eva L. R. Meyerowitz takes the fact that the Akan have adopted the vulture as the symbol of self-creation to be a proof of Egyptian influence.[2] She also stresses the links between the god Ptah and the Akan god Odomankoma, both bisexual, who, after creating themselves

1. See J. Leclant, 1956a, pp. 31–2.
2. E. L.-R. Meyerowitz, p. 31.

created the world with their own hands. Although an interesting association,[3] it is not conclusive evidence that contacts existed between ancient Egypt on the one hand and the ancient Akan or the region of the Bight of Benin on the other. In the same way the serpent cult, studied in all African civilizations by many distinguished scholars, was considered from early times likely to be derived from an Egyptian origin. But this view discounts the fact that ancient cultures observed their environment very closely and were perfectly capable of drawing their cults from their own observation. There are other hypotheses. J. Leclant,[4] for instance, refers to the suggestion sometimes made that the serpent cult had come to Meroe, and perhaps to other parts of Africa, from India. So much for the importance of adopting a cautious approach.

Before turning to the traces, whether certain, hypothetical or improbable, of Egypt's links with the rest of the continent in ancient times, we should note that whatever the thesis finally adopted concerning the ancient people of Egypt,[5] there is apparently a considerable chronological and technological discrepancy between the latter and its peripheral civilizations.[6] Even though it is technically a part of Africa, Egyptian culture detached itself from its western and southern environment. Egypt obviously distrusted its northern neighbours still more when they became a threat. Culturally, Pharaonic Egypt felt out of step with its neighbours. That it outpaced them is certain, but why it did so is difficult to see. From then onwards, gradually, even if technical solidarity persisted, profound differences in their way of life set the Egyptians apart from their neighbours. Above all, if we take the ethnical identity of the Egyptians and their southern neighbours into account, it is of prime importance that we consider the reasons for this – if we succeed in discovering them – which would shed light on the extent to which writing was adopted as an instrument of social and cultural cohesion in the Nile valley. Research should be focused on this problem. Are the adoption and use of writing facts simply connected with biological and natural phenomena, an essential accident linked to the spirit of a people, or are they merely the inevitable product of a culture at a certain stage of its political and social integration?

The Cairo Symposium (1974) stressed the ethnical and cultural stability of Egypt during the 3000 years of Pharaonic rule. The lower Nile valley was like a sponge absorbing, for over thirty centuries, infiltrations or

3. It should be noted here that the self-creation problem is not limited to Ptah (a demigod, but all the craftsmen's patron). It also extends to Re and other deities. A subjacent general myth apparently existed in Egypt, among various local groups and perhaps at different periods.

4. See J. Leclant, 1956b, ch. 10.

5. See Chapter 1 and the summary of the Cairo Symposium.

6. H.-J. Hugot, 1976, p. 76, points out that when Egypt was unified, about −3200, the Saharan Neolithic age was at its peak. He categorically rejects the hypothesis occasionally formulated that Egyptian Neolithic man could be of Saharan origin (p. 73).

immigrations from various peripheries, except in some difficult times of intensified pressure by foreign peoples. To the west, but also to the south, people related to one another in varying degrees were either kept within their habitat by Egyptian frontier fortifications or were regarded as available at will to the valley to provide food or men for its defence. Save for this feeling of Egyptian particularity, which may have been characteristic only of the upper classes of society and which developed gradually, it is hard to know how the Egyptians behaved towards their immediate neighbours. The latter – like all the other peoples with whom the Egyptians came into contact – were regarded as obliged as a matter of course to make their contribution in men and riches to Pharaonic civilization. Tribute, from the outset, was one of the signs of submission of Egypt's neighbours, and non-payment was followed by punitive expeditions. However, the attitude of the neighbours was not resigned and passive all the time. Egypt was not always able to dictate to them and her relations with Africa varied with the centuries.

## Western neighbours: Saharans and Libyans[7]

It is generally agreed that in the predynastic period frequent human exchanges with the Sahara declined. Very little is known about these exchanges and it is sometimes claimed that they did not exist.[8] In the dynastic period it is certain that Egypt exerted an influence on the Sahara, although again very little is known about it.[9]

In fact, for the Egyptians, according to the latest research, the Saharans during the dynastic period were mainly the Libyans who had gradually concentrated in the north of one of the most vast and inhospitable deserts in the world. The situation was different in the Neolithic period when the rapid spread of the desert, which increased during the dynastic period, forced the Libyans, shepherds and hunters, back to the periphery of their former habitat, or led them, starving, to knock at the door of the Nilotic paradise which had to be defended against them. Their pressure continued unremittingly but was seldom crowned with success, except perhaps in the western part of the Delta where the Saharan population

7. I would here express my thanks to Professor T. Gostynsky, the author of a monograph on ancient Libya which he kindly communicated to Unesco to facilitate the drafting of this chapter. I have drawn on it several times.

8. In several passages of the *Final Report* of the Cairo Symposium (1974). One of the most promising current investigations is based on rock engravings and paintings 'from the Atlantic to the Red Sea'. Although apparently concerning the prehistoric era in particular, this study contains a wealth of precise data.

9. H.-J. Hugot, 1976, p. 73. However, note the warning (p. 82) against the hasty conclusions of those who, for example, detect in certain themes of Saharan rock paintings (ram with sun discs, sorcerers with zoomorphic masks, etc.) traces of an eighteenth-dynasty influence. He says: 'This means working over-hastily and too easily overlooking the manner of applying the scientific proof required for the validity of a hypothesis.'

is undoubtedly ancient and homogeneous. In the great oases encircled by their desert – Khariyah, Dakhilah, Farafirah and Siwah – the Egyptian nobility took to hunting. In so doing, they assumed an obligation which had originally fallen to the king. To fight against and destroy the inhabitants of the desert (even the harmless hare) meant helping to maintain the cosmic order, because the desert belonged to Seth and to primary chaos that constantly threatened to return to earth and to destroy the order (Ma'at) which was willed by the gods and for which Pharaoh was responsible. Therefore hunting was not simply a pleasurable pastime of the privileged classes. It had a profound religious significance.

These oases had to be crossed in order to go southwards towards Chad or northwards towards the Fezzan and the Niger. However, we have today no proof that these routes were used regularly during the dynastic period.

Research on these routes, apart from their inherent interest, should certainly be undertaken. Archaeology and toponymy should make it possible to find out whether or not the Egyptians used these major African traffic routes to go to Tibesti, Darfur, Bahr el Ghazal and Chad or to the Fezzan and Ghudamis.

At all events, at least from the nineteenth dynasty onwards, the Libyans formed a reserve of manpower and soldiers for Egypt. Libyan captives, recognizable by the feathers they wore as a head-dress, had a good reputation as soldiers, particularly as charioteers. Often branded with a red-hot iron, they were not used as labour for the great collective operations, or for domestic work.[10] They were enrolled in the army where their proportion grew with the passing of centuries and where they met those other immigrants, the Nubians. As cattle-breeders they supplied livestock for Egyptian consumption,[11] either as tribute or seized from them as booty during raids. Thus they played an economic role comparable to that of the Nubians.

Of course, Egyptian historiographers judged the Libyan encroachments very harshly when they occurred.[12] In the thirteenth and twelfth centuries before our era, as under the Old Kingdom, the Libyans were driven by necessity to try to penetrate into Egypt. Seti I and Ramses II erected a network of fortifications against them and captured the boldest invaders. After two vain attempts to return to the western part of the Delta whence they had been chased, the Libyans obtained from Ramses III, in the twelfth century before our era, permission to settle there. In exchange, they played a greater part in the military defence of Egypt. In the tenth century, and for

10. Snefru boasted of capturing 11 000 Libyans and 13 100 head of cattle.

11. The inscriptions mention imports of several tens of thousands of horned cattle, sheep, goats and donkeys.

12. From − 3000 to − 1800 the Egyptians were able, according to their chroniclers, to check Libyan invasions. All the expeditions mentioned during this long period were from Egypt to Libya. The very fact that they occurred reveals a problem in Egyptian–Libyan relations. From − 1800 to − 1300, Egyptian sources are silent on this point.

nearly two centuries thereafter, Libyans ruled Egypt under the twenty-second and twenty-third dynasties. This new state of affairs aroused strong reactions in Upper Egypt where attempts were made to oust them with the support of the kingdom of Napata. This rivalry between black and white warriors and politicians was the beginning of a situation which was to prevail for a long time in the life of Egypt. The immediate Nubian response was to set up the Ethiopian dynasty created by Peye (Piankhi).

When considering the relations between Egypt and other nations, whether African or not, the still almost unknown part played by the Delta should never be forgotten. Archaeological excavations in this region of Egypt are still so inadequate that all we can do is to put forward a few suppositions.

During the dynastic period, the Delta was often and sometimes massively over-run by the migrations of neighbouring peoples from the west, north or north-east.[13] This always affected the life of Egypt to a greater or lesser degree. It will suffice to recall Egypt's relations with Byblos (vital for timber supplies), the Hyksos episode, the exodus of the Hebrews, the attacks of the Libyans and the Sea Peoples, in order to understand that the Delta was always a trouble spot in the days of Pharaonic Egypt. In particular, when seeking to develop additional foreign trade with Africa, Asia and the Mediterranean, Egypt had to exercise a firm control over the Delta seaboard. From the beginning of the Pharaonic period, the commitment of Egyptian commercial and military policy to the north and the north-east ran counter, to some extent, to the desire to make contacts with and penetrate into the interior of the African continent. When dealing with the history of Egypt throughout the ages, this important contradiction should be kept in mind. Egypt, a Mediterranean and maritime nation, had to control a serviceable space open to the Mediterranean and to the north of the Red Sea; well-built portages between the latter and the Nile, north of the First Cataract, sufficed to ensure the indispensable junction between the western and eastern economic basins. However, as an African nation, the Egyptians may have been tempted to penetrate a long way inland along the Nile, at least as far as the Fourth Cataract. They would then have come up against difficulties of the kind dealt with in other chapters of this work. They may also have been attracted to Chad, passing through the ancient valleys which lead to the left bank

13. As the Cairo Symposium strongly emphasized, the ancient history of the Delta has still to be discovered. In fact, what is known about northern Egypt in prehistoric and proto-historic times does not go much farther down than present-day Cairo. Nor was the Old Kingdom better informed. The coastal strip may have remained for a very long time and over a widespread area outside the Egyptian sphere. In fact, in the fourth millennium, when the Egyptian state was formed, Lower Egypt spread from Heliopolis to Al Fayyum inclusive and Upper Egypt from south of Al Fayyum to Al Kab. Therefore the Delta is scarcely involved, and Upper Egypt, said to be more African, stopped when sandstone, rightly qualified as Nubian, appeared marking the entry into another world, whether ethnical or political, of Ta-Seti, the Land of the Bow.

of the Nile, and to Ethiopia with its wealth of ivory. Southwards a major obstacle would probably have been the extensive marshlands which the Egyptians would have found difficult to reach or cross, and which throughout antiquity protected the secret of the very high Nile valleys. Although we can today follow the history of Egypt's northern relations and of the portages between the Red Sea and the Nile fairly easily, archaeological data concerning the ancient Egyptians' land-ward relations with the distant south are sadly lacking.

Therefore, for the time being we have to resort to more or less probable suppositions, based on texts, linguistics, ethnology or simply common sense. But the history of Egypt has been considered for so long by the Egyptologists themselves as Mediterranean and white that it is now necessary to change research techniques and materials, and especially the research workers' mentality in order to replace the land of the Pharaohs in its African context.

## Southern neighbours: the Egyptians, the upper Nile basins, their links with Africa

The most recent archaeological excavations, the findings of which are often as yet unpublished, highlight similarities between the Khartoum area and the lower Nile valley in the Neolithic age; similarities which are very difficult to explain.

With the Old Kingdom, however, this apparent similarity ceased to exist. Already in the first dynasty forts protected the south of Egypt against its southern neighbours. More and more, throughout their long common history, political and cultural differences and conflicting interests separated the territories north of the First Cataract from those that lie south of the Fourth Cataract. Nevertheless, relations, which were complex and diverse, were never completely broken off between the Egyptians and their southern neighbours whom they called the Nehesi.

At all events, Lower Nubia interested the Egyptians on account of the gold it produced, and the more southerly Nilotic regions because of the routes leading to the African interior by the White Nile, the Saharan valleys or Darfur. Throughout the history of Egypt, access to the south was a predominant concern. This probably also explains the importance attributed to the control of the western oases, another access route parallel to the Nile.

From the beginning of the Old Kingdom, the Sudan, like Libya, represented for the Egyptians a source of manpower,[14] livestock and

---

14. Pharaoh Snefru stated that he had brought back 7000 men from the south, from a land called Ta-Seti. Seti = archaic type of bow. A. H. Gardiner, 1950, p. 512. Ta-Seti = Land of those who carry the Seti bow. It is interesting to note that all the Sudanese tribes up to the Congo basin carry this same bow.

minerals.[15] The Nubians, famous for their archery, held a prominent place in the Egyptian army. They were brought in, too, as agricultural labourers (during the Middle Kingdom, for instance, at Al Fayyum, where villages are identifiable by their name: Villages of the Nubians), but were fairly quickly assimilated into Egyptian socio-cultural life. Probably at the end of the first dynasty, changes occurred in Nubia which in all likelihood upset relations with Egypt. The slow emergence of Group G, which appears not to have been fully constituted until the fifth dynasty, leaves a gap of five centuries in our knowledge of these relations.

The Egyptians began to organize their links with the Sudan at the end of the fifth dynasty. During the same period, a new political and economic post was established known as the Governor of the South. The holder was responsible for guarding the southern gate of Egypt, for organizing commercial exchanges and facilitating the circulation of trading expeditions. This post required certain qualifications, among which was a knowledge of trade and of the languages of the inhabitants of the regions. Unas, a Governor of the South under the sixth dynasty, was in command of recruits from different parts of Nubia: Nehesi (Nubians) from the land of Irhtet, Madja, Yam, Wawat and Kau.

At the end of the Old Kingdom trade relations between Egypt and the Sudan were interrupted. However, the prince of Edfu relates on the wall of his tomb at Mealla that grain was sent to Wawat to prevent famine. This is evidence that relations between Egypt and Nubia continued at that time. Furthermore, Nubian soldiers played an important part in the battles in Middle Egypt during the First Intermediate Period. There exist painted wooden models of a company of Nubian archers, forty-strong, which show the importance accorded by the Egyptians to the Sudanese soldier.

However, the development at this time of Group C in Lower Nubia was probably responsible, like the troubles during the First Intermediate Period, for the decline in relations between Egyptians and Sudanese.

The peoples of Group C are still little known. It was long thought that they had slowly infiltrated into the Nile valley, but it is now believed that they were simply the successors of the Group A peoples. Whatever the reason, the relations between these peoples and the Egyptians were always awkward. Several pieces of pottery discovered near Jebel Kekan, beside the Khor Baraka at Agordat (Eritrea), are in the museum at Khartoum. They are similar to the Group C pottery discovered in Lower Nubia. Had these Group C peoples, for some unknown reason (drought, Egyptian forces arriving in Nubia), been led to abandon Lower Nubia, probably during the twelfth dynasty? These peoples would then have left their homes in the Wadi el Allaqi Valley for the Red Sea mountains where the Beja tribes live today. Likewise, some peoples speaking a Nubian language now

15. As from −2500 furnaces designed to melt the local copper were set up by the Egyptians at Buhen, south of Wadi Halfa.

live in the Nuba hills south of Kordofan. Hence, it may be assumed that the Sudan witnessed a migration of Group C southwards and westwards from the north.

In the south, the empire of Kerma, less directly affected by the Egyptian invasion, had been influenced by Egypt in the cultural sphere since − 2000. However, it retained its own identity until its end in about − 1580. Little by little, the Egyptians were to give the name of Kush to this culture, known since − 2000, but used by them to characterize the kingdom set up south of the Second Cataract after − 1700.

At the beginning of the Middle Kingdom the kings of Egypt, threatened by Asiatic Bedouins, appear to have asked the inhabitants of the Sudan for help. Menthuhotep III, founder of the eleventh dynasty, was perhaps black-skinned. If so, this might be why he asked the Sudan for help and it would tend to prove that relations between Egypt and the Sudan, interrupted during the First Intermediate Period, had been resumed. In all likelihood, some Egyptians crossed into the Sudan. From the stelae[16] found at Buhen, we know that several Egyptian families lived in Nubia for a long time during the Middle Kingdom. They had Egyptian names and worshipped the local gods.[17] The kings of that period built fourteen forts in Nubia to safeguard their frontiers and trading expeditions.

When the Hyksos seized the northern and middle parts of Egypt, Kush increased its independence and power. The kingdom of Kush was a potential danger to the Pharaohs. A recently discovered Egyptian text reveals that during the war to overthrow the Hyksos, Kamose, the last Pharaoh of the seventeenth dynasty, was informed of the capture of a messenger from the Hyksos king inviting the king of Kush to be his ally against the Egyptians. With the eighteenth dynasty, pressure on the Sudan once again became very strong and relations were expanded on an unprecedented scale.[18] Simultaneously the egyptianization of the regions between the Second and the Fourth Cataracts gathered momentum. In the reign of Thutmose III, the shape of the tombs in this region changed. Instead of tumuli, Egyptian-shaped tombs were built, and instead of rock tombs, small pyramids like those found at Deir el Medina were constructed. Hence the similarity of the cities of Buhen and Aniba to Egyptian cities. Likewise ushabtis and scarabs were found in tombs in the Sudan.

16. J. Vercoutter, 1957, pp. 61–9. The dating system adopted by J. Vercoutter in this article has recently been disputed. J. Vercoutter now believes that these stelae belong rather to the Second Intermediate Period and are practically contemporary with the Hyksos.

17. G. Posener, 1958, p. 65: 'This country [Kush] was colonized by the Pharaonic State. For many centuries, it was under the ascendancy of Egyptian civilization, its customs, language, beliefs and institutions. The whole course of Nubia's history bears the stamp of its northern neighbour.'

18. This is the period when, for reasons that are still not clear today, Egyptian iconography shows a major change in its portrayal of black Africans. Various hypotheses have been framed, including one to the effect that contacts with the rest of the continent were extended at that time.

The drawings and names on the princes' tombs were inscribed in a typically Egyptian way. The tomb of Heka-Nefer,[19] prince of Aniba during the reign of Tutankhamun, is like the rock tombs in Egypt. Simpson even supposed that this tomb was covered by a pyramid in the style of those at Deir el Medina. The tomb of Dhuty-Hetep, Prince of Debeira under the reign of Queen Hatshepsut, resembles those in Thebes.

Nubia and Egypt had never been so close before. In − 1400, the temple of Soleb was built. The military and sometimes the administrative part played by the Sudanese was greater than ever before and reached its culmination when the Ethiopian dynasty dominated Egypt. Nevertheless, although egyptianized, the inhabitants of the high valleys did not become Egyptian. A distinct culture continued to express itself, albeit in Egyptian form, even at the time of the thirtieth dynasty.

The latter restored to Egypt an African depth recorded in the Bible, first when the Lord protects the Hebrews from the assault of the Assyrians, by inspiring their king in a dream with the fear of an attempt against him by Tir-hakah,[20] the king of Ethiopia, and, second, when the Hebrew King Hezekiah sought an alliance with the Pharaoh and his people.[21]

These were the last great moments of unity.

The conquest of Thebes by the Assyrians coincided with the rise in the south of the Meroitic empire. The defence of this region against the assaults from the north became all the more necessary in that the Egyptian armies henceforth included large contingents of Hebrew, Phoenician and Greek mercenaries. In the absence of the necessary research, the relations, certainly difficult, between the new Nilotic empire and Egypt are little known.

## Punt

As in the case of other problems of African history, a great deal of ink, not always of excellent quality, has flowed in order to locate the fabled land of Punt, with which the Egyptians had relations, at least during the New Empire; and which the images at Dayr al Bahri reveal. Attempts were made to place this country in Morocco, Mauritania, the region of the Zambezi, and so on.[22] Today, agreement has almost been reached on the location of Punt in the Horn of Africa, although much hesitation as to its exact boundaries still exists.[23] One tempting theory is that it was situated

19. W. K. Simpson, 1963.
20. 2 Kings, 19: 9, and Isaiah, 37: 9.
21. W. Reichhold. The author provided an interesting translation from a passage of Chapter 17 of the Book of Isaiah, concerning the sending of an envoy to the black Pharaoh: 'Go, you swift messengers to the tall and bronzed people, to a people always feared, to a nation mighty and conquering, whose land the rivers divide.'
22. R. Herzog, 1968, pp. 42–5, gives a full list of the theories on this subject.
23. ibid.

on that part of the African coast which stretches from the Poitialeh river in northern Somalia to Cape Guardafui. It is a mountainous area with terraced plantations reminiscent of those depicted at Dayr al Bahri. Many trees, including the incense-producing balsam, grow on these terraces.

In the region which is today called Goluin there is an inlet where Queen Hatshepsut's vessels may have been moored and it is there that the ancient River Elphas flowed into the ocean. This location and the reference to Queen Hatshepsut's ships heading for Punt suggest the Egyptians' use of the sea route to the foreign land. Recently, R. Herzog tried to show this had not been so and that the Egyptians' relations with Punt were maintained over land. This theory aroused strong reactions.[24]

Very recent research[25] led to the discovery on the Red Sea coast, north of Al Qusayr at the mouth of the Wadi Gasus, of traces of Egyptian connections with Punt. One of the inscriptions found has been transcribed by the discoverer as follows: 'King of Upper and Lower Egypt, Kheperkare[26] beloved of the God Khenty-Khety, son of Re, Sesostris beloved of Hathor mistress of Pwenet [Punt].' Another includes the passage: '... the Mine of Punt to reach it in peace and to return in peace'. These inscriptions, supported by others, confirm that expeditions to Punt went by sea. Unfortunately, owing to the locality where they were found, they do not supply indications as to the geographical position of the land itself.

Agreement therefore seems to have been virtually reached to the effect that Egyptian vessels sailed to Punt to seek precious incense and many other products formerly provided by southern Arabia. An attempt has been made to trace the route taken by these vessels.[27]

It is claimed that several Pharaohs tried to reach more distant regions. An expedition to Punt under Ramses III is described in the Papyrus Harris: 'The fleet ... crossed the Muqad Sea.' Its vessels arrived south of Cape Guardafui, perhaps as far as Cape Hafun on the Indian Ocean. But this route was somewhat dangerous because of the storms that rage in that area. Probably, therefore, we can conclude that Cape Guardafui was the southernmost point for ships bound for Punt and that the latter's southern boundaries were near this Cape. As for its northern boundaries, they may be said to have changed from century to century.

According to P. Montet, there is another way of looking at the problem. He writes:[28] '... the land of Punt was certainly in African territory be-

24. See for instance K. A. Kitchen, 1971. However, recent archaeological discoveries in countries which lie between Punt and Egypt do not justify the rejection without a thorough study of R. Herzog's hypothesis.
25. Abd el-Halim Sayyd (Mana'im), 1976.
26. This refers to Sesostris I (c. −1970 to −1930) and Egyptian texts mention expeditions to Punt well before that date, during the Old Kingdom.
27. This has been done by K. A. Kitchen, 1971.
28. P. Montet, 1970, p. 132.

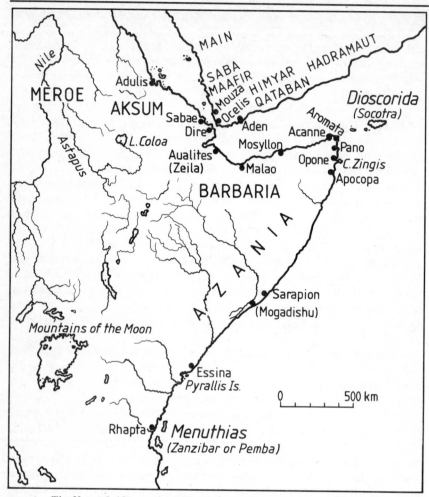

FIG. 4.1 *The Horn of Africa and neighbouring areas in antiquity*

cause according to a stele of the Saite Period, if it rains on the mountain of Punt, the region of the Nile was affected: the area also extended into Asia, because Punt of Asia, was a geographical expression – the only (and as yet unpublished) example of which is to be found at Soleb. In the light of these two indications, we can identify the two shores of the land of the god, with the two banks of the Trait of Bab el Mandeb. Further proof is supplied by the fact that the incense-bearing tree grew equally well at Arabia Felix and in Africa.'[29]

29. K. A. Kitchen, 1971, p. 185, pointed out that this theory is unacceptable, if only because of the presence of the *giraffe* among the animals characteristic of Punt.

We can trace successive stages in the relations between Egypt and Punt. The first preceded the reign of Queen Hatshepsut. At that time, the Egyptians had very little information about Punt. They obtained incense from middlemen who spread legends about this country in order to raise the price of incense. The few Egyptians known to have completed the voyage to Punt were bold men. A man of Aswan, under the Old Kingdom, says: 'I went forth with my lord, the count and treasurer and my lord, the count and treasurer of the god Khui, of the god Theti to Kush, to Byblos and Punt eleven times.'[30] The second period began with Queen Hatshepsut. A fleet of five ships, according to the artist who decorated the temple at Dayr al Bahri, was sent to bring back incense-bearing trees. Perehu and his wife – who was deformed[31] – his daughter and a group of natives are shown receiving the expedition and exchanging compliments, presents and products known to come from Punt and clearly depicted: three great trees planted in the garden of the god Amon, so tall that cattle could walk under them.[32] Under these great trees, the other gifts are shown heaped together, such as ivory, tortoise shells, cattle with short and long horns, 'myrrh trees with their roots wrapped in their original soil, as a good gardener does today, dry incense, ebony, panther skins, baboons, chimpanzees, greyhounds, a giraffe, and the like ...'.

In a room of the same temple at Dayr al Bahri, there is a picture of Hatshepsut's divine birth in which her mother, Ahmose, is awakened by the scent of incense from the land of Punt. Here, the association of the name of Punt with her divine origin is evidence of the friendship between the Queen of Egypt and Punt, whose inhabitants worshipped Amon.

The pictures of this expedition have taught us about life in the land of Punt, its plants, animals and inhabitants, and its cone-shaped huts, built on piles amidst palm, ebony and balsam trees.

To judge by the pictures of Punt on the temples, there is nothing new to report after Queen Hatshepsut's reign. Then the texts mention the Puntites' arrival in Egypt. Punt is henceforth listed among the vanquished peoples which, considering how far away it was, sounds rather unlikely. The Puntite chieftains were required to bring gifts to the Pharaoh, who ordered one of his subordinates to receive them and their gifts. There is

30. J. H. Breasted, 1906, I, para. 361.
31. Mainly by her steatopygia.
32. D. M. M. Dixon, 1969, p. 55, finds that the success of the planting of the myrrh trees brought back by Hatshepsut's expedition to her temple was only temporary. 'Notwithstanding a partial and temporary success, the transplantation experiments were a failure. The precise reasons for this failure will be clear only when the botanical identity of tree(s) producing the incense has been established. This cannot be done on the basis of the conventionalized Egyptian representations. In the meantime, it is suggested that for reasons of commercial self-interest, the Puntites may have deliberately frustrated the Egyptian experiment.' If the success was short-lived, the kings who succeeded Hatshepsut would not have continued to import these trees, as, for example, Amenhotep II did (see Tomb No. 143 at Thebes), or Ramses II and Ramses III, who both ordered them to be imported.

some evidence of trading in Red Sea ports between Puntites and Egyptians and of the transporting of goods from Punt by land between the Red Sea and the Nile (Tomb of Amon-Mose at Thebes and Tomb No. 143).

Towards the end of the reign of Ramses IV, relations with Punt came to an end. But the memory of Punt remained in the minds of the Egyptians.

Perhaps we should include among the testimonies to these relations in ancient times the fact that a headrest in modern Somali is called a barchi or barki, which is similar to its name in ancient Egyptian. Moreover, the Somalis call their New Year the Feast of Pharaoh.

## The rest of Africa

Endeavours by a people or its leaders to establish relations with other countries arise from diverse motives which can, in the last resort, generally be reduced to simple terms. Needs are a powerful spur to exploration and efforts to establish stable relations. Egypt needed African products: ivory, incense, ebony and, more generally, timber. For the last the Near East provided an obvious alternative source. To be sure that timber from the interior of Africa was in fact used it would be necessary to assess the whole range of Egyptian evidence.

Egypt's relations with Africa are too often thought of as a one-way flow, as the spreading of her culture abroad. This is to overlook the fact that she depended materially on the sale of certain African products. Consequently, influences may well have been reciprocal. In this field, everything has still to be done and investigation is very arduous. Ecology changed between the far-off times of the kingdom and the Greeks' appearance in Egypt; long, painstaking research, based on archaeology and linguistics, is required to reconstitute the ancient exchange of goods from texts and images that may at best only provide very indirect evidence. What we have learnt in recent years from archaeology, for instance, about trading long ago in obsidian, which was a much-prized mineral in prehistoric times, should incite us to patience and caution but also give us the hope of obtaining results undreamed of today.

A naval exploration of the African coasts at the time of Pharaoh Necho II, −610 to −595, has attracted the attention of research workers, but not all agree on the historical accuracy of the facts reported a century later by Herodotus.

> Libya shows clearly that it is encompassed by the sea, save only where it borders on Asia; and this was proved first (as far as we know) by Necos, King of Egypt. He, when he had made an end of digging the canal which leads from the Nile to the Arabian Gulf, sent Phoenicians in ships, charging them to sail on their return voyage past the Pillars of Heracles till they should come into the

northern sea and so to Egypt. So the Phoenicians set out from the Red Sea and sailed the southern sea; whenever autumn came, they would put in and sow the land, to whatever part of Libya they might come, and there await the harvest; then having gathered in the crop, they sailed on, so that after two years had passed, it was in the third that they rounded the Pillars of Heracles and came to Egypt. There they said (what some may believe, though I do not) that in sailing round Libya they had the sun on their right hand.

Thus the first knowledge of Libya was gained.[33]

In this text, Libya, of course, means the whole African continent, the Pillars of Heracles are the Straits of Gibraltar, and the Phoenicians came from their own country, which had been recently conquered by Necho II. Therefore, the problem remains unsolved. J. Yoyotte[34] believes in the authenticity of this tale and of the events it describes. A body called the Punt Association has recently been formed in France for the purpose of carrying out again, on a ship specially built according to ancient Egyptian techniques, the tour of Africa as described by Herodotus. But there are plenty of sceptics who explain such passages from Herodotus otherwise than by the circumnavigation of the continent, or who even contest the authenticity of this affair from start to finish. As in the case of the voyage of Hannon, the battle between research workers on this subject is probably by no means ended.

Necho II, who comes very late in the line of Pharaohs, undertook many other operations. To him is attributed the first great work of constructing a canal along a course which is still a matter of doubt among historians. It might have been intended to link the Mediterranean to the Red Sea. It was more likely the canal joining the Nile to the Red Sea, which was actually open to navigation for several centuries and which, in the Islamic area, was of major importance for the relations between Egypt and Arabia.

Should we also attribute to curiosity and a taste for the exotic the expedition which Harkhuf undertook on behalf of Pepi II and which gave rise to conclusions both contradictory and difficult to accept? Harkhuf, as mentioned below,[35] brought back a dwarf dancer for Pepi II from the Land of Yam. The conclusion is sometimes drawn on the unsupported assumption that the dwarf was a Pygmy,[36] that this example, unique of its kind, proves the existence of relations between Egypt, the upper Nile

---

33. Herodotus, IV, 42.
34. J. Yoyotte, 1958, p. 370.
35. See Chapters 8, 9, 10, 11.
36. P. Montet, 1970, p. 129, makes a far more cautious statement on this subject: 'Before Harkhuf, a traveller called Bawerded brought back a dwarf dancer, a native of the Land of Punt.'

and Chad. Harkhuf's expedition belongs to history, whereas many others are more or less in the realm of legend or fiction.[37] In the first place very little is known about the ancient habitat of the Pygmies and it is dangerous to assume that they were found in large numbers in the upper regions of the Nile basins.[38] Secondly, there is no proof that the dwarf concerned was a Pygmy, and, lastly, it is still not known for certain where the Land of Yam was situated.[39]

As we have seen, the evidence is neither certain nor consistent as far as scientific curiosity or a taste for the exotic is concerned. The observation often made, that African fauna is present in Egyptian iconography, is by no means conclusive evidence, in the present state of knowledge, of the existence of Egyptian relations with the heart of Africa. The ape, the sacred animal of Toth and the panther skins required for the priestly vestments for the rites of the cult of Osiris performed by Horus and also for the garb of the Pharaohs, may have come from bordering countries or from occasional chance exchanges between merchants. Before we can form a clear idea of the extent of the Egyptians' knowledge of Africa a great deal of research must be done to investigate the chronology as well as the quantative and qualitative significance of the many references to animals found in Egyptian texts and images.

Whether relations with Africa were impelled by need or by curiosity, the evidence assembled is very flimsy and its interpretation too difficult and too controversial for any conclusion to be reached in the present state of our knowledge. Yet there are many ways open for rewarding research.

Therefore, although it is perfectly justifiable to record a few hypotheses and to stress the desirability of some further research, the reader should not be left with the impression that what follows is accepted or, still less, proved.

It is permissible to wonder, and so far hardly anyone has, whether the Egyptians were able to use Nigerian tin. In ancient times there were two known and remote sources of tin production: Cornwall and the East Indies. Is it totally unreasonable to suppose that Nok could have originated from ancient tin mines in Bauchi with a market in the Nile valley?[40] This is a mere academic hypothesis for the moment, but one which deserves to be investigated because if the results were positive they would shed so

37. M. Girgüs.

38. For variations regarding the location of the Pygmies, see C. Préaux, 1957, pp. 284–312.

39. R. Herzog, 1968, is of the opinion that Harkhuf reached the Swaddi swamps or the Darfur hills. T. Säve-Söderbergh, 1953, p. 177, situates the Land of Yam south of the Second Cataract and thinks that the 'Libyan' oases south of the Nile might have served as relay stations for the southward-bound expeditions which foreshadow the future Darfur caravans.

40. Against this supposition, see Schaeffer's article in *JEA*. In his opinion, the tin used by the Egyptians came from Syria.

much light on aspects of the relations between ancient Egypt and Africa farther south that are now hard to understand. For this it would be essential to examine very closely, at every level and with the aid of all disciplines, any vestiges that may remain in transit areas such as Darfur and Bahrel Ghazal. In this field, as in so many others, almost everything remains to be done. Ethnologists, by undertaking long and arduous investigations, might add more evidence on this difficult subject.

The question has often arisen whether the column-based headrest invented by the Egyptians has not spread with their civilization to other regions of Africa.[41] Again, caution is advisable and the temptation to be diffuse must be avoided. Are this and other headrests exclusively African, originating from Egypt? Do they exist in other cultures far from Africa? Are they not rather of a functional nature and therefore likely to have been invented at different places very far apart?

In another field, should it be concluded, as some research workers have perhaps been too quick to do, that any form of sacred royalty in Africa is of Egyptian origin, the result of a physical and historical relationship between ancient Egypt and its African creators?[42] Should we not think of spontaneous developments more or less spaced out in time?

What were the routes taken by the cult of the ram, the sacred animal of Amon, which is honoured in Kush, in the Sahara, among the Yoruba and among the Fon? For the time being, all these resemblances and presences must be listed, without leaping to conclusions.[43]

In many fields, it is possible to point to the similarity between ancient Egyptian techniques, practices or beliefs and African ones of more or less recent origin. One of the most attractive examples at first sight is that of the doubles (known as Kas in ancient Egypt) of the physical person to which the Egyptians and many present-day African societies attach importance. The after-life forms of these doubles among the Bantu, Ule or Akan, for instance, make it very tempting to associate them with Egyptian conceptions in Pharaonic times.[44]

It has long been pointed out that the Dogon bury voodoo pottery and they are by no means the only ones. This custom has been compared with that of the Egyptians, who placed potsherds bearing the names of their enemies in bowls which they buried at specific points. A comparison has also been drawn between Egyptian inhumation rites and those described by al

41. An entry on the column-based headrests of the ancient Egyptians and the ethno-graphic affinities revealed by their use, by E. T. Hamy in G. Parrinder's book, p. 61, gives us a good example of an African headrest. It is on show in the British Museum. Another was discovered in Fezzan: C. M. Daniels, 1968b.

42. See G. W. B. Huntingford, in R. Oliver and G. Mathew, pp. 88–9, and B. Davidson, 1962, p. 44.

43. G. A. Wainwright, 1951.

44. S. Sauneron, Paris, 1959, p. 113, pointed out the interest of this association but urged caution.

Bakri for the kings of Ghana in the eleventh century of our era.

There would be no end to the list that could be made of practices of a similar nature accumulated for decades in studies of a more or less scientific nature. Linguistics also provides an enormous area for research, where probabilities at present outnumber certainties.

All this leads to the conclusion that Egyptian civilization very probably had an influence on more recent African civilizations, though to what extent is still little known. In trying to assess the latter, it would be wise also to consider how far influence was exercised in the opposite direction, that is to say, on Egypt. An influence extending over 5000 years is not proof of synchronological contacts, just as traces of contacts are not proof of their continuity. This is a fascinating inquiry which has only just been begun.

Generally speaking the links between Egypt and the African continent in Pharaonic times is one of the most important matters facing African historiographers today. It calls in question a great many scientific or philosophical postulates: for instance, the acceptance or refusal of the supposition that the most ancient peoples of Egypt were black-skinned, without exception, and the acceptance or refusal of the theory of diffusionism. It also calls in question the methodology or research, for instance, concerning the circulation of inventions, of copper or iron, or of the textiles on which it was customary to write. It sheds doubt on the possibility, hitherto calmly assumed, that an isolated research worker can achieve success in such a broad field without the aid of related disciplines.

From every point of view, this problem is a major test of the scientific conscientiousness, accuracy and openness of mind of the Africans who will endeavour to unravel it, with the help, more enlightened than in the past, of foreign research workers.

PLATE 4.1 *The tribute of Libyan prisoners of the Ancient Empire*

PLATE 4.2 *Seti I killing a Libyan chief*

PLATE 4.3 *Nubian tribute of Rekh-mi-Re*

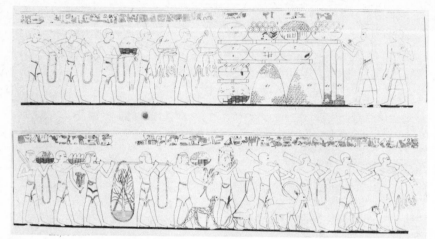

PLATE 4.4 *The tribute of Punt*

PLATE 4.5 *Houses of the Land of Punt*

154

# The legacy of Pharaonic Egypt

R.-EL-NADOURY
*with the collaboration of* J. VERCOUTTER

Pharaonic Egypt's valuable contributions to the world can be traced in many fields including history, economics, science, art, philosophy. Specialists in these, and many other fields, have long realized the importance of this legacy, even though it is often impossible to determine in what way it was passed on to neighbouring or subsequent cultures.

Indeed, that legacy or, at least, the evidence we have of it, which is so important for the history of mankind, was transmitted in large part by classical antiquity (first by the Greeks and later by the Romans) before passing to the Arabs. Now, the pre-Hellenes and Greeks did not come into contact with Egypt before −1600 or thereabouts and close ties were not established until the seventh century before our era, with the spread of Greek adventurers, travellers and, later, settlers into the Mediterranean basin, particularly into Egypt. At the same time, the Greeks and their forerunners in the second and first millennia before our era were in contact with the civilizations of Asia Minor and through them, with the ancient Mesopotamian world of which they were the continuation. It is, accordingly, often very difficult to ascertain the exact cultural milieu, whether Asian or Egyptian, both so closely linked, in which this or that invention or technique first appeared.

In addition, the difficulty of establishing the chronology of the remote periods of antiquity makes attributions of the paternity of ideas very hazardous. Carbon 14 datings are too vague to determine to the nearest century or two whether, in a milieu where knowledge was always rapidly transmitted, it was the Asian or African world that was the originator. Lastly, the possibility of convergences cannot be disregarded. To cite but one example: there is good reason to believe (see the Introduction) that writing was discovered at about the same time both in Egypt and Mesopotamia without there necessarily having been any influence of one civilization on the other.

For all that, the legacy bequeathed by Egypt to succeeding civilizations, and to the ancient civilizations of Africa in particular, is not to be underestimated.

## Contributions of prehistoric Egypt

One of the earliest and most remarkable advances made by Egypt was in the field of economics. At the end of the Neolithic period, around −5000, the ancient Egyptians gradually transformed the Nile valley (see Chapter 1), enabling its inhabitants to progress from a food-gathering economy to a food-producing one, and this important transition in human development in the valley had great consequences, material as well as moral. For the growth of agriculture made it possible for the ancient Egyptian to adopt a settled, integrated village life and this development affected his social and moral development not only in prehistoric but also during the dynastic periods.

It is not certain that Asia played the predominant and unique role in the Neolithic revolution that was formerly attributed to it (see Unesco *General History of Africa*, Vol. I, ch. 27). However that might be, one of the first results of this Neolithic revolution in the valley was that the ancient Egyptian started to think of the natural forces around him. He saw these, especially the sun and the river, as gods, who were symbolized in many forms, especially in the animals and birds with which he was most familiar. In developing agriculture he also established the principle of co-operation within the community, for without such co-operation among the people of the village, agricultural production would have been limited. This led to another important development: the introduction of a new social system within the community; that is, the specialization of labour. Specialized workers appeared in farming, irrigation, agricultural industries, pottery-making and many other related fields and the large number of archaeological remains attest to their long-lasting traditions.

Pharaonic civilization was remarkable for the continuity of its development. Once a thing was acquired, it was passed on, with improvements, from the dawn of the history of Egypt to its close. This was how Neolithic techniques were transmitted and enriched in the predynastic period (−3500 to −3000) and were subsequently preserved when the historical period was in full flower. The art of stone-cutting is sufficient evidence.

As early as −3500, the Egyptians, the heirs to the Neolithic period in the valley, used the flint deposits there, especially those at Thebes, to carve instruments of incomparable quality, of which the Gebel-el-Arak Knife (see Chapter 1) is one example among hundreds. Produced by pressure, the fine and regular grooves of the stone gave the knife an inimitable gently rippled and perfectly polished surface. To make such weapons required uncommon manual dexterity. This art remained alive in Egypt and a scene painted in a tomb at Beni Hasan depicts artisans of the time of the Middle Kingdom (*c.* −1900) still fashioning these same knives with incurvate blades.

This craftsmanship is also found in the carving of stone vases. Here, too, the technique of the Neolithic period carried through the predynastic period and the Old Kingdom and continued to the end of ancient Egyptian history. The Egyptian stone-carver used every kind of stone, even the hardest varieties, working with basalt, breccia, diorite, granite, porphyry as readily as with the softer calcareous alabasters, schists, serpentines and soapstones.

From Egypt, stone-carving techniques later passed to the Mediterranean world. The carvers of Cretan vases must surely have learned their skills, if not in Egypt itself, at least in a milieu that was thoroughly steeped in Egyptian culture like the Syro-Palestinian Corridor. Even the shapes of the vases that were carved in ancient Minoa betray their Egyptian origins.

The dexterity of the cutters of hard stone passed to the sculptors. This can be seen in the great Egyptian hard stone sculptures, from the diorite Chefren of Cairo to the large black basalt sarcophagi of the Apis bulls. The skill then passed to the sculptors of the Ptolemaic period and later found expression in the statuary of the Roman empire.

These changes in Neolithic times are characteristically reflected in the growth of town planning in Egypt. A striking example of this can be found in one of the oldest villages in the Nile valley: Merimda Beni Salama on the western edge of the Delta.

In conjunction with the very ancient Egyptian belief in the after-life and immortality, we have here a combination of important cultural and social developments which can be traced throughout the Neolithic and Chalco-lithic periods from the predynastic down to the protodynastic period. They led to the establishment and development of the Egyptian Pharaonic tradition.

## Historical times

In the Egyptian Pharaonic civilization of historical times two main currents can be discerned. The first is the material legacy. The second, also descended from the most distant past, is the more abstract cultural legacy. They are inter-related and together comprise the Egyptian cultural pheno-menon. The material legacy includes crafts and sciences (geometry, astronomy, chemistry), applied mathematics, medicine, surgery and artistic productions. The cultural side covers religion, literature and philosophic theories.

### Craft contributions

The ancient Egyptians' contribution in the crafts can be traced in stone, as we have just seen, but also in metal, wood, glass, ivory, bone and many other materials. They explored and exploited the various natural resources of the country and gradually refined the techniques required in making stone and copper tools such as axes, chisels, mallets and adzes designed with great skill for use in building as well as in industry for such purposes as drilling holes or fixing blocks. They also fashioned bows, arrows, daggers, shields and throwing-clubs.

For a long period, and even during historical times, the tools and arms inherited from the Neolithic period continued to be made of stone. The chalk cliffs bordering the Nile are rich in flints of large size and excellent quality which the Egyptians continued to use long after the discovery of the use of copper and bronze. Furthermore, religious rites often required the use of stone instruments, a fact that contributed largely to the perpetuation of stone-cutting techniques and especially of flint knapping.

Very little use was made of iron for metal vases until the very end of the Pharaonic period, so Egyptian metal-working techniques were confined to the use of gold, silver, copper, and copper alloys such as bronze and brass. Traces of the mining and processing of copper ore by Egyptians have been found in Sinai as well as in Nubia and Buhen where the Pharaohs of the Old Kingdom possessed copper-smelting plants.

In Sinai and in Nubia, the Egyptians worked with the local populations, and the techniques used in the processing of metal could, therefore, pass easily from one culture to the other. This was perhaps the time when Pharaonic script, through the intermediary of proto-Sinaitic script, which it influences, played an important part in the invention of the alphabet. It was perhaps the occasion when copper working became widespread, first in the Nile basin and then beyond.

As long ago as the early dynastic period (*c.* − 3000), the Egyptians knew, and employed in making their copper tools, all the basic techniques of metal working such as forging, hammering, casting, stamping, soldering, and riveting techniques which they mastered very rapidly. As well as tools, large Egyptian copper statues have been found which date from − 2300. Texts of an earlier time, dating back to − 2900, note the existence of statues of the same type, and scenes from mastabas of the very earliest period depict workshops where gold and electrum, which is a blend of gold and silver, are being fashioned into jewellery. Although gold and copper working did not originate in Egypt, there is no doubt that Egypt contributed a great deal to its improvement and extension.

As we stressed at the beginning of this chapter, it is often difficult to determine whether a particular technique originated in an Asian or African culture. But, thanks to the representations found in tombs, Egypt at least provides us with a wealth of information on the techniques used by craftsmen. In the workshops depicted in paintings or bas-reliefs on the tomb walls, both above and below ground, one sees, for example, carpenters and cabinet-makers at work making furniture, weapons and boats, and the tools they used, such as pliers, hammers, saws, drills, adzes, chisels and mallets, all faithfully represented and with infinite detail, as well as the manner in which they used them. As a result, we know that the Egyptian saw was a pull-saw and not a push-saw, like the modern saw. There is a mine of information for students of the history of techniques and the way they came down to us, which has not yet been fully studied.

As well as these pictorial representations the ancient Egyptians left in their tombs models of workshops with model craftsmen making various objects. These models are also invaluable to the historian in interpreting the techniques and the manner in which they developed. Furthermore the large quantities of artisan objects which have been found, manufactured either by hand or with the aid of tools, attest to the variety of industries in ancient Egypt. For example, in the making of jewellery they used precious and semi-precious stones such as gold, silver, felspar, lapis-lazuli, turquoise, amethyst and cornelian, fashioning them with remarkable precision into crowns, necklaces and other items of adornment.

The cultivation of flax rapidly led to great ability in hand-spinning and linen-making. The latter was known from the start of the Neolithic period (*c.* −5000), and its beginning coincided with the emergence of civilization in the Nile valley. The women spun the linen, doing so with great skill since they frequently handled two spindles simultaneously. Characteristic of Egyptian spinning was the length of the thread produced and this required a technique which placed the spindle some feet away from the raw fibre. To make the distance even greater, the women perched on high stools. Their looms were at first horizontal, and then, beginning in the Middle Empire, vertical which enabled them to produce the very long fabrics required for the loose-fitting everyday clothing, as well as for the funerary ritual mummy wrappings and shrouds.

For the Pharaohs, woven fabrics constituted a commodity particularly appreciated abroad. The finest cloth of all, byssus, was woven in the temples and was especially renowned. The Ptolemies supervised the weaving shops and controlled the quality of the manufacture, and their central administration, doubtless following the pattern set by the earlier Pharaohs, organized sales abroad which brought the king huge revenues because of the superior quality of the goods produced by Egyptian weavers. Here we have a graphic example of one of the ways in which the Egyptian legacy was handed down.

The wood, leather and metal industries were also perfected and the products of these industries have survived in good condition to the present day.

Other objects produced by Egyptian craftsmen included silver vases, wooden coffins, combs and decorated ivory handles. The ancient Egyptians also had a special talent for weaving wild reeds into mats and the spun fibre of the palm-tree made possible the production of sturdy nets and ropes. Pottery manufacture which started in prehistory in a rough form developed into the finer red, black-rimmed pottery, and then polished and incised pottery. These vessels were used for storing various materials but

159

some were for decorative purposes. The Egyptian belief in certain values and especially in eternal life necessitated the manufacture of a great number of often decorated objects for the dead and led to a high standard of perfection and artistic production.

Egypt contributed, if not the invention, at least the distribution of glass-making techniques to world civilization. While it is true that Mesopotamia and the civilizations of the Indus were likewise familiar at a very early time with glazing, the technique which is the basis of glass-making, there is no evidence to suggest that they spread it abroad. The most one can suppose, therefore, is that once again there was a phenomenon of convergence and that glass-making was discovered independently both in Asia and in the Nile valley.

It is certain that the Egyptians demonstrated their aptitude in the art of glass-making in a relatively short time. The presence of glass beads seems to be attested in the predynastic period (*c.* −3500), although it is not certain that they were deliberately made by the craftsman. Glass, as such, was known in the fifth dynasty (*c.* −2500) and began to spread from the time of the New Kingdom (*c.* −1600). It was then used not only for beads but also for vases of a great variety of shapes, from the graceful stemmed chalice to vases in the form of fishes. They were usually polychromatic and always opaque. Transparent glass made its appearance under Tutankhamun (*c.* −1300). Starting about −700, Egyptian polychromatic glass vases, in the form called alabaster, spread throughout the Mediterranean area. They were copied by the Phoenicians, who developed their manufacture into an industry.

In the later period, hieroglyphic signs, moulded in coloured glass, were set in wood or stone to make inscriptions. The techniques of the Pharaonic glass-makers were handed down to craftsmen of the hellenistic period, who invented blown glass. Alexandria then became the main centre for the manufacture of glass-ware, exporting its products as far as China. Aurelius levied a tax on Egyptian glass-ware imported into Rome. The Meroitic empire later imported some glass-ware from Alexandria but, above all, adopted its manufacturing techniques and spread them to the upper Nile valley.

One of the most important industries was that of the production of papyrus invented by the ancient Egyptians. No plant played a more significant role in Egypt than papyrus. Its fibres were used for boat-making and for caulking, for the wicks of oil lamps, for mats, baskets, ropes and hawsers. The hawsers which served to moor the pontoon bridge that Xerxes tried to lay across the Hellespont were made in Egypt out of papyrus fibres. When tied together in bundles, papyrus stems served as pillars in early architecture until classical architects took them as a model for their simple or clustered columns whose capitals were shaped like closed or open flowers. But, above all, papyrus was used to make 'papyrus', from which the word 'paper' is derived, undoubtedly a cognate of the ancient

Egyptian word *paperaâ* which means 'He of-the-Great-Residence' (Royal Palace) which has come down to us from classical antiquity.

Papyrus was made by placing crosswise successive layers of fine strips taken from the stem of the plant which, after pressing and drying, formed a large sheet.

Twenty sheets of papyrus joined together while they were still moist formed a scroll 3 to 6 metres in length. Several scrolls could be joined together and reach a length of 30 or 40 metres. It was this scroll that constituted Egyptian books. They were held in the left hand and unrolled as the reading proceeded. The volumen of classic antiquity is a direct heir of this scroll.

Of all the writing materials employed in antiquity, papyrus was certainly the most practical. It was supple and light. Its sole drawback was its fragility. Over a long period it stood up poorly to humidity, and it burnt very easily. It has been estimated that to maintain the inventory of a small Egyptian temple, 10 metres of papyrus were required each month. Provincial notaries, during the Ptolemaic dynasty, used from six to thirteen scrolls or 25–57 metres *each day*. Every large estate and royal palace and all the temples maintained registers, inventories and libraries, which indicates that hundreds of kilometres of papyrus must have existed at that time whereas only a few hundreds of metres have been rediscovered.

The papyrus used in Egypt from the time of the first dynasty (*c.* −3000) until the end of the Pharaonic period was later adopted by the Greeks, the Romans, the Copts, the Byzantines, the Aramaeans and the Arabs. A large part of Greek and Latin literature has come down to us on papyrus. Papyrus scrolls were one of the principal exports of Egypt. Papyrus was, unquestionably, one of the major legacies bequeathed to civilization by Pharaonic Egypt.

All these industries depended on techniques and skills and led to the creation of a body of artisans and improved techniques. The museums and private collections throughout the world contain hundreds, even thousands, of archaeological examples of the various products of ancient Egypt.

Not the least of their technical contributions to the world were their tradition and ability in stonemasonry. It was no easy task to transform huge blocks of granite, limestone, basalt and diorite from raw material into well-shaped polished masonry required by various architectural designs.

Moreover, the search for stone to build their monuments, no less than prospection for ores and efforts to discover fibres, semi-precious stones and coloured pigments, contributed to the spread of Egyptian techniques to Asia and Africa.

The Egyptians did not hesitate to fetch their stone from the open desert, sometimes going as far as 100 kilometres from the Nile. The quarry from which the diorite came for the famous statue of Chephren in the

Cairo Museum lies in the Nubian desert some 65 kilometres to the north-west of Abu Simbel. Quarries were worked from the dawn of Egyptian history (*c.* −2800).

Egyptian quarrying techniques depended on the kind of stone being extracted. For limestone, they hollowed out galleries in the broad band of Eocene cliffs that border the Nile and extracted the magnificent blocks of fine stone used to construct the Great Pyramids which were then faced with blocks of granite. The sandstone deposits in the region of El Kob, in Upper Egypt and in Nubia, were mined by open-face techniques. For hard stone, the quarriers first cut a groove around the block to be extracted, and then at various points along the groove made deep notches into which they inserted wooden wedges. These they wet and the swelling of the wood was sufficient to split the block along the groove. This technique is still used today in granite quarries. Is it a legacy from Egypt?

The only tools used by the Egyptian stoneworker were the wooden mallet and copper chisel for soft stones like limestone and sandstone, and the pick, chisel and hard stone hammer for metamorphic rocks like granite, gneiss, diorite and basalt. When the quarry was located far from the Nile, an expedition was launched with sometimes as many as 14 000 men comprising officers and soldiers, porters and quarrymen, scribes and doctors. Such expeditions were equipped to remain for long periods out of Egypt and must have contributed to the spread of Egyptian civilization, especially in Africa.

The skills acquired by stoneworkers in the early dynastic period led the Egyptians, by the time of the Old Kingdom (*c.* −2400), to hew their final resting-places in solid rock. Much before this date, from −3000 to −2400, the building of tombs, planned as the dwelling-places of the dead, had already led them to build imposing superstructures which, in time, with the changes which occurred in architecture, led first to the step pyramid and then to the pyramid proper.

The Egyptian expertise in woodworking is brilliantly manifested in their shipbuilding. The necessities of daily life in the Nile valley, where the river is the only convenient thoroughfare, made expert boatmen of the Egyptians from the earliest times. Boats occupied a prominent position in their earliest works of art from prehistoric times on. Since in their belief an after-life was closely modelled on earthly life, it is not surprising that they placed models of boats in the tombs, or represented scenes of boat construction and river scenes on tomb walls. They would even sometimes bury actual boats near the tombs ready for use by the dead. This was the case at Heluan in a burial ground of the first two dynasties, and at Dahshur, near the pyramid of Sesostris III. But a more recent discovery is extraordinary. In 1952, two great pits dug into the rock and covered with huge limestone slabs were discovered along the southern side of the Great Pyramid. In the pits, partially disassembled, but complete with oars, cabins, and rudders, were discovered the very boats used by Cheops. One of these boats has been removed from the pit and restored. The other one is still waiting to be taken out of its tomb.

Cheops' boat, now in a special museum, has been rebuilt. When found it consisted of 1224 pieces of wood which had been partially disassembled and stacked in thirteen successive layers in the pit. The boat measures 43·4 metres long, 5·9 metres wide, and has a capacity of about 40 tons. The side planks are between 13 and 14 centimetres thick. Its draught is difficult to calculate precisely, but was clearly very slight in relation to the ship's mass. Although it does possess a rudimentary frame of timbers, Cheops' boat has no keel, and is flat-bottomed and narrow. The most remarkable fact is that it was built without any nails: the pieces of wood are held together solely by the use of tenon and mortise joints. The constituent elements, planks, timbers and cross members, are tied to each other with ropes. This facilitated their reassembly. The ship contained a large, spacious central cabin, as well as a covered shelter in the bow. There was no mast, and it was either propelled by oars or was towed, even though the sail had been in use in Egypt long before Cheops' reign. Amphibious military expeditions far from Egypt on the Red Sea and the Euphrates were made possible by this method of construction, assembling separate sections which were then tied to one another. In fact, the Egyptian army carried with it, in a piecemeal form, the boats which it might need.

We can see from their width in relation to their length and from their shallow draught, that these Egyptian boats were designed for use on the river. Their primary object was to achieve maximum capacity while avoiding running aground. None the less, beginning with the fifth dynasty, and probably even before, the Egyptians knew how to adapt their ships for ocean-going voyages. The boats of Sahure show that for use at sea the height of the prow and the poop were greatly reduced. In Cheops' boat, these were raised high above the waterline. This made the ship difficult to manage in the waves of the Mediterranean or the Red Sea. In addition, Egyptian naval engineers lent great solidity to the whole structure by equipping the ship with a torsion-cable passing over the bridge and tying the stern firmly to the bow. This cable also acted as a keel, ensuring the rigidity of the entire structure and reducing the danger of its breaking in the middle.

With these modifications, the Egyptian ship was capable of plying the farthest maritime routes opened up by the Pharaohs, whether on the Mediterranean in the direction of Palestine, Syria, Cyprus and Crete, or on the Red Sea towards the distant country of Punt. There is no reason to believe that the Egyptians had been influenced by the Phoenicians in this field. On the contrary, it is quite possible, although it cannot be proved, given the current level of knowledge, that it was the Egyptians who pioneered the use of sails in maritime voyages (Egyptian yards and sails were adjustable, allowing various speeds) and invented the rudder. Certainly from the time of the Old Kingdom the large directional oars located in the stern were provided with vertical bars, transforming them in effect into rudders.

## Scientific contributions

The Pharaonic contribution to science and applied mathematics has left a valuable legacy in the fields of physics, chemistry, zoology, geology, medicine, pharmacology, geometry and applied mathematics. In fact, they gave to humanity a large store of experience in each of these fields, some of which were combined in order to execute a specific project.

### MUMMIFICATION

One outstanding example of the genius of the ancient Egyptians is mummification. It shows their mastery of a number of sciences including physics, chemistry, medicine and surgery. Their ability in each branch was an accumulation of long experience. For example, they exploited their discovery of the chemical characteristic of natron, which was found in certain areas of Egypt, particularly in the Wadi el Natrun, by using the chemical attributes of this substance for use in the practical fulfilment of the demands of their beliefs in the after-life. For the ancient Egyptians believed in the continuity of life after death and emphasized this belief in a practical way by preserving the human body. The compounds of natron have been analysed in modern times as a mixture of sodium carbonate, sodium bicarbonate, salt and sodium sulphate. The ancient Egyptian, therefore, was aware of the chemical functions of these substances. In the process of mummification he soaked the body in natron for seventy days. He drew the brain out through the nostrils and he also removed the intestines through an incision made in the side of the body. Such operations as these necessitated an accurate knowledge of anatomy and the good state of preservation of the mummies illustrates this intimate knowledge.

### SURGERY

It was, undoubtedly, the knowledge they acquired from mummification that enabled the Egyptians to develop surgical techniques at a very early period in their history. We have quite a good knowledge of Egyptian surgery, in fact, thanks to the Smith Papyrus, a copy of an original which was composed under the Old Kingdom, between $-2600$ and $-2400$. This papyrus is virtually a treatise on bone surgery and external pathology. Forty-eight cases are examined systematically. In each case, the author of the treatise begins his account under a general heading: 'Instructions concerning [such and such a case]'; followed by a clinical description: 'If you observe [such symptoms]'. The descriptions are always precise and incisive. They are followed by the diagnosis: 'You will say in this connection a case of [this or that wound]', and, depending on the case, 'a case that I can treat' or 'the case is without remedy'. If the surgeon can treat the patient, the treatment to be administered is then described in detail, for example: 'the first day you will apply a bandage with a piece of meat; afterwards you will place two strips of cloth in such a way as to join the lips of the wound together ...'.

Several of the treatments indicated in the Smith Papyrus are still used today. Egyptian surgeons knew how to stitch up wounds and to set a fracture using wooden or pasteboard splints. And there were times when the surgeon simply advised that nature should be allowed to take its own course. In two instances, the Smith Papyrus instructs the patient to maintain his regular diet.

Of the cases studied by the Smith Papyrus, the majority concerned superficial lacerations of the skull or face. Others concerned lesions of the bones or joints such as contusions of the cervical or spinal vertebrae, dislocations, perforations of the skull or sternum, and sundry fractures affecting the nose, jaw, collar-bone, humerus, ribs, skull and vertebrae. Examination of mummies has revealed traces of surgery, such as the jaw dating from the Old Kingdom which has two holes bored to drain an abscess, or the skull fractured by a blow from an axe or sword and successfully reset. There is also evidence of dental work such as fillings done with a mineral cement, and one mummy had a kind of bridge of gold wire joining two shaky teeth.

By its methodical approach, the Smith Papyrus bears testimony to the skill of the surgeons of ancient Egypt, skill which it would be fair to assume was handed on gradually, in Africa as well as in Asia and to classical antiquity, by the doctors who were always attached to Egyptian expeditions to foreign lands. Moreover, it is known that foreign sovereigns, like the Asian prince of Bakhtan, Bactria, or Cambyses himself, brought in Egyptian doctors, that Hippocrates 'had access to the library of the Imhotep temple at Memphis' and that other Greek physicians later followed his example.

## MEDICINE

Medical knowledge can be considered as one of the most important early scientific contributions of the ancient Egyptian to the history of man. Documents show in detail the titles of Egyptian physicians and their different fields of specialization. In fact the civilizations of the ancient Near East and the classical world recognized the ability and reputation of the ancient Egyptians in medicine and pharmacology. One of the most significant personalities in the history of medicine is Imhotep, the vizier, architect and physician of King Zoser of the third dynasty. His fame survived throughout Egyptian ancient history and through to Greek times. Deified by the Egyptians under the name Imouthes, he was assimilated by the Greeks to Askelepios, the god of medicine. In fact, Egyptian influence on the Greek world in both medicine and pharmacology is easily recognizable in remedies and prescriptions. Some medical instruments used in surgical operations have been discovered during excavations.

Written evidence of ancient Egyptian medicine comes in medical documents such as the Ebers Papyrus, the Berlin Papyrus, the Edwin Smith Surgical Papyrus and many others which illustrate the techniques of the operations and detail the prescribed cures.

These texts are copies of originals dating back to the Old Kingdom (*c.* −2500). In contrast to the Edwin Smith Surgical Papyrus, which is highly scientific, the purely medical texts were based on magic. The Egyptians regarded sickness as the work of the gods or malevolent spirits, which provided justification for resorting to magic and which explains why some of the remedies prescribed on the Ebers Papyrus, for example, resemble more a magical incantation than a medical prescription.

Despite this aspect, common to other ancient civilizations as well, Egyptian medicine was a not inconsiderable science which contained the beginnings of a methodical approach, especially in the observation of symptoms, and this method doubtless passed to posterity by reason of its importance. The Egyptian doctor examined his patient and determined the symptoms of his complaint. He then made his diagnosis and prescribed treatment. All the extant texts describe this sequence, from which it may be concluded that it was standard procedure. The examination was made in two stages some days apart if the case was unclear. Among the ailments identified and competently described and treated by Egyptian doctors were gastric disorders, stomach swelling, skin cancer, coryza, laryngitis, angina pectoris, diabetes, constipation, haemorrhoids, bronchitis, retention and incontinence of urine, bilharzia, ophthalmia, etc.

The Egyptian doctor treated his patient using suppositories, ointments, syrups, potions, oils, massages, enemas, purges, poultices, and even inhalants whose use they taught to the Greeks. Their pharmacopoeia contained a large variety of medicinal herbs, the names of which, unfortunately, elude translation. Egyptian medical techniques and medicines enjoyed great prestige in antiquity, as we know from Herodotus. The names of nearly one hundred ancient Egyptian physicians have been passed down to us through these texts. Among them are oculists and dentists, of whom Hesy-Re, who lived around −2600 under the fourth dynasty, could be considered as one of the most ancient. Among the specialists were also veterinarians. The physicians used a variety of instruments in their work.

MATHEMATICS (arithmetic, algebra and geometry)

Mathematics is an important field of science in which the ancient Egyptians worked. The accurate measurements of their enormous architectural and sculptural monuments are worthy proof of their preoccupation with precision. They would never have been able to reach this pitch of perfection without a minimum of mathematical capacity.

Two important mathematical papyri have come down to us from the Middle Kingdom (−2000 to −1750), those of Moscow and Rhind. The Egyptian method of numeration, based on the decimal system, consisted of repeating the symbols for numbers (ones, tens, hundreds, thousands) as many times as necessary to obtain the desired figure. There was no zero. It is interesting to note that the Egyptian symbols for the fractions $\frac{1}{2}$, $\frac{1}{3}$, $\frac{1}{4}$, and so on originate in the myth of Horus and Seth, in which one of Horus' falcon eyes was torn out and cut into pieces by Seth. It is these pieces that symbolize certain fractions.

Egyptian mathematics may be considered under the three headings of arithmetic, algebra and geometry.

Egyptian administrative organization required a knowledge of arithmetic. The efficiency of the highly centralized administration depended on knowing exactly what was happening in each province, in all spheres of activity. It is not surprising, then, that the scribes spent an enormous amount of time keeping records of the area of land under cultivation, the quantities of products available and their distribution, the size and quality of the staff, and so on.

The Egyptian method of calculation was simple. They reduced all operations to a series of multiplications and divisions by two (duplication), a slow process which requires little memorization and makes multiplication tables unnecessary. In divisions, whenever the dividend was not exactly divisible by the divider, the scribe introduced fractions, but the system used only fractions whose numerator was the number 1. The operations on fractions were also done by systematic doubling. The texts contain numerous examples of proportional shares obtained in this way, with the scribe adding at the end of his calculations the formula 'it is exactly that', which is equivalent to our 'QED'.

All the problems posed and solved in Egyptian treatises on arithmetic have one trait in common: they are all material problems of the type that a scribe, isolated in some remote outpost, would have to solve daily, like the apportioning of seven loaves of bread among ten men in proportion to their rank in the hierarchy, or the calculation of the number of bricks required to build an inclined plane. It was, then, basically an empirical system, with little in it of an abstract nature. It is difficult to judge what elements of such a system might have passed into neighbouring cultures.

It is not exactly clear whether one may properly speak of an Egyptian algebra and specialists in the history of science hold different views on this matter. Certain problems described in the Rhind Papyrus are formulated as follows: 'A quantity [*ahâ* in Egyptian] to which is added [or subtracted] this or that increment ($n$) results in quantity ($N$). What is this quantity?' Algebraically, this would be expressed as $x \pm \dfrac{x}{n} = N$, which has led some historians of science to conclude that the Egyptians used algebraic calculations. However, the solutions proposed by the scribe of the Rhind

Papyrus to this type of problem are always reached by simple arithmetic, and the only instance in which algebra might have been used is a problem of division which implies the existence of a quadratic equation. The scribe solved this problem as a modern algebraist would do, but instead of taking an abstract symbol like $x$ as the basis of calculation, he took the number 1. The question whether Egyptian algebra existed or not depends therefore on whether one accepts or rejects the possibility of doing algebra without abstract symbols.

The Greek writers Herodotus and Strabo concur in the view that geometry was invented by the Egyptians. The need to calculate the area of the land eroded or added each year by the flooding of the Nile apparently led them to its discovery. As a matter of fact, Egyptian geometry, like mathematics, was empirical. In ancient treatises, the task was first and foremost to provide the scribe with a formula that would enable him to find rapidly the area of a field, the volume of grain in a silo or the number of bricks required for a building project. The scribe never applied abstract reasoning to the solution of a particular problem but just provided the practical means in the shape figures. None the less, the Egyptians knew perfectly well how to calculate the area of a triangle or a circle, the volume of a cylinder, of a pyramid or a truncated pyramid, and probably that of a hemisphere. Their greatest success was the calculation of the area of a circle. They proceeded by reducing the diameter by one-ninth and squaring the result which was equivalent to assigning a value of 3·1605 to $\pi$, which is much more precise than the value 3 given to $\pi$ by other ancient peoples.

Knowledge of geometry proved of considerable practical use in land-surveying, which played a significant role in Egypt. There are many tombs with paintings showing teams of surveyors busy checking that the boundary-stones of fields have not been shifted and then measuring with a knotted cord, the forerunner of our surveyor's chain, the area of the cultivated field. The surveyor's cord or *nouh* is mentioned in the earliest texts (*c.* −2800). The central government possessed a cadastral office, the records of which were ransacked during the Memphite revolution (*c.* −2150) but were restored to order during the Middle Kingdom (*c.* −1990).

ASTRONOMY

The documentation we possess on Egyptian astronomy is not at all comparable to the material available on mathematics (the Rhind and the Moscow papyri) or surgery and medicine (the Edwin Smith and the Ebers papyri). There is reason to believe, however, that treatises on astronomy did exist. Although the Carlsberg 9 Papyrus, which describes a method for determining the phases of the moon, was undoubtedly written during the Roman period, it derives from much earlier sources and is devoid of any hellenistic influence; the same is true of the Carlsberg 1

Papyrus. Unfortunately the earlier sources are not extant and the Egyptian contribution to astronomy must therefore be deduced from practical applications made on the basis of observations. This contribution is, however, far from insignificant.

As we have seen (see Introduction), the Egyptian calendar year was divided into three seasons of four months, each having thirty days; to these 360 days, five were added at the end of the year. The 365-day calendar year, the most accurate known in antiquity, is at the origin of our own calendar year in as much as it served as the basis of the Julian reform ( − 47) and of the Gregorian reform of 1582. Side by side with this civil calendar, the Egyptians also used a religious, lunar calendar and were able to predict the moon's phases with adequate accuracy.

Ever since the Napoleonic expedition to Egypt, Europeans have been struck by the accuracy of the alignment of structures built at the time of the Pharaohs, particularly the pyramids, the four façades of which face the four cardinal points. The Great Pyramids deviate from true North by less than one degree. Such accuracy could have been achieved only by astronomical observation either of the direction of the Pole Star at the time; or the culmination of a fixed star; or the bisectrix of the angle formed by the direction of a star at twelve-hour intervals, the bisectrix of the angle of the rising and setting of a fixed star; or the observation of the maximum deviations of a fixed star (which would have been 7 from Ursa Major, according to Z. Zorba). In all these cases, precise astronomical observation is required to calculate the alignment. The Egyptians were perfectly capable of such observations because they possessed a corps of astronomers working under the authority of the vizier whose job it was to observe the night sky, to note the rising of the stars, especially of Sirius (*Sóthis*), and, above all, to determine the passage of the hours of darkness. These, for the Egyptians, varied in length according to the seasons: night, which was supposed to contain twelve hours, always commenced at sunset and ended at sunrise. Tables have come down to us which indicate that each night hour was marked, month by month, at ten-day intervals, by the appearance of a constellation or a star of the first magnitude. The tables distinguished thirty-six such constellations or stars which constituted *decans*, each one of which inaugurated a ten-day period.

This system dates back at least to the third dynasty (*c*. −2600). Apart from the tables, the priest-astronomer possessed simple observation instruments: a sighting-rod and a square to which a plumb-line was attached and which required a team of two observers. Despite the rudimentary nature of this technique, the observations were precise, as evidenced by the accuracy of the orientations of the pyramids. Certain tombs have paintings representing the sky. The stars are represented in picture form which has made it possible to identify some of the constellations recognized by the Egyptians. Ursa Major is called the Ox Leg; the stars surrounding Arcturus are represented by a crocodile and hippopotamus coupled together; Cygnus is represented by a man with his arms extended; Orion by a person running with his head turned back; Cassiopeia by a figure with outstretched arms; and Draco, Pleiades, Scorpius and Aries by other figures.

To determine the daytime hours, which also varied according to the seasons, the Egyptians used a *gnomon*, a simple rod planted vertically on a graduated board with a plumb-line attached. This instrument served to measure the time spent on the irrigation of the fields, since the water had to be distributed impartially. As well as the *gnomon*, the Egyptians had water clocks which were placed in their temples. These water clocks were borrowed and perfected by the Greeks and are the clepsydras of antiquity. They were made in Egypt as early as −1580.

### ARCHITECTURE

The ancient Egyptians applied their mathematical knowledge to the extraction, transportation and positioning of the huge blocks of stone used in their architectural projects. They had a long tradition in using mud-bricks and various kinds of stone from very early times. Their first use of heavy granite was during the beginning of the third millennium before our era. It was used for the flooring of some tombs belonging to the first dynasty at Abydos. In the second dynasty they used limestone in constructing the walls of tombs.

A new phase was started in the third dynasty. This was a vital develop-ment in the history of Egyptian architecture, for it was the construction of the first complete building in stone. This is the step pyramid at Sakkara, which forms a part of the huge funerary complex of King Zoser.

Imhotep, who was probably the vizier of King Zoser (*c.* −2580), was the architect who built the ensemble containing the step pyramid where hewn stone was used for the first time. The blocks were small and looked very much like a limestone imitation of the sun-dried brick used earlier in funerary architecture. Similarly, the imbedded columns and the ceiling joists were stone copies of the bundles of plants and beams used in earlier construction. Thus, there is every indication that Egyptian architecture was amongst the first to use hewn stone in coursed work.

Egypt developed a wide variety of architectural forms, of which the pyramid is, undoubtedly, the most characteristic. The first pyramids were step pyramids and it was not until the fourth dynasty (*c.* −2300) that they gradually became triangular in form. From that period, the architects gave up the use of the small stones of the third dynasty in favour of large blocks of limestone and granite.

Until the Roman conquest, civil architecture continued to use sundried bricks even in the building of royal palaces. The outbuildings of Ramses in Thebes and the great Nubian fortresses provide a very good idea of the versatility of this material. It could be used with the utmost refinement, as can be seen from the Palace of Amenhotep IV at Tell-el-Amarna with its pavements and ceilings decorated with paintings. Another contribution in the field of architecture was the creation of the column. This was at first attached to the wall, but later became free-standing columns.

In developing this architectural skill the ancient Egyptian was much influenced by the local environment. For example, in arriving at the idea of a column, he was inspired by his observation of wild plants such as reeds and papyrus. He cut the capitals of the columns into the shape of lotus flowers, papyrus and other plants, and this was another architectural innovation. The lotus papyrus palm and fluted columns of ancient Egypt were adopted in the architecture of other cultures.

It is likely that the ancient Egyptians invented the vault during the second dynasty (*c.* −2900). To begin with it was a vault of bricks but by the sixth dynasty the Egyptians were building stone vaults.

The Great Giza Pyramid was one of the seven wonders of the ancient world. A building of such great proportions stands proof of the architectural and administrative ability of the ancient Egyptians. The construction of the ascending corridors, leading to the granite chamber of the king, and the existence of two openings or vents, on both the northern and southern sides of the royal chamber, extending to the outside to provide ventilation, are good examples of their ingenuity.

The exact proportions, measurements and orientation of the chambers and corridors of the pyramids, to say nothing of the cutting and erection of giant obelisks in solid stone, indicate the possession of great technical skills from very early times.

To transport and position the stone blocks, the Egyptians used levers, rollers and wooden cross-bars. Their architectural achievements despite their considerable dimensions were accomplished solely through the strength of human arms, without the use of any mechanical means other than the principle of the lever in its diverse forms.

The technical knowledge acquired by the Egyptians in construction and irrigation as the result of digging canals and building dikes or dams manifested itself in other fields allied to architecture.

By −2550, they had sufficient skill to build a dam of hewn stone in a wadi near Cairo. Somewhat later, their engineers cut navigable channels in the rocks of the First Cataract at Aswan. By all evidence, towards −1740, they seem to have succeeded in erecting a barrage on the Nile itself at Semna, in Nubia, to facilitate navigation to the south. And finally, during the same period, they built a ramp, parallel to the Second Cataract, over which they slid their boats on the fluid mud of the Nile. The ramp extended over several kilometres, a predecessor of the Greek *diolkos* of the Isthmus of Corinth, and ensured that the rapids of the Second Cataract were never a hindrance to navigation.

Garden design and town planning are other aspects of Egyptian architecture. The Egyptians had a great fondness for gardens. Even the poor managed to plant a tree or two in the narrow courtyard of their houses. When they were rich, their gardens rivalled their residences in size and luxury. Under the third dynasty (*c.* −2800), a high official would expect to possess a garden of more than two-and-a-half acres which always contained a pool, which was a distinctive feature of Egyptian gardens. The garden was arranged around the pool or pools, for there could be several of them. They served as fish ponds, as reservoirs for watering and as a source of cooling fresh air for the house nearby. Frequently, the master of the house had a light wooden pavilion built near the pool where he could come for a breath of fresh air in the evening and receive friends for cold drinks.

These artificial pools were occasionally quite large. Snefru's palace lake was large enough for him to sail upon it accompanied by young, lightly clad girls plying the oars, and Amenhotep III had a vast pool built in his Theban palace. This very Egyptian taste for garden parks later passed to Rome.

There are earlier examples of town planning than those attributed to Greek genius. As early as −1895, under the reign of Sesostris II, the city of Kahun was built inside a rectangular wall. The city had both administrative and residential buildings. The workers' houses, nearly 250 of which have been excavated, were built in blocks along streets 4 metres wide which ran into a central thoroughfare 8 metres wide. Each house occupied a ground area of 100 to 125 square metres and contained a dozen rooms on a single level. Located in another quarter of the city were the houses of the leading citizens – town houses which sometimes had as many as seventy rooms, or more modest homes which were, nevertheless, considerably larger than those of the workers. These houses were also built along rectilinear avenues running parallel to the city walls. These avenues had a drain running down the centre.

The large fortresses in Nubia were patterned on the same lines, and the same urban plan was adopted, under the New Kingdom, at Tell-el-Amarna, among other places, where the streets crossed at right angles though the city itself did not have the geometrical severity of Kahun.

It would, of course, be hazardous to suggest that all Egyptian cities were laid out like Kahun or Tell-el-Amarna. Those cities were built at one go under the orders of a sovereign. Cities which grew up over a long period of time must have had a more haphazard appearance. The fact of the matter remains, however, that the geometric plans of the city and the standardized type of houses that were built shed light on the trends of Egyptian town planning. Were they the forerunners of the town planning of the Hellenes? The question is worth asking.

While Egypt unquestionably made a major contribution in the field of architecture, it is nevertheless more difficult to judge the impact it had on the world as a whole in this sphere. Architects in many cultures, to be sure, have used, and are still using, colonnades, pyramids and obelisks which are undeniably of Egyptian origin. But was there not, in addition, an influence that goes back even farther and comes down to us through the intermediary of the Greeks? It is difficult not to discern in the clustered columns of Sakkara and the proto-Doric columns at Beni Hasan the remote ancestors of the columns of Greek and, later, Roman classical art. One fact, at least, seems established: the architectural traditions of the Pharaohs made their way into Africa first via Meroe and then Napata, which transmitted forms such as pyramids and pylons, among others, as well as techniques such as building with small, hewn, well-shaped masonry.

## Cultural contributions

This side of the Egyptian Pharaonic legacy is an abstract one. It includes their contributions in the fields of writing, literature, art and religion.

### LITERATURE

The Egyptians developed a hieroglyphic writing system in which many of the symbols came from their African environment. For this reason it can be assumed to be their original creation rather than borrowed (see Introduction).

The ancient Egyptian at first expressed himself in pictorial ideograms which were soon formalized into symbols reflecting phonetic sounds which, in their later abbreviated form, could be considered as a step towards an alphabetic script.

Cultural contacts with the Semitic script developed in Sinai, where there appeared distinctive forms of writing which borrowed forms possessing affinities with hieroglyphics, may have contributed to the invention of the true alphabet which was borrowed by the Greeks and had its influence on Europe. Apart from this, the ancient Egyptians invented the tools of writing (which we have already described in the section on crafts). Their discovery of papyrus, handed down to classical antiquity, thanks to its light weight, flexibility and the almost unlimited dimensions that could be papyrus 'scrolls', certainly played a role in the diffusion of thought and knowledge. There is an extensive literature dating from Pharaonic times covering every aspect of Egyptian life, from religious theories to literature, such as stories, plays, poetry, dialogues and criticism. This literature can be considered as one of the most vital cultural legacies of ancient Egypt. Even though it is impossible to determine what parts of it were taken over by neighbouring African cultures, a modern ethnologist was able to recognize a legend of Egyptian origin, one also found in a text of Herodotus, among the Nilotes of the province of Equatoria in the Sudan.

Some the most impressive examples of Egyptian literature are those written during the First Intermediate Period and during the early Middle Kingdom. One eminent scholar of Egyptology, James Henry Breasted, considered this literature as an early sign of intellectual and social maturity.

He described this period as a dawn of conscience when a man could debate with his own soul on metaphysical matters. Another example of the literature of this period was a work written by the Eloquent Peasant which expresses dissatisfaction with the community and with the condition of the land. This could be considered as an early step towards a social revolution and democracy.

A good example of the sentiments expressed in Egyptian literature is seen in the inscription on four wooden coffins found in El-Bersheh in Middle Egypt: 'I created the four winds so every man could breathe ... I caused the flood so the poor could benefit as well as the rich ... I created every man equal to his neighbour ...'

Lastly, it is conceivable that certain specimens of Egyptian literature have survived to our day thanks to the marvellous stories of Arabic literature. The latter, indeed, seem at times to have their source in Egyptian oral tradition. It has, for example, been possible to establish a parallel between the story of 'Ali Baba and the Forty Thieves' from *The Arabian Nights* and a Pharaonic story, 'The Taking of Joppe', and between 'Sinbad the Sailor' and 'The Shipwrecked Sailor', a Pharaonic tale of the Middle Kingdom.

ART

In the field of art the ancient Egyptians expressed their ideas in a great many techniques including sculpture, painting, reliefs and architecture (see Pls 4–6). They combined worldly affairs and activities with hopes for the after-life, and their art was particularly expressive because it gave representation to beliefs that were deeply held. For them, there was only a semblance of death when all signs of life ceased, for the human being still continued to exist in every way. But to survive they required the support of their body, through mummification or, failing that, through an image. Statues and statuettes, bas-reliefs and tomb paintings are there to perpetuate the life of the individual in the afterworld. This is why the details of the human body are shaped with such precision. To heighten the intensity of his gaze, the eyes of the statues were inlaid, and even the eyebrows were fashioned in copper or silver. The eyeballs were made of white quartz and the pupils were made of resin. Sometimes the Egyptian artists manufactured gold statues or hammered copper ones on a wooden base. This required great skill and experience in the shaping of metal. This skill can be seen in a large number of statues dating from every historical period which have been found in various archaeological sites.

In the field of minor arts, the ancient Egyptians produced a very large number of amulets, scarabs and seals and also ornamental objects and jewellery, which are no less beautiful for their smaller size. It is undoubtedly these small objects which were most widespread and esteemed in Africa, the Near East and even in Europe. It is often the wide distribution of these objects that makes it possible to discover the bonds which linked Egypt to other nations long ago.

All artistic objects in ancient Egypt were made, not for the sake of art alone, but above all as an expression of the Egyptian belief that life relating to the living world would be repeated after death.

## Religion

This can be considered as one of the philosophical contributions of Egypt. For the ancient Egyptians developed a number of theories concerning the creation of life, the role of the natural powers, and the response of the human community towards them; also the world of the gods and their influence on human thought, the divine aspect of kingship, the role of the priesthood in the community and the belief in eternity and life in the netherworld.

It was their profound experience in such abstract thought that influenced the Egyptian community to such an extent that it had a lasting effect on the outside world. Particularly apparent to the historian is the Egyptian religious influence in certain Graeco-Roman religious objects, as can be seen by the popularity of the goddess Isis and her cult in classical antiquity.

## Transmission of the Pharaonic legacy. Role of the Syro-Palestinian Corridor

Phoenicia played a special and important role in transmitting the Pharaonic legacy to the rest of the world.

Egypt's influence on Phoenicia can be traced through the economic and cultural contacts between the two areas. Such a relationship became‹ apparent when trade and exploration started to expand during the pre- and protodynastic times, in order to fulfil the vast needs of those periods. Even the invention of writing as an essential means of communication developed partly as a result of economic and religious factors. That is to say, the contacts with Phoenicia were indispensable to import vital raw materials like wood, for example, which were necessary for the erection and construction of shrines and religious monuments.

Egyptian traders established a shrine of their own at Byblos, a city with which they had very close trade contacts. Egyptian culture and ideas were spread throughout the Mediterranean basin by the intermediary of the Phoenicians.

The influence of Egyptian culture on biblical wisdom, among other things, is noteworthy (see Chapter 3). With regard to the Levant, commercial and cultural relations existed throughout the second and first millennia before our era, which include the Middle and New Kingdom as well as under the late dynasties. Relations naturally increased following Egyptian political and military expansion, and Egyptian artistic patterns occur in various Syrian and Palestinian sites such as Ras Shamra, Qatna and Megisso, as can be seen from statues, sphinxes and decorative patterns. The exchange of gifts helped in expanding the cultural and commercial relations.

It should be stated that it was the Egyptian artistic influence that affected Syrian local art and this was a direct result of the contacts between Egypt and the Levant. In Mittani, in the north-east of Syria, Egyptian artistic elements can also be observed. For example, the Egyptian goddess Hathor is represented in mural paintings. It seems that Egyptian artistic influence spread from Syria to neighbouring communities; this is indicated by the number of ivory handles and plaques of Egyptian motifs in the decoration of some bronze bowls and especially in attempts to imitate Egyptian dress, the winged scarabs and the falcon-headed sphinxes.

Egyptian artistic influence, which has been observed in Phoenician and Syrian art, is actually combined with local artistic motifs, as well as other foreign elements, both in sculpture in the round and in reliefs. This phenomenon can be observed not only in Syria but also among the Phoenician objects found in Cyprus and Greece, since the Phoenicians played an important cultural and commercial role in the Mediterranean world and carried elements of the Egyptian culture to other areas.

Egyptian hieroglyphic writing has been traced in the Semitic scripts of the Levant. This can be observed by comparing some typical Egyptian hieroglyphs, the proto-Sinaitic signs, and the Phoenician alphabet. The proto-Sinaitic elements were influenced by the Egyptian hieroglyphic ideograms, and they simplified these ideograms in a way which may be considered as a step towards alphabetical signs. Proto-Sinaitic writing could be taken as a step towards the Phoenician alphabet and hence towards the European alphabet.

This vast Pharaonic legacy, disseminated through the ancient civilizations of the Near East, has in turn transmitted to modern Europe a civilization by way of the classical world.

Economic and political contacts between Egypt and the eastern Mediterranean world in historical times resulted in the distribution of objects of the Pharaonic civilization as far as Anatolia and the pre-Hellenic Aegean world. Thus, a cup bearing the name of the solar temple of Userkaf, first Pharaoh of the fifth dynasty, was found on the island of Cythera, while pieces of a gold-plated armchair, carrying Schure's titles, were found at Dorak in Anatolia.

Besides these relations between Pharaonic Egypt and the Mediterranean world, there were also the cultural ties which linked Egypt with the African interior. These relations existed during the earliest stages of prehistory as well as in historical times. Egyptian civilization under the Pharaohs permeated the neighbouring African cultures. Comparative studies prove the existence of common cultural elements between black Africa and Egypt, such as the relationship between royalty and natural forces. This is clear from archaeological findings in the former territory of the land of Kush: royal pyramids were built in El-Kurru, Nuri, Gebel Barkal and Meroe. They bear witness to the significance of Egyptian influence in Africa.

Unfortunately, our ignorance of the Meroitic language, and of the extent of the Meroitic empire, prevents us from judging the impact it had on the cultures of ancient Africa as a whole to the east, west and south of the Meroitic empire.

PLATE 5.1 *The goddess Hathor*

PLATE 5.2a *Karnak: the resting place of Amon's boat*

PLATE 5.2b *Giza: the resting place of Cheop's boat*

PLATE 5.3 *Discoveries made by the French Archaeological Mission to the Sudan*

PLATE 5.4 *The pyramids of Snefru at Dahshur*

PLATE 5.5 *Columns of the Temple of Sakkara*

PLATE 5.6 *Proto-Doric columns of Deir el Bahari*

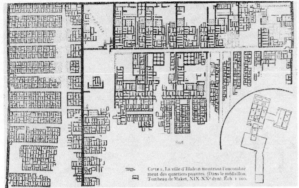

PLATE 5.7 *Town planning:
layout of the town of
Illahun (Kahun), after
Petrie, showing the crowding
of the poorer districts. (Inset:
tomb of Maket, XIX–XX
Dynasties.)*

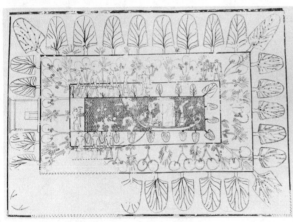

PLATE 5.8 *An Egyptian
garden*

PLATE 5.9 *Manufacture of metal vases*

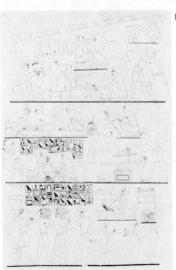

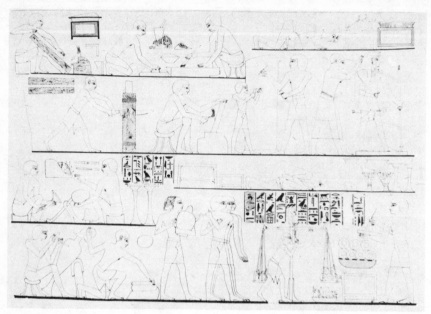

PLATE 5.10 *Cabinet makers at work*

PLATE 5.11 *The manufacture of bricks*

PLATE 5.12 *Model of a weaver's workshop, twelfth dynasty, about −2000*

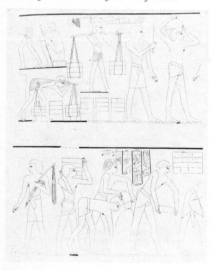

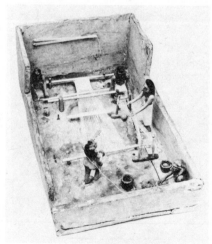

PLATE 5.13 *Ramses II (fluids technique)*

PLATE 5.14 *Beer-making, Old Kingdom*

PLATE 5.15 *Model of a house during the Middle Empire*

# Egypt in the hellenistic era

**H. RIAD**

*with the collaboration of* J. DEVISSE

At the death of Alexander the Great, his empire comprised Macedonia, a large part of Asia Minor, the eastern shores of the Mediterranean, and Egypt, extending into Asia to the east as far as the Punjab. After his death in −323, three dynasties founded by three of his generals were already well established to control the empire: the Antigonids in Macedonia, the Seleucids in Asia in what had been the Persian empire, and the Ptolemies in Egypt.

The Ptolemies reigned over Egypt for three centuries, initiating a period that was very different from preceding periods in the country's history, at least in the outward aspects of its life and political geography. Egypt was subsequently to fall under Roman domination.[1]

## A new type of state in Egypt

Under rather more than a dozen Ptolemies, Egypt was initially strongly marked by the stamp of the foreign rulers and the demands of the new policy, with subsequent slow assimilation, as before, of the new masters[2] of the Delta.[3]

The forward defence of the capital which, probably from the time of Ptolemy II onwards, was situated on the sea coast for the first time in Egypt's history, in Alexandria, necessitated military and naval ascendancy in the eastern Mediterranean. The twofold danger of attack from their Syrian rivals and from the Nubians compelled the Ptolemies to adopt a very costly military policy. First, they had not only to distribute land to the mercenaries but also to meet heavy expenses in cash; and, secondly,

---

1. These are conventional limits. See: W. Tarn, 1930, pp. 1ff.; M. Bieber, pp. 1ff. gives −330 to −300 as the limit; she mentions other authors such as Droysen (from −280 up to the time of Augustus) and R. Lagueur, who gives −400 as the beginning of the period.

2. This was particularly true under the founder of the line, Ptolemy Soter I (−367 to −283), his son Ptolemy II Philadelphus (−285 to −246) and Ptolemy III Euergetes (−246 to −221), who were the most remarkable warriors − and possibly the most remarkable statesmen as well − of the entire line.

3. C. Préaux, 1950, p. 111, rightly draws attention to the Delta's quite unprecedented importance in Egypt's foreign relations.

they had to seek the basic materials for adequate military strength some considerable distance from Egypt. To ensure an adequate supply of timber for shipbuilding, it was necessary to limit construction work in Egypt, to develop royal plantations in the Nile valley, and to import timber from the Aegean and the islands; it was also necessary to import the tar, pitch and iron needed for the shipyards.[4] Hence was created what was to be a permanent feature of Egyptian economic life for more than a thousand years. The most spectacular aspect of this maritime development was the establishment of bases for elephant-hunting all along the African coast as far as Somalia,[5] and the construction, at enormous expense, of ships designed for transporting the beasts. Elephants were needed to combat the rival Seleucids, who used to obtain theirs from Asia.[6] It was also necessary to send to India for mahouts to train the captured elephants. Of this effort the only lasting trace is to be found in its cultural consequences: Hippalus' discovery, in the reign of Ptolemy III, of the pattern of the monsoons shortened the journey to the Indies and made it less dangerous and less expensive. Trade relations with Asia naturally increased.[7] The Ptolemies spared no effort to improve relations between the Red Sea and the Delta. The canal driven by Darius I from the eastern arm of the Nile towards the Bitter Lakes was deepened in the reign of Ptolemy Philadelphus and made more easily navigable by large vessels. Ptolemy Philadelphus also established a route between Coptos in the Thebaid and Berenice on the Red Sea.

The foreign policy of the Ptolemies involved them in heavy expenditure, which had to be balanced by a very large income into the royal coffers. A partial solution to the problem was provided by strict control over the economy and by the supervision of exports, some of which were systematically developed under royal monopoly. Corn was stored in immense granaries in Alexandria providing the king with produce that could be exported to the north in exchange for strategic raw materials and also serve as the means of rewarding the enormous population of Alexandria by distributing grain from time to time, especially when there was a shortage. Increased production of exportable commodities led to a systematic policy of bringing virgin soil under cultivation at royal expense, but the ruler remained indifferent to the welfare of the Egyptian farmers.

4. C. Préaux, 1939, emphasizes the magnitude of the undertaking: in − 306 Ptolemy I possessed 200 vessels, while Ptolemy Philadelphus had over 400 ships deployed throughout his empire.

5. J. Leclant, 1976b, Vol. I, p. 230. Ptolemy Philadelphus opened ports at Arsinoë, Myos Hormos and Berenice. He also laid out roads between the Nile and the Red Sea (C. Préaux, 1939).

6. C. Préaux, 1939.

7. 'Ptolemy Philadelphus attempted to divert from the Arabian caravan route the merchandise which was transported along it from Ethiopia, Arabia itself, and, via the Arabs, from India. Again it was Alexandria that benefited from this policy': quoted in A. Bernand, pp. 258–9.

Initially, at least, he no longer co-ordinated production as the Pharaohs had done but merely seized the products needed for his treasury.[8]

Another way of meeting the vast cost of armaments and imports was the export to the Mediterranean of African products: ivory, gold, feathers and ostrich eggs were bought in places to the south of Egypt and in the Horn of Africa, for resale in the Mediterranean. Other merchandise was brought from the Indian Ocean: rare woods, dyes, silks and precious stones were re-exported (in some cases after processing by the Alexandrians) to Greece, the Greek colonies, Italy, the whole of the eastern Mediterranean, and even as far as the Black Sea. It will be seen, once again, that this commercial activity had considerable cultural repercussions.

It is even very probable that the Ptolemies sold slaves, although certainly to a lesser extent than Carthage during the same period.[9]

An attempt was also made to reduce the amount spent on purchasing special items demanded by the large Greek colony living in Egypt. So, in order to satisfy the tastes and the customs of the Greeks, the Ptolemies tried forcibly to introduce the cultivation of new species such as balsam into Egypt, but the Egyptian peasants resisted these novelties.

These policies were to bear fruit only at the cost of constant military preparedness and permanent control over the eastern Mediterranean, the Red Sea and the Indian Ocean. The Ptolemies were never able to keep all the cards firmly in their hand for any length of time and, from the fourth of the line onwards, their grip gradually loosened and Egypt slowly slipped back once more into its traditional type of economy.

The fact remains that the Ptolemies gave the Egyptian economy a vigorous, if probably highly artificial, boost to the benefit of the state and the Greek ruling class.

The processing industry was particularly well developed in the Delta and the region of Alexandria. A special effort was made to obtain wool and to introduce Arab and Milesian sheep. The cloth mills learned to work this new raw material in addition to flax, and it became possible to produce fourteen different varieties of cloth. Alexandria had the monopoly of the manufacture of papyrus, a plant peculiar to Egypt which grew in the marshes of the Delta not far from the capital. The art of glass-making, which was already known during the time of the Pharaohs, reached a very high degree of refinement, new methods being perfected under the Ptolemies. For centuries Alexandria was renowned as a centre for the making of glass-ware. Alexandria also possessed great skill in the working of metals such as gold, silver and bronze, its inlaid vases being highly valued.

Alexandria not only exported the merchandise it produced (cloth, papyrus, glass and jewellery) but also re-exported goods from Arabia, East Africa and India.

8. Papyrus was of course among these products.
9. J. Leclant, 1976b, p. 230.

Part of the price paid for the development of this kind of industrial production in the Delta was necessarily the growth of slavery.[10]

In order to deal with all these financial problems, a strong currency[11] was needed. To expand trade with the rest of the hellenistic world, the currency had to be tied to that world's monetary standards, which were alien to Egypt. A complete, new financial system was therefore built up. Banks played an important part in the economic life of the country. A central state bank was set up in Alexandria, with branches in the capitals of the nomes and sub-branches in the major villages. These royal banks carried on every kind of banking transaction. There were also private banks, which had a secondary role in the country's economic life. The operation of the royal monopolies and the ponderous fiscal administration were extremely costly and imposed a very heavy burden on the population.[12] This highly structured economy brought no financial benefit whatsoever to the Egyptians themselves.

In agriculture, conflicts between the indigenous population and the foreigners were frequent. Some of these conflicts ended in the peasants seeking sanctuary in the temples or fleeing far from their homes.

The Ptolemies were looked upon as the wealthiest kings of their time. Their wealth was certainly shared by a large number of those Greeks who belonged to the ruling class, who all lived comfortably. The Ptolemies and the Greeks of Alexandria, for example, were easily able to obtain a variety of flowers and fruits when the fancy took them, even outside the capital.[13]

Ptolemy Philadelphus was the first to realize that the weight of this system might be too heavy for the Egyptians to bear. He wanted to become a true Egyptian sovereign and heir to the Pharaohs: we know, for example, that he visited the land development works in the Fayyum. This trend was intensified by his successors following their failures abroad.

The Ptolemies none the less never succeeded in eliminating the basic inequality of the society over which they reigned.

Foreigners were socially, politically and economically in a very different position from that of the native population and had far greater advantages. The high officials of the palace and the members of the government were foreigners, as were also the army officers and the soldiers. In agriculture, foreigners had a better chance than Egyptians of becoming landowners.

---

10. C. Préaux, 1939.

11. Under the Ptolemies the search for gold in the valleys of the tributaries of the Nile towards Ethiopia was increased. Strabo described the mining conditions as appalling. The amount of gold produced was insufficient to meet the demand and its price continually rose (ibid.).

12. As nearly always happens, this tax burden became heavier when the initial successes gave way to reverses (ibid.).

13. For the Ptolemaic economy as a whole, see the recent publication by E. Will, pp. 133ff. pp. 133ff.

In industry they were the contractors, not the workers. Most of the royal and private banks were managed by them. In short, they were rich while the natives were poor. If an Egyptian wanted to borrow money or corn he generally had to borrow it from a foreigner; when he rented a plot of land it was usually land owned by foreigners, and so it was with everything. Hence the natives became docile tools in the hands of the foreigners. Besides their normal work, the native Egyptians had numerous obligations to fulfil. They were required to perform compulsory work on the canals and embankments and, from time to time, in the mines and quarries. Foreigners, as a special favour, were probably exempted from compulsory labour, and some classes of foreigners enjoyed special tax privileges as well. This view of the situation, however, must not be exaggerated. Some native-born Egyptians such as Manetho, for example, by becoming rich and collaborating with the Greeks did manage to achieve a place among the ruling classes.

Archaeology sometimes yields finds in connection with this society which are difficult to interpret: E. Bernand has published an epitaph of a black slave, written by a local Greek-educated poet.[14]

One of the most unexpected consequences of the arrival in Egypt of large numbers of Greeks was the spread of certain Egyptian cults throughout the Greek world.

The Greeks, when they first came, had their own gods and their own religious beliefs, which were very different from those of the Egyptians. Very soon, however, there grew up a tendency to associate certain Greek gods with certain Egyptian gods and a new trinity was created, consisting of Serapis as the father-god, Isis as the mother-goddess, and Harpocrates the son-god. For the Egyptians, Serapis was their old god Osir-Hapi or Osirapis (whence the name Serapis was derived). For the Greeks, Serapis, who was depicted as an old man with a beard, resembled their god Zeus. Each of the two communities worshipped him in their own fashion. Isis, a purely Egyptian goddess, was henceforth depicted clad in a Greek robe with the characteristic knot at the breast. Harpocrates was the infant Horus, son of Isis, and was depicted as a child with his finger in his mouth.

The focal point of this new religion was the Serapeion of Alexandria, which was erected to the west of the city. We have very little information about the appearance of this temple, but we know from Roman historians that it stood on a high platform reached by a stairway of a hundred steps. As early as the third century before our era, the cult of Serapis was rapidly spreading to the islands of the Aegean sea. By the first century, people everywhere were invoking Serapis and Isis as saviours. Worship of them spread far afield, the cult of Isis reaching Uruk in Babylonia and that of Serapis reaching India. Of all the gods of the hellenistic world, Isis of the Myriad Names was probably the greatest. A hymn to Isis, found at Zos,

14. E. Bernand, pp. 143–7.

runs: 'I am she whom women call goddess. I ordained that women should be loved by men, brought wife and husband together, and invented marriage. I ordained that women should bear children, and that children should love their parents.'[15] When Christianity triumphed, Isis alone survived; her statues served as images of the Madonna.

Jean Leclant, in stressing the role of the black Africans in spreading the cult of Isis, [16] remarks in a recent work that the sculpted head of a priest of Isis, found at Athens and dating from the first century, is perhaps that of a half-caste.[17]

## A renowned capital on the coast 'beside Egypt'

It was during the reign of the Ptolemies that Alexandria was founded, a city so prosperous that it became not only the capital of Egypt but also the most important city of the hellenistic world. It must be stressed that Egypt, which had suffered military defeat and been politically incorporated into the Macedonian empire, exerted a matchless fascination on Alexander, who wanted to make it the site of one of his most renowned urban schemes and perhaps thought of establishing the capital of his empire there. Furthermore, Egyptian learning was held in such esteem that the scholars of the empire soon began coming to live in Alexandria. Under the Ptolemies, Alexandria may be regarded as the intellectual capital of the Mediterranean world. It was spoken of as though it were situated not *in* Egypt but *near* Egypt (Alexandria ad Aegyptum). Strabo described it as follows: 'the city's main advantage is that it is the only spot in the whole of Egypt equally well-placed for sea trade, by virtue of its fine harbours, and for inland trade, since the river makes it easy to transport all the merchandise there and bring it all together in that place, which has become the greatest market place of the inhabited world'.[18] In those few lines, however, Strabo both exaggerates the excellence of the site chosen and falls far short of painting a complete picture of Alexandria.

The construction of the city and of its harbours, in point of fact, required an immense amount of labour over a long period.[19]

The site of the new city had been chosen by Alexander the Great while on his way from Memphis to the oasis of Ammonium (Siwa) to consult the famous oracle at the temple of Zeus-Ammon in −331. He had been struck by the excellent position of the strip of land lying between the Mediterranean to the north and Lake Mareotis to the south, well

15. W. Tarn, 1930, p. 324.

16. J. Leclant, 1976b, p. 282; see also F. M. Snowden, Jr, 1976, pp. 112–16.

17. J. Leclant, 1976b, note 80.

18. Cited by E. Bernand, p. 92.

19. To give but one example, there were enormous cisterns to hold fresh water for the inhabitants. At the beginning of the nineteenth century, three hundred of these could still be seen (ibid., p. 42).

away from the marshes of the Delta and yet close to the Canopic branch of the Nile. The site was occupied by a small village called Rhacotis, well protected from the waves and storms by the island of Pharos. Plans for the future city which was to immortalize the name of Alexander were drawn up by the architect Dinocrates, and work began immediately. At the time of Alexander's death, the work was not very far advanced, and the city does not seem to have been completed until the reign of Ptolemy II (−285 to −246).

The architect devised a plan to connect the island of Pharos with the mainland by means of a wide mole called the Heptastadion because it was seven stadia (approximately 1200 metres) long. This has now disappeared beneath the alluvial deposits that have built up from both sides.

The building of the Heptastadion resulted in the formation of two harbours: the one to the east – the 'Portus Magnus' – being larger than the one on the west side, which was called 'Portus Eunostos' or the port of safe return. There was also a third harbour on Lake Mareotis for inland trade.

The new city was planned on the lines of the most modern Greek cities of the time. Its main characteristic was a predominance of straight lines. Most of the streets were straight and intersected at right angles.

Under Ptolemy I Soter, the major political role was still held by Memphis, but after the body of Alexander had been transported (it is said) to the new capital,[20] Ptolemy II established the seat of power of the dynasty permanently there.

The city was divided into districts. Philo of Alexandria (−30 to +45) says that there were five districts called by the first five letters of the Greek alphabet. Unfortunately, we know very little about these districts. The royal quarter occupied nearly one-third of the city adjoining the eastern harbour. It was the most attractive part of the city, with the royal palaces surrounded by gardens with magnificent fountains and cages containing animals brought from all over the known world. This district also contained the famous museum, the library and the royal cemetery.

The inhabitants of the city lived in communities. The Greeks and foreigners lived in the eastern part, the Jews in the Delta district close to the royal quarter, and the native Egyptians to the west in the Rhacotis district. The population as a whole had a reputation for instability, though the various ethnic or social groups differed greatly.

The city's social spectrum was very broad. First, there were the king and his court, the high officials and the army. There were also scholars, scientists and men of letters, rich businessmen, modest shopkeepers, artisans, dockers, sailors and slaves. The native Egyptians, however, formed the main body of the population of Alexandria and included peasants, artisans, small shopkeepers, shepherds, sailors, etc.

20. ibid., p. 299: the tomb, if it existed, has never been found.

In the streets of the city many languages were spoken; Greek in its various dialects was, of course, the most widespread. Egyptian was the language of the inhabitants of the native quarters, while in the Jewish quarter Aramaic and Hebrew were the prevailing tongues and other Semitic languages might also be heard.

Alexandria was particularly famous for certain monuments whose location is now difficult to determine. Some of the most important parts of the hellenistic city are today below sea-level, and the rest is buried deep below the modern city. When speaking of the monuments of the ancient city, therefore, we often rely as much on the descriptions of ancient authors as on what archaeologists have uncovered.

In the south-eastern part of the island of Pharos, at the entrance to the eastern harbour, stood the famous lighthouse (*Pharos*), which ranked as one of the seven wonders of the world. The Alexandrian lighthouse gave its name and its basic form to all the lighthouses of antiquity.

This lighthouse was completely destroyed in the fourteenth century, so that our knowledge of its shape and arrangement is derived from a few classical references and some descriptions by Arab historians.[21]

Ancient coins and representations on mosaics give us an idea of its shape. It was designed by Sostratus of Cnidus in about −280 in the reign of Ptolemy Philadelphus. It was about 135 metres high and constructed chiefly of limestone. The friezes and ornamental work were partly in marble and partly in bronze.

The lighthouse continued to function until the time of the Arab conquest in +642. This marked the start of a series of disasters culminating in the nineteenth century. In +1480, the Mameluke Sultan Kait Bey used stone from the ruins to build a fort as part of his coastal defences against the Turks who were threatening Egypt at that time. This fort is still standing and bears the Sultan's name.

The Arabic word *al-manarah* means both lighthouse and minaret, and the Alexandrian lighthouse has often been held to be the prototype for the minarets of mosques. The truth of this has not been established beyond all doubt, but there are nevertheless interesting similarities between the proportions of the lighthouse and those of certain minarets.

The museum, with its enormous library, was by far the most important achievement of the Ptolemies in Alexandria. It was started by Ptolemy I Soter on the advice of an Athenian refugee, Demetrius of Phalerum. The museum derived its name from the Muses, whose worship symbolized the

---

21. In +1166 Abu-l-Hajjy Yussuf Ibn Muhammad al-Balawi al-Andalusi went to Alexandria as a tourist. He has given us an accurate description of the lighthouse's dimensions. In plan, the base was a square with sides of 8·35 metres; the first stage stood 56·73 metres high; the second, which was octagonal in section, rose another 27·45 metres above the first, while the third was a drum 7·32 metres in height (see ibid., 1966, p. 106). The measurements supplied by this Arab author do not agree with those traditionally associated with the Alexandrian lighthouse.

scientific mind. The buildings have been described by Strabo as follows: 'The royal palaces also comprise the Museum, which contains a walk, an exedra and a vast hall in which the Museum's philologists take their meals together. There are also general funds for the maintenance of the college and a priest set over the Museum by the kings, or, at the present time, by Caesar.'[22] Thus scientists and men of letters lived in this institution. They were housed and fed and were able to give themselves up entirely to their research and studies, with no menial duties to perform. Its organization was similar to that of modern universities, except that the resident scholars were not required to give lectures.[23]

In the second century of our era, fellowships in the Alexandrian museum were still coveted.

Demetrius of Phalerum had advised Ptolemy Soter to create a library which would bring together the whole of contemporary culture by means of purchases and systematic copying of manuscripts and very soon more than 200 000 volumes had been collected. The management of this cultural repository was entrusted to illustrious specialists of the contemporary Greek world.[24]

A smaller library in the Serapeion held 45 000 volumes.

No institution like the museum of Alexandria existed anywhere else in the hellenistic world. The only library that could compete with that of Alexandria was the one at Pergamon. We are largely indebted to the library of Alexandria for the survival of the tragedies of Aeschylus, the comedies of Aristophanes, the odes of Pindar and Bacchylides and the histories of Herodotus and Thucydides.

Cultural facilities such as these attracted the scholars of the Greek world. Many of them, in fact, came to Alexandria and made some of the most important discoveries of antiquity at the museum.

Certain poets acted both as secretaries and as courtiers. Callimachus composed his famous elegy 'The Lock of Berenice' there, as well as many other works. Berenice, the wife of Ptolemy III Euergetes, vows to give the gods a lock of her hair if he returns safely from the war in Syria. On his return, the queen fulfils her vow. On the following day the royal lock has vanished from the temple. At that time, Conon, the astronomer, had just discovered a new constellation and so he christened it 'Berenice's Hair' and invented the myth that the gods themselves had carried off the lock from the temple and placed it in the heavens. The constellation still bears

---

22. Strabo, 17.1.8.

23. Like our universities, the museum sometimes came in for criticism. One Alexandrian complained that 'in densely populated Egypt, scribes, great lovers of books of gramarye [*sic*], are waxing fat and carrying on their interminable squabbles in the aviary of the Muses': quoted by E. Bernand, 1966.

24. One of these, Callimachus of Cyrene (−310 to −240), prepared a 120-volume catalogue of the library's entire contents.

the name Coma Berenices to this day. Callimachus honoured the astronomer's courtly tribute in an elegy which we possess only in the Latin translation by Catullus (*c.* −84 to −54).

Geographers, cosmographers and astronomers played a large part in Alexandrian scientific development. We shall see, however, that certain discoveries of theirs they owed essentially to Egypt and not only to the library of Alexandria.

Eratosthenes, the father of scientific geography, was born at Cyrene in about −285. In about −245, Ptolemy offered him the post of librarian, which he held until his death. His most remarkable achievement was his attempt to measure the circumference of the earth, basing his calculations on the relationship between the shadow cast at the summer solstice on the sundial at Alexandria and the absence of shadow at Syene (Aswan). He concluded that the circumference of the entire earth was 252 000 stadia (i.e. 46 695 kilometres), which is greater by one-seventh than the actual circumference (40 008 kilometres). It was also Eratosthenes who catalogued 675 stars.

The geographer Strabo (*c.* −63 to +24), to whom we owe the oldest systematic account of the geography of Egypt, was born in Cappadocia, spent most of his life in Rome and Asia Minor, and finally settled in Alexandria. Although Strabo belongs to the Roman period, the core of his work was hellenistic. His treatise on geography comprises seventeen volumes, with his description of Egypt taking up nearly two-thirds of the final volume.

Geography and astronomy presuppose a very advanced knowledge of mathematics. Among the museum's eminent men was the famous mathematician Euclid (−330 to −275), who was the first to be given charge of the mathematics department and wrote an important work on astronomy (the Phaenomena) as well as the famous treatise on geometry (the Elements), which remained the basic work on the subject and was translated into Latin and Arabic. Archimedes of Syracuse (−287 to −212), one of the greatest mathematicians of Euclid's school, discovered the relationship between diameter and circumference, the theory of the spiral and the law of gravity. His most important contribution to mathematics and mechanics, however, was his invention known as the Archimedean screw, a device still used in Egypt for raising water.

Apollonius of Perga, the great geometer, came to Alexandria from Palmyra in about −240 to work in the mathematics school and owes his renown to his remarkable treatise on conic sections. He was the founder of trigonometry.

At first heavily dependent on the disciples of Eudoxus and Pythagoras, from the third century onwards the mathematics school of Alexandria took on its own distinctive characteristics and became the principal focus of Greek mathematics.

Theophrastus, who lived at the time of Ptolemy I, is regarded, on account of his work on the history and physiology of plants, as the founder of scientific botany.

Diodorus Siculus, the historian, visited Egypt in −59. The first book of his historical work 'Library of History', written in Greek, is given over to an account of the myths, kings and customs of Egypt. According to Diodorus, the first appearance of man on earth took place in Egypt. He says (1, 10): 'At the beginning of the world, man first came into existence in Egypt, both because of the favourable climate of the country and because of the nature of the Nile.'

Physicians, too, came to work at the museum and at the library, the intellectual freedom which reigned there enabling them to make progress in the study of anatomy by dissecting corpses.

Herophilus of Asia Minor, who came to Egypt in the first half of the third century before our era, was the first to discover the connection between the heartbeat and the pulse and to distinguish between arteries and veins. Some of the names he gave to parts of the body are still in use today, e.g. the duodenum and the torcular Herophili.

Erasistratus, another eminent surgeon who was also born in Asia Minor, threw new light on the anatomy of the heart while working at Alexandria.

Here again, the renown of the medical school of Alexandria was to be long-lived. There is an obituary verse preserved in Milan which says of the physician to whom it relates: 'Egypt the all-sublime was his fatherland.'[25]

In the course of time, the native Egyptian element made its presence felt more and more. Manetho, an Egyptian from Samanud in the Delta, was one of the most famous scholar-priests of the beginning of the third century before our era. His chief work, the 'Aegyptiaca', would have been our best source of information on the history of ancient Egypt had it reached us in its entirety. The fragments which still exist contain lists of the names of kings arranged in dynasties and mentioning the duration of each king's reign, a method adopted by modern historians.

The museum and its library, however, came to a sad end. It is believed that the first disaster occurred during Julius Caesar's Alexandrian campaign, when he set fire to the ships lying in the harbour to prevent their falling into the hands of his enemies. The flames raged so fiercely that they reached the book repositories, although some think the fire did not reach the library itself but merely destroyed the booksellers' shops.

After the Roman conquest of Egypt, the decline and ruin must have been progressive. The museum and library suffered from the troubles of that time. Many of the scholars left the country, and the books found their way to Rome. In +270, the emperor Aurelian destroyed much of the Bruchion, the district of Alexandria in which the museum and library were situated. The spread and triumph of Christianity, moreover, dealt them a mortal blow. There are absolutely no grounds for supposing that they continued to

25. A. Bernand, 1966, p. 263.

exist after the fifth century. There is therefore no basis for the accusation made by the thirteenth-century Christian Syrian historian Abu al-Faraj ibu al-Ibri (known in Europe as Berbebraeus) that Amru Ibn-al-As burned down the library of Alexandria.

## Egyptian influence on hellenistic culture

We have seen that the Ptolemies strove to develop relations between Egypt and the Indian Ocean. Where land exploration is concerned there is still much discussion as to whether they had a systematic policy to trace the course of the Nile and make use of the river, far to the south, as a route for penetration and commerce. Be that as it may, it is certain that exploration to the south of Egypt took place. Timosthenes, navarch of Philadelphia, visited Nubia; Aristo reconnoitred the Arabian coasts;

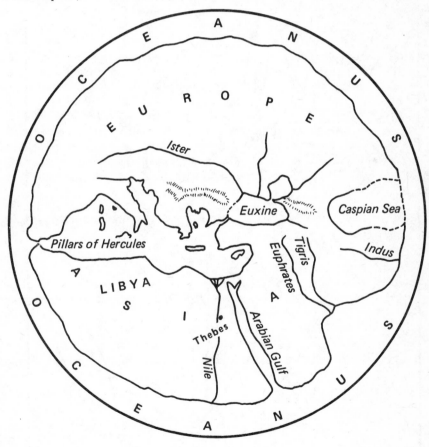

FIG. 6.1 *Map of the world according to Hecataeus*

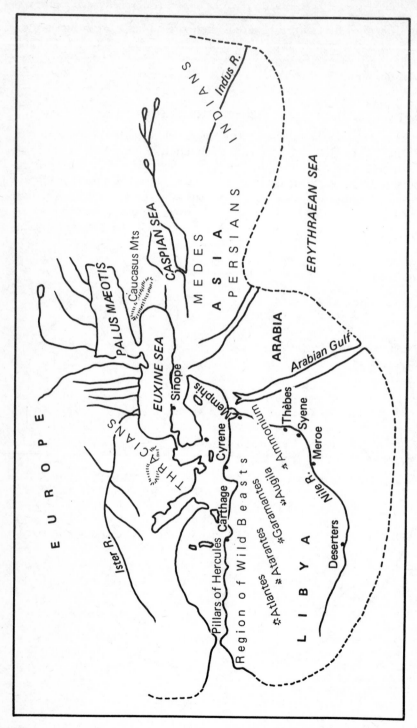

FIG. 6.2 *Map of the world according to Herodotus*

Satyrus followed the African coast to a point south of Cape Guardafui. The accounts of these explorations have been recorded and provide material for the works of scholars such as Agatharchides.[26]

These explorers, furthermore, were following in illustrious footsteps. In about −500, Hecataeus of Miletus, the first Greek geographer to visit Egypt, wrote the first systematic description of the world. Unfortunately only fragments of his geographical treatise have survived. In Egypt he travelled as far as Thebes, and it seems very probable that he included a detailed description of Egypt in his treatise. Hecataeus considered the earth to be a flat disc with Greece at its centre. He divided the world into two continents, Europe and Asia, the latter consisting of Egypt and the whole of North Africa, known at that time under the name of Libya. He imagined that in the south the Nile connected with the River Oceanus, which encircled the whole world. Herodotus of Halicarnassus had visited Egypt in about −450. He went as far south as Elephantine, which he described as the frontier between Egypt and Ethiopia. Herodotus devoted the second of the nine books of his *History* to Egypt. He was the first geographer to mention Meroe by name, having actually met Meroites at Aswan.

Herodotus also thought that the earth was flat but, unlike Hecataeus, he did not think it was circular, nor did he believe that it was encircled by the River Oceanus. He divided the world into three continents: Europe, Asia and Libya (i.e. Africa), stating that the last was surrounded on all sides by the sea except at the point where it was joined to Asia.

Much later, in −59, Diodorus visited Egypt and described the course of the Nile in the first book of his work. He was of the opinion that the Nile rose in Ethiopia and contained a large number of islands including the one called Meroe. Diodorus devoted the whole of his third book to Ethiopia, that is, to what is now called the Sudan. Strabo, like him, referred to the Meroe region as an island and also gave details of its inhabitants.

While the Greeks in general considered it an achievement to visit the First Cataract and venture a little farther south, an exploit which they commemorated by carving their names on the Egyptian monuments,[27] scholars showed great interest in the valley of the Nile to the south of Aswan (known then as Syene). The exact latitude of Meroe was already known at the time of Ptolemy Philadelphus.[28] Eratosthenes, who, as we have seen, worked at Syene, calculated the distance from Meroe to the Equator. He also described with a wealth of detail the conditions of

26. See C. Préaux, 1939, p. 356. At that time the descriptions of the people visited concentrated on what was observed of their customs, and the names used to describe them reflected their eating habits; these characteristics later found their way into antique and medieval Latin texts and, to some extent, into Arab sources.

27. C. Préaux, 1957, pp. 310ff.

28. ibid.

navigation on the Nile, and had at least indirect knowledge of the Blue Nile and the Atbara. His discoveries and those of many other explorers found their way into later works, first those of Strabo and later those of Pliny, who was very fond of picturesque details about the interior of Africa and the valley of the Nile, and finally into the works of the great cosmographer, Ptolemy, who later compiled a systematic record of the material comprising the hellenistic Egyptian heritage. These authors in turn passed on this information, sometimes embellished with partly or wholly legendary details or observations, to the Byzantine, western or Muslim cultures. The essential body of knowledge about the middle valley of the Nile was therefore set for a long time to come at the time of the Ptolemies. It is true to say that this middle valley was the 'pole of attraction for astronomers and ethnographers' and that military expeditions were regularly accompanied by scientific missions.[29]

Even more surprising was the slow absorption of the Greek milieu by the Egyptian. It would seem that the Egyptians did not give way to cultural pressure. They kept an independent attitude towards the Ptolemies, unlike the Greeks, who displayed a striking adulation of the sovereign.[30] Yet the Greek language at that time enjoyed international status and was easier to write than Egyptian. Officially, everyone spoke Greek. It has been noticed by archaeologists, however, that almost as many papyri are found in Demotic as in Greek.[31] Greek law was very slow to be reflected in Egyptian legal instruments, while the Egyptian calendar gradually prevailed over the Greek. What is more, by means of the Greek language an entire Egyptian heritage became available to a world it would never have reached without the new linguistic medium which served to convey it.

Art can probably be said to be the sphere in which the Egyptian and even black African impregnation of hellenistic culture was the most surprising and spectacular. The Greeks, lovers of the theatre as they had been in Athens, built monuments in Egypt which reflected their taste. Contact with the Egyptian temples, however, had given them a sense of the colossal. The same tendency also crept into their sculpture: a head of Serapis measuring 51 centimetres has been found and there are numerous gigantic statues in the Graeco-Roman museum in Alexandria.

At first, naturally enough, artistic techniques and tastes among the Greek community in Egypt were similar to those in other Greek communities of the far-flung empire. It is also true that products from the Alexandrian

29. ibid.

30. C. Préaux, 1939.

31. The major difference between them lies in the subjects with which they deal: the Greek papyri treat of a large variety of subjects while the others cover very few. They can be regarded, however, as constituting an abundant source of information on the management of the temples and on the lives of Egyptian families.

workshops resembled those of Greece to some extent and showed the influence of fashions foreign to Africa. There are a great many examples of this imported art in the Alexandria museum. One of the most remarkable is the head of Alexander, which belongs to the tradition of the school of Lysippus. But innovation was also taking place in Alexandria, the most important new technique being that described by archaeologists by the Italian term *sfumato*, which is a blending of light and shade on the softened contours of the facial features, not much attention being paid to the representation of hair or cheeks. The latter were usually modelled in stucco, which lends itself to the soft modelling preferred by the Alexandrian artists. When these parts were added they were usually coloured. Sculptors and painters looked to Egyptian models for inspiration at all levels, as may be seen from the representation of the gods. Isis wears a very tight-fitting dress with the characteristic knot between the breasts and on her head she wears an Egyptian crown, but the modelling of the body is typically Greek. A favourite among the Greek goddesses was Aphrodite. Figurines often represented her naked in various attitudes: rising from the sea, braiding her hair, stooping to unfasten her sandal from one foot uplifted, or gathering her mantle about the lower half of her body with both hands.

Among the Greek heroes, Heracles was frequently represented. Bowls and lamps found at Alexandria depict his labours, showing him fighting the lion, the bull and the Amazons.

In Pharaonic Egypt, the Nile had been depicted as a fat man with breasts bearing lotus or papyrus, the plants growing in the Nile valley. The Greeks represented him as a strong, bearded man either seated or reclining with hippopotamuses, crocodiles or a sphinx, the symbols of Egypt. Representations of royal personages followed the same pattern. Painting, which remained very faithful to the Greek models throughout the fourth and third centuries, began in the second to include scenes that were Egyptian in style side by side with others in Greek style, as, for example, in one of the tombs of Anfushi in Alexandria. The main burial chamber is decorated from the very entrance in a mixture of Egyptian and Greek styles, both in its architecture and in its painted decoration.

The sketchy rendering of the palm trees painted in another Anfushi tomb is characteristic of the first century. The redecoration of the second Anfushi tomb contains many more Egyptian elements, with new scenes in the Egyptian style.

Mosaics appeared first in the eastern Mediterranean and possibly in Alexandria itself. Several mosaic pavements with pictorial motifs have been discovered in and around Alexandria. The most important is inscribed with the name 'Sophilos' and, inside the central rectangle, shows the head of a woman with a mast and yardarm. This head is crowned with a head-dress in the form of a ship's prow and is thought to have been a personification of the city of Alexandria. Around the central rectangle is a series of ornate decorative borders. It was found in the east of the Delta and dates from the second century.

No doubt the most surprising aspect of Egypt's hellenistic production, however, in the richness of its invention and tastes, was the proliferation of humorous, grotesque[32] or realistic statuettes representing scenes from daily life and depicting Egyptians and black Africans. The small figurines in bronze, marble, terracotta or plaster were made for the common people, but the existence of more valuable pieces attests to the general popularity of these themes.

Bes, the most thoroughly Egyptian of the Gods adopted by the Greeks, was given a grotesque appearance and was later given an equally comical and ugly wife, Besa or Beset. The attraction for the Greeks in Egypt of everything non-Greek prompted them to order objects for daily use, luxury articles, or ornaments showing negroes. The faithfulness of the rendering sometimes attained a high artistic quality, but more often it demonstrated the sculptor's powers of observation rather than his taste. Sometimes the subject is some street scene, like the statuette of a young negro asleep next to an amphora. Negroes were depicted on all kinds of daily objects such as water jars. The way in which they were depicted shows no sense of fear or of unhealthy exoticism. Negroes were often shown with elephants, or fighting crocodiles, while the inclusion of dwarfs is a muted echo of the ancient literary themes relating to Pygmies. Black wrestlers, dancing girls, jugglers, orators and musicians bear witness to the fact not only that scenes were taken from life by sculptors but also that such scenes were popular with the public. Some very fine heads and portraits of negroes prove that personages of higher social rank from black Africa lived in or passed through Ptolemaic Alexandria.[33] The interest in negroes shown by the Alexandrians may perhaps be partly explained by the Ptolemies' interest in the great pre-Saharan oases which gave access to the black African world.

Through the hellenistic art of Egypt, the figure of the negro spread into the Mediterranean world to a greater extent than ever before.

## Egypt in the hellenistic era: relations with Libya

Through Cyrenaica (the eastern part of Libya), certain aspects of hellenistic civilization found their way from Egypt into North Africa.[34] This was not the first time that Greek civilization had appeared in Cyrenaica, for we know that Greeks from the Dorian island of Thaenae emigrated to Cyrenaica, where they founded Cyrene, their first colony, in −631. This was followed by the founding of four more colonies: the port

32. A. Badawy, 1965, pp. 189–98.
33. On this subject see F. M. Snowden, Jnr 1976, pp. 187–212.
34. The author of this chapter was assisted on the subject of Libya by Dr Mustapha Kamel Abdel Alim.

of Cyrene (later Apollonia), Tauchira, Barca (present-day Al-Merg) and Euhesperides. These colonies, especially Cyrene, were products of Greek civilization and underwent the normal political changes that took place in every Greek city. With the founding of Cyrene began the reign of the Battiad dynasty, which came to an end as a result of internal strife in about −440. Then followed the usual conflict between aristocracy and democracy, and Cyrenaica became a land of confusion and strife.

The whole of the ancient world was at this time on the eve of a great upheaval with the coming of Alexander the Great, who invaded Egypt in the autumn of −332 and pressed westwards to Praetorium (present-day Marsa-Matrûh) on his way to the Siwa oasis to consult the oracle of Zeus-Ammon. Cyrene, and probably the other cities too (having in fact misunderstood Alexander's intentions and wishing to prevent his invasion of Cyrenaica), attempted to safeguard their independence by sending ambassadors to meet him at Praetenium and protest their cities' loyalty. But they could not preserve their independence for ever, for in −332, after Alexander's death, Ptolemy, while still satrap of Egypt, seized the opportunity provided by the internal struggles at Cyrene and annexed Cyrenaica, thus initiating the hellenistic period in that country. Except for a brief period of independence (*c.* −258 to −246), the domination of Cyrenaica by the Ptolemies lasted from −322 to −96, when Ptolemy Apion (son of Ptolemy Euergetes II), who was ruling over Cyrenaica, bequeathed it to the Roman people and it was combined with Crete into a Roman province.

At the beginning of the hellenistic era, Cyrenaica was a country of small villages with very few towns. Under the Ptolemies, the towns were given new names, some of which were Ptolemaic dynastic names. Cyrene kept its name, but Tauchira was rechristened Arsinoë (present-day Tokra), and Barca's port was given the name of Ptolemaïs (present-day Tolmeta) and superseded Barca as the official city centre. Euhesperides gave way to a new city which received the name of Berenice (present-day Benghazi) in honour of Berenice, the Cyrenaean princess and wife of Ptolemy III. Cyrene's port was raised to city rank and given the name of Apollonia (present-day Susa).

Cyrenaica was peopled by a mixture of races. In the cities, besides the Greeks (who were either full citizens or enjoyed certain limited rights) there was a non-Greek population composed mainly of Jews and many other foreigners. Outside the cities, the rural population ('georgoi') consisted of native Libyans and mercenary soldiers who had settled there as cleruchs.

These 'georgoi' tilled the arable lands of Cyrenaica, made up of the royal lands (*gêbasilikê*), the city lands (*gê politikê*), and the land left to the native Libyans. This social structure resulted in a clash between the native Libyans and the Greek settlers.

Cyrenaica in the hellenistic period was a country of great economic importance, being regarded as one of the granaries of the ancient world. It has been said that Cyrene sent a gift of 800 000 medimni of grain to the Greek cities in metropolitan Greece during the famine of −330 to −326. Much has been said about its wool, its horse-breeding, and the famous silphium of Cyrenaica, which was a monopoly of the battiad kings and probably remained a monopoly of the Ptolemies.

This gift of grain is not the only evidence of the close relations existing between the Greeks of Cyrenaica and those in Greece itself. It is well known that Cyrene contributed greatly to the intellectual life of the Greeks, especially in the fourth century, through its renowned philosophers and mathematicians. As a result of its close intellectual contacts with Athens, Cyrene made it possible for philosophy and a great many branches of learning to flourish on the Cyrenaican plateau. It was here that the philosophical school known as the Cyrenaics developed. This was a minor Socratic school founded by Aristippus (*c.* −400 to −365), the grandson of the Aristippus who was friend and companion to Socrates. This intellectual activity and fertility were still evident in the hellenistic era. We need only cite in evidence the names of Callimachus (−305 to −240) and Eratosthenes (−275 to −194), who were among those to leave Cyrene for Alexandria to enrich the latter's activity in the development of the sciences and literature. At the academy, the museum and the library, they added to the sum of creative intelligence in Alexandria and enabled the city to become the main pole of intellectual attraction in the hellenistic era. Even in Athens itself, it was Carneades the Cyrenaean (−305 to −240), one of the leaders of the sceptics school of philosophers, who founded the New Academy. At Cyrene, as in other Greek cities, the Greek system of education was preserved. There are a great many inscriptions referring to the gymnasia and ephebia.

Many statues of philosophers, poets and the nine Muses have been discovered at Cyrene. The discovery of a bust of Demosthenes, albeit a Roman copy, is very significant since it shows the high esteem in which such a great Greek orator was held by the Greek population of Cyrene.

Some fine examples of Alexandrian sculpture have been found among the numerous marble statues at Cyrene. The few original portraits from hellenistic times show very close affinities with what is known as the hellenistic art of Alexandria. It is not surprising that the technique used in Alexandria was copied to a certain extent at Cyrene. Another similarity between the Greek sculpture of Cyrenaica and that of Alexandria can be seen in the Cyrenaean busts. A comparison of Cyrenaean funerary busts with Egyptian mummy portraits clearly reveals the close similarity between them. Even when the pieces in question are from the Roman era, there is no denying their Ptolemaic origin.

From Cyrene came painted hellenistic pottery and terracotta figurines. These figurines were produced in local workshops which had started by reproducing and imitating Greek terracottas but gradually evolved their own characteristic style. Study of these figurines is rewarding as they reflect the daily lives of the inhabitants of Cyrenaica, especially in the cities.

In the sphere of religion, the dynastic Ptolemaic cult found its way to Cyrenaica, as can be seen from the large number of dedicatory inscriptions to the Ptolemaic kings and queens. The cities of Cyrenaica also adopted the cult of Serapis, and temples to Isis and Osiris have been found at Cyrene and Ptolemaïs.

From Cyrenaica, this Graeco-Egyptian cult probably reached Tripolitania, which was never ruled by the Ptolemies in pre-Roman times. The sanctuary of Serapis and of Isis was discovered at Leptis Magna, and it is interesting to note that at Sabrata the cult of Isis was combined with Isiac rites. The cults of Isis and Serapis must have extended farther west as the cult of Isis became more general and as the Serapis cult started giving the ancient world a new hope of a better life.

Much of what has been said about hellenistic Cyrenaica concerns only the Greeks, since information concerning the native Libyans and the extent to which they were influenced by hellenistic civilization is scarce and hard to find. We know that the native Libyans, driven away from the fertile coastal lands and contained in the interior, did not welcome the presence of the Greeks. Hellenistic civilization, nevertheless, owed much to this region of North Africa which enabled it to develop and flourish for three centuries.

The great prosperity of Meroe, especially during the reigns of Ergamenes and his successors, was due essentially to its friendly relations with Egypt. Few traces of hellenistic influence have to date been found in the temples and pyramids of Meroe.[35] The temple built by Ergamenes at Dakka in Lower Nubia is purely Egyptian in conception. When he died, his mummy was entombed in a pyramid near Meroe, decorated with scenes taken from the Book of the Dead. His successor, Azekramon (Ezekher-Amon), built a temple in the Egyptian style near Debod, not far from Philae.

The life of the people of Meroe was very like that of the Egyptians. Our knowledge of the life and society of those times has to be derived from a study of archaeological finds since we are not yet able to read the Meroitic language[36] and have no such rich source of information about daily life as is furnished by the tomb paintings of ancient Egypt.

As in Egypt, the king was regarded as divine. Queens played an important part in the life of the country and sometimes ruled in their own right. Considerable influence was wielded by the priests, and the temples had rich possessions. The Meroitic people derived most of their official religious ideas from Egypt but also had their own gods.

35. See F. and U. Hintze, 1967, pp. 23–8.
36. See Chapter 10 below.

Meroitic burial customs show a mixture of local and Egyptian traditions. We know from furniture found that the beds were of the style known as *angareeb*, similar to the beds of ancient Egypt that are still used today in the Nile valley.

The main activity of most of the Meroitic peoples was agriculture. To irrigate their lands, they used the *shadouf* and the *sakkieh*, two devices still used in both countries for raising water from lower to higher land.

Similar tools and weapons such as adzes, hoe blades, axes, chisels, and many small articles such as tweezers have been found in both countries. All these implements were made of bronze. Large iron tools have, however, also been found in Meroe. The presence of large mounds of iron slag near the city shows that the production and use of iron was very common. The ore was smelted in simple furnaces fired by charcoal produced from the acacia trees growing along the Nile.

Resemblances have been noted between objects which have been found in Egypt and in the Sudan. Some of these, however, such as headrests and musical instruments, are strikingly Egyptian in appearance, and it is possible that they are Meroitic in origin.

PLATE 6.1 *Lighthouse at Alexandria*

PLATE 6.2 *Relief representing Goddess Isis with her son Harpocrates in the background*

PLATE 6.4 *Cleopatra VII*

PLATE 6.3 *Head of Alexander the Great*

PLATE 6.5 *Ulysses escaping from Polyphemus by hiding beneath a ram's belly*

PLATE 6.6 *Painting from a tomb at Anfushi, Alexandria*

206

PLATE 6.7 *A fragment of a bronze balsa-marium*

PLATE 6.8 *Grotesque head*

PLATE 6.9 *Statuette (fragment) of a black 'street-lighter', upright, walking, wearing a tunic and carrying a short ladder on the left arm (right arm and feet missing)*

207

# Egypt under Roman domination

## S. DONADONI

## Rome: from alliance to domination over Egypt

Egypt passed from the rule of the Ptolemies to that of Rome almost imperceptibly. Relations between Alexandria and Rome had for a long time, since Ptolemy Philadelphus, been very friendly. He was the first of the line to sign a treaty of friendship with Rome and send an embassy there, in −273. Half a century later Ptolemy Philopator had remained friendly to Rome during its war with Hannibal (−218 to −201) and Rome had reciprocated by saving Egypt's independence when Antiochus III invaded it in −168. Nevertheless, after establishing that position the republic had in practice become able and accustomed to control Egyptian affairs in a way that became all too obvious in the Ptolemies' last years. The aim of Cleopatra VII's intrigues with Roman generals between −51 and −30 had probably been to make them espouse her kingdom's interests, but her unconditional support of her friend Mark Antony lost her the throne for good as soon as Octavian conquered him in −31.

The attitude towards Egypt of its new master showed clearly the importance which Rome attached to this new province of its empire. It stationed three legions there, nearly 15 000 men. Their duty was to restore control over the country, in which anarchy had raged during the Ptolemies' final reigns and led to the destruction of Thebes in −88. The first Roman prefect, Cornelius Gallus, led troops into Upper Egypt beyond the First Cataract. After him the prefect Petronius reconquered the province of Lower Nubia called the Dodecaschene (because it measured twelve schenes), about 120 kilometres from Syene (Aswan) to Hiera Sycaminos (Muharraqa). It had belonged to the Ptolemies, but the rulers of Meroe (now in the Sudan) had long since added it to their kingdom. The excessive trust that the prefect Gallus, the Roman emperor's confidant, placed in his successes finally cost him his life, an event which proved the very special importance that Octavian, by then called Augustus, attached to its conquest. He very jealously retained the province of Egypt under his direct administration, and gave the senate no jurisdiction of any kind over it. Later, in fact, senators were expressly forbidden even to set foot in it, a rule that was very severely enforced. The Roman emperor therefore succeeded the Ptolemies in Egypt, and tried to take their place in its structure. He took charge of its religion, and was soon known as the builder of numerous temples, the best preserved of which are those of Nubia, in Debod, Talmis, Dendur and Pselkis. He also took charge of its everyday well-being, and used the army not only to keep public order but also to repair the canal system, badly damaged during the disorders of the last Ptolemies. This exception became the rule, and troops were also used in this way in the reigns of Mero ($+54$ to $+68$), Trajan ($+98$ to $+117$) and Probus ($+276$ to $+282$).

## Roman administration

The Roman emperor, however, copied the Ptolemies' administration of Egypt as a kind of vast personal estate, the whole income from which was managed by the crown. This exploitation by Augustus soon became the starting-point of the whole policy he devised for Egypt, which continued even though his successor reproached the prefect with excessive taxation, reminding him that sheep ought to be shorn but not flayed.

The emperor's direct authority was shown by his personal appointment of the prefect, who was always a knight (not a senator), to the highest office in the country, and of the other officers (the *procuratores*)[1] who acted in his name. A small administrative detail clearly illustrates Egypt's special character: it was the only country in the whole empire where years were counted by the emperor's reign and not named after the consuls holding office. This perpetuated the ancient Ptolemaic and Pharaonic practice and invested the Roman head of state with an aura of royalty unrecognized anywhere else in the empire's organization.

This imperial exploitation, however, contained a new factor which the Ptolemies did not have. Whereas under them the produce of Egypt's fields and industry had enriched a dynasty whose various interests were all in Egypt, the emperors regarded the country as the storehouse of the wheat they were accustomed to distribute to the plebs of Rome to obtain its goodwill. Egypt's function as the empire's granary took away the fruit of its soil without giving it any substantial counterpart in regular trade. Its change from an independent state to a province actually brought other and more important differences of structure. We can describe these in considerable detail because we have learnt a great deal about every aspect of daily life in Egypt from some precious documents peculiar to itself, its papyri. These are public and private charters which its dry soil has preserved for thousands of years and passed down to scholars who for a century and a half have studied the philology and history they contain. Thus our knowledge is based on original texts which illumine the narratives of the historians with a precision of detail rarely attained in other fields of the ancient world.

1. Or 'representatives': 'pro' = instead of; 'curare' = take care of.

The government's geographical unit was the *nome* (nowadays known as a mudiria) which was subdivided into two *toparchiai* each containing a number of villages (*kome*). The nomes of Upper Egypt formed together a higher unit, the *Thebaid*, which resembled the Heptanomis (the seven nomes of Middle Egypt) and the nomes of the Delta. A nome was governed by a *strategos* (the old Ptolemaic military title), who had beside him as an administrative technician a *royal scribe* (also a Ptolemaic title). Junior officials administered lesser units, according to even older traditions.

The central government, however, was new. Its kernel was established in Alexandria, the old royal city, which now became the capital instead of Memphis. This general staff of the government was composed entirely of Roman citizens nominated directly by the emperor. First came the prefect, the head of all the departments, including the treasury, the army and the courts. His power was limited only by the power of appeal against his decisions to the emperor in person. The prefect, to enable him to perform his duties, had a council which also consisted of Roman knights. The *juridicus*, the *dikaiodotes* and the *archidikastes* helped him to administer justice; the *procurator usiacus*[2] helped him to administer financially the funds which accrued to the emperor in person; and a knight had charge of the temples. The groups of nomes also came under the authority of the three *epistrategoi*, who were knights with the rank of procurator. According to the tradition of Roman organization, a person who had military command must also be the head of the administration in general and of jurisprudence in particular. This idea profoundly affected the older judicial machinery, which under the local Egyptian law gave the judges jurisdiction in cases where the documents were in the language of the country, and in other cases gave it to Greek judges. Now the only judge was the prefect, who could obviously delegate his power to others, especially to the strategos, but who alone was responsible. He made a circuit of the country each year to settle the most difficult cases; it was called the *conventus* and was held at Pelusium near Alexandria, at Memphis, and at Arsinoe in the Fayyum. He applied Roman law to Roman citizens and to others he applied the aliens' law, which took account of the manners and customs of the country but with a number of exceptions.

These examples alone show that the Roman presence had the capacity to change the structure of Ptolemaic Egypt. Since the beginning of the period of Augustus, however, other factors had still greater potentiality for change. The Ptolemaic administration was highly centralized and mostly consisted of paid officials, whose salaries came from their right to manage farms differing in size according to the importance of their duties. The army, likewise, was a hereditary organization which carried with it the right, also hereditary, to cultivate properties whose size was fixed according certain criteria (whether the official was Greek or Egyptian, whether he

2. From *ousia*, 'estate'.

had a horse to feed or not, and so on). During the Ptolemaic period the system had already suffered from the inevitable exploitation. In the Roman period it changed completely. The paid official gave way to the honorary magistrate. At the same time colleges were formed of persons who all had the same duties and were all collectively responsible. Beside the *strategos* stood the *archontes* and commandants; beside the *komogrammateus*, the village scribe, stood the elders, the *presbyteroi*.

Although the state no longer maintained the government or paid its expenses, the small and middle-sized private estate was enlarged by the distribution of land which until then had been royal or usufructuary (the *kleroi* had paid the public servants). There grew up therefore a class of property holders from whom were elected the unpaid magistrates who fulfilled their functions as a duty, a *munus*, for which they had been reimbursed in advance by the property rights which they had been given. To this class of property owners and potential administrators the empire entrusted the defence of its interests, choosing one social group to favour and setting it against the others. Under the first Ptolemies the Greeks had, *de facto*, occupied a privileged position which had declined considerably after the battle of Raphia in −217, when Egypt's national troops had been soundly beaten, and even more during the difficult times of the dynasty's last kings.

The Roman occupiers, in their need to set group against group, resorted to the ancient custom and restored to the Greeks their privileged position, this time not only in fact but also in law. The Egyptians paid a poll-tax (the *laographia* to which a man was liable merely by existing) from which the Greeks were exempt. The inhabitants of the provincial capitals, the *metropoles*, paid less than villagers; peasants might not leave the land they tilled, the *idia*. So the important thing was to belong to a Greek-educated family. A man could claim this only if he could show by documents that his two grandfathers had both attended a *gymnasion*, a Greek school. Under the Ptolemies this was a free institution; after them it became restricted to metropolitans and was controlled by the state. A man could only call himself a graduate of a gymnasium (*apo tou gymnasiou*) after a scrutiny (*epikrisis*) of his genealogical title. If he proved his claim he was regarded as one of a Greek-speaking urban bourgeoisie as opposed to country folk, who were mostly peasants and Egyptians. The right of the Egyptians as such disappeared in this new social setting, the chief purpose of which was to organize a solid middle class with a stake in the future of the empire.

It will be convenient here to mention the particular status of the autonomous cities (*poleis*) under the Ptolemies, such as Ptolemais in Upper Egypt and the ancient and glorious Naucratis[3] in the Delta. The third *polis*, Alexandria, was still the greatest port in the Mediterranean, rivalling

3. A Greek colony dating from the Saitic period.

Rome in population and importance. Nevertheless it lost its senate and became the base of the naval unit known as the Augusta Alexandrina fleet, while quite close to the city the Roman army was encamped at Nicopolis. The Alexandrians, whose scathing and forceful wit was famous, were never on good terms with their new masters and lost no chance of showing it.

## Egypt under Roman domination

For quite a long time these bases of the Roman dominion were left alone. Provincial life went on in a *pax Romana* paid for by the taxes based on the wheat levy, the *annona*, which was a source of periodical rebellion and protest. Tiberius (+14 to +37), who succeeded Augustus, was able to reduce to two the number of legions stationed in Egypt. It was under his successor that disorders between the Greeks of Alexandria and the many Jews who lived in the city broke out for the first time. A rivalry thus grew up which alternated between copious bloodshed and official complaints to the emperor at Rome. A body of literature called the Acts of the Martyrs of Alexandria related in defensive tones the trials of Jews. Attempts were made at Rome to impose settlements, but these contented neither of the parties, each of which thought itself sacrificed.

The relations between the government and the Jews of Egypt were embittered during the revolt in Judaea. Vespasian (69–79), who had become emperor in Syria and was acclaimed in Alexandria, recalled the legions from Nicopolis for the siege of Jerusalem. After its destruction in Trajan's reign (98–117) the Jews of Egypt rose in rebellion and besieged Alexandria, in troubles which were long remembered as the Jews' War. When the general Marcius Turbo defeated the rebels the Jewish colony in Alexandria ceased to exist.

Apart, however, from these particular events, the empire's first century and the early years of its second were a period of relative calm and prosperity. The emperor Nero (54–68) sent explorers into the kingdom of Meroe, with which Rome had peaceful trading relations; Vespasian became very popular in Alexandria, which attributed miraculous powers to him; Trajan (98–117) reduced the legions stationed in Egypt to one only, which indicates that the situation was calm. He also drove a canal between the Nile and the Red Sea to increase trade with the East and compete with the caravan routes which led to Syria through country outside Roman control. These measures all benefited Alexandria, which was still the chief port in the whole Mediterranean. Moreover, when famine devastated the country Trajan sent in much-needed wheat, reversing for once the principle that Egypt had to pay the *annona* to Rome.

Trajan's successor, Hadrian (117–38), showed still greater interest in the country, and in 130 and 131 made a fairly long journey there with his wife. Egypt owed to him the repair of the destruction caused in Alexandria by the Jews' War and the foundation in Middle Egypt of the town of

Antinopolis to commemorate his favourite Antinous, who had voluntarily drowned himself there to save his master – so it was said – from some obscure danger announced by the oracles. The young martyr was deified and identified with Osiris, well within the Egyptian tradition of apotheosis by drowning. There were, however, also practical reasons for founding that city, which was given the rank of a *polis*, or free city, and became a centre friendly to Rome in the interior of Egypt and the starting-point of a caravan route between the Red Sea and the Nile valley.

The economic situation of the peasants and smallholders, which is documented in detail in papyri, nevertheless showed that the discrimination in favour of the middle class which had been a principle of Roman policy would bear bitter fruit. The humble folk became poor and unrest began to stir. One of its first signs was the murder of the prefect at Alexandria in the reign of Hadrian's successor, Antoninus Pius (138–61), who had to go to Egypt to restore order. His son Marcus Aurelius, the philosopher and philanthropist (161–80), faced a still more critical situation when the *boukoloi*, the cattlemen of the Delta, broke out in a ferocious revolt. It was headed by an Egyptian priest called Isidor and the rebels were united by a mystical enthusiasm due, as some said, to the practice of ritual cannibalism; but they fought heroically for their right to a less miserable life and to racial recognition. The Alexandrians were this time on the Roman side because they had privileges which the Egyptians had not. The rebellion held out against the garrison forces. The general Avidius Cassius had to bring his legions from Syria and even then could not beat the cattlemen in battle until he had set them against each other. He was the Avidius Cassius who, in 175, when rumours went about that the emperor was dead, had himself proclaimed emperor by his troops in Alexandria. This was the first attempt of its kind in Egypt and ended without much trouble, since Marcus Aurelius pardoned the rash general.

The tension between Rome and Egypt went on growing in spite of the reforms of Septimus Severus (193–211), who gave the Alexandrians back their senate, *boule*, which signified autonomy and which Augustus had dissolved. When Caracalla, his successor (211–17), visited Alexandria he was so enraged by its citizens' jeers that he promptly ordered a general massacre of its youths after he had assembled them on the pretext of wishing to enrol them in the army. After the slaughter the troops left their quarters in Nicopolis and stayed in the city to force it into submission.

These episodes of blood and violence partly offset the importance of the emperor's best-known action which was the grant of the Antoninian constitution in 212. This supreme document made citizens of all the inhabitants of the empire and removed the barriers which until then had separated Roman citizens from provincials. Until then, except for officials from abroad, Roman citizens had been very rarely found in Egypt. They were mostly Egyptians who had served in the Roman army, had gained their citizenship on retirement after twenty or twenty-five years' service, and had gone back to their home towns as notables in the little group of metropolitans.

The constitution did away, in principle, with the dual status of the empire's inhabitants. The ordinary law became that of Rome and the general structure of society was accordingly completely changed. Nevertheless, if any country felt this social revolution less than the rest, it was Egypt. An article in the constitution barred from citizenship the *dediticii*, those who had surrendered after a military defeat, which the Egyptians were deemed to have done. Once more the emperors favoured the hellenized urban middle class against the indigenous peasantry. An edict of Caracalla actually forbade Egyptians to enter Alexandria except to bring in fuel for the public baths or cattle for slaughter. It exempted, however, those who wished – and were able – to live there to acquire an education that assimilated them to the Greeks. Nothing could show more clearly the economic base of the discrimination.

Together with the constitution the general administrative system was also changed. When Alexandria recovered its senate, a general reform altered the standing of the towns. The metropoles became cities (*poleis*) and took over the direct administration of their provinces. Public office was no longer conferred on rich and capable (*euporoi kai epitedeioi*) persons whom the epistratege chose by lot, but on members of the senate (*boule*) which every town now had. In return, each senator was bound to perform his spell of administration and contribute towards its expenses. Some papyri contain full reports of meetings of the high-ranking boards on which the *prytanes* (senators) decided who should hold public office. Some eligible candidates tried to avoid it. Indeed these honours became unbearably burdensome in an economy hard hit by the revolt of the cattlemen and the ensuing decay of the system, which thus lost most of its former splendour.

Egypt was no longer the empire's granary. That function was performed by *Africa* (the present Maghrib), from the end of the second century onwards. This could only mean that Egypt was exhausted. A movement that started, spread and became increasingly dangerous was the flight (*anachoresis*) of cultivators from their fields into the desert because they could no longer pay the taxes the state demanded of them.

Towards the middle of the third century a series of highly dramatic events happened. A prefect of Egypt, Marcus Julius Aemilianus, had himself proclaimed emperor in 262 and was heavily defeated by Gallienus after reigning a few months. Foreign peoples appeared on the frontiers, raided the country and even occupied tracts of it for some time. It was not by chance that in the reign of Claudius II (268–70) an Egyptian named Thimagenes called the Palmyrians into the country. These people lived in a rich caravan town and were allied to the empire but independent of it. Their queen Zenobia, without an open breach with Rome, sent in an army 70 000 strong which gave the legions a great deal of trouble because victories were useless when the people sided with the invaders. Even when Aurelian took the situation in hand and drove the Palmyrians out, some anti-Roman sections of the population led by one Firmus joined those of the invaders who still remained in Egypt. They also linked themselves to a race which began to be spoken of with terror, the Blemmyes. These were nomads who were spreading into Lower Nubia and often appeared in Upper Egypt out of the desert, which they dominated, and terrorized the cultivators.

The general who succeeded in dominating the Palmyrians, the Blemmyes and their allies the Egyptian guerillas was Probus (276–82), who succeeded Aurelian after commanding his forces. He made serious efforts to improve the situation of the country, which was well on the road to ruin and no longer reacted to a social life centred in a traditional administration. The welcome given even the Blemmyes, who behaved like nomad raiders, showed clearly that the community would have to be strengthened from inside by giving its members new confidence. This was doubtless Probus' aim when, having beaten the invading barbarians and become emperor, he set his army to dig canals and improve agriculture.

Egypt's crisis merely reflected in a clearly defined setting the much larger crisis of the empire itself. The man who had the courage to face this larger problem was Diocletian (284–305), who remoulded the whole system of the state. This subject is too vast to touch on here except so far as it concerns Egypt. The new emperor saw the situation clearly and gave up Nubia which was open to invasion by the Blemmyes and to the Nomads, who were an African people akin to them, on condition that they should undertake to guard the empire's southern frontier. For this service they were paid sums which their petty kings (*reguli*, *basiliskoi*) enjoyed calling tribute.

Egypt itself was now divided into three provinces, each of which had formerly been an epistrategy. The two northern provinces, the Delta and Heptanomis (the seven nomes), were now named Aegyptus Jovia and Aegyptus Herculia and administered by a civil governor (*praeses*) who had no authority over the armed forces. The southern province, the Thebaid, which was more exposed to invasion, was placed under a *dux*, who held both the civil and the military power. Egypt lost its character as a separate province and struck the same coinage as the rest of the empire. Its administration was brought into line with that of other provinces by the appointment of a *curator civitatis*, the city taxation officer, who had charge of fiscal problems. At the same time a new taxation system came into force which, broadly speaking, fixed taxes for fifteen years at a stretch (*indictiones*). This was an advance on the chaos of arbitrary and unexpected taxation, but to be a significant change, required that a balance be struck between taxation and the whole wealth-producing system. The community tended, slowly at first and later more and more obviously, to fall into fixed patterns which provided a refuge for the taxpayer when taxation became too heavy. One consequence was that the state had to enforce immobility: no one was allowed to leave his post. Peasants had to remain peasants and stay on the same land, so that they became serfs of the glebe, but also the *honestiores* (the respectable citizens) were bound fast to their duties as taxpayers and administrators. *Anachoresis* soon became a necessity for all social levels. Only persons with clear-cut political authority could defend their position. Naturally the less fortunate tended to join the groups surrounding these potentates, relying on their protection against the tax gatherer and handing over their property to them to look after. The government used every legal means of opposing this slide towards a society dominated and organized by large landowners; but the law was powerless because it took no account of the causes underlying the trend it was trying to stop. When the large landowners had became entitled to regard themselves as the collectors of the taxes which they owed to the state (*autopragia*), the property system had become completely different. The smallholding which at the beginning of the empire had been the strength of the middle class disappeared before the baronial estate – and baronial authority – which broke up the old municipal administrative units into other economic units.

## The impact of Christianity on Egyptian society

This process obviously took a long time to grow and ran parallel with another development: the rise of Christianity in Egypt. Taken in a wide enough historical perspective, this may be regarded as one of the movements of religious exchange between Egypt and the rest of the ancient world. The extent and importance of the Nile valley cults in the Roman empire are well known. Isis and Osiris, or Serapis, another form of the same concept, became gods who were worshipped everywhere and gave widely separated peoples the same mystical hopes of salvation, the same experiences of ardent faith.

Such cults, whose influence over the conscience and feeling of the masses the political authorities found hard to control, were often under attack. Augustus, although he built temples in Egypt, did not conceal his distrust of its gods. They had upheld his enemy Antony, whose relations with Cleopatra had, so the rumour went, even threatened the imperial position of Rome. Antony's defeat at Actium had also been officially a defeat for the Egyptian gods. Caligula changed his attitude towards foreign divinities; Titus (+ 79 to + 81) had consecrated a bull to Apis, and his successor Domitian (+81 to +96) was an ardent worshipper of the gods of Egypt, to whom he had been bound by a debt of superstitious gratitude ever since he had escaped from danger by disguising himself as a priest of Isis. Since then the passion of Osiris, the mourning of Isis and her spouse's resurrection had become promises for sufferers, who had recognized in them a deep harmony with human nature as well as qualities transcending it.

In this way the religious experience of Egypt may have helped to spread another religion of salvation, which Christianity in some of its aspects could be considered to be, especially in a country where concern with the hereafter had always been a powerful factor in religious speculation. Egypt, moreover, had for long centuries had a Jewish colony whose presence had as early as Ptolemy Philadelphus been a motive for the Greek translation of the Bible called the Septuagint. A knowledge of the scriptural root of Christianity was therefore likely in Egypt from an early period and among different communities and may have helped to spread the new religion at its outset.

Very little is really known about all this. What seems important is that the spread of Christianity was similar to that of other religious experiences such as those of the Gnostics or the Manichaeans, whose original texts Egypt has preserved on papyrus or parchment found in its soil. All this points to a crisis in the pagan world, whose traditional religion no longer satisfied the spiritual needs of the people. In Egypt religious precept demanded that the language of the country be adopted as the ritual tongue. Christianity as well as Gnosticism and Manichaeism adopted Coptic in one or other of its various provincial or regional dialects. Not only did this mean that preachers spoke to the humblest classes of the people, who had been shut out of the Greek culture of the ruling classes, but also that in religion the first place was given to the native population and to that national culture which had virtually been denied the benefits of the constitution of Antoninus and shut out of the new categories of citizens of the empire. Whereas in the official view the native Egyptian was a *dediticius* not worth the trouble of assimilating, for the Christians the word *Hellena* meant a pagan and therefore an object of contempt.

The number and importance of the Christians was reflected, by a strange but not uncommon paradox, in their frequent persecution by the emperors. That of Decius (249–51) left a series of peculiar records in Egypt. Certificates were issued to persons who had made in the presence of the authorities a pagan sacrifice by burning a few grains of incense as a greeting to the emperor. Those who refused were presumed to be Christians and were liable to be punished as disloyal subjects. But the persecution which eclipsed all others in the popular memory and started the Coptic or the martyrs' era was that which Diocletian (303) unleashed with all the energy and rigour of which that prince was capable. It was the final test, which showed the futility of opposing a movement which had already taken permanent hold. A few years later Constantine acknowledged at Milan (313) the right to be a Christian, and began the long task of assimilating the Christian society to the needs of the empire. From that moment the history of Christianity in Egypt was bound up firmly with the relations between Alexandria and Constantinople, the new imperial capital.

## The distinctive role of Egypt within the Christian empire

From the time when the empire officially became Christian under Theodosius, the history of Egypt was directly affected by the official attitude of the emperors, who increasingly claimed the right to lay down, from Constantinople, the dogma to be taught and accepted throughout the empire. The desire for juridical unity was soon combined with an insistence on the religious uniformity known as orthodoxy.

As a religion, Christianity rests on certain articles of faith, and from the earliest centuries of its existence, differing views and interpretations of these articles have brought Christians into fierce conflict with one another.

As long as the church was unable to come out into the open, quarrels among the faithful had no political significance, but as soon as the Christian community finally became representative of the majority of the subjects of the empire, their feuds became affairs of state. Even Constantine frequently had to intervene to settle discussions which were poisoning relations between groups of Christians and which, in the guise of theology, often threatened public order. To Constantine's practical and authoritarian mind, religious discussion – heresy – ought to disappear and give way to an ordered and definitively acknowledged conception of what was true and hence lawful. His successors followed his example, and this attitude was at the root of the constant tension that existed between the Constantinople court and the bishopric of Alexandria, each considering itself responsible for maintaining the true faith, or orthodoxy.

These religious debates frequently brought deeply felt, carefully preserved and venerated local traditions into conflict with the abstract and remote decisions of the authorities. In both Alexandria and Antioch, the prestige of Christianity's most ancient episcopal sees was reinforced by the personal qualities of some of the prelates who occupied them. What is perhaps even more important, the two intellectual capitals of the Graeco-Roman world gave the theological debates which developed there a slant that was difficult to reconcile with imperial ideas – and sometimes even with the ideas of the Bishop of Rome.

In Alexandria, Christianity acquired, at a very early date and by the normal processes of growth, a character that was rather different from that of Christianity in the rest of the country. The Greek culture with which the city was impregnated was visible even in the way the new religion had been received. The change to Christianity took the form not of a revolutionary act of faith but of an attempt to justify certain new concepts and integrate them into the broad framework of the philosophy and philology of antiquity. The Alexandrians had before them the example of what Philo the Jew had accomplished in their own city in the first century of our era, when he attempted to give scripture a Greek and universal meaning. They therefore organized a *Didaskaleion*, which is thought to have been founded by a man called Panthenus, a converted Stoic and therefore well versed in Greek philosophy. The persecution by Septimus Severus forced the school to close for a time, but it reopened under the leadership of figures such as Clement of Alexandria (*c.* 145–210), a man of prodigious erudition; and his pupil Origen (185–252), under whom philosophical speculation and philological interest reached their summit. Origen managed to reconcile being a Christian with following the teaching of the founder of neo-Platonism, Ammonius Sacca. It was these eminent personalities who did most to graft Christianity, which was still taking shape, on to the classical tradition, enabling it to take over the succession of a civilization, that of Greece and Rome, which had seemed basically incompatible with it. This was Egypt's most important contribution to nascent Christianity. This attitude, however, had little appeal for the non-Greek population of the country, whose type of religious experience was more instinctive. As for the Bishop of Alexandria, his situation in relation to his priests (*presbyteroi*) was a very special one since they formed, as was usual in the early church, a very powerful college. To maintain his authority he therefore had to rely on the provincial bishops (the *chorepiskopoi* or *bishops* of the *chora*, i.e. Egypt outside Alexandria) who depended on him for their consecration.

In this conflict of interests and attitudes, very serious disputes broke out. The first of these began when Bishop Melecius of Lycopolis (Asyut) supported the advocates of rigorism in refusing to admit into the bosom of the church those who had proved wanting during the persecutions.

Another dispute, which had much more serious consequences, arose from differences of opinion between scholars and between philosophical schools concerning the dual human and divine nature of Christ. Did he have two indissociable natures, a single divine nature – his humanity being but an outward show – or two separate natures? The priest Arius, in Syria, opted for the second solution to the problem, stinging the church into an official rejoinder condemning him. The most ardent defender of orthodoxy was Saint Athanasius (293–373), Patriarch of Alexandria, who in the midst of this storm successfully stood up even to those emperors who supported Arianism and who was recognized as the champion of the church both by the Greeks and by the Romans. Half a century later, another Patriarch of Alexandria, Cyril (412–44), opposed the doctrines of Nestorius, the Patriarch of Constantinople, and successfully stood up to the emperor Theodosius II. On this occasion, Cyril corrected the previous affirmations of the theologians by stressing that there were in Christ one person and two natures. After his death, the monk Eutyches, backed by Cyril's successor, Dioscurus, went a stage farther by maintaining that there was but one nature in Christ. The Council of Chalcedon condemned this doctrine in 451. It subsequently became a self-evident truth for the Alexandrians, with their pride in the learning and holiness of their patriarchs. This philosophico-theological movement was later to be known as Monophysitism.

The decisions of the Council of Chalcedon (451), which definitively settled the matter by declaring belief in the intimate union of two natures in Christ to be an article of faith, started a crisis in Alexandria which lasted until the Muslim conquest. From the time of the Council there were two patriarchs in Alexandria. There was the Melchite Patriarch (from the Arabic *malik* meaning king), who was appointed by Constantinople, was responsible to the king and exercised administrative, judicial and law-enforcement powers, and side by side with him there was a rival Monophysite Patriarch, who, in the eyes of the Egyptians, was the defender of the sole acceptable theological truth: the oneness of the nature of Christ. The power of the Melchite Patriarch, which was based on imperial legitimacy and strength, was matched by that of the Monophysite Patriarch, who had behind him a national feeling which was becoming more and more anti-Byzantine.

The bitter and sometimes bloody feuds between the faithful took place mainly in the city of Alexandria. Echoes of the often scandalous events which took place in that city reached the provinces, but the Christianity of the Nile valley, in point of fact, succeeded in demonstrating its practical flavour, in contrast to the speculations of the Alexandrians, in an experiment that was to prove fundamental in the development of the church. Considering wordly life to be the source and occasion of sin, the Christians of Egypt systematically practised withdrawal from the world, forming religious communities which perhaps had precedents both in pagan Egypt and among the Jews in Egypt (such as the *Therapeutes* whose virtuous practices Philo described) but which now became pillars of the new religion. Different phases can be distinguished in the history of this movement known as monasticism. Its first outstanding representative was Paul of Thebes (234–347), a hermit who with his disciple Anthony (251–356) fled the world and organized a group of anchorites. Last but not least there was Pachomius (276–349), who with great practical sense devised groups who shared certain tasks and responsibilities, were subject to a code of discipline and lived together in a highly developed communal life (*Koinobia*). This brings us to Shenout of Atripa (348–466) who, at the White Convent (Deir-el-Abyad), subjected men and women to the strictest discipline and perfected in Egypt the system which was further developed in medieval Europe.

Clearly this withdrawal from the world and this gathering together in large groups were not simply acts of faith. They were rather a transference to a religious setting of factors which, as we have already seen, were present in Byzantine Egypt. *Anachoresis* has both a religious and a fiscal meaning (*anachoretes* means both a hermit and someone who flees to evade taxes he can no longer pay); and people's eagerness to go and live in the desert was an indictment of the hardships of daily life. Moreover, many of the documents relating to life in the convents show that they were great organizations owning land, cattle, workshops, store-houses and farm installations. A convent may be rich and active while its monks are individually poor and devoted to the contemplative life. It can easily be seen that this solution was similar to that which led to the disappearance of the smallholding in favour of the latifundium. The monks living in convents found fulfilment not only for their religious aspirations but also for another deep desire of those times, which was for a refuge from the difficulties of everyday life and protection against an overweening authority. This explains the very large numbers of the monastic population, running into tens of thousands, to which contemporary records refer. The effect of the use of the monasteries as a shelter from the state, or at least as a mitigation of its incapacity to fulfil its responsibilities to its citizens, led the ecclesiastical authorities increasingly to take the place of the civil authorities. In these circumstances the emperors had good reason in trying to prevent administrators from becoming monks.

It is easy to see that this society was less inclined than in the past to adopt the traditions of hellenism, either in its classical form or in its new forms manifested in Constantinople. The figurative traditions of the Roman era were developed locally in what is rather vaguely called Coptic art. The national literature, which now dealt only with religious subjects, used the vernacular of the country, and the rich proliferation of pious texts bears witness to the development of a tradition to which historians have in the past perhaps not done full justice.

In the end, however, the Alexandrian spirit of resistance, which was essentially theological, coincided in the sixth century with that of the anchorites. Constantinople was exerting increasingly heavy pressure to impose on a reluctant Egypt the doctrines of the Council of Chalcedon and many others subsequently laid down in Constantinople. Circumstances combined to discredit, in Egypt, the rich and authoritarian official church, which was responsible for keeping order, and to confer popularity on the persecuted Monophysites, who in the fifth century received tremendous doctrinal support from Syria and were joined in the sixth century by other persecuted Syrians. A general feeling of lassitude overcame Egyptians of all social classes. The firm belief that the Egyptian position was right and just was reinforced by many incidents in the growing number of apocryphal texts relating to episodes of Christ's life in Egypt. The Byzantines had become undesirable aliens, representing an unwelcome political occupation.

The papyri have preserved very precise information on the mood of the population at its various levels. The same feeling of fear, privation and weariness was everywhere. No wonder that the country, exhausted by a rapacious and ineffectual administration, divided internally by disputes and estranged from Constantinople by mutual distrust, was drained of its economic strength.

Not many years were to pass before the vulnerability of Byzantine rule was shown up by two military defeats.

The Sassanid king Chosroes II wanted to weaken the power of

Byzantium. The Sassanids already dominated the southern part of Arabia and were hindering Byzantine trade in the Red Sea. They struck in three directions: towards Anatolia and Byzantium, towards Aleppo and Antioch, and towards Aqaba and Egypt, reaching the Nile Delta in 615. The Persian occupation was marked by the insurrection of the Jews, finally liberated from the long Roman oppression, and by the open reappearance of the Monophysite church, which for some years became the only official church.

The reconquest of Egypt by Heraclius in 629 gave the Byzantines only a brief respite, compelled as they were to exercise close surveillance over a colony which had by then become virtually ungovernable. Terror reigned in 632, under the Melchite Patriarch, when Byzantium decided to impose a new orthodoxy which was neither that of the Council of Chalcedon nor that of Rome nor yet Monophysitism. From 639 onwards the Muslims adopted a threatening posture, and in 642 the Egyptians gave themselves up to the new conquerors, who had promised to establish more equitable economic and fiscal conditions. The Arab conquest marked the beginning of a new era in Egyptian history.

*a) Roman baths and hypocaust*

*b) Roman theatre, with marble seats and columns (partly restored)*

*c) The corridor around the Roman theatre*

PLATE 7.1 *Polish excavations at Kôm el-Dikka, Alexandria*

PLATE 7.2 *Head of a statue of Vespasian*

223

PLATE 7.3 *Statuette of a black gladiator, standing, wearing a tunic, cuirass and helmet, and armed with a shield and dagger*

PLATE 7.4 *Statuette of a black warrior holding a double axe*

PLATE 7.6 *Head of Tetrarch*

PLATE 7.5 *Earthenware tile: black figure kneeling and blowing a musical instrument*

100 Himmelfahrt Christi mit stillender Maria, *Apsismalerei aus Baouit*

PLATE 7.7 *Baouit painting*

PLATE 7.8 *The ancient residence which served Mari-Mina Monastery*

# The importance of Nubia: a link between Central Africa and the Mediterranean

S. ADAM
*with the collaboration of* J. VERCOUTTER

A glance at a physical map of Africa is enough to bring out the importance of Nubia as a link between the Great Lakes and the Congo basin of Central Africa on the one hand and the Mediterranean on the other. The Nile valley, much of which runs parallel to the Red Sea down the Nubian 'Corridor', with the Sahara to the west and the Arabian or Nubian desert to the east, brought the ancient civilizations of the Mediterranean into direct contact with black Africa. The discovery of a fine bronze head of Augustus at Meroe, less than 200 kilometres from Khartoum, need cause no surprise.

Although the Nile is a reliable means of crossing these desert regions, the journey is not as easy as it might appear at first sight. From Aswan almost to Omdurman, the cataracts make north–south progress up the Nile difficult, and at times navigation is quite impossible. Moreover, the river's two enormous bends add greatly to the distance and are sometimes a major difficulty in themselves: between Abu Hamed and Wadi al-Malik, for example, the Nile flows south-west instead of north, so that for much of the year upstream traffic has to struggle against both wind and current, though the downstream trip is, of course, much easier. Farther south lie the extensive marshlands of the Sudds which, though not impassable, do not facilitate cultural or economic exchange.

Nevertheless, all things considered, Nubia is one of the regions of Africa where contacts are very easy, not only between north and south but also between east and west. In the southern part of Nubia, the Blue Nile, the Atbara and their tributaries, the piedmont plains of Ethiopia and the depression which strikes down from the Red Sea coast offer convenient access to the Ethiopian highlands and also to the Red Sea and the Indian Ocean. To the west, Wadi al-Malik and Wadi Huwar, now dry but not so formerly, join the Nile between the Third and Fourth Cataracts and, with the Kordofan and Darfur plains, provide Nubia with an easy route to the Chad depression, and thence to the valley of the Niger and West Africa.

Nubia thus stands astride an African crossroads; it is a meeting-place for civilizations to the east and west, to the north and south of Africa,

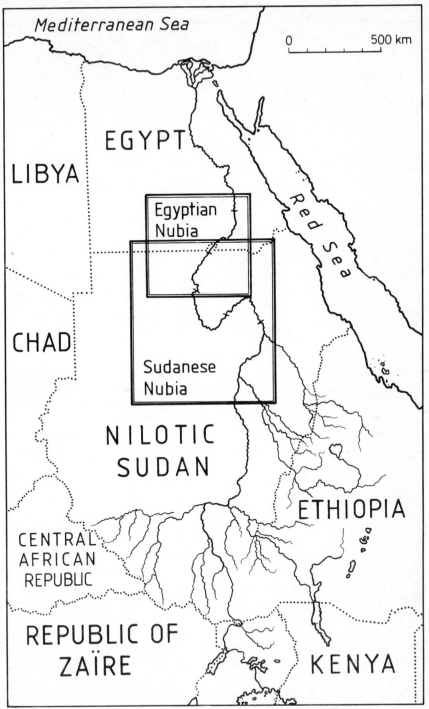

FIG. 8.1 *The Nile Valley and the Nubian 'Corridor'*

227

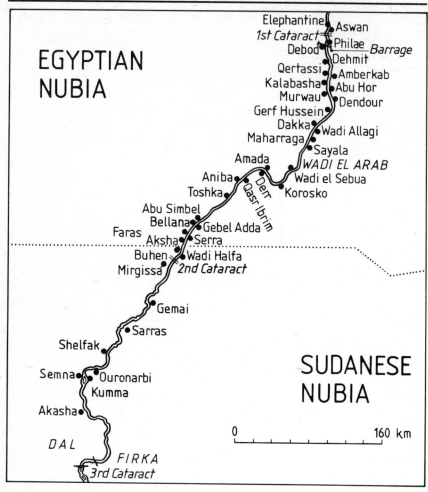

FIG. 8.2 *Ancient Nubia* (after K. Michalowski, 1967b, p. 29)

as well as those of the Near East, distant Asia and Mediterranean Europe.

In the last few years there has been a tendency to use the word 'Nubia' for the northern part of the country only, the area between the First and Second Cataracts. The Unesco 'Save Nubia' campaign reinforced – if it did not create – this trend. But Nubia does not end at the arid and stony Batn el-Hagar; it stretches much farther south. As far back as 1820, Costas in his 'description of Egypt', defined it as 'that part of the Nile valley between the First Cataract and the Kingdom of Sennar', whose capital is more than 280 kilometres south of Khartoum. But even this more generous view understates the true extent of Nubia.

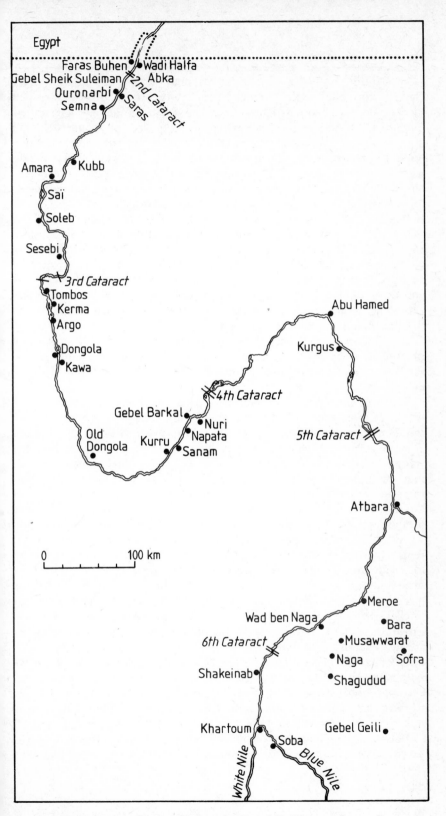

FIG. 8.3 *Upper Sudanese Nubia* (after F. and U. Hintze, 1967, p. 26)

Historically, as the most ancient Egyptian texts bear out, travellers coming from the north entered Nubia a little south of Al-Kab. The Egyptian province situated between Thebes and Aswan was long called Ta-Seti, the 'Land of the Bow', in ancient Egyptian, and the hieroglyphic documents traditionally apply this term to what we call Nubia. Greater Nubia, in earliest times, thus began with the sandy areas of the Nile valley, where the 'Nubian sands' take over from the limestone to the north. Originally it included the First Cataract. Its southern limit is more difficult to determine, but archaeological research has shown that from the fourth millennium before our era the same or related cultures extended throughout the whole region from the edge of the Ethiopian highlands in the south to the Egyptian part of the Nile in the north. Thus, to give more precision to Costas' phrase, we could define historical Nubia as that part of the Nile basin lying between the west-north-west frontier of present-day Ethiopia and Egypt. This includes the Nile valley itself, parts of the White Nile and Blue Nile, and all their tributaries above 12° north, such as the Atbar, the Rahad and the Dindor (see maps).

It is important to clarify the geographical limits of Nubia so that we can review what is known about this country and gain a better understanding of its historical role in linking Central Africa with the Mediterranean world.

There is, however, an enormous disparity between our knowledge of the different parts of Nubia. Archaeological investigation carried out before the dams were built or raised at Aswan has provided us with far more archaeological knowledge of Lower Nubia, that is, the region between Aswan and Batn el-Hagar (Second Cataract), than of any other part of the Nile valley. Yet it should be observed that no excavations were made before the first dam was built at Aswan, in 1896: all the ancient sites close to the river and within range of the first reservoir were destroyed before any idea of their number, nature or importance could be obtained. It was only when this dam was raised for the first time, in 1902, that the archaeological remains were investigated, and this then became normal practice before each subsequent elevation. After the last occasion, 1928–38, more than fifty volumes, many of them folio, were produced which dealt with the monuments and archeology of 'Egyptian' Nubia. Before the new dam at Shellal, the Sadd-al-Ali, was filled, a further series of investigations was carried out as far as Batn el-Hagar; the full reports of this final undertaking are just beginning to appear.

It is therefore reasonable to say that the history and archaeology of Lower Nubia are fairly well known; once all the historical, archaeological and anthropological studies under way have been published, we shall be able to form an accurate picture of the role this part of Nubia once played in linking north and south. However, the situation as regards Nubia south of Batn el-Hagar is quite different and much less satisfactory. With the exception of a few very small regions, much of the country is still a *terra incognita* from the archaeological, and therefore historical, point of view. It is true that the important 'Pharaonic' sites between the Second and Fourth Cataracts have been or are about to be excavated. The same can be said of a number of more specifically 'Sudanese' sites, such as (from south to north) Jebel Moya, a few Neolithic settlements at or near Khartoum, Naqa, Mussawwarat es-Sufra, Wad-ban-Naga, Meroe, Ghazali Napata, Dongola and Kerma. Yet none of these sites has been thoroughly explored, and some major sites such as Kerma and Meroe, which were important political centres and are vital to the study of Nubian influence in Africa, have hardly been touched.

Apart from archaeological research, ancient Pharaonic texts, as well as some in Latin and Greek, yield a little information about the early history of civilization in Nubia, and give us some idea of its role in the evolution of Africa. But these sources cannot make up for the lack of archaeological and literary information concerning the greater part of Nubia. This is true of the great valleys – the Nile itself south of the Second Cataract, the Blue Nile, the White Nile and the Atbara – outlying regions such as Darfur and Kordofan, and the eastern itineraries towards the Red Sea and Ethiopia.

In short, Nubia is so situated that it ought to provide more well-dated information than any other African country concerning the historical links between Central and North Africa and between the east and west of the continent. But we have so little to go on, except for the northern part of the country, that our knowledge of their nature, importance and duration is necessarily very inadequate.

One fact struck all observers from the ancient Mediterranean world: Nubia was and is a land of black people. The Egyptians always depicted its inhabitants with a much darker skin than their own. The Greeks, and later the Romans too, called them 'Ethiopians', i.e. those with a 'burnt skin', and the first Arab travellers referred to Nubia as 'Baled-as-Sudan', the 'land of black people'. In medieval texts the title 'Prefect of the Nubians' is written 'Praefectus Negritarum' and the inhabitants are called 'Nigrites'. And finally, in the wall paintings of Faras the dark skin of the Nubians stands out from the light skins of the heavenly beings – Christ, the Virgin Mary and the saints.

But, even if we were able to do so, we should not wish to join in the purely anthropological debate as to whether the Nubians are of 'negro' or 'hamitic' origin. Egyptian drawings from before −1580 make a clear distinction between the physical type of the Nehesyu from Lower Nubia, who only differ from the Egyptians in the colour of their skin, and that of the 'Kushites' who appear in the Nile valley at this time either as invaders or, more probably, because Egyptians and Nehesyu Nubians had by now come into contact with them farther south. These new 'Kushites' were not only very dark-skinned; they also had many of the facial traits still to be observed in Central and West Africa; they were quite different from both ancient and contemporary Nubians.

African in language and civilization, the inhabitants of Nubia were well placed to serve as useful intermediaries for the closely related neighbouring cultures. As Nubia's long history, from about −7000 to +700, is related in detail in the following chapters (9–12), we shall give only a brief account of certain aspects of its history which cast light on Nubia's relations with adjacent civilizations.

From about −7000, and above all during the humid periods towards the end of Neolithic times, there seems to have been a common material culture throughout Nubia, from the edge of the Ethiopian highlands to the Al-Kab region and even as far north as Middle Egypt. It was only towards −3000 that there is a distinct difference between the civilization of the lower Egyptian part of the Nile valley and that of the upper, Nubian, part. Until this time very similar, if not identical, funeral customs, pottery, stone and, later, metal instruments are found from Khartoum in the south to Matuar, near Asyut, in the north. They show how similar the various regions were as regards social organization, religious beliefs and funeral rites, as well as the general way of life, in which hunting, fishing and animal husbandry were associated with an as yet crude form of agriculture.

Towards −3200 the art of writing appeared in Egypt, whereas Nubia south of the First Cataract remained attached to its own social systems and its oral culture. By −2800 writing was in general use in Egypt, probably because of the demands of a highly centralized political organization, and contributed to the development of irrigation and so of a common agriculture which took over from hunting, fishing and stock-breeding; and this gradually reinforced the differences between the civilizations of Greater Nubia and Egypt.

In the south, the Negro populations of Nubia, with their oral culture, maintained a social and political organization based on small units, and felt no need for writing; they must, however, have known of its existence, because they still had contact, and sometimes violent contact, with the Pharaonic world. Egypt, driven by the requirements of irrigation, gradually evolved a highly centralized monarchic type of organization, since a powerful central authority was the only means of compelling the population, when necessary, to carry out the collective tasks that had to be done in order to make the whole of the lower Nile valley suitable for cultivation: building and maintaining dykes parallel to the river, levelling the 'basins', digging canals and making dams so that the ever-variable level of flood water could be used as efficiently as possible (see above). It was thus natural for two very distinct types of society to come into being and coexist in the Nile valley; one, in Nubia, pastoral and perhaps still semi-nomadic though not without agricultural skills, the other essentially agricultural, bent upon the intensive cultivation of the land, and politically centralized. These two 'specialized' civilizations, which had been similar and autonomous up to about −3000, gradually came to complement each other economically, a development which facilitated exchange between them.

Unfortunately it is extremely difficult to find out details of the links which grew up between these two societies. Our knowledge of their relations from the end of the third millennium onwards depends entirely on Egyptian sources. Moreover, the literary texts give a false impression, because they tend to deal only with military expeditions, and the archaeological evidence, except for Lower Nubia, is quite inadequate, for it is limited to Nubian articles found in Egypt or, at best, to Egyptian objects discovered in Nubian sites between Aswan and the Second Cataract.

Such as it is, this information suggests that the upper and lower Nile valley were in quite close touch. Their common cultural origin must not be overlooked, and it was, after all, an asset. Protodynastic and Thinite Egyptian pottery ware is found in areas as far south as, and beyond, the Dal Cataract, and this shows that manufactured articles were exchanged between north and south, for while Egyptian objects – vases, pearls, amulets – have been discovered in Nubia, a great deal of ebony, ivory, incense, and perhaps obsidian from the south was used in Egyptian tomb furniture of this period. This commerce may have helped ideas and techniques to spread from one region to the other, but our knowledge is still too patchy for us to gauge the importance or even the direction of such influences. To take but two examples: did the technique of enamelling, as applied to beads and amulets, for instance, originate in the north or in the south? It appears at almost the same time in both societies.

The same is true of the red pottery with a black border which is so characteristic of the potter's art throughout the ancient Nilotic world. It seems to appear first in the upper Nile valley between the Fourth and Sixth Cataracts, before we have evidence of it in the lower valley, in Egypt. But again dating is too hazardous for us to be sure.

On the other hand, the pottery made from a buff-coloured fossil clay, known to specialists as 'Qena ware', is unquestionably Egyptian; both the raw material used and the technique of manufacture leave no room for doubt. A great deal was imported, at least into Lower Nubia, from the end of the fourth millennium until the beginning of the third millennium before our era. It is often found at Nubian sites south of the First Cataract, which suggests that there was a brisk trade between the Theban region and Lower Nubia. The Qena clay was suitable for making large vessels capable of holding liquids or solids, but unfortunately we have no idea of what they contained – oils, fats, cheese? However, they are a clear sign that exchanges between Egypt and the Nubian Corridor were frequent, and probably of greater historical importance than the occasional raids which from about −3000 onwards the Pharaohs were in the habit of launching against the Ta-Seti – the Land of the Bow – between the First and Second Cataracts.

These raids, however, which are referred to in the earliest Egyptian texts (see Chapter 9), provide the first indication of the dual aspect – military and economic – of north–south contacts along the Nile valley. Despite their ambiguity, these contacts reveal the importance of the

'Nubian Corridor' in providing a link between Africa and the Mediterranean.

By −3200, under the first dynasty, the Egyptians already had sufficient knowledge of the country to risk sending a body of troops as far as the beginning of the Second Cataract. We can hazard a guess as to the reasons for this expedition. First, there was the need to find raw materials which were lacking or becoming scarce in Egypt – especially wood. The belt of forest which, in former times, must have lined the banks of the river was becoming sparser and would progressively disappear as the lower Nile was increasingly brought under control and the irrigation system, with its networks of 'basins', was gradually extended.

A second important reason for the Egyptian army to intervene in Nubia was the desire to keep open the passage southwards: incense, gum, ivory, ebony and panthers come not from between the First and Second Cataracts, but from much farther south. At this time, however, Lower Nubia was densely populated, as we can see from the number and size of A-Group burial grounds (see Chapter 9).

These people did not come from the north, as was believed until a few years ago. They were the descendants of Neolithic groups which had settled in the valley between the First and Third Cataracts, but they were probably related to those which occupied the upper valley between the Fourth and Sixth Cataracts, judging by the household objects discovered by archaeologists in both areas. Some of these people were still hunters and fishermen, but those near the river were mainly engaged in agriculture, whereas the inhabitants of the outlying savannah on both sides of the Nile led an essentially pastoral and perhaps even semi-nomadic life. For the climate was still in the humid phase which ended the African Neolithic period, and the 'Nubian Corridor' was not restricted to the narrow river valley, but probably extended a considerable way from each bank, so that its inhabitants could if they wished intercept the Egyptian caravans heading south overland as well as along the river.

In any case, evidence of the Egyptians' interest in Lower Nubia is to be found in the many ethnic terms or place names referring to this region which are preserved in the most ancient Pharaonic texts. But these concern no more than about 325 kilometres of the valley, from Elephantine in the north to the first rapids of the Second Cataract at Buhen (such sites are now submerged under the waters of the High Dam), which the Egyptians certainly reached under the reign of King Djer of the first dynasty if not in the time of King Scorpion himself, at the very end of the predynastic period.

Around −2700, information on north–south contacts obtained from excavations on A-Group sites suddenly dries up, at least in Lower Nubia: there are no longer more than a very few Nubian tombs or settlements. It is as if the inhabitants had suddenly deserted their land. Why the formerly dense population between the First and Second Cataracts should disappear in this way has not yet been fully explained. Was it because the Pharaohs had stripped the country of its produce, or did the Nubians withdraw of their own accord – either towards the savannah on each side of the valley or farther south? These questions are particularly difficult to answer because there has been practically no archaeological investigation of the region south of the Second Cataract, or of the approaches on either side of the Nile.

For knowledge of this period, between about −2700 and −2200, we therefore have to rely on the very few hints to be found in Egyptian literary sources. These report military campaigns in the Ta-Seti region of Nubia – which might explain why the country was abandoned. Thus we learn that under Snefru (about −2680) the Pharaoh's forces captured 110 000 prisoners and 200 000 head of cattle, figures which confirm both the size of the population at the end of the A-Group period before the country was deserted, and the large scale of animal husbandry in their society, sometimes compared to the present-day 'cattle-complex' in north-east Africa. Yet we cannot account for such a vast quantity of livestock unless these people exploited much of the steppe or savannah, which then extended far on each side of the river, as well as the Nile valley itself.

An important archaeological find in 1961–2 has helped to cast a little more light on the background of the history of the Nubian Corridor during this obscure period. A settlement of the Egyptian Old Kingdom was discovered at Buhen, with Pharaonic seals, some dating from the end of the fourth dynasty, but most from the fifth dynasty. This settlement was linked to a group of furnaces used for smelting copper.

The discovery reveals, first, that the Egyptians did not depend solely on Asian copper – from Sinai in particular – and that they had already thoroughly prospected for metals in African Nubia. Secondly, it indicates something of great importance: that the Egyptians had been able – or had been obliged – to introduce smelting techniques in the upper Nile valley. The Buhen find proves that African copper was produced at this time. But to produce copper you must first discover and then mine the vein, build special furnaces and supply them with a suitable fuel, make melting-pots, cast the metal and refine it at least to a certain extent before finally making it into ingots. The Nubians could hardly have watched all this going on, even if they were not actively engaged in it, without acquiring at least a basic knowledge of metallurgy. This early introduction to metallurgy, in the middle of the third millennium before our era, is probably the best explanation for the skill they showed some 500 years later (around −2000) in making copper objects as well as in handling gold.

A little before −2200, this obscure period drew to a close, and we again come across information from both archaeological and literary sources. The Egyptian documents of the sixth dynasty, the last dynasty of the Old Kingdom, include several accounts of expeditions into Upper Nubia (see Chapter 9). At the beginning of this dynasty these expeditions were clearly of a commercial nature, and peaceful: the Egyptians sought to obtain in Nubia the scarce types of stone needed for royal buildings, or simply wood. They employed a technique which was to be used again later: they looked for scarce or bulky goods and wood at the same time. Wood from the upper valley was used to build boats which then transported the heavy goods back to Egypt, where the fleet of boats was dismantled and the wood reused for other purposes. Clearly this commerce also furthered the circulation of ideas and techniques in both directions. The Egyptian pantheon even acquired a new African deity, Dedun, provider of incense. To improve their communications with the south, the Egyptians dug out navigable channels in the rapids of the First Cataract at Aswan; this policy, initiated in the third millennium before our era, was to be continued by the Pharaohs of the Middle Kingdom and later by those of the New Kingdom.

Egyptian expeditions also took the land routes as well as routes along the river valley. At that time these were certainly not desert tracks, because the Neolithic humid phase had barely ended; the journey south, if not in the shade, must have abounded with springs and water-holes, since pack-animals such as asses, which need regular supplies of water, were in normal use. It was along one of these tracks, the so-called oasis route, that asses transported incense, ebony, certain oils, leopard-skins, ivory and so forth to Egypt. Recent discoveries suggest that at least one such road began at the Dakhilah oasis, the oasis of Khargah being still a lake. Unfortunately, Egyptian texts do not tell us what the Egyptians gave in exchange for the goods they brought back, nor do they state exactly where they got their supplies, which is still more unfortunate. They mention a number of African place names, but specialists are still uncertain where these are located. Here, too, much could emerge from the systematic archaeological exploration not only of the Nubian part of the Nile valley south of the Second Cataract but also – and this is perhaps more important – of the land routes to the west of the valley, which link the chain of 'Libyan' oases with Selima and the valleys or depressions leading to Ennedi, Tibesti, Kordofan, Darfur and Lake Chad.

Whether they followed the valley or went overland, it seems very likely that, from these early times, the Egyptians were already in touch with Africa south of the Sahara, and that the 'Nubian Corridor' played an important part in these contacts. Under Pepi II, towards −2200, an Egyptian expedition brought back from the distant south a 'dwarf for the sacred dance' (see Chapter 9). The word used to describe this person is *deneg*, whereas the usual term employed for a dwarf in the hieroglyphic texts is *nemu*. We might well wonder – and the answer is likely to be positive – whether *deneg* refers in fact to a Pygmy. If this is so – and the translation deneg = Pygmy is now broadly accepted – the Egyptians of the Old Kingdom must have been in direct or indirect contact with this race from the equatorial forest. Even if the Pygmies' habitat extended much farther north than it does today, which is possible and even likely, because of the different climate during the third millennium, this area would still have been very far to the south of Nubia. We can therefore conclude that the Egyptians of the Old Kingdom had contacts with Central Africa, and that Nubia and its inhabitants did much to make such contacts possible.

In any case, contacts between Egypt and Central Africa probably go back a very long way, since the word *deneg* occurs in the Pyramid texts. Admittedly, there is a great deal of disagreement as to when these texts were written, but even if we take the most conservative estimate they could not be later than the fifth dynasty, and it is very probable that they are much older.

Thus, in the sixth dynasty at the very latest, the Egyptians knew of the existence of Pygmies. This is confirmed by a sixth-dynasty text which relates that a *deneg* had already reached Egypt in the time of the Pharaoh Isesi, the last king but one of the fifth dynasty. This Pygmy had been found in the land of Punt, which suggests that his homeland must have been very far to the south of Nubia, since Punt must be somewhere along the coast of Eritrea or Somalia. Here, too, the 'dwarf dancer' must have been acquired for the Egyptians by a third party. In each case the probable presence of Pygmies in Egypt implies that there were contacts between the lower Nile valley and sub-equatorial Africa.

At the end of the sixth dynasty, in the reign of Pepi II, the peaceful relations between Egypt and Nubia, based on mutual interest and the Pharaohs' need to have free access to the resources of the distant regions of Africa, appear to deteriorate. Texts written towards the end of Pepi II's reign hint at conflicts between Egyptian expeditions and inhabitants of the Corridor. For example, an Egyptian leading an expedition was killed during his journey south, and his son had to mount an attack to recover the body and bring it back for ritual burial in Egypt.

It is difficult not to see a connection between this tension and the changes which began to affect the climate towards −2400, which certainly led to population movements. Up to −2400, the whole area between 15° and 30° north was more humid than today and hence habitable. Even if it was not densely populated in relation to its size, this area must have supported a large number of inhabitants.

But the climate gradually became dry, and drove these people to take refuge in more hospitable regions: the south and, of course, the Nile valley, Egyptian iconography seems to have perpetuated the memory of these migrations. It is about −2350, at the time of the fifth dynasty, that the theme of cadaverous shepherds first appears in the scenes of daily life painted on the mastabas. It is tempting, indeed more than tempting, to see in these famished figures nomadic or semi-nomadic shepherds who had fled the encroaching desert to find food and work in Egypt.

There thus seems no point in looking – as has been done – for a distant origin of the so-called C-Group peoples (see Chapter 9) who appear towards −2300 in the Nubian Corridor. These people had in fact been close by and were only driven to settle in the valley by the change in climatic conditions. But these migrants from the encroaching desert must have had to struggle against those already living by the river – and the texts from the end of the sixth dynasty might well be an echo of this antagonism.

However this may be, these new peoples were descended directly from the A-Group as archaeological sources make clear. They kept up the tradition of mutual exchange with the lower Nile valley, and later served as intermediaries between Africa and the Egyptian and Mediterranean civilizations.

From −2300, so far as archaeology can tell, the population of the Nubian Corridor split up into several 'families'. Though closely related, they each had their own material culture – pottery, types of instruments, weapons and tools – and their own burial rites – type of tomb, the arrangement of the tomb, furniture inside and outside the sepulchre, etc. The similarities, however, far outweigh the differences: the important place of livestock-breeding, the widespread use of the red pottery with a black border, 'tumulus'-type graves, and so forth.

From −2200 to −1580, the C-Group peoples between Aswan and Batn el-Hagar (see map) remained in close contact with Egypt, either because Egypt administered the region directly (c. −2000 to c. −1700), or because many Egyptians became permanent residents in the country (c. −1650 to c. −1580), very probably in the service of the new kingdom of Kush (see below and Chapter 9). As they continued to keep in touch with their home region, Thebes, they helped to spread Egyptian ideas and techniques.

Farther south, from Batn el-Hagar onwards, lay the kingdom of Kerma, named after the most important centre so far discovered (see Chapter 9). Its civilization differs only in detail from that of the C-Group and archaeological finds in the very few sites so far excavated reveal links not only with Egypt but also, from −1600 onwards, with the Asiatic Hyksos, who appear to have been in direct contact with them.

It is quite easy to determine the northern limit of the area administered by 'Kerma': it is Batn el-Hagar. But the southern boundary is quite another matter. Recent finds (1973) of Kerma pottery between the White Nile and the Blue Nile south of Khartoum appear to suggest that, even if the kingdom of Kerma itself did not extend as far as present-day Gezira, its influence did, and so brought it into close touch with the Nilotic world of the Sudds (see map).

It is particularly unfortunate that we cannot be certain how far the kingdom of Kerma extended towards equatorial Africa, since this kingdom, probably the first African 'empire' known to history, had achieved a high degree of civilization which enabled it to exert a profound influence on countries situated to its south, along the upper Nile and in Central Africa, as well as to the east and west. If we accept the hypothesis that the kingdom of Kerma stretched from the Third Cataract up to the White Nile, it would have controlled not only the great north–south artery formed by the Nile valley but also the east–west routes from Atlantic Africa to the Red Sea and the Indian Ocean. It was therefore well placed to pass on techniques and ideas from Egypt or from the Hyksos with whom, as we have seen, they had contacts to the African cultures of these regions.

This is not the place to discuss the question whether the large buildings which still dominate the Kerma site are of Egyptian or Nubian origin (see Chapter 9); though the bricks are made according to a Pharaonic technique, the plan of the buildings is quite different from that of contemporary structures in the lower Valley. Until we know more, it is preferable to regard them as 'Kushite' work which underwent Egyptian influence. Kerma seems to have been the most important urban centre in the kingdom of Kush whose name appears in Pharaonic texts from −2000.

We need only emphasize that this kingdom may have greatly influenced neighbouring cultures through its techniques, especially in metallurgy, and that its political strength, to which the size of its capital bears witness, may have enabled it to project its influence far afield. Unfortunately there has been little or no archaeological exploration in the outlying areas of the kingdom, so that we are not yet in a position to do more than speculate about the role of the kingdom of Kerma in transmitting ideas, techniques or languages.

We have just stressed one point which appears certain: the material power of the kingdom of Kush. This is proved by the precautions taken against it by the Pharaohs of the twelfth dynasty, from Sesostris I to Amenemhat III. The potential threat of 'Kerma' to Egypt is vividly illustrated by the chain of fortresses which, from Semna north to Debeira (see map), were built to defend the southern frontier of Egypt against the Kushite armies. All these fortresses, eleven in number, their walls from 6 to 8 metres thick and 10 to 12 metres high, with rounded bastions jutting out and their access on the riverside well protected, not only defended the Nile but also served as military bases for campaigns in the desert or towards the south. Such expeditions were commonplace throughout the reigns of the first six Pharaohs of the dynasty, and are proof of the boundless energy of the Kerma peoples, who were perhaps themselves under the pressure of ethnic groups coming from much farther south. It is one of the tragic consequences of building the new Aswan dam that these masterpieces in the art of fortification inevitably disappeared.

The improvements made by the Egyptians to the north–south route from −2000 to −1780, prove conclusively that the Nubian Corridor was still the principal artery between Africa, the lower Nile valley and the Mediterranean world: the navigable channels through the First Cataract were kept clear, a *doilkos* – a track for hauling boats over land – was constructed parallel to the impassable rapids of the Second Cataract, and a dam was built at Semna to facilitate navigation of the minor rapids of

Batn el-Hagar. All this shows that the Pharaohs of the twelfth dynasty were bent on making the passage south as satisfactory as possible.

When Sesostris III fixed the Egyptian frontier at Semna, he further reinforced the military defences against the possibility of attacks by a powerful aggressor from the south, but a famous text records his command that these fortifications should not hinder the commercial traffic from which both Egyptians and Nubians had much to gain.

Not much is known about the troubled period from −1780 to −1580, which Egyptologists call the Second Intermediate Period, but it seems to have been a golden age for the kingdom of Kush, the capital of which, Kerma, appears to have taken advantage of the weakening grip of Egyptian rulers to increase the amount of trade between the lower and upper Nile valley, from which it profited.

The importance of this trade should not be underestimated. Countless marks of sigillarian earth, which were used to seal letters, and various other articles transported from the north, have been found at Kerma as well as in the Egyptian fortresses; the latter, contrary to what used to be thought, were not abandoned during the Second Intermediate Period, or were abandoned at a relatively late stage, and not for long. Whereas during the Middle Kingdom the garrisons had been relieved at regular intervals, during the Second Intermediate Period those occupying the fortresses became permanent residents in Nubia; they had their families with them, and were buried there. It is even likely that they gradually recognized the suzerainty of the king of Kush. Of Egyptian origin, they must have done a great deal to spread their culture throughout the society of which they were members.

Contact between the African kingdom of Kush and Egypt seems to have been closest during the Hyksos period (−1650 to −1580). All along the Nubian Corridor scarabs and seal-marks bearing the names of the Asiatic kings then ruling Egypt have been found. There are so many at Kerma itself that at one time Nubia was thought to have been over-run by the Hyksos after the submission of Upper Egypt. We now know that this did not happen, but the Africans of the middle Nile had such close links with the Asiatics, of the Delta, that when the Theban Pharaohs of the seventeenth dynasty embarked upon the reconquest of Middle and Lower Egypt, the Hyksos king naturally turned for help to his African ally and proposed taking joint military action against their common enemy, the Pharaoh of Egypt (see Chapter 9).

In any case, the relations between Theban Upper Egypt and the Kushites of Kerma were both hostile and complementary. From −1650 to −1580 Thebans serving the king of Kush brought their technical expertise to Middle Nubia, and the presence of many Egyptians stationed in the fortresses of Lower Nubia ensured that Kush would maintain contact with the Hyksos rulers in the north. Moreover, the last Pharaohs of the seventeenth dynasty employed Medja mercenaries both in their internal struggles to unify Upper Egypt and in the war to drive out the Hyksos. These African soldiers from the Nubian desert were of the same race and practically the same culture as the sedentary Nehesyu people settled along the river.

Thus throughout the Second Intermediate Period Nubians were to be found in Egypt and Egyptians in Nubia – and this certainly aided both commercial and cultural exchanges. Gradually the Nubian Corridor became a melting-pot in which African and Mediterranean elements intermingled and produced a mixed culture. Yet these very close contacts had dramatic repercussions on the development of the first kingdom of Kush at Kerma.

The Pharaohs of the eighteenth dynasty, the Thutmosids, the heirs and descendants of those who had reunified Egypt and expelled the Hyksos invaders, realized that a united African kingdom on the other side of its southern border could be dangerous for Egypt: a Hyksos–Kushite alliance had almost reduced Theban ambitions to nothing. Besides, the Asian threat was still real, even after the Hyksos had retreated to Palestine. To protect itself, Egypt embarked on a policy of systematically intervening in the Near East.

Egypt's own resources – both of manpower and raw materials – were inferior to the potential strength of Asia Minor, as subsequent history made clear. The Theban Pharaohs knew that Africa south of Semna was richly endowed with the raw materials and manpower Egypt lacked, and they would not rest until they had complete control of the Nubian Corridor, the sole means of reaching that part of Africa whose resources were so essential to their Asian policy.

It has often been held that the Egyptian armies had little difficulty in gaining control of the Nubian Corridor. This is not so. Campaign followed campaign, under each Pharaoh of the New Kingdom, from Ahmosis to Seti I and Ramses II, before they achieved success.

Nubian resistance seems to have taken two forms: revolts against the Egyptian control of their country, and also a more or less general abandonment of their land as they fled towards the south. The country gradually became depopulated, as we can see by the decreasing number of tombs in both Upper and Lower Nubia. This obliged the Pharaohs to push on farther and farther towards the south in order to obtain the African supplies which were vital to their policy of dominating the Near East.

By the time of Thutmosis I the entire region between the Second and Fourth Cataracts had been conquered. The Egyptians now had direct control of the desert roads to Darfur, Kordofan and Chad, either from Sinai by way of Selima and Wadi Huwar or from present-day Debba via Wadi al-Malik. But they could also advance towards the Great Lake region of Africa, either by simply following the Nile from Abu Hamad – stone inscriptions including cartouches of Thutmose I and Thutmose III have been found in this area – or by cutting across the Bayuda desert from Korti to rejoin the main course of the Nile, via Wadi Muqaddam and Wadi Abu Dom, at the Fifth Cataract. Besides being far shorter, this route avoided the difficulties of the south-west–north-east upstream journey between Korti and Abu Hamad, as well as those of navigating the Fourth and Fifth Cataracts.

Did the Pharaohs of the New Kingdom really take advantage of these exceptional opportunities to penetrate deep into Africa? We cannot be sure that they did. Once again, no thorough archaeological survey of these itineraries – the western Wadis (Huwar and Al-Malik), the Nile between the Fourth and Fifth Cataracts, the Bayuda – has been carried out. Nevertheless, from the reign of Thutmose IV (about −1450) a striking change in the iconographic representation of negroes in tombs and on monuments suggests that either Egyptian expeditions or intermediaries on their behalf did indeed use these routes.

The negro figures depicted on the Pharaonic tombs and monuments are of a completely new physical type, which sometimes bears a resemblance to the Nilotic Shilluks and Dinkas of today (the tomb of Sebekhotep) or to the inhabitants of Kordofan and the Naba Mountains of modern Sudan.

The few thorough anthropological studies of the peoples that stayed in the Nile valley between the Second and Fourth Cataracts, despite the Pharaonic occupation, throw up no evidence of important ethnic changes in Nubia at this time. On the contrary, they reveal that the physical type of the people living in the region has displayed a remarkable continuity. This means that until we know more, we can accept that the negroes who appear in the iconography of the New Kingdom met the Egyptians in their own country; and we may conclude that direct contacts, even if only during brief military expeditions, existed between Egyptians and negroes in the heart of Africa between −1450 and −1200.

This short survey has shown that Nubia's special and sometimes involuntary role as an intermediary, which arose from its geographical position between Central Africa and the Mediterranean, was well established by −1800. It also brings out some constant features – the fact that it was important for Egypt to have access to African resources, together with Nubia's interest in the northern cultures – which brought about a continuing interchange that went on with varying degrees of intensity throughout the succeeding periods from −1200 to +700.

The kingdom of Napata ( − 800 to − 300) and the empire of Meroe ( −300 to +300), the civilizations of Ballana and Qustul (X-group) ( −300 to +600) and the Christian kingdoms after +600, all saw Nubia as the essential link between Central Africa and the Mediterranean civilizations. Like the Hyksos before them, the Persians, Greeks, Romans, Christians and Muslims all discovered the world of black Africa in Nubia. Different cultures met and blended at this crossroads, just as they had done from

−7000 to −1200, when little by little a civilization had come into being whose fundamentally Nubian aspects were suffused with unmistakable Egyptian influences.

Through Nubia artefacts, techniques and ideas found their way from north to south and doubtless from south to north. Unfortunately – and once again this needs to be stressed – this account of mutual interchange cannot be filled out until the archaeology of Africa south of 20° north is more thoroughly explored; as things are it is very incomplete, and even misleading, for the role of the north is obviously exaggerated, simply because we know so little about the south. There have been many theories concerning the diffusion of languages and cultures between the two sides of the Nile, as well as between north and south, but theories they will remain until we possess more detailed knowledge about the 'black' cultures which existed from −7000 to +700, in the Nilotic Sudds, Kordofan, Darfur, Chad, the eastern approaches to Ethiopia and the area between the Nile and the Red Sea.

PLATE 8.1 *Nubian monuments of Philae being re-erected on the neighbouring island of Agilkia*

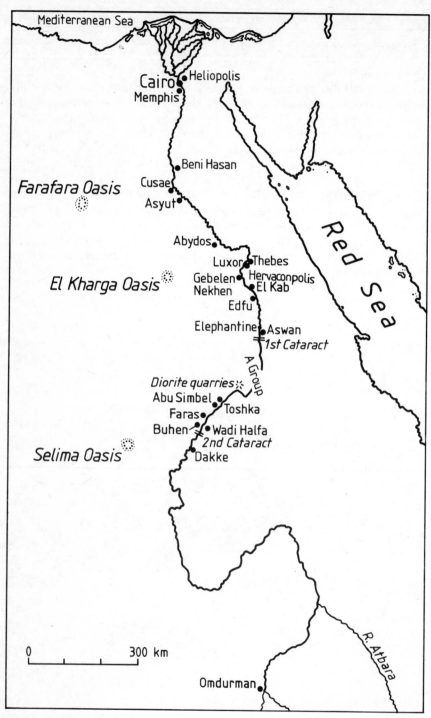

FIG. 9.1 *Nubia and Egypt*

# Nubia before Napata (− 3100 to − 750)

**N. M. SHERIF**

## The A-Group period

Around the end of the fourth millennium before our era there flourished in Nubia a remarkable culture known to archaeologists as the A-Group.[1] The copper tools (the earliest metal tools so far discovered in the Sudan) and the pottery of Egyptian origin unearthed from A-Group graves show the flowering of the A-Group culture to have been contemporary with the first dynasty in Egypt (− 3100). This culture is denoted, as are also some other Nubian cultures, by a letter of the alphabet because it was non-literate, no specific references to it exist on the part of literate peoples, nor can it be associated with any particular place of discovery or important centre. Yet it was a period of prosperity marked by a considerable increase in population.

Definite A-Group archaeological remains have so far been discovered in Nubia between the First Cataract in the north and Batn-el-Hagar (Belly of Stones) in the south. But pottery similar to that of the A-Group has been found on the surface in various sites farther south in the northern Sudan. A grave near Omdurman Bridge[2] yielded a pot indistinguishable from another pot found at Faras in an A-Group grave.[3]

Ethnically the A-Group was very similar in physical characteristics to the predynastic Egyptians.[4] They were semi-nomadic people, probably herding sheep, goats and some cattle. They usually lived in small camps, moving whenever a pasturage became exhausted.

The A-Group belongs to the Chalcolithic culture. This means that essentially they were Neolithic, but with a limited usage of copper tools, all of which were imported from Egypt. One of the important characteristics of the A-Group culture is the pottery found in the graves of the people associated with it. Several types can be recognized but the 'constant feature

1. G. A. Reisner, 1910–27.
2. A. J. Arkell, 1949, pp. 99, 106 and Plates 91–100.
3. F. L. Griffith, 1921, No. 8, pp. 1–13.
4. W. B. Emery, 1965, p. 124.

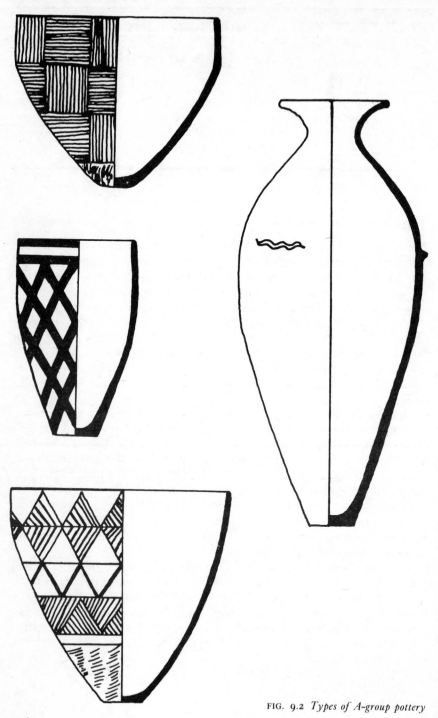

FIG. 9.2 *Types of A-group pottery*

FIG. 9.3 *Types of A-group burials (after W. B. Emery, 1965)*

of the A-Group pottery is the skilful craftsmanship and the artistic decoration and design, which set this ceramic art high above that of most of the contemporary cultures'.[5] Typical of the A-Group culture is a fine thin pottery with a black-burnished inside while its outside has red-painted decoration in imitation of basketwork. With this type of pottery are also found large bulbous jars with a pointed base[6] and pots with 'wavy ledge' handles and deep pink ware conical jars of Egyptian origin.[7]

As for the burial customs of the A-Group people, two types of grave are known to us. The first type was a simple oval pit about 0·8 metres deep while the other was an oval pit 1·3 metres deep with a sunk chamber on one side. The body, which was enclosed in a leather shroud, was placed in a contracted position on the right with the head normally to the west. Besides pottery, articles deposited in the grave included stone palettes in the form of oval or rhomboid plates, ostrich-feather fans, alabaster grinding-stones, copper axes and borers, wooden boomerangs, bone bracelets, female idols made of clay and beads of shell, carnelian and blue-glazed steatite.

5. B. Schönbäck, p. 43.
6. W. B. Emery, 1965, p. 125
7. ibid., p. 125.

## The end of the A-Group

The A-Group, which is thought to have continued in Nubia to the end of the second dynasty in Egypt (−2780), was followed by a period of marked cultural decline and poverty. This period lasted from the beginning of the Egyptian third dynasty (−2780) to the sixth dynasty (−2258). That is to say, it was contemporary with what is known in Egypt as the Old Kingdom period.[8] The culture found in Nubia during this era was termed the B-Group by the early archaeologists, who worked in the area. They claimed that Lower Nubia during the Egyptian Old Kingdom was inhabited by a distinct native group different from the preceding A-Group.[9] Though some scholars[10] still consider it valid,[11] this hypothesis has been rejected by others.[12] However, the existence of the B-Group as such is now generally held to be doubtful.[13]

The continuity of A-Group features in the graves of the so-called B-Group culture makes it probable that they were simply graves of impoverished A-Group people when their culture was on the decline. These new features, recognizable in the B-Group and which differentiate it in some aspects from its predecessor, were perhaps the outcome of the general decline and poverty. The cause of this decline may be found in the repeated hostile activities against Nubia of Egypt since its unification, and the formation of a strong centralized state under one sovereign.

## Egypt in Nubia

From very early times the ancient Egyptians were dazzled by Nubia because of its riches in gold, incense, ivory, ebony, oils, semi-precious stones and other luxury goods, and they continuously endeavoured to bring the trade and economic resources of that land under their own control.[14] Thus we see that the history of Nubia is almost inseparable from that of Egypt. An ebony tablet from the time of Hor-aha, the first king of the Egyptian first dynasty, seems to celebrate a victory over Nubia,[15] but the exact nature of the king's activity against the Nubians is as yet unknown. It might have been only a military movement planned to safeguard his southern frontier at the First Cataract.[16] The Egyptian artefacts discovered

8. ibid., pp. 124, 127.
9. G. A. von Reisner, 1910–27, pp. 313–48.
10. W. B. Emery, 1965, pp. 127–9.
11. B. G. Trigger, 1965, p. 78.
12. H. S. Smith, 1966, p. 118.
13. F. Hintze, 1968.
14. B. G. Trigger, 1965, p. 79.
15. W. M. F. Petrie, 1901, p. 20 and Plates 1 and 2.
16. T. Säve-Söderbergh, 1941.

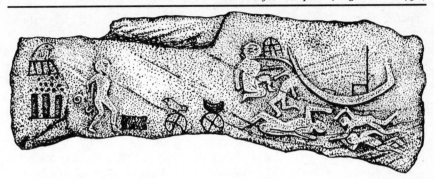

FIG. 9.4 *The inscription of King Djer at Jebel Sheikh Suliman*

at Faras[17] in the A-Group graves which belong to the reign of Djer and Ouadji, the third and fourth rulers of the first dynasty, also indicate contact between the two countries even in that remote time.

However, the earliest record of Egyptian conquest in Nubia is the very important document now exhibited in the Antiquities Garden of the Sudan National Museum in Khartoum. This was a scene originally engraved on a sandstone slab on the top of a small knoll, known as Jebel Sheikh Suliman, about seven miles south of Wadi Halfa town on the west bank of the Nile.[18] It belongs to the reign of King Djer, the third king of the first dynasty already mentioned. The scene records a battle in the Nile waged by King Djer against the Nubians.

At the extreme right of the scene there is a first-dynasty-style boat, with its vertical stern and high prow. Many corpses float below the boat, while a figure (a Nubian chieftain perhaps) hangs from its prow. To the left of this are two wheel-like designs, which are the hieroglyphic signs portraying a village with crossroads which signify a town. To the left of the town signs we see the ripple sign of water (probably denoting that the cataract region was the field of battle). Then a figure of a man is seen with his arms tied behind his back and holding a bow which in Egyptian is called Zeti, and which personifies Ta-Zeti, the land of the bow, meaning Nubia. Behind this figure is the name of King Djer on what is probably a palace façade.[19]

Another record of Egyptian hostile actions in Nubia is a fragment of an inscribed stone from Hierakonpolis (El-Kom-el-Ahmar on the left bank of the Nile north of Idfu) which shows King Kasekhem of the second dynasty kneeling on a prisoner representing Nubia. But the actual subjugation of Nubia seems to have come in the reign of Snefru, the founder of the fourth dynasty. The Palermo Stone[20] tells us that King

17. F. L. Griffith, 1921, pp. 1–18.
18. A. J. Arkell, 1950, pp. 27–30.
19. N. M. Sherif, pp. 17–18.
20. J. H. Breasted, 1906, Vol. I, p. 146.

Snefru destroyed Ta-Nehasyu, the Land of the Nubians,[21] and captured 7000 prisoners and 200 000 cattle and sheep.

After the military operations of Khasekhem and Snefru the Nubians seem to have accepted Egyptian supremacy, for it is evident that the Egyptians found no difficulty in exploiting the vast mineral resources of Nubia. The diorite deposits west of Toshka were quarried for stone for royal statues, and inscriptions of Cheops, the owner of the great pyramid at Giza, Dedefre, and Sahure of the fifth dynasty (−2563 to −2423) were engraved on the rocks there by successive expeditions. To exploit effectively the mineral resources of the land they conquered, the Egyptians colonized Nubia. Recent archaeological discoveries at Buhen, just below the Second Cataract, have shown the existence of a purely Egyptian colony at Buhen in the fourth and fifth dynasties. One of the industries of this Egyptian settlement was working copper, as is shown by the furnaces and remains of copper ore found in it. This indicates the existence of copper deposits somewhere in the region. The names of several kings of the fourth and fifth dynasties were found there on papyrus and jar sealings.[22]

Moreover, it is very probable that the Egyptians extended their authority even over the land south of the Second Cataract at least as far as Dakka some 133 kilometres south of Buhen. An Old Kingdom inscription discovered by the author at Dakka shows that the Egyptians were searching for minerals in that part of Nubia.[23]

Two records of King Merenre discovered at the First Cataract[24] may be taken as an indication that Egypt's southern border was at Aswan during the sixth dynasty (−2434 to −2242); yet it seems that the Egyptians even at that period exerted some sort of political influence over the Nubian tribes, for these records show that King Merenre came to the district of the First Cataract to receive the homage of the chiefs of Medju, Irtet and Wawat, which were presumably tribal regions south of the First Cataract.

Peace reigned in Nubia during the sixth dynasty and the Egyptians recognized the great importance of the commercial potentialities of that land and its significance for the economic well-being of their own country. Trade was well organized and conducted by the able monarch of Aswan, the importance of which increased enormously both as a trading centre between the north and the south and also as a frontier control post. The records of these monarchs inscribed in their tombs on the west bank of the Nile at Aswan furnish researchers with much interesting information on the conditions existing in Nubia at that time. This evidence shows that Nubia seems to have been divided into a number of regions with independent rulers.

21. A. H. Gardiner, 1961.
22. W. B. Emery, 1963, pp. 116–20.
23. F. Hintze, 1965, p. 14.
24. J. H. Breasted, 1906, Vol. I, pp. 317–18.

The most revealing of the inscriptions of these Aswan nobles relates to the life of Harkhuf, the famous caravan leader who served in the reigns of Merenre and Pepi II. He led four missions to the land of Yam, a region not yet identified but certainly beyond the Second Cataract to the south. Three of these expeditions[25] were made during the reign of King Merenre and the fourth under King Pepi II. On the first journey Harkhuf and his father were commissioned to 'explore a road to Yam', a mission that took them seven months to accomplish. The second journey, which Harkhuf made alone, lasted for eight months. In this journey he took the Elephantine road (the desert road starting on the west bank at Aswan) and returned through Irtet, Mekher and Tereres. Here Harkhuf makes it clear that the lands of Irtet and Setu were under the jurisdiction of a single ruler. His third journey was undertaken along the oasis route. During this journey he learned that the chief of Yam had gone to Libya to conquer it. He followed him into that country and managed to appease him. He returned from this journey 'with 300 donkeys loaded with incense, ebony, oil, panther skins, elephant tusks, tree trunks and many other beautiful objects'. When he passed north through the territories of Irtet, Setu and Wawat, which were now united under one chief, Harkhuf was conducted by a military escort from Yam. On the fourth and last expedition Harkhuf brought back from the land of Yam a dancing dwarf for the young King Pepi II, who was extremely delighted with it.

But from the tombs of Pepinakht, another monarch of Elephantine who held office under King Pepi II, we learn that in spite of the general good relations between the Egyptians and the Nubians (which certainly was profitable to both) during the sixth dynasty peace was at times seriously disturbed in Nubia. It seems that there were periods of trouble when Egypt was compelled to resort to force of arms. Pepinakht was sent once to 'hack up Wawat and Irtet'. He may be regarded as successful in his errand for he killed large numbers of Nubians as well as capturing prisoners. He made a second expedition to the south with the aim of 'pacifying these countries'. This time he was able to bring two Nubian chiefs to the Egyptian court.

## The C-Group period

Towards the end of the Egyptian Old Empire[26] or sometime during the period of Egyptian history called by Egyptologists the First Intermediate Period ( − 2240 to − 2150)[27] there appeared in Lower Nubia a new independent culture (with different characteristic objects and different burial traditions) known to archaeologists as the C-Group. Similar to its

25. ibid., Vol. I, pp. 333–5.
26. B. G. Trigger, 1965, p. 87.
27. A. J. Arkell, 1961, p. 46.

forerunner, the A-Group, this culture was also a Chalcolithic culture. It lasted in this part of the Nile valley up to the time when Nubia was completely egyptianized in the sixteenth century before our era. The northern limit of the C-Group culture was at the village of Kubanieh North in Egypt[28] but the southern border has not yet been demarcated for certain, though some remains of the culture have been found as far south as Akasha at the southern end of the Second Cataract region. This makes it probable that the southern boundary of the C-Group was situated somewhere in the Batn-el-Hagar area.

Of the origin of the C-Group culture or the ethnic group to which it belonged, nothing definite is yet known. Owing to the lack of any substantial evidence on this problem, archaeologists have been led to put forward various hypothetical theories.[29] One of these theories suggests that this culture might be a continuation of its predecessor the A-Group, for they were related to each other.[30] Another theory claimed that the culture grew out of influences introduced into Nubia by the arrival of a new people. The supporters of this theory differed among themselves on the question of the original home of these new people and on the direction from which they came. Cultural and anatomical data have been cited to support the various arguments. Some claim that the new people immigrated into Lower Nubia from the eastern desert or the region of the river Atbara.[31] Others believe that they came from the west, specifically from Libya.[32] A recent theory rejects the migration hypothesis and sees the C-Group culture as the outcome of a cultural evolution. However, a great deal is yet to be discovered about the archaeology of the areas concerned and until extensive scientific research is carried out there, these theories will remain hypotheses only.

It seems clear that the C-Group were essentially cattle-herding people who lived in small camps or occasionally settled in villages. The houses discovered in the region of Wadi Halfa were of two types: one had round rooms, the walls of which were built of stones plastered with mud, and the other type had square rooms built of mud-brick.[33] Their basic characteristics are inferred from the large number of rock pictures of cattle and the prominence of cattle in their burial rites.

The earliest burials of the C-Group culture are characterized by small stone superstructures over round or oval pits. The semi-contracted body was laid on its right side with the head oriented east and often placed on a straw pillow. The body was frequently wrapped in a leather garment. This type of grave gave way to another of large stone superstructures over

28. H. Junker, 1919–22, p. 35.
29. M. Bietak, 1961–65, pp. 1–82.
30. G. A. Reisner, 1910–27, p. 333.
31. C. M. Firth, pp. 11–12.
32. W. B. Emery and L. P. Kirwan, 1935, p. 4.
33. T. Säve-Söderbergh, 1965, p. 48.

rectangular pits, often with rounded corners and sometimes lined with stone slabs. A third type, which is later in date, is also found among the C-Group. Now we find brick chapels often built against the north or east of the stone superstructures. Burials were commonly oriented north to south. Animals were buried in the graves. Sometimes skulls of oxen or goats painted with patterns in red and black were placed all around the superstructures. The grave-goods consisted of different forms of pottery, stone, bone and ivory bracelets, shell ear-rings, bone and faience beads, leather sandals, mother-of-pearl discs for armlets and Egyptian scarabs. Sometimes bronze mirrors as well as weapons (daggers, short swords and battle-axes) are found in the C-Group graves.[34]

Despite increasing contact with Egypt, the C-Group culture continued to develop along its own lines, adopting neither Egyptian technology, nor religious beliefs, nor literacy. One of the most important characteristics of this culture is its pottery. It is handmade and is normally in the form of bowls, frequently decorated by impressed or incised geometric patterns, which were often filled with a white pigment. A typical C-Group stone tool is the polished colt of green stone (nephrite).

FIG. 9.5 *Typical C-group graves (after Steindorff)*

34. ibid., pp. 49–50.

FIG. 9.6 *Types of C-group pottery*

# The Middle Kingdom

The rulers of the Egyptian Middle Kingdom put an end to the internal troubles of their country and united it under their sway. They then directed their attention to the land south of Egypt, namely, Nubia. This move began under the kings of the Theban eleventh dynasty. On a fragment from the temple of Gebelein in Upper Egypt, Menthuhotep II is depicted striking his enemies, among whom we find Nubians. A rock inscription of Menthuhotep III at the First Cataract refers to an expedition 'with ships to Wawat' which is the Shellal–Wadi Halfa reach of the Nile. Moreover, there are references which make it probable that the Egyptians of the eleventh dynasty had occupied Nubia as far south as Wadi Halfa. There are, for instance, several graffiti on two hills west and north of Abdel Gadir village on the west bank of the Nile just below the Second Cataract which mention Antef, Menthuhotep and Sebekhotep (names common in the eleventh dynasty), and which relate to quarrying, hunting and clerical work.[35] However, whatever the situation in Nubia might have been during the eleventh dynasty, it was under the twelfth dynasty ( − 1991 to − 1786) that Nubia was effectively occupied as far as Semna, where the southern border of the kingdom was firmly established. It was here that the remarkable stele of Senusret III, the fifth king of the dynasty, was set up to provide an unmistakable boundary mark. The stele forbade any Nubian to pass 'downstream or overland or by boat, [also] any herds of Nubians, apart from any Nubian who shall come to trade in Iken or upon any good business that may be done with them'.[36] Iken is now known to be the fortress of Mirgissa, about 40 kilometres north of Semna.[37]

Several pieces of evidence indicate that the permanent occupation of this part of Nubia was begun by Amenemhet I, the founder of the twelfth dynasty. He is thought to be partly of Nubian origin. The descent of King Amenemhet is deduced from a papyrus now in the museum of Leningrad, the sole aim of which was to make legitimate his coming to the throne of Egypt. According to this papyrus, King Snefru of the fourth dynasty called in a priest to amuse him. When the king asked him about the future, the priest foretold a time of hardship and misery in Egypt which would end when 'a king shall come belonging to the south, Ameny by name, the son of a woman of Ta-Zeti [Nubia]'. The name Ameny is the abbreviation of the name Amenemhet.[38] A rock inscription found near Krosko in Lower Nubia dating from the twenty-ninth year of Amenemhet's reign states that his troops reached Krosko in order to 'overthrow Wawat'. In the teachings he left to his son we hear Amenemhet say: 'I seized the

35. A. J. Arkell, 1961, pp. 56 and 58–9.
36. A. H. Gardiner, 1961, p. 135.
37. J. Vercoutter, 1964, p. 62.
38. A. H. Gardiner, 1961, p. 126.

people of Wawat and captured the people of Medju.'[39] Once again, inscriptions of the same king west of Abu Simbel show quarrying activities in Lower Nubia during the last part of his reign.

The occupation of Nubia commenced by Amenemhet I was completed by his son and successor Senusret I.[40] On a large inscribed stone put up in the eighteenth year of Senusret I at Buhen by an officer with the name Mentuhotep, the Theban war-god Montu is shown presenting to the king a line of bound war-prisoners from ten Nubian localities. The name of each locality is contained in an oval frame beneath the head and shoulders of the captive who represents the people of the said locality. Amongst the conquered lands mentioned on this sandstone stele are Kush, Sha'at and Shemyk. Sha'at is the present island of Sai,[41] some 190 kilometres south of Buhen, while Shemyk, according to a recently discovered inscription, is the Dal Cataract region 40 kilometres downstream of Sai Island.

Kush, though soon used by the Egyptians to describe a large southern land, was originally a restricted Nubian territory first heard of during the Middle Kingdom.[42] If the Buhen stele enumerates place names from north to south as do other known documents from the same period,[43] then Kush was not only north of Sha'at but also north of Shemyk. Now, we know that the latter is Dal Island or the Dal Cataract region north of Sai Island; and thus we can safely locate Kush somewhere north of Dal and south of the Second Cataract or Semna.[44]

A second indication of the victory over Nubia won by Senusret I, which left the Pharaohs of the twelfth dynasty in full control of the country north of Semna, is provided by an inscription found in the tomb of Ameny, the monarch of Beni Hassan in Egypt. This tells us that Ameny sailed southward in the company of the king himself and 'passed beyond Kush and reached the end of the earth'.[45]

The reasons which prompted the Egyptians to occupy part of Nubia were both economic and defensive. Economically they wanted, on the one hand, to secure skins, ivory and ebony and, on the other hand, to exploit the mineral wealth of Nubia.[46] The security of their kingdom necessitated the defence of its southern frontier against the Nubians and the desert dwellers to their east. The strategy was to maintain a buffer between the border of Egypt proper in the region of the First Cataract and the land south of Semna, which constituted the source of real menace to them,

39. J. H. Breasted, 1906, Vol. 1, p. 483.
40. A. J. Arkell, 1961, pp. 59–60.
41. J. Vercoutter, 1958, pp. 147–8.
42. G. Posener, 1958, p. 47.
43. ibid., p. 60.
44. ibid., p. 50.
45. A. H. Gardiner, 1961, p. 134.
46. B. G. Trigger, 1965, p. 94.

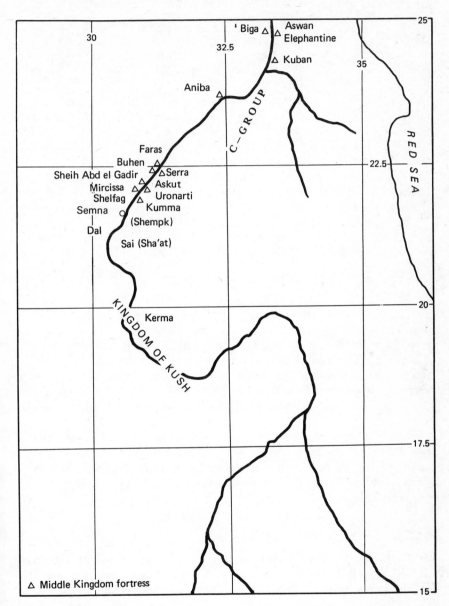

FIG. 9.7 *Nubia, 1580 before our era*

in order to control traffic along the Nile and eradicate any threat to their country from Kush.

The defensive nature of the Egyptian occupation of Nubia during the Middle Kingdom period is clearly manifested by the number and the strength of the fortresses the kings of the twelfth dynasty were compelled to build in the occupied territory. A late Middle Kingdom papyrus discovered in a tomb near the Ramesseum at Luxor[47] names seventeen Nubian forts between Semna in the south and Shellal in the north. They fall into two groups, those to the north of the Second Cataract intended to maintain a strong grip on the native population,[48] namely, the C-Group people, and those built on eminences between the Second Cataract and Semna to protect boats in trouble in the shoals and defend the frontier.[49] That these forts were clearly built for defence is even shown by the names assigned to them, such as 'Repelling the Tribes', 'Repressing ...', 'Curbing the Deserts', 'Repelling the Inu' and 'Repelling the Mazaiu'.[50]

The strength of these forts and the effort made to render them impregnable can be seen from the fortress at Buhen, which was one of the best-preserved forts in Nubia before it was flooded by the waters of the new Aswan High Dam. This formidable Middle Kingdom fortress consisted of an elaborate series of fortifications within fortifications built on a rectangular plan measuring 172 by 160 metres.[51] The defence system consisted of a brick wall 4·8 metres thick and at least 10 metres high with towers at regular intervals. At the bottom of this main wall was a brick-paved rampart, protected by a series of round bastions with double rows of loopholes. The whole fort was surrounded by a dry ditch cut into the bed rock 6·5 metres deep. The ditch was 8·4 metres wide and the other scarp was heightened by brickwork. There were two gates on the east side facing the Nile, and a third, heavily fortified, on the west side facing the desert.

Following the collapse of the Middle Kingdom and the Hyksos (Asiatic tribes) invasion, the Egyptians lost their control over Nubia. The forts were ransacked and burnt by the natives, who seem to have seized the opportunity of the collapse of the central government in Egypt to regain their independence.

## Kerma (−1730 to −1580)

We have already noticed that the southern boundary of the Egyptian Middle Kingdom was unquestionably fixed at Semna by Senusret III. But the important excavations carried out by the American archaeologist

47. W. B. Emery, 1965, p. 143.
48. A. H. Gardiner, 1961, p. 135.
49. A. J. Arkell, 1961, p. 61.
50. A. H. Gardiner, 1961, p. 135.
51. W. B. Emery, 1960, pp. 7–8.

G. A. Reisner between 1913 and 1916 at Kerma, a short distance above the Third Cataract and 150 miles south of Semna as the crow flies, revealed what has come to be known as the Kerma culture. This culture has since been the subject of conflicting interpretations from scholars.

The ancient site of Kerma comprises two remarkable edifices locally known as the Western Dufufa and the Eastern Dufufa. The former is a solid mass of sun-dried brick and the latter is a funerary chapel, also in mud-brick, surrounded by a large cemetery of mound graves. Both buildings are typical of Middle Kingdom construction. In the Western Dufufa, Reisner found fragments of broken alabaster vases with the cartouches of Pepi I and II of the sixth dynasty together with those of Amenemhet I and Senusret I. Beside the Eastern Dufufa was unearthed an inscribed stone relating that the king's sole companion Antef had been dispatched to repair a building in Inebu, using the word *Amenemhet maa kheru* which means the walls of Amenemhet the Justified. In a burial mound near this funerary chapel were found the lower part of a statue of Hepzefia (prince of Asyut in Egypt, whose tomb has been found there), a statue of his wife Sennuwy and fragments of other statues of officials and kings. In the light of these discoveries, Reisner concluded[52] that: (*a*) the walls underneath the Western Dufufa are those of an Old Kingdom trading post; (*b*) the Western Dufufa was, in the Middle Kingdom, the southernmost stronghold in the chain of forts built by the Egyptians, between Aswan and Kerma, to safeguard their interests in Nubia; (*c*) Kerma was the headquarters of Egyptian Governors-General, the first of whom might have been Hapidjefa; (*d*) the Egyptian Governors-General were buried in the cemetery near the Eastern Dufufa in an Egyptian fashion; and (*e*) when the Hyksos invaded Egypt the fortified outpost at Kerma was destroyed by the Nubians.

Reisner's interpretation of the archaeological evidence discovered at Kerma was first questioned by Junker.[53] The Western Dufufa was too small for a fort and was also dangerously isolated, being situated 400 kilometres away from the nearest Egyptian fort at Semna. Moreover, the raw materials, such as graphite, copper oxide, hematite, mica, resin, rock crystal, carnelian, ostrich egg-shell, discovered in the various rooms indicate that the Western Dufufa was a fortified trading post rather than an administrative centre.

As for the cemetery, Reisner's view, that it was the burial place of Egyptian Governors, was based solely on the discovery of the statues of Hapidjefa and his wife in one of the large burial mounds. The mode of burial in these large graves of Kerma was entirely Nubian. Here mummification was not practised and the dead man was buried on a bed with his wives, children and attendants in the same grave. Now, bearing

---

52. G. A. Reisner, 1923a.
53. H. Junker, 1921.

in mind that these graves are Egyptian neither in their construction nor in their method of burial, and knowing that the Egyptians dreaded being buried abroad mainly because they might lose the appropriate burial rites, it becomes peculiarly difficult to believe that a person of Hapidjefa's social and political status would have been buried in a foreign land in a fashion utterly alien to Egyptian religious beliefs. Moreover, among the things found in the supposed tumulus of Hapidjefa were numerous grave-goods unquestionably dating from the Second Intermediate Period or the Hyksos period.[54] From this, Säve-Söderbergh and Arkell[55] concluded that the statues found in this mound grave had been exchanged by Egyptian traders for Nubian commodities from the local princes of Kerma during the Second Intermediate Period.

Thus Reisner's theory concerning the Western Dufufa and the cemetery around the Eastern Dufufa has been generally rejected. Instead most scholars advocated the view that the Western Dufufa was only an Egyptian trading post, while the cemetery was the burial ground of the native princes.

Hintze, re-examining the different theories put forward regarding the Kerma problem, sees that they 'contained inner contradictions making their correctness dubious'.[56] In the first place he notes that the arguments raised by Junker, rejecting Reisner's interpretation, hold good also to refute Junker's own assumption that the Western Dufufa was a fortified trading post. Hintze also considers it unlikely that an Egyptian fortified trading post would have existed in this part of Nubia at this time, particularly if Kerma is taken as the political seat of Kush (as some of Reisner's opposers hold),[57] which was the traditional enemy of Egypt during the Middle Kingdom. And as all the scholars whose views he has re-examined agree that the cemetery is a Nubian cemetery and that the Eastern Dufufa is a funerary chapel attached to it, Hintze points out the improbability of the Pharaoh sending an Egyptian official to 'vile Kush' in order to repair a chapel to a Nubian cemetery. Lastly, Hintze stresses what has already been shown by Säve-Söderbergh, namely, that the cemetery belongs to the Second Intermediate Period; that is to say, that it is later than the Western Dufufa and therefore the supposed Governors of the Western Dufufa in the Middle Kingdom could not be buried there.

All these considerations led Hintze to abandon once and for all the 'conception of an Egyptian trading post' at Kerma. To him Kerma is simply the 'centre of a native Nubian culture and the residence of a native dynasty'. The Western Dufufa was the residence of the native ruler of Kush and it was destroyed by the Egyptian troops at the beginning of the New Kingdom.

54. T. Säve-Söderbergh, 1941.
55. A. J. Arkell, 1961, p. 71.
56. F. Hintze, 1964.
57. A. J. Arkell, 1961, p. 72.

This is a simple theory which sounds nearer to the truth especially as regards the evidence from the cemetery. The date of the objects found in the graves and the mode of their construction and burial rites clearly show that they were not built for the Middle Kingdom Egyptian Governors-General. But substantial evidence is still needed to prove that the Western Dufufa was the residence of the native ruler of Kush. The existence of an ordinary Egyptian trading post at Kerma during the Middle Kingdom cannot be ruled out as easily as Hintze contends. The site dug by Reisner is the only site so far excavated in the Dongola region, and even this single site is not yet fully excavated. The Dongola area is rich in Kerma sites, and until systematic archaeological research is carried out there, a great deal will remain unknown regarding the Kerma culture.

## The Kingdom of Kush

As the geographical name Kush is connected with Kerma[58] and as the tumuli at Kerma clearly show that they were the burials of strong native rulers who had commercial and diplomatic relations with the Hyksos kings in Egypt, it seems more likely that Kerma was the capital of the kingdom of Kush. This kingdom flourished during what is known in Egyptian history as the Second Intermediate Period ( − 1730 to − 1580). The existence of this kingdom, whose ruler was called the Prince of Kush, is now known from a variety of documentary evidence. The first stele of Kamose,[59] the last king of the Egyptian seventeenth dynasty and probably the first king who raised the banner of organized struggle against the Hyksos, depicts the political situation in the Nile valley at that time. This stele shows the existence of an independent kingdom in Kush, with its northern frontier fixed at Elephantine, an Egyptian state in Upper Egypt, situated between Elephantine in the south and Cusae in the north and finally the Hyksos kingdom in Lower Egypt. Another stele[60] tells us that Kamose captured on the oasis route a message sent by Apophis, the Hyksos king, to the ruler of Kush seeking his aid against the Egyptian king. Moreover, two stelae discovered at Buhen show that two officials by the names of Sepedher[61] and Ka[62] served under the ruler of Kush. The kingdom of Kush, which controlled the whole of Nubia south of Elephantine after the collapse of the Middle Kingdom in Egypt following the Hyksos invasion, came to an end when Tuthmose I conquered Nubia beyond the Fourth Cataract.

58. G. Posener, 1958, p. 39; A. J. Arkell, 1961, p. 72.
59. L. Habachi, 1955, p. 195.
60. T. Säve-Söderbergh, 1956, pp. 54–61.
61. Philadelphia, 10984.
62. Khartoum, No. 18.

FIG. 9.8 *Types of Kerma pottery*

## Kerma culture

Typical sites of the Kerma culture have been discovered in Nubia only as far north as Mirgissa,[63] indicating that the Second Cataract was the boundary between the Kerma and C-Group cultures. The characteristic features of the Kerma culture were a thin highly polished black-topped red ware that was made on a potter's wheel; animal-shaped vessels and others decorated with animal motifs; special copper daggers, woodwork decorated with patterns of inlaid ivory figures and mica figures and ornaments sewn on leather caps. Although many of the wares discovered at Kerma undoubtedly manifest a native cultural tradition, the influence of Egyptian techniques of craftsmanship and design cannot be overlooked.[64] It has been suggested that a great deal of the material in question was actually manufactured by Egyptian craftsmen,[65] but it could equally be said that it was produced to meet local taste by native craftsmen who had acquired Egyptian techniques.

Regarding the religious aspect, the characteristic feature of the Kerma culture is the burial rites. A Kerma grave is marked by a dome-shaped

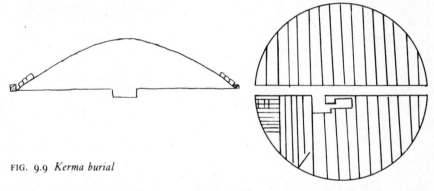

FIG. 9.9 *Kerma burial*

tumulus of earth outlined by a ring of black stones sprinkled over with white pebbles. One of the big tumuli at Kerma Cemetery (K III) consisted of circular brick walls, 90 metres in diameter.[66] Two parallel walls running across the middle of the mound from east to west formed a central corridor which divided the mound into two sections. Other parallel walls ran out at right angles from the two sides of this corridor to the circumference of the circle to the north and south. In the middle of the southern wall of the corridor a doorway opened into a vestibule leading to the

63. J. Vercoutter, 1964, p. 59.
64. B. G. Trigger, 1965, p. 103.
65. A. J. Arkell, 1961, p. 74.
66. G. A. Reisner, 1923a, p. 135.

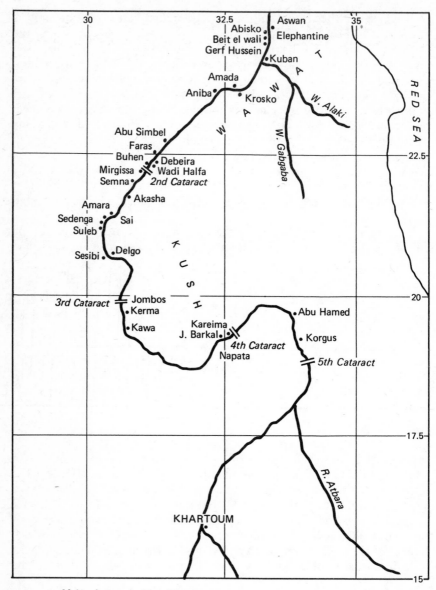

FIG. 9.10 *Nubia during the New Kingdom*

main burial chamber to the east side of it. At Kerma the main burial lay on a bed on the right side. On this bed were put a wooden headrest, an ostrich-feather fan, and a pair of sandals. A large number of pottery vessels were placed beside the bed and round the walls of the chamber. The most striking burial custom at Kerma was the use of human sacrifices. The owner of the grave was accompanied by 200 to 300 persons, the majority being women and children. They were buried alive in the central corridor.

## The New Kingdom ( − 1580 to − 1050)

When the Egyptians had re-established themselves after the liberation of their country from the Hyksos, they once again began to turn their attention to their southern frontier and this led to the largest conquest of Nubia ever achieved by Egypt throughout its ancient history.

The first stele of Kamose, already referred to, describes how he was situated between a king in Lower Egypt and another in Kush. It also states that his courtiers were satisfied with the state of affairs on Egypt's southern frontier as Elephantine was strongly held. But a passage in the second stele[67] shows that Kamose waged war against the Nubians before attacking the Hyksos. In view of the courtiers' statement that the frontier at Elephantine was safe and strong, it is likely that Kamose had just mounted a punitive expedition against the Nubians and this may explain the existence of the royal names of Kamose near Toshka in Lower Nubia.

The occupation of Nubia was accomplished by Amosis, successor of Kamose and founder of the Egyptian eighteenth dynasty. The main source of our information on his military activities in Nubia and also those of his immediate followers is the autobiography of the Admiral Ahmose, a simple shipmaster-captain, son of Ebana, inscribed on the walls of his tomb at El Kab in Egypt. Here we are told that 'His Majesty went up to Khent Hennefer [an unidentified region in Nubia] to overthrow the Nubians after he had destroyed the Asiatics'. Amosis was able to rebuild and enlarge the fortress of Buhen and erect a temple there. He may even have advanced to Sai Island, 190 kilometres upstream from Buhen, for a statue of him was found there together with inscriptions relating to himself and his wife.[68]

However, it was Tuthmose I ( − 1530 to − 1520) who accomplished the conquest of the northern Sudan; thus bringing the independence of the kingdom of Kush to an end. On his arrival at Tumbus, the southern end of the Third Cataract, he set up his great inscription. From there he continued his push southwards, effectively occupying the whole reach between Kerma and Kurgus, 50 miles south of Abu Hamed, where he

67. T. Säve-Söderbergh, 1956, p. 57.
68. J. Vercoutter, 1956; 1958.

left an inscription and perhaps built a fort.[69] Thus Nubia came to be fully controlled by Egypt and a new and remarkable era in its history began, which left permanent marks on its cultural life throughout the following periods.

## Nubia under the eighteenth dynasty

From a rock inscription between Aswan and Philae dating from the first year of Tuthmose II[70] we know that there was a revolt in Nubia after the death of Tuthmose I. According to this inscription a messenger arrived to bring to His Majesty's ears the news that Kush had started to rebel and that the chief of Kush and other princes to the north of him had conspired together. It also informs us that an expedition had been sent and the rebels quelled. After this punitive mission peace was restored and firmly established in Nubia for some years.

Peace prevailed throughout the reign of Queen Hatshepsut who succeeded Tuthmose II. The most important monument of her time in Nubia is the magnificent temple she built inside the Middle Kingdom citadel walls at Buhen.[71] It was dedicated to Horus, the falcon-headed god, Lord of Buhen. The importance of this temple lies in its great historical and artistic interest. Here one finds reliefs of the finest eighteenth-dynasty style and execution, and the colours on the walls are still well preserved. Later, the temple was usurped by Tuthmose III, who distorted the original design and systematically and ruthlessly defaced the cartouches and the portraits of Queen Hatshepsut.

The temple is built of Nubian sandstone and consists of two principal parts: a forecourt, and a rectangular building with a row of columns on its north, south and east sides. Queen Hatshepsut also built a temple dedicated to the goddess Hathor at Faras, on the west bank of the Nile; just on the modern political border between Egypt and the Sudan.[72]

The Annals of Tuthmose III inscribed on the walls of the great temple of Amen at Karnak show us the payment of the tribute of Wawat for eight years and of Kush for five years. This clearly indicates that the tribute of Nubia regularly flowed into the King's Chest,[73] and that peaceful conditions continued in the reign of Tuthmose III. In his second year he rebuilt in stone the ruined mud-brick temple of Senusret III at Semna West and dedicated it to the Nubian gods Dedwen, Khnum and to the deified Senusret III. This temple ranks among the best-preserved free-standing temples of pre-Ptolemaic date in the whole Nile valley. The walls are covered with scenes in relief, hieroglyphic inscriptions and painted

69. A. J. Arkell, 1961, p. 84.
70. J. H. Breasted, 1906, Vol. 1, pp. 119–22.
71. D. R. MacIver and C. L. Woolley.
72. F. L. Griffith, 1921, p. 83.
73. A. J. Arkell, 1961, p. 88.

work. The text and scenes are undoubtedly the work of first-class crafts-men.[74] He also built small temples in the forts of Semna East, Uronarti, Faras and perhaps Sai Island.

Tuthmose III was succeeded by Amenophis II during whose reign Nubia was at peace. He finished building the temple of Amada (an important town in Lower Nubia) started by his father Tuthmose III. On a stele dating from the third year of his reign and set up in that temple Amenophis II records his victorious return from his campaign in Asia with the bodies of seven princes 'whom he had slain with his own club'. Six captive princes were ordered to be hanged before the walls of his capital at Thebes. And the stele tells us that the seventh prince 'was sent by ship to Nubia and hanged upon the enclosure wall surrounding Napata in order that the victorious might of His Majesty be seen for eternity'.[75]

From the reign of Tuthmose IV, who followed Amenophis II, we have a record at the island of Konosso near Philae of one successful expedition to quell a revolt in Nubia. This record is dated the year eight of Tuthmose IV.

Tuthmose IV was succeeded by his son Amenophis III who led a campaign against Nubia as far as Karei in the fifth year of his reign. He erected at Soleb, on the west bank of the Nile 220 kilometres south of Wadi Halfa, the most magnificent temple in the whole of Nubia. The temple was dedicated to his own living image. Amenophis III also built a temple for his queen, Teye, at Sedeinga, 13 miles north of Soleb on the same side of the Nile.

The political upheaval in Egypt caused by the religious revolution of Amenophis IV ( − 1370 to − 1352) did not disrupt peace in Nubia and building activities continued as before. At Sesebi south of Soleb opposite Delgo, Amenophis IV, before he changed his name to Akhenaton, built a group of three temples on a common substructure.[76] They were inside a small walled town which included a small shrine dedicated to Aton the new god. It seems that he also founded the town of Gem-aten which was situated at Kawa opposite modern Dongola. At Kawa a small temple was also built by his successor Tutankhamun.[77] At Faras, Huy, viceroy of Nubia under Tutankhamun, built a temple and a walled settlement.[78]

The end of the eighteenth dynasty brought trouble in Egypt but seems to have had no effect on peace and stability in Nubia. On the whole Nubia developed peacefully during the whole of the eighteenth dynasty.

## Nubia under the nineteenth dynasty

From the time of Akhenaton onwards Egypt became continuously weaker

74. R. A. Caminos, 1964a, p. 85.
75. A. H. Gardiner, 1961, p. 200.
76. H. W. Fairman, 1938, pp. 151–6.
77. M. F. L. Macadam, 1949, p. 12.
78. F. L. Griffith, 1921, p. 83.

internally and externally. Akhenaton was a man of dreams and his religious movement brought much harm to the empire. Moreover, he was succeeded by feeble Pharaohs who were completely unable to find a solution to the problem of the time. The entire land was in a state of unrest. There was every reason to fear open civil war and general anarchy. At this critical moment Egypt was lucky enough to find a deliverer in the person of a general named Horemheb, who was an able and experienced leader. During the reign of Tutankhamun, Horemheb toured Nubia after the restoration of the old regime.[79] When later he usurped the throne of Egypt he appeared again in Nubia. Although this occasion is described, on the walls of his commemorative rock temple at Silsila in Upper Egypt, as a military expedition, it appears to have been rather a visit by a usurper to make sure of his position in a region of vital importance to him. However, Horemheb won the loyalty of the Egyptian administration of Nubia; and this is shown by the fact that Paser, viceroy of Nubia in the previous reign, continued to fill the same post under him.

Ramses I (−1320 to −1318), the real founder of the nineteenth dynasty, succeeded Horemheb. In the second year of his reign he put up a stele in the temple of Hatshepsut at Buhen on which he tells us that he increased the number of the priests of that temple and its slaves, and that he added new buildings.

After the death of Ramses I, his son Seti I (−1318 to −1298) ascended the throne. He exploited the Nubian gold mines to bring money into his treasury to pay for his enormous building schemes. To increase the output of the Wadi-el-Alaki mines he dug a well on the road leading south-east from Kuban in Lower Nubia, but he failed to reach water, and the attempt to improve the gold supply from this region was not successful. In Upper Nubia Seti I built a town at Amara West, some 180 kilometres south of Wadi Halfa. He probably also built the great temple of Amon at Jebel Barkal (the ancient Egyptian dw-w3b: The Holy Mountain) near Kereima. There is very little evidence of military activities in Nubia during the reign of Seti I. It seems that nothing necessitated serious military expeditions, but this does not mean that small punitive missions may have been dispatched to Nubia.

Seti was succeeded by his son Ramses II (−1320 to −1318). We have numerous references to military activity in Nubia during the rule of this Pharaoh who reigned for a long time, but as they give no dates or place names they are not very useful.[80] In general, peace seems to have prevailed in Nubia during the time of Ramses II and this is supported by the enormous building activities undertaken by him throughout Nubia.

In the third year of his reign we find Ramses II at Memphis consulting with his officials about the possibility of opening the Alaki country to

79. A. J. Arkell, 1961, p. 94.
80. W. B. Emery, 1965, p. 193.

develop the gold mines there, which his father had unsuccessfully attempted to exploit. The viceroy of Kush, who was present, explained the difficulty to the king and related the fruitless attempt of his father to supply the route with water. However, another attempt was ordered by the king and it proved successful, for water was reached only twelve cubits below the depth dug by his father, Seti I. At Kuban, where the road leading to the Wadi-el-Alaki mines left the Nile valley, a stele was erected commemorating this achievement.

Ramses II initiated enormous building activities in Nubia. He built temples at Beit-el-Wali, Gerf Hussein, Wadi-es-Sebua, Derr, Abu Simbel and Aksha in Lower Nubia, and at Amara and Barkal in Upper Nubia.

As for Amara, the excavations carried out there[81] have shown that the town was founded by Seti I, while the temple was the work of Ramses II. This town was continuously occupied during the nineteenth and twentieth dynasties. Amara is thought to have been the residence of the viceroy of Kush.[82]

The temple of Abu Simbel, one of the largest rock-cut structures in the whole world, is no doubt a unique piece of architectural work.[83] It is hewn into a great head of sandstone rock on the left bank of the Nile. The site of this great temple was perhaps selected because the place was considered sacred long before the temple was cut there. It was dedicated to Re-Harakhte, the god of the rising sun, who is represented as a man with the head of a falcon wearing the solar disc.

On the façade of the temple of Abu Simbel are four colossal seated statues cut out of the living rock. The seated statues, two on each side of the entrance, represent Ramses II wearing the double crown of Egypt. The entrance opens directly into the great hall where two rows of four-square pillars are seen. On the front of these pillars are gigantic standing statues of the king, again wearing the double crown. On the walls of the great hall, which are 30 feet high, there are scenes and inscriptions concerning religious ceremonies and the Pharaoh's military activities against the Hittites in Syria and the Nubians in the south. In the north and west walls of the same hall are doors leading into several storerooms with only religious reliefs on their walls. From the great hall and through the central door in the west wall, there is a small hall. Its roof is supported by four square pillars and the reliefs on its walls are again of a religious nature. There is another room just before the sanctuary. This room has three doors in its west wall; the two on either side give access to smaller rooms without inscriptions on their walls, and the one in the middle leads into the Holy of Holies in which Ramses II is enthroned as a god beside the three most powerful gods of Egypt, namely, Amon-Re of Thebes, Re-

81. H. W. Fairman, 1938; 1939, pp. 139–44; 1948, pp. 1–11.
82. A. J. Arkell, 1961, p. 94.
83. W. B. Emery, 1965, p. 194.

Harakhte of Heliopolis, the City of the Sun, and Ptah of Memphis, the old capital.

## Administration of Nubia

At the head of the Egyptian administrative machinery in Nubia during the New Kingdom period was the viceroy of Nubia. From the beginning this official bore the title 'Governor of the southern countries' side by side with his title 'King's son'. The former title was the title which really determined his function. At the time of Tuthmose IV, the viceroy of Nubia had the same name as the Crown Prince, who was called Amenophis. In order to distinguish one from the other, the viceroy of Nubia was called the King's son of Kush. Afterwards the new title was given to all viceroys who followed Amenophis. This title might not mean that the viceroys of Nubia were from the royal family; but it might be an indication of the importance of this office and the high authority the viceroy enjoyed. These officials were chosen from reliable men obviously devoted to the Pharaoh to whom they were directly responsible. They were capable administrators.

Nubia was divided into two vast territories. The land between Nekhen (in Upper Egypt) and the Second Cataract, which was known as Wawat, and the whole area south between the Second and Fourth Cataracts was called Kush. The viceroy was at the head of many administrative departments which were clearly modelled on counterparts in Egypt. He was assisted by officials in charge of the various administrative departments needed to rule Nubia. The Nubian towns were under governors responsible to the viceroy. His staff included a Commander of the Archers of Kush and two deputies, one for Wawat and the other for Kush. Under him there were police forces for internal security as well as the garrisons of the various towns and a small army to protect expeditions to the gold mines. An important responsibility of the viceroy of Nubia was the punctual delivery of the tribute of Nubia personally to the vizier in Thebes.[84] In addition, the viceroy of Nubia was also the religious head of the country.

The native tribal chiefs also took part in the administration of Nubia. The Egyptian policy of the time was to win the loyalty of the local princes[85] by allowing them to maintain their sovereignty in their districts.

## Egyptianization of Nubia

The early stages of the Egyptian occupation of Nubia during the New Kingdom encountered resistance. But the Nubians soon settled down under the new Egyptian administration to a peaceful development of their country never before experienced. We have already seen that temples were built all over Nubia by the kings of the eighteenth and nineteenth dynasties.

84. A. J. Arkell, 1961, p. 98.
85. B. G. Trigger, 1965, p. 107.

Then towns important as religious, commercial and administrative centres grew around those temples. Nubia was entirely reorganized on purely Egyptian lines and a completely Egyptian system of administration was set up entailing the presence of a considerable number of Egyptian scribes, priests, soldiers and artisans. This ultimately resulted in complete egyptianization of Nubia. The natives adopted the Egyptian religion and worshipped Egyptian divinities. The old burial customs gave way to Egyptian rites. No longer was the body laid out on its side in a semi-contracted position. Instead, we find the deceased extended on his back or placed in a wooden coffin. The graves of this period were of three types:[86] a plain rectangular pit, a rock-cut shaft with a subterranean end burial chamber, and a rectangular pit with a lateral niche dug on one of the long sides. The grave-goods deposited in these tombs are typically Egyptian of the period. The techniques applied by the Egyptians in arts and architecture were also adopted by the Nubians.

The process of egyptianization which had actually started in Nubia during the Second Intermediate Period was now accelerated to reach its climax. Amongst the important factors which helped to promote speedily the cultural assimilation of the Nubians to the Egyptian mode of life was the policy followed by the Pharaonic administration in Nubia during the New Kingdom. As already mentioned the official policy was to gain the loyalty and support of the native chieftains. Their sons were educated at the royal court in Egypt where 'they heard the speech of the Egyptians in the retinue of the King. This caused them to forget their own language.'[87] Thus they were strongly egyptianized and this of course helped to ensure the loyalty of the Nubian princes to Egypt and to Egyptian culture. It naturally follows that once a chief has been converted to a foreign religion and has accepted for his everyday life the rules of a certain culture, his subjects will follow his example. Egyptianization was first aimed at the indigenous upper class which paved the way for the quick egyptianization of the simple population of Nubia.

One of these local princes who lived in the same way as an upper-class Egyptian of the age was Djehuty-hotep, Prince of Serra (the ancient Teh-Khet), north of Wadi Halfa. He lived during the reign of Queen Hatshepsut and inherited the princedom from his father and was later succeeded by his brother Amenemhet. From a small statuette belonging to Amenemhet (now in the Sudan National Museum) we know that he worked as a scribe at the town of Buhen before he became Prince of 'Teh-Khet'. This shows that during the New Kingdom the native educated class took part in the administration of Nubia along with Egyptians.

The tomb of Djehuty-hotep was discovered one mile east of the Nile

86. W. B. Emery, 1965, p. 178.
87. T. Säve-Söderbergh, 1941, p. 185.

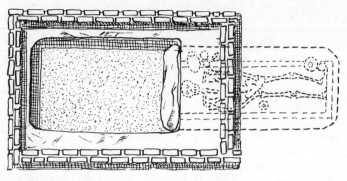

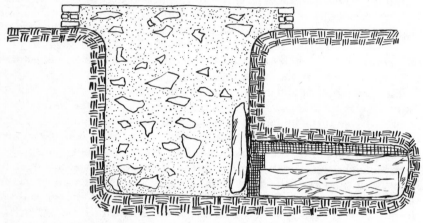

FIG. 9.11 (a) *Type of New Kingdom burial (after W. B. Emery, 1965)*
FIG. 9.11 (b) *Type of New Kingdon burial (after W. B. Emery, 1965)*

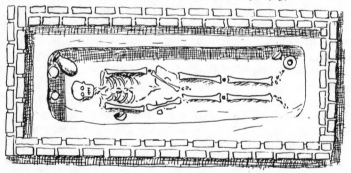

at the village of Debeira, some 20 kilometres north of Wadi Halfa town.[88] It was hewn into a small sandstone hill, and was planned and decorated in an entirely Egyptian fashion. Its scenes depict Prince Djehuty-hotep inspecting work on his farm, receiving homage in the Egyptian way from his serfs, hunting with bow and arrow from a horse-drawn chariot and enjoying a banquet with his guests. It would have been impossible to distinguish him from an Egyptian noble of the New Kingdom had he not inscribed his Nubian, as well as his Egyptian, name. The hieroglyphic inscriptions on the door jambs of the entrance to the tomb depict Horus, probably the goddess Hathor, Lady of Faras, the ancient Ibshek[89] and Anubis, the dog-headed god of the necropolis.

## The Economy of Nubia

The economic importance of Nubia during the New Kingdom is mostly inferred from the lists of tribute on the walls of temples and also from pictorial representation of Nubian goods in the tombs of Egyptian officials responsible for bringing them to the Pharaoh. At this time the Egyptians intensified mining in Nubia, in a manner exceeding any previous exploitation, in order to procure carnelian, haematite, amason stone, turquoise, malachite, granite and amethyst. But the principal product of Nubia was gold. During the reign of King Tuthmose III the annual tribute of Wawat only amounted to 550 pounds.[90] The gold of Nubia came from the mines of the region rich in precious metals around Wadi-el-Alaki and Wadi Gabgada in the eastern desert and also from those mines scattered along the Nile valley as far south as Abu Hamed.[91]

Other Egyptian imports from Nubia consisted of ebony, ivory, incense, oils, cattle, leopards, ostrich eggs and feathers, panther-skins, giraffes and giraffe-tail fly-whisks, greyhounds, baboons and grain. By the end of the eighteenth dynasty we see manufactured goods figuring as part of the tribute of Nubia. In the tomb of Huy, viceroy of Nubia during the reign of Tutankhamun, we find that the tribute from the south included shields, stools, beds and armchairs.[92]

## The End of the New Kingdom

On account of its wealth and also because of the importance of its troops, Nubia towards the close of the New Kingdom started to play a significant role in the internal political affairs of Egypt itself. Disorder, weakness,

88. H. T. Thabit, pp. 81–6.
89. T. Säve-Söderbergh, 1960, p. 30.
90. F. Hintze, 1968, p. 17.
91. J. Vercoutter, 1959, p. 128.
92. N. de G. Davies and A. H. Gardiner, p. 22.

corruption and struggles for power were the characteristic features of the time in Egypt. The competing parties in those struggles, fully appreciating the importance of Nubia in their dealings, endeavoured to win the support of the administration there. King Ramses-Siptah of the nineteenth dynasty went himself to Nubia in the first year of his reign in order to appoint Seti as the viceroy of Nubia.[93] His delegate brought gifts and rewards from the king to the higher officials of Nubia. Merneptah-Siptah, the last king of the nineteenth dynasty, was even forced to send one of his officials to fetch the tribute of Nubia,[94] although dispatching the tribute was the duty of the viceroy of Nubia when the Pharaoh exercised real power and actual control of his empire.

During the twentieth dynasty the situation in Egypt deteriorated enormously. There was a harem conspiracy in the time of Ramses III (−1198 to −1166) which aimed at deposing the reigning sovereign. One of the conspirators, the sister of the commander of the bowmen in Nubia, persuaded her brother to assist in the execution of the plot. But it is evident that the viceroy of Nubia remained loyal to the Pharaoh. Under Ramses XI, the last king of the twentieth dynasty, a rebellion broke out in the region of Asyut. The king with the help of Pa-nehesi, the viceroy of Kush, and his troops succeeded in quelling the revolt and in restoring order in Upper Egypt. Following this rising a certain Heri-Hor became the Chief Priest of Amar in Thebes. It seems that he was made the Chief Priest by Pa-nehesi and his Nubian soldiers and one supposes that he was one of his followers. In the nineteenth year of Ramses XI, after the death of Pa-nehesi, Heri-Hor was appointed viceroy of Nubia and vizier of Thebes. Thus he became the actual master of Upper Egypt and Nubia. Following the death of Ramses XI, he became king (−1085) and with him started a new line of rulers in Egypt. Then chaos reigned in Egypt and with it a dark age commenced in Nubia, to continue until the eighth century before our era when Kush suddenly emerged as a great power.

93. J. H. Breasted, 1906, Vol. III.
94. D. R. MacIver and C. L. Woolley, p. 26, Plate 12.

PLATE 9.1 *A selection of Kerma pottery*

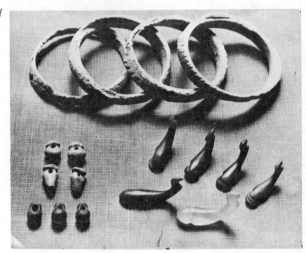

PLATE 9.2 *Personal ornaments*

PLATE 9.3 *Kerma pottery*

275

PLATE 9.4 *Kerma
pottery*

PLATE 9.5 *Kerma
pottery*

PLATE 9.6 *Kerma
pottery*

PLATE 9.7 *Kerma
pottery*

PLATE 9.8 *Kerma pottery*

PLATE 9.9 *The western fortifications of the Middle Kingdom fortress at Buhen*

PLATE 9.10 *The eastern Dufufa at Kerma with a grave in the foreground*

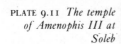
PLATE 9.11 *The temple of Amenophis III at Soleb*

# The empire of Kush: Napata and Meroe

**J. LECLANT**

Though today the region is extremely isolated behind a barrier of deserts and the difficult hurdles of the Second, Third and Fourth Cataracts of the Nile, Dongola and the adjacent basins of the Middle Nile were formerly the centre of rich and powerful political structures. In the first half of the second millennium the so-called Kerma culture marked a rich and prosperous kingdom, the Kush of the Egyptian records. The extremely patchy archaeological prospection of this still little-known zone is quite inadequate for fixing the history of this sector after the brilliant but relatively short phase of Egyptian domination under the New Empire (−1580 to −1085); for nearly three centuries, the link between Africa and the Mediterranean world seems to be broken and almost total silence blankets Nubia. But from the end of the ninth century before our era we get a re-awakening: G. A. von Reisner's excavation of the El-Kurru necropolis[1] near Napata below the Fourth Cataract revealed the tombs of a succession of princes: initially mounds and later masonry structures of mastaba type.

## Sudanese domination in Egypt: the twenty-fifth or 'Ethiopian' dynasty

These are the royal ancestors of the line which effected the union of Egypt and the Sudan, known in general history as the twenty-fifth or 'Ethiopian' dynasty of Egypt.[2] It was long thought that this dynasty descended from Egyptian refugees from the Theban region, on the strength of the similarity of certain names and the position of the god Amon and his priesthood. Later some arrow-heads of Saharan type led to a belief in the dynasty's Libyan origin. In actual fact it sprang from the soil and may perhaps represent the succession of the ancient sovereigns of Kerma.

The names of the earliest rulers are unknown. Then one Alara was succeeded by Kashta, whose name seems to be formed from 'Kush', and his Egyptian-style cartouches appear on a stele discovered at Elephantine,

1. D. Dunham and O. Bates.
2. J. Leclant, 1965b, pp. 354–9.

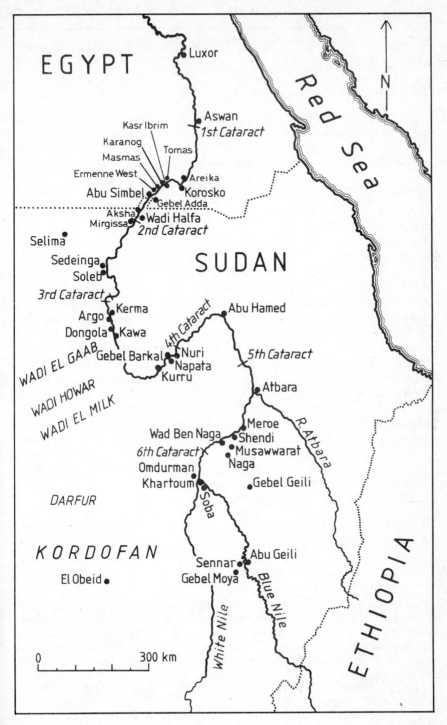

EGYPT

Luxor

Aswan
*1st Cataract*

Kasr Ibrim
Karanog          Tomas
Masmas
Ermenne West          Areika
Abu Simbel          Korosko
          Gebel Adda
Aksha
Mirgissa          Wadi Halfa
          *2nd Cataract*

Selima

Sedeinga
Soleb
*3rd Cataract*

SUDAN

Kerma          Abu Hamed
Argo          *4th Cataract*
Dongola          Kawa          *5th Cataract*
WADI EL GAAB          Gebel Barkal          Nuri
          Napata
          Kurru
WADI HOWAR          Atbara

WADI EL MILK

          Meroe
Wad Ben Naga          Shendi
*6th Cataract*          Musawwarat
Omdurman          Naga          R. Atbara
Khartoum          Gebel Geili

DARFUR          Soba

KORDOFAN          Abu Geili
El Obeid          Sennar
          Gebel Moya

White Nile          Blue Nile

ETHIOPIA

Red Sea

N

0          300 km

FIG. 10.1 *Meroitic sites*

at a time (around −750) when the Nubians occupied at least part of Upper Egypt.

## The Stele of Peye (Piankhi)

With the succeeding monarch, the illustrious Piankhi, whose name should henceforth be written as 'Peye',[3] we enter the mainstream of history: one of the inscriptions which he caused to be carved at Napata, and which, rediscovered in the middle of the last century, is now preserved in the Cairo Museum and known as the Stele of Victory,[4] is one of the longest and most detailed texts of ancient Egypt; on front, back and sides are 159 lines of hieroglyphs describing the deliberations of the king in his palace and the phases of his campaign against the Libyan princes who were masters of Middle Egypt and the Delta. Pious episodes and orations succeed one another: Peye knows how to be merciful: a great lover of horses, he is angered, at Hermopolis, to find all the horses dead in the stables but he forgives. On the other hand he refuses to meet 'those who were defiled', the dynasts of the Delta who ate fish; and suddenly in the middle of the jubilation we get a withdrawal southwards right back to the Sudan. However, we also note the installation at Thebes as Divine Votaress of Amon of Amenirdis the Elder, daughter of Kashta himself.[5] Another great stele of Peye's,[6] discovered in 1920, defines the federative character of the Kushite empire conjointly with proclamation of the supremacy of the god Amon: 'Amon of Napata has made me sovereign over every people; he to whom I say "thou art a king" shall be a king; he to whom I say "thou shalt not be a king" shall not be a king. Amon of Thebes has made me sovereign over Egypt; he to whom I say "be clothed as a king" is clothed as a king; he to whom I say "thou shalt not be clothed as a king" shall not be clothed as a king . . . the gods make a king, the people make a king, but it is Amon who made me.'

## King Shabaka

Towards −713, Shabaka, brother of Peye, ascended the throne. He brought the entire Nile valley as far as the Delta under the empire of

---

3. The name formerly written Piankhi contains in hieroglyphic writing the sign of the 'croix ansée', which was read as *ankh* as in Egyptian, but this sign seems to have been considered by the Meroites as merely an ideogram, that for 'life', corresponding to the meaning of the Meroitic root *p* (*e*) *y* (*e*) which gives us the form 'Peye' usually adopted today. Cf. A. Heyler and J. Leclant, p. 552; K. H. Priese, 1968, pp. 165–91; G. Vittmann, pp. 12–16.

4. J. H. Breasted, 1906; K. B. Priese, 1970, pp. 16–32; J. Leclant, 1974, pp. 122–3.

5. J. Leclant, 1973b.

6. Khartoum Museum, No. 1851: G. A. Reisner, 1931, pp. 89–100 and Plate V.

Kush[7] and is reputed to have had Bocchoris, dynast of Sais, who resisted him, burnt to death; the compilers of the lists of the kings of Egypt regard him as the founder of the twenty-fifth dynasty. The Weltpolitik of the Middle East drew the Kushites towards Asia where Assyrian pressure was beginning to make itself felt; the appeals from princes and cities of Syria–Palestine and in particular from Jerusalem[8] become urgent. But to begin with, Shabaka seems to have preserved good relations with Assyria. In the Sudan and Egypt, he launched a policy of monument building which was expanded under his successors, the two sons of Peye, first Shabataka (−700 to −690), and then the glorious Taharqa (−690 to −664).[9]

## King Taharqa: the struggle against the Assyrians

Taharqa's name is found on numerous monuments throughout the whole length of the valley. He built his sanctuaries at the foot of the holy mountain of Gebel Barkal, a kind of sandstone table formation which dominates the large fertile basin of Napata. His name is to be seen at several other places in Nubia such as Kawa. In the Theban region he erected colonnades on the four main faces of the Temple of Karnak and constructed in them large numbers of small chapels where the cults of Amon and Osiris were associated. We have evidence of his presence at Memphis and in the Delta. Abandoning the traditional necropolis of El-Kurru, Taharqa built at Nuri what appears to be a cenotaph comparable to the Abydos Osireion;[10] a tomb inscribed with some of his styles and titles has been discovered at Sedeinga.[11] Several firmly striding statues of exceptional quality show us how he looked; the beautifully sculpted granite was embellished with gold ornamentation. The face is heavy, with a fleshy nose, a wide thick-lipped mouth and a short, strong chin enhancing the extraordinary power of the face. Various texts, in particular a number of large stelae discovered by Griffith at Kawa, throw more light on the king's policy: shrine building, sumptuous offerings of plate, sanctuary equipment, and precious materials and endowments and personnel. The sixth year of the reign is particularly celebrated, when a high flood of the Nile waters

---

7. The Egyptians and the Nubians gave this political organization the name 'Kush', which had been traditionally used for the region of the Middle Nile since the Middle Kingdom. As this name is found in the Bible, English-speaking authors use the adjective 'Kushite', whereas in the French historiographical tradition the corresponding dynasty, the twenty-fifth of Egypt, is called the 'Ethiopian' dynasty (cf. note 2 above). We shall avoid any reference to Ethiopia here in order to do away with any risk of confusion with present-day Ethiopia.

8. H. von Zeissl, pp. 21–6.

9. J. Leclant, 1965b, index, p. 407.

10. D. Dunham and O. Bates, 1955, Vol. II, pp. 6–16.

11. Tomb WT 1, Sedeinga: M. S. Giorgini, pp. 116–23.

lowering afforded an occasion for stressing the prosperity of the kingdom:[12] in recounting the coming of the queen-mother, Abale,[13] the king enlarges on the situation at the time.

Taharqa had accepted the challenge of war with the Assyrians. His name looms large in the Bible[14] where the terror caused by the black warriors of the land of Kush is evident. Assarhaddon (−681 to −669) failed in his attempt to invade Egypt and it was his successor Assurbanipal who, at the head of an extremely strong army, captured and sacked Thebes in −663.

# King Tanoutamon:
# the end of Sudanese domination in Egypt

By that time Taharqa had already been succeeded by his nephew Tanoutamon, son of Shabataka. The so-called Stele of the Dream shows successively the appearance of two serpents – an obvious allusion to the double Uraeus of the Ethiopian sovereigns – the crowning of Tanoutamon at Napata, his march to the north, the taking of Memphis, building works at Napata, a campaign in the desert and the ensuing submission of the local princes. But in actual fact, with the defeat inflicted by the Assyrians, the Kushites withdrew southward and their dynasty in Egypt ended. Thenceforward that country was to be Mediterranean-oriented, its unification being the work of a Delta dynast, the Saite Psammetik I, who freed it from the Assyrians. In the ninth year of the reign of Psammetik I (−654), he procured the selection of his daughter Nitokris as divine votaress at Thebes.[15]

# A twin monarchy

We shall do well to pause over this fifty-year period during which Egypt and the Sudan combined with a great African power. The Kushite kingdom presents itself as a twin monarchy; its symbol is the double Uraeus, the two snakes which rise above the forehead of the Pharaoh and protect him. In their general style, their clothing and their attitudes the sovereigns of the twenty-fifth dynasty copy the Pharaohs of Egypt who preceded them and whose successors, if not descendants, they claim to be. The style of their monuments is typically Pharaonic. The inscriptions are Egyptian, recalling the pure classical tradition. But features are more akin to those of

12. Brought on by very heavy rainfall, this 'flood which carried away cattle' submerged the whole country; but the providential will of Amon prevented other related catastrophes, destroying rodents and serpents, warding off the ravages of locusts and preventing the winds from the south blowing in fury.

13. M. F. L. Macadam, 1949, Inscr. IV, pp. 18–21.

14. 2 *Kings*, 19: 9; *Isaiah*, 37: 9.

15. R. A. Caminos, 1964b, pp. 71–101.

Hamitic pastoralists with an undoubted strain of black blood: marked cheekbones, heavy chins, thick lips. They also wear ornaments characteristic of the Sudan. A popular head-dress is a kind of close cap fitting tightly to the neck with a sidepiece protecting the temple; a thick knotted head-band holds it in place leaving two streamers hanging behind the shoulders. Ear-rings and the pendants of necklaces are adorned with rams' heads, the ram being the sacred animal of Amon. Amon is in fact the great god of the dynasty, worshipped in four major sanctuaries – Napata, Tore (probably Sanam), Kawa and Pnubs (Tabo in the isle of Argo). For the service of each of these sanctuaries princesses were consecrated as musicians of Amon. In the Sudanese part of their empire the entourages of Kushites frequently included their mothers, wives, sisters and female cousins. This was not so in Egypt proper, though the Kushite Pharaohs were assisted at Thebes by the divine votaresses – princesses vowed to virginity, with the god Amon as their only spouse. Conceded quasi-royal privileges, the Amenirdises and Shepenoupets formed a kind of parallel dynasty with succession from aunt to niece; but they were not eponymous and had no functions in connection with the Nile floods. While they headed an important establishment, their power was nevertheless limited by the presence in Thebes itself of a prefect of the city representing the Pharaoh.

The glory of the twenty-fifth dynasty was great; a whole tradition about it developed among the classical authors. And in fact the art of this epoch shows great vigour. Taking over the best of the past tradition the Kushites gave it new power and notable force.

## Napata, the first capital of the Kushite Empire

After the retreat of the Kushites from Egypt under the assaults of Assyrians, their history is much more difficult to determine; even the chronology is extremely vague. For a millennium a state survived, becoming ever more African, the kingdom of Kush, the name of its own choice from the ancient native name for the territory. In the eyes of conventional Egyptology this represents a long period of decadence during which the Pharaonic influences became progressively corrupted. In actual fact it is a culture out of Africa which alternately entrenches itself in its specificity or seeks to align itself with the Egyptian civilization – itself, for that matter, African properly speaking; from time to time echoes reach it from the Mediterranean, in particular after the foundation of Alexandria.

To begin with, the capital remained at Napata at the foot of the sacred mountain, Gebel Barkal. Later, almost certainly in the sixth century before our era, it was transferred much farther south to Meroe. There is little certainty as to the extent of the Kushite kingdom and so far the differences between its component regions are still unclarified. In the far north, Lower Nubia, a kind of no man's land, remained in dispute between the Meroites and whoever were masters of Egypt: Saites, Persians, Ptolemies and latterly Romans. A zone of silence exists from the end of the Egyptian New Empire (around −1085), and this little-favoured region in the solitude of the tropical deserts seems to have remained largely uninhabited until the opening of the Christian era. Its revival then was probably due to the introduction of the *saqia* (water wheel) (cf. Chapter 11). In the heartland of the empire, Nubia proper, extending along the river (Napata, Dongola and Kerma basins), appears always to have been appreciably different from the steppe region of the 'Island of Meroe'. Eastward in Butana there are numerous unexcavated sites, while the caravan routes and the Red Sea littoral are still awaiting exploration. Archaeological exploration has not been carried far enough for us to be able to indicate the limits of the Kushite kingdom to the south in the savannahs and highly fertile lands of the Gezira; it is accepted, however, that it included the central Sudan and extended at least as far as Sennar on the Blue Nile and Kosti on the White Nile; the objects dug up at Gebel Moya must also be taken into account. Westwards, its influence must have reached Kordofan at least and we can hope for much from explorations carried out across the wide band of the Nilo-Chadian savannahs.

At Napata the tombs of the Nuri cemetery[16] are among the essential elements for determining the history, still very inadequately known, of the kings of the Napatan dynasty. The first few rulers are still very much egyptianized. As in the case of the twenty-fifth dynasty kings, their burial places are surmounted by Egyptian-style pyramids whose form is more reminiscent of those of the high dignitaries of the last days of the New Empire than of the royal pyramids of the fourth dynasty; the decoration of their burial chambers and their solid granite sarcophagi follow the Egyptian style in every particular: religious inscriptions in a tradition going back to those of the pyramids cover their sides, and those items of the grave furnishings which have escaped the tomb robbers – libation jars, ushabtis and figurines – are likewise just as in Egypt.

Of the first two kings barely more than the names are known; they were Atlanarsa (−653 to −643), son of Taharqa, and the former's own son, Senkamanisken (−643 to −623), of whose statues fragments of great beauty have been found in the Gebel Barkal. The two sons and successors of Senkamanisken, first Anlamani (−623 to −593), succeeded by Aspelta (−593 to −568), are better known. At Kawa a stele of Anlamani[17] describes the king's progress through the provinces and his provision for their temples, a campaign against a people who could be the Blemmyes, the coming of the queen-mother, Nasalsa, and the consecration of the king's sisters as sistrum-players before the god Amon in each of his four great sanctuaries.

16. D. Dunham and O. Bates.
17. M. F. L. Macadam, 1949, pp. 44–50, Plates 15–16.

This king's brother and successor, Aspelta (− 593 to − 568), left two great inscriptions discovered years ago. The Enthronement or Coronation Text dates from the first year of the reign[18] and shows the army mustered near the Gebel Barkal, the decision of the leaders to consult Amon of Napata and the god's designation of Aspelta, whose descent through the 'Royal Sisters' is particularly distinguished, the king's assumption of the royal emblems and his thanks to and invocation of the god, his joyful reception by the army and his gifts to the temples. So much for the military and religious bases of the Kushite monarchy. The stele of the Appanaging of the princesses, of the third year of the reign, is preserved in the Musée du Louvre: it is the description of the investiture of a princess as priestess. A further text discovered by G. A. Reisner in the Gebel Barkal narrates the foundation by the sovereign of a chantry in honour, long after his death, of Khaliut, son of Peye. On the other hand, some scholars' attribution to Aspelta of the Stele of Excommunication is more doubtful, the names of the king having been defaced. The rather obscure text describes how the members of a family which had planned a murder were excluded from the temple of Amon of Napata; the god condemns them to be burned and the king warns the priests against more crimes of this king.

## The expedition of Psammetik II and the fall of Napata

Aspelta was a contemporary of Psammetik II. This is one of the few really secure synchronisms, almost the only one in a thousand years of history. In − 591, or the second year of the king's reign, the land of Kush was invaded by an Egyptian expedition, stiffened with Greek and Carian mercenaries, under two generals, Amasis and Potasimto,[19] and Napata was captured.

## Transfer of the capital to Meroe

Thenceforward the Kushites aimed at keeping a greater distance between themselves and their powerful northern neighbours; it is undoubtedly to this Egyptian raid, whose importance has long been underestimated, that we must attribute the transfer of the capital from Napata to Meroe, i.e. much farther south, at no great distance from the Sixth Cataract. Aspelta is in fact the first attested Meroe sovereign. This notwithstanding, Napata unquestionably remained the religious capital of the kingdom: the monarchs continued to be buried in the Nuri necropolis down to the end of the fourth century.

18. I. Hofmann, 1971a.

19. S. Sauneron and J. Yoyotte, 1952, pp. 157–207. A new version of this text has been published by H. S. K. Bakry, pp. 225ff., Plates 56–9.

In −525 a Persian danger developed. We know the reply of the Nubian king to the ambassadors of Cambyses[20] (Herodotus, III, 21): 'when the Persians bend, as easily as I, bows as big as this, then let them march against the Ethiopians in superior numbers'. Cambyses did not take this advice: his army was unable to effect a crossing of the Batn el-Hagar and had to retire with heavy losses. For all that, the Persians counted the inhabitants of Kush as their subjects. A shield is set aside for them on the pediment, inscribed with the peoples of the empire, of the magnificent statue of Darius recently brought to light at Susa.[21] It is conceivable that a narrow belt of Nubian territory remained under their sway and there were Kushite contingents in the armies of Darius and Xerxes. There are also references to gifts of gold, ebony, elephant tusks and even children, with the ancient tributes formerly levied by Egypt seemingly going to Persepolis and Susa.

A further possible explanation for the transfer of the capital may have been climatic and economic considerations. At Meroe the steppes were much more extensive than in the basins around Napata, hemmed in by deserts. To livestock were added agriculture, cultivation being perfectly possible in this zone of summer rainfall. Enormous irrigation basins (hafirs) were dug out adjacent to the principal sites. Commerce must have been brisk, as Meroe was an ideal entrepôt for the caravan routes between the Red Sea, the upper Nile and Chad. Above all, the comparative abundance of trees and shrubs supplied the necessary fuel for the working of iron from the ore found in the Nubian sandstone. The slag heaps evidence the extent of manufacturing activities but the most recent authorities condemn the description of Meroe as the Birmingham of Africa as exaggerated.[22]

For long centuries, which remain obscure, historians have little more to go on than royal tombs. Their excavator, G. A. von Reisner, set about matching the list of attested royal names which the pyramids brought to light, with chancy results which have undergone many revisions since then and may be still liable to amendment. The last king buried at Nuri was Nastasen (a little before −300). Thereafter royal and princely internments took place in the Meroe cemeteries. Nevertheless a number of kings did go back to the Gebel Barkal, which may have been why some historians have believed in the probable existence in northern Nubia of two dynasties parallel to the Meroe dynasties, one of them immediately after Nastasen, and the other in the first century before our era.[23]

Only a few major inscriptions provide some light, and that patchily, to say the least. The Egyptian used degenerates; more accurately perhaps, behind the hieroglyphic symbols, which may take on aspects bordering on

20. Herodotus, III, 21.

21. J. Perrot *et al.*, pp. 235–66.

22. See bibliographical references below, in particular: B. G. Trigger, 1969, pp. 23–50, and H. Amborn, pp. 74–95.

23. For Meroitic chronology see bibliographical references below.

the fantastic, we need to look for 'notes' of the contemporary state of the language – in point of fact Demotic – and also echoes of Meroitic, the Kushites' own language.

We have several inscriptions of King Amannoteyeriké (a little before −400). The best describes the election of the king, a 'strong man of 41', and for the most there are accounts of military expeditions, religious festivities, a torchlight tattoo, the visit of the queen-mother, restoration work on buildings and donations to sanctuaries.

Next·we get Harsiotef, whose famous inscription is devoted partly to ceremonies and partly to campaigns against a multitude of different enemies. It is the same with the stele of Nastasen carried off by Lepsius to Berlin. This stele may, incidentally, give us a synchronism if one of the inscriptions is indeed the name of Khababash, fleetingly kinglet of Egypt (second half of the fourth century). In one of his campaigns Nastasen captured 202 120 head of cattle and 505 200 of small livestock. One would like to be able to 'place' all the peoples mentioned in the inscriptions; the spoils are often enormous and quite obviously we need to look in the Nilo-Chadian savannah for certain ethnic groups. The engraving of the stele is of high quality and evidences the subsistence or renewal of direct Egyptian influence.

## The philhellene Ergamenos

The renaissance which appears to mark the succeeding decades is confirmed in Greek historiography's account of 'Ergamenos'. After writing of the all-powerful position of the Kushite priests, who could even constrain the king to commit suicide if he had ceased to please the people, Diodorus of Sicily[24] relates how a sovereign steeped in Greek culture, Ergamenos, dared to fight back and had a number of priests put to death. Doubts nevertheless subsist as to the identity of Ergamenos; which of the three Meroitic sovereigns was he, Arkakamani, Arnekhamani or Arquamani? Arnekhamani was the king who built the Lion temple at Mussawwarat es-Sufra,[25] where hymns can be read composed in good Ptolemaic Egyptian and Egyptian artists and scribes must have worked. At the same time, we also find reliefs in purely Meroitic style: head-dress, ornaments and royal regalia are of local inspiration and the faces do not conform to the Egyptian canon. Along with the Pharaonic divinities, worship is paid to purely Meroitic gods, Apedemak the Lion-god[26] and Sbomeker. Undoubtedly relations with Egypt subsisted, since we have sanctuaries of common Egyptian and Nubian dedication at Philae and at Dakka in Lower Nubia. However,

---

24. Diodorus Siculus, III, 6. There is no corroboration for his assertion that the priests could actually bring about the king's death.

25. F. Hintze, 1976.

26. L. V. Zabkar.

FIG. 10.2 Saqia (*from* Archaeology, *Autumn 1977, Vol. 17, no. 3*)

the revolts in the south of Ptolemaic Egypt at the end of the third century before our era may have been backed by the Nubian kinglets: Ptolemy V had to campaign in the country and Ptolemy VI established colonies in the Triacontaschone.[27]

## The Meroitic language and form of writing

With Queen Shanakdakhete (around −170 to −160) we appear to get the accession to full power of a typically local matriarchy.[28] It is on an edifice in her name at Naga that we find inscriptions engraved in Meroitic hieroglyphs which are among the most ancient known.

27. The Greeks gave the name Dodecaschene to the area south of Philae, some '12 schenes' long, i.e. approximately 120 kilometres. There has been some argument as to whether the 320-odd kilometres of the 'Triacontaschene' should also be counted starting from Philae, or on the contrary starting from the southernmost end of the area previously defined.

28. cf. B. G. Haycock, pp. 461–80; I. S. Katznelson, 1966, pp. 35–40 (in Russian); M. F. L. Macadam, 1966, pp. 46–7; J. Desanges, 1968, pp. 89–104; July 1971, pp. 2–5.

These hieroglyphs are borrowed from Egyptian but differ in their values. They are written and read the other way round from Egyptian ones; this may attest a deliberate desire to be different. With these hieroglyphs there goes a cursive form of writing often abbreviated; the signs seem to be derived in part from the demotic writing used in Egypt at that period for administrative and private documents. Whatever the case may be, the Meroitic language, whose nature is still not known, and the graphic system are completely different from the Egyptian: the twenty-three signs used represent the consonants, some vowels and syllabics; groups of 'colons' usually separate the individual words. In 1909 the English scholar F. L. Griffith found the key to transliteration. Since then the texts have been classified into different types, with comparable expressions set side by side in parallel, particularly those taken from funerary texts. Beginning with an invocation to Isis and Osiris, these contain the name of the deceased, of his mother (usually at the top of the list) and father, some names of relations by blood or marriage, which abound in titles and high ranks, and the names of places and divinities. It is, however, difficult to go any farther. Study, in particular of how the article is used, has made it possible to cut the texts up into units known as stichs, which are of convenient length for analysis. An effort has also been made with verbs, where a system of affixes has been discovered. In recent years computer techniques have made possible the systematic recording of texts which have been transliterated, together with their detailed analyses.[29] For the time being, however, the translation as such of the 800-odd texts recovered remains as a whole impossible.

The first long Meroitic texts appear on two stelae of King Taniydamani, who is dated about the end of the second century before our era. The uncertainties of Meroitic chronology are particularly serious for this period, to such a point that – as we have seen – certain scholars have taken the view that there was an independent state at Napata, which seems highly improbable. Thereafter a preponderant place falls to two queens, Amanirenas and Amanishakheto. Their husbands remain forgotten and we do not even know the name of Amanishakheto's. The throne was also occupied for some years by a king, the former prince Akinidad, son of Queen Amanirenas and King Teriteqas. Nevertheless, it is important which of these two queens came first, both of them 'Candace', which is the transcription of the Meroitic title *Kdke* according to the tradition of the classical authors.[30]

---

29. The Paris Groupe d'Etudes Méroitiques has begun a computer-based recording of the Meroitic texts grouped together in the *Répertoire d'Epigraphe Méroitique*. See bibliographical references below, in particular the articles published in Khartoum, 1974, pp. 17–40.

30. See note 28 above.

## Rome and Meroe

One of the two queens had dealings with Augustus in a famous episode, one of the rare occasions when Meroe appears on the stage of universal history. Following the sack of Aswan by the Meroites (which was probably when the statue of Augustus was captured, the head of which has been discovered buried under the threshold of one of the palaces of Meroe), the prefect of Roman Egypt, Petronius, mounted a punitive expedition and captured Napata in −23. A permanent garrison was established by the Romans at Primis (Qasr Ibrim), which held off the Meroites.[31] In −21 or −20 a peace treaty was negotiated at Samos, where Augustus was staying at the time. The Roman garrison appears to have been withdrawn; the exaction of a tribute from the Meroites was renounced and the frontier between the Roman and Meroitic empires was fixed at Hiera Sycaminos (Muharraqa). Shall we ever know whether Amanirenas or Amanishakheto was the one-eyed, 'mannish-looking' Candace who, according to Strabo, Pliny and Dion Cassius, conducted the negotiations with the Roman invaders?

## The Meroitic empire at its height

This period around the start of the Christian era is one of the peaks of Meroitic civilization, as a number of buildings attest. The names of Akinidad and of the Queen Amanishakheto are inscribed in Temple T at Kawa, and a palace discovered of late years at Ouad ben Naga close by the river has been attributed to the queen.[32] Her fine tomb is still to be seen in the Northern Cemetery of Meroe.[33] The pyramid, with the traditional eastern approach of pylon chapel, is one of the most imposing in the old city and in 1834 yielded to the Italian adventurer Ferlini the elaborate jewels which are today the glory of the Munich and Berlin museums. Similar ornaments adorn the reliefs, where queens and princes display a rather flashy luxury which is to some degree reminiscent of that of another civilization – of rich merchants – on the frontiers of the hellenized world, namely, Palmyra. To the luxury is added a touch of violence, with cruel scenes of prisoners being torn to pieces by lions, impaled on pikes or devoured by birds of prey.

Natakamani, son-in-law and successor of Amanishakheto, and his wife, Queen Amanitere (−12 to +12) were also great builders, and their names are indisputably those recurring most frequently on the Kushite monuments. Throughout the major cities of the empire, these monuments

31. J. Desanges, 1949, pp. 139–47, and J. M. Plumley, 1971, pp. 7–24, 1 map, 11 illustrations.
32. J. Vercoutter, 1962, pp. 263–99.
33. D. Dunham and O. Bates, IV, pp. 106–11.

speak of the power of a dynasty at its apogee. In the north, at a site south of the Second Cataract, the king and queen built a temple at Amara in which the reliefs are Egyptian work, the only non-Egyptian element being the detail of the royal Meroitic head-dress, a close cap girdled by a head-band hanging loose behind. In the isle of Argo just above the Third Cataract, the two colossi have long been accepted as Natekamani's.[34] The royal couple also put in hand the restoration of Napata, devastated by Petronius' expedition, and in particular of the temple of Amon. At Meroe itself the names of Natekamani and his consort appear in the great temple of Amon jointly with the name of the prince Arikankharor. At Ouad ben Naga, the South Temple is their work. They devoted particular attention to Naga, the great centre of the steppe-country south of Meroe: the frontal approach to the temple of Amon became a pylon whose decoration combines Egyptian influences and purely Meroitic features, while the most famous building is the Naga lion temple whose reliefs are among the most representative examples of Meroitic art. The pyramids of the king, the queen and the princes have been identified at Meroe. The king and queen liked to be portrayed with one of the royal princes, Arikankharor, Arikakhatani or Sherkaror, varying according to the monument; perhaps the princes were viceroys of the provinces in whose principal temples they were pictured. Sherkaror seems to have ascended the throne in succession to his parents shortly after the opening of the Christian era; a rock carving at Gebel Qeili in the south of Butana shows him triumphing over innumerable enemies under the protection of a solar deity.

## Meroe and the surrounding countries

It is in the next few years that we get the famous episode recorded in the Acts of the Apostles (8:28–39) of the deacon Philip's conversion, on the road from Jerusalem to Gaza, of 'an Ethiopian, an eunuch, a minister of Candace, the Queen of the Ethiopians, in charge of all her treasure . . .'[35] Whatever the value and significance of this evidence it does show that Meroe was known afar.

There is quite another direction in which researchers were long tempted to look for connections with the outer world: one representation of Apedemak, the Lion-god, shows him with a threefold lion's mask and four arms;[36] this has suggested India, just as have reliefs at Naga which show a lotus flower with a serpent rising from it. The neck of the serpent becomes a human body with one arm which is the mask of Apedemak

34. S. Wenig suggests that these should now be recognized as the gods Arensnuphis and Sebiumeker: 1967, pp. 143–4.

35. In the French translation of the Bible (the 'Jerusalem version') the footnotes state that the area referred to is 'above the First Cataract: Nubia or the Egyptian Sudan', i.e. the Kush country we defined above in note 7.

36. See above, note 26.

wearing a triple crown. In the ruins of Mussawwarat es-Sufra numerous elephant figures are to be noticed; one of the more curious is an elephant figure which serves to cap a broad wall. The most recent research is inclined to abandon the Hindu hypothesis and to look for strictly local, and thereby the more interesting, origins in the kingdom of Kush.[37]

This distant country continued to intrigue the Romans. Towards +60 Nero sent two centurions up the Nile; on their return they stated that the land was too poor to be worth conquering.[38] An inscription in Latin is carved on one of the walls of Mussawwarat, while Roman coins, though in very small numbers, reached parts of Nubia and the Sudan; a coin of Claudius has been found in Meroe, one of Nero at Karanog, a coin of Diocletian far into Kordofan (El Obeid), and another of the middle of the fourth century of our era at Sennar. These modest remains take their place alongside the discoveries of the Meroe baths, the bronzes of hundreds of tombs or the magnificent parcel of glass-ware quite recently discovered at Sedeinga.[39]

The most constant relations maintained by Meroe were with the temple of Isis at Philae: embassies were sent regularly with rich gifts for the sanctuary of the goddess, where quantities of graffiti have been preserved in Demotic, in Greek and in Meroitic. They enable us to establish the sole synchronism of one of the last Meroitic reigns, that of Teqorideamani (+246 to +266), who sent ambassadors to Philae in +253. We know very little of the last centuries of Meroe. The indigenous component in the culture becomes more and more important. The control of the caravan routes between the Nile valley, the Red Sea and the Nilo-Chadian savannah – the economic cornerstone of this empire – was probably not easy to maintain. The royal pyramids become progressively smaller and poorer; while the rarity of Egyptian or Mediterranean objects indicates a cutting-off of outside influences, a cause or a consequence of the country's decadence.

## Decline and fall of Meroe

The Meroites, who until then had beaten back the raids of the nomad tribes, thenceforward became a tempting prey for their neighbours, Aksumites to the south, nomadic Blemmyes to the east and Nubas to the west. It is almost certainly this last group, mentioned for the first time by Eratosthenes in −200, to which should be ascribed the overthrow of the Meroitic empire.

On this we have no more than indirect evidence. Towards +330, the

37. See bibliographical references below. On possible links with India, cf. A. J. Arkell, 1951; I. Hofmann, 1975.

38. For source material on Nero's expedition, see F. Hintze, 1959a.

39. cf. *Orientalia*, 40, 1971, pp. 252–5, Plates XLIII–XLVII; J. Leclant, 1973a, pp. 52–68, 16 Figs; J. Leclant, in K. Michalowski, 1975, pp. 85–7, 19 Figs.

kingdom of Aksum, which had grown up on the high table-lands of present-day Ethiopia, had rapidly attained the summit of its power; Ezana,[40] the first monarch to embrace Christianity, reached the confluence of the Atbara and boasts of having mounted an expedition yielding much booty 'against the Nubas'. From this we may conclude that the Meroitic kingdom had already collapsed at the time of Ezana's campaign. From then onwards inscriptions in Meroitic ceased and it may be that this was when Meroitic language gave place to the tongue ancestral to present-day Nubian. Even the pottery, while remaining faithful to its millennary tradition, acquires new characteristics.

Some authorities have theorized that the Kushite royal family fled westward and settled at Darfur where there would seem to be traces of the survival of Meroitic traditions.[41] In any event, explorations in these regions and in the southern Sudan should afford us a better understanding of how Egyptian influences were transmitted towards inner Africa through the intermediary of Meroe. The glory of Kush is quite surely reflected in certain legends of Central and West Africa. The Sao have legends of the bringing of knowledge by men from the east. Knowledge of techniques spread; certain peoples cast bronze by the 'cire perdue' method, as in the Kushite kingdom; but above all, and of vital importance, it would seem to be thanks to Meroe that the working of iron spread over the African continent.[42]

Whatever the importance of this penetration of Meroitic influences through the rest of Africa, the role of Kush should never be underestimated: for over a thousand years, first at Napata and then at Meroe, there flourished a strongly original civilization which, beneath an Egyptian-style veneer fairly constantly maintained, remained profoundly African.

## Nubia after the fall of Meroe: 'Group X'

It can be taken that the Nubas from the west or south-west were the 'carriers' of the Nubian language, whose offshoots even today are living tongues both in certain mountainous regions of Darfur and in the various sectors of Upper and Lower Nubia.

As we have just seen, a proportion of Nuba groups had installed themselves in the southern part of the Meroitic kingdom. Archaeologically they are there identifiable by pottery of a rather African type. Their tombs are tumuli, of which some have been excavated at Tanqasi[43] near the Gebel Barkal and at Ushara, while others remain to be explored, in particular

40. L. P. Kirwan, 1960, pp. 163–73; I. Hofmann, 1971b, pp. 342–52.
41. In particular, A. J. Arkell, 1961, pp. 174ff., put forward this hypothesis on the basis of the existence of ruins and onomastic traces. It does not appear, however, to have gone beyond the realm of pure hypothesis.
42. See above, note 22, and bibliographical references below.
43. P. L. Shinnie, 1954b; L. P. Kirwan, 1957, pp. 37–41.

along the west bank of the Nile. It appears to have been about +570 that these Nubas were converted to Christianity by the Monophysite Bishop Longinos. In the north the date of the survivals of the Meroitic kingdom appears to have been different, up to a point. Since G. A. Reisner's 1907 survey, the cultural phase succeeding the fall of Meroe has been designated by one letter as Group X, a frank admission of ignorance. This culture extended over all Lower Nubia as far as Sai and Wawa to the south towards the Third Cataract. In this area it pursued its evolution from the first part of the fourth century to the middle of the sixth, i.e. up to the introduction of Christianity and the rapid rise of the Christian kingdoms of Nubia.

The barbarian luxury of the Group X kinglets was revealed in the period 1931–3, when the English archaeologists Emery and Kirwan, at Ballana and Qustul[44] a few miles south of Abu Simbel, excavated enormous tumuli which J. L. Burckhardt, the unwearying pioneer surveyor of Nubia, had already noted at the start of the previous century. Surrounded by their wives, their servants and their richly caparisoned horses, the dead reposed on litters as in the old days of Kerma. Their heavy diadems and silver bracelets set with coloured stones have a wealth of reminders of Egypt or Meroe, such as the ram's head of Amon bearing a huge crown *atef*, the fringes of *uraei* or the busts of Isis. Alexandrian influences are clearly apparent in the treasures of silverware which strewed the floor: among the ewers, cups and patens, there was an incised plate showing Hermes seated on a globe with a griffin by his side; there are also huge bronze lamps and a wooden chest inlaid with panels of carved ivory. But the pottery is still of the traditional Meroitic type so that the qualities of a truly Nubian technique persist over the millennia.

## Nobades or Blemmyes

Which were the populations of Group X – Nobades or Blemmyes? The Blemmyes[45] were warlike nomads customarily identified with the Bedja tribes of the eastern desert. As regards the Nobades or Nobates, after much disputation they are accepted as Nubas; the writer is inclined to think them the lords of Ballana and Qustul. In any event Blemmyes and Nobades are barely more than names for us, and it seems preferable to use the term 'Group X' or 'Ballana culture'.

Ancient literary evidences and epigraphic documents enable us to tie the main historical outlines. The historian Procopus claims that, towards the end of the third century, when the Roman emperor Diocletian pulled back the frontier to the First Cataract, he encouraged the Nobates to leave the

44. See bibliographical references below, and in particular W. B. Emery and L. P. Kirwan, 1938.
45. L. Castiglione, 1970, pp. 90–103.

Oasis region and to establish themselves on the Nile, reckoning on their serving as a screen for Egypt against the incursions of the Blemmyes. In actual fact, under Theodosius towards 450, Philae was attacked by the Blemmyes and the Nobades; they were driven back eventually by forces commanded by Maximinus, and then by the prefect Florus.

After the advent of Christianity they were permitted to continue to visit the sanctuary of Isis at Philae and for certain major feasts were allowed to borrow the statue of the goddess. Qasr Ibrim may have been one of the staging posts for this pilgrimage, for what seems to have been a statuette of Isis in painted earthenware was found there. It was only under Justinian, between +535 and +537, that his general, Narses, closed the temple of Philae and expelled the last priests.

The same period saw the undertaking of the evangelization of Nubia. If we are to believe John of Ephesus, the Melkite Orthodox envoys of the emperor were outdistanced by the Monophysite missionary Julian, backed by the empress Theodora, and he succeeded, in +543, in converting the king of the Nobades. In a corrupt Greek inscription, unfortunately undated, in the temple of Kalabsha, the Nobatian king Silko boasts of having, by God's help, conquered the Blemmyes, who thus vanish from history.

PLATE 10.1b *Detail of head of statue*

PLATE 10.1a *Ethiopian black granite statue of King Aspelta*

PLATE 10.2 *Queen Amanishakheto: relief from the pyramid at Meroe*

PLATE 10.4 *Painted blue glassware of Sedeinga, Khartoum*

PLATE 10.3 *Crown of Ballana*

# The civilization of Napata and Meroe

A. A. HAKEM
*with the collaboration of* I. HRBEK *and*
J. VERCOUTTER

## Political organization

### The nature of kingship

The most outstanding feature of political power in Nubia and central Sudan from the eighth century before our era to the fourth century of our era seems to have been its remarkable stability and continuity. Unlike many of ancient kingdoms, the country escaped the upheavals associated with violent dynastic changes. Indeed one can say that basically the same royal lineage continued to rule uninterruptedly under the same traditions.

Until recently theories prevailed that the Napatan dynasty was of foreign origin, either Libyan[1] or Egyptian derived from the High Priests of Thebes.[2] But the arguments on which these theories are founded are weak and most modern scholars are inclined to consider the dynasty as of local origin.[3] Apart from the somatic features depicted on statues of the kings[4] many other traits – the system of their election, the role of queen-mothers, burial customs and some other indications – clearly point to an indigenous culture and origin uninfluenced from outside.

Some of these traits are significant in helping us to sketch the character and nature of the political and social structure of the empire of Kush.

One of the peculiar features of the Meroitic political system was the choice of a new sovereign by election. Classical authors, from Herodotus, fifth century before our era, to Diodorus of Sicily, first century before our era, express their surprise about this usage, so different from that in other ancient kingdoms, in their accounts about the 'Aethiopians', as the inhabitants of the Kush empire were then generally called. They insist on the oracular choice of the new king; Diodorus affirms that 'the priests previously select the best of candidates and from those that are summoned the people take as a king the one whom the god chooses as he is carried round

---

1. G. A. Reisner, 1918–19, pp. 41–4; idem, 1923b, pp. 61–4; and many of his other papers; cf. also F. L. Griffith, 1917, p. 27.
2. G. Maspero, p. 169; E. Meyer, p. 52; S. Curto, 1965.
3. An account of the controversy is given by D. M. M. Dixon, 1964, pp. 121–32.
4. cf. J. Leclant, 1976b.

in procession ... Straightway they address and honour him as if he were a god since the kingdom was entrusted to him by the will of the divinity.'[5]

Diodorus describes here, undoubtedly from hearsay, only the formal ceremony which initiated a new reign and which incorporated religious symbols. The procedures of the actual choice remained hidden from him and his informants.

Fortunately we are able to reconstruct the succession procedures from Napatan inscriptions which describe the choice and coronation ceremonies in great detail. The earliest of them relate to King Piankhi (Peye) (−751 to −716) and the latest to Nastasen (−335 to −310). Coronation inscriptions may have been made after that date, but since the script and language used are Meroitic, which is still undeciphered, we cannot be certain. The Napatan coronation inscriptions are our best source for the understanding of the political institutions, in particular the features of kingship and the other related institutions. Although they are written in the contemporary style of the Egyptian hieroglyphic they show great differences from the usual run of similar New Kingdom inscriptions. Thus they have to be regarded as a product of their own culture.[6]

Among these inscriptions the three latest, those of Amani-nete-yerike (−431 to −405), Harsiotef (−404 to −369) and Nastasen (−335 to −310) show that the kings were anxious to observe strict traditional practices and proclaim their insistence on the traditions and customs of their ancestors. At the same time, these texts give more details than the earlier ones, though their language is difficult to follow. They show a remarkable consistency in their subject matter and even sometimes in their phraseology. Thus, in all three cases, the king before his appointment was described as living among the other royal brethren at Meroe. He first succeeded to the throne at Meroe and then he journeyed northward to Napata for the ceremonies. In fact, Amani-nete-yerike says categorically that he was elected by the leaders of his armies to be king at the age of 41 and that he had fought a war before he could proceed to Napata for the coronation. Even when he reached Napata he went into the royal palace where he received the crown of *Ta-Sti* as a further confirmation of his assumption of kingship. After this he entered the temple for the ceremony where he asked the god (addressing his statue or shrine) to grant him his kingship, which the god did as a matter of formality.

Earlier inscriptions confirm the conclusion that the succession to the throne was fixed before the king entered the temple. Thus, the succession

5. Diodorus Siculus, III, 5; J. Desanges, 1968, p. 90.
6. For the Conquest Stele of Piankhi and Tanwetamani's Dream Stele, see J. H. Breasted, 1906, pp. 406–73. The Stele of Taharqa, the Stelae of King Anlamani and the Great Inscription of King Amani-nete-yerike, have been translated by M. F. L. Macadam, 1949, Vol. I, pp. 4–80. For the Election Stele of Aspelta, the Dedication Stele of Queen Madiqen, the Excommunication Stele of King Aspelta, the Annals of Hersiotef and the Annals of King Nastasen, see E. A. T. Wallis Budge, 1912.

of Taharqa (−689 to −664) was decided by Shebitku (−701 to −689) who lived in Memphis in Egypt. Taharqa was summoned from among his royal brethren and journeyed northward no doubt visiting Napata en route, and paid homage at Gematon (Kawa) before proceeding to Thebes.[7]

The highlights of the ceremonies as given in Tanwetamani's (−664 to −653) stele are that he lived somewhere outside Napata, perhaps among his other royal brothers with his mother Qalhata; there he was first proclaimed king and then started a festival procession journeying northward to Napata and farther on to Elephantine and Karnak. It seems thus that the place where he had been before the start of the procession was south of Napata, i.e. Meroe. Consequently, the decision regarding the succession was made outside Napata, according to normal practice. Anlamani (−623 to −593) describes the episodes of his festivals at Gematon, where the stele was found, in similar terms and adds that he had brought his mother to attend these ceremonies like Taharqa before him.[8]

In his famous stele Aspelta (−593 to −568) adds more details about this ceremony. He confirms that he succeeded his brother Anlamani and that he was chosen from among his royal brothers by a group of twenty-four high civil officials and military leaders. Justifying his claims to the throne, Aspelta refers to the will of god Amun-Re and also his own ancestry to assert his hereditary right of succession through the female line of descent. In spite of the lengthy exultation to the god Amun-Re it is evident that the role of the priesthood was limited. Aspelta also adds many details of entering into the inner part of the temple where he found the sceptres and crowns of his predecessors and was given the crown of his brother Anlamani. This is similar to the accounts of Amani-nete-yerike and Nastasen.

Important conclusions emerge from these inscriptions. One is that the journey northward to visit various temples was an important part of the coronation ceremony which every king would have to make on his accession to the throne; the second is that the temple of Amun in Napata had a special role in this ceremony and that this remained unchallenged. All this has a direct bearing on G. A. Reisner's theory of the existence of two independent kingdoms of Napata recently restated by Hintze.[9]

This theory was put forward by G. A. von Reisner to explain the number of royal cemeteries. His basic assumption was that a royal burial was closely connected with the capital: a king would be buried not very far from his royal residence. Hence, the cemetery of El-Kurru, the earliest royal cemetery, and the cemetery of Nuri, which succeeded El-Kurru, were royal burials up to the time of Nastasen when the capital was Napata. Subsequently, the two cemeteries of Begrawiya South and North became royal

7. M. F. L. Macadam, 1949, Vol. I.
8. ibid., p. 46.
9. F. Hintze, 1971b.

cemeteries when the capital was moved to Meroe around −300, after the reign of Nastasen. At Gebel Barkal, in Napata, however, there are two groups of pyramids. Archaeological and architectural considerations convinced Reisner that the first group fell immediately after Nastasen and the second group dated from the first century before our era and ended when the Romans raided Napata in −23 or soon after. Each group was assigned to a branch of the royal family ruling at Napata independently from the main ruling family at Meroe.[10]

However, the majority of scholars has abandoned this notion of the division of the kingdom.[11] A detailed study of the succession procedures and the ceremonies of coronation shows that Reisner's hypothesis is untenable. For it is inconceivable that a sovereign should be proclaimed king at his capital and then go to the capital of an independent kingdom to be crowned, in particular when it is the capital of a very insignificant kingdom as suggested by Reisner's hypothesis. On the other hand, there is no evidence to suggest that the ceremony was abandoned since the Greek authors confirm that it continued during the third and second centuries before our era, as Bion[12] indicated, and during the first century before our era, as Diodorus Siculus relates. However, one can safely say that Napata played an important role in the Meroitic kingdom. Kings went thither to receive their insignia of rule in accordance with an established tradition and they were sometimes buried there.

An analysis of all the relevant texts shows that the office of king was hereditary in the royal lineage, in contrast to the Pharaonic or any other ancient Oriental system where the succession normally followed the father-son pattern. In Napata and Meroe the king was chosen among his royal brethren. The initiative in choosing a new sovereign came from the army leaders, high officials and clan chiefs. Any claimant of doubtful ability or unpopular with the electors might well be passed over. The oracular confirmation was merely a formal ratification of a previous choice and had rather a symbolic character designed for the public, which was persuaded that god himself had elected the new ruler. Further, it is plain that in theory the crown was to pass to the brothers of a king before descending to the next generation: from among twenty-seven kings ruling before Nastasen, fourteen were the brothers of preceding kings. There were, of course, exceptions when this or that king usurped the throne, but in such cases he tried to justify and legalize his action. There are also some signs that the right to the throne might depend even more on claims through the maternal line than on royal paternity. The role of the queen-mother in the choice of a new king is seen from many inscriptions. Some of these traits have

10. G. A. Reisner, 1923b, pp. 34–77.

11. S. Wenig, 1967, pp. 9–27.

12. Bion is the author of several treatises on geography and natural history of which only a few fragments are known by different ancient authors. Pliny the Elder mentions in particular, in his *Natural History*, book VI, a list of cities along the Nile drawn up by Bion.

close parallels among kingdoms and chiefdoms in various parts of Africa.[13]

All the coronation ceremonies point to a sacral kingship in Napata and Meroe: the king was considered to be an adopted son of various deities. How far he himself was regarded as a god or as the incarnation of a god is not clear but since he was chosen by the gods his actions were directed by them through the precepts of customary law. We have a highly developed concept of a divinely appointed king who dispenses judgement and justice in accordance with the will of a god or gods, a concept which forms the essence of all absolute kingships ancient and modern. Although in theory his power was absolute and undivided the king had to rule strictly according to customary law from which he was not permitted to deviate. He was, moreover, limited by many taboos. Strabo and Diodorus Siculus relate cases where priests, acting avowedly under divine instructions, ordered the king to commit suicide.[14] They state that this custom persisted until the time of Ergamenos (about −250 to −125), who had had a Greek education which freed him from superstitions and who executed the leading priests for their presumption. After that time the custom of royal suicide disappeared.[15]

The rulers of Napata and Meroe used traditional Pharaonic titles in their inscriptions. Nowhere in their titulature do we encounter a Meroitic word for king. The title *kwr* (read *qere*, *qer* or *qeren*) appears only in Psammetik II's account of his conquest of Kush when he mentions the king Aspelta.[16] Though this title must have been the usual form of address of Kushite sovereigns, it was not allowed to intrude into the monuments of Kush.

## The candace: the role of the queen-mother

The exact role played by royal ladies in the earlier periods is not quite clear but there are many indications that they occupied prominent positions and important offices in the realm. During the Kushite rule over Egypt the office of the chief priestess (*Dewat Neter*) to god Amun in Thebes was held by the daughter of the king and gave her great economic and political influence. Even after the loss of Egypt, and consequently of this office, royal ladies continued to hold prominent positions coupled with considerable power among the temple priesthood of Amun at Napata and elsewhere.

The queen-mother's important role at the election and coronation ceremonies of her son is mentioned by Taharqa and Anlamani in such a way

13. For instance in Kaffa, Buganda, Ankola, among the Shilluk, in Monomotapa and elsewhere.

14. Strabo, XVII, 2, 3; Diodorus Siculus, III, 6.

15. Diodorus, loc. cit. There are many parallels to the ritual killing of kings on the order of priests or elders in Africa; cf. L. Frobenius.

16. S. Sauneron and J. Yoyotte, 1952, pp. 157–207, recognized for the first time '*kwr*' as the Meroitic title for 'King'. The modern Alur word *ker*, 'the quality of chiefliness', is probably etymologically related to the Meroitic word; cf. B. G. Haycock, p. 471, no. 34.

as to leave no doubt about her decisive influence and specific status. She also exercised an influence through a complicated system of adoption, whereby the queen-mother, designated by the title Mistress of Kush, adopted the wife of her son. Thus Nasalsa adopted Madiqen, wife of Anlamani, who soon died and was succeeded by his brother Aspelta, whose wife Henuttskhabit was eventually adopted by both Nasalsa and Madiqen. On the stele of Nastasen (− 335 to − 310) the upper scene shows his mother Pelekhs and his wife Sakhakh each holding a sistrum which seems to have been the sign of their office. The inscription of Anlamani says that he had dedicated each of his four sisters to one of the four temples of Amun to be sistrum players and to pray for him before this god.

The iconography confirms the enhanced status of queen-mothers. In religious scenes on temple walls they occupy prominent positions, second only to the king himself, whereas on the walls of the pyramid chapels the queen appears behind the deceased king participating as the principal person in the offerings presented to him.

In the later period these queens – either mothers or wives – started to assume political power and proclaim themselves sovereign, even adopting the royal title Son of Re, Lord of the Two Lands (*sa Re, neb Tawy*) or Son of Re and King (*sa Re, nswbit*).[17] Many of them became famous, and in Graeco-Roman times Meroe was known to have been ruled by a line of *Candaces, Kandake* or queens regnant.

This title is derived from Meroitic *Ktke* or *Kdke*[18] meaning queen-mother. Another title – *qere* – meaning ruler, was not used until the Meroitic script appeared. As a matter of fact we have only four queens known to have used this title, namely Amanirenas, Amanishekhete, Nawidemak and Maleqereabar, all by definition being candaces.[19] It is noteworthy that in the royal tombs of Nuri, from Taharqa (died − 664) to Nastasen (died about − 310) there is no evidence of a queen having the full burial of a reigning monarch and during this period no reigning queen is known. The earliest attested reigning queen was Shanakdekhete, early in the second century before our era, and she was allowed a full royal burial in Begrawiya North. Most probably, in the beginning, the title and the office did not mean more than queen-mother. She was entrusted with bringing up the royal children, for Taharqa mentions in his stele that he was with his mother Queen Abar till the age of 21, living among other royal brothers, the godly youth from which the heir to the throne was chosen. She was thus in a position to exercise great power and influence, which were manifested by her special role in the ceremony of coronation and her adoption of the wife of her son. At some stage the queens would outgrow their sons or husbands and take a favourable moment to assume all power

17. F. Hintze, 1959a, pp. 36–9.
18. The *n* is often elided in Meroitic proper names; cf. F. L. Griffith, 1911–12, p. 55.
19. M. F. L. Macadam, 1966.

for themselves. From Shanakdekhete onwards we have a series of reigning queens but beginning with Amanirenas in the first century before our era there seems to be another development. This was the close association of the first wife of the king and, perhaps, their eldest son on many of the important monuments. This suggests some degree of co-regency since the wife who survived her husband often became the reigning candace. However, this system did not last for more than three generations and seems to come to an end after Natakamani, Amenitere and Sherakarer in the first half of the first century of our era. All this points to the internal development of a local institution which was not a copy of a foreign practice such as that of the Ptolemies in Egypt: an example is Cleopatra. Indeed we can observe how these institutions grew in complexity over the centuries.

This kingship system which developed in Kush had some advantages over a rigid system of strict direct succession since it eliminated the danger of an unsuitable successor, whether a minor or an unpopular personality. The injection of new blood into the royal family was assured by the system of adoption. The various checks and controls inherent in this system, the prominence given to the queen-mother and the insistence on rightful descent ensured the rule of the same royal family. All this may have contributed to the continuity and stability enjoyed by Napata and Meroe for such long centuries.

## Central and provincial administration

Our knowledge of the structure of the central and provincial administration is as yet fragmentary. There is a marked absence of records of a biographical nature about private persons, from which it would be possible to collect information about titles and offices, their significance and functions.

At the centre of the administration stood the king, an absolute autocratic ruler whose word was law. He did not delegate his power to any person, nor did he share it with anyone. In fact, there is a total absence of one administrator, such as a High Priest for all the temples, or a vizier in whose hands some degree of power was concentrated. The royal residence formed the centre of the administrative system. According to a recent survey of the evidence[20] it seems that Meroe was the only town which can be regarded as the royal residence and centre of administration. Piankhi was rather vague as to his place of residence, while it is obvious that Memphis was the capital of his immediate successors of the twenty-fifth dynasty of Egypt. However, Taharqa clearly indicates that he was living among his royal brothers with his mother. From other inscriptions it is clear that these royal brothers lived at Meroe. In this respect, it is remarkable that it is only at Meroe, and in particular at Begrawiya West cemetery, that one finds

20. A. M. Ali Hakem, 1972a, pp. 30ff.

children's or infants' graves with funerary objects showing that they were of court status. There is a marked absence of such graves at the other royal cemeteries at El-Kuru and Nuri. Hence one may conclude that the royal family lived at Meroe and this must have been the permanent residence of the king.

The central administration was run by a number of high officials whose Egyptian titles are preserved in two stelae of Asyelta. Among them we find – apart from army commanders – the chiefs of the treasury, seal bearers, heads of archives, chiefs of granaries, the chief scribe of Kush and other scribes.[21] Whether these titles corresponded to the real functions of their bearers or whether they reflect only Egyptian models is difficult to decide. Whatever the case these officials played an important role in the election of a new king as well as in the administration of the kingdom. Perhaps the deciphering of Meroitic writing will throw light on this important question.

Military leaders appear several times on these inscriptions at critical points. They were charged with proclaiming the succession of a new king and carrying out the traditional ceremonies of coronation. In fact, they may have had some significant role in the choice of the successor. From this one can suppose that most probably the majority were members of the royal family, and perhaps even senior members.[22] It was customary for the king not to go into battle but to stay in his palace assigning the conduct of the war to one of the generals. This was the case in Piankhi's campaign in Egypt, Amani-nete-yerike's war against the Reherehas in the Butana and Nastasen's campaign. Yet we do not know what happened to these generals. Even after a successful campaign they disappeared and the king reaped all the honours of victory.

As for the administration of the provinces, there are traces of royal palaces to be found in many localities. Each palace formed a small administrative unit headed perhaps by a chief seal bearer who kept the stores and accounts of the residence.[23]

However, in the later period starting perhaps towards the end of the first century before our era, we have enough records of provincial administrators to reconstruct at least the skeleton of the northern province of the kingdom which seems to have developed very fast in response to the unsettled conditions following the Roman conquest of Egypt and their unsuccessful attempt to advance farther south into Nubia. To meet this situation on the frontier a special administration for Lower Nubia was created. At its head was the *Paqar*, *qar*, a prominent court personality, possibly a royal prince, if the first holder may be considered to have established the rule. The first was Akinidad, the son of Teritiqas and Amanirenas, who fought against the

21. G. von Steindorff, Vol. III; H. Schäfer, 1905–8, pp. 86, 103, 104.
22. E. A. T. Wallis Budge, 1912, pp. 105ff.
23. M. F. L. Macadam, 1949, Vol. I, p. 58.

Roman invasion of Nubia. The same title was also borne by Arkankharor, Arikakhatani and Sherekarer (the king of the Jabel Qayli rock pictures)[24] and the three sons of Natakamani and Amanitere ( − 12 to + 12). Their names with the title *pqr* have been found on inscriptions from Napata, Meroe and Naqa.[25] However, none of these was associated with Lower Nubia and the term seems to have been a generic title for a prince and not a specific title for the viceroy of the north.

However, the title *Paqar* appears several times in connection with other lesser offices, such as the *taraheb* and the *anhararab* in the little town of Taketer, or the *harapen*, the chief of the Faras region.[26] We can deduce that the holder of the title was the provincial head of Meroitic Lower Nubia. Under the *Paqar* the leading officer in charge of the administration was the *peshte*,[27] which title is first recorded in the first century before our era and which seems to become more prominent during the third century of our era.

The area under the *peshte* jurisdiction was Akin, corresponding to all Meroitic Nubia as far south as Napata itself. How the rank of *peshte* was attained is not clear, whether through inheritance or by royal decree or by appointment by the *Paqar*. However, their large number points to a shorter tenure of office. With the title of *peshte* were associated other titles, sometimes of very high religious status, not only in the local hierarchy but even at Napata or Meroe. Two other important posts under the *peshte* were the *pelmes-ate* (general of the water) and *pelmes-adab* (general of the land). These two officers seem to have been responsible for looking after the meagre yet vital communications of Nubia by land and by water, to ensure the flow of trade with Egypt, to control the frontiers and check the dangerous movements of the nomads both to the east and west of the Nile. These officials were helped by other minor officials, scribes, priests and local administrators. Whether a similar system of provincial administration existed in other provinces we do not know. However, it is certain that the different environment and settlement pattern in the Butana would have needed a different type of administration from that of Lower Nubia along the Nile valley. Unfortunately we possess no records except the imposing temples which must have formed good bases for administrative units, besides their function as religious institutions.

The Meroitic kingdom at its height was so vast and means of communication probably so poor that provincial governors must have been obliged to decentralize authority for administration to function at all. In a much looser relationship to the central government were the chiefs of various ethnic groups on the fringes of the kingdom. In later periods the state included

24. F. Hintze, 1959a, pp. 189–92.
25. A. J. Arkell, 1961, p. 163.
26. F. L. Griffith, 1911–12, p. 62.
27. ibid., p. 120 and Index. It corresponds to the Egyptian *p. s. nsw, psente*; M. F. L. Macadam, 1950, pp. 45–6.

a number of princedoms. Pliny writes that in the Island of Meroe forty-five other Ethiopian kings held sway[28] apart from the candaces. Other classical authors speak about tyrannoi, who were subject to Meroitic kings.[29]

To the south of Meroe were settled the Simbriti, who were allegedly Egyptian refugees, ruled by a queen under Meroitic sovereignty, but on the left bank of the Nile (in Kordofan) lived numerous groups of Nubai under several princelings independent of Meroe.[30] A similar situation seems to have existed in the eastern desert, which was inhabited by many nomadic groups different in culture and languages from the Meroites.

Many inscriptions indicate that the Meroitic kings often led military expeditions against these independent or semi-independent ethnic groups, partly in order to subdue them or as reprisals for raids, or to obtain booty consisting of cattle and slaves. The peoples most often named were the Reheres and the Majai, who probably lived between the Nile and Red Sea and could have been the ancestors of the Beja.

All this indicates that Kush was not a centralized state, and during the later period the kingdom included a number of principalities in some kind of dependency on the Meroitic kings.[31]

## Economic and social life

### Ecology

The kingdom of Kush depended on a broad basis of economic activity. It was as varied as the geographical diversity of the region which extended from Lower Nubia to the south of Sennar and to Gebel Moya region in the southern Gezira plain and included extensive areas between the Nile valley and the Red Sea. Similarly large areas on the west of the Nile were probably under the Meroitic influence though their extent is still unknown. This wide area ranges from the arid to those which receive appreciable summer rainfall. In Nubia economic activity was based on the type of agriculture usual in the Nile valley where the river with its single course provides the only source of water. Although in some places the arable land ranges from nothing at all to a narrow strip along the river, yet in others in Upper Nubia the arable land widens out into basins. This type of riverine cultivation extends farther south along the banks of the Nile and its tributaries. Such geographical conditions in Lower Nubia had a direct influence on political and socio-economic life. Recent archaeological work has indi-

28. Pliny, 186.

29. cf. Bion and Nicholas of Damascus, in C. Muller, Vol. 3, p. 463, Vol. 4, p. 351; Seneca, VI, 8, 3.

30. Strabo, XVII, 1, 2, quoting Eratosthenes.

31. Even in the Napatan period the Kushitic empire had a federal character; cf. Chapter 10.

cated that the levels of the Nile were low and since Nubia lies outside the rainbelt, the ecological conditions were not suitable for an agriculture designed to support an appreciable population. In fact it has been suggested that during the early part of the Natapan period Lower Nubia was for a considerable length of time entirely depopulated and that it was only from the third or second century before our era, and as a result of the introduction of the *saqiya*,[32] that it became repopulated.

In Upper Nubia flood plains, such as the Kerma basin, the Letti basin and Nuri, made cultivable thanks to the Nile flood or, where possible, by the use of water-lifting devices, permitted the growth of large urban centres of considerable historical importance such as those at Barkal, Kawa, Tabo, Soleb or Amara. In this area agrarian economy played a greater role and plantations of dates and vines, in particular, are referred to several times in the inscriptions of Taharqa, Hersiotef and Nastasen.

However, from the middle of the fifth century before our era, this area suffered from droughts and the encroachment of sand, which indicate ecological changes which reduced the grazing area of the hinterland. Such conditions might have tempted the nomads of the eastern desert to move into the Nile valley and so into conflict with its people. Perhaps this was the reason for the wars which extended even to the northern parts of Meroe by the reign of Amani-nete-yerike ($-431$ to $-404$) and subsequent kings. These factors made Upper Nubia lose much of its former significance in the later period of the Meriotic kingdom.

From the junction of the River Atbara with the main Nile southward, the Nile is no longer that decisive single course which cuts through desert land. Instead, each of the Nile tributaries (the Atbara, Blue Nile, White Nile, Dinder, Rahad and so on) is equally important and offers the same agricultural and other economic possibilities but with a wider area of cultivation. Furthermore, the land between these tributaries has an appreciable rainfall during summer, creating extensive pasture and land suitable for cultivation as well. As a matter of fact, the Butana, the Island of Meroe between the Atbara, the Blue Nile and the White Nile, formed the heartland of the Meroitic kingdom and the main type of economic activity was nomadic or semi-nomadic pastoralism.

## Agriculture and animal husbandry

At the time of the rise of the Napata kingdom animal husbandry had a millenary tradition and, together with agriculture, formed the main source of subsistence of the people. Apart from long-horned and short-horned cattle the people bred sheep, goats and to a lesser extent horses[33] and

32. B. Trigger, 1965, p. 123.
33. There is a horse-cemetery at El-Kurru; D. Dunham and O. Bates, pp. 110–17.

donkeys, too, as beasts of burden. Camels were introduced only comparatively late, at the end of the first century before our era.[34]

Cattle-breeding played such an important role in the economic life of the country that the transfer of the royal residence from Napata to Meroe could be explained by the need to be nearer to the main grazing area, for the rainfall zone begins to the south of the new capital. Another reason for the move may be seen in the fact that intensive grazing in the northern parts gradually led to soil erosion on both banks of the Nile. In any case the transfer of the centre of the state in the fourth century apparently gave a new impulse to the development of cattle-breeding. After a period history repeated itself because the cattle destroyed shrubs and trees as well as the grass, initiating another cycle of desiccation. From the first century of our era onwards the grazing lands south of Meroe were not able to sustain the former dense population of pastoralists, who were forced to move westwards or southwards. In the long run this development was probably one of the main reasons of the decay and later the fall of the Meroitic kingdom.

The primacy of cattle-breeding in the empire of Kush is attested in many ways: in iconography, in burial rites, in metaphors – an army without a leader is compared to a herd without a herdsman,[35] and so on.

Offerings to the temples consisted mainly of livestock and it seems that the wealth of the kings, the aristocracy and the temple priests was measured in cattle. The accounts of classical authors, Strabo and Diodorus of Sicily, leave no doubt about the pastoralist character of the Meroitic society, which in many respects was similar to later African cattle-breeding societies.

Throughout the whole history of Napata and Meroe the development of agriculture in the northern parts was influenced by both climate and the scarcity of fertile land in the very narrow valley of the Nile. The lack of land was one of the reasons why the inhabitants – unlike their northern neighbours, the Egyptians – did not feel the need to create a single irrigation system with all its social and political consequences. This does not mean that irrigation was not known in this part of Nubia. Vestiges of ancient irrigation works have been discovered on the Kerma plateau dating from the fifteenth century before our era. The chief irrigation machines at this time were the *shadūf*, to be superseded later by the *saqiya*. The latter, called in Nubian *Kolē*,[36] appeared in Lower Nubia only in Meroitic times but a more precise date is difficult to determine. The sites at Dakka and at Gammai, dating from the third century before our era, seem to be the oldest to contain remains of *saqiya*.[37] The introduction of this irrigation machine

34. A bronze figure of a camel was found in the tomb of King Arikankharer, −25 to −15. cf. D. Dunham and O. Bates, Table XLIX.

35. M. F. L. Macadam, 1949, Vol. I, Inscr. IX.

36. Many place names between Shellal and As-Sabua are formed from this word, such as Koledul, Loleyseg, Arisman-Kole, Sulwi-Kole, etc.; cf. U. Monneret de Villard, 1941, pp. 46ff.

37. O. Bates and D. Dunham, p. 105; R. Herzog, 1957, p. 136.

had a decisive influence on agriculture, especially in Dongola, as this wheel lifts water 3 to 8 metres with much less expenditure of labour and time than the *shadūf*, which is driven by human energy; the *saqiya*, on the other hand, by buffalo or other animals.

Even the southern parts of the country, at least at the end of the sixth century before our era, were predominantly pastoral if we can believe Herodotus, who describes the Island of Meroe as inhabited mostly by cattle-breeders and the agriculture as rather underdeveloped.[38] Archaeology seems to substantiate this view since in the B-level in Gebel Moya, dating from the Napata period and later, sixth to fifth centuries before our era, no traces of agricultural activity were found.[39]

With the gradual shifting of the empire's centre southward and the increase of acreage of irrigated land the situation changed. At the height of the Meroitic kingdom the Island of Meroe was intensively cultivated. The network of canals and *hafirs*, irrigation basins, bears witness to this. One of the emblems of Meroitic kings and priests at this time was a sceptre in the form of a plough, or perhaps a hoe, similar to that widely used in Egypt.

The main cereals cultivated were barley, wheat and, above all, sorghum or *durra* of local origin, and also lentils, *Lens esculenta*, cucumbers, melons and gourds.

Among technical crops the first place belongs to cotton. It was unknown in ancient Egypt but there are many indications that its cultivation in the Nile valley started in the empire of Kush before the beginnings of our era. Evidence from earlier times is scanty but about the fourth century before our era the cultivation of cotton and the knowledge of its spinning and weaving in Meroe reached a very high level. It is even maintained that the export of textiles was one of the sources of wealth of Meroe.[40] The Aksumite King Ezana boasted in his inscription that he destroyed large cotton plantations in Meroe.[41]

Our sources are silent about the forms of land tenure and land exploitation, but since the village community continued its traditional existence well into the nineteenth century we can assume that it existed in the same form in the Napatan and Meroitic periods. The king was considered the sole owner of the land. This was a characteristic common to many ancient societies and gave rise to various forms of land tenure. So the system of land tenure throws no useful light on the relations between the king, as owner, and the cultivators of the soil.

An important branch of agriculture was the cultivation of fruit in orchards and grapes in vineyards. Many of these belonged to temples and were cultivated by slaves.

38. Herodotus, III, 22–3.
39. F. S. A. Addison, p. 104.
40. J. W. Crowfoot, 1911, p. 37, Memoir No. 19.
41. E. Littmann, 1950, p. 116.

Generally speaking there existed in the Napata and Meroe periods the same branches of agriculture as in ancient Egypt but in another relationship. Animal husbandry dominated over agriculture, and garden and orchard cultivation were less developed. But cotton started to be cultivated here much earlier than in Egypt. So far as is known the agricultural products were not exported as they were hardly sufficient for local consumption.

## Mineral resources

During antiquity the empire of Kush has been considered one of the richest countries of the known world. This renown was due more to the mineral wealth of the border lands to the east of the Nile than to the core of the kingdom itself.

Kush was one of the main gold-producing areas in the ancient world. Gold was mined between the Nile and the Red Sea, mostly in the part to the north of the eighteenth parallel where many traces of ancient mining are to be found. Gold production must have been an important occupation in the Meroitic empire and the temples seem to have owned large quantities of it. Taharqa endowed one of his numerous temples with 110 kilogrammes of gold in nine years.[42] Recent excavations at Meroe and Mussawwarat es-Sufra revealed temples with walls and statues covered by gold leaf. Gold and its export were not only one of the main sources of the wealth and greatness of the kingdom but greatly influenced foreign relations with Egypt and Rome. It has been computed that during antiquity Kush produced about 1 600 000 kilogrammes of pure gold.[43] Gold must also have been prized by the nomadic peoples according to various reports. King Nastasen, for instance, exacted nearly 300 kilogrammes of gold from various peoples he fought near Meroe.[44]

Although numerous silver and bronze objects have been found in burial places, and offerings to temples very often comprised silver artefacts, sometimes of high artistic quality, it seems that neither silver nor copper were mined locally and must have been imported from outside.

On the other hand, the eastern desert was rich in various precious and semi-precious stones such as amethyst, carbuncle, hyacinth, chrysolith, beryl and others. Even if these mines were not all controlled by the Meroitic kingdom, in the last resort all their products went through Meroitic trade channels, and so increased the fame of Meroe as one of the richest countries in the ancient world.

## The problem of iron working

The large mounds of slag found near the ancient town of Meroe and

42. J. Vercoutter, 1959, p. 137.
43. H. Quiring, p. 56.
44. H. Schäfer, 1901, pp. 20–1.

elsewhere in the Butana have been the cause of much speculation on the importance of iron in Meroitic civilization. It has been maintained that the knowledge of iron smelting and iron working in many parts of sub-Saharan Africa was derived from Meroe. Already in 1911 A. H. Sayce declared that Meroe must have been the 'Birmingham of ancient Africa'[45] and this view was current until quite recently among scholars and became accepted theory in the majority of works dealing with African or Sudanese history.[46]

In recent years this generally accepted view has been contested by some scholars who raised a number of serious objections to it.[47] These pointed out that the iron objects found in graves are extremely few in number. Wainwright had already realized that there were only a few traces of iron in about −400 and that iron is by no means frequent until the fall of the Meroitic kingdom in about +320. On the other hand, Tylecote has stated positively that there are traces of iron smelting before −200 whereas Amborn in a painstaking analysis of all metallic objects found in the necropolis demonstrated the prevalence of bronze objects over iron ones even in the later period. He concluded that it is more likely that all the finds were imported iron which was possibly worked up in Nubia by local blacksmiths whose existence, however, is certainly known only from the post-Meroitic X-Group culture. In any case one cannot deduce a knowledge of the smelting of iron from examples of its working-up into objects.

Amborn is of the opinion that the slag heaps of Meroe are remains of industries other than iron. If these dumps were in fact the waste products of iron smelting, the areas around Meroe should be littered with iron-smelting furnaces. Instead, until very recently no traces had been found of such a furnace.[48]

The controversy is far from being concluded and more archaeological work is needed to arrive at a positive proof of iron smelting at Meroe. The scarcity of iron tools and artefacts in burial sites does not point to a large-scale iron production and throws doubt on the theory that Meroe was the Birmingham of Africa. On the other hand, this does not mean that iron smelting was quite unknown in this region nor that it was not practised in neighbouring parts of Africa. The problem of iron in Meroe is one of the most crucial in African history and merits thorough investigation by all the modern techniques at the disposal of archaeologists and historians.

45. A. H. Sayce, p. 55.

46. G. A. Wainwright, 1945, pp. 5–36; A. J. Arkell in mány of his writings, lastly 1966, pp. 451ff.; P. L. Shinnie, 1967, pp. 160ff.; I. S. Katznelson, pp. 289ff. and others.

47. cf. B. G. Trigger, 1969, pp. 23–50; R. F. Tylecote, pp. 67–72; H. Amborn, pp. 71–95.

48. H. Amborn, pp. 83–7 and 92. P. L. Shinnie and F. Y. Kense have just issued a communication at the Third International Meroitic Conference in Toronto, 1977, in which they contest Amborn's assertion: in fact, iron-smelting furnaces were discovered at Meroe (Begrawiya) during recent excavations.

Only then will we be able to assess the role of Meroe in the African iron age.

## Towns, crafts and trade

The Nile valley, regulated by the unfailing annual inundation, favoured the development of permanent settlements and the eventual growth of towns. And this in turn encouraged the development of crafts. Some of these Nile valley urban centres were so situated that they grew into outlets for trade with the hinterland and other trading communities. Many of them played a role also as administrative and religious centres.[49]

It has been suggested that urban development in Lower Nubia followed political development and the growing interest of the Meroites in their northern borders with Egypt. Meroitic armies were repeatedly sent in to Lower Nubia and the soldiers tended to settle down to develop a self-supporting economy. They benefited from trade relations with Egypt and consequently large towns and thriving local communities located in strategic positions such as Qasr Ibrim or Gebel Adda grew up in Lower Nubia. Political and religious life centred round a local magnate or a family with hereditary administrative or military office. This aristocracy lived in castles like that at Karanog or in palaces like the Governor's Palace in Mussawwarat es-Sufra.

Pliny, quoting as his authorities Bion and Juba, has preserved the names of many Meroitic towns on both banks of the Nile, situated between the First Cataract and the town of Meroe.[50]

The most northerly Meroitic monument is Arqamani's chapel in Dakka, the ancient Pselchis, but the nearest frontier town seems to have stood south of Wadi as-Sabua, where traces of a large settlement with a cemetery have been found. Other important urban settlements in this region were Karanog near the modern town of Aniba and opposite it the great fort of Qasr Ibrim, although the surviving buildings are mostly post-Meroitic.

The town of Faras, Pakhoras, was the main administrative centre of the province called *Akin*, which corresponded to Lower Nubia. Some official buildings have been excavated, among them the so-called Western Palace dating from the first century of our era and built of sun-dried bricks and a fortification situated on the river bank.

South of Faras Meroitic settlements are rare. The region is inhospitable and the valley too narrow to meet the needs of a large population. Only in the vicinity of Dongola do we find wider lands and increased signs of ancient occupation. Opposite the modern town of Dongola lies Kawa, where a large town with many temples indicates a long history and where excavations revealed many important Meroitic monuments and inscriptions.

49. A. M. Ali Hakem, 1972b, pp. 639–46.
50. *Hist. Bat.*, VI, 178, 179.

Upstream from Kawa there are no sites of importance until Napata is reached. Its place in royal ceremonies and religious customs has already been stressed. The importance of this town derived from its location at the northern end of the caravan route which skirted the three scarcely navigable cataracts. All goods from the southern and central parts of the kingdom as well as from the interior of Africa had to go through Napata. Though the town site of Napata remains partly unexplored the royal cemeteries at El-Kurru, Nuri and Gebel Barkal, as well as the temples of Gebel Barkal and at Sanam, have all been investigated. We can thus assess the importance of Napata as a royal and religious centre in the earlier period of Kush history. Until the time of Nastasen the cemeteries around Napata were used for royal burials, and even afterwards, when the kings were normally buried at Meroe, some preferred to be interred at Gebel Barkal.

The next important urban centre in the Nile valley was at Dangeil, 5 miles north of Berber, where the remains of brick buildings and walls were discovered. The site itself seems to lie on an important route leading from Meroe to the north.

In the Island of Meroe, which corresponds roughly to the modern Butane plain lying between the Atbara and the Blue Nile, many traces of Meroitic settlement were found.[51]

Although the city of Meroe is mentioned for the first time in the last quarter of the fifth century before our era in the inscription of Amannateieriko in the Kawa temple under the name of *B.rw.t*, the lowest excavation strata show that a large settlement existed on this site already in the eighth century. Herodotus, II, 29, calls it a big city and excavations have confirmed that the town occupied a large area with a central part surrounded by suburbs and perhaps also by a wall. Apart from being for many centuries the capital and royal residence, Meroe was one of the main economic and trade centres of the country, lying at the crossroads of caravan routes and serving as a river port too. The greater part of the town area, consisting of many mounds covered with red brick fragments, still awaits its archaeologists.[52] But the part hitherto excavated and examined is sufficient to show that Meroe at its height had been an enormous city with all the attributes of urban life. As such Meroe must be numbered among the most important monuments of early civilization on the African continent. The main elements of the excavated parts of the city are the royal city with palaces, a royal bath and other buildings, and the temple of Amun. In the vicinity were found the temple of Isis, the Lion temple, the Sun temple, many pyramids and non-royal cemeteries.

Not far away from Meroe lies the site of Wad ben Naqa, consisting of ruins of at least two temples. Recent excavations have revealed a large

51. A. M. Ali Hakem, 1972b.

52. The recent excavations (1972–5) have been carried out by the Universities of Calgary and Khartoum during which numerous new temples have been discovered.

building which was perhaps a palace, and a beehive structure which may have been an enormous silo. This and many scattered mounds in the vicinity indicate the importance of this town, the residence of the candaces and a Nile port.[53]

Among other important sites, the following should be mentioned. Basa, lying in Wadi Hawad, has a temple and an enormous *hafir* surrounded by stone statues of lions. The most interesting feature is that this town did not grow haphazardly but was strictly planned according to the terrain then covered by trees and shrubs.[54] Of exceptional importance from many points of view is Mussawwarat es-Sufra in the Wadi el-Banat at some distance from the Nile. Its main feature, the Great Enclosure, consists of many buildings and walled enclosures surrounding a temple built in the first century before our era or a little earlier. The number of representations of elephants suggests that they were in some way important to the country. There is a number of temples, the most important of them being the Lion temple dedicated to the god Apedemak. The recent excavations by F. Hintze[55] threw new light on many aspects of Meroitic history, art and religion but much remains enigmatic.

Apart from their administrative and religious functions the Meroitic towns were also important centres of crafts and trade. So far no special studies have been devoted to these aspects of Meroitic economic history but the existing evidence indicates a high technological and artistic level of crafts. Specialized building crafts were necessary for the erection and decoration of the numerous monuments, palaces, temples, pyramids, and so on. Although in the earlier period Egyptian influence is unmistakable, from the third century before our era many autochthonous elements show that Meroitic craftsmen and artists freed themselves from foreign models and created a highly original and independent artistic tradition.

Pottery is the best-known of all the products of the Meroitic civilization and owes its fame to its quality both in its texture and its decoration. There are two distinct traditions: the handmade pottery made by women which shows a remarkable continuity of form and style and reflects a deep-rooted African tradition,[56] and the wheel-turned ware made by men which is more varied and responsive to stylistic changes. These differences lead to the conclusion that already from early times wheel-made pottery developed as a separate craft producing wares for market and thus subject to changing fashions and the demands of the middle and higher classes of Meroitic society, whilst the people continued to use the traditional utility pottery made at home by women.

Jewellery was another highly developed craft. It has been found in con-

53. cf. J. Vercoutter, 1962.
54. J. W. Crowfoot, 1911, pp. 11–20.
55. cf. F. Hintze, 1962; 1971a.
56. P. L. Shinnie, 1967, p. 116, points out that this ware is still made today in the same style not only in the Sudan but in many other parts of Africa.

siderable quantities mostly in royal tombs. As with other artefacts the earlier jewellery was closely modelled on Egyptian styles and only later examples are characteristically Meroitic in style and ornamentation. The main materials were gold, silver, semi-precious stones, and the range of artefacts goes from plaques to necklaces, bracelets, ear-rings and finger-rings. The design of the jewellery shows considerable variety: some are of Egyptian inspiration but others show clearly that they are in the tradition of Meroitic craftsmen and artists. An allied craft was in carving ivory. Owing to the abundance and accessibility of this material in Meroe it is not surprising that the carvers evolved their own techniques and traditions, with motifs drawn chiefly from animals (giraffes, rhinoceroses and ostriches).

Cabinet-makers produced various kinds of furniture, especially beds but also wooden caskets, strong-boxes and even musical instruments. Weavers made cotton and linen textiles. Tanners processed hides and leather. The remnants of the work of all these crafts have been found in various tombs.

All this indicates that in Meroe there existed a comparatively large class of craftsmen to which belonged also artists, architects and sculptors. How these crafts were organized is so far unknown as the names of crafts in Meroitic inscriptions remain undeciphered. It is likely that workshops for the temple services existed as in Egypt[57] and perhaps *ergasteries* were organized at the royal court.

The empire of Kush formed an ideal entrepôt for the caravan routes between the Red Sea, the Upper Nile and the Nile–Chad savannah. It is therefore not surprising that foreign trade played an important role in the Meroitic economy as well as in its politics. Evidence of commercial relations with Egypt is sufficiently abundant to allow an assessment of the magnitude of the trade, its commodities and routes. On the other hand trade with other parts of Africa can only be surmised and many problems are still unsolved. Since ancient times the main exports from Nubia were gold, incense, ivory, ebony, oils, semi-precious stones, ostrich feathers and leopard skins. Although some of these goods originated on Meroitic territory, the origin of others is clearly from countries far to the south.

Foreign trade was directed mainly to Egypt and the Mediterranean world and later perhaps to southern Arabia. The chief trade route went along the Nile, although in some parts it crossed the savannah, for instance, between Meroe and Napata, and Napata and Lower Nubia. The Island of Meroe must have been criss-crossed by many caravan routes and it was also the starting-point for caravans to the Red Sea region, northern Ethiopia, Kordofan and Darfur. The control of this large network of routes was a constant worry for the Meroitic kings, for the nomadic peoples very often raided the caravans. The rulers built fortresses at strategic points in the Bajude steppe – between Meroe and Napata, for instance – to protect the trade routes and also dug wells along them.

57. Such workshops were found at the temple T in Kawa dated from the seventh or sixth century before our era; cf. M. F. L. Macadam, 1949, Vol. I, pp. 211–32.

The evidence is too scanty to deal fully with the development of the foreign trade of Meroe during its whole history. It can be only surmised that this trade reached its peak at the beginning of the hellenistic period with the increased demands of the Ptolemaic dynasty for exotic goods from Africa. Later, at the beginning of the first century before our era, the main route was transferred from the Nile axis to the Red Sea. This diminished the volume of goods directly exported from Meroe since many could be obtained in northern Ethiopia where Aksum had just started to rise. The last centuries of the Meroitic Kingdom coincided with the crisis of the Roman empire which led at first to a sharp decline and later to a quasi-total interruption of trade relations between Meroe and Egypt. Many towns in Lower Nubia dependent on this trade were ruined. Moreover, neither Rome nor Meroe were at this time able to defend the trade routes against the raids of nomadic Blemmyes and Nobades.[58]

## Social structure

In the absence of any direct information it is almost impossible to present a coherent picture of the social structure in Meroe. So far we know only about the existence of a higher or ruling class composed of the king and his relatives, of a court and provincial aristocracy that fulfilled various administrative and military functions and of a very influential temple priest-hood. At the opposite end of the social scale our sources often mention the existence of slaves recruited from prisoners of war. From indirect evidence we can surmise that, apart from cultivators and cattle-breeders who must have formed the majority of the Meroitic population, there existed a middle class of craftsmen, traders and various minor officials and servants, but nothing at all is known about their social status. Until more evidence becomes available any attempt to characterize the type of social and production relationships would be premature.

Epigraphic and other documents hint that warlike activities played a not unimportant role in the kingdom but how the armies were raised and organized it is difficult to say. It seems that apart from a standing royal guard all male inhabitants were mobilized in time of need. Accounts from the Roman period indicate that the army was divided into infantry and cavalry but that Meroitic soldiers were not very disciplined in comparison with the Roman legions. Wars were fought against nomadic groups in-habiting the eastern desert, never fully subjected and ready to invade the cultivated lands on favourable occasions. At the same time many aggressive wars were made to increase the territory and to seize booty (cattle and slaves), which must have formed an important source of wealth for the ruling classes and the priesthood.

A large proportion of prisoners of war was regularly given by the kings

58. For an analysis of the causes of decline see I. S. Katznelson, pp. 249ff.

to the temples and sometimes even the newly occupied territory. The number of slaves must have been proportionally very high, and in Roman times many black slaves were exported to Egypt and to Mediterranean countries. Slave labour was exploited in building pyramids, temples, palaces and other monumental buildings as well as in the orchards and gardens of the temples. The slaves were perhaps employed for digging and repairing irrigation canals and basins (*hafirs*). Slavery in Meroe developed as in other Oriental tyrannies but rather slowly and never constituted the main base of production since slave labour had a comparatively narrower sphere of application. In inscriptions a greater number of women than men is always mentioned, which indicates that domestic slavery was the prevailing form.

# Religion

## General features

The Meroitic peoples derived most of their official religious ideas from Egypt. The majority of gods worshipped in Meroitic temples correspond to those of Egypt, and earlier Meroitic kings considered Amun the highest god, from whom they derived their rights to the throne. The priests of the temples of Amun exercised an enormous influence, at least to the time of King Ergamenes, who seems to have broken their former absolute control. But even later kings showed – at least in their inscriptions – a veneration for Amun and his priests, who were variously favoured by gifts of gold, slaves, cattle and landed property.

Along with Pharaonic divinities such as Isis, Horus, Thoth, Arensnuphis, Satis, with their original symbols, purely Meroitic gods were worshipped like the Lion-god Apedemak or the god Sebewyemeker (Sbomeker). The official cult of these gods began as late as the third century before our era. It seems that they were formerly local gods of the southern parts of the empire and came to prominence only when the Egyptian influence began to fade and was replaced by more particularly Meroitic cultural traits. It should be remembered that it was also about this time that Meroitic cultural script and language were introduced into inscriptions.

Apedemak, a warrior god, was a divinity of great importance to the Meroites. He is depicted with a lion head and lions played some part in the ceremonies of the temple especially in Musawwarat es-Sufra.[59] At the same place we find another Meroitic god unknown to the Egyptians, Sebewyemeker, who was perhaps the chief local god since he was considered as creator. Some goddesses are also depicted at Naqa but their names and place in the Meroitic pantheon remain unknown.

The presence of two sets of divinities, one of Egyptian and the other of local origin, is reflected also in temple architecture.

59. L. V. Zabkar.

## Amun temples

Religious symbolism played an important role in the designing of temples in ancient Egypt. The act of worship was expressed in elaborate and complex rituals and each part of the temple had a specific role in the progress of the ritual. These various parts, e.g. halls, courtyards, chambers, chapels, etc., were laid out axially producing a long corridor of procession. Such temples were built in the Dongol region by Piankhi and Taharqa and their successors. The most important of these temples dedicated to Amun-Re in Napata was built at Gebel Barkal. On the other hand Meroe does not figure in earlier coronation inscriptions as having a temple to Amun.

However, towards the end of the first century before our era the city of Meroe was honoured with the building of one of these temples and a long inscription in Meroitic script was set up in front. The earliest names associated with it are King Amanikhabale (−65 to −41) and Queen Amanishakhete (−41 to −12). This temple became perhaps the leading temple of Amun-Re in the later period of the kingdom. It is noticeable that from this period onwards, other similar Amun temples of a smaller size were built at Meroe, Musawwarat es-Sufra, Naqa and Wad ben Naqa. The Aksum temple at Meroe played a similar role to that of Napata at Gebel Barkal and must have formed a formidable challenge to Napata prominence, eventually superseding it. Even during the earlier period, before the building of the Amun temple of Meroe, Napata had not an entire monopoly as the religious centre, for there existed other types of temple, which dominated the religious life throughout the Butana and radiated from there northward. These are the lion temples to which we must now turn.

## Lion temples

The name lion temple is suggested by a marked preponderance of lion figures, whether sculptured in the round, guarding the approach and the entrance of temples, or in relief in a prominent position. The figure of the lion represents also the chief Meroitic god Apedemak. This does not mean that every temple of this kind was dedicated solely to Apedemak. The existence of this type has been observed by different authorities[60] but in the description of individual temples various names have been given to them.[61] Thus, we hear of the Apis temple, Isis temple, Sun temple, Augustus-head temple, Fresco Chamber, and so on. The use of such terms led, in some cases, to misunderstanding and mistaken conclusions.[62] The

60. J. Garstang *et al.*, p. 57; M. F. L. Macadam, 1949, Vol. I, p. 114; F. Hintze, 1962, 1971a.

61. B. Porter and R. Moss, pp. 264ff.

62. E.g. the Sun temple so called by Sayce who relied on Herodotus; report of the presence of a 'Table of the Sun' has led some to suggest special Sun worship at Meroe. Terms like Isis-temple and Apis-temple might lead to similar mistaken conclusions.

use of the term lion temple would eliminate further misunderstanding, the figure of the lion being its most distinctive feature. Statues of rams are associated with Amun temples at Barkal, Kawa, Meroe, Naqa, where the lion statues are entirely absent even when the lion-god Apedemak was probably one of the deities worshipped and when his figure appeared among those of the other deities. Although ram-headed deities, Amun-Re and Khnum, appear quite often on the reliefs of these lion temples there is no single instance of a ram statue being found associated with any of the lion temples.

## Distribution and types of lion temples

Besides thirty-two recorded lion temples there are fourteen other sites in which the presence of lion temples is almost certain. If we add to this the occurrence of priestly titles associated with temples in localities such as Nalete, Tiye, etc., the number of these temples must have been very great indeed. They seem to have been distributed throughout the whole realm of Meroe. From a study of this distribution two facts clearly emerge; the first is that there are four localities where several temples have been discovered: Naqa with eight temples, Musawwarat es-Sufra and Meroe with six temples at each site and Gebel Barkal with three temples.

Several temples in one locality indicate the religious importance of a site. The most elaborate and perhaps the leading temples of the kingdom were those at Musawwarat es-Sufra and the Sun temple at Meroe (M 250). On the other hand, Naqa has more temples than any other single site whilst Barkal provides the earliest datable examples of lion temples. The first one (B 900), built by Piankhi ($-750$ to $-716$), had originally two chambers which were later transformed into a pyloned single-chamber lion temple. The second temple is B 700 started by Atlanersa ($-635$ to $-643$) and finished by Senkamanisken ($-643$ to $-623$).

The second fact is that the regions where the two types were built do not coincide. It is possible to argue that on the whole the Amun temples are found in the Napatan region, while the lion temples are found in the Island of Meroe, where Amun temples were built only from the first century before our era onwards.

All lion temples can be divided into two basic types. The first is a two-chamber temple, the earliest examples of this type being built of plain mud-brick without a pylon. The second type has a single chamber only and the majority of these temples has a pylon in front although the earlier examples are without it.

Two local sources can be suggested for the appearance of the second type of lion temple. That it had developed from the first type seems evident from the fact that B 900 was reconstructed at a subsequent date with the plan of the second type. On the other hand, there are several small single-chamber structures at both Barkal[63] and Kerma[64] from which the second type might have derived its origin. The earliest examples of this type can be found perhaps below Meroe M 250, possibly dating from Aspelta, and below temple 100 of Musawwarat es-Sufra dating from before −500.[65]

The other influence on the plan of the lion temple might have been Egypt. Chapels exist which were built at various periods, either inside other temple enclosures or on the edge of the desert. They were the resting-places for the barque or the statue of the god during various processions. The majority are elaborate and multi-chambered,[66] and even though a feature of the twenty-fifth dynasty at Thebes is the building or addition of various small chapels at Karnak and elsewhere,[67] these do not normally reflect lion temple design. An indigenous origin would therefore seem more likely. In its simplicity it was suitable to areas like the Butana where the lack of skill and materials made an elaborate building such as the Amun temples unlikely, at least in the very early period. Perhaps the simplicity of the temple reflects a simple type of worship as one would expect among nomad communities of the Butana and other regions.

Although the two types of temple – Amun and lion temples – suggest at first glance two kinds of religion, a careful reconsideration shows that in fact there was only one religion in Meroe. For the coexistence of two religions would presuppose either a considerable degree of religious tolerance which can hardly be expected at that time, or fierce conflict and continuous religious wars and this does not appear on any form of record. On the contrary, the pantheon worshipped in the Amun temples seems also to have been worshipped in the lion temples except that certain gods were given more prominence in one temple than in another. The gods are after all a mixture of Egyptian gods such as Amun-Re or the Osirian triad or indigenous local gods such as Apedemak, Mandulis, Sebewyemeker.[68] The differences in the temple plans indicate differences rather in the rituals than in the religion. The rituals connected with coronation ceremonies needed an Amun-temple type to accommodate processions and festivities. This form of religious practice made it possible to incorporate various local gods and beliefs without conflict and hence helped to give coherence for a very long period to a kingdom composed of very diverse elements.

63. G. A. Reisner, 1918, p. 224.
64. G. A. Reisner, 1923a, p. 423.
65. F. and U. Hintze, 1970.
66. A. Badawy, 1968, p. 282.
67. J. Leclant, 1965b, p. 18.
68. J. Leclant, 1970b, pp. 141–53.

PLATE 11.1 *Pyramid of King Nate-kamani at Meroe with ruins of chapel and pylon in foreground*

PLATE 11.2 *Granite ram at Naqa*

PLATE 11.4 *Gold jewellery of Queen Amanishekhete (−41 to −12)*

PLATE 11.3 *Sandstone plaque showing Prince Arikhankerer slaying his enemies (possibly second century of our era)*

PLATE 11.5 *Various pieces of Meroitic pottery*
      *Top left*  } *Painted pots showing figures in caricature*
      *Top right* }
      *Centre: Painted pot showing a lion eating a man*
      *Bottom left: Painted pot with heads of lion-god Apedemak*
      *Bottom right: Red-ware pot with band seated frogs with plants between them*

323

PLATE 11.6 *Various bronze bowls from Meroe*

PLATE 11.8 *The Meroitic God Sebewye-meker, Lion Temple at Mussawwarat es-Sufra*

PLATE 11.7 *King Arnekhamani: from the Lion Temple at Mussawwarat es-Sufra*

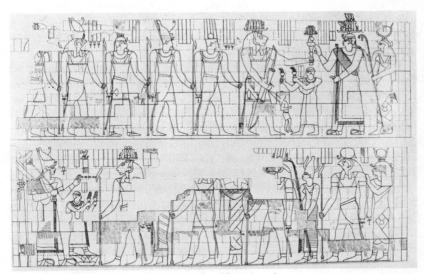

PLATE 11.9 *The god Apedemak leading other Meroitic gods*

325

# The spreading of Christianity in Nubia

## K. MICHALOWSKI

The social structures and historical events of Nubia's early Christian period were shaped by two main factors. One of these was the decline of the kingdom of Meroe, which occupied Nubia from the third century before our era to the third century of our era. The other was the romanization and then the christianization of Egypt, its northern neighbour. After the kingdom of Meroe fell, a Nobadian state was formed in northern Nubia between the First Cataract and the Dal, i.e. the area between the Second and the Third Cataracts. It emerged after a long series of struggles between the Blemmyes and the Nobades, who finally gained control of the Nile valley and pushed the Blemmyes (Bega or Buga) out into the eastern desert.

The excavations carried out by various international missions as part of the campaign to save the Nubian monuments yielded much fresh information on this period of Nubian history.

The Polish excavations at Faras confirmed that ancient Pachoras was the capital of the kingdom of the Nobades towards the end of its existence. It was the site of their sovereigns' palace, which was transformed later into the earliest cathedral.[1]

The remains of their material culture show that the contrasts in their society's living standards were extreme. The masses were relatively poor. Their humble burial places made the British archaeologist G. A. von Reisner,[2] who first discovered their civilization, use the term 'the X-Group Culture' – for lack of a more exact historical definition. In contrast to the common people's low level, the ruling classes, princes and court cultivated the traditions of Meroitic art and culture. The most representative remains of the material culture of that tenuous upper crust of society are the lavish tomb furniture of the well-known tumuli of Ballana, discovered in 1938 by W. B. Emery,[3] and the Sovereigns' Palace of Nubia at Faras mentioned earlier.

The interdependence between the Ballana culture and that of the

1. K. Michalowski, 1967b, pp. 49–52.
2. G. A. Reisner, 1910–27, pp. 345.
3. W. B. Emery and L. P. Kirwan, 1938.

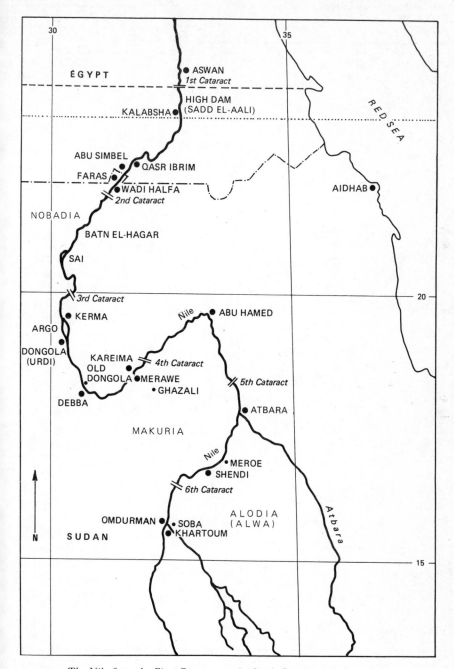

FIG. 12.1 *The Nile from the First Cataract to the Sixth Cataract*

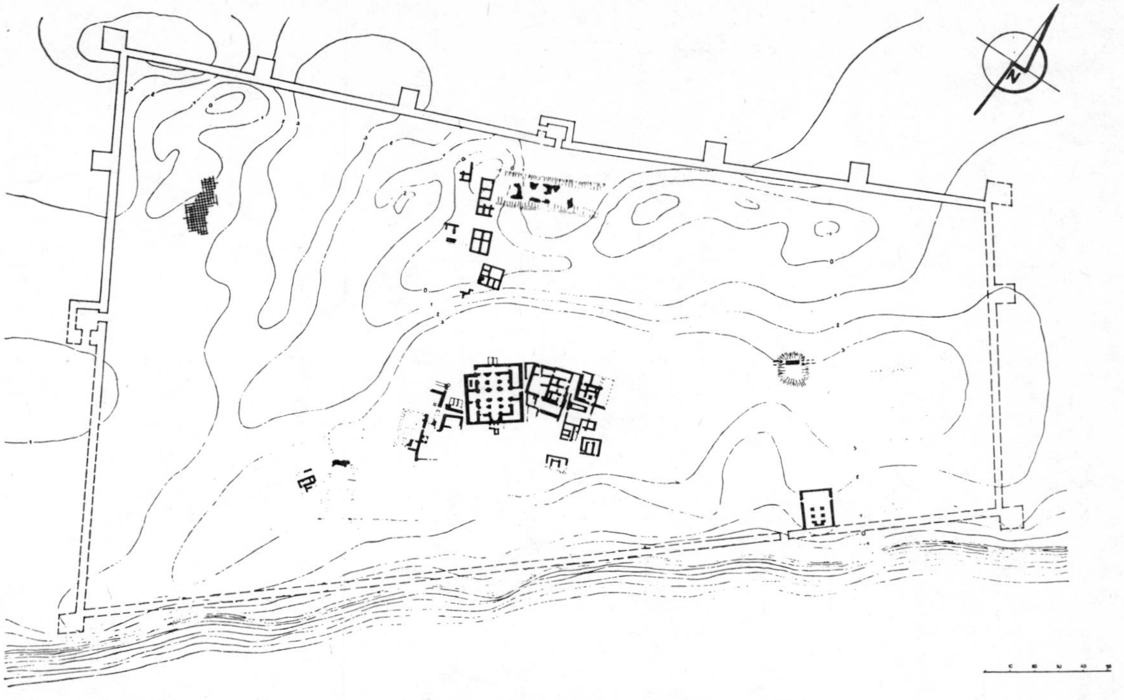

I. Faras. General plan of the site within the Enclosure Walls

In the middle — the Great Kom; top left corner — remains of the Great Church; bottom right corner — the Rivergate Church

FIG. 12.2  *Plans of Faras I*

X-Group was not elucidated until quite recently.[4] A short time ago scholars were still disputing it. Some of them held that the X-Group was an enigma[5] in Nubia's history and attributed the Ballana tumuli to chiefs of the Blemmyes,[6] and the other objects of that period to late Meroitic art and culture.[7] Others were inclined to call the whole of that period the 'Ballana civilization'.[8]

The Polish excavations at Faras led to the discovery under the Nobadian Sovereigns' Palace of a Christian church built of unbaked bricks that must have antedated the end of the fifth century. This early dating has, it is true, recently been contested[9] but the facts are that among 'X-Group' tombs there have been found Christian graves[10] and that Christian oil lamps and pottery decorated with the sign of the cross appear in X-Group settlements on Meinarti Island.[11] This is strong evidence that very early, even before the official christianization of Nubia by the mission headed by the priest Julianos which was sent out by the empress Theodora of Byzantium, the Christian faith had reached the Nobades and readily made converts among the poor. A further argument for an early penetration of Nubia by the Christian faith is the existence there of monasteries and hermitages since the end of the fifth century.[12] It can therefore be confidently stated that the Christian religion had gradually infiltrated into Nubia before its official conversion which, according to John of Ephesus,[13] took place in +543.

Many factors explain this early christianization of the country of the Nobades. Both the Roman empire, still hostile to Christianity in the third century, and the Christian empire of the fourth, fifth and sixth centuries persecuted those who did not obey official injunctions with regard to religion. Hence many Egyptians perhaps, and also Nubians fleeing from Egypt, may have brought their faith to the Nobades dwelling south of Aswan. The traders' caravans passed through Aswan on their southward route, carrying beliefs along with the rest. Byzantine diplomacy, too, played anything but a minor role in the fifth and sixth centuries, Byzantium being anxious to remain on good terms with Aksum in the face of the Persian threat in the Red Sea. In 524 a formal treaty enabled Aksum to send Blemmyes and Nobades to take part in the projected expedition in the Yemen. The priests were certainly not inactive in these transactions and relationships.

4. K. Michalowski, 1967a, pp. 194–211.
5. L. P. Kirwan, 1963, pp. 55–78.
6. W. B. Emery, 1965, pp. 57–90.
7. F. L. Griffith, 1926, pp. 21ff.
8. B. G. Trigger, 1965, p. 127.
9. P. Grossman, pp. 330–50.
10. T. Säve-Söderbergh, 1963, p. 67.
11. W. Y. Adams, 1965a, p. 155; 1965b, p. 172.
12. S. Jakobielski, 1972, p. 21.
13. L. P. Kirwan, 1939, pp. 49–51.

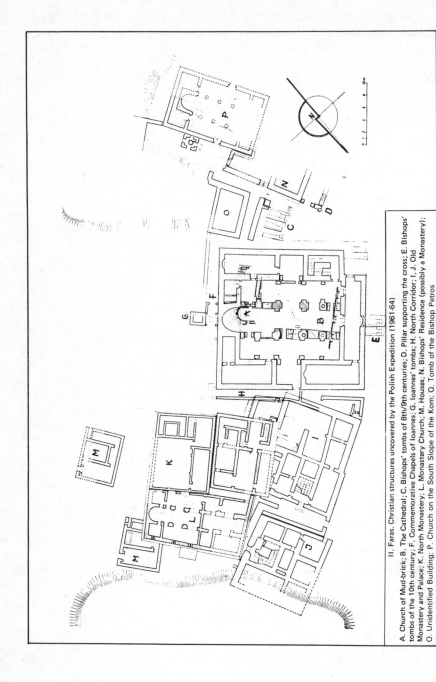

II. Faras. Christian structures uncovered by the Polish Expedition (1961-64)

A. Church of Mud-brick; B. The Cathedral; C. Bishops' tombs of 8th/9th centuries; D. Pillar supporting the cross; E. Bishops' tombs of the 10th century; F. Commemorative Chapels of Ioannes; G. Ioannes' tombs; H. North Corridor; I, J. Old Monastery and Palace; K. North Monastery; L. Monastery Church; M. Houses; N. Bishops' Residence (possibly a Monastery); O. Unidentified Building; P. Church on the South Slope of the Kom; Q. Tomb of the Bishop Petros

FIG. 12.3  *Plans of Faras II*

By order of the empress Theodora the priest Julianos gave Monophysite baptism only to the sovereigns of the country. Under the influence of Christian Egypt most of its people had been strongly attracted to the new faith and had adopted it much earlier. A church on the banks of the Nile in an outlying district was serving a humble Christian community back in the sixth century. The conversion of the Nobadian rulers to Christianity was for them an important political act. They no longer had a well-defined religious ideology with which to hold the people's allegiance and Christianity now gave them access to Egypt, where since the fourth century bishops had resided on the island of Philae.[14] Through Egypt they could reach the Mediterranean and the centre of the civilization of that era – Byzantium.

The kingdom of the Nobadae (Nūba in Arabic), known as Nobadia, extended from Philae to the Second Cataract. Its capital was Faras. In the south, as far as ancient Meroe, another Nubian kingdom emerged in the sixth century with Old Dongola (Dungula in Arabic) as its capital. This kingdom was later called Makuria (Muqurra in Arabic). In contrast to northern Nubia, which had adopted the Monophysite doctrine, Makuria was converted to orthodox Melkite by a mission which the emperor Justinian sent out in 567–70.[15]

As a result of the Polish excavations carried out at Old Dongola since 1964, four churches and the Christian royal palace have been identified.[16] One of these buildings dates back to the end of the seventh or the beginning of the eighth century. Beneath it the remains of an earlier church built of unbaked bricks have been discovered. This religious building, which was not the cathedral, had five naves and was supported by sixteen granite columns 5·20 metres in height. In view of the magnitude of the remains discovered, there is reason to think that the enthusiastic descriptions given by an Arab traveller in the eleventh century were historically accurate: Dongola was an important capital, at least as regards its monuments.

Finally, between 660 and 700 the Makurites also adopted the Monophysite doctrine and the fact was not without important consequences. Towards 580, with the support of the Nobadae, a Byzantine mission came to Alodia and its leader, Bishop Longinos, noted that the country had already been partly converted by the Aksumites. Towards the end of the sixth century Nubia was therefore a Christian country consisting of three kingdoms: Nobadia in the north, Makuria in the centre and Alodia in the

14. U. Monneret de Villard, 1938; H. Munier, 1943, pp. 8ff.

15. U. Monnerèt de Villard, 1938, p. 64; L. P. Kirwan, 1966, p. 127.

16. K. Michalowski, 1966, pp. 189–299; 1969, pp. 30–3; S. Jakobielski and A. Ostrasz; S. Jakobielski and L. Krzyzaniak; K. Michalowski, pp. 163–6; S. Jakobielski, 1970, pp. 167ff.; pp. 70–5; M. Martens, 1973, pp. 263–71; S. Jakobielski, 1975b, pp. 349–60.

south. Their mutual relations are not even yet entirely clear, at any rate in respect of the first period of their independence.[17]

Until recently the history of Christian Nubia was a part of Egyptology, ancient history and palaeo-Christianity, and most often of the history of Coptic Egypt. Ugo Monneret de Villard's standard work[18] contains all that was known about Christian Nubia in 1938. His four-volume survey of medieval Nubia[19] provided a wealth of illustrative material when it appeared, and still helps research workers to study many points of detail. He deals in his books with the results of archaeological excavation, but he has meticulously combed Arabic texts, which are still often the only sources of confirmation about important facts of Nubian history and the chronology of Nubian kings. Some of the most important of these are the writings of Al-Yáqûbi (874), Al-Mas'udi (956), Ibn Hawqal (c. 960), Selim al-Aswāni (c. 970), Abu Sālih (c. 1200), Al-Makīn (1272), Ibn Khaldun (1342–1406) and, in particular, Maqrizi (1364–1442).[20]

Since Monneret de Villard's research, many archaeological discoveries have been accumulated, particularly through the 'Nubian campaign' organized under the auspices of Unesco in 1960–5 to explore ground that was to be flooded by the Nile water above the Sadd al-'Āalī, the High Dam. In some parts of northern Nubia the slow rise of the water level in the storage basin has allowed digging to continue until 1971, and at Qasr Ibrim, which is not flooded, until now.

The results of the research of the last few years have often been exceptionally valuable and have brought the problems of Christian Nubia back into the foreground. The first reports of the diggings were published in *Kush* for Sudanese Nubia, and in the *Annales du Service des Antiquités de l'Egypte* for Egyptian Nubia. Some reports have appeared in independent series of publications.[21] New summaries have appeared, and archaeological research has been transferred south of the threatened area.

A new approach to the problem of Christianity in Nubia appears particularly in the works of W. Y. Adams (mainly as regards ceramic classification),[22] B. Trigger,[23] L. P. Kirwan,[24] P. L. Shinnie,[25]

17. W. Y. Adams, 1965, p. 170.

18. U. Monneret de Villard, 1938.

19. U. Monneret de Villard, 1935–57.

20. A list of the most important Arab and Christian texts on the history of Christian Nubia has recently been given by G. Vantini.

21. T. Säve-Söderbergh, 1970; M. Almagro, 1963–5; K. Michalowski, 1965c.

22. W. Y. Adams, 1961, pp. 7–43; 1962a, pp. 62–75; 1962b, pp. 245–88; W. Y. Adams and H. A. Nordström, pp. 1–10; W. Y. Adams, 1964a, pp. 227–47; 1965a, pp. 148–76; 1965b, pp. 87–139; 1966a, pp. 13–30; 1968, pp. 194–215; 1967, pp. 11–19; T. Säve-Söderbergh, 1970, pp. 224, 225, 227, 232, 235; 1972, pp. 11–17.

23. B. G. Trigger, 1965, pp. 347–87.

24. L. P. Kirwan, 1966, pp. 121–8.

25. P. L. Shinnie, 1965, pp. 263–73; 1971a, pp. 42–50.

J. M. Plumley,[26] K. Michalowski,[27] S. Jakobielski[28] and W. H. C. Frend.[29] The detailed news of recent discoveries in Nubia published each year by J. Leclant in *Orientalia* deserves special attention.[30]

Copious information, some of it hypothetical, was supplied by the First Symposium on Christian Nubia held in 1969 at the Villa Hugel in Essen. It has been published in a separate volume edited by E. Dinkler.[31] The results of the Second Symposium, held in Warsaw in 1972, were issued in 1975.[32]

Although Nubia, unlike Egypt, was not part of the Byzantine empire, there undoubtedly existed between them definite links forged by the missions of the priests Julianos and Longinos. The organization of the Nubian government, as its nomenclature shows, was strictly modelled on the Byzantine bureaucracy. Though the Persian invasion of Egypt in 616 stopped at the northern frontier of Nubia, evidence exists that the northern kingdom was invaded by Sassanid detachments stationed south of the First Cataract. In any case the invasion by Chosroes II broke the direct links between Nubia and Egypt, by then Christian, and in particular the contacts between the Nubian clergy and the patriarchate of Alexandria, which officially supervised the church of Nubia. In 641 Egypt came under the rule of the Arabs. Christian Nubia was severed from the Mediterranean culture for centuries to come.

At first the Arabs did not consider the conquest of Nubia important, and only made raids into the north. Therefore, as soon as Egypt submitted, they signed with Nubia a treaty called a *baqt*, which bound the Nubians to pay an annual tribute of slaves and certain goods and the Arabs to provide a suitable quantity of food and clothing. During the seven centuries of Christian Nubia's independence, both sides regarded the treaty as valid in principle, but more than one armed clash occurred. Thus, almost as soon as the *baqt* was signed, the Emir Abdallah ibn Abu Ṣarh raided Dongola in 651–2; but that did not interrupt the constant trade between Nubia and Muslim Egypt.[33]

Northern and Central Nubia united to form one state, doubtless in consequence of the first skirmishes between the Arabs from Egypt and the Nubians. Maqrizi, quoting earlier Arab sources, states that in the middle of the seventh century the whole of central and northern Nubia as far as the Alodian border was ruled by the same king, Qalidurut.[34] The

26. J. M. Plumley, 1970, pp. 129–34; 1971, pp. 8–24.
27. K. Michalowski, 1965a, pp. 9–25; 1967b, pp. 194–211; 1966b.
28. S. Jakobielski, 1972.
29. W. H. C. Frend, 1968, p. 319; 1972a, pp. 224–9; 1972b, pp. 297–308.
30. J. Leclant, 1954.
31. K. Michalowski, 1975.
32. K. Michalowski, 1975.
33. W. Y. Adams, 1965c, p. 173.
34. K. Michalowski, 1967b.

Christian sources seem to prove that the union of Nubia was the work of King Merkurios, who came to the throne in 697 and is said to have introduced Monophysitism into Makuria. He set up the capital of the united kingdom in Dongola.

To this day the question of Monophysitism in Nubia is not entirely clear, especially as regards the kingdom's relations with the orthodox Melkite church. It is still possible that the Melkite doctrine persisted in some form in the interior of the kingdom. It is known that as late as the fourteenth century the province of Maris, the former kingdom of northern Nubia, was subject to a Melkite bishop who, as metropolitan resident in Tafa, ruled over a diocese which included the whole of Nubia. Moreover, except in the eighth century, Alexandria always had two patriarchs, a Mono-physite and a Melkite.[35]

The union of the two Nubian kingdoms led to vigorous economic and political development of the country. King Kyriakos, who succeeded Merkurios, was regarded as a 'great' king: he ruled through thirteen governors. Like the Pharaohs of the Old Kingdom in Egypt, the kings of Nubia were also high-ranking priests. They were not only empowered to settle religious questions, but could also perform certain religious functions, on condition that their hands were not stained with human blood.[36]

When King Kyriakos learned that the Ummayyad governor had imprisoned the Patriarch of Alexandria, he attacked Egypt on that pretext and penetrated as far as Fustat.[37] As soon as the Patriarch was released, the Nubians went home. Kyriakos' expedition to Fustat proves that Nubia did not confine itself strictly to defence but also took offensive action against Muslim Egypt.

Important papyri shedding light on the relations between Egypt and Nubia during this period were recently discovered at Qasr Ibrim. They comprise correspondence between the king of Nubia and the governor of Egypt. The longest scroll, dated +758, contains a complaint in Arabic lodged by Mūsa K'ah Ibn Uyayna against the Nubians because they did not observe the *baqt*.[38]

Military expeditions, however, are not the sole evidence of the vigour of the Nubian state after the beginning of the eighth century. Archaeological discoveries have also proved the extraordinary development of culture, art and monumental architecture in Nubia during that period. In 707 Bishop Paulos rebuilt Faras Cathedral and decorated it with splendid murals.[39]

35. U. Monneret de Villard, 1938, pp. 81, 158–9; P. L. Shinnie, 1954a, p. 5.

36. U. Monneret de Villard, 1938, p. 99.

37. ibid., p. 98.

38. J. P. Plumley and W. Y. Adams, pp. 237–8; P. Van Moorsel, J. Jacquet and H. Schneider.

39. K. Michalowski, 1964, pp. 79–94; J. Leclant and J. Leroy, pp. 361–2; F. and U. Hintze, 1968, pp. 31–3, Figs 140–7; K. Weitzmann, pp. 325–46; T. Golgowski, pp. 293–312; M. Martens, 1972, pp. 207–50; 1973; K. Michalowski, 1974.

Some important religious buildings in Old Dongola date from that period.[40] Other Nubian churches, such as those of Abdallah Nirqi[41] and Al-Sabu'a,[42] were splendidly decorated with murals which became a constant feature of ceremonial decoration.

Excavation of sites known for some time or recently discovered have also revealed how widely Christianity was established at a more humble level, that is, in the villages, as early as the eighth century.[43]

Probably at the end of the eighth and the beginning of the ninth centuries the Nubian King Yoannes added to the united kingdom of Nubia the southern province of Alodia.[44]

The Christian period was a time of rapid economic development in Nubia. The population of northern Nubia alone was about 50 000.[45] The introduction of *saqiya* (water-wheel) irrigation in the Ptolemaic and Roman periods enlarged the area under cultivation by watering it between the abundant Nile floods of that time[46] and it produced wheat, barley, millet and grapes. The abundant date harvests from the palm plantations also raised the country's living standards.

Trade with neighbouring countries increased but extended far beyond them. The inhabitants of Makuria sold ivory to Byzantium and copper and gold to Ethiopia. Their merchants' caravans went to the heart of Africa, to the lands which are now Nigeria and Ghana, in rowing boats and on camels. The well-to-do classes preferred Byzantine dress. The women wore long robes, often decorated with coloured embroidery.[47]

As has already been said, the organization of power in Christian Nubia was modelled on Byzantium. The civil governor of the province was the eparch, whose authority was symbolized by the horned crown which he wore on a helmet decorated with a crescent.[48] He usually wore a full robe held in by a scarf. The fringes of the bishops' stoles, which they wore over their rich and complex liturgical vestments, were adorned with small bells.

That the Nubians were famous archers is attested by many ancient and Arab authors. In addition to the bow they used the sword and the javelin.

Private houses were built of unbaked bricks and had several rooms; they were vaulted or had flat roofs of wood, thatch and clay. At the height of Nubia's prosperity their walls were more massive and were whitened.

40. See note 16 above.
41. A. Klasens, 1964, pp. 147–56; P. Van Moorsel, 1967, pp. 388–92; 1966, pp. 297–316; idem, *Actas del VIII Congreso Internacional de Arqueologia Cristiana*, Barcelona, 1972, pp. 349–95; idem, 1970, pp. 103–10.
42. F. Daumas, Cairo, 1967, pp. 40ff.; 1965, pp. 41–50.
43. J. Vercoutter, 1970, pp. 155–60.
44. U. Monneret de Villard, 1938, p. 102; K. Michalowski, 1965a, p. 17.
45. B. G. Trigger, 1965, p. 168.
46. ibid., p. 166.
47. I. Hofmann, 1967, pp. 522–92.
48. K. Michalowski, 1974, pp. 44–5.

Houses of more than one storey were perhaps intended to be used for defensive purposes. Some districts had piped water. House walls of ashlar stone have been found on the islands at the Second Cataract. In northern Nubia villages were surrounded by walls to protect the inhabitants from Arab raiders. Sometimes the villagers built up communal stores against siege. Near the centre of the village stood the church.

Sacred buildings, with a few rare exceptions, were built of unbaked bricks. Only in the cathedrals of Qasr Ibrim, Faras and Dongola were the walls made of stone or burnt bricks. Most churches were built in the basilical style, but cruciform or central-plan churches are sometimes found in Nubian architecture. The decoration of the first period, that is, until the end of the seventh century, can only be deduced from the monumental cathedrals mentioned above.

Except for parts of converted pagan buildings, for example at Faras, the decoration was of sandstone and repeated the traditional scroll-work pattern borrowed by Meroitic art from the hellenistic art of the Roman east. Mention should be made of the beautiful sculptured volutes of the foliated capitals. Icons painted on wooden panels or carved were probably used at that time as ritual images.

The oldest monuments of Christian art in Nubia are powerfully influenced by Coptic Egypt.[49] This is chiefly shown by their subjects, e.g. the frieze of doves or eagles recalling their images on Coptic stelae.[50]

From the eighth century onwards Nubian churches were decorated with *fresco secco* paintings. Thanks to the Faras discoveries of 1961–4, it is possible, from more than 120 mural paintings in perfect condition, including portraits of bishops whose dates of office can be found in the List of Bishops, to deduce a general evolution of style in Nubian paintings,[51] which is confirmed by fragments of murals from other Nubian churches.

Faras was at that time undoubtedly the artistic centre at least of northern Nubia.[52] The style of the paintings found north of Faras at Abdallah Nirqi[53] and Tamit,[54] and south of it at Sonqi Tino,[55] is definitely provincial by comparison with the great works at Faras.

From the beginning of the eighth century to the middle of the ninth,

49. P. Du Bourguet, 1964b, pp. 221ff.; K. Wessel, 1964, pp. 223ff.; 1963; P. Du Bourguet, 1964a, pp. 25–48.

50. J. M. Plumley, 1970, pp. 132–3, Figs 109–19; N. Jansma and M. de Grooth, pp. 2–9; L. Török, 1971.

51. K. Michalowski, 1964, pp. 79–94; see also note 39 above.

52. K. Michalowski, 1966.

53. A. Klasens, 1967, pp. 85ff.; L. Castiglione, 1967, pp. 14–19; P. Van Moorsel, 1966, pp. 297–316; 1967, pp. 388–92; 1970, pp. 103–10; idem, *Actas del VIII Congreso Internacional de Arqueologia Cristiana*, Barcelona, 1972, pp. 349–95; P. Van Moorsel, J. Jacquet and H. Schneider.

54. Archaeological Mission to Egypt of the University of Rome, Rome, 1967.

55. S. Donadoni and G. Vantini, pp. 247–73; S. Donadoni and S. Curto, 1968, pp. 123ff.; S. Donadoni, 1970, pp. 209–18.

Nubian painters preferred violet tones in their pictures. This period of Nubian painting was strongly influenced by Coptic art, the traditions of which were derived from the expressive style of the Fayum portraits. One of the most representative works of that period is the head of St Anne of Faras (now in the Warsaw museum),[56] but the influence of Byzantine art and its themes can also be seen.[57]

Later that style developed, and until the middle of the tenth century white is clearly predominant. This may be due to the influence of Syro-Palestinian painting which is distinguished by a characteristic way of rendering double folds of vestments and certain iconographic features.[58] Perhaps the fact that Jerusalem was at that time a goal of pilgrimage for all the countries of the Christian East may account for this development in contemporary Nubian painting.

Very close ties between the Monophysite kingdom of Nubia and the Monophysite sect of the Jacobites of Antioch are also known to have existed at that time. Deacon John[59] and Abu Salih[60] both mention that in the reign of King Kyriakos the Monophysite (Jacobite) Patriarch of Alexandria was the head of the Nubian church. A very strong realist trend then appeared for the first time in Nubian painting; its best example is the portrait of Bishop Kyros of Faras (now in Khartoum Museum).[61]

Excavation has unearthed a vast quantity of artefacts, pottery being of course the most abundant. W. Y. Adams has made a systematic study of them.[62] He finds that they yield evidence of interesting technical, stylistic and economico-social developments. After the successes of the X-Group period, the local production of modelled ceramics proved to be less inventive, as is shown by the relatively few forms and decorative patterns of the early Christian period with which we are concerned here. Wheel-turned ceramics evolved too: owing to the interruption of relations with the Mediterranean, the number of vessels designed to hold wine for storage and drinking purposes seems to dwindle; on the other hand, various refinements were introduced; for example, it became general practice to provide receptacles with stems to make them easier to handle.

Even before 750, Aswan supplied the south with an appreciable propor-

56. K. Michalowski, 1965b p. 188, Pl. XLI b; 1966b, Pl. II, 2; 1967b, p. 109, Pl. 27 and 32; T. Zawadzki, p. 289; K. Michalowski, 1970, Fig. 16; M. Martens, 1972, p. 216, Fig. 5.

57. K. Michalowski, 1967b, p. 74; S. Jakobielski, 1972, pp. 67–9; M. Martens, 1972, pp. 234 and 249.

58. K. Weitzmann, p. 337.

59. *Patrologia Orientalis*, pp. 140–3.

60. B. T. A. Evetts and A. J. Butler, 1895; U. Monneret de Villard, 1938, pp. 135–6; F. L. Griffith, 1925, p. 265.

61. K. Michalowski, 1966b, p. 14, Pl. VI, 2; 1967b, p. 117, Pl. 37; S. Jakobielski, 1966, pp. 159–60, Fig. 2 (abbr. list); K. Michalowski, 1970, Pl. 9; M. Martens, 1972, pp. 240–1, 248ff.; S. Jakobielski, 1972, pp. 86–8, Fig. 13.

62. Most recently, W. Y. Adams, 1970, pp. 111–23.

tion of the ceramics used there. This trade was not interrupted when the Muslims settled in Egypt.

To sum up, until the ninth century, Nubia enjoyed an initial period of prosperity which was not greatly disturbed by their usually peaceful Muslim neighbours. The cultural unity of early Christian Nubia is difficult to discern. In Faras, the aristocracy and administrative officials spoke Greek, as did the dignitaries of the church. The clergy also understood Coptic, which was perhaps the language of many refugees. As for Nubian, while it was widely spoken by the population, the only traces remaining of a written form of the language date from a later period, probably not earlier than the middle of the ninth century.

Christian Nubia's golden age, around 800, was yet to come.

PLATE 12.2 *Sandstone capital from Faras*
*(first half of seventh century)*

PLATE 12.1 *Faras Cathedral*

PLATE 12.3 *Early Christian*
*decorated door lintel from Faras*
*(second half of sixth century or*
*early seventh century)*

PLATE 12.4 *Head of St Anne: a*
*mural in North Aisle of Faras*
*Cathedral (eighth century)*

339

PLATE 12.5 *Fragment of a decorative sandstone frieze from the apse of Faras Cathedral (first half of seventh century)*

PLATE 12.6 *Terracotta window from the Church of Granite Columns at Old Dongola, the Sudan (late seventh century)*

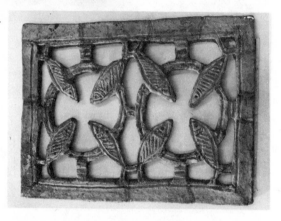

PLATE 12.7 *Christian Nubian ceramic*

PLATE 12.8 *The east wall of the church of Qasr Ibrim: 'The Arches'*

# Pre-Aksumite culture

### H. DE CONTENSON

The northern regions of Ethiopia, which were to emerge from prehistoric times about the fifth century before our era, do not seem to have been very densely populated in an earlier age. Very little is known about their original inhabitants; the scant information we have, however, indicates that human groups developed there in much the same way as in the rest of the Horn of Africa.

During the last ten millennia before our era, the few stone tools that have survived resemble the collection of artefacts dating from the late stone age of southern Africa. In this period, pastoral peoples seemed to have lived here, who made drawings of their humpless, long-horned cattle on the rocky crags that stretched from the north of Eritrea to the land of the Hareri; their herds resembled those that were raised at the same period in the Sahara and in the Nile basin. These peoples were in contact with the Egyptian world from a very early date.

Linguistically, the Kushite element is also of importance; it was of local origin, and was beginning to be perceptible in other spheres. The recent discoveries made at Gobedra, near Aksum (Phillipson, 1977), show that the practice of millet-growing and the use of pottery began in the third or fourth millennium. Thus there is reason to believe that, alongside pastoral activities, a recognizably Ethiopian type of agriculture began to develop from this time. The new techniques were probably associated with a more settled way of life, which created more favourable conditions for the development of a higher civilization.

While the founding of the city of Aksum and the appearance of a royal Aksumite dynasty can be dated from the second century before our era, from the evidence of the geographer Claudius Ptolemy,[1] corroborated a hundred years or so later by the *Periplus Maris Erythraei* ('Circumnavigation of the Erythrean Sea')[2] and by archaeological discoveries,[3] ancient Greek and Latin writers tell us almost nothing about the centuries leading up to these events.

1. Claudius Ptolemy, 1932; H. de Contenson, 1960, pp. 77, 79, Fig. 2.
2. H. de Contenson, 1960, pp. 75–80; J. Pirenne, 1961, pp. 441, 459.
3. H. de Contenson, 1960, pp. 80–95.

FIG. 13.1 *Ethiopia in the intermediary pre–Aksumite period*

They merely tell us that, in the middle of the third century before our era, Ptolemy II founded Philadelphus, the port of Adulis, which was enlarged by his successor Ptolemy III Euergetes, and which Pliny, around +75, said he considered one of the most important ports of call on the Red Sea (*maximum hic emporium Troglodytarum, etiam Aethiopum*). He also mentions the numerous Asachae tribes who lived by elephant-hunting in the mountains which were a five-day journey away from the sea (*Inter montes autem et Nilum Simbarri sunt, Palugges, in ipsis veri montibus asachae multis nationibus; abesse a mari dicuntur diem V itinere: vivunt elephantorum venatu*).[4] The association that is frequently suggested between this ethnic term and the name of Aksum is highly conjectural.

The other written sources of the period, particularly the south Arabian texts which have come to light, make no mention whatever, as far as one can judge, of events on the African side of the Red Sea at this period.

Apart from legendary accounts, which are not dealt with in this chapter, information must therefore be sought in the series of archaeological discoveries that have been made since the beginning of the twentieth century. They enable us to reconstruct the pre-Aksumite period, which, as we know from the studies of F. Anfray, consists of a south Arabian period and a transitional period.[5]

## The south Arabian period

This is the period when 'South Arabian influence was strong in northern Ethiopia'. The chief sign of this influence is the existence in Eritrea and Tigre of monuments and inscriptions which are akin to those current in south Arabia during the supremacy of the kingdom of Saba. Thanks to the palaeographic and stylistic studies of J. Pirenne, the parallel examples found in south Arabia can be dated from the fifth and fourth centuries before our era. This chronology has been accepted by all the specialists in this field of research.[6] It is generally agreed that the same dates apply to the finds made in Ethiopia, although the hypothesis put forward by C. Conti-Rossini of a time-lag between the two shores of the Red Sea cannot be definitely ruled out;[7] according to F. Anfray, 'there is reason to think that in future it will be necessary to reduce the time-span, and perhaps to advance the dates of the south Arabian period'.

The only remaining architectural monument of this period is the temple of Yeha, which was later converted into a Christian church. The temple is built of large blocks, carefully fitted together, with bossage and cornerstones, and consists of a rectangular cella about 18·6 metres by 15 metres resting on an eight-tiered pyramidal base. As J. Pirenne points out, the

4. Pliny; H. de Contenson, 1960, pp. 77, 78, Fig. 1.
5. F. Anfray, 1967, pp. 48–50; 1968, pp. 353–6.
6. J. Pirenne, 1955, 1956.
7. C. Conti-Rossini, 1928, pp. 110–11.

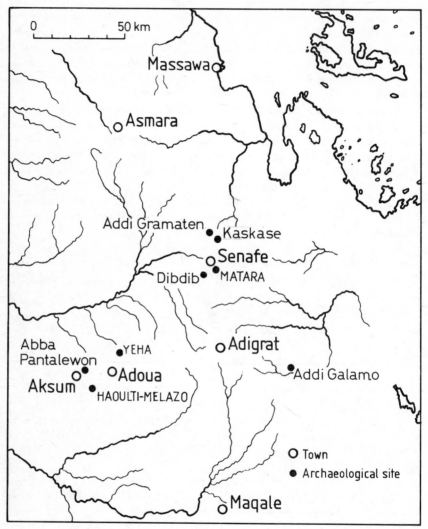

FIG. 13.2 *Ethiopia in the south Arabian period*

façades, which are preserved up to a height of about 9 metres, are treated in a similar way to several buildings found in Mârib, the capital of the kingdom of Saba, including the principal temple, which also stands on a tiered base, but the plan of Yeha is not like that of any of the south Arabian sanctuaries known to us.[8] Another building in Yeha, badly ruined, comprises rectangular megalithic pillars standing on a high terrace; it is situated at Grat-Beal-Guebri and is now being excavated. This building seems to date back to the same period.[9] Similar pillars exist at two other sites. Some are to be seen at the top of the hill of Haoulti, south of Aksum, where they are set up in no apparent order and may not be in their original position.[10] At Kaskasé, on the road from Yeha to Adulis, there are six pillars whose arrangement is not yet understood as the site has not yet been excavated.[11] These pillars are reminiscent of the rows of gigantic four-cornered pillars that adorn the sanctuaries of Mârib (Awwam, Bar'an) and Timna (the temple of Ashtar).

The sculptures found at Yeha also point to Mârib, as for example the frieze of ibexes and the fluted and denticulated plaques, which are also found in the Melazo region, at Haoulti and Enda Cerqos, and which may have served as wall coverings. The Melazo area, about 8 miles south of Aksum, has proved to be rich in sculptures dating back to the south Arabian period: as well as the stelae of Haoulti and the decorated plaques mentioned above, there are a number of works that were used again later in modified forms. The most outstanding examples are the naos and the statues discovered at Haoulti.

The monument that is called a naos on a proposal by J. Pirenne – a better term than the previously suggested 'throne' – is carved from a single block of fine local limestone about 140 centimetres high. It has four feet shaped like a bull's hooves, two pointing forward, two back; they support a base decorated with two bars, which is surmounted by a niche covered with ornamentation except for the back, which is quite smooth. The niche is topped by a dais in the shape of a depressed arch 67 centimetres wide and 57 centimetres deep; along the edge, which is 7 centimetres high, there run two rows of reclining ibexes that converge towards a stylized tree standing on the tip of the naos; similar ibexes, pointing inwards towards the niche, cover the edges of both sides in superimposed metopes 13 centimetres wide.

The external surface of each side is decorated with the same scene in bas-relief: a small beardless figure holding a staff precedes a large bearded man holding a sort of fan; both seem to be walking. Their noses are slightly aquiline, giving them a Semitic appearance, and their hair is

8. D. Krencker, pp. 79–84, Figs 164–76; J. Pirenne, 1965, pp. 1044–8.
9. D. Krencker, pp. 87–9, Figs 195–9; F. Anfray, 1963, pp. 45–64; 1972a, pp. 57–64; R. Fattovich, pp. 65–86.
10. H. de Contenson, 1963b, pp. 41–86; J. Pirenne, 1970a, pp. 121–2.
11. D. Krencker, pp. 143–4, Figs 298–301.

represented by small lozenges. The small figure wears a plain robe flaring right down to the ankles, and a mantle covering his shoulders; on the right-hand side of the naos, a masculine proper noun is written over his head in Sabaean script: 'RPS' (Rafash). The large figure wears a baggy loin-cloth with a flap falling down behind, held in at the waist by a belt that appears to be knotted at the back with one end hanging free; a cloak thrown over his shoulders is held in place by two corners tied in a large flat knot on his chest. On the left-hand bas-relief, he is holding the object described as a fan with both hands, but on the right-hand bas-relief, he is wearing a quadruple bracelet on his left wrist and holding a sort of club in his right hand. These few differences between the two bas-reliefs do not seem significant enough for us to doubt that the two depict the same scene, the interpretation of which will be discussed later.

The same site at Haoulti yielded several statues of a similar type, only one of which is almost complete. It was broken when it was found, and its pieces were scattered among those of the naos. The statue is of fine white local limestone veined with mauve, and is 82 centimetres high. It represents a seated woman with her hands on her knees, dressed in a long robe with narrow vertical pleats shown by grooves that follow the lines of her body; the neck, slightly V-shaped in front, is edged with piping, and round the hem of the robe a narrow band of plain material is edged by another line of piping. Over the robe she wears a wide necklace composed of three thick, ringed strands from which hangs a scutiform pectoral; this is counter-balanced between her shoulder-blades by an ornament in the shape of a trapeze with six vertical stems. Round each wrist is a quadruple toric bracelet. Her hands lie flat on her knees, and her bare feet rest on a little rectangular base. Her head, also bare, is intact except for her nose and right ear, and her hair is represented by rows of little lozenges. Her eyes are accented by a line in relief, her chin is fleshy, and her full cheeks form dimples round the mouth, giving it a beak-like shape and producing the effect of a smiling expression that is perhaps unintended. The statue was meant to fit into a seat, for the backs of the legs are flattened and have a vertical lug, badly damaged, in the middle.[12]

Apart from the fragments of at least two similar statues, there was a headless statue, less delicately executed than the one described above but otherwise differing from it only because its sole ornament was the three-stranded necklace and it was seated on a small stool decorated with a bar.

The posture of the Haoulti statues recalls that of a statuette discovered accidentally with miscellaneous other antiquities at Addi Galamo, on the western edge of the Tigre plateau (a site formerly known as Azbi Dera, or Haouilé Assaraou).[13] The statuette is only about 40 centimetres high,

---

12. H. de Contenson, 1962, pp. 68–83; J. Pirenne, 1967, pp. 125–33.
13. A. Shiferacu, pp. 13–15; A. Caquot and A. J. Drewes, pp. 18–26, Plates V–VIII; J. Doresse, 1957, pp. 64–5.

and is much more roughly fashioned. The hands rest on the knees, but hold two cylindrical cups that were probably intended to serve as receptacles for offerings. The hair too is represented by lozenges, and there are grooves bearing the traces of a necklace with a counterweight and of bracelets that may have been made of some precious metal. The robe is not pleated, but is decorated with rosettes, probably inlaid, that may represent embroidery, and it ends in a fringe. The seat is simply a stool decorated with a bar.

When F. Anfray excavated Matara, an important site in the neighbourhood of Kaskasé, a fragment of a head of the same type as the Haoulti head was unearthed in a pre-Aksumite stratum of Mound B, but the workmanship is much more rudimentary and the details are in high relief.[14]

Another statuette, on show at the National Museum of Rome (MNR 12113), has many points in common with the Haoulti statues. It represents a seated woman in yellowish limestone, whose head and arms have broken. Its height as it stands at present is 23·7 centimetres. The woman wears a long, fluted robe, a ringed double-stranded necklace from which there hangs a row of beads, a pectoral and a counterweight. The lower part is in the shape of a base on which is inscribed a south Arabian name, Kanan. According to J. Pirenne, the script dates from the end of the fourth century before our era.[15] This rather crude statuette is believed to come from south Arabia, but as its place of origin cannot be located more precisely, it is permissible to wonder whether it was not really produced in Ethiopia during the south Arabian period.

South Arabia has so far only yielded objects presenting such general similarities as the seated position, which is not a particularly specific feature: statuettes known as ancestor statues, some of which are feminine; representations of seated women on the funerary bas-reliefs of Mârib, Hâz and the Aden Museum; the statue of 'Lady Bar'at at Timna', in which J. Pirenne sees the great south Arabian goddess.[16]

As early as the ninth and eighth centuries before our era, the type of the sea woman or goddess, often holding a goblet, is very common in the area under Syro-Hittite control (Tell Halaf, Zindjirli, Marash and Neirab). There seems to be a real relationship between the Ethiopian statues and those of Asia Minor in the late seventh and early sixth centuries before our era (for example, the Branchides and the funerary effigies of Miletus), which represent rather corpulent seated figures, their hands on their knees, wearing long robes. We find in that region that faces of the same period have protuberant eyes, rounded cheeks and mouths in the shape of an upturned arc, very similar to those of the face of the Haoulti statue. These features appear in a Phrygian goddess from Boghaz Keuy, to which our

14. F. Anfray and G. Annequin, pp. 60–1.
15. A. Jamme, 1956, p. 67; H. de Contenson, 1962, pp. 74–5, Fig. 9; J. Pirenne, 1965, pp. 1046–7.
16. H. de Contenson, 1962, p. 76; J. Pirenne, 1967, p. 131.

attention has been drawn by H. Seyrig, a head from Miletus, and other Ionian sculptures. The expression becomes a real smile in the Attic works of the first half of the sixth century.[17] J. Pirenne has already pointed out certain affinities between the orientalized Greek art of the sixth century or the derived styles of the fifth century and south Arabian art.

A head from the Acropolis also shows a stylization of the hair that recalls the Haoulti statue. The same treatment of the hair is found in a small Graeco-Persian head from Amrit and in the Apadana of Persepolis, where it is used indiscriminately to depict the woolly hair of the negroid Kushites and the carefully waved and curled locks of the Medic usher leading them.[18] It is therefore difficult to tell whether lozenged hair is a stylization of curls or a faithful representation of woolly hair and to draw any ethnic conclusions from this feature.

While analogies with the seated statues are found mainly in the Semitic Near East and in the orientalized hellenic world, there is evidence of an Egyptian, and more specifically Meroitic, influence in the counter-weighted necklaces, inspired by the *mankhit*, and in the pleated robes which, as J. Pirenne has observed, recall the tunics of the queens of Meroe and the corpulence that they inherited from Ati of Punt, a contemporary of Hatshepsut.[19]

Such comparisons highlight the diversity of the influences reflected in these seated women of Tigre, but they provide no definite answer to the question of what they represent. Neither can any conclusive argument be drawn from the inscribed base found at Addi Galamo which seems to be associated with the statuette. We do not know whether the text means 'In order that he may grant a child to YMNT', as A. J. Drewes thought, or 'To the one who brings help to Yamanat. Wâlidum', as G. Ryckmans thought, or even 'To the protection [divinity] of the Yemen. Wâlidum', as suggested by J. Pirenne. One might even hesitate to regard them as queens or dignitaries, or, as J. Pirenne maintains, as representations of the great goddess. Despite the difficulty raised by the simultaneous presence of several almost identical effigies, the fact that the debris of the complete statue was mingled with that of the naos militates in favour of the last interpretation, as does the fact that their sizes match; when the two monuments were excavated, these facts led us to suppose that they were made to go together.

We would be inclined, then, to reject the hypothesis of an empty throne of the type found in Phoenicia, Adulis or Tacazzé, and to return to our first impression, considering, like J. Pirenne, that the object is 'a stone reproduction of a processional naos', in which a cult statue rested. Apart from a few fragments found at Haoulti which might come from a similar monument, this naos is unique of its kind. Although nothing analogous has come

17. H. de Contenson, 1962, p. 77.
18. ibid., p. 82.
19. ibid., p. 78; J. Pirenne, 1967, p. 132.

to light in south Arabia – which might merely be due to the present state
of archaeological research in the Yemen – some of its features have been
found there, treated in a rigorously identical fashion.

The same bull's hooves are seen on stone furniture identified by G. van
Beek and on a marble statuette from Mârib.[20] Reclining ibexes, often
arranged in superimposed metopes and on the edge of a flat stele, an
example of which was recently discovered at Matara, occur frequently in
the Sabaean region (Mârib, Ház).[21] We also find ibexes associated with a
stylized tree, the fruits of which they seem to be eating, on an altar from
Mârib. The religious significance of these ibexes, whether associated with a
'tree of life' or not, appears to be in no doubt: Grohmann seems to have
proved that the ibex symbolized the god of the moon, Almaqah, to whom
the bull was also dedicated.[22]

While the technique of the lateral bas-reliefs is closer to the Persian
Achemenidean style than to the south Arabian works known to us at
present, which are apparently of later date, there are parallels between the
figures represented and the bronze sculpture in the round from Mârib:
hair, eyes, ears, loin-cloth and sandals.[23] The treatment of the hair, eyes
and mouth hardly differs from that of the Haoulti statue, and the nose –
missing in the latter – accentuates the Semitic type of the large figure, a
type still quite common in Tigre. He closely resembles the king of Punt
from Deir el Bahari with his graceful bearing, short hair, pointed beard,
aquiline nose, the belt tied at the back, and the loin-cloth with a flap falling
down behind.[24]

The interpretation of the scene represented still gives rise to discussion.
Two hypotheses were put forward in the very first publication. One
suggested that the scene should be seen in a realistic light as depicting
a servant carrying a fan or a standard and, in his right hand, a club or a
fly whisk, preceded by a child whose sex was determined by the masculine
noun RFŚ. The other hypothesis conformed more closely to ancient con-
ventions and suggested that the scene represented an important figure,
either a deity or a powerful human being, protecting an inferior person.[25]
A. Jamme adopted the latter point of view and attributed the noun RFŚ
to the large figure which, he believed, represented a god holding a
winnowing-fan and a club and extending his protection to a pregnant
woman, who was none other than the seated woman closely associated with
the 'throne'.[26] J. Pirenne, for her part, has concluded that the figure

20. H. de Contenson, 1962, p. 79.
21. ibid., p. 80; F. Anfray, 1965, p. 59, Pl. LXIII, 2.
22. A. Grohmann, 1914b, pp. 40, 56–67.
23. F. P. Albright, 1958.
24. H. de Contenson, 1962, pp. 82–3.
25. ibid., p. 73.
26. A. Jamme, 1963, pp. 324–7 (it is not clear on what basis the author maintains that
the woman on the right-hand side is pregnant but not on the left, as the two figures are
exactly identical).

represents an important person, 'even a *mukarrib* or a chief', bearing the name of RFŠ, who is presenting to the goddess whose statue rested inside the naos the insignia of power – a fan or parasol and a club – and who is preceded by a buxom woman, presumed to be his wife who is offering a staff.[27] Although this explanation seems at present to be the most plausible, it is difficult to allow that the noun RFŠ applies to the large figure, given its position. Furthermore, the association between the mother-goddess and the symbols of the male moon-god would have to be explained.

The sculpture of the south Arabian period is also represented by sphinxes, although, apart from a small fragment discovered at Melazo,[28] they have so far been found only in Erythrea. The best-preserved sphinx comes from Addi Gramaten, north-east of Kaskasé. Its hair is plaited, as it is in some Aksumite pottery heads of a later period and as it is worn by the women of Tigre today, and round its neck is a three-stranded necklace.[29] The necklace is also found on the forequarters of two sphinxes with hammer-wrought facets that stand out from a stone plaque found at Matara.[30] Another sphinx, very badly damaged, has been found at Dibdib, south of Matara.[31] J. Pirenne points out that these lions with human heads have nothing in common with the griffins and winged sphinxes of the Phoenician tradition which were produced in south Arabia at a later period.[32] Perhaps we should look for Egyptian or Meroitic prototypes, origins already suggested for a south Arabian head with plaited hair and a necklace.[33]

One category of objects carved in stone that is particularly well represented in northern Ethiopia is that of incense altars. Most of these belong to a type that is well known in south Arabia: a cubic altar with architectural decoration, often standing on a pyramidal base. The most beautiful example, which, according to J. Pirenne, surpasses all the south Arabian examples, is the altar of Addi Galamo, but a series of altars in various states of preservation has been found at Gobochela in Melazo, several have been found at Yeha, and fragments have been found at Matara or at unidentified places.[34] A group of four altars found at

27. J. Pirenne, 1967, p. 132.

28. J. Leclant, 1959b, p. 51, Pl. XLII, a.

29. A. Davico, pp. 1–6.

30. F. Anfray, 1965, p. 59, Pl. LXIII, 4.

31. C. Conti-Rossini, 1928, p. 225, Pl. XLIII, Nos 128–9; V. Franchini, pp. 5–16, Figs 7–8, 11–1.

32. J. Pirenne, 1965, pp. 1046–7.

33. A. Grohamm, 1927, Fig. 55.

34. *Addi Galamo*: A. Caquot and A. J. Drewes, pp. 26–32, Plates IX–XI; *Gobochela*: J. Leclant, 1959b, pp. 47–53; A. J. Drewes, 1959, pp. 90–7, Plates XXX, XXXI, XXXIV, XXXVIII; J. Pirenne, 1970, p. 119, Pl. XXIV, b; *Yeha*: A. J. Drewes and R. Schneider, 1970, pp. 58–9, Pl. XVI, p. 62, Pl. XIX; *Matara*: F. Anfray and G. Annequin, pp. 59, 75, 89–91, Plates LXIII, 3, LXXI; *unidentified sites*: R. Schneider, 1961, p. 64, Pl. XXXVIII, b.

Gobochela represents a hitherto unknown variety: the cylindrical incense altar on a base in the shape of a truncated cone.[35] Here the decoration is confined to the south Arabian divine symbol of a crescent surmounted by a disc and to a frieze of triangles. As for the small cubic altar of south Arabia, we only have two objects which, despite their rough workmanship, seem to belong to the south Arabian period. One, unearthed at Matara, is the first in Ethiopia to be referred to specifically as a perfume-burning altar, a *mqtr*.[36] The second, found near the preceding site at a place called Zala Kesedmai, differs in the bas-reliefs that decorate its sides. On one side is the divine symbol of the disc and crescent, and on the opposite side a stylized 'tree of life' that recalls the 'tree of life' of Haoulti. The ibexes on the two remaining sides are turned towards this tree.[37]

As in south Arabia, beside these incense-burning altars we find libation altars, which can be recognized by the channel allowing the offered liquid to run out. At Yeha were found several platforms similar to those at Hureidha or the Mârib region, with a drainage channel in the shape of a bucranium. An animal's head was undoubtedly represented on one of them, but it is so worn that it is impossible to identify it.[38] On others, there are fine inscriptions in relief and friezes of beam-ends like those of the perfume-burning altars.[39] The first specimen mentioned, one of the second group and a unique libation altar at Matara all bear the local name of this series of objects, *mtryn*, a term which is not corroborated in south Arabia. The Matara site also yielded thick sacrificial tables similar to the first one from Yeha.[40] The libation altar of Addi Gramaten bears a much closer resemblance to the more elaborate type with a frieze of beam-ends and a tiered base.[41] The altar at Fikya, near Kaskasé, which is in the shape of a bowl with protomes of sphinxes or lions, is rather more reminiscent, according to J. Pirenne, of shapes common in Meroitic art.[42]

All that the archaeological excavations have given us in the way of material remains apart from these sculptures is a type of pottery which is as yet little known. F. Anfray attributes to this period tulip-shaped vases and large jars with handles and horizontal ridges that come from Matara and Yeha. He compares this material with what was found at Es-Soba, a few miles north of Aden, which seems to date from the sixth century before our era.[43]

The epigraphic documents that palaeography allows us to attribute to the

35. J. Leclant, 1959b, pp. 48–9; A. J. Drewes, 1959, pp. 88, 89, 91, 94, Plates XXXV–XXXVII.
36. A. J. Drewes and R. Schneider, 1967, pp. 89–91, Pl. XLIII, 1–2.
37. F. Anfray and G. Annequin, p. 76, Pl. LXXIV.
38. A. J. Drewes and R. Schneider, 1970, pp. 59–60, Pl. XVI, b–e.
39. ibid., pp. 60–2, Pl. XVIII, a–b.
40. F. Anfray and G. Annequin, pp. 59, 75, 90, Pl. LXXII, 1–3.
41. A. Davico, pp. 1–3.
42. A. J. Drewes, 1956, pp. 179–82, Pl. I; F. Anfray, 1965, pp. 6–7, Pl. III.
43. F. Anfray, 1966, pp. 1–74; fasc. 1, 1970, p. 58.

most ancient period are all in south Arabian script but, according to A. J. Drewes, they fall into two groups. The first group consists of inscriptions on monuments written in the authentic Sabaean language with a few local peculiarities; the second includes inscriptions on rocks written in a script which imitates that of the first group but in fact transcribes a Semitic language thought to be only related to Sabaean.[44] In the present state of research, the geographical extent of the second group seems to be limited to the Erythrean district of 'Acchele Guzaï in the northern part of the high plateau. While the inscriptions as a whole yield information mainly bearing on onomastics, from which we see that proper names of south Arabian appearance predominate, the first group also gives glimpses of the religious beliefs and social structure of the period.

The texts mention not only the terms used for cult objects such as perfume-burners or sacrificial tables, as we saw above, but also the names of a number of deities who constitute a pantheon almost identical with that of the kingdom of Saba. The most comprehensive list known at present appears on a block that was re-utilized in the church of Enda Çerqos at Melazo: '... 'Astar and Hawbas and Almaqah and Dât-Himyam and Dât-Ba'dan ...'[45]

'Astar appears in two other inscriptions, one from Yeha and the other of unknown origin.[46] It is simply the Ethiopian form of the name of the star-god Athtar who is also associated with Almaqah in three votic texts, one at Yeha and two at Matara.[47] At the latter site there is an altar dedicated to Shron, which is an epithet of this god who is identified with the planet Venus.[48]

Apart from the Enda Çerqos inscription, Hawbas, the moon-god, seems only to be mentioned in Ethiopia on the sphinx and altar at Dibdib.[49]

The moon-god, who seems to have been most venerated in Ethiopia as well as in Saba, is Almagah (or Ilumguh according to A. Jamme). In addition to the inscriptions of Matara, Yeha and Enda Çerqos we have already mentioned, all the texts found at Gobochela in Melazo, as well as the altar at Addi Galamo and a libation altar at Yeha, are dedicated to him alone.[50] The Temple of Yeha was probably dedicated to him too, as were the great sanctuaries of Awwâm and Bar'an at Mârib. Finally, it is Almaqah who is symbolized by the ibexes of Matara, Yeha and Haoulti, the bull's hooves carved on the naos at Haoulti, and the alabaster bull at Gobochela.[51]

44. A. J. Drewes, 1962.
45. A. J. Drewes, 1959, p. 99; R. Schneider, 1961, pp. 61–2.
46. R. Schneider, pp. 64–5 (JE 671, script B 1–B 2); A. J. Drewes and R. Schneider, 1970, pp. 60–1.
47. A. J. Drewes, 1959, pp. 89–91; A. J. Drewes and R. Schneider, 1970, pp. 58–9.
48. A. J. Drewes and R. Schneider, 1967, pp. 89–90.
49. C. Conti-Rossini, 1928, p. 225, Pl. XLIII, Nos 128–9; V. Franchini, pp. 5–16, Figs 7–8, 11–14; A. J. Drewes, 1954, pp. 185–6.
50. A. J. Drewes, 1959, pp. 89–94, 97–9; A. J. Drewes and R. Schneider, 1970, pp. 61–2.
51. G. Hailemarian, p. 50, Pl. XV; J. Leclant, 1959b, p. 51, Pl. LI.

The solar cult is represented by a pair of goddesses, Dât-Himyam and Dât-Ba'dan, who seem to correspond to the summer sun and the winter sun. The former is also mentioned on the libation altar at Addi Gramaten, as well as at Yeha and Fikya. The latter appears in fragmentary inscriptions at Matara and Abba Pantalewon, near Aksum.[52]

Other deities vouched for on libation altars at Yeha seem to play a far less important role. Nrw, associated in one instance with 'Astar, is mentioned twice and corresponds to the south Arabian Nawraw, who is also a star-god.[53] The same altar that mentions these two deities also adds Yf'm which, according to Littmann, is the name of a god. Another altar is dedicated to Sdgn and Nsbthw.[54] Finally, A. Jamme considers the noun RFŠ inscribed on the naos of Haoulti to be the name of a deity. Such an elaborate religion implies a complex social structure.

Whereas dedicatory texts usually give only the filiation of the high-ranking persons concerned, the Gobochela texts reveal that the population was organized in clans. Four texts from this site and one from Yeha mention 'Lhy, of the Grb clan, of the family of [or son of] Ygdm'l Fqmm of Mârib'; this person is associated with his brother SBHHMW on some of the dedications; at Yeha, he consecrates his worldly goods and his son Hyrmh to 'Astar and Almaqah.[55] It is probable that the terms YQDM'L and FQMM denote ethnic groups, but we are sure that GRB does. The expressions 'of Mârib' and 'of Hadaqan' in the two Matara texts[56] refer to toponyms rather than to tribes; they may concern places founded in the north of Ethiopia by south Arabian colonists, but, according to L. Ricci, these terms would rather seem to indicate that these groups came originally from Arabia proper.[57]

The political organization of northern Ethiopia during the south Arabian period is known to us through a few inscriptions, in particular those on the altar of Addi Galamo and on a block found at Enda Çerqos in Melazo.[58] It seems to have been a hereditary monarchy, two of whose dynasts, Rbh and his son Lmm, bear the same title: 'King Sr'n of the tribe of Yg'd *mukarrib* of D'iamat and of Saba''; the first of these two sovereigns added on the altar of Addi Galamo: 'descendant of the tribe W'rn of Raydan'. The second is also mentioned on the altar of unknown origin dedicated to 'Anstar; the same Lmm, or another sovereign bearing the same name, is mentioned in two texts at Matara, in one of which he is associated with a certain Sumu'alay, the name borne by a Sabaean *mukarrib*.[59] The fact

52. R. Schneider, 1965, p. 90.

53. A. J. Drewes and R. Schneider, 1970, pp. 61 and 62.

54. ibid., pp. 59–60.

55. A. J. Drewes, 1959, pp. 89, 91, 97–9; A. J. Drewes and R. Schneider, 1970, pp. 58–9.

56. R. Schneider, 1965a, pp. 89–91.

57. L. Ricci, 1961, p. 133; A. J. Drewes and R. Schneider, 1970, p. 59.

58. A. Caquot and A. J. Drewes, pp. 26–33; R. Schneider, 1965b, pp. 221–2.

59. R. Schneider, 1961, pp. 64–5; R. Schneider, 1965a, p. 90; A. J. Drewes and R. Schneider, 1967, pp. 89–91.

that the link with the Waren tribe of Raydan is explicitly mentioned shows the importance which these kings attached to their south Arabian descent. The title of mukarrib of D'iamat and of Saba' may be explained in various ways: it might refer to south Arabian regions whose princes had extended their rule to northern Ethiopia; these terms might represent African districts to which south Arabian colonists had given the names of their home provinces; or they might have a purely political and non-territorial significance. The first hypothesis seems most improbable and we must agree with A. J. Drewes that these dynasts no doubt exercised the power of mukarrib of Saba' over their subjects from south Arabia or of south Arabian extraction. The titles of 'King Sr'n, of the tribe of Yg'd' might be read: 'King of the Tsar'ane, of the tribe of the Ig'azyan'; they would show that they also ruled the native part of the population and that they were descended from the local tribe of Yg'd (or Igz) in which A. J. Drewes sees the ancestors of the Ge'ez.

Three fragmentary inscriptions, those of Abba Pantalewon, the altar at Addi Galamo and the pantheon of Enda Çerqos, allude to a historical event that seems to have taken place during the reign of Rbh. It concerns the capture and sacking of D'iamat, 'its eastern part and its western part, its reds and its blacks'. Unfortunately, the identification of this region and of the aggressors remains in doubt.

Architecture, works of art, epigraphy and the data provided by the texts on religious beliefs and social organization in northern Ethiopia all afford evidence of a strong south Arabian influence in the fifth and fourth centuries before our era. As F. Anfray reminds us, the emergence of this predominantly Semitic culture was preceded by several centuries of silent penetration; 'small groups of immigrants peddled south Arabian culture', no doubt under the pressure of economic and demographic circumstances which we do not yet understand.[60] It is not impossible, as the same investigator suggests, that these colonists introduced new agricultural techniques, in particular the use of the swing-plough, and built the first stone villages of Ethiopia.

From the work of L. Ricci and A. J. Drewes, we get the impression that the south Arabian element was preponderant in certain centres where an embryonic form of urban life grew up around a sanctuary, for instance, at Yeha, in the Melazo region, and perhaps also at Addi Galamo and Matara, whereas the basic local culture, with certain Nilotic additions, was better represented in the Erythrean region with the sites of 'Acchele Guzaï, Addi Gramaten and Dibdib.

The appearance of a cultural unit whose internal coherence is evident, however, throughout the northern part of the Ethiopian plateau must certainly have coincided with the rise to power and the survival as a dominant class of one group, but we shall probably never know whether

60. F. Anfray, 1967, pp. 49–50; 1968, pp. 353, 356.

this group consisted of descendants of south Arabian colonists or of indigenous inhabitants who had assimilated this superior culture so well that they had made it their own. C. Conti-Rossini focused attention on the predominance of south Arabian characteristics in this first Ethiopian civilization. Reacting against this tendency, J. Pirenne and F. Anfray have emphasized the original aspects of this culture, which represents a synthesis of various influences and which, when it draws its inspiration from south Arabian forms, shows that it is superior to its models. Perhaps the term Ethiopo-Sabaean period would convey the specific nature of this culture more effectively. As F. Anfray admits, however, the apparent superiority of the African works may only be an impression resulting from the lack of continuity which has hitherto been typical of archaeological research in the Yemen. New discoveries beyond the Red Sea and in Ethiopia as well as in the ancient kingdom of Meroe will probably give us a clearer idea of the acculturation processes that may have occurred during the second half of the last millennium before our era. There can be no doubt that from then on Ethiopia was a crossroads of trade routes and cultural influences.

## The intermediary period

A much stronger impression of a local culture having assimilated foreign influences is conveyed by material dating from the second pre-Aksumite period, which has been called the intermediary period.

Some characteristics of south Arabian origin are no doubt still perceptible but, as F. Anfray has made clear, it is no longer a case of direct influences but of internal developments growing from earlier contributions. Inscriptions in a much rougher script are used to transcribe a language less and less like the original south Arabian dialect.[61] *Mukarribs* are no longer mentioned, but a text found at Kaskasé refers to a king bearing a south Arabian name, Waren Hayanat (W'RN HYNT), descendant of Salamat.[62] The GRB clan, well vouched for at Gobochela in Melazo during the south Arabian phase, still exists, although its links with Mârib are no longer stated, for one of its members dedicates a cube-shaped incense altar with a pyramidal base to Almaqah:[63] a crude shale statuette of a bull is also dedicated to the same deity.[64] At Addi Gramaten, a later hand has added to the altar a second dedication to Dât-Himyam, and to the sphinx a name: Wahab-Wadd. The epigraphic documentation is completed by inscriptions composed of cursive south Arabian letters, such as those of Der'a and Zeban Mororo, and by the inscribed tile of Tsehuf

61. L. Ricci, 1959 pp. 55–95; 1960, pp. 77–119; A. J. Drewes, 1962, *passim*.
62. *DAE*, pp. 62–3.
63. J. Leclant, 1959b, p. 47; A. J. Drewes, 1959, p. 92, Plates XXXII–XXXIII.
64. A. J. Drewes, 1959, pp. 95–7, Plates XXXIX–XL.

Emni, which seems to be written neither in the south Arabian nor in the Ethiopian language.[65]

The architecture of the intermediary period is hardly represented except by the religious buildings unearthed in the region of Melazo. All the objects from Gobochela were found, either re-utilized for other purposes or else *in situ*, by J. Leclant in a rectangular structure oriented on an east–west axis; it consists of a surrounding wall 18·1 by 7·3 metres which encloses an esplanade leading to a cella 8·9 by 6·75 metres. The latter opens by a door in the middle of the western side, and the eastern part is occupied by a bench on which the sacred objects were placed.[66]

The statue and the naos of Haoulti were found in a corridor between two badly ruined buildings likewise oriented on an east–west axis.[67] Only the east–west dimensions are certain: 11 metres for the northern building, 10·50 metres for the southern building. Each has a flight of steps on its eastern side, probably situated in the middle, which would mean that from north to south the northern building measured 13 metres and the southern building 11 metres. Each flight of steps led up to a terrace; whether the terraces were covered or not is hard to tell. Both are surrounded by a bench which breaks off only at the flight of steps and on which ex-voto offerings in pottery and metal were laid. Most of these pottery ex-votos are animals, generally highly stylized but in some cases quite naturalistic: cattle, sometimes fitted with miniature yokes, beasts of burden carrying a load, strange quadrupeds with their tongues hanging out, a few seated women and, near the flights of steps, sphinxes likewise made of pottery.[68] Apart from their east–west orientation, another feature that the structures of this period have in common is that they are built, not of limestone as before, but of blue granite or local shale. This characteristic recurs in Aksumite architecture and it appears in Erythrea in Matara Period 2 and in the still untouched ruins of Fikya, which may also belong to the intermediary phase.[69]

Another characteristic of this period is the great accumulation of objects in underground deposits such as the well tombs of Yeha and Matara or the pits of Sabea and Haoulti.[70] It should be noted that at Sabea, the name of which seems to be evocative of south Arabia, two out of three pits excavated appear, according to the description of J. Leclant, to have the same shape as the contemporary well tombs. The large number of metal objects found in these deposits as well as on the hill of Haoulti around the

65. C. Conti-Rossini, 1947, p. 12, Plates II–III; A. J. Drewes and R. Schneider, 1970, pp. 66–7.

66. J. Leclant, 1959, pp. 44, 45, Plates XXIII–XXVI.

67. H. de Contenson, 1963b, pp. 41–2, Plates XXVI–XXIX.

68. ibid., pp. 43–4, Plates XXXV–XL.

69. F. Anfray, 1965, pp. 6–7, Pl. III and pp. 59, 61, 72, 74.

70. *Yeha:* F. Anfray, 1963, pp. 171–92, Plates CXIV–CLVI; *Matara:* F. Anfray, 1967, pp. 33–42, Plates IX–XVII, XXX–XXXIV, XLII; H. de Contenson, 1969, pp. 162–3; *Sabea:* J. Leclant and A. Miquel, pp. 109–14, Plates LI–LXIII; *Haoulti:* H. de Contenson, 1963b, pp. 48–51, Plates XLIX–LX.

sanctuaries is quite remarkable and suggests that the local metal-working industry expanded considerably from the third century before our era onwards.

Iron implements, the manufacture of which was probably introduced during this phase, are mainly represented at Yeha by rings, scissors, swords and daggers; a sword and some rings have also been found at Matara. Several fragments of iron objects have also been collected round the temples at Haoulti.

However, bronze is much more prevalent than iron, perhaps because of its greater resistance to corrosion. A large number of thick open rings with a rectangular section was found at Sabea, and an object of the same type was lying on the bench of one of the sanctuaries at Haoulti. These rings were possibly worn as bracelets or anklets in the Meroitic fashion, but it may be asked whether they were not also used as money.[71] At Yeha and Matara, lighter rings are found which could be considered as bracelets or ear-rings. A number of broad-ended tools may have been used for wood-working: axes at Haoulti and Yeha; curved spur-headed adzes at Yeha and Sabea, to which we may add the instrument found at Maï Mafalu in Erythrea;[72] straight scissors at Yeha; curved scissors from the same site, the use of which is not very clear. As for agricultural implements, there are riveted sickles at Yeha, Haoulti and Gobochela. Weapons are repre- sented by a crescent-shaped axe or halberd and two riveted daggers from Haoulti, as well as two knives from Matara, one riveted and the other with a crescent-shaped pommel. The Yeha tombs have further yielded cooking- pots, balance-pans and a small bell; fragments of receptacles were also collected on the hill-top at Haoulti. Needles and pins come from Haoulti, Yeha and Matara. Small bronze beads are reported from Sabea, Haoulti and Yeha.

There is one last category of bronze objects that reflects a south Arabian tradition, namely, the pierced plaques called identity badges.[73] A. J. Drewes and R. Schneider distinguish between two classes. The first in- cludes small thin objects in geometrical shapes, fitted with a ring and decorated with a symmetrical pattern in which monograms or isolated letters can sometimes be recognized; this class contains the plaques from Sabea and Haoulti and most of those from Yeha. The second class, which is only found at the Yeha site, is composed of larger, thicker plaques, fitted with a handle and shaped somewhat like a stylized animal, a bull, an ibex, a lion or a bird; the plaques in this class contain proper names written in cursive south Arabian script; here again, the language seems to be midway between Sabaean and Ge'ez; the name most clearly read is 'W'RN HYTW', which is precisely the name of the king mentioned at Kaskasé. It is note- worthy that similar devices have been found in rupestral inscriptions and on

71. O. Tufnell, pp. 37–54.
72. C. Conti-Rossini, 1928.
73. A. J. Drewes and R. Schneider, 1967, pp. 92–6, Pl XLIV.

potsherds at Haoulti, but instead of being in the form of stamp-impressions they are in relief. Outside Ethiopia, only a few similar bronze objects are known to us in south Arabia.

When we consider the high technical level revealed by these objects, it seems plausible to attribute to the Ethiopian bronze-workers of this inter-mediary stage – as F. Anfray suggests – other works such as a miniature pair of bull's hooves found near the Haoulti sanctuaries, and the powerful figurine of a bull from Mahabere Dyogwe,[74] which would appear to afford further evidence of the cult of Almaqah. F. Anfray judiciously deduces that the figures of humped cattle, such as those found at Addi Galamo, Matara and Zeban Kutur, are no earlier than the Aksumite period; at Addi Galamo, they are probably contemporary with the three-footed alabaster altars and the bronze sceptre of Gadar.

Gold is used for ornaments such as finger rings at Yeha and Haoulti, ear-rings, beads and coiled wire at Haoulti. Countless little pieces of neck-laces of various colours, made of glass paste or frit, are found on all the sites of this period, and pieces made of stone are also found at Sabea and Matara.

Other stone objects include small sandstone mortars or incense burners, disc-shaped or rectangular, found at Yeha, Matara and Haoulti, a seal found at Sabea, an alabaster vase and an incised ring made of serpentine found at Yeha.

Lastly, the deposit at Haoulti contained two earthenware amulets representing a Ptah-patec and a Hathoric head, while in the lower levels at Matara a cornelian amulet representing a Harpocrat was found. Among the finds at Addi Galamo were four bronze vessels, including a bowl decorated with finely engraved lotus flowers and frogs, and a fragment of a vase with an embossed line of cattle. This group of objects is particularly interesting as they are of Meroitic origin and provide evidence of relations between ancient Ethiopia and the Nile valley.[75]

Some Meroitic influence can also be seen in the pottery of this period, which is highly characteristic.[76] There is an elegance and variety of form that is not found again in Ethiopia. The clay is usually micaceous, black or red in colour, and the surfaces are often glazed. The geometrical designs with which they are decorated are usually incised, but are sometimes applied with red or white paint. Incised decorations filled in with clay, usually white but sometimes blue or red, are also found. As well as the

74. H. de Contenson, 1961, pp. 21–2, Pl. XXII; F. Anfray, 1967, pp. 44–6.

75. H. de Contenson, 1963, p. 48, Pl. XLIX, b, c; L. P. Kirwan, 1960, p. 172; J. Leclant, 1961, p. 392; J. Leclant, 1962, pp. 295–8, Plates IX–X.

76. R. Paribeni, pp. 446–51; J. Leclant and A. Miquel, 1959, pp. 109, 114, Plates LI–LXIII; H. de Contenson, 1963, pp. 44, 49–50, Plates XLI, LIII, b, LX; F. Anfray, 1963, pp. 190–1, Plates CXXVIII–CXLV; F. Anfray, 1968, pp. 13–15, Plates XLVII–L, Figs I, 2, II; F. Anfray, 1967, p. 42, Plates XXX–XXXIX, XLII.

material found in the pits there is a wealth of evidence, still largely unpublished, on the hill-top at Haoulti, in the deeper layers at Yeha and Matara, and probably also in the oldest pottery of Adulis.

While the ex-votos of Haoulti indicate that the basis of the economy was mainly agricultural and pastoral, the rapid progress made by metal-working in bronze, iron and gold, by the quantity production of stone or glass-paste objects, and by pottery, shows that a class of specialized crafts-men had now appeared. It certainly seems that the process of urbanization was under way in a number of centres founded during the south Arabian period, such as Melazo, Yeha and Matara, or in more recent settlements such as Adulis. While the memory of the south Arabian traditions had not yet died out, the new stimulus seems to have come from the kingdom of Meroe, which played a primary role in the diffusion of metal-working techniques over Africa.

It is quite possible that the decline of Meroe, on the one hand, and the waning power of the south Arabian kingdoms, on the other hand, allowed the Ethiopians to control all trade in gold, incense, ivory and products imported from the Indian Ocean.

PLATE 13.1 *The 'throne' or 'naos' of Haoulti*
a) *The right side*        b) *The front*        c) *The left side*

PLATE 13.2a *Statue of Haoulti*        PLATE 13.2b *Detail of head and shoulders*

PLATE 13.3 *Incense altar of Addi Galamo*

PLATE 13.4 *Bronze bull, Mahabere Dyogwre*

PLATE 13.5 *Bronze identification marks of Yeha:*
  *a) a bird*
  *b) a lion*    *c) a bouquetin*

# The civilization of Aksum from the first to the seventh century

F. ANFRAY

According to primary sources, the history of the kingdom of Aksum extends from the first century of our era over almost a thousand years. It includes two armed incursions into south Arabia in the third, fourth and sixth centuries, an expedition to Meroe in the fourth century, and, during the first half of that same century, the introduction of Christianity.

A score of kings, most of them known only from their coinage, succeeded one another on the Aksum throne. The names of Ezana and Kaleb are particularly illustrious. Those of other monarchs have been handed down by tradition, though here tradition is unfortunately very unreliable. The earliest king actually recorded is Zoscales, mentioned in a Greek text belonging to the end of the first century, but it is still an open question whether he is the same as the Za-Hakalé who occurs in the traditional lists of monarchs.

Our knowledge of Aksumite civilization comes from various sources, from authors of antiquity, such as Pliny, who mentions Adulis, to Arab chroniclers such as Ibn Hischa, Ibn Hischam and Ibn Hawkal. But these texts are mostly somewhat vague, and the greater part of our evidence comes from local epigraphy and the gradually increasing amount of archaeological material. Inscriptions, which are few, began to be collected in the nineteenth century. Among the most important are texts by Ezana, engraved in stone. The discovery of other inscriptions by Ezana, by Kaleb, and by one of the latter's sons (Waazelia), in Greek, Ge'ez and pseudo-Sabaean, yielded all kinds of information, added to in the last twenty years by other evidence of a similar kind, including cave inscriptions and texts on sheets of schist found in Eritrea. These date from the second century, and are the earliest writings of the Aksumite period.

But archaeological observation and excavations are undoubtedly the major source of evidence on Aksumite civilization. In the nineteenth century, travellers began to record the existence of sites, buildings and inscriptions. Various studies were published, some of them of the greatest interest, as for example the amply documented work produced by the German mission to Aksum in 1906. The Ethiopian Institute of Archaeology was founded in 1952, and systematic work was begun. Several sites were thoroughly examined, including Aksum, Melazo, Haoulti, Yeha and Matara. At the same time, the map of ancient settlements was considerably extended. We now know of about forty major sites, and further prospecting will certainly add to the list. But research is still inadequate, so that on the whole our knowledge remains patchy. Most of the remains so far discovered have not been dated with certainty. Inscriptions are practically the only evidence with a real chronology, and even that is not always definite. So much data is still missing that we can give no more than a general outline of Aksum civilization.

## Area

Archaeology shows the Aksumite kingdom as a tall rectangle roughly 300 kilometres long by 160 kilometres wide, lying between 13° and 17° north and 30° and 40° east. It extends from the region north of Keren to Alagui in the south, and from Adulis on the coast to the environs of Takkaze in the west. Addi-Dahno is practically the last-known site in this part, about 30 kilometres from Aksum.

## Proto-Aksumite period

The name of Aksum appears for the first time in the *Periplus Maris Erythraei* ('Circumnavigation of the Erythrean Sea'), a naval and commercial guide compiled by a merchant from Egypt. The work dates from the end of the first century. Ptolemy the Geographer, in the second century, also mentions the place.

The *Periplus* also supplies information about Adulis, now covered with sand, about 50 kilometres south of Massaoua. It describes Adulis as 'a large village three days' journey from Koloè, a town of the interior and the chief market for ivory. From this place to the city of the people called the Aksumites is another five days' journey. Here is brought all the ivory from the land beyond the Nile, across the region called Cyenum and thence to Adulis.' So this village served as an outlet for Aksum, especially for ivory. The text says rhinoceros horn, tortoise-shell and obsidian were also sold there. These things are among the exports from Adulis mentioned by Pliny before the *Periplus*; the name of Adulis is thus referred to before that of Aksum. According to Pliny, Adulis is in the land of the Troglodytes. 'Maximum hic emporium Troglodytarum, etiam Aethiopum . . .' Since the first century the Romans and the Greeks knew of the existence of the Aksumite people and of their 'towns' in the hinterland of Adulis.

Archaeology gives us little information about the material culture of the early centuries of the period. A few inscriptions of the second and third centuries are practically the only datable evidence. But although they are both few and brief, they do have some striking features. They offer the earliest forms of the Ethiopic alphabet, the use of which has survived to the present day. Even so they are not the oldest inscriptions found in the

Aksumite area: several others, of south Arabian type, belong to the second half of the last millennium before our era. The south Arabian script was the model for the Ethiopic. The shape of the letters changed considerably in the second century of our era, moving away from the south Arabian script.

It is certain that other vestiges of these early centuries exist, apart from the writing; remains of buildings, pottery and other objects. But in the present state of research it has not been possible to identify them. Several monuments of the third or the beginning of the fourth century, such as the stelae at Matara and Anza, show that Aksumite civilization did not break completely with the culture of the pre-Aksumite period. They show, engraved or in relief, the lunar symbol of a disc over a crescent in the same form as on the perfume-braziers of the fifth century before our era. The same symbol is also found on the coins. Writing with south Arabian affinities is still to be seen on the great stones of Ezana and Kaleb. But there are important changes. The inscriptions show that religion had altered. The old gods were no longer invoked, and all the other emblems – ibex, lion, sphinx and so on – had been abandoned, with the exception of the lunar symbol. For at this period a new form of civilization was coming into being, quite distinct from that of the preceding period, for this reason known as the pre-Aksumite. In so far as the sites reveal it, this phenomenon can be observed in many other aspects of cultural life.

## Aksumite sites

Adulis and Aksum which, according to the *Periplus*, were at the two ends of the route used in antiquity, are the most important of these sites, and also the only ones where the ancient name, attested in texts and inscriptions, has been preserved locally down to the present. Adulis is a deserted site, but the people of the nearby villages still call the ruins Azuli. All, or nearly all, the other ancient sites have names which are certainly not those of Aksumite antiquity. They are mainly concentrated in the eastern part of the area, from Aratou in the north to Nazret in the south, and include Tokonda, Matara, Etch-Marè and the great sites at Kohaito, which is identified not implausibly with Koloè. (See the map included in Chapter 16.)

### Aksum

The city of Aksum, and the kingdom of the same name, enjoyed a great reputation in the third century of our era, according to a text of the period attributed to Mani, which describes the kingdom as the 'third in the world'. And indeed in the town itself, great buildings and much other material evidence preserve the memory of a great historical epoch. Gigantic stelae (one of them the tallest carved monolith there is), a huge stone table, massive throne bases, fragments of columns, royal tombs, what appear to be extensive remains underneath an eighteenth-century basilica – all these, together with legends and traditions, tell the visitor of a glorious past.

At the beginning of this century a German mission sketched and photographed all the visible monuments. In the western part of the town they uncovered the ruins of three architectural complexes which they rightly identified as the remains of the palace. Subsequent work, in particular that of the Institute of Archaeology, has brought new buildings to light and revealed a wealth of facts about the ancient royal city.

Of the three edifices known to tradition as Enda-Semon, Enda-Mikael and Taakha-Maryam, all that remained were the basements, but today they can only be seen in the sketches and photographs of the German mission. The biggest of these palaces or castles, Enda-Semon, was 35 metres square; Enda-Mikael was 27 metres square, and Taakha-Maryam, 24. The castles were surrounded by courtyards and outbuildings forming rectangular complexes which measured, at Taakha-Maryam, for example, about 120 by 85 metres.

The ruins of another imposing building lie under the church of Maryam-Tsion, to the east of which, below the level of the terrace, the remains of a basement varying in width from 42 to 30 metres still survive.

To the west of the town, from 1966 to 1968, the Ethiopian Institute of Archaeology discovered and studied another architectural complex. These ruins, situated at Dongour, to the north of the Gondar road, are those of another castle belonging to about the seventh century.

The ground sloped away from the foot of a hillock with a flat top. According to a local tradition, this mound of earth and stones covered the tomb of the Queen of Sheba. The uncovered remains of the castle occupy an area of about 3000 square metres. The walls form an irregular quadrilateral with one side 57 metres long and another half a metre shorter. The walls in the centre of the ruins still stand 5 metres high.

Four irregular groups of buildings containing about forty rooms in all are so arranged as to form a square enclosure around the main part of the castles. This stands on a tiered base 1·8 metres high and consists of seven rooms reached by three outer staircases. Three courtyards separate this dwelling from its outbuildings. The outer walls comprise projecting parts alternating with recessed parts. Solid masonry piers, grouped in twos or fours, were found buried in several rooms both in the main building and in the ancillary living quarters. They served as bases for stone pillars, or more probably wooden posts, supporting whatever structures were above. In the vestibules of the main building, broad stone bases covered by geometrical pavement served this purpose. Special features of the layout of the north-eastern and south-western parts of the site suggest that at those points staircases led to an upper floor which was the main dwelling area.

Three ovens of baked brick have been uncovered in the western part of the site. In one room in the outbuildings, to the south, a brick structure bearing traces of flames seems to have been a heating device.

The Dongour site is the finest example of Aksumite architecture that can be seen today. On account of its peripheral position and comparatively modest size, Dongour does not seem to have been a royal residence. It was more probably inhabited by some leading citizen.

Another outstanding building, the remains of which are attributed by tradition to Kaleb and his son Guebra-Masqal, once stood on a hill to the north-east of Aksum. A pair of what might be called chapels were raised over crypts consisting of several vaults built of and covered by stone flags: there are five vaults in the crypt of Guebra-Masqal to the south, and three in that of Kaleb to the north. The upper part of the building is relatively recent and indeed shows signs of having been frequently altered. There is reason to think that the crypts are older, and that the vaults were brought back into use in about the seventh or eighth century. The flight of steps leading to Kaleb's tomb has large polygonal blocks of stone reminiscent of certain north Syrian buildings of the second or third century. The monument was surrounded by a large necropolis, and several shaft tombs have lately been discovered nearby. There are others some distance away towards the east.

At Bazen, to the east of the town, some oven-type tombs are hollowed out of the rocky hillside. Some have a shaft, and vaults on each side at the bottom. The same sector contains a multiple tomb with a stairway of seventeen steps, also hollowed out of the rock, and dominated by a stele which in ancient times did not stand alone, since an English traveller at the beginning of the nineteenth century tells of having seen fourteen fallen 'obelisks' here.

The ancient city covered the area between the giant stelae and the Dongour site, and ruins lie everywhere under the surface. Here and there, outcrops of walls point to the existence of Aksumite buildings. When excavations can be undertaken in the places traditionally called Addi-Kiltè and Tchaanadoug, they will bring to light a vast stretch of Aksum's past.

## Adulis

There are few remains on the surface of this site, which is not on the coast but about 4 kilometres inland. Rock, sand and vegetation cover a considerable expanse of ruins, however. As far as can be judged from the evidence above ground, they lie within a rectangle roughly 500 metres long and 400 wide. In some places, heaps of debris show where various archaeological expeditions have been at work. Towards the north-east the ground is scattered with fragments of pillars and large quantities of shards. In 1868 a British expeditionary force which landed nearby dug up some remains of buildings, but of the work undertaken since little remains apart from the walls uncovered by Paribeni's mission in 1906, and those found in 1961–2 by the mission of the Ethiopian Institute of Archaeology.

At the beginning of 1906, Sundstrom, a Swede, discovered a large edifice in the northern sector, and shortly afterwards Paribeni uncovered two smaller ruins, to the east and the west. All these ruins consist of the tiered and stepped basements of rectangular structures which are surrounded by outbuildings. Sundstrom called the one he uncovered a 'palace'. It is a vast complex 38 metres long and 22 wide, and thus covers an area more extensive than that of Enda-Semon, the castle in Aksum, where the central dwelling was 35 metres long. Over the basement, two rows of pillars divide the building lengthwise into three sections, and two more rows of pillars divide the width in the same fashion. Such a basilical plan suggests not a palace but a Christian sanctuary.

The basement revealed to the west of this complex by Paribeni displays the same architectural features. It is about $18\frac{1}{2}$ metres long. The upper part was covered by a pavement, and comprised the remains of the pillars of a nave. At the eastern end, a semi-circular apse between two rooms was a sufficient indication that the ruins were those of a basilica. A lower level of the building belonged to an older structure which the Italian archaeologist called the Altar of the Sun. In the light of other evidence, we may now regard it as the remains of a building, probably religious, belonging to an earlier period than the basilica constructed over it.

To the east of Sundstrom's discovery, Paribeni found the basement of another church 25 metres long, with traces of a semi-circular apse. There were two striking features: a baptismal tank in the room south of the apse and, in the centre of the building, the remains of eight pillars arranged octagonally. A square plan and a rectangular plan are thus combined in the same building.

On the Erythrean plateau, 135 kilometres south of Asmara, near Sénafé, there is one of the oldest archaeological sites in Ethiopia: its lowest levels belong to a large building of the south Arabian period.

The Institute of Archaeology carried out systematic excavations of the Matara site between 1959 and 1970, but there is still a great deal to discover. The pre-Aksumite levels have only been subjected to soundings, mainly because there are many other structures of architectural interest lying above them. About half the Aksumite level has been explored. These digs have revealed four large villas, three Christian churches, and an ordinary residential quarter consisting of some thirty houses. The four villas are of the now familiar type, with a main dwelling constructed over a tiered basement and surrounded by outhouses. As elsewhere, masonry piers buried under the rooms of the main building served as bases for the posts supporting the vestibules. The steps leading up to the main entrances must have been protected by porch roofs: there are cavities at the corners of each flight of steps which may have held wooden uprights.

The ordinary houses consist of two or three rooms. The walls are of an average thickness of 70 centimetres. Remains of hearths, brick ovens and numerous receptacles have made it possible to locate the living quarters.

There is another type of house intermediate in size between the villas and the ordinary dwellings. This type has some features in common with the central building of the villas – a similar lay-out and stepped walls.

There is reason to think that this typology in the architecture reflects a social hierarchy.

To the south and east of the town there are religious edifices which are outwardly very much like the other structures: they have a central building surrounded by courtyards and outhouses; the method of construction was exactly the same. One of these edifices is a sort of funerary chapel rather like Kaleb's Tomb at Aksum, though not so large. It is 15 metres long and 10 wide, and stands over a crypt which is reached by a flight of fourteen steps.

To the east another church – the third from the bottom of four distinct layers of ruins – had a central nave and side-aisles divided from the nave by two rows of four pillars, of which the bases are still extant. An apse with a room on either side lies on the same axis as the nave, which is oriented in the same direction in all buildings of this kind. The outer walls are 22·4 metres long and 13·5 metres wide. A baptismal tank has been found in a room on the east side of the church, behind the apse. Water was delivered into the tank by a series of amphoras fitted into each other so as to form a conduit running down the wall outside.

There was another church on the hill of Goual-Saim, to the south of the site, but here most of the walls have been destroyed and the lay-out is scarcely visible. However, there are some vestiges of a schist pavement and of the bases of pillars. It was a comparatively small building.

## Kohaito

On this site, which lies north of Matara at a height of 2600 metres, many ruins of architectural interest can be seen. Ten or so mounds scattered over quite a large area contain the remains of large buildings belonging to the end of the Aksumite period and, in all probability, fragments of still older structures. Several pillars are still standing on the mounds. It is thought that most of them belonged to churches of about the same size as those at Matara. The walls on all the hillocks display the features of Aksumite masonry work and are laid out on the same rectangular pattern as those visible on other sites of the period. Seven of these architectural complexes can easily be discerned. As well as these ruined buildings, to the north-north-east there was a dam consisting of regular courses of perfectly fitted blocks of stone. Its function was to impound the water on the south-eastern side of a natural basin commonly known as the Safra basin. The dam is 67 metres long and stands about 3 metres high in its central section, where two sets of projecting stones form steps leading down from the top of the dam to the water.

To the east there is a rock-hewn shaft tomb which comprises two rooms or burial-vaults. A cross of the Aksumite type cut into the rock adorns one of the sides of the tomb.

In a ravine near the site the rock is painted and carved with figures representing oxen, camels and other animals.

## Towns and markets

The big settlements – and that applies to those places already mentioned as well as several others – formed compact and crowded communities where dwellings stood close together and clustered round large buildings designed for various purposes. Excavations at Aksum, Adulis and Matara have shown that these places were real urban centres. In the quarter of Matara inhabited by the common people there is a narrow winding alley between the houses. All this points to a comparatively large population whose activities were not wholly confined to agriculture. The presence of coins sheds light on the development of the economy. Further evidence is afforded by the nature of the objects which have been unearthed: glass-ware, Mediterranean amphoras. Works of art (such as a bronze lamp and various articles made of gold) suggest that luxury was not unknown.

One point should be noted: most of the buildings that are usually visible, or that have been uncovered by excavation, belong to the late Aksumite period. However, there are remains which, though they cannot always be accurately dated, are older, and upon which the buildings of the last period were erected. These show that even at the period to which they belong the situation could not have been very different. The author of the *Periplus*, in the first century, calls Koloè a 'town of the interior'. He also says that it is 'the chief market for ivory'. He describes Adulis as a market-town, which gets ivory from 'the city of the people called the Aksumites', where the ivory is first collected. So Adulis must be identified as a market-town, too. And the other urban centres should also be regarded as markets and trading places (Aratou, Tokonda, Etch-Maré, Degonm, Haghero-Deragoueh, Henzat, etc.). It is not certain that the trading took place inside the towns themselves; in fact, it is much more likely that business was transacted in the outskirts, for we know that these ancient towns were not surrounded by ramparts. But so far no evidence has been found to settle this question.

## Aksumite architecture – general characteristics

The chief characteristics of Aksumite architecture are the use of stone, a square or rectangular lay-out, the regular alternation of projecting parts and recessed parts, tiered basements with large buildings erected over them, and a type of masonry which uses no other mortar but clay. In addition, there is the striking fact that these distinctive features are reproduced practically everywhere. It has already been noted that the same architectural formulas are applied in all the major edifices, religious or otherwise. They all stand on the same type of tiered base and are reached by monumental stairs, often comprising seven steps. They are all surrounded by out-buildings from which they are separated by small courtyards.

It may be taken as certain that the castles and villas comprised at least one storey above the ground floor, which, given its height, ought rather to be called the first floor. Given the smallness of the rooms at this level, and the fact that they were cluttered with pillars or posts, it is probable that the real living quarters were on the floor above. It is an open question whether the big castles of Aksum had several upper storeys. At the beginning of this century the architect of the German mission attempted a reconstitution, and the sketch of the building at Enda-Mikael shows towers of four storeys at the corners of the central structure. As almost nothing of the building has survived (even less today than in 1906), it is not easy to decide whether the attempted reconstitution is plausible, but judging by the masonry work as shown in photographs and drawings and as exemplified in other buildings, the comparatively thin walls, made of stones bound together only with cob-mortar, were not very strong, and we may doubt whether Enda-Mikael, or any of the other castles, had more than two storeys. Although rather unlikely, it is just possible that some particularly stout ones may have had three; but to imagine more than that seems far-fetched. In the sixth century, Cosmas Indicopleustes, in his *Christian Topography*, says that in Ethiopia (he does not specify Aksum, but it is probable that he went there) he saw a 'royal dwelling with four towers'. Although this terse remark does not give the position of the towers, it refers to high buildings, and this is the important point.

The Aksumites included timber among their building materials. The frames of doors and windows were of wood and at certain points in the walls, especially at the corners of rooms, joists were let into the masonry to strengthen it. The beams supporting the floors of rooms in upper storeys or the roofs, which were probably flat, were of course wooden. The carved stelae which show the projecting butt-ends of beams undoubtedly give a faithful picture of the practices of the time.

It was also the custom to make the basements of large buildings as solid as possible by laying large blocks of hewn stone at the corners or along the top in long rows. Many of these blocks are to be seen in buildings of the late Aksumite period, some of them having been used before in a previous structure. There can be no doubt that the builders of the first Aksumite period, especially those of the third and fourth centuries, were very fond of large blocks of stone. This is strikingly illustrated by the stelae, and the giant slab in front of them.

## Monolithic monuments

The stelae of Aksum are of several types. Many of those to be seen in the area are just large, roughly trimmed stones, as at Goudit in the southern sector of the Dongour site. They are scattered about a field and there is no doubt that in antiquity they marked the places of graves. Other stelae have smooth sides and a curved top. Some are over 20 metres high. This type of stele too is found in various places, though they are most plentiful near the group of giant stelae. There are seven stelae in this group. They are remarkable for their decorative carvings. Only one is still standing. Five lie broken on the ground. The seventh was taken to Rome and in 1937 it was erected near the Caracalla Theatre where it still stands.

The carvings imitate many-storeyed buildings. The tallest of the stelae, which was about 33 metres high, depicts nine superimposed storeys on one of its sides: a lofty dwelling complete with door, windows, butt-ends of beams, is perfectly carved in hard stone. The meaning of this imaginary architecture is entirely unknown. There are practically no points of comparison between it and any other examples elsewhere. One of these stelae has lances carved on the pediment. Another, which is not one of those representing architecture, displays a sort of shield – if it *is* a shield – under a two-sloped roof – if it *is* a roof. Holes or metal nails were used to fix emblems into position, but the emblems are no longer there and we do not know what they were, nor even whether they were not added later. It can hardly be doubted that these monuments are funerary cippi. One hesitates to say whether they marked the seat of some divine power or commemorated the existence of some human being. The symbolism of the decoration shrouds the whole question in mystery. As to the difference between the dimensions of the stelae, one can hardly be wrong in thinking that they corresponded to a hierarchy of social status.

The same uncertainty prevails as to the significance of the enormous stone slab in front of the big stelae, which was placed, originally at least, on thick pillars. Its dimensions (length: over 17 metres, width: 6·5 metres, thickness: 1·3 metres) make the mind boggle if we try to assess the amount of energy needed to move this slab over what must have been hundreds of metres. We do not know where such blocks of stone were quarried. There is an ancient stone-cutting shop near a high hill west of Aksum, where a big block about 27 metres long was being given a rough dressing. But we cannot be sure that the huge slab or the carved stelae came from that place, over 2 kilometres away. Whatever the transport problem, the mere fact that these stones were erected suggests the existence of a powerful collective organization.

At Matara and Anza, on the eastern plateau, there are two round-topped stelae about 5 metres high. They display two distinctive features: a crescent which is the symbol of the south Arabian religion; and an inscription in Ge'ez. Such inscriptions have a commemorative significance; this has been definitely established, at least at Matara. Palaeographic factors indicate that they date from the third or the beginning of the fourth century. The workmanship of these monoliths is the same as that of the smooth stelae at Aksum.

At Aksum, monoliths of yet another kind are scattered about in various places. These are big stone platforms, a dozen of which can be seen standing in a row in the area occupied by the giant stelae near the basilica of Maryam-Tsion. Most probably they were the bases of thrones. Some are more than 2·5 metres long and have an average thickness of 40 to 50 centimetres. The central part of the upper surface forms a bulge which comprises holes for holding the legs of a seat. There used to be one of these bases on the Matara site. So far twenty-seven such monoliths have been listed.

These thrones loomed large in Aksumite culture. They are mentioned in two inscriptions of Ezana. In the sixth century, Cosmas noted the presence of a throne close to a stele at Adulis. 'The throne has a square base.' 'It is made of excellent white marble' and 'entirely ... hewn out of a single block of stone'. Both throne and stele were 'covered with Greek characters'. The inscription on the throne was composed by an Aksumite sovereign who ruled in about the third century. The significance of these monuments is not clear. Are they thrones commemorating victories? Votive seats? Symbols of regal power? They are as much of an enigma as the great stelae.

The group near Maryam-Tsion is arranged so that all the thrones face east, in the same direction as the carved sides of the stelae. If this arrangement is the original one, it is possible that they were turned towards a temple which may have stood at that time on the site of the present church, where there are many ruins.

The inscriptions themselves are cut into the hard stone, a kind of granite. One of Ezana's texts, which is in three different scripts – Ethiopic, south Arabian and Greek – is engraved on both sides of a stone over 2 metres high.

This fondness for large-scale monuments appears to have prevailed in the case of statues too. At the beginning of the century, a flat stone was discovered at Aksum which displayed hollowed-out footprints 92 centimetres long. The stone had been used as the plinth for a statue, probably of metal. Ezana's inscriptions say that he erected statues in honour of the divinity. One such text reads: 'As a token of gratitude to Him who begot us, Ares the Unvanquished, we have raised statues, one of gold, another of silver, and three of bronze, to His glory.' No Aksumite statue has yet been recovered, but the archaeological investigations are far from complete. Few representations of animals have been discovered, either in stone or in metal. Cosmas tells us that he saw 'four bronze statues' of unicorns (no doubt rhinoceroses) 'in the royal palace'.

## Pottery

Aksumite sites yield large quantities of terracotta vessels, some broken and others intact.

Such pottery is mainly utilitarian, and has been found in both red and black terracotta, the former easily predominating. In many of the pots, the outer surface is finished in matt colour; in several cases, it has been smoothed with stone; some are coated with red slip. There is no evidence at all of the use of the wheel.

The vessels vary in size, ranging from tiny cups to vats 80 centimetres high. The jars, bowls, jugs, pans, basins and cups are not always decorated. When they are, the decoration usually consists of geometric designs, either carved, painted, moulded or stamped. The patterns are simple, for the most part – festoons, zigzags, grouped discs, checks, helices, bars and so on. The motifs are rarely taken from nature; just a few ears of corn; moulded birds and snakes. Some of the decoration has an obvious symbolic significance, as in the case of the mould-made arms added to the rims of basins. The Christian cross appears over and over again on the rims, sides or bottoms of vessels.

There is a difference between the pottery from the east of the plateau and that from the west. In the Aksum area we find a kind of vessel with linear incisions on its sides, but this type is rare on the eastern plateau. There is a bowl from Matara, with a boss and ribs under the rim, of which no counterpart has so far been discovered in the Aksum area, but here, on the other hand, we find a jar with a spout in the form of a human head which has not yet been paralleled elsewhere.

The information yielded by current investigations enables us to classify groups of pottery finds according to chronological series, but more excavation will have to be done before we have anything like accurate datings.

Imported pottery, mainly jars with handles and ribbed sides, is also found in the Aksumite layer of all the sites. These amphoras, of which there are a large number at Adulis, are of Mediterranean origin. They were sometimes used as burial urns for babies, as has been established at Adulis, Matara and Aksum. There is no trace of such amphoras in the pre-Aksumite levels. In the Aksumite layer are also found many fragments of glass phials, bottles and cups, and blue-glaze vessels dating from the end of the Aksumite period and mostly imported from the Indian Ocean. (They are admittedly unearthed more often in fragments than whole.) There are also little cups which look like *terra sigillata* and were probably imported from Egypt.

The abundance of pottery on the sites implies the consumption of large quantities of wood. The landscape must have had more trees in antiquity than it has now.

## A few special objects

Archaeological research has led to the discovery of various objects such as seals fashioned in stone or terracotta and engraved with geometric motifs or profiles of animals; little tools made of various metals; terracotta dice; fragments of blades; figurines of animals; female statuettes similar to the fertility figures of prehistory; and so on. Of special interest are a bronze lamp and a treasure hoard brought to light during excavations at Matara.

The first consists of an oblong bowl resting on a stem made to resemble a colonnade of stylized palm-trees. On top of the bowl is a round boss decorated with a pattern which represents a dog wearing a collar in the act of catching an ibex. On the reverse of the bowl a bucrane is modelled in light relief. The lamp stands 41 centimetres high; the bowl is 31 centimetres long. To judge by its symbolism – which seems to be that of the ritual chase, especially in view of the presence of the bucrane – the lamp probably came from south Arabia, where similar objects have been discovered.

The treasure was found in a bronze vessel 18 centimetres high. It consists of two crosses, three chains, a brooch, sixty-eight pendants, sixty-four necklace beads, fourteen coins of Roman emperors of the second and third centuries (mainly the Antonines), and two bracteates. All the articles are of gold, and in a remarkably good state of preservation. Judging from where they were found, they must have been gathered together in about the seventh century. (The coins are not a guide to the dating in this case, for all except one are fitted with rings, which indicates that they were used as jewellery.)

Sometimes Aksumite levels yield south Arabian inscriptions and fragments of perfume-braziers from the fifth century before our era. The stones are usually broken and have been reused by Aksumite builders. These levels also produce a few articles imported from Egypt or Nubia, or, as at Haoulti, terracotta figurines which, according to Henri de Contenson, the explorer of this site, 'seem related to those met with in India in the Mathura and Gupta periods'. He also points out, in this connection, that 'the first two centuries of our era were precisely the heyday of the traders who established contacts between India and the Mediterranean via the Red Sea'.

## Numismatics

Aksumite coins are of special importance. It is through them alone that the names of eighteen kings of Aksum are known.

Several thousand coins have been found. The ploughed fields around Aksum throw up a good many, especially during the rainy season when the water washes away the soil. Most are of bronze, and they vary in size from 8 to 22 millimetres. They depict kings, often showing the head and shoulders, sometimes with and sometimes without a crown. Only one is represented sitting on a throne, in profile. The coins carry various symbols. Those of the early kings (Endybis, Aphilas, Ousanas I, Wazeba, Ezana) bear the disc and crescent. All coins made after Ezana's conversion to Christianity depict the cross, either in the middle of one side, or among the letters of the legend inscribed round the edge. In some cases the bust of the king is framed by two bent ears of corn or one straight ear is represented in the centre, as on the coins of Aphilas and Ezana. Perhaps the ears of corn were emblems of a power to ensure the fertility of the land.

The legends are written in Greek or Ethiopic, never in south Arabian. Greek appears on the very earliest coins; Ethiopic begins only with Wazeba. The words of the legend vary: 'By the grace of God', 'Health and happiness to the people', 'Peace to the people', 'He will conquer through Christ', and so on. And of course the name of the king is shown, with the title 'King of the Aksumites', or 'King of Aksum'.

The coins bear no dates, and this gives rise to many conjectures when it comes to classification. The oldest type – probably the one minted in the reign of Endybis – goes back no farther than the third century. The latest, bearing the name of Hataza, dates from the eighth century.

## Script and language

The earliest alphabet used in Ethiopia, which dates back to the fifth century before our era, is of a south Arabian type. It transcribes a language that is akin to the Semitic dialects of south Arabia.

Aksumite writing differs from this south Arabian script but is nevertheless derived from it.

The first examples of Ethiopic script properly so-called date from the second century of our era. They are consonantal in form. The characters are still reminiscent of their south Arabian origin, but they gradually evolve their own distinctive shapes. The direction of the writing, which was initially variable, became fixed, and it then ran from left to right. These first inscriptions were engraved on tablets of schist. They are not numerous and comprise a few words. The oldest was discovered at Matara, in Erythrea. An inscription engraved on a metal object has been found which dates from the third century. It mentions King Gadara and is the first Ethiopic inscription known to bear the name of Aksum. Other texts were engraved on stone. The great inscriptions of King Ezana belong to the fourth century. It is with them that syllabism first appears, soon becoming the rule in Ethiopic script. Vocalic signs become integrated into the consonantal system, denoting the different tone qualities of the spoken language.

This language, as revealed in the inscriptions, is known as Ge'ez. It is a member of the southern group of the Semitic family. It is the language of the Aksumites.

During the Aksumite period, south Arabian and Greek scripts were in use, albeit to a limited extent. South Arabian script is still to be found in the sixth-century inscriptions of Kaleb and of one of his sons, Waazeba. About the fifth century, the Bible was translated into Geez.

## The rise of Aksumite civilization

Five centuries before our era a special form of civilization marked by south Arabian influences was established on the northern Ethiopian plateau. It was essentially an agrarian civilization, and it prospered during the fifth and fourth centuries before our era. In the course of the following centuries it declined, at least judging by the present lack of archaeological documentation. But the culture did not die out. Some of its characteristics were preserved in the Aksumite civilization. Certain features of the language and writing, a religious emblem, the name of a god (Astar still appears in one of Ezana's inscriptions), architectural and agricultural traditions (probably, among others, the use of the swing-plough), show that in the early centuries of our era an ancient heritage was still alive. It is also noteworthy that, especially on the eastern plateau, most Aksumite buildings occupy the same sites as those of the pre-Aksumite period. This betokens a kind of continuity.

However, the archaeological finds dating from the first centuries of our era reveal many aspects that are new. Although the writing used in the inscriptions was derived from a south Arabian script, a considerable change is now apparent. Religion too has altered. The names of all the ancient gods have disappeared except for that of Astar. They are replaced in the Ezana texts by the names of the triad Mahrem, Beher and Meder. As regards architecture, while it continues to be characterized by the use of stone and wood and by the tiered basement of its buildings, it displays various new features. Pottery is very different in workmanship, shape and decoration, and imported ceramics are also found, while glass-ware occurs in all sites. Where there used to be only villages, small towns and cities are now developing. The name of Aksum appears (for the first time in the historical records of this period), and it is probably significant that the site seems to have had no appreciable past before the first century.

## Economic factors

During the Aksumite era, as in the preceding centuries, agriculture and animal husbandry formed the basis of economic life. But in Aksumite times this developed along quite distinctive lines, no doubt because of two factors in particular.

All ancient sources indicate that maritime trade increased in the Red Sea in the course of the first two centuries. This is attributable to the Roman expansion in this area, which was facilitated by progress in navigation. We know that navigational methods improved at the beginning of the first century. The pilot Hippalus showed how sailors could make use of the winds to the best advantage, and this undoubtedly gave an impetus to sea traffic. Strabo records that 'every year, in the time of Augustus, a hundred and twenty ships set out from Myos Hormos'.

Commercial connections multiplied. Ships brought cargoes, and made it possible to trade with India and the Mediterranean world. Adulis was the meeting-point for maritime trade, as it was – and this is the second factor – for inland trade. In the interior, a traffic was growing in a very valuable commodity: ivory. In fact, Pliny and the author of the *Periplus* place it first on the list of exports from Adulis. Aksum was the great collecting-centre for ivory from various regions. It was an article which was indispensable to the luxury-loving Romans. In the age of the Ptolemies the Ethiopian elephant was already highly prized. Armies used it as a sort of tank. Later it was hunted for its tusks. Whenever the authors of antiquity talk of Adulis, Aksum or Ethiopia (East Africa), they always give prominence to elephants and their ivory. They mention other goods – hippopotamus hides, rhinoceros horn, tortoise-shell, gold, slaves, spices – but they take a special interest in elephants. According to the *Periplus*, elephants lived inland, like the rhinoceros, but sometimes they were hunted 'on the shore itself, near Adulis'. In the reign of Justinian, Nonnosus visited Aksum and on the way saw a herd of 5000 elephants. Cosmas notes that there is 'a multitude of elephants with large tusks; from Ethiopia these tusks are sent by boat to India, Persia, the land of the Himyarites, and Romania' (*Christian Topography*, XI, 33). In 1962, the mission from the Ethiopian Institute of Archaeology found an elephant's tusk in the Aksumite ruins at Adulis, and in 1967, they discovered pieces of a terracotta figurine of an elephant in the walls of the castle at Dongour.

## The African roots

The civilization of Aksum developed in the first centuries of our era, but its roots lie deep in prehistory. It was foreshadowed in the culture of the last five centuries before our era. Archaeology is attempting to define its characteristic features, but only a few aspects of the subject have been investigated so far, and the cataloguing of the data of antiquity is by no means complete. The main task ahead is to determine what comes from external influences and what is really indigenous: like other civilizations, that of Aksum is the result of an evolutionary process aided by geographic conditions and historical circumstances. The indigenous contribution is naturally of great importance, for there can be no doubt that Aksumite civilization is, above all, the product of a people whose ethnic identity is progressively emerging from the study of its inscriptions, language and traditions. Archaeology is gradually revealing the unique character of Aksum's material achievements. Much remains to be done, and future research will concentrate on interpreting the significance of the evidence dug out of the soil. But already we know that the civilization of Aksum owes its particular qualities to its African roots.

PLATE 14.1 *Aerial photograph of Aksum*

PLATE 14.2 *Neck of a bottle*

PLATE 14.3 *Lioness sculptured on the side of a rock, Aksumite period*

PLATE 14.4 *Foot of a throne*

PLATE 14.5 *Elephant tusk*

PLATE 14.7 *Perfume-pan, Alexandrian style*

PLATE 14.8 *Matara: base of an Aksumite building*

PLATE 14.6 *Matara: inscription of the third century of our era*

# Aksum: political system, economics and culture, first to fourth century

## 15

### Y. M. KOBISHANOV

Historical sources of the second and third centuries record the rapid rise of a new African power: Aksum. Claudius Ptolemy (around the middle of the second century), the first to mention the Aksumites as one of the peoples of Ethiopia, knows the cities of Meroe and Adulis but not that of Aksum. This situation in north-east Africa resembles that described in *Aethiopica*, the novel by Heliodoros, a Graeco-Phoenician author of the third century, who describes the arrival of the Aksumite ambassadors, not as subjects and tributaries, but as friends and allies of the Meroitic king. The *Periplus Maris Erythraei* ('Circumnavigation of the Erythrean Sea'), where one can find data on different periods from before 105 to the beginning of the third century of our era mentions the 'metropolis of the so-called Aksumites' as a little-known city and the kingdom of its ruler Zoscales (obviously Za-Hecale of the Aksum kings' list) as very young. Zoscales ruled all the Red Sea coast of Erythrea, but the hegemony in the Beja desert belonged to Meroe. The balance between these two powers – the old metropolis of the Meroites and the young metropolis of the Aksumites – recalls the novel by Heliodoros. The *Periplus* makes no reference to the Aksumites' expansion to south Arabia. The earliest sources to mention it are the Sabaean inscriptions of the end of the second and the beginning of the third centuries which report on the 'Abyssinians' or Aksumites who wage war in Yemen and occupy some of its territories. Between 183 and 213 the Aksumites' kings, Gadara and his son, seem to have been the most powerful rulers in southern Arabia and the real leaders of the anti-Sabaean coalition. At the end of the third and in the early years of the fourth centuries, 'Azbah, an Aksumite King, also waged war in South Arabia'.[1]

Subsequently, the Himarites united the country but the Aksumite kings claimed to be their sovereign, as can be seen from their titles.

---

1. The main inscriptions in *Corpus inscriptionum semiticarum ab Academiae inscriptionum ... Pars quarta*, 1889–1929; A. Jamme, 1962; G. Ryckmans, 1955, 1956. For some remarks on the inscriptions see G. Ryckmans, 1964. For an account of the events see also H. von Wissmann, 1964. For the chronology see A. Loundine and G. Ryckmans, 1964.

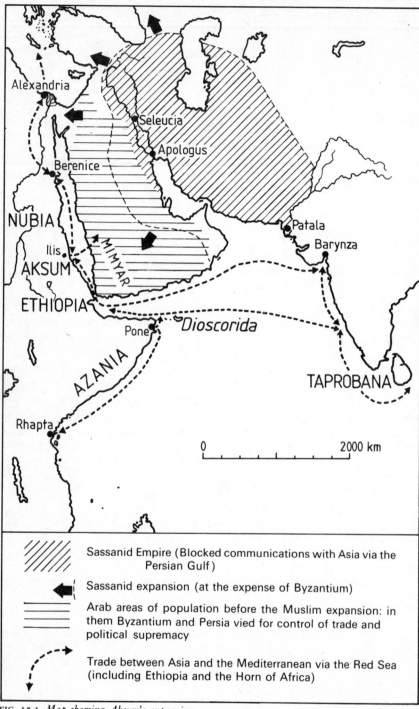

FIG. 15.1 *Map showing Aksum's expansion*

Wars in southern Arabia are also reported in two Greek inscriptions by Aksumite kings whose names and dates of reign are unknown. The longer inscription was copied in the middle of the sixth century by Cosmas Indicopleustes. Its author conquered the coastal parts of Yemen 'till the land of the Sabaeans' and vast territories in Africa 'from the frontiers of Egypt' to the land of incense of Somali.[2]

By about 270 the fame of the new state had reached Persia. The 'Kephalaia' of the prophet Mani (216–76) calls Aksum one of the four greatest empires of the world.

What resources and organization did Aksum have to achieve such successes?

## Occupations

For the most part the Aksumites were engaged in agriculture and stock-breeding, practically the same types of occupation as those of the present-day Tigre peasants. The mountain slopes were terraced and irrigated by the water of mountain streams channelled into the fields. In the foot-hills and on the plains, cisterns and dams were constructed as reservoirs for rainwater and irrigation canals were dug. Inscriptions indicate that wheat[3] and other cereals were sown; viticulture also existed. Ploughs drawn by oxen were used. Large herds of cattle, sheep and goats were kept; other domestic animals were asses and mules. Like the Meroites, the Aksumites had learned to capture and domesticate elephants, but these were reserved for the use of the royal court.[4] According to inscriptions, the diet consisted of flat wheaten cakes, ale, wine, hydromel, honey, meat, butter and vegetable-oil.[5]

The crafts and trades of blacksmiths and other metal-workers, potters, builders, stone-masons and carvers, among others, attained a very high level of skill and artistry. The most important technical innovation was the use of iron tools, which became far more widespread than in the first millennium before our era and inevitably influenced the further development of agriculture, trades and military science. Another innovation was the introduction of a cohesive cementing solution in building, which led to the development of a form of stone and timber construction.

## Political structure

Aksum may have been initially a principality which in the course of time became the capital province of a feudal kingdom. History confronted its

2. E. O. Winstedt, pp. 74–7.
3. *Deutsche Aksum Expedition* 4: 21; *DAE* 6: 10; *DAE* 7: 12; E. Littmann, 1910–15; A. J. Drewes, 1962, pp. 30ff.
4. L. A. Dindorff, 1831, pp. 457–8; E. O. Winstedt, p. 324.
5. *DAE* 4: 13–21; *DAE* 6: 7–11; *DAE* 7: 9–13; A. J. Drewes, 1962, p. 73.

rulers with various tasks, the most urgent of which was the establishment of their power over the segmentary states of northern Ethiopia, and the assembling of these into one kingdom. Success depended upon the Aksumite ruler's strength and the degree to which it exceeded that of other princes of ancient Ethiopia. It sometimes happened that a new ruler, on ascending the throne, was obliged to inaugurate his reign with a countrywide campaign to enforce at least formal submission on the principalities. Although this action was taken by an Aksum monarch whose name has not survived, but who established the Monumentum Adulitanum, Ezana was obliged to assert his authority anew at the outset of his reign.[6]

The founding of a kingdom served as the basis on which to build an empire. From the close of the second century up to the beginning of the fourth, Aksum took part in the military and diplomatic struggle waged between the states of southern Arabia. Following this, the Aksumites subjugated the regions situated between the Tigre plateau and the valley of the Nile. In the fourth century they conquered the Meroe kingdom, which by that time had declined.

In this way was built an empire extending over the rich cultivated lands of northern Ethiopia, Sudan and southern Arabia, which included all the peoples who inhabited the countries south of the boundaries of the Roman empire, between the Sahara to the west and the inner Arabian desert of Rub' el Hālī to the east.

The state was divided into Aksum proper and its vassal kingdoms, the rulers of which were subjects of the Aksum king of kings, to whom they paid tribute. The Greeks called the Aksumite potentate the basileus (only Athanasius the Great and Philostorgius termed him tyrant); the vassal kings were known as archontes, tyrants and ethnarchs. Syrian writers such as John of Ephesus, Simeon of Beth-Arsam and the author of the 'Book of the Himyarites', accorded the title of king (mlk') to the Aksumite 'king of kings' and also to the kings of Himyar and 'Alwa, who were his subjects. But the Aksumite term for all these was 'negus'. Only in particular cases, where the writing was intended for a foreign reader, were terminological distinctions introduced.[7] Each 'people', kingdom, principality, city and tribe had its own negus.[8] Mention is made of army neguses (nägästa särāwit) (*DAE* 9:

---

6. E. O. Winstedt, pp. 72–7; *DAE* 8; *DAE* 9.

7. For instance, in the Greek text of 'Ezānā's bilingua (*DAE* 4, 6, 7), the Aksum ruler is entitled the king of kings, as well as the king of the Aksumites and others, while the Beja rulers are called little kings. In the pseudo-Sabaean text, the king of Aksum is referred to in terms of Sabaean origin – mlk, mlk mlkn – while the Beja rulers are given the Ethiopian term – nägäšt. In the Greek inscription recording his Nubian campaign, 'Ezānā calls himself simply king, and not king of kings, possibly for reasons connected with his foreign policy (A. Caquot and P. Nautin, pp. 270–1). But this title in itself denoted a very high rank accorded even to Roman–Byzantine emperors: *DAE* 9, 13–nägastat Sarawit.

8. *DAE* 8: 7–12, 27, 29; *DAE* 9: 9–12; *DAE* 11: 36; A. J. Drewes, 1962, pp. 30ff., 65–7; R. Schneider, 1974, pp. 771, 775.

13). Apart from leading armies in time of war, these neguses assumed command of building operations.[9] Among the neguses, the inscriptions name kings of four tribes of Bega (Beja), each ruling over about 1100 subjects (*DAE* 4: 19–2; *DAE* 6: 7–17; *DAE* 7: 6–18) and the ruler of the Agabo principality whose subjects numbered scarcely more than between 200 and 275 grown men, or a total of 1000–1500 persons. Vassal kingdoms were situated on the Tigre plateau and in the region of Zula Bay (Agago, Metin, Agame, etc.), beyond the Taqqaze river (Walqa'it, Samēn, Agaw), in the arid regions around the Ethiopian uplands (Agwezat) and likewise in the Arabian peninsula. After Ezana's victory, these kingdoms extended to Upper Nubia, between the Fourth Rapids and Sennar. Certain vassal kings (for example those in southern Arabia and Upper Nubia) possessed their own vassals – hereditary rulers of a lower rank. A power-hierarchy was thus created, from the Aksum king of kings down to the chiefs of separate communities.

Two methods of collecting tribute existed: either the vassal rulers (such as Abraha, king of Himyar) sent a yearly tribute to Aksum, or the king of Aksum, accompanied by a numerous retinue, travelled round his domains gathering tribute and victuals for his attendants on the way. The vassal king followed the same method. A compromise between these two methods was achieved by the vassals delivering tribute at appointed stages along the king's route.

The sources contain no information on the administrative system of Aksum, which appears to have been poorly developed. Near relatives of the king assumed an important part in the direction of affairs. It is understandable, therefore, that the Roman emperor Constantine II addressed his letter not only to Ezana, but also to Šē'azana, his brother.[10] Military expeditions were led as a rule by the king, his brother,[11] or other kinsmen.[12] Armies of less importance, commanded by army kings, were made up of warriors from the communities or tribes; the expression 'my people', uttered by an Aksum king, is synonymous with 'my armies'.[13]

The rulers of Aksum settled warlike tribes along the borders of the state: Abyssinians in southern Arabia;[14] four tribes of Bega in the Matlia region, or in the Byrn land (which possibly lay in Begemdir) (*DAE* 4, 6, 7). Furthermore, the king of kings evidently had at his disposal an armed retinue which in peacetime consisted of his court, but in wartime of his guards (as in fourteenth-century Ethiopia). Apparently, court officials carried out the functions of government, serving, for instance, as envoys.

9. A. J. Drewes, 1962, p. 65; A. A. Vasilyev, pp. 63–4.

10. J. P. Migne, p. 635.

11. *DAE* 4: 9; *DAE* 6: 3; *DAE* 7: 5.

12. Procopius, p. 275.

13. *DAE* 9: 12–34; *DAE* 10: 9–10, 23; *DAE* 11: 18, 30–5, 37–8; A. Caquot, 1965, pp. 223–5; R. Schneider, 1974, pp. 771, 774, 778, 781, 783–4, 785; *DAE* 4; *DAE* 6; *DAE* 7.

14. Procopius, p. 274; A. Møberg, p. cv; *Martyrium sancti Arethae et sociorum in civitate Negran*, Acta sanctorum, Octobris, T. X., Brussels, 1861, p. 7; G. Ryckmans, 1953.

The hellenized Syrians, Aedesius and Frumentius, who had been made royal slaves, were later promoted, one to the office of wine-pourer, the other to the position of secretary and treasurer to the Aksum king.[15]

Far too little is known about the history of this kingdom to enable us to trace the development of its political system. It may be assumed, however, that at the time when the Aksum monarchy flourished, something like a centralizing process took place in its structure. In the fourth century Ezana's activities were concentrated on subjugating or taking captive rebellious vassals who were the hereditary rulers of separate principalities. But by the sixth century an Aksum king was already appointing the south Arabian kings: Ma'dikarib and Sumayia' Ašwa' at Himyar, Ibn Harith (St Aretha's son) at Nagran. Furthermore, by founding warriors' settlements in vassal kingdoms, the king of kings secured their commanders' direct submission to Aksum.

The common norms of law that prevailed in the kingdom may be studied in the first juridical records of Aksum: in the four laws from the Sāfrā (Drewes, p. 73).

## Commerce and commercial policy

The position held by the Aksum kingdom in world commerce was that of a first-rate trading power, as evidenced by the minting of its own gold, silver and copper coinage. It was the first state in tropical Africa to introduce a coinage; none existed in any of the vassal states, not even those of Himyar and 'Alva. The minting of coin, especially gold, was not only an economic but also a political measure, proclaiming to the whole world the independence and prosperity of the Aksum state, the names of its monarchs and the mottoes of their reign. The first Aksumite king to put his own coinage into circulation was Endybis (in the second half of the third century). The Aksumites' monetary system was similar to the Byzantine system; in weight, standard and form, Aksumite coins bore a basic resemblance to Byzantine coins of the same period.

Although natural domestic production predominated, a certain connection existed between the productive and the commercial importance of Aksum. This connection tended to be indirect rather than direct, and was maintained by means of the political superstructure. An idea of export items from Aksumite Ethiopia may be gained from the accounts of Roman–Byzantine authors. Pliny refers to shipments from Ethiopia's Red Sea ports of obsidian, ivory, rhinoceros horns, hippopotamus hides, monkeys (sphingia) and also slaves. The *Periplus* contains an enumeration of exports from Adulis which includes turtle, obsidian, ivory and rhinoceros horns. Nonnosius alludes to gold dust as one of Aksumite Ethiopia's exports. Cosmas Indicopleustes writes of perfumes, gold, ivory and live animals sent

15. T. Mommsen, pp. 972–3.

abroad from Ethiopia, and recounts that the Aksumites acquired emeralds from the Blemmyes in the Nubian desert and sent them to be sold in northern India. He further asserts that he purchased a hippopotamus tusk in Ethiopia.[16]

The wares enumerated, with the exception of gold and emeralds, were only such as could be obtained by hunting, trapping and collecting. Agricultural and dairy produce, and goods produced by craftsmen or tradesmen, are not mentioned. If these were exported, it must have been in very limited quantities, and to places within the bounds of the Roman–Byzantine empire. The famous Ethiopian wheat may possibly have been exported to neighbouring countries, although the earliest, extremely vague, information about this dates from the tenth century. On the contrary, to judge from the accounts in the *Periplus*, Adulis imported certain foodstuffs such as small quantities of Laodicean (Syrian) and Italian wine and olive-oil; the ports of the Horn of Africa received cereals, wine and the juice of the young Diospolis grape from Egypt, wheat, rice, bosmor, sesame oil and sugarcane from India. Apparently, some of these products, such as sugar-cane, must have been shipped to Adulis as well.[17]

In those times, export of cattle to relatively distant lands was out of the question. Cosmas Indicopleustes informs us that the Aksumites supplied oxen, salt and iron for trading with Sasu, where there were goldfields (evidently in the south-west of Ethiopia). But the incident of the exchange of a piece of meat for nuggets of gold must have found its way into Cosmas' account from some widely known fable.[18] Isolated references to the discovery of samples of Aksumite metalwork in Arabia are available: they include an alabaster lamp,[19] coins, and a Samharian spear mentioned in the mu'allaqa of the pre-Islamic Arabian poet Labīd.[20]

Rather more is to be learned about Aksumite imports of wares made by foreign craftsmen. The *Periplus*, referring to the domains of King Zoscales, says:

> To those places they bring rough unfulled cloth himation made in Egypt for the barbarians, imitation dyed abolla, lention sheared on both sides, many different things made of transparent glass, other vessels of murrhine [moulded from glazed paste] produced in Diospolis, as well as brass ... copper ... iron. Among other things brought here are hatchets, axes, knives, large round copper bowls, some denarii for the use of foreigners residing here, a small quantity of Laodicean and Italian wine and of olive oil. For the king himself

16. Cosmas, *Periplus Maris Erythreae*, 3–6; E. O. Winstedt, pp. 69, 320, 322, 324, 325; L. A. Dindorff, 1870, p. 474.
17. Cosmas, *Periplus* ..., 6, 7, 17.
18. E. O. Winstedt, pp. 71–2.
19. A. Grohmann, 1915, pp. 410–22.
20. Labīd ibn Rabī'ah, p. 74.

they bring silver and gold vessels made in the local fashion. The outer garments they bring – abolla and kanakes [burnows] – are not very dear. From the interior of Ariaka [Middle India] they bring Indian iron and steel, and cotton fabrics (particularly the wider and coarser kinds known as molokhina and sygmatoghena); belts, cloaks, a few molokhinese sindoni garments and material coloured with a kind of varnish.

It is possible that some kinds of goods imported into Aksumite Ethiopia have been omitted from this list. For instance, in the *Periplus* it is noted that 'a small quantity of tin', some glass-ware, tunics and 'various woollen himation in the barbarian taste', Arsinoian woollen mantles, products of Egypt, arrived at the ports of the Horn of Africa. Objects of iron and glass produced in Muza (al-Mūha) in southern Arabia[21] were brought to Azania.

In the course of time, the general trend in imports underwent a change. By the end of the fifth century and the beginning of the sixth, the ban imposed by Roman emperors on exports of precious metals, iron and foodstuffs 'to the Omerites [Himyarites] and Aksumites'[22] must have caused considerable alteration in the list of Roman–Byzantine imports to Adulis, although the restrictions had been somewhat relaxed during the Byzantine–Aksumite alliance in Justinian's time. Goods that were not allowed to leave the bounds of the empire had to be obtained by the Aksumites from other sources.

In general, archaeological data confirm and supplement the accounts left by the *Periplus*. Excavations in strata dating from the period under review at Aksum, Adulis and Matara, and the finds at Hawila-Asseraw (in the Asbi-Derā district) and Debre-Dāmo, yielded many objects of non-Ethiopian origin, some of which must have reached that country through trade. Most of the foreign wares came from the Roman–Byzantine empire, especially from Egypt; they included amphoras which evidently served as vessels for wine or oil; fragments of glass-ware, gold ornaments and necklaces of Roman silver coins (Matara), a beautiful gem (Adulis), lamps of bronze and a bronze balance and weights (Adulis and Aksum).[23]

Objects of Indian origin have also been found: a seal in Adulis,[24,25] terracotta figurines in Aksum,[25] 104 gold coins dating from the reigns of the Kushana kings before the year 200 in Debre-Dāmo.[26] Pre-Islamic Arabia yielded silver and bronze coins found accidentally in Erythrea and during

21. Cosmas, *Periplus* ..., 6, 7, 17.
22. *Codex Theodosianus,* XII, 2, 12.
23. F. Anfray, 1972b; F. Anfray and G. Annequin, p. 68; H. de Contenson, 1963c, p. 12, Pl. XX; F. Anfray, 1972b, p. 752.
24. R. Paribeni, Fig. 49.
25. H. de Contenson, 1963c, pp. 45–6, Plates XLVII–XLVIII a–c.
26. A. Mordini.

excavations at Aksum[27] and a lamp of bronze from Matara.[28] Examples of Meroe workmanship are numerous: fragments of ceramic vessels have been found in many places, statuette-amulets in faïence of Hathor and Ptah in Aksum and in cornelian of Horus in Matara,[29] sculptured stelae showing figures of Horus on crocodiles (seen at Aksum and described by James Bruce in the eighteenth century[30]) and bronze bowls found at Hawila-Asseraw.[31] Some of these objects may have reached Ethiopia from Sudan in the course of trade, but probably most of them were spoils of war, or tribute. The Aksumites may have received from the Meroe region a fairly large proportion of the cotton materials and iron they needed. Other African countries sent gold to Aksum from Sasu and perhaps from the Bega country, and incense and spices from northern Somalia.

The unification of a considerable part of north-east Africa by the Aksumites soon enriched their nobility. Among these wealthy people, the Roman, Arabian and Indian merchants found customers for their luxury goods, which were the most profitable of all.

Some of the wares listed in the *Periplus* of Pseudo-Arrianus were reserved, as has been pointed out, for the Aksum king's use. At the beginning of the third century, foreign merchants were apparently obliged to send gifts commensurate with their wealth to the king of Aksum and the ruler of Adulis; in the lifetime of Pseudo-Arrianus, these presents were 'inexpensive' gold and silver vessels, 'coarse and imitation' abolla and kaunakes. It is interesting to note that about the year 524, the Alexandrian patriarch sent the king of Aksum the gift of a silver vessel.[32] The increase of wealth and the spread of luxurious habits at the Aksum royal court (according to descriptions left by Cosmas, John Malalas and Nonnusius) meant that gifts of higher quality and value were expected. It is possible that at this time a system of customs duties was established.

The profits accruing from the creation of the powerful Aksum kingdom enriched not only the nobility but also the whole of the privileged ethno-social group of Aksumites who were the citizens of the capital community. Many of the goods enumerated in the *Periplus* were imported for a wider stratum of the population. Bracelets of imported brass worked by local smiths, spears of imported iron and other metal articles in local use, as well as clothing made of foreign fabrics were transformed into saleable wares for local markets, by this means becoming available to both the urban and the rural populations. Finally, foreign merchants and other foreign groups

27. A. Gaudio, pp. 4–5; H. de Contenson, 1963c, p. 8, Plates XIV; p. 12, Pl. XIV.
28. F. Anfray, 1967, pp. 46ff.
29. H. de Contenson, 1963c, p. 43; J. Leclant, 1965c, pp. 86–7, Pl. LXVII, 1.
30. B. van de Walle, pp. 238–47.
31. J. Doresse, 1960, pp. 229–248; A. Caquot and J. Leclant, 1956, pp. 226–34; A. Caquot and A. J. Drewes, pp. 17–41.
32. *Martyrium sancti Arethae et sociorum in civitate Negran.* Acta sanctorum, X, Octobris 24. Antwerp, 1861, p. 743.

settled in Adulis, Aksum and different Ethiopian towns, and brought in quantities of imported goods. It is among these groups that wine and olive-oil found a ready sale. Excavated objects such as the balance and weights, the seal, Roman and Kushana coins were obviously traces left by Roman–Byzantine and Indian merchants who had lived in Adulis and Aksum. The *Periplus* states plainly that denarii were brought to Adulis for foreigners living there, that is to say, neither African nor Roman subjects. As is well known, the drain of Roman currency to southern Arabia, India, Ceylon and other eastern lands assumed catastrophic proportions. The foreigners who brought in denarii may have been merchants from India, Ceylon and Arabia. Among those who traded with the Aksum kingdom, Arab tradition recalls the Banu-Kuraish from Mecca, Cosmas Indicopleustes speaks of islanders from Socotra, and 'Pseudo-Calisthenes' mentions Indians. The relative importance of overseas cities and countries for Ethiopian trade in the early sixth century may be judged by the number of ships that entered the Ethiopian harbour of Gabaza in the summer of 525. This list is to be found in the 'Martyrdom of Aretha',[33] and a detailed analysis of it has been made by N. V. Pigulevskaya.[34] Nine ships are described as Indian – a term that admits of various interpretations. Seven vessels arrived from the isle of al-Farasan al-Kabir, inhabited by the Farasan, a southern Arabian Christian tribe who played a leading part in Red Sea commerce. Fifteen ships arrived from Palestinian Elat, the chief port of the Syrian–Palestinian region. Twenty-two vessels came from Egyptian ports – twenty from Clysme, and only two from Berenice. Another seven came from the island of Iotaba (Thiran). All the Roman citizens whose journeys to Adulis or Aksum are authentically known were born in either Egypt or Syria.

The leading contractors who dealt with foreign merchants were Aksumite monarchs and vassals of separate domains in the kingdom of Aksum, particularly Adulis and southern Arabia. These were the men who had at their disposal sufficient goods for export. In this kingdom, as in neighbouring southern Arabia and also in Byzantium, trade monopolies may have existed at that time. Elephant-hunting and the sale of ivory and gold could easily have been largely the monopoly of the ruler. Only the king and the archontes of Aksum possessed sufficient wealth to purchase foreign goods.

The rulers owned vast herds. In Ezana's inscriptions, mention is made of spoils obtained in two Aksumite campaigns in Afan and Nubia, which altogether comprised over 32 500 head of cattle and more than 51 000 sheep, as well as many hundreds of pack animals. It is not quite clear whether these were the spoils of the entire army or only the king's share, but the latter seems the more likely supposition. In the inscriptions concerning the resettlement of four Bega ethnic groups, Ezana declared that he en-

33. *Martyrium sancti Arethae*, p. 747.
34. N. V. Pigulevskaya, 1951, pp. 300–1.

dowed them with 25 000 head of cattle,[35] a figure which enables us to judge the extent of the herds concentrated on the king's own farms. It is noteworthy that every number recorded in these inscriptions is written first in words, then in figures – just as in modern times. It was possibly during the Aksumite period that a court appointment known as a cattle-clerk (sahafeham) was created and remained an honourable title for governors of certain provinces until the fourteenth century.

In Aksum, as in other African kingdoms of antiquity, herds constituted wealth but it was extremely difficult to transform them into saleable merchandise. The systematic export of herds by sea was out of the question although the Aksumites contrived to send some animals singly, even some elephants belonging to the army of Abraha. Cattle could, of course, be driven into the African interior for sale to the people there – Cosmas Indicopleustes mentions that caravans of Aksumites drove cattle into Sasu – but a considerable proportion of these animals must inevitably have been needed for victualling the caravan itself.

One kind of merchandise for which the demand never slackened throughout the centuries was that of slaves. There are references in the Ezana inscriptions and sources connected with Aksumite–Himyarite wars to prisoners taken in warfare who were regarded as desirable merchandise by foreign slave-traders. Gold and silver seized as spoils of war, or as tribute sent from Nubia, from the Beja, Agaw, Himyar and other countries were brought by caravans from Sasu and minted as coin which went to pay for the foreign goods required by the king and his nobles.

Although industry in Aksum did not result in any important volume of saleable commodities, the abundance of agricultural and animal products permitted the Aksumites to load trading vessels and caravans. Thus they provided their own food and commodities for home consumption and also for some trade with other countries.

Some idea of how they organized their commerce is given by Cosmas Indicopleustes in his account of how Sasu supplied gold to Aksum from its many goldfields. 'From year to year (or perhaps they should read once in two years?) the Aksumite king sends, through the archon of Agaw, people to bring back gold. Many travel with these people for the same purpose, so that altogether there might be more than five hundred.' Cosmas further points out that all the members of the caravan were armed and endeavoured to reach their destinations before the big rains. He gives the exact period when these rains were to be expected. The gold conveyed from Sasu was in nuggets the size of the wolf-beans known as tankaras.[36]

It seems that the nucleus of a caravan consisted of the king's agents, accompanied by some other people, who might be noblemen's agents and rich Aksumites, but not foreigners. At that time, Ethiopian rulers were no

35. *DAE* 10: 17–22; *DAE* 11: 43–4; *DAE* 4: 13–15; *DAE* 6: 7–8; *DAE* 7: 9–10.
36. E. O. Winstedt, pp. 70–1.

strangers to commercial interests. In the *Periplus*, King Zoscales is termed 'miserly and mercenary'. Trading was regarded as a state enterprise, and it appears that the archon of Agaw, whose business it was to fit out and dispatch the Aksumite caravan to Sasu, took full responsibility for it. The Ēzana inscription concerning the campaign in Afan, where the defeat of four Afan tribes and the capture of the ruler are described, records the fate that befell those who attacked the Aksumite caravans, the people of Afan having slaughtered the members of the Aksumite trading caravan.[37]

The political hegemony of the Aksumite kingdom on the world's trade-routes proved no less profitable than direct participation in trade.

When he had subjugated Upper Nubia, southern Arabia, the Lake Tana region, and the tribes of the deserts surrounding Ethiopia, the king of Aksum controlled the routes linking Egypt and Syria with the countries of the Indian Ocean, and also with the interior of north-east Africa. The Straits of Bab-el-Mandeb which, like the Straits of Malacca and Gibraltar, constituted one of the three main sea highways of the ancient world, also came under Aksumite control. In antiquity, Bab-el-Mandeb was a busy sea-route linking the Red Sea to the Persian Gulf, India, Ceylon, the Straits of Malacca, and the countries of South-East and eastern Asia. From the Gulf of Aden another route branched out along the coast of Somali to East Africa (the Azania of Claudius Ptolemy and Pseudo-Arrianus). This route was explored and used by mariners from southern Arabia and in the earliest centuries of our era – by those of India and the Roman empire as well.

During the period under review the Red Sea trade flourished, though stories of piracy were current at about the same time. Tribes from the African and the Arabian coasts of the southern Red Sea and the Gulf of Aden engaged in piracy. Roman authors characteristically attributed piratical attacks in this region to changes in the political attitude of Aksum and other Red Sea states towards the Romans.[38]

Roman merchants had a vital interest in the establishment of security along the trade-routes within the sphere of Aksumite hegemony, and consequently in its unifying policy. For this reason they supported the union of the Roman–Byzantine empire with the Aksumite kingdom. It would not, however, be correct to represent the Aksum kings simply as promoters of Roman–Byzantine policy, including its religious and commercial aspects. They pursued an independent political course that corresponded with Byzantine policy particularly when the predominantly economic interests of the two powers coincided. An instance of this may be drawn from the sixth century when, despite the frequent voyages of the Byzantines to India, they considered that the Ethiopians had more stable trade relations with that country.[39]

37. *DAE* 10.
38. Cosmas, *Periplus* ..., 4; T. Mommsen, p. 972.
39. Procopius, pp. 275–7.

The Aksumites' trade with Sasu was a secret jealously guarded from the Byzantines. Indeed, Cosmas Indicopleustes knew of that country solely by hearsay, through Ethiopians. We find Ethiopian (Aksumite) deacons evidently in charge of the trading colony of Ethiopians in Libya[40] and Nagran[41] from the beginning of the fifth century to the beginning of the sixth. When Bishop Moses of Adulis sailed to India[42] at the outset of the fifth century, he was probably on a visit to his spiritual flock, who by that time had formed trading colonies at ports in India and Ceylon. The commercial voyages of the Adulis townsmen in particular, and Ethiopians in general, to Ceylon, south and north India, are recorded by Pseudo-Callisthenes and Cosmas Indicopleustes.[43] The growth of the town of Adulis and the strengthening of its position in world trade reflected the expansion of the Aksumite kingdom and its might. In the opinion of Pliny (*c.* 60) and of Claudius Ptolemy (*c.* 150)[44] Adulis was merely one of the small trading markets of Africa, and Pseudo-Arrianus termed it a village.

In the fourth century and the beginning of the fifth, the harbours of Adulis and the Horn of Africa scarcely attracted the attention of Roman geographers. Between the fifth and sixth centuries, however, Adulis became the leading port between Clysme and the ports of India and the names of other African ports vanished from written sources.[45]

The fact that Adulis then reached a peak of prosperity which it never achieved before or after was due, not to successfully resisting any type of competition, but solely to the active patronage of the early feudal Aksum state. It was understandable, then, that Adulis should be called 'the officially established market' in 'The Circumnavigation of the Erythrean Sea'.

## Culture

The development of the early feudal empire was reflected in the ideology and culture of Aksum over a period lasting from the second to the fourth centuries. The brief inscriptions devoted to the gods underwent a gradual transformation into detailed accounts of the victories won by the king of kings. Particularly interesting in this respect are the Ethiopian and Greek inscriptions of Ezana, who attained the peak of epigraphic style in an inscription giving the fullest account of his Nubian campaign.[46] The inscription reveals genuine eloquence, religious feeling and a free use

40. A. Caquot and J. Leclant, 1959, p. 174.
41. A. Møberg, p. 14, b, cx. S. Irfan, 1971, p. 64.
42. B. Priaulx, 1863.
43. ibid.; E. O. Winstedt, p. 324.
44. Pliny, VI, 172; Claudius Ptolemy, IV, 7, 10.
45. B. Priaulx, p. 277; J. Desanges, 1967, pp. 141–58.
46. *DAE* 11.

of complex conceptions. The basic underlying ideas are the glorification of a mighty, invincible monarch, whose wrath it would be madness to provoke, and praise of the God, whose special and enduring protection the king enjoys. Well-reasoned arguments are advanced for the need of Aksumite campaigns in Nubia and other reprisals. King Ezana is represented as irreproachably fair-minded and magnanimous. This inscription may be justifiably termed a literary achievement. It has points in common with folk-poetry and Ethiopian literature of a later period.

A parallel evolution took place in the mottoes on Aksum coinage. Coins dating from the third to the mid-fourth century bear the ethnic sobriquet peculiar to each monarch, which consists of the word be'esi (man) and an ethronym relating to the name of one of the Aksumite 'armies'. It was in some way associated with the tribal and military structure of the Aksum state and possibly stemmed from the military democracy of the Ethiopians of antiquity. Currency coined in the time of Ezana and his successors bore a Greek motto signifying 'May the country be satisfied!' It is evident that this demagogic device reflects an official doctrine, the first traces of which may be discerned in the inscriptions of Ezana.[47] Clearly, the king aimed at making himself popular with the nation, a purpose in keeping with the nature of a power which was undergoing transformation into a monarchy. Later on, this motto in its Greek and Ethiopian versions gave place to pious Christian formulas.

In the recurrent change of mottoes on coins, and in the royal inscriptions of Aksum, two warring tendencies can be seen in the ideology of officialdom: the monarchical idea bound up with Christian unity and the demagogic notion stemming from local traditions.

With the idea of empire came the development of the gigantesque in architecture and the figurative, such as the colossal monolithic stelae, 33·5 metres in height, erected on a platform 114 metres in length; the monolithic basalt slab measuring 17·3 by 6·7 by 1·12 metres; the huge metal statues (the base of one of these has been preserved but the dimensions of the others are known from inscriptions); the vast royal palaces of the Aksum kings Enda-Mikael and Enda-Simeon; and particularly the palatial set of buildings, Taaka-Maryam, extending over an area of 120 metres by 80 metres – all these are unparalleled in tropical Africa. The mania for the gigantic reflected the tastes of the Aksumite monarchy and the monuments were the concrete realization of its ideological purpose, which was to instil awe-inspiring admiration for the greatness and strength of the potentate to whom the monuments were dedicated. With the taste for the gigantesque, a tendency towards the decorative became noticeably stronger in architecture. The combination of stone and wood in building, with alternate stone blocks worked to a greater or lesser extent at various points in the edifice, with wooden beams and rubble filling cemented with a

47. *DAE* 7: 24; *DAE* 11: 48.

cohesive solution, greatly simplified the builders' task and made it possible to achieve a highly decorative effect. The synthesis of rough and squared stone in the wall-surfaces and the heavy wooden crossbeams ending in so-called monkey's heads created a natural plastic richness and a striking arrangement of varied textures. The decorative effect was enhanced by alternating projections and retractions; by recessed doorways with heavy wooden doors terminating a flight of steps; by the rain gutters, with terminals in the form of lions' heads. Greater attention than in the past was paid to interiors. The marked trend towards a more decorative style of building answered the growing tastes for comfort and luxury among the ruling strata of Aksumites who had become rich through the founding of the empire. During this period architecture and sculpture in Ethiopia were of a striking originality which, however, did not exclude adaptation of different cultural influences from the Roman empire, southern Arabia, India and Meroe. Especially significant were the Syrian influences that stemmed from the spread of Christianity.

The four-towered palace of the Aksumite kings is mentioned by Cosmas Indicopleustes.[48] According to the reconstruction made by Dr Krenker, it was a castle, and the arrangement of the adjacent buildings – palaces, temples and other sanctuaries – made it the most inaccessible part of the city. This quarter, to judge from the results of the excavations by H. de Contenson, continued to be fortified into Christian times.[49]

The paganism of the Aksumites closely resembled the religion of ancient southern Arabia. It was a complex polytheism with the characteristics of agricultural and stock-breeding cults. The deities worshipped were Astar, the embodiment of the planet Venus, and the chthonic deities Behēr and Meder, both symbolizing earth. The Astar cult enjoyed equal popularity in the pre-Aksumite period, and continued in pagan Aksum.[50] Traces of it survived into later times. Behēr and Meder (as a simple deity) followed Astar in inscriptions.[51] A relic of this form of worship was the Ethiopian Christian term Egzi'abhēr (God; or, literally, the god Behēr, or god of earth).[52]

The moon deity Hawbas had been worshipped in southern Arabia and in pre-Aksumite Ethiopia. Conti-Rossini produced evidence to show that the god Gad and his cult, against which medieval saints struggled, was none other than the god of the moon.[53] Conti-Rossini connected this cult of the moon with the fact that the taurine antelope was held sacred in modern Eritrea. A study of tribal beliefs in that country in the twentieth century

48. E. O. Winstedt, p. 72.
49. D. Krencker, 1913, p. 107ff., 113ff.; H. de Contenson, 1963c, p. 9, Pl. IX.
50. *DAE* 6: 20; *DAE* 7: 21; *DAE* 10: 25; *DAE* 27: 1; A. J. Drewes, 1962, pp. 26–7, Plates VI, XXI.
51. *DAE* 6: 21; *DAE* 7: 21; *DAE* 10: 25–6.
52. W. Vycichl, 1957, pp. 249, 250.
53. C. Conti-Rossini, 1947, p. 53.

revealed that in northern Ethiopia cults of antiquity survived and that the moon is still worshipped as a deity.[54] Possibly the Aksumites connected the features of the moon-deity with the image of the god Mahrem.

Symbols of the sun and moon are found on stelae from Aksum, Matara and Anza, and on the coinage of the Aksumite kings of pre-Christian times. They refer probably to Mahrem, the dynastic and tribal deity of the Aksumites. In the pagan bilingua of Ezana, the Mahrem of the Ethiopian text[55] is given the Greek name, Ares.[56] All the pagan Greek inscriptions of the Aksum kings,[57] with the exception of the Sembrythes' inscriptions in which the name of the god is absent, use the name Ares. As is well known, the Athenian Ares was worshipped as the god of war. It follows, then, that his double, Mahrem, was also worshipped as the god of war. In the Aksumite inscriptions Ares-Mahrem, in his capacity of War-god, is termed 'invincible', 'unconquerable by his enemies' and ensuring victory.[58] In his capacity as the tribal progenitor, Ares is called the 'god of the Aksumites'[59] in the inscriptions from Abba-Pantalewon. As the dynastic deity, the kings called Mahrem-Ares their 'greatest god', ancestor of kings.[60] Mahrem was considered first of all as the god-progenitor and protector of the Aksumites; secondly, as the invincible god of war; thirdly, the forefather and father of the king; fourthly, he seems to have been regarded as the king of gods. It was to him that the kings of Aksum consecrated their victorious thrones in Aksum itself as well as in the regions they had conquered.

It is clear that Mahrem, god of war and monarchy, reigned supreme over the astral and chthonic deities in the same way that a consecrated monarch dominated a people; at the same time, war, personified by Mahrem, predominated over peaceful labour and was looked upon as a more sacred task, more honourable than peasants' toil, sanctified though this might be by the precepts of their forefathers. Plainly discernible in the religion of Aksum are the characteristic features of early class ideology, that of a feudal society in the process of formation.

The Aksumites offered sacrifices to their gods. Domestic animals constituted the bulk of these offerings. One of Ezana's inscriptions[61] records that a dozen oxen were offered up to Mahrem at a single sacrifice.

54. E. Littman, 1910–15, pp. 65 (no. 50), 69 (no. 52).

55. *DAE* 6: 2, 18, 26; *DAE* 7: 3, 19, 21, 25.

56. *DAE* 4: 6, 29.

57. *DAE* 2: 8; *Monumentum Adulitanum* (E. O. Winstedt, p. 77); A. H. Sayce, 1909, pp. 189, 190.

58. *DAE* 2: 8; *DAE* 4: 6, 29; *DAE* 6: 2–3; *DAE* 7: 3–4; *DAE* 8: 4–5; *DAE* 9: 4; *DAE* 10: 5–6.

59. *DAE* 2: 8.

60. E. O. Winstedt, p. 77; *DAE* 10: 5, 29–30; *DAE* 8: 4; *DAE* 9: 3–4; *DAE* 6: 2; *DAE* 7: 3.

61. *DAE* 10: 29–30.

According to a search carried out by A. J. Drewes [62] on the Safra inscription, sterile cows and ewes were the offerings (a sacrifice still widespread among some Ethiopian peoples). This inscription, the scholar notes, contains specific terms used during the ritual, at which a priest-immolator officiated. References to the slaughter of beasts used in burnt-offerings to Astar are found in other inscriptions. According to ancient Semitic custom, some kinds of donation for sacrifice were brought in ritually immaculate clothing; for others this was not obligatory. But already in the pre-Aksumite period the living sacrificial animal was supplanted by its consecrated image. Bronze and stone images of sacrificial bulls, rams and other animals, many bearing inscriptions, have been preserved.

Ancestor-cult, especially of dead kings, occupied an important place in the religion of the Aksumites. It was customary to dedicate stelae to them: häwelt, a word stemming from the root *h-w-l*, means 'to go round', or 'to worship' and is comparable to the Islamic worship of the Qaaba. Sacrifices were brought to the altars and to the pedestals of stelae carved in the form of altars, and the blood of the sacrifices flowed down into hollows hewn in the form of bowls. The graves of Aksumite kings were regarded as the city's holy places. Vessels and other objects found in burial grounds indicate belief in a life beyond the grave. Some indirect references suggest the existence of a cult of 'lords of the mountains' reminiscent of corresponding cults in Arabia.

Although information on the religion of the Aksumites is still extremely fragmentary, it may be considered a relatively developed religion, linked to a complicated ritual and a professional priesthood.

During the early Aksumite period religious ideas from countries near and far penetrated into Ethiopia. In the *Monumentum Adulitanum* mention is made of Poseidon, a Sea-god who was evidently worshipped by the inhabitants of Adulis and along the southern part of the Red Sea coast.[63] The holy places of Almaqah, 'national' god of the Sabaeans, worshipped by king Gadara of Aksum,[64] were situated at Melazo and perhaps at Hawila-Asseraw. The newly discovered stele at Aksum, with the Egyptian symbol of life ankh,[65] and objects pertaining to the cult of Hathor, Ptah and Horus, as well as scarabs, suggests that adherents to the Egyptian–Meroe religion were residing at some time in Aksum, Adulis and Matara. The small images of Buddha found at Aksum[66] were probably brought there by Buddhist merchants from India. Numerous groups professing the Judaic religion were living in southern Arabia and some must have come to settle in Ethiopia prior to the sixth century, when Christianity became of leading importance (see Chapter 14 and Chapter 16).

62. A. J. Drewes, 1962, pp. 50–4.
63. E. O. Winstedt, p. 77.
64. A. Jamme, 1957, p. 79.
65. F. Anfray, 1972b, p. 71.
66. H. de Contenson, 1963b, pp. 45, 46, Plates XLVII–XLVIII, a, c.

As a result of the influence exerted by Christianity and other mono-theistic religions in Ethiopia and Arabia, these countries evolved a mono-theistic outlook peculiarly their own, which is reflected in the Ge'ez inscriptions: for instance, those of Ezana that concern the Nubian cam-paign (*DAE* 11), and of Abreha Täklä Aksum from Wadi Menih[67] (a personage not to be confused with king Abreha), and the same is true of later Sabaean inscriptions from southern Arabia.

No irreconcilable contradictions existed between this form of mono-theism and Christianity; Ezana in the aforementioned inscription, Wa'azab in a newly discovered inscription and Abreha, king of Himyar, in his in-scriptions use the terms and concepts of an 'indefinite monotheism' for the propagation of Christianity.

As a result of foreign cultural influences, the subculture of the Aksumite monarchy was not only national but also international in character. Side by side with Ge'ez, the Greek language was used as a state and international language. Apparently, kings like Za-Hekale and Ezana knew Greek (the *Periplus* reports that 'king Zoscales' was literate in Greek, and Ezana's mentor, a Graeco-Phoenician, Frumentius, later the first bishop of Aksum). The majority of Aksumite kings of the third and fourth centuries minted coins with Greek mottoes. We know of six royal Greek inscriptions of Aksum.

We have no reason to think that Sabaean was one of the official languages of the early Aksumite kingdom. One of the three texts of Ezana pseudo-trilingual (in fact, Ge'ez Greek bilingual) is written in later Himyaritic script and has some exaggerated peculiarities of Sabaeo-Himyaritic orthography. The same script is used in three other royal inscriptions of Aksum by Ezana, Kaleb and Wa'azab.[68] Thus together with an inscrip-tion at Tsehuf-Emni (Erythrea)[69] we have five 'pseudo-Himyaritic' texts from Ethiopia. Their language is Ge'ez with very few Sabaean words.

It is not clear why Aksumite kings used the 'pseudo-Himyaritic' texts side by side with those of normal Ethiopic in their inscriptions of definitely official character. But in all cases it is evidence of south Arabian influence.

Perhaps the use of the Himyaritic script as well as that of vocalized Ethiopic, and the introduced figures, were innovations of Ezana's rule, and these innovations were inter-related.

The basic principles of vocalized Ethiopic script have no analogy in the whole Semito-Hamitic world, but are typical of Indian alphabets. In the nineteenth century B. Johns, R. Lepsius and E. Glaser connected the Ethiopic alphabet with India. In 1915 A. Grohmann pointed out the principal similarities between the idea of the vocalized Ethiopic alphabet

---

67. E. Littman, 1954, pp. 120, 121.
68. *DAE* 8: 18–19; R. Schneider, 1974, pp. 767–70.
69. C. Conti-Rossini, 1903.

and that of Brahmi or Karaoshti, as well as some common details such as similar signs used for 'u' and 'short'.[70] The hypothesis of Indian influence on the reformers of the old consonant Ethiopic alphabet seems to be quite probable.

The hypothetical Greek influence on the creation of the Ethiopic alphabet has not been proved, although the Greek origin of the system and the main signs of Ethiopic figures, as they first appeared in Ezana's inscriptions, is certain.

The vocalized Ethiopic alphabet so closely reproduces the phonematic system of Ge'ez that it is inconceivable than any but an Ethiopian could have been its creator. This alphabet, with the addition of some signs, has been in continuous use in Ethiopia till this day and is generally regarded as the outstanding achievement of the Aksumite civilization.

Soon after its creation, the Ethiopic vocalized script began to influence the scripts of Transcaucasia. D. A. Olderogge suggested that Mesrop Mashtotz used the vocalized Ethiopic script when he invented the Armenian alphabet. Not long before this time (at the end of the fifth century) the Ethiopian script may have been introduced into Armenia by the Syrian bishop Daniel.[71]

It was through the mediation of north Syria that Aksum and Armenia had cultural relations at this time. We have some evidence about the Syrians in Aksum and about Syrian influence on Aksumite architecture,[72] particularly in the grand monolithic stelae in the form of multi-storey buildings. Some analogy with south Arabian and Indian architecture of the time can also be seen. During the second and third centuries we may reasonably suggest that Meroitic influence predominated. All the articles of Meroitic handicraft found in Ethiopia belong to this period. A bronze warder with the inscription of Gadara, a king of Aksum, recalls similar warders of the Meroitic kings.[73] Elephants may have been introduced into the Aksumite royal ritual under the influence of India as well as that of Meroe.

The Aksumite kingdom was not only an important trading power on the routes from the Roman world to India and from Arabia to north-east Africa, but also a great centre of culture which seeped down these routes. In their turn, many of the ancient civilized countries of north-east Africa and south Arabia determined many features of the Aksumite culture under whose domination they lived.

70. A. Grohmann, 1915, pp. 57–87.
71. D. A. Olderogge, 1972, pp. 195–203.
72. F. Anfray, 1974, pp. 761–5.
73. A. Caquot and A. J. Drewes; J. Doresse, 1960.

PLATE 15.1 *Gold money from the reign of King Endybis (third century of our era)*

PLATE 15.2 *Greek inscription from Ezana (fourth century)*

PLATE 15.3 *Greek Inscription from Wa'Zaba (sixth century)*

PLATE 15.4 *Gold money from the reign of King Ousanas*

# 16

# Christian Aksum

TEKLE TSADIK MEKOURIA

## Traditional pre-Christian cults in Aksum

Up to the eighteenth century, religion, whatever its form, played a major part in every human society. In general, polytheism preceded monotheism. Present-day Christian centres were once cradles of paganism. No nation has adopted Christianity without first passing through a period of paganism.

Ethiopia is no exception to that rule; it was not privileged to accept monotheism directly, without first practising the most diverse forms of worship. In a country like Ethiopia, which never experienced long periods of foreign rule, it was natural for several cults to exist and to be transmitted from father to son.

Among the inhabitants of ancient Ethiopia the Kushitic groups (Beja and Aguew), unlike the ruling classes, had escaped assimilation to Semitic culture, and worshipped different natural objects such as giant trees, rivers, lakes, high mountains or animals. All these were believed to shelter good or evil spirits, to whom various annual or seasonal offerings and sacrifices had to be made.

The tribes of Semitic origin who had not inherited the Kushitic cult, and the Semitized Kushites, fairly advanced as compared with the previous groups, worshipped nature in its celestial and terrestrial forms (the sun, moon and stars, the land and the earth) under the names of the triad Mahrem, Behēr and Meder. These were in rivalry with foreign or seminational gods of south Arabia or Assyro-Babylonia such as Almuqah, Awbas, Astart, who in turn were assimilated to the Greek gods Zeus, Ares and Poseidon.[1]

This somewhat arbitrary assimilation, fostered by influential travellers who proselytized on behalf of their own gods, was allowed by certain kings of Aksum whose culture was Greek. But it did not shake the foundations of the divinity of Mahrem, regarded as the national god. The Mahrem of the Aksumites could be called Zeus by a Greek and Amon by a Nubian of Egyptian culture, since every man spoke in his own language. It will be

---

1. E. Littmann and D. Krencker, pp. 4–35; C. Conti-Rossini, 1928, pp. 141–4; E. A. Drouin; A. de Longpérier, p. 28.

remembered that when Alexander the Great, who called himself the son of Zeus, made his triumphal entry into Egypt in − 332, he was received by the priests as the son of Amon.

Old Ethiopian texts, based on oral tradition and investigations and dating from the time of King Amde Tsion ( + 1313 to + 1342), report the existence of a cult of the serpent 'arwe', side by side with the practice of the Law of Moses.[2] This serpent was sometimes considered as a dragon-god and sometimes as the first reigning king Arwe-Negus, father of the queen of Sheba – a claim that no present-day reader would take seriously.

This popular belief surely belongs to the legendary history of ancient Ethiopia, before the dawn of its authentic history. All nations have some such legend preceding their ancient and medieval histories: the she-wolf suckling the two first kings of Rome is an example among many others. Even more often, genuine history is so embellished with miracles that it is difficult to distinguish truth from legend.

The Semites who came from south Arabia and are the ancestors of the Tigre and the Amara, living on the high plateau, were said to have brought with them several south Arabian cults. The existence of these creeds, quoted confusedly by travellers, is confirmed by epigraphic and numismatic documents.

Following the research done by Bruce, Salt, A. Dillman, among others, the monumental work of the German mission of 1906 (printed in 1913) and the successive discoveries of the archaeologists of the Ethiopian Institute of Archaeology, founded in 1952 at Addis Ababa, form the basis of our in-depth knowledge of pre-Christian Aksumite cults. The practice of such cults at the court of Aksum before its conversion to Christianity is attested by the temple of Yeha (which is still standing), scattered stelae, castle sites and votive objects.

However, a point to be clarified is whether this comparatively developed religion was a royal and aristocratic preserve or was practised also by the people at large. As for the existence of Judaism in Ethiopia, several factors testify to the presence of a group which professed the Jewish religion; the history of the kings, *Tarike Neguest*, mentions it briefly. This was a group which perhaps even ruled for a certain time.

Even if we leave aside the fantastic story of Kbre Neguest (Glory of the Kings) which the Ethiopian clerics consider as a basic work of history and literature and where all the kings of Aksum are wrongly said to be linked with Solomon and Moses, certain traditions handed down through the centuries refer to the presence of believers of the Jewish faith. Indications of this are circumcision and excision at an early age, while the relative respect for the Sabbath, the sacred chants and liturgical dances accompanied by drums, sistra and hand-clapping all recall the dance of

2. Degiazmetch Haylon Collection, *Tarike Neguest*, deposited in Paris, No. 143, pp. 23–35. T. Tamrāt, pp. 21–30.

the Jews and that of King David before the Ark of the Covenant.

But with the introduction of Christianity, which was either preceded or followed by a transfer of power into the hands of other groups (Sabaeans, Habesan and others), the Jews, as everywhere else, were victims of prejudice and violence and withdrew into less accessible areas. The massacre of the Najrah Christians in south Arabia in the sixth century and the uprising of the Palasha in the tenth century seem to be linked with the ill-treatment inflicted on Jews living in the most Christian empire of Aksum, or to be reactions to the political and economic hegemony of the latter in Arabia.

## The coming of Christianity to Aksum

The new religion founded in Palestine by Christ and spread by his militants throughout all the empires of East and West arrived, in its turn, at the court of Aksum, in the midst of a polytheistic cult followed by the Kushites and of a sub-Arabic religion practised by the Semites and the Semitized Kushites.

On the basis of the apocryphal texts of the Acts of the Apostles drawn up by a certain Abdia, part of the population mistakenly believes that Saint Matthew was the first to bring Christianity to Ethiopia. This view, however, is supported by no document worthy of belief.

The history of the kings, *Tarike Neguest*, attributes to the famous Frumentius the privilege of having introduced Christianity into the country. Frumentius is later called the Enlightener (Kessate Brhan) or Abba Selama, which means Father of Peace. The arrival of Frumentius in Ethiopia, his depature for Alexandria and his return to Aksum are described in detail by Eusebius and Rufinus. The work of the latter, which deals particularly with the arrival of Christianity in Ethiopia, was later translated into Ge'ez and subsequently into Amharic.

According to Rufinus, a certain Meropius of Tyre wished to go to the Indies (following the example of the philosopher Metrodorus) with two young relatives, Frumentius and Aedesius. On their return, his boat was attacked by the population of a port (on the Red Sea?). Meropius died and the two young brothers were taken to the king of Aksum. The younger one, Aedesius, became a cup-bearer, whilst Frumentius, owing to his Greek culture, became the king's counsellor and treasurer, as well as tutor to the royal children. According to the date of arrival of the two young men, this king seems to have been Ella Amida, father of King Ezana. After the death of Ella Amida, his wife became regent and asked the two young men to remain with her to administer the country until her son was old enough to reign.

So Frumentius brought up the young prince to love the new Christian religion. Having thus prepared the ground, he then departed with his brother Aedesius. While Aedesius returned to Tyre to help his aged parents, Frumentius went to Alexandria to visit the Patriarch Athanasius, and told him of the favourable attitude of the royal family of Aksum towards Christianity, urging Athanasius to send a bishop there. The patriarch, being unwilling to send a bishop who knew neither the language nor the customs of the country, therefore consecrated Frumentius himself as bishop of the church of Aksum and sent him back to Ethiopia. Frumentius then baptized the king and all the royal family.[3]

It is from this date, therefore, that Christianity spread in Aksum. The first Christian king, educated and then baptized by Frumentius, appears to have been Ezana, the son of Ella Amida. And there is every reason to believe that the example of the king and the royal family was widely followed. However, it is none the less difficult to see how a man who was merely the king's secretary and treasurer and later became the assistant of the queen-mother (Sophie?) could have taught the new Christian religion – which was not the court religion, nor the state religion – to the royal children, to the detriment of the invincible Mahrem, the greatest of the gods and the king's ancestor. Perhaps Frumentius was an able secretary and a talented administrator and therefore, as Rufinus claims, indirectly influenced the young princes under his tutelage to embrace the Christian religion. Yet this influence could not have been strong enough to overthrow and replace, without causing a stir, a religion that had been firmly ensconced for a long time.

While recognizing the part played by Frumentius, we suggest that the change of religion should be attributed to another cause. Thanks to epigraphic and numismatic documents, and to travellers' reports, we know that the court of Aksum was on friendly terms with Constantinople. There were considerable commercial and cultural exchanges between the two countries. Eusebius, in his *Vita Constantini*, mentions the presence of Ethiopians in Constantinople during the reign of Constantine. The use of the Greek script and the Greek language at the court of Aksum is also very significant. King Zoskales in the first century of our era spoke and wrote Greek, as did Ezana himself. All this clearly indicates the preponderance of Greek culture in the Aksumite kingdom.[4]

Now the emperor of Constantinople, Constantine the Great, who conquered Maxentius in 312 and presided over the Council of Nicaea in 325, was the contemporary of King Ella Amida and of Ezana. The splendour of Constantine's court, and his leaning towards Christianity, were doubtless recounted and enlarged upon by other travellers besides Frumentius, who are not mentioned in the annals. All this must have made a deep impression on the court of Aksum and on Frumentius himself, a Graeco-Phoenician by birth and a product of this culture and religion, who finally found the king and his family ready to embrace the new Christianity which was already widespread at the court of Constantinople.

3. Cosmas Indicopleustes, pp. 77–8; E. A. T. Wallis Budge, 1966, pp. 142–50; Ç. Conti-Rossini, 1928, pp. 145–60.
4. W. H. Schoff, 1912, pp. 60–7.

But probably the Aksumite court did not take this step without some embarrassment. The departure of Frumentius for Alexandria, and his return to Aksum as bishop, seem to have occurred in a climate of doubt and apprehension of which the bishop took full advantage.

At all events, betrayed by his own son, the Mahrem described as invisible to the enemy was vanquished by Christ. The triumph of the sign of the cross over the lunar crescent is attested by both inscriptions and coins.

The transfer from one religion to another is of course never easy, and it must have been even less so for the kings, who loved their god as their own father. A king's honour was always linked to his god. The interests of the court and of the religious leaders were almost everywhere identified with one another. When a king like Ezana called his god 'unconquerable', he was in fact thinking only of himself. Through the attribute he was seeking his own invincibility.

We can therefore imagine the difficulties that Ezana had to face, as did his contemporary, Constantine the Great. For indeed the emperor of Constantinople, although he presided over Christian councils and arbitrated in the religious disputes of the patriarchs, was baptized only on his deathbed, since he feared betrayal by the believers in the old cults of Zeus and Ares.[5]

Similarly, as Guidi and Conti-Rossini have pointed out, King Ezana and his family – through fear or pride – did not suddenly abandon their old god in favour of the Christian religion. The famous inscription registered by Deutsche Aksum expedition (DAE) in Volume II, which begins with the words 'with the help of the Lord of Heaven and Earth ...' and which is considered by all Ethiopians as Ezana's first indication of his Christianity, clearly shows his desire to assimilate the new religion to the old belief in the gods Bēher and Meder, by avoiding any mention of the name of Christ, Christ's unity with God and the Trinity which he forms with the Father and the Holy Spirit.[6] The expression 'Lord of Heaven and Earth' – Igzia Semay Wem, first pronounced in the fourth century by the first Christian king – has remained in use down to the present day.

Neither foreign works not local accounts so far published give any specific date for the introduction of Christianity to Aksum. The history of the kings, *Tarike Neguest*, as well as the *Guedel Tekle Haymanot*, state that the brothers Frumentius and Aedesius arrived in +257 and that Frumentius returned to Aksum as bishop in +315.[7] Other sources of the same kind give the dates +333, +343, +350, and others. All these dates seem to be arbitrary. Certain foreign works state that King Ella Amida, father of Ezana, died about +320–35. Taking fifteen years as the

5. Eusebius of Pamphylia, pp. 65, 366–8, 418–22.
6. E. Cerulli, 1956, pp. 16–21.
7. E. A. T. Wallis Budge, 1928, pp. 147–50; I. Guidi, 1896, pp. 427–30; 1906, Vol. II.

age of majority, and allowing for the departure and return of Frumentius, the baptism of King Ezana must therefore have occurred between +350 and +360.[8]

Lacking authentic documents, contemporary authors simply state cautiously that Christianity was introduced into Ethiopia in the fourth century.

In fact an inscription in Greek characters, discovered at Philae, mentions the visit in 360 of an Aksumite viceroy, a Christian named Abratoeis, to the Roman emperor, who received him with all the honours due to his rank.[9] This emperor must have been Constans II (+341–68), the son of Constantine the Great. Although a Christian, he had adopted the doctrine of Arius, who denied the unity and the consubstantiality of the three persons of the Holy Trinity and consequently the perfect equality of Jesus Christ with the Father. The Council of Nicaea, held in +325 and presided over by the father of Constantine II, had condemned this doctrine.

An implacable enemy of Arius was precisely Athanasius, who had consecrated Frumentius bishop of Aksum. This patriarch was himself later ousted on the orders of the semi-apostate emperor, who nominated a certain George, very favourable to Arianism, to replace him.

The news of the arrival in Aksum of Frumentius, a fervent supporter of the Patriarch Athanasius, who had consecrated him, was not likely to please the emperor of Constantinople. He immediately dispatched a letter to King Aizanz (Ezana) and to his brother Saizana, generously calling them his 'greatly honoured brothers'. In a friendly manner, he requested them to send back Frumentius to the new patriarch, George, in Alexandria, so that his case could be examined by the latter and his colleagues, who alone had the power to decide whether or not Frumentius was worthy to head the bishopric of Aksum.

Unfortunately, we do not possess the document that might have revealed the reaction of the two brothers on receipt of this letter. Although the national interest forced them to maintain friendly relations with the powerful emperor of Constantinople, it would seem that they did not comply with his request. All the local sources affirm that Frumentius carried out his episcopal duties peacefully to the end of his life. *The Synaxarium* (a sort of biography of saints) which described his apostolate ends: '... He [Frumentius] arrived in the land of Ag'Azi [Ethiopia] during the reign of Abraha and Atsbaha [Ezana and his brother Atsbaha] and preached the peace of our Lord Jesus Christ throughout the country. That is why he is called Abba Selama [Father of Peace]. After leading the people of Ethiopia to the [Christian] faith, he died in the peace of god...'[10]

8. C. Conti-Rossini, 1928, pp. 148–9.
9. Congresso Internazionale di Studi Etiopici, Accademia dei Lincei, 1974, Vol. I, p. 174.
10. T. T. Mekouria, 1966–7, Vol. II, pp. 203–17.

# The spread of Christianity

The introduction and spread of Christianity by Bishop Frumentius and the two brother-kings (Abraha–Atsbaha) are widely recognized. All the local sources confirm this. A curious fact is that in the many texts dating from this period and written before the end of the nineteenth century, there is no trace of the name Ezana, which appears to be the king's pagan name. Nor, to my knowledge, does any epigraphic or numismatic inscription mention the name Abraha, which is presumably the king's baptismal name. So we have different names for the same man who, by good or bad fortune was, like Constantine the Great, a semi-pagan and a semi-Christian during his reign. The texts are often in flagrant contradiction. The names of several kings, clearly engraved on the stelae and the coins of Aksum, do not feature in the lists drawn up by the local authors. A man who was a pagan for some authors was, for others, a believer according to the Law of Moses.

While some consider Abraha to be the baptismal name of Ezana, the famous inscription in vocalized Ge'ez, registered No. II in the DAE and considered by all Ethiopian scholars to be the epigraph dating from the time of his conversion to Christianity, mentions only the name Ezana. In that case, Abraha cannot have been the king's baptismal name. Of course, we are not familiar with the onomastics prevailing in the kingdom of Aksum in the fourth century. Neither do we know whether the Aksumite kings also had a proper name in infancy apart from their baptismal name and their royal name, as was the case for the emperors of the Amara dynasties of so-called Solomonian origin (in the thirteenth and twentieth centuries).

The influence of the two brothers, and especially that of Abraha, was enormous in the country. He built the city of Aksum and its first cathedral. Several churches and convents claim to have been founded by him, though we should not forget how much help was given in this work by his brother Atsbaha and by Bishop Frumentius, as well as by other religious leaders not mentioned in the sources.

It appears that the Christian kingdom of Aksum was ruled by a kind of theocratic triumvirate 'ABRAHA–ATSBAHA–SELAMA', Selama being the name given by churchmen to Frumentius.

The first proselytism in favour of the new religion seems to have been well received by a part of the population linked to the court by ethnic and cultural ties. These were Sabaean, Habesan, Himyard of Semitic stock, ancestors of the Tigre and the Amhara, who accepted their masters' religion without difficulty.

After the introduction of Christianity, and as those converted to the faith increased in numbers, journeys to the holy places became frequent. In a letter sent from Jerusalem in the year 386, a certain Paola wrote to her friend Marcella who lived in Rome: 'What should we say of the Armenians ... of the Indian and Ethiopian people, who hasten to this place

[Jerusalem]; where they show exemplary virtue . . . ?' Saint Jerome, doctor of the Latin church, also mentions the continual arrival of Ethiopians at the holy places.[11]

The spread of Christianity in the kingdom of Aksum during the fifth and sixth centuries was the work of churchmen whom all the traditional texts describe as TSADKAN (Just) or TESSEATOU KIDOUSSAN (Nine Saints). But their arrival in the kingdom of Aksum involved the latter in the theological quarrels current at the time in the large cities of the Byzantine empire.

Though it was born in a small village of Palestine and seemed to be the religion of the poor and persecuted, from the time Constantine promulgated the Edict of Liman in 313, Christianity became a religion of states. The churches organized themselves, supported by the Christian emperors. Popes and patriarchs divided up the regions of the Christian empire of East and West. The persecutions and witch hunts of the Diocletian period were gone for ever. Peace reigned in Rome, Alexandria, Damascus, Antioch and all the places where the most violent persecution has formerly occurred.[12]

The patriarch and doctors of the church led comparatively pleasant lives, spending most of their time in reading the holy books and in examining certain passages likely to shed light on the nature of the founder of the Christian religion. Reading and meditation inspired ideas of a kind that sowed discord among Christians. Thus it was that a faith founded on love, peace and brotherhood transformed itself into a battleground, to the point where the successors of the apostles and martyrs sometimes came to blows.

Profound reflection on the nature of Christ God-Man and on the Trinity became a great source of controversy, as we shall see.

After the condemnation of Arius in 325, it was the turn of the Patriarch of Constantinople, Nestorius, to arouse a great polemic by publicly professing the humanity of Christ in opposition to the doctrine established at Nicaea on the divine nature of Christ.[13] According to Nestorius the two natures of Christ (human and divine) were quite distinct and separate. The Virgin Mary was the mother of Christ as a man, not as God, and therefore should not be called Theotokos, or Mother of God, but merely Christotokos, Mother of Christ.

This proposition met with strong opposition from Cyril, Patriarch of Alexandria, and from Pope Celestine of Rome. Nestorius was condemned in Ephesus (431) as a heretic and thrown into prison.

His successor Flavian, Patriarch of Constantinople, put forward another idea on the two natures of Christ (human and divine), without, however,

11. E. Cerulli, 1943, pp. 1–2.

12. It should not be forgotten that the fifth, sixth and seventh centuries were marked by extremely violent theological controversies accompanied by fresh persecutions of minority groups that had been condemned.

13. This is of necessity a highly condensed summary of church history during that period.

denying that Christ was true man and true God. In Flavian's view, each of Christ's two natures was perfect and distinct, and united only in the person of Christ. Dioscoros, Patriarch of Alexandria, at once opposed this viewpoint. Christ, he said, had but one nature, which was at once human and divine. This was the Monophysitism whose chief defender was the scholar Eutyches. Close argument degenerated into uproar during the Council held at Ephesus in 442. Dioscoros and Eutyches emerged victorious from this stormy debate; the loser, having been soundly flogged by his opponents, died very soon afterwards and Dioscoros returned triumphant to Alexandria.

But this Pyrrhic victory of the Monophysites was short-lived. When their imperial ally, Theodosius II, died his general, Marcian, seized power, and the burning question of the nature of Christ was once more raised. A council composed of 636 prelates and doctors of the church was held in 451 in Chalcedon, under the presidency of the emperor Marcian. The discussion became so confused that it was impossible to discern either victor or vanquished, and the question had to be put before the Pope of Rome, who was considered to be the supreme head of all the churches. Pope Leo the Great declared in a letter that he was in favour of the doctrine of the two separate natures of Christ. The Council therefore condemned Dioscoros. His opponents, armed on the one hand by the opinion of the supreme head of the universal church, and on the other by the support of the emperor Marcian, went so far as to manhandle and beat Dioscoros in revenge for the ill-treatment of the Patriarch Flavian. Dioscoros was then banished to an island in Galatia.

Now, ever since the time of Frumentius, the kingdom of Aksum had, as we know, come under the jurisdiction of the patriarchate of Alexandria, whence it received its bishop and canon law. The kings and bishops of Aksum were therefore naturally upholders of the Monophysite cause, which was later, in Ethiopia, to take the name of TEWAHDO. The news of the ill-treatment inflicted on their patriarch filled them with great hatred of the supporters of the doctrine of the two natures of Christ. For the Monophysites life became unbearable throughout the whole empire of Constantinople, since the conquerors of Chalcedon threatened and insulted them incessantly. To escape from this intolerable existence, the Monophysites fled towards Egypt and Arabia. It was at this time that the famous Nine Saints arrived in the kingdom of Aksum, where they sought refuge with others who professed the same doctrine as themselves.

The history of the kings, *Tarike Neguest*, refers briefly to the arrival of the Nine Saints: 'Sal'adoba gave birth to All'Ameda, and during his reign the Nine Saints came from Rome [Constantinople]. They built up [Asterat'ou] the religion and the monastic laws ...'[14] According to some

14. Emin Bey, manuscript deposited at the Bibliothèque Nationale, Paris.

local sources, All'Ameda reigned between 460 and 470, and between 487 and 497 according to others; so the arrival of the saints must be situated between these dates. Certain authors believe they arrived at the beginning of the sixth century (in the era of Kaleb and of Guebre Meskel), but this seems less likely.

The arrival of the apostolate of some of these saints – Aregawi, Penteleon, Guerima and Aftse – were described later by monks in detailed biographies. Unfortunately, the latter contain so many miracles and manifestations of austerity and penitence that present-day readers remain somewhat sceptical.

They carried out their apostolate in various places: Abba Aregawi went up to Debre-Dāmo, where the cult of the Python appeared to have taken root among the local population. Abba Guerima settled at Mettera (Madera) near Senafe, and Abba Aftse at Yeha, where one can still see the ancient temple dedicated to the god Almuqah (fifth century). Penteleon and Likanos remained in the city of Aksum, while Alef and Tsihma went to Bhzan and to Tseden Tsedeniya; Ym'ata and Gouba settled in the region of Guerealta.

In the places where they lived, convents and churches dedicated to them are still to be seen today. Some are carved into giant rocks, and are accessible only by means of a rope. In the convent of Abba Ym'ata, also built on a rock, at Goh (Guerealta), there is a circular painting representing the Nine Saints.

Christianity, as introduced in the fourth century by Frumentius, was therefore consolidated by these saints. They were, of course, helped by the successors of King Ezana, such as Kaleb and Guebre Meskel, who were fervent Christians. In their teaching of the Gospel, the Nine Saints upheld the Monophysite doctrine for which so many Christians had suffered ill-treatment and exile.

However, the spreading of Christianity was not due solely to these nine monks who came from the Byzantine empire. Guided by bishops such as the famous Abba Metta'e, hundreds of native and foreign monks certainly helped to propagate the Christian faith although they did not have the privilege, like the Nine Saints, of being mentioned by name in the annals.[15] Starting from the northern regions, Christianity was implanted in other provinces such as Beguemdr, Gogiam and Choa, among the Beja and the Amhara. The Christian religion benefited from the faithful support of kings, queens, princes, governors and dignitaries of the church, who had many convents and churches built in places where the traditional cults had flourished.

The temples of the gods of the pre-Christian Aksumite or pre-Aksumite period were often built on high ground where there were tall trees and streams. Debre-Dāmo, Abba Penteleon, Abba Metta'e de Chimzana and

15. I. Guidi, 1896, pp. 19–30.

Yeha bear witness to this fact. After the conversion of the Aksumite kings all these temples were transformed into churches.

And now we come to the question of the language in which these monks, who came from all corners of the Byzantine empire, taught the Gospel. The people of the upper classes close to the court were more or less polyglot and spoke Greek, Syriac or Arabic; in their case there does not seem to have been any linguistic problem. But the foreign monks were obliged to study the language of the country before they could make themselves understood by the people in general. Possibly some of the pilgrims who went to the holy places in Jerusalem, Constantinople and Alexandria spoke Greek or Syriac and could act as interpreters, or could teach the people themselves, directly.

This would explain why we find Greek-style names and Syriac words in several of our religious texts, such as: Arami (Aramene), Arb, Haymanot, Hatti, Mehayn, Melak, Melekot, etc. (pagan, Friday, faith, sin, believer, angel, divinity).

## The kingdom of Aksum and south Arabia

It has long been known that groups of peoples of Semitic origin crossed the Red Sea and settled in northern Ethiopia, probably seeking more fertile and richer lands than their own desert country. The newcomers possessed a higher form of civilization than that of indigenous peoples (most of whom were Beja, Aguew, and so on, of Kushitic origin) and ended by taking over the central power and founding the cities of Yeha, Matara, Aksum and other places.

Other groups of the same origin (Sabaeans, Himyarites) remained in their native land, while those who had crossed the Red Sea became more and more powerful, to the point where the central government of Aksum seemed strong enough to some to be considered the third world power. Royal castles, temples, circles and crescents, symbolizing the gods Mahrem and Almuqah, all confirm the identity of the two peoples who lived on either side of the Red Sea.[16]

This ethnic and cultural kinship explains to a large extent the Aksumite conquest of south Arabia which the Aksumites considered their ancestral home, and why in his formal titles King Ezana laid great stress on that of king of Aksum, of Mimyar, of Saba, as distinct from those who called themselves Kasu, Siyamo and Beja, and who came from the western regions, or were simply natives of Kushitic areas.

Until the beginning of the fourth century the Semitic people on the opposite shores of the Red Sea practised the same traditional religions, that is, the worship of the moon, with the crescent as its symbol, which is still honoured today by the Muslim Arab states. Perhaps the Prophet

16. C. Conti-Rossini, 1928, ch. 4.

Muhammad did not require converts to abandon this symbol, whereas the bishops of Aksum put pressure on the Christian kings to replace it by the Christian symbol of the cross.

## Struggle between Christians and Jews in south Arabia

Other groups of Hebraic religion had been living in this same region of south Arabia for a long time, perhaps since the destruction of Jerusalem by Nebuchadnezzar in $-587$ and its occupation by the Lagidae. But their numbers increased greatly after the third destruction of Jerusalem by the emperor Titus in $+70$, when Jews persecuted by the Romans received a welcome from their compatriots settled in south Arabia.

Furthermore, many Monophysites left the Byzantine empire and sought refuge in Arabia after the Council of Nicaea and even more after that of Chalcedon, when Arians were condemned and persecuted. There, with the help of the kings and the Christians of Aksum, they founded a powerful community. Under the rule of the emperor Justin I ($+518$–27), many Syrian Monophysites were expelled by order of the emperor, and left for Hira (Najaf, now in Iraq) and from there reached south Arabia and settled in Najran.[17]

Between these two communities of Jews and Christians was the whole Arab group, among them Yemenites, Cataban, Hadramut, who clung to the traditional cult of the moon and were quite naturally attracted to the flourishing precincts of the KA'ABA. Muhammad, the founder of Islam and the destroyer of idols, was not yet born. The three religious confessions had, perforce, to live side by side. But the Christians, thanks to the unfailing help of the Aksumites increased in number and developed and organized their community. Many churches were built. Najran and Zafar (Tafar) became great Christian cultural centres[18] and major trading posts.[19]

The Jews too, with the talent they show in all fields, had formed a community in Saba and in Himyar and sought to control trade there. So a sharp rivalry developed between Christians and Jews. The Christians considered the Jews to be deicides destined to burn in hell; and the Jews outraged the Christians by calling them 'Goyim', Gentiles and pagan adorers of man.

The successes of the Christians allied to Aksum and Byzantium, as well as the ill-treatment meted out in Byzantium and the Aksumite world to those who practised the Jewish religion, developed a capacity for fierce

---

17. E. A. T. Wallis Budge, 1928b, Vol. I, pp. 261–9.
18. E. A. T. Wallis Budge, 1928a, pp. 743–7.
19. On this point see the very important study by N. Pigulevskaya, 1969. This work is translated from the Russian.

retaliation among the Jewish communities of south Arabia. The Arabs who were faithful to traditional cults were also threatened by the monopoly of trade relations by the Christians[20] and ended by siding with the Jews. The proselytism of the Christians may also have served to bring the other two religions together, threatened as they were by the cultural and religious imperialism of Christianity.

## Massacre of the Christians of Najran by the Jews

While the emperor Justin I reigned in Byzantium (+ 518–27), Kaleb was emperor of Aksum. It was at this time that the Jews, with the help of the Himyarites, massacred the Christians of Zafar and Najran. This event is recorded mainly by the religious authors of the period, Procopius and Sergius.[21] In their texts, the king who is called Kaleb in our Ge'ez text is given the Greek name of Hellesthaios. Sometimes this name becomes Elle Atsbaha, perhaps an arabized form. One also finds the variant Hellesbaios. Similarly, the Jewish king of Himyar, who was known as Zurah or Masruc, took the Jewish name of Yussuf when he came to power, and the Arab authors called him Dhu-Nuwas, or Dunaas, Dimnos, Dimion or Damianos.[22] In the Ethiopian text that tells the story of the Najran massacres he bears the name of FINHAS. In order not to create confusion in the reader's mind, I shall, in this chapter, call the king of Aksum Kaleb and the Jewish king Dhu-Nuwas.

Sergius, who claims to have gathered his information from eye-witnesses, gives the following version of the event which Conti-Rossini has translated into Italian in his *Storia di Ethiopia*. Dhu-Nuwas or Masruc, king of the Himyarites, persecuted the Christians, with the support of the Jews and the pagans. Bishop Thomas therefore went to Abyssinia to seek aid, and found it. The Abyssinians, led by a certain Haywana, crossed the Red Sea and prepared to attack Dhu-Nuwas. The latter, not being able to withstand so strong a force, signed a peace treaty with the Abyssinian leader Haywana who, after leaving part of his army behind him, returned home. With the bulk of the troops gone, Dhu-Nuwas treacherously massacred the Christians of Zafar and burned all the churches, together with the 300 Christian soldiers left as a garrison.

But the worst massacre described by the authors of this period took place in + 523 at Najran, the most highly developed of the Christian centres. Among the martyrs was a much revered old nobleman, Harite (Aretas), whom the Ge'ez text refers to as Hiruth.[23]

20. N. Pigulevskaya, 1969, pp. 211ff.
21. N. Pigulevskaya, relies on other sources.
22. C. Conti-Rossini, 1928, pp. 171–3.
23. ibid., p. 172.

## King Kaleb's maritime expedition

Kaleb or Elle Atsbaha, son of Tazena, was the most famous emperor of his time, perhaps comparable to Ezana. One of the reasons for his fame was his maritime expedition which is related below.

After the massacre of +523, a nobleman named Umayyah managed to get back to Aksum and told King Kaleb and the bishop what had happened to the Christians. Other Christians escaped to Constantinople to inform the emperor Justin. Through the Patriarch Timothy of Alexandria, Justin sent a letter to Kaleb urging him to avenge the bloodshed of Christians.

We can imagine the effect that the news of the Christian massacre had on the two emperors. However, as we know, the country of Saba and Himyar was linked more closely, ethnically and culturally, to the empire of Aksum than to that of Byzantium. So King Kaleb hastily assembled an army that would guarantee victory. He is said to have obtained 120 000 men and 60 warships[24] from the emperor Justin.[25] However, other authors state that he left with his own ships which were anchored at Adulis, and that his army numbered no more than 30 000 soldiers.[26]

Traditional sources report that the king, after concluding his military preparations, went to the convent of Abba Penteleon – one of the Nine Saints who was still alive – to ask for the saint's blessing for himself and for the success of the battle upon which he was about to engage. The old monk promised him victory, and the king left for the shores of Gabazas, near Adulis, where intense preparations for war were being made.

Towards the end of May +525, Kaleb embarked and set sail with all his ships for south Arabia where the Himyarite king awaited them. In fact, when the king and his army arrived they found the enemy port blocked by chains and guarded by soldiers ready to defend themselves.

Without waiting for the end of the battle, King Kaleb looked for a more propitious place to land his troops. By chance, one of the family of Dhu-Nuwas, who had been captured in battle, told them of such a place and the king, accompanied by some twenty boats, succeeded in disembarking. This enabled him to put the rest of the king of Himyar's soldiers to flight. It was while the main part of the contingent continued to fight that Dhu-Nuwas fell into King Kaleb's hands, with seven of his companions. Kaleb, wishing to avenge the shedding of Christian blood, unhesitatingly killed him on the spot.

When the battle ended, the Christian troops invaded first the town of Tafar (Zafar) and then Najran. In their turn, the Christian soldiers laid waste the land and massacred the enemies of their religion. During

---

24. These figures are rightly considered inaccurate by N. Pigulevskaya, 1969, p. 243.
25. Other views concerning the origin of this fleet are to be found in N. Pigulevskaya, 1969, p. 243.
26. A. Coquot, 1965, pp. 223–5.

this slaughter, Christians who could not talk the soldiers' language drew the sign of the cross on their hands to show that they, too, were Christians, and that their lives should be spared.[27]

At Najran, the king was present at a ceremony to commemorate the martyrdom of the Christians who had lost their lives in the massacre, and before he returned to Aksum he had a monument built in Marib in memory of his victory.[28] Kaleb also erected a monument in Marib, so that his name might be remembered by future generations.[29]

Before his return to Aksum the king left a certain Summyapha Awsa at Zafar, under the orders of Abreha, who was the best-known Christian general at the court of Aksum, as also in south Arabia.

A contingent of 10 000 men was left as a garrison. After his successful campaign Kaleb received a triumphal welcome, as one can well imagine, on his return to Aksum. Yet, instead of savouring the fruits of victory, this king, who was both religious and warlike, retired to the convent of Abba Penteleon to lead a monastic life and swore never to leave it. He sent his crown to Jerusalem, begging Bishop Yohannes to hang it before the door of the Holy Sepulchre in accordance with a vow he had made before the campaign.

The ancient sources, some of Greek and others of Arabic origin, and a third collection, drawn up locally from the sixteenth century onwards, contradict each other on what occurred during the military expedition and on the names of those who played a part in this vengeful maritime campaign. Furthermore, while certain texts state that there was only one expedition, others relate that Kaleb returned to Arabia and was not finally victorious until after a second expedition. But this is of no great importance to present-day readers.

The king's decision to abdicate after such a victory is admirable in itself, if the facts reported in the traditional texts are accurate. But another text states that Kaleb remained on his throne until 542. It is quite possible that if his war against Dhu-Nuwas took place in Arabia in 525, that he reigned for another seventeen years, unless there is an error of dating, after his return to Aksum.[30]

## Literature

Aksum had several alphabets which were used by men of letters and by the court for its administration. Among the stelae of Aksum, some carry inscriptions only in Sabaean, or in Ge'ez or sometimes in Greek, but seldom in all three languages together. Sabaean was the alphabet of the Sabaean tribes, which are thought to be one of the ancestors of the Aksumites,

27. S. Irfann, pp. 242–76.
28. C. Conti-Rossini, 1928, pp. 167–201.
29. E. A. T. Wallis Budge, 1966, pp. 261–4.
30. T. T. Mekouria, 1966b, pp. 2–7; C. Conti-Rossini, 1928, pp. 108–9.

described in the traditional text as Neguede Yoktan (tribe of Yoktan)[31] and from whom the present-day Amhara, Tigre, Gouraghe, Argoba and Harrari (Aderes) are descended.

Greek, like English today, was the vehicular language of that period, a foreign tongue introduced into Aksum because of the kingdom's cultural, economic and political relations with the Byzantine empire, especially under a number of kings who seem to have had Greek names: Zoskales, Aphilas, Andibis, Sombrotus, and so on. In the end, it was Ge'ez, at first without vowel signs and later vocalized, that became from the sixth and seventh centuries onwards the official national language of the Aksumites, the language of the Aga'izyan – another name given by the natives, which means liberators.[32]

In general, the language provides research workers with useful pointers, but does not in itself enable the ethnic group to be identified. For a native might be of Semitic origin, of Aksumite nationality and Greek culture and another might be of Beja or Blemmye stock, a Nubian by birth or nationality, and of Egyptian culture. Therefore a person who spoke or wrote Ge'ez was not necessarily an Aksumite.

After the Arab conquest in the Middle East and North Africa during the seventh century, Greek and Sabaean gave way to Ge'ez, which began to be used in all circles – civil, military and religious. Greek maintained its influence only through translation of the Bible from Greek into Ge'ez, and through certain works of the Fathers of the Church such as Cyril of Alexandria or St John Chrysostom. As always happens, translators who could not find the exact word they wanted in Ge'ez sometimes used Greek words. This is how the Greek developed that is used in Ethiopia to this day.

Since parchment manuscripts prior to the thirteenth century are totally lacking, the true, authentic Aksumite literature that is known at present is limited to epigraphic and numismatic inscriptions. Sometimes a few epigraphs, half obliterated or badly carved, fail to give the literary meaning that would make possible an unbroken reconstitution of a real literature.

The first inscription which marks the beginning of Christian Aksumite literature is the one which the DAE registered under No. II, in which King Ezana, newly converted, described his victory over the people of Noba (the Nubians), who had dared to dispute his power beyond the River Takazi and had put his emissaries to death. One can believe in the moral sense of this conquering emperor when he accuses 'the Noba of ill-treating and oppressing the people of Mengourto, Hasa and Baria, the people of black and red colour (SEB'A TSELIME, SEB'A QUE'YH), of having twice broken the oath they had taken . . .' Was this the result of his new religion?

31. E. Cerulli, 1956, pp. 18–21.
32. E. A. T. Wallis Budge, 1966, pp. 136–7; C. Conti-Rossini, 1928, Monete axumite Tabola LX.

Yet, Ezana boasts of having killed 602 men, 415 women and a number of children thanks to the power of his new God, whom he calls, 'Lord of Heaven and Earth, who was the conqueror', but without himself committing any injustice. By this he seems to imply that the perfidious people of Noba, who had provoked the war, had deserved their punishment.[33]

The influence of Christianity appears also on the numerous coins of the kings of Aksum, where the Christian symbol of the cross replaced the crescent, symbol of the ancient religion. Certain Aksumite kings, wishing for publicity or to gain the sympathies of their people, had unusual legends inscribed on their coins. The coinage of King Wazed or Wazeba (son of King Kaleb – sixth century) had his effigy on one side and on the other the inscription: 'Let the people be joyful'. Most significant are the coins of King Lyouel, which bear his crowned head on one side (to the right of the crown there is a small cross) and a cross on the other, which would seem to indicate that he was a fervent Christian. On another coin of the same king the inscription 'Christ is with us'[34] figures in Ge'ez, without a vowel sign. This is the first time the name of Christ is mentioned.

The Old Testament was gradually translated from Greek into Ge'ez during the fifth and sixth centuries. The Bible came into use in Ethiopia, and its teaching assumed vital importance in the court and in ecclesiastical circles, until it eventually became the sole basis of science and philosophy without, however, overshadowing certain works of the fathers of the church.

After the Council of Chalcedon in +451, the Nine Saints and their disciples arrived in Ethiopia and strengthened the influence of Monophysitism among the Ethiopian clergy. That is why the Ethiopian church systematically avoided all other works, of whatever value, that came from the West. One remembers the agreement between Amr Ibn Alas, the companion of the Prophet Muhammad, on one hand, and on the other, the Patriarchs Benjamin and Chenouda, at the siege of Heliopolis in 640 during the conquest of Egypt. Their hatred of the Patriarch Mukaukis and of all those who professed the doctrine of the two natures of Christ led the Egyptian Monophysites to rally to the side of the Muslims.

As remarked earlier, the Bible became the fount of all knowledge. From the time when Christianity took root until the beginning of the twentieth century, any Ethiopian scholar worthy of the name was not one versed in Graeco-Roman science or philosophy, but a man who knew the Bible and the works of the Patriarch Cyril, St John Chrysostom and other founders of the church, and who could comment on different versions; a man who could interpret suitably the mysteries of the incarnation of Christ and the Trinity of the Godhead.

For the Amhara dynasty who were said to have descended from Solomon

33. E. Cerulli, 1956, pp. 222–3.
34. J. B. Coulbeaux, pp. 59–60; T. T. Mekouria, 1967.

and were the legitimate heirs of the kings of Aksum, the most revered kings were David and his son Solomon. Then followed Alexander the Great, Constantine the Great and Theodosius II, the two latter because of the help they had given to Christianity. They knew nothing of Charlemagne, Charles Martel or Charles the Fat. The biblical persons of most renown for the monks were Joshua, Samson and Gideon. The Song of Songs, the Proverbs, the Book of the Wisdom of Solomon, the Wisdom of the Son of Sirach, etc., were considered works of true philosophy, more than the writings of Plato or Aristotle. Virgil, Seneca and Cicero and the medieval scholars of the West were totally unknown.

The Christian society of Ethiopia loves and admires David more than anyone else, considering him to be the ancestor of Mary and of the so-called Solomian dynasty. The Ethiopian religious adore the Psalms and believe that by reading each morning the Psalm for the day they will be protected from all evil. By reading the Psalms constantly they, like David, believe that Almighty God is their exclusive ally.

The Book of Psalms plays a pre-eminent part in Ethiopian Christian society; Psalms are recited on the most diverse occasions. At funerals, for instance, the *Debterotches* or cantors divide the Psalms between them and recite them beside the coffin, while other priests concentrate on reading from the book of burial, the Quenzete, which is very similar to the ancient Egyptian Book of the Dead.

Whilst some religious use the Psalms as prayers, others employ them for magico-religious purposes. The scholar knows by heart the appropriate Psalms for each circumstance, to gain happiness or to avoid misfortune, to ward off a threatening plague or to be protected from gunfire. Generally they quote Psalms 6, 7, 10, 57 and others.

To illustrate the constant recourse to the Psalms I will cite but two examples. A peasant who has lost his cow, his ewe or his ass and cannot find it will recite, or have recited for him, Psalms 1–16, 18 and 10–12.

In 1927, the arrival of the first aeroplane in Addis Ababa was considered a great event. The following day, a ceremony was organized in the presence of the empress Zauditu and the Ras Teferi, the future Haile Selassie. All the priests and cantors were there, attired in their ceremonial vestments. When a religious leader was asked what should be sung on this occasion he immediately suggested the following verses: 'Thou stretchest out the heavens like a curtain ... makest the clouds thy chariot ... and walketh upon the wings of the wind ... bowed the heavens also, and came down ... thou rodest ... and didst fly, didst fly upon the wings of the wind ... and made darkness thy secret place' (Psalms 104 and 18).

Part of the heritage that Ethiopia received from Christian Aksum are the liturgical chants assembled in a work known as the Degoua. According to fourteenth-century local sources, the author was a native of Aksum called Yared, a contemporary of King Guebre Meskel and of Abba Aregawi, one of the Nine Saints.

In reading this book of religious chants in all its details, one sees that the texts are drawn from the Bible, from the works of the early patriarchs, from the famous theologians of the third to the eighth centuries, and from the apocryphal books. They are arranged poetically and concisely and form a great collection divided into several books, chapters and verses. Then all the verses are separated (the first line is usually written in red) and there is a verse for each annual and monthly feast. They are all written in praise of angels, saints, martyrs, the Virgin Mary and God, and are used for the morning and evening services.

The liturgical chant is divided into four sections with cadences which symbolize the four beasts around the throne of God (Revelation 4:6) in such a way that the same text, to be used for any particular feast, can be sung and danced in several different ways. I will try to give an idea of these four sections.

(1) *Kum-Zema* is the basic chant, in its simplest form.

(2) *Zemane-oscillating:* this is the longest chant, where the cantors manipulate their long batons, held in the right hand; they wave them and twist their own bodies in all directions, according to the rhythm of the chant.

(3) *Meregde-skip* (up and down): this chant goes a little faster than the two previous ones. Here the monk-cantor holds his baton in his left hand and sometimes leans on it, while in his right hand he holds his sistrum which is made of iron, silver or gold according to his rank. He moves the sistrum up and down. Two youths sitting nearby beat their drums to accompany the monk, being careful to follow the regular rhythm of the chant. Anyone carelessly producing a wrong note is sent away and replaced at once.

(4) *Tsfat* (hand-clapping) is the quickest chant, which can be continued for a certain time to the accompaniment of the sistra. Towards the end, the Tsfat is followed by a Werebe, a kind of varied and charming modulation which is sung by a single, very gifted cantor, who has a pleasant voice; the others listen attentively before joining him in chorus and in unison, passing gradually from moderato (Lezebe) to allegro (Dimkete) and from presto to prestissimo (Tchebtchedo). This time, the two youths rise to their feet, passing the cord of their drums round their necks, striking hard and so imparting warmth and gaiety to this sacred chant.

The cantors, their heads covered with muslin togas and wearing their feast-day robes, hold their batons on their left shoulders and their sistra in their right hands and begin to sing and dance at a faster rhythm.

This is the most lively part of the chant, where the chief cantor makes spectacular movements and now and then the delighted women, from their places in the congregation, utter cries of joy, 'ILILILI'.

All this takes place either within or outside the church during religious feasts or else to celebrate the traditional exposure of the famous *Tabot* or sacred tablet which, following the example of Moses' Ark of the Covenant, represents the saint to whom the church is dedicated. This takes place in the presence of the emperor, the bishop and the civil, military and ecclesiastical authorities.

When the head of the church, in agreement with the grand master of ceremonies – who at the same time is the chief ecclesiastical LIKE KAHNAT – decides that the people present are satisfied, he gives the sign for the chant to stop. Whereupon a great silence replaces all the religious tumult. The bishop then rises and gives his final blessing. The return of the *Tabot* to its place is greeted by the same chants and 'ILILTA' as when it was brought out, and everyone prostrates himself.

Biblical literature and liturgical chants have a long traditional history, part authentic and part legend, which I have not ventured to do more than summarize. They form part of the inheritance that Christian Aksum has generously bequeathed to the Ethiopians over the centuries.

PLATE 16.1 *Painting from the church of Guh: the Apostles (fifteenth century)*

PLATE 16.3 *Debre-Dāmo seen from a distance*

PLATE 16.2 *King Frumentius Abraha (Izana) and his brother Atsbaha, from the church of Abraha we Atsbaha (seventeenth century)*

PLATE 16.4 *The approach to the monastery church at Debre-Dāmo*

421

PLATE 16.5 *Choristers bowing religiously*

PLATE 16.6 *Church of Abba Aregawi at Debre-Dāmo*

# The proto-Berbers

## J. DESANGES

## The Berbers in Africa Minor: genesis of a people, drying up of the Sahara, and early Mediterranean influences: the 'Ethiopians' of Africa Minor, a residual ethnic element

The ethnic components of the Libyan population were more or less settled before the arrival of the Phoenicians on the African coasts at the beginning of the first millennium before our era, they were not to alter at any time during the whole of antiquity, for it would not seem that the Phoenician and Roman demographic accretions were of any consequence. In fact the demographic contribution of the Phoenicians to Africa Minor cannot be assessed precisely. It is unlikely, however, that the Carthaginians would have such constant recourse to mercenaries on the battlefield if those of Phoenician origin had been more numerous. The demographic contribution of the Romans is also difficult to evaluate. The number of Italians settled in Africa in the time of Augustus, when colonization was at its peak, has been estimated at 15 000.[1] To this figure should be added a few thousand Italians who settled in Africa of their own free will. In our view some 20 000 colonists would be the maximum for the Augustan period, for Roman Africa was in no way a mass-settlement area. The demographic contributions of Vandals and Byzantines were undoubtedly far more modest.

At least thirteen millennia before our era[2] there existed a culture very improperly known as Ibero-Maurusian (although navigation across the Straits of Gibraltar was not to open until 9000 years later). Its bearers, the race of Mechta el-Arbi, were tall (1.72 metres on average) and dolichocephalic. They had a low forehead and long limbs (they would be the first race to represent *homo sapiens* in the Maghrib),[3] and were addicted to removal of the incisors. A trend towards mesobrachycephalism and signs of slenderness have been detected on certain sites, notably at Columnata in

1. P. Romanelli, 1959, p. 207.
2. G. Camps, 1974b, pp. 262–8.
3. See L. Balout, 1955, pp. 435–57; also G. Camps, 1974d, pp. 81–6.

western Algeria[4] towards − 6000. The Ibero-Maurusian culture, properly so called, disappeared at the end of the ninth millennium. This did not happen suddenly everywhere, however. It was supplanted by the Capsian culture in Cyrenaica, but yielded more indecisively to local cultures in western Algeria and Morocco. No evidence of its existence is to be found on the north-eastern coasts of Tunisia or on the small offshore islands,[5] and it left few traces in the Tangiers area. It is most unlikely to have reached the Canaries as is commonly thought, for the Guanches, although anthropologically similar to the men of Mechta el-Arbi, in no way resembled the latter as regards industries and customs. This culture could not have come from Europe since it arose before the beginnings of navigation across the Straits and from and to Sicily. It is tempting to think that its origins were eastern but it may have come rather from the north of the Nilotic Sudan, as J. Tixier claims. Subsequently as they came under pressure from migrating peoples, the Ibero-Maurusians doubtless took refuge in the hills and may be regarded as constituting one of the anthropological components of the population of the djebels.

In about −7000[6] there appeared men of fairly tall stature, of Mediterranean race but not devoid of negroid characteristics.[7] They are known as Capsians after the site of Capsa (now Cafsa). They flourished in an area which has not been exactly defined but which certainly lay inland without, apparently, extending to the westernmost borders of North Africa or to the southern Sahara. They settled usually on a hillock or a slope near a source of water, but sometimes in plains featuring lakes or marshes, and their diet included snails. This culture also came from the east and it could not have spread by sea. It must be reckoned to have come to an end by about the year − 4500. Although the Capsian crania are identical with many contemporary types, it is thought that true proto-Berbers were not in evidence until the Neolithic age, since Capsian funeral rites do not appear to have survived in the Libyco-Berber world.[8] It will be noted, however, that the custom of using and decorating ostrich eggs which characterized the Capsian way of life – to use the vivid expression of Camps-Fabrer[9] – persisted throughout the Neolithic era up to the time of the Libyan peoples mentioned in historical records, such as the Garamantes. The latter, according to Lucian, used the eggs for countless purposes and this is confirmed by excavations at Abou Njem (inland Tripolitania).[10] Nevertheless, Neolithic man in Africa Minor can doubtless be regarded as a cousin of the Capsian. At all events, the historical

4. M. C. Chamla, 1970, pp 113–14.
5. L. Balout, 1967, p. 23.
6. G. Camps, 1974b, p. 265.
7. For G. Camps's reservations, see 1974d, p. 159.
8. L. Balout, 1955, pp. 435–7.
9. H. Camps-Fabrer, 1966, p. 7.
10. R. Rebuffat, 1969–70, p. 12.

peopling of the Maghrib is certainly the result of a merger, in proportions not yet determined, of three elements: Ibero-Maurusian, Capsian and Neolithic.

It is generally agreed that the Neolithic age began with the appearance of ceramics. Recent Carbon 14 measurements indicate that the use of ceramics spread outwards from the central and eastern Sahara. Within that area the oldest Neolithic examples are of Sudanese inspiration. The beginnings of ceramics may be dated to the seventh millennium before our era in the region stretching from the Ennedi to the Hoggar.[11] The makers were probably black or negroid people related to the Sudanese of early Khartoum. The ox had undoubtedly become domesticated by −4000 at the latest. It is not impossible that cattle were domesticated earlier in the Acacus.[12] Evidence of a Neolithic culture in the Capsian tradition dates from a somewhat later period – in about −5350 at Fort Flatters,[13] even a little earlier in the valley of the Saoura – and does not become established in the northern part of the Capsian area before −4500. In the region lying between these two currents which affect 'the Maghreb of the high lands and the Northern Sahara', Neolithic characteristics do not emerge until much later. European influence is out of the question except in the case of a third Neolithic culture which came to the fore on the Moroccan and Oranian coasts in the sixth millennium before our era[14] although we hesitate to date the beginnings of navigation across the Straits of Gibraltar so far back. Balout would agree to place the beginnings of navigation across the Straits of Gibraltar in the fourth millennium before our era.

The humid period of the Neolithic age came to an end towards the middle of the third millennium, as attested by the dating of guano from the Taessa (Atakor in the Hoggar).[15] Arkell's work on the fossil fauna and flora on Mesolithic and Neolithic sites in the Khartoum region gives some support to this finding as regards the valley of the upper Nile. From this time on North Africa, almost totally cut off from the whole continent by desert, found itself virtually an island, only able to communicate easily with the rest of Africa through the narrow corridor of Tripolitania. This drastic reduction of the former unity of Africa was, however, compensated for by new relationships established precisely at that time on the two wings of the Maghreb, on the one hand with the south of the Iberian peninsula, and on the other with Sicily, Sardinia, Malta and southern Italy.[16]

As early as the close of the third millennium before our era the painted

11. H. J. Hugot, 1963, p. 134; cf. ibid., p. 138 and note 3, p. 185. On recent Carbon 14 datings, see G. Camps, 1974b, p. 269.

12. W. Resch, p. 52; see also P. Beck and P. Huard; F. Mori, 1964, pp. 233–41; J. P. Maître, 1971, pp. 57–8.

13. G. Camps, G. Delibrias and J. Thommeret, p. 23.

14. L. Balout, 1967, p. 28; G. Camps, 1974b, p. 272.

15. A. Pons and P. Quézel, pp. 34–5; G. Delibrias, H. J. Hugot and P. Quézel, pp. 267–70.

16. G. Camps, 1960a, pp. 31–55; 1961.

potsherds of Gar Cahal, in the Ceuta area, bear a resemblance to the Chalcolithic ceramics of Los Millares. We must therefore assume sea-route contacts[17] which may perhaps take us back to the fourth millennium. From −2000, ivory and ostrich eggs were imported into Spain, while bell-shaped vessels of Iberian origin make their appearance in the Ceuta and Tetuan areas. Towards −1500, copper and bronze arrow-heads are to be found in the west of Africa Minor, no doubt first imported by Iberian hunters; but they do not appear to have spread westward beyond the region of Algiers. Because of the lack of tin, the use of bronze is hardly noticeable in North Africa. At the other end of Africa Minor, from Korba to Bizerta, the presence of flakes of obsidian originating from the Lipari islands and worked in Sicily and Pantellaria provides evidence of the beginnings of navigation in the Messina Straits. G. Camps[18] has drawn attention to the numerous borrowings made from then onwards by eastern Africa Minor from European neighbours: rectangular tombs with short access passages and right-angled bays, cut into the cliffs and known as 'Haounet', existed in Sicily as early as −1300; the Algerian and Tunisian dolmens are of a type similar to those widely found in Sardinia and Italy; the Castellucio ceramics which were common throughout Sicily towards −1500, with geometrical designs painted in brown or black on a paler background, are the forerunners of Kabyle pottery; and so forth. More distant influences, from Cyprus or Asia Minor, came through Malta, Pantellaria and Sicily as soon as Aegean, and then Phoenician, sailors began to reach those islands. By such means did this land of North Africa, long before the foundation of Carthage, assume its place in the Mediterranean complex as a gigantic peninsula, receiving nevertheless through the Tripolitanian corridor other cultural contributions such as those funerary monuments with recesses and chapels which were common on the southern slopes of the Atlas range in remote antiquity and in which the incubation ritual may have been practised. The tomb of Tin Hinan is a variant of this type of monument.[19]

The deep originality of Africa Minor, lying on the borders of the continent, the result both of the drying-up of the Sahara and of the appearance of navigation, needs to be stressed. However, not all links with deeper Africa were broken. While the climate of North Africa in ancient times was very much the same as it is today, the marginal belt of the Sahara continued for a long time to be better watered and more wooded in its hilly expanses,[20] with aquifers lying much closer to the surface so

17. G. Souville, Vol. III, pp. 315–44.
18. G. Camps, 1974d, p. 206.
19. G. Camps, 1974d, pp. 207 and 568; 1965, pp. 65–83.
20. K. W. Butzer, p. 48. This writer believes that there was a slight improvement in climate during the first millennium before our era. There is a contrary opinion in P. Quézel and C. Martinez, p. 224, which is that the drying-up process was continuous from −2700 onwards.

that water was more accessible and the horse could therefore be used for Saharan travel. In the Fezzan in particular, surface overspills from aquifers persisted for a long time according to Pliny the Elder (*Natural History*, XXXI, 22), who mentions the salt lake Apuscidamo (i.e. *apud Cidamum*), and El Bekri (*Description de l'Afrique septentrionale*, tr. Slane, p. 116), who mentions the swamp areas from Nefzaoua to Ghadames. We can regard as living evidence of the original African unity the fact that, in ancient times, dark-skinned men whom the Greeks were later to call Ethiopians, that is, 'burnt faces', were in contact with the Libyco-Berber world, in most of the oases of the Sahara, in the Fezzan and on all the Saharan slopes of the Atlas range.[21] They led a peaceful existence and engaged not only in food-gathering and hunting, but also in agriculture based on extremely ancient methods of irrigation.[22]

It would certainly be a mistake to imagine a wholly Ethiopian Sahara in the Neolithic and protohistorical ages, even if we are careful to give the term 'Ethiopian' its broadest sense of 'man of colour' and refrain from interpreting it as 'Negro'. M. Cl. Chamla has recently thought it possible to establish[23] that only one-quarter of the skeletons of this period could be identified with black men, while over 40 per cent show no negroid characteristics. On the other hand, the remains of a child discovered in a rock-sheltered deposit in the Acacus,[24] and dated approximately between −3446 and −180, are negroid. In the Punic burial grounds, negroid remains were not rare and there were black auxiliaries in the Carthaginian army who were certainly not Nilotics. Furthermore, if we are to believe Diodorus (XX, 57.5), a lieutenant of Agathocles in northern Tunisia at the close of the fourth century before our era overcame a people whose skin was similar to the Ethiopians'. There is much evidence of the presence of 'Ethiopians' on the southern borders of Africa Minor. Throughout the classical period, mention is also made of peoples belonging to intermediate races, the Melano-Getules or Leuco-Ethiopians in particular in Ptolemy. The Garamantes themselves were occasionally described as somewhat or even wholly black. They are somewhat black in Ptolemy, I.9.7, p. 25, and they

---

21. Regarding the North African Ethiopians, cf. S. Gsell, 1913–28, pp. 293–304. On the notion of 'Ethiopians' (the name is thought to figure already on the Pylos tablets in the form ai-ti-jo-qo), see F. M. Snowden, Jnr, 1970, pp. 1–17 and 15–16, and the comments of J. Desanges, 1970, pp. 88–9.

22. Concerning irrigation and cultivation in the southern Tunisian oases, where the population was part-'Ethiopian', see Pliny the Elder, 188; El Bekri, p. 116. On the importance of the underground canals (foggaras) of the Garamantes, a mixed population, see C. M. Daniels, 1970, p. 17. There are reservations, however, by H. Lhote, 1967, pp. 67–8, who believes that food-gathering continued for a long time to be the principal resource of these 'Ethiopians'.

23. M. C. Chamla, 1968, p. 248 and Pl. 8.

24. F. Sattin and G. Gusmano, p. 8.

are 'more likely Ethiopians' in Ptolemy, I.8.5, p. 31 A. Garamantian slave is described as having a body the colour of pitch'.[25] An anthropological survey carried out in their burial grounds confirms the composite nature of their racial characteristics;[26] it is pure prejudice and an improbable assertion to claim that the negroid skeletons are those of slaves, for it is an arbitrary conclusion to say that two groups of white skeletons out of four represent the proportion of Garamantes in antiquity.

These coloured people do not appear to be related in any degree to most of the contemporary populations of the banks of the Senegal and Niger rivers. We are dealing here with an original ethnic group which has today been largely overlaid by a steadily growing accretion of western Africans owing to the medieval traffic in slaves. St Gsell,[27] following R. Collignon, gives the following description of the 'Ethiopian' of antiquity as deduced from the posterity he supposedly left behind him in the oases of southern Tunisia:

> height above average, very long and narrow skull with the crown sloping backward, slanting forehead, prominent brows, strongly marked cheekbones below which the face forms a narrow triangle, deeply-indented nose, short and *retroussé* but not flat, large and thick-lipped mouth, receding chin, broad and square shoulders, a thorax shaped like an inverted cone, narrowing to the pelvis. The skin is very dark, or a reddish-brown colour, the eyes and the slightly frizzy hair are jet black.

In short, the type is not unlike certain Nilotics, but the physique of these herdsmen, the ancestors of the Saharan 'Ethiopians', is far from uniform. Some, according to H. Lhote[28] and G. Camps,[29] resemble today's Fulani, others the Tooboos. H. von Fleischhacker[30] assumes the presence among them of Khoisanides and of descendants of an undifferentiated *homo sapiens* (neither black nor white) of Asian origin.

Libyco-Berbers (Maurii and Numidians on the coast, Getules on the plateaux), white or half-bred Saharans on the borders of the desert – such as Pharusians, Nigrites or Garamantes, 'Ethiopians' scattered from the Sous to the Djerid – these were the peoples of Africa Minor at the time of the first Phoenician sea voyages, and such they remained throughout antiquity.

25. Frontinus; *Strat*, 1.11.18: during the Sicilian campaign in 480. Claudius Ptolemaeus, 1901, pp. 743, 745; A. Riese, pp. 155–6; Diodorus, XX, 57.5.
26. S. Sergi.
27. S. Gsell, 1913–28, p. 294.
28. H. Lhote, 1967, p. 81.
29. G. Camps, 1970, pp. 39–41.
30. H. von Fleischhacker, pp. 12–53.

# The proto-Berbers in their relations with the Egyptians and the Peoples of the Sea

Libya's historical sources in the second millennium before our era, whether inscriptions or figured objects, are essentially Egyptian in character and concern Libyan populations in contact with Egypt[31] who were able to settle in the north-west of the Delta before the unification of the Nile valley.

As early as the predynastic era, towards the middle of the fourth millennium, the ivory handle of the Djebel-el-Arak knife may perhaps have portrayed long-haired Libyans, naked except for a belt holding up the phallic covering. This interpretation has, however, been contested and we cannot be certain of the Libyan identity in an iconography before the emergence of the first name given to the Libyans by the Egyptians, that of Tehenou. According to W. Hölscher,[32] this name appears on a fragment of a schist *palette* belonging to King Scorpio, and next on an ivory cylinder from Hierakopolis dating from the reign of Narmer (third millennium). This second object pictures the Pharaoh's booty and prisoners. But it is a bas-relief of the funeral temple of Sahouré (fifth dynasty, *c.* −2500) that enlightens us about the physical aspect and clothing of the Tehenou.

These men were tall, with sharp profiles, thick lips, full beards and a characteristic hair-style, with a heavy growth on the back of the neck, locks reaching to the shoulders and a small quiff upright above the forehead. Apart from the belt and phallic covering already mentioned, they wore distinctive broad ribbons around their shoulders, crossing on the breast, and necklaces hung with pendants. They inhabited the Libyan desert and its oases during the third millennium.

Under the sixth dynasty, towards −2300, reference was made to the Temehou. These were not a branch of the Tehenou, as O. Bates surmised,[33] but a new ethnic group with paler skins and blue eyes, including a considerable proportion of fair-haired individuals.[34] Their leather cloaks often leave one shoulder uncovered. According to an account of Hirkhouf's third journey, it would seem that their land was adjacent to Lower Nubia and must have included the Great Oasis of Khargah.[35] It has been suggested that they are identical with the Group-C people who settled in Nubia during the Middle Empire and the beginnings of the New Empire,[36] and this hypothesis is strengthened by a resemblance between the pottery of that group and the pottery found in Wadi Howar, 400 kilometres south-west of the Third Cataract.[37]

31. F. F. Gadallah, pp. 43–76 (in Arabic, English summary pp. 78–81).
32. W. Hölscher, p. 12.
33. O. Bates, p. 46.
34. G. Möller, p. 38; W. Hölscher, p. 24.
35. O. Bates, pp. 49–51.
36. ibid., p. 249, note 3; p. 251 as regards vocabulary; cf. W. Vychichl, 1961, pp. 289–290.
37. W. Hölscher, pp. 54–7; A. J. Arkell, 1961, pp. 49–50; reservations by B. G. Trigger, 1965, pp. 88–90.

These Temehou appear to have been keen warriors, and the Middle Empire Pharaohs often had to fight them. They are frequently portrayed under the New Empire and easily recognized by their tresses hanging in front of the ears and curling back over the shoulders. They often wore feathers in their hair and were sometimes tattooed. Their weapon is the bow, or sometimes a sword or boomerang. These features are also noted among the Syrtes Libyans of the fifth century by Herodotus. Hence it can be deduced that the Temehou are indeed the ancestors of the Libyans known to the Greeks in Cyrenaica. This, however, cannot in itself justify G. Möller's[38] bold theory that they are identical with the Adyrmachidae, close neighbours of the Egyptians according to Herodotus (IV, 168), even though the latter were regarded by Silius Italicus (*Punica*, IX, 223, 225) as Nile-bank dwellers – not unlike the Nubae – who perhaps on occasion occupied southern oases. According to the same author (*Punica*, III, 268–9), their bodies were blackened by the sun as were those of the Nubae, and this would bring them close to the Adyrmachidae of Lower Nubia, whose neighbours the Temehou were; but this does not tally with the clear complexions of the Temehou. Their presence at Kawa is a hypothesis which has been advanced.[39]

The forays of the Temehou became more menacing during the nineteenth dynasty. After Seti I had driven them back *c.* −1317, Ramses II incorporated Libyan contingents into the Egyptian army and organized a defence line along the Mediterranean shore as far as el-Alamein.[40] The stele at the latter spot confirms the occupation of the region by Ramses II and is the first object referring to the Libou. From the name of these people the Greeks derived the geographical term Libya, which then applied to their area of movement, and then step by step to the whole of Africa. Under Merneptah, in −1227, mention is made of the Meshwesh as western neighbours of the Libou.[41] Both the Libou and the Meshwesh appear to have formed part of the broader group of the Temehou;[42] but the figured representations show that the Meshwesh wear the phallic covering (no doubt because they were circumcised), whereas the Libou wear a loincloth. Having occupied the oases of Bahariya and Farafra, the combined tribes were defeated north-west of Memphis by the Egyptians.

38. G. Möller, p. 48; a philological refutation by W. Hölscher, p. 50.
39. M. F. L. Macadam, 1949, Vol. I, p. 100, Nos. 20, 21: ADRMKDE and ADRMLKD.
40. J. Y. Brinton, pp. 78–81, 163–5 and Pl. XX, Fig. 4; A. Rowe, pp. 6–7, Fig. 4. On six new stelae, showing victory scenes of Ramses II over the Libyans, found later at Zawyet-el-Rakkam by Labib Habachi, see J. Leclant, 1954, p. 75 and Pl. XVIII.
41. G. A. Wainright, pp. 89–99. Concerning the names of Libou and Meshwesh chiefs, see J. Yoyotte, 1958, p. 23. Yoyotte considers the Libou to be closer to the Delta. F. Chamoux, p. 55, locates them, on the contrary, west of the Meshwesh, but we think he is wrong. Libya in the strict sense remained a region close to the Mareotis; see Claudius Ptolemaeus, 1901, pp. 696–8. The Libou must therefore have settled very close to Egypt. For the subsequent fate of these peoples, see J. Yoyotte, 1961, pp. 122–51.
42. W. Hölscher, pp. 47–8; cf. note 34 above.

An inscription on the temple of Karnak notes the presence by the side of the Libyans of various northern peoples, the Akaiwesh, Toursha, Shardanes and Shakalesh, belonging to the group of Peoples of the Sea who were then devastating Palestine. Their appearance on the western side of Egypt is somewhat unexpected, and it has sometimes been supposed that the Karnak inscription confused two almost contemporaneous campaigns, conducted one to the east and the other to the west of the Delta,[43] or simply that these northern contingents were mercenaries, having deserted from the Egyptian army.

The two best-known Egypto-Libyan wars, however, are dated — 1194 to — 1188, in the reign of Ramses III. They are recorded in the Harris Grand Papyrus and in inscriptions and reliefs of the Pharaoh's funeral temple at Medinat-Habou. First the Libou, then the Meshwesh, tried in vain to overcome Egyptian resistance on the Nile, and were defeated one after the other. Many prisoners were pressed into the Pharaoh's army, where their military qualities were so greatly appreciated that the Libyan officers, towards the close of the New Empire, had acquired a dominant influence in it. Mention is made of the Esbet and the Beken among the Libyans on whom Ramses III made war. It would be tempting to relate these ethnic groups to the Arbytes (or Asbystes) and the Bakales of Herodotus (IV, 170, 171), but the Esbet reading is disputable[44] and the connection thus becomes fragile. At all events, it is hardly justifiable to identify the Meshwesh with Herodotus' Maxyans (IV, 191), who were long-established settlers in Tunisia.[45]

One of the consequences of the victories of Ramses III was of special significance in that he was thereby enabled to control the western oases through which the cult of the Theban Amon was spreading, particularly the oasis of Siwa, gradually reaching Tripolitania along the 'thirst tracts'[46] and, in the Punic period, exerting an undoubted influence on the cult of the god Ba'al Ammon,[47] a near homonym.

Such are the first pieces of evidence which tell us something about the Libyans in the most easterly part of their wide area of settlement. It should

43. F. Chamoux, p. 52.

44. H. Gauthier, 1927, Vol. I, pp. 104, 117; J. Leclant, 1950b, p. 338; W. Hölscher, p. 65, note 2. Reading suggests the Isebeten of Tuareg tales; see W. Vychichl, 1956, pp. 211–20.

45. See the well-founded reservations of S. Gsell, 1913–28, Vol. I, p. 354; idem, 1915, pp. 113–34.

46. J. Leclant, 1950b, pp. 193–253; R. Rebuffat, 1970, pp. 1–20. On the cult of Ammon in the Syrtes region, cf. S. Gsell, 1913–28, Vol. IV, p. 286.

47. M. Leglay, 1966, pp. 428–31. This writer does not believe that the Amon of Siwa provides a link between the Theban Amon and Ba'al Ammon. He considers that the Libyco-Berbers of Africa Minor, up to the Oran region, fell under the Egyptian influence at a time preceding the foundation of the sanctuary at Siwa. Worship of the Punic Ba'al Ammon would then have become superimposed upon a local worship of the ram, already identified with the Egyptian Ammon.

be noted that the Peoples of the Sea, for their part, are only mentioned once in an inscription at Karnak, as being in constant contact with the Libyans during the reign of Merneptah in − 1227, and that this inscription itself may be the result of an amalgam of several campaigns.[48] But even if we grant that there were detachments of Peoples of the Sea among the Libyans, can we go on to assert that these were the peoples who taught the Libyans the use of chariots, first in the confines of Egypt and then throughout the Sahara?

This proposition has the support of some first-rate Sahara specialists,[49] although there are few similarities between the Aegean and the Saharan portrayals of chariots, as is well demonstrated by an archaeologist of classical antiquity such as G. Charles-Picard[50] and a specialist of the horse such as J. Spruytte.[51] The Saharan chariots are seen in a horseman's perspective and not in profile; the platform is not raised and rests on the centre of the axle, well away from the wheels, thus limiting the passenger load in practice to one driver, whose hands hold a kind of short whip and not a weapon. The horses, mostly Barbaries, are harnessed by means of a collar-yoke, not a yoke resting on the withers. Although they are indeed shown in an extended position ('flying gallop'), neither their hocks nor their knees appear. In the Aegean documents, moreover, the 'flying gallop' is not the stance of harnessed horses. Thus the Saharan chariots would seem to be strongly characterized as somewhat fragile 'sporting' vehicles.

Therefore, we should probably distinguish the Saharan chariots from the war chariots of antiquity identified among the foes of Ramses III and later among the Garamantes (four-horse chariots), the Arbytes, the Zoeces, the Libyans in the service of Agathocles in the neighbourhood of Carthage, the Pharusians and the Nigretes. Rather than assume a borrowing from the Peoples of the Sea, we will be closer to the truth in allowing, with W. Hölscher,[52] that the Libyans borrowed the chariot from the Egyptians who had used it ever since the Hyksos invasion four or five centuries earlier.

48. Similarly the figures' representations of Medinet-Habou mingle the Libyan assaults of −1194 and −1188 with the invasion by the Peoples of the Sea in −1191, see E. Drioton and J. Vandier, pp. 434–6.

49. R. Perret, pp. 50–1.

50. G. Charles-Picard, 1958a, p. 46. It will, however, be noted that while the author's comments on the originality of Saharan portrayals of chariots are entirely judicious, his argument according to which this iconography was influenced by Roman imperial art is unacceptable, as pointed out by G. Camps, 1960b, p. 21, note 46, and H. Lhote, 1953, pp. 225–38. From the time of Ramses III to the time recorded by Diodorus, XX, 38, 2, and Strabo, XVII, 3, 7, both of whose sources preceded the Roman empire, chariots were used by the Libyans from the neighbourhood of the Syrtesto in southern Morocco; cf. O. Bates, p. 139, and note 41 above.

51. J. Spruytte, 1968, pp. 32–42.

52. W. Hölscher, p. 40; G. Camps, 1961, p. 406, note 3. It is impossible to distinguish a representation of a Libyan chariot under Ramses III from that of an Egyptian chariot. See W. M. Müller, 1906–20, Vol. II, p. 121.

The origins of the Saharan chariots remain a mystery. They were made entirely of wood, the design was very simple, and they may have been constructed according to an original technique.[53] Moreover, the Barbary (or Mongol) horse, of small size, having a convex face and forehead line, a prominent and hollow backbone with five lumbar vertebrae, and sloping hindquarters, cannot be derived from the Arab–Oriental breed with its square-cut profile, as ridden by both the Hyksos and the Aegeans.[54] It may perhaps have spread from East Africa and the Sudan,[55] but this is only a hypothesis. We may note that both in the Saharan rock carvings and in carvings of the Roman era within the *Limes*, portrayals of the Arab–Asiatic horse are exceedingly scarce, although they exist.[56] However, even supposing we are not confronted in these cases with a stylized image foreign to African realities, it remains true that until the arrival of the Arabs the Barbary horse remained the dominant species in Africa Minor.

Although we may agree that the eastern Libyans borrowed the long sword from the Peoples of the Sea, the use of that weapon does not seem to have been widespread.[57] Altogether, it would not appear that the Peoples of the Sea exerted as great an influence on the Libyan civilization as many scholars claim. On the other hand the Egyptian influence, fostered in the Delta by ethnic affinities during the protohistorical epoch, must not be discounted even if little is known about the pattern of dissemination.

## Life of the Berbers before the foundation of Carthage

As H. Basset[58] and G. Camps[59] have rightly underlined, agriculture was not revealed to the Libyco-Berbers by the Phoenicians, but had been practised by them since the close of Neolithic times. To suppose that the Canaanites imported agriculture into Africa Minor during the second millennium before our era is a very hazardous hypothesis. Engravings and paintings of the metal age represent a swing-plough in a more or less diagrammatic form at La Cheffia (eastern Constantine region) and in the High Atlas.[60] West of Tebessa, in the region of the Douar Tazbent, a pattern of squares is what remains today of primitive hydraulic installations

53. J. Spruytte, 1967, pp. 279–81. But P. Huard and J. Leclant, 1972, pp. 74–5, assume that the chariots of the Saharan Equidians began as imitations of Egyptian chariots but quickly became sporting and prestige vehicles, following a process which has not been elucidated.

54. J. Spruytte, 1968, pp. 32–3. The author's judicious comments lead, however (p. 35), to an unlikely assumption, namely that the Barbary horse came at a remote period from Spain or even from south-western France and was brought across the Straits of Gibraltar.

55. P. Beck and P. Huard, p. 225.

56. G. Espérandieu, p. 15.

57. G. Camps, 1960b, p. 112 and notes 371–3.

58. H. Basset, pp. 340ff.

59. G. Camps, 1960b, pp. 69ff.

60. J. Bobo and J. Morel, pp. 163–81; J. Malhomme, pp. 373–85.

dating from much earlier than the epoch of native kingdoms. Users of these installations had equipment still partly made of stone.

At the time when the Phoenicians were about to introduce a triangular metal-shared plough, the Berbers were already using their own type of plough, which was admittedly less effective, for it consisted of a simple wooden share drawn through the soil.[61] This plough must have brought to an end the exclusive use of the hoe, for the Guanches who used the latter never knew the plough. It appears that at first the Libyans often drew the plough themselves by means of ropes slung over their shoulders. But they had already been familiar for a very long time with the harnessing of oxen, which is depicted both in Egyptian frescoes and in High Atlas engravings. On the other hand they do not appear to have known any mechanical method of threshing their crops before Punic times[62] and were content to let the grain be trodden out by heavy cattle.

Botanists have shown that hard wheat (perhaps brought from Abyssinia) and barley[63] were grown in North Africa long before the arrival of the Phoenicians, together with beans and chick-peas,[64] although the latter derived their Berber name, *ikiker*, from the Latin *cicer*.

In sylviculture, on the contrary, the Phoenician–Punic influence was decisive. However, the Berbers may have known how to graft the oleaster well before the Carthaginians spread the cultivation of the olive. On the other hand, there is no evidence that the vine, which had existed in the Algiers region ever since the beginning of the Quaternary period, was cultivated before the arrival of the Phoenicians. The pre-Saharan Berbers such as the Nasamonians of Herodotus (IV, 172, 182) and the 'Ethiopians', cultivated the date-palm, which was less common on the borders of Africa Minor than it is today. But the fig was the Berbers' favourite fruit[65] even though Cato the Elder displayed a fresh fig in Rome to symbolize the destruction of a rival city which was all too close.

Archaeological research into funerary monuments confirms the existence in remote antiquity of large sedentary groups practising agriculture in Africa Minor. It is true that the dating of protohistorical monuments is peculiarly difficult in this region owing to the fact that Berber ceramics are highly conservative. In any event, as long as we lack other evidence to which an acceptably accurate date can be attached, we shall consider as representative of the 'pre-Carthaginian' life of the Berbers the material collected in the burial grounds of the remote pre-Roman period, which are free from Carthaginian influences.

61. G. Camps, 1960b, pp. 82–3, with a bibliography at p. 82, note 287.
62. Concerning the plostellum poenicum originating in Palestine and Phoenicia, see most recently J. Kolendo, pp. 15–16.
63. J. Erroux, pp. 238–53.
64. G. Camps, 1960b, p. 80.
65. G. Camps, 1960b, p. 90.

Such tomb furniture testifies, as is well demonstrated by G. Camps,[66] to the great antiquity of the Berber rural culture. We can agree with this scholar that a map of the distribution of the protohistorical burial grounds containing ceramics will give us a reasonably accurate notion of the geographical spread of agriculture. It is noteworthy that the tumuli of south Africa Minor contain no pottery; nor is any found in the Saharan encroachments lying between the Zahrez and the Hodna; nor again in eastern Morocco, between the Muluya and the Algerian border. A study of ceramic shapes has enabled G. Camps to throw some light on the way of life of the Libyco-Berbers at this time. The typology is very close to that of contemporary ceramics: bowls, basins and goblets to contain liquids and broths, more or less shallow plates, large dishes somewhat similar to those used in our day for baking unleavened bread, griddlecakes and pancakes. A kind of fruit-dish on a stem base is also found from the protohistorical age up to the present day. Perforations show that from the earliest times the Berbers hung their eating-vessels on the wall. On the other hand, there are no modern equivalents of the ancient filtering-pots, and G. Camps has wondered whether they were not used for separating honey or for preparing infusions.

Archaeologists have also established that the nomads of the southern sites carried ornamental weapons and wore bracelets, metallic pendants or porcelain beads more often than the sedentary inhabitants. Some scraps of fabric indicate the use of striped cloth. Garments made of leather appear frequently in Saharan rock paintings and confirm what Herodotus says (IV, 189). Rock engravings found near Sigus attest to the existence in ancient times of the burnous, which is perhaps the origin of legends concerning headless men or men with their faces in their chests. Such cloaks were apparently also worn by the Blemmyes of the Arabian desert on the borders of Upper Egypt.

The Numides and Maurii were armed with a long narrow javelin and a hunting-knife, whereas the sedentary settlers, in contrast to the population farther south, were seldom buried with their weapons. 'Ethiopians' and mixed peoples, Nigrites and Pharusians in particular, carried bows and arrows, as Strabo states (XVIII, 3, 7). Pliny the Elder (*Natural History*, VI, 194) mentions a desert population 'above' the Great Syrtis: the Longonpori – a name taken from the Greek and meaning 'javelin-bearers'.

The chief source of wealth of the nomads was the raising of sheep, goats and cattle. An engraving showing a milking scene has been found at Djorf Torba, west of Colomb Béchar,[67] in an area now completely bare. According to Elien (NA, VII, 10.1) these nomads did not have slaves, but used dogs instead; the same comments have been made regarding the Red Sea Troglodytes and the Ethiopians of the Nile swamps. But Elien

66. ibid., pp. 96, 97, 101–4, 107–11.
67. ibid., pp. 115, 116, Fig. 13.

(VII, 40) says that other Ethiopians made a dog their king. (Aristocreon seems to be the source of this statement.) Hunting was naturally a common activity, and Ptolemy mentions some Oreipaei hunters living in southern Tunisia near the Ethiopian border, who were neighbours of the Nybgenite Ethiopians roaming the lands south of the Djerid.[68]

Of the social organization of the Libyco-Berbers in times preceding those described in classical sources we know very little, at least if we ignore recurrent attempts at reconstitution based on later evidence. The imposing size of the mounds of the Rharb in Morocco, or of the mausoleum of the Medracen in the Constantine region, suggest that in those parts of both the western and eastern Maghreb which were independent of Carthage monarchies had sprung up at least as early as the fourth century. Nothing more can be asserted, for the brilliant picture of Libyan social organization painted by St Gsell is mainly based on Roman documents of the imperial age, and even on the evidence of the poet Corippus who was a contemporary of Justinian.

## Religious beliefs of the Libyco-Berbers

It is difficult to gain an insight into the religious beliefs of the Libyco-Berbers before the impact of the Punic Phoenicians and later that of the Romans. Protohistorical archaeology never allows us to reconstitute more than rites, and even then, in the case of Africa Minor, the possibility is confined to funerary rites.[69] We must therefore resort once again to the evidence of the classical authors and glean what we can from inscriptions of the Roman epoch without being certain that the customs to which they attest existed in the remoter period with which this chapter is concerned. There is all the more reason to remember that it is always hazardous to project into the past pre-Islamic survivals which we think we can detect in Berber societies of medieval and modern times.

Among the Libyans, the sense of holiness appears to have crystallized around a great variety of objects. Supernatural power was often thought to be manifested in the surrounding countryside, hence the many fluvial or mountain genie worshipped in the inscriptions of Roman times.[70] More precisely localized, divine power could reside in the commonest objects. Round or pointed stones, such as granite pebbles, symbolizing the human face or phallus, were an object of worship.[71] Pomponius Mela (Choz. I.39), and Pliny (*Natural History*, II, 115) knew of a rock in Cyrenaica which it was forbidden to touch for fear of unleashing the south wind. Sources of

68. J. Desanges, 1962, pp. 89–90, 129, 228–9. The Oreipaei Eropaei are perhaps the ancestors of the dark-skinned Rebäya.

69. G. Camps, 1961, p. 461.

70. See the recent work of M. Leglay, 1966, p. 420 and note 7, p. 421 and note 1; W. Vychichl, 1972, pp. 623–4.

71. E. Gobert, pp. 24–110; W. Vychichl, 1972, p. 679.

fresh water, in particular springs and wells, were also worshipped. In the fourth century of our era, St Augustine tells us that on Midsummer Day the Numides practised ritual immersion in the sea. Tree-worship was not unknown: a fourth-century African synod requested the emperor to abolish idolatry 'even in forests and trees'. Sea-bathing at the summer solstice and the worship of waters or trees were manifestations of a glorification of fecundity which, according to Nicholas of Damascus (C. Müller, *Fragmenta Hist. Graec.*, III, p. 462, *Frag. 135*), a contemporary of Augustus, is expressed in the most direct manner by the Dapsolibues: soon after the Pleiades had set, as night darkened, the women withdrew, extinguishing their lights. The men then joined them, each mating with the partner to whom chance had united him. There is reason to believe that these 'Dapsolibues' were in reality the Dapsilo-Libues or 'rich-Libyans', which would amply explain their taste for fertility rites on 'the night of errors'.

Animals symbolizing most obviously the power to procreate – the bull, the lion and the ram – are precisely those which the Libyans venerated. Corippus tells (*Iohannis*, IV, pp. 666–73) how the Laguantan (or Lewâta) of Syrtis would let loose a bull representing their god Gurzil, son of Ammon, on their enemies. Both the royal tomb of Kbor Roumia near Cherchel and the princely mausoleum at Dougga are decorated with images of lions. But it was the ram that was the main object of a cult.[72] which probably spread throughout Africa before the Sahara became a desert. Athanasius (*Contra gentes*, 24) informs us that the ram was considered as a divinity by the Libyans under the name of Amon. Mention should also be made of the fish-cult characteristic of the area which is now Tunisia: it partly explains the wealth of fish images found in Tunisian mosaics. The fish – a phallic symbol – warded off the evil eye. A fish-shaped phallus ejaculating between two female pudenda is shown in a mosaic from Susa. Alongside the fish, the shell was widespread as a symbol of the female sex throughout Africa Minor; it served the living as a charm and comforted the dead in their tombs.

Other parts of the human body were regarded as the receptacles of supernatural powers, in particular the hair. G. Charles-Picard[73] has drawn attention to the custom among Libyans of wearing the hair in a single braid piled in a crest on top of the head. This is in evidence from the time of the Egyptian frescoes to that of the Libyan hermes of the Antonine baths, not overlooking the Macae of Herodotus (IV, 175). If we believe Strabo (XVII, 3, 7) the Maurusians avoided getting too close to each other while out walking so as not to disarrange their hair-styles. Rather than being a sign of coquetry, this doubtless indicated a religious fear of a threat to their virility. Probably for the same reason, among the women

72. G. Charles-Picard, 1954; M. Leglay, 1966; W. Vychichl, 1972, pp. 695–7.
73. G. Charles-Picard, 1954, p. 14.

of the Adyrmachidae delousing was accompanied by a vengeance rite (Herodotus, IV, 168).

A man was surrounded with care after death. It is in the religious realm that archaeology is most revealing about the Libyco-Berbers. G. Camps's monumental thesis[74] gives us material for a brief sketch. The body was generally buried on its side and bent or folded up. Before this was done, the bones were often stripped of the flesh and even more frequently bones or flesh were coated in red ochre which was thought to restore life to the corpse. Food was supplied, and amulets were placed to protect him in his after-life. There were animal offerings, such as a horse, and occasionally a ritual murder was perpetrated so that the dead might retain a faithful servant. Members of his family joined him in his tomb when they died, including in many cases, especially in Orania and Morocco, the spouse, thus showing that monogamy, or at least selective polygamy, was widely practised.

Sacrifices in honour of the dead were performed in front of their tombs in a reserved area facing the rising sun. Sometimes the vital force of the dead man was symbolized by means of a monumental stone in the form of an obelisk or a stele. Herodotus (IV, 172) informs us that the Nasamonians consulted their ancestors about the future by sleeping on their tombs. G. Camps believes that this incubation ritual is the reason for the existence of the bazinas and tumuli of platform shape, but the Saharan monuments incorporating a chapel and chamber appear to be the best adapted to this custom. It was probably widespread throughout the Saharan populations, since they expressed astonishment at the fact that the Atlantes (Herodotus, IV, 184) never had any visions in sleep.

Herodotus also reports (IV, 172) that the Nasamonians, when taking an oath, laid a hand on the tomb of one considered to have been pre-eminently just and good. This seems to be a sign of an emergent cult of the dead. Protohistorical archaeology shows that entire cemeteries were built up around certain tombs. Men held in particular esteem while living could thus gather around them a host of sepulchres, and no doubt living crowds also. G. Camps rightly wonders[75] whether the worship of the famous dead did not lead to the building or remodelling of the population groupings of which there is evidence in the Punic and Roman periods. As soon as a kingdom was founded, a cult of its dead sovereigns would naturally spring up.

The Libyans do not appear to have worshipped major god figures represented in a more or less human form. According to Herodotus (IV, 188) they only sacrificed to the sun and the moon. However, those of the Djerid area were more inclined to offer sacrifices to Athena, Triton and

74. G. Camps, 1961, pp. 461–566. We can only attempt here to give a very brief summary of this survey of archaeological data.
75. G. Camps, 1961, p. 564.

Poseidon, while the Atarantians (IV, 184), the westerly neighbours of the Garamantes, cursed the sun. Cicero relates (*Rep.*, VI, 4) that Massinissa gave thanks to the sun and other divinities in the sky. The sun continued to be worshipped in several towns of Roman Africa such as Maktar, Althiburos, Thugga and Sufetula, but some Punic influence may have been at work here and there.[76]

Apart from the two major heavenly bodies, both epigraphy and literary sources reveal a profusion of divinities, often mentioned only once, and sometimes even referred to collectively, e.g. the Dii Mauri.[77] A carving found near Baja appears to picture a kind of pantheon of seven divinities. But this no doubt reflects a kind of polytheism introduced under Punic influence, which led the Libyans to personalize the divine powers. Left to themselves, the Libyans were always drawn more to the sacred than to the gods.[78]

PLATE 17.1 right *Lions from Kbor Roumia*

PLATE 17.2 left *Libyan stela from Abizar* (*southeast of Tigzirt*): a bas-relief sculpture of an armed horseman. The left hand holds a round shield and three javelins; the right arm is extended, with an indeterminate round object between the thumb and the index finger. Seated on the horse's rump is a small figure whose left hand is touching the warrior, and whose right hand, which is also raised, holds a weapon. The horseman has a triangular, pointed beard down to his chest. Around its neck, the horse has an amulet, possibly a phallus. In front of the horse are two animals, one a quadruped, perhaps a dog, the other apparently a bird, perhaps an ostrich.

76. G. Charles-Picard, 1957, pp. 33–9.
77. G. Camps, 1954, pp. 233–60.
78. Concerning the theory that there was one major god for the Libyco-Berbers, see M. Leglay, 1966, pp. 425–31. After ruling out Iolaos, Baliddir and Iuch, the author expresses the view, that the Theban Amon was on the way to becoming the prevailing god in Saharan Africa and Africa Minor when the Phoenicians made their appearance on the continent. This is an attractive theory, but we do not find it fully proven.

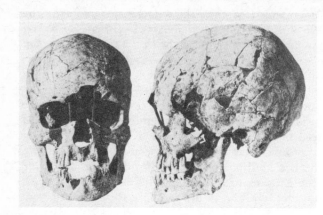

PLATE 17.3 *Skull of Champlain man: left,* norma facialis; *right,* norma lateralis sinistra

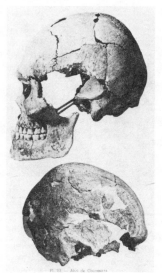

PLATE 17.4 *Skull of Columnata man: top,* cranium norma lateralis; *bottom,* calva norma lateralis dextra

PLATE 17.5 *Skull of Capsian man: left,* norma facialis; *right,* norma lateralis sinistra

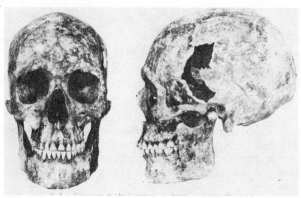

# The Carthaginian period

## 18

### B. H. WARMINGTON

The entry of the Maghrib into recorded history begins with the arrival on its coasts of sailors and settlers from Phoenicia. The reconstruction of the history of this period is complicated by the fact that the sources are almost all Greek and Roman, and for these two peoples the Phoenicians of the west, especially under the leadership of Carthage, were for most of it bitter enemies. Hence the picture in the sources is a hostile one. No Carthaginian literature has survived;[1] the contribution made by archaeology is also limited because in most cases the Phoenician settlements are overlaid by much more substantial Roman towns, though in the last two decades some progress has been made. There are a large number of inscriptions in various forms of the Phoenician language but almost all are tomb or votive inscriptions which tell us little.

The development of the indigenous Libyan cultures before the third century is likewise to some degree obscure. The Neolithic in the Capsian tradition continued in the Maghrib well into the first millennium before our era and there was little that could be described as a separate Bronze Age. The archaeological picture of the first millennium is therefore one of continuing slow evolution but with Phoenician influences operating with increasing effect from about the fourth century. The particular phenomenon of widespread large stone-built surface tombs appears to have no connection with the much earlier megalithic cultures of northern Europe, and it seems probable that they are to be dated to our period. The largest, such as the tumulus of Mzora and the Medracen, are probably connected with the growth of larger tribal units in the fourth or third centuries. There is a marked degree of uniformity throughout the Maghrib.

---

1. S. Moscati, p. 113: 'Greek and Latin authors chiefly concentrated their attention on the wars first between Carthage and Syracuse and later between Carthage and Rome. Here the accounts are comprehensive, detailed and written soon after the events. With regard to the rest of Carthaginian history the information is sporadic. Aristotle's observations on the Punic Constitution, Polybius' account of the revolt of the mercenaries, the Greek version of Hanno's inscription, the list of Carthage's dominions in Africa in the middle of the fourth century given by Pseudo-Skylax, are examples taken from a scattered and disorganized documentation, full of lacunae and frequently difficult to assemble.'

Greek and Roman authors refer to a large number of different tribes by name, but for the period under review generally divide the non-Phoenician inhabitants of the Maghrib into three main groups. In the west, between the Atlantic and the Mulucca (Moulouya), were the Mauri, and the name Mauretania, earlier Maurousia, was given to their territory, but later the designation was extended much farther east beyond the Chelif. Between the Mauri and the maximum western extension of the Carthaginians' inland territory (see below) were the Numidae with their territory Numidia. Although the Greeks and Romans incorrectly derived the name Numidae from a Greek word meaning 'to graze' and held it to be descriptive of their way of life, i.e. nomadic, there appears to be no essential difference between the inhabitants of the two areas; semi-nomadic pastoralism dominated both, though there were already areas of sedentary life and regular agriculture, which continued to increase. There was in addition fairly close contact between Mauretania and southern Spain where similar cultures existed. The third group were the Gaetuli, the name given to true nomads along the northern fringes of the Sahara. The classical names for these groups, and for individual tribes, are used throughout this chapter.

## The earliest Phoenician settlements

The universal tradition of antiquity was that Tyre was the Phoenician city responsible for the expeditions of the Phoenicians to the west, leading to numerous settlements. The pre-eminence of Tyre among the cities of Phoenicia in the period following the destruction of the Bronze Age civilizations in the Near East in the thirteenth century is attested by biblical and other sources. Tyre and the other cities (such as Sidon and Byblus) from about − 1000 were the most active trading cities in the eastern Aegean and Near East, little interrupted by the growth of the Assyrian empire. The motive which sent Phoenician traders into the western Mediterranean was the search for sources of metal, in particular gold, silver, copper and tin. This led them at an early date to Spain, which remained one of the chief sources of silver in the Mediterranean world even in the Roman period. The general picture is probably correctly summarized for us by the historian Diodorus Siculus (first century) who says that 'the natives [i.e. of Spain] were ignorant of the use of silver till the Phoenicians on their trading voyages acquired it in exchange for a small quantity of merchandise; carrying it to Greece, Asia and other countries they gained great wealth. Their power also increased through this commerce, carried on for a long time, and they were able to send out numerous colonies to Sicily and the neighbouring islands, to Africa, Sardinia and Spain itself.' Traditionally the earliest Phoenician foundation in the west was on the site of the modern Cadiz, the name itself deriving from the Phoenician Gadir, meaning a fort, presumably representing its origin as a trading post.

The long sea route to the new markets of Spain needed protecting, especially in the sailing conditions of antiquity when it was the general practice to hug the coast and anchor or beach the ship at night. The Phoenicians used both a northern route, along the southern coasts of Sicily, Sardinia and the Balearic Islands, and a southern one, along the coast of North Africa. Along the latter route it has been estimated that there was probably an anchorage used by the Phoenicians every 30 miles or so, though the development of such anchorages into permanent settlements depended on various factors; the classic sites were offshore islands or promontories with landing-places on either side. Utilization of such sites was not particularly difficult for the Phoenicians since the cultural and hence political and military level of the inhabitants of the Maghrib, and for that matter of most of the western Mediterranean, was inferior to theirs. In addition, general strategic factors led to the advancement of some sites as opposed to others; it is significant that three of the most important, Carthage and Utica (Utique) in North Africa, and Motya (Mozia) in Sicily, are all well placed on the narrows leading from the eastern into the western Mediterranean and dominate both the southern and northern routes.

## Foundation of Carthage

The name Carthage (Latin: *Carthago*) represents the Phoenician name Kart Hadasht, meaning New City. This may imply that the place was destined from the start to be the chief settlement of the Phoenicians in the west, but we know too little of the archaeology of its earliest period to be certain of this. The traditional date for the foundation is −814, long after the traditional dates for Cadiz (−1110) and Utica (−1101). These latter dates have a legendary appearance. As for the date of Carthage, the earliest uncontested archaeological material is of the middle of the eighth century before our era, that is, within a couple of generations of the traditional date. Nothing of historical value can be derived from the foundation legends transmitted to us in various versions by Greek and Roman authors. Material of about the same date comes from Utica, and of seventh- or sixth-century date from Leptis Magna (Lebda), Hadrumetum (Sousse), Tipasa, Siga (Rachgoun), Lixus (on the Oued Loukkos) and Mogador, the last being the most distant Phoenician settlement so far known. Finds of parallel date have been made at Motya in Sicily, Nora (Nuri), Sulcis and Tharros (Torre di S. Giovanni) in Sardinia and at Cadiz and Almunecar in Spain. The general coherence of the archaeological evidence indicates that, while individual voyages may have been made earlier, permanent settlements on the coast of the Maghrib were not made before − 800. It must be emphasized that unlike the settlements which the Greeks were making in Sicily and Italy and elsewhere in the eighth and seventh centuries, all the Phoenician settlements, including Carthage itself, remained small places, with perhaps no more than a few hundred settlers at most, for

443

generations; further, they long remained politically subordinate to Tyre, as was to be expected having regard to their prime function as anchorages and supply points.

## Carthaginian leadership of the western Phoenicians

The emergence of Carthage as an independent city, followed by her leadership of the rest of the Phoenicians in the west and the creation of an empire based in North Africa, with profound historical consequences for the whole of the western Mediterranean area, began in the sixth century before our era. One reason was the weakening of the power of Tyre and the Phoenician homeland and their subjection to the Babylonian empire. More significant appears to have been growing pressure from the Greek settlements in Sicily. The most important of these, such as Syracuse, had grown in wealth and population with great rapidity; they had been founded primarily as a result of population pressures in Greece itself. During the seventh century there appears to have been no great conflict between Phoenicians and Greeks, and Greek imports are known from many Phoenician sites in the Maghrib; but in − 580 the city of Selinus (Selinunte) and other Sicilian Greeks tried to drive the Phoenicians from their settlements at Motya and Palermo. Carthage appears to have taken the lead in repelling this attack, which if successful would have led the Greeks on to threaten the Phoenician settlements in Sardinia and opened the Spanish trade from which they had so far been excluded. Following this success the Phoenician settlements on Sardinia were consolidated. Also during this century an alliance was formed between Carthage and Etruscan cities on the west coast of Italy. A joint victory in about − 535 prevented Greeks from settling on Corsica. A final success in this period was in Africa itself; a Spartan named Dorieus tried to found a settlement at the mouth of the Kinyps river (Oued Oukirri) in Libya. Carthage regarded this as an intrusion and within three years was able to drive out the Greeks with help from the native Libyans.

The burden of leadership of the Phoenicians of the west seems to have been too heavy for the manpower available for Carthage. Up to the sixth century they relied, as did the city states of Greece, on their own citizens. In the middle of the century under the leadership of Mago, founder of a dominant family in the city, the policy of hiring mercenary troops on a large scale was initiated, a policy followed for the remainder of Carthaginian history. Of the non-Carthaginian elements which were hired, the Libyans provided the biggest share, which became still larger when Carthage acquired territory in the interior and levied troops compulsorily (see below). They were particularly useful as light infantry. As mercenaries, or under treaties of alliance at a later date, Numidian and Mauretanian cavalry from the northern parts of modern Algeria and Morocco were a significant part of all large Carthaginian armies; Spanish, Gallic, Italian and finally Greek mercenaries are found in the service of Carthage at various dates. The policy was more successful than is normally admitted and it is unlikely that Carthage could ever have sustained the long wars in which she was engaged on the basis of her own limited population.

The generation after the success against Dorieus saw profound changes among the Greek cities of Sicily, which reacted seriously on Carthage. Gelon, ruler of Gela and from −485 of Syracuse, initiated a war to avenge Dorieus and planned a campaign to conquer the area of Phoenician settlement around the Gulf of Gabes. As a result, Carthage sought friends in Sicily among those opposed to Gelon and in −480 put a large mercenary army into the island, perhaps taking advantage of the fact that the same year saw the invasion of Greece by Persia. A figure for the Carthaginian fleet at this date is given as 200 ships, which puts it on a par with that of Syracuse and not much less than that of Athens. However, the intervention ended in complete disaster with the destruction of the army and the fleet at a great battle at Himera. Gelon was unable or unwilling to follow up this success and allowed peace on a moderate war indemnity.

## Expansion in North Africa

The defeat was followed by seventy years of peace in which Carthage avoided conflict with the Greeks but yet was able to maintain her trading monopoly. More important, she turned towards the acquisition of territory in Africa itself. This change occurred as Carthage was increasingly isolated by Greek success elsewhere, first against the Persians, in which the Phoenicians lost heavily, and against the Etruscans in Italy. It is possible that the Carthaginians sought to restrict their own trade with the Greek world – certainly the grave contents of the fifth century look poor and austere, with little imported material. This does not imply, however, that the community as a whole was more impoverished than before, since grave-goods are not in themselves indicators of wealth or poverty. The new policy is associated with the Magonid family, led at this time by Hanno, son of the Hamilcar who had been defeated at Himera, and is loosely described by the late Greek writer Dio Chrysostom as 'transforming the Carthaginians from Tyrians into Africans'.

While the amount of land conquered in the fifth century and the number of settlements now grown to towns, even if small, is uncertain, it began to approach the maximum which Carthage ever controlled. Most important was conquest of the Cap Bon peninsula and a considerable area of land to the south of Carthage, at least as far as Dougga. This included some of the most fertile land in Tunisia, an area where later Roman settlement was particularly dense. It provided the essential supply of food and the possibility of a much larger population in the city. Many Carthaginians had estates in Cap Bon at a later date. Land in Cap Bon counted as city land and the inhabitants were presumably reduced to servile or semi-servile status. Inhabitants of the rest of the conquered territory were obliged to pay tribute and provide troops.

The number of Phoenician settlements on the coast was added to by those now sent out by Carthage herself, though we are ignorant of some of their names. Like the original settlements, they were small places, of a few hundred, established where native inhabitants came to trade their goods, as is indicated by the fact that the Greeks called them *emporia* – markets.

The boundary between the Carthaginian empire and the area of Greek colonization in Cyrenaica was on the Gulf of Sidra, but settlements on the coast of Libya were few. The most important was at Lepcis where it is probable that permanent settlement was made when the expedition of Dorieus to the vicinity showed that there was a danger of Greek intrusion. At Sabratha, there was a settlement by the early fourth century. Lepcis became the administrative centre of the settlements round the Gulf of Gabes and is known to have been a wealthy place at the end of the Carthaginian period, and its Phoenician culture even remained dominant for over a century under Roman rule. The source of its wealth is generally held to be trans-Saharan trade, since the area was the terminus of the shortest route by way of Cidamus (Ghadames) to the Niger. However, we do not know in what this trade consisted, except that semi-precious stones are mentioned. The agricultural wealth of the area in Roman times owed its origin to the Carthaginian settlers. Further sites on the Gulf of Gabes were Zouchis, which became well known for its salted fish and purple dye, Gigthis (Bou Ghirarah) and Tacapae (Gabes). Continuing north- wards, Thaenae (or Tina) was where the southern limit of the city's inland territory reached the sea. Traditionally Lepcis Minor and Hadrumetum were founded from Phoenicia, not Carthage, and the latter became the largest town on the east coast of Tunisia. From Neapolis (Nabeul) a road ran across the base of Cap Bon to Carthage.

West of Carthage lay Utica, second only to Carthage in importance; it was, like Carthage, a port though now seven miles inland. It retained at least a nominal independence of Carthage till a late stage. Beyond it, the coast as far as the Straits of Gibraltar offered a number of anchorages but few of them developed to the same degree as those on the Tunisian coast, no doubt primarily because of the greater difficulty of access into the interior. Known or probable sites include Hippo Acra (Bizerta), Hippo Regius (Bone), Rusicade (Skikda), Tipasa and Icosium (Algiers). A number of places in Roman times (besides Rusicade) contained the Phoenician element *rus* meaning 'cape', e.g. Rusucurru (Dellys) and Rusguniae (Natifou). Tingi (Tangiers) is referred to in the fifth century but was presumably known to the Phoenicians as soon as they regularly sailed to Cadiz.

# The empire of Carthage

Carthage was criticized by its enemies for the harsh treatment and exploitation of her subjects, and there were certainly several categories among these. The most privileged were doubtless the old Phoenician settlements and those established by Carthage herself, whose inhabitants were called Libyphoenicians (the African Phoenicians) by the Greeks. They appear to have had local officials and institutions similar to those of Carthage herself (see below), as did (it is known) Gades (Cadiz), Tharros and the Phoenicians of Malta. They had to pay dues on imports and exports and sometimes troops were levied from them; it is also likely that they took part in the manning of the Carthaginian fleet. After −348 they seem to have been forbidden to trade with anyone except Carthage. The position of Carthaginian subjects in Sicily was affected by their proximity to Greek cities; they were allowed their own institutions and issued their own coinage throughout the fifth century in a period when Carthage herself did not coin. Their trade does not seem to have been restricted; on the analogy of Roman practice when Sicily fell to Rome, a tribute of one-tenth of the produce was levied.

The Libyans of the interior were the worst off, though tribal structures appear to have been permitted to them. It seems that Carthaginian officials directly supervised the collection of tribute and the enrolment of soldiers. The normal exaction of tribute seems to have been one-quarter of the crops, and at a critical point in the first war with Rome 50 per cent was taken. According to the Greek historian Polybius (second century), many Libyans took part in the destructive mercenary revolt which followed Carthage's defeat in the war out of hatred for this and other actions; 'the Carthaginians had admired and honoured not those governors who had treated their subjects with moderation and humanity but those who had exacted the greatest amount of supplies and treated the inhabitants most ruthlessly'. This appears to have been a justified criticism, as there were a number of Libyan revolts apart from the one mentioned and the Carthaginians seem to have failed to pursue policies aimed at inducing the conquered populations to acquiesce in their condition.

# Carthaginian trade and exploration

## West Africa

There was general agreement among Greeks and Romans that Carthage depended more on trade than any other city, and when they thought of a typical Carthaginian they thought of a merchant. Further, it was believed that Carthage was the wealthiest city in the Mediterranean world. However, it must be said that both the trade itself and the alleged wealth have left remarkably few traces for the archaeologist, much less, for example, than in the case of major Greek and Etruscan cities of the same era. Undoubtedly one major reason in the case of Carthage is that the bulk of her trade was in items which left no trace, primarily metals in unworked state – the primary object of Phoenician exploration in the first place – textiles, slaves and, increasingly as her fertile lands were worked, foodstuffs. The profits from the trade with backward tribes, from whom gold, silver, tin and presumably iron (since Carthage is known to have made her own weapons) were obtained in exchange for cheap manufactures, are indicated by the vast mercenary armies she could raise in the fourth and third centuries and a mintage of gold coinage far in excess of that of other advanced cities. The active leadership of the state in major trading enterprises is indicated in our sources, particularly those concerned with West Africa. According to Herodotus (fifth century), the Egyptian King Necho (*c.* −610 to −594) sent Phoenician mariners to sail down the Red Sea and thence to circumnavigate Africa. They are said to have taken two years on the journey, having twice halted to sow and reap a crop of wheat. Herodotus believed that the voyage had been successful and it is not impossible, but it had no repercussions at the time; if it took place, the vast size of the continent thus revealed must have removed any ideas of a route from the Red Sea to the Mediterranean. The Carthaginians who, again according to Herodotus, believed that Africa could be circumnavigated, must have known of the venture, and of another of the early fifth century. A Persian prince procured a ship in Egypt on orders to attempt the circumnavigation in the opposite direction; he appears to have sailed down the Moroccan coast a good distance beyond Cape Spartel but was forced to return. Herodotus also gives an account of Carthaginian trade on the Moroccan coast. Writing about −430 he says:

> The Carthaginians also inform us about a part of Africa and its inhabitants beyond the Straits of Gibraltar. When they reach this country, they unload their goods and arrange them on the beach; they then return to their ships and send up a smoke signal. When the natives see the smoke, they come down to the sea and place a quantity of gold in exchange for the goods and then retire. The Carthaginians then come ashore again and examine the gold that has been left; if they think it represents the value of the goods they collect it and sail away; if not, they return to their ships and wait until the natives have added sufficient gold to satisfy them. Neither side tricks the other; the Carthaginians never touch the gold until it equals in value what they have brought for sale, and the natives do not touch the goods till the gold has been taken away.

Such is the earliest description we have of the classic method of dumb barter. This gold trade is normally associated with a much discussed Greek text which claims to be a translation of the report of a voyage down the Moroccan coast by one Hanno, identified as the leader of the Magonid family in the middle of the fifth century and the statesman also responsible for Carthaginian expansion elsewhere in Africa. The difficulties of interpretation preclude a full discussion; in general it may be said that in view of the known Carthaginian policy of excluding all other traders from the area the likelihood of their producing for public view a report which was in any way revealing is unlikely. Furthermore the document does not even mention any purpose for the voyage. The most concrete part deals with the planting of settlements on the Moroccan coast. That there were such settlements is known; Lixus, at the mouth of the Oued Loukkos, was certainly one – it is not mentioned by Hanno – and the later history of the tribes of the area (see below) shows the cultural influence of Carthage. The most southerly settlement mentioned in the report is called Cerne, generally identified with Hern Island at the mouth of the Rio de Oro. This name is mentioned in another Greek geographical source known as Pseudo-Scylax of about −338. 'At Cerne, the Phoenicians [i.e. Carthaginians] anchor their *gauloi* as their merchant ships are called and pitch tents on the island. After unloading their goods they take them to the mainland in small boats; there live Ethiopians with whom they trade. In exchange for their goods they acquire the skins of deer, lions and leopards, elephant hides and tusks ... the Phoenicians bring perfume, Egyptian stones [? faience] and Athenian pottery and jars.' Again there is no mention of gold; Cerne appears as an anchorage rather than a settlement. The goods brought from Carthage look correct, but the acquisition of wild animal skins has been doubted on the grounds that these were obtained much nearer Carthage. Hanno's report concludes with an account of two voyages even farther south than Cerne, with graphic descriptions of ferocious inhabitants, drums in the night and rivers of fire, presumably designed to inspire alarm among any possible competitors. The southern limit of the voyage has been put as far distant as Mount Cameroon, but this seems altogether too far. The most southerly point producing archaeological evidence of Carthaginian visits is Mogador, but the evidence is of seasonal visits confined to the sixth century and it cannot be identified with any place in the report.

If gold was the objective, it is remarkable that all knowledge of the trade disappeared with the fall of Carthage even though some settlements on the Moroccan coast survived. The Greek historian Polybius sailed beyond Cerne after −146 but discovered nothing worthwhile, and in the first century of our era the Roman writer Pliny wrote of the report of Hanno, 'many Greeks and Romans on the basis of it tell of many fabulous things and of many foundations of cities of which in fact neither memory nor trace remain'. Oddly enough Mogador began to be visited again by sailors from the Roman client state of Mauretania (see below), but it seems that fish rather than gold was the purpose.

## The Atlantic

A report of another voyage led by Hanno's contemporary Himilco was known in antiquity but only scattered references survive. It explored the Atlantic coast of Spain and France, and certainly reached as far as Brittany. The object was probably to increase direct control of the trade in tin obtained from various sources close to the Atlantic coasts. A number of ancient writers were interested in the trade, no doubt because the Carthaginians allowed so little information to emerge. In fact, the Carthaginian period was the last stage in the trade in tin along this coast which went back to prehistoric times, with south-west Britain as one of its most important sources. However, there is no evidence that any Phoenician ever reached Britain; no Phoenician object has ever been found there (nor, for that matter, in Brittany). If tin from Britain was obtained it was probably through the intermediary activity of tribes in Brittany. There is the likelihood that most tin from British sources was transported across Gaul to the Rhône Valley and the Mediterranean, and that the Carthaginians got most of theirs from northern Spain. In any case, the most valuable mineral produce in Spain was silver; we know that in the third century the production reached impressive levels and it was undoubtedly of far greater importance than tin. It was from the fifth century that Cadiz grew rapidly in importance. It was the only Carthaginian dependant in the west apart from Ibiza to issue its own coins, and according to the Greek geographer Strabo its shipbuilders excelled all others in the vessels they built for both Mediterranean and Atlantic waters.

## Mediterranean trade

As stated, Carthage exercised a monopoly of trade within her empire, either sinking any intruding vessel or arranging commercial treaties with possible competitors like the Etruscan cities and Rome. Normally foreign traders were not allowed to trade west of Carthage; this meant that goods they brought to that city were then moved and traded in Carthaginian vessels. It was by these ways that products from Etruria, Campania, Egypt and various Greek cities reached a large number of North African sites. The manufactures of Carthage are not easy to identify archaeologically because they lack individual style and merit. This may even have been an economic asset in the fourth century, particularly after the major economic and political changes in the western Mediterranean brought about the conquests of Alexander the Great. These created larger markets of a more cosmopolitan kind for cheap manufactures which the Carthaginians were well placed to exploit. It was only in the fourth century that Carthage began to issue her own coins as her trade with advanced powers increased, and as the changed economic scene made it necessary also to pay mercenaries in coin.

## Saharan trade

The problem of Carthaginian contacts with Saharan peoples, and people living even farther south, is obscure. If communications or contacts existed they must have been based on Leptis Magna and Sabratha, since it is in this region that there are the fewest natural obstacles. Carthaginian concern to keep Greeks from the area has been cited as evidence that trade of some substance with the interior existed, since suitable agricultural land for settlement is scarce. In the fifth century Herodotus knew of two tribal groups, the Garamantes and Nasamones, in the regions south of the Syrtic gulf; he also said that it took thirty days to get from the coast to the region of the former tribe, presumably the population of Garama (Germa). It was via the Garamantes that the Romans obtained more knowledge of the interior of Africa centuries later. A late story says that a Carthaginian named Mago crossed the desert three times. Unfortunately, up to the present such trade as existed has left no archaeological trace whatever, and in literature only carbuncles are mentioned as an article of desert commerce. Slaves were perhaps traded – the Garamantes are said to have pursued Ethiopians (i.e. Negro peoples) in four-horse chariots; ivory and skins are suggested, though these were readily available in the Maghreb; and gold from the Sudan is still more problematical, though not impossible. Recent archaeological evidence from Germa indicates that the earliest population growth is from the fifth or fourth century and that over succeeding centuries a considerable sedentary population based on agriculture grew up. This may be due to cultural influences extending from the Carthaginian sites on the coast. After the destruction of Carthage the Romans penetrated both to Germa and Ghadames and occasionally farther south, and there are some archaeological traces of imports from the Mediterranean world into the interior, but on a modest scale. The lack at this time of camels in North Africa explains the difficulty and irregularity of trans-Saharan travel. Even if Saharan conditions were not so severe in ancient as they have been in more recent times, this absence would make trade on any large scale extremely difficult. The integration of the Sahara and trans-Saharan regions into a wider cultural environment must therefore be dated to the early Arab period.

## The city of Carthage

Although Carthage had the reputation of possessing enormous wealth this is not manifested for us in the archaeology, even allowing for the complete destruction of the city by the Romans. This is not to say that there were no important buildings as in other ancient cities of similar size. Carthage had an elaborate double artificial harbour, the outer for the use of merchant ships – how many could use it at one time is not known – and the inner which had quays and sheds for 220 warships, together with a control building sufficiently high to give a view over intervening buildings out to sea. The city walls were of exceptional dimensions and held out against every attack till the final Roman assault. The total length (including that along the sea) was about 22 miles, the crucial sector of the two-and-a-half miles across the isthmus of Carthage being 40 feet high and 30 feet thick. An inner citadel with an *enceinte* of about two miles enclosed the hill known as Byrsa, no doubt the oldest part of the city. Between the harbour and the Byrsa was an open public space equivalent to a Greek *agora*, but it does not seem that it ever had the regular planned or monumental aspect which came to characterize Greek cities. The city seems to have developed unplanned, with narrow winding streets, and we hear of buildings up to six storeys in height, as at Tyre itself and at Motya in Sicily. As for temples, although these are said to have been numerous, they are unlikely to have been substantial till the later stages of Carthaginian history when Greek cultural influence became pronounced, since most of the evidence goes to show that the Carthaginians were essentially conservative in religious matters and long remained faithful to the concept of simple enclosures without monumental buildings. The population at its height can only be the subject of an educated guess; a figure of 700 000 given by Strabo is an impossible density but may refer to the city and the whole of the Cap Bon area. A more likely figure of 400 000, including slaves, would put Carthage on a par with Athens of the fifth century.

## Carthaginian political institutions

The only aspect of Carthage to receive praise from Greeks and Romans was its political constitution which seemed to ensure the stability so highly cherished in antiquity. Details are obscure, and it is not always certain that they have properly understood the facts, but the main outlines seem to be as follows. Hereditary kingship prevailed in the Phoenician cities till hellenistic times, and all our sources likewise refer to kingship at Carthage; for example, Hamilcar, defeated at Himera, and Hanno, the leader of the African expansion, are so described. It is probable that in calling them kings the classical authors were thinking as much of their sacral and judicial as their political and military powers. The position was in principle elective, not hereditary, but several generations of the Magonid family held the position. During the sixth and fifth centuries they appear also to have been the military leaders of the state when occasion demanded. During the fifth century a process began whereby the power of the kings was diminished. This appears to be associated with the rise to power of the *sufets*, the only Carthaginian political term transcribed for us by Roman writers. The word combines the meaning of judge and governor and since in the third century two (perhaps more) were elected annually, it was easy to compare them with Roman consuls; and the term *sufet* remained in use in North Africa in areas of Carthaginian culture for at least a century after the Roman conquest, to denote the chief magistrate of a town. The reduction in the power of the kings was similar to developments in Greek cities and in Rome. At the same time the power of a wealthy aristocracy increased. In addition to their exclusive membership of a council of state like the Roman senate, the aristocracy established a court of 100 members apparently with the specific function of controlling all organs of government. Although the citizen body had some say in election of kings, *sufets* and other officials, it is certain that Carthaginian politics were always dominated by the rich – Aristotle considered the part played by wealth at Carthage to be a bad feature. Both birth and wealth were essential for election. All matters were decided by kings or *sufets* and council in concert, and only if they disagreed were assemblies of the citizens consulted. In the fourth or third century command of the armed forces was entirely divorced from other offices; generals were appointed only as needed for specific campaigns, since the state had no standing army requiring a permanent commander; several families, the Magonids in early history, and the Barcids (see below) later, developed a military tradition. It is notable that Carthage never succumbed to a *coup d'état* led by an ambitious general, as was the frequent fate of Greek cities especially in Sicily; presumably the organs of supervision and control were effective. The fact that from the early fifth century Carthaginian citizens were immune from military service except at rare intervals probably prevented them from developing a sense of their own strength which was such a potent factor in the growth of democratic tendencies in Greece and Rome.

## Carthaginian religion

While their political institutions were praised, Carthaginian religious life was severely criticized by classical authors above all because of the persistence of human sacrifice. The intensity of religious beliefs was likewise commented on. Naturally the cults at Carthage have similarities with those of Phoenicia from which they derived. The supreme male deity of the Phoenician world was known in Africa as Baal Hammon, the meaning of the epithet Hammon apparently being fiery and expressive of his solar aspect. He was identified in Roman times with Saturn. In the fifth century he was outstripped, at any rate in popular worship, by a goddess named Tanit. The name is apparently Libyan and the growth of her cult is associated with the acquisition of territory in Africa, because it had pronounced fertility aspects, owing much to the Greek goddesses Hera and Demeter. Crude representations of a female figure with arms raised occur on hundreds of stelae from Carthage and elsewhere. These two deities overshadowed the rest, though we know also of Astarte, Eshmoun (identified with Aesculapius the divine healer) and Melkart, the particular protector of the mother city Tyre. The institution of human sacrifice is proved archaeologically by discoveries not only at Carthage and Hadrumetum but also at Cirta, in Libyan territory but much influenced by Carthaginian culture, and at a number of settlements outside Africa. The discoveries are of sacred enclosures containing urns with the calcined bones of children, often marked by stelae referring to a sacrificial offering generally to Baal Hammon but often to Tanit as well. According to our sources (which have doubtful features) the sacrifices were always of males, were annual, and an obligation on the leading families. The practice certainly declined but an incident in − 310 shows that it could be revived in moments of crisis when its neglect was held responsible for divine displeasure. There is no doubt that the emphasis of Carthaginian religious ideas was on the necessity of appeasing the capricious power of the gods. The great majority of Carthaginian names were theophoric, no doubt with the same intention; for example, Hamilcar means favoured by Melkart and Hannibal favoured by Baal. Besides human sacrifice, there was an elaborate sacrificial system involving other victims, and a priesthood including both full-time priests and others who were not members of a separate caste. In spite of their contacts with Egypt the Carthaginians appear to have attached little importance to the idea of life after death, in this respect being like the early Hebrews. Inhumation was the general rule and the grave-goods moderate; many tombs contained small grotesque masks of terracotta which are assumed to have an apotropaic significance.

The Carthaginians were far less influenced even at a late date by Greek civilization than the Etruscans and Romans though they were by no means altogether untouched by it. The cult of Demeter and Kore was officially installed in the city but there was no widespread hellenization of the traditional cults. Artistically the minor crafts of Carthage show little influence, but the few remains of the second century show that by that date architectural influences emanating from the Greek world were being felt not only at a Carthaginian site (Dar Essafi in Cap Bon) but also in Libyan territory (Dougga). Phoenician was used as a literary language, but none of its products has survived. We know of a treatise on agriculture by a certain Mago which was translated into Latin, and it is clear that Mago made use of Greek books on the subject; we hear also of some Carthaginian followers of Greek philosophy.

## Conflicts with the Sicilian Greeks

The period of expansion in Africa and peace elsewhere which had lasted since the disaster at Himera ended in −410. The Greek states in Sicily had become involved in the great struggle for supremacy in Greece between Athens and Sparta; and though an Athenian expedition to Sicily had met total disaster the aftermath finally embroiled Carthage. The city of Segesta, a native Sicilian community but allied to Carthage, had been in part responsible for bringing the Athenians into Sicily and was now subject to a major punitive attack by the Greek city of Selinus, and appealed to Carthage. The appeal was accepted, presumably because if Segesta were defeated, Greek control would reduce the Phoenician settlements to a mere toe-hold on the west of the island. In addition, the Carthaginian leader Hannibal turned the expedition into a war to avenge the defeat at Himera in which his grandfather had perished. In $-409$ a mercenary army of perhaps 50 000 laid siege to Selinus and took it by storm after nine days; shortly afterwards Himera was also taken and razed to the ground, with the massacre of all the inhabitants who had not previously fled. Hannibal then returned and disbanded the army, which indicated that there was no thought of extending her territory, though it is clear that from this date the Phoenicians here, together with other territory in Sicily which they dominated, created in effect a Carthaginian province. However, in $-406$ Carthage was tempted to try for the first and only time to conquer the entire island after attacks on her territory by some Syracusans. An even larger force was sent and Acragas, the second largest Greek city, was taken in $-406$, and in $-405$, Gela. But Hannibal was unable to crown his victories with the capture of Syracuse itself; it appears that an epidemic destroyed half his army, and the new ruler of Syracuse was happy to make peace in order to consolidate his own position. The terms confirmed Carthaginian rule over the west of Sicily including both a number of native Sicilian communities and the survivors of Selinus, Acragas and Himera. This left Carthage with a larger territory than she had had before, and more tribute. Furthermore it broke the isolation in which she had been living during most of the fifth century and from this date we find that imports and trade in general with the Greek world revived, in spite of the frequent periods of war. The fact is that the Greeks were not united, being divided among a number of proudly independent cities. Although on a number of occasions calls were made to all of them in Sicily to combine to drive out the Carthaginians from the island they never succeeded, since such calls tended to be opportunistic moves in the interests of individual states or personalities. This was the case with Dionysius of Syracuse, who tried on three occasions, from $-398$ to $-392$, $-383$ to $-375$ and $-368$, to expel the Carthaginians. On each occasion there were remarkable reversals of fortune; in $-398$, for example, the Phoenician city of Motya was taken and destroyed, but in the very next year Syracuse in turn was threatened but saved a second time by an epidemic. Most of the time the Carthaginians were able to maintain the River Halycus (Platani) as the eastern boundary of their territory. Their heterogeneous and hastily raised armies of mercenaries usually proved a match for classical Greek hoplites, and their fleet was generally superior. More significantly she could never be isolated from the Greek world again. There were no Greeks residing in Carthage and the way was open for Carthage to be invited by Greek politicians themselves to intervene, and in general to become a recognized part of the hellenistic world. During the $-350$s she was well on the way to dominating the whole of the island by peaceful means, as internal political strife weakened the Greek cities still further. Only the expedition of an idealistic Corinthian named Timoleon saved the Greek position. It may be noted that at the battle of the river Crimisos ( − 341) an élite force of 3000 Carthaginian citizens was destroyed. This is said to have been the worst loss Carthage ever suffered, which shows how dependent she was on mercenaries.

Africa itself was naturally immune from destruction except that we hear of a revolt in − 368/7 which was easily suppressed. Some time in the 340s, a certain Hanno tried to stage a *coup d'état* by calling on the slave population, African subjects and Mauretanian tribes to join him, but it does not appear that there was a serious threat. Very different was the situation from − 310 to − 307 when Carthage was engaged in yet another war with Syracuse, now ruled by Agathocles. When his city was under siege, the Greek tried a desperate venture; eluding the Carthaginian fleet he landed 14 000 men on Cap Bon, burned his ships and made for Carthage. Except at Carthage itself there were no strong points or garrisons, and a vast amount of damage was done within Carthaginian territory in the three years before he was forced to leave Africa.

## The first war with Rome

These conflicts were, however, on a minor scale compared with the revolutionary changes in the east during the same period, when Alexander the Great created an empire stretching as far as India. But Carthage was soon herself to be engaged in a struggle of at least as great a world-historical importance, namely, with Rome. A treaty existed between them as early as − 508 when Rome was just one of many Italian communities of moderate size. Another treaty was signed in − 348, again regulating trade between the two powers, and though Rome was by now much stronger the treaty was very favourable to Carthage, simply because Rome's trading interests were negligible. In the next decades Rome broke through with dramatic rapidity to become the dominating power throughout Italy. The gap between the areas in which the two powers were interested closed even further when in − 293 Carthage's old enemy Agathocles operated in southern Italy. A few years later, King Pyrrhus of Epirus was invited into Italy to try to liberate the Greek cities of southern Italy, led by Tarantum, from Roman domination. Although he was unsuccessful, he was approached by the Sicilian Greeks to be their protector against Carthage. To try to prevent this, Carthage sent an impressive fleet to Rome to encourage Rome to continue the war with Pyrrhus. She was successful, but Pyrrhus came to Sicily in any case and had some modest but not decisive successes before he returned to Greece in − 276. Thus Carthage and Rome up to this date had no conflict of interests, yet a decade later were involved in a conflict which produced the heaviest losses on both sides of any known war up to that time. Though the result was of geopolitical significance, there is little doubt that the cause of the war was relatively trivial and that neither side had deep-seated aims. In −264 Rome accepted the submission of Messana (Messina) which had previously been an ally of Carthage against Syracuse. Roman politicians at the time were brimming with self-confidence; it appears to have been expected that Carthage would not react, and that there was easy booty to be obtained from the Greek cities of Sicily. Some also played on Roman fears that Carthage, if she held Messana, could dominate Italy, in which in fact she had never had any interest whatever. Carthage determined to resist Roman intervention because it would mean a complete change in the balance of power which had existed in the island for a century and a half, and also no doubt because they felt that Roman policy was dangerously adventurist. The ensuing war (first Punic war) lasted till −242 with massive losses on both sides. Contrary to what one might expect the Carthaginian fleet did not prove superior even though the Romans never had a fleet of any size till −261. Roman naval victories included Mylae in 260, where 10 000 rowers from the Carthaginian fleet were lost, and Cape Ecnomus in −256. But in −255 a Roman fleet was lost in a storm off Cape Camarina with 25 000 soldiers and 70 000 rowers, and there were other defeats to follow on both sides. For some years both were in a state of exhaustion and operations were limited. In another paradox, the Roman legions, already the finest infantry force known, failed to drive the Carthaginians out of Sicily. In −256 the Romans tried the tactic of Agathocles and put an army into Africa. The Carthaginians were defeated at Adys (or Oudna) and the Romans seized Tunis as a base from which to attack Carthage. They failed, however, to take advantage of revolts among Carthage's Numidian subjects. In −255 Carthage hired an experienced Greek mercenary, General Xanthippus, and the Roman force was destroyed. The war finally ended in −242 when the Carthaginian fleet was defeated off the Aegates Islands. This meant that Sicily could no longer be supplied, and a peace of exhaustion followed, in which Carthage gave up Sicily and agreed to a substantial indemnity.

## Hannibal and the second war with Rome

The economic difficulties caused by the war made it difficult to pay the mercenaries, half of whom were Libyans. A revolt took place in Africa characterized by ferocious atrocities on both sides. Some 20 000 mercenaries were involved, one of the most effective leaders being a Libyan named Matho. Carthage itself was at risk and the rebels for a time controlled Utica, Hippo Acra and Tunis; they were well enough organized to issue their own coins with the legend 'Libyon' (meaning of the Libyans) in Greek. The intensity of the struggle, which ended in −237, testified to the harshness of Carthaginian treatment of the Libyans. At the same time the Romans highhandedly seized Sardinia while Carthage was in no position to resist. Resentment at this no doubt stifled any opposition to the projects of Hamilcar Barca, a general who had distinguished himself in Sicily. He set out to extend Carthage's direct control in Spain, where it had previously been limited to coastal stations. The object was twofold – to exploit directly the mineral resources, thus compensating for the loss of Sicilian revenues, and to mobilize the manpower of Spain into an army which could match Rome in the field. Over a period of less than twenty years he and his son-in-law Hasdrubal won control of over half the Iberian peninsula and created an army of some 50 000 men. In −221 Hasdrubal was succeeded in command of the new empire in Spain by Hamilcar's son Hannibal. There is little evidence to support the later Roman view that the whole venture was a private scheme of the Barcids, as the family were called, to take vengeance on Rome, and that they were not supported by the home government. In −220 Rome became anxious about the Carthaginian recovery and engaged in a manoeuvre designed to prevent the consolidation or extension of Carthaginian control in Spain. Hannibal (and his government) rejected Rome's threats and decided, in the light of the adventurist Roman policies in 264 and 237, that war was inevitable. In −218 Hannibal crossed the Ebro on his way to the Alps and the road into Italy. The strategy was based on the assumption that Rome could only be finally defeated in Italy itself, and in any case it was necessary to forestall a Roman invasion of Africa, which could easily be mounted since she now controlled the sea. This war (the second Punic war) lasted till −202, again with tremendous losses on the Roman side. Hannibal's military genius welded together a superb fighting force, largely of Spaniards but also with Gallic and African contingents. Notable victories were won at Lake Trasimene (217) and Cannae (216), Rome's greatest single defeat. He could not, however, break the will of the Roman senate and people, or the strength of Rome's Italian alliance, which largely remained loyal to Rome in spite of years of devastation of their country, and provided the Roman army with seemingly inexhaustible reserves of manpower which Hannibal could never match. While in Italy the defensive policy of Fabius Maximus was pursued, never allowing Hannibal again to exercise his genius in the field, Spain was won for Rome by the young Scipio Africanus in −206. Rome then prepared for an attack on Africa.

In this they were assisted by the situation in Numidia. The native tribes had now been exposed to Carthaginian civilization for several centuries. Much larger political units had evolved than before, and repeated service in Carthage's wars had increased their strength and sophistication. Syphax, chief of the largest Numidian tribe, the Masaesyli, whose territory extended from the Ampsaga (Oued el Kebir) in the east to the Mulucha (Moulouys) in the west, had defected from Carthage in −213 but had rejoined her in −208 when he married a daughter of a leading Carthaginian. Conversely Gaia, the chief of the Massyli, sandwiched between the Masaesyli and Carthaginian territory, had been loyal to Carthage during the period of

Syphax's defection, and his son Masinissa rendered good service in Spain. When Rome was victorious Masinissa decided to back what must have seemed to be the winning side and made his peace with Scipio. On returning to Africa he could not establish himself as head of his tribe but gathered a private force and after two years of epic adventures was waiting to fight for Scipio when he landed. He played a major part in initial successes in −203 before Hannibal was finally recalled from Italy. The final battle took place at Zama (Sab Biar) in 202 when Hannibal suffered defeat. Masinissa, who had meanwhile driven Syphax out of his territory, provided 4000 cavalry, contributing decisively to the Roman victory. Under the peace terms, Carthage gave up her fleet and had her territory in Africa limited by a line roughly from Thabraca to Thaenae; but she was also to return to Masinissa any land his ancestors ever held, a fruitful cause of disputes, and was forbidden to make war outside Africa or even within it without Rome's permission.

## Masinissa and the kingdom of Numidia

Carthage survived another fifty years, but this period of the history of the Maghrib is primarily that of a rapid advance in the economy and society of most of the tribes close to the Mediterranean. It was a historical paradox that the chief figure in this, which involved a more rapid spread of Carthaginian civilization than ever before, should have been Carthage's great enemy Masinissa. An epic figure of enormous physical vigour and natural talents he had been educated at Carthage, and undoubtedly assessed correctly the use that he could make of Carthaginian civilization in his own territory. His personality was such that later, instead of merely being regarded as a useful deserter by the Romans after −206, he established close ties of friendship with a number of the most influential Roman politicians. He was rewarded after Zama with the eastern, more fertile parts of Syphax's territory, and thus ruled from Cirta (Constantine) a territory which extended from somewhere west of that city to the new Carthaginian boundary. (The less developed area between Masinissa's kingdom and the Moulouya was left to Syphax's son.) Several ancient writers stressed that it was Masinissa who substantially increased the agricultural production of Numidia, Strabo claiming that he converted the nomads into farmers. Like all generalizations this is exaggerated, but there is no doubt that there was a substantial increase in the area of cereal production, with a surplus for export, even if stock-rearing continued to predominate. This was of great significance for the future and still more expansive development in Roman times. Trade in other products was limited and the only coins issued were of bronze and copper. Masinissa's capital would appear to have grown into a real city (though the population of 200 000 attributed to it under Masinissa's son must be a gross exaggeration). The archaeology is not well known but its urban aspect will have been almost entirely Carthaginian; more Punic stelae have been found there than in any other African site except Carthage itself and there can be no doubt that the language of Carthage became increasingly used in Numidia and Mauretania.

## The destruction of Carthage

At this period, to be a Roman ally was to be a Roman dependant, and the prime requirement was obedience to Roman will and the avoidance of any action which might arouse Roman suspicion, however unjustified. Masinissa's political skill is demonstrated by his understanding of these facts. Over a period of fifty years he sought to exert increasing pressure on Carthaginian territory and probably hoped that in the end Carthage itself would fall to him with Roman assent. At first, Rome had no interest in further weakening Carthage, which was also naturally a dependant, and down to −170 his gains in territory were small. From −167, however, Rome pursued increasingly ruthless policies, not only in Africa, and favoured Masinissa, who fed their suspicions of Carthage and was also exemplary in sending supplies and men whenever Rome called on him. By these means he added to his kingdom the *emporia* on the Gulf of Gabes and much of the Bagradas Valley. Opinion in the Roman senate gradually came round to the view of the elder Cato that Carthage must finally be destroyed. Although it was true that Carthage had shown a remarkable recovery from the second Punic war, any idea that she could ever again be a threat to Rome was irrational. The Carthaginians were given the choice of abandoning their city and moving into the interior or facing war and its consequences. When they chose the latter alternative, a Roman army was sent to Africa in −149. In spite of overwhelming superiority, Carthage held out till −146. Some Libyans still supported her, and Masinissa himself resented the Roman action which deprived him of his cherished hope, but had to acquiesce. Most of the old-established Phoenician and Carthaginian settlements, such as Utica, Hadrumetum, Thapsus and others, went over to the Romans and avoided inevitable destruction. Carthage itself was razed to the ground and the site ceremonially cursed, a symbolic action by Rome testifying to the fear and hatred which she had accumulated over a century for the power which most sternly resisted her domination over the Mediterranean world.

## Post-Carthaginian successor states

### Numidia

Yet it was more than another century before Rome properly supplanted Carthage as the dominant political and cultural power in the Maghrib. For various reasons (see Chapter 20) Rome only took over a small part of north-eastern Tunisia after the destruction of Carthage and even this was largely neglected. In the rest of North Africa she recognized a series of client kingdoms who were generally left to their own devices. Within these kingdoms the cultural influence of Carthage continued and even increased as the older coastal settlements continued to flourish and many refugees from the last years of Carthage's struggle fled there. The Phoenician language in its later form known as Neo-Punic spread ever more widely. We are told that the Romans even handed over to the Numidian kings libraries saved from the destruction of Carthage. It may be that some of the books were of practical value like the treatise of agriculture, by Mago. None of the later kings was as powerful as Masinissa, but there can be little doubt that the main lines of development in the Numidian and Mauretanian kingdoms continued. It should be stressed that to some extent the two kingdoms continued as merely geographical expressions, since within them a large number of tribes retained their identity well into Roman times, some even beyond, and political unity remained tenuous. This was exacerbated by polygamy within the royal houses (Masinissa was said to have had ten sons who survived him) and later by Roman interference. In Numidia, Masinissa died in − 148 at the age of about 90 and was succeeded by Micipsa (− 148 to − 118). During his reign trade between Numidia and Rome and Italy increased and we hear of numerous Italian traders at Cirta. On his death the kingdom was jointly ruled by two of his brothers together with Jugurtha, a grandson of Masinissa, who had the support of the Roman statesman Scipio Aemilianus, just as Masinissa had had that of an earlier Scipio. Jugurtha was a man of great vigour and sought to establish himself as sole ruler. The Romans then attempted a formal division of the kingdom but when Jugurtha captured Cirta from one of his rivals and killed the Italian residents, Rome declared war. Jugurtha sustained a formidable resistance, causing some military humiliation to Rome until he was betrayed to the Romans by Bocchus, ruler of Mauretania. Rome then established as king another member of Masinissa's dynasty named Gauda who was followed by his son, Hiempsal. After briefly being exiled by a rival between −88 and −83, Hiempsal reigned till −60; he is known to have written a book about Africa in the Punic language, and presumably continued the civilizing work of his dynasty. In its last years as an independent state Numidia became embroiled in the civil wars which destroyed the Roman republic. Hiempsal's son Juba (−60 to −46), who had been publicly insulted as a young man by Julius Caesar, joined the Pompeian cause in −49 and rendered it a great deal of assistance in Africa, to the extent that he was said to have been promised the Roman province in Africa if the Pompeians won. He committed suicide after Caesar's victory at Thapsus, which was followed by the establishment of direct Roman rule over Numidia.

## Mauretania

The Mauretanian kingdom is generally considered to have developed more slowly than Numidia but this may be due to lack of information. Obviously the mountain massif of the Atlas remained as immune to Phoenician as it later did to Roman civilization but there was some development of sedentary life in fertile regions such as the Moulouya Valley and along the Atlantic coast. It was in the mountainous regions that individual tribes retained their identity into Roman times and even beyond. Mauri are referred to as early as the expedition to Sicily of −406, in Hanno's revolt in the −350s and the Roman invasion of Africa in −256. A king of the Mauri helped Masinissa at a critical point in his fortunes but there were also Mauri in Hannibal's army at Zama. At a later date, Bocchus I at first helped Jugurtha against Rome but later betrayed him, and was rewarded with substantial territory east of the Moulouya. In the next generation the area seems to have been divided. Bocchus II ruled the eastern part and in association with an Italian adventurer, P. Sittius, fought against Juba in the interest of Caesar, who was also supported by Bogud II, who ruled west of the Moulouya. Both were rewarded, Bocchus with further extension of his territory at the expense of Numidia. A few years later Bogud II supported Mark Antony against Octavian in the Roman civil war, and was driven out of his territory by Bocchus II in the interest of Octavian. As Bocchus died in −33 and Bogud was killed in −31, the whole vast area was now without a ruler. However, the emperor Augustus decided that the time was not opportune for Rome to take direct control, fearing perhaps formidable military problems from the mountain tribes. In −25 he installed as king Juba, son of the last Numidian king, who had spent his boyhood since the age of 4 in Italy, and for whom the Numidian kingdom had been temporarily reconstituted from −30 to −25. Ruling for over 40 years as a completely loyal client king, Juba did to some degree in Mauretania what Masinissa had done in Numidia. He was a man of largely peaceful interests, fully hellenized in culture, and the author of many books (now lost) written in Greek. There is no doubt that his capital Iol, renamed Caesarea (Oherchell), and probably also an alternative capital, Volubilis, became fully urbanized in his reign. He was succeeded by his son Ptolemaus who ruled till +40 when he was summoned to Rome by the emperor Gaius and executed, no reason being known. This action, preliminary to the provincialization of the area, sparked off a revolt which was suppressed after several years. In +44 Mauretania was made into two provinces, thus completing the organization of the Maghrib under direct Roman rule.

# The Phoenician heritage in the Maghrib

In general, the period of the independent Numidian and Mauretanian kingdoms saw the evolution and entrenchment of a culture of mixed Libyan and Phoenician character, the latter element being culturally dominant though naturally representing only a minority of the population as a whole. The agricultural development in Numidia already discussed occurred in more distant areas where geographical conditions were appropriate. Outside of Cirta and, later, Iol-Caesarea, urban development did not extend far but was sufficient in some areas to prepare the ground for a considerable extension in the Roman period. The strength of the mixed culture may be seen by the fact that the use of Neo-Punic on inscriptions lasted into the second century of our era, and that over the same period the term *sufet* is known to have been used in at least thirty different towns as far apart as Volubilis in western Morocco and Leptis Magna in Libya. The strong persistence of Phoenician/Libyan religion in Roman times is also a fact with wide ramifications. That to a certain degree there was a superficial cultural unity throughout the Maghrib at this time is also attested by the mysterious Libyan script. Developing, it seems, in the second century before our era when it was used on two inscriptions at Dougga, it was later used in the Roman period on stelae (probably in imitation of Punic custom), of which a number have been found in Morocco, on the Algerian/Tunisian border and in Libya. As written languages both Libyan and Neo-Punic gave way to Latin in the Roman period; a spoken form of Punic still widely current in late Roman times but it is impossible to determine the status and extent of spoken Libyan. The similarity of the Libyan script to that used in modern times by the Touareg is a fact which baffles explanation.

In general historical terms, the establishment of the Phoenician settlements in the Maghrib constituted the only extension into the western Mediterranean area of the older civilizations of the ancient Near and Middle East, all of which Carthage outlived. This, along with the spread of the Greeks to the west, was part of the movement by which the entire western Mediterranean, and to a degree north-western Europe, till then inhabited by tribal peoples of great variety, were brought within the range of influence of the civilizations of the Aegean and the East. In the history of Africa, the Phoenician period brought the Maghrib into the general history of the Mediterranean world, emphasizing its connections with the northern as well as the eastern shores. The geographical conditions which, till modern times at least, already associated the Maghrib with the Mediterranean world were emphasized. In view of the limitations of our historical sources, growth of more exact knowledge of the evolution of the native Libyan culture and its response to the introduction of Phoenician civilization must await the further work of the archaeologist.*

* *Note*: It is intended to give a more detailed account of the legacy and role of Libya during the period covered in this volume in the next edition.
    It is planned to hold a symposium which will deal with the contribution

of Libya in classical Antiquity, with particular reference to the role of Cyrenaica during the Greek era, Libya during the Phoenician period and the civilization of the Garamantes.

# 19

## The Roman and post-Roman period in North Africa

*Part I: the Roman period*   A. MAHJOUBI

### The Roman occupation and the resistance of the indigenous population

After the destruction of Carthage in −146 and the reduction of her territory to the status of a Roman province, the fate of North Africa lay in the hands of Rome and the indigenous kingdoms. It would have been desirable to devote a special chapter to the study of the latter, from the advent of the Numidian kingdoms up to the end of the reign of the last king of Mauretania in +40. Thereafter, the whole of North Africa became Roman and remained so until the Vandal invasion.

However, neither the occupation of the country, nor, above all, what is euphemistically referred to, in the language of colonialism, as its pacification, was easily achieved. The Roman thrust southward and westward from the former territory of Carthage and the former kingdom of Juba I met with obstinate resistance. Unfortunately, we only have records of the most outstanding episodes of the struggle. After Rome had established and consolidated her domination, the economic and cultural unity which she had worked so hard to bring about in North Africa was eventually undermined by an endless resistance taking a military form, and also having political and ethnic, social and religious aspects. Everything we know about this resistance and these revolts is gathered from literary and epigraphic sources presenting a purely Roman point of view, and the difficulties of historical analysis are further aggravated by some of the lines of approach adopted by modern historiography. At the beginning of the century, in particular, and until very recently, historiographers were unable or unwilling to discard certain views influenced in varying degrees by the prevailing ideology of the colonial period.[1]

The distinctive nature of the African wars emerges, more particularly,

1. See in this connection the Introduction to the work by M. Bénabou, 1976, particularly pp. 9–15.

from the accounts of the phase of conquest. During the last quarter of the first century before our era, a long series of triumphs celebrated by Roman generals over the Maurusiani, Musulamii, Gaetulians and Garamantes afford indisputable evidence that the indigenous populations were never completely subjugated despite the Roman victories.[2]

The best-known of these wars is that of the Numidian Tacfarinas, which lasted for eight years under the reign of Tiberius, and extended to all the southern confines of North Africa, from Tripolitania as far as Mauretania. It is often summarily presented by modern historians as a struggle between civilization and the Barbaric world, an effort by the nomadic and semi-nomadic indigenous population to halt the Roman advance and the process of settlement, thereby rejecting the benefits of a superior form of civilization and a better social order.[3] However, the demands attributed by Tacitus to Tacfarinas give a clearer idea of the deep-seated causes of the resistance of the indigenous inhabitants. The Numidian leader took up arms to force the all-powerful emperor to recognize his people's right to land, for the Roman conquest had been immediately followed by the sequestration of all the fertile land. The fields of the sedentary Numidians were laid waste; the areas traditionally roamed by the nomads were steadily reduced and limited; veterans and other Roman and Italian colonists established themselves everywhere, starting with the richest parts of the country; tax-collecting companies and members of the Roman aristocracy, senators and knights, carved out huge estates for themselves. While their country was being exploited in this way, all the autochthonous nomads, and all the sedentary inhabitants who did not live in the few cities spared by the succession of wars and expropriation measures, were either reduced to abject poverty or were driven into the steppes and the desert. Their only hope therefore lay in armed resistance, and their principal war aim was to recover their land.

Military operations continued throughout the first two centuries of our era, and the Roman thrust towards the south-west stirred up the tribes which assembled and dispersed in the area stretching from the valley of the Moulouya to the Djebel Amour and the Ouarsenis. Having easily established themselves in the coastal strip and in the north-east, the Romans advanced by stages in the southern part of what is modern Tunisia, as well as in the High Plateaux and the Saharan Atlas. Under the Julio-Claudian emperors, the frontier of the conquered territory stretched from Cirta in the west to Tacape in the south, and included Ammaedara, which was the headquarters of the Legio III Augusta, Thelepte and Capsa. Under the Flavian emperors, the legion established itself at Theveste and the boundary was pushed forward as far as Sitifis; the Nementcha region

2. P. Romanelli, 1959, pp. 175ff.
3. ibid., pp. 227ff.

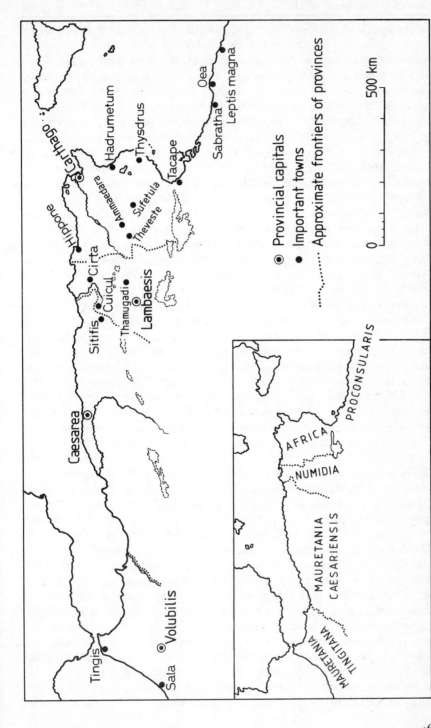

FIG. 19.1 *Roman provinces in North Africa at the end of the second century of our era\(after A. Mahjoubi, 1977)*

467

was incorporated under Trajan and the colony of Timgad was founded in +100; finally, in 128, the legion set up a permanent garrison at Lambaesis and roads were driven through the Aures mountains, which were defended against the tribes by a camp at Gemellae. Between the Roman provinces and the desert regions lying to the south into which the tribes had been driven, a frontier zone was created – the *limes*; this was gradually advanced in a south-westerly direction and consisted of a network, from 50 to 100 kilometres deep, of trenches and roads defended by a string of military posts and small forts. The aerial archaeological research work done by J. Baradez has revealed, among other things, the segments of a *fossatum*, bordered by an earth-bank or a wall and guarded at irregular intervals by square or rectangular towers. In order to keep watch on the movements of the nomad tribes and prevent them from pillaging agricultural areas and the caravans that proceeded northwards to the trading cities of the Gulfs of Gabès and Sidra, the Serer people had, at the end of the second century, established a series of small forts in front of the *limes* properly speaking, such as Dimmidi (Messad), Cidamus (Ghadames) and Golas (Bu-Njem). The southern boundaries of the African provinces were eventually equipped in this way with an effective defence system during the first two centuries of our era.

However, Rome was powerless to root out the resistance of the Berbers, and never succeeded in keeping the nomads of the south and west permanently in check. Despite the efforts of Trajan and Hadrian, and notwithstanding the firm policy pursued by Septimius Severus on the borders of Tripolitania, the crisis of the third century put an untimely end to this enterprise. The desert, the mobility of the camel-mounted nomads and the ease with which communications could be kept open from west to east along the Saharan Atlas range, assured the indomitable Berbers of great freedom of movement. In this respect, the tribes which finally succeeded in wearing down the domination of Rome found their reservoir of manpower in Mauretania Tingitana and, later on, in the vast stretches of desert in the hinterland of Tripolitania. Up to the first quarter of the third century, the centre and south of the country were defended from local raiders by the Legio III Augusta, whose theoretical strength of 5000 to 6000 men was reinforced as necessary by large numbers of auxiliaries. It has been calculated that the maximum number of soldiers may have amounted to between 25 000 and 30 000 in the second century. This is not by any means a high figure, although it is necessary to take account of the veterans still liable for service who settled on the lands cleared for cultivation along the *limes*; in time of need, troops were also transferred from the legions stationed in the other provinces of the empire, and particularly from those in Spain, in order to defend Mauretania Tingitana. For the maintenance of law and order, the proconsul of Africa could also call on the thirteenth city cohort stationed at Carthage, as well as a small cavalry corps, while the repression of piracy and the patrolling of the coasts were the duties of the fleet of Alexandria. The composition of the African legion was very varied at first, but subsequently nearly all the recruits came from the local population. There were, however, some eastern corps – the *cohors Chalcidenorum*, the Palmyrian archers – which were made up of Syrians accustomed to desert warfare.

## Administrative organization and military problems

On 13 January −27, Octavian, on whom the title of Augustus was conferred three days later, divided the provinces of the empire, in accordance with the approved principle, between himself and the senate. Africa, which had long since been conquered and pacified and was bound to the senatorial class by many traditions of an economic as well as a political nature, fell among the provinces to be administered by the senate. Its western boundary ran through Ampsaga – Cuicul – Zarai – Hodna, and in the south-east its territory included a coastal plain in Tripolitania stretching as far as the altars of the Philaeni which marked the frontier with Cyrenaica. This *provincia Africa*, to which the epithet *proconsularis* was also applied, combined the two provinces successively established by Rome in North Africa: one had consisted of the Punic territory conquered in −146, and was known as Africa Vetus, and the other had been created by Caesar after his African campaign against the Pompeians and their ally, King Juba I of Numidia, and was called Africa Nova. In addition to these territories there were the four Cirtean colonies which Caesar had assigned to the Italian adventurer P. Sittius.

As in republican times, the Roman senate continued during the imperial period to delegate a governor in Africa. He was a very high-ranking official, for he was one of the two senior ex-consuls present in Rome at the time of drawing lots for the provinces; he therefore bore the title of proconsul and, unless his term of office was prolonged as an exceptional measure, he held his appointment in Carthage for only one year. In addition to his judicial prerogatives, by virtue of which he was the supreme judge of the province both in civil and in criminal cases, he was invested with administrative and financial powers: he supervised the administration and the municipal authorities, autonomous though they were in principle, and notified them of imperial laws and regulations; he directed the execution of major public works and sanctioned expenditure; he exercised supreme control over the department responsible for keeping Rome supplied with African corn, and over the operation of the fiscal system, the proceeds of which were earmarked for the *aerarium Saturni*, the treasury of the senate. He was assisted by propraetor legates, one of whom resided in Carthage itself, and the other at Hippone, and by a quaestor, who was in charge of the financial administration. Furthermore, as already mentioned, he was provided with a small contingent of troops, about 1600 strong, for the maintenance of law and order.

The emperor could intervene in the affairs of the senatorial province either directly or, as was most often the case, through a resident equestrian procurator, who was an imperial official responsible for the management of the vast imperial domains and for the collection of certain indirect taxes, such as the *vicesima hereditatium*, which supplied the military treasury controlled by the emperor. The procurator also had a measure of judicial power, limited in principle to the settlement of tax disputes. From the year 135 he was assisted by a *procurator Patrimonii*, for the administration of the domains, and a *procurator IIII Publicorum Africae*, for the administration of the fiscal revenues. These officials of the imperial administration often came into conflict with the proconsul, although there is no evidence that they had instructions to keep him under supervision.

Meanwhile, proconsular Africa, unlike the majority of senatorial provinces, could not be deprived of troops. While the north-eastern part, which corresponded to the old province of Africa Vetus, was very quiet, this was not the case in the southern regions, where the Roman authorities needed a military garrison to guard and gradually to extend the supposedly pacified zone. These troops, consisting mainly of the Legio III Augusta, were commanded by an imperial legate subordinate to the proconsul, who was therefore in the position of being able to assert the military authority of the republican governors responsible to the senate. However, this situation could not last indefinitely without arousing the emperor's distrust. It was not long before Caligula decided, in pursuance of a general policy of restricting the powers of the civil governors and reducing the authority and autonomy of the senate, to make an important politico-military change in the organization of proconsular Africa: the military command was taken out of the hands of the civil government, and this resulted in the creation, *de facto* if not *de jure*, of a military territory of Numidia under the authority of the legate in command of the Legio III Augusta. As early as +39, the status of the official entrusted with this special command must have stood halfway between that of the legates who were governors of provinces and that of the legates who were deputies of the general of the legions.[4]

The situation was not very clear, however, and inevitably gave rise to disputes between the proconsul and the legate of the legion concerning their respective fields of competence and authority. Septimius Severus eventually regularized the position by raising the military territory to the dignity of a province: this was the province of Numidia, probably created in +198 to +199.[5] It was administered by the legate of the legion, who was also called the *praeses* and was directly nominated and transferred by the emperor, and its western frontier still followed the left bank of the Ampsaga (Oued-el-Kébir), passed to the west of Cuicul and Zarai, cut across the Hodna plain and dipped southwards in the direction of Laghouat.

4. M. Bénabou, 1972, pp. 61–75.
5. H. G. Pflaum, pp. 61–75.

The eastern frontier ran from a point north-west of Hippone to the west of Calama, followed the right bank of the Oued Cherf, passed to the west of Magifa, and advanced towards the north-west edge of the Chott-el-Jerid.

Between the Ampsaga and the Atlantic there lay the kingdom of Mauretania which had been bequeathed by King Bocchus the Younger to the Roman empire as far back as −33.[6] Octavian, the future Augustus, accepted the legacy and availed himself of the opportunity to plant eleven colonies of veterans in the country, but in −25 he gave up the kingdom to Juba II, who was succeeded by his son Ptolemy in +23. The cautious Octavian probably thought that the country was not ripe for a Roman occupation and that it was necessary to prepare the way through the intervention of indigenous leaders. In +40 Caligula, judging that the time for direct administration had arrived, caused Ptolemy to be assassinated.[7] Finally, Claudius decided, at the end of +42, to organize the two provinces of Mauretania: Caesariensis to the east and Tingitana to the west, separated by the Mulucha (Moulouya). Like Numidia, both Mauretanian provinces came directly under the authority of the emperor. They were governed by ordinary equestrian procurators, one of whom resided at Iol-Caesarea, and the other probably at Volubilis, where they commanded auxiliary troops and at the same time were invested with certain civil and military powers.

No further major changes were made in the military and administrative organization of the African provinces until the reign of Diocletian. Although it suffered less than other provinces, Africa could not escape the repercussions of the general crisis which affected the whole of the Roman world from many different aspects – political, economic, religious and ethical. It was already a potential threat at the end of the Antonine period and the gathering clouds were not by any means dispersed by the transformations of the Severan period. From 238 onwards, the situation deteriorated until a storm of alarming violence broke out at the end of the third century. In North Africa, the waning of Roman power was already foreshadowed by the attacks of the Moorish tribes, which were resumed with renewed vigour between 253 and 262, and again under the reign of Diocletian.[8] Imperial authority was gradually undermined by the stresses arising from the protracted financial and economic crisis on hitherto prosperous provinces (effects both dramatic and stealthy in the case of the proconsular province and Numidia during the second century and the first quarter of the third) and the growing disequilibrium between the social classes. To this should be added the consequences of usurpations and military anarchy. So the power of Rome crumbled into a multitude of successive or concurrent regimes.

6. P. Romanelli, 1959, pp. 156ff.
7. J. Carcopino, 1958, pp. 191ff.; 1948, pp. 288–301; M. I. Rostovtzev, 1957, pp. 321ff.; T. Kotula, 1964, pp. 76–92.
8. See, lastly, M. Bénabou, 1976, pp. 218ff. and pp. 234ff.

However, the empire reacted against these evils in time to save itself. In the reign of Gallienus, the first of a wide range of measures were taken, step by step and empirically, which affected every field of activity, transformed the army and the command structure, reformed the government and administration of the provinces, and extended to social policy, religion and the imperial cult. This was the beginning of the work of restoration which progressed under Aurelian and Probus and culminated in a system rooted in the far-reaching reforms of Diocletian. Lastly, the innovations of Constantine, which brought a new world into being, might be said at the time to amount to a coherent synthesis of the successes and failures of these reforms, as well as the religious trends of the age.

The separation of civil and military powers was one of the salient features of the provincial administration of the later empire. It was gradually achieved between the reign of Gallienus and that of Constantine, who organized it in its definitive form.

The remodelling of the military system in North Africa became a necessity when the African legion, the III Augusta,[9] was disbanded under Gordian III. The command was finally entrusted to the count of Africa, who had the troops of all the African provinces under his authority. This army of the fourth century was very different from that of the earlier empire; the attacks by the Moorish tribes made it essential to build up a mobile army, a striking force always ready to take swift action in zones of insecurity. It was composed of legionary infantry units and cavalry detachments recruited mainly from the romanized peasants living in the vicinity of the camps. However, military service gradually became a hereditary and fiscal obligation, and this inevitably impaired the value of the contingents. In addition to this mobile army, regarded as crack troops, there were the *limitanei*, peasant-soldiers who were allotted plots of land situated along the *limes*. They were exempted from the payment of taxes and were required, in return, to guard the frontier and repulse any raiding tribes. Like those in the east, the *limitanei* of Mauretania Tingitana were organized in traditional units – wings, cohorts – but all those of the other African provinces were divided, instead, into geographical sectors, each taking its orders from a *Praepositus limitis*. Archaeological evidence of various kinds, found particularly in the eastern sector of the *limes*, shows that the *limitanei* were grouped around fortified farms and lived from the land, frequently introducing irrigation by canals. They thus contributed to the development of agriculture and human settlements on the confines of the Sahara and made the *limes* much more into a zone of trade and cultural contacts than a line of separation between the Roman provinces and the independent part of the country which had remained Berber. This explains how Romano-African civilization and Christianity

9. ibid., pp. 207ff., and for the reconstitution of the legion under the reign of Valerian, pp. 214ff.

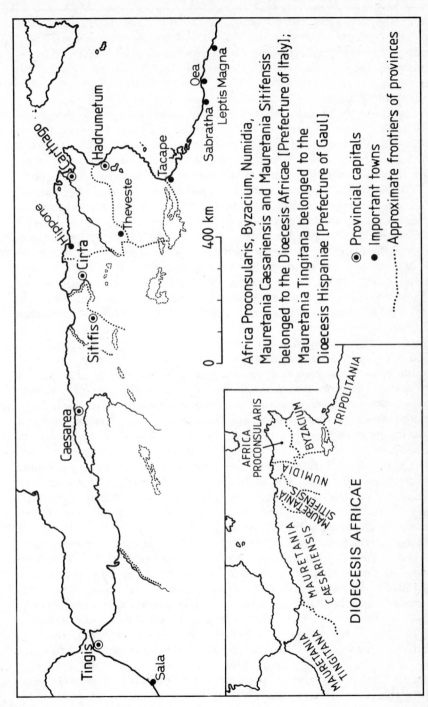

Labels on the map:

Carthago
Hadrumetum
Oea
Sabratha
Leptis Magna
Tacape
Theveste
Hippone
Cirta
Sitifis
Caesarea
Tingis
Sala

400 km
0

Africa Proconsularis, Byzacium, Numidia,
Mauretania Caesariensis and Mauretania Sitifensis
belonged to the Dioecesis Africae [Prefecture of Italy];
Mauretania Tingitana belonged to the
Dioecesis Hispaniae [Prefecture of Gaul]

⊙ Provincial capitals
● Important towns
......... Approximate frontiers of provinces

DIOECESIS AFRICAE

AFRICA PROCONSULARIS
BYZACIUM
NUMIDIA
MAURETANIA SITIFENSIS
MAURETANIA CAESARIENSIS
MAURETANIA TINGITANA
TRIPOLITANIA

FIG. 19.2  *Roman provinces in North Africa in the fourth century of our era (A. Mahjoubi, 1977)*

473

were able to reach regions lying outside the scope of direct administration by Rome. It must be added that the Roman government had always maintained relations with the tribal chieftains, who often agreed, in exchange for subsidies and the conferment of an imperial investiture recognizing their local powers, to supply contingents of men assigned to guard duties along the *limes*.

Concurrently with the military reforms, there was a radical revision of the territorial organization of the provinces. It is now established, however, that the reorganization was carried out gradually, having regard to the needs and conditions prevailing in each province. In order to strengthen the imperial authority, while at the same time curtailing the authority of the proconsul whose power often played into the hands of usurpers, and to increase the revenue from taxes to finance defence measures against the threatened onslaughts on the frontiers, proconsular Africa was split into three autonomous provinces, in the north, Zeugitana, or the proconsular province in the proper sense of the term, extended southwards as far as a line running between Ammaedara and Pupput, near Hammamet; westwards, it included Calama, Thubursian Numidarum and Theveste. However, the proconsul in Carthage was still an important official. He was a *clarissimus* who, after his term of office, often reached the top of the consular hierarchy and ranked among the *illustres*. These proconsuls of the fourth century were not infrequently of African extraction. They were always assisted by two legates, who generally had family connections with them and resided one at Carthage and the other at Hippone. The proconsul retained his judicial and administrative prerogatives but the supervision of municipal affairs was exercised in an increasingly tyrannical manner, and the work of administration tended to become more complicated owing to the proliferation of departments and officials responsible to the proconsul and his legate.

The province of Byzacium was an offshoot of the proconsular province. It stretched from the Ammaedara–Pupput line as far as the gates of Tacape. Westwards, it included the regions of Mactar, Sufetula, Thelepte and Capsa. However, in the south, the guard posts of the *limes* did not come under the authority of the governor of the province of Byzacium, which, like the proconsular province, was without troops; the posts situated near the Chott el-Jerid were therefore the responsibility of Numidia, while those in the south-west were under the authority of Tripolitania. The governor of Byzacium, who resided at Hadrumet, was at first of equestrian rank and held the title of *praeses*; but possibly during the reign of Constantine and, in any case, after 340, he acceded to consular status.

In the south-east, the new province of Tripolitania comprised two different zones: a coastal strip stretching from Tacape to the altars of the Philaeni, which came under the proconsul and very probably the legation at Carthage; in the interior, the *limes* region of Tripolitania was placed, until the third century, under the authority of the commander of the

Legio III Augusta, governor of the province of Numidia. This region included the Djeffara and the Matmatas, and extended as far as the northern tip of the Chott el-Jerid. Recent research has shown that, contrary to previous impressions, whereas the Romans had evacuated certain advanced positions, such as Golas (Bu-Njem), they had maintained their positions south of the coast during the fourth century and up to the beginning of the fifth century.[10] This was why the governors of Tripolitania were able to play an important military role on various occasions: up to 324–6, they enjoyed the title of *praeses* together with the attendant military powers, and resided at Leptis Magna. Subsequently, the command of the troops stationed on the *limes* was assigned to the count of Africa, who did not keep it, however, without interruptions: shortly before 360 and in 365, the command of the *limes tripolitanus* was provisionally withdrawn from the *Comes Africae* and assigned to the *praeses* of Tripolitania, possibly owing to the restlessness of the Austuriani tribe.

The province of Numidia had a narrow outlet to the sea between the Edough mountains on the east and the mouth of the Ampsaga on the west, but towards the south its territory widened out and stretched from the eastern end of the Chott el-Hodna to the gates of Theveste. It was divided at first into two zones, one comprising the quiet region of the towns of the old Cirtean confederation around the capital city Cirta, and the other consisting of the turbulent mountainous region in the south with Lambaesis as the principal settlement, but was reunified as early as 314. However, it continued to be ruled by a governor of equestrian rank exercising both the civil and the military powers, and holding the title of *praeses*, up to 316. In that year, the civil government was entrusted to senators bearing the new title of *consularis provinciae*, and then given the rank of *clarissimi*; the great majority belonged to the Roman aristocracy, on account of the landed interests which linked the latter to this rich province. Cirta became the only capital and took the name of Constantine, in honour of the emperor.

The problem of the administrative reorganization of the provinces of Mauretania in the fourth century is dominated by a question of prime importance: were the interior of Tingitana and all the western part of Caesariensis evacuated by Diocletian just before his accession? In the light of recent research, it appears to be very doubtful whether the region lying to the west of Mauretania Caesariensis was relinquished.[11] On the other hand, it is agreed that Diocletian evacuated all the territories south of the Oued Loukkos in Mauretania Tingitana in 285; Rome seems, however, to have maintained purely maritime relations with the coastal towns, which

---

10. The withdrawal from inner Tripolitania, affirmed by C. Courtois, 1955, pp. 70–9, is contradicted by archaeology. See A. di Vita, 1964, pp. 65–98 and G. Clemente, pp. 318–42.

11. See P. Salama, 1954a, pp. 224–9, and 1954b, pp. 1292–1311.

would explain how places like Sala could continue, under Constantine, to live within the Roman orbit.[12] Furthermore, Diocletian detached the eastern part of Mauretania Caesariensis to make a new province: this was Mauretania Sitifensis, with Sitifis, the modern Sétif, as its capital. Lastly, Mauretania Tingitana was separated for administrative purposes from the rest of Africa and was attached to the diocese constituted by the Spanish provinces.

To ensure liaison between the central government and the provinces, which had thus become smaller and more numerous, Diocletian increased the number of high officials who exercised the once extraordinary but now permanent functions of praetorian vice-prefects; in principle, these *vicarii* were *equites perfectissimi*, but they were promoted to the rank of *clarissimi* when they were set over governors of the senatorial class. Each *vicarius* was in charge of a specific diocese, composed of a certain number of provinces. The diocese of Africa comprised the provinces of North Africa, excluding Mauretania Tingitana; the governors of these provinces were placed under the authority of the *vicarius* who resided in Carthage and was answerable to the praetorian prefect of Italy–Africa–Illyria, except for the proconsul of Africa who was directly responsible to the emperor.

## Colonization and municipal organization

Like Greek civilization, Roman civilization was essentially an urban phenomenon. The degree to which a province was civilized and Romanized was therefore determined by the closeness of the towns.[13] In the African provinces, and particularly Africa Proconsularis, urban life was highly developed; at least 500 cities have been counted in North Africa as a whole, 200 of which existed in the proconsular province alone[14] but it has not been made sufficiently clear that this urban civilization was largely inherited from the Punic–Numidian age.[15]

In the Republican period, no cities had yet been admitted to a share of Roman citizenship; there were only seven cities of Phoenician origin, enjoying a measure of autonomy which was not invulnerable to political vicissitudes: these were the cities which had sided with Rome during the last Punic war. Their traditional institutions were formally recognized and they were also exempted from the land tax, the *stipendium*. Meanwhile,

12. J. Boubbe, pp. 141–5, and A. Jodin.

13. For the role and development of urban structures, see M. Clavel and P. Levêque, pp. 7–94. As Courtois wrote, everything took place 'as though the only criterion for valid participation in civilisation was the extent to which daily life reflected more or less exactly daily life in Rome': 1955, p. 111.

14. G. Charles-Picard, 1959, pp. 45ff.

15. See, for example, in the article by G. Camps, 1960b, pp. 52–4, the list of cities anterior to the second Punic war, and that of the cities of the Numidian Kingdom between the *fossa regia* and the *Mulucha*, pp. 275–7.

Roman rule tolerated, but did not legally protect, the institutions of the other African cities, which continued to apply the Phoenician administrative system and to be headed by suffetes and councils of notables, while paying the *stipendium*.[16] The first official attempt at colonization was made by G. Gracchus, under the provisions of the *Lex Rubria*, in − 123, 6000 settlers, both Romans and Latins, were to be assigned large tracts of land, on the basis of 200 *ingera* per capita, i.e. 50 hectares; the total area, to which the common land must be added, presupposed the availability of a vast stretch of territory. Consequently, it is thought that the allotments extended southwards from the Medjerda as far as the *fossa regia*, the frontier of the first Roman province of Africa. Colonists cannot, therefore, have lived only in Carthage; later on, at all events, they must have been scattered in a number of small towns. It was also necessary, no doubt, to expropriate the previous landowners and move them elsewhere. The fate of Rome's first attempt at colonization in Africa is well known: for political motives rooted in the hatred felt by the Roman aristocracy for G. Gracchus, the reformer and leader of the popular party, and also for economic reasons arising out of the fact that the settlers were humble and impecunious folk and rarely of peasant stock, the venture failed; so it was that this colonization project merely served, in the last analysis, as a pretext for overthrowing the popular party and permitting wealthy men, senators and knights, to carve vast estates out of the African territories conquered by the republic.

After the Jugurthine war in − 103, Marius assigned to his veterans and members of the Gaetulian tribe plots of land situated possibly along the *fossa regia*, between Acholla and Thaenae, and, in any case, certainly in the west, in the middle valley of the Medjerda; from the epigraphical evidence it seems that these allotments of land are commemorated in the Thurburnica inscriptions which refer to Marius as the *conditor* of this colony, and in the appellations of *Mariana* and *Marianum* given later to the colony of Uchi Maius and the *municipium* of Thibar. Also in − 103, it seems that colonists were settled in the Kerbena Islands by the father of Julius Caesar. But the colonization movement did not get really under way until the Colonia Julia Carthago was founded either by Octavian alone, or by the triumvirate in − 42, or more probably in − 44, according to the generally accepted opinion. The first century of Roman occupation was therefore a period of retrogression for Africa, distinguished, in particular, by the shameless exploitation of the fertile land; the slow progress of colonization was thus due to the greed of the businessmen, chiefly knights, and senators who conducted their affairs through middle-men when they could not obtain political missions taking them to Africa.[17] In reviving

16. G. Charles-Picard, 1959, pp. 22ff.

17. On the colonization of the African province during the republican era, see S. Gsell, Paris, 1913–28, and P. Romanelli, 1959, pp. 43–71.

the plans of his adoptive father Julius Caesar, Augustus Octavius initiated a new epoch in the history of Africa, a new political pattern, and a far-reaching administrative, military and religious programme. According to the list supplied by Pliny, whose sources still give rise to much controversy,[18] there were soon six Roman colonies, fifteen *oppida civium romanorum*, one *oppidum latinum*, one *oppidum immune* and thirty *oppida libera*. An epigraphic text at Dougga[19] lends support, at least partially, to the theory of the German Kornemann about the beginnings of colonization and municipal organization:[20] in −29, when the Colonia Juliana was rounded into final shape by a fresh influx of colonists to Carthage, or possibly even earlier, the Roman citizens who had arrived with large or small bands of immigrants to settle in the vicinity of the peregrine cities, grouping themselves into *pagi* and acquiring rural estates, found that their properties were contiguous with the territory (*pertica*) of the colony of Carthage. Augustus also founded no fewer than thirteen colonies between the years −33 and −25 in Mauretania.

The emperors who succeeded Augustus continued to apply his policy; under Marcus Aurelius there were more than thirty-five colonies distributed throughout the African provinces. As a general rule, the immigrants were veterans who had served in legions disbanded as a result of the reorganization of the army; there were also Italians who had been evicted or ruined by the agricultural crisis in the peninsula. The number of the latter was not so large, however, as to turn the African provinces into resettlement areas. But the rational implantation of these colonies took well into account defensive and economic considerations.

The attitude towards the indigenous inhabitants which left them a large measure of actual self-government in their municipal affairs, taking account of their linguistic, ethnic and religious characteristics, was not at all incompatible with a policy of eventual assimilation; for the economic and political benefits and privileges enjoyed by Roman citizens never lost their attraction for the upper classes of African society. The latter, who belonged to the peasant communities at whose expense the colonies of immigrants became established and developed, regarded the town much more as a centre of repression than a centre of romanization.

The question of municipal status raises problems of great complexity which we can only summarize here.[21] In the first place, there were the peregrine cities, which were very numerous and whose inhabitants were not Roman citizens. Most of these cities were liable to the *stipendium*, but

18. Moreover, the information provided by Pliny the Elder (V, 22–30) on the status of these towns is difficult to interpret. The problem is reviewed by P. A. Brunt, pp. 581–3.

19. C. Poinssot, pp. 55–76.

20. E. Kornemann.

21. The problem of Roman municipal policy in Africa is the subject of two recent studies which bring up to date former studies on the question: L. Teutsch, and J. Gascon.

some enjoyed the *libertas*, which signified that their autonomy was legally recognized, and a few were even *immunes*, in other words, exempted from the *stipendium*, the tax levied by the conquerors. Secondly, there were the Latin cities: they had been granted, by a general charter, or because they had been populated by Latin colonists, either the *ius latii maioris*, which extended Roman citizenship both to the municipal magistrates and to the members of the assembly of decurions, or the *ius latii minoris*, which restricted citizenship to individuals holding a civil office or a *honor*; the other inhabitants, however, enjoyed civil rights very similar to those conferred on Roman citizens. Thirdly, in the *coloniae iuris Romani*, whose status was defined by a posthumous law of Caesar's all the inhabitants were Roman citizens except, of course, the slaves, the *incolae* (foreign residents) and the *adtributi*, that is to say, the indigenous population of the sectors attached for administration purposes to these colonies. Alongside the colonies of immigrants there developed therefore an increasing number of honorary colonies, which were former indigenous communities, whose constant evolution towards the Roman way of life became officially recognized through the benefits of Roman law.

In addition, there were the *vici*, *pagi*, which usually formed part of the *pertica* of a city: on the large imperial domains, the farmers rarely had any contact with town-dwellers, and administration was in the hands of the imperial procurators. Lastly, in the south of the African provinces, and particularly in the Mauretanian provinces, the townless regions subject to the tribal system were kept under supervision by small military detachments commanded by *praefecti*.

However, many points concerning municipal institutions are still obscure. As regards the definition of the *municipium iuris Romani*, for example, it was long believed, with Mommsen's authority, that communities of Roman citizens were called *municipia* or *coloniae*, and that the distinction between the terms was mainly a question of their relative status, the title of colony being the greater honour. Virtually no difference was detectable, therefore, between the two types of community, the explanation being thought to lie in the adoption of increasingly uniform constitutions for such corporate bodies. According to a theory propounded by C. Saumagne, which has not by any means been unanimously accepted, however, there is reason to think that *municipia iuris Romani*, existed only in Italy; it would follow that all provincial *municipia* were in the *iuris Latini* class and that there would be no communities in the *iuris Romani* class in Africa other than the colonies and the *oppida civium romanorum*. This would have helped to clarify the problem of the naturalization process in the provinces: the *ius Latii*, which conferred Roman citizenship on the rich, would then appear to have represented an essential step towards the integration of whole communities.[22]

22. C. Saumagne. His thesis is refuted by J. Desanges, 1972, pp. 253–73.

Due allowance being made for these fine distinctions, it is clear that the African cities came to bear an ever closer resemblance to the Italian *municipia*; everywhere we find a popular assembly, a senate, magistrates appointed for a term of office limited to one year and on a collegial basis, *duoviri, quattuorviri, aediles, quaestores*. It has been noticed, however, that the *populus* was particularly long-lived in Africa, whereas the popular assembly had fallen into abeyance elsewhere. The citizens composing the *populus* were grouped into smaller bodies known as *curiae*; one school of thought holds these to be a survival of an ancient Carthaginian institution; the African *curiae* would then have had nothing but the name in common with those of the other parts of the empire. However, the real power did not lie in the hands of the *populus*, but in those of the municipal senate, consisting of about a hundred members forming the *ordo decurionum*, a senatorial order at local level. These decurions were selected from among former magistrates over the age of 25 and also, occasionally, from among the wealthy citizens. They administered the city finances, decided on new expenditure, managed municipal property. They were organized in a hierarchy based on social rank; at the top were the honorary members who were entrusted with the defence of the city's interests: they were generally men of local birth who had climbed the social ladder until they had been admitted by *adlectio* to the highest orders of the empire; ideally, a knight or a senator made a career in Rome, moved in circles close to the emperor and was thus in a good position to represent the interests of his town by submitting a personal request to the emperor for an improvement in its legal status or a remission of taxes, and likewise to intercede in favour of a young fellow-citizen embarking upon his career. There followed, in order of precedence, the former *duumvirs*, the former *aediles*, the former *quaestors*, and last of all the ordinary decurions who had not yet acceded to high office. All were required to possess a fortune amounting to a figure fixed by a kind of rating system which was moderate in the very numerous small towns but extremely high in the large towns, and particularly in Carthage, where it was equal to the property qualification for admission to the equestrian order. This meant that only wealthy men could play a role in the city where the magistrates presided over the Popular Assembly and the senate, dispatched current business, maintained relations with the provincial authorities and exercised judicial powers limited to petty offences and minor litigation.

To discharge the duties of public offices it was necessary to have ample means and leisure: far from receiving a salary, the magistrates were required, on taking up their office, to pay into the municipal treasury a sum varying with the rank of the office and the size of the town: in addition it was the custom to display generosity in several ways, by giving banquets, organizing games, financing the construction of monuments. Most of the public edifices (baths, markets, fountains, temples, theatres) of African towns thus owed their existence to a real spirit of competition among the notables. The highest civil office in a city was that of the *duoviri quinquennales*, who were elected every five years and were responsible for carrying out the census; this meant that they had to count the total number of inhabitants and that of the Roman citizens, evaluate fortunes and thereby determine the position of individuals in the social scale and in relation to tax assessment.

This fiscal responsibility was to become an increasingly decisive factor, compelling the central authorities to interfere in municipal affairs. City finances, which were sometimes in a precarious position, were gradually subjected from the second century onwards to inspection by *curatores civitatis* as a remedial measure for difficulties arising from squandered funds and expenditures incurred for prestige-enhancing purposes. This was the first sign of a trend towards centralization and the imposition of a bureaucratic system of state control which came into force with the crisis of the third century and was firmly established in the fourth century, having superseded liberalism and municipal self-government.

## Economic life

### The population

We have no contemporary estimate, however approximate, of the size of the population in Roman times. It was necessary, of course, to organize a census periodically for fiscal purposes, but the returns have not come down to us. In this field, therefore, we are reduced all too often to barely adequate methods of arriving at possible figures: the application of a mean density coefficient in computing the total number of inhabitants, and, especially, the use of the topographical argument, in combination with various considerations, in attempting to assess, in particular, the number of town-dwellers. C. Courtois, for example, has taken the episcopal registers as his starting point and has concluded, after discussion, that there were 500 African cities; after giving much thought to the density figure and mean area to be adopted, he has settled on an average of 5000 inhabitants per city, which represents 2 500 000 town-dwellers out of a total of 4 million inhabitants of the African provinces as a whole under the early empire, which had fallen to 3 million under the later empire. The latter figures are based on the estimates of J. Beloch who had calculated the size of the population of the Roman empire from the census returns obtained by Augustus in Italy. However, C. Courtois had formed the opinion that the density of 16 inhabitants to a square kilometre regarded as probable by the German scholar was too high for North Africa, which had only about 8 million inhabitants in the middle of the nineteenth century; he had therefore reduced it to 11 inhabitants to a square kilometre, while reckoning that the towns had 250 inhabitants to a hectare, like the French towns of the eighteenth and nineteenth centuries.[23] G. Charles-

23. C. Courtois, 1955, pp. 104ff.

Picard has raised many objections to C. Courtois' figures for various reasons which have led him to two conclusions, namely, that the density of the African population exceeded 100 inhabitants to the square kilometre in certain regions and that, notwithstanding the large number of towns, the majority of inhabitants of this primarily agricultural country lived in small market-towns and on the large rural states of widely dispersed villas. Proconsular Africa would then seem to have had a total of 3 500 000 inhabitants; the addition of the population of Numidia and the Mauretanian provinces would result in a figure of 6 500 000 inhabitants for the period between the middle of the second century and the first third of the third century, when Africa was at the height of its prosperity.[24]

More recently, A. Lézine has presented a point of view regarding the urban population which is at variance with that of G. Charles-Picard; arguing, like the latter, that living conditions and density of population in the Tunisian Sahel were very similar during the Middle Ages to those existing in ancient times, he has attempted to calculate the size of the population of Sousse towards the end of the tenth century, and that of the population of Carthage between 150 and 238. He has finally arrived at the number of 1 300 000 town-dwellers; if we were to accept this conclusion, while retaining the figure proposed by C. Courtois for the total population, the figure for country-dwellers would appear more reasonable.[25] However, a fresh approach to these demographic problems has been suggested by recent research work; instead of relying only on the data yielded by the *census* of ancient times, the density of population, the relative numbers of *domus* and *insulae*, and the number of recipients of doles of corn, we now also take into account the number of tombs per generation and the *summae honorariae* paid by newly appointed magistrates at a rate varying according to their rank and the size of the town.[26]

## Agriculture

It is common knowledge that agriculture was the mainstay of the economy of ancient times; in Africa during the Roman period, the land was the principal and most highly prized source of wealth and social consideration. It is also a platitude to say that Africa was the granary of Rome; this expression has sometimes been used to imply that it once enjoyed proverbial abundance contrasting with the poverty of modern times, so as to bring in an ill-informed verdict relating to the degeneration of the

24. G. Charles-Picard, 1959, pp. 45ff.
25. A. Lézine, 1960, pp. 69–82.
26. See in particular the criticism of population evaluation methods by R. P. Duncan-Jones, pp. 85ff. From an inscription at Siagu, which mentions a legacy to be distributed to the citizens of the towns the author concludes that the number of citizens was 4000 whereas that of the whole population of the city was between 14 000 and 17 000.

For the treatment of population problems, see M. Bénabou, 1976, pp. 385ff.

population, totally disregarding the complex problems which have created the conditions of underdevelopment. Here we are really obliged to repeat a truth which cannot have been overlooked by historians: in point of fact, Africa was the granary of Rome because, being a vanquished country, it was forced to keep the conqueror supplied with corn by way of tribute. Under Augustus, for instance, 200 000 Romans received a free ration of 44 litres of corn per month, totalling about a million bushels. In any event, the theory of Africa's remarkable prosperity and exceptionally high yields of corn in Roman times has been demolished by the geographer J. Despois.[27]

At first, the Roman conquest brought in its wake a decline in agriculture, as in the African economy as a whole. The Carthaginian *Chora* was laid waste and its arboriculture was abandoned, for Italy was then in control of the wine and oil market and saw to it that there was no competition in these lucrative branches of husbandry. Corn-growing was the only one to be carried on, and in the reign of Augustus it started to expand for a political reason which was to prevail up to the end of the Roman rule, namely, the need to ensure food supplies for the Roman plebs. After Rome had pushed the frontiers farther to the west and south and had embarked upon the policy of confining the tribes to circumscribed areas, while pursuing an active land development policy, particularly through the extension of the great hydraulic projects, there was a sharp rise in the figures for corn production. By the time that Nero was on the throne, Africa, we know, was already keeping the capital of the empire supplied with corn for eight months of the year: it has thus been calculated that the African contribution was 18 million bushels, or 1 260 000 quintals.

In view of the fact that this figure represented the amount of the *annona* – that is, the yearly produce from the imperial domains recently enlarged very substantially as a result of Nero's confiscation of the great estates of the Roman senators – to which was added the levy in kind raised on the other lands, G. Charles-Picard reckoned that the *annona* accounted for a little over one-seventh of the average output of African corn-growers. This therefore amounted to about 126 million bushels, or 9 million quintals. The quantity of corn left in Africa was therefore too small, once the seed-corn had been set aside, to satisfy the local demand: 'a good many peasants were obliged to live on millet or barley, and drought necessarily brought famine in its train'.[28] During the period of great prosperity in Africa, from the middle of the second century until 238, the position improved, owing, in particular, to the cultivation of the virgin lands of Numidia and also those of the Mauretanian provinces, but Africa had to meet new fiscal exactions, as when the military *annona* was converted, under Septimius Severus, into a regular pecuniary charge. From the second

27. J. Despois, pp. 187ff.
28. G. Charles-Picard, 1959, p. 91.

century onwards, however, large investments in public buildings are a sign of prosperity among the upper classes and, in particular, among the urban middle class. The truth is that, in this period, the imperial government allowed the provinces more freedom of action in developing their economy, whereas Italy was suffering from a crisis which had already become a problem under the Claudian emperors and was still unsolved. The cultivation of the olive and the vine, however, was only encouraged, at first, as a means of making use of the *'subsiciva'* or lands unsuitable for corn-growing, but the profitability of the wine and oil trade stimulated the trend in this direction, so that olive groves and vineyards spread at a spectacular rate, the former being particularly prolific, even in steppe-like regions.

Rural estates and landscapes are depicted on mosaics produced between the end of the first century and the middle of the fourth; the landowner's villa generally stands in the middle of a great orchard or park, and is sometimes surrounded by utilitarian buildings where slaves are busily at work. The property is occasionally represented, but is more often symbolized by typical activities or a background suggesting the natural features of the region: hills, scenes illustrating the work of ploughing, sowing, harvesting, transplanting or grape-gathering, flocks of sheep, farmyard fowls, bee-hives, and so on.

From the very beginnings of the occupation, the mark of Roman colonization was a chequer-work of agrarian units – the centuriation; the soil of Africa was divided into squares measuring 710 metres across which formed a perfectly symmetrical chessboard pattern.[29] Having become the property of the Roman people (*ager publicus populi romani*) by right of conquest, these lands were classified in several categories under complicated property laws which were constantly changing. Except in Mauretania, where no restrictions were placed on rights of way, tribal property steadily lost ground to the ever-expanding area occupied by colonists. A huge operation designed to contain the tribes within certain areas was unremittingly pursued under the early empire, and was even stepped up in the Severan period when the *limes* was pushed forward in Tripolitania, Numidia and Mauretania, involving violent expropriation action against the tribes, who were driven into the desert. However, indigenous landowners living in the cities, whose property was not expropriated for the benefit of Roman or Latin settlers, generally kept their estates on condition that they paid the *stipendium* from which very few of the peregrine cities were exempt. Another real property category was composed of lands distributed to the Roman citizens – veterans, Roman or Italian immigrants of small means – who settled in the colonies, the *oppida civium romanorum*, the *pagi*. In course of time, however, the legal status of the lands of the indigenous cities and that of the properties of the Roman cities became

29. See R. Chevallier and A. Caillemer, pp. 275–86.

indistinguishable as municipal constitutions developed a tendency to integrate the autochthonous communities. The last category comprised the huge estates which members of the Roman aristocracy had succeeded in acquiring, particularly at the end of the republican period and at the times when Africa offered a vast field of opportunity for investments in real property. In the first century before our era, for instance, six Roman senators owned half the soil of the African provinces between them, but Nero put them to death and incorporated their *fundi* into the imperial *patrimonium*. Under the later empire, however, quite a number of large private estates belonging to the Roman aristocracy still existed, especially in Numidia, and there was a general tendency for large properties to absorb small ones, particularly under the later empire.

The status and organization of the great imperial domains are known to us thanks to four major inscriptions and other evidence yielded by the rich store of African epigraphs.[30] They have handed down to us texts of prime importance, such as the *Lex Manciana* and the *Lex Hadriana* which are not 'laws' within the meaning of Roman public law, but working regulations. In the opinion of many writers, they applied to the whole of the *ager publicus* existing throughout the empire, according to J. Carcopino, or only in Africa, according to M. Rostovtseff. Others believe them to be regulations applying specifically to the region comprising the imperial *saltus* of the middle valley of the Medjerda, although this interpretation has been refuted by recent finds. In any event, we only have detailed knowledge of the management methods applying to the imperial domains. These were leased to contractors known as *conductores*, who employed *villici* to run them. The *villicus* developed the resources of part of the domain himself; he probably used slaves and farm labourers, as well as the compulsory services demanded of the colonists. These *coloni* were free men who farmed the greater part of the domain as sub-tenants of the *conductores*. The main purpose of the *Lex Manciana* and the *Lex Hadriana* was to determine the rights and duties of the *conductores* and their managers (*villici*), on the one hand, and those of the farmers (*coloni*), on the other hand; the principle was that, in return for the delivery of one-third of their annual crops and a specified number of days of labour on the land which was under the direct management of the *villicus*, the farmers enjoyed, on their respective plots of land, the right of use, which they could bequeath to their heirs and even sell, on condition that the new holder of the right left the farming cycle undisturbed for two consecutive years. The management of the domains was supervised by a strictly graded body of imperial officials: at the top, the *procurator of the patrimonial department* who resided in Rome with his staff, prepared the general regulations and implementary memoranda. He was a senior member

30. Substantial bibliography is available on this question. See G. Charles-Picard, 1959, pp. 61ff. and note 31, pp. 371–2.

of the equestrian order. In each province, a resident procurator, who was likewise a high-ranking *eques*, supervised the procurators of the districts (*tractus*), which comprised a number of estates (*saltus*); at the lowest level, the procurators of the estates were, in most cases, ordinary freedmen. The task of these procurators of *saltus* was to conclude contracts with the *conductores*, ensure that the regulations were observed, act as an arbitrator in disputes between *conductores* and *coloni*, and assist the former in the collection of rents. We see from the Souk-el-Khemis inscription which dates from the reign of Commodus that the *conductores* and the procurators responsible for supervising their management of the estates collaborated to cheat the tenant farmers of their statutory rights and took arbitrary decisions to increase their burden of obligations. These *conductores* were, in fact, men to be reckoned with, powerful capitalists, to whose influence the procurators were not immune. Many writers believe, like A. Piganiel, that the future condition of the farmers under the Byzantine empire was already foreshadowed by that of the tenants described by the Souk-el-Khemis inscription. From the fourth century onwards, the term *coloni* denoted all peasants cultivating imperial or privately owned estates throughout the empire. They were free men, in principle, but their freedom was increasingly curtailed by laws forbidding them to leave the land they were working on. The landowner was responsible for the payment of the taxes levied on the tenant's produce, and could only discharge his responsibility if the farming cycle was undisturbed: this induced him to tie the peasant to the land, so that the latter's legal status tended to resemble that of the slave. This trend resulted in the serfdom which prevailed in the West during the Middle Ages as the common lot of the descendants of colonists and of the descendants of rural slaves.

The pattern of development of agriculture in Africa under the later empire continues to be a controversial subject; generally speaking, modern historians have been struck by the large number of properties not subject to levies and therefore uncultivated, from which they have inferred that there was a fairly rapid extension of areas of land allowed to run to waste. C. Lepelley has recently shown that the problem is a more complex one, and that the situation was not as alarming as it was thought to be, at least in proconsular Africa and the province of Byzacium. It cannot be said that there was a mass flight from the land or a disastrous decline in agricultural output. Until the invasion of the Vandals, Africa was to remain the source of the food supplies of Rome, which was deprived, after the foundation of Constantinople, of the Egyptian quota of corn; moreover, the prosperity of Ifriqiya in the eighth, ninth and tenth centuries, which is vouched for by Arab sources, cannot be explained if we accept the proposition that the typical symptoms of a recession are discernible.[31] However, food shortages were not unknown, mainly owing to natural

31. C. Lepelley, 1967, pp. 135–44.

causes, and it must be said that the economic importance of cereals seems to have waned while that of olive-trees increased, except in Numidia which remained a corn-growing country.

## Industry and trade

It has generally been noticed that epigraphs and figures carved on monuments yield much less information in Africa than in other Western provinces about the life of craftsmen and hired workmen. However, while metal-working seems to have been less prevalent in the African provinces, we must not be tempted to indulge in generalizations; it could be pointed out, for example, that the epigraphical material contains very few references to builders and architects although their works cover innumerable archaeological sites in Africa. In any event, the technological stagnation of the Roman period was not conducive to any large-scale development of the industries of antiquity. In these circumstances, the leading industries were concerned with the processing of agricultural products, and particularly the manufacturing of olive-oil; the ruins of olive-presses, which are found in such profusion in the area stretching from *Sefetula* to Thelepte and Tebessa, testify to the importance of oil in the economy of ancient times, not only as the staple fat for human consumption, but also as the sole fuel for lamps and an essential toilet requisite.[32]

The pottery industry, which was associated to a variable degree with the olive-oil industry, met the demand for lamps and containers, in addition to producing domestic utensils. In Punic times, the local industry concentrated on turning out everyday articles, and the most delicate specimens of the potter's art were imported at first from Greece and Etruria and later from southern Italy. With the Roman conquest, Africa became more dependent on foreign production centres: Campania was superseded by Tuscany and then by the Gallic workshops, which exported their goods mainly to Mauretania; however, in the proconsular province, a new pottery industry started to develop àt the beginning of the second century of our era along with a general economic recovery.

The work of J. P. Morel, who has detected the African imitations of the black glazed pottery of Campania,[33] and that of P. A. Février and J. W. Salomonson on the *terra sigillata*, together with the latest excavations conducted by the research workers of the Archaeological Institute of Tunis, have shown that there was a steady increase in the number and size of the African workshops.[34] Besides the ordinary run of articles, they produced the fine-quality pottery coloured orange-red, at first, and pale orange, later, which had become popular throughout the western Mediter-

32. See H. Camps-Fabrer, 1953.
33. J. P. Morel, 1968 and 1962–5.
34. See for example, A. Mahjoubi, A. Ennabli and J. W. Salomonson.

ranean countries; from the first half of the third century, they decorated beautiful cylindrical amphoras and biconic vases with applied ornamentation in the form of raised figures inspired mainly by the games of the amphitheatre: they fashioned high-quality lamps, and statuettes which were placed in tombs or private shrines. The fourth century saw the widespread production of yet another type of pottery known to specialists as 'light sigillate D'. Foreign imports in the primordial economic sector constituted by the pottery industry soon disappeared, even in the Mauretanian provinces, and sales of African manufactures and raw materials (oil, earthenware, purple-dyed cloth, glass-ware, wooden ware, the produce of quarries, such as Numidian marble), to which must of course be added corn, as well as slaves, timber, wild beasts for the amphitheatre games, must have greatly exceeded those of imported products, which consisted probably of finished goods, and particularly those made of metal.

Africa has thus succeeded in breaking free from its economic dependence, and its foreign trade regained some of the importance of Punic times. Port facilities were extended to keep pace with the development of the exportable resources of the hinterland and to handle the quantities of grain and oil to be shipped to Italy; the main dealings were with Ostia, the harbour which was Rome's outlet to the sea; on the site of Ostia have been found, among the *scholae* (offices) of the shipping corporations, no fewer than nine buildings which belonged to the African corporations of Mauretania Caesariensis, *Musluvium, Hippo Diarrhytus*, Carthage, *Curubis, Missus, Gummi, Sullectum* and *Sabratha*. These *domini navium* or *navicularii*, who formed corporations, were collectively responsible for the transport of commodities to Italy;[35] they were granted special privileges as early as the reign of Claudius, and they were organized, up to the time of Septimius Severus, according to the principle of free association. Soon, however, state control was introduced in this field as in the other sectors of the economy, especially as the victualling of Rome was a far too important matter to be left to purely private enterprise; the *navicularii* were accordingly considered to be performing a public service. The trade with Italy remained, however, in African hands. As regards commerce with the East, which was a flourishing business in Carthaginian times, it was in the hands of Eastern merchants under the empire and in the fourth century they were still visiting African ports to conduct their negotiations. While we do not know exactly what kind of products were unloaded by these merchants, who were called Syrians, it is not difficult to imagine the diversity and abundance of the cargo of their return journey, judging from the large numbers of gold coins bearing the effigy of the Eastern emperors which have been unearthed, and which they must have left in Africa to balance their accounts. Lastly, the trans-Saharan trade must be considered, but it will be dealt with below in the context of the

35. G. Calza, pp. 178ff.

relations between the African provinces and the peoples of the Sahara.

Texts surviving from ancient times, as well as archaeological and epigraphical finds, have a great deal to tell us about Africa's internal trade. We know from such sources that *nundinae*, sorts of fairs, were held in rural centres on different days of the week, like the present-day Souks. In villages, *macella* (provision-markets) were established on a site consisting of a square surrounded by porticoes on to which there opened the booths of the various merchants. A number of such sites have been excavated, notably at Leptis, where sorts of kiosks were equipped with standard instruments for measuring length and capacity which were inspected by the municipal *aediles*. Other deals and transactions were concluded on the *forum* or in the shops and covered markets of the towns (occupied by bankers and money changers, tavern-keepers, cloth-merchants, and so on). The roads which were originally designed to serve the purposes of conquest and colonization soon had a stimulating effect on trade because, of course, they facilitated the transport of goods. Under Augustus and his successors, two roads of strategic importance linked Carthage with the south-west, via the valley of the Miliana, and with the south-east via the coast. The third side of the triangle was constituted by the Ammaedara–Tacape strategic highway, which was the first route attested by milestones. Under the Flavians and the first Antonines, the road system was greatly extended, in particular by the construction of the Carthage–Theveste highway; around the former military centres of Theveste and Lambaesis, a network of roads encircled the Aures and Nementcha mountains and stretched northwards towards Hippo-Regius. From then on, an ever-increasing number of roads were built up all over proconsular Africa and Mauretania where the fortified sector of Rapidum was linked, in one direction, with Gemellae and Lambaesis, and in the other, with the coastal cities of Caesarea and Saldae. After 235, however, the maintenance and repair of the obsolescent road system raised many problems.[36]

Much research has been done on the various technical questions relating to Roman roads: lay-out, structure, bridges and viaducts, auxiliary buildings for the use of travellers. These surveys make it abundantly clear that the Roman rulers were very conscious of the strategic and colonizing importance of the highways, their administrative role as illustrated by the relay posts of the messenger service run by the *cursus publicus*, and also their economic role; in this connection, special attention has been devoted, for example, to the route of the marble trade between Simitthu and Thabraca, and a study has been made of the sites of the *horrea* and *mansiones* (barns and warehouses) situated at crossroads and at various points along the roads for the storage of the grain and oil delivered to the tax-collectors.

36. P. Salama, 1951.

## The relations between the African provinces and the peoples of the Sahara

It has long been known that the Romans had three great Saharan fortresses on the confines of the desert, in the south of Tripolitania: they were those of Bu-Njem, Gheria el-Gherbia and Ghadames, which was called Cidamus in ancient times. Until fairly recently they were regarded merely as advanced post of the *limes*, but it has now been established that they were situated on the borderline between the desert and a zone under Roman control inhabited by sedentary peasants who lived in fortified farms and were mainly engaged in the cultivation of olive-trees in the drainage basins of the wadis. In this region, an original type of civilization developed, bearing the mark of strong local traditions on to which Punic influences had been grafted; the indigenous traditions and the Punic imprint, illustrated, in particular, by the numerous inscriptions in local alphabets, and by the survival of the Punic language up to the eve of the Arab invasion, proved adaptable, however, to the new way of life introduced by the Romans. The fortresses commanded the main routes linking the coast with the Fezzan, the land of the Garamantes. As far back as −19, Cornelius Balbus had attacked these Garamantes and, according to Pliny, had subdued several of their towns and fortresses, including Garama and Cidamus. Later, possibly in the reign of Domitian, an expedition led by Julius Maternus set out from Leptis Magna and reached Garama; accompanied by the king of the Garamantes and his army, the expedition then travelled as far as the country of the Ethiopians and the region of Agisymba where, we are told, rhinoceros were to be seen. This shows that the Romans were primarily interested in the Fezzan in so far as this permanent caravan base enabled them to approach the fringe of trans-Saharan Africa. It also explains why the crises and reconciliations recorded in laconic texts were a constant source of anxiety for the Romans in their relations with the kingdom of the Garamantes. By adding their findings to the scrappy information gleaned from such texts, the exploratory surveys and archaeological digs of the last few years have gradually widened our knowledge about the caravan routes leading to the confines of black Africa, and have given us a clearer idea of the progress made by the Romans in this direction; they have yielded copious details about the military, civil and commercial aspects of life in this border country, particularly at Bu-Njem.[37] In the first place, the trans-Saharan lands were suppliers of gold: between Punic times and the Muslim–Arabic period, various different routes were followed by the traders conveying the gold from the placers in Guinea to the shores of the Mediterranean, but each route left its own mark on the history of North Africa. The caravan

---

37. See in particular, in *the Comptes-rendus de l'Académie des inscriptions* for 1969, 1972, 1975, the communications by R. Rebuffat concerning the excavations of Bu-Njem (*Goleas*).

trade also brought black slaves, ostrich feathers, wild beasts, emeralds and carbuncles from the Sahara. In exchange, the Roman provinces supplied wine, metal objects, pottery, textiles and glass-ware, as has been shown by the excavations carried out, in particular, at the necropolises of the Fezzan.

The increasingly widespread use of the dromedary, from the second and third centuries, in the zone lying on the confines of the Sahara which is traversed by the routes running southwards and eastwards, probably had the effect of reviving a nomadic way of life by facilitating travel, so that wandering tribes had less difficulty in finding pasture for their flocks and herds and in plundering caravans and sedentary communities influenced in various degrees by Roman civilization. At first, the same tribe was probably divided into sedentary groups, which were established along the regular routes and on the *limes*, and camel-herding nomadic groups in the south; then, towards the middle of the fourth century, the imperial government became less and less capable of policing the desert and, although it did not follow a deliberate policy of withdrawal, the small settlements on the confines of the desert, which had flourished in the third century, found that they could only just survive and were in serious danger of extinction by the fifth century. It is not, therefore, because of a sudden influx of large numbers of dromedaries in the third century, as was systematically argued by E. F. Gautier, that the camel-herding nomads became a threat to the security of the southern frontiers. It is more likely that these animals were gradually introduced. The growing tendency to use them as a means of transport at first served the purposes of Roman policy, which had succeeded in adapting itself to the environmental conditions and thus in creating true centres of penetration operations, but ultimately had the opposite effect by enabling the nomadic tribes to acquire the necessary mobility for a fresh wave of attacks on the regions from which they had been driven back.[38] A further question of some interest is whether the intelligent Saharan policy of the Severan emperors may not be explained by the fact that the founder of the dynasty was born in Leptis Magna; owing to these origins, they may well have had access to first-hand information regarding the conditions, resources and routes existing in the arid hinterland.

## The rise of Romano-Berbers and problems of African society

Under Augustus and his successors, the population of the African provinces was composed of three groups distinguished from each other by the laws that governed them, as well as their languages and customs: Roman

38. E. Demougeot, pp. 209–47.

or Italian immigrants; Carthaginians and sedentary Libyans who had incorporated Punic institutions and practices into their own traditions, the latter being in the majority; nomadic Libyans who were severely restricted to certain areas or were banished entirely from the regions containing the usable land they had been forced to surrender.

It has often been said, quite correctly, that the African provinces were not regarded as resettlement areas: in the reign of Hadrian, colonies of veterans ceased to be founded in proconsular Africa, and those in Numidia were henceforth established for the benefit of soldiers recruited in African towns. As we have seen above, the status of the latter rose steadily until it had become completely romanized: virtually all indigenous town-dwellers had been integrated, and particularly the most wealthy – who sought by this means to escape from the socio-economic and juridical inferiority imposed upon them as a result of the Roman conquest – by the time that the *constitutio Antonina* was promulgated in 212. This granted Roman citizenship to all the free inhabitants of the empire who had not yet acquired it, except for the *dediticii*. Septimius Severus had already followed the example of the Antonines in elevating an immense number of communities to the rank of *municipium* or even *colonia*; non-citizens came to be in the minority, so that the existence of inferior juridical rights became less and less defensible by comparison with the need to simplify the administrative and fiscal systems, and with the trends in favour of political, legal, ethical and religious universalism. However, anyone who did not live in a large or small community of a municipal type, and particularly the members of tribes relegated to steppe-like or mountainous regions, had to be classified among the *dediticii* whose institutions and autonomy had not been recognized, even implicitly, when they had capitulated; they remained, therefore, outside the pale of romanized society.

Thus, ethnical distinctions tended to disappear only in the cities, which, however, were very numerous, especially in proconsular Africa. Social distinctions took their place in urban communities. The two highest social classes, namely, the senatorial and equestrian orders, enjoyed a status defined by the property qualification and reflected in insignia and titles. Although the property qualification was necessary, it was not sufficient in itself, whereas the principle of heredity was always applied; unless the emperor conferred the rank of senator or knight as a special favour, it was acquired solely by right of birth. Nevertheless, it is clear, from the study of individual careers as recorded in the available texts and, especially, in epigraphs, that this aristocracy frequently recruited new members; the families of the old Roman *nobilitas*, who dilapidated their fortunes in maintaining princely establishments, were more and more willing to open their ranks, first, to natives of the Western provinces of the empire, and later, to Graeco-Orientals. The first senator of African stock came from Cirta; he lived in the reign of Vespasian. A century later, around the year 170, the number of African senators had risen to about a hundred, forming the second largest group, after the group composed of men of Italian stock. Similarly, the first African knight known to history, who came from Musti, was given the gold ring by Tiberius, and by Hadrian's time there were several thousand knights in proconsular Africa and Numidia. Under the early empire, it was from the semi-noble equestrian order that the vast majority of officials were recruited to perform a dual function, the two branches of which later came to be separated, one being concerned with civil affairs and the other with military affairs. By the third century, a career in the latter branch had become hardly distinguishable from a purely military career. We see, then, that the rise of the Romano-Berbers was a prominent feature of the Antonine–Severan period, when Africans were playing an important role in Rome and the empire.

The main social force which had made it possible, under the early empire, and in the interests of the emperors themselves, to infuse fresh blood into the aristocratic orders, ensuring that the equestrian order, in particular, maintained the high standard of professional competence and personal qualities required for the performance of its dual function, was undoubtedly the urban middle class, which might be called the municipal bourgeoisie. Individuals thrown up by this decurion class became assimilated by the imperial aristocracy from which the emperors recruited the officials to fill key posts, one of the determining factors in these appointments being the spirit of solidarity prevailing, in Rome, between natives of the same province: this accounts for the predominance of Spaniards at the beginning of the second century, followed by that of the Africans, whose place was taken by the Syrians and then by the Pannonians.

The decurion middle class constituted, as has often been said, the very backbone of romanized communities in Africa. Under the early empire, it recruited its members almost entirely from a certain stratum of the land-tenure structure: the decurion lived in town on the income derived from his property, but he did not own a *latifundium* nor was he a peasant, and even if he felt attached to his land, he preferred a bourgeois style of living; he might be very rich: to make a name for himself in the city and earn the gratitude of his fellow-townsmen, he had to be lavish with gifts, which he distributed on a scale dictated by his vanity as much as by his generosity: he organized municipal games, gave doles of food and money to the poor, or erected and maintained public buildings. So it was that even the least significant of cities displayed a passion for architectural embellishment out of all proportion with their size. They were all determined to have their forum, complete with statues on their pedestals, their senate-house, their basilica for the courts of justice, baths, libraries, magnificent and costly edifices for the municipal games, as well as a multitude of temples in honour of official or traditional gods. Although offering certain advantages, such as the legal protection afforded by the municipal institutions and a higher standard of living, the proliferation of cities both great and small, like the wealth of the urban élite, was inevitably based on the exploitation of the peasants.

Even though the theory on the decline of the towns in the fourth century now has to be revised, since there is epigraphical evidence of relatively intense building activity and archaeology has revealed sumptuously decorated dwellings even during the third century, the social pattern of urban life was very different under the late empire from that prevailing under the early empire. Agriculture was still the main source of the incomes of the best people in the towns, but the decurions, representing the middle class which had hitherto governed through the city councils, were supplanted by an oligarchy of great landowners, the municipal *primates* or *principales*, who had made their fortune by exporting the corn and oil of their estates and had thus gained admission to the imperial nobility. These men of substance, who enjoyed the support of the imperial government, acceded to the highest positions in municipal and provincial government; they reconstructed public buildings destroyed in the third century or restored those falling apart with age, and embellished their cities, knowing that such liturgical activities opened the way to a career. The emperors adapted their urban policy to these social changes; the essential aim was to encourage the growth of towns, not only because it was one of the principal factors on which the empire's taxation system was based, but primarily because towns formed a solid rampart against the menace of the alleged barbarians. As for the general body of *curiales*, this being the term applied under the later empire to the *ordo decurionum*, it grew steadily poorer. It was collectively required to discharge increasingly onerous duties. As they were compulsorily invested with the responsibility for the municipal *munera* (food supplies, public services, upkeep of public buildings and cults, and so on), the *curiales* became in fact the local collectors of the taxes due by the city, and their properties were regarded as the security for the community's fiscal obligations. The richest *curiales* sought to rise to the rank of *primates*, and thus to take refuge in the privileged orders, namely, the senatorial or equestrian nobility. Others evaded the burden of municipal duties by joining the army or the administrative *militae*, or alternatively by insinuating themselves into the ranks of the clergy. The imperial government had to resort to drastic counter-measures against the desertion of the *curiae*, which was harmful to municipal life, in other words, to the very foundations of Roman rule. The *curiales* were further obliged to impose membership of their body on whoever possessed a fortune of the appropriate magnitude, which meant virtually all *possessores*. These made up a true hereditary class whose steady decline was reflected in that of the Roman way of life. Thus, by according privileges to a small group of *principales*, who ended, moreover, by deserting the cities, the empire crushed the general body of *curiales* out of existence, and this acerbated the social crisis and aggravated its repercussions on the development of the cities themselves.

Whereas under the principate townsmen who had grown rich through trade could eventually accede to the magistratures and become members of the *ordo decurionum*, while professional men such as physicians or architects were highly respected, this was no longer the case under the later empire. All the categories of the urban population below the *curiales* were reduced to the level of the 'plebs'. Every essential occupation, such as those concerned with food and transport, became a hereditary calling from which all legal channels of escape had been closed.

In rural areas, it was still unusual, during the fourth century, for great African landowners to live permanently on their estates in isolation from the rest of the world; as we have seen, they continued to take some interest in the embellishment of the cities and in municipal life. But at the end of the century the first signs appeared of a trend towards a seigneurial type of agriculture; the *dominus*, who had become progressively more independent on his lands, appropriated more and more of the prerogatives of the defaulting state, policing his own domain and even exercising the power of low justice within its boundaries. With the introduction of the taxation system of the *iugatio-capitatio*, it was in the interests both of the imperial treasury and of the large landed proprietors that there should be no change, on a given property, in the productive units of labour and land. Lay and ecclesiastical landlords were thus able, with the aid of the imperial administration, to debar the *coloni* from attempting to improve their lot, and succeeded in tying them to the land. As for the owners of small and medium-sized properties who lived in the cities, we have seen that they sought to escape from their position of *curiales*; they had a clear-cut choice between returning to the urban plebs, and accepting a kind of feudal relationship with the great estate neighbouring their own. A general tendency towards a concentration of the land in the hands of a few proprietors had, indeed, been in evidence for a long time; Cyprian had already recorded in the middle of the third century that 'the rich acquire one estate after another, ousting their needy neighbours and there is no end to the inordinate extension of their lands'.[39]

There is no space in this brief account to discuss the circumcellion movement which has always been a subject of controversy among specialists. It should simply be noted that these rebel bands were reported in Numidia in the fourth century and that this movement which developed in country areas, although violently anti-Catholic, had an obvious social character.

## Religious life and the advent of Christianity

The Roman domination had practically no inhibiting effect upon the worship of the traditional deities venerated by the indigenous population.

39. On these social questions see J. Gagé.

The old Berber cults of genii often continued, in humble rural sanctuaries, to be observed in their ancestral forms, but in some cases they were absorbed into the cults of the Graeco-Roman deities: for instance, the cult of the genii of fecundating or health-giving waters was sometimes masked by that of Neptune, Aesculapius or Serapis. In the regions which had belonged to the Numidian kingdoms, where Punic influence was profourd and durable, a pantheon of native gods was even adumbrated. But the majority of the population of the African provinces practised the cults of Saturn[40] and the Graeco-Roman equivalents of the old gods of Carthage; the religion of this African Saturn was merely a continuation of that of Baal Hammon, just as Juno-Caelestis, the chief deity of Roman Carthage, was none other than Tanit, the great goddess of Punic Carthage. The cult of the agrarian deities – the *Cereres* – had likewise been introduced in Numidian–Punic times. Romanization changed the African religion to some extent, of course: the Punic language disappeared from the ex-voto offerings, the abstract symbols inscribed on the stelae were frequently replaced by figures typifying deities generally derived from Graeco-Roman art, places of worship reflected the influence of Roman architecture. But where its inner meaning was concerned, the African religion kept its particularism alive, and this found expression in the ritual, the figures represented on the stelae, and even the wording of the Latin dedications, which echoed the time-honoured formulas with remarkable consistency.

As regards the empire's official cults, it was not long before they were honoured in the cities; loyalty to Rome had to be expressed, in particular, through the observance of religious practices, which was an integral part of Roman civilization. Members of the *ordo decurionum* who reached the zenith of their municipal career earnestly aspired to be invested with the dignity of flamen in perpetuity, so as to become a member of the priesthood which enjoyed the privilege of offering the prayers and vows of the citizens to the deified imperial couple. Furthermore, the provincial assembly, composed of the delegates of all the municipal assemblies, met once a year in Carthage to choose the provincial flamen – the high priest whose office it was to solemnize the official cult in the name of the whole province. Lastly, in each city, the cult of the Capitoline triad, Jupiter, Juno and Minerva, that of Mars, father and protector of the Roman people, of Venus, Ceres, Apollo, Mercury, Hercules and Bacchus were other official forms of the empire's religion and of Graeco-Roman spiritual life. Temples and statues, altars and sacrifices were everywhere to be found in honour of these deities, and of many others as well, such as Peace, Concord, Fortune, the genius of the empire, the genius of the Roman senate, and so on.

The deities of the eastern regions of the empire, readily accepted in

40. M. Leglay, 1966 and 1967.

Rome, were also honoured in Africa where they were introduced by officials, soldiers and merchants, who spread the cult of Isis, Mithra or Cybele, these being sometimes identified with local gods, as, for example, Isis with Demeter or Cybele with Caelestis. The great wave of mysticism which was invading the whole Roman world reached Africa in this way, although the salvation-seeking eastern religions did not appeal to the African élite as strongly as the *thiasus* of the worship of Bacchus or Demeter. Similarly, spiritualistic doctrines, and especially Neo-Platonism, gained ground in some circles and were even reconciled with certain Punic traditions: the Chorfa stelae, for example, illustrate tendencies influenced by Neo-Platonism. Certain authors even think that the idea expressed by these monuments, namely, that there is a supreme deity who acts upon the terrestrial world through hypostases, had probably prepared the way for Christian monotheism.

Does this explain why Christianity developed in Africa earlier than in the other Western provinces of the empire? The rapid introduction of the new religion was promoted, of course, by the close relations with Rome, and possibly also by the existence of small Jewish communities living in the ports, and particularly at Carthage. It is remarkable, however, that Latin should have won recognition as the language of African Christianity from the outset, while the Roman church was still using Greek. According to Tertullian, who lived at the end of the second and the beginning of the third century, there were large numbers of Christians in Africa at that time, belonging to all classes and all occupations. It was possible to hold a synod of seventy-one bishops at Carthage around the year 220; ninety bishops attended another synod convened about 240. This shows that small Christian communities were scattered in many African cities, constituting what the empire no doubt regarded as a serious danger. It was true that by rejecting the imperial ideology and particularly by refusing to participate in the cult of the emperor, the Christians were resolutely adopting the stance of an opposition movement. In spite of its broadminded outlook and its usually tolerant attitude towards new cults, Rome could not compromise with a sect which aimed to create an ever-widening network of groups pursuing a different ideal outside the framework of the official institutions. Harsh penalties were therefore inflicted upon the Christians: in 180, twelve Christians of the town of Scilli were decapitated by order of the proconsul, and the year 203 saw the martyrdom of Saints Perpetua and Felicity and their companions, who were delivered to the beasts in the arena of the Carthage amphitheatre. But the repressive measures, which, it must be added, were only sporadically enforced, failed to stifle the zeal and fervour of the faithful, many of whom were avidly bent on martyrdom.

There is no room in this brief account for a review of the history of African Christianity, which was at its zenith in the period between the peace won by the church in the fourth century and the establishment of the Arabs in North Africa. A special study might be devoted to this complex question, which involves more especially a survey of the Donatist schism and, of course, of Christian literature from Tertullian to Saint Augustine, whose personality and work were the last brilliant product of the Roman way of life in Africa. The West is indebted to him for preserving and handing down the heritage of Latin culture, as Christianity throughout the ages has been for the legacy of his doctrine, whose richness has seldom been paralleled.

## African culture

After being long neglected by writers of Roman history, the art of the provinces and outlying cultures have now become the centre of attention. This is due to a clearer understanding of the limits of romanization and the different forms it took in its contacts with indigenous societies. Furthermore, there is no denying the truth that the art of a given province cannot be dissociated from its economic, social and religious life. In this connection, it became necessary, in order to study and appreciate the art developed in the African provinces under Roman rule, to take account of the enduring Libyco-Punic substratum which, moreover, continued to follow its own pattern of life and evolution for centuries.

There can be no question of dealing here with the complex problems which are being tackled mainly by archaeologists. We need only refer the reader to G. Charles-Picard's book entitled *La Civilisation de l'Afrique romaine*, which devotes an important chapter to African literature and art. We shall merely draw attention to a few points. The first is that this African culture is not indebted solely to the Phoenicians and Carthaginians for its early inspiration. When sea-faring peoples of the east began to frequent the coasts of Africa at the beginning of the first millennium before our era the country had already been penetrated, through contacts with the Mediterranean islands, by various techniques such as the one which gave rise to the painted pottery known as Kabyle or Berber. The existence at that time of sedentary populations ready to accept the rudiments of an urban form of civilization has now been demonstrated by the Algerian–Tunisian dolmens and the haounets of northern Tunisia, as well as by the objects found in the funeral monuments excavated in north-west Morocco.[41] Later the Phoenician and Punic culture, mixed with Egyptian and Oriental elements, and impregnated with hellenistic influences after the fourth century before our era, was adopted and adapted by the native population before, but mainly after, the destruction of Carthage. Lastly, the Italo-Roman contributions, being more significant and more directly imposed, inevitably generated hybrid varieties which are often difficult to

41. Recent work has completely transformed traditional views. See, for example, G. Camps, 1960b and 1961, E. G. Gobert, pp. 1–44; J. Tixeront, pp. 1–50; P. A. Février, 1967, pp. 107–23.

define. It has become customary, however, to distinguish between two cultures in Africa, one being official and Roman, and the other popular, indigenous and provincial. But there are monuments, of course, in which the two trends meet and contaminate each other, so that they lose their separate identities.

African architectural works generally reproduced types of public monuments which were prevalent throughout the Roman world, and accordingly derived their inspiration from an essentially Roman technique and ideal. Nor were ornamental sculptures and the great statues of gods, emperors and prominent men very different in style from their counterparts in Italy or in other provinces. However, architectural or sculptural creations linked with the religious or funeral traditions of the population, as well as certain special construction or decoration techniques, bore the stamp of local characteristics: this is evident in the temples raised to deities who retained their native individuality despite their apparent identification with Roman gods, in certain monumental sepulchres, in a special wall-building technique known as 'opus africum', in domestic architecture and, lastly, in the votive stelae still imbued with pre-Roman influences. In the Severan period, the sculptures of Leptis Magna and those of other towns in Tripolitania and proconsular Africa were strongly influenced by a significant artistic trend originating in Asia Minor, which was all the more readily assimilated because it was in keeping with ancient, but still vigorous tendencies in African art.

The countless mosaics brought to light since the beginning of this century also display local tendencies and characteristics. Here again, we can only refer the reader to the specialized periodicals and to the above-mentioned book by G. Charles-Picard who brings his chapter on the 'African baroque' to a close with the following words: 'To say the very least, therefore, Africa fully repaid her debt to Rome, and showed that she was capable of reaping benefits from her borrowings in a spirit which is neither that of Greece nor that of the hellenized Levant.'[42]

## Part II: From Rome to Islam  P. SALAMA

When Roman domination ended in North Africa, after holding sway for four centuries in some regions, up to five in others, the internal situation presented a complex picture. Regional risings, religious conflicts, social unrest, all led to a worsening climate, but the soundness of administrative experience and the prestige of Latin culture gave this imported civilization a good many chances of survival.

Split into vanquished or independent zones according to the vicissitudes

42. G. Charles-Picard, 1959, p. 353.

of foreign conquest or local resistance, post-Roman and pre-Islamic North Africa experienced one of the most distinctive periods in its history.[43]

# The regions under foreign occupation

Over a period of close on three centuries, two foreign invaders in turn took over the tutelage of Rome without ever succeeding in entirely reconstituting its frontiers.

## The Vandal episode

Nothing could have been more unexpected in North Africa than these conquerors of Germanic origin. No domination was less in keeping with the actual circumstances of the country. Outstripping the other Germanic peoples who, like them, had swarmed over western Europe in +406, the Vandals settled first of all in the south of the Iberian peninsula which has seemingly perpetuated their name (Vandalusia = Andalusia).

Whether invited or not to intervene in the internal quarrels of Roman power in North Africa, they crossed the Straits of Gibraltar, 80 000 strong, under the leadership of their king Gaiseric (or Genseric) in +429. Their advance made lightning progress. In +430 they were already besieging the town of Hippone and the Romans acknowledged their possession of the Constantine region in +435. Three years later they took Carthage and, after a brief withdrawal in +442, commenced three large-scale operations in +455: the final annexation of all the eastern zone of Roman Africa, the conquest of the majority of the major islands in the western Mediterranean – the Balearics, Sardinia and Sicily – and an audacious expedition to sack Rome itself. The eastern empire, hoping to oust these intruders, suffered a naval disaster in +468 and acknowledged the *fait accompli* – a treaty in +474 finally established good relations between Byzantium and the Vandals who represented a major maritime power in the western Mediterranean.

Did this Germanic occupation of a part of North Africa over a century prove beneficial? In reading literary sources of the time, openly hostile to the usurpers, one is appalled at their brutality. But modern criticism has succeeded in removing the subject from its inflammatory context. The term 'vandalism', synonymous with the spirit of destruction, was coined only at the end of the eighteenth century, and today, in the light of much archaeological evidence, it seems clear that in their poor management of the territory, the Vandals sinned more through omission than intention.

We are getting an increasingly clear idea of the legal structure of the Vandal state: royalty springing from a military aristocracy, both holding authority over the great public and private domains of the old Roman

43. Our title 'From Rome to Islam' is taken from a study, mainly of a bibliographical character, by C. Courtois, *Revue Africaine*, 1942, pp. 24–55.

Africa; the maintenance of Roman administration, regional and local, including even the use, in support of the new royal cult, of the old provincial assemblies of imperial tradition. Carthage thus became the rich metropolis of the new state. This same concern for Latin traditionalism affected the agrarian structure where the old Roman laws governing the organization of peasant life, particularly the *Lex Manciana*, were ingeniously preserved. The phenomenon of population drift away from the towns, which had already begun, as everywhere, under the later empire, was intensified, bringing with it the decay and retrenchment of many towns. On the other hand, certain others, such as Ammaedara, Theveste or Hippone, kept on building. It seems, in fact, and the maintenance of the monetary economy bears this out, that during this period neither agriculture nor trade experienced any obvious decline. External relations seem to have been prosperous and the whole group of Vandal possessions was termed the 'grain empire'. Symbolizing the wealth of the well-to-do classes, fine jewellery, Germanic in style, has been found at various times in Hippone, Carthage, Thuburbo Maius and Mactar.

On the political and religious sides the picture is darker. On the southern and western flanks of their North African domain, the Vandals experienced such assaults from the 'Moors', the general term for the North African rebels, that it is virtually impossible to fix a definite frontier to their zone of control. It was no doubt a fluctuating one and probably at no time extended westwards beyond the region of Djemila–Cuicul.

In religion there was a constant climate of crisis. The Vandals were Christian, but professed the Arian creed, a heresy that was intolerable to the traditional Catholic clergy. This led to the virtually systematic repression of the clergy by a central authority which was little inclined to put up with resistance on questions of dogma. Anti-Catholic fury reached its climax following a pseudo-council held in Carthage in +484.

This situation of moral and social crisis thus brought about a process of collapse, hastened, in fact, by the excesses or incompetence of Gaiseric's successors. In +530 the supplanting by Gelimer of King Hilderic, ally of Justinian, emperor of the eastern empire, sparked off the Byzantine conquest.[44]

---

44. Ancient literary texts concerning the Vandal period in North Africa are mainly by three 'partisan' authors who are clearly hostile: first, the Catholic bishop, Victor de Vita (*Histoire de la persécution dans les provinces africaines*) and Fulgentius of Ruspe (*Opera*); and second, the Byzantine historian Procopius (*The Vandal War*). Latest editions: J. Fraipont and O. Veh.

The basic modern study is that of C. Courtois, 1955, a major work, corrected and supplemented on certain points by many archaeological contributions. The question as a whole is taken up by H.-J. Diesner, 1965, pp. 957–92, and 1966.

The land tenure problem has been illustrated by the discovery of legal deeds inscribed

## The Byzantine episode

The court at Constantinople, regarding itself as the legitimate successor of the Roman empire, resolved to expel the new Germanic states in the west from the territories they had usurped. It was in North Africa that this operation proved least ineffective.

In + 533, on Justinian's orders, an expeditionary force commanded by Belisarius wiped out Vandal authority in three months and this people as such disappeared from history. The first Byzantine measure, the famous edict of +534, which reorganized the country's administrative structures, set the pattern that was to be followed: a policy of both a military and legal kind, too closely based on that of the Romans. There was failure to realize that after a hundred years and more of slackened discipline, the rural masses would no longer accept the rigidity of administrative conservatism; and what in fact the century and a half of Byzantine occupation in North Africa produced was some undeniable achievements in the field of building against a backcloth of perpetual insecurity.

Reconquest of the country was, in itself, difficult, and its process appears to anticipate to a certain extent, the Arab and French interventions in the seventh and nineteenth centuries respectively. Once the mirage of Vandal power – comparable to the future Turkish administration – was removed, the conquerors came up against the resistance of the indigenous chieftains, and vanquishing them was a slow task, achieved either by force or subterfuge. From + 534 to + 539, the patrician Solomon, a talented but violent general, was checked and then killed by the mountain people of Iavdas in the Aurès, and the nomads of Coutzina and Antalas in the Tunisian–Tripolitanian steppes. His successor, Johannes Troglita, adopting a more flexible attitude *vis-à-vis* the Berber princes, divided them by intrigue or got rid of them by assassination, but the pacification he obtained was illusory (+544–8). Agitation persisted then, until the end of the seventh century. One need only study a map showing the Byzantine strongholds in North Africa to understand that this 'strategy of fortresses' barring the invasion routes, occupying all the crossing points and defending the country to its very heart, was evidence of a perpetual state of alert

on wooden tablets or fragments of pottery: C. Courtois, L. Leschi, J. Miniconi, C. Ferrat, C. Saumagne; P. A. Février and J. Bonnal, pp. 239–59.

Concerning the territorial expansion of the Vandal kingdom to the south and west of Numidia: P. A. Février, 1962–7; idem, 1965, pp. 88–91; H.-J. Diesner, 1969, pp. 481–90.

Concerning institutions: A. Chastagnol, pp. 130–4; A. Chastagnol and N. Duval, pp. 87–118. Concerning the state of the kingdom and urban decline in particular: L. Maurin, pp. 225–54. Concerning the religious question: C. Courtois, 1954; C. Lepelley, pp. 189–204; many works by Diesner quoted in the Desanges–Lancel analytical bibliography, 1970, pp. 486–7; J.-L. Maier.

for the enemy loomed everywhere. The old offensive spirit was accordingly replaced by defensive tactics evincing an anxious state of mind.

It was in vain that, at the end of the sixth century and the beginning of the seventh, the emperors Maurice Tiberius and later Heraclius attempted to shorten the front by reducing the area of territory occupied. It was to no avail. Byzantine expansion was never able to extend westwards beyond the region of Setif. Only a few of the most outlying coastal towns were garrisoned; but closely blockaded by the 'Moors', they also foreshadowed a famous military situation, that of the Spanish *presidios* in the sixteenth century.

In this context it is to the credit of the Byzantines that they managed to exercise their authority in the administrative and economic domains. The Roman towns in the past continued to decline and their populations dwindled, in the shelter of the powerful fortresses which constituted their citadels, as at Tebessa, Haïdra or Timgad. The old provinces, sometimes reconstituted artificially, received governors who were under the authority of a praetorian prefect established in Carthage; but this was quite separate from the military power. At the end of the sixth century a supreme head, the exarch or patrician, concentrated virtually all power in his hands.

Domestic policy, stemming from Roman methods, naturally sought to restore the tax revenue of old. The *annona*, the annual tax payable in wheat, was accordingly reintroduced. Following confiscation of the royal domains of the Vandals, private estates were given back to their former owners, the search extending, if necessary, to the third generation of their descendants. One can imagine the number of legal and material disputes this operation gave rise to. In every domain, taxation was regarded as a crushing burden. Economic life was, however, relatively prosperous. Maintenance of the monetary economy for all transactions, and the handing over of external trade to official agents, gave Carthage and its hinterland a reputation of great wealth in the Mediterranean world, all the more so since the two sides of the straits of Sicily were under Byzantine authority. It is to be doubted whether the North African rural population benefited to any great extent from this general situation.

As regards religious affairs, the new masters re-established the traditional cult, i.e. Orthodox Catholicism, and proscribed Arianism. A fresh revival of Donatism, which had formerly been rife in Roman Africa, was severely repressed; it was, quite rightly, regarded as a phenomenon of social strife. Byzantium even indulged in a dogmatic crisis, that of monothelitism, a futile discussion on the divine and human natures of Christ and, on the event of the Mohammedan conquest, the North African clergy was torn apart by this question.

From this time on, the widespread administrative or military insubordination, abuse of power and corruption in high places, in the face of the constant Berber threat, portended sooner or later inevitable collapse. It took some fifty years, from +647 to +698, for a new and unexpected

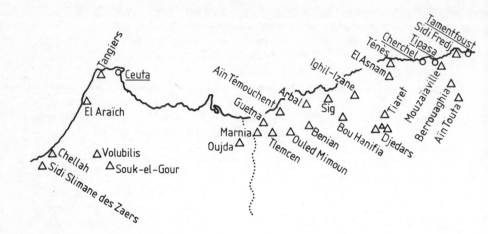

KEY

1. Main military constructions and fortresses in Byzantine territory

| | | | |
|---|---|---|---|
| 1 | Lebda = former Leptis Magna | 29 | El Kef = Sicca Veneria |
| 2 | Tripoli = Oea | 30 | Henchir Djezza = Aubuzza |
| 3 | Sabratha = Sabratha | 31 | Ebba = Obba |
| 4 | Bou Ghrara = Gigthis | 32 | Lorbeus = Laribus |
| 5 | Gabès = Tacapes | 33 | Sidi Amara |
| 6 | Bordj Iunca = Macomades Minores | 34 | Ksar Lemsa = Limisa |
| 7 | Ras Kaboudia = Justinianopolis | 35 | Henchir Sguidam |
| 8 | Ras Salakta = Sullecthum | 36 | El Kessra = Chusira |
| 9 | Ras Dimass = Thapsus | 37 | Djelloula |
| 10 | Lemna = Leptiminus | 38 | Henchir = Ogab |
| 11 | Sousse = Hadrumetum Justiniana | 39 | Sbiba = Sufes |
| 12 | Hergla = Horrea Caelia | 40 | Haïdra = Ammaedara |
| 13 | Henchir Fratis = Aphrodisium | 41 | Gastel |
| 14 | Aïn Tébornok = Tubernuc | 42 | Tébessa = Theveste |
| 15 | Carthage = Carthago Justiniana | 43 | Henchir Bou Driès |
| 16 | Béja = Vaga | 44 | Sbeïtla = Sufetula |
| 17 | Hamman Darradji = Bulla Regia | 45 | Fériana = Thelepte |
| 18 | Bordj Hellal | 46 | Gafsa = Capsa |
| 19 | Aïn Tpunga = Tignica | 47 | Négrine = Ad Maiores |
| 20 | Henchir Dermoulia = Coreva | 48 | Badès = Badias |
| 21 | Henchir Tembra = Thaborra | 49 | Thouda = Thabudeos |
| 22 | Téboursouk = Thubursicu Bure | 50 | Biskra = Vescera |
| 23 | Dougga = Thugga | 51 | Tolga |
| 24 | Aïn Hedja = Agbia | 52 | Tobna = Thubunae |
| 25 | El Krib = Mustis | 53 | Ksar Bellezma |
| 26 | Kern el Kebch = Aunobari | 54 | Aïn Zana = Diana Veteranorum |
| 27 | Henchir Douamis = Uchi Maius | 55 | Aïn el Ksar |
| 28 | Sidi Bellaoui | 56 | Lambèse = Lambaese |

FIG. 19.3 *The Byzantine episode in North Africa showing military constructions, fortresses, towns*

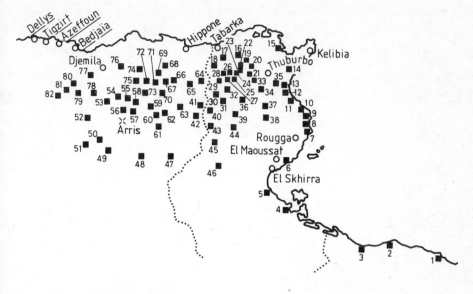

57    Timgad = Thamugadi
58    Henchir Guesses
59    Baghaï = Bagai
60    Khenchela = Mascula
61    Henchir Oum Kif = Cedias
62    Ksar el Kelb = Vegesela ?
63    Henchir Cheragreg
64    Taoura = Thagora
65    Mdaourouch = Madauros
66    Tifech = Tipasa
67    Khamissa = Thubursicu Numidarum
68    Guelma = Calama
69    Announa = Thibilis
70    Ksar Adjeledj
71    Ksar Sbahi = Gadiaufala
72    Aïn el Bordj = Tigisis
73    Djebel Ferroukh
74    Constantine = Constantina
75    Fedj Sila = Sila
76    Mila = Milev
77    Sétif = Sitifis
78    Zraïa = Zarai
79    Kherbet Zembia = Cellas
80    Aïn Toumella = Thamallula
81    Oued Ksob
82    Béchilga = Zabi Justiniana

FIG. 19.3 *Key continued*

2. *Place-names underlined:* Towns occupied by the Byzantines lying outside protected territory

Bedjaïa = Saldae, probably occupied
Azeffoun = Ruzasus, probably occupied
Tigzirt = Iomnium, Byzantine rampart
Dellys = Rusuccuru, Byzantine objects
Tamentfoust = Rusguniae, Byzantine inscriptions
Tipasa = Tipasa, Byzantine coins
Cherchel = Caesarea, texts
Sebta (Ceuta) = Septem, texts

3. *Place-names not underlined:* Last dated evidence of towns and monuments in independent Africa

| | Date |
|---|---|
| Sidi Fredj (Sidi Ferruch): church inscription | 449/538 |
| Mouzaïaville: Funerary inscription (also 6th-century objects) | 495 |
| Berrouaghia = Zaba: church inscription | 474 |
| Aïn Touta: church inscription | 461 |
| El Asnam = Castellum Tingitanum: church inscription | 475 |
| Ighil Izane = Mina: ecclesiastical text | 525 |
| Tiaret: funerary inscription | 509 |
| Djedars de Frenda: funerary monuments | 5th to 7th centuries (?) |
| Sig = Tasaccura: funerary inscription | after 450 |
| Arbal = Regiae: funerary inscription | 494 |
| Bou Hanifia = Aquae Sirenses: Funerary inscription | 577 |
| Bénian = Alamiliaria: funerary inscription | end of 5th century |
| Aïn Témouchent = Albulae (Safar?): funerary inscription | 544 |
| Ouled Mimoun = Altava: funerary inscription; | 599 |
| epigraphic context | 655 |
| Tlemcen = Pomaria: funerary inscription | 651 |
| Guetna: funerary inscription | 524 |
| Marnia = Numerus Syrorum: funerary inscription | 460 |
| but occupation comparable with that of Tlemcen | |
| Vicinity of Oudja: coins | first half of 7th century |
| Volubilis (Walili): funerary inscription | 655 |
| concerning a dignitary of Altava | |
| Souk el Gour: funerary monument | 7th century |
| Sidi Slimane des Zaers: coins | first half of 7th century |
| Chellah = Sala: Byzantine weight | 6th century |
| El Araich (Larache) = Lixus: coins | first half of 7th century |
| Tangiers = Tingis: coins | first half of 7th century |

.......................... Present day frontiers between Morocco, Algeria, Tunisia and Libya.

visitor, the Arab conqueror, to wipe out the Byzantine rule for ever.

Apart from the historical interest of the period, splendid archaeological remains have been preserved. The building of large-scale fortresses, the creation or decoration of churches, sometimes in sumptuous style, as at Sabratha or Kelibia, display a remarkable spirit of perseverance and faith.[45]

## The independent regions

If we bear in mind that Roman Africa of the later empire had already experienced a number of political and social transformations, we can realize the extent to which the arrival of the Vandals served as a liberating channel for these old tendencies. 'Eternal Africa' regained its rights and the foreign presence, near or far, was no longer regarded as a burden. It would be a delusion, then, to differentiate, in psychological terms, between the regions governed by Berber princes and nominally owing allegiance to Vandal or Byzantine sovereignty and those regions which were completely independent. The former, situated on the periphery of the zones under foreign occupation, were decentralized to such a point that they were constantly breaking away from the central authority. The Byzantine rulers in fact approved the grant of official investiture to Iavdas in the Aurēs, to Guenfan, Antalas and Coutzina in the High Tunisian steppes and to Carcazan in Tripolitania; all these 'vassals' freely administered the territories settled on them, and there was virtually no question of their ever being taken back from them.

45. Literature from ancient times concerning Byzantine Africa is basically represented by the Greek historian Procopius, who was a veritable 'war correspondent' during the reconquest: *The Vandal War* (see note 44 above) and *The Buildings* (ed. B. H. Dewing); and by the Latin poet Corippus, who recounted the military epic of Johannes Troglita against the Moors: the *Iohannis* (ed. Partsch and ed. Diggle-Goodyear). The fundamental critical work on the period is still that of C. Diehl. Since that date archaeological discoveries and publications on points of detail have multiplied. We quote only the most recent.

On history properly speaking: K. Belkhodja. On the geographical limits of the occupation: J. Desanges, 1963, pp. 41–69.

The fortifications are being studied in greater detail: R.-G. Goodchild, 1966, pp. 225–50; A. H. M. Jones, 1968, pp. 289–97; S. Lancel and L. Pouthier, pp. 247–53; J. Lassus, 1956, pp. 232–9; 1971; 1975, pp. 463–74; P. Romanelli, 1970, pp. 398–407.

On religious questions: P. Champetier, pp. 103–20; A. Berthier, pp. 283–92, and more particularly Y. Duval and P.-A. Février, pp. 257–320.

Religious architecture, mosaics and epigraphy during the same period are dealt with fundamentally, as regards Haidra and Sbeitla, by N. Duval, 1971; cf. N. Duval and F. Baratte, 1973, 1974, which refer back to the complete bibliography; cf. P. Cintas and N. Duval, pp. 155–265; M. Fendri; N. Duval, 1974, pp. 157–73; G. de Angelis d'Ossat and R. Farioli, pp. 29–56. Money hoards and the Byzantine coinage issued by the Carthage mint have been catalogued by C. Morrisson. A hoard of gold coins has recently been discovered in excavations at Rougg-a, near El Djem in Tunisia, which was undoubtedly buried at the time of the first Arab foray into the country, in 647: R. Guery, pp. 318–19.

As regards the zones which were quite free from external interference, some of them remote from Vandal or Byzantine strongholds, in the former Mauretania Caesariensis and Mauretania Tingitana they enjoyed absolute independence from +429 onwards and their rulers did not interfere in their neighbours' affairs unless it was to gain some personal advantage.

Here we again come up against one of the main constants in the history of the Maghrib of classical times – the tendency towards territorial division and rivalry the moment a centralizing force has disappeared. Political division is then governed by geographical considerations.

Very little is unfortunately known of the structure of this post-Roman independent North Africa. Some kingdoms were formed there by large socio-political federations, only revealed to us by rare literary allusions or chance archaeological findings. There was, for instance, at the beginning of the sixth century, in the Altaya and Tlemcen region, the government of Masuna, 'king of the Moors and the Romans'; a little later, in the Aurès, the reign of a certain Masties, '*dux* for sixty-seven years, *imperator* for forty years', who never repudiated his faith 'either towards the Romans or the Moors'. Vartaia, another local ruler, pays his tribute; he is perhaps ruler of the zone of Hodna. There is no doubt that the town of Tiaret, a former citadel of the Roman *limes*, admirably situated at the junction of the nomad and sedentary worlds, was also, as far back as the fifth century, the capital of a dynasty whose power is still symbolized by the Djedars of Frenda, great tombs of impressive majesty. The powerful Garmul, king of Mauretania, who destroyed a Byzantine army in 571 ought also perhaps to be considered in this connection. Lastly, during the sixth and seventh centuries, an indigenous principality existed in distant Tingitana in the northern part of where is now Morocco, whose vitality is attested by the inscriptions at Volubilis and the Mausoleum of Souk el Gour.

In most cases, the socio-political organization reveals a structure that is neither sketchy nor anarchical. Original institutions combined Berber traditions and the Roman administrative model. 'Moors' and 'Romans' were associated, a formula which certainly implies collaboration between the peasant element, non-romanized, and the city-dwellers, with several centuries of Latin influence behind them. There was, then, no kind of challenge to an administrative and cultural heritage which was foreign in origin, and which at times was a source of some pride. The historical map which we have drawn for these regions shows the survival of small urban centres such as Tiaret, Altaya, Tlemcen and Volubilis, still Christian in character, where the use of Latin was still current practice until the seventh century.

But we must not delude ourselves concerning the existence of these lingering effects. The future lay not in the nostalgic attachment of petty kings to defunct prestige but in the irresistible drive towards independence and breaking away with which the rural masses were inspired. The area as a whole was irrevocably committed to the process of de-romanization, and even de-Christianization, a process which was to assume different forms and involve varying periods of time according to the locality. The most immediate and elementary manifestation of this phenomenon was the assault launched everywhere by the mountain-dwellers and nomads on the traditional symbols of wealth, that is to say, towns and estates. We know that Djémila, Timgad, Thelepte and several famous cities were devastated before the arrival of the Byzantine armies. The cross-checking of archaeological and literary sources and, more especially, the discovery of several hoards of coins, has revealed among other disorders, a general rebellion which occurred at the very end of the fifth century. At the same time, operations by the major nomad tribes in south Tunisia and Tripolitania, such as the Levathes or Louata tribe, show the considerable part played by camels in the general economy and military tactics of the fifth and sixth centuries. To vanquish these nomads in the open country, the Byzantine army had to face a triple ring of animals attached to one another, a veritable living bastion that had to be cut down with the sword. However, these were all hostile operations against foreigners, Vandals or Byzantines. In addition the independent regions themselves experienced comparable turmoil, inter-regional wars or local forays.

Behind these tumultuous events, which fanned violence over a long period until ultimately a balance was reached, we can imagine an economic and social background which led to the gradual impoverishment of the people in general. In statistics which we have, for example, for the number of dioceses in the year + 484 in Mauretania Caesariensis we still find the names of most of the towns of classical Roman Africa. Even supposing that many of these had already been reduced to village status, they none the less existed. The fact that churches were still being built, often adorned with fine mosaics as at El Asnam, points to creative activity, necessarily based on remaining sources of wealth. No doubt benefit was still being reaped from the momentum of the previous epoch. Archaeology, however, reveals virtually nothing comparable in the sixth and seventh centuries. The abandonment of the towns thus continued at the same time as this new society, of a basically rural type – one that was to be found everywhere in the Upper Middle Ages – became consolidated.

What monumental remains did this final period bequeath to us? The districts close to the Mauretanian littoral, where the Byzantines were ensconced, were readily open to influences. For example, fine bronze candelabra dating from the sixth century were found in the ruins of Mouzaiaville to the south of Tipasa. The very site of Ténès was made famous by the discovery of one of the most remarkable treasures of gold and silver ware in the ancient world, including more especially the official regalia of imperial dignitaries. Their existence in this remote place is still a mystery. It is the author's belief that all these jewels were stolen and are perhaps related to the sack of Rome which was perpetrated, the texts tell us, in +455 by Vandal troops with Moorish contingents.

But once we move away from the coastal areas and the districts under foreign occupation, building activity ceases at the end of the fifth century. There are, however, two important exceptions to this rule, represented by the famous colossus-type tombs in which the art of building recovered its pristine excellence without necessarily being affected by any foreign influence. Thus in Morocco, the Mausoleum of Souk-el-Gour, which can be dated to the seventh century, and in Algeria, the Djedars of Frenda, extending chronologically from the fifth to the seventh (?) centuries, display an architectural vigour that would be inexplicable if the local context had been one of utter destitution. It is hardly surprising that the first Muslim kingdoms in the central and western Maghrib, that of Rostemides of Tiaret, and then of the Idrissids of Walili (Volubilis), should have taken root precisely in these very places.

And so the ancient period came to an end in these regions, a hybrid episode in which the action of social and political transformations gradually eroded Latin influence, revealing that unquenchable spirit of independence and immense steadfastness of purpose which is the constant hallmark of the history of North Africa.[46]

46. There are only sporadic references to the situation in the independent regions in ancient literary sources: there are allusions by Procopius and Corippus, for example, when the political intervention of the Vandals and the Byzantines involves the Moors. For example, the *Iohannis* contains hundreds of details on indigenous sociology. But our main evidence is drawn from archaeological findings. There is an eminently intuitive analysis of the problem by C. Courtois, 1955, pp. 325–52. Several writers have commented on the inscription in honour of Masties, found in 1941 in Arris in the Aurès; cf. latterly J. Carcopino, 1956, pp. 339–48, in reply to Courtois' conclusions. The 'roumis' of Volubilis have been studied by J. Carcopino, 1948, pp. 288–301. For the most recent epigraphic evidence, J. Marcillet-Jaubert.

On the great rebellion at the end of the fifth century, P. Salama, 1959, pp. 238–9.

The economic and monetary situation of the independent regions is described by R. Turcan, pp. 201–57; J. Heurgon, 1958, gives a remarkable study of the jewels and advances the theory that these belonged to a wealthy family established in Ténès. But the eclectic nature of the collection seems more in keeping with the mentality of a thief. As regards the continuance of building activity after 429 see, for example, P.-A. Février, 1965.

The great post-Roman dynastic tombs have been the subject of a very recent analytical study: G. Camps, 1974a, pp. 191–208, and more especially F. Kadra.

Concerning the survival during a large part of the Muslim Middle Ages – and more particularly in Tlemcen, Bedjaïa, Kairouan and Tripoli – of Christian communities which generally still spoke Latin: C. Courtois, 1945, pp. 97–122 and 193–266; A. Majoubi, 1966, pp. 85–104.

PLATE 19.1 *Mosaic from Sousse: Virgil writing the* Aeneid

PLATE 19.2 *Mosaic from Chebba: The Triumph of Neptune*

PLATE 19.3 *Aqueduct from Zaghouan, which supplied Carthage*

PLATE 19.4 *Sabratha (Libya):*
frons scaenae *of the Roman theatre*

PLATE 19.5 *Tripoli (the ancient town of
Oea, Libya): triumphal arch of Marcus
Aurelius; detail of the Triumph*

PLATE 19.6 *Maktar (ancient town
of Mactaris Tunisia): arch of
Trajan, entrance to the forum.*

PLATE 19.7 (*left*) *Djemila (ancient town of Cuicul, Algeria): centre of the town*

PLATE 19.8 *Timgad (ancient city of Thamugadi, Algeria): avenue and arch of Trajan*

PLATE 19.9 *Haïdra (Tunisia): Byzantine fortress, 6th century, general view*

PLATE 19.10 *Lebda (ancient town of Leptis Magna, Libya): work being carried out in the Roman amphitheatre*

PLATE 19.11 *Sbeitla (Tunisia); oil press installed in an ancient street of the Roman town (6th–7th centuries)*

PLATE 19.12 *Haïdra (Tunisia): Byzantine fortress, 6th century, detail*

PLATE 19.13 *Timgad (Algeria): Byzantine fortress, 6th century: south rampart, officers' living quarters and chapel*

PLATE 19.14 *Jedar at Ternaten, near Frenda (Algeria): burial chamber, 6th century*

PLATE 19.15 *Timgad (Algeria): Byzantine fortress, 6th century*

# The Sahara
# in classical antiquity

P. SALAMA

The traditional notion of 'classical antiquity' may appear *a priori* incompatible with the study of Saharan problems. These have a very particular classification. To take only one example: in Mediterranean archaeology, classical antiquity covers a period of roughly a thousand years, from the fifth century before our era to the fifth century of our era, but in the protohistory of the Sahara it would cover the end of the 'caballine' period and part of the 'Libyco-Berber', neither of these periods, moreover, being exactly datable. Any absolute chronology would therefore seem to be ruled out in this case.

Nevertheless, during that same millennium, the Saharan universe was the scene of highly important events which were connected in large part with the history of the Graeco-Roman world. So I have no hesitation in using classical chronological criteria, which are valid for the whole of the known world.

How is the question of the Sahara of antiquity approached by the historian? First, Graeco-Latin textual sources must be examined: while the information collected is not always reliable, and may induce error, it is in principle of value. The next step is to bring modern methods of scholarship to bear so as to correct the raw data little by little and shed light on the problem as a whole. That done, the Sahara of 'antiquity' will no longer be judged only from the outside. It will reveal its own personality.

## Contemporary textual sources and their overinterpretation

We know the analytical methods of the ancient geographers and historians. Unable to visit inaccessible regions themselves, they gathered second-hand information which had a goodly share of error and fable. *Terra incognita*, the great desert, was not even given a name. Not until the Arabs came was the term 'Sahara' applied to that vast region which was like an enormous basin. The Greeks, and later on the Romans, spoke only of Inner Libya, a very vague geographical expression signifying what lay beyond the North African territories, or Inner Ethiopia, a zone still farther south which derived its name from the dark skins of its inhabitants. Descriptions

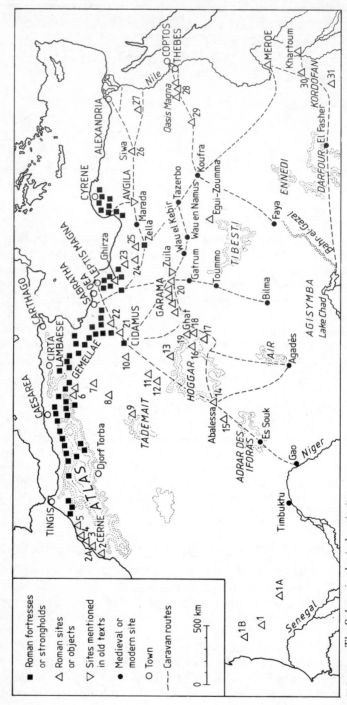

FIG. 20.1  *The Sahara in classical antiquity*

KEY

1 Resseremt, near Akjoujt, Mauretania: 2 *denarii* AR Roman Republic (Mauny, 1956a, p. 255)

1A Tamkartkart, Mauretania: Roman *denarius* 2nd century of our era (*Notes Africaines*, No. 115, 1967, p. 101)

1B Akjoujt, Mauretania: Roman bronze *fibula* (*Antiquités africaines*, 1970, pp. 51–4)

2 Essaouira-Mogador, Morocco: Punic and Roman material, 7th century before our era to 5th century of our era (Jodin, 1966)

2A Cape Rhir, Morocco: Punic ceramics, 3rd century before our era (Rebuffat, *Antiquités africaines*, 1974, pp. 39–40)

3 Safi, Morocco: Roman coin treasure, 4th century (*PSAM*, 1934, p. 127) Jorf el Youdi (15 km south of Safi): Foot of Punic statue (*Antiquités africaines*, 1974, pp. 38–9)

4 Azemmour, Morocco: Punic ceramics; Roman coins, 2nd century of our era (Mauny, 1956a, p. 250: *Antiquités africaines*, 1974, p. 35) El Djedida (Mazagan) (15 km south of Azemmour) and Meharza (30 km south of Azemmour): Roman coins, 1st and 2nd centuries of our era (*Antiquités africaines*, 1974, p. 36)

5 Casablanca, Roches Noires: treasure of *denarii* AR Roman Republic from shipwrecked galley (Mauny, 1956a, p. 250) Fedala, Sidi Slimane of the Zaers, Bouznika, Skhirat, Dchira, Temara, Dar el Soltane (all on 80 km of coast east of Casablanca): Roman ceramics; Roman and Byzantine coins (*Antiquités africaines*, 1974, pp. 29–32)

6 Oued Itel, Algeria: Roman ceramics in indigenous tombs (*CRAI*, 1896, p. 10)

7 Ghourd el Oucif: treasure of *denarii* AR Roman Republic, 2nd century of our era (Mauny, 1956a, p. 252)

8 Hassi el Hadjar, Algeria: Roman ceramics and coins (unedited, Favergeat)

9 Fort Miribel, Algeria: fragment of lamp with long neck (Byzantine?) (H.-J. Hugot)

10 El Menzeha, Algeria: bronze bell; Roman ceramics (J. P. Morel, *Bull. Soc. Préhist. Française*, 1946, p. 228)

11 Erg el Ouar, near Temassinine (formerly Fort Flatters), Algeria: Roman bronze rose (unedited, Spruytte)

12 Issaouane Tifernine, near Tabelbalet, Al-geria: 2 bronze bracelets (uned., J. Spruytte)

13 Ilezi (formerly Fort Polignac), Algeria: Roman coins (Lhote, *Bull. liaison saharienne*, April 1953, p. 57)

14 Abalessa, Algeria, Tin Hinan group of monuments: Roman jewellery and objects, 3rd and 4th centuries (Camps, 1965)

15 Timmissao, Algeria: Roman coins (Mauny, 1956, p. 252)

16 Chaaba-Arkouya, Djanet, Algeria: Roman ceramics and bronze bracelet in tumulus (Lhote, *Libyca A*, 1971, p. 187)

17 Dider and Tadrart, Tassili N'Ajjar, Algeria: Roman coins, 4th century (Mauny, 1956, p. 251); Roman ceramics (uned., J. Spruytte)

18 Tin Alkoum, Algeria: Roman ceramics and glass in tombs, 4th century of our era (Leschi, 1945)

19 Ghat, Libya: Roman ceramics and glass in tombs, 4th century (Pace-Caputo, S.)

20 Garamantic group: Djerma, Zinchera, Tin Abunda, Taghit, El Charaïg, El Abiod, Libya: late Punic ceramics; Roman ceramics and glass, 1st to 5th centuries of our era (M. Reygasse, H. Lhote, 1955, G. Camps, 1965, M. Gast, 1972)

21 Materes, Libya: site Romanized 2nd century of our era (Rebuffat, 1972, pp. 322–6)

22 Sinaouen, Libya: De La Tène II *fibula* (Camps, *Libyca/A*, 1963, pp. 169–74); site Romanized 2nd century of our era (Rebuffat, 1972)

23 Oued Neina, Libya: Romanized site (Brogan, *Libya antiqua*, 1965, pp. 57–64)

24 Ouaddan, Libya: Romanized site (Rebuffat, 1970)

25 Tagrift, Libya: Romanized site (Rebuffat, ibid.)

26 Siwa, Ammon Oasis, Egypt: Hellenized then Romanized site

27 Ouadi Rayan, Egypt: Romanized site (Caton Thompson, 1929–30)

28 Dakhla-Mehatta-Kharga, Egypt, Oasis Magna of the ancients: Hellenized then Romanized sites

29 Abu Ballas, Egypt: Late Roman ceramics (Mitwally, *Amer. Journal of Arch.*, 1952, pp. 114–26)

30 Kordofan, Sudan: Romanized site (Arkell, 1951, p. 353)

31 El Obeid, Sudan: Roman coins (Mauny, 1956a, p. 254)

of these regions, which frightened contemporaries by their sheer mysteri-
ousness, are therefore full of fabulous details in which men and animals
often take on the aspect of ludicrous or terrifying monsters.

However, even if they could not always steer away from legends, serious
authors did record valuable information and with time we find the quality
of their work improves, in proportion, doubtless, as the progress of
Graeco-Roman colonization in Africa made people aware of the realities.

As early as the middle of the fifth century before our era, Herodotus
obtained first-rate information, in Egypt, as to the existence and the customs
of Saharan populations on the southern borders of Tripolitania and
Cyrenaica. In his writings we find the Garamantes hunting Troglodytes
in four-horse chariots (IV, 183). We find the Nasamonians (IV, 172–5)
pushing beyond the wilderness of sand to discover in a country of men
with black skins, a great river full of crocodiles, like the Nile.[1] We further
learn (IV, 43) of the extraordinary exploit of Phoenician sailors who
managed to circumnavigate the entire African continent, east to west, for
Pharaoh in about −600, and then of the Persians' failure to do the same
thing, but in the opposite direction, after venturing into the Atlantic
(IV, 43). Finally, we see the Carthaginians exchanging their trade goods
for precious gold dust, on the West African coast (IV, 196).

At this point in our sources comes a celebrated document which can
be dated from the first half of the fourth century before our era, the *Periplus*
of Hanno, a narrative of the voyage of a Carthaginian charged with
exploring and colonizing that same coast (*Geographici Graeci Minores*, I).
Full of picturesque scenery, savages, crocodiles and hippopotamuses, this
short recital nevertheless gives two important landmarks: the Island of
Cerne, known from another source as a depot for ivory and skins of wild
beasts (*Scylax Periplus*, fourth century before our era, para. 112), and a
great volcano called 'the Chariot of the Gods', the final stage of Hanno's
voyage along the African coast. The existence of these two points was to
be confirmed in the second century before our era by the voyage of
the Greek historian Polybius, though his narrative is only known at
second hand, through another text (Pliny the Elder, *Natural History*,
V 9–10).

Such are our main sources of information previous to Roman colonization
in Africa. Paradoxically, it is the most ancient source that is the least
open to criticism. Except for the circumnavigation of Africa, which calls
for some reserve, Herodotus' documentation is solid and for the most
part moderate, and does not lend itself to overinterpretation.[2] By contrast
the *Periplus* of Hanno, with its lavish topographical detail, has been the

---

1. On the subject of this expedition, cf. R. Lonis, confirming S. Gsell's theory about
the Nasamonians' routes in the direction of the Saoura valley.
2. J. Leclant, 1950b, pp. 193–253; R. Carpenter, 1965, pp. 231–42.

occasion for euphoric commentaries; and traditional historians have readily assigned to the Carthaginians a knowledge of the entire coast of West Africa as far as Cameroon.[3]

With the Romans the situation changed. Firmly ensconced in Mediterranean Africa and Egypt, the conquerors lost no time in making first-hand contact with the adjoining regions. This involved – in no colonizing spirit – military campaigns of intimidation and commercial, and even scientific, reconnaissance.

For example, a most valuable text of Pliny the Elder's (*Natural History*, V, 5) tells of a raid in −19 by the proconsul of Africa, Cornelius Balbus, against the unruly kingdom of the Garamantes of the Fezzan. Along with a few toponyms that are perfectly identifiable, like Rhapsa (Gafsa), Cidamus (Ghadames) or Garama (Jerma), the list of Roman victories contains many others that are ambiguous and recall the sound of modern Saharan place names. This was taken as proof sufficient that the Romans reached the Niger.[4]

More eloquent still, so it seemed, were narratives in literature of the Latin period which implied that the Romans made sizeable incursions into the interior of the African continent. The writer Marinus of Tyre (late first century of our era) and his commentator the celebrated geographer Claudius Ptolemy, whose African documentation goes back to the years +110 to +120, report that the Governor Septimius Flacchus, 'campaigning from a base in Libya, covered the distance from the country of the Garamantes to the Ethiopians in a three-months' journey southwards; while on the other hand Julius Maternus, coming from Leptis Magna and journeying from Garama on in the company of the King of the Garamantes, who was marching against the Ethiopians, reached Agisymba, an Ethiopian land where rhinoceros abound, after four months' unbroken travel southwards' (Ptolemy, *Geography*, I, 8, 4). This story took on the more importance in that Ptolemy backed up his seemingly vast knowledge of African geography with a mathematical system, longitudes and latitudes authenticating the places mentioned. His map of the interior was furbished out with hundreds of names of mountains, rivers, tribes and cities and, what with the aid of phonetic similarities, his work produced such an impression that once again people believed they had proof that the Romans were fully acquainted with the tropical regions of Africa, especially Niger and Chad.[5]

Today this overgenerous, exaggerated view no longer holds. Modern methods of analysis oblige us to rethink the history of the Sahara.

3. S. Gsell, 1918, pp. 272–519; J. Carcopino, 1948, pp. 73–163; H. Deschamps, 1970, pp. 203–10.
4. H. Lhote, 1954, pp. 41–83; 1958.
5. A. Berthelot.

# The approach of present-day scholarship

## The new textual criticism

Modern historians have clearly seen that three major works were in question: the *Periplus* of Hanno, the episode of Cornelius Balbus, and Ptolemy's *Geography*.

For several years the veracity of the *Periplus* has been under quasi-decisive attack. First, it has been established that ancient ships venturing beyond Cape Juby but exposed on the return voyage to the full force of strong trade winds would never have been able to get back to their base.[6] This has therefore limited the geographical range of Hanno's voyage to the Atlantic coast of Morocco, where recent archaeological work has identified the ancient island of Cerne with the island of Essaouira-Mogador.[7] What is more, a subtle method of philological comparisons goes to show that the tale of the *Periplus* is simply an unskilful plagiarism from a passage in Herodotus, hence an out-and-out forgery.[8]

Second victim: Pliny's story of the raid by Cornelius Balbus. Analysis of manuscripts makes it possible to refute systematically any toponymic identification with regions of the central and southern Sahara. The Roman victory therefore covered only the south of the Maghrib and the Fezzan.[9] Moreover, a proconsul, whose office only lasted for one year, could scarcely have gone any farther.

Finally, Ptolemy's *Geography*, an imposing work, turns out to be singularly restricted territorially. Its longitudes and latitudes, calculated according to the norms of antiquity, like its mountains, rivers, cities and tribes, bring us to the southern confines of the Maghrib; and its Niger, for example, is no longer anything but a waterway in southern Algeria. The Fezzan, then, would have been the most southerly zone known to the Romans, the problem of Agisymba, on the borders of *terrae incognitae*, remaining open.[10]

The results of these modern experiments in textual criticism are highly interesting, but still they stop, in general chronology, at the beginning of the second century of our era. No geographical work of a later date has come down to us. Now there is archaeological proof that in the third and fourth centuries objects of Roman origin penetrated far more deeply into the middle of the desert. Ancient geographical knowledge must have been improved and we can be sure that Roman documentation was no longer unaware of the existence of humid zones beyond the great desert.

6. R. Mauny, 1945, pp. 503–8; thesis resumed in *Mémoires IFAN*, 1961, pp. 95–101.
7. A. Jodin.
8. G. Germain, 1957, pp. 207–48. The authenticity of the work is still upheld by G. Charles-Picard, 1968, pp. 27–31.                                        —
9. J. Desanges, 1957, pp. 5–43.
10. R. Mauny, 1947, pp. 241–93, with a good map; J. Desanges, 1962.

Now that we are freed of textual constraints which were sometimes burdensome, we can try to see what the Sahara of antiquity itself has to show us.

What were its ecological, anthropological, sociological frameworks? What archaeological remains has it revealed to us?

## The ecological problem

Palaeoclimatically, the Sahara is known to have reached the final phase of its desiccation in the era we are considering.[11] But we have to qualify. Patches of resistance – mainly the mountainous regions and the great valleys – still preserved enough humidity for the life there to be far more intense than it is in our time. The Ahaggar, the Fezzan, the Tibesti and the northern Sahara still had a fairly high level of habitability. This may explain the survival of a wild fauna which has now disappeared: crocodiles in the wadis and gueltas (permanent water-holes), felines in hill country: but it is doubtful that large herbivores like the elephant or the rhinoceros could have gone on living this side of the Tibesti or even of the Kuar country, the northern fringe of the great tropical savannahs of Chad, where, naturally, they were plentiful.[12]

Domestic animals except for the camel, of which I shall speak later, held out along with men in the refuge-zones of habitation. There were modern bovine breeds and flocks of goats and sheep. But it is odd to find the donkey, beast of all work of the Saharan oases, virtually un-represented in rock pictures.

## The anthropological problem

For lack of scientific criteria, contemporary literature generally used 'Ethiopians' for all the peoples of the African interior. Ancient writers cannot be blamed for this. Even modern anthropologists and historians have not always analysed the problem very well, the criterion of Negritude being ill-defined,[13] and for a long time it was supposed that the presence of a white population in the Sahara was a recent phenomenon only, a regular conquest, a result of the Romans' driving the steppe Berbers out of Maghrib territory.[14]

11. J. Dubief, R. Furon.

12. R. Mauny, 1956b, pp. 246–79; cf. pp. 124–45.

13. The Greek *Aethiops* is usually translated 'man with a sunburnt face'; there was a very frank discussion at the symposium held at Dakar from 19 to 24 January 1976 on 'Black Africa and the Mediterranean world in antiquity', but views on the subject have not changed substantially.

14. S. Gsell, 1926, pp. 149–66; an erudite analysis of the entire literature and icono-graphy of antiquity by F. M. Snowden, 1970, 364 pp.; cf. J. Desanges, 1970, pp. 87–95; L. Cracco-Ruggini, 1974, pp. 141–93.

Here too the situation is becoming clearer in the light of recent work both in the Fezzan and in Saharan Algeria. It is now considered that during the protohistorical period – of which antiquity was merely the final stage – the central and northern Sahara was peopled mainly by white elements: 'Tall, of Mediterranean aspect ... with large cranial capacity ... face rather long and narrow ... slender limbs' – the very same morphological characteristics as those of the modern Tuaregs. Now, it seems that the origin of this physical type is no longer to be looked for towards the Maghrib but rather towards the north-east of the African continent.[15] As for the modern Haratin of the Saharan oases, it would seem that despite some crossbreeding they are primarily local descendants of the sedentary 'Ethiopians' in Herodotus who were enslaved by the rich Garamantes.[16] We may know more about this when definite conclusions are obtained by the technique for studying blood-groups.[17] On the other hand, it is probable that the population of the southern Sahara, to the extent that it was inhabited on any considerable scale, consisted only of black-skinned people from the tropical savannah.

## Civilization

In the absence of absolutely reliable chronology, it seems *a priori* difficult to assess the progress of Saharan civilization in antiquity, especially since it is not certain that the different zones of this vast territory developed along the same lines. A good means of studying the problem is to start from the cultural situation of the Sahara at the end of the Neolithic period[18] and, on this basis, to follow the line of development in various fields.

### LANGUAGE AND WRITING
It is indisputably during antiquity that we first find evidence of an important event in the history of Saharan civilization: the appearance of a language. This language is still to be found in our day, profoundly changed from its far-off original form. The mother-language, which was pluridialectal and which for practical convenience is called 'Berber', belongs to the Hamitic–Semitic common trunk, but branched off from it long ago. Its ancient form, 'Libyan', is attested in all Mediterranean African

---

15. Pace-Caputo and Sergi, 1951, pp. 443–504; L. G. Zohrer, pp. 4–133; L. C. Briggs, pp. 195–9; M. C. Chamla, 1968, pp. 181–201, with an analysis of the skeleton of 'Queen Tin Hinan', p. 114; J. Desanges, 1975, 1976, 1977. See the use of medieval Arabic literature for interpreting Tuareg origins in B. Hama.

16. G. Camps, 1969a, pp. 11–17.

17. R. Cabannes.

18. The situation has been well defined by G. Camps, 1974d, pp. 221–61, 320–41, 345–7.

territories and in the Canary Islands, through written examples.[19] There is no doubt that this language was introduced into the Sahara from the north or the north-east with the immigration of white populations. No date can be put to the event, but Saharan writing, called 'Tifinagh', deriving from the Libyan alphabet of the Maghrib, is a fairly late phenomenon. In the northern territories there seems to be no unimpeachable evidence of Libyan writing before the third or second century before our era, and it is accepted that the Berbers came to write their language down under Carthaginian influence. The word 'Tifinagh' – 'Tifinar' in French transliteration – is itself based on the root FNR which in all Semitic languages designates the Phoenician people.

In the Sahara, Tifinagh writing gradually moved away from its Libyan ancestral form, 'Old Tifinagh' still being fairly close to it. We must therefore be particularly cautious in the dating of rock drawings called 'Libyco-Berber' with written characters on them. Very serious mistakes can be made. Moreover, the Berber language and alphabet may also have been used by negroid populations.

## SOCIO-POLITICAL ORGANIZATION

Climatic constraints certainly reduced most of the Saharan populations to the nomadic style of life, with centres of sedentation such as the first Arab conquerors knew. Tribal organization, inherent at that stage of evolution, was the basic political rule,[20] but it gave rise to incessant wars – reported with exactitude in Herodotus and Ptolemy.

For two regions, however, we have more solid data: the Ahaggar and the Fezzan zone.

In the Ahaggar, in the second half of the fourth century of our era, the socio-political pyramid culminated in a woman. When her tomb was discovered, intact, at Abalessa, the association was immediately made with the local legend of a Queen Tin Hinan who had come from Moroccan Tafilet in distant times and was ancestress of the Tuareg people. 'Tin Hinan' she will therefore be down to eternity.[21] In the Berber world there were several examples of supreme authority being attributed to a holy woman; in any case the attitude towards women in Tuareg society is a liberal one. The funerary equipment of this 'princess' – seven gold bracelets, eight silver bracelets, several other precious jewels – can be approximately dated by the impression of a Roman coin of the emperor Constantine going back to +313 to +324. As for the wooden bed on which the body was resting, when submitted to the radio-carbon test it revealed the date +470 (±130).

19. L. Galand, 1969, pp. 171–3 – general bibliography; yearly chronicles by the same author: 1965–70; J. R. Applegate, pp. 586–661; J. Bynon, pp. 64–77; S. Chaker; L. Galand, 1974, pp. 131–53; G. Camps, 1975.

20. R. Capot-Rey, pp. 204–367.

21. M. Reygasse, pp. 88–108; H. Lhote, 1955; G. Camps, 1965, pp. 65–83; 1974c; M. Gast, pp. 395–400.

As we shall see, this dignitary's wealth can only be explained by her privileged position both in the social hierarchy and in trans-Saharan trade.

In the narrow, fertile valley between the Ubari Erg and the Erg of Murzuq, a series of oases were spaced out from El Abiod to Tin Abunda. Garama, present-day Jerma, was the chief town. From the safety of this lair, the Garamantes soon wielded supremacy over the whole of the Fezzan, ancient Phazania, and levied tribute on many surrounding tribes, both nomadic and sedentary. The great regional entity called the Kingdom of the Garamantes in Graeco-Latin literature appears as the only organized state in the interior of Africa, south of the lands that were the possession first of Carthage and then of Rome. Its prestige and its wealth, borne out by archaeology, have made it renowned in our day, and in the most diverse fields we hear tell of Garamantic civilization. This civilization probably involved a hierarchical organization of tribes along Berber socio-political lines, culminating in the authority of a supreme agueklid. The Garamantes – mentioned by Herodotus as early as the fifth century before our era – opposed the Roman advance on the southern borders of the Maghrib. Defeated by Cornelius Balbus in − 19 and then, finally, by the legate Valerius Festus in +69 they seem to have become a sort of client-state of the empire. Archaeological research at and around Garama has revealed nearly ten centuries of a civilization which was partly founded on foreign relations, from the last Punic era (second century before our era) to the coming of the Arabs (seventh century of our era).[22]

Thus in the Ahaggar and the Fezzan, but also throughout the northern Sahara, in Tassili n'Ajjer during its last period and perhaps even in the Adrar des Iforas, supreme political power in antiquity was indisputably in the hands of an aristocracy of a white or near-white race, armed with javelins, daggers and swords, wearing warrior garb, mounted on processional chariots, and engaging in hunting and warring, to the detriment of Negro or negroid groups, who were kept in a state of subjection. In the absence of documents, it is impossible to say whether the position was the same on the edges of the Sahara bordering on the Niger–Chadic savannahs. It is very likely that white influence had not penetrated to those parts.

As regards religion, there is no doubt that the whole of the central and southern Sahara remained animist. Only the people of northern Sahara, in direct contact with the Mediterranean world, may have been converted to Christianity in late antiquity. One classical author asserts categorically that the Garamantes and the Macuritae were converted at the end of the sixth century;[23] but archaeological research has so far not confirmed this.

22. Pace-Caputo and Sergi; S. Aiyub, 1962; 1967a; 1967b, pp. 213–19; C. M. Daniels, 1968b, pp. 113–94; II. von Fleischhacker, pp. 12–53; C. M. Daniels, 1965–73; 1972–3, pp. 35–40.

23. J. Desanges, 1962, pp. 96 and 257.

## SAHARAN ART OF ANTIQUITY

The finest monuments of Jerma, funerary for the most part, show a Roman influence which partly deprives them of originality. To appreciate the Saharan personality, we must research elsewhere.

A good number of funerary monuments known as 'pre-Islamic' date from our era. In the great edifice of Abalessa which is preserved in the Ahaggar, we find disposed around the tomb of Tin Hinan an ambulatory which is peculiarly African in architecture.[24] At Tin Alkoum, at the south-eastern opening of the Tassili n'Ajjer, a series of circular tombs of traditional Saharan workmanship can be dated through Roman funerary equipment of the fourth century, as can similar monuments at the nearby necropolis of Ghat.[25]

Though they cannot be dated precisely, the funerary or cult monuments of dry stone found in Tassili and the Ahaggar – pavings, circular walled enclosures, ornamental basins, 'key-holes' – date from the whole of the period until Islam came to replace them by flat tombs and simple stelae. As to the most original of them, those at Fadroun, their stylistic origins must be sought in the Fezzan and the area along the borders of Egypt.

In the north-west Sahara, in the necropolis of Djorf Torba near Bechar – unfortunately ravaged by tourists – there were even to be found inside the edifices, curious figurative ex-votos; flat slabs, either carved or painted, some with Libyan inscriptions or drawings of horses or human figures, in a style similar to that of late antiquity in the Maghrib, and as yet devoid of Islamic elements.

It is more difficult to put a date to the large circles of standing monoliths found in the Ahaggar (were they perhaps already Muslim?) and more particularly those at Gona Orka and Enneri-Mokto, to the west of the Tibesti. It is in my opinion unnecessary to seek for foreign influences, since the erection of menhirs, both funerary and cult objects, is common to all early civilizations. In this respect there is nothing in the Sahara to equal the site of Tondidarou, near Niafunké, 150 kilometres south-west of Timbuktu.[26]

But for the most impressive Saharan art we must above all look at the rock drawings. According to the traditional classification of the pre-historians, antiquity corresponds to the penultimate stage of rock art, the Libyco-Berber period which follows the caballine era and precedes the Arabo-Berber.[27] While this sequence is correct in itself, it lacks precise

24. G. Camps, 1961, *passim*, 1965.

25. L. Leschi, 1965, pp. 183–6; Pace-Caputo and Sergi, pp. 120–440.

26. J. P. Savary. About the figurative stelae of Djorf Torba virtually nothing has been written; M. Reygasse, pp. 104 and 107–8; supplementary information kindly provided by L. Balout. With regard to the standing megaliths in Tibesti: P. Huard and J. M. Massip, pp. 1–27; for Tondidarou: R. Mauny, 1970, pp. 133–7.

27. The generally adopted classification (Breuil, Graziosi, Huard, Lhote, etc.); cf. R. Mauny, 1954. *Contra*: J. P. Maître, 1976, pp. 759–83.

chronological bases, and dating of the Libyco-Berber as between −200 and +700 is still precarious. The presence of Old Tifinagh characters is perhaps the least uncertain criterion, though this type of writing carries over into the Muslim era. Since the horse and the wheeled vehicle were still coexisting, it is very hard to differentiate them chronologically. Are the war chariots at the flying gallop of the Fezzan and Tassili in an egyptianizing tradition which might go back to the fourteenth century before our era, or in a Graeco-Cyrenaican tradition acquired, at earliest, towards the sixth? Drawings of camels cover almost all Saharan regions, but their age, too, it is hard to estimate. It is to be feared that very few of them fall within our historical frame of reference. Libyco-Berber works, residuum of the admirable Neolithic works on whose traditions they drew, prove how vigorous pictorial art was in the Sahara at the moment when it was dying out in the lands to the north.

## Economic life. Internal communications and foreign relations: a camel revolution?

From time immemorial economic life in the Sahara has been linked with the problem of communications. For classical antiquity, therefore, the enrichment of certain regions like the Fezzan is related to their sphere of influence, presupposing the existence of a fair amount of trading. Since internal trafficking, we know, was already limited, the cause of this prosperity must be sought in their relations with the outside world. This new situation was a fundamental contrast to that of the humid Sahara of prehistoric times.

But what means can be used for the study of the problem as a whole? We possess, for assessment of the economic position and influence of a territory, one reliable criterion: we only have to examine the archaeological material unearthed in the surrounding regions. Thus Roman coins in considerable quantities have been discovered in Scandinavia and northeast Europe – throughout the northern periphery of the classical world – and also, farther away still, on the banks of the Indus and in Vietnam, bearing witness to the vast area covered by Rome's foreign trade. But what can be learned about the region with which we are dealing? As we move away from North Africa proper, the amount of Roman archaeological material diminishes until, in the southern Sahara, it disappears completely. So far, none at all has been found in the Niger–Chadic savannahs.[28] This indicates that there were, in classical antiquity, virtually no contacts between the Roman and the Negro-African worlds.

This is of course not absolutely certain: future archaeological excavations

---

28. J.-P. Lebeuf, 1970, with full scientific commentary and bibliography. Certain regions of tropical Africa had already possessed their own culture for a long time (Nok civilization in northern Nigeria): R. Mauny, 1970, pp. 131–3; J. Ki-Zerbo, pp. 89, 90.

may provide new information, but there will always be considerable uncertainty on the subject.

The writers of antiquity, for example, made very little reference to Saharan products and their appraisal is borne out by archaeology. Some Greek or Latin texts mention carbuncles or chalcedonies, precious stones from the country of the Garamantes, Troglodytes or Nasamones, territories lying to the south of present-day Libya. It is possible that there were the precious stones, called amazonite, a deposit of which has been found at Egusi Zumma in the Dohone massif, north-east of Tibesti.[29]

In my opinion, the capture of wild animals was the principal source of profit for the territory. Of course at that time North Africa too still teemed with lions and tigers, antelopes and ostriches; but such was the scale of Roman demand that the hunt had to be extended to the interior of Africa. We have eloquent statistics on this subject. At the inauguration of the Flavian amphitheatre in Rome at the end of the first century 9000 were fought; for his triumph in 106 the emperor Trajan exhibited 11 000. Most of these wild animals were 'Libycae' or 'Africanae' – that is, were exported from North Africa.[30] In this inventory elephants and rhinoceroses came from the southernmost parts of the Sahara or even from Chad and Bahr el Gazal.[31] In any event ivory must have had a place in trans-Saharan trade, the North African elephant having almost entirely disappeared by the second century of our era. It will not be forgotten, however, that Nubia supplied Rome with a quota of wild animals.

I find it hard to believe that there was a trade with Europe in black slaves. The Western Roman world was not looking for black slaves. It has often been made out that convoys of gold dust from Mali and the Gulf of Guinea supplied the European market, prefiguring the trade situation of the Middle Ages.[32] This opinion is mere hypothesis. We have the inventories of all the gold-producing regions of the Roman and Byzantine eras, and Africa is never listed there. But one may well suspect that a more or less secret traffic in gold existed between Senegal and the south of Morocco, a region which was itself gold-producing and was very isolated from the Roman frontiers, since the Arabs very quickly established contact with this market, as early as 734.

29. T. Monod, 1948, pp. 151–4; 1974, pp. 51–66. Identical stones also exist in the Nile valley.

30. G. Jennison; J. Aymard; J. M. C. Toynbee.

31. R. Mauny, 1955. At Leptis Magna, capital and port of Tripolitania, the city totem was in fact an elephant: 1940, pp. 67–86. J. Desanges, 1964, pp. 713–15: coins of the emperor Domitian, contemporary with the Flavian amphitheatre and representing a two-horned African rhinoceros. It has been suggested that Agisymba may be connected with the word Azbin, the local name for the Aïr Massif, but it is not certain that the rhinoceros could still have been extant, at this time, in this part of the Sahara. It is possible, moreover, that the names Agisymba and Azbin may have phonetic doublets spread over a large geographical area.

32. J. Carcopino, 1948.

These few trade relations, which are not yet well understood, cast doubt on the use of Saharan itineraries. Here again one must be prudent. The only elements we have to go on in attempting to reconstruct the communications network are certain points like Ghadames or Phazania where natural arteries have their outlet, the territorial dispersal of Roman objects in the Sahara, and finally comparison with caravan routes before or after the period we are considering. Only the last two elements present a difficulty.

Of course the discovery of an isolated Roman object, particularly a coin, is in itself inconclusive; the northern Saharan populations were still using Roman coins in the nineteenth century.[33] But when the point where those objects were discovered fall into a co-ordinated spatial pattern, and trace, with good probability, a caravan route which is known from other sources, we have grounds for taking them into consideration; for it is not only coins that are involved but also pottery in tombs. The area over which these pieces of evidence are dispersed accordingly shows that the Garamantic civilization, a civilization itself depending on its relations with Rome, extended its influence over hundreds of kilometres. It must be made plain that this was purely a Garamantic influence and not, strictly speaking, a Roman one though it provided a route of secondary importance for the distribution of Roman objects. Here we have the clearest and most distinctive characteristic of the Sahara of antiquity. The local peoples knew one another from neighbouring group to neighbouring group, whatever the reason may have been which originally provoked their relations and the reason may quite well have been a quest for goods for sale in Rome. In such a context the funerary equipment of Tin Hinan is symptomatic; it can be seen as a set of exotic objects collected for a local chief who doubtless levied a toll on people who crossed her territory. The Tuaregs of later days certainly had this pattern of behaviour.

It seems that, generally speaking, Saharan lines of communication for foreign trade were mostly oriented towards the north and the north-east, with the Garamantes and their satellites siphoning traffic towards the Fezzan zone. From there, well-attested itineraries led towards the great Syrtic ports (Sabratha, Oea and Leptis Magna), which were cities of great wealth as early as the Punic era. From Garama one could also join up with the valley of the Nile, either by a northern route through the oases of Zuila, Zella, Aujila and Siwa, all of them points already known to writers of antiquity; or by a more southerly route where Kifra served as a crossroads.[34] In these eastern regions of the Sahara, inevitably, we come back to the old problem of Neolithic and protohistorical communications for which Tibesti provided a staging post.[35] But it seems that relations

33. R. Mauny, 1956a, pp. 249–61.
34. J. Leclant, 1950b; R. C. Law, pp. 181–200; R. Rebuffat, 1970, pp. 1–20.
35. P. Beck and P. Huard. T. Gostynski, pp. 473–588.

declined first with hellenistic, then with Roman Egypt, trade being increasingly diverted to the Mediterranean coast.[36]

It is probably in the eastern Sahara, too, that we should seek the link which brought iron into the black world, in so far as this did not occur independently. The problem of the transition from the stone age to the metal age in the Saharan and Niger regions, which undoubtedly occurred in the period under consideration, is of immense importance. Here again, geographical uniformity is lacking. In the same region – such as, for instance, Mauretania – evidence is found of the simultaneous existence, in the last centuries preceding our era, of stone and metal implements. Stone implements have been found at Zemeilet Barka, Hassi Bernous and Wadi Zegag (carbon 14 dating of accessory materials and of copper working in the Akjujit area).[37] The latter may have been influenced by the industry of Sous (south Morocco) which might have existed earlier; but it is not impossible that the incidence of metal working, at least as regards gold and copper, may have been a local phenomenon.

The question of the iron industry, which requires the use of higher temperatures and more complex techniques, is different. It will be remembered that iron metallurgy took several centuries to spread from the Caucasus as far as Western Europe. Thus the problem of how iron metallurgy made its appearance in the black world is extremely controversial, some maintaining that it was a specifically African invention, others that it was brought there by foreign intervention. The upholders of the second theory are themselves divided into two camps: some assume a Mediterranean influence, across the central Sahara; whilst others trace the origin of this technique to the land of Kush and assume that it followed the natural route linking the Niger to the Nile Valley via Kordofan and Darfur. Be this as it may, carbon 14 datings indicate that iron metallurgy existed in the area of Chad and northern Nigeria in the second and first century before our era. The possibility of its having evolved locally is not to be rejected out of hand; but if such was not the case, it was probably transmitted by the Meroitic civilization,[38] so that the central Saharan routes were not involved.

Study of the means of transport can also help us better to locate the Saharan routes and check certain hypotheses. We know that the great desert was conquered by the horse before it was conquered by the camel. Here as in other places the 'caballine' period had as its first consequence the use of wheeled vehicles. We do not know when wagons and chariots disappeared, but according to Herodotus, the Garamantes were still using them. Archaeology confirms his testimony. The most diversified drawings

36. Unesco, 1963–7; G. Camps, 1978.
37. N. Lambert, 1970, pp. 43–62; G. Camps, 1974d, pp. 322–3 and 343.
38. General survey with bibliography in R. Mauny, pp. 66–76; cf. J. Leclant, 1956b, pp. 83–91; B. Davidson, 1959, pp. 62–7; P. Huard, pp. 377–404; R. Cornevin, pp. 453–4.

of wheeled vehicles abound in the Sahara. Systematic inventories have even made it possible to give a cartographic reconstruction of trans-Saharan wagon routes.[39] Though we must not let ourselves be too dazzled by such clues, we must recognize that apart from the western route, parallel to the Atlantic coast line, which does not play an active part in our classical sources, the path of several ancient journeys attested by texts or by archaeological material turn out to coincide with these famous proto-historical routes. It should be added that any Saharan itinerary used by horses, whether in harness or no, required either a system of watering-places, which we know the Garamantes had, or else the transport of a large store of provisions.

As for the camel – more exactly, the one-humped dromedary originating in the Near East – it appears in Saharan Africa only belatedly. This event has been discussed *ad infinitum*.[40] On the continent itself, in fact, the camel was a late arrival. It is not found in Egypt until the Persian and hellenistic periods (fifth and fourth centuries before our era) and it is a likely supposition that it spread to the Sahara from the lower Nile valley. The event seems very hard to date. All we have to go on are Libyco-Berber Saharan rock drawings which are of little use for accurate chronology and a large number of inscriptions and sculptures from Roman North Africa, all apparently subsequent to the second century of our era. On the other hand, a graphic monument of Ostia, the port of Rome, dating from the last thirty years of the first century of our era, shows the elephant and the camel in use in games in the arena. In −46 Caesar had already captured in Africa twenty-two camels of the Numidian King Juba I, whose states extended to the Saharan frontiers. Perhaps they were still rare animals. But if 150 years later the ones imported to Rome were really African, camels, since they were not yet common in Maghreb territory, must already have been living in the Sahara in considerable numbers and been obtained there for the games.

Let me note in passing the symbolic presence of camels on the well-

---

39. General bibliography in R. Mauny, 1970, pp. 61–5; Add. H. Lhote, 1970, pp. 83–5. These drawings are not sufficiently clear and detailed or sufficiently homogeneous for any sure conclusions to be based on them. The only definite point to emerge is the Garamantic style of the horse-drawn chariots, found only in the Fezzan and in Tassili n'Ajjar. These seem, moreover, to be only parade vehicles, made of wood and leather and, according to Spruytte's reconstitution, weighing not more than about 30 kilogrammes – unsuited, therefore, for the transport of merchandise (G. Camps, 1974d, pp. 260–1 and J. Spruytte, 1977). I am not convinced that the style of these Garamantic chariots is due to the influence of Cretan invaders who got lost in the Libyan desert some time about the end of the second millennium before our era. The routes themselves are problematical: they were probably nothing more than general directions, and quite aside from the wild theories about Romans on chariots reaching the Niger (H. Lhote, 1970), some writers have even disputed their existence altogether: R. Cornevin, p. 453, after P. Huard; G. Camps, 1974d, pp. 346–7.

40. C. Courtois, 1955, pp. 98–101; K. Schauenburg, pp. 59–94; E. Demougeot, pp. 209–47; H. Lhote, 1967, pp. 57–89; J. Kolendo, pp. 287–98.

known Roman coins called 'spintrian', which were probably struck for the use of courtesans, the ancients believing that these ruminants had lascivious instincts which were quite exceptional!

I am inclined to agree with those historians who attach quite exceptional importance to the increasing use of camels in the Sahara. Supple-footed, adaptable to all terrains, amazingly abstemious thanks to the metabolic water secreted by his organism, this animal proved providential for all the nomads, who were handicapped by the drawbacks of the horse at a time when the climate was becoming alarmingly drier. Camels meant increased mobility for individuals and for groups, an advantage which had been recognized for a long time in Arabia. It is even thought that changing the method of harnessing especially by altering the position of the saddle made it possible to train 'meharis', camels for racing and for use in battle.[41]

For several centuries the use of these animals spread slowly but systematically, to judge by the abundance in all regions of the great desert of 'cameline' rock drawings, hard to date, alas, and obviously of far later workmanship than the fine 'caballine' pictures. Though no classical text mentions their possessing the camel, the Garamantes and their subjects must eventually have come to this invaluable auxiliary – hence, probably, the regularity of their trade relations with the most distant zones. It is perhaps not merely by chance that all the Roman material in the region of Ghat and Abalessa is fourth century. In this period camels were also plentiful in northern Tripolitania, where the Roman authorities could normally requisition 4000, to the cost of the city of Leptis. The supply of camels also greatly strengthened the nomads' potential for attack on Roman territories.

## Rome's 'Sahara policy'

For lack of documents, we do not know whether Punic Carthage was much alarmed at the presence of powerful tribes on her southern frontiers. Excavations at Garama prove that at least during the second and first centuries before our era, the ports of the Syrtic coast, which then belonged to the kingdom of Numidia, had trade relations with the Fezzan, relations on which their wealth was largely dependent.

Roman history is better known. The main lines of Latin policy can be briefly summarized as follows: occupation of the agricultural lands of the Maghrib required strategic cover to the south. In these regions the Saharan nomads were a nuisance. Their seasonal migrations into the colonized territory, ineluctable because essential to their survival, had their uses in that they made the products of the steppe and the desert available to the settlers, but there was always the risk of their creating conflict with the sedentary tribes. Even the distant Garamantes seemed dangerous, in

41. T. Monod, 1967.

as much as they could at any moment reinforce the aggressive potential of the nomads. The mere fact of their power was a challenge.

Roman history, throughout four centuries and more particularly in the late period, provides abundant examples of Saharans from the southern borders of Tripolitania and Cyrenaica, camel-borne nomads such as the Austurians, the Marmarides and above all the Mazices, causing anxiety both to coastal Libya and to the Egyptian oases.[42] This is an indication both of their mobility and of their striking range.

To avert this double peril, the first step in Roman strategy was to cut the nomads off from their rear bases by swiftly destroying the strongest Saharan states. The Nasamones and Garamantes were completely reduced by the height of the empire. From then on, in the second and third centuries, all that was needed was to protect the colonized territory by careful organization of a mighty network of fortresses, glacis and lines of communication, sited to take the utmost advantage of terrain. This explains the irregular configuration of the Roman *limes* which protected all the provinces of Mediterranean Africa with amazing strategic virtuosity.[43] It also seemed to afford good hopes that north Saharan nomadism could be kept under control.

However, pacification proved only temporary. From the fourth century on the nomads with their camels were knocking at the gates even more threateningly than before, daily wearing down the resistance of the *limes* garrisons.

We know the sequel. In the eviction of Rome, a process which was due to multifarious causes, the Sahara had played a role.

So, as we have seen, we are not entirely without knowledge of the Sahara of Antiquity, even though the information we have is incomplete. Several points are certain. The desiccation of the climate did not kill the desert. Human activity went on. Languages and writing were consolidated there. The increasing use of camels eased problems of transport and communication. The region played its own part in the history of the great Mediterranean states. Did the same perhaps hold true of tropical Africa? It is in this context of continued development that the medieval renaissance undoubtedly had its roots.

42. Literature and epigraphy collected by J. Desanges, 1962, and L. Cracco-Ruggini, 1974.
43. On the question of Roman–Saharan contacts in terms of the limes: for Mauretania, see P. Salama, 1953, pp. 231–51, and 1955, pp. 329–67; 1976, pp. 579–95; idem. For Numidia: J. Baradez. For Tripolitania: A. di Vita, pp. 65–98; R. Rebuffat, 1972, pp. 319–39.

PLATE 20.2 *The tomb of 'Queen Tin Hinan' at Abalessa*

*a) Main entrance*
*b) Flagstones used for covering the ditch trench*

PLATE 20.1 *The criteria for understanding the age of rock paintings are based on style and patina. Later periods, however, are difficult to date. These three examples, which come from the Sefar region (Tassili n'Ajjers) are said to originate from the 'libyco-berber' period. In fact, the inscriptions which are in 'ancient tifinar' show the Islamic names of Hakim and Mohamed*

PLATE 20.3 *Skeleton of 'Queen Tin Hinan'*

PLATE 20.4 *Persons of 'garamantean' physique on a Roman mosaic from Zliten, Tripolitania. In general the scene of captives being thrown to wild animals is interpreted as an epilogue to the crushing of the Garamantes by the Romans in +69*

PLATE 20.5 *Gold bracelet belonging to 'Queen Tin Hinan'*

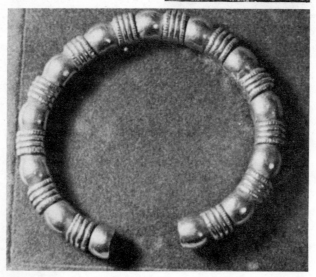

# 21

## Introduction to the later prehistory of sub-Saharan Africa

### M. POSNANSKY

## Information obtained from archaeology

One of the main achievements of recent research in sub-Saharan African archaeology is the realization that peoples at different stages of technological development were living contemporaneously in different parts of Africa. There was no single end to the stone age, agricultural practices were adopted at different times and many of the communities with whom we will be concerned in the next few chapters were still living by hunting and food-gathering and using a stone age technology right up to the end of the first millennium of our era. But no societies were ever static and there was in most cases active culture contact across quite long distances. Contact was strongest paradoxically across what might have been thought of as the most impenetrable of barriers, the Sahara desert, and provided a unifying force in African history. It is impossible to assign an exact closing date for the period under discussion in an area for which we have no fixed historical dates. Dates we have, but they are largely obtained from radiocarbon determinations (Carbon 14). The dates obtained are relatively accurate but the variability for the period under review may range over several centuries. Rather than fix a definite date for the close of the period, the chapters on sub-Saharan Africa deal largely with what is commonly known as the 'Neolithic' and early iron age period. The period thus defined ends in most areas around −1000. The 'Neolithic' in sub-Saharan Africa is a term which has been used in various inconsistent ways in the past either to denote an agricultural economy and/or to distinguish tool assemblages which include polished or groundstone cutting tools, pottery and in many instances querns or grindstones. Early farming communities were not necessarily characterized by the same tool assemblages. Recent research in many parts of Africa has demonstrated the time-trangressive nature of tools like the ground stone axe which made its first appearance in parts of Africa amongst hunter and food-gatherer tool kits of more than 7000 to 8000 years ago, whilst similar tools were probably still used in parts of the Zaïre basin (Uelian) probably less than a thousand years ago. Pottery seems similarly to have been used by hunter-gatherers in contact with their agricultural neighbours long before its users became farmers themselves. Grindstones first appeared regularly on late stone age sites in several parts of Africa and are an indication of the more intensive use of plant remains. By the early iron age we mean the period during which there was a persistent use of an iron technology as opposed to the occasional use of iron tools. By and large the early iron age in sub-Saharan Africa was characterized by the presence of small, relatively dispersed settlements and not by the development of states which first arose in the late iron age (Posnansky, 1972).

Unfortunately our knowledge of the physical nature of the inhabitants of sub-Saharan Africa is very limited. In West Africa there were certainly peoples who possessed some physical features similar to the present-day inhabitants of the area as early as the tenth millennium before our era (Iwo-Eluru in Nigeria) and have been termed 'proto-Negroes'.[1] Negro skeletal remains have also been described from both the Sahara and the Sahelian belts dating from contexts as early as the fifth millennium before our era.[2] In southern Africa the ancestors of the present-day Khoisan hunter-food-gatherers and herders of Namibia and Botswana (San and Khoikhoi) were larger than their descendants and occupied areas as far north as Zambia for certain, and possibly even as far as the Semliki river in eastern Zaïre. Excellent evidence for this came from the Gwisho sites in Zambia at which the tool kit and the inferred diet clearly indicate that the groups involved were ancestral San, but the average height of the 4000-year-old group was much greater than that of the present-day San immediately to the west in Botswana.[3] From largely Rift valley locations in Kenya skeletal remains from the sixth millennium before our era onwards were interpreted by Leakey (1936) as being closer to some of the physical types of the Ethiopian area than to those of the present Bantu- and Nilotic-speaking peoples, but these were studied nearly half a century ago and a new evaluation has for long been due. Biogenetic studies by Singer and Weiner[4] have indicated that the San and the Negro are closer to one another than they are to any outside group, which suggests that they are the lineal descendants of the original stone age inhabitants of Africa. They have also indicated the biological homogeneity of the African populations stretching from West Africa right through to South Africa. Hiernaux,[5] in a penetrating and exhaustive analysis of existing genetic data, largely obtained through the expansion of medical research in Africa, has indicated the mixed nature of most African populations which testifies to the long period of physical and cultural contact which has been going on in the sub-Saharan area. Only in the remote areas, e.g. the Zaïre forest home of the pygmies or the

1. E. W. Brothwell and T. Shaw, pp. 221–7.
2. M. C. Chamla, 1968.
3. C. Gabel.
4. R. Singer and J. S. Weiner, pp. 168–76.
5. J. Hiernaux, 1968a.

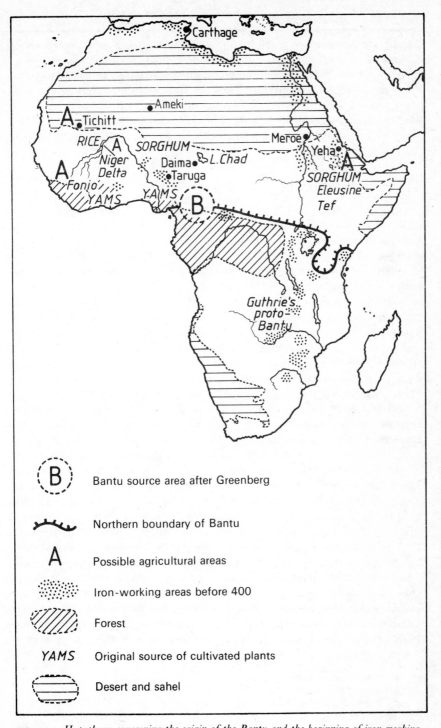

FIG. 21.1 *Hypotheses concerning the origin of the Bantu and the beginning of iron working*

Kalahari environment of the San, were the populations significantly different and there the difference must be explained by genetic isolation. In areas like the Sahelian belt and on the fringes of north-east Africa and in Madagascar there is a mixture between largely Negro populations and populations which developed independently of those to the south such as the Malayo-Polynesians in the case of Madagascar, and peoples akin to those of the Mediterranean periphery and south-west Asia in north-eastern Africa and the Sahara.

## The contribution of linguistics

Crucial to an understanding of the early iron age in sub-Saharan Africa is an appreciation of the linguistic background. Most archaeologists have had to cite linguistic evidence in order to interpret their own data. Two principal sets of events concern us in the period under review: first, the fragmentation of the Congo–Kordofanian language family, to use Greenberg's term,[6] and secondly, the dispersion of the Bantu-speaking peoples, who now comprise more than 90 per cent of the peoples south of a line drawn from the Bight of Biafra to the East African coast around Malindi. We know very little about the first set of events. All that can be said about them is that the Kordofanian languages are old, relatively numerous, often spoken by very small, in some cases minuscule, groups of people, with each language distinct from its neighbours and with the whole comprised within the modern province of Kordofan in the republic of Sudan and principally concentrated around the Nuba Hills. The Kordofanian languages have diverged widely from the Niger–Congo languages and are isolated from the linguistic groups around them. Nothing useful can be said about the time scale involved in the separation of the Kordofanian from the Niger–Congo dialects of the proto-Congo–Kordofanian family except that it probably predates −10 000 to −8000.

The fragmentation of the Niger–Congo languages may be related to the gradual expansion of peoples south from the Sahel with the growing desiccation of the Sahara. Painter[7] has put a time scale of around −6000 to −3000 on the fragmentation but there are other views. Armstrong[8] has suggested that the languages of southern Nigeria are as much as 10 000 years old which implies a much earlier movement to the south. Both views could of course be right with some of the Niger–Congo language speakers having broken away from the main group and later having become isolated in a forest environment. These are perhaps the linguistic counterparts of the Iwo-Eluru proto-Negro inhabitants. Other Niger–Congo speakers spread later from the Sahel, once an agricultural way of life was

6. cf. Volume I, Chapter 12.
7. C. Painter, pp. 58–66.
8. R. G. Armstrong.

established. A problem about this interpretation is that the earliest food producers in the Sahel appear to have been pastoralists rather than arable agriculturalists. The suggestion made by Sutton in Chapter 23[9] may be a solution to the problem since there is evidence of Sahelian pastoralists being associated with harpoons and other items identified as diagnostic of the aquatic culture. The linguistic divergence within the Niger–Congo family would, however, appear to be related to the geographical separation of different, largely agricultural groups, a separation far enough back in time for the individual components of the Niger–Congo family to have become linguistically very distinct.

When we turn to the Bantu languages we are faced with a different situation. There are more than 2000 Bantu languages in eastern, southern and central Africa which have vocabulary items and a structural framework in common and are thus related, a relationship which was recognized as early as 1862 by Bleek who coined the name Bantu for them because of their common use of the word 'Bantu' for people. As long ago as 1889 Meinhof recognized that the Bantu languages are related to those of West Africa, then known as the Western Sudanic languages. The divergence between the different Bantu languages is nowhere near as great as that between the different West African languages and most estimates put the divergence back to around 2000 to 3000 years. There are however various linguistic theories about how the Bantu separated from the other West African languages, of which two have been more often accepted. Joseph Greenberg[10] approached the problem from the macro-level in his study of African languages as a whole and used grammatical as well as lexical evidence taken from some 800 languages. From these languages he distinguished an average of 200 morphemes or core words which he considered as basic elements within the vocabulary, the sort of words that a child learns from its mother such as the low numerals, parts of the body, simple bodily functions like sleeping, eating, urinating, etc., and the basic components of the physical world around a child such as the earth, water and fire. Using core words he discovered that the Bantu languages are closer to the other West African languages than is, for example, English to proto-German which is a relationship which linguists have always regarded as close. He worked out that 42 per cent of the vocabulary of Bantu is present in the nearest West African languages, compared to only 34 per cent of the English words in proto-German. He thus concluded that 'Bantu does not even form a single genetic sub-family ... but belongs within one of ... [the] sub-families ... Benue-Cross or Semi-Bantu.'[11] He thus placed the source area of the Bantu

9. cf. also J. E. G. Sutton, 1974. Sutton thinks that 'there was a former spread of an aquatic way of life in the period of optimum wet conditions and that the people responsible were the original Nilo-Saharan people'.

10. J. H. Greenberg, 1963; idem, 1972, pp. 189–216.

11. J. H. Greenberg, 1963, p. 7.

firmly in the Nigerian Cameroon border area. The late Professor Guthrie[12] worked on the micro-level after years of immersion in comparative Bantu studies and analysed some 350 Bantu languages and dialects. He isolated the roots of cognate words which had to have the same meaning in at least three separate languages. From the 2400 sets of roots that he isolated he found that 23 per cent of them were 'general'; that is, they were widely dispersed over the whole Bantu area whilst 61 per cent of them were 'specific' to a more restricted area. Using the general sets he worked out a Common Bantu Index which indicated the percentage of the general words in any Bantu language. The isoglosses (or lines connecting equal Bantu indices) thus constructed, indicated a nuclear area where the retention rate was over 50 per cent situated in the grasslands south of the Zaïre forest in the Zambezi–Zaïre watershed area. It was in this nuclear area that he assumed the proto-Bantu had developed. The main spread or fragmentation of the proto-Bantu took place from this proto-Bantu source area. He also worked out two proto-Bantu dialects, Eastern and Western Bantu, which contain more than 60 per cent of his specific cognates. Using individual words he tried to throw light on the environment in which proto-Bantu was spoken and he found that words for 'fishing with a line', 'canoe', 'paddle' and 'to forge' are all fairly common, whilst the proto-Bantu word for forest refers to thickets rather than to dense forest. He thus suggested that the proto-Bantu people were able to forge iron, lived south of the true forest and were familiar with boats and rivers before they dispersed. In Guthrie's scheme the north-west Bantu languages (Greenberg's source area) score only 11–18 per cent on his Bantu Index and are thus distant descendants of the proto-Bantu and not ancestral Bantu languages. He does, however, agree that far back in time there was a pre-Bantu population situated in the Chari–Chad area. Oliver[13] diagrammatized the Guthrie theory and has postulated a small group of pre-Bantu, using boats, working their way through the forest to the southern grassland where they multiplied and from where they eventually dispersed in all directions.

There is thus agreement on the ultimate ancestry of the Bantu languages in West Africa but disagreement on the immediate centre of dispersion. Ehret[14] and several other linguists have supported Greenberg in general as they feel that on linguistic grounds the area of greatest linguistic diversity (in this case the area to the north-west of the main Bantu zone) was most likely to be the area of earliest settlement. Ehret has also suggested that Guthrie's roots should be weighted, as some must be of greater significance than others in trying to determine the source area of the Bantu. Ehret, partly on the basis of the assumed core vocabulary of the

12. M. Guthrie, 1967–71, pp. 20–49.
13. R. Oliver, pp. 361–76.
14. C. Ehret, 1972, pp. 1–12.

early Bantu speakers, is in favour of a before −1000 forest source where the early Bantu had farmed and also fished. Dalby,[15] who has strong disagreements with Greenberg in matters of detail, has developed the theory of a Fragmentation Belt in West Africa in which the Bantu are placed. Outside this belt there is some uniformity but within it diversity suggestive of the movements of peoples which resulted in the dispersion of both the Niger–Congo and the Bantu speakers. Those authorities who are willing to propose a chronology would place the Bantu expansion somewhere between 2000 and 3000 years ago and accept that iron was in use by those who expanded, and all would agree to the rapid, some would say explosive, expansion of the Bantu.

## The role of agriculture

Before discussing the importance of iron in this equation of the dispersion of peoples there is a further element to be taken into consideration and that is agriculture. This will be dealt with in some detail on a regional basis in later chapters but some general features should be discussed. In an introductory chapter of this nature, though, only generalizations can be made and for details the reader is referred to the proceedings of the 1972 symposium on Early Agriculture in Africa.[16]

Agriculture implies some control over one's food supply and a relatively settled existence in contrast to the more constant movement of the hunter-gatherers. Group size increased and more complex social, and ultimately political structures were able to develop. Agriculture, particularly arable agriculture and horticulture, also normally involved a higher population density and an increase in the total population figure. Archaeologists identify agricultural societies by both direct and indirect evidence. Direct evidence includes the discovery of seeds or grains in a carbonized state on archaeological sites or by their retrieval using advanced archaeological recovery techniques such as flotation analysis; palynology which identifies the fossil pollen of cultivated plants; and the identification of seed impressions in pottery. Indirect evidence, or circumstantial evidence, involves the discovery of implements and utensils assumed to have been used for cultivation, harvesting and the preparation of plant foods. Unfortunately the climatic conditions in much of sub-Saharan Africa militate against the discovery of very much in the way of direct evidence. Organic matter normally disintegrates within days of its disposal. The soils on most tropical sites are on the whole aerobic and do not allow for the preservation of pollen. Where pollen is found, as in the high-altitude swamps and lakes, the location is too far removed from land suited for

15. D. Dalby, 1970, pp. 147–71.
16. J. R. Harlan, et. al.

539

arable cultivation to provide evidence for past agriculture.[17] A further problem is that many of the tools and implements for agriculture are of an equivocal nature. A knife for peeling vegetable foods can be used for other purposes, grindstones can be used for pulverizing ochre for paint or for pounding and grinding non-cultivated foodstuffs, and are commonly found in many late stone age contexts. Many of Africa's food crops like bananas, yams and other roots do not produce pollen and many are cultivated using wooden digging sticks to avoid damage to the tubers. The actual food for eating prepared from such plants is very often pounded in wooden mortars using pestles which have a very limited life and stand little chance of survival in the soils of the areas in which they are used. Archaeologists thus have to reply on even more circumstantial evidence for inferring agriculture, such as the existence of large settlements sites, the presence of what appear to be permanent houses, the use of pottery or the existence of regular cemeteries. As will appear obvious from Chapter 26 the hunter–food-gatherers in Africa occasionally lived in large communities, often used pottery and if their fishing or other specialized hunting or food gathering occupation was successful, would indulge in the making of relatively permanent settlements such as those at early Khartoum or Ishango of late stone age date. It is thus possible, regretfully, to conclude that as yet our evidence for untangling the story of early agriculture in sub-Saharan Africa is somewhat thin and that our conclusions can only be speculative, but in the course of time, with more advanced retrieval techniques and intensified botanical and palynological research into the genetic background and distribution of Africa's cultivated plants, it should be possible to provide more substantial information.

Up to the end of the 1950s it was commonly assumed that agriculture was late in date in most of sub-Saharan Africa, in fact largely contemporaneous with the introduction of an iron technology in all but parts of West Africa and that the idea had dispersed from south-western Asia to the Nile valley and ultimately to the rest of Africa. New evidence from the Sahara and elsewhere is indicating, however, that the story is not so straightforward. The first question-marks against this orthodox view of the origins of African agriculture were placed by Murdock[18] who postulated a source area for much of Africa's agriculture in the west of West Africa around the headwaters of the Niger and the Senegal in the Futa Jallon. Though much of Murdock's hypothesis cannot now be substantiated in detail, nevertheless it is apparent that yams, one form of rice (*Oryza glaberrina*), sorghum, the oil palm and many lesser staples were indigenous

17. There are, however, occasions when palynological studies have provided valuable information, as with the core from Pilkington day of Lake Victoria which indicated a vegetational change between 2000 to 3000 years ago with the forest species giving way to grasses which is suggestive of extensive clearance activities consequent upon the advent of agricultural peoples (R. L. Kendall and D. A. Livingstone, p. 386).

18. G. P. Murdock.

to West Africa. The main question, however, is whether the existence of such crops in West Africa points to an early development of agriculture independent of that outside Africa? Some archaeologists[19] have argued strongly for vegeculture based on yam cultivation but there are no cogent arguments against the evidence so far produced.[20] It is clear that villages, like Amekni, did exist in the Sahara as early as the sixth millennium before our era, that Neolithic communities in the forest utilized oil palms, cowpeas and such-like local staples, and that sorghum and certain *pennisetum* (millet) varieties are of fairly widespread distribution in their wild state in a broad belt of the savannah and Sahelian vegetational zones stretching from the Atlantic to Ethiopia. It is also clear that Ethiopia had several staples like tef and other grains, as well as the wild non-fruiting banana (*Musa ensete*), and that agriculture developed there at an early date, probably by at least the third millennium before our era. Though there is circumstantial evidence for Sudanic agriculture as early as the fourth millennium the earliest direct evidence comes from second millennium contexts like Tichitt in Mauretania and Kintampo in northern Ghana.[21] Pastoralism, if the testimony of rock art[22] is a reasonable guide, may have sixth-millennium origins and actual cattle remains have come from several well-dated early fourth-millennium Sahelian contexts.

Though the origins, date and mode of development of most African agriculture are somewhat controversial, it is generally agreed that, except for the possibility of some highly localized millet-growing communities in the Rift Valley of Kenya, the beginnings of arable agriculture, at least in most of Bantu-speaking Africa, are contemporaneous with the first appearance of an iron technology. It is also fairly widely agreed that many of the early staples of agriculture in Bantu Africa like the fruiting banana, the colocasias (coco yams), eleusine (finger millet) and sorghum were introduced ultimately either from West Africa, or in the case of the bananas indirectly from south-east Asia. The earliest cattle were pre-iron age in date and are found in East Africa as early as the beginning of the first millennium before our era, and it would seem from the evidence referred to by Parkington in Chapter 26 that sheep had diffused as far south as the Cape in South Africa by the beginning of the first millennium of our era. It may be that the spread of pastoralism had something to do with the dispersal of the aquatic culture described by Sutton in Chapter 23, as Ehret[23] has convincingly indicated the evidence for the social influence of the Central Sudanic languages on the Bantu languages. He has described for instance how words for 'cow' and terms used for milking activities were borrowed by the Bantu from their Central Sudanic neighbours, presumably

19. O. Davies, 1962, pp. 291–302.
20. M. Posnansky, 1969, pp. 101–7.
21. P. J. Munson and C. Flight in J. R. Harlan, 1976.
22. Mori, 1972.
23. C. Ehret, 1967, pp. 1–17; 1973, pp. 1–71.

along with the cattle and milking practices. On the basis of linguistic differentiation amongst the presumed proto-Central Sudanic speakers, Ehret[24] infers that the cattle-keepers preceded the arable agriculturalists. He also sees this interaction as first taking place around the middle of the first millennium before our era. He further suggests[25] that the area around Lake Tanganyika was important for the eventual dispersal of the eastern group of proto-Bantu as it is an area suited to sorghum and eleusine cultivation as well as cattle-keeping. Ehret[26] has also indicated that the proto-Bantu words for 'hoe' and 'sorghum' were derived from the Central Sudanic languages and we must therefore envisage a social interaction between Nilo-Saharan peoples and the ancestors of the Bantu and a diffusion southwards of hoe agriculture and sorghum cultivation particularly into the Bantu world. Though some expansion of population may have taken place as a result of these developments by the first millennium before our era, the archaeological evidence described in later chapters clearly indicates that the main expansion of agricultural peoples took place in the first millennium of our era in most of Bantu Africa.

## Iron

An important question in any discussion of the early expansion of agricultural people into the southern half of Africa is that of the origin of the diffusion of iron working. To clear scrub and bush, forest fringe and woodland a slashing tool is the easiest implement to use. Stone age Iran did not have such tools and though the ground and polished stone axe of the 'Neolithic' industries could be used for felling trees, or more probably for woodworking, it is not an all-purpose clearing tool as is the present-day iron cutlass or *panga*. In sub-Saharan Africa there was no bronze age. The earliest evidence for the use of copper comes from Mauretania and would appear to be a result of the exploitation of the limited copper resources around Akjoüjt by either Maghrebis or peoples in contact with the bronze age peoples of north-west Africa. The copper workings date from a period between the ninth and fifth centuries before our era,[27] which is only a little earlier than the earliest proven iron workings in West Africa at Taruga in the Jos plateau of Nigeria which date from the fifth or fourth century before our era.

Considerable speculation (and here it should be stressed that the arguments are highly speculative and that firm data is non-existent for early furnace and bellow types) has arisen over the question of the origins of early African iron working. There are several acceptable schools of

24. 1973, p. 19.
25. 1972, p. 14.
26. 1973, p. 5.
27. N. Lambert, 1970.

thought but none can as yet be proved correct. The older school for a spread of iron working from the Nile valley particularly Meroe, termed by Sayce[28] the 'Birmingham of Africa'. Trigger[29] has more recently indicated that iron objects are relatively rare in Nubia before −400 and even afterwards only small implements such as light ornaments characterize the Meroitic period, whilst Tylecote[30] has positively stated that there were no trace of iron *smelting* before −200. In Egypt iron objects, though found occasionally in early deposits, and presumably obtained by trade or worked from meteoric iron, were of no importance until the seventh century before our era.[31] The objects of meteoric iron were worked laboriously in methods more commonly used for stone.[32] There is, however, no firm evidence of a direct diffusion of iron working from the Nile valley either westwards or southwards. Iron in Ethiopia, dating from the fifth century in several of the Aksumite centres such as Yeha, probably came from south Arabia, as is suggested by the designs on cattle brands; alternatively it could have come from the Ptolemaic ports on the Red Sea such as Adulis, with which these centres were in contact. On the basis of a furnace at Meroe, Williams[33] has postulated that the typical furnace consisted in a fairly narrow shaft with forced draught by bellows. By implication he interprets the present wide distribution of the shaft furnace to indicate the importance of the Nile valley source. In addition there are in the Tibesti, Ennedi and Borkou highland areas of the Sahara engravings and paintings of warriors with shields and spears which have been termed 'Libyco-Berber' whilst others certainly have Nile valley affinities.[34] There are, however, very few well-dated paintings of this nature and those that are datable seem to postdate the earliest iron working in Nigeria.

The discovery of the early dates for Nigerian iron working focused the attention of scholars on the possibilities of a North African source. The Phoenicians spread iron technology from the Levant to parts of the North African coast in the early part of the first millennium before our era.

The distribution pattern of paintings and engravings of wheeled chariots pulled by horses which extends from the Tripolitanian coast through the Tassili and Hoggar to the middle Nile, and from the Moroccan coast to Mauretania, indicates that there was certainly contact between North Africa and the Sahara by the middle of the first millennium before our era. The chariots and horses are clearly not indigenous to the Sahara, and Lhote[35]

28. E. A. Sayce, 1912, pp. 53–65.
29. B. G. Trigger, 1969, pp. 23–50.
30. R. F. Tylecote, pp. 67–72.
31. A diametrically opposed point of view is to be found in C. A. Diop, 1973, pp. 532–47.
32. R. J. Forbes, 1950; idem, 1954, pp. 572–99.
33. D. Williams, pp. 62–80.
34. P. Huard, pp. 377–404.
35. H. Lhote, 1953a, pp. 1138–1228.

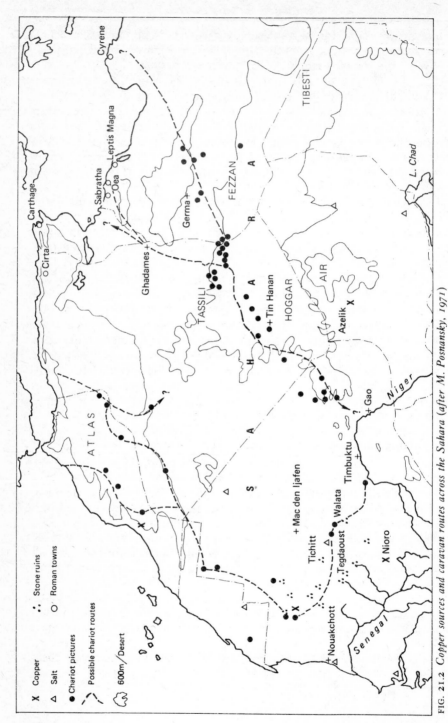

FIG. 21.2 *Copper sources and caravan routes across the Sahara (after M. Posnansky, 1971)*

Stone ruins
Roman towns
X Copper
△ Salt
● Chariot pictures
Possible chariot routes
600m/Desert

Cyrene
TIBESTI
L. Chad
Leptis Magna
Sabratha
Oea
Carthage
Germa
FEZZAN
R        A
Cirta
Ghadames
TASSILI
H   A
Tin Hanan
HOGGAR
AIR
Azelik
X
Niger
+ Gao
A
Gao
ATLAS
?
S
Mac den Ijafen
Timbuktu
Walata
Tichitt
Tegdaoust
X Nioro
Nouakchott
Senegal

has even suggested that the flying gallop attitude of the horses has links with the Aegean area. Connah[36] has postulated that as iron working is late, around +500 at Daima, near Lake Chad, which is situated on the likely corridor route from the Nile valley, iron must have come from the north; otherwise one would expect to find evidence of iron technology earlier in the Chad area than in the Jos area. Other relatively early dates for iron working come from Ghana, Hani (+80) and Senegal. It is just as possible, of course, to suggest that iron working could have come from North Africa via Mauretania in the trail of the copper workers and spread along the Sudanic belt westwards and southwards, though in that case the dates should be earlier in Senegal and Mauretania than in Nigeria. It is of course possible to suggest multiple lines of influence bringing iron working to tropical Africa with a line to Mauretania from the Maghreb, another across the Sahara to Nigeria and a third one across the Red Sea to Ethiopia, as well as others via the east coast from the Red Sea area, India or south-east Asia to East Africa.

The suggestion has recently been made that iron working may have developed indigenously in Africa. A strong proponent of this view is C. A. Diop[37] who is supported by Dr Wai Andah in Chapter 24 of the present volume. The main argument in favour of indigenous development is that for far too long archaeologists have looked for evidence of iron working based on the Mediterranean model whereas iron in Africa may have been worked rather differently. Iron smelting requires high temperatures (up to $1150°C$ to turn the ore into a bloom compared to $1100°C$ for the actual melting-point of copper), and it also requires a knowledge of the chemistry in so far as iron is the result of carbon and oxygen to the ores being smelted. Those who argue in favour of a single origin for iron working adduce evidence that this specialized knowledge developed as a result of experience in copper and in the kiln firing of pottery. They further argue that chronology is on their side in that there is abundant evidence for iron working in Anatolia in the early second millennium before our era, whereas it is scarce outside western Asia until the turn of the first millennium before our era. The proponents of the indigenous development theory, however, argue that knowledge of smelting could have been obtained through the experience of pot firing in pits and that the surface lateritic ores of Africa were easier to work than the hard rock ores of the Middle East. It is further suggested that as many of the early sites for iron technology in West Africa, such as those associated with the Nok culture or in Upper Volta, are associated with stone tools then the possibility must remain open that iron working took place in predominantly late stone age contexts.

The apparently recent kilns which are now being investigated in the

36. G. Connah, 1969a, pp. 30–62.
37. C. A. Diop, 1968, pp. 10–38.

Congo have unfortunately added nothing new to our knowledge and will probably never yield any traces of the first period of their use. But, having been found and dated, they might give some indication of the route followed by the iron trade between Shaba and the sea and make it possible to establish some dates for this late development.

Unfortunately it is impossible to prove any of the theories about early iron working. None of the early furnace sites tell us sufficient about the nature of the kilns and still less about the types of bellows employed. Far too few kiln sites have been excavated and it is obvious that the picture must remain very fluid until more are discovered and investigated. Vast areas remain unexplored, and iron smelting sites are very commonly located away from settlements, so that they may go undetected until discovered by lucky accident. The advent of the proto-magnetometer for prospection may speed up the discovery, but it is a feature of the early iron age everywhere that reconstructable furnaces are exceptional. Far too few dates have so far been obtained for early iron age sites as a whole to be certain even about the dates of the introduction of iron working into the various parts of tropical Africa. In the early 1960s, for instance, it was thought that iron working began in East Africa around +1000, and now the date has been pushed back by at least 750 years; the same is true of Ghana where until the discovery of the Hani furnace dating to the second century of our era the normally quoted date was around +900. Nevertheless, certain conclusions can be drawn. First, there is not a great deal of evidence to suggest direct spread from the Nile Valley to West Africa so that the idea of dispersion from Meroe has the least evidence to support it. Secondly, there is no positive evidence of kiln or pit-fired pottery in West Africa in the period before +0, and the ethnographic evidence for an indigenous development for iron working has not been extensively presented and refers at best to second millennium of our era situations so that we must reluctantly keep an open mind about the origins of iron working. The sparse evidence which does exist indicates earlier dates for West Africa than are available for East or Central Africa, which further suggests a spread from West Africa southwards and eastwards. Iron working spread remarkably rapidly, since the earliest dates in South Africa[38] are around +400, i.e. a few centuries later than most of those for West Africa.

This rapid spread of iron working, some would call it explosive, thus matches the evidence from linguistics. The archaeological evidence from East or Central Africa, which further suggests a spread from West Africa of the first millennium of our era shows definite similarities of shape and decoration over a wide area of tropical Africa, which can only be explained by postulating a common origin for the various wares (Soper, 1971, for East Africa, and Huffman, 1970, for southern Africa). After the initial similarities, strong regional diversity developed. This trend is well observed

38. R. J. Mason, 1974, p. 211–16.

in Zambia[39] where perhaps a more intensive study of iron age pottery has been made than elsewhere in tropical Africa. The conclusion of Ehret[40] who on the basis of linguistic evidence thinks in terms of 'loose collections of independent but mutually interacting communities' coexisting with un-assimilated hunter-gatherers, is also very acceptable on archaeological grounds. As these Bantu communities became adapted to specific environments, so their interactions with more distant communities grew less and their languages and material cultures diverged.

## Exchanges between the different regions of the continent

A further feature of the history of tropical Africa at this period which needs to be stressed is the continuing and intensifying influence of North Africa on the Sudanic belt. Influence is perhaps a misleading term, as the flow of commodities and ideas was very much a two-way process. The Sahara, as has been seen in the earlier chapters, was neither a barrier nor a no man's land but an area with a detailed history of its own, much of which still needs to be unravelled. By its very nature as a desert its population was sparse and nomadic, and in the period under review the majority of its population probably consisted of pastoralists who moved from the desert to the highlands, like the Hoggar, the Tassili, the Tibesti, and from the Sahelian belt northwards and southwards with the passage of the seasons. It is very difficult either to quantify the actual contact that existed or to describe its effects, though in recent years archaeological work in the Sudanic belt is clearly indicating that contact there was, both indirect such as that provided by the effects of nomadism and direct such as may have grown up through trade contacts and mineral exploitation.[41] Our information at present consists of classical literary sources, rock paintings and engravings in the Sahara and archaeological evidence. Some of the evidence has already been dealt with in Volume I and in earlier chapters, but some recapitulation is called for at this stage.

Before dealing with the literary evidence for contact across the Sahara it is necessary to mention the two direct sea contacts reported to have been made from the Mediterranean to West Africa. The first is the voyage of nearly three years said to have been made by Phoenician sailors in the service of Necho. This has been discussed in Chapter 4. It is recorded in Herodotus, who somewhat doubted the story because of the fact that they had the sun on their right, which is one of the reasons for accepting the story. The scanty facts presented by the literary sources make it impossible to verify. It is of some significance that Strabo and other classical writers

39. D. W. Phillipson, 1968a.
40. C. Ehret, 1973, p. 24.
41. We must no doubt resist the temptation to exaggerate the importance of the few results which have been obtained.

rejected the story altogether. A voyage certainly seems to have taken place but whether they circumnavigated Africa is uncertain. Mauny (1960)[42] has suggested that it is very improbable that the slow-moving oared ships then plying from Egypt could have managed the currents either of the Cape or of the north-western coast of Africa, where they would also have found the utmost difficulty in obtaining sufficient water or food along the largely desert stretch of coast, a stretch which would have taken months rather than weeks to navigate in a northwards direction. Circumstantial evidence against the voyage is very strong. The second voyage is said to have been made by the Carthaginian, Hanno. The tale contained in the *Periplus* is highly exaggerated[43] and fanciful and its topographical details are ambiguous and often contradictory; nevertheless, many writers have accepted the story at face value. They have suggested that the description of a flaming mountain refers either to the volcanic Mount Cameroon or to bush fires in Sierra Leone, whilst the mention in the *Periplus* of hairy people called 'gorillas' has been taken literally as the first description of gorillas.[44] Germain's (1957) research into the textual context and details of the *Periplus*, however, suggests that it is not genuine and that most of it is quite a late classical fabrication. Ferguson,[45] however, aware of Germain's objection and knowing the West African geography, feels that the voyage did take place and that the Gabon estuary was the farthest point reached. Mauny (1960) has indicated that the same circumstantial evidence that adduced against Necho's reign would apply equally well to Hanno's voyage. If the voyages were made, they certainly had no impact on West Africa. No undoubted or well-authenticated and dated Carthaginian, Phoenician or Egyptian artefacts have been found along the West African coast.

The Carthaginians certainly obtained gold along the Atlantic coast of Morocco as the account of the 'dumb barter' trading in Herodotus implies but it is doubtful whether classical sailors reached further south than the Senegal river, which Warmington[46] suggested is the 'Bambotum'

42. At a symposium held in Dakar in January 1976 ('Black Africa and the Mediterranean World in Antiquity') Mr Raoul Lonis presented an important paper in this field on the conditions of navigation off the Atlantic coast of Africa in Antiquity: the problem of the 'return'. Supported by a mass of written or iconographical evidence, Mr Lonis set out to prove that R. Mauny's thesis was probably formulated in too categorical a manner, and that the ships of Antiquity were technically quite capable of making the voyage from south to north along the African coasts.

43. For example, his fleet is said to have comprised sixty vessels and 30 000 passengers and crew.

44. V. Reynolds argues that the classical writers were familiar with baboons and that the creatures were apes with which they were not familiar, and that it is quite likely that gorillas which are as tall as man, unlike the chimpanzees, may have had a former distribution as far west as Sierra Leone.

45. p. 7.

46. B. H. Warmington, 1969, p. 79.

referred to by Polybius, a late second-century Greek writer in the employ of Rome, and even that ascription is not without reservation. Most contemporary sources about the Carthaginians indicate that they were highly secretive, and it is probable that if they had made successful voyages of exploration or trade they would not have announced them to the world for the benefit of their trading competitors. There is no evidence that they ventured overland any farther south than the Romans whose limit of active contact, except for the expeditions of Septimus Flaccus and Julius Maternus in +70, appears to have been the Hoggar. There are various classical references to the Garamantean movements but they do not appear to have affected the area south of the Fezzan.

Much more evidence of contact in pre-Islamic times comes from the rock art and archaeological evidence. Rock art indicates that regular lines of communications were open to the Sudanic belt as early as −500. Herodotus' tale of the Nasamonians' journey to what appears to be the Niger may be a literary reference to an actual journey. Of particular interest in this tale is the mention of a negro city which Ferguson[47] identifies as being in the region of Timbuktu. The drawings are mainly of chariots or carts, some horse-drawn and some bullock-drawn.[48] Lhote (1953) has noted that there are no chariots in Aïr or the Tibesti except near the Fezzan. Most of the pictures of bullocks are found near the western route. We should perhaps not draw too many conclusions from the chariots. Daniels[49] has suggested that they 'indicate the widely spread usage of a common type of vehicle rather than any complex system of Saharan roadways'. Where datable, as in the case of those associated with late Neolithic villages,[50] they belong to the period −1100 to −400. We have to assume from the rock art that the routes across the Sahara were negotiable by horse, bullock and almost certainly by the versatile donkey. The eastern route has a strong concentration in the Tassili, and Lhote has indicated possible termini on the Tripolitanian coast in such centres as Leptis, Oea and Sabratha. Bovill[51] argues that the three towns of Carthaginian origin were situated closer to one another than the natural resources of the coast or the immediate hinterland would warrant, and suggests that they commanded the Garamantean road to the Fezzan. 'Carbuncles', perhaps a form of chalcedony for beads, as well as emeralds and other semi-precious stones[52] are assumed to have been one of the objectives of this trade. Slaves, though not very important at this period, may have been another element in the trade; negro skeletons have come from Punic cemeteries and there were certainly negro soldiers in the Carthaginian

47. p. 10.
48. P. J. Munson, J. Ferguson, 1969.
49. 1970, p. 13.
50. P. J. Munson, 1969, p. 62.
51. p. 21.
52. B. H. Warmington, 1969, p. 66.

armies. Other items may have been of such tropical products as civet, ostrich eggs and feathers.

Earlier in this chapter we have considered the evidence for copper working in Mauretania. The archaeological evidence would indicate that the western route was of greater direct importance than the eastern across the Tassili. The exploitation of the copper may have provided the incentive for a contemporaneous working of gold to the south. The evidence of Senegambian megaliths, referred to in Chapter 24, indicates that before the rise of the state of Old Ghana gold and iron working were well established there and may well have been an important factor in its rise. Mauny (1952) has pointed out that the Wolof, Serer and Dyula words for gold ('urus') in the western Sudan are similar to the Puni 'haras', and it is possible that prospectors encouraged by the gold trade on the Atlantic coast of Morocco pushed south to exploit known Mauretanian sources and thus spread their own terminology. From the finds in the Senegal tumuli there is abundant evidence of Maghribian influence and one must infer that trade contacts slowly increased from their beginnings in the first or second millennium before our era. It is even possible that camels were used in the trade on this western route before the arrival of the Arabs in the late eighth century of our era: after all, camels were known in North Africa from at least the first century before our era (Caesar mentioned their capture in −46 and they were quite common by the fourth century. The wealth exhibited by the builders of the tumuli and megaliths of the Senegambian and upper Niger areas (Posnansky, 1973) by +1000 is perhaps one of the strongest pointers to the existence and scale of the pre-Islamic trade. Until more archaeological research is undertaken it is difficult to know just how old much of the trade was or how important the outside contacts may have been.

To sum up, particularly as regards contacts between the different regions, most of the information available scarcely allows us to advance beyond the stage of cautious speculation. The existence of early megaliths in the Bouar region of the Central African Republic and the presence of other standing stones in many other regions of Africa point to the conclusion, for example, that patient research work needs to be done by experts on megalithic structures.

# The East African coast and its role in maritime trade

A. M. H. SHERIFF

One of the outstanding characteristics of the East African coast has been its relative accessibility, not only from the interior but also from the sea. Accessibility from the interior has been a vital factor in population movements into the coastal belt, and helps to explain its ethnic and cultural complexity. The sea, on the other hand, has been a means of contact with the outside world. One of the main features of the history of the East African coast over the last 2000 years has therefore been not isolation but the interpenetration of two cultural streams to produce a new amalgam, the coastal Swahili civilization. The vehicle of that process has been trade, which facilitated the assimilation of the East African coast into the international economic system with its attendant consequences.

A dearth of historical sources, however, makes it difficult to reconstruct the history of the East African coast before the seventh century of our era. All the available sources, both documentary and numismatic, are the products of international trade, and we have little material on the history of the coast before the establishment of international contacts. The earliest Graeco-Roman documentary sources make only indirect (though often valuable) references to the east coast of Africa. Strabo ($-29$ to $+19$), who witnessed the period of Roman expansion under Augustus, not only gives contemporary and sometimes eye-witness accounts of the Red Sea region and Indian Ocean trade, but also incorporates fragments of earlier geographies now lost.[1] Pliny ($+23$ to $+79$) describes the Roman empire at its height, and is most valuable for his descriptions of trade and navigation in the Indian Ocean, and of the luxurious and decadent style of imperial Rome.[2]

The most important source for the Indian Ocean during this period, and the first direct, though meagre, account of the East African coast, is the

1. Strabo, Vol. II, pp. 209–13.
2. Pliny, Vol. II, pp. 371–2.

*Periplus Maris Erythraei*, 'Circumnavigation of the Erythraean Sea'[3] written apparently by an unknown Greek commercial agent based in Egypt. The *Periplus* is basically an eye-witness account. The dating has for long been controversial. Many scholars, including Schoff and Miller, have argued that the *Periplus* seems to be a description of a still-prosperous Roman trade in the Indian Ocean at the height of the Roman empire, i.e. roughly contemporaneous with Pliny's description in the second half of the first century of our era.[4] J. Pirenne, on the other hand, is alone in suggesting an early third century date.[5] An intermediate view suggesting a date early in the second century is proposed by Mathew, who argues that although the *Periplus* is earlier than Ptolemy's *Geography*, the East African material in the latter was not written in the mid-second century of our era with the rest of the work but was added later.[6] As will be shown below, there is no reason to accept Mathew's assertion, and we are thus forced to the conclusion that the *Periplus* cannot be later than the end of the first century of our era.

A considerable increase in knowledge of the Indian Ocean in general and of East Africa in particular is noticeable in Ptolemy's *Geography*, written about $+156$. Mathew has suggested that the *Geography* was later edited, and that 'it seems safest to treat the East African section as representing the sum of knowledge acquired in the Mediterranean world by the close of the fourth century AD'.[7] But Ptolemy is fairly specific in acknowledging his indebtedness for the East African material to Marinus of Tyre who was definitely his contemporary.[8]

The last documentary source for the period is the *Christian Topography* of Cosmas Indicopleustes written during the first half of the sixth century of our era. It obviously belongs to the period when the Roman empire, and Roman trade in the Indian Ocean, had already entered a period of precipitate decline. It is most useful for its information on Ethiopia, on the ascendency of the Persians in the Indian Ocean, and for the ignorance

3. English translations by W. Vincent; J. W. McCrindle; W. H. Schoff, 1912, whose translation has generally been used; J. I. Miller; more recently, J. Pirenne, 1970b; also Chapter 16 of this volume. Erythraean Sea was the term used by Graeco-Roman geographers at least from the time of Herodotus in the fifth century before our era to refer to the Indian Ocean. See W. H. Schoff, 1912, pp. 50–1; E. H. Bunbury, 1959, Vol. I, pp. 219–221; cf. also J. Pirenne, 1970.

4. W. H. Schoff, 1912, pp. 8–15, suggested *c.* $+60$, but later revised it to $+70$–89. See Schoff as to the date of the *Periplus*: 1917, pp. 827–30; E. H. Warmington, 1928, p. 52 ($+60$); R. E. M. Wheeler, 1954, p. 127 (third quarter of the first century of our era); M. P. Charlesworth, 1966, p. 148 ($+50$–65); J. I. Miller, pp. 16–18 ($+79$–84).

5. Quoted in G. Mathew, in R. I. Rotberg and N. Chittick; cf. also J. Pirenne, 1970.

6. G. Mathew, in R. Oliver and G. Mathew, 1963, pp. 94–6; G. Mathew, 1974, *passim*. Against this opinion, J. Pirenne, 1970.

7. G. Mathew, 1963, p. 96.

8. E. L. Stevenson, ss. 1.9, 1.17. Relevant passages are reproduced in J. W. T. Allen, pp. 53–5. E. H. Bunbury, pp. 519–20, 537, 610–11.

it displays about the coast of East Africa south of Cape Guardafui.[9]

Unfortunately we still lack firm archaeological evidence about the East African coast during this period to confirm and complement the available documentary sources. What we do have are a number of coin collections which have come to light on the coast over the last three-quarters of a century. It should be pointed out, however, that none of these collections was found at a known or excavated archaeological site, and that the circumstances under which they were found have unfortunately been poorly recorded. At best we can say that numismatic evidence does not conflict with the available documentary sources, and that it is valuable as a pointer to the rhythm of international trade along the East African coast.

The earliest find consisted of six coins discovered at Kimoni, north of Tanga, 'in a mound "under" trees about 200 years old', apparently buried for a long time. The find covered a span between the third and the twelfth centuries of our era. Therefore it could not have been deposited as a hoard before the latter date, but whether the earlier coins were brought to East Africa in pre-Islamic times remains uncertain.[10] The second find consisted of a single gold piece of Ptolemy Soter (−116 to −108), which in 1901 was offered for sale to a German merchant in Dar-es-Salaam by an African street vendor, and may have come from somewhere along the coast.[11]

A number of collections of unknown provenance came to light in the Zanzibar Museum in 1955. The first, in an envelope marked Otesiphon (capital of the Parthian and Sassanid empires near Baghdad) consisted of five Persian coins ranging from the first to the third centuries of our era. According to Freeman-Grenville, when he examined them they still had the 'especial type of dirt' typical of Zanzibar sticking to them, and he was in no doubt that they had been found somewhere in Zanzibar. The other two groups of coins also had this dirt sticking to them and were probably found in Zanzibar or Pemba. They covered a wider range, from the second century before our era to the fourteenth century of our era, which suggests that they were not hoards but collections of chance finds.[12]

The remaining two finds pose similar problems of interpretation. Haywood claimed to have found a large collection of coins and a vessel shaped like a Greek amphora at Bur Gao (Port Dunford) in 1913. The vessel got broken during a storm and he unfortunately threw away the pieces. The coins remained unpublished for twenty years and were not even mentioned in his account of his visit published in 1927. The collection seems to fall into two distinct portions. The first, which seems to form the core of the collection, consists of seventy-five coins of Ptolemaic Egypt, imperial Rome and Byzantium, covering the period from the third

9. J. W. McCrindle.

10. N. Chittick, 1966, pp. 156–7. These coins could even have been buried only in the sixteenth century.

11. G. S. P. Freeman-Grenville, 1962a, p. 22.

12. ibid., p. 23.

century before our era to the first half of the fourth century of our era. The second portion consists of thirteen coins of Mameluk and Ottoman Egypt ranging from the thirteenth century of our era onwards. When the site was briefly visited by Wheeler and Mathew in 1955, and by Chittick in 1968, nothing was found on the surface that could be ascribed to a date earlier than the fifteenth century, though archaeological excavations have not yet been carried out. Chittick argues that if the coins were found as a hoard, they could not have been deposited before the sixteenth century. Wheeler, on the other hand, suggests that 'the significance of the discovery is not necessarily vitiated' by the addition of the later Egyptian coins.[13] These could have been added to the collection in the long interval before they passed into the hands of the numismatist. The core of the collection could thus have been deposited some time after the first half of the fourth century.

The other collection is reputed to have been dug up at Dimbani in southern Zanzibar by an old farmer, Idi Usi, now dead; and it passed into the hands of an amateur collector. The coins have been only tentatively identified. The core appears to consist of twenty-nine Roman coins and one Parthian coin of the first to the fourth centuries of our era. The collection also includes a late twelfth-century Chinese coin and some later Islamic, European and even colonial African coins of the period down to the late nineteenth century.[14] It may be suggested that, as in the case of the Haywood collection, the later coins were perhaps added to the core at a later stage.

These, then, are the meagre sources for the reconstruction of the history of the East African coast before the seventh century. The reconstruction attempted below, though not timid, can therefore be only tentative in many respects until some success is achieved in archaeological work for this early period on the coast.

## The continental factor

The East African coastal region forms a fairly distinct geographical entity, bounded on the west by a belt of poor, low-rainfall scrub known as the *nyika*. It runs close behind the coast in Kenya, receding farther inland in Tanzania, where it is also broken by the basins of the Ruaha, Rufiji and Pangani rivers and by the eastern rim of the mountains. Population movements, therefore, probably followed corridors of more favourable environment around or across the *nyika*, such as that along the Tana in Kenya and the Pangani and associated mountain chains in north-eastern Tanzania.

13. ibid., pp. 21–2; N. Chittick, 1969, pp. 115–30; R. E. M. Wheeler, 1954, p. 114.

14. The present owner of the collection wishes to remain anonymous but I am grateful to him for letting me examine the coins. Tentative identification by Mrs S. Urwin, in a letter dated 23 August 1972.

The earliest evidence about the population of the East African coast comes from the *Periplus* which describes the inhabitants of the coast as 'very great in stature'.[15] Oliver suggests that they were Kushites comparable to the late stone age agriculturists who inhabited the Kenya highlands from about — 1000, who according to the available archaeological evidence were men of 'tall stature'. The fact that iron objects figure among the imports suggests that the coastal peoples did not yet know how to work iron. There are several Kushitic-speaking pockets close to the coast and within the above-mentioned corridors, such as the Sanye people near the Tana and the Mbugu in Usambara, who may be remnants of this early coastal population.[16]

Archaeological evidence indicates a rapid infiltration of iron-using, probably Bantu-speaking people, into the coastal hinterland during the early centuries of our era. They may well have moved up the coastal belt from the south and occupied the south Pare and Kwale areas behind Mombasa. Subsequently they appear to have moved up the coast as far as Barawa, and up the Pangani corridor to the north Pare and Kilimanjaro region by the middle of the first millennium of our era. In their expansion they probably assimilated the pre-existing population of the coastal belt.[17]

From the available evidence it is difficult to obtain an adequate picture of the coastal economy and society before international commercial links were established. The people may have been agriculturalists, like the late stone age Kushites of the interior. From the *Periplus* it is clear that fishing played an important role in the economy, and the document gives a very accurate description of fish-trapping using 'wicker baskets', a method still common along the coast. But the population appears to have been essentially coast-bound. They had dug-out canoes and small 'sewed boats', but not apparently deep-sea dhows. As late as the twelfth century of our era, al-Idrisi comments that 'the Zanj have no ships to voyage in, but use vessels from Oman and other countries'.[18] Unfortunately we have no evidence about socio-political organization in this period, for though the *Periplus* mentions chiefs at each of the market-towns, international trade may have been a crucial factor in the rise of the chiefs and also of the market-towns.[19] It thus appears that the population of the East African coast before the establishment of international commercial links was at a rather low level of technological, and probably also of socio-political, development. Hence,

15. *Periplus*, 16.

16. R. A. Oliver, p. 368; J. E. G. Sutton, 1966, p. 42. The *Periplus* does not provide any evidence of Indonesian immigrants on the coast, and Jones's musicological evidence has not been accepted widely: A. H. M. Jones, 1969, pp. 131–90.

17. R. C. Soper, 1967a, pp. 3, 16, 24, 33–4; N. Chittick, 1969, p. 122; K. Odner, 1971a, pp. 107, 1971b, 145.

18. *Periplus*, 15, 16; G. F. Hourani, 1963, pp. 91–3; G. S. P. Freeman-Grenville, 1962b, p. 19.

19. *Periplus*, 16.

when international trading links were established, the initiative lay with the mariners from the northern rim of the Indian Ocean, with all the consequences that followed from that situation.

## The oceanic factor

If accessibility from the land has made the East African coast historically an integral part of Africa, accessibility from the sea has subjected it to a long history of commercial contact, cultural influence and population movements from the lands across the Indian Ocean. In considering that history it is necessary to examine both the potential and the opportunities for inter-regional communication. Kirk defines in broad terms three geographical environments around the Indian Ocean: the south-western 'forest' region, comprising the coastlands of Kenya, Tanzania, Mozambique and Madagascar; the intermediate 'desert' region extending from the Somali Horn to the Indus basin; and the south-eastern 'forest' region from India to Indonesia.[20] Obviously the potential for exchange between the two 'forest' regions is small in staples, though it may be enlarged if we include luxuries or manufactured goods whose provenance is more localized by natural or historical circumstances. On the other hand, the potential for exchange between the 'desert' and the two 'forest' regions is much greater for, besides the exchange of luxuries and manufactured goods, the 'desert' region is often seriously deficient in the foodstuffs and timber obtainable from the 'forest' regions. Moreover the 'desert' region occupies a strategically intermediate position between the two 'forest' regions, and also between them and the Mediterranean world. The history of the western Indian Ocean until the seventh century is therefore to a considerable extent the history of interaction along two distinct lines, between East Africa and the Middle East, and between the latter and India; and also of the intermediary role played by the Middle East between the Indian Ocean and the Mediterranean.

Such interaction was made possible by the development of a suitable marine technology and the harnessing of the winds and currents of the Indian Ocean. The most important geographical characteristic of the Indian Ocean is the seasonal reversal of the monsoon winds. During the northern winter the north-east monsoon prevails steadily as far as Zanzibar but with decreasing constancy southwards, and is seldom reliable beyond Cape Delgado. This pattern of circulation is reinforced by the Equatorial current, which flows southwards after striking the Somali coast and thus facilitates the voyage of the dhows from the Arabian coast. Arab dhows can leave their home ports in late November, though the majority leave in early January, when the monsoon is fully established, and take twenty to twenty-five days for the voyage. By March the north-east monsoon begins to break

20. W. Kirk, pp. 265–6.

down, and since East Africa is at the edge of the monsoon system it breaks up earlier in the south. By April the wind has reversed to become the south-west monsoon. The equatorial current at this time strikes the coast near Cape Delgado and splits into the strong north-flowing current which facilitates the northward journey, and the south-flowing current which hinders exit from the Mozambique channel. This is the season of departure of the dhows from East Africa, but there is an interruption between mid-May and mid-August when the weather is too boisterous for Indian Ocean shipping. Dhows therefore sail either with the 'build-up' of the monsoon in April, if commercial transactions can be completed in time, or with the 'tail-end' in August which becomes increasingly necessary as the voyage is lengthened to the south of Zanzibar. It is clear that by the beginning of the Christian era Indian Ocean mariners were already acquainted with the use of these winds.[21] They had also overcome the technical problem of building a large enough vessel in an area without iron by resorting to 'sewing' planks together with vegetable fibres.[22]

The spatial extent of reliable monsoons and the level of commercial organization in East Africa thus help to define the normal radius of action of the monsoon dhows. With a rather simple commercial organization involving a more direct exchange between foreign vessels and the market-towns, which appears to have been the case before the seventh century, the northern dhows are unlikely to have gone much farther south than Zanzibar. It was not until the medieval period that an elaborate entrepôt developed at Kilwa for the more effective exploitation of the southern coastlands.

## Development of trade in the western Indian Ocean

The earliest historical evidence about the western Indian Ocean suggests that, contrary to common assertion in textbooks, there was no commercial intercourse, direct or otherwise, between East Africa and India before the seventh century of our era. Even trade between India and the Middle East until the time of the *Periplus* appears to have been confined to a few luxuries.[23] It seems likely that apart from gold and some other precious goods India was largely self-sufficient, especially in the staple 'forest' products that East Africa could have supplied. Indeed, India appears to have been an active exporter of ivory at this time, which probably delayed the exploitation of African ivory resources.

That exploitation appears to have been stimulated by the intense rivalry among Greek successor states after the death of Alexander. The firm control

21. ibid., pp. 263–5; B. A. Datoo, 1970a, pp. 1–10; D. N. McMaster, pp. 13–24; B. Datoo and A. M. H. Sheriff, p. 102.

22. G. F. Hourani, 1963, pp. 4–6.

23. R. E. M. Wheeler, 1966, p. 67; G. F. Hourani, 1963, pp. 8–9; A. L. Basham, p. 230; *Periplus*, 49, 56, 62.

exercised by the Seleucids over the land-routes to India induced the Ptolemies of Egypt to seek ivory from elsewhere. The immediate need was to secure war elephants, but the Ptolemies also wished to break the Seleucid monopoly over the supply of Indian ivory to the Mediterranean. They therefore turned to the African coast of the Red Sea, establishing a series of elephant-hunting posts as far as the mouth of the Red Sea. The effect of the Ptolemies' policy was thus a tremendous expansion of the ivory trade.[24]

The loss of Syria under Ptolemy V ( − 204 to − 181), and the growing demand in Italy for Arabian and Indian commodities at a time when the immediate hinterland of the Red Sea coast was apparently being depleted of ivory, forced Egypt to turn to the southern sea-route in order to maintain some commercial contact with India. By the end of the second century before our era, Socotra was inhabited by foreign traders including Cretans, and Eudoxus took advantage of a shipwrecked Indian pilot to make the first direct voyage to India. Indian trade continued to grow sufficiently in importance for officers to be appointed 'in charge of the Red and Indian Seas' between − 110 and − 51.[25] But Eudoxus' initiative does not seem to have been followed up regularly. Strabo implies that this was due to the weakness and anarchy of the later Ptolemies when 'not so many as twenty vessels would dare to traverse the Arabian Gulf [Red Sea] far enough to get a peep outside the straits.[26] Egyptian trade with India at that time was therefore largely indirect, through the south-west Arabian entrepôts. Speaking of Aden, the *Periplus* says: 'In the early days of the city, when the voyage was not yet made from India to Egypt, and when they did not dare to sail from Egypt to the ports across this Ocean, but all came together at this place, it received cargoes from both countries.[27] South-west Arabia thus occupied a crucial middleman's position and appropriated its share of commercial profit which became proverbial.[28] The Sabaeans were superseded in *c.* − 115 by the Himyarites, who gradually came to concentrate the entrepôt traffic at the port of Muza which was governed by the vassal state of Maafir.[29]

The south-west Arabians also appear to have controlled the other branch

24. H. F. Tozer, pp. 146–7; Strabo, Vol. VII, pp. 319, 331; Pliny, Vol. II, pp. 465–569; G. F. Hourani, 1963, pp. 19–20; W. Tarn and G. T. Griffith, pp. 245–6; H. G. Rawlinson, pp. 90–2.

25. Strabo, Vol. I, pp. 377–9; Diodorus Siculus, pp. 213–15; *Periplus*, 30; W. Tarn and G. T. Griffith, pp. 247–8; H. G. Rawlinson, pp. 94, 96; E. H. Bunbury, Vol. I, p. 649; Vol. II, pp. 74–8; E. H. Warmington, 1963, pp. 61–2; G. F. Hourani, 1963, p. 94.

26. Strabo, Vol. VIII, p. 53.

27. *Periplus*, 26.

28. Strabo, Vol. VII, p. 349, Vol. I, pp. 143–5. See also Diodorus, Vol. II, p. 231; Pliny, Vol. II, p. 459; Not all the wealth of the south Arabians was derived from trade, for they had also developed a sophisticated irrigation system: G. W. Van Beek, 1969, p. 43.

29. *Periplus*, 21–6; W. H. Schoff, 1912, pp. 30–2, 106–9; *Encyclopaedia Britannica*, 11th edn, 1911, Vol. 2, p. 264, Vol. 3, pp. 955–7; E. H. Warmington, 1928, p. 11.

of trade which led down the East African coast. It has already been suggested that one of the driving forces for Ptolemaic commercial expansion down the Red Sea was the increasing demand for Oriental luxuries, including ivory. It is therefore possible that the Arabs extended their commercial activities to the East African coast at this time to supply that demand for ivory. It is significant that when, at the end of the second century before our era, the north-east monsoon apparently blew Eudoxus on to the African coast somewhere south of Cape Guardafui, he was able to obtain a pilot, probably an Arab, who took him back to the Red Sea.[30] These trading connections undoubtedly preceded the establishment of any formal Arab suzerainty* on the East African coast which the *Periplus* in the second half of the first century of our era describes as 'ancient'.[31] Exactly how early and how far down the coast these trading connections extended in the pre-Roman period is difficult to determine in the absence of archaeological evidence. To date only one Ptolemaic gold coin of the late second century before our era has been allegedly found in the vicinity of Dar-es-Salaam, while the twenty-two Ptolemaic coins in the Haywood collection could not have been deposited before the fourth century of our era at the earliest.[32]

On present evidence, therefore, we can date Arab commercial expansion to the East African coast to perhaps as early as the second century before our era. Miller, however, argues that East Africa formed a vital link in the cinnamon trade between east Asia (the spice's natural habitat) and the northern coast of Somalia, where not only the Graeco-Romans but also the ancient Egyptians obtained it from the second millennium before our era. On the strength of Pliny's reference to the transport of cinnamon 'over wide seas on rafts', Miller postulates trans-oceanic voyages by Indonesians to Madagascar and the East African coast, followed by coastal and overland routes ending at the Somali ports.[33] While Indonesian migration to Madagascar may have taken this form, it is now held to have taken place during the first millennium of our era. Moreover, there is nothing to link that migration with the trade-route described by Pliny, which quite clearly appears to follow the northern coast of the Indian Ocean, terminating at the South Arabian port of Ocilia.[34] There is thus no support for Miller's circuitous cinnamon route, or for his enormous extension of the time when East Africa was linked commercially with the lands across the Indian Ocean.

30. Strabo, Vol. I, pp. 377–9.

31. *Periplus*, p. 16; B. A. Datoo, 1970b, p. 73, adopts a later date based on a later dating of the *Periplus*; 1963, G. Mathew, 1963, p. 98, suggests third century before our era, but this is based on the Haywood collection of doubtful historical significance. See p. 553 above.

32. See pp. 553–4 above.

33. J. I. Miller, pp. 42–3, 53–7, 153–72. Professor N. Chittick, consulted by the Committee, expressed reservations about the existence of this commerce of cinnamon.

34. B. A. Datoo, 1970b, p. 71; Pliny, Vol. XII, pp. 87–8.

* It has been suggested that 'vassal' be replaced by 'dependant' and 'suzerainty' by 'domination'.

## Expansion of trade under the Romans

The establishment of the Roman empire under Augustus resulted in a tremendous increase in the demand for Oriental commodities in the Mediterranean. A large number of separate economies, both within the empire and beyond, were gradually integrated into a vast system of international trade in which the producers of raw materials and luxuries were locked in an exchange relationship with the consumers at the centre. The system thus expanded the market and permitted the transfer of wealth to the centre of the empire.[35] The concentration of wealth in the hands of the warlike ruling class, leaving commerce and industry to the subject peoples, led merely to intense competition in extravagance. As Pliny complained: 'By the lowest reckoning India, China and the [Arabian] peninsula take from our empire 100 million sesterces every year – that is the sum which our luxuries and our women cost us.'[36]

The expansion of the market under Augustus brought about a more aggressive policy in the Red Sea designed to break the Arab monopoly over the Oriental trade. The Romans sought to establish a direct sea-route to India, and to control the southern end of the 'incense route' with an expedition in −24 under Gallus. Though the expedition failed, Roman trade was able to forge ahead rapidly, probably partly because the direct sea-route could compete fairly successfully with the Arab route. Strabo learnt in *c.* − 26 to − 24 that 'as many as 120 vessels were sailing from Myos Hormos to India, whereas formerly under the Ptolemies only a very few ventured to undertake the voyage to carry on traffic in Indian merchandise.'[37] It is reasonable to assume that such a heavy annual traffic presupposed a regular use of the monsoon for a more direct voyage from the mouth of the Red Sea to northern India. Over the next three-quarters of a century a better acquaintance with the alignment of the west coast of India enabled Roman navigators to cut across the Arabian Sea to Malabar, the source of pepper, the prime Indian luxury.[38]

Despite the Roman entry into the Indian Ocean trade, however, the *Periplus* itself gives a picture of a very lively trade still in the hands of the Indians and Arabs. The Indians traded actively in the Persian Gulf and the Red Sea, but apparently not south of Cape Guardafui. They exported pepper from the Malabar coast, ivory from north-west, south and east India, and large quantities of cotton cloth for the Roman market and also iron and steel, cloth and foodstuffs for the north Somali and Ethiopian ports. In return they took a variety of metals, clothing of 'inferior sorts', wine and 'a great quantity of coins'.[39] The Arabs, on the other

35. F. Orteil, 1952, pp. 382–91.
36. Pliny, Vol. IV, p. 63.
37. Strabo, Vol. I, pp. 453–5, Vol. VII, pp. 353–63.
38. Pliny, Vol. II, pp. 415–19.
39. *Periplus*, 6, 14, 36, 49, 56, 62; J. I. Miller, pp. 136–7.

hand, apart from exporting frankincense and myrrh, were largely the intermediaries in the trade between the Indian Ocean and the Mediterranean. While they shared the Indian trade with the Indians and increasingly the Romans, they seem to have enjoyed a virtual monopoly over the trade with the East African coast: a fact which is corroborated by Roman ignorance of the African coast south of Cape Guardafui before the *Periplus*. Moreover, though the latter document is undoubtedly an eye-witness account of the East African coast, the fact that only four paragraphs are devoted to it suggests that the region still lay beyond the normal range of Graeco-Roman activities.[40]

## Assimilation of the East African coast into the Roman economic system

Whatever the level of Arab commercial activity along the East African coast in the pre-Roman period, it is almost certain that it received a fresh stimulus as a result of the economic unification and increased opulence of the Roman empire. The demand for ivory grew enormously as the Romans began to use it not only for statues and combs but chairs, tables, bird-cages and carriages; there was even an ivory stable for the imperial horse.[41] By the first century of our era, ivory could be obtained only from far into the interior in the Upper Nile region, coming down to Adulis. Consequently, the supply of ivory from the East African coast, though it was considered to be of a lower quality than that of Adulis, assumed a greater importance.[42] It served to integrate the region even further into the international system of trade centred on the Mediterranean through the south-west Arabian state of Himyar. The *Periplus* states that though each of the market-towns down the East African coast had its own chief, Himyar exercised suzerainty through the subordinate chief of Maafir, who in turn farmed it out to the people of Muza. The latter 'send thither many large ships, using Arab captains and agents, who are familiar with the natives and intermarry with them, and who know the whole coast and understand the language'.[43] The assimilation of the East African coast into the international system was therefore not only at the level of commerce, but also involved political domination and social penetration. The latter may thus have begun the process of creating a class of coastal sea-going and trading people of mixed parentage, who acted as local agents for the international system of trade.

40. Strabo, Vol. VII, p. 333; *Periplus*, 15–18.
41. E. H. Warmington, 1928, p. 163.
42. *Periplus*, 4, 17.
43. ibid., 16.

Azania,[44] as the Romans called the east coast of Africa south of Ras Hafun, was probably not economically unified. It consisted rather of a series of market-towns each with its own chief, each dependent on its own narrow hinterland for export commodities and each visited directly by the monsoon dhows. The *Periplus* mentions a number of places such as Sarapion, probably a few miles north of Merca, Nikon, probably Burgao (Port Dunford), and the Pyralean Islands which have been identified with the Lamu archipelago. At these places ships could lie at anchor but there is as yet no reference to any commercial activities at them. South of the Lamu archipelago there is indeed a change in the character of the coastline, as the *Periplus* so accurately described. Two days' sail beyond lay the island of Menouthias, 'about 300 stadia [about 55 kilometres] from the mainland, low and wooded'.[45] Pemba is the first major island that the northern mariners would encounter, and probably the only one that could have been reached in two days from Lamu. Moreover, Pemba is in fact 50 kilometres from the mainland, as against 36 kilometres in the case of Zanzibar. Menouthias, however, was not a commercially important port. It provided a kind of tortoiseshell which was in greatest demand after that from India, but the island's only major economic activity described in the *Periplus* was fishing.[46]

The only market-town along the coast south of Ras Hafun mentioned in the *Periplus* was Rhapta. According to that document the emporium was two days' sail beyond Menouthias, and Ptolemy says that it was located on a river of the same name 'not far from the sea'.[47] Baxter and Allen argue that if the two days' voyage began from the northern end of Pemba and ended at a river some distance from the sea, the most probable location of Rhapta would be somewhere up the Pangani river, which formerly had a northern mouth. Datoo argues that in view of sailing conditions Rhapta was probably located between Pangani and Dar-es-Salaam.[48] Rhapta was apparently governed by a local chief but under the overall suzerainty of the south-west Arabian state. The *Periplus*, however, gives the impression that that suzerainty consisted of little more than a monopoly of external

44. The term first occurred in Pliny, Vol. VI, p. 172, where it seems to refer vaguely to the sea outside the Red Sea. In the *Periplus*, 15, 16 and 18, and in Ptolemy, Vol. I, pp. 17, 121, the term definitely refers to the east coast of Africa. It has been suggested that it is a corruption of Zanj which was later used by Arab geographers and which appears in Ptolemy and Cosmas as Zingisa and Zingion respectively; G. S. P. Freeman-Grenville, 1968. See also W. H. Schoff, 1912, p. 92. I have excluded from consideration the parts on the Gulf of Aden which formed a separate economic region whose major economic activities included the export of frankincense and myrrh, and the re-export of cinnamon from southeast Asia, neither of which characterized the coast south of Ras Hafun: see B. A. Datoo, 1970b, pp. 71–2.
45. *Periplus*, 15; B. A. Datoo, 1970b, p. 68; G. Mathew, 1963, p. 95.
46. *Periplus*, 15.
47. ibid., 16; Ptolemy, Vol. I, p. 17, quoted in J. W. T. Allen, p. 55.
48. H. C. Baxter, p. 17; J. W. T. Allen, pp. 55–9; B. A. Datoo, 1970b, pp. 68–9.

trade exercised by Arab captains and agents of Muza. The most important economic function of the port was the export of 'a great quantity of ivory', rhinoceros horns, high-quality tortoise-shell and a little coconut-oil. These were exchanged primarily for iron goods, particularly 'lances made at Muza especially for this trade', hatchets, daggers and awls, various kinds of glass and 'a little wine and wheat, not for trade, but to serve for getting the goodwill of the savages'.[49]

That trade was growing rapidly in the early centuries of our era is indicated by Ptolemy during the first half of the second century. Along the Somali coast a new emporium had arisen called Essina, and Sarapion and Nikon (Toniki) are now described as 'port' and 'emporium' respectively. But the most spectacular development had occurred at Rhapta which is now described as a 'metropolis' (in Ptolemaic usage implying the capital of a state) and there is no longer any reference to Arab suzerainty. Though this is a negative piece of evidence, it is quite likely that the growth of trade had permitted the acquisition of enough wealth and power to overthrow Arab suzerainty and establish a politically independent state. That growth of trade was probably made possible by the expansion of the hinterland of Rhapta by the time of Ptolemy. He located to the west of Rhapta not only the famous snow-capped Mountains of the Moon but also Mount Maste near the headwaters of the river on which Rhapta stood, and the Pylae mountains somewhat to the north-west of it.[50] The information about these mountains must have reached the Graeco-Roman mariners through local Arabs or Africans, and would suggest some form of commercial penetration into the interior from Rhapta. The most obvious corridor through the *nyika* wilderness from the northern half of the coast of Tanzania, and the most natural hinterland for any major port in the region, consists of the Pangani valley and the chain of mountains from Usambara and Upare to the snow-capped Kilimanjaro from which the Pangani in fact rises. Recent excavations in the Pare hills have yielded sea-shells and shell beads at Gonja which suggest commercial links with the coast, though the present evidence cannot be dated earlier than *c.* +500.[51] All these considerations would favour the location of Rhapta on the Pangani.[52] Trade also seems to have spread southward along the coast as far as Cape Delgado. Whereas to the author of the *Periplus* Rhapta was the end of the known world, Ptolemy quotes a Greek mariner for the distance as far south as Cape Prason at the end of a wide shallow bay, probably the concave coast of southern Tanzania, around which lived 'men-eating savages'.[53]

49. *Periplus*, 16, 17.
50. Ptolemy, Vol. I, pp. 17, 121, Vol. IV, pp. 7, 31; E. H. Warmington, 1963, pp. 66–8.
51. R. C. Soper, 1967b, pp. 24, 27; personal communication dated 13 October 1972.
52. By no means all authors agree on this location. To date, no ancient ruin has been found near Pangani. There have been occasional attempts to identify Rhapta with a vanished site on the estuary of the River Rufiji.
53. *Periplus*, 16, 18; Ptolemy, Vol. I, pp. 9, 1–3, Vol. II, pp. 17, 121.

Thus, by the middle of the second century a large part of the East African coast and at least part of the Pangani corridor had been drawn into the international system of trade. The momentum which had pushed the commercial frontier into East African waters began to weaken as the Roman empire entered its long period of decline in the third century. As the wealth of the ruling class was dissipated by the economic decentralization of the empire and confiscations by the emperors, the urban consumer class decayed and the bourgeois middle class became impoverished, leading to a considerable contraction of the market, especially for luxuries, and a reversion to a subsistence rural economy. A shift occurred in international trade from spices, precious stones and ivory to cotton and industrial products. Direct trade may have ceased altogether, as the marked gap in numismatic evidence suggests, but there was a brief revival at the end of the third and the beginning of the fourth centuries with the political re-consolidation of the empire. Existing numismatic evidence for East Africa is unsatisfactory, though it seems to show a similar fluctuation. The Haywood collection mentioned earlier included six imperial Roman coins dated to the mid-second century of our era, followed by a gap until the end of the third and the fourth centuries which is represented by seventy-nine coins. In the Dimbani collection there seems to be only one coin of the first century, while the rest of the identified Roman coins seem to belong to the third and fourth centuries of our era.[54]

What were the consequences of East Africa's involvement in that system of trade? First, it may at its height have stimulated economic growth by supplying iron goods (though most of them appear to have been weapons of war), and perhaps the knowledge of iron-working which would have been of seminal significance to the history of East Africa.[55] Secondly, the demand for ivory, rhinoceros horns and tortoise-shell gave value to resources which had probably had little local value previously, and thus widened the range of East Africa's sources of wealth; while the reference to the export of coconut-oil suggests both the introduction of that important plant from the east and the stimulation of some industrial activity for the extraction of oil. International trade may also have brought about the incipient urbanization of the market-centres, which were visited by foreign traders but were apparently settled primarily by Africans and the growing class of racially mixed coastal peoples, both increasingly outward-looking and dependent on foreign trade, for which they were the local link. The wealth accruing from that trade enriched that class, and may have led to the concentration of enough wealth and power to enable Rhapta to declare its autonomy. But it was by no means trying to withdraw from international trade, on which it thrived. To the extent that it had become dependent on international trade, its economy may have been distorted and unbalanced

54. F. Orteil, 1956, pp. 250, 266–7, 273–5, 279; M. P. Charlesworth, 1926, pp. 61, 71. For East African numismatic evidence see pp. 533–4 above.

55. M. Posnansky, 1966a, pp. 87, 90.

with undue reliance on the export of a few luxuries to the opulent Roman empire, and therefore vulnerable to fluctuations in international trade. When the Goths began to close in on Rome (Rome fell in +410), they were also strangling the economic system centred on Rome, with far-reaching consequences for all the regions that may have come to depend on it. Distant Rhapta may have withered as a result. No trace of the 'metropolis' has so far been found on the East African coast.

## The realignment of East Africa's external relations

The disintegration of the system of international trade probably had a similarly catastrophic effect on another state which had become dependent on it: Himyar in south-west Arabia. The decline in the Roman demand for the frankincense it produced, and for other Oriental luxuries for which it was the middleman, undoubtedly affected its well-being, and laid it open to invasions from Ethiopia, and later Persia. On the sea it may have lost much of its middleman's role partly to the Ethiopians whose port of Adulis emerged as a centre for the export of upper Nile ivory not only to the Mediterranean but also eastwards to Persia and even to the hitherto self-sufficient India, which marks an important shift in the direction of the ivory trade.[56]

The Ethiopians, however, do not appear to have been able to step fully into the shoes of the Arabs as carriers of trade in the western Indian Ocean. Farther east, Persia was emerging as a significant maritime power. The Sassanids began in the third century of our era to encourage native Persian navigation, monopolized the trade as far as India during the sixth, and extended their commerce to China at the latest by the seventh century. They also expanded westwards to acquire control over the other artery of trade through the Red Sea, conquering both south-west Arabia and Egypt by the early seventh century. Though the Persian empire collapsed under the Muslim onslaught in *c.* +635, there is considerable evidence to show that Persian navigators continued to dominate the Indian Ocean trade for a considerable period thereafter, bequeathing a significant nautical and commercial vocabulary to the whole Indian Ocean world.[57]

Such a command of the western Indian Ocean by the Persians in the sixth and seventh centuries, especially in view of the decline of the Arabs and the inability of the Ethiopians to replace them, strongly suggests that they had a dominant commercial influence over the East African coast. Though the coast may not have fallen under the political hegemony of the Persians, as was once believed, it is not improbable that the strong

56. G. W. Van Beek, 1969, p. 46; R. K. P. Pankhurst, pp. 26–7; Cosmas, p. 372; G. F. Hourani, 1969, pp. 42–4.

57. H. Hasan; G. F. Hourani, 1969, pp. 38–41, 44–65; Procopius of Caesarea, Vol. I, pp. 193–5; T. M. Ricks, pp. 342–3. A ninth-century Chinese source speaks of Persian commercial activities on the Somali coast: J. L. Duyvendak, p. 13.

tradition of Shirazi (Persian) migration to the East African coast may have originated during this period. Unfortunately there is a hiatus in the documentary sources between the Graeco-Roman authors and the Arab writers of the ninth century; and no archaeological evidence from the pre-Islamic period has so far been unearthed along the coast except for the five Parthian and Sassanid coins of the first three centuries of our era which may have been dug up somewhere in Zanzibar. Nevertheless, there is evidence for commercial contact between East Africa and the Persian Gulf at least as early as the seventh century, admittedly already in the Islamic period, though it may have extended into the pre-Islamic period. Already there are references to the importing of slaves from East Africa (Zanj) and elsewhere as soldiers, domestics and agricultural labourers to reclaim the marshlands of southern Iraq. By the end of the century they were apparently numerous enough to revolt for the first time, though the more spectacular revolt occurred nearly two centuries later. There are also reports of Zanji slaves reaching China as early as the seventh century.[58]

The Persians and the Persian Gulf may also have begun to play an important role as an intermediary between East Africa and India. The collapse of the Roman empire had deprived East Africa of its major ivory market at a time when India was still largely self-sufficient. But already by the beginning of the sixth century Indian demand for ivory for the manufacture of bridal ornaments seems to have begun to outstrip local supply. That demand was securely based on the regular ritual destruction of these ornaments upon the termination of the Hindu marriage by the death of either of the partners. By the tenth century India and China were the most important markets for East African ivory.[59]

By the end of the seventh century, therefore, firm commercial links had been re-established between the East African coast and the northern rim of the Indian Ocean. The growing demand for ivory in India had at last permitted the forging of commercial links between the two 'forest' regions, and the Indian market was to serve East Africa until the nineteenth century. In return the East Africans probably received a wide range of manufactured goods, including cloth and beads. This exchange underpinned the city-states which were founded along the coast. But during this second phase of its history the East African coast experienced a change predominantly in the direction of its trade rather than in its character: it diversified the market for its ivory, but did not divert its economy from reliance on the exchange of a few raw materials for manufactured luxuries. The export of slaves, though not horrific or in an unbroken stream, still meant a drain on East Africa's human resources that may have been of critical significance

58. T. M. Ricks, pp. 339, 343; S. A. Riavi, pp. 200–1; G. Mathew, 1963, pp. 101, 107–8. For coin finds see p. 554 above.

59. Cosmas, p. 372; G. S. P. Freeman-Grenville, 1962a, p. 25; Al-Mas'udi, in G. S. P. Freeman-Grenville, 1962b, pp. 15–16.

at certain times and places in the history of East Africa even before the nineteenth century. The trade, however, was under the control of a class of coastal peoples themselves a product of international trade and dependent for their prosperity on its continuance. They could hardly have been expected to initiate a move to withdraw from this relationship of dependence and underdevelopment.

# East Africa before the seventh century

## 23

J. E. G. SUTTON

It is easier to acquire knowledge of the situation of the peoples and societies in East Africa after +100 than during the earlier periods. A great deal of research is now being done on these latter periods and the findings are leading to a constant revision of all or parts of the previous conclusions.

Study of the 2000 years from −1000 to +1000 is difficult. It calls for sophisticated methods and a vast amount of information which archaeology has so far been unable to furnish in its entirety.

The study which follows is therefore conjectural, hypothetical or even provocative on more than one point, in order to stimulate reflection and research.

The approach to the early history of East Africa is therefore a cultural one essentially, an attempt to reconstruct the way or ways of life as far as the combined archaeological, anthropological and linguistic evidences will allow. Reference is frequently made to language groups. In themselves these may be less important than broader cultural and economic considerations; but language is a part of culture and a historical thing, something handed down (albeit continually modified) from generation to generation in a community, and a means by which people clearly identify themselves as groups and distinguish themselves from others. (These others they may recognize as related in some way, should the languages be partly intelligible or share certain common features, or conversely, should no relationship be obvious, they may regard them as completely alien.) Largely for these reasons, linguistic definitions and classifications of peoples are commonly the most clear and convenient for anthropologists and historians. Those used in this chapter are clarified in the accompanying chart and map. They follow in general the scheme originally laid down in *Zamani* (edited by Ogot and Keiran, 1968), which was based on Greenberg's classification of African languages.

## The southern savannah hunting tradition

Throughout the savannahs and light woodlands which cover most of Africa to the east and south of the great equatorial forest belt, the main population for many thousands of years before the Iron Age consisted of hunter-

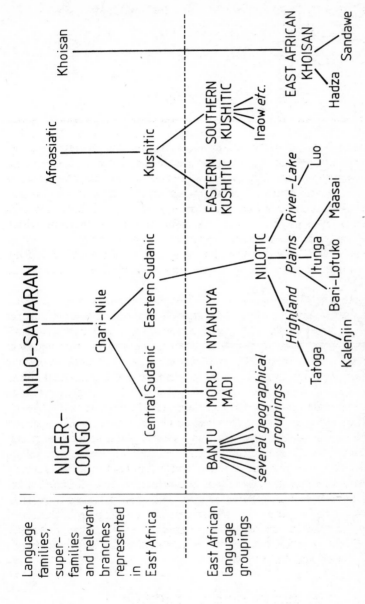

FIG. 23.1  *East African language groupings and relationships*

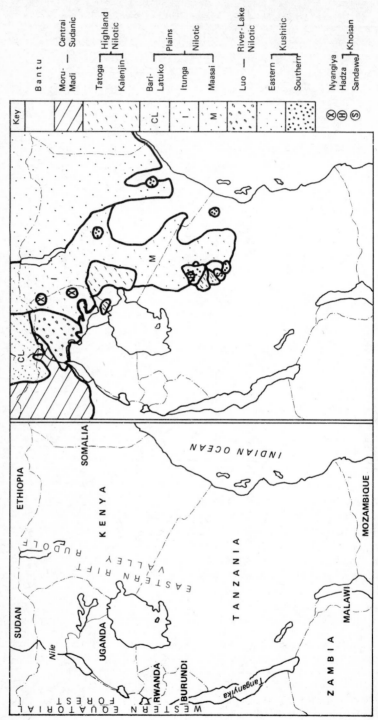

FIG. 23.2 *East Africa: Political map and map showing the distribution of languages and peoples*

gatherers using bows and arrows and advanced stone-working techniques (principally of the broad tradition which archaeologists have called Wilton, for which see Volume I). These people were generally of a physical type which is represented now by the so-called San and Khoi-Khoi inhabiting the Kalahari and its margins. Their language would have been of the Khoisan family, distinctive for its 'clicks'. Nowadays these languages are confined to the Khoi and San of southern and south-western Africa, and in East Africa to two small separate groups living in north-central Tanzania – the Sandawe and Hadza.[1]

The Hadza remain hunters and gatherers, few in number, fairly mobile and expert in finding and winning the wild food resources of their territory.[2] The Sandawe, on the other hand, have for some time been growing crops and keeping goats and cattle, but they maintain a marked cultural attachment to the bush and an instinctive knowledge of its potential. Physically, both of these tribes are negroid, in general type; however, some observers detect traces of another ancestry in the Sandawe and possibly in the Hadza too. Their intermarriage with the surrounding negroid peoples would explain a drift in the latter's direction.

Interesting again is the observation that this very territory of the Hadza and Sandawe and that which lies between them contains, unlike the rest of eastern Africa, numerous examples of hunter rock art, painted on the inner walls of natural shelters which were used from time to time during the late stone age as temporary camps and family bases. These paintings[3] have a social and often religious significance which is as yet poorly understood; but they also provide valuable indications of hunting methods, diets and daily life. Now, hunter art of this same period similarly painted on rock-shelter walls occurs again in several parts of southern Africa; and, though there are some obvious regional differences, a number of parallels in style, subject matter and technique are observable between the southern African and central Tanzanian examples. These artistic parallels are complemented by the general relationship of the Wilton stone-working techniques employed by the rock-shelter occupants of the two regions. Although neither Hadza nor Sandawe are known to paint in a serious way these days – just as both have given up making stone tools – the message of the evidence is that at some time during the late stone age this region shared an ethnic and cultural tradition with the countries to the south.

This extensive savannah hunter-gatherer way of life had a cultural sophistication and economic viability of its own. If it was the gathering side which produced the bulk of the food consumed (as recent studies

1. These Hadza are often known by the less precise name 'Tindiga'. The classification of their language as Khoisan has been disputed, but is probably correct. There are no serious doubts about the classification of Sandawe in the Khoisan family.

2. A 'villagization' scheme with agricultural instruction is presently being attempted by the Tanzanian government for the Hadza.

3. See Volume I, Chapter 26.

of San and other groups indicate), the more difficult and respected task of winning meat was essential for a balanced diet and for satisfying the appetite. All this depended on a degree of mobility, with seasonal camps but no permanent settlements, as the groups followed the game or exploited the vegetable resources of a territory, and this would have restrained population growth and perhaps inhibited change. It helps to explain why this old savannah population has in recent millennia been assimilated in most regions by the fishing, pastoral and agricultural communities, whose more intensive and productive methods of obtaining food allowed them to maintain more permanent bases and to increase their numbers and enlarge their territories.

So the greater part of the vast region once occupied by the hunter-gatherers become afterwards the domain of Bantu cultivators. In a number of these Bantu regions stories are told of chance encounters with small strange folk who once lived and hunted in the bush and forest. These stories are not historically precise; yet they very likely reflect a core of vague memory handed down from the period a thousand years ago and more when the Bantu were colonizing this expanse of south-central Africa and gradually confining and assimilating the sparser Sandawe population with its very different way of life. A contrasting way in which this old hunting tradition may be reflected in later agricultural times is the prominence accorded to hunting feats and skills in Bantu legend. The founder of a royal line is often a wandering archer or the leader of a band. This seems to derive from an ancient ideology which respected the strength and courage, the judgement and persistence of the successful hunter who could bring home the prized meat.

But not the whole of East Africa became part of the Bantu world. As will be explained below, northern Uganda, much of Kenya and parts of north-central Tanzania have long been occupied by a range of distinct populations, with Kushitic, Nilotic and other languages, some of whom became established there during the iron age, others earlier. Here, as further south, there are clear ethnographic and archaeological evidences of the existence in both recent and ancient times of numerous hunter-gatherer communities. For the most part these were probably not representatives of the bush tradition of the southern savannahs. Although the northern limit of this tradition is not easily defined, there is no strong reason to place it beyond Lake Victoria and the equator. It is sometimes suggested in the literature that San-type populations extended formerly as far as the Horn of Africa and the middle Nile; but this view is based on rather flimsy evidence or presumption – on skeletal finds, few and fragmentary, which are insufficiently distinctive or belong to much more ancient periods before the full differentiation of the later African physical types; on stone tool assemblages of the late stone age from northern Uganda and Kenya, Ethiopia and Somalia which exhibit some vague or general similarities to the Wilton industries of the countries to the south; and on the existence of these small latter-day hunting communities and backwoodsmen in several scattered places. The point about these present groups is that few of them are socially or economically independent. Often they live beside if not actually within the territory of agricultural and pastoral Kushites and Nilotes whose language they speak and whom they supply with products of the bush and forest – honey, skins, meat, and so. Some of these groups – certain of the Dorobo bands in the Kenya highlands, for instance – need not be aboriginal hunter-gatherers at all, but the result of more recent opportunities for specialization as well as for reversion to the forest by individuals who fail to get on in society. In certain regions of Kushitic speech or strong Kushitic influence in Kenya and Ethiopia, such groups tend to comprise distinct castes of the main group rather than peoples with a full identity of their own, and commonly undertake unclean activities, notably potting and smithing, for the good of the broader community. Such crafts were of course totally alien to the old hunting and gathering tradition of the savannahs.

All the same, these northerly regions of East Africa may well have constituted during much of the late stone age a fluctuating frontier zone, partly determined by climatic changes, between the cultures of San-type populations of the southern savannahs and others of north-eastern and middle Africa. Of these regions much remains to be learned. However, at least two other distinct cultural traditions and broad ethnic entities, also lacking either agriculture or livestock, are identifiable within or bordering East Africa in recent millennia. They are the subjects of the following two sections.

# The collecting and trapping tradition of the equatorial forest

In the rain-forest of the Congo basin, and especially its easterly edges abutting on Rwanda and south-western Uganda, there live Pygmy Negroes. Their range and numbers are smaller than in earlier times, because of the gradual expansion of settled agricultural peoples, Bantu mainly, who have cleared much of the forest and reduced the natural food resources on which the pygmies used to live. Many of the latter have been assimilated, but others survive as independent bands, though maintaining relations with the neighbouring Bantu and speaking the latter's languages.

Although this forest life of the pygmies was, like that of the San, based economically on the hunting and collecting of wild animals and vegetables, it demanded a very different type of ecological adjustment and technological specialization. To include both pygmies and San under the same 'hunter-gatherer' label is to overlook their distinct ways of living and thinking, as alien to each other as either is to that of Bantu cultivators. The pygmy way of life, like that of the San, must represent an ancient cultural and economic tradition attached to a special environment, in this case the dense forest whose nature helps explain the distinctive physical features and short stature of these people.

However, historical evidence of any sort bearing on the pygmies and their former geographical extent is extremely scant, although in the Congo basin some very tentative attempts have been made at correlating certain late and middle stone age remains (the Lupembo-Tshitolian complex). The distribution and dating of this complex does at least indicate an important forest and woodland tradition, ancient in origin and persisting into quite recent times. Its later phases are not well represented eastward of Rwanda; so, should it be the work of pygmies, it would not support a view of their extension into East Africa during the late stone age, even at times when rainfall was higher and forests greater. There are, it is true, allusions to the former presence of pygmies in scattered parts of East Africa in random historical and anthropological writings. Some of these appear to be based on ethnographic misconceptions, others on folklore or vague oral-traditional evidence mentioning small hunter-gatherer peoples in the past. In so far as these accounts relate to specific peoples and relatively precise periods of time, they probably refer in most cases to San-type hunters of the savannah tradition or in the northerly portion of East Africa to separate groups, so-called Dorobo and other backwoodsmen, which were discussed above.

Among these legendary forest peoples, the Gumba, spoken of by the Kikuyu in the eastern part of the Kenya highlands, deserve special mention. There is considerable confusion over who the Gumba were and the sort of life they led. This is due first to the inherent vagueness of the evidence and the tendency of informants to rationalize from the legends, and secondly to muddled recording and analysis by historical investigators. Nevertheless, there exists clear archaeological evidence in Kikuyu country of people who, some time during the last two thousand years, lived in the high forests where they constructed, and apparently inhabited, clusters of curious circular depressions on the ridges. Although these people worked stone, they were probably not just a local and retiring late stone age relic. Their pottery and the possibility of a connection with iron suggest that they maintained some cultural connections with the early highland Bantu, for whom they very likely fulfilled special economic functions. These people may or may not have much to do with the vanished Gumba of the legends; but they promise, when more fully studied, to provide a valuable example of a localized population developing a distinctive forest culture, albeit in quite recent times and in some form of symbiosis with nearby agriculturalists. At this very general level of environmental adjustment there may be some room for comparison with the pygmies of the Congo basin. But, despite the speculations of certain writers, there are no good grounds for assuming that these former inhabitants of the forests of Kikuyuland, Gumba or whoever, were themselves of the pygmy stock.

# The aquatic tradition of Middle Africa

This question, which has been neglected for so long, is taken up in the previous volume of this history.[4] It will suffice here, therefore, to consider the final development of this interesting way of life.

By −5000 the climate had turned markedly drier and the lakes had fallen far below their previous high stands, being fed by fewer and smaller rivers. Thus the geographical continuity and in places the economic basis of the aquatic way of life was undermined. The days of its cultural dominance were over. However, around −3000 conditions turned more humid again for a while and lake levels correspondingly rose (but not as high as in the seventh millennium). In the eastern rift valley in Kenya a modified aquatic culture was resuscitated at this time, perhaps through new migrations or contacts with the middle and upper Nile. Remains of this late aquatic phase, with unusual pottery styles and shallow stone bowls, have been found above Lakes Rudolf and Nakuru, dating generally, it seems, around −3000. Despite the apparent absence of harpoons from sites of this period, these people certainly fished. But very likely the diet was less predominantly aquatic than in the main phase of between three thousand and five thousand years earlier. By −2000, with the dry trend re-established, the viability of an aquatic culture was finally undermined in much of the eastern Rift valley.

It appears that the population of this later aquatic phase was also basically negroid. Direct clues on its language are lacking. But the most reasonable argument is that it belonged to one branch or other of the Chari–Nile family (the eastern division of Nilo-Saharan).

One would expect the great aquatic civilization, both its main phase between −8000 and −5000 and its later revival around −3000, to be represented by the rivers and swamps of the upper Nile basin and in particular along the old shore-lines of East Africa's biggest lake, Victoria Nyanze. Oddly, signs of this seem to be lacking for the millennia in question. However, by the first millennium before our era there were people who camped on islands and in rock-shelters and open stations and by the lake itself and by rivers in the region, whose diet included fish and molluscs, but also the flesh of bush game and perhaps of cattle and sheep. Whether some of these people cultivated at all is very uncertain; but there is some interesting evidence of forest clearance around Lake Victoria at this time, which is indicative at the least of some new and relatively intensive form of land use. The pottery of these people, known as Kansyore ware, bears some striking affinities to the much older dotted wavy-line wares of the early aquatic tradition. As far as is known, these wares had been superseded long before in the Nile valley; and it is unlikely therefore that the Kansyore types were simply introduced to Lake Victoria as late as the first or second

4. See Volume I, Chapter 20.

millennium before our era. More likely, the aquatic tradition stretches back several millennia here as elsewhere, but all that has been recognized of it so far is its most recent and run-down phase immediately before the iron age. In which case one may wonder whether signs of the old aquatic life await discovery by the more southerly East African lakes too – notably the length of Lake Tanganyika.

While there are no direct clues to the language-group to which these Lake Victoria people of the first millennium belonged, it is possible that it was Central Sudanic (a division of Chari–Nile). This region and that to its south was from the beginning of the iron age populated by Bantu; and, according to one linguistic school of thought, these Bantu in their process of settlement assimilated an older and smaller population of Central Sudanic speakers from whom they learned about sheep and cattle and how to keep them. Having no words of their own for these things, the early Bantu borrowed them from these earlier inhabitants of these regions whose own languages become extinct. Southwards of Lake Victoria no reasonable archaeological support for this hypothesis has yet been found; but around the lake itself a case can be made for identifying the sites with Kansyore ware with the Central Sudanic language-group, especially if the association in some places with remains of sheep and cattle in the first millennium be correct. Maybe, an isolated and very declined aquatic tradition was at this time reinvigorated by contact on its eastern side with a new pastoral tradition which established itself in the Kenya highlands.

## The Kushitic pastoral tradition

For, as the drier climatic regime became firmly established by the second millennium, not only did the lakes retreat to approximately their present levels (and the fish become extinct in some cases), but the forests receded also, leaving in their place, most notably in the eastern Rift and across the adjacent plateaus, fine upland pastures. And, though around Lake Victoria and by several other lakes and rivers one could still fish and maintain some of the elements of the old aquatic life, this tradition had now lost its great geographical continuity and the cultural assurance which formerly went with this. The new prestige in much of the Middle African belt, and especially its eastern end, was cattle-keeping, and to continue to live by and off the waters was commonly seen as backward and intellectually stagnant. It was not only an archaic way of life: it was, in the view of the more successful pastoral groups, uncouth and unclean. The first pastoralists in East Africa identified themselves by not only their Kushitic speech and insistence on circumcision, but also a taboo against fish.

For a long time now cattle have, in those parts of East Africa with grass of sufficient quality and quantity and free from tsetse and endemic diseases, been an object of prestige and an indication of wealth. But it is important to understand that this cattle ideology is based on hard economic sense. Cattle provide meat and, more important, milk; and even among people who rely on their fields for most of their food, livestock are an important source of protein and also a safeguard against famines periodically caused by drought or pests. Moreover, one should not overlook the important role of goats and sheep, which commonly provide the main sources of meat to communities concentrating on cattle-keeping and on agriculture alike.

The first East African cattle were introduced into the highland and Rift valley region of Kenya no less than three thousand years ago. It was probably a long-horned humpless breed. Bones of both cows and of goats (or sheep) have been found at several pre-iron age archaeological sites dated throughout the first millennium. Although a few of these were living places, the more frequent discoveries are of burials, both in caves and more commonly in or under cairns (stone mounds). Clearly a fuller picture of the economy of these people of the first millennium must await the discovery and meticulous examination of more occupation sites: nevertheless, the objects deposited in graves, though doubtless specially selected and of religious significance, are often much better preserved and must in some way reflect the way of living or attitude to life. Among the finds to date are grindstones and pestles, deep stone bowls and pots, calabashes and wooden vessels probably for milk-drinking, baskets and string, ground stone axes and worked pieces of ivory, and necklaces made of beads of various stones, bone, shell and hard vegetable materials. As a cultural complex this is roughly the equivalent of what was formerly described as the 'stone bowl culture' (its main and later phase); but it will probably be found to comprise in fact a series of communities and cultural variants.

The economy was not exclusively pastoral. Antelopes and other game were hunted, especially perhaps by some of the poorer communities. It is not yet known for certain whether types of sorghum or millet or other foods were cultivated by these people, but the likelihood is strong. To begin with, the amount of pottery at some of the sites suggests that part at least of the population was more settled than would have been the case in a purely pastoral community, while the grinding equipment also hints at the cultivation, preparation and consumption of grain. However, these big flat grindstones and the accompanying pestles could have been used for crushing wild vegetables or even non-food items. For instance, some of those left in the graves are stained with red ochre with which the corpses had been adorned. But this observation need not rule out a utilitarian purpose in everyday life. A more persuasive argument for assuming some cultivation is that, without the ability to turn to alternative sources of food in times of severe crisis following prolonged droughts or cattle epidemics, it is unlikely that such societies could have survived long; and hunting and gathering would have sufficed as a temporary stop-gap and main source of food for only very small and dispersed groups.[5] Nevertheless, a cultural accent on cattle-keeping and a predominant economic reliance on livestock is illustrated by the geographical distribution of these people, virtually confining themselves to those regions with fine extensive grasslands. The Crater highlands in northern Tanzania, containing the green bowl of Ngorongoro with its cemeteries of this period, were the essential southern limit of this long pastoral zone. A people more committed to combining their stock-raising with agriculture would have spread out farther into fertile districts on their eastern and western sides and could have continued farther southwards.

The pottery styles and certain other features of the material culture of these early pastoralists of the highlands and Rift valley of Kenya and northern Tanzania seem to betray influences from the middle Nile region. But the reflection is a pale one, the influences probably indirect. They do not necessarily mean that the cattle and their herders originated in that region. Rather, they may result from contact with and assimilation of the late aquatic population with its own more ancient Nile connections which was previously established by the Rift valley lakes. An illustration of this is the continuity of the strange stone bowls in this region through some two thousand years, from late aquatic times to early pastoral ones.

The regional contrasts are equally significant. For, since the second millennium, there has developed a cultural divide running north–south between the highlands of Ethiopia and Kenya (with the intervening arid plains) on the eastern side, where the pastoral tradition entrenched itself, and, to the west, the upper Nile basin with Lake Victoria, where an aquatic economy remained viable for smallish populations. This line constituted at no time an iron curtain or a barrier to people and ideas, which have in fact moved across in either direction both before and during the iron age. But it does represent the meeting of two broad and generally distinct cultural traditions. This is reflected in linguistic comparisons and analyses and, less precisely, by physical–anthropological observations.

Difficult though it is to generalize on physical types, one gets the clear impression that the populations to the west of this line are very typically negroid and that those in the highlands and plains to the east are rather less so. Language studies point to influences from Ethiopia to the East

5. It is true that in recent centuries some pastoral societies have managed to avoid cultivation completely (and even to despise hunting too). But this has been possible through reliance on either obtaining grains and other vegetables by barter with agricultural neighbours in order to survive the dry season, or on raiding other peoples with a mixed agricultural–pastoral economy. The latter practice was essential for the central Masai divisions who, despite their control of expanses of fine highland pastures, often felt their own meat supplies insufficient for their appetites, and more important, were compelled after losses or bad years to acquire new breeding bulls and to replenish without delay their herds of milch-cows, if their way of life and their community were to continue. Neither of these solutions was open to the original East African cattle-keepers of the first millennium before our era.

African highlands, keeping all the time a little to the east of the cultural divide. Ethiopia is the ancient home of the Kushitic language-family; and most of the present Bantu and Nilotic languages of Kenya and of north-eastern and north-central Tanzania reveal evidence of borrowing from Kushitic tongues. In a few places, notably at the southern end of this zone, such southern Kushitic languages actually persist, though of course highly diverged from the old Kushitic forms. Among the important cultural-historical messages which the word-borrowings provide is the contribution to cattle-keeping made by the early Kushitic populations in East Africa.

The Kushitic cultural element in East African history is reflected in other ways, and up to a point in the non-chiefly social and political institutions, based on age-organization, of the peoples of the plains and highlands of Kenya and parts of northern Tanzania. But this observation is a very general one, and not all aspects of these systems need be traceable to the original Kushitic settlement.[6] Of more specifically Kushitic origin must be the custom of circumcision in initiation, whose distribution coincides remarkably closely with that of substantial word-borrowings from Kushitic and the normal aversion to fish in the same broad region, whose significance in the East African historial experience was argued above.

We gain then a picture of a pastoral Kushitic-speaking people, tall and relatively light-skinned, expanding southwards and making themselves masters of the rich grasslands, the plains and more especially the plateaux, of Kenya and northern Tanzania about three thousand years ago. All this may sound just like a restatement of the now rejected Hamitic myth. The point is that, while the more illogical and romantic aspects of the various and vaguely stated Hamitic hypotheses do derive from prejudiced European scholarship and grotesque attitudes towards Africa and black peoples, the factual bases of these views were not entirely fictitious. Some of the observations were acute and certain of the historical interpretations very judicious. The error of the Hamitic school lay in its presuppositions and its obsession with *origins* of peoples and ideas. Failing to appreciate the local scene, it emphasized a particular set of external influences, that is the Kushitic element and the pastoral prestige rather than seeing this as but one of many parts of the East African historical and cultural experience – an experience in which the old savannah hunting tradition, the aquatic one established during the wet millennia, and more recently the Bantu with their attachment to iron and agriculture, have been equally important complements.

6. Some may result from later contact with eastern Kushitic peoples of southern Ethiopia and the Kenya border, notably the region of Lake Rudolf. In the present millennium certain eastern Kushitic peoples, notably groups of Galla and Somali, have extended a long way into northern and eastern Kenya. Such movements should be distinguished from the much more ancient southern Kushitic expansion discussed here.

## The Bantu agricultural and iron-using tradition

While pastoralism and the associated fish taboo provided the cultural and ethnic hallmark of the Kushites in one zone of East Africa during the first millennium, that of the early Bantu during the following millennium was the working and use of iron. How or whence this knowledge was obtained is still unclear: this question is discussed in Chapter 21. Much more important than this question of origin is the evident fact that the early Bantu depended on iron and were identified as the people who possessed its secrets. Probably the earlier peoples of East Africa were unfamiliar with it. For tools and weapons they had taken suitable stones and worked them by ancient techniques. For instance, the eastern Rift Valley in the Kushitic zone is blessed with sources of an unusually fine stone called obsidian (opaque volcanic glass), from which excellent blades of different sizes were readily producible for all sorts of purposes, including spear-heads and probably circumcision-knives. The contemporaneous but distinct communities living around Lake Victoria, among whom the aquatic tradition persisted in part, were less fortunate than those in the Rift Valley in the stones available to them, but succeeded none the less in manufacturing complex tool-kits from quartz, cherts and other stones with good flaking properties, as also did the savannah hunters in the regions southward. To all such varied peoples, the first contact with strangers practising an iron technology must have been a shattering intellectual experience.

The main expansion of the Bantu was vast and fast, not a series of gradual stages as some have argued. But neither was it a matter of purposeless nomadic wandering, nor of organized military conquest. It was a remarkable process of *colonization* – in the true sense of the word – the opening up of essentially empty lands. This Bantu expansion did not engulf the whole of the area considered here. About one-third of East Africa has remained non-Bantu on account of the resilience and adaptability of some of the earlier populations especially in the long zone of the eastern Rift with its old Kushitic populations, augmented during the iron age by the arrival of certain Nilotic divisions. (See the linguistic map and the preceding and succeeding sections.)

This is not to say that there has been no interaction between the Bantu and various of the Kushites and Nilotes in East Africa during these two thousand years. From time to time considerable intermarriage and assimilation in both directions must have occurred, as well as cultural borrowings and economic enrichment of several kinds. The Bantu soon began supplementing their agricultural diet with the milk and meat of cattle in those regions with suitable grass and free of tsetse. Among those Bantu living around Lake Victoria and in the lush upland pastures to the west, cattle have long been especially important. Conversely the role of grain agriculture among the Kushitic and Nilotic populations of the Kenya and northern Tanzania highlands has in time been enhanced, owing to the sheer need to feed larger numbers of people, combined with the influence or example of neighbouring Bantu and their techniques. Some parts of the highlands have become Bantu linguistically, while reflecting in various cultural and social features the assimilation of a substantial Kushitic substratum. This is most striking among the highly populous and compact Kikuyu. Their language is Bantu, and the intensive agriculture in these fertile hills and forest-clearings can be seen as a local adaptation of traditional Bantu ways. But the Kikuyu political system based on age-sets with circumcision, together with an aversion to fish, belongs more to the older Kushitic usage of the highlands.

The Kushitic zone of the highlands and Rift Valley, while retaining its basic shape (through becoming during the iron age more Nilotic than Kushitic in terms of actual linguistic distributions), did therefore suffer some Bantu encroachment, especially in wet forest areas with their unusually rich agricultural potential (and hence, eventually, the densest populations). On the other hand, there are places where in the second millennium of our era the extent of Bantu speech has been pushed back. This has happened along parts of the coast and hinterland of southern Somalia and north-eastern Kenya; and again in the regions of Lwoo expansion in central and eastern Uganda and by the Kenya shores of Lake Victoria. These movements and assimilating processes are highly important for the later history of these regions and will be discussed in greater detail in the ensuing volumes. But, relatively speaking, these are minor adjustments. More significant here is the observation that the main elements of the linguistic map and of the seminal cultural traditions of East Africa were already established. The Bantu expansion was basically over and the northern Bantu line in East Africa was roughly drawn 1500 years ago. At this flexible irregular line Bantu colonization was contained by the prior establishment of virile and sufficiently adaptable cultures and economies. Around Lake Victoria, however, and all the way southward the situation was different.

The communities of the shores of Lake Victoria and the river-side all around at the eve of the Bantu expansion were, as argued above, descended from the old aquatic population. Lately it had combined some hunting and possibly a little stock-raising and even agriculture, while remaining distinct from the Kushitic highland pastoralists to the east. However versatile these people may or may not have been, they seem to have been quite quickly absorbed into the societies of Bantu settlers. Their legacy may have been a substantial one, nevertheless. In particular, several aspects of the fishing techniques and beliefs of the Bantu around the shores and on the islands of Lake Victoria very likely derive from these preceding inhabitants. Definitely ancient is the cult of Mugase, god of the lake and creator of storms, whose goodwill ensures a successful catch, whose anger brings disaster.

Equally interesting is the message of the archaeological finds and dates as they accumulate, indicating that it was around Lake Victoria and in the highlands above the western Rift valley that the easterly Bantu consolidated themselves and developed their savannah way of life. Here, in a zone of good rainfall close to the forest edge, experimentation with sorghum and millet cultivation (suitable for large-scale savannah expansion) would have been pioneered, acquaintance made with stock-raising, the distinctive Bantu pottery given its special features and decoration (dimpled bases, etc.), and the arts of metallurgy perfected, if not first encountered. Significantly, in north-western Tanzania, Rwanda and the Kivu province of Zaïre, comprising the fertile districts along the eastern edge of the great rain forest, there have come to light brick-built iron-working furnaces, evidence of a highly sophisticated and productive industry. Should it prove possible to discern two stages in the spread of the Bantu beyond the original forest base, this would be the first or formative one, beginning perhaps somewhat more rather than less than two thousand years ago.[7]

Further south, in Tanzania and beyond, the situation confronting the expanding Bantu in the early and middle centuries of the first millennium of our era was a wilder but perhaps simpler one. Radiating from a quite populous base region in the westerly part of East Africa, armed with the necessary tools, skills and seeds, they were now penetrating woodlands and savannahs hitherto only lightly populated and exploited by hunter-gatherers of the bush tradition. Though not inconsequential, the influence of these hunters upon the Bantu would have been less than that of the peoples they had found in Uganda and Kenya. Nevertheless, flexibility and adaptation were necessary in every new district colonized, depending on soils and altitude, the rainfall and its annual distribution.[8] However far one went, one retained that sense of Bantu-ness: being Bantu indeed meant continually to hive off, carrying a sack of seed and a few tools with which to clear and cultivate, to settle for a while rather than to settle *down* in permanent villages. This process did not end immediately the Bantu had reached the opposite coasts of the sub-continent and the borders of the Kalahari desert; for there remained within the regions traversed plenty of land uncleared, so that population increases could for some time be accommodated without resort to more intensive agricultural methods. So often in Bantu local history the guiding theme is one focusing on the senior clan, whose founder is supposed to have come and first cleared that piece of bush.

The hunters may not have been forcibly driven out or persecuted; more likely they were respected for their knowledge of the land and skill with

7. Whether this was a phenomenon of the eastern side of the forest only, or equally of its long southern side lying between Lake Tanganyika and the Congo mouth, must await fuller investigation of the latter region (see Chapter 25).

8. In northerly and near-coastal regions of East Africa two distinct planting seasons would have been normally possible. But the prevailing climatic regime farther south would have allowed only one.

the bow. But as settlement became denser, there was less and less scope for organized hunting and gathering as a full means of subsistence and a communal way of life. Many of the hunters were sooner or later absorbed into Bantu society. But they would have been absorbed as individuals, through marriage or possibly clientage: it was not possible for a hunting band or tribe as such to make the cultural change, to 'Bantuize' itself.

With the new technology, the magical control of the soil which thus began yielding grain foods,[9] pots in which to cook them palatably, and iron tools and arrow-heads (which, incidentally, could be traded to the hunters), the Bantu success and superiority were assured. They could afford to assimilate hunters without any fear of losing their identity or diluting their culture. There does not seem to have been any need to maintain artificial distinguishing marks or prohibitions: bodily mutilations or taboos of a general Bantu sort are not obvious. Their new speech which codified their way of life was enough. The economy, as seen, was flexible and, depending on the local situation, could include hunting, fishing or cattle-rearing. Where none of these was possible or sufficient for protein requirements, this need was presumably satisfied by keeping goats or growing certain pulses. The normal staple was probably sorghum: this assumption is based on the observation that this grain with its numerous varieties suited to different terrains is an ancient traditional one in eastern Africa and Bantu-land, while in Zambia charred seeds of sorghum have been recognized in archaeological excavations of early iron age settlements.[10]

This interpretation of Bantu expansion and settlement in East Africa (and in countries to the south and west) at the beginning of the iron age is based on a combination of linguistic and archaeological evidences, as well as general ethnographic considerations. The obvious point about the numerous Bantu languages, especially those outside the Congo forest, is their close common relationship which points to a quite recent separation and differentiation, of the order of some one or two thousand years. Another thing which emerges from a comparative study of Bantu languages is an acquaintance with iron and the skills of working it from early times. This

9. Rain-making being commonly essential.

10. In some of the previous literature there has been considerable discussion of the role of bananas in the Bantu expansion. This crop originated in south-eastern Asia and is unlikely to have been introduced to the east coast of Africa until some time in the first millennium of our era. It would have become known to Bantu communities therefore after the great expansion was over. It is, of course, a crop of settled rather than of colonizing peoples, and in later Bantu history permanent banana gardens have become increasingly important in wet regions with dense sedentary populations, notably the northern and western sides of Lake Victoria and several highland masses. In fact, during the last thousand years or so bananas have been utilized and developed in East Africa more than anywhere else in the world.

American starch foods – notably maize and cassava – were unknown in East Africa until very recently.

is one reason for associating the early iron age archaeological sites, dating from the early and middle parts of the first millennium of our era, in many districts of eastern and south-central Africa with the Bantu colonization. But a more compelling reason for confidently identifying these sites as those of the early Bantu is simply that their distribution agrees so nicely with that of present Bantu peoples. There are no sensible grounds for theorizing that a quite different population covered this same broad region only to disappear completely no more than a thousand years ago.

The most frequent and diagnostic objects found on these early Bantu sites are not iron tools and weapons (for these were usually too valuable to be discarded and even if they had been, would normally have corroded completely), but the broken pieces of earthenware pots. These were referred to above. From the very beginning these pottery wares were by no means identical region by region throughout the enormous span of Bantu settlement. New types are being recognized continually by archaeologists. Perhaps the best known are the dimple-based (or Urewa) wares found around Lake Victoria and further west, extending moreover to the northern end of Lake Tanganyika and the woodlands south of the forest in Zaïre. Besides the dimples on the bases of some of these vessels, many have elaborately shaped rims and remarkable decoration in scrolls and other patterns. To the south and east of the dimple-based zone, the early iron age wares fall into two main groupings. In north-eastern Tanzania and south-eastern Kenya, that is beyond the great Kushitic bulge, Kwale ware, as it is called, occurs from the highland edges down to the coastal plain. At the southern end of Lake Tanganyika, and in the countries farther south, a whole plethora of regional wares has been identified. (These include those in Zambia previously known as channelled.)

What is not disputed is that all these wares have a general family relationship; and there has been considerable discussion of what might be deduced from this about the directions of the Bantu expansion. It is not the average or most typical pots which are likely to be the most revealing, but the extreme and more peculiar features. And, in glancing at a range of early iron age pottery collections from sites scattered between the equator and the borders of South Africa, the immediate impression is that the northerly wares, especially the dimple-based from around and west of Lake Victoria, have a stamp of originality which becomes less striking the further south one scans. It is as though the northern potters consciously signed their wares 'Bantu', whereas the southerly ones, separated from the mainstream of tradition, took this point for granted so that a progressive simplification of the original Bantu shapes, rims and decorative patterns set in. This was natural enough anywhere from central Tanzania southward where potting seems to have been a new art introduced by the first Bantu settlers: any pot was automatically 'Bantu' here. But in the Kenya highlands and around Lake Victoria other peoples had long been making their own pottery. Therefore the Kwale ware of the east, though perhaps less original than the 'dimple-based', needed to retain and emphasize special Bantu features. In fact in some places in north-eastern Tanzania, where the wooded hills meet the open plains, both Kwale and a completely distinct ware of the same date occur together. Is this where Bantu and Kushitic met?

A detailed map of the Bantu expansion cannot be reconstructed from this pottery evidence, especially since there are some regions on which virtually nothing is known archaeologically. These include southern Tanzania and Mozambique. Nevertheless, the picture indicated is that of radiation through the savannahs from a general nucleus somewhere to the west of Lake Victoria near the forest edge. The most recent reassessments of the language relationships of the present non-forest Bantu describe an essentially identical pattern of Bantu historical development and dispersal from the forest. It certainly appears that, wherever the successful egress from the forest was made, whether on its southern or its eastern side, the first movement was to expand around its edge in one or both directions and into the similarly humid country surrounding Lake Victoria. The bolder strike southwards and south-eastwards into the almost limitless savannahs came after.

The region around the southern end of Lake Tanganyika, or the corridor between that and Lake Nyasa, may have acted as a secondary dispersal centre, both for the southerly Bantu and for the north-easterly, that is the makers of 'Kwale ware'. But a useful reconstruction of the history of the latter region must await information of what was happening in southern Tanzania during the first millennium of our era. One theory is that Kushitic-speakers extended right through the middle belt of Tanzania from the northern to the southern highlands.

Among the present East African Bantu, pottery is usually a woman's craft. But there are ethnographic clues in countries to the west and south that the original Bantu potting tradition was diffused by male craftsmen accompanying the colonizing bands. This is bold speculation, but is possibly deducible from the archaeological and ethnographic evidence gathered by D. W. Phillipson in Zambia.[11] In which case it was very likely closely associated with the other important Bantu craft, that of smelting iron-ore and forging tools. No new colony could succeed if it lacked specialists versed in the secrets of potting and smithing. There is likely, however, to have been some trade, even if rather slight at this early stage. For iron ore, while not rare in fact, is certainly not universally available, and really rich sources are few. Its distribution may have influenced the pattern of initial Bantu settlement. The very early exploitation of fine ores and the elaborate smelting furnaces in Rwanda and the adjacent part of Tanzania have already been noted. In north-eastern Tanzania, similarly, the early sites in and below the Pare hills may reflect interest in the plentiful

11. See *Journal of African History*, XV (1974), pp. 1–25, esp. 11–12.

ores of that district. Not far away, in the foothills of Kilimanjaro, where iron ore is unknown, there are more sites of this period. Maybe, the pattern of trade of recent times, by which bars of smelted iron (and pots too) were traded from Pare to Kilimanjaro to be exchanged for food and livestock, is some 1500 years old. All the same, large-scale and long-distance trade should not be imagined for these early Bantu colonizing communities. The accent was on settlement and subsistence. It is not till the middle period of Bantu history, around a thousand years ago, that signs of commercial development become at all apparent. For the early period not even the Kwale ware sites, some of them very close to the Indian Ocean, have yielded objects of coastal or foreign provenance.

Another household necessity to such agricultural communities would have been salt. In recent times this commodity has been obtained in many areas of East Africa by a variety of methods. These include the burning of certain reeds and grasses which take in salt from the soil. The ashes are dissolved in water, and the resultant brine filtered and evaporated. The same extracting processes are used for salty soils in some places. Soda for cooking hard vegetables is obtained by similar techniques. Their productivity is usually low and the quality of the salt often poor. And some districts lacked opportunities for these even, and must have depended on trade for their bare requirements. It is here that the richer sources of salt which exist in a few places in the East African interior, in the form of concentrated salt-soils, brine-springs and Rift valley mineral lakes, became important. Of these only the springs of pure brine at Uvinza in western Tanzania are so far known to have been exploited during the early iron age. Investigations at other salt centres – Kibiro by Lake Albert in Uganda, Ivuna in south-western Tanzania – did not reveal evidence of activity before the present millennium. But it is possible that further work at such sites, and especially at the salt lakes of Kasenyi and Katwe in south-western Uganda, will prove more informative on the early period. The more easterly Bantu, moreover, could doubtless have been supplied from the coastal creeks.

## The Nilotes: adaptation and variation

Beside the Bantu, another language group – or rather series of distantly related language groups – occupied much of East Africa during the iron age. These were the Nilotes. While their physical features differ in certain general respects from those of the Bantu, the Nilotes are very pronouncedly negroid. It is true, nevertheless, that those Nilotic-speakers who have moved furthest eastward and southward into the old Kushitic zone of Kenya and northern Tanzania have assimilated some of the previous Ethiopoid population. This helps account for the original negroid features of the present Itunga, Masai, Kalenjin and Tatoga groupings. These are the people who were in the past classified as 'Nilo-Hamites'. Their partly

Kushitic ancestry is further shown – but in a variety of ways among these different groups – in their cultural heritage. This has involved considerable word-borrowing from Kushitic tongues. But basically their languages remain Nilotic.[12]

Nothing concrete is known about the early history of the Nilotes. Nevertheless, the distribution and internal relationships of their three existing branches point to the low grasslands and watersides of the upper Nile basin as their original homeland. One could speculate that their emergence as the dominant group within the eastern Sudanic division of the Chari–Nile language-family and their periodic rapid, if not explosive expansions in several directions result from their adoption of cattle in this part of the old aquatic zone some three thousand or so years ago. The cattle could have been obtained either from the Kushites in the Ethiopian highlands to the east or more probably from people further down the Nile. Here in the White Nile basin fishing remained in vogue alongside stock-raising as well as the development of grain cultivation. This three-sided economic exploitation of the environment is maintained by the present peoples along the White Nile and its tributaries.

The divisions within the Nilotic languages – between the Highland, River-Lake and Plains[13] Nilotes – are deep and ancient (considerably more so than those in Bantu, for instance). And, while a date for the break-up of 'parent Nilotic' cannot be accurately estimated, it could not have been less than two thousand years ago. This would have occurred somewhere in the southern Sudan, possibly towards the Ethiopian border. From this general region representatives of each of the three divisions have moved into northerly and even central parts of East Africa during the last two thousand years. However, the extensions of Plains Nilotes (notably the Itunga group in eastern Uganda and north-western Kenya, and the Masai in Kenya and northern Tanzania) and the River-Lake Nilotes (the Lwoo of Uganda and the Kenya lake-shore) belong to the present millennium and are therefore the concern of later volumes of this History. In this volume our main concern is limited to the Highland division of Nilotic, represented nowadays by the Kalenjin of the western Kenya highlands and the Tatoga scattered over various grasslands in northern Tanzania.

The early Highland Nilotes are not yet known archaeologically; but their present distribution and internal linguistic comparison show that they must have established themselves in Kenya quite a thousand years ago. It is possible that their emergence as a group with an identity, culture and language of their own had begun with the coming of iron to the upper

12. The original use of the word 'Nilotic' was, of course, geographical – 'of the River Nile'. But as used here, and as generally used in historical writing these days, 'Nilotic' refers to a group of languages defined strictly by linguistic criteria, regardless of location. See the accompanying map.

13. These are the terms used in B. A. Ogot and J. A. Keiran. They correspond to Greenberg's 'Southern', 'Western' and 'Eastern' Nilotic respectively. See Bibliography.

Nile basin and the Ethiopian borderlands. In these regions and in the Kushitic zone it is likely that the knowledge of iron and the skills of working it derived from a northerly source.[14] This would have been independent of its adoption by the early Bantu, with whose expansion iron-working was, as discussed above, probably in westerly and southerly parts of East Africa.

Whatever may be the explanation of the success of the early Highland Nilotes in the first millennium of our era, they took over a considerable part, but certainly not all, of the Rift Valley and adjacent highlands and plains which had previously been Kushitic territory. This was largely a process of assimilation as much as of invasion and expulsion: it probably continued well into the second millennium. Already these Nilotes had herded cattle and cultivated grains: nevertheless, they doubtless had much to learn from the Kushites on how to pursue these activities most successfully in their new highland environment. Their social organization with cycling age-sets, moreover, appears to be an amalgamation of Nilotic and Kushitic elements, while the custom of circumcision as a mark of initiation into a named age-set is specifically Kushitic. So is their prohibition against fish. By climbing the escarpments with one's cattle, one was consciously turning one's back on the lakes, swamps and rivers of the west.

The majority of the Nilotes remained in the Nile basin, in the southern Sudan mainly. Here they were not directly influenced by Kushitic ways, and they usefully combined stock-keeping, grain cultivation and fishing. However, the Plains division eventually split into three principal branches, and it is instructive to observe their range of cultural and environmental adaptations from north-west to south-east. Among the Bari–Lotuko cluster in the southern Sudan and the borders of northern Uganda a fairly typical Nilotic life has been maintained. In the rather dry hills and plains which cross from northern Uganda into Kenya, herded by the Itunga grouping (Karamojong, Turkana, Teso, etc.), fishing is infrequent, though this may be attributable to the scarcity of opportunities as much as to a cultural prohibition. Beyond the Itunga, the third branch of the Plains Nilotes, the Masai, has extended across a very large part of the highlands and plateau grasslands of Kenya and northern Tanzania. Here in recent centuries they have assimilated and been strongly influenced by the earlier settled Highland Nilotes and, directly or indirectly, the southern Kushitic. They have adopted then not only the fish taboo, but circumcision too. In these fine pastures, in fact, the central Masai sections succeeded recently in pursuing the pastoral ethic to its ultimate extreme.

These are by no means all the examples that could be cited of Nilotic

14. In northern Ethiopia and on the middle Nile iron became known around the middle of the first millennium before our era. Iron trade goods are recorded as being imported on the East African coast in the earliest centuries of our era (see Chapter 22) . But there is no indication that the skills of working iron were learned from such external sources or carried inland.

expansion and assimilation often of a seemingly haphazard sort – assimilation of other Nilotic divisions and subdivisions as well as of non-Nilotes, and processes of expansion frequently demanding both ecological and cultural adaptations. In the southern Sudan and in northern and eastern Uganda the interactions which have taken place during the present millennium, and probably the preceding one too, between certain branches of the Plains and River-Lake Nilotes have been quite as complex as those just noted between Nilotes and Kushites and between older Nilotes and newer Nilotes in the Kenya and northern Tanzania highlands. Better covered in the historical literature are the pressures of the Lwoo, a branch of the River-Lake Nilotes, upon the northerly Bantu in Uganda and by the Kenya lake-shore during the last six or seven centuries. Less attention has been paid to two other non-Nilotic groupings, the one in north-eastern Uganda, the other in north-western Uganda and adjacent countries, which are now confined but were clearly much more extensive and important a thousand years ago and more.

The first of these consists of the Nyangiya-speakers (who include the present Tepeth and Teuso or Ik), some of whom hunt, others of whom cultivate quite intensively on isolated mountains close to the north-eastern border of Uganda. This has certainly been a region of cultural diversity, where it is believed, moreover, that some of the late stone age tool-making techniques survived among hill communities into the present millennium. The surrounding country, mostly rather dry, is herded by the Plains Nilotic Itunga peoples, who, together perhaps with other Nilotic groupings before them, have been responsible for confining and largely assimilating these Nyangiya. The latter's language may be distantly related to Nilotic (in the eastern Sudanic branch of the Chari–Nile family).[15] Maybe, before the Nilotic movements, the Nyangiya constituted an important agricultural and pastoral population filling some of the territory between the Kushitic zone to the east and that of the later aquatic peoples of the upper Nile.

These late representatives of the old and rather decayed aquatic tradition may, it was hinted above, have belonged to the Central Sudanic language group (which constitutes a separate division of the Chari–Nile family). Nowadays this is a fragmented sub-family, consisting of separate clusters spaced around the north-eastern edge of the equatorial forest. One of these clusters (the so-called 'Moru-Madi') cuts across the borders of north-western Uganda. It is likely that, before the expansion of the Bantu into central Uganda nearly two thousand years ago and the Nilotic movements from the north and north-east, such Central Sudanic-speakers were much more extensive in the upper Nile basin and by Lake Victoria. Some of

15. This classification has been disputed, one suggestion being that the affinities of Nyangiya lie rather with the Afro-Asiatic super-family (to which Kushitic, among other families, belongs).

the cultural foundations of this highly populous zone of East Africa are more ancient than its present Bantu and Lwoo languages.

## The East African 'megalithic' problem

In the older literature on eastern Africa and its history there was considerable discussion of advanced civilizations in Antiquity. These were posited in the interlacustrine region and more particularly in the highlands of Kenya and northern Tanzania (the old Kushitic zone, interestingly), among others. Such historical views were based on a mixture of ethnographic traits, unscientifically collected 'oral traditions' and archaeological observations, the last consisting of the remains of supposed 'engineering' works and the ruins of buildings and terraces of dry-stone (that is 'megalithic'). Unfortunately, much of the primary evidence was inaccurately recorded, or even where accurate, was illogically interpreted or correlated with quite irrelevant materials to please fanciful historical outlooks which were fashionable at the time, notably the notorious Hamitic ideas. This tendency was all too eagerly taken up by secondary writers who uncritically accepted and in some cases irresponsibly exaggerated the supposed primary evidence. Equally illogical was the presumption so often made that various types of archaeological features, whether genuine or bogus, whether with or without stonework, distributed over a wide region, should be attributable to a single people or culture at a particular period of the past. Such a presumption underlay Huntingford's theory of an Azanian civilization in Kenya and northern Tanzania, which he attributed to Hamites, and equally Murdock's hypothesis of megalithic Kushites having once inhabited the same general region. (Murdock, by the way, was specifically opposed to the Hamitic prejudices of earlier writers.)

The word megalithic is thus a loaded one which serves no cultural or historical purpose in East Africa. It is worth, nevertheless, briefly noting and commenting on those features which have been cited as evidence of ancient megalithic cultures. Not all are in fact stone constructions. In this chapter mention was made of the cairns (or stone mounds), which represent graves, frequently encountered in the pastures of Kenya and northern Tanzania. Many, if not most, of these date to the end of the late stone age between two and three thousand years ago and are probably the work of Kushitic-speaking peoples. But some may be more recent. It is possible, but by no means certain, that some of the rock-cut wells which occur in the drier pastures of southern Masailand in Tanzania and also of eastern and northern Kenya may date back to the same period, when cattle were introduced. So perhaps may some of the so-called ancient roads in the highlands, which are in fact nothing more than cattle-tracks accidentally eroded by the continual passing of herds across ridges and down slopes to water over periods of time. Many of these are still being enlarged, and new ones started. Less likely to extend back so far are the practices of irrigated agriculture pursued on and below several of the Rift escarpments and mountain passes of northern Tanzania and Kenya. On the other hand, it can be demonstrated that these are at least a few centuries old in places. Much more rare and much less important for historical argument, despite what has been written, are hillside agricultural terraces. Only in very peculiar or marginal situations were these constructed. Some accounts even speak of monoliths and stone phalli in the East African interior: it is highly doubtful whether any such things ever stood there!

There is, however, a little more to the East African megalithic issue than this. One also reads of stone houses and enclosures and pit-dwellings. Though here again there has been some inaccurate description and misinterpretation, there are some bases of archaeological fact to be faced. The features in question consist of types of dry-stone walling and revetting and lie in two separate areas. Culturally too, these two complexes were quite separate from each other, interesting though it is that they were roughly contemporary, each dating essentially to the middle centuries of the present millennium (incidentally, well outside the period properly covered in this volume).

The first of these complexes comprises the so-called Sirikwa Holes, which are extremely numerous over the whole of the western highlands of Kenya. These represent defended, sunken cattle-kraals of the earlier Kalenjin peoples: they were not pit-dwellings, as was once believed. But houses were attached to the kraals, being built of wood and thatch, not of stone. In fact even the kraals were normally stoneless, being enclosed with banked earth and fences: only in stony localities were slabs and boulders employed to revet neatly the enclosure banks and entrance devices. This observation demonstrates effectively how the presence or absence of stonework has to be explained in environmental terms as much as in cultural ones.

The second complex lies similarly on the western side of the great Rift Valley, but some distance to the south beyond the Tanzania border. It consists of several sites – of which the biggest and most famous is Engaruka[16] – lying by rivers suitable for irrigation at the feet of the escarpments of the Crater highlands. Here stonework was used for a variety of purposes. These include several sorts of defensive works, notably stock plus village walls. Within these compact villages, sited on the escarpment face, each house stood in a beautifully stone-revetted platform-enclosure and was approached through a revetted terrace-pathway. Yet here again the actual houses were not built of stone, but of wood and thatch. More remarkable at Engaruka is the use of stone to line and revet the sides of hundreds of irrigation furrows, and to divide and level thousands of fields covering 20 square kilometres.

16. For recent reappraisal of Engaruka and related sites, see the articles by N. Chittick and J. E. G. Sutton, 1976.

The identity and language affiliation of the inhabitants of Engaruka have not been definitely established. For it was a group which was broken up and assimilated piecemeal some 200 years ago. Despite the remarkable quality and extent of the dry-stonework, it seems that the people who lived and cultivated here had stagnated in relative isolation, by being forced to over-exploit the resources of their soil and their water supplies in very restricted areas. Theirs was a way of life which had specialized so far in a particular direction that it could not adapt.

This then is the answer to romantically inclined historians who would make so much of Engaruka. It cannot be used to support theories of wide-ranging megalithic civilizations. Nor was it a city of 30 000 or more people, as was once conjectured – and as has been repeated in several books. Rather, it was a concentrated peasant community depending for subsistence on an unusually intensive agricultural system. It is remarkable, but in its local context and as an example of rural cultural development and collapse in a very special situation. Moreover, its main dating in the second millennium of our era now seems clear enough following recent investigations and radio-carbon tests. A first millennium date for some of the remains here, which was suggested in the 1960s as a result of some unexpectedly early radio-carbon determinations, is now believed to be an error, or at least un-representative of the remains as a whole.

# West Africa before the seventh century

## B. WAI ANDAH

Critical appraisal of the available archaeological and other relevant data does not support the popular belief that outside cultural influence was mainly responsible for the origins, development and overall character of the Neolithic and 'iron age' societies of West Africa. In particular, it is wrong to claim that ideas and peoples from outside, usually from the north across the Sahara, stimulated or generated most major developments pertaining to early food production or the earliest working of iron and copper. The data suggest rather that complex regional, sub-regional and local factors were variably important and that West African Neolithic and iron age sites explicable to a greater or lesser extent within systems of sites integrated as much as possible with the major ecological constraints at work.

# The origins of agriculture and animal husbandry

It cannot be overemphasized that to obtain a proper understanding of the history of plant/animal domestication in the tropics, traditional (i.e. European) concepts and contexts need to be drastically reviewed and in some instances completely abandoned. Experiments need to be conducted to find out how long it must have taken to develop the present African cultigens from their various wild ancestors, and in the various ecological niches. Furthermore the scope of archaeological work needs to be widened. Plant succession and soil studies of prehistoric sites (hitherto grossly neglected) have a major role to play in understanding how and when the change from hunting and gathering occurred in West Africa – especially as 'direct' evidence is often lacking.

Domestication in this context means the process of withdrawing animals from natural selection processes; directing their reproduction; making them serve man (by their work and/or their products); and modifying their

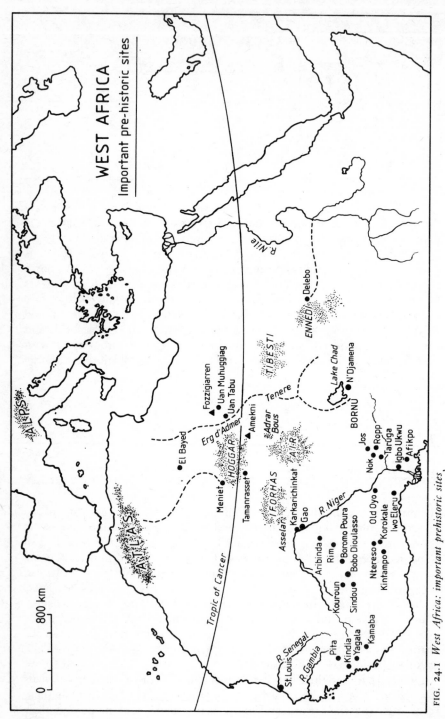

FIG. 24.1 *West Africa: important prehistoric sites.*

594

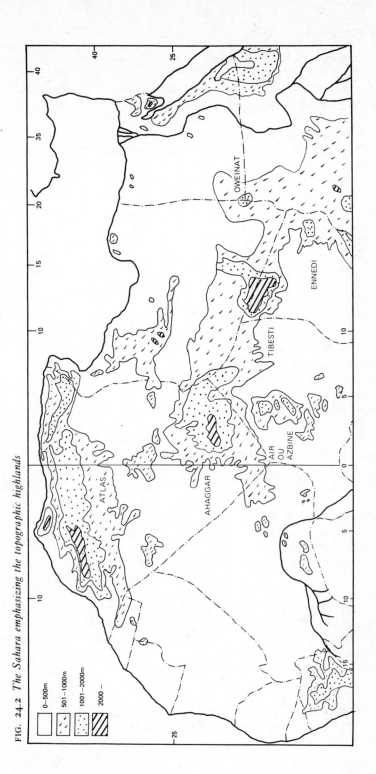

FIG. 24.2 *The Sahara emphasizing the topographic highlands*

characteristics by selective breeding, while losing some old character traits. Plant cultivation here refers to the deliberate planting of tubers or seeds and the protection of fruit trees, vines, etc., with a view to obtaining for human use an appreciable quantity of these tubers, seeds and fruits.

Terms such as *'vegeculture'* and *arboriculture*, common in the literature, are avoided here because they carry connotations of evolutionary sealing of cultural superiority. So also is the definition (e.g. Spencer, 1968)[1] of agriculture in the technological sense as 'systems of food production that involve *advanced* tools, draught animals or mechanical power, *developed* cropping systems and *mature* technologies of production'. Certain words are italicized in order to emphasize the subjective nature of such a definition.

Ecological studies indicate, first, that animal domestication if feasible in the semi-arid tropical and subtropical savannah areas (Bonsma, 1970)[2] because the soil PH is fairly high ($\pm 7 \cdot 0$), and consequently the macro-elements (nitrogen and phosphorus) are relatively readily assimilable and pastures have a relatively high protein content. Secondly, and in contrast, such studies indicate that domesticated animals are not an important feature of food production in the humid tropical regions partly because the soil PH and the assimilability of the macro-elements nitrogen, phosphorus and calcium are generally low; hence the pasturage is high in cellulose and crude fibre, and has a high heat increment value. Heat production and dissipation by the animals are thus real problems for livestock in the humid tropics. To maintain thermal equilibrium in such regions cattle are usually small, giving them a large surface area per unit weight and facilitating heat dissipation. Where some domesticated animals were in fact kept, the problem of high temperatures appears to have been overcome by the selection of small livestock which could adapt to tropical conditions.

Thirdly, ecological studies show that the annual plants cultivated in most of West Africa, in complete contrast to those of the Middle East, were and still are adapted to growth in a season of high temperature and high humidity. Except in the cool and relatively dry highlands, Middle Eastern cereals fail completely because of their inability to withstand pathogens that flourish at high temperatures. Botanical investigations (Portères, 1950, 1951, 1962; Doggett, 1965; Havinden, 1970)[3] indicate that cereal crops such as millet (*Pennisetum typhoideum*), fonio (*Digitaria exilis*) and rice (*Oryza glaberrima*), vegetable crops like cow pea (*Vigna Sinensis*) and earth pea (*Vcandzeia subterranea*), tubers such as Guinea yams (*Dioscorea cayenensis* and *D. Rotundata*) and the oil palm (*Elaies guinensis*) and the ground nut (*Kerstingiella geocarpa*) are indigenous and probably have a long history of cultivation in various parts of West Africa.[4]

1. J. E. Spencer, pp. 501–2.
2. J. C. Bonsma, pp. 169–72.
3. A. Portères, 1950, pp. 489–507; 1951a, pp. 16–21; 1951b, pp. 38–42; 1962, pp. 195–210; H. Doggett, pp. 50–69; M. A. Havinden, pp. 532–55.
4. See Volume I, Chapter 25.

Palaeontological, botanical, ecological, ethnographic and archaeological data, all combined, suggest that at the general level the food-producing complexes first adopted were farming (crop cultivation), pastoralism and mixed farming (i.e. a combination of animal rearing and plant cultivation). At the specific level, these food-producing complexes varied according to the kinds of crops cultivated, the animals kept and the ways in which these were cropped or reared and the settlement and social systems adopted.

Indeed, archaeological and ethnographic data suggest the existence in West Africa of (i) early cattle herding in the northern and eastern Sahara; (ii) early seed-crop complexes, possibly practising permanent field systems, on the slopes and scarps of the central Saharan highlands; (iii) seed-cropping complexes in parts of the Sahel and northern savannah regions, with influences impinging on these from both north and south (in this connection, it appears that the inland delta of the Niger, the edge of the Futa Jallon hills in the upper basin of the Senegal, Niger and Gambia rivers, and the Sudanic environments in general, may have been nuclear areas for crops like rice (*Oryza glaberrima*), millets (*Digitaria*), guinea corn and bulrush millets); (iv) mixed farming and cattle herding in the central and eastern Sahel regions and parts of the northern savannah regions, where the desiccation of the Sahara may have played an important role; and (v) root and tree crop complexes in the forest fringe regions to the far south (Alexander and Coursey, 1969).[5]

These early 'Neolithic' complexes were characterized by distinctly different artefact complexes, as well as (largely inferred) different settlement and social patterns and land use methods. In some areas, however (e.g. Tiemassas, Senegal and Paratoumbian, Mauretania), two or more traditions met and overlapped.

Generally, the hunting and pastoralist complexes in the north have stone industries based on blades, and contain geometrical microliths, projectile points, very few or no heavy tools, engravings on stone or ostrich-egg shells, and a limited range of rather plain pottery types. On the other hand, the seed-cropping complexes of central parts of the Sahara and the northern grasslands have rich polished and ground stone tools, a variety of flaked tools, a varied range of morphologically distinctive pottery, but few or no microliths or projectile points. The vegetable (root) crop complexes to the south also contain polished and ground tools, but are characterized principally by flake-based industries containing heavy flaked biface tools and choppers. Such technological specificity is apparent also at the present day in the use of the hoe or the digging-stick for cultivation, as well as in the ways farms are tilled (deep or shallow tillage) and prepared, taking full account of the type of crop, the nature of the soil and the water supply available.

5. J. Alexander and D. G. Coursey, pp. 123–9.

## Early cattle-herding Neolithic complexes of the north

Remains of domestic shorthorn have been found at Uan Muhuggiag, south-west Libya (Mori, 1965) and Adrar Bous Aïr, (Clark, 1972)[6]; and the dates obtained suggest domestication of cattle from −5590 (±200) in the former area and −3830 to −3790 in the latter. At Uan Muhuggiag sheep remains were also found. The short-horned type of cattle does not, however, appear, to have existed in the Nile Valley before the eleventh dynasty (−2600) although there is evidence for the long-horned type at Kom Ombo in Egypt during the Pleistocene.

The fact that the shorthorn existed in the central Sahara for at least 1200 years before their appearance in the Nile Valley rules out any possibility of their having come from Egypt or the Near East. At the moment it is not clear whether the progenitors of the Saharan shorthorn came from the Sahara or the Maghrib or both. But measurements of the metapodials of these animals from both regions (A. B. Smith, 1973)[7] indicate a reduction in their size through time, the Pleistocene animals having much larger metapodials.

Cultural evidence, however, suggests that in Libya there may have been an early instance of transition from hunting and gathering to pastoralism, which extended as far to the south-east as Adrar Bous (Tenereen, −4000 to −2500) and as far to the south-west as Tichitt (Khimiya phase, post-1500). In these areas the pastoralists appear to have been direct descendants of earlier inhabitants, and the new way of life (especially at Tichitt) probably replaced or was combined with a seed-cropping Neolithic. If so, it means either that the concept of cattle domestication was transferred to these areas or that they were on the outskirts of a large nuclear zone of cattle domestication. Radio-carbon dates from sites reporting domesticated *Bos* indicate possible expansion of cattle from the Saharan heartlands into the southern Sahara and Sahel zones of West Africa, and some form of relationship with the desiccation of the desert region.

## Early seed-cropping Neolithic complexes

### The central Saharan highlands

Such evidence as exists suggests that seed-cropping, but *not any other form of cultivation*, probably occurred much earlier here than anywhere to the south. The earliest evidence for this early form of Neolithic comes mainly from rock-shelter sites at Amekni and Meniet in the Hoggar. At Amekni in contexts dated to −6100 and −4850, Camps[8] recovered two pollen

6. F. Mori, 1965; J. D. Clark, 1972.
7. A. B. Smith.
8. G. Camps, 1969a, pp. 186–8.

grains which are considered, because of their size and shape, to represent a domesticated variety of *Pennisetum*. From Meniet, Pons and Quezel[9] identified two pollen grains belonging to a level dated to about −3600 which may be a cultivated cereal. Hugot[10] suggests that these are wheat.

Other less conclusive evidence for seed-crop cultivation in this area comes from the rock shelter at Sefar in the Tassili, radio-carbon dated to about −3100. Paintings in this shelter[11] appear to depict cultivation, while linguistic evidence suggests a considerable antiquity for sorghum cultivation in the central Sahara.[12] Apart from occupying rock shelters, the prehistoric people of this region also occupied relatively large permanent villages or settlements on hillsides and the edges of escarpments overlooking lakes or wadis,[13] and used an industry particularly rich in polished and flaked axes, grinders and querns, dimple stones, rubbers, pottery and nondescript flake tools.

It has often been suggested, with little or no justification,[14] that this crop complex represents stimulus – diffusion from the Near East via Egypt. First, the cultural complex associated with the possible seed-crops found in central Saharan sites is very different from those of Egypt and the Near East. Secondly, the dates for the archaeologically earliest cultivated crops in Egypt appear to be later at least than those of Amekni. Thirdly, the cultural similarities (e.g. numerous millstones) between the central Saharan complex and the pre-ceramic complex discovered by Hobler and Hester (1969)[15] in the vicinity of the Dungal and Dineigi oases in south-western Libya are nowhere near enough to suggest any close relationship. Unlike the Hoggar complex, the Libyan one is a blade industry and not a flake industry and contains several sickle-blades, a variety of projectiles, drill-like piercing tools and biface knives. This complex, which dates from at least −6000 and may go back to as early as −8300, bears more similarity to the Mesolithic industries of north-east Africa and the Nubian region of the Nile. Thus although the Libyan complex occurs at the north-eastern end of the large semi-circular plateau running through the central Sahara, it cannot possibly be the direct precursor of the Hoggar 'Neolithic' which occurs at the south-western end of the same plateau. Archaeologists working in the area might do better to look for the precursor first in the latter area (i.e. the Hoggar).

9. A. Pons and P. Quezel, pp. 27–35.
10. H. J. Hugot, 1968. p. 485.
11. H. Lhote, 1959, p. 118.
12. G. Camps, 1960b, p. 79.
13. J. P. Maître, 1966, pp. 95–104.
14. P. J. Munson, 1972.
15. P. 1. Hobler and J. J. Hester, pp. 120–30.

## The southern Sahara, the Sahel and parts of the savannah regions of West Africa

The Neolithic in these parts of West Africa has often been regarded as the result of northern influences; and there may well be some justification for this view since some of the late stone age industries in this area show affinities with the post-Palaeolithic complexes of the Hoggar or of the eastern Sahara and the Maghrib. But the main archaeological traditions characteristic of the early Neolithic (late stone age) in this area show distinctive traits, especially in pottery, tool complexes and settlement size and pattern. Most settlements at that time were located on escarpments or flats near former lakes or wadis. Three main traditions may be discerned, probably reflecting differences in economic and social patterns:

> (i) At the northern fringe of this region are industries, such as those of the Tenereen and Bel-air (Senegal), which have a blade base, a variety of geometrical microliths and/or projectiles, few or no polished or ground stone items, and relatively small settlement areas.
>
> (ii) In the central areas, such as Borkou, Ennedi, Tilemsi, Ntereso and Daima, industries are found which lack geometrical microliths but have a variety of projectiles, fish-hooks and harpoons, some polished and ground stone items and relatively large settlement areas.

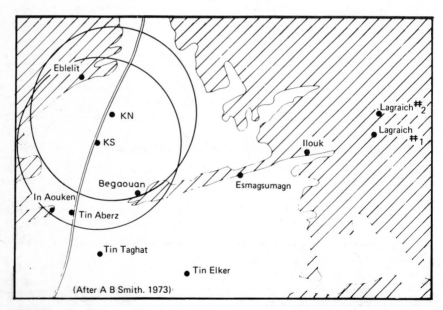

FIG. 24.3 *The Tilemsi valley complex*

(iii) The third group of industries to the south, represented principally by Nok and Kintamp, is virtually devoid of blades, geometrical microliths and projectiles, but is rich in polished and ground stone tools. They are characterized by relatively larger and apparently more permanent settlements.

## THE TILEMSI VALLEY COMPLEXES

Evidence from the Karkarichinkat sites[16] shows that during at least the later part of the most recent wet phase of the Sahara (−2000 to −1300), this area was inhabited by pastoral peoples with a way of life not very dissimilar from that of some present-day semi-nomadic pastoralists such as the Nuer of the Sudan[17] and the Fulani of West Africa.[18] The Karkarichinkat South sites resemble fishing and herding camps, as witness the abundance of bivalve shells, fishbones and *Bos* remains with few or no stone artefacts except fish-hooks. In contrast the abundance of pottery, clay figurines of animals and stone artefacts (especially a great variety of

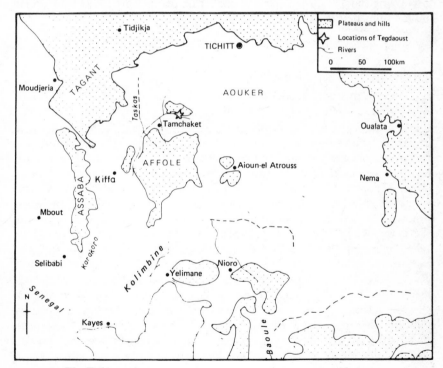

FIG. 24.4 *The Tichitt region*

16. A. B. Smith, pp. 33–55.
17. E. E. Evans-Pritchard, 1940.
18. M. Dupire, 1962.

projectiles) at Karkarichinkat North all suggests a shift away from standing water and a greater involvement in herding, hunting and possibly some plant cultivation.

The cultural groups who lived in northern Tilemsi, around Asselar, had an industry similar to the Tenereen of the Sahara region (Tixier, 1962) and at least as old (skeletal material has been dated to −4440). Both groups contain grindstones, polished axes and scrapers; geometrical microliths are rarer in the Lower Tilemsi, although their projectile elements and pottery appear different. At Asselar and Karkarichinkat it would seem that besides herding cattle the people also hunted wild animals (gazelle, warthog, giraffe, etc.), fished, and gathered both mollusca and plants (*Grewai sp.*, *Celtis integrifolia*, *Vitex sp.* and *Acacia nilotica*). The present ecology of these plants suggests a rainfall around 200 mm, which is double the present precipitation in the Lower Tilemsi Valley. Studies by Camps[19] in the Admer Erg south of Tassili-n-Ajjer suggest that pastoralists with industries similar to the Tenereen existed as far north as this as well as occupying the Tassili-n-Ajjer and bordering plains from at least the fourth millennium before our era.

## THE DHAR TICHITT REGION

Research in this part of southern Mauretania has revealed an eight-phase, well-dated, late stone age sequence[20] containing subsistence data which sheds some light on the problem of early food production in this area in particular and in the region of the Senegal/Niger headwaters generally.

A plausible explanation for the development trend reported at Tichitt, because it fits the archaeological data much better, would be as follows – special rearing and propagation of *Cenchrus biflorus* in the Khimiya phase (−1500), then intensification and expansion of this practice of incipient production and propagation of plants to include several other plants during the dry Naghez phase (−1100). Munson and many other archaeologists seem to forget that a cultivated form of plant represents the *end*, not the beginning of the process of ennobling. Cultigens differ in length of time according to the plant and the special local cultural and ecological factors involved. The fact that only *Pennisetum* and *Brachiaria deflexa* showed ultimate indications of man's efforts at domestication merely indicates that man was most successful with these plants; it does not mean that they were the only plants reared. This fact readily accounts for the marked increase of *Pennisetum* and the continued presence of *Brachiaria deflexa* in the subsequent phases.

19. G. Camps, 1969a.

20. P. J. Munson, 1967, p. 91; 1968, pp. 6–13; 1970, pp. 47–8; 1972; R. Mauny, 1950, pp. 35–43.

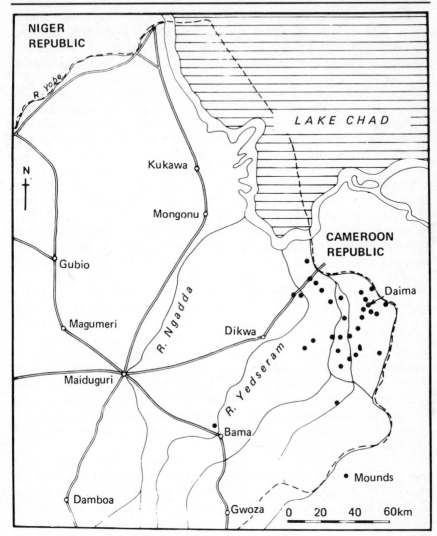

FIG. 24.5 *Settlement mounds of the* Firki

## THE REGION SOUTH OF LAKE CHAD

This region, known as the *Firki*, comprises black clay plains which stretch away from the southern margins of Lake Chad and are thought to have been formed from lagoon deposits on the edge of a formerly larger lake.[21] It is also the area in which Portères thinks *Sorghum arundinaceum* and *Pennisetum* (bulrush or pearl millet) were first domesticated. This zone

21. R. A. Pullan.

is comparatively fertile and well watered. Although the mean annual rainfall is low (655 mm at Maiduguri) and the dry season sufficiently long and intense (up to 43°C) to dry most of the rivers, the area is flooded and impassable during the rains, primarily because of the impermeability of the absolutely level plains. On the other hand, the soil is very retentive of moisture once it has absorbed it; and this retentiveness is now artificially increased by the construction of low banks round the fields. Seasonal inundation rendered this area attractive for settlement by both farmers and herders, while seasonal extremes considerably restricted habitable sites and the constant use of such areas in the past resulted in the accretion of occupation mounds and tells.

Excavation of some of these mounds in northern Nigeria, Cameroon and Chad has so far revealed successive occupations over periods of time known in some cases to approach and exceed 2000 years. Lebeuf,[22] working principally in Chad, is convinced that the mounds are connected with the Sao of oral traditions. Even if this term has much cultural or ethnic value, this writer shares Connah's[23] reluctance to use oral tradition to identify peoples some of whom lived 2500 years ago.

Connah[24] also carried out a systematic study of one of the most impressive of these mounds, that at Daima (14° 30′ E, and 12° 12·5′ N). The Daima evidence suggests that by the early sixth century before our era there were late stone age herdsmen living in this area, keeping cattle and sheep or goats, using polished stone axes the material for which had to be carried many miles into this completely stoneless region, and making tools and weapons of polished bone. Among the outstanding finds at this level were large quantities of animal bones which reflect the strong pastoral element, and many small clay figurines apparently representing domestic animals. These earliest occupants of the site probably built only in grass and wood, and lacked metals of any kind.

Findings from sites like Rop[25] and Dutsen Kongba[26] strongly suggest that a fully stone-using Neolithic level also immediately preceded the famous Nok iron age culture (i.e. before −2500) of the savannah mosaic of the Jos Plateau. If so, such a level probably also contained a microlithic industry apart from the polished and ground stone equipment also found in the late iron age levels. The Nok people may well have traded such tools to peoples occupying the stoneless regions to the north, and perhaps also the pottery, which often decorated at Daima is best represented by a fine ware with burnished red surfaces with toothed comb or roulette.

22. J.-P. Lebeuf, 1962.
23. G. Connah, 1969b, p. 55.
24. G. Connah, 1967a, pp. 146–7.
25. E. Eyo, 1964–5, p. 5–13; 1972, pp. 13–16.
26. R. York *et al.*

THE KINTAMPO–NTERESO COMPLEXES, CENTRAL GHANA
Archaeological evidence indicating the existence of a negroid group practising food production at least as early as − 1300 to − 1400 has so far been found in four main areas of Ghana: east of the Banda hills, the high ground around Kintampo, riverine sites scattered among the open woodlands of the inner Volta basin, and the Accra plains to the far south.

These groups of sites can now be distinguished from one another more by environmental setting than by evidence of material culture. Burnt daub is fairly common at the Kintampo site and points to more or less fixed abodes. The widespread distribution of polished axes and 'rasps' (also called 'terracotta cigars' into areas where suitable rocks are absent, points to the practice of some kind of inter-regional trade. Evidence at three of the Kintampo sites also shows that the Kintampo complex was preceded by another with a distinctly different pottery tradition, stone tools and animal remains, reflecting intensive hunting and gathering and/or incipient cultivation.

Ntereso is a highly unusual Kintampo site whose significance is difficult to determine. It lies on a low ridge overlooking a riverain site where aquatic resources (e.g. shells and fish) were of great importance. The presence of harpoons and fish-hooks in this industry therefore probably reflects a special adaptation to a riverain situation. There were also a wide variety of well-made arrowheads, unique in the area and showing Saharan affinities. Radio-carbon dates (averaging − 1300) place this site at roughly the same period as Kintampo (i.e. after − 1450). Animal bones recovered are mostly of wild species, especially antelopes; but dwarf goats have also been identified.[27] Davies[28] also claimed that ears of *Pennisetum* were used as roulettes for decorating some of the pottery, but this identification remains inconclusive since it has been pointed out[29] that a tight rockering with a small toothed comb can give a similar effect.

## The forest fringe areas

A distinctly local industrial complex, different in character from the preceding late stone age industries, directly succeeded the latter in the forest fringe areas of West Africa, as well as in the open grassland regions of north central Upper Volta. The same industry overlaps with a more northern Neolithic complex in parts of Senegal, Mali and Mauretania (Vaufrey's Paratoumbien).

The early food-producing peoples of the forest region (the so-called Guinea Neolithic) occupied rock shelters and caves as well as open air

27. P. L. Carter and C. Flight, pp. 277–82.
28. O. Davies, 1964.
29. C. Flight.

sites. Examples of shelters are Yengema,[30] Kamabai and Yagala, all in Sierra Leone;[31] Kakimbon, Blande and Monkey Caves in Guinea; Bosumpra in Ghana; and Iwo Eleru and Ukpa in Nigeria. From Iwo Eleru also comes evidence suggesting that the predecessors as well as the Neolithic peoples were negroid. The best-known open sites include the valley and hill slope sites of Rim in north central Upper Volta, and the Senegal coastal sites of Rarenno, Tiemassas and Cap Manuel.

In many of these 'Guinea Neolithic' areas the people occupied or exploited rocky terrains containing outcrops of quartz, dolerite and cherty metavolcanic rocks. Furthermore, at sites such as Rim, the hill slopes were apparently used for terrace farming. Heavy bifacially flaked pick-like tools, semi-circular bifaces (Davies' hoes) and other crude biface tools, a large number and wide variety of polished axes, grindstones, some pestles, small quartz elements – especially *outils esquilles*, and roulette decorated pottery are the commonest features of this complex. The pick-like and semi-circular bifaces seem to be derived from Sangoan core axes and picks, and it has been suggested[32] that they were probably used for gathering and propagating tubers and digging hunting traps. The pestle and mortar (which probably had its wooden counterpart) was probably for pounding fibrous tropical tubers in much the same way as is done today.[33]

Where this complex meets a more northern type of tradition, such as in the Paratoumbien of Mali and Mauretania and in Senegal (between Pointe Sarenne and Tiemassas), the above-mentioned types of artefacts are usually found in association with foliate points, notched blades and blades with retouched edges. At sites such as Tiemassas, the local complex (southern Neolithic), dated by natural stratigraphic means to between −6000 and −2000,[34] clearly precedes the intrusive northern (Belairien) Neolithic, and directly follows from local late stone age traditions.

Significantly, this archaeological evidence from the Mali–Mauretania–Senegal nexus seems to lend support to Portères' thesis that the red-skinned African rices (*Oryza glaberrima* and *Oryza stapfili*) could have been first domesticated by an indigenous wet cultivation method at least 3500 years old in the extensive flood plains of the upper Niger between Segu and Timbuktu in Mali, an area where the Niger divides into several streams and lakes (the inland Niger delta); and from there such cultivation may have spread down the Gambia and Casamance rivers to the coastal peoples of Senegambia. It is worth noting also that the botanical evidence clearly rules out the idea of rice cultivation having resulted from the introduction of knowledge of cereal cultivation. Portères[35] has pointed out that whereas

30. C. S. Coon.
31. J. H. Atherton, pp. 39–74.
32. O. Davies, 1968, pp. 479–82.
33. T. Shaw, 1972.
34. C. Deschamps, D. Demoulin and A. Abdallah, pp. 130–2.
35. A. Portères, 1962, pp. 195–210.

the ancestral form of wheat (emmer) gave edible seeds so that cultivation could have developed from grain collection, this was not possible for African rice, since its ancestral forms did not yield a collectible crop.

Further east, especially at the Sierra Leone sites, Iwo Eleru and Bosumpra, both dating evidence and the nature of the archaeological sequence in the forest fringe areas suggest that major changes in technology (i.e. pottery, polished ground stone tools, etc.) were probably associated with an indigenous incipient cultivation of local plants such as yams and coco-yams, as well as the oil palm. Such changes may have spread northwards from here.

All in all, then, the data suggest that the central Saharan and adjoining Sahel highland areas were the centre for the earliest and an independent cultivation of some grain crops, especially *Pennisetum* and sorghum, whilst the forest fringe areas of Nigeria saw the earliest indigenous cultivation of certain root (yams, coco-yams) and tree (oil palm) crops. On the other hand the forest fringe area to the extreme west was the nuclear area for rice cultivation. Dealing specifically with sorghum, Portères[36] noted that of the three regions which possessed basic wild stocks of sorghum (West Africa, Ethiopia and East Africa), West Africa was of special significance because unlike East Africa (and Asia) its current types are unique instead of being crosses between the three primary forms. But more recently Stemler and his colleagues[37] have suggested that *Caudatum* may be a relatively new strain of sorghum, first developed some time after about + 350 by Chari–Nile-speaking peoples of the Sudan Republic.

While radio-carbon data indicate that the 'Neolithic' of the central Saharan area (*c.* −7000) was the earliest of all the primary farming Neolithics, it also shows that the transition to food production in the forest fringe areas was much earlier than the same event in the Sudanic and Sahel zones to the north. At Iwo Eleru this change dates to just after − 4000 (− 3620) and continued until − 1500. At Ukpa rock shelter near Afikpo (5° 54′ N, 7° 56′ E; Shaw, 1969b)[38] the Neolithic pottery and hoe-containing level dates to −2935 (± 140) continuing to −95.

The Guinea Neolithic occurs slightly later in Sierra Leone to the east and in Upper Volta to the north. At Yengema cave, thermoluminescent dating of pottery representing 'more or less the beginning and the end of the ceramic Neolithic' indicates a period from −2500 to −1500. At Kamabai the Neolithic levels span a period from −2500 to +340 (± 100). In the north central region of Upper Volta (Rim), the same type of industry has been dated to between − 1650 and + 1000.

But the distinctive character of the Guinea Neolithic of the forest fringe areas, and its dating in relation to the early food-producing cultural

36. A. Portères, 1962.
37. A. B. L. Stemler, J. R. Harlan and J. M. J. Dewet, pp. 161–83.
38. T. Shaw, 1969b.

complexes in the savannah and Sahel zones, suggest not only that the change to food production occurred earlier in the forest areas but that it was independent of northern influences. Such evidence thus supports the idea that the cultivation of indigenous crops such as rice (to the west) and yams and oil palm (to the east) in the forest region were old and an independent achievement of the local peoples. It is worth noting also in this respect that the wear on the teeth of the Iwo Eleru skeleton[39] is explained as the result of tearing at sand-covered tubers such as yams. Also significant is the fact that the Guinea Neolithic sites are most prominent in forest fringe zones, in gallery forests along streams, and in clearings in the forest, all of which are also the yam's natural habitat.

The fact that the Guinea Neolithics extend as far north as Upper Volta as well as being there later (while they overlap with northern elements in parts of Mali, Mauretania and Senegal), indicates that southern influences did travel north. Like many present-day tropical forest cultivators, Neolithic root and tree crop cultivators may have practised land shifting, at least initially, and consequently lived in relatively small rather than in large groups and settlements.

Thus to say that the West African 'early Neolithic' complexes had distinctly local features, many of which reflect independently evolved economic and social adaptation measures for uniquely local ecologies, is not to say that each was an isolated enclave. The scanty skeletal evidence available suggests that the populations of most of these areas were negroid.

In the Sahara, Neolithic man seems to have been a mixture of the Mediterranean and Negro races who settled in the Tassili area in Neolithic times. In moving southward, they probably gave rise to several of the dark-skinned groups who inhabit what is now savannah.

That the early Neolithic negroid peoples of West Africa were not living in isolated cultural enclaves is also illustrated by similarities in pottery features (e.g. rockering technique and comb-stamped decoration). If the dating is correct, then it is likely that these pottery features probably spread from the central Sahara (together with knowledge of grain crop cultivation) to parts of the Sahel and savannah. On the other hand, rouletting was a more specifically southern feature; while the dotted wavy-line and wavy-line decorations typical of the Nilotic regions were completely absent in the south, but were just present in some eastern and central Saharan complexes (e.g. Hoggar, Bornu–Chad and South Ennedi).

It is also important to stress that the transition to food production need not always have involved *visibly* new tools. Ethnographic examples strongly suggest to this author that such a transition may have been mainly associated with changes in labour habits and land-use methods, without necessarily involving a change of tools. Examples of such changes include terrace building and elaborate ridging; the maintenance of domestic animals for

39. T. Shaw, 1971.

manure; hoeing and weeding, transplanting, multi-cropping, water control and soil conservation. Such changes may have been resorted to at various times and places when real land scarcity was for one reason or another experienced. Such modification of agricultural systems had some effect on social organization and settlement patterns, but we cannot generalize about this since this factor acted in concert with others which probably varied in type and character from one area to another.

It now appears that there were at least four primary areas of Neolithic development, two of which were in the far north of West Africa. Particularly in the open plains of the northern region, the pastoral form of transhumance was established very early. In lacustrine areas and the valleys and surrounding hill slopes, seed-cropping and in some cases mixed farming were prominent. On the other hand, the lowlands and forest fringe areas of the south were primary hearths for root and tree crop cultivation.

Two main nuclear areas have been identified in West Africa, one to the north in the Sahel/Sudanic transitional zone, the other to the south on the fringes of the forest area. Both were thus located in regions with contrasting seasons, one season being unfavourable to growth (heat, drought or cold). Plants in such habitats store up reserves to enable them to resume vigorous new life when the 'favourable' weather returns. These reserves were in the form of roots and tubers in the south and seeds in the northern Sudanic zone.

In the forest and savannah areas with little or no seasonal climatic variation on the other hand, plants grew at a slow and regular pace. They did not need to struggle for survival, nor to accumulate reserves – a feature which by example probably encouraged domestication ventures in both nuclear areas. The central savannah zone, sandwiched between the two nuclear areas, appears to have been a meeting-point for influences from both of them.

It is significant that the growing season for crops was longer in the lowland forest regions, whilst the soils of the lacustrine and riverain regions of the north were more fertile and just as easily worked. For these reasons, man's way of life in these areas differed to some extent, as did also the effect of his activities. In the latter regions it was enough to clear small areas of bush to practise hoe agriculture. In the forest regions, however, increased agricultural activity often meant more intensive (extensive) forest clearance though this did not necessarily go with an increase in the size of permanence of settlements. Whereas under the former system a limited area of land could be farmed continuously, under the latter a shifting basis of cultivation would often be employed. These general differences in exploitative systems often had far-reaching implications for both the size and the character of West African social groups, and also for the nature of their settlements, throughout the prehistoric and historic periods. But both the dynamics of early food production and also the implications varied to some extent according to the habitat.

In all three main cultural regions, however, the transition from food gathering to food growing modified man's attitude towards his natural environment and his human group in several ways. From being a gatherer, he became a producer and 'storer', and subsequently (through long-distance trade) exchanged some of the resources which his neighbours lacked for commodities which his own group needed. The economic change also encouraged the development of handicraft activities and new technologies (ceramics, metal working, etc.) as well as active and complex trading networks, in addition to more profound social changes. But these social changes varied in kind and degree according to the type of agricultural base that was established.

## The early iron age

Iron age developments do not seem to have differed markedly from Neolithic trends, except that the earliest instances of transition to metal/iron age in West Africa occurred at both ends of the Sahel/savannah zone rather than in the forest regions to the south. In this respect, as with early food production, all the cultural and chronological evidence strongly suggests that there was much that was indigenous in this venture into metal working.

As set out in detail elsewhere,[40] the evidence about the early iron age in West Africa may be typologically and to some extent chronologically and stratigraphically divided into assemblages containing: (i) pottery, iron and ground stone tools; (ii) pottery, iron and/or other metals, sometimes in conjunction with special (pot) burial practices; and (iii) pottery alone.

Sites where traces of iron working are mixed with a more or less flourishing stone industry are usually the oldest types of iron age assemblage, and probably reflect the transition from stone to iron age. Sites belonging to such transitional industries have been identified in several parts of West Africa, as well as elsewhere (e.g. in the Great Lakes region of East Africa). Such industries generally contain iron slag, knife blades, fragments of arrow and spearheads, hooks and bracelets, hammerstones, a variety of axe/adze forms, stone discs (rings), querns and rubber stones. There are also distinct regional trends. For instance, terracotta figurines seem to be particularly characteristic of northern Nigeria, but they also occur in some sites in Ghana. Iron-smelting tuyeres and pieces of presumed furnace wall are known from northern Nigeria. On the other hand, crudely flaked biface tools are most characteristic of the Sierra Leone sites of Kamabai and Yagala. At Rim in Upper Volta such heavy biface tools together with axe/adzes occur in association with pot burials and indicate links with the preceding Guinea Neolithic.

Regional variation is also evident in pottery from the early iron age. For example, Bailloud's[41] sequence from Ennedi of two related styles,

40. B. W. Andah (formerly B. Wai-Ogosu).
41. G. Bailloud, 1969, pp. 31–45.

Telimorou and Chigeou which span the late Neolithic/early iron age transition, appear to be related to Coppens'[42] *céramique cannelée* from Chad and Courtain's[43] Taimanga style from Borkou. Telimorou is associated with the earliest open village sites, and has been tentatively dated to the first millennium before our era. Both Bailloud and Courtin point out the resemblance of these pottery styles to that of the C-group in Nubia, though the dating of the latter seems likely to be considerably earlier (starting about −2000) in Nubia. Most of the characteristics of the decorations of these styles − bands of oblique comb stamping, incised cross-hatching, interlocking, incised hatched triangles, false relief chevron, parallel grooving, etc. − are also typical of early iron age complexes at Early Taruga, Lebeuf's Lake Chad sites, Sindou and Ntereso levels 2 and 3, as well as the Sierra Leone cave sites. Certain early Taruga style features also seem to foreshadow the 'Ife Complex' in respect of both pottery and figurine traditions.

In contrast to the above, later Taruga pottery styles are more similar to those of Neolithic/iron age levels at Rim. At both, a wide variety of decorations obtained by twisted and carved roulettes are prominent and there are isolated examples of the maize cob roulette. Perhaps the best known of early iron age societies in West Africa so far is that of Nok, which also seems to have been one of the earliest and most influential. The Nok people were certainly working iron by −500, and probably some time before. The culture is best known for its very impressive artistic tradition, particularly the terracotta figurines. Notwithstanding their knowledge of iron working, the Nok people still continued to use stone tools where these were considered more efficient. Examples of stone tools still in use included grinders and dimple stones as well as polished and flaked axes. Even within the same period, and when circumscribed by the same artistic tradition, some Nok sites contained unique features suggesting regional variation. For instance, polished axes were entirely absent from Taruga and there are differences in domestic pottery between Samun Dukiya, Taruga and Katsina Ala.[44]

Not only was Nok culture firmly established well over 2500 years ago, but its influence appears to have been far reaching. For instance, some of the stylistic features of Nok culture are paralleled in the clay figurines at Daima, where iron working started about the fifth/sixth century of our era.

Connah suggests that around the eighth century the original people at Daima were replaced by others who were fully iron-using and predominantly cereal-cultivating people with rather wider contacts than their predecessors. But the tradition of burial by crouched inhumation was continued, as was the making of clay figurines. At no stage did they

42. Y. S. Coppens, 1969, pp. 129–46.
43. J. Courtain, 1966, pp. 147–59; 1969.
44. A. Fagg, pp. 75–9.

bury their dead inside the enormous pottery jars usually referred to as So pots, although this type of pottery is present in the upper part of the mound.

Many important ancient village mound sites, some up to half a kilometre long, were found on artificial or natural hillocks on the banks of rivers in the lower Chari valley in the Chad Republic, within a radius of 100 kilometres from Fort Lamy. These yielded some of the same finds as at Nok and Daima, including fine terracotta figurines, both human and animal, stone ornaments, copper and bronze weapons, and many thousands of potsherds. Huge funerary pots were also used here and the villages were surrounded by defensive walls. Radio-carbon dates ranging from −425 to +1700 have been obtained by Lebeuf (1969) for these Sao sites and would seem to date the entire span of Sao I, II and III. Shaw,[45] however, thinks that the divisions are not satisfactorily defined in terms of stratigraphy and cultural material. Should the −425 determination date an iron-containing level, its importance would be obvious.

## Southern Nigeria

Willett[46] observes that 'so many features of the Nok culture, particularly of its art, are found in later cultures elsewhere in West Africa, that it is difficult not to believe that the Nok culture as we know it represents the ancestral stock from which much of the sulptural traditions of West Africa derives'. True or not, there are certainly many similarities between Nok and Ife art which are unlikely to be coincidental.[47] As at Nok, a naturalistic sculpture tradition dates back to at least +960 (±130), and an elaborate bead-work was present at Ife and Benin and to a lesser extent at other ancient Yoruba towns.

Domestic pottery at Ife represents a further elaboration of Nok types, especially in the sense that decoration was more varied, including incision (straight lines, zigzags, stabs and curvilinear designs), burnishing, painting and rouletting (with both carved wood and twisted string). Strips of clay were also used or applied for decoration, while potsherds were similarly used for house pavements.

The Igbo Ukwu excavations[48] clearly indicate that iron working in southeastern Nigeria is at least as early as the ninth century of our era but there is nothing to suggest that it could not have been earlier. Because iron smithing was a highly skilled occupation, it remained exclusive to certain communities and lineages. The most famous of the Igbo smiths are those from Awka, east of Onitsha, who apparently first obtained iron (ore?) from the Igbo

45. T. Shaw 1969a, pp. 226–9.
46. F. Willett, p. 117.
47. ibid., 120.
48. T. Shaw, 1970a.

smelters of Udi, east of Awka, and only much later received supplies of European iron. Other foci of metal working among the Ibo were the Abiriba iron smelters, among the Cross river (eastern) Igbo; the iron and brass smiths located near the Okigwe–Arochuku ridge, and the Nkwerre smiths in the southern part of this region.

Because insufficient archaeological work has been done in this area, it is difficult to elaborate on the development of iron working. The proximity of the Awka to the Igbo Ukwu sites, and the general similarity of many of the items suggest possible relationships; but the time difference between the two complexes is vast, and the Awka smiths have not, at least in more recent times, exhibited certain of the artistic and technical traits, including brass casting, typical of the Igbo Ukwu work.

One excavation in the Awka area[49] yielded fifteen iron gongs and an iron sword similar to those still made by the Awka smiths, as well as a large number of cast bronze bells and other objects dated to $+1495$ ($\pm 95$) which cannot be so readily attributed to Awka smiths.

It is also not clear what the time/cultural relationship is between Ife and Igbo Ukwu, although Willett thinks it possible that Ife may be much earlier than is at present supposed and may even be much nearer Nok than present evidence (*c*. thirteenth to fourteenth centuries of our era) suggests. If the Ife beads are indeed the same as the 'akori' beads of the Guinea coast, as both Frobenius and ethnographic evidence from southern Nigeria suggest, then it is conceivable that the Igbo Ukwu glass beads were manufactured at Ife. If so, it would mean that Ife culture dates at least as far back as the Igbo Ukwu finds (ninth century of our era). In this connection it may also be significant that a discontinuity of tradition at Ife in the stone sculpture, glass industry and clay figurines is largely paralleled at Daima,[50] and that the cultural discontinuity at Daima dates from between the sixth and ninth centuries of our era. As some burial goods at Daima could also indicate trade contacts between Ife and Daima, it is quite likely that the cultural parallel may have a time significance. Thus there is a real possibility that Ife dates back to at least the sixth century of our era.

## The iron age in the extreme west

The iron age in the extreme western section is even less well known than that of Nok and neighbouring areas. For instance, such information as exists for Mauretania relates not to an iron age but to a 'copper age'. In the middle Niger region, and particularly in Senegambia, only a partial chronological sequence has so far been obtained.[51]

49. D. Hartle, 1966, p. 26; idem, 1968, p. 73.
50. G. Connah, 1967a, pp. 146–7.
51. O. Linares de Sapir, pp. 23–54.

Excavations by N. Lambert at Akjoujt[52] indicate that copper smelting in the western Sahara dates as far back as −570 to −400; this may also have been the probable date of the trans-Saharan trade in copper. Estimates at one of the sites suggest that 40 tons of copper were extracted from it, and it is possible that some of this output was exported from the western Sahara to the Sudan. Although Akjoujt declined in importance in early historic times, perhaps because of the depletion of timber supplies for smelting (as happened at Meroe), the trans-Saharan trade apparently continued to maintain supplies of copper and copper goods across the central Sudan.

The vast number of copper objects from sites and museum collections, and also those mentioned in written sources, suggest that the use of this metal, scarce though it was, was widespread in West Africa for a very long time – although it was not as important as wood, iron or clay. Copper and its alloys, when imported, came in a number of forms which changed little over the centuries, such as bars, manillas, rings, wires, bells and basins. These were probably used without alteration as the raw material for local industry, for casting by means of the lost-wax process, and for hammering, drawing, twisting, etc.

African peoples made a distinction between red copper, that is, copper in its pure form, bronze and yellow copper or brass. Unfortunately such precision is lacking in much of the literature. Spectrographic analysis needs to be carried out to establish the actual metal content of an object and the preferences of the earliest users of copper and its alloy (bronze).

## The middle Niger region

Artificial earth mounds, either settlement sites or graves (tumuli) are known from three main areas in this region. They are:

(i) the Niger–Bani confluence in the Bani valley;
(ii) north and north-east of Masina and Segu; and
(iii) far to the east of the bend, in Upper Volta.

A large thick-walled ware decorated chiefly with a twisted-string roulette was consistently present in all three areas, and often served as a burial pot. In places burial pots occur in twos and threes, with accompanying domestic equipment. In Upper Volta (Rim), the main associated tools were iron, polished and ground stone tools and domestic pottery. Bronze and copper objects were also present in the Niger bend area. Also present in the Masina and Segu areas, but not at Bani or Rim (Upper Volta) far to the east, is a distinctive slipware having polymorphic forms; fine thin-walled dishes and bowls, some of which were carrinated, pedestalled or flat based; footed cups; and jugs and conical jars.[53]

52. E. W. Herbert, pp. 170–94.
53. G. Szumowski, pp. 225–57.

In Segu and Timbuktu some of these 'iron age' people were mainly farmers cultivating millet and rice, while others were mainly fishermen using nets with terracotta weights instead of bone harpoons. There were impressive pre-Islamic monuments, with artistically dressed stones, and some of the finds cover several acres, indicating major settlements. But very few, if any, of these sites have been investigated, and then only superficially, although many were extensively looted by the French.[54]

The exact size and nature of these settlements and the type of economy of their inhabitants have yet to be determined through extensive excavation. A chronological sequence has also not yet been obtained. Monod's suggestion that these pot burial cultures were part of a wider 'lehim complex', which was concentrated on the Mediterranean coast and spread to the region of the Niger bend, implies that such iron age cultures in West Africa postdate the advent of the Arabs (i.e. +1000 and +1400). But the results of recent research do not support this view.

At Kouga, for example, excavations of a tumulus yielded a date of −950 (±120) at a relatively late level containing a traditional white-on-red painted ware. Surface sherds bore impressions of millet, wheat and perhaps maize. Both at this site and at several others in this part of West Africa the indications are that there was an earlier iron age level mostly characterized by impressed or undecorated sherds, bone and stone tools, and bracelets. A related cultural tradition in Upper Volta yielded even earlier dates in the fifth/sixth century of our era.[55]

## The Senegambia region

Burial tumuli have also been discovered in parts of this region, especially at Rao at the mouth of the river Senegal[56] and in northern Senegal along the river. Again, although most of these are yet to be investigated closely, superficial study indicates that burials were made in wooden chambers covered by mounds at least 4 metres high, and that they contained iron tools, copper bracelets, beads, gold, jewellery and several simply shaped pots, bowls, beakers and jars, unpainted but closely decorated with elaborate designs, largely scorings and jabs but and without comb impressions. Recent excavations date these burials to +750[57] which is later than the period which concerns us in this chapter.

Of greater relevance to our period are the main coastal sites in this region, which consist mainly of shell middens. Near St Louis and in Casamance these middens sometimes have large baobabs growing on them. The St Louis middens studied by Joire,[58] as well as several others, yielded an

54. O. Davies, 1967a, p. 260.
55. B. W. Andah.
56. J. Joire, 1955, pp. 249–333.
57. C. Deschamps and G. Thilmans.
58. J. Joire, 1947, pp. 170–340.

industry with occasional comb-impressed sherds, a ring of twisted copper and iron, a bone axe and a few other bone artefacts. Among other things, the shell midden people harvested oysters and traded them to the inland peoples. The area of coastal dunes and rocks between St Louis and Joal, reported not to be a breeding ground for oysters,[59] was also thickly inhabited from Neolithic to iron age times. At a few sites at Dakar (e.g. Bel-Air), iron age material is distinctly stratified above the Neolithic. Pottery shapes and ornamentation appear to have varied little over many centuries; and consequently unstratified sites cannot be satisfactorily classified.

A study of several shell middens in an area 22 by 6 kilometres in lower Casamance has revealed a cultural sequence extending from −200 to +1600 overlapping with early modern Dyola material culture. Sapir believes that the earliest phase so far known (−1200 to +200), found only in the Loudia and Quolof sites, represents a late rather than an early Neolithic phase. Cultural contacts and/or influences are indicated by the pottery of this period, which shares decorative techniques such as wavy-line incision with Neolithic pottery widely distributed from Cap Vert[60] to southern Algeria[61] and even Central Africa. No stone tools were present, but nodules of bog iron were common, suggesting the possible use of iron. Prehistoric stone axes have, however, been reported from the vicinity of Bignona, supposedly found in shell middens.

Archaeological data of this period reflect sparse settlements in small encampments on low sandy ridges, probably covered by grass and shrubs and surrounded by forest. Shellfish gathering was not practised, and as the only animal bones reported are a few unidentifiable mammal remains, the means of subsistence is not clear.

The complete absence of mollusc remains or fishbones (from four sites spanning about 400 years of occupation), and the presence of sherd rather than shell-tempered pottery, are considered by the original investigator as indications that these 'early inhabitants' of the coast were not in fact adapted to coastal life. Aubreville[62] considers that thick forests once covered the whole area surrounding the Cussouye Plateau until it was ravaged by fire and converted into open paddy fields. If correct, this may mean that these Period I inhabitants were already farmers, perhaps of mountain or dry rice.

During the subsequent occupations (Periods II to IV, i.e. after +300), the rich fauna of the mangrove channels and marigots was exploited, and agriculture may also have been practised, although a systematic search for the remains of rice or other plants has yet to be carried out. The findings

59. O. Davies, 1967a; 1967b, pp. 115–18.
60. R. Mauny, 1951, pp. 165–80.
61. H. J. Hugot, 1963.
62. A. Aubreville, p. 131.

from these levels are also described by the investigator as 'fitting well with historic and modern Dyola practices', while the sequence of pottery types links the ancient and the nearby modern middens.

On our present view, this sequence seems too recent to shed much light on the origins of wet rice agriculture in the area. It may be useful, however to note here that according to Portères,[63] Senegambia was a secondary centre of *Oryza glaberrima* propagation, the primary centre being somewhere near the middle Niger.

The lower Casamance sites appear to represent an advanced stage of wet rice cultivation. At this time the use of iron tools makes it possible to reclaim mangrove swamps and ridge heavy alluvial clay soils for paddy fields. We may in fact do well to look for the first centres of *Oryza glaberrima* cultivation in the looser soils of drained inland valleys where it would have been possible to cultivate dry land or mountain rice by broadcasting or punch-hole planting after clearing by girdling the trees with stone implements.

What actually happened can only be discovered, if at all, by means of more full-scale archaeological investigations of key areas. In any case it is now known that recognizable aspects of Dyola culture were already present from Period II onwards. Groups lived on sandy ridges in or near alluvial valleys, just as they do today, depositing their rubbish in particular spots. There it accumulated in regular middens, which contain pottery fragments and other refuse comparable with Dyola material culture. Throughout the sequence the ceramic tradition of lower Casamance emphasized incised, punctuated and impressed rather than painted decorations and utilitarian rather than ornamental or ceremonial shapes. Whether or not these Casamance people buried pots with their dead remains unknown, since no graves were found in or near the sites.

It has been suggested by scholars such as Arkell that the West African iron working traditions described above were derived from Egypt or Nubia, whilst others, such as Mauny, favour Carthage. But the proponents of such views fail to appreciate, among other things, the fundamental difference in the way iron metallurgy developed in the two areas. In Egypt and Nubia the transition to the iron age was achieved through the working of copper, gold, silver and meteoric iron in the predynastic period, and then of terrestrial iron. In contrast, the centres of ancient iron working in Africa south of the Sahara appear to have progressed straight from stone to iron, with little or no copper or bronze except perhaps in Mauretania. In fact copper and bronze were later worked in much the same way as iron, whereas in Egypt and Nubia copper and iron were worked by very different methods. Available dating evidence gives no more support to either variant of the diffusion theory of iron working than does directly retrieved cultural evidence. It appears, for instance, that the Garamantes

63. A. Portères, 1950.

of Libya and the Meroitic people began using chariots, and probably iron tools, at about the same time ($-500$) as iron working started in the Nok region of northern Nigeria. Indeed, dates from some sites suggest that iron working may even have occurred in the Nok region as early as $-1000$.

The diffusion theory for iron working in West Africa does not give proper consideration to the many problems connected with the process: viz., how, when and in what places (not necessarily in one place) steps were taken to change rock or earthy material into new, tough, durable metals which would be more effective than stone for weapons and also have a wide variety of other uses. In this respect Diop[64] and Trigger[65] have correctly noted that 'the early dates for Iron Age sites in West Africa and in Southern Africa should serve to remind us that the possibility should be kept open that iron working may have developed independently at one or more points south of the Sahara'. The subject of the beginnings has too often been confused with that of the degree of refinement of the working techniques. Worse still, the scholars who suggest that iron working spread from the Near East to Africa have usually mistakenly assumed that the stages of metallurgy observed in the Near East and Europe must necessarily apply to all parts of Africa.

# Prehistoric trade and the earliest states of West Africa

Goods recovered from Fezzan tombs indicate that Roman items were being imported between the first and fourth centuries of our era. It seems that after replacing the Carthaginians on the Tripolitanian coast in the late second century before our era, the Romans in their turn imported ivory and slaves from the Sudan, with the Garamantes acting as intermediaries. Literary sources also refer to hunting expeditions and raids into the south, and finds of Roman material have been made along the 'chariot route' south-west of Fezzan. After the decline of Roman rule trade declined, but later revived with the Byzantine reconquest after $+533$ and before the Arab overran the Fezzan.[66] Recent archaeological research thus clearly shows that an important element of long-distance trade in prehistoric times was carried on with the peoples of the Sahara and North Africa. But this by no means justifies claims such as those made by Posnansky[67] that 'to discover the origins of long-distance trade in West Africa our search has to

64. C. A. Diop, 1968, pp. 10–38.
65. B. G. Trigger, 1969, p. 50.
66. Note by the Volume editor: an opposing point of view is presented in Chapters 17, 18 and 20 of the present volume.
67. M. Posnansky, 1971, p. 111.

begin in the sands of the Sahara'. However well-intentioned such a claim may be, the emphasis is wrong and the far-reaching implications false. For one thing, it ignores the fact that an internal system of long-distance trade existed in West Africa which much preceded (and indeed made possible) the development of trans-Saharan trade.

In the view of this author, existing evidence points to the existence from early iron age times of a complex and extensive network of long-distance trade, thriving on local complementary craft industries, especially (e.g. in fish and salt) between coastal peoples and inland farming peoples on the one hand, and also between the latter peoples to the south and more pastoralist societies to the north on the other. Important local products traded included iron and stone (for tools and weapons), leather, salt, grains, dried fish, cloth, pottery, woodwork, kola nuts and stone and iron personal ornaments.

As Posnansky himself admits, among many early farming communities in West Africa polished stone axes, known locally in Ghana as *nyame akume*, and pottery were traded over distances of hundreds of miles from Neolithic and iron age times. The stone rasps of the Kintampo 'culture' dated to about $-1500$, were made from a dolomitic marl which was evidently traded over substantial distances for it has been found both on the Accra plain and in northern Ghana. At Rim, near Ouahigouya, Neolithic iron age levels are associated with axe factories and the site appears to have been a major centre for the supply of axes to areas lacking the raw material.

From the iron age further evidence of a local raw material is provided by the recognition in the fabric of pots of clays foreign to the areas in which the pots themselves have been found. Such local trade probably also explains some aspects of the economic, social and political developments that were an integral part of the foundation of the early ancient state of Ghana. Its importance certainly goes beyond the mere indication of cultural contacts on a regional basis and the proof that very few agricultural societies were entirely self-contained.

The patterns of internal trade and crafts (industry) developed within West Africa shaped and sustained trade routes between the West African and the Saharan worlds. Such internal trade also fostered the growth of larger villages and towns in the late Neolithic and iron age times. Archaeological information which is now accumulating even for the forest areas of West Africa, continues to indicate that the subsequent emergence of the Ashanti, Benin and Yoruba states, as well as the Igbo Ukwu culture, depended essentially on a highly successful exploitation of their environment by earlier iron-using (and in some cases non-iron-using) peoples.

# Central Africa

F. VAN NOTEN
*with the collaboration of* D. CAHEN
*and* P. DE MARET

## Introduction

Two problems fundamental to the history of Africa are the diffusion of metallurgy and the amazing spread of the Bantu languages.

For a long time there has been a distinct tendency to link the two questions and explain them in terms of one another. The diffusion of metallurgy is seen as a consequence of the spread of the Bantu-speaking peoples, and, conversely, this expansion is supposed to have been facilitated by the possession of iron tools which made it possible to tackle the equatorial forest.

Language specialists were the first to put forward the theory that the Bantu languages originated on the plateaux of Nigeria and Cameroon. Archaeologists, historians and anthropologists followed suit and tried to make the findings in their respective fields fit in with that hypothesis. But the areas covered by these sciences do not exactly coincide, and it is a pity that the word Bantu, a linguistic term, should have come to be used for the ethnological concept of the Bantu peoples and their societies, and thence for the archaeological concept of a Bantu iron age.[1]

## Geographical background

The region dealt with in this chapter is Central Africa, i.e. the republic of Zaïre and the neighbouring countries of Gabon, Congo, the Central African Republic, Rwanda, Burundi and northern Zambia.

It forms a huge basin with an average altitude of 500 metres. Around this vast inner plain the ground rises in steps to become mountains or high plateaux.

The regions near the Equator have abundant rainfall all the year round. To both north and south are belts which have two rainy seasons that merge into one; from about latitudes 5° or 6° there is one rainy season.

Mean annual temperatures are fairly high, the range widening with distance from the Equator.

1. In this chapter 'Bantu' will be used only in the linguistic sense.

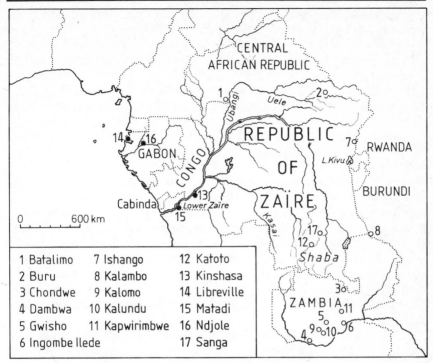

FIG. 25.1 *Map of Central Africa showing places mentioned in the text*

| | | |
|---|---|---|
| 1 Batalimo | 7 Ishango | 12 Katoto |
| 2 Buru | 8 Kalambo | 13 Kinshasa |
| 3 Chondwe | 9 Kalomo | 14 Libreville |
| 4 Dambwa | 10 Kalundu | 15 Matadi |
| 5 Gwisho | 11 Kapwirimbwe | 16 Ndjole |
| 6 Ingombe Ilede | | 17 Sanga |

The central basin is covered by dense equatorial forest bordered with savannah. In areas with a definite dry season, grass predominates, but there are often strips of forest along the rivers.

## Late stone age

Late stone age societies of hunter-gatherers used increasingly specialized tools. A distinction is generally made between two opposing traditions, that of the Tshitolian industrial complex and that of the complex of microlithic industries of which the Nachikufan and the Wilton are the best-known examples.

The late stone age is often contrasted with the Neolithic, either in technological terms (polished tools, whether or not in association with pottery) or in socio-economic terms (animal husbandry and agriculture, the settlement of nomad peoples and possible growth of cities). At present, socio-economic data are so scanty that we are reduced to inferring this distinction on the basis of technological factors alone, and these turn out to be inconclusive. Polished axes and pottery are already to be found in late stone age archaeological contexts.

The Tshitolian stands out fairly clearly from the other late stone age industries of Central Africa. Geographically it belongs to the southern and above all the south-east areas of the Zaïre basin.

The Tshitolian seems to continue the tradition of the Lupembian complex, from which it is separated mainly by a tendency to reduce the size of instruments and by the appearance of new forms: leaf-shaped and tanged flaked arrowheads, geometric microliths (segments, trapeziums). Some polished tools are also found towards the end of the Tshitolian.

Chronologically, the Tshitolian appears to have stretched roughly from −12 000 to −4000 – perhaps to −2000 or even, locally, to the beginning of our era.

The Nachikufan is an essentially microlithic industry which seems to have been established in the north of Zambia over 16 000 years ago. It had three successive stages. The oldest produced microlithic tools in association with a large number of pierced stones and grinding equipment. The second stage, which began about −8000, is characterized by the presence of polished tools. The last stage of this industry, beginning about −2000, is marked by a great abundance of small segments, pottery and a few articles made of iron – these last probably the result of trade. The Nachikufan tradition appears to have lasted down to the nineteenth century.

There is evidence of the Wilton, a purely microlithic industry, in southern Zambia and a large part of South Africa. Polished tools also appeared towards the end of its development.

It is generally attributed to proto-San groups. At Gwisho in central Zambia, where conditions are exceptionally favourable to the preservation of remains, it has been possible to reconstruct the way such a population lived during the second millennium before our era.

Skills were extremely widespread and complete and included the making of stone, wood and bone instruments. Microlithic tools were designed mainly for working in wood and for making arrow-tips, harpoons and knives. Microlithic tools include among other things some polished axes, grinders and bedstones. Among the wooden tools are found digging-sticks and arrow-tips comparable to those found today among the San. Bone tools include needles, perforators and arrow-tips.

Houses seem to have consisted of huts of branches and grass similar to those of the San of the Kalahari desert. The dead were buried on the spot, with no goods in their graves. The bodies lay in various positions.

Neither agriculture nor animal husbandry was practised. Excavations have shown that the food was comparable to that of present-day peoples and consisted basically of a large variety of vegetable products, gathered from wild plants supplemented by hunting and fishing.

The inhabitants of Gwisho lived off quite a large area, and hunted animals both of the plain and of the forest.

There are a large number of microlithic industries in Central Africa which have been inadequately described and cannot be classed with those listed above. Probably some of them are merely local variants, adapted to special materials or activities.

As we have mentioned, there is little evidence to justify a distinction between the late stone age and the Neolithic. However, the technological features traditionally attributed to the Neolithic do predominate in certain regions, for example Uele, Ubangi, and, to a lesser extent, Lower Zaïre. This led the early archaeologists of Central Africa to distinguish a Uelian, a Ubangian and a Leopoldian Neolithic. But these so-called industries are practically unknown except for their polished tools collected on the surface of the ground or acquired by purchase. Whenever more extensive research has been carried out it has appreciably modified previous ideas. In this way the Uelian, known for its fine axes of polished hematite (Fig. 25.2) would seem to belong at least partly to the iron age. A workshop for shaping tools was recently discovered at Buru in Uele. Two calibrated radio-carbon dates indicate that this workshop, where the beginnings of axes

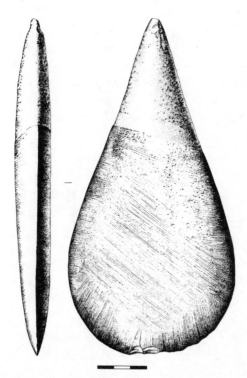

FIG. 25.2 *Uelian polished axe (hematite)*

were found alongside fragments of pipes, iron slag and pottery, belongs to the first half of the seventeenth century.

As regards Ubangian, there is now an excavated site at Batalimo, south of Bangui, in the Central African Republic. This site has produced hewn hatchets or adzes, an axe with a partly polished cutting edge, an abundant non-microlithic industry, and richly decorated pottery; tall wide-necked jars (Fig. 25.3) and flat-bottomed pots and bowls. Thermoluminescent

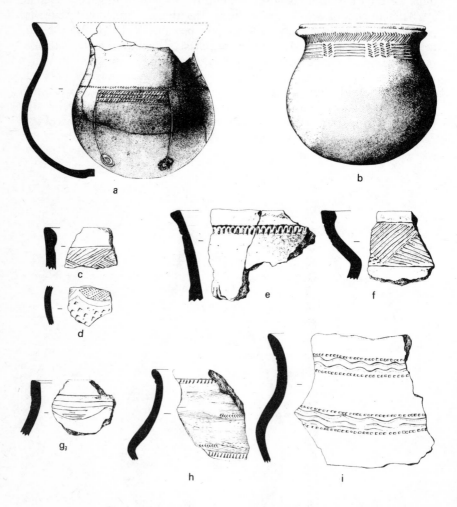

FIG. 25.3 *Objects found at the Batalimo site, south of Bangui (Central African Republic): (a) Urewe-type pot (after Leakey, Owen, Leakey, pl. IV); (b) Kalambo pot; (c), (d) Shards from Kangonga (Chondwo site) (after Phillipson, 1968a, fig. 4); (e), (f) Shards found at Kapwirimbwe; (g) Shard from Kalundu (after Fagan, 1967, fig. 122); (h), (i) Shards from Dambwa*

dating places the pottery around + 380 ( ± 220). This date may seem too recent to some, but in the absence of other evidence it cannot be rejected.

In Lower Zaïre, from Matadi to Kinshasa, axes with more or less polished edges are found, sometimes in association with flat-bottomed pottery. During a recent sondage in a cave of this region a polished axe was found in association with this pottery and with wood ash, and a sampling of it, radio-carbon dated, gave a calibrated age of −390 to −160. Sondage of another cave about 6 miles away also yielded a polished axe in association with this same pottery.

In Gabon the stratigraphy of various sites, such as that of Ndjole, 120 miles east of Libreville, has revealed a Neolithic level containing axes with polished edges, pottery and fragments of quartz.

## Early iron age

There were contacts between the peoples of the stone age that was drawing to an end and the first workers in metals. That fact is generally established.

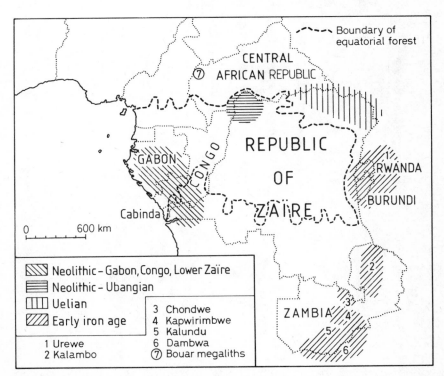

FIG. 25.4 *Map of Central Africa showing areas of 'Neolithic' and 'early iron age' occupation*

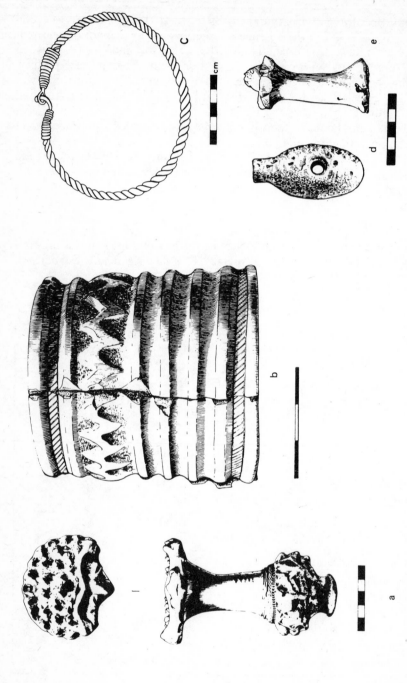

FIG. 25.5 Objects found at Sanga: (a) Vessel with anthropomorphic decoration, view from above and side; (b) Ivory bracelet; (c) Copper necklace; (d) Iron whistle; (e) Terracotta counter

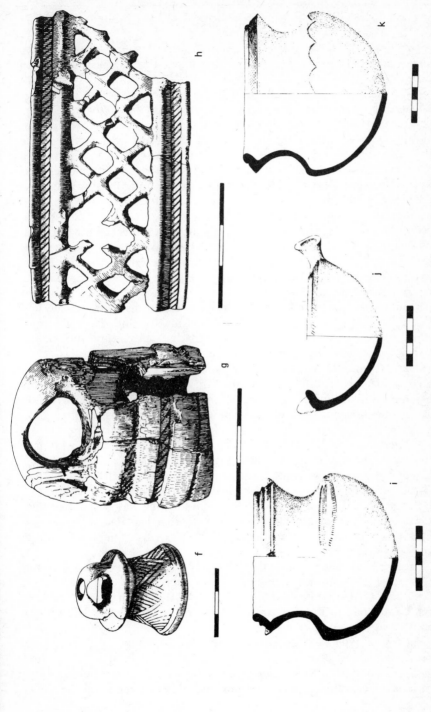

FIG. 25.5 cont. (*f*) *Stone pendant*; (*g*) *Ivory pendant*; (*h*) *Fragment of ivory half necklace*; (*i*), (*j*), (*k*) *Types of pottery. (Tervuren Museum: J. Hiernaux, E. De Longrée and J. De Buyst, 1971)*

But we do not know if this technological change brought about far-reaching changes in the societies concerned.

For Central Africa we have neither historical sources (such as the *Circumnavigation of the Erythraean Sea*) nor anthropological sources to throw light on the period corresponding to the early iron age. Therefore our only evidence is archaeological.

The early iron age is customarily associated with dimple-based pottery. This pottery (Fig. 25.3a), described for the first time in 1948, is now known as Urewe. It is attested in part of Kenya, in Uganda and in the lake region. Some examples found at Kasaï also seem to belong to this vast area of distribution. Most dates for these ceramic types fall between +250 and +400. But in at least one site at Katuruka, in Buhaya, Tanzania, considerably earlier dates have been obtained. Unfortunately it is still hard to assess the implications of this discovery.

Urewe ware presents a very homogeneous appearance, and it has often been suggested that the various examples had a common origin and that the differences they present are local variants rather than different chronological stages. It is true that they are never found stratigraphically superimposed on one another.

From the very beginning, iron working seems to have been associated with certain cultural traits such as pottery making and the building of daub villages. It is also generally agreed that agriculture and animal husbandry were practised at the same period.

The presence of Urewe pottery is well attested in the lake region (Kenya, Uganda, Rwanda, Burundi, Tanzania) and also in Zaïre, in the region of Kivu. For a long time Zambian pottery of the early iron age (channel-decorated ware) was grouped with dimple-based pottery. But in fact it seems it can be broken down into several regional types.

J. Hiernaux and E. Maquet are practically the only persons who have studied the early iron age in these regions. They first published (1957) a description of two sites in Kivu. At Tshamfu, a typical Urewe pottery was associated with remains of smelted iron and with handmade bricks. At Bishange, a furnace designed for iron smelting has been excavated. It was built with handmade bricks which often had one side that was slightly concave and was decorated with impressions of fingers. Bishange pottery is also of the Urewe type.

Later (1960) these authors described several iron age sites discovered in Rwanda and Burundi. The pottery has been classed in three groups: A, B and C. Only the first group, A, identical with Urewe pottery, seems to belong to the early iron age, the others apparently being more recent.

Pottery of type A is associated with iron slag, pipes and handmade bricks, sometimes decorated, like the ones at Kivu. In at least two sites these bricks seem to have belonged to a furnace for iron smelting. Two dates have been published: the Ndora site, +250 ($\pm$100), and the site of

Cyamakuza, a locality in the commune of Ndora, in the prefecture of Butare, +380 (±80).

At Mukinanira, pottery of type A was lying just above and partly mingled with a stone industry of the late stone age. At Masangano, likewise, the two groups of remains were mingled. From this we might deduce that the makers of type A pottery brought metallurgy to this part of Africa at a time when the region was still inhabited by hunter-gatherers of the late stone age. The coexistence of groups of people so technologically different is fairly widely attested. In our day, the Twa still lead a life as hunters in the equatorial forest of this region.

Recent excavations at places which oral tradition points to as the sites of Tutsi royal graves have sometimes revealed early iron age structures. For instance, at Rurembo a hole dug in laterite contained wood ash dated −230 (±50). Above the hole was a jar of type A. A similar hole at Rambura yielded iron slag, fragments of pipes, a few shards which looked like Urewe ware, some shaped stones of the late stone age, and wood ash dated +295 (±60). This last result corresponds nicely with those previously obtained by J. Hiernaux.

The craftsmen in this industry seem to have arrived in the Kalambo valley around +300 and to have stayed there for 600, possibly even 1000 years. The population, which seems to have been rather dense, led a peaceful life in villages which had neither palisades nor trenches. The area occupied, according to a plan which is not known, covered roughly from 10 to 42 acres.

Some vestiges of structures for habitation or storage have been preserved. A series of eight pits with straight parallel edges, something over 1 metre in diameter and nearly 2 metres in average depth, contained pots and potsherds, fragments of moulds, objects made of iron, and iron slag. Four of the pits were surrounded by a circular trench, possibly the remains of a superstructure.

There is only indirect evidence that there were agricultural activities. Nor is there any sure trace of animal husbandry.

Many pieces of iron slag, especially one great block of dross from the base of a furnace, and several fragments of pipes show that iron-smelting was practised, if not in the living sites, at least in their neighbourhood.

Among the iron objects unearthed from the pits may be mentioned many spear- and knife-tips, arrow-tips, bracelets or anklets, rings for fingers or toes. Bracelets or anklets and other ornaments were also made of copper.

The use of stone continued, as is evidenced by many millstones and pestles, stampers, hammers (including a smith's hammer), an anvil, and many crude artefacts which were used for scratching, cutting or rubbing.

White clay and red ochre were used as pigments.

The lip of pottery in most cases is rounded and flaring, thickened at the rim. All the bases are rounded except on two pots which have a dimple pressed in by the fingers. Decoration, which was applied before firing, is most often seen on or above the shoulder. The patterns consist of bands of parallel horizontal grooves broken by herring-bones and spirals. A network of slanting and criss-cross incisions of rows of triangular impressions and punctuations occasionally form the pattern of false relief covering the neck and shoulder.

Examples of pottery similar to that at Kalambo Falls have been found in eleven sites in the northern province of Zambia, distributed over an area of more than 37 thousand square miles.

Except for the necropolises at Sanga and Katoto (which are so important that we shall consider them separately below), no early iron age site has yet been discovered in Shaba. However, the whole of the remains un-earthed in those two burial grounds seem so highly developed that it would be most surprising if they were not preceded by an earlier iron age. Moreover, in the copper-bearing area of north-west Zambia, along the Zaïre border, several open-air habitats have been explored, some of which would seem to go back to the fourth century of our era.

In the absence of extensive excavations and absolute datings, the few data we have are very conjectural. Four pots, two of them dimple-based, found near Tshikapa seem to belong to the Urewe type; on the other hand many jars and shards found in a cave near Mbuji-Mayi rather closely recall the pottery of the Kalambo Falls industry.

Apart from Zambia and the lake regions, Lower Zaïre is the only region where remains have been discovered which it seems possible to attribute to the early iron age. On evidence collected in caves, six kinds of pottery have been provisionally distinguished, and a few objects made of iron.

Further study of the pottery reveals the existence of many groups, some of them quite widely diffused. None of these groups is related to Urewe ware.

Since excavation has not been extensive, we cannot attempt a chronology of this pottery or of the objects in metal.

At Kinshasa, near the sources of the Funa, wood ash accompanied with a small atypical shard has been dated −270 (±90). Though this date undeniably falls within the iron age, it has to be viewed very cautiously, the association of the dated ash with the shard being no more formally established than that for another date relating to Kinshasa – from Mimosas Island, in mid-river. There examples of wood ash in association with pottery have been dated +410 (±100). Unfortunately the shards thus dated have never been published.

Mimosas Island has, however, yielded pottery identical with that found in the upper layers at Gombe Point (formerly Kalina Point), the eponymous site of the Kalinian, excavated by J. Colette in 1925 and 1927. Re-excavated in 1973 and 1974, this site revealed an important level of iron age occupation, vestiges of which are found all over the promontory. At the top of most of the cuts were alignments of wood ash, pottery, stones and burnt earth, some pieces of slag, and bits of millstones, lying on the soil of a habitat which had various archaeological structures, large hearths and, especially, pits that were sometimes over 2 metres deep. These pits occasionally contained a more or less complete pot, and two of them had tiny fragments of an iron object. This may therefore be an early iron age habitat. Here too we shall soon know more, thanks to radio-carbon datings now in progress.

In the Bouar region of the Central African Republic there are several barrows of various sizes with squared stones on top sometimes 3 metres high. Sometimes there are rows of vaults, and it seems that these cairns were intended for burial places. No bones have been found, however,[2] though articles made of iron have been discovered. Six radio-carbon datings are available. Two belong to the sixth and fifth millennia before our era and the other four range from the seventh century before our era to the first century of our era. The first date seems to be that of the building of the barrows, the second that at which they came into use again in the iron age.

The cemeteries of Sanga and Katoto are in the Upper Zaïre valley, in the Upemba tombs, and are the best known early iron age sites in the republic of Zaïre.

Situated on the edge of Lake Kisale, near Kinkondja, the Sanga burial ground, discovered quite a long time ago, was systematically excavated in 1957 and 1958. New excavations were undertaken in 1974. A total of 175 graves have been opened, but it is clear that a large part of the cemetery has still to be explored.

After the excavations of 1958 three groups of pottery were distinguished and it looked as if a chronology could be worked out for them. The Kisalian group (the most abundant) seemed the oldest, followed by the Mulongo group (from the name of a place north-east of Sanga), and finally by red slip ware.

The 1958 excavations revealed that these three groups were at least in part contemporary with one another.

In the absence of internal chronology, two radio-carbon datings enable us to estimate the age of the cemetery:

$$+710 \ (\pm 120)$$
$$+880 \ (\pm 200).$$

The older date was obtained from a grave in which the position of the body was quite unusual and the single pot, though Kisalian, untypical. The other date comes from a grave without goods characteristic of any of the three cultures.[3] Therefore we do not know exactly what is dated.

2. Except under very rare conditions, the acidity of the soil in Central Africa destroys bones in open-air sites very quickly.

3. Furthermore, it seems that in the laboratory, bones from a grave in the Mulongo group were added to the sample.

Moreover, the vagueness of these dates detracts considerably from their value. All we can safely say is that, to within a couple of hundred years, some of the graves at Sanga go back to between the seventh and ninth centuries of our era.

The excavations give us an idea of the burial ground itself, and, through that, a glimpse of ancient Sanga society.

Despite the fact that the three groups of pottery were contemporaneous, they apparently did not all belong to the same population. The graves containing Mulongo or red slip ware are almost the only ones to contain little crosses of copper. These are practically absent from Kisalian graves. On the other hand, all the graves are equally rich in well-worked iron and copper objects. It may be supposed that the minority who were buried with crosses were different from the Kisalian population, and perhaps were the source of the copper, of which the nearest deposits are about 180 miles to the south.

Burial rites seem to have been rather complex. Most of the graves are pointed towards the north or north-east – the Mulongo – red slip ones, towards the south. The dead person usually lay *decubitus dorsal* and was accompanied with objects presumably intended to make things easier for him in the other world. The pottery shows no signs of wear and the strong resemblance among certain vessels in a given tomb seem to indicate that it was made for exclusively funerary purposes. These jars were probably filled with food and drink. The corpse was adorned with jewels of copper, iron, ivory. It seems as if premature infants, too, were buried. In some cases the dead person has a bundle of little crosses in his hand. There is a clear tendency for the size of the jars to be in proportion to the age of the dead person.

The general picture one gets of Sanga is of a civilization where the people attach more importance to hunting and fishing than to agriculture. However, hoes and bedstones have been found in the graves, as have remains of goats and fowl.

No grave is rich enough to indicate that it belonged to an important chief, but the fineness of the grave-goods shows the great skill of the Sanga craftsmen, who worked in bone, stone and wood, made iron and copper wire, and practised open-mould casting. Their pottery seems very original.

As the bones have not been analysed, the only anthropological datum we possess is an odontological study of some of the human remains. This study shows in particular the frequency of mutilated teeth. We do not know the whole extent of the burial ground, which would have given some idea of the size of the population.

The Sanga civilization, then, seems to have been a brilliant phenomenon, but, so far as our present knowledge goes, an isolated one. Probably the discoveries as a whole cover a longer period than that suggested by the two radio-carbon datings.

New excavations were undertaken in 1974. The main purpose was to learn just how long the burial ground has been in use and establish its internal chronology, to delimit its area, and to try to find the habitat site. Thirty new graves were explored; they will probably enable us to complete the chronology and form some idea of the size of the burial ground. But because of the expansion of the modern village the habitat site could not be found.

However, at Katongo, 6 miles from Sanga, excavations seem to have revealed a habitat level at the foot of a hill less than half a mile from a cemetery; excavations also revealed the existence of pottery groups recognized at Sanga.

Situated on the right bank of the Lualaba, near Bukama, some 80 miles upstream from Sanga, the Katoto burial ground was partially excavated in 1959, when forty-seven graves were uncovered.

Three different archaeological finds were made. First the graves; then pits containing material different from that in the graves; then an upper layer containing pottery distinct from that found in the graves and the pits.

The first difference between the burial grounds at Sanga and Katoto is that in the latter there are graves for multiple burials containing up to seven people. Some of them have yielded such articles as a smith's hammer, anvils, heaps of iron tips, and a battle-axe. These must have been the graves of important personages, blacksmiths very likely, in whose honour were sacrificed two women and four children in one case and two women and one child in another.

The grave-goods are just as rich as at Sanga, and here too suggest a prosperous society with a high level of technical development. The presence of numerous hoes and millstones indicates that agriculture was important, but hunting and fishing must have been practised too.

Completely absent from Katoto are the little copper crosses, Mulongo pottery and red slip ware. But three Kisalian bowls were found – the only evidence of any contact between Sanga and Katoto.

The presence of glass beads and ornaments made of shells from both the Atlantic and the Indian Ocean indicates fairly far-flung trading activities.

Katoto pottery is original, like that at Sanga, and seems somewhat less stereotyped. Some decorative motifs are reminiscent of Urewe ware, but as none of the latter has been found in the Shaba area it cannot be said that Katoto pottery is a development of the Urewe type rather than a simple case of convergence. As a matter of fact most of these common motifs, such as the spiral, strapwork, herring-bone and concentric circles, are very widespread.

The pits are later than the graves, and sometimes disturb them. One of them has been given a radio-carbon dating: +1190 (±60).

Few shards have been found in the pits, but some of those that have been dug up have a dimpled base, which again suggests Urewe pottery.

The burial ground at Katoto completes the picture suggested by the excavations at Sanga. But it seems astonishing that two such large settlements, quite close to each other and apparently contemporary, should have had so little to do with each other.

Despite the abundance of grave-goods, we do not know very much about the people buried in these necropolises. We do not know who they were, where they came from or what they died of, and we have but scant means of imagining how they lived. The size of the two burial grounds suggests that towards the end of the first millennium of our era the banks of the upper Lualaba were the site of large concentrations of people, which gave rise to brilliant civilizations. The excavations now under way at several new sites should teach us more about those civilizations.

## Origin of the Bantu

As we have said, the word 'Bantu' designates in the first place a group of languages. But it has gradually acquired an ethnographical, and even an anthropological connotation. In fact it was linguistic classification that served as a basis for researchers in other disciplines.

In the absence of written evidence, archaeology does not enable us to establish direct correlations between existing evidence of the iron age and the linguistic notion of Bantu.

Excavations reveal pottery, articles of iron and copper, culinary remains and a few skeletons. But just as it is impossible to say one pot is more specifically Indo-European than another, so it is impossible to point to a 'Bantu' jar.

Up till now it is linguistics which has provided most details about the origin and expansion of the 'Bantu'. According to certain linguisticians, mainly following the work of Greenberg and of Guthrie, the Bantu languages, which now spread over nearly half Africa, originated in the middle Benue area, on the borders of Nigeria and Cameroon.

Many attempts have been made to link the success of 'Bantu' groups to the knowledge of working in iron. But one observes, comparing metallurgical terms in the Bantu languages, that there is great diversity in the basic vocabulary of forging. However, certain reconstructions suggest the use of iron at proto-Bantu level, for instance the expressions for forging, hammer, and bellows. Were these words in the language before the division, or did they enter it as borrowings at some unknown stage in the ramification process? It is not impossible that those words which are widely attested result from a shift in meaning from proto-Bantu to the present-day languages. Thus the word for 'forge' would be only a special application of the word for 'beat'. Finally, other metallurgical terms seem to have the same origin in both Bantu and non-Bantu languages, which seems to indicate that in both instances it is a matter of borrowings.

When one thinks of how important the ability to work metals was in traditional African societies, it is difficult to see why, if the 'Bantu' worked in iron before their expansion, we find no obvious linguistic traces of it.

Looking at the work of different ethnologists, one sees that although certain cultural areas can be distinguished in the 'Bantu' world, it is not possible to find a collection of characteristics common to the 'Bantu' and differentiating them from other African peoples.

Finally, very little research in physical anthropology has been done on the 'Bantu'. An article by J. Hiernaux (1968) is alone in supplying a few facts. Hiernaux shows the biological resemblances between Bantu-speaking peoples. But his conclusions are drawn from the evidence of present-day peoples. So little work has been done in this area of human palaeontology that it is very difficult to distinguish a complete present-day 'Bantu' skeleton from one belonging to some other African, or even European group. What can be said, then, of the damaged or fragmentary skeletons which are often all that archaeology affords?

The only human fossil remains that have been properly studied come from Ishango, in Virunga Park in Zaïre. Unfortunately the age of these remains cannot be accurately determined, and it has not been possible to ascribe them to a definite physical type.

## Nature of societies in the early iron age

Little is known about the kind of life people lived at the beginning of the iron age. Such evidence as there is varies with the extent of the research that has been carried out: the sites in Zambia and the burial grounds at Sanga and Katoto, in Shaba, provide the most concrete data.

Remains of habitats are rare in Central Africa. The only ones known are at Gombe, Kalambo Falls and perhaps Katongo.

The only proof of agricultural activity at the beginning of the iron age consists of iron hoes practically identical in form with modern ones. Holes dug in the ground have been regarded as store pits, and small daub constructions as granaries. The fact that there are numerous remains of millstones is less convincing, as societies which lived by hunting and food gathering also had grinding implements.

As in the case of plants, early iron age remains of domestic animals are very rare and difficult to identify. We have no concrete evidence for Central Africa except the remains of cannon-bones of goats in some graves at Sanga.

The presence of tsetse fly in certain areas is a serious obstacle to animal husbandry, and these areas must have varied in the course of time. This makes it difficult to say where animal husbandry may have been practicable in such distant periods.

Hunting and fishing were still major sources of food.

Excavations have yielded arrowheads and spearheads, and remains of what must have been hunting dogs. Snares and nets were probably also used.

The importance of fishing is shown by the hooks found in the graves at Sanga and Katoto. The trefoil braseros of Sanga are very much like those used in their canoes by boatmen in the equatorial part of Zaïre.

A certain number of objects which have been excavated show that extensive trade networks existed in the early iron age.

Trade seems to have been limited chiefly to areas near the big rivers, the Zaïre and the Zambesi. Sites a long way from the rivers or the lake region yield very few imported articles.

A distinction needs to be made between two kinds of trade: regional trade, mostly in metals, pottery, basketwork, dried fish and salt, and long-distance trade, the latter dealing in shells (cowries and conuses), glass beads, and metals like copper. In Zaïre, at Sanga and at Katoto, all the shells and beads came from the east coast, with the exception of a conus at Katoto from the Atlantic, a distance of some 900 miles as the crow flies. Little copper crosses, used as a sort of coin, have been found quite a long way from copper-producing areas.

Despite the gaps in our knowledge, it seems probable that the economy of the peoples of the early iron age differed little from that of traditional societies today.

It was based on agriculture and animal husbandry, but probably still relied to a large extent on hunting and fishing and food that grew wild. Economically they were practically self-sufficient societies.

Even the most ancient excavated remains of metallurgy do not differ fundamentally from those of societies described to us by ethnographers. But within a given region there are contemporaneous variations in technique and type of goods produced. Differences in metal objects or forge tools are therefore not necessarily chronological, but may quite as well be cultural.

Brick furnaces for iron smelting have been found in association with dimple-based ware in Kivu, Rwanda, Burundi and Buhaya in north-west Tanzania. It should be noted that in the only description of iron smelting in Rwanda, given by Bourgeois (1957), a circle of baked bricks is used in the building of a furnace rather similar to the remains found by Hiernaux and Maquet.

Up to now the use of copper has always appeared in association with that of iron. Copper was mined in Shaba, in the north of Zambia and probably in Lower Zaïre. As the objects found at Sanga and Katoto show, working in copper had already attained a high degree of refinement. Lead also appears to have been used at this period. The Kongo were still mining lead at the beginning of the present century.

Pottery remains are not decisive evidence of the iron age since, as we have seen, pottery is also found in the context of the late stone age and the Neolithic. It is generally impossible to distinguish iron age pottery as such from that of the earlier periods.

In the lake regions and in Zambia, however, there are some kinds of pottery typical of the iron age, such as those of Urewe, Kalambo, Chondwe, Kapwirimbwe, Kalundu and Dambwa.

Jars were made by patting and pulling the clay into strips or cords which were often arranged in a coil. The variety of shapes and decorations is so great that we show here only a few of the most characteristic.

As far as archaeology enables us to judge, societies of the early iron age were not essentially different from those of today and must have presented the same sort of diversity.

The agricultural techniques then practised were not favourable to the establishment of large settlements, and involved a certain mobility.

The burial grounds at Sanga and Katoto are exceptional in that they are the result either of very long occupation or of a large concentration of people on the banks of the Lualaba. The richness of the goods in some graves, especially at Katoto, may be a sign of social inequalities.

The abundance and workmanship of objects of iron, copper, stone, wood, bone and clay reflect not only the skill of the craftsmen but also, probably, some degree of specialization.

All the graves discovered give evidence of elaborate burial practices. The dead wore many ornaments – bracelets, rings, necklaces, pendants, strings of beads and shells. Cowries, conuses, and beads of glass or stone may have served, among other things, as coin in the same manner as the small crosses. Lastly, the most ancient dated wood sculpture of Central Africa comes from Angola and has been dated +750.

## Conclusion

I have several times stressed the danger of using the provisional findings of one science to back the conclusions of another. Hasty correlation too often leads to general theories which within the rigorous framework of their proper discipline would be difficult to maintain. Nevertheless, any attempt at describing the nature of early iron age societies or the origin of the Bantu-speaking peoples involves collating archaeological and non-archaeological data.

Certain theories, such as Guthrie's, put forward an extremely elaborate general explanation. The historical and geographical theory built up by Guthrie has clearly influenced, perhaps unconsciously, many archaeologists and anthropologists.

The anthropological–archaeological–linguistic explanation which linked the spread of the Bantu languages to the diffusion of working in iron chimed very well with the idea of evolution from beginnings in the Fertile Crescent, while denying that Africa could have arrived at discoveries independently.

637

Recent developments have caused these theories to be reconsidered. Linguisticians call in question the methods and results of glottochronology. New datings throw fresh light on the origin of metallurgy in Central Africa. Vestiges of iron workings at the Katuruka site have been dated as belonging to about −500 or −400.[4]

In the present state of our ignorance, and taking the new evidence into account, it is clear that the problems connected with the diffusion of iron and the origin of the Bantu languages are more complex than was thought, and cannot be reduced to an oversimple explanation beset by contradictions.

It therefore seems pointless to go on constructing new hypotheses for migrations and for the origin of metallurgy each time that an excavation results in new datings. We can nevertheless attempt to relate certain relevant facts. In regard to the origin of iron working, the new dates proposed for Katuruka seem to imply a connection with the almost contemporaneous dates put forward for Meroe. It is therefore possible to conceive of metal working having spread southwards from Meroe, but in that case it would appear to have taken place very quickly. One cannot consequently at present rule out another origin which could even be local.

It is hard to see how the idea of an indissoluble link between the diffusion of iron working and the expansion of the 'Bantu' can persist, even though it is not yet proved that the two phenomena are completely unconnected. Could we not suppose that the 'Bantu' were ignorant of iron at the start of their perigrinations, but discovered it in the course of their expansion?

As the reader will have observed, our information about the early iron age in Central Africa is of unequal value and very fragmentary; early research led to the construction of theories that now totter beneath the accumulated weight of new data. Much work – more extensive, more systematic and better co-ordinated – must be done before we can arrive at a convincing explanation of the events of this crucial period in the history of Central Africa.

4. The dates given here are calculated in radio-carbon years, which do not correspond exactly to calendar years. Dates before our era need to be increased in proportion, which varies with the period concerned.

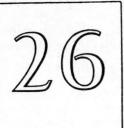

# Southern Africa: hunters and food-gatherers

J. E. PARKINGTON

## Note by the International Scientific Committee

The International Scientific Committee would have preferred this chapter like all the others to have been presented within the chronological framework strictly laid down for Volume II. It therefore requested the volume editor to put this point to the author. The latter did not consider it possible to make any radical alteration to his text. The Committee is therefore publishing it in the form agreed after discussion with the author. It nevertheless maintains serious reservations regarding the method used, particularly in paragraph 1, and regarding the resulting confusion for the reader, who is presented at one and the same time with information on the Palaeolithic and the contemporary periods.

Recent research has shown that iron-using peoples had moved south of the Limpopo by at latest the fourth or fifth century of our era.[1] Although much detail remains unpublished, it seems clear that the iron age inhabitants of the Transvaal and Swaziland were agriculturalists and herdsmen, and manufactured pottery similar to that known from Zimbabwe, Zambia and Malawi at about the same time.[2] It is not known whether the apparently rapid diffusion of iron age peoples continued farther south at the same pace, but the earliest dates for iron-working in Natal are somewhat later, around −1050.[3] Nor is it yet possible to say at what time the iron-using groups reached the most southerly extent of their distribution, around the Fish river in the eastern district of the Cape. Despite these uncertainties, which will no doubt be the focus of much further work, it is known that the iron age populations disrupted and displaced indigenous groups of hunter-gatherers who were largely ignorant of metal-working, stock-breeding and plant domestication. Only in areas unsuitable for occupation by mixed farmers, such as the rugged Drakensberg escarpment, were hunters able to

---

1. P. B. Beaumont and J. C. Vogel, pp. 66–89; R. J. Mason, 1973, p. 324; M. Klapwijk, 1974, pp. 19–23.
2. See Chapter 27 of this volume.
3. O. Davies, 1971, pp. 165–78.

survive the expansion of the early iron age. Even these retreats were ineffective against the deprivations of today.

A second, and in many ways more destructive, population expansion began from the Cape in the middle of the sixteenth century. The earliest contacts were made by the Portuguese voyagers of the late fifteenth century, but were intensified by the decision of the Dutch East India Company to establish a revictualling station in Table Bay in 1652. Within sixty years most of the inhabitants of the Cape within a radius of 100 kilometres of this station had abandoned their traditional settlement pattern and either migrated, drifted into the growing colony as servants or succumbed to diseases introduced by the colonists.[4] Before the end of the seventeenth century the revictualling station had become a colony and the colonists had fought at least two prolonged engagements with indigenous groups over land-ownership. Indigenous peoples were initially lumped together under the term 'Ottentoo' or 'Hottentot', but gradually the distinction between herdsmen (Hottentots, many of whose tribal names were known) and hunters (bushmen, or bosjesmen, also known as Sonqua Hottentots) was recognized and used. These groups were obviously closely related since they spoke similar languages, shared a good deal of subsistence technology and material culture, and were physically not unlike one another. Since in these respects they were clearly distinct from the other indigenous population group, the iron-using farmers farther to the north and east, they were generally identified as a separate element and would now be known as Khoi Khoi herdsmen and San hunters, often fused to produce the term 'Khoisan'.[5]

It seems impossible in this case to keep within the chronological limits strictly laid down for this volume, but the author has attempted to describe the lasting and relatively stable aspects of a way of life, leaving it to the authors of the other volumes concerned with these regions to draw attention to the changes which have occurred over the centuries in the life of these groups as a result of contact with the outside world, and to the part they themselves have played in the general history of southern Africa. In this way the risk of overlapping will be minimized.

## The Khoisan

This chapter will describe what is known of the way of life of hunters and herdsmen trapped between iron age farmers and European colonists in the southern parts of southern Africa. Since the colonists were literate and the iron age farmers were not, the documentation on traditional San and Khoi Khoi life and Khoisan relations with other groups is heavily biased towards the western Cape. In some ways this bias has been compounded

4. R. H. Elphick; S. Marks, pp. 55–80.
5. I. Schapera, 1930.

by the rich archaeology of the Cape mountain belt as compared with many other parts of southern Africa. But the descriptions offered, though often relating to the south and west, should illuminate Khoi Khoi and San life-styles throughout the region, though much detail of local conditions will, of course, be missing.

For various reasons there is a good deal of evidence as to how the Khoisan groups lived. Because they survived until fairly recently, there is much archaeological evidence in the form of artefactual remains and plant and animal food residues. Because they came into contact with literate societies, there is a body of historical documentation on their indigenous ways of life. In addition, at least some of the indigenous groups left their own documents in the form of rock paintings and engravings, which are a valuable source of social, economic, technological and probably religious information. An important fact is that the environment in many parts of southern Africa has not changed radically since the time when it was first occupied by hunters and herdsmen. After 250 years of agricultural activity, it is still possible to document and monitor the spatial and seasonal factors in the environment which must have to some extent determined the nature of prehistoric settlement.

The availability of important food resources, the location of outcrops of raw material and cyclical changes in pasture and water supply all help to suggest the sorts of settlement patterns to which hunters and herdsmen may have resorted. Finally, although no hunters or herdsmen remain in the Cape, there are related groups in Namibia and Botswana which have survived long enough to have been methodically studied by anthropologists. Their studies of the technology, economy and social organization provide archaeologists with invaluable general models for interpreting the remains of extinct peoples in other areas.

Since neither the Khoi Khoi herdsmen nor the San hunters used metals for their cutting, scraping or chopping tools, they fall within the scope of stone age studies, and have been viewed in the past very largely in terms of the stone artefacts they produced. This has meant that historians or anthropologists wishing to make use of the archaeological record have had to use artefact lists and fit Wilton and Smithfield industries into their picture of settlement before contact with Europeans. For the purposes of the discussion which follows, minor differences between artefact assemblages from site to site will not be emphasized or used as criteria for subdividing hunters or herdsmen into cultural groupings. Instead it will be assumed that all the later stone age occupants of southern Africa made some use of microlithic stone artefacts in the form of scrapers, missile tips, adzes and drills. The varying proportions of these tools from site to site and the appearance occasionally of other tool forms will be interpreted as reflecting the different tool requirements of populations as they moved about their various daily tasks. People in widely separate areas may have had quite different raw materials available to them, or may have been engaged in significantly different subsistence activities, and so may have produced quite dissimilar stone tool assemblages. Nevertheless, they were similar communities linked by a generally similar technology and a number of non-technological characteristics such as language, physical type and economy.

## San hunter-gatherers

Recent ethnographic studies of hunter-gatherers have shown the very considerable importance of the gathered or collected component of the diet of groups in this economic category.[6] It is clear from the accounts of the Kung and the G/wi of the Kalahari[7] that the foods collected by the women tide the group over from day to day, though men and children also gather such 'veldkos'. The importance of gathered foods, much but not all of which may be vegetable, is that they are predictable in their location and may be relied upon on a daily basis. High-protein meat, hunted or snared by men, is also of importance but being less predictable is not part of the daily staple food. The implication is not that hunters should be renamed gatherers, but that the balance between the food resources available to hunting and gathering groups needs to be recognized. Such groups keep themselves alive on collected foods but benefit periodically from successes in the hunt.

That this pattern was once widespread throughout southern Africa is clear both from the first-hand descriptions of European travellers of the seventeenth and eighteenth centuries and from the fragmentary archaeological record. For example, Paterson wrote in Namaqualand in August 1778 of some 'bush Hottentots', that: 'they had no cattle and ... they lived upon roots and gums; and sometimes feasted on an antelope which they occasionally shot with their poisoned arrows';[8] and Thompson, travelling through the Cradock district near the upper Orange river in June 1823, visited a 'bushman kraal' of whose occupants he wrote: 'these poor creatures subsist chiefly upon certain wild bulbs which grow in the plains and also upon locusts, white ants, and other insects ... This is all they have to subsist upon, except where now and then the men succeed in killing game with their poisoned arrows.'[9]

Similar quotations, spanning a geographical range from Cape Town to the edges of the Cape colony at the time, and from as early as the 1650s to the 1820s, are unanimous in their assessment of the San subsistence diet. Few descriptions mention game without qualifying it as 'occasionally taken' and all mention roots and bulbs as being particular staples. In fact, whilst the authors mention many plant foods, including herbs, berries and

6. R. B. Lee and I. Devore.
7. R. B. Lee, 1972.
8. W. Paterson.
9. G. Thompson.

gum, it is the 'uyntjes' – literally onions, or 'bulbous roots' – which appear most commonly in the historical record. These are not strictly onions but the corms of various plants of the iris family, such as *Iris* itself, *Gladiolus*, *Ixia* and *Moraea*, all of which are mentioned by name. Along with these plant foods there are numerous references to collectable animal foods such as caterpillars, ants, locusts and tortoises, and to honey, all of which must be considered as of importance in the day-to-day quest for food.

The archaeological record is, of course, likely to be biased towards those foods which, when eaten, leave durable residues. It is for this reason that archaeology has stressed the hunting of game by San groups in southern Africa. But where favourable conditions for preservation have allowed organic materials to be recovered and analysed, the importance of plant foods can be recognized. Rock shelters and caves in Namibia,[10] the south-western Cape,[11] the eastern Cape,[12] Natal[13] and Lesotho[14] contain many plant remains, prominent amongst which are stems, corm tunics and corm bases from a number of iridaceous plants. Of course the types of plant foods available varies from site to site depending on what grows in the locality, but generally speaking there is a clear pattern of rootstocks such as corms and tubers, supplemented by the seeds of fruit-bearing species.[15]

Most of the historic accounts of the animal part of the prehistoric diet mention 'game' generally and the implication is that a wide range of species were taken. This is confirmed by the faunal lists from large excavations such as those at Die Kelders[16] and Nelson Bay Cave,[17] where the range extends from shrews to elephants and even whales. But the fauna from these sites show a strong bias towards smaller animals such as tortoises, dassies, dune mole rats and small territorial herbivores such as the steenbok, the grysbok and the duiker. The bones of carnivores are rare, perhaps reflecting occasional kills to obtain pelts; the larger herbivores such as hartebeest, eland and buffalo are much rarer than the smaller animals, and only occasional traces of elephant, hippo or rhino have been recovered. Whilst the proportions in part reflect a tendency for the prehistoric groups to bring back smaller animals to their home base and to butcher larger game where hunted, there is no doubt that ground game and the smaller herbivores were the prime targets or most frequent victims in the hunt.

Marine resources were fully exploited by San groups, as the large number

10. W. E. Wendt, pp. 1–45.
11. J. E. Parkington and C. Pöggenpoel.
12. H. J. Deacon, 1969, pp. 141–69; H. J. and J. Deacon, 1963, pp. 96–121.
13. O. Davies, personal communication.
14. P. L. Carter, personal communication.
15. H. J. Deacon, 1969, J. E. Parkington, pp. 223–43.
16. F. R. Schweitzer, pp. 136–8; F. R. Schweitzer and K. Scott, p. 547.
17. R. G. Klein, pp. 177–208.

of coastal shell middens, both in and out of caves, demonstrates. The relationship between 'strandløpers' and San and Khoi Khoi groups will be discussed later, but there is convincing evidence that many of the coastal caves and open midden stations were occupied by San groups. Although shells are the most prominent feature of these sites, the faunal assemblages show that a wide range of marine animals was eaten, notably seals, lobsters, fish and birds. The remains of plant foods are rare on coastal sites. Farther inland there is evidence from both the eastern and western Cape that freshwater shellfish were collected,[18] and freshwater fish have been recognized both in the western Cape and in Lesotho.[19] Fishing is in fact portrayed in a number of rock paintings in Lesotho and east Griqualand.[20]

The diet of San groups is thus well documented, both historically and archaeologically, although the distribution of excavations is very uneven and some areas are virtually unexplored or lacking in well-preserved deposits. In general terms, the day-to-day staples were collectable items, including rootstocks, other plant foods, honey, and insects such as locusts, grasshoppers, termites and caterpillars. These were supplemented by small animals such as tortoises, dassies and dune mole rats, by the smaller herbivores, and less frequently by larger animals. The groups along the coast caught fish, rock lobsters, seals and sea-birds, and gathered quantities of shellfish, notably limpets and mussels. Riverine resources, including freshwater molluscs and fish, were utilized, and there is one historical reference to dried fish.[21] Thunberg, recording his observations in the western Cape in the 1770s, describes as follows a drink made by either hunters or herdsmen, or both:

> Gli is, in the Hottentot language, the name of an umbelliferous plant, the root of which, dried and reduced to powder, they mix with cold water and honey in a trough, and after letting it ferment for the space of one night, obtain a species of mead which they drink in order to throw themselves in the state of intoxication.[22]

The technology by which these resources were exploited is reflected in the assemblages of stone, bone, wood and fibre from caves and shelters throughout southern Africa, and in the descriptions of early travellers in the region. The corms and tubers were dug up with a wooden digging-stick, shaped to a spatulate point by shaving and charring, and weighted with a perforated stone which was jammed down on to the mid-shaft.

18. H. J. and J. Deacon, 1972; J. Rudner, pp. 441–663.
19. J. E. Parkington and C. Pöggenpoel, p. 6; P. L. Carter, 1969, pp. 1–11.
20. L. Smits, pp. 60–7; P. Vinicombe, 1965, pp. 578–81.
21. H. B. Thom.
22. C. P. Thunberg, p. 31.

These implements have been described by a number of travellers,[23] and fragments have been recovered from De Hangen and Diepkloof in the western Cape[24] and from Scotts Cave in the southern Cape.[25] There are many rock paintings depicting women with weighted digging-sticks (see Fig. 26.1) who often seem to be carrying leather bags, no doubt to transport the foodstuffs home. Leatherwork is fairly commonly found in the dry environments of the rock shelters and caves of the Cape, but it is usually not clear whether bags of karosses or leather aprons are involved. Two sorts of string bags or nets are known: the first type, found at Melkhoutboom and Windhoek Farm Cave,[26] is fine-meshed and may have been used to carry roots and tubers (mesh size about 10 millimetres); the second is a larger mesh, known only from a fragment at the Diepkloof Cave in the western Cape[27] and an illustration in Paterson's Narrative.[28] Judging from this excellent drawing, this type may have been used to carry ostrich eggshell water-bottles. All the archaeological specimens are made from twine manufactured from the stem fibres of the rush *Cyperus textilis*, so named by Thunberg in the eighteenth century because of its use for this purpose. Perforated or bored stones are among the commonest surface finds throughout southern Africa.

Almost all commentators on San hunting refer to the bow and poisoned arrows as being the principal weapon. Barrow visited parts of the present eastern Cape in 1797 and wrote:

> The bow was a plain piece of wood from the guerrie bosch, apparently a species of *Rhus* ... the string, 3 feet long, was composed of the fibres of the dorsal muscles of the springbok twisted into a cord. The stem of an aloe furnished the quiver. The arrow consisted of a reed in one extremity of which was inserted a piece of highly polished solid bone from the leg of an ostrich, round and about five inches in length ... The whole length of the arrow was barely two feet ... the poison taken from the heads of snakes, mixed with the juices of certain bulbous-rooted plants is what they mostly depend upon.[29]

Though complete implements are rarely met in excavations, there are examples of all components of this equipment from caves in the western and eastern Cape. Possible bow fragments, reed mainshafts, notched reed lengths, polished bone points and linkshafts, knotted sinew and painted aloe

---

23. A. Sparrman, p. 219; G. Thompson, Vol. I, p. 57; cf. J. de Greverboek (who gives the length as 3 feet); Schapera 1933.

24. J. E. Parkington and C. Pöggenpoel, J. E. Parkington, unpublished PhD.

25. H. J. and J. Deacon, 1963.

26. H. J. Deacon, 1969; C. S. Grobbelaar and A. J. H. Goodwin, pp. 95–101.

27. J. E. Parkington, unpublished PhD.

28. W. Paterson.

29. J. Barrow.

FIG. 26.1 *Rock painting: women with digging-sticks weighted with perforated stones. It was the women's task to collect roots and corms as well as other reliable foods, on their daily excursions into the veld (scale 2/3; colour faded red)*

fragments represent the discarded or lost remnants of San hunting equipment. Small lunate or segment-shaped stone artefacts may indicate a second type of missile point, set into vegetable mastic as the cutting edge of arrows as demonstrated in Cape Town by bushmen captives in the 1920s.[30] Bows, arrows and quivers are very commonly depicted in rock art throughout southern Africa (see Fig. 26.2).

Many animals, however, were not shot with the bow but caught in snares made of vegetable twine and set out in the veld. Paterson saw 'several snares laid for the wild beasts'[31] whilst travelling near the Orange river in 1779 and almost certainly much of the two-stranded twine recovered

30. A. J. H. Goodwin, p. 195.
31. W. Paterson, p. 114.

FIG. 26.2 *A group of men with bows, arrows and quivers. It was the men's job to hunt and snare animals to complement the largely vegetable contribution of the women*

from sites such as De Hangen,[32] Scotts Cave[33] and Melkhoutboom[34] represents discarded lengths which once formed rope snares. This technique was presumably most effective against small territorial herbivores such as steenbok, which tend to follow well-worn tracks and could be guided by brush fences into the snares set for them. Two curious forked wooden objects from Windhoek Farm Cave[35] and Scotts Cave[36] have been interpreted as triggers used in snares.

Other hunting techniques have been mentioned in historical accounts, but have not yet been supported by archaeological evidence. For example, a number of travellers in the eighteenth century described large pits dug close to river-banks with pointed stakes set upright within them. These were usually interpreted as designed to trap larger game such as elephant, rhino, hippo and buffalo, and have a wide geographical distribution extending south from the Orange river and east as far as the Gamtoos.

32. J. E. Parkington and C. Pöggenpoel.
33. H. J. and J. Deacon, 1963.
34. H. J. Deacon, 1969.
35. C. S. Grobbelaar and A. J. H. Goodwin.
36. H. J. and J. Deacon, 1963.

Whilst visiting the colonial frontier near Graaff Reinet, Barrow described another hunting technique whereby San hunters built 'drives of piles of stones with gaps in places or lines of sticks with ostrich feathers tied on top' into which they drove the more gregarious game species of the inland plateau.[37]

Obviously a number of fishing techniques were used by hunter-gatherers and most of them are documented archaeologically. Perhaps the most spectacular are the funnel-shaped reed-basket traps of the lower Orange river described by both Lichtenstein and Barrow and ascribed by them to 'bosjesmans', almost certainly San.[38] These traps were placed in the streams and were described as having been made from 'osiers, twigs of trees, and reeds' in a pointed or funnel-shaped design, no doubt similar to that still used in the Kafue and Limpopo rivers.[39] Though no traces of these have been excavated, a number of rock paintings from Lesotho and east Griqualand undoubtedly depict sets of these traps connected by reed or wooden fences and catching large numbers of freshwater fish, notably the yellowfish, *Barbus*.[40] Freshwater fish bones have been found at sites as far apart as the western Cape and Lesotho, but the techniques used are not always obvious. Carter has tentatively described a number of V-shaped slender bone hooks as fish-hooks, but admits that other interpretations are possible.[41] In the fishing scenes from Tsoelike in Lesotho, the fishermen appear to be using long, possibly barbed spears and to be standing in boats (see Fig. 26.3). Perhaps for this reason Vinnicombe felt that the scenes were of a late date; but their dating remains an enigma. No form of boat is documented by excavation, but this is perhaps unlikely anyway.

In the lower Orange river, at the same location as the basket traps, Lichtenstein reports that 'if they [bosjesmans] expect a swelling of the stream, while the water is still low they make upon the strand a large cistern as it were enclosed by a wall of stones which serves as a reservoir, where, if fortune be favourable, a quantity of fish are deposited at the subsiding of the water'.[42] This form of rock fish-trap designed to use the rise and fall of the river parallels the tidal fish-traps reported from around the cost of southern Africa from St Helena Bay to Algoa Bay.[43] Since many coastal examples are still in working order (and some still in use) it seems reasonable to suppose that coastal stone age populations used them until very recently. The large number of inshore fishes usually found in sites close

37. J. Barrow, Vol I, p. 284.
38. H. Lichtenstein, Vol. II, p. 44; J. Barrow.
39. L. Smits.
40. ibid.; P. Vinicombe, 1960, pp. 15–19; 1965.
41. P. L. Carter, 1969; P. L. Carter, personal communication.
42. H. Lichtenstein.
43. A. J. H. Goodwin.

FIG. 26.3 *Fishing scene from Tsoelike, Lesotho. The hunter-gatherers of southern Africa were also fishermen, catching both marine and freshwater species using a number of different techniques, this one apparently involving small boats or rafts*

to fish-traps suggest they were highly effective where there was sufficient tidal rise to cover the walls adequately.

Goodwin reported the discovery of a small bone fish gorge attached to a line of in the wall of one rock fish-trap, suggesting that other fishing techniques may have been used in the immediate prehistoric past. Small slivers of bone from two to six centimetres long and ground to a point at both ends have in fact been found in very large numbers at both Elands Bay Cave[44] and Nelson Bay Cave.[45] But in both cases the artefacts were located in layers 7000–10 000 years old and became extremely rare, though not absent, in more recent layers. They may have been used as baited fish-gorges, but it is worth noting that the Ona of Tierra del Fuego made similar artefacts of wood in the last century to catch cormorants, which are very common at both the cave sites referred to above.

44. J. E. Parkington, unpublished PhD.
45. R. G. Klein, unpublished.

There are no undoubted fish-hooks at coastal sites in southern Africa, and no convincing harpoon heads, though wooden versions of the latter are mentioned by Barrow from the lower Orange river.[46] His actual words are: 'we found several harpoons of wood, some pointed with bone, and fixed to ropes made apparently of some sort of grass'. These appear to have been wooden-shafted and bone-pointed but not necessarily barbed. Two barbed bone points have been found in the dunes of the Agulhas area, but the contexts are not published, though one was found to have penetrated the lumbar vertebra of an adult female skeleton of 'Khoisan' affinities.[47] Perforated ceramic and stone objects from sites along the southern Cape coast have been described as net sinkers which if accurate would document net fishing by coastal San. In view of the abundance of fibrous twine and the undoubted existence of netting at inland sites, this is perhaps not surprising.

The techniques used to catch or collect other coastal resources are not well documented. Spatulate bone artefacts are found at some sites and may have been the implements used to detach limpets from their rocky perches, but there is no compelling evidence. Nor can it be demonstrated how lobsters, sea-birds or seals were caught, though there is one historical record of the shooting of seals with the bow[48] and another of Khoi Khoi clubbing seals to death at an isolated rocky point near Saldanha Bay.[49] Perhaps the highly fragmented nature of the skull parts found at Elands Bay Cave and other sites reflects the latter practice.

Although the San were generally not given to domestication and cultivation, there seems to be some evidence that at least by the seventeenth century they kept dogs, apparently for hunting. Dapper, who never visited the Cape but was well informed by those who had, reported in 1668 that the Sonqua 'keep many hunting dogs trained to hunt the rock rabbits which are their principal food'.[50] There certainly are quantities of dassie or rock rabbit bones in excavated rock shelters of the western Cape, and there is some indication[51] that there may be domestic dog bones amongst the larger faunal assemblages.

In addition to foods actively hunted, there seems little doubt that scavenging played a useful part in San subsistence. In particular, dead fish or stranded whales are reported to have been eaten by those living along the coast. Another, obviously important, technique is the making of the variety of containers used to carry water. Ostrich eggshell water-bottles, sometimes decorated with incisions, are described in the historical accounts and have been recovered, albeit usually fragmented, from numerous sites.

46. J. Barrow, p. 300.
47. J. E. Parkington, unpublished PhD.
48. W. Paterson.
49. H. B. Thom.
50. I. Schapera, 1933.
51. K. Scott, personal communication.

Whole examples, and even nests of several bottles which have obviously been buried at some strategic place, are known, but have usually been recovered by amateurs and consequently are not fully recorded. Animal bladders were also used to carry water but ceramic vessels are never described for the purpose. Pottery will be discussed in some detail in the section on Khoi herdsmen.

All in all, San technology seems to have included a wide range of hunting and gathering techniques, using implements made from materials such as stone, bone, wood, fibre, reed, leather, shell, ivory, sinew and leaf[52] and often including composite tools in which raw materials were combined. Stone seems to have formed only the tip or cutting or scraping edge of more complex tools, and stone artefacts were clearly as often as not mounted in mastic on a wooden or bone handle.[53] For these artefacts, fine-grained homogeneous rocks such as chalcedony, agate, silcrete or indurated shale were preferred, whilst the more brittle quartz was also used and quartzite pebbles and boulders were turned into upper and lower grind-stones for grinding pigments or foodstuffs. It is interesting that few of the seventeenth- and eighteenth-century travellers specifically mention or describe the manufacture of stone artefacts, perhaps indicating the gradual replacement of at least some stone artefacts by bone, wooden or metal versions. The implications of this picture of wide raw material usage are obvious for those who wish to classify and distinguish between groups on the basis of stone assemblage comparisons alone.

Archaeological research is increasingly directed as the conditions which governed the settlement of San groups. The result is that it is becoming possible to describe the patterns of need of hunter-gatherers in ecological terms which were not familiar to early travellers. Nevertheless, historical records and information from rock paintings can obviously add to the evidence now emerging from large-scale excavation and detailed analyses of animal bones and plant remains.

Compared with the hunter-gatherers of the Kalahari and farther afield, it is likely that San groups would have been small and highly mobile units. In this connection it is not surprising to note that the early expeditions sent out by Van Riebeeck came across very large numbers of unoccupied windbreaks, and that Paterson recorded the same phenomenon a hundred years later near the mouth of the Orange river.[54] These shelters were brush screens intended to protect the occupants from the elements, and were obviously abandoned after use, probably for only a few days. Nor is it surprising that by and large San groups rarely numbered more than twenty individuals, and in most cases were either small work-parties of under ten men or women, or larger groups at a camp site with both

52. J. E. Parkington and C. Pöggenpoel.
53. H. J. Deacon, 1966, pp. 87–90; H. J. Deacon, 1969.
54. H. B. Thom; W. Paterson, p. 117.

FIG. 26.4 *Rock painting showing a group of hunters in their cave, surrounded by a range of digging sticks, bags, quivers and bows. The perforated stone digging-stick weights are clearly visible*

sexes and children represented. The only exceptions to this are, for example, the groups of 150 and 500 people described by Barrow and a camp of fifty huts reported by Thunberg, both in the late eighteenth century when hunters were gathering in unusually large numbers to defend themselves against European raiding commandos.[55] The size of groups represented in rock paintings seems to confirm that the most frequent social unit was under twenty people, though larger groupings are found (see Figure 26.4).

Many authorities reported that the 'boschiesmen' occupied caves and rock shelters where they were available, and these sites figure prominently in the archaeological literature. At the Great Elephant shelter in the Erongo mountains in Namibia, three or perhaps four windbreaks, similar to those described in the veld by early travellers, have been mapped and described.[56] From many sites in the Cape there is evidence that San groups brought in bundles of grasses as bedding, and that this was laid around the back and side walls of the caves to form a spongy mattress. In at least two cases a shallow hollow was scraped out of bedrock or previously accumulated deposits to hold the grass.[57] At coastal sites estuarine grasses, especially *Zostera*, were used as bedding, and these sites show that sleeping, cooking, fire-making and refuse areas were clearly separated.

There is good evidence, in the form of a high correlation between women and digging-sticks and between men and bows in rock art, that there was a fairly strict division of labour amongst the San groups. This is con-

55. J. Barrow, pp. 275, 307; C. P. Thunberg, p. 174.
56. J. D. Clark and J. Walton, pp. 1–16.
57. J. E. Parkington and C. Pöggenpoel.

firmed repeatedly in historical literature, for example by Thompson who in the 1820s 'saw numbers of Bushwomen on the plains digging up roots', and by Dopper who described a species of bulb which 'is their daily provender which the women go every day to dig from the rivers'.[58] No doubt men also collected vegetable foods whilst on hunting expeditions, but the crucial role of the women in guaranteeing a daily food supply needs to be underlined.

There is good reason to suppose that the supply of most of the food-stuffs collected or hunted by San, as well as the water they needed, would have been subject to seasonal fluctuations. For example, the winter rainfall of the south-western Cape is a highly seasonal phenomenon in which 70 to 80 per cent of the annual rainfall falls in the months of May to October, a period which coincides with that of the lowest monthly temperatures and localized frosts. There are important consequences of this situation, not least of fairly rigid vegetation cycle of winter growth, spring flowering, summer fruiting and perennation or dormancy of underground storage organs through a hot, dry summer. More obvious, perhaps, is the marked variation between the dry summer and the wet winter in the amounts of surface water and pasturage. In addition to seasonal fluctuation of resources, there is the fact that not all resources can be found everywhere. Again using the western Cape as an example, many plants and animals are unevenly distributed through geographical microzones such as the coastal fringe, the coastal forelands, the mountain belt, the inter-montane river valleys and the inland arid basin. San groups occupying this or any other region of southern Africa must obviously have adopted settlement patterns designed to take into account local or temporary abundances and to ensure a varied and sufficient food supply throughout the year. There is some evidence in the historical accounts, in the results of archaeological excavations and in the body of rock art data, to illustrate some of these patterns.

Given the importance of corms in the San diet, their uneven availability must have had considerable influence in determining settlement patterns. The fluctuations are hinted at in some historical accounts, and arise from the vegetation cycle described above. Since corms are in fact stores of food maintained by the plants through the summer to support the new season's growth and flowering the following winter and spring, they are logically bound to vary in size, visibility and palatability throughout the cycle. More specifically, when the food store is used up by the growth of green parts and flowers, the corms are shrivelled and unlikely to make a significant contribution to the food supply. That there was such a dearth in the supply of corms is suggested by Lichtenstein, who wrote of 'bonjesmen' that: 'he will live for months together upon a few little bulbs which at certain times of the year are to be found in the low part of the

58. G. Thompson, Vol. I, p. 58; I. Schapera, 1933, p. 55.

country'.[59] Speaking of a particular 'bulb', he said: 'it is most in order to be eaten when the flower is just gone off'.[60] Further corroboration of this interpretation is provided by the unique system of time reckoning amongst the Cape populations (ascribed to 'Hottentots' but perhaps used by both Khoi Khoi and San) recorded by Sparrman, Barrow and Thunberg in the late eighteenth century.[61] In the words of Barrow, 'the season of the year is indicated by being so many moons before or after the uyntjes tyd [literally "onion time"] or the time that the roots of the *Iris edulis* are in season; a time particularly noticed by him as these bulbs once constituted a considerable part of his vegetable food'. These comments, when read in conjunction with the results of modern observations on corm growth and development, suggest that at least in the Cape Folded Belt of mountains there were important fluctuations in basic foodstuffs.

In other parts of southern Africa, where rainfall is low and evenly distributed throughout the year, or where the maximum rainfall coincides with summer high temperatures, there may have been quite different but equally important supply peaks and troughs. The movement of herds such as eland, hartebeest and springbok in and out of the karroo regions or between summer and winter rainfall pastures would undoubtedly have influenced the distribution of the San population. Evidence exists of various patterns intended to meet these changes in food supplies. They include seasonal mobility, restrictions in the use of certain foods to particular times, alterations in the size of the social unit, the storage of foodstuffs and the establishment of a wide-ranging network of kinship ties as a safeguard against failures in local supplies.

The seasonal occupancy of sites has been postulated in both Lesotho[62] and the south-western Cape[63] on the basis of the potential of the sites to meet the required needs and the analysis of plant remains and animal bones. It seems likely that in the western Cape groups of San turned to collectible coastal foods such as shellfish at times of minimal supplies of corm and fruit, that is, during winter and early spring. Although the evidence is far from complete, analysis of the ages at death of the remains of seals and dassies is suggestive. Further documentation of this seasonal movement is provided by the results of Shackleton's work on the shells from the Nelson Bay Cave in the extreme southern Cape.[64] Measurement of the oxygen isotope ratios in midden shells and comparison with modern ocean surface temperature fluctuations persuaded Dr Shackleton that the middens analysed accumulated only during the winter. There is much work to be done to document more precisely the movements employed by the

59. H. Lichtenstein, p. 193.
60. ibid., p. 45.
61. A. Sparrman, p. 104; A. Barrow, p. 159; C. P. Thunberg, p. 197.
62. P. L. Carter, 1970, pp. 55–8.
63. J. E. Parkington, 1972, pp. 223–43.
64. N. J. Shackleton, pp. 133–41.

San to even out the year's resources, but some comments in Lichtenstein, who recognized the importance of ecology, illustrate the point. He described how 'even the leanest, most wretched figures imaginable' could become quite different beings simply by 'changing their quarters'.[65]

Both the Kung and the G/wi of the Kalahari restrict their use of certain resources to those times of the year when less uniformly available alternative cannot be found. As may be expected, the value of a resource is intimately related to the number of alternatives available, and also to its palatability, nutritional value and ease of collection. It seems likely that San groups farther south would have used their resources in a similar way, restricting the sets of foods gathered so that an even supply was maintained. Few instances of this are, as yet, documented in the archaeological record, but one example may be found in the differences in the supply of small game such as dassies and tortoises in coastal and inland sites in the western Cape. At inland sites such as De Hangen, tortoises and dassies are the most common animals represented, yet at the coastal site of Elands Bay Cave both are extremely uncommon by comparison.[66] This may in part reflect seasonal variation in availability, especially in the case of the hibernating tortoise, but probably also results from the presence at the coast of a range of small-animal alternative foods such as fish, crayfish and sea-birds. Other examples among plant foods remain so far undetected, though they may be reflected in the different composition of the plant remains at inland sites such as De Hangen and Diepkloof in the western Cape.[67]

It has been shown repeatedly[68] that hunter-gatherer groups tend to move in units of variable size in order to increase the efficiency of their use of resources: fission into small family groups when resources are spread thinly, and fusion into larger gatherings when the type of subsistence requires the use of considerable manpower, or when resources are highly concentrated and thus capable of supporting large gatherings. This pattern also serves to maintain the kinship web between neighbouring groups who use the occasional large gathering to pass on news, exchange items, technological innovations and perhaps women, through whom the web of kinship obligations is traced. In times of catastrophes, these obligations are a lifeline allowing one group to survive by temporarily using another's resources. Moreover, personal difficulties can be solved by one or other party leaving a group and either temporarily or permanently joining another in which there are relatives. Though the recognition of these features remains a goal of archaeological research, the most explicit information about them, at present, comes from historical records and, perhaps questionably, from rock art.

65. H. Lichtenstein, p. 45.
66. J. E. Parkington, 1972.
67. J. E. Parkington, unpublished PhD.
68. R. B. Lee and I. Devore.

FIG. 26.5 *Rock painting: a large group of figures, most of them recognizable as male, depicted in what might be a dancing scene. Scenes such as these involve large numbers and perhaps relate to non-economic activities, suggest that small groups occasionally came together perhaps seasonally, to engage in exchange and other ceremonial activities*

Lichtenstein, perhaps the most acute observer of San social organization among the early travellers, noted that 'families alone form close associations in single small hordes ... the hardships that attend on satisfying the most urgent necessities of life preclude the possibility of forming larger societies: these families even are sometimes obliged to separate since the same spot will not afford sustenance for all'.[69] Still referring to a hunter-gatherer group, he said:

> 'a horde commonly consists of the different members of one family only, and no one has any power or distinction above the rest ... everyone leaves his horde, and attaches himself to another entirely at his own pleasure ... very little intercourse exists between the separate hordes; they seldom unite unless in some extraordinary undertaking, for which the combined strengths of a great many is required. For the most part the hordes keep at a distance from each other, since the smaller the number, the easier is a supply of food procured.'[70]

It is remarkable that these comments on group size, group composition, the fission and fusion of groups, territorial arrangements and the egalitarian social system are virtually identical to those of trained anthropologists made 200 years later amongst obviously related groups in the Kalahari.[71]

One study of the size of groups depicted in the rock art of the western Cape resulted in a mean group size of about fourteen persons, a figure very similar to that recorded in the diaries of the late eighteenth-century commandos.[72] This probably reflects the 'horde' of Lichtenstein, which might have varied between ten and thirty persons, whilst the very low numbers occasionally encountered were apparently work-groups of either men or women about their daily tasks. However, there are examples of rock paintings which illustrate up to thirty or forty men in a single scene, which

69. H. Lichtenstein, p. 193.
70. ibid., pp. 48–9.
71. E. M. Thomas.
72. T. M. O'C. Maggs, pp. 49–53.

FIG. 26.6 *Occasionally when groups met, the result was marked by conflict rather than co-operation. Here is a conflict scene between two evenly matched groups, apparently males*

must mean a gathering of around a hundred persons or more (see Fig. 26.5). It is very tempting to interpret such occasional paintings as a reflection of the periodic fusion of groups referred to above. It would be particularly interesting if large painted groups tended to be engaged in non-economic activities such as dancing and to be located in areas suspected of high seasonal food potential. Unfortunately, this information is not yet available, and the possibility remains unsubstantiated. The mountain belt of the western Cape is one such area, where the rich collectible resources such as honey, caterpillars, fruits, corms and tortoises may have allowed groups to camp near to one another during the summer months in order to maintain old ties and exchange material gifts. A small parcel of mussel-shells wrapped in leaf at the cave De Hangen seems to have been a valued exchange item destined to be transported farther inland.[73] Certainly the winter potential of the Karroo basin and strandveld complement the summer potential of the mountain belt which divides them. Whether such systems can be recognized depends upon the success of plant and animal studies now in progress.

The storage of foodstuffs from times of plenty to times of scarcity is not characteristic of recent Kalahari groups, who seem to have regarded the environment as a natural larder which always provided some combination

73. J. E. Parkington and C. Pöggenpoel.

of foods and which required little supplementing. It seems that, by carefully planning an annual beat around the available resources and conserving the more common foods for difficult times, the need to store food was minimized. Food was usually collected and consumed the same day, or over a few days in the case of unusual bounties such as large game. The situation farther south seems to have been similar, since evidence of storage pits is rare in the archaeological record and the early travellers never describe storage as an important aspect of San subsistence. Kolb, who had access to the information of many observers of Khoi Khoi and San life at the end of the seventeenth century, noted that 'though the fields abound with wholesome and very nourishing fruits and roots which they might lay up in plenty against a rainy day, yet it is the custom of the women to ... gather only such a quantity ... as will serve their families for the day'.[74] Other early authorities mention the storing of dried grasshoppers, the pounded roots of the canna plant (a species of *Salsola*) and dried apricots, items which were probably not as economically important as the roots, tubers and corms. In the southern Cape there is evidence, as yet unpublished, of large numbers of storage pits associated with San cave sites.[75] As yet unconfirmed reports suggest that the seeds recovered from these pits may have been collected for their oil content rather than as food.

From the evidence that has been presented, it seems clear that San groups were highly organized small mobile groups with an intimate knowledge of the resources available to them and how these resources varied through time and space. The subsistence base, the range of hunting, fishing and gathering techniques and the settlement patterns employed are becoming increasingly better documented, using data from a variety of sources. As Lee has pointed out, the impression that hunter-gatherers subsisted on the brink of disaster has been shown to be generally far from the truth. An old woman (it is not known whether she was Khoi Khoi or San) was questioned by Barrow in the Bokkeveld in 1798, of which he said:

> on being asked if her memory could carry her back to the time when the Christians first came among them, she replied, with a shake of her head, that she had very strong reasons to remember it, for that before she had ever heard of the Christians, she knew not the want of a bellyful, whereas it was now a difficult matter to get a mouthful.[76]

## Khoi Khoi pastoralists

The picture of hunting and gathering within defined environmental contexts is, of course, seriously incomplete when dealing with the

74. I. Schapera, 1933, p. 205.
75. H. J. Deacon, personal communication.
76. J. Barrow, pp. 398–9.

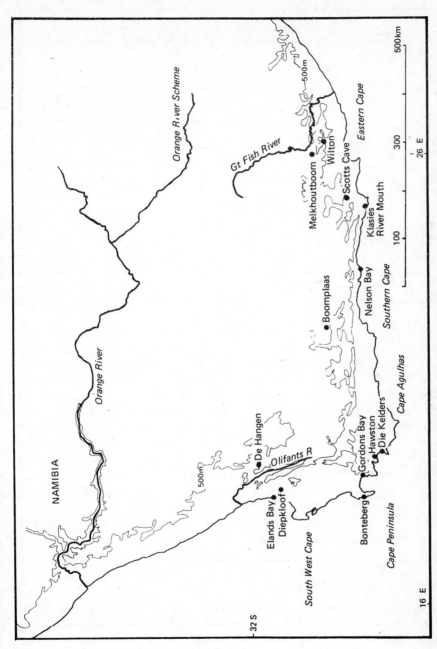

FIG. 26.7 *A map of southern Africa showing the distribution of late stone age sites, most of them revealing potsherds or domestic stock in the first centuries of our era*

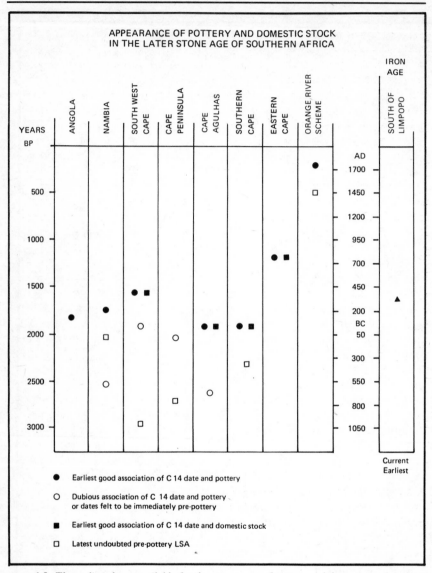

APPEARANCE OF POTTERY AND DOMESTIC STOCK
IN THE LATER STONE AGE OF SOUTHERN AFRICA

● Earliest good association of C 14 date and pottery

○ Dubious association of C 14 date and pottery
   or dates felt to be immediately pre-pottery

■ Earliest good association of C 14 date and domestic stock

□ Latest undoubted pre-pottery LSA

FIG. 26.8 *The earliest dates available for the appearance of pottery and domestic stock in later stone age contexts in southern Africa*

immediate precolonial period, say, since −2000. At every site marked on Fig. 26.7, with the exception of Bonteberg and Gordons Bay (where they have not been actively sought), there are the remains of domestic stock in a later stone age context. Since there are no indigenous sheep, goats or cattle, and since these assemblages predate contact with European or Negro herdsmen, it must be assumed that this records the appearance of

660

herded stock from another source. The earliest radio-carbon dates associated with domestic animals and the potsherds at sites from Angola to the eastern Cape are summarized in Figure 26.8. Also included is the rather sparse information on these items from inland areas and, for reference, the earliest dates presently available for the penetration of iron-using, Bantu-speaking mixed farmers into southern Africa. Although the apparent pattern may change with further research, it seems worthwhile risking some interpretations in terms of the origin and speech of Khoi Khoi herdsmen (see Fig. 26.9).

The most obvious point is that potsherds appear for the first time in sites from Angola to the southern Cape during the period −2000 to −1600. As more shards are found, dating will become more accurate, and it may be that radio-carbon dating will ultimately point to the same dates for the appearance of patterns throughout the whole region. Only four dates before −2000 have been reported, and there are reasons for supposing that all of these are either seriously contaminated[77] or pre-pottery.[78]

A second and no less important observation is that wherever a search from traces of domestic animals has been specifically made, they appear as early in the archaeological record as potsherds. This may not be true in *every site*, but when dates from neighbouring sites are combined to form local sequences, then they appear concurrently. Although this approach may seem unjustified, it can be defended as ironing out problems raised simply by sampling phenomena. The implication is that potsherds and domestic stock diffused quickly, at the same time and through the same area. The word 'diffused' seems inescapable since, whereas pottery could be independently invented, domestic animals obviously could not. Moreover, the pottery shows no signs of being crude or early inefficient attempts at a technological innovation.

A point of considerable though as yet not over-riding importance is that the association of dates linking early domestic animals and pottery relates to the coastal plain and adjacent mountain chains along the Atlantic and western Indian Ocean coasts. Whilst this may in part arise from the understandable preoccupation of archaeologists with the depositional sequences of caves in the sandstone of the Cape Folded Belt, there is some reason to suppose that the absence of early dates east of the Gamtoos river and north of the Folded Belt is significant.[79] In any case, the association coincides well with the historically documented pastoralists known collectively as Khoi Khoi.[80]

Although research continues into the spread of iron and domestic

77. C. G. Sampson.
78. F. R. Schweitzer, and K. Scott; T. M. O'C Maggs, personal communication; Wadley, personal communication.
79. C. G. Sampson; R. M. Derricourt, 1973a, pp. 280–4; P. L. Carter, 1969; P. L. Carter and J. C. Vogel.
80. L. F. Maingard, pp. 487–504; R. H. Elphick.

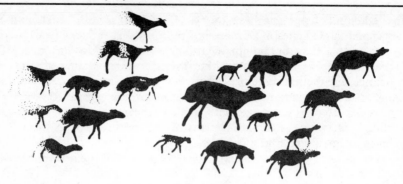

FIG. 26.9 *A herd of bat-tailed sheep, the sort of sheep herded by the Khoi pastoralists and observed by the early colonists at the Cape*

animals into southern Africa along an easterly route, present evidence suggests the fourth or fifth century of our era for their introduction south of the Limpopo.[81] Thus the set of late stone age dates associated with both pottery and domestic stock predates that of the iron age farther north and east by fully two to three hundred years, an interval surely not accountable to radio-carbon dating.

The implication of this contextual, distributional and chronological pattern seems to be that herding peoples with pottery spread rapidly into the southern Cape along a westerly coastal route around −2000. No doubt groups of hunters were integrated into the pastoralist societies and there must have been some important readjustments in demographic and economic patterns, though these remain largely undocumented. It seems inescapable that these intruders were the Khoi Khoi pastoralists.

It is of course of considerable interest to speculate on the origins, causes and circumstances of this intrusion, but with so little data such speculation must be very imprecise. Research in Zambia and Zimbabwe has tended to be rigidly divided into iron age and stone age, with the result that surface levels in cave, shelter or open sites containing pottery have often been written off as stone age with iron age contamination. The fact is that in these areas there may well have been populations of a technically stone age character but whose economy included the herding of some domestic stock, and who manufactured pottery recognizably different from local iron-using agriculturists. In Zimbabwe the so-called Bambata pottery is fairly generally recognized as distinct from iron age pottery and was often recovered with 'Wilton', that is late stone age, artefacts. Whether this reflects a pre-iron age spread of pastoralists or not remains contentious, but corroboration for the idea may be sought in the distribution of paintings of fat-tailed sheep from Zimbabwe generally believed to be of stone age associations. These were the sheep herded

81. M. Klapwijk, pp. 19–23; R. J. Mason, 1973, p. 324; P. B. Beaumont and J. C. Vogel.

662

by Khoi Khoi pastoralists at the Cape in the fifteenth, sixteenth and seventeenth centuries of our era.

Should the distribution of stone age sheep-herding peoples be extended through Zimbabwe and Zambia, the possibility arises of some origin in East Africa where cultural, linguistic and even biological antecedents have been postulated. The existence of herding peoples who make pottery with lugs, the survival of 'click languages' in the Hatsa and Sandawe and the claimed 'Hamitic' features of 'Hottentot' populations have all at one time or another been quoted as evidence of a north-eastern origin for the herding, non-iron-using populations of southern Africa. Whilst these connections may be dubious or in some cases rejected, the continuity of traits such as ceramics, sheep-herding, sheep and cattle types, non-iron technology, ground stone artefacts and possibly language, if proven, would argue strongly for an ultimate east African origin for Khoi Khoi pastoralists. This in turn would suggest that the disruptions which caused the movements of Bantu-speakers in a predominantly eastern wave southwards, may also have prompted a western move, perhaps slightly earlier or simply faster, of herding non-agriculturalist peoples towards the Cape. The absence of 'Hottentot' or 'Cape Coastal' pottery from the Transvaal, Swaziland, Natal, the Orange Free State or the Transkei may merely reflect the facts that agriculture is a more feasible pursuit in these better-watered summer rainfall areas and that highly mobile herding peoples without crops were more capable of spreading through the dry landscapes of Namibia and the northern Cape and thence to the pastures of the western and southern Cape. It is conceivable that sheep were brought along the western route but that cattle were obtained by Khoi Khoi pastoralists from the east, from Bantu-speaking populations by then resident in the Transkei region. Support for this may come from the abundance of presumed later stone age paintings of fat-tailed sheep in the western Cape but the absence of similar paintings of cattle, although cattle were painted in the areas now settled by Bantu-speakers. Furthermore the presence of cattle-bones as early as sheep-bones in later stone age excavations in the southern Cape is not yet firmly documented.

Thus, there are grounds for speculating that sheep-herding peoples, related to stone-using hunters and distinct physically from Bantu-speakers, having received stock and pottery from neighbours in east Africa, migrated west and then south in search of pasture, to arrive finally at the Cape soon after −2000. Such populations may have incorporated, fought with or simply learned to live with locally existing hunters and subsequently met with and interacted with Bantu-speakers in what is today the Transkei. The sparse distribution of pottery, ground stone artefacts and animal bones along the route just described may mean nothing more than that they were highly mobile, leaving debris so thinly dispersed as to be archaeologically practically invisible.

Unfortunately, the number of undoubted herdsmen sites excavated remains very small, unless some of the open shell middens, surface scatters of stone artefacts or rock-shelter occupations turn out to be the residues of herdsmen the ecology of Khoi Khoi groups remains a subject for future archaeological research. For information on diet, technology and organization it is necessary to rely heavily upon the accounts of early European settlers and travellers. For example, referring to the Cape Khoi Khoi, Willem Ten Rhyne, a botanist and physician in the service of the Dutch East Indian Company, wrote the following whilst on a short visit to the Cape in 1673:

> Their diet is a vegetable one . . . from marshes and mounds they root up sword-lilies; with the leaves of this plant they roof their huts, the bulbs they use for bread . . . The only interruption to this diet is in the event of a marriage or a birth when they slaughter an ox or at least a sheep to provide a feast for their friends, unless some wild animal should happen to be taken. They drink the milk of cows and sheep.[82]

There are other such references which suggest that Khoi Khoi were loath to kill their stock except on special occasions and which illustrate the milk and vegetable basis of their diet. To a considerable extent it was the same as that of the San, being based on the gathering of rootstocks supplemented by occasional meat, either domestic or wild, but with the addition of regular milk supplies. This latter may well explain the fact that hunters with no access to milk and its nutritional value were consistently described by early travellers as smaller than herders.[83]

Because the Khoi Khoi depended so much upon collected food staples and supplemented these with hunted meat, it is not surprising to find a technology very similar to that of the San although the relative dependence upon particular techniques may be expected to have varied with the differences in their economy. Thus, mention of the bow and arrow is more frequent in descriptions of San but there is no doubt that the Namaqua in the late seventeenth century and the Gonaqua in the late eighteenth century used bows, poisoned arrows and quivers.[84] However, it is significant that in both of these accounts 'assegays' were mentioned as of equal importance, whereas this is never the case in accounts of San. Le Vaillant recorded that the Gonaqua use 'gins and snares', which they placed in convenient spots to catch large animals,[85] and large pit traps near the Brak river in the southern Cape and elsewhere were ascribed to 'Hottentots', probably, Khoi Khoi pastoralists.[86] Similarly some early travellers specifically cite herding groups as using basket traps for fishing in the

82. I. Schapera, p. 129.
83. H. B. Thom, Vol. I, p. 305.
84. H. B. Thom, Vol. III, pp. 350–3; F. Le Vaillant, pp. 306–9.
85. F. Le Vaillant, p. 306.
86. C. P. Thunberg, p. 177.

Orange, digging sticks for rooting out corms and bulbs, bags for carrying foodstuffs, and wooden clubs for killing seals. All this technology was held in common with San hunter-gatherers.

Perhaps the three traits not necessarily shared with hunters are the building of more substantial huts from rushes, the manufacture of pottery and the knowledge of the shaping of metals. Since Khoi Khoi moved about pastures in fairly large numbers, they did not use caves and seem to have built domed huts with a sapling structure across which mats of rushes and perhaps skins were laid. These huts were usually arranged in a circular village plan and it is frequently stated that the domestic animals were kraaled overnight within the village circle. When the time came to move, the saplings and mats were simply packed on to the back of oxen and transported to the new site.[87] The situation as regards pottery and metal-working is not so straightforward. Several early writers mention the manufacture of 'earthenware, exceedingly brittle and ... almost all shaped alike',[88] but no accounts specifically ascribe them to San. In fact Ten Rhyne observed that only 'the richer among them make pots' though his meaning is obscure.[89] The Namaqua of the late seventeenth and the Gonaqua of the late eighteenth centuries both made pottery, and it is probable that the remarks of Kolb, Grevenbroek and Ten Rhyne refer to Cape Khoi Khoi in the late seventeenth century.[90] It is tempting to assume that the appearance of pottery in the rock shelters and caves of the Cape of the early centuries of our era marks the spread of pot-making pastoralists into the area. Perhaps the conical-necked pots with the characteristic internally reinforced lugs are the standard pattern referred to by Le Vaillant. This is one of the recurrent pot forms from coastal and near-coastal sites in the Cape[91] and in its shape and lugs might reflect the need for containers with handles to carry milk. Other uses, including the melting of grease, are mentioned in the early literature.[92]

There is no evidence that the Cape Khoi Khoi were habitual metalworkers before the arrival of European settlers, but the Namaqua were quite obviously able to work copper into beads and discs in the seventeenth century. When Van Meerhoff made the first contact with the Namaqua from the Cape colony in 1661, he mentioned 'copper discs ... chains of copper and iron beads',[93] but offers no comments on where or how they were made. In his review of the Cape Khoi Khoi, Elphick has persuasively argued that the Namaqua probably knew how to work copper and were

87. A. Sparrman, pp. 138–9.
88. F. Le Vaillant, p. 311.
89. I. Schapera, 1933.
90. P. Kolb, p. 251.
91. J. Rudner.
92. F. Le Vaillant, p. 311.
93. H. B. Thom, p. 353.

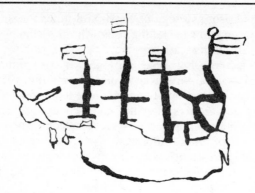

FIG. 26.10 *A galleon painted in the mountains of the Western Cape, presumably seen at Saldanha Bay or Table Bay where such ships put in regularly from the beginning of the seventeenth century of our era*

actively exploiting the copper ores of Namaqualand.[94] He adds that 'the same may be said, with only slightly less certainty, about the Cape Khoi'.[95]

The size of the Khoi Khoi pastoralist groups may well have varied seasonally, but there is no doubt that they were consistently larger than those of San hunter-gatherers. Paterson noted villages of nineteen, eighteen, eleven and six huts among the Namaqua,[96] and Le Vaillant described a Gonaqua 'horde' near the Great Fish river in which about 400 persons lived in '40 huts, built on a space about 600 feet square' which 'formed several crescents and were all connected together by small enclosures belonging to each'.[97] The Cochoqua, observed Dapper, 'dwelt mostly near and in the valleys of Saldanha Bay ... they are settled in fifteen or sixteen different villages about a quarter of an hour's distance from one another, and all told inhabit four hundred or four hundred and fifty huts ... each village consists of 30, 36, 40 or 50 huts, more or less, all placed in a circle a little distance apart'.[98] He estimated their joint stock at about 100 000 cattle and 200 000 sheep. Living as they did in fairly large communities, the Khoi Khoi obviously needed to keep on the move to maintain a supply of pasture for their animals and plant foods for themselves. Forty Khoi Khoi women would deplete a locality much more rapidly than five of their San counterparts. Le Vaillant recorded 'those indispensable emigrations to which they [Khoi Khoi] are compelled by the difference of the seasons',[99] and, with reference to the Namaqua,

94. R. H. Elphick.
95. R. H. Elphick, p. 115.
96. W. Paterson, pp. 57, 104, 122, 125.
97. F. Le Vaillant, p. 289.
98. I. Schapera, 1933, p. 23.
99. F. Le Vaillant, p. 328.

Governor van der Stel noted that 'according to the season of the year they go into the mountains and then back to the valleys and the shore, wherever they find the best pasture'.[100] In the early days of the settlement at Table Bay it was clear that the powerful 'Saldanhamen' used the pastures of the bay in the dry summer but moved north towards Saldanha Bay at other times. The Khoi Khoi, in short, were continually on the move and had at their disposal large tracts of grazing land, especially the coastal plain and intermontane valleys. Movement into the Karroo pastures, probably after the winter rain, is mentioned by Sparrman, who noted that 'the constant and unequivocal experience of the colonists with regard to this point agrees with the practice of the Hottentots'.[101]

Whilst in the Longkloof beyond Swellendam in 1775, Sparrman made a detailed observation which suggests that Khoi Khoi pastoralists regularly burnt the veld in order to stimulate the growth of animal grasses and geophytic plants. This form of veld management had the effect of maintaining a preclimax vegetal pattern in which useful elements were more prevalent than would normally be the case. His comment mentions

> fire, which is made use of by the colonists and the Hottentots for the purposes of clearing their fields of weeds. The ground is, it's true, by this means ... stripped quite bare; but merely in order that it may soon afterwards appear in a much more beautiful dress, being decked with various kinds of annual grasses, herbs and stately lilies which had before been choked up by shrubs and perennial plants ... thus forming with their young shoots and leaves a delightful and verdant pasturage for the use of game and cattle.[102]

This practice seems to have preceded colonial settlement, since many early visitors to the Cape noted the prevalence of large bush fires and Commander Van Riebeeck learnt to correlate fires on the distant mountains with the imminent arrival of Khoi Khoi groups.

Relations between San and Khoi Khoi were characterized by both conflict and co-operation. In the early years after the founding of the settlement at Table Bay, Van Riebeeck heard often of 'a certain people of very small stature, subsisting very meagrely, quite wild, without huts, cattle or anything in the world'.[103] These people, known then as Sonqua or Soaqua, lived in part by stealing stock from pastoralists and one group based on the Berg river were specifically known as Obiqua, which means 'robber men'. However, as the colonists penetrated farther inland and learnt more of the inter-relations between groups, there are occasional

100. G. Waterhouse.
101. A. Sparrman, p. 178.
102. ibid., p. 264.
103. H. B. Thom. p. 305.

FIG. 26.11 *Wagons, horses and trekkers observed moving into the inter-mountain pastures of the Western Cape in the very early eighteenth century of our era.*

references to a form of clientship whereby San hunters became attached to larger groups of Khoi Khoi. Van der Stel wrote: 'these Sonquas are just the same as the poor in Europe, each tribe of Hottentots having some of them and employing them to bring news of the approach of a strange tribe. They steal nothing from the kraals of their employers, but regularly from other kraals.'[104] Kolb, writing some twenty years later, confirmed that 'the Sonquas ... for a livelihood take up for the most part the military profession, and are mercenaries to the other Hottentots nations in their wars, serving barely for food from day to day'.[105] These Sonquas were San who had become integrated into Khoi Khoi society. Elphick argues convincingly that the expansion of Khoi Khoi groups into previously San territories would have involved a cycle of integration passing through warfare, clientship, intermarriage and assimilation.[106] It seems

104. G. Waterhouse, p. 122.
105. P. Kolb, p. 76.
106. R. H. Elphick.

668

FIG. 26.12 *A group of small stock raiders armed with bows and arrows defending their booty against larger figures carrying shields and spears. The distinction presumably reflects that between San hunters and Negro cattle owners, in the central and eastern districts of southern Africa*

likely that the introduction of herding into southern Africa would have involved both population movements *and* the assimilation of indigenous hunter-gatherers, as Elphick suggests, but the documentation of both processes remain a difficult archaeological exercise.

Relations between San, Khoi Khoi and other groups such as immigrant colonists or iron-using agriculturalists were probably as varied as those between San and Khoi Khoi. In the west both San and Khoi Khoi were driven from their lands and exterminated or assimilated into colonial society. A number of rock paintings from the western Cape depict the covered waggons, mounted horsemen and weapons of the trekking farmers (see Fig. 26.11). In the east the conflict between iron age farmers and hunters is largely undocumented but again rock paintings depict cattle thefts in which small bowmen steal from larger figures with spears and shields (see Fig. 26.12). The later stages of this interaction are recorded when literate colonists moved into Natal and on the slopes of the Drakensberg mountains. Khoi Khoi herdsmen, perhaps having more in common with Bantu-speaking mixed farmers than did the San, seem to have established more harmonious relations with, for example, Xhosa and Tswana groups. The description of the Gonaqua by Le Vaillant suggests a history of

669

close ties between them and nearby Xhosa, including considerable inter-marriage.[107] It is probably quite wrong to imagine clear economic, linguistic, physical or cultural distinctions between the various prehistoric peoples of southern Africa. Even more unlikely, perhaps, is the possibility that any such distinctions would have coincided exactly.[108]

107. F. Le Vaillant, p. 264.
108. R. M. Derricourt, 1973b, pp. 449–55.

# 27

# The beginnings of the iron age in southern Africa

## D. W. PHILLIPSON

## Introduction

The cultural episode in southern Africa[1] known to historians as the early iron age saw the introduction into the area of a way of life which contrasted sharply with those which had gone before, and one which established the character of subsequent historical developments throughout the region. Early in the first millennium of our era a substantial population movement brought to southern Africa a negroid farming people whose economy, settlement-type, perhaps even their physical appearance and their language, were in marked contrast with those of the earlier inhabitants, and who introduced knowledge of the arts of metallurgy and potting which were, in this area, previously unknown. It is with the nature, origin and development of these early iron age societies that this chapter is concerned.

Archaeologists now recognize a broad cultural similarity among the communities who introduced iron age material culture into southern Africa. The remains of these communities are attributed to a common southern African early iron age industrial complex[2] which is distinguished from other later, iron age industries, both by its chronological integrity and by the clear designation of its associated pottery to a common tradition. The distribution of this early iron age industrial complex extends far beyond the southern African region here discussed.[3] Numerous regional subdivisions within the complex may be recognized primarily on the basis of ceramic stylistic variation, and in many areas these groupings may be confirmed by further unrelated cultural traits. The early iron age ceramic tradition appears to have been introduced throughout its area of

1. The geographical area covered by this chapter (see map, Fig. 27.1) comprises Angola, the southern half of Zambia, Malawi, Mozambique, Botswana, Zimbabwe, Swaziland and parts of Namibia and South Africa. Readers should also note that dates have been given in uncorrected radio-carbon years.

2. R. C. Soper, 1971, pp. 5-37.

3. For the most recent statement, see ibid.

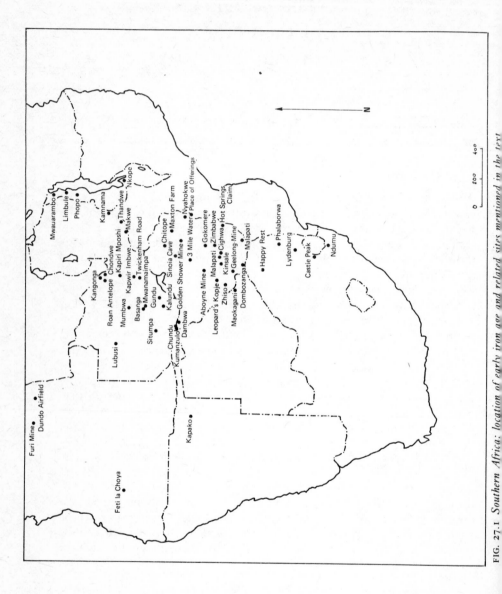

FIG. 27.1 *Southern Africa: location of early iron age and related sites mentioned in the text*

N

0        200      400

Mwaurambo
Limbule
Phopo
Kamnama
Thandwe
Nkope
Makwe
Maxton Farm
Nyahokwe
3 Mile Water Place of Offerings
Chitope
Sinoia Cave
Chondwe
Roan Antelope
Kapiri Mposhi
Kangonga
Kapwir Imbwe
Twickenham Road
Mumbwa
Mwanamaimpa
Basanga
Gundu
Kalundu
Golden Shower Mine
Situmpa
Dambwa
Chundu
Kumanzulo
Lubusi
Aboyne Mine
Leopard's Kopje
Zhiso
Malapati
Kinsale
Maokagani
Geelong Mine
Dombozanga
Gokomere
Zimbabwe
Cighwa Hot Springs
Claim
Malapati
Happy Rest
Phalaborwa
Lydenburg
Castle Peak
Ndumu
Furi Mine
Dundo Airfield
Kapako
Feti la Choya

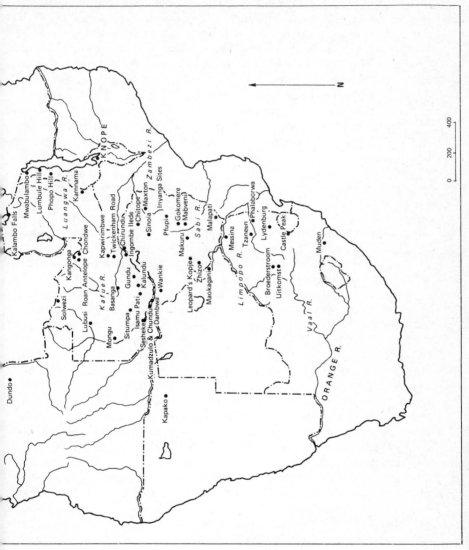

FIG. 27.2 *Southern Africa: sites*

distribution during the first few centuries of our era and to have survived in most areas until its displacement by distinct and more heterogeneous later iron age traditions, most frequently around the beginning of the present millennium. This terminal date varies in some areas, the early iron age being displaced by the eighth century in certain regions, while in others there may be demonstrated a considerable degree of typological continuity between the early iron age and the modern traditional ceramic industries.[4] For convenience, in the context of the present multi-volume work, I have taken it upon myself to discuss the early iron age cultures up to the time of their displacement or until the eleventh century of our era, whichever is the earlier in each region. I have thus left the later survivals of the early iron age cultures for discussion elsewhere in the context of their later iron age contemporaries.

It is in the milieu of the early iron age industrial complex that a number of cultural traits of paramount importance make their first appearance in southern Africa.[5] These traits are, primarily, food production, metallurgy, the making of pottery and settlement in semi-permanent villages with houses made of mud applied to a wattle or lathe framework (pole-and-*daga*). Subject to the variable suitability of the terrain and the distribution of the mineral deposits, these four traits appear to be ubiquitous on early iron age sites in this region. The material culture of the early iron age societies is in sudden and marked contrast with that of their 'late stone age' predecessors and contemporaries. Both in its different components and as a viable entity it can be shown to have been introduced into southern Africa in a fully fledged form; and it is clear that its antecedents are to be sought, not within this region, but far away to the north. For example, no southern African site has yielded pottery which can be regarded as in any way ancestral to the early iron age wares; metallurgy appears to have been introduced as a fully developed and efficient technology into an area where previously even a rudimentary knowledge of its techniques was totally lacking. The domestic animals and cultigens of the early iron age were of species not previously known in the southern part of the subcontinent. In view of this, and of its broadly contemporaneous appearance over an enormous area, it is hard to escape the conclusion that the early iron age was introduced into southern Africa by means of a substantial and rapid movement of population which brought with it a full-fledged but alien culture, the formative processes of which had taken place elsewhere.

It is thus clear that the early iron age represents but one sector of human activity in southern Africa during the first millennium of our era. In many areas 'late stone age' folk continued to practise their traditional way of life throughout this period; while some of their counterparts farther to the

4. D. W. Phillipson, 1974, pp. 1–25; 1975, pp. 321–42.
5. Some of these traits rapidly spread beyond the area of early iron age culture.

south, beyond the southernmost penetration of the early iron age, appear to have adopted certain new cultural traits which are best seen as derived from contact, both direct and indirect, with early iron age settlers. These 'late stone age' and related populations are discussed by J. E. Parkington in Chapter 26 of the present volume.

Reconstruction of the early iron age in southern Africa must be based first and foremost on archaeological evidence. Unlike events of the later periods of the iron age, those of this time – which corresponds broadly with the first millennium of our era – lie effectively beyond the range of oral tradition. As has been shown in an earlier chapter, attempts have been made to base historical reconstructions of the pre-literate early iron age societies of this region on purely linguistic evidence. In the present state of our knowledge, however, it seems preferable generally to admit the conclusions of historical linguistics as secondary evidence for comparison with a sequence which has first been established on the basis of archaeology.

## Regional survey of archaeological evidence

### Southern Zambia, Angola, Malawi

A regional survey of the Zambian early iron age has recently been undertaken by the present writer; and a number of distinct groups have been recognized primarily on the basis of the typology of the associated pottery.[6] Here, we are only concerned with the evidence from the southern part of the country. Two closely related groups may be discerned in the Copperbelt region and on the Lusaka plateau. The Chondwe group of the Copperbelt is characterized by pottery vessels with thickened or undifferentiated rims, the most frequent decorative motifs being lines of alternately facing triangular impressions forming a chevron design in false relief and also chardate areas of comb-stamping delineated by broad grooves. The score of village sites which have so far yielded pottery of this type are distributed alongside rivers and streams, generally close to the tree-lines of the dambos which fringe the upper reaches of the Kafue head-water tributaries. Radio-carbon dates for the Chondwe group sites of Kangonga and Chondwe cover the sixth to the eleventh centuries of our era, but study of pottery typology suggests that certain other sites may be earlier. Iron and copper working is evident throughout the time range of the known sites. However, exploitation of the area's copper deposits appears to have been on a small scale in early iron age times, although it attracted widespread trade contacts.[7]

To the south, centred on the Lusaka plateau, are the early iron age sites attributed to the Kapwirimbwe group, the pottery of which is distinguished

6. D. W. Phillipson, 1968a, pp. 191–211.
7. E. A. C. Mills and N. T. Filmer, pp. 129–45; D. W. Phillipson, 1972a, pp. 93–128.

from that of the Chondwe group by the greater degree and frequency of rim-thickening and by the extreme rarity of all comb-stamped decoration, the place of which is taken by a variety of incised designs. At the village of Kapwirimbwe, 13 kilometres east of Lusaka, the apparently brief occupation has been securely dated from around the fifth century of our era. There were extensive remains of collapsed *daga* structures, many of which appear to have been iron-smelting furnaces. Enormous quantities of iron slag and bloom confirmed that extensive iron-working had been conducted in the immediate vicinity. Iron tools were more common than is usual on sites of the Zambian iron age but copper appears to have been unknown. Bone fragments indicated the presence of domestic cattle.[8] The later development of the Kapwirimbwe group is best illustrated at the Twickenham Road site in an eastern suburb of Lusaka. Here, domestic goats were kept and wild animals hunted. Iron-working, as at Kapwirimbwe, was on a substantial scale, but only in the final phase of the early iron age at Twickenham Road does copper make its appearance.[9] The distribution of the Kapwirimbwe group extends to the south-east into the Zambezi valley near Chirundu and beyond on to the Mashonaland plateau around Urungwe, where it is best known from a site adjacent to the Sinoia Cave, dating from the second half of the first millennium of our era.[10]

In western Zambia few early iron age sites have so far been discovered. At Sioma Mission on the upper Zambezi, a settlement is dated from the middle centuries of the first millennium;[11] another, beside the Lubusi river west of Kamoa, belongs to the last quarter of that millennium. These sites have yielded pottery which, although undoubtedly belonging to the early iron age, is markedly distinct from that of the groups recognized farther to the east. There was evidence for iron-working at both sites.[12] Physically, the upper Zambezi area is best regarded as an extension of the Kalahari Sand country of Angola. Here, hardly any dated archaeological pottery assemblages are available for comparison, but the small collection from Dundo Airfield, dating from between the seventh and the ninth centuries and therefore virtually contemporary with Lubusi, shows many features in common with the latter material.[13] In the Dundo area pottery appears to have been made since the early centuries of our era, if the evidence of a radio-carbon date from the stream gravels at Furi Mine can be relied upon.[14] We can be reasonably sure that iron age communities were present over wide areas elsewhere in Angola during the first millennium of our era but little detail is available.

8. D. W. Phillipson, 1968b, pp. 87–105.
9. D. W. Phillipson, 1970a, pp. 77–118.
10. K. R. Robinson, 1966a, pp. 131–55; P. S. Garlake, 1970a, pp. 25–44.
11. J. O. Vogel, 1973.
12. D. W. Phillipson, 1971, pp. 51–7.
13. J. D. Clark, 1968b, pp. 189–205.
14. C. J. Ferguson and W. F. Libby, p. 17.

At this point it is convenient to note that iron age sites dating from the first millennium of our era are now known from more southerly areas of Angola, as at Feti la Choya where the earliest iron age occupation is dated from the seventh or eighth century.[15] The relationship of this site to the early iron age industrial complex cannot be determined since no details of the associated artefacts, beyond the bare fact that iron and pottery were present, have so far been made available.[16] In the extreme north of Namibia, the site of Kapako has yielded pottery, described in a preliminary and provisional account as akin to that from Kapwirimbwe, associated with a radio-carbon date in the late first millennium.[17]

South of the Kafue, in the fertile plateau regions of the Southern Province of Zambia, several sites of large early iron age villages have now been discovered. Individual sites were apparently settled for much longer than was general elsewhere; the earliest such occupations apparently took place around the fourth century. This early iron age settlement seems to have been denser than in most other populations whose counterparts elsewhere long survived the arrival of agriculture and metallurgy.[18] The material culture of the early iron age Kalundu group of the Batoka plateau has much in common with that of the Kapwirimbwe group but the pottery is readily distinguished, primarily by the rarity of false-relief chevron stamping and of bowls with pronounced internal thickening of the rim. Cowrie shells indicate contacts with the coastal trade but glass beads are absent. The lowest levels of the Kalundu site near Kalomo yielded a large assemblage of animal bones of which less than two-fifths were of domestic cattle and small stock; hunting evidently continued to play an important part in the economy. Iron was used for the manufacture of such objects as razors, arrowheads and probable thumb-piano keys. Copper fragments were also recovered.[19] On the plateau, the Kalundu group occupation lasted until the ninth century;[20] in the Kafue valley around Namwala the early iron age occupations at Basanga and Mwanamaipa have been dated from between the fifth and the ninth centuries.[21]

The Zambezi valley area around Livingstone is probably the best-explored region of southern Africa from the point of view of iron age archaeology. The early iron age Dambwa group of this area shares features both with the Kalundu group and with the Gokomere sites in Zimbabwe.[22]

15. B. M. Fagan, 1965, pp. 107–16.

16. J. Vansina, 1966.

17. J. E. G. Sutton, 1972, pp. 1–24.

18. For discussions of interaction between early iron age and late stone age populations, see D. W. Phillipson, 1968a, pp. 191–211; 1969, pp. 24–49; S. F. Miller, 1969, pp. 81–90.

19. B. M. Fagan, 1967.

20. As, for example, at Gundu: B. M. Fagan, 1969b, pp. 149–69.

21. Basanga and Mwanamaimpa were excavated by Dr B. M. Fagan. For the radio-carbon dates see D. W. Phillipson, 1970b, pp. 1–15.

22. S. G. H. Daniels and D. W. Phillipson, Vol. II.

It has been suggested that, after an initial and little-known phase best illustrated by the small assemblage of shards from the Situmpa site near Machili, the main florescence of the Dambwa group may have been derived from a secondary centre of dispersal of iron age culture situated south of the Zambezi.[23] At Kamudzulo, dated between the fifth and seventh centuries, were found traces of sub-rectangular pole-and-*daga* houses. A small piece of imported glass found inside one of these houses indicates that contact with the coastal trade had begun by the seventh century. Burial customs of this period are best illustrated at Chundu where the corpses were interred individually in pits; they were buried in a tightly contracted posture with the knees drawn up to the chin. Grave-goods appear to have been deposited in separate pits nearby; these generally contained pairs of pottery vessels forming a container for the funeral cache, which at this site invariably included an iron hoe often with the addition of other objects such as iron or copper bangles, cowrie shells or shell disc beads. One of these caches also contained two seeds, tentatively identified as being of squash and a bean.[24] Dambwa group settlements, like those of the Kalundu group to the north, have yielded osteological evidence for the herding of domestic cattle as well as sheep and/or goats, but the preponderance of bones of wild species confirms the continued importance of hunting. Locally made iron tools included bodkins, knives, hoes and axes, bangles, and points for spears and arrows. Copper does not occur in the region and must have been brought in by trade, the two nearest known sources being in the Kafue Hook region of Zambia and around Wankie in Zimbabwe. Copper artefacts found on Dambwa group sites include bangles and trade-bars.

During the eighth century an increased tempo of ceramic typological change lead to the appearance of the Kalomo pottery tradition which is now seen as a local development within the Victoria Falls region from the early iron age Dambwa group pottery. Around the middle of the ninth century makers of the Kalomo tradition pottery introduced their wares on to the Batoka plateau and appear rapidly to have displaced the remaining Kalundu group population there.[25]

In the Eastern Province of Zambia the early iron age population appears to have been established by the third century of our era, but to have been sparse; the majority of the inhabitants of this area probably retained their 'late stone age' way of life well into the present millennium, until long after the inception of the later iron age.[26] The pottery of these Kamnama group sites of eastern Zambia is clearly closely related to that from contemporary

23. This account of the early iron age in the Victoria Falls region is largely based on the research of Mr J. O. Vogel, whose published accounts include Lusaka, 1971, and others cited elsewhere.
24. J. O. Vogel, 1969, p. 524; 1972, pp. 583–6.
25. J. O. Vogel, 1970, pp. 77–88.
26. D. W. Phillipson, 1973, pp. 3–24.

settlements in adjacent regions of Malawi, where an outline iron age archaeological sequence is now available for the greater part of the country lying to the west of the lake.

In northern Malawi, a site on the South Rukuru river beside Phopo Hill has yielded evidence for prolonged early iron age occupation dated to between the second and fifth centuries of our era. Potsherds, wild-animal bones and evidence for iron-smelting were recovered, together with shell disc beads. Glass beads were not recovered. The pottery is clearly akin to that from Kamnama; and the general affinities of this material to the early iron age wares of East Africa, especially that from Kwale inland from Mombasa,[27] are clear. Comparable material from Lumbule Hill near Livingstonia is dated to about the middle of the first millennium. In northern Malawi the Mwavarambo site appears to represent the local form of the early iron age, showing some affinities with the Malambo group of northern Zambia.[28] Mwavarambo is dated from the eleventh to the thirteenth centuries.[29] In southern Malawi, the finds from the numerous sites attributed to the Nkope group[30] indicate comparable settlements of the period from the fourth to the eleventh centuries.

The early iron age ceramics from Malawi and adjacent regions of Zambia form a clear typological link between the contemporary wares of East Africa and those of Zimbabwe, but they are markedly distinct from those of the Chondwe, Kapwirimbwe and Kalundu groups in the trans-Luangwan regions to the west. Unfortunately, no data are available on early iron age sites, if any do indeed occur, in the country to the east of Lake Malawi.

## Africa south of the Zambezi

In Zimbabwe the same general picture of regionally differentiatied early iron age industries belonging to a common industrial complex is continued. We have already referred to the industries of two northern regions of the country, which are closely related to Zambian groups. Over most of the rest of Zimbabwe the early iron age cultures show considerable basic similarity. There is general acceptance for a tripartite division of the associated pottery. Ziwa ware appears centred on the eastern highlands around Inyanga and extending both westwards towards Salisbury and southwards along the Mozambique border areas towards the Lowveld. Zhiso ware (formerly known as Leopard's Kopje I)[31] is found in the south-west around

27. R. C. Soper, 1967a, pp. 1–17.
28. D. W. Phillipson, 1968a, pp. 191–211.
29. This account of the early iron age of Malawi is based on the research of Mr K. R. Robinson, which he has described in the following publications: 1966, pp. 169–88; with B. Sandelowsky, 1968, pp. 107–46.
30. K. R. Robinson, 1973.
31. For the Leopard's Kopje culture, see K. R. Robinson, 1966b, pp. 5–51.

Bulawayo. Gokomere ware is widely distributed in the south-central area. The typology shows that the three groups are intimately related; indeed recent work has shown that in several areas there is considerable typological overlap between the groups and suggests that they may not always be so sharply defined as are some of the Zambian early iron age groups.[32]

A clear picture of Zimbabwean early iron age settlement is obtained at Mabveni in the Chibi district, where remains of three pole-and-*daga* structures have been investigated; one of these was interpreted as a storage bin which was originally raised above the ground on stones. Traces of dry stone walling could not be linked unequivocally with the early iron age settlement, but are architecturally distinct from structures of more recent date. The pottery was characterized by necked vessels with diagonal comb-stamped decoration on the thickened rim-band, and a variety of open bowls. Clay figurines of sheep and humans were also recovered, as were beads made of iron, copper and shell. Contact with coastal trade is demonstrated by the presence of marine shells and glass beads.[33] Sheep were the only domestic animals represented. The site is dated from some period within the first two-thirds of the first millennium. Confirmatory evidence for much of the above comes from a rock shelter at Gokomere Mission north of Fort Victoria, where the animal bones included a horn-core of domestic goat. The early iron age settlement at Gokomere is dated from between the fifth and seventh centuries.[34] The earliest iron age occupation of the 'Acropolis' at Great Zimbabwe is a further example of the Gokomere early iron age industry, dated between the third and fifth centuries for its end.[35]

The early iron age of Ziwa ware of north-eastern Zimbabwe was first recognized in the Inyanga area;[36] the earliest Ziwa pottery shows many points in common with Gokomere ware, but tends to be more elaborately decorated. Such pottery is at present best known from the 'Place of Offerings', a large undated open site on Ziwa Mountain near Inyanga. Associated finds include iron tools, copper objects, shell beads and part of an imported cowrie shell. Millet and pumpkin seeds are apparently associated with the early iron age occupation.

Later versions of the Ziwa pottery tradition show a general moderation of the more flamboyant features, while the use of haematite and graphite finishes is introduced. Radio-carbon dates indicate that the Ziwa wares cover the greater part of the first millennium. A date of the tenth or eleventh century, from the lowest levels of the stone-built enclosure at Nyahokwe beside Ziwa Mountain, is attributed to a final phase of the Ziwa

32. T. N. Huffman, 1971a, pp. 20–44.
33. K. R. Robinson, 1961b, pp. 75–102.
34. T. Gardner, L. H. Wells and J. F. Schofield, pp. 219–53; K. R. Robinson, 1963, pp. 155–71.
35. R. Summers, K. R. Robinson and A. Whitty.
36. R. Summers, 1958. For the 'Place of Offerings', see also D. R. MacIver, 1906.

tradition. Several human skeletons have been found on early iron age Ziwa sites in this area and appear to show negroid physical characteristics.[37]

Pottery apparently related to the final phases of the Ziwa tradition shows a far more extensive distribution than does its earlier counterpart, being recorded from a wide area of north-eastern Zimbabwe as far to the west as the Salisbury district. The pottery recovered from the Golden Shower gold mine at Arcturus appears to be best attributed to a late manifestation of the Ziwa tradition, possibly belonging to the last quarter of the first millennium, but this attribution and dating should be regarded as tentative pending further investigations.[38] The association of this type of pottery with prehistoric mines is discussed in greater detail below.

The final phase of the early iron age in northern Mashonaland is best represented by the sites at Chitope, some 100 kilometres north-north-west of Salisbury, and at Maxton Farm near Shamva Hill.[39] Both sites are attributed to around the eleventh century and are thought but briefly to antedate the introduction into the area of the later iron age Musengezi ware. The Maxton Farm site is situated on a kopje, the summit of which is surrounded by a low stone wall 'built of large, loosely piled diorite blocks, untrimmed, unselected and without packing or wedging'.[40] Upright monoliths were set into the top of the wall at frequent intervals along its length. There is no reason to doubt the association of the wall with the occupation of the settlement which it encloses.

Significant economic development is thus indicated in this area during the later centuries of the early iron age. It is only in its later forms that Ziwa ware is found associated with imported glass beads. Comparable pottery is also found on sites with simple terraces and stone walling, as well as on gold and copper mines, indicating that its makers were involved in the more comprehensive exploitation of their territory's natural resources than had been their predecessors, and also that they were in contact with the trade network of the Indian Ocean.

It is at this time, too, that domestic cattle are first attested in the archaeological record of Zimbabwe. Remains of these animals are markedly absent from sites of the earliest phase of iron age settlement south of the Zambezi, where the only domestic species represented are sheep and goats. Cattle are first recorded on sites dated to the eighth century. They do not, however, become frequent before the inception of the later iron age.[41]

Centred on Bulawayo, the sites yielding Zhiso-type pottery have much

---

37. F. O. Bernhard, 1961, pp. 84–92; 1964; H. de Villiers, pp. 17–28.
38. J. F. Schofield; T. N. Huffman, 1974, pp. 238–42.
39. P. S. Garlake, 1967, 1969.
40. P. S. Garlake, 1967, p. 3; 1969.
41. T. N. Huffman, 1973.

in common with the early iron age industries farther east. It now appears that this pottery does not represent the initial early iron age occupation of the area; this is probably seen in such sites as Mandau and Madiliyangwa in the Matopo hills, where the sherds have close typological connections both with the early Gokomere wares and with the earliest iron age pottery of the Dambwa group in the Victoria Falls region.[42] It seems probable that in much of south-western Zimbabwe the early iron age population remained sparse until the development of the Zhiso industry late in the first millennium. Rock art studies indicate the substantial survival of late stone age peoples throughout this time, especially in the Matopo hills.[43]

Excavations at Zhiso Hill in the Matopos have yielded fragments of pole-and-*daga* structures and settings of stones which are interpreted as the supports for grain storage bins, together with pottery decorated primarily with comb-stamped motifs; this material is dated between the ninth and twelfth centuries.[44]

At other sites which have yielded Zhiso pottery, notably Pumbaje and Ngwapani, stone terrace-walling may be contemporary, but the association is uncertain.[45] An eighth- or ninth-century Zhiso horizon represents the earliest iron age occupation at the Leopard's Kopje site, 24 kilometres west of Bulawayo. Associated finds included shell and glass beads, iron slag, copper bangles, teeth of sheep or goats and, less certainly associated, remains of cow-peas. Cattle bones, which were common in the overlying deposits of the Leopard's Kopje industry (Mambo phase), were not represented in the comparatively small faunal assemblage from the basal Zhiso horizon.[46]

In the extreme south-east of Zimbabwe an early iron age village site at Malapati on the Nuanetsi river has been dated from the last quarter of the first millennium.[47] Cattle bones were recovered, and the pottery from this site shows affinities with both Gokomere and Zhiso wares and, through the latter, with material recovered in eastern Botswana, as at Maokagani Hill.[48]

The spread of the early iron age industrial complex south of the Limpopo during the first millennium is now indicated, but the evidence is sparse and incomplete. Pottery similar to that from Malapati has been discovered at Matakoma in the Soutspansberg of the northern Transvaal; no absolute dates for the site are available, but the similarity with the dated Malapati assemblage makes a date in the second half of the first millennium

42. N. Jones, pp. 1–44.
43. See Chapter 26 above.
44. K. R. Robinson, 1966b, pp. 5–51.
45. ibid.
46. T. N. Huffman, 1971b, pp. 85–9.
47. K. R. Robinson, 1963, pp. 155–71; 1961a.
48. J. F. Schofield.

appear probable.[49] Near Tzaneen in the north-eastern Transvaal, pottery of early iron age type has been dated from the third or fourth century, indicating that the spread of this complex south of the Limpopo did not long postdate its introduction into Zimbabwe.[50] More comprehensive remains have recently been recovered at Broederstroom, west of Pretoria. Here, R. J. Mason has unearthed the remains of thirteen collapsed huts together with traces of iron-working. The early iron age pottery from this site, which is dated from around the fifth century, is associated with bones of domestic cattle, sheep and goats.[51]

Even farther to the south, several occurrences of iron age artefacts have been dated from the first millennium, but their attribution to the early iron age industrial complex remains uncertain.[52] At Castle Peak, Ngwenya, in western Swaziland, an iron age presence is securely dated from the fourth or fifth century. The excavators' preliminary note[53] indicates that the pottery, which was found associated with stone mining tools, occasional iron objects and artefacts of 'late stone age' type, may be attributable to the early iron age. From a broadly contemporary site at Lydenburg has been recovered a remarkable terracotta representation of a life-sized human head, associated with pottery of a type, designated NC3 by J. F. Schofield, whose relationship to the early iron age industrial complex remains to be elucidated. The distribution of NC3 pottery extends southwards into Natal where, at Muden, it is found on a site which has also yielded bones of domestic cattle and small stock.[54]

## Archaeological synthesis

Despite the uneven distribution and quality of archaeological research into the early iron age which will have become apparent from the foregoing summary, several broad overall trends may be discerned. Within the area under review, study of the pottery typology permits the recognition of two major divisions within the early iron age. One, best known in central and southern Zambia where it is represented by the Chondwe, Kapwirimbwe and Kalundu groups, extends for a considerable but unknown distance to the west. The other occupies Malawi, eastern Zambia and the area of known early iron age settlement south of the Zambezi.[55] The Dambwa group

49. J. B. de Vaal, pp. 303–18.
50. M. Klapwijk, 1973, p. 324.
51. R. J. Mason, 1973, pp. 324–5; 1974, pp. 211–16.
52. I here exclude from the early iron age industrial complex such finds as those at Uitkomst and Phalaborwa, the typological affinities of which appear to be with later material. There is likewise no evidence for the cultural associations of the seventh-century iron-smelting furnace from northern Natal described by T. P. Dutton, pp. 37–40.
53. Quoted in B. M. Fagan, 1967, pp. 513–27.
54. J. F. Schofield, R. R. Inskeep and K. L. von Bezing, p. 102; R. R. Inskeep, p. 326; T. M. O'C. Maggs.
55. D. W. Phillipson, 1975, pp. 321–42.

in the Victoria Falls area of the Zambezi valley shares features in common with both divisions. This classification is confirmed to a certain extent by the study of selected economic aspects of the early iron age, as is attempted below.

## Food-producing economy

Detailed evidence for the food-producing economy of the early iron age societies has only rarely been recovered. The presence of relatively large, semi-permanent villages is, of course, suggestive of an economy based to a substantial extent on food production, while the discovery of occasional iron hoes and large numbers of grindstones is indicative of some form of agriculture. More specific evidence for the identity of the cultigens and domesticates involved has, however, only been forthcoming from comparatively few sites.

Within the area and time period covered by this chapter the only early iron age sites to have yielded physical identifiable remains of cultivated plants are Chundu (where the finds were provisionally identified as of squash and a bean), the 'Place of Offerings' at Inyanga (which yielded seeds of millet and pumpkin), and Leopard's Kopje (where cow-peas are reported). Seeds of sorghum were recovered from Kalomo tradition levels at Kalundu and Isamu Pati.[56] The Ingombe Illede site near Kariba (not culturally attributed to the early iron age) also produced remains of sorghum which have been directly dated to the seventh or eighth century.[57] This scanty evidence indicates some of the crops which were raised by early iron age farmers in southern Africa, but there is no reason to believe that the list is comprehensive.

When we turn to consider the physical remains of domestic animals, the evidence is slightly more substantial. Remains of sheep and/or goats are recorded from Twickenham Road, Kalundu, Kumadzulo, Mabveni, Gokomere, Leopard's Kopje, Makuru and Broederstroom. These widely scattered sites cover the whole time span of the early iron age in southern Africa. Bones of domestic cattle, however, come from early contexts only at the southern Zambian sites of Kapwirimbwe, Kalundu and Kumadzulo. South of the Zambezi cattle do not appear to occur before the eighth century, as at Coronation Park, Makuru and Malapati.[58] That sheep were introduced into Zimbabwe before cattle may also be inferred from the study of the rock paintings of that country, where fat-tailed sheep are frequently represented but cattle never.[59] Recent evidence from Broederstroom, however, suggests that cattle may be of earlier occurrence in the Transvaal,

56. B. M. Fagan, 1967.
57. B. M. Fagan, D. W. Phillipson and S. G. H. Daniels.
58. T. N. Huffman, 1973.
59. C. K. Cooke, pp. 7–10.

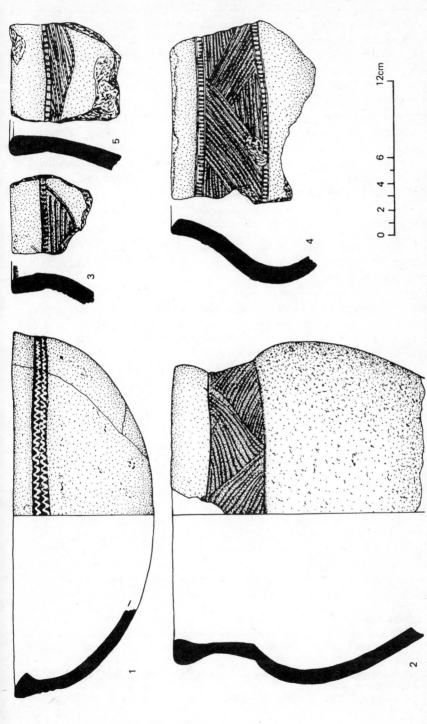

FIG. 27.3 *Early iron age pottery from Twickenham Road: nos. 1, 2, after D. W. Phillipson (1970) and Kalundu; nos. 3–5 after B. M. Fagan (1967)*

where they were probably derived from a westerly source.[60]

Even in the southern Zambian region, cattle in early iron age times appear to have been relatively uncommon, in contrast to the importance which they assumed in the economy of later periods. During the second half of the first millennium, a gradual change of emphasis in the local iron age economy may be discerned. At Kalundu, the period saw a steady increase in the proportion of domestic animal bones of those of wild species in successive horizons, indicating a gradual shift from hunting to animal husbandry.[61] In the Victoria Falls region iron hoes become markedly less frequent at much the same time, and it seems reasonable to assume a corresponding change of emphasis away from agriculture in favour of increased herding of domestic animals.[62]

## Mining and metallurgy

Only three metals were worked on any substantial scale during the southern African iron age: these, in decreasing order of importance, were iron, copper and gold.[63]

Iron ore in one form or another is extremely widespread throughout the region; where richer ores were not available, ferricrete or bog iron appear to have been smelted, despite their low yield. Iron-working seems to have been introduced throughout the region contemporaneously with the arrival of the other diagnostic traits which constitute iron age culture as here defined. There is no evidence that iron was generally mined other than by the excavation of shallow pits; often the ore was simply collected from the surface. Details of the iron-smelting furnaces of the southern African early iron age are not known,[64] but it is interesting to note that smelting appears frequently to have been conducted within the confines of the villages, as if the taboos, which in later periods ensured that smelting operations were carried out away from all contact with women, did not at that time apply. Tewels appear to have been used in the smelting process; this does not prove the use of bellows since tewels are also used in natural-draught furnaces.[65] The objects made of iron were generally of domestic utilitarian purpose; knives, arrow and spearheads and the like. There was probably little long-distance trade in iron or iron objects.

60. R. G. Welbourne, p. 325. The presence of cattle in late stone age South Africa may date from the first millennium of our era, possibly predating their arrival in Zimbabwe. Their introduction to South Africa by a westerly route therefore seems probable. This is in keeping with linguistic evidence quoted by C. Ehret, 1967, pp. 1–17; C. Ehret *et al.*, 1972, pp. 9–27.

61. B. M. Fagan, 1967.

62. This was probably a gradual process extending over several centuries.

63. Tin was also worked on a small scale, at least in the nineteenth century in southern Zambia.

64. It is not clear whether a furnace at Inyanga discovered by Bernhard should be attributed to the early iron age.

65. For example, D. W. Phillipson, 1968c, pp. 102–13.

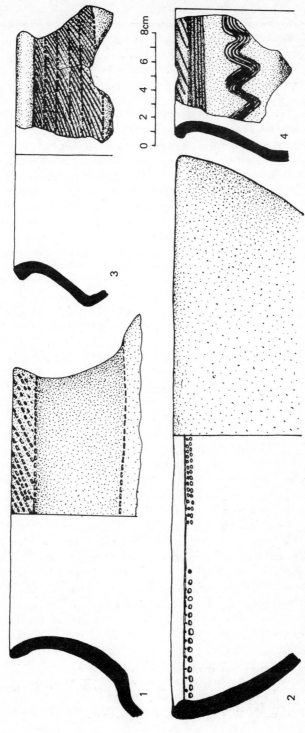

FIG. 27.4 Pottery from Mabveni: nos. 1, 2, after K. R. Robinson (1961) and Dambwa; nos. 3, 4, after S. G. H. Daniels and D. W. Phillipson (1969)

Copper deposits have a far more restricted distribution than do those of iron. The main areas in southern Africa where such deposits occur are on the Zambezi/Congo watershed stretching from the modern Copperbelt westwards to Solwezi, in the Hook of the Kafue area, in the Sinoia and Wankie areas of Zimbabwe, in eastern Botswana adjacent to the Zimbabwean border, in the Limpopo valley around Messina, and in the Phalaborwa area of the eastern Transvaal. Deposits farther to the west in Angola and Namibia need not be considered here because of the virtual absence of archaeological research in these areas. It is probable that copper deposits in all the regions noted above were exploited in iron age times, but considerable difficulty is experienced in determining early, as opposed to later, activity. Many prehistoric workings have been destroyed or substantially modified by recent mining. Copper artefacts are, however, widely distributed on early iron age sites, although they are not so common as they are on those of later periods. It cannot be demonstrated that copper-working technology was practised in all areas at such an early date in the early iron age as were the corresponding techniques for iron; in the Lusaka region, for example, copper appears to have been known until a late phase of the early iron age. Knowledge of copper in areas closer to the ore deposits was considerably earlier, as on the Chondwe group sites, and in most of Zimbabwe. Copper was clearly regarded as a relative luxury and its use was largely restricted to the manufacture of small items of personal adornment such as beads and bangles of thin twisted strip. The metal was traded in the form of bars, of which the best example from an early iron age context is that from Kumadzulo. No copper-smelting furnaces of the early iron age have been investigated. Since potsherds characteristic of the wares of several far-flung regions are recorded from early iron age sites adjacent to Zambian Copperbelt mines, notably at Roan Antelope, it may be inferred that people came from great distances to obtain copper from these sites, a practice which continued into later iron age times.[66] It may be concluded that in much of southern Africa copper was worked on a small scale in early iron age times, but that the large-scale exploitation of this metal was a phenomenon of the later iron age.[67]

Iron age gold-mining in southern Africa appears to have been restricted largely to Zimbabwe and immediately adjacent regions.[68] Small-scale prehistoric workings in Zambia, South Africa and elsewhere have been reported, but no detailed investigations have been conducted. In contrast, well over a thousand prehistoric goldmines have been recorded in Zimbabwe and closely bordering regions of Botswana and the Transvaal.[69] Most of the ancient workings have been destroyed by further mining

66. D. W. Phillipson, 1972b, pp. 93–128.

67. Research into prehistoric copper-working in south-central Africa, with particular reference to Zambia, is currently being undertaken by Mr M. S. Bisson.

68. The following account is largely based on that of R. Summers.

69. The actual number of mines must have been several times this figure.

within the past eighty years and only in very few cases are detailed descriptions available. Dating the prehistoric exploitation of the Zimbabwean gold deposits is correspondingly difficult. The earliest radio-carbon dates for ancient mines in this region are from the Aboyne and Geelong mines, both around the twelfth century. There are four reports of early iron age pottery having been recovered within or immediately adjacent to ancient mines: in each case the pottery concerned is best attributed to a late manifestation of the Ziwa tradition. The occurrence of such pottery at the Golden Shower mine near Arcturus has already been noted; similar material comes from the Three Skids claim. Both these sites are in the Mazoe valley region. Farther to the south near Umkondo in the Sabi valley region, comparable pottery has been recovered from the Hot Springs claim. Finally, late Ziwa pottery comes from an ore-processing site with dolly holes and crushing depressions at Three Mile Water near Que Que, the closest such site to the extensive ancient workings at the Gaika, Globe and Phoenix mines. All these mines were worked in prehistoric times by means of open stopes; this is indeed by far the commonest type of ancient working in Zimbabwe. Golden Shower mine and Hot Springs claim each had only one such stope; the Que Que mines were far more extensive, over 160 stopes being present at Gaika mine, while those at Phoenix reached a depth of almost 40 metres. It is, however, clear that the latter sites were operated over many centuries and there is no evidence that early iron age mining was on other than a very small scale.

Although substantial quantities of gold objects have been recovered from Zimbabwean iron age sites, the great majority of these were removed by treasure-seekers during the early years of the European occupation; in hardly any cases, therefore, are data available concerning the provenance and archaeological associations of such discoveries. The few finds of gold which have been made in controlled archaeological excavations have all come from later iron age contexts.[70]

In view of the exiguous dating evidence from ancient goldmines it is possible to draw only tentative conclusions from the evidence of the four such sites which have yielded early iron age artefacts. None of these sites is dated, but the pottery would appear to indicate a date not earlier than the ninth century and probably not later than the eleventh.[71] There is no convincing evidence for the exploitation of the Zimbabwean gold deposits before this time. This conclusion is in keeping with the evidence of Arabic written records in which the first mention of gold from this region bought on the East African coast occurs in a tenth-century context.[72]

The four gold-mining sites which have yielded early iron age pottery all

70. The burials at Ingombe Illede which included gold objects among the grave-goods are now known not to be associated with the late first-millennium occupation of that site: D. W. Phillipson and B. M. Fagan, pp. 199–204.

71. R. Summers and T. N. Huffman suggest that a somewhat earlier date may be possible.

72. Al-Mas'udi, in G. S. P. Freeman-Grenville, 1962b, p. 15.

occur in the eastern parts of Zimbabwe, in the valleys of the Mazoe and the Sabi. Both these rivers provide relatively easy communications between the interior and the coast. The writings of Arab geographers leave no doubt that, from this initial period of gold-mining, the metal was exported. Whether it was also used locally at this period is not yet clear. In this context it is significant that the commencement of gold-mining and the introduction of imported glass beads appears to have been broadly synchronous. If the two events are indeed connected, the stimulus for the development of gold-mining may well have been primarily external. Summers's contention[73] that it was specifically from India that the techniques and, by implication, some of the miners were derived, is, however, unconvincing in the present state of our knowledge. Although the initiation of the exploitation of Zimbabwean gold may safely be attributed to a late phase of the early iron age, it was not until yet later times that mining was undertaken on a really substantial scale.

## Architecture

Only a few sites have yielded information permitting the reconstruction of architectural plans and structural details attributable to the early iron age in this region; and there must remain some doubt as to the extent to which these sites are characteristic of the architecture of southern Africa as a whole during this period. Kumadzulo produced evidence of the plans of eleven houses of pole-and-*daga* construction. These were sub-rectangular in outline with substantial corner posts; the maximum wall-length was only 2·3 metres. No comparable evidence has been recovered from other early iron age sites in southern Africa, but fragmentary traces from a number of other sites such as Dambwa and Chitope suggest that the general method of construction illustrated at Kumadzulo was frequently used, although the sub-rectangular shape of the Kumadzulo houses cannot be paralleled elsewhere.

Building in stone was widespread in the iron age in regions south of the Zambezi, but the practice seems not to have spread into Zambia except on a very small scale during the closing centuries of the later iron age.[74]

As has been noted above, there is, however, some evidence that in Zimbabwe building in stone was widespread during the early iron age although on a much smaller and less elaborate scale than was subsequently attained. Stone building, as has been shown, may be associated with the Gokomere, later Ziwa and Zhiso sites. Undressed stone was mainly employed at this time for building terrace and field walls and

73. R. Summers.

74. In Zambia, terrace walling has been reported from near Mazabuka on the southern Province plateau; this, and the rough stone walling found on defensive sites in the Lusaka area and in the southern part of the Eastern province, are probably all attributable to the eighteenth or nineteenth centuries.

simple enclosures. The most elaborate form attained by early iron age builders was probably of the type described above from Maxton Farm. The later iron age brought greater elaboration and expansion to the stone-building tradition which was, however, securely established well before the close of the first millennium. The stone-building sequence at Great Zimbabwe itself is attributed exclusively to the later iron age.[75]

The above summary has been able only to cover selected aspects of early iron age economy and technology. It has, however, been adequate to emphasize the extent to which the early iron age provides the foundation to subsequent iron age cultural development in the southern African region.

## Conclusion

Such, in outline, is the present state of our knowledge concerning the early iron age in southern Africa. Elucidation of the events of this cultural episode is here regarded as primarily an archaeological exercise. Historical linguistic investigations can clearly also make a major contribution to early iron age studies; these have been discussed in an earlier chapter.

Within the southern African region here discussed, two major divisions of the early iron age may be recognized in the archaeological record. They may best be regarded as primary divisions of the common early iron age industrial complex but they may be readily distinguished from each other by the typology of the associated pottery. One division displays a distribution extending southwards between the Luangwa valley and Lake Malawi to Zimbabwe and the northern Transvaal; its people were herders of sheep and goats but appear initially to have lacked cattle. The second division is best known from central and southern Zambia but there are indications that it also extended over an enormous area farther to the west. In this region cattle were known in early iron age times and it was probably from those folk that cattle were passed to the early Khoisan pastoralists of the most southerly regions of the continent, to which the early iron age industrial complex itself did not penetrate.

The very uneven distribution of archaeological research prevents a more detailed view of the broader subdivisions of the early iron age. In particular, the whole of Mozambique is a complete blank on the distribution maps, so events throughout the area between the Indian Ocean and Lake Malawi remain entirely unknown. Most of Angola and much of South Africa have so far been very inadequately investigated. When these deficiencies have been remedied it is probable that very major revisions will be required to the synthesis here proposed.

It has been shown that the culture introduced to southern Africa by the early iron age people was responsible for establishing many of the main trends in the subsequent culture-history of the region until quite

75. R. Summers, K. R. Robinson, A. Whitty and P. S. Garlake, 1973.

recent times. Of particular interest to the historian in this context is the extent to which the regionally differentiated characteristics of later times may be traced back to the early iron age. The stone-building tradition of Zimbabwe and the Transvaal, the gold-mining of Zimbabwe and the copper-working of the Copperbelt area, for example, are all seen to have their inception in the context of the early iron age in their respective regions, although they did not reach their full florescence until later times. Continuity between the early and later iron ages in many areas was thus presumably more marked than has often been assumed; but it is only when more intensive research has been conducted, particularly in those areas which remain virtually unexplored by archaeologists, that the full contribution of the early iron age to southern African history may be evaluated.

# Madagascar

**28**

P. VÉRIN

## Cultural investigations

The population of Madagascar has been the subject of many studies, yet despite several often valid hypotheses, its origins are still veiled in mystery. Most authors agree that while the neighbouring African continent has made ethnic contributions to Madagascar, the Malayo-Polynesian elements, that are just as obvious, especially in the central highlands, should also be stressed. The double ethnic origin of the Malagasy would explain the physical differences amongst the inhabitants of the island, who all speak an Indonesian language. Although this language is divided into three dialects, its linguistic unity is unquestionable.

Archaeological discoveries of historical importance first began to be made from 1962 but previously important results had been gained from research in the fields of comparative linguistics, ethnology, musicology and physical anthropology. It is therefore appropriate to summarize briefly the investigations into Malagasy cultural history made in these auxiliary sciences before examining the data that we possess on the first settlements.

## Linguistics

The Dutchman de Houtman was the first scholar to suggest that Malagasy belongs to the Malayo-Polynesian linguistic group. In 1603 he published some dialogues and a Malay–Malagasy dictionary,[1] and his theory was reaffirmed by Luis Mariano who a few years later recognized the existence in the north-west of a 'Kaffir' language (Swahili) that was spoken on the north-west coast, as distinct from a 'Buki' language (Malagasy) spoken 'throughout the interior of the island and on the rest of the coast ... that is very similar to Malay'.

Van der Tuuk[2] later established scientifically the relationship between Malagasy and the Indonesian languages. His research was followed by that of Favre, Brandstetter, Marre, Richardson and, especially, Demp-

1. R. Drury, pp. 323–92.
2. Van der Tuuk.

FIG. 28.1 *Madagascar showing important sites*

wolf. Dempwolf's reconstruction of Proto-Indonesian shows that Merina, which he called Hova, does not differ significantly from other languages of the Indonesian family. Dahl later pointed out that Malagasy had been influenced by Bantu, not only in its vocabulary but also in its phonology. This fact is of prime importance for the discussion of African–Indonesian interactions, which will be described later. Hébert has shown in several of his works that there is often a bipartition among the Indonesian terms in Malagasy that demonstrates the hetero-geneity of its south-east Asian origins. Dez has made an analysis of the vocabulary of Indonesian origin that allows us to infer what type of civilization was brought to Madagascar by the emigrants.[3] And lastly glottochronology has confirmed the deeply Indonesian nature of the basic vocabularly (94 per cent) and provides an idea of the length of time that separates Malagasy from the proto-language.[4] But although the main elements of the basic Malagasy linguistic corpus belong to the Indonesian subgroup, we should not forget that other elements, Indian, Arabic and

3. J. Dez, pp. 197–214.
4. P. Vérin, C. Kottak and P. Gorlin.

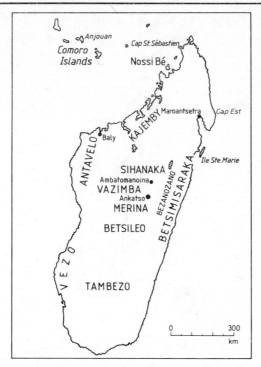

FIG. 28.2 *Madagascar showing places mentioned in the text*

African, have also been incorporated into the language. The contacts implied by these elements help us to understand the contacts and admixtures of the Indonesian diaspora westwards.

## Physical anthropology

Research in this field has confirmed that the Malagasy belong both to the mongoloid and to the negroid stock. Rakoto-Ratsimamanga has come to important conclusions on the distribution and nature of the pigmentation most frequently found among the inhabitants of the central highlands. He distinguishes four morphological types among which the population is divided in the following proportions:[5]

| | |
|---|---|
| Indonesian–mongoloid type | 37% |
| Negro–Oceanic type | 52% |
| Negro–African type | 2% |
| European type | 9% |

5. In defining his categories, Rakoto-Ratsimamanga was highly influenced by Grandidier's 'south Asian' theories. He does not clearly indicate the parameters used to define these types.

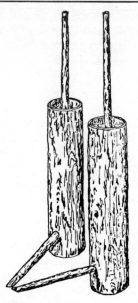

FIG. 28.3 *Double-valved bellows of the type found in Indonesia*

One might question whether such a large proportion of the negroid element is really of Oceanic origin. More recently Mrs Chamla has proposed, on the basis of measurements taken from the skulls preserved in the Musée de l'Homme, that three morphological types should be distinguished:

a light brown Asiatic type similar to the Indonesians;
a dark type, African rather than Melanesian;
a mixed type, that seems to be generally most frequent.

Haematological research carried out by Pigache[6] shows very clearly that the Malagasy negroids are of African and not Melanesian origin.

The Indonesian physical type is dominant among individuals descended from the ancient Imerina free castes. However, the descendants of former captives who came from the coastal regions or from Africa are of a clearly negroid type. The Indonesians also seem to have contributed to the biological complexity of the Sihanaka, the Bezanozano, of some Betsimisaraka and of the northern Betsileo. Whether they also contributed to the constitution of the biological stock of the other coastal groups, where the negroid type is widespread and often more or less general, is still a matter for discussion.

The study of the skeletal remains found in Madagascar should help us to understand the process of racial intermixture. In particular it should

6. J. P. Pigache, pp. 175–7.

indicate whether the fusion between the African and the Indonesian elements actually took place on the island or elsewhere. However, an almost total absence of skeletons found in archaeological contexts has so far hindered the collection of such data.[7]

## Ethnology and musicology

It was H. Deschamps[8] who first attempted to distinguish between the Indonesian and the African contributions to Malagasy civilization. African cultural features are found such as elements of the cattle complex, the snake-cult addressed to dead kings in the west and in Betsileo, and some features of the socio-political organization found in the coastal regions. However, the social organization of Imerina is completely Indonesian in character.

Malagasy civilization owes much to the east, including most house forms, rice culture on irrigated terraces, some aspects of ancestor-worship, and a whole technological complex including the double-valved bellows, the outrigger canoe, the underground oven containing porous volcanic rock, and less well known objects, such as the rotating bow drill and the mounted file for opening coconuts, that have been studied on the west coast of Madagascar and that are found as far away as eastern Polynesia, identical in form, under the names of *hu* and *'ana* (in Tahitian dialect).

Hornell and the Culwicks have studied Indonesian cultural echoes on the East African coast, and more recently G. P. Murdock has referred to a 'Malaysian botanical complex', which he considers includes those plants introduced in ancient times from south-east Asia. Among them he mentions rice (*Oryza sativa*), Polynesian arrow-root (*Tacca pinnatifida*), the taro (*Colocasia antiquorum*), the yam (*Discorea alata, D. bulbifera* and *D. esculenta*), the banana (*Musa paradisiaca* and *M. sapientium*), the bread-fruit tree (*Artocarpus incisa*), the coconut palm (*Coco nufera*), the sugar cane (*Saccharum officinalum*), etc. Murdock believes that migrations from Indonesia bringing this botanical complex to Madagascar took place during the first millennium before our era and travelled right along the coasts of southern Asia before reaching the coast of East Africa.

Murdock is certainly right to exclude the idea of a non-stop migration straight across the Indian Ocean, and the date he attributes to these migrations is quite reasonable. But as far as ethno-botanical evidence is concerned, Deschamps, and more recently Hébert, have shown that some plants imported to Madagascar a long time ago sometimes bear Indonesian names, sometimes African names, and sometimes both at once. Hébert,

7. Apart from studies of the skeletal remains found at Vohemar and on the north-western sites which date from a later (Arabic) period than the first settlements.
8. H. Deschamps, 1960.

however, stresses that 'identical nomenclatures between different countries is no proof of a botanical loan'. To give an example, the fact that on the western coast of Madagascar the banana is known by an Indonesian name (*fontsy*) does not prove conclusively that the plant was brought by Indonesian immigrants, for in the central highlands the banana has a Bantu name (*akondro*). Thus either theory of its origin may be put forward with valid arguments. Hébert goes on to quote Haudricourt whose point of view is even more explicit. In his study on the origin of Malagasy cultivated plants, Haudricourt writes: 'the existence of a name of Indonesian origin does not mean for certain that it [the plant] originated in Indonesia, for the emigrants recognized among the indigenous flora plants similar to those of their native land, and gave them the same names'. It should be added that new and unknown plants might well have been given names inspired by their similarity to species found in the immigrants' native land.

The arguments quoted above indicate how delicately ethno-botanical evidence should be handled. The same is true in the field of musicology. C. Sachs has shown that several different influences combined in Madagascar: Indonesian, African and Arabic. But Jones went much further. He believed that Indonesian influence spread not only as far as Madagascar but right through Africa. I feel that, while several of Jones' theories should not be rejected, the possibility that similar discoveries were made independently on both sides of the Indian Ocean should not be excluded.

One can conclude from the above evidence that the ancestors of the Malagasy are both Indonesian and African in origin, and that the predominantly Indonesian nature of the language need not minimize the role played by Africa in the settlement of Madagascar. That great neighbouring continent contributed physically to the majority of the population and also gave Madagascar many features of its culture and its socio-political organization. Such a hybrid situation is not to be found in the Comoro Islands or on the coast of Africa where Indonesian influxes are also supposed to have occurred.

The different theories as to the origins of the Malagasy in fact hover between two extremes, Africa and Indonesia, though it is true that some authors such as Razafintsalama (who maintained, on the basis of several thousand suspect etymological derivations, that great island had been colonized by Buddhist monks) hold completely deviant points of view. A. Grandidier attributed an exaggerated importance to Asia, believing that apart from the recent Makua arrivals all the ancestors of the Malagasy came from south-east Asia, including the negroids that he calls – for this purpose – Melanesians. G. Ferrand[9] accepted this view which is in defiance of the geographical evidence, though less unreasonably, and stressed the more African aspects of the origins of the Malagasy. He distinguished the following historical phases:

9. G. Ferrand, 1908, pp. 353–500.

a possible pre–Bantu-speaking period;

a Bantu-speaking period dating to before the Christian era;

a pre-Merina Indonesian period from the second to the fourth century with emigration from Sumatra during which the newcomers established their supremacy over the Bantu-speaking peoples;

arrival of the Arabs from the seventh to the eleventh centuries;

a new wave of Sumatrans in the tenth century, among whom we find Ramini, the ancestor of the Zafindraminia, and Rakuba, the ancestor of the Hova;

lastly, the Persians and, in about 1500, the Zafikasinambo.

G. Julien[10] also assigned the principal role to Africa, whereas Malzac[11] believed that the Hova had taught their language to all the Bantu of Madagascar.

## The first settlements in Madagascar

Before going more deeply into the Indonesian and African origins of the Malagasy people, we should evaluate the theories that attempt to credit Madagascar with very ancient migrations from the Mediterranean region.

### Phoenicians, Hebrews or people of the *Periplus?*

In dealing with countries beyond the fringes of the ancient world the Phoenicians, Egyptians, Sabaeans, Greeks and Hebrews are often credited with clearly exaggerated contributions to the history of those countries. For instance Bent (1893) attributed the founding of Zimbabwe to the Phoenicians, and C. Poirier identified the region of Sofala with the countries of Punt and Ophir.

According to some authors ancient voyagers even reached Madagascar. F. de Mahy thought he had found Phoenician remains at Majunga, but Ferrand and I are unable to confirm his hypothesis. A. Grandidier[12] in his account states that the Greeks, and of course the Arabs, visited Madagascar. According to him, 'ever since ancient times this island was known to the Greeks and the Arabs, by the names of Menuthias, Djafouna and Chezbezat which they gave it, and the accurate but very short description which they have left us of it, did not catch the attention of European geographers, who only learned of its existence through the Portuguese in 1500'.

In fact the only Greek name, 'Menuthias', which occurs in Ptolemy[13]

---

10. G. Julien, pp. 375, 644.
11. V. Malzac.
12. A. Grandidier, p. 11.
13. Ptolemaeus Claudius.

and the *Periplus* is more likely to denote the island of Pemba, or perhaps Zanzibar or Mafia. A certain F. Du Mesgnil[14] took it into his head to write a work with the title, *Madagascar, Homer and the Mycenaean civilization*, which gives a clear picture of the speculations that the work contains.

The legends of Jewish migrations are more difficult to dismiss. Father Joseph Briant,[15] in his slim volume *The Hebrew in Madagascar*, is convinced that there were, not one, but two Jewish migrations to Madagascar. He supports his arguments with several hundred comparisons between Malagasy and Hebrew words. Such devious theories, based on a facile linguistic comparison between words that might possibly be alike, are unfortunately only too common in Madagascar where J. Auber developed them in many dubious works which were, however, printed by the government press.

Such researches into the Jewish origins of certain of the Malagasy go back to Flacourt, who believed that the first foreigners to come to the east coast of Madagascar were 'the Zaffe-Hibrahim, or those of the lineage of Abraham, the inhabitants of the Isle of the Blessed Mary and the neighbouring lands', and in his foreword to the *History of the Great Isle of Madagascar* Flacourt[16] justifies his hypothesis by the existence of biblical names, the practice of circumcision and the fact that working on Saturday is forbidden.

G. Ferrand denies the possibility of these Jewish migrations. He believes that the few Semitic names on the island can be attributed to the Malagasy who were converted to Islam,[17] and as for the fact that working on Saturdays is forbidden, Saturday is simply a 'fady' (taboo) day, a common occurrence in Malagasy custom: on the east coast fady still occurs on Tuesdays, Thursdays or Saturdays according to the region. Moreover it seems that in the seventeenth century the existence of circumcision among several exotic peoples led Christian French authors to try to find a Jewish origin for them. Another seventeenth-century example of such research from another region is to be found in the French–Carib dictionary compiled by Father Raymond Breton.

A different theory as to the origins of the pre-Islamic Malagasy has recently been put forward by Poirier, who sees a duality in the Muslim contributions to Madagascar. While his predecessors felt that the attenuated Muslim practices that survive in Madagascar suggested a Jewish origin, Poirier considers that they are a primitive form of religion that came to Madagascar from Arabia. However archaeological data from East Africa and Madagascar give no support to this theory. The massive Arab infiltrations that fertilized Swahili culture commenced in the eighth

14. F. du Mesgnil.
15. J. Briant, 1945.
16. E. Flacourt.
17. G. Ferrand, 1891–1902.

century, and although there was traffic along the East African coast in the second century of our era, the final port of call after Menouthias (which cannot have been Madagascar) was Rhapta. According to the author of the *Periplus*, the very last market-city of the country of Azania was called Rhapta because of its sewn boats (rapton plorarion); there, large quantities of ivory and tortoise-shell were to be found.

Rhapta has not yet been located, but it is thought that it must be between Pangani and the Rufiji river delta. It is probable that Madagascar was not interested in this coastal trade, not merely because it did not extend as far as Rhapta, but also because the island was uninhabited.

On the basis of the available historical and archaeological evidence it is reasonable to suppose that Madagascar was reached by Indonesians and Africans some time between the fifth and the eighth centuries, and in any case no later than the ninth century. We should therefore examine the vicissitudes of what is known of these first Afro-Asiatic settlements.

## The first Indonesian immigrants

Although it would be rash to attempt to put a definite date to the migration of the first Indonesians, for reasons that we shall go into later we can conjecture that their departure took place from the fifth century of our era. They may have continued moving until the twelfth century, as Deschamps thinks. The name Palaeo-Indonesians is given to the first migrants who made contact with the Africans and who probably also made alliances with them. The later arrivals, known as Neo-Indonesians, were the ancestors of the Merina. This last wave has preserved its original biological identity better, possibly because it followed a more direct route, but it is probable that because of its smaller numbers it adopted the language of Palaeo-Indonesians who arrived earlier in Madagascar.

The dichotomy between the Palaeo-Indonesians and the Neo-Indonesians is not only chronological and biological, but is also reflected in their social organization. Ottino has shown that the central highland societies were originally organized very much like those of Indonesia. The foko, an Imerina kinship unit that Bloch calls a deme, is found in a very similar form in Timor under the name of fukum. However, the coastal Malagasy societies have many points in common with Bantu-speaking Africa.

Hébert has observed an east–west division for a number of Malagasy terms of Indonesian origin, and makes some very interesting remarks on the subject of calendars (1960): Sakalava calendars contain few Sanskrit words, whereas those of the descendants of the Neo-Indonesians contain many more.[18]

18. This argument will appear questionable to those who contend that the spread of calendars can take place without there being any migration. Besides, it is possible that, in modifying their calendar, the Sakalava were influenced by the Muslims.

The Neo-Indonesians seem to possess traditions, even if they are rather vague, as to their Indonesian origins. The *Tantaran'ny Andriana*, the 'Chronicles of the History of the Merina' collected by Father Callet, alluded to a landing on the east coast somewhere between Maroantsetra and Mangoro. Ramilison, in his 'History of the Zafimamy', takes up this tradition of a landing, which he situates in Maroantsetra.

The country of origin of the Indonesians who emigrated westwards across the Indian Ocean, whether of those who left in the very earliest times or those who left much later, is still a mystery. In my opinion, a glottochronological comparison of Malagasy (or rather of its various dialects) with a large number of the Indonesian languages of the Archipelago and the Indo-Chinese mainland would be very fruitful. The language that possessed the highest number of terms in common with Malagasy would indicate the common south-east Asian stem from which the various languages diverged. O. Dahl has shown the close relationship between Malagasy and the Manjaan language of Borneo, and I. Dyen has confirmed this with glottochronological calculations, pointing out that there is a higher common retention of the Malagasy–Manjaan word-pair than for the Malagasy–Malay word-pair. This does not necessarily mean that Malagasy originated in Borneo, for other languages may be closer to it. Ferrand, in his *Notes on Malagasy Phonetics*, held that there was a close similarity between Malagasy and Batak, and he went on to make comparisons with Kawi and Javanese.

The Proto-Malagasy from south-east Asia, who created the Indian Ocean equivalent of the Polynesian epic, may, according to Solheim,[19] have led a very similar life to the Ibans of Borneo, who divide their year into a sedentary period devoted to slash-and-burn agriculture, and a period of navigation – and sometimes even of piracy. Hébert[20] wonders whether these intrepid navigators may not have been Bukis whose deformed name was later used to denote Madagascar in the Arabic accounts right up to the present day (Swahili Buki or Bukini).

I have been struck by the similarity between the moated fortified villages of Neo-Indonesians (A. Mille has counted 16 000 sites in Imerina), and those found in Indo-China and Thailand. These fortified sites appear in Indo-China as early as the Neolithic period, but some date from the middle of the first millennium of our era. It is in any case quite reasonable to look for the origins of the Malagasy Indonesians in northern south-east Asia, for 1500 years ago the Indonesian civilizations were expanding well into the Indo-Chinese peninsula. Later generations of this tentative proto-culture may well have ended up on islands, some in Borneo and some in Madagascar.

Although we are unable to say for certain which country or countries

19. W. Solheim, pp. 33–42.
20. J. C. Hébert, 1971, pp. 583–613.

in Indonesia gave rise to the Malagasy proto-culture, this does not mean that we are reduced to mere speculation. From the fifth century on, and probably far earlier, the Indonesians undertook many sea-journeys, in particular to India, and from the seventh to the twelfth centuries great maritime powers grew up in Indonesia, notably the Hindu empires of Crivijaya in Sumatra (seventh to thirteenth centuries), of the Cailendra (eighth century), of Mataram (ninth to eleventh centuries) and of Mojo-pahit (thirteenth century) in Java and of Jambi (twelfth century) in Malaya.

In our present state of knowledge it is no easier to give a precise date to the Indonesian migrations than to establish their geographical origin. Ferrand, and later Dahl, noticed that although there are many Sanskrit words in Malagasy they are far fewer than in the languages to which they are closely related (Malay or rather Maajan). From this it may be deduced that the migrations towards Madagascar did not start until the sanskritiza-tion of Indonesia had begun.[21] This process of sanskritization is much in evidence from the fourth century of our era on, and must therefore have begun earlier, but its influence was felt much more in some parts of Indonesia and south-east Asia than in others.

Glottochronological comparisons between Malay and Malagasy, and within the various dialects that derive from Proto-Malagasy, provide us with a series of chronological possibilities ranging from a little before to well into the first millennium of our era.[22] The most profitable aspect of studies of vocabulary divergence lies in the possible classifications of different dialects, and in what one may infer from them concerning migrations within Madagascar itself. Deschamps has noted that the sea-routes east of India were well established long ago whereas those to the west of India were known only in the first centuries of our era and this, to my mind, bears far more weight than the uncertainties of glottochronology.

If some stone artefacts were found, they would enable us to know more about the earliest phase of Malagasy history. Up to now none has been found, and I am of the view that the first Malagasy to live on the island were acquainted with metal. We know that on the African coast the stone age was superseded by the iron age between the first and fourth centuries of our era. The bronze age in Indonesia was far earlier,[23] and what is more important, very different civilizations coexisted there; there were even a few isolated groups in Indonesia that continued to use stone tools after the tenth century.

Whether or not stone objects exist in Madagascar is a matter of controversy. Two adze-like objects have so far been found, one by Bloch in the region of Ambatomanoina,[24] the other by Marimari Kellum-Ottino

21. O. Ch. Dahl, p. 367.
22. P. Vérin, C. Kottak and P. Gorlin, pp. 26–83.
23. H. R. Van Heekeren.
24. M. Bloch and P. Vérin, pp. 240–1.

at Tambazo, east of Malaimbandy. For the moment no definite conclusion can be reached, for these two worked pieces come from places where gun flints may have been worked; but if any confirmation were forthcoming this could place the arrival of the first Indonesians at least halfway through the first millennium of our era. Grandidier's announcement[25] that worked stones resembling gun flints had been found in the sub-fossil layer of Lamboara is extremely interesting, for when the sub-fossils became extinct firearms had not yet been introduced to Madagascar, and the stone might really be a product of lithic industry.

Malagasy pottery from the centre and the east is similar in many respects to the objects found in the Bau–Kalanay complex, but the pottery found in Africa belonging to this archaic period is not yet well enough known for it to be possible to distinguish precisely the African features from the Indonesian.

The raised stone monuments of the Malagasy ancestor-cult are highly reminiscent of Indonesia. Ferrand uses solid etymological techniques to link the word used to denote the divinity (Zanahary) with Malay and Cham homologues.

As far as means of transport are concerned, it has often been asked whether the Indonesians of the first millennium of our era had ships capable of covering such long distances. We know that at that period sewn boats, 'mtepe', were in use in the west Indian Ocean. These mtepe were perhaps one of the ancestors of the dhow, though the hull of the mtepe was joined by ligatures whereas the hull of the dhow is pegged together. The sails of the two vessels differed, however. In the east Indian Ocean, as Deschamps has shown, there were ships that could be taken on the high seas; the earliest picture of such a ship appears in the sculpture of the Borobudur temple (Java, eighth century) depicting a ship with an out-rigger, two masts and sails.

Having recognized the Indonesian contribution to the settlement of Madagascar, it remains to discover the routes that they may have taken. Many authors have pointed out the existence firstly of the great south Equatorial route which, in theory, might lead from Java to Madagascar; this south Equatorial current is strong between the southern coasts of Java and the neighbouring region of the Amber Cape from August to September. Sibrée has pointed out that the pumice stones which came from the Krakatoa explosion travelled along such a route that brought them eventually to the coast of Madagascar.

Although not absolutely untenable, the idea of a direct route from Insulindia to Madagascar remains unlikely for reasons that Donque explains perfectly: although *a priori* a direct route between Java and Madagascar meets with no insurmountable obstacles during the southern winter, when tropical cyclones are absent from the region, yet we should

25. Dyen; and A. Grandidier.

note the existence of factors that might invalidate such a hypothesis, for the direct journey covers a distance of nearly 4000 miles over a marine desert without a single port of call. We should, therefore, rather envisage a route that called in at southern India and Ceylon. Deschamps alludes to references made to pirate incursions in these regions in the first half of the first millennium of our era.

The journey from southern India to Madagascar does not pose any great problem. The route along the southern coasts of West Africa had been known since the period of the *Periplus*, and the abundance of Chinese coinage found later at Siraf testifies to the importance of trade between the Far East and the Middle East by sea. From the Middle East travellers went down the African coast as they had done in the days of Rhapta's prosperity, and it is probable that the discovery of the Comoro Islands was an intermediary step to that of Madagascar. From off Cape Delgado one can make out the silhouette of Kartala on the Great Comoro in clear weather, the contours of Moheli can be seen from the Great Comoro, and so on all the way to Mayotte. It is easy to imagine that a boat heading for one of the islands in the Comoro Archipelago might have missed its destination and ended up in the Nosy-Be or Cape Saint Sebastian, as often happened to Zanzibar dhows forced off route by bad weather in the nineteenth century.

It is in fact very likely that the Comoro Islands were settled a long time ago. The chronicles of local writers such as Said Ali note the presence there of pagan populations during the Beja period that preceded the arrival of the Muslims. Although we do not know whether they were Africans or Indonesians, it is nevertheless an interesting clue. According to some authors such as Repiquet and Robineau,[26] the population of the Heights of Anjouan, the Wamatsa, include a certain proportion of the descendants of the first pre-Islamic inhabitants. This hypothesis has not yet been properly examined. We may admit to the possibility that the Proto-Malagasy immigrants were Indonesian in origin on toponymical evidence (for example Antsahe can be compared to the Malagasy 'Antsaha') or on the evidence of traditional technology. At Ouani a traditional type of pottery survives that bears a marked resemblance in the shape and decoration of its cooking-pots to the corresponding Malagasy utensils.[27] Hébert has shown that in Anjuan there are also taboos on the eels of the mountain lakes that are very similar to the taboos observed by some Malagasy with respect to the same eel, which in Madagascar, as in Anjuan, bears a name that is of Indonesian derivation. Barraux[28] points to a tradition, that may be Malay–Polynesian in origin, found in Voueni. Of course, the culture of the Comoro Islands, like that of the east African coast, possesses objects from

26. C. Robineau, pp. 17–34.
27. P. Vérin, 1968, pp. 111–18.
28. M. Barraux, pp. 93–9.

south-east Asia such as the outrigger canoes and the file for opening coconuts.

The Indonesian substratum of Anjuan may one day be brought to light by the excavations being carried out at Old Sima. A road runs through this site, where there is still a fifteenth-century mosque underneath which lies an archaeological stratum containing sherds of red ochre pottery and an abundance of sea-shells – kitchen refuse. A Carbon 14 test on a *tridacnis* from the deeper strata shows that the site is 1550 years old, plus or minus 70 (Gakushuin Laboratory). This site should be excavated although it is difficult of access, for the pre-Islamic strata of Sima probably contain clues to the mystery of Proto-Malagasy.

The Indonesians who stayed on the African coast may, as Deschamps believed (as also did Kent, in a different but quite as hypothetical a form), have formed a nucleus for the settlement of Madagascar. The impact of the Indonesians on the African coast has been exaggerated, for the 'Malaysian complex' of plants imported into Africa from south-east Asia is not necessarily linked to Indonesia: according to the *Periplus* sugar-cane, and probably the coconut-palm, arrived independently.

The fact that the outrigger canoe is found throughout the Indian Ocean is certainly an indication of the extent of Indonesian influence, as Hornell realized; Deschamps believes that it shows the route taken by the migrations to Madagascar, a plausible idea which is, however, still under discussion, for the close links between Swahili and Malagasy culture may have encouraged such loans.

When we try to evaluate the extent of Indonesian influence on the East African coast we realize that it was relatively weak. If there had been any Indonesian settlement on the eastern coast, traces should have been found but none has so far been discovered. This leads us to believe that Asian impact on the coast – if it existed at all – was relatively localized and never constituted a colony of any size. In this context, we should discuss the information provided by the first Arab geographers. The oldest and most stimulating text to deal with the subject is undoubtedly that which recounts the incursions of the Waqwaq people on the African coasts in the second half of the tenth century. J. and M. Faublée[29] and R. Mauny[30] all justifiably consider this text to be extremely important, but they interpret it differently. The text comes from the 'Book of the Marvels of India' by Bowork ibn Chamriyar, a Persian from Ramhormoz.[31] The pertinent reference is as follows:

> Ibn Lakis has told me that the people of Waqwaq have been observed to do stupefying things. Thus in 334 AH [+945–6]

29. J. and M. Faublée.
30. R. Mauny, 1965.
31. L. M. Devic, 1878; Van der Lith, 1883–6, quoted by G. Ferrand, 1913–14, pp. 586–7.

they arrived there in a thousand landings and fought them with extreme vigour, though without being able to vanquish them, for Qanbaloh is surrounded by a strong wall around which stretches the estuary full of sea water, so that Qanbaloh stands in the midst of this estuary like a powerful citadel. When later people from Waqwaq landed there they asked them why it was that they had come to this place rather than another, and they replied that it was because they could find there goods which were required in their country and in China, such as ivory, tortoise-shell, leopard skins, and ambergris; also they were seeking out the Zeng, because they bore slavery with such ease and because they were so strong. They said that they had come a whole year's journey and that they had pillaged islands situated six days' sailing from Qanbaloh, and had made themselves masters of a number of villages and towns in the Zeng land of Sofala, not to speak of other towns which were not known to them. If these people spoke the truth and their account was accurate, that is, if they really had come a whole year's journey, then this would bear out what Ibn Lakis said of the islands of Waqwaq; that they are situated opposite China.[32]

Qanbaloh is probably the island of Pemba, and from the account of these incursions we may infer that the pirates came from south-east Asia, perhaps via Madagascar 'six days' sailing away'. It is true that during the first half of the tenth century the Indonesians were to be found in this area of the Indian Ocean, but at present we have no means of confirming that these arrivals took place well before the beginning of the tenth century.

If we refer to the other Arabic texts found and translated by Ferrand, it becomes obvious that the inhabitants of Waqwaq were negroids, but they may have included Indonesians, and they already had the mixed biological and linguistic structure of the Proto-Malagasy complex. In any case, Indonesian journeys to the African coast seem to have continued into the twelfth century, as a passage from Idrisi shows:

> The Zendju have no ships in which they can voyage, but boats land in their country from Oman, as do others that are heading for the islands of Zabadj [Zabedj, that is Sumatra] which belong to the Indies. These foreigners sell their goods and buy the produce of the country. The inhabitants of the islands of Zabadj call at Zendj in both large and small ships and trade their merchandise for them, as they understand each others' language.[33]

In another passage of the same manuscript[34] Idrisi states: 'the people

---

32. J. Sauvaget, quoted in J. and M. Faublée.
33. Idrisi Manuscript 2222 in the Bibliothèque Nationale, fol. 16, Vol. L, 9–12; also G. Ferrand, 1913–14, p. 552.
34. Fol. 21, Vol. L, 1–12.

of Komr and the merchants of Maharadja [Djaviga] call there [in Zendj], and are made welcome and trade with them'.

In the Arabic accounts Waqwaq and Komr sometimes seem to be confused, but the fifteenth-century charts of Ibn Majid and Suleyman el Mahri show unequivocally that the geographical term Komr denotes Madagascar, and sometimes even the Comoro Islands and Madagascar together. The confusion is interesting because it was probably the Waqwaq who settled the country of Komr.

## The end of Indonesian migration to the west

It is possible that it was the increased influence of Islam from the beginning of the second millennium that put a stop to the voyages of the Indonesians. A passage in Ibn el Mudjawir (thirteenth century) recounts an interesting Arabian tradition on this subject. The passage has been translated by Ferrand[35] and Deschamps rightly considers it to be fundamental:

> The site of Aden was inhabited by fishermen after the fall of the empire of the Pharaohs [probably the Roman empire, with its eastern capital of Alexandria]. The people of Al Komr invaded Aden and took possession of it, driving out the fishermen and setting up stone buildings on the mountains. They all arrived during a single monsoon. Now these people are dead and their migrations are finished. From Aden to Mogadiscio there is one monsoon, from Mogadiscio to Kiloa there is a second monsoon, and from Kiloa to Al Komr there is a third. The people of Al Komr had made use of these three as one, and a ship from Al Komr had arrived this way in Aden in Hejira 626 [+1228]: it had been on its way to Kiloa and had arrived in Aden by mistake. Their ships have outriggers because their seas are dangerous and shallow. But the Barabar drove them out of Aden, and now no one knows of the sea voyages of this people, or can tell how they lived and what they had done.

The Indonesian voyages to the coast of Africa ceased quite early, but this does not mean that relations were broken off between the Far East and the west Indian Ocean. On the contrary, there are indications of the expansion of Indian Ocean trade that was probably largely in the hands of the Muslims who became more and more familiar with the trade-routes. Ibn Majid's chart gives precise latitudes for the towns on the African coast and for the Indonesian territories and entrepôts across the ocean, which could, in those times, be crossed in thirty to forty days.

It is not inconceivable that though the Indonesians had stopped frequenting the coast of Africa, they continued to sail straight to

35. G. Ferrand, 1913–14.

Madagascar, perhaps from the southern regions of India. The Neo-Indonesians may have also followed this route. We know that it is quite practicable, for in 1930 some fishermen from the Laocadive Islands arrived alive and well at East Cape, having come directly to Madagascar from their own archipelago. The Neo-Indonesians learned the Malagasy dialect of the eastern inhabitants and were in contact with the Muslims, who at that time owned entrepôts on the eastern coast.

The pioneer Neo-Indonesians do seem to have made landings on the east coast but the region where the first Indonesians actually settled is still under discussion. Dahl has discovered that the names of the points of the compass in Malagasy and in the Indonesian languages are very closely related, but only coincide if the Malagasy compass is turned 90 degrees. Thus in Maanjan *barat* means west and *timor* east, whereas the corresponding Malagasy words, *avaratra* and *atsimo*, mean north and south respectively. This deplacement can easily be explained if we consider that for sea-going peoples the points of the compass are defined in terms of the winds: the north wind that brings the thunderstorms to the north-west coasts of Madagascar corresponds to the wet west wind of Indonesia, while the dry south wind has been identified with the dry east trade winds in Indonesia. Dahl's explanation is only valid for the north-west coast of Madagascar where he considers the immigrants would first have landed. But according to Hébert this pleasing hypothesis does not stand up to critical examination. If one pays more attention to the general characteristics of the winds (such as rainy and dry seasons) than to their actual direction, one understands that the Proto-Malagasy, who gave the name of 'barat laut' to the rain-bearing west wind in Indonesia, should have given the name 'avaratra' to the north where the rains come from, adopting a common measure between east and west in Madagascar, where in fact the rains and thunderstorms of the hot season blow from a north-easterly direction on the east coast and from a north-westerly direction on the west coast. There is nothing that allows us to presume that the Malagasy settled first of all on the north-west coast.[36]

## The African and Swahili immigration

This discussion of the various hypotheses as to the Indonesian origins of the Malagasy should not allow us to forget that an important – and possibly major – contribution to the settlement of Madagascar was from Africa. Deschamps has put forward two hypotheses to explain this Afro-Asian symbiosis, firstly that there was ethnic and cultural mixing on the east coast of Africa itself, and secondly that the Indonesians may have raided the neighbouring coast from Madagascar. Kent also sees the symbiosis in terms of strong Indonesian influence in Africa and a subsequent

36. J. C. Hébert, 1968a, pp. 809–20; 1968b, pp. 159–205; 1971, pp. 583–613.

colonization of Madagascar. However, at present we have no archaeological information whatsoever from the southern coastal sites of Africa (Tanzania–Mozambique), and I personally refuse to consider such theories except as mere hypotheses. It is quite possible that the Afro-Indonesians symbiosis may have begun in the Comoro Islands or in north Madagascar.

The often-repeated idea that Madagascar was originally inhabited by pygmies defies all geological and navigational evidence since Madagascar has been an isolated island since the Tertiary era and the pygmies are no sailors and did not share in the expansion of the Swahili maritime civilization. Moreover, such tribes as the Mikea who were once thought to have been the last of the pygmy inhabitants are not particularly small.

In my opinion the Malagasy of African origin are Bantu-speaking people; it is probable that they started arriving in the island at the latest from the ninth century on, as did the Indonesians, but it is unlikely that the African migration continued until the dawn of recent historical times (sixteenth century). We may suppose that most of the Africans arrived at the same time and in the same way as the Muslims or the non-Muslim Swahili.

Though the Malagasy vocabulary is predominantly Indonesian, we should not forget the Bantu contribution. Similarly the Creole spoken in the Antilles consisting of 95 per cent French with some African elements. The Bantu contribution to Malagasy is on two levels, principally that of vocabulary but also that of word structure. The fact that Bantu words occur in all the dialects of Madagascar shows that the African settlement of the country was not particularly belated; their influence is found in the very roots of Malagasy civilization. The Malagasy language bears traces of a very pronounced Bantu influence. This influence is so great, and of such a character, that it is inexplicable unless a Bantu substratum is assumed. Moreover, O. Dahl has clearly demonstrated that the change-over from consonant finals (Indonesian) to vowel finals was caused by the Bantu substratum, and if this is the case then this change must have taken place soon after the Indonesians settled down among the Bantu-speaking people, during the period when the latter were adapting to the new language.[37]

There are consequently grounds for seeking the cause of the transformation of Malagasy into a language with vowel finals not in Indonesia but in Madagascar itself.

If the language spoken in Madagascar before the arrival of the Indonesians was a Bantu language, this transformation is very easy to understand. Among the Bantu languages, those which allow of final consonants are rare exceptions, and I personally do not know of any in East Africa. People who speak a language without final consonants always find it difficult to pronounce the final consonants of another language, at

37. O. Ch. Dahl, pp. 113–14.

least when there is no supporting vowel. All those who have taught French in Madagascar will have discovered this for themselves!

I therefore assume that the changeover from consonant finals to vowel finals was caused by a Bantu substratum. And if this is the case then this change must have taken place soon after the Indonesians settled down among the Bantu-speakers, during the period when the latter were adapting to the new language. It was thus one of the first phonetic changes after the immigration to Madagascar. We know little about how Madagascar fitted into the general picture of the expansion of Bantu-speaking people. That many of them were sea-going is known, as for example the Bajun of Somalia, studied by Grottanelli, the Mvita of Kenya and the ancient Makua of Mozambique, but it is difficult to establish any links between them and Madagascar in the absence of archaeological evidence. It has recently been discovered that the linguistic foundations of the language spoken on the island of Anjuan can be linked to Pokomo on the coast of Kenya (in the region of the mouth of the Tana river), and this Comoro Island may have been a stopping place on the way, as perhaps also the island of Juan de Nova, that is frequented nowadays by turtle-hunters and by dhows.[38] The Bantu-speaking people must have passed through the Comoro Islands to get to Madagascar. It is therefore natural to think that the Bantu language or languages formerly spoken in Madagascar were closely related to those of the Comoro Islands.

The ancient Bantu words which exist in Malagasy support this hypothesis. From Ibn Battuta we know that at the beginning of the fourteenth century the Swahili civilization, though not totally Muslim, was expanding. It is my opinion that these early sailors from the primitive Swahili civilizations, whether Muslim or not, played a fundamental role in African migration to Madagascar.

Although it is at present impossible to unravel the succession of cultural contributions, many authors have been conscious of the heterogeneous character of the settlement of north and west Madagascar. Mellis, throughout his book on the north-west, stresses the contrast between the people of the sea-coast (antandrano) and the people of the interior (olo boka antety); this contrast is reflected in some of their funerary rites.

Some of the inhabitants of predominantly African physique recognize that they came originally from beyond the sea, and this appears in their customs. This is the case with the Vezo-Antavelo along the western and north-western coast, and the Kajemby who still have their cemeteries on the dunes of the beaches and acknowledge that they are related to Sandangoatsy. The Sandangoatsy now live in the interior, near Lake Kinkony, but this was not always the case, for charts and Portuguese accounts from the beginning of the seventeenth century show the name *Sarangaco* or *Sangaco* (a corruption of Sandangoatsy) on the edges of Marambitsy bay.

38. Nautical Instructions, 1969, p. 159.

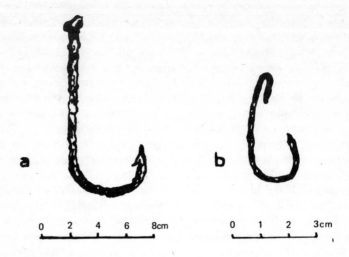

FIG. 28.4 *Fish-hooks from Talaky* (*twelfth century*)

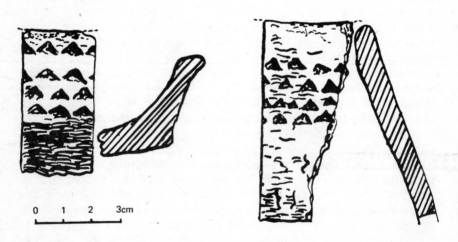

FIG. 28.5 *Ceramics from Kingany and Rasoky* (*fifteenth century*)

In the last three and a half centuries, however, the Sandangoatsy have turned their backs on the sea which was their first home, and it is probable that the Vazimba of central west Madagascar and the central highlands have done the same.

The movements of the coast-dwelling Bantu-speakers from the ninth century account for the African contribution to the settlement of Madagascar, but we still have to explain why the Indonesian language became the *lingua franca*. Some of the Bantu-speakers must have come into contact with the Indonesians, and it is possible that between different Africans speaking different languages or dialects Indonesian may have been a language of convenience. However, Madagascar must have continued to be the linguistic and ethnic chequerboard for quite a while, at least on the coast around Baly and Maintirano (Mariano's Bambala), on the Tsiribihina (according to Drury), and among certain Vazimba tribes in the interior (according to Birkeli and Hébert). The ancient Vazimba led a rather primitive life economically. They lived as fishermen on the coasts, but in the interior they probably depended to a great extent on a crude use of the natural resources at their disposal. Gathering berries, hunting and collecting honey were probably sufficient for their needs. According to Drury, the Vazimba of the Tsiribihina were river fishers, and excavations have shown great heaps of shells eaten by these berry-gathering peoples near Ankazoaka and Ankatso.

The symbiosis between the Indonesian and Africans started at the very beginning of the settlement of Madagascar. By the tenth century a few of the coastal Bantu-speakers must have converted to Islam. I find striking the fact that the Muslims of Madagascar share with all the peoples of the west and north-west coasts the same myth as to their origins, the myth of Mojomby, or 'the lost island'. Elsewhere[39] I have recounted the myth in literary form as it was told to me by the Antalaotse of Boina Bay. According to my informants, Selimany Sebany and Tonga, the ancestors of the Kajemby and the Antalaotse, once lived together on an island between the African coast and the Comoros. They lived by trade and practised the Muslim religion. But when impiety and discord appeared on the island, Allah decided to punish them: the island sank beneath a raging sea and only a few righteous men escaped. Some say that they were miraculously saved, others say that God sent a whale to carry them away. Kajemby and Antalaotse were descended from righteous men. It seems likely therefore that the Muslims did not superimpose their culture on Madagascar, but rather played a catalytic role among the Africans who had migrated there.

39. P. Vérin, 1970a, pp. 256–8.

PLATE 28.1 *Stone pot, Vohemar civilization*

PLATE 28.2 *Chinese pottery, Vohemar civilization*

PLATE 28.3 *Antalaotse tomb of Antsoheribory*

PLATE 28.4 *Ancient door of Miandrivahiny Ambohimanga (Imerina)*

PLATE 28.5 *Fishing canoe 'vezo' of Indonesian balancing type*

PLATE 28.6 *Village of Andavadoaka in the south-west; the thatched huts are identical to the first constructions erected here*

PLATE 28.7 *Terraced rice fields near Ambositra, which might be compared to those of Luçon in the Philippines*

PLATE 28.8 *Cemetery of Marovoay near Morondava*

PLATE 28.9 *Cemetery of Ambohimalaza (Imerina); the 'cold-houses' on the graves imitate the style of traditional homes*

PLATE 28.10 *Statue of Antsary: Antanosy art near Fort-Dauphin*

PLATE 28.11 *A lesson in geomancy: extreme south*

# The societies of Africa south of the Sahara in the early iron age

## M. POSNANSKY

In the last few chapters we have looked at the archaeology of different regions of sub-Saharan Africa in the closing millennium before our era and during the first millennium of our era. The purpose of this chapter is to try to assess some of the major trends which seem to have been developing in the history of Africa during the period under review. The changes which took place in all areas were of a fundamental nature. The economy was transformed from one which was largely parasitic on the landscape to one which was in control of its means of food production from both plants and animals. The technology was equally transformed from a simple one based largely on stone and wood to a far more complex one based on various metals as well as stone. During the period the foundations had been laid for the African societies we know today – the boundaries between different linguistic groups were to alter slightly, the population was to expand radically, and social and political groupings were to become more complex as states emerged, but by and large many of the fundamental demographic and economic aspects of sub-Saharan Africa had been established by the last quarter of the first millennium of our era.

One of the problems in trying to delineate the emergent trends lies in the unevenness of the archaeological coverage. Vast areas still remain archaeologically unexplored, particularly in some of the largest countries such as Angola, Mozambique, Zaïre, the Central African Republic, Cameroon, Dahomey, the Ivory Coast, Mali, Upper Volta, Niger, Sierra Leone and Madagascar. Even where significant research has been undertaken it is highly localized, as in Senegal or Chad. It is important to note that whereas organizations concerned with antiquities date from the nineteenth century for parts of North Africa (e.g. Egypt, 1858) many sub-Saharan countries have only initiated research with independence and the establishment of national museums and universities. Nevertheless the establishment within the last ten years of radio-carbon chronology has revolutionized our knowledge of the early iron age and allows some broad generalizations to be made about the time scale involved in the various economic developments.

# Mineral exploitation

Four minerals of more than local significance were exploited during the period: copper, salt, iron and gold in the probable order of their initial exploitation. Stone was, of course, still in use even after metals were used for the more important tools and weapons.

## Copper

Copper was first mined in Mauretania probably by the first quarter of the first millennium before our era. The form of the copper artefacts found in the area suggests that the stimulus for the mining came from contact with Morocco. Very little is known of the form that the original mines took, though it is believed that they were relatively shallow undertakings.[1] The Mauretanian mines were the only ones that we know for certain were operational before + 1000. Other sources of copper occur in Mali and Niger in the Nioro and Takedda areas and were certainly being exploited by the second millennium of our era but when they were first discovered or worked is unknown.

There is evidence from Arab writers and also classical sources[2] to suggest that copper was an element in trans-Saharan trade as early as the first millennium of our era, coming south, perhaps, in return for the gold going to the north. The finding of ingots at Macden Ijafen in the western Sahara is evidence of the importance of the trade at a slightly later period (eleventh or twelfth century of our era). Of vital importance for an appreciation of the scale of the trade is the material from Igbo Ukwu in eastern Nigeria. If really of the ninth century, as claimed by the excavator Thurstan Shaw,[3] and also by Dr Wai-Andah in Chapter 24, it clearly indicates that the trade must have been large scale by the eighth or ninth centuries of our era, in order to account for the large number of cuprous objects and for the implied even larger numbers which still await discovery in similar sites. But many other scholars[4] are unwilling to accept such an early date and suggest one well within the second millennium of our era. As the distribution of copper ores in Africa is highly localized on account of geological factors, only trade can explain the abundance of the Igbo material. Shaw feels that the technology involved in making the *cire-perdue* castings was northern-inspired and probably Arab in origin. Apart from the possibility of Igbo Ukwu, there are surprisingly few copper objects in West Africa before + 1000, except in Senegal and Mauretania, which are close either to the

---

1. N. Lambert, 1971, pp. 9–21.
2. M. Posnansky, 1971, pp. 110–25.
3. T. Shaw, 1970, pp. 503–17.
4. B. Lawal, pp. 1–8; M. Posnansky, 1973b, pp. 309–11.

Akjoujt mines or to the western Saharan trade-route. One area from which copper objects can be dated to the end of the millennium is the Niger valley above Segu, in which spectacular tumuli like El Ouladji and Killi are situated. The copper in these objects could either have been obtained from the Sahelian sources in Mali or Niger or derived from trade. Unfortunately most of the objects from these tumuli were found in the early part of this century and have now been lost so that they only remain as tantalizing illustrations in the excavators' reports. Spectographic analyses should help in determining the original copper sources but the problem with cuprous objects is that they are often made up of an amalgam of new metal and melted-down scrap. Nevertheless, eventually some trace elements should be able to be detected which can indicate whether the Nioro and Takedda ores were being exploited at the time the tumuli were built.

Another copper source worked at this time was that in the Shaba region of Zaïre, where the excavations at Sanga and Katoto have revealed an abundance of copper objects. Nevertheless, it is worth noting that in the tripartite cultural division suggested by the excavator Nenquin[5] the earliest phase, the Kisalian, is represented by twenty-seven graves, of which only two contained copper ingots. This suggests that during the Kisalian period, dating from the seventh to the ninth centuries of our era, copper, though being exploited and made into ornaments, was not really abundant. The copper belt in northern Zambia was also exploited at this time with a date for copper-mining of $+400 \pm 90$ being reported from Kansanshi.[6] Copper items, however, were more numerous in southern than in northern Zambia at this time. The first and far from numerous copper items in southern Zambia were probably obtained from the Sinoia area of Zimbabwe and sources in eastern Zambia. So far we know nothing about the exploitation methods in either of these areas. Elsewhere in Africa copper was a very scarce resource: it has not been found on sites in Eastern Africa until a much later date.

## Salt

Salt is a mineral that was in great demand particularly with the beginning of an agricultural mode of life. Hunters and food-gatherers probably obtained a large amount of their salt intake from the animals they hunted and from fresh plant food. Salt only becomes an essential additive where fresh foods are unobtainable in very dry areas, where body perspiration is also normally excessive. It becomes extremely desirable, however, amongst societies with relatively restricted diets as was the case with arable agriculturalists. We have no idea when the salt resources of the Sahara at

5. J. Nenquin, 1957; 1963, p. 277.
6. M. S. Bisson, pp. 276–92.

Taghaza and Awlil were first extracted. That they were an element in the trade of the Sahara by the first millennium of our era is evident from Arabic texts of the last quarter of the millennium. It is probable that some of the salt extraction is as old as the copper-mining and the development of the Tichitt settlements in Mauretania, both areas where a sedentary life would have imposed the need for salt supplies. We know quite a lot about mining activities in the medieval period, which will be discussed in later volumes, but nothing about them at this time. It is probable that at this period the mining operations were of a fairly simple kind. Salt would have been available as a surface deposit in various parts of the Sahara as a result of the desiccation process after −250. Perhaps man noted which dried-up lakes, swamp or pond beds attracted wild animals. Surface salts are often quite obvious from their colour.

There are several known early salt-workings in East Africa at Uvinza,[7] east of Kigoma in Tanzania, at Kibiro[8] on the shores of Lake Mobutu Sese Seko in Uganda, at Basanga in Zambia[9] and probably also at Sanga[10] in Zaïre and in the Gwembe valley in Zambia. The salt extraction at Uvinza was probably rudimentary as the fifth- and sixth-century finds at the salt springs were not associated with the stone-lined brine tanks which characterized the second-millennium occupation. Salt springs were also the source of the salt at Kibiro where an elaborate boiling and filtration process may date from the first millennium of our era; as there would be very little *raison d'être* for occupation at the site otherwise. At Basanga the salt flats were occupied from as early as the fifth century and suggest an early, though so far not definitely established, exploitation of the salt, probably by evaporation processes. Salt elsewhere was probably made in the variety of ways which persisted until the nineteenth century which involved burning and boiling grasses, or even goat droppings, from areas of known high soil-salt content, and then evaporating off the brine so obtained and filtering out all the large impurities. Colander vessels used in such processes are common throughout iron age contexts but unfortunately such perforated vessels could also be used for other food preparation processes, which makes the certain ascription of salt-making often very difficult.

## Iron

Iron ores were worked as early as middle stone age times in Swaziland[11] for use as pigments. It is clear that body pigments and iron oxides ochres for body pigments and later for decorating rock surfaces were eagerly sought after from early stone age times. A piece of haematitic colouring matter

7. J. E. G. Sutton and A. D. Roberts, pp. 45–86.
8. J. Hiernaux and E. Maquet, 1968, p. 49.
9. A. D. Roberts, p. 720.
10. B. M. Fagan, 1969a, p. 7.
11. R. A. Dart and P. B. Beaumont, 1969a, pp. 127–8.

was even brought into the Olduvai Basin by very early stone age tool-users. By late stone age times manganese,[12] specularite,[13] and haematite were being regularly mined at localities in Zambia, Swaziland and in the northern Cape.[14] An excavation in some of the workings at Doornfontein indicated regular mining operations involving galleries and chambers from which up to 45 000 metric tons of specularite may have been obtained, probably by Khoisan-speaking groups from the ninth century of our era onwards. It is likely that the existence of such mines and the implied knowledge of metallic ores and their properties helped the rapid growth of an iron technology in the first half of the first millennium of our era.

Elsewhere in sub-Saharan Africa we do not have such clear indications of mining for iron and it seems that the lateritic crust of the tropical areas was the most likely source of iron ores. Bog iron, however, was used in the lower Casamance valley in Senegal[15] and at Machili in Zambia.[16] The iron so obtained would have been broken down into very small pieces and hand-selected for smelting. A region where the mining, as opposed to the surface collecting, of laterites may have been undertaken was to the north of the Gambia river in the area of the Senegambian megaliths, which are themselves upright blocks of laterite. Their use there as ritual structures and the growth of an iron technology in the area during the first millennium of our era would indicate that it would be a small step towards the actual mining of the laterites for smelting. It is possible that extensive smelting of the laterites was an essential preliminary to the idea of quarrying the laterite for building purposes. A similar process may have developed in the Central African Republic where megaliths also occur. It has been suggested by Wai Andah in Chapter 24 that the ease of laterite-digging as opposed to haematite-quarrying may be one of the clues to a hitherto unsubstantiated claim for an indigenous development of an iron technology in Africa. Laterite, when damp and buried beneath a soil profile, is relatively crumbly and far easier to dig through than normal rock. Unfortunately, except for the southern African mines, no other certain iron-'mining' areas have been either found or accurately dated. It is possible that the Uelian stone axes of haematite in north-eastern Zaïre and Uganda may be of iron age date and fashioned in haematite in imitation of wrought iron.

## Gold

Gold was almost certainly mined in West Africa during the period under review, as well as being collected by alluvial panning. Though implied by

12. R. A. Dart and P. Beaumont, 1969b, pp. 91–6.
13. A. Boshier and P. Beaumont, 1972, pp. 2–12.
14. P. B. Beaumont and A. K. Boshier, pp. 41–59.
15. O. Linares de Sapir, p. 43.
16. J. D. Clark and B. M. Fagan, pp. 354–71.

the Arabic sources, no actual goldmines have been located, excavated or dated, nor has evidence for the refining processes been recovered. These were probably similar to those well documented for later periods.[17] The main areas for which there is evidence of gold exploitation – largely from non-contemporaneous sources – were located near the headwaters of the Niger and Senegal rivers in present-day Guinea and Mali and are known as Bambouk and Bouré. There is rather better evidence (discussed by Phillipson in Chapter 27) for gold-mining by means of shallow adits or stopes in north-eastern Zimbabwe, but there is no undisputed evidence that the activity is older than the eighth or ninth century of our era. The ores seem to have been crushed using pounding stones.

It is possible that experimentation with different ores from stone age times laid the foundation for the later larger-scale extraction of both copper and gold. Whereas many copper objects have been found on excavations thus enabling us to date the introduction of copper as a material for both tools and ornaments, very little gold has been found in contexts of the first millennium of our era. It was too valuable to be lost without a search. The only gold objects of an early date are those from the Senegalese tumuli which date from towards the end of the period.

## Stone

Stone was almost certainly quarried for various purposes, the most important of which was to provide the raw material for ground and polished stone tools and for the manufacture of querns. Many societies used fixed querns, taking their grains to a rocky outcrop where they could also lay out foods to dry and where they could grind grains or pound vegetable foods. But such outcrops are not available everywhere and it is evident that rock for grindstones, both the upper and lower varieties, had to be searched for and often moved over considerable distances. Unfortunately this aspect of archaeology has attracted only scant attention in Africa so far. In years to come, when the number of archaeologists and geologists increases and the geology of the continent has been adequately mapped, it will be a routine job to section all strange rock-types and undertake a petrological analysis as an aid in tracing them to their geological source areas. Axe factories have occasionally been found, as at Buroburo[18] in Ghana, whilst a quern factory dating to the first century before our era has been discovered at Kintampo[19] in Ghana. At this latter site large numbers of partially made rubbers for grinding, as well as querns, were found in a rock shelter which was largely man-made by extensive fire 'setting' to dislodge the stone. The curious oval-sectioned rasps (also termed 'cigars') which are such a distinctive

17. N. Levtzion, pp. 283.
18. R. Nunoo, pp. 321–33.
19. P. A. Rahtz and C. Flight, pp. 1–31.

feature of Ghanaian archaeology appear in part to be fashioned from a single rock-type[20] which was traded over a wide area. All over sub-Saharan Africa grooves normally 10–12 centimetres wide and up to 50 centimetres long mark the spots where suitable flaked stone roughouts were ground to make axes, adzes and chisels. It is probable that the process of quarrying, albeit on a small scale, grinding, polishing and trading of either the roughouts or the finished products went on throughout the period in diminishing intensity as iron replaced stone. In some areas ground-stone tools were, however, still in use in the second millennium of our era. Surprisingly few groundstone tools have been found in East and southern Africa though they are extremely common in West Africa.

Grey vesicular lava, which like laterite is easier to shape on first exposure to the air, was quarried for stone bowls in Kenya and possibly Tanzania during the first millennium before our era. Their use is unknown: many of those found were associated with burials. They are too soft for grinding anything but soft vegetable foods. Similar bowls have been found in Namibia, but elsewhere they are rare.

Another relatively unexplored activity which certainly took place was the search for suitable semi-precious stones to make into beads: cornelian and various forms of chalcedony such as agates and jaspers, as well as crystalline quartzes or rock crystal, were the most common. Beads of these materials are found all over sub-Saharan Africa – often in graves such as those at the Njoro river cave site in Kenya, dated to the tenth century before our era and also on habitation sites. At Lantana in Niger[21] a mine for red stone (jasper) which is still traded to Nigeria for bead-making is believed to be very old, but it is impossible to date its origin. Rarely abundant, stone beads nevertheless indicate a deliberate search for well-known rock types. Such beads were, of course, made as long ago as stone age times and were to continue being made right throughout the iron age until gradually replaced by the cheaper, more easily made and eventually more accessible glass trade-beads.

## Trade[22]

Some form of exchange has gone on between communities probably from relatively early stone age times. The exchange of bright or useful stones and honey for meat and occasionally even womenfolk probably marked the gatherings of foraging peoples, if models based on the study of modern hunters and food-gatherers are any guide. Such exchanges, which were of both a ritual and economic significance, would have become regular as societies entered into an agricultural existence, though even in late

20. M. Posnansky, 1969–70, p. 20.
21. G. de Beauchêne, 1970, p. 63.
22. See Chapter 21 and M. Posnansky, 1971.

stone age times specialized fishers, seafood collectors or hunters must have led relatively settled lives and thus required for their tools stones and other materials which were not locally available. It is possible that certain bone implements, such as harpoons, which required more than average expertise, may have been traded. But it is fair to conclude that agriculture, implying a sedentary or a seasonal or periodically shifting existence, would have involved an increase in trade. Much of this trade was probably on a relatively restricted scale and local in scope but would have included such commodities as salt, certain types of stone and later iron tools, beads, shells, possibly plants for medicinal or ritual use, meat for arable communities and grains and root crops for pastoral groups, specialized utensils or substances like poisons for fishing or hunting, dried fish and all sorts of objects with a scarcity value such as strange seeds, animal claws, teeth, curious stones, bones, etc., which might have had a magical significance and which even today are the stock-in-trade of certain stalls in West African markets. Except for the polished stone tools, quern stones and salt which have been referred to in the previous section, nothing is known about this trade.

With the advent of metals, however, trade took on a different character. Copper and gold are more localized than stones and were in demand by communities both to the north of the Sahara and to the east around the Indian Ocean. Cowries and other Indian Ocean marine shells found on excavation sites in Zambia such as Kalundu and Gundu from the fourth to the sixth centuries of our era in Gokomere sites in Zimbabwe and at Sanga in the heart of the continent, indicate the beginnings of more than a local trade. True, such objects often found singly could have been curiosities handed from group to group from the coast to inland, but it is significant that they occur in areas which had resources of value to the outside world. The presence of copper ingots in the Central and southern African sites indicates a growing complexity in the trade, whilst the wealth of objects both in the Senegalese tumuli and at Sanga points to the success of the trade and the growth of social or political structures which took advantage of the wealth generated. There is no reason to suppose that the trade was on a very big scale at this date even across the Sahara but the networks had been established. We also have little evidence of markets or distribution centres in sub-Saharan Africa, though Arabic references to the old Ghana capital suggest that they probably existed before the acceleration of the trade brought about by the Arab conquest of North Africa. The chiefs' courts probably served as redistribution centres, a suggestion which is supported by the varied objects from the Malian and Senegalese tumuli. But unfortunately for this period we can only speculate from the barest of scattered information.

Glass beads have come from several sites in Zambia, Shaba (Zaïre) and Zimbabwe from contexts in the last half of the first millennium and they were certainly imports. A recent attempt[23] to both date and find the origin

23. C. C. Davidson and J. D. Clark, pp. 75–86.

of the 'trade wind' beads of the Indian Ocean has proved somewhat disappointing. They are found all around the Indian Ocean from the Philippines to the East African coast. Sources for their manufacture in the Levant, where Hebron was an ancient bead-making centre, India and Alexandria, have all been suggested. Trade wind beads are small, normally reheated cane beads in a variety of single colours. Though certain factories in India are known to have exported them from the ninth century onwards it is very difficult to assign beads to precise factories without exhaustive analyses. More than 150 000 similar beads have come from Igbo Ukwu and if an early date is accepted for that site it implies an extensive trade in beads across the Sahara by the late first millennium of our era.

Summers[24] has suggested that it was the Indian Ocean trade that led to Indian prospecting and mining methods being adopted in the Zimbabwe gold industry but his ideas have gained very little support. The gold was probably being mined by or before the time when the trade from the East African coast affected the Zimbabwe area. Far too little is known either about early mining methods or about first millennium gold trade to link either with any outside influence. The trade of the East African coast has been discussed in Chapter 22 and clearly indicates the extensive contacts around the Indian Ocean which affected Africa. Though the trade was extensive it was not intensive and hardly affected the interior of the continent before +1000 except up the Mazoe and Ravi river valleys in Mozambique leading to Zimbabwe.

## Emerging themes in African history: sub-Saharan Africa in the last quarter of the first millennium of our era

It is now necessary to see whether, from the mass of descriptive data presented in the last eight chapters, any conclusions can be drawn about the state of African society at the end of the early iron age. The period witnessed the transformation of the economy of sub-Saharan Africa from one of hunting and gathering to one mainly dependent on agriculture. Population certainly grew and settled life, villages and larger social units were the outcome. It is difficult to ascertain the social structures involved but it is likely that over most of Africa we are dealing with relatively small villages consisting of one or more lineage groups with wider affinities based on clan relationships. Population densities must have been small in most areas: probably only a handful to the square kilometre. Following the initial rapid movements consequent upon the advent of iron, allowing clearance of the more wooded areas of Africa, communities had settled down. We have evidence of their isolation in the divergence of different members of the same language families and in the increasingly varied pottery forms and decorations which were developing in most areas around

24. R. Summers, pp. 256–7.

+600 to +1000. Demographic estimates, based both on the historical evidence available in North Africa and on extrapolation from ethnographic data and colonial census figures, indicate a population of well under 10 million for the whole of sub-Saharan Africa before +1000. If indications from oral traditions of change from matrilineal to patrilineal societies in the past five hundred years, particularly in East Africa, are any guide, we are dealing very much with matrilineal societies over most of the areas of tropical Africa.

From the distribution of archaeological artefacts it would appear that the West African forest zone was probably only very lightly settled, though an exception here may have been parts of southern Nigeria. Areas which are now less popular because of their thinner soil and lower rainfall, such as the Jos plateau, seem at that time to have been more attractive to peoples with a less sophisticated technology. The densest settlement was largely in the savannah woodland and in the so-called 'dry forest' areas. The large number of sites in the Niger Delta area of Mali between Segu and Timbuktu, where over 10 million square kilometres is inundated annually bringing water (and increased fertility) to an otherwise marginal environment, indicates that it was also an area favourable for both early agriculturalists and pastoralists. This was an area where fishing continued to be important and trade developed rapidly. The latter activity was facilitated by the ease of river movement and the need to transport such basic commodities as firewood and building timber or grass to areas which had little vegetation cover. There seems little indication that in Africa the drier 'bush' country of central Tanzania, northern Uganda and Kenya was occupied by agriculturalists; and the same is certainly true of the more arid parts and high-altitude zones (like Lesotho) of South Africa. River valleys like the Zambezi, the Kafue and the upper Nile, and parts of the shores of Lakes Nyasa, Victoria and Kivu, as well as smaller ones, seem to have attracted settlement. Particularly favoured, however, were ecotone situations where the food resources of two or more ecological zones (forest and savannah, plain and foothills, etc.) could be exploited. This was particularly advantageous on the southern edge of the savannah in West Africa or around the Zaïrean forest, from where it was easier to cut slowly into the forest fringes for land for cultivation whilst at the same time taking advantage of its natural resources such as game, wood products, including bark cloth, and wild fruits. The forest presented very much a moving frontier and new groups penetrated it slowly, first for hunting and collecting and later for settlement. On the whole we are dealing with agricultural settlements mainly in areas with rainfall figures of 600–1400 millimetres per annum. Pastoral activities and short seasonal cultivation was of course possible in area like the Sahel with rainfalls as low as 150 millimetres. Though there were sheep as far south as the Cape by the beginning of the millennium and there must have been herders there and also in parts of the Sahelian and Sudanic belts, this was not an era when purely pastoral societies were dominant. Kraals when found are small. It would appear that the northern cultivators were better adapted to coping with lower rainfall regimes than those in the Bantu world, which is possibly a reflection of their 'Neolithic' ancestry and their early cultivation of such crops as millet and sorghum. The coasts nowhere seem to have been settled extensively and there are no long traditions of coastal fishing activities using boats. There are midden deposits of shells, fish bones and (in some localities) animal bones, as along the Casamance river and other inlets of the Senegambian regions; along the sea-lagoons of the Guinea coast as far as the Ivory Coast; around the Cape and on the eastern shore of Lake Victoria (the old Wilton C of L. S. B. Leakey). Such strandlopers, however, were never numerous and had very little impact on the peoples of the interior. There must have been some scattered settlements on the East African coast, according to the documentary sources discussed in Chapter 22, but there are virtually no archaeological traces of settlement until the eighth century of our era, when it would appear that more permanent colonists were arriving from the Persian Gulf area and/or the Benadir coast of Somalia.

Curiously it is more difficult to discover details about the religious beliefs of this time than about those of the preceding hunter-gatherers of the late stone age. The latter provided many clues in their rock art.[25] The earliest agriculturists possibly painted the rocks and may have been responsible for the stylized art of much of East and Central Africa, particularly of the area around Lake Victoria[26] and of Zambia.[27] Though we have some idea when this art tradition was finishing, we have no idea when it originated. The practice of burial is in itself often an expression of religious belief and the goods that were buried with the dead would in many cases indicate a sense of the need for such items in the after-life. This is not of course, the only possible explanation. The size of the grave, the splendour of the grave-goods and the munificence of the accompanying ceremony can also serve to demonstrate the status, whether political, ritual, economic or social, of the family of the bereaved. The scale of the funeral activities would also help to establish the genealogy of the chief mourners. It should be remembered however, and we have excellent twentieth-century parallels for the practice, that non-religious societies often build very striking mausolea. The existence of impressive burial mounds or funerary monuments need not necessarily imply a belief in a given god or group of gods; but it certainly indicates confidence in the future on the part of society, and represents a political gesture of continuity by a ruling or elite group. Nevertheless the cemeteries by Lake Kisale in the Shaba region of Zaïre, the huge tumuli along the middle Niger and the Senegambian megaliths and burial mounds are all evidence, not just of settled peoples,

25. M. Posnansky, 1972a, pp. 29–44.
26. J. H. Chaplin, pp. 1–50.
27. D. W. Phillipson, 1972a.

but of peoples willing to invest part of their wealth and much of their labour in funerary monuments and/or grave goods. The full interpretation of these manifestations must await further detailed excavations and the publication of adequate site reports. The consistency of some of the burial practices with regard to body orientation or grave alignment indicates a regulated canon of beliefs. The sheer size of the Malian tumuli probably indicates the establishment of the institution of kingship, which, if not necessarily divine, was certainly endowed with many of the powers of the supreme ruler. Such rulers could evidently obtain, whether freely or by coercion we are in no position to determine, the labour of large numbers of people in an area of limited population to erect tumuli 65 metres in diameter and 12 metres high, like that at El Ouladzi.[28]

It is apparent that in the period under review states of some kind were emerging. The two key areas were the Sudanic belt and the area of central Africa around the headwaters of the Lualaba. In the Sudanic belt there were possibly three nuclear area, around Ghana in southern Mauretania and Senegal, in the inland Niger Delta above Segu and around Lake Chad. All were areas where long-distance trade was beginning to be important and where agriculture probably developed earlier than in areas farther to the south. Several hypotheses have been advanced for the emergence of states. A popular view based initially on ideas first advanced by Frazer[29] in *The Golden Bough* more than eighty years ago, was that divine kingship, which many would claim is a characteristic feature of centralized African societies, spread from ancient Egypt, possibly via the office of rainmaker. The first chiefs were thus charismatic spiritual leaders, who obtained their inspiration from neighbouring societies where similar systems operated and ultimately from a common source, namely, Egypt. The theory was later refined by Baumann[30] who described the characteristic features of the Sudanic state, and more recently by Oliver.[31] The concept of the Sudanic state which has thus been elaborated is supported by eye-witness descriptions in medieval Arabic of Ghana and other West African states and by sixteenth-century Portuguese descriptions of Central African states. All these accounts stress the mystery surrounding the king, the extreme deference of his subjects and the practice of regicide in the case of imperfection or ill health. For Oliver the spread of horse-borne, iron-using warriors is a crucial factor in the diffusion of the idea of the state, in the creation of the ruling élite and in the control and expansion of the frontiers. There are, however, other views, and most African scholars see in diffusionist views an attempt to bring in more advanced cultural elements from outside without investigating the possibilities of an in-

28. R. Mauny, 1961.
29. J. G. Frazer.
30. H. Baumann and D. Westermann.
31. R. Oliver and B. M. Fagan.

dependent development of statehood. The critics of diffusionist views, of which the writer is one,[32] feel that though there are similarities between the ceremonial and ritual of many African states there are very substantial differences. Many of the similarities may be later accretions, particularly when trade expanded following the spread of Islam into Africa. Other reasons advanced for state formation include the effects of long-distance trade and scarce mineral exploitation, which were probably factors in the rise of Ghana, and also the results of competition for scarce resources in areas of marginal fertility. This latter view has been advanced by Carneiro[33] for the rise of ancient Egypt, but it could equally well apply in a Sahelian context. According to this theory one group, often with the help of superior military technology, would expand at the expense of weaker neighbours, who would thus become the dependants of the conquering group. In time other areas would be absorbed, and eventually the conquering group would be left controlling a large area in which it was in a minority. It would need to reinforce its authority not only by military prowess but also by creating a social structure with the elite military group at the top. The oral traditions and rituals of the ruling group would provide the state religion, which would thus help to ensure and rationalize the mystique of its authority. The head of the elite group, if he were not so in reality, would become the supposed unilineal descendant or reincarnation of the original conqueror, with definite divine characteristics. The divinity of the ruler in such a model is not original but is acquired, often slowly, mostly deliberately, but often probably incidentally, as a defence mechanism to preserve the distinctive integrity of the chief.

The idea that the development of trade led to states has been widely discussed. Basically the theory is that trade leads to increased wealth, and that increased wealth is eventually manifest in social stratification. Wealth leads to powers of patronage and the ability to control other activities, such as the exploitation of minerals, the manufacture of consumer goods or the production of food. All these activities led to further wealth and the centralization of more powers. Several of these elements, such as the acquisition of wealth and the social stratification which are apparent in the Sanga area of Shaba, can of course be discovered by the archaeologist. Bisson,[34] however, claims that eighth- or ninth-century of our era evidence from Sanga predates the advent of long-distance trade in the area. Though there is apparent wealth in the area, there is a dearth of imports. He feels that the copper ingots in the form of crosses were used as a general-purpose currency which enhanced the prestige and status of the ruling group. In such a case the ruling group may have become established because of its extra expertise in metallurgy, its control of key craftsmen, or the communal

32. M. Posnansky, 1966b, pp. 1–12.
33. R. L. Carneiro, pp. 733–8.
34. M. S. Bisson, pp. 288–9.

need for leadership consequent upon a population increase in a particularly favourable environment.

Turning from hypothesis to fact, the only area in which we can convincingly assert that a kingdom existed in the period under review was at the western edge of the Sudan, where the kingdom of Ghana was certainly in existence by +700 and could have been emerging for up to a thousand years. The reasons for its growth must have been its control of valuable mineral resources (copper, iron and gold, in the probable order of their exploitation); its control of the salt trade; and possibly its location in an area of primary development of an agricultural mode of life, as represented by the Tichitt sequence. A detailed account of the state will be found in the next volume; but it is probably no coincidence that the growth of ancient Ghana, the building of the Senegambian megaliths and the rich burial mounds of Senegal were contemporaneous developments. They were probably related parts of the same pattern of economic growth.

As we have seen in the preceding chapters, there is no uniform ending to the period under review as there is for North Africa; nevertheless the arrival of the Arabs in North Africa was ultimately to affect either directly or indirectly much of West and East Africa. We have seen that by +800 most of Africa was firmly in the iron age. The forest margin was being slowly eroded by the advance of agriculture, both in West Africa and in southern Central Africa. Population was increasing. The first phase of the agricultural revolution had involved the rapid expansion of small groups of arable cultivators, who probably obtained a great deal of their protein by using the age-old, well-tried methods of their stone age hunting and gathering ancestors. Much of their hunting equipment was the same as their predecessors'; nets, bone and horn fish-hooks and wooden spears and arrows, perhaps still barbed at times with microliths or the sharpened ends of antelope horns or similar natural substances. In a few cases it was supplemented by more efficient, though costly, iron arrowheads and more quickly made fish-hooks. Much of their mythology and religion must also have been derived from their foraging forebears, but as life became more settled they developed new beliefs based on the mysteries of agriculture and metal-working. Some of these beliefs had probably been passed on by the people who transmitted the new mysteries. The iron age farmers were more creative, moulding pots, carving drums, making baskets, smelting iron, forging tools. Their religion was becoming centred on creative deities, and their systems of belief were aimed at ensuring salvation from the vicissitudes of a Nature to which the agriculturalist is more vulnerable. Their ritual and music were probably more elaborate, their material culture was more varied and their sense of tradition and social continuity was more firmly established. Fundamental changes had taken place in society which ultimately affected all the succeeding periods of African history.

# Conclusion

G. MOKHTAR

In this volume an attempt has been made to show, as far as possible, the main trends in the early history of Africa: the major changes that occurred, the fundamental contacts between its various regions, and the state of African societies and groups during the period under review.

The volume outlines a general framework for research, and the main lines along which studies should be directed. However, it already seems possible to reach some conclusions and to adopt some hypotheses although it should be clearly and strongly emphasized that a great deal remains to be done and long, in-depth studies are needed.

The chapters on ancient Egypt demonstrate that before the third millennium before our era, Egypt had achieved a high intellectual, social and material standard, compared with most other parts of the world. The ancient Egyptian civilization, besides being old, original and rich in initiative, lasted for almost three thousand years. It resulted not only from favourable environment factors, but also from the efforts to control those factors and put them to beneficial use. There is no doubt that the natural elements played an important and remarkable role in the development of the ancient Egyptian civilization. But, on the other hand, this role was supplemented and became effective only through the Egyptians' struggle to tame their environment, to overcome the difficulties and problems it posed, and so to render it beneficial for their own prosperity.

The ancient Egyptians, through the invention of writing in their pre-dynastic period, made a considerable advance towards civilization. Writing extended the range of man's communications, developed his mentality and widened his knowledge. The invention of writing was more important and effective than any battle the ancient Egyptians fought or any other achievement they accomplished. The first writing appeared about −3200, and in its last stage – the Coptic language – is still used today in Coptic churches in Egypt. So, we can consider this rich life of almost fifty centuries of the ancient Egyptian language as the longest of any of the world's languages. Finally, we can say that the invention of writing was the main stage passed by the Egyptians on their long road towards civilization and prosperity.

Our knowledge of ancient Egypt is due mostly to the discovery of writing and the establishment of a kind of chronology. It is not the same system of chronology we use today, because the ancient Egyptians dated the events they desired to record according to the rule of the king reigning at the time. But with the aid of this system the historian Manethen of Sebennytos was able to arrange the rulers of Egypt from Menes to Alexander the Great in thirty dynasties. Modern scholars have grouped several dynasties together under the name of Empire or Kingdom: old, modern and new.

Although Egypt was open to cultural currents coming especially from the East, this volume shows how the Egyptian civilization rested to a great extent on an African foundation and also that Egypt, which is a part of Africa, was one of the main centres of universal civilization in ancient times and that a great deal of scientific knowledge, art and literature emanated from that region, and influenced Greece in particular. In the fields of mathematics (geometry, arithmetic, etc.), astronomy and the measurement of time (the calendar), medicine, architecture, music and literature (narrative, poetry, tragedy, etc.), Greece received, developed and transmitted to the West a great part of the Egyptian legacy – from Pharaonic and Ptolomaic Egypt. Through Greece and Phoenicia, the ancient Egyptian civilization entered into contact not only with Europe, but also with North Africa and even the Indian sub-continent.

Wide differences of opinion exist about the peopling of Egypt, which is still a subject of serious and deep study. It is hoped that the great progress in the methodology of physical anthropology will enable definitive conclusions on this subject to be reached in the near future.

According to records mentioned in this volume, Nubia has been closely connected with Egypt since the earliest times as a result of various factors: physical factors, particularly similar geographical features, especially between Nubia and the extreme southern part of Upper Egypt; historical and political factors, which are important in themselves and were greatly strengthened by the physical aspect; social factors, which are reflected in culture and religion. Thus, since the beginning of the first Egyptian dynasty, and through the Old Kingdom, the Egyptians paid a great deal of attention to the northern area of Nubia, which they considered as a complementary part of their own country. They organized a flow of trade with the Nubians, exploited Nubian natural resources, and when any Nubian resistance was shown they sent military missions to end it. Some of the Old Kingdom expeditions which were led by some of the earliest travellers and pioneer explorers, such as Ony, Mekhu, Sabni and Khuefeher (Harkuf), penetrated into the Sahara and possibly into Central Africa.

Egyptian interest in Nubia was reflected particularly in the construction of numerous temples which, besides being religious centres, were meant to show Egypt's civilization and power, and the mightiness and holiness of its king. The main reason for such interest was the fact that Nubia – since

733

the remotest ages – had been the passage for trade between the Mediterranean and the heart of Africa. So, Nubia contained also the remains of a number of fortresses from the Pharaonic and Roman periods, which were built to protect trade and enforce peace in those regions.

However, since prehistoric days Nubia had constituted a geographical and social unit. Since the dawn of history, it had been inhabited by people whose culture was identical with that of the northern valley of the Nile. But, starting from about −3200, the Egyptians began to outstrip their southern neighbours in the cultural domain, and made vast strides towards civilization, while Nubia remained stationary at the prehistoric level for a considerable time. In the first half of the second millennium before our era, the so-called Kerma culture, a rich and prosperous civilization, flourished in Nubia. Although greatly influenced by Egyptian culture, it possessed its own local characteristics. But, after the beginning of the first millennium before our era, when the power of Egypt waned, a native monarchy began to be established, with Napata as its capital, which later ruled Egypt itself. The fifty-year Nubian domination in Egypt during the seventh period (the first part of the twenty-fifth dynasty) effected a union of Egypt and Nubia. The glory of this great African power was outstanding, as shown by classical writers.

After the transfer of the capital to Meroe, Nubia experienced a period of progress and prosperity and resumed contacts with its neighbours, until nearly the ninth century. The expansion of the Meroitic monarchy to the west and south, its role in diffusing its ideas and techniques and its transmission of Eastern and Western influences are still under study and discussion. Also, even after the publication of this volume, further stimulus should be given to the efforts to decipher the Meroitic script. The 900 documents which exist would reveal information of many kinds. It would also make available, side by side with the Pharaonic language, a new classical language that was strictly African.

From the fourth century of our era, Christianity began to spread to Nubia, where the temples were converted into churches. The role of Christian Nubia was also great, its achievements were numerous, and its influence on its neighbours was remarkable.

Christian Nubia's golden age was during the eighth century, when it enjoyed an initial period of development and prosperity. Nubia remained under the rule of a Christian monarchy until Islam spread all over the country. From that time, it began to be swept by Arabic Islamic culture, losing to a great extent its traditional character.

Nubia, because of its geographical location, played a special and sometimes involuntary role as an intermediary between Central Africa and the Mediterranean. The kingdom of Napata, the empire of Meroe and the Christian kingdom showed Nubia as a link between North and South. Through it, culture, techniques and material found their way through surrounding regions. It is by the stubborn pursuit of research that we may discover that the Egypto-Nubian civilization played a similar role in Africa to that of the Graeco-Roman civilization in Europe.

Interest in the history of ancient Nubia was resurrected recently when the Egyptian project of a high dam over Aswan took shape. From the first moment, it became obvious that the dam would mean the submersion of sixteen temples, all the chapels, churches, tombs, rock inscriptions and other historical sites in the area of Nubia, which would be flooded. These monuments had mostly been left intact by time. At the request of Egypt and the Sudan, Unesco launched in 1959 an appeal asking all nations, organizations and men of goodwill to help technically, scientifically and financially to save the Nubian monuments. At once there began a successful international campaign which has saved most of the Nubian monuments, representing centuries of history and holding the keys to early cultures.

Further archaeological excavations around the Kerma site where funeral rites were identical with those in Ghana, in the region of Dongola and the south-west oases in particular, would give us a better idea of certain archaic cultural affinities and perhaps reveal other links in the cultural chain between the valley of the Nile and the interior of Africa. In any case, it would give us a clearer idea of the itinerary followed by explorers of the ancient Empire, such as Harkuf.

Although Ethiopia was influenced at the beginning by various motives, it established a cultural unit whose central coherence could be identified as coming from south Arabia. Material sources dating back to the second pre-Aksumite period indicate that a local culture existed which had assimilated foreign influences.

The kingdom of Aksum, which lasted from the first century of our era for about one thousand years, adopted a quite distinct form, different from that of the pre-Aksumite period. The civilization of Aksum, like that of ancient Egypt, was the result of a cultural development, whose roots went back to prehistory. It was an African civilization, which was produced by its people, although some Meroitic influence can be traced in the pottery of the second pre-Aksumite period.

During the second and third centuries, the Meroitic influence pre-dominated in Ethiopia. The newly discovered Stele of Aksum with the Egyptian symbol of life (Ankh), and objects connected with Hathor, Ptah and Horus, as well as scarabs, show the influence of the Egyptian Meroe religion on Aksumite beliefs.

The Aksumite kingdom was an important trade power on the routes from the Roman world to India and from Arabia to North Africa, and also a great centre of cultural dissemination. So far, only a few aspects of Aksumite culture and its African roots have been investigated and much still remains to be done.

The arrival of Christianity in Ethiopia – as in Egypt and Meroe – brought great changes in the culture and life of the people. The role of Christianity and its continuity in Ethiopia, its influence inside and outside

735

that country, are interesting subjects which deserve in-depth study in the near future.

In view of the limitations of our historical sources, increased knowledge about the evolution of the native Libyan culture and its reaction to the introduction of the Phoenician civilization must wait until the archaeologists and historians have carried out further studies.

In the present state of our knowledge we must therefore consider that the entry of the Maghrib into recorded history begins with the arrival of the Phoenicians on the coast of North Africa, although Carthaginian contacts with the peoples of the Sahara and even with people living farther south remains obscure. At the same time, it should be pointed out that the culture of North Africa is not indebted solely to the Phoenicians for its early inspiration, which was mainly African.

The Phoenician period brought the Maghreb into the general history of the Mediterranean world, since the Phoenician culture was mixed with Egyptian and Oriental elements and depended on trade relations with other Mediterranean countries. Nevertheless, the later period of the Numidian and Mauretanian kingdoms saw the evolution of a culture of mixed Libyan and Phoenician character.

Although we have very scarce and incomplete knowledge about the Sahara and its culture in antiquity, several points can be made. It is certain that the desiccation of the climate did not kill the desert and that human activity continued there; that languages and writing were consolidated; that with the increased use of camels, means of transport were developed which allowed the Sahara to play an important role in cultural exchanges between the Maghrib and tropical Africa.

We can therefore conclude that the Sahara was neither a barrier nor a dead zone, but an area with its own culture and history which still needs to be studied to discover the continuing influence of the Maghrib on the Sudanic belt. There were always active cultural contacts across the Sahara with sub-Saharan Africa which greatly affected African history.[1]

Hitherto, it has often been customary to situate the beginning of the history of Africa south of the Sahara at approximately the fifteenth century of our era[2] for two main reasons, namely, the dearth of written documents and the dogmatic cleavage which historians have made mentally between that part of the continent on the one hand and ancient Egypt and North Africa on the other.

This volume, despite the gaps and incompleteness of the research so far undertaken, has helped to demonstrate the possibility of a cultural unity of the entire continent in the most widely varying fields.

1. See Chapter 29, 'The societies of Africa south of the Sahara in the early iron age', by Professor Merrick Posnansky. It deals with the results obtained in the last ten chapters of this volume concerning sub-Saharan Africa.

2. Some writers in both Anglophone and Francophone Africa paid a good deal of attention to sub-Saharan Africa before the fifteenth century.

The theory of the genetic kinship between ancient Egyptian and the African languages has been discussed. If research confirms this theory, it will prove the deep-rooted linguistic unity of the continent. The similarity of royal structures, the relationship of rites and cosmogonies (circumcision, totemism, vitalism, metempsychosis, etc.), the affinity of material cultures (tilling equipment is one example), are all matters to be deeply studied in the future.

The cultural heritage left to us by the societies which lived in Egypt, Nubia, Ethiopia and the Maghrib is of great importance. The monotheism imposed by the Christians, and before them by the Jews, in these regions was strong and expressive and no doubt facilitated the entry of Islam into Africa. These well-known facts stand on the credit side of the Africans; on the debit side are unclear areas where a vast amount of work remains to be done, and many uncertain points to be clarified.

Likewise, completion of the third condition for the writing of Volumes I and II, i.e. the reconstruction of the ancient African road network since protohistorical times, and a determination of the extent of cultivated areas during the same period from the analysis of photographs taken from satellites for that purpose, would singularly broaden and deepen our knowledge both of the intra-continental cultural and trade relations of the time and the degree to which the land was occupied.

More extensive work on ethnonyms and toponyms should make it possible to determine migratory currents and unsuspected ethnic relationships from one end of the continent to the other.

I hope this volume will persuade the African countries to show more interest in, and give more help to, the archaeology of ancient Africa.

737

# Members of the International Scientific Committee for the Drafting of a General History of Africa

*The dates cited below refer to dates of membership.*

Professor J. F. A. Ajayi
(Nigeria), from 1971
Editor Volume VI

Professor F. A. Albuquerque Mourao
(Brazil), from 1975

Professor A. A. Boahen
(Ghana), from 1971
Editor Volume VII

H. E. Boubou Hama
(Niger), 1971–8

H. E. M. Bull
(Zambia), from 1971

Professor D. Chanaiwa
(Zimbabwe), from 1975

Professor P. D. Curtin
(USA), from 1975

Professor J. Devisse
(France), from 1971

Professor M. Difuila
(Angola), from 1978

Professor H. Djait
(Tunisia), from 1975

Professor Cheikh Anta Diop
(Senegal), from 1971

Professor J. D. Fage
(UK), from 1971

H. E. M. El Fasi
(Morocco), from 1971
Editor Volume III

Professor J. L. Franco
(Cuba), from 1971

Mr M. H. I. Galaal
(Somalia), from 1971

Professor Dr V. L. Grottanelli
(Italy), from 1971

Professor E. Haberland
(Federal Republic of Germany), from 1971

Dr Aklilu Habte
(Ethiopia), from 1971

H. E. A. Hampate Ba
(Mali), 1971–8

Dr I. S. El-Hareir
(Libya), from 1978

Dr I. Hrbek
(Czechoslovakia), from 1971

Dr A. Jones
(Liberia), from 1971

Abbé A. Kagame
(Rwanda), from 1971

Professor I. M. Kimanbo
(Tanzania), from 1971

Professor J. Ki-Zerbo
(Upper Volta), from 1971
Editor Volume I

M. D. Laya
(Niger), from 1979

Dr A. Letnev
(USSR), from 1971

Dr G. Mokhtar
(Egypt), from 1971
Editor Volume II

Professor P. Mutibwa
(Uganda), from 1975

Professor D. T. Niane
(Senegal), from 1971
Editor Volume IV

Professor L. D. Ngcongco
(Botswana), from 1971

Professor T. Obenga
(People's Republic of the Congo),
from 1975

Professor B. A. Ogot
(Kenya), from 1971
Editor Volume V

Professor C. Ravoajanahary
(Madagascar), from 1971

Mr W. Rodney
(Guyana), from 1979, deceased

Professor M. Shibeika
(Sudan), from 1971, deceased

Professor Y. A. Talib
(Singapore), from 1975

Professor A. Teixeira da Mota
(Portugal), from 1978

Mgr T. Tshibangu
(Zaïre), from 1971

Professor J. Vansina
(Belgium), from 1971

Rt Hon. Dr E. Williams
(Trinidad and Tobago), 1976–8

Professor A. A. Mazrui
(Kenya)
Editor Volume VIII, not a
member of the Committee

*Secretariat of the International
Scientific Committee*
Mr Maurice Glélé, Division of Cultural
Studies, Unesco, 1 rue Miollis, 75015 Paris

# Biographies of Authors

CHAPTER 13   H. de Contenson (France); specialist in African history; author of works on Ethiopian archaeology and Christian Nubia; engaged in research at the Centre National de la Recherche Scientifique (CNRS).

CHAPTER 14   F. Anfray (France); specialist in archaeology; author of a number of articles on archaeological research in Ethiopia; Head of the French Archaeological Mission to Ethiopia.

CHAPTER 15   Y. M. Kobishanov (USSR); historian, author of numerous articles on African anthropology; member of the USSR Academy of Sciences.

CHAPTER 16   Tekle Tsadik Mekouria (Ethiopia); historian; writer; specialist in the political, economic and social history of Ethiopia from its origins to the 20th century; retired.

CHAPTER 17   J. Desanges (France); specialist in the history of Ancient Africa; author of numerous works and articles on Ancient Africa; lecturer at the University of Nantes.

CHAPTER 18   B. H. Warmington (United Kingdom); specialist in the history of ancient Rome: author of many works on North Africa; lecturer in Ancient History.

CHAPTER 19   A. Mahjoubi (Tunisia); specialist in Ancient History of North Africa; author of numerous works and articles on Tunisian archaeology; assistant professor at the University of Tunis.

P. Salama (Algeria); archaeologist; specialist in the history of the ancient institutions of the Maghrib; professor at the University of Algiers.

CHAPTER 20   P. Salama

CHAPTER 21   M. Posnansky (UK); historian and archaeologist; author of a number of important works on the archaeological history of East Africa.

CHAPTER 22   A. M. H. Sheriff (Tanzania); specialist in the history of the East African slave trade; lecturer at the University of Dar-es-Salaam.

CHAPTER 23   J. E. G. Sutton (United Kingdom); specialist in prehistory; author of numerous works and articles on African history; former President of the Department of Archaeology at the University of Oxford.

CHAPTER 24   B. Wai-Andah (Nigeria); specialist in archaeology; author of works on the archaeology of West Africa; lecturer at the University of Ibadan.

CHAPTER 25   F. Van Noten (Belgium); specialist in prehistory and archaeology; author of numerous works and publications on prehistory of Central Africa; Curator at the Royal Museum of Prehistory and Archaeology.

CHAPTER 26   J. E. Parkington (UK); archaeologist; author of works on the prehistory of Southern Africa; professor of archaeology.

CHAPTER 27   D. W. Phillipson (UK); archaeologist; author of works on the archaeology of East and Southern Africa.

CHAPTER 28   P. Verin (France); specialist in history and archaeology; author of numerous publications on Madagascar and the civilizations of the Indian Ocean; engaged in research on Madagascar.

CHAPTER 29   M. Posnansky.

CONCLUSION   G. Mokhtar.

# Bibliography

*The publishers wish to point out that while every effort has been made to ensure that the details in this Bibliography are correct, some errors may occur as a result of the complexity and the international nature of the work.*

## Abbreviations and List of Periodicals

*ÄA   Ägyptologische Abhandlungen*, Wiesbaden, Harrassowitz
*AA   American Anthropologist*, Washington, DC
*AAW   Abhandlungen der Königlich Preussischen Akademie der Wissenschaften*, Berlin
*AB   Africana Bulletin*, Warsaw University, Warsaw
*ACPM   Annals of the Cape Provincial Museums*, Grahamstown
*Actas VIII Congr. Intern. Archeo. Crist.   Actas del VIII Congresso Internazionale di Archeologia Cristiana*, Barcelona, 1972
*Actes Coll. Bamako I   Actes du 1er Colloque International de Bamako Organisé par la Fondation SCOA pour la Recherche Scientifique en Afrique Noire* (Projet Boucle du Niger), Baomako, 27 Jan.–1 Feb. 1975 1 February 1975
*Actes Coll. Intern. Biolog. Pop. Sahar.   Actes du Colloque International de Biologie des Populations Sahariennes*, Algiers, 1969
*Actes Coll. Intern. Fer.*   Actes du Colloque International. Le Fer à travers les âges, Nancy, 3–6 October 1956, Annales de l'Est, Mém. no. 16, Nancy, 1956
*Actes 1er Coll. Intern. Archéol. Afr.   Actes du 1er Colloque International d'Archéologie Africaine*, Fort Lamy, 11–16 December 1966, Études et documents tchadiens, Mém. no. 1, Fort Lamy, 1969
*Actes 7e Coll. Intern. Hist. Marit.   Actes du 7e Colloque International d'Histoire Maritime* (Lourenço Marques, 1962), published 1964, Paris, SEVPEN
*Actes 8e Coll. Intern. Hist. Marit.   Actes du 8e Colloque International d'Histoire Maritime* (Beirut, 1966), published 1970, Paris, SEVPEN
*Actes Coll. Nubiol. Intern.   Actes du Colloque Nubiologique International au Museé National de Varsovie*, Warsaw, 1972
*Actes Conf. Ann. Soc. Phil. Soudan   Actes de la Conférence Annuelle de la Societé Philosophique du Soudan*
*Actes 2e Conf. Intern. Afr. Ouest   Comptes Rendus, 2nd International West African Conference*, Bissau, 1947
*Actes XIV Congr. Intern. Ét. Byz.   Actes du XIVe Congrès International d'Études Byzantines*, Bucharest, 1971
*Actes 2e Congr. Intern. Ét. N. Afr.   Actes du 2e Congrès International d'Études Nord Africaines* (*Congresso Internazionale de Studi Nord Africani*), *Revue de l'Occident Musulman et de la Méditerranée* (Aix-en-Provence, 1968), published Gap, Ophrys, 1970
*Acts III Cong. PPQS   Acts of the Third Pan-African Congress of Prehistory and Quaternary Study*, Lusaka, 1955
*Acts IV Congr. PPQS   Acts of the Fourth Pan-African Congress of Prehistory and Quaternary Study*, Leopoldville, 1959, *AMRAC* 40
*Acts VI Congr. PPQS   Acts of the Sixth Pan-African Congress of Prehistory and Quaternary Study*, Dakar, 1967, Chambéry, Impr. réunies
*Acts VII Congr. PPQS   Acts of the Seventh Pan-African Congress of Prehistory and Quaternary Study*, Addis Ababa, 1971
*AE   Annales d'Éthiopie*, Paris, Institut Éthiopien d'Études et de Recherches, Section d'Archéologie
*AEPHE   Annuaire de l'École Pratique des Hautes Études*, IVe section (Section des Sciences Historiques et Philologiques), Paris
*AFLSD   Annuales de la Faculté des Lettres et Sciences humaines de Dakar, Hamburg*
*ÄFU   Ägyptologische Forschungen* (ed. A. Scharff), Glückstadt, Hamburg, New York
*AHS   African Historical Studies*, Boston University African Studies Centre (became *IJAHS* in 1972)
*AI   Africana Italiana*, Rome
*AIESEE   Revue des Études Sud-Est Européennes*, Academia Republicii Populare Romine, Association Internationale d'Études Sud-Est Européennes, Bucharest

*AJA    American Journal of Archaeology* (journal of the Archaeological Institute of America), Boston, Mass.

*AKM    Abhandlungen für die Kunde des Morgenlandes*, Deutsche Morgenkindlische Gesellschaft, Leipzig

*Akten XI Intern. Limeskong.    Akten des XI Internationalen Limeskongresses*, Budapest, Akademia Kiado, 1976

*ALOS    Annual of the Leeds Oriental Society*, University of Leeds

*ALS    African Language Studies*, School of Oriental and African Studies, London University

*AMRAC    Annales du Museé Royal de l'Afrique Centrale*, Series in 8°, Sciences humaines, Tervuren, Belgium

*Ann. Afr.    Annuaire de l'Afrique du Nord*, Paris (Centre d'Études Nord-Africaines; Centre de Recherches sur l'Afrique Méditerranéene; Centre de Recherches et d'Études sur les Sociétés Méditerranéennes)

*Annales    Annales. Économies, sociétés, civilisations*, Paris

*Ant. Afr.    Antiquités, Africaines*, Éditions du Centre Nationale de la Recherche Scientifique, Paris

*Antananarivo    Antananarivo*, Annual, Tananarive

*Anthropologie    Anthropologie*, Paris

*Antiquity    Antiquity*, Gloucester

*AQ    African Quarterly*, New Delhi

*Archaeology    Archaeology*, Archaeological Institute of America, Boston, Mass.

*Archaeometry    Archaeometry*, Research laboratory of Archaeology and the History of Art, Oxford

*ARSC    Académie Royale des Sciences Coloniales, Classe des Sciences Morales et Politiques*, N.S., Brussels

*AS    African Studies*

*ASAE    Annales du Service des Antiquités d'Égypte*, Cairo

*ASAM    Annals of the South African Museum*

*Asian Perspectives    Asian Perspectives*, Far Eastern Prehistory Association, Hong Kong

*ASR    African Social Research*

*AT    L'Agronomie Tropicale*, Nogent-sur-Marne

*Atti IV Congr. Intern. Stud. Et.    Atti del IV Congresso Internazionale di Studi Etiopici*, Rome, 10–15 April 1972, Rome, Accademia nazionale dei Lincei

*AUEI    Avhandlinger Utgitt av. Egede Instituttet*, Oslo, Egede Instituttet

*Azania    Azania*, Journal of the British Institute of History and Archaeology in E. Africa, Nairobi

*BAA    Bulletin d'Archéologie Algérienne*, Algiers

*BAM    Bulletin de l'Académie Malgache*, Tananarive

*BA Maroc.    Bulletin d'archéologie marocaine*, Casablanca

*BHM    Bulletin of Historical Metallurgy*

*BIFAN    Bulletin de l'Institut Français* (later re-named *Fondamental*) *d'Afrique Noire*, Dakar

*BIFAO    Bulletin de l'Institut Français d'Archéologie Orientale*, Cairo

*BM    Bulletin de Madagascar*, Tananarive

*BO    Bibliotheca Orientalis*, Leyden, Netherlands instituut voor Het Nabije Oosten

*Bonner Jahrbücher    Bonner Jahrbücher*, Verein von Alterthumsfreunden im Rheinlande, Bonn

*BS    Bulletin Scientifique*. Ministère de la France d'Outre-Mer, Direction de l'agriculture

*BSAC    Bulletin de la Société d'Archéologie Classique*

*BSA Copte    Bulletin de la Société d'Archéologie Copte* (Jam'lyat al-Athar al Q'ibtiyah), Cairo

*BSFE    Bulletin de la Société Française d'Egyptologie*, Paris

*BSHNAN    Bulletin de la Société d'Histoire Naturelle de l'Afrique du Nord*

*BSNAF    Bulletin de la Société Nationale des Antiquaires de France*, Paris

*BSNG    Bulletin de la Société Neuchâteloise de Géographie*, Neuchâtel

*BSPF    Bulletin de la Société Prehistorique Française*, Paris

*BSPPG    Bulletin de la Société Préhistorique et Protohistorique Gabonaise*, Libreville

*BSRA    Bulletin de la Société Royale d'Archéologie*

*BWS 56    Burg Wartenstein Symposium no. 56 on the origin of African domesticated plants*, 19–27 August 1972

*Byzantinische Zeitschrift    Byzantinische Zeitschrift*, Leipzig

*Byzantinoslavica    Byzantinoslavica*, Prague

*Byzantion    Byzantion*, Brussels

*CA    Current Anthropology*, Chicago

*CAMAP    Travaux du Centre d'Archéologie Mediterranéenne de l'Académie Poionaise des Sciences* (ed. K. Michalowski), Warsaw

CC   *Corsi di Cultura sull'Arte Ravennate e Bizantina*, Ravenna 1965
CEA   *Cahiers d'Études Africaines*, Paris, Mouton
*Chronique d'Égypte   Chronique d'Égypte*, Fondation Égyptologique de la Reine Élizabeth, Brussels
*Cimbebasia   Cimbebasia*, State Museum, Windhoek
CM   *Civilisation Malgache*, Tananarive, Université de Madagascar, Faculté des Lettres et Sciences Humaines
CQ   *Classical Quarterly*, London
C-RAI   *Compte-Rendu des Séances de l'Académie des Inscriptions et Belles Lettres*, Pairs, Klincksieck
C-RGLCS   *Compte-Rendu des Séances du Groupe Linguistique d'Études Chamito-Sémitiques*, École Pratique des Hautes Études, Sorbonne, Paris
C-RSB   *Compt-Rendu Sommaire des Séances de la Société de Biogéographie*, Paris
CSA   *Cahiers de la Société Asiatique*, Paris
CSSH   *Comparative Studies in Society and History*, The Hague
CTL   *Current Trends in Linguistics*, The Hague
DAE   *Deutsche Axum Expedition*, Berlin
EAGR   *East African Geographical Review*, Kampala
EEFEM   *Egypt Exploration Fund Memoirs*, London, Trübner & Co.
EHR   *Economic History Review*, London, New York, CUP
*Encyclopédie berbère   Encyclopédie berbère. Laboratoire d'Anthropologie et de Préhistoire des Pays de la Méditerranée occidentale*, Aix-en-Provence
*Gazette des Beaux Arts   Gazette des Beaux Arts*, Paris
GJ   *The Geographical Journal*, London
GNQ   *Ghana Notes and Queries*, Legon
HAS   *Harvard African Studies*, Cambridge, Mass., Harvard University Press
HBZAK   *Hamburger Beiträger zur Afrika-Kunde*, Deutsches Institut für Afrika Forschung, Hamburg
*Hesperis   Hesperis*, Institut des Hautes Études Marocaines, Rabat
*Homo   Homo*, University of Toulouse
HZ   *Historische Zeitschrift*, Munich
IJAHS   *International Journal of African Historical Studies*, New York (formerly *AHS*)
JA   *Journal Asiatique*, Paris
JAH   *Journal of African History*, London, New York, CUP
JAOS   *Journal of the American Oriental Society*, New Haven, Conn.
JASA   *Journal of African Science Association*, Paris
JARCE   *Journal of the American Research Center in Egypt*, Boston, Mass.
JCH   *Journal of Classical History*, London
JEA   *The Journal of Egyptian Archaeology*, London
JHSN   *Journal of the Historical Society of Nigeria*, Ibadan
JGS   *Journal of Glass Studies*, Corning, NY
JRAI   *Journal of the Royal Anthropological Institute of Great Britain and Ireland*, London
JRAS   *Journal of the Royal Asiatic Society of Great Britain and Ireland*, London
JRS   *Journal of Roman Studies*, Society for the Promotion of Roman Studies, London
JS   *Le Journal des Savants*, Paris
JSA   *Journal de la Société des Africanistes*, Paris
JSAIMM   *Journal of the South African Institute of Mining and Metallurgy*, Johannesburg
JTG   *Journal of Tropical Geography*, Singapore
*Karthago   Karthago*, Revue d'Archéologie africaine, Tunisia
*Kush   Kush*, Journal of the Sudan Antiquities Services, Khartoum
LAAA   *Liverpool Annals of Archaeology and Anthropology*, Liverpool
*Lammergeyer   Lammergeyer*, Journal of the National Parks Game and Fish Preservation Board, Pietermaritzburg
*Latomus   Latomus*, Brussels
*Libyca   Libyca*, Bulletin of the Service d'Antiquités of Algeria, Direction de l'Intérieur et des Beaux Arts, Algiers
MADP   *Malawi Antiquities Department Publications*, Zomba
MAGW   *Mitteilungen der Anthropologischen Gesellschaft in Wien*
MAI   *Mitteilungen des deutsches Archäologischen Instituts*, Wiesbaden, Harvasowitz
*Man   Man*, New York
*Mém. CRAPE   Mémoires du Centre de Recherches Anthropologiques, Préhistoriques et Ethnographiques*, Institut Français des Sciences Humaines en Algérie
MEJ   *Middle East Journal*, Washington, DC
MIOD   *Mitteilungen des Instituts für Orientforschung Deutsche*, Akademie der Wissenschaften, Berlin

*MN Meroitic Newsletter*
*Le Muséon Le Muséon, Revue d'Etudes Orientales*, Louvain
*NA Notes Africaines*, Bulletin d'Information de l'IFAN, Dakar (See *BIFAN* above)
*NADA The Rhodesian Native Affairs Department Annual*, Salisbury
*NAS Nigerian Archaeology Seminar*, 3–5 July 1974
*Nature Nature*, London
*NKJ Nederlands Kunsthistorisch Jaarboek*, Bussum, Van Dishoek
*Numismatic Chronicle Numismatic Chronicle*, Numismatic Society, London
*OA Opuscula Atheniensia*, Lund
*Objets et Mondes Objets et Mondes*, Musée de l'Homme, Paris
*OCA Orientalia Christiana Analecta*, Rome
*Odù Odù*, Journal of Yoruba and Related Studies, Western Region Literature Committee, Nigeria
*OL Oceanic Linguistics*, Department of Anthropology, Southern Illinois University, Carbondale, Illinois
*OPNM Occasional Papers of the National Museums of Southern Rhodesia*, Bulawayo
*Optima Optima*, Johannesburg
*Oriens Antiquus Oriens Antiquus*, Centro per le Antichità e la Storia dell' Arte del Vicino Oriente, Rome
*Orientalia Orientalia*, Amsterdam
*PA Problème de Ägyptologie*, Leiden
*Paideuma Paideuma, Mitteilungen zur Kulturkunde*, Frankfurt am Main
*Plaisirs équestres*, Paris
*Proc. PS Proceedings of the Prehistoric Society*, Cambridge
*QAL Quaderni di Archeologia della Libia*, Rome
*RA Revue Africaine, Journal des Travaux de la Société Historique Algérienne*, Algiers
*RAC Rivista di Archeologia Cristiana della Pontificia*, Commissione di archeologia sacra, Rome
*Radiocarbon Radiocarbon*, Annual Supplement to the American Journal of Science, New York
*R. Arch. Revue Archéologique*, Paris
*R. Anth. Revue Anthropologique*, Paris
*RE Revue d'Égyptologie*, Paris
*REA Revue des Études Anciennes*, Bordeaux
*REL Revue des Études Latines*, Paris
*RESEE Revue des'études du sud-est européen*, Bucharest
*RFHOM Revue Française d'Historie d'Outre-Mer*, Paris
*RH Revue Historique*, Paris
*Rhodesiana* Publication of the Rhodesiana Society, Salisbury
*RHR Revue de l'Histoire des Religions, Annales du Musée Guimet*, Paris, Leroux
*ROMM Revue de l'Occident Musulman et de la Méditerranée*, Aix-en-Provence
*RRAL Rendiconti della Reale Accademia dei Lincei*, Rome
*RSE Rassengna di Studi Etiopici*, Rome
*RSO Rivista degli Studi Orientali Scuola Orientale della università di Roma*, Rome
*RUB Revue de l'Université de Bruxelles*, Brussels
*SA Scientific American*, New York
*SAAAS South African Association for the Advancement of Science*, Johannesburg
*SAAB South African Archaeological Bulletin*, Cape Town
*Le Saharien Le Saharien*, Revue d'action touristique, culturelle, économique et sportive, Paris, Association de la Rahla et des Amis du Sahara
*SAJS South African Journal of Science*, Johannesburg
*SAK Studien zur Altägyptischen Kultur*, Hamburg, H. Buske Verlag
*SAs Société Asiatique*, Paris
*SASAE Supplément aux Annales du Service des Antiquités d'Égypte*, Cairo
*Sc. South Africa Science South Africa*
*SJA Southwestern Journal of Anthropology*, Albuquerque, New Mexico
*SLS Society for Libyan Studies*
*SM Studi magrebini*, Naples, Istituto Universitario Orientale
*SNR Sudan Notes and Records*, Khartoum
*Syria Syria*, Revue d'art oriental et d'archéologie, Paris
*TJH Transafrican Journal of History*
*TNR Tanganyika (Tanzania) Notes and Records*, Dar es Salaam
*TRSSA Transactions of the Royal Society of South Africa*
*Trav. IRS Travaux de l'Institut de Recherches Sahariennes*, University of Algiers, Algiers
*Ufahamu Ufahamu*, Journal of the African Activist Association, Los Angeles

*UJ  Uganda Journal*, Uganda Society, Kampala
*WA  World Archaeology*, London
*WAAN  West African Archaeological Newsletter*, Ibadan
*WAJA  West African Journal of Archaeology*, Ibadan
*WZKM  Wiener Zeitschrift für die Kunde des Morgenlandes*, Vienna
*ZÄS  Zeitschrift für Ägyptische Sprache und Altertumskunde*, Osnabrück, Zeller
*ZDMG  Zeitschrift der Deutschen Morgenländischen Gesellschaft*, Leipzig
*Zephyrus  Zephyrus*, Crónica del Seminario de Arqueologia, Salamanca
*ZK  Zeitschrift für Kirchengeschichte*, Gotha
*ZMJ  Zambia Museum Journal*, Lusaka
*ZMP  Zambia Museum Papers*, Lusaka
*ZZSK  Zbornik Zastite Spomenika Kulture*


**Abel, A.** (1972) 'L'Ethiopie et ses rapports avec l'Arabie préislamique jusqu'à l'émigration de ca. 615', *IVth CISE*. **(Chap. 14)**

**Abraham, D. P.** (1951) 'The principality of Maungure', *NADA*, 28. **(Chap. 27)**

**Abraham, D. P.** (1959) 'The Monomotapa dynasty in Southern Rhodesia', *NADA*, 36. **(Chap. 27)**

**Abraham, D. P.** (1961) 'Maramuca, an exercise in the combined use of Portuguese records and oral tradition', *JAH*, II, 2, pp. 211–25. **(Chap. 27)**

**Abraham, D. P.** (1962) 'The early political history of the kingdom of Mwene Mutapa, 850–1589', *Historians in Tropical Africa* (Salisbury: University College of Rhodesia and Nyasaland). **(Chap. 27)**

**Abraham, D. P.** (1964) 'The ethnohistory of the empire of Mutapa, problems and methods', in J. Vansina, R. Mauny and L. V. Thomas (eds), *The Historian in Tropical Africa* (London/Accra/Ibadan: Oxford University Press for the International African Institute), pp. 104–26. **(Chap. 27)**

**Abu Saleh** (1969) *The Churches and Monasteries of Egypt and some Neighbouring Countries*, tr. B. T. Evetts and A. J. Butler (Oxford: Clarendon Press). Reprint.

**Adams, W. Y.** (1962a) 'Pottery kiln excavations', *Kush*, 10, pp. 62–75. **(Chap. 12)**

**Adams, W. Y.** (1962b) 'An introductory classification of Christian Nubian pottery', *Kush*, 10, pp. 245–88. **(Chap. 12)**

**Adams, W. Y.** (1964) 'Sudan antiquities service excavations at Meinarti 1962–3', *Kush*, 12, pp. 227–47. **(Chap. 12)**

**Adams, W. Y.** (1964a) 'Post-pharonic Nubia in the light of archaeology', *JEA*, 50, pp. 102–20. **(Chap. 12)**

**Adams, W. Y.** (1965a) 'Sudan antiquities service excavations at Meinarti 1963–4', *Kush*, 13, pp. 148–76. **(Chap. 12)**

**Adams, W. Y.** (1965b) 'Architectural evolution of the Nubian church 500–1400 AD', *JARCE*, 4, pp. 87–139. **(Chap. 12)**

**Adams, W. Y.** (1965c) 'Post-pharaonic Nubia in the light of archaeology II', *JEA*, 51, pp. 160–78. **(Chap. 12)**

**Adams, W. Y.** (1966a) 'The Nubian campaign: retrospect', *Mélanges offerts à K. Michalowski* (Warsaw), pp. 13–20. **(Chap. 12)**

**Adams, W. Y.** (1966b) 'Post-pharaonic Nubia in the light of archaeology III', *JEA*, 52, pp. 147–62. **(Chap. 12)**

**Adams, W. Y.** (1967) 'Continuity and change in Nubian cultural history', *SNR*, XLVIII, pp. 11–19. **(Chap. 12)**

**Adams, W. Y.** (1968) 'Invasion, diffusion, evolution?', *Antiquity* (Gloucester), XLII, pp. 194–215. **(Chap. 12)**

**Adams, W. H.** (1970) *Nubische Kunst* (Recklinghausen), pp. 111–23. **(Chap. 12)**

**Adams, W. Y. and Nordström, H. A.** (1963) 'The archaeological survey on the west bank of the Nile, third season 1961–2', *Kush*, 11, pp. 10–46. **(Chap. 12)**

**Adams, W. Y. and Verwers, C. J.** (1961) 'Archaeological survey of Sudanese Nubia', *Kush*, 9, pp. 7–43. **(Chap. 12)**

**Addison, F. S. A.** (1949) *Jebel Moya* (*The Wellcome Excavations in the Sudan*), 2 Vols (London: Oxford University Press). **(Chap. 11)**

**Aeschylus,** *Works*, ed. H. Weir Smyth (1922–57) (London: Heinemann; Cambridge, Mass.: Harvard University Press). **(Chap. 1)**

**Albright, F. P.** (1958) *Archaeological Discoveries in South Arabia* (Baltimore). **(Chap. 13)**

**Albright, W. F.** (1973) 'The Amarna letters from Palestine', *Cambridge Ancient History* (Cambridge: CUP), Vol. II, pt 2, ch. XX. **(Chap. 2)**

Aldred, C. (1952) *The Development of Ancient Egyptian Art from 3200 to 1315 BC.* Contains 3 works: *Old Kingdom Art in Ancient Egypt* (1949), *Middle Kingdom Art in Ancient Egypt 2300–1590 BC* (1950), *New Kingdom Art in Ancient Egypt during the Eighteenth Dynasty, 1590–1315 BC* (1951) (London: Tiranti). (**Chap. 3**)

Aldred, C. (1965) *Egypt to the End of the Old Kingdom* (London: Thames & Hudson). (**Chap. 5**)

Aldred, C. (1968) *Akhenaten, Pharaoh of Egypt: A new study* (London: Thames & Hudson). (**Chap. 2**)

Alexander, J. and Coursey, D. G. (1969) 'The origins of yam cultivation', in P. H. Ucko and G. W. Dimbleby (eds), *The Domestication and Exploitation of Plants and Animals* (London: Duckworth), pp. 123–9. (**Chap. 24**)

Ali Hakem, A. M. (1972a) 'The city of Meroe and the myth of Napata. A new perspective in Meroitic archaeology', in S. Bushra (ed.), *Urbanization in the Sudan*, Proceedings of Annual Conference of the Philosophical Society of the Sudan, Khartoum. (**Chap. 11**)

Ali Hakem, A. M. (1972b) 'Meroitic settlement of the Butana, central Sudan', in P. H. Ucko, R. Tringham and G. W. Dimbleby (eds), *Man, Settlement and Urbanism* (London: Duckworth), pp. 639–46. (**Chap. 11**)

Allen, J. W. T. (1949) 'Rhapta', *TNR*, 27, pp. 52–9. (**Chap. 22**)

Allen, T. G. (1960) *The Egyptian Book of the Dead. Documents in the Oriental Institute Museum at the University of Chicago*, Vol. LXXXII (Chicago: University of Chicago Press). (**Chaps 2, 3**)

Almagro-Basch, A. (ed.) (1963–5) *Unesco, Spanish Committee on Nubia: Report of the Archaeological Mission* (Madrid: Dirección General de Relaciones Culturales). (**Chap. 12**)

Amborn, H. (1970) 'Die Problematik der Eisenverhüttung im Reiche Meroe', *Paideuma*, XVI, pp. 71–95. (**Chaps 10, 11**)

Amélineau, E. (1908) *Prolégomènes a l'étude de la religion égyptienne*, Vols 21, 30 (Paris: Bibliothèque de l'École Pratique des Hautes Études. Sciences religieuses). (**Chap. 1**)

Ammianus Marcellinus, *Ammien Marcellin, ou les dix-huit livres de son histoire qui nous sont restés*, tr. G. Moulines (1778), 3 Vols (Lyons: Bruyset). (**Chap. 1**)

Ammianus Marcellinus, *Works*, 3 Vols, tr. S. C. Rolfe (1935–40) (London: Heinemann; Cambridge, Mass.: Harvard University Press). (**Chap. 1**)

Andah, B. W. (1973) 'Archaeological reconnaissance of Upper-Volta', thesis (Berkeley: University of California). (**Chap. 24**)

Anfray, F. (1963) 'Une campagne de fouilles à Yeha', *AE*, 5 (February–March 1960), pp. 171–92. (**Chap. 13**)

Anfray, F. (1965) 'Chronique archéologique (1960–64)', *AE*, 6, pp. 3–48. (**Chap. 13**)

Anfray, F. (1966) 'La poterie de Matara', *RSE*, 22, pp. 1–74. (**Chap. 13**)

Anfray, F. (1967) 'Matara', *AE*, 7, pp. 33–97. (**Chaps 13, 15**)

Anfray, F. (1968) 'Aspects de l'archéologie éthiopienne', *JAH*, 9, pp. 345–66. (**Chaps 13, 14**)

Anfray, F. (1970) 'Matara', *Travaux de la Recherche Coordonnée sur Programme RCP 230*, fasc. 1 (Paris: CNRS), pp. 53–60. (**Chap. 13**)

Anfray, F. (1971) 'Les fouilles de Yeha en 1971', *Travaux de la Recherche Coordonnée sur Programme RCP 230*, fasc. 1 (Paris: CNRS), pp. 53–60. (**Chap. 13**)

Anfray, F. (1972a) 'Les fouilles de Yeha (mai–juin 1972)', *Travaux de la Recherche Coordonnée sur Programme RCP 230*, fasc. 3 (Paris: CNRS), pp. 57–64. (**Chap. 13**)

Anfray, F. (1972b) 'L'archéologie d'Axoum en 1972', *Paideuma*, XVIII, p. 71, plate VI. (**Chap. 15**)

Anfray, F. (1974) 'Deux villes axoumites: Adoulis et Matara', *Atti IV Congr. Intern. Stud. Et.*, pp. 752–65. (**Chap. 15**)

Anfray, F. and Annequin, G. (1965) 'Matara. Deuxième, troisième et quatrième campagnes de fouilles', *AE*, 6, pp. 49–86. (**Chaps 13, 15**)

Anfray, F., Caquot, A. and Nautin, P. (1970) 'Une nouvelle inscription grecque d'Ezana, roi d'Axoum', *JS*, pp. 260–73. (**Chap. 14**)

Angelis D'Ossat, G. de and Farioli, R. (1975) 'Il complesso paleocristiano de Brevigliere-Elkhadra', *QAL*, pp. 29–56. (**Chap. 19**)

Apollodorus, *The Library*, tr. Sir J. G. Frazer (1921), 2 Vols (Cambridge, Mass.: Harvard University Press; London: Heinemann). (**Chap. 1**)

Applegate, J. R. (1970) 'The Berber languages', *CTL*, VI, pp. 586–661. (**Chap. 20**)

Aristotle, *Works* (tr. 1926–70), 23 Vols (London: Heinemann; Boston: Harvard University Press). (**Chap. 1**)

Aristotle, *The Works of Aristotle*, translated into English, J. A. Smith and W. D. Ross (eds) (1908–52), 12 Vols (Oxford: OUP). (**Chap. 1**)

Aristotle, *Opera*, ed. O. A. Gigon (1961–2) (Berlin: de Gruyter). (**Chap. 1**)

Arkell, A. J. (1949) *Early Khartoum. An Account of the Excavations of an Early Occupation Site*

*Carried Out by the Sudan Government Antiquities Service 1944–1945* (Oxford: OUP). (Chap. 9)

Arkell, A. J. (1950) 'Varia Sudanica', *JEA*, 36, pp. 27–30. (Chap. 9)

Arkell, A. J. (1951) 'Meroë and India, aspects of archaeology in Britain and beyond', essays presented to O. G. S. Crawford (London). (Chap. 10)

Arkell, A. J. (1961) *A History of the Sudan from the Earliest Times to 1821* (London: University of London, Athlone Press), 2nd edn revised. (Chaps 6, 9, 10, 11, 17)

Arkell, A. J. (1966) 'The iron age in the Sudan', *CA*, 7, 4, pp. 451–78. (Chap. 11)

Armstrong, R. G. (1964) *The Study of West African Languages* (Ibadan: Ibadan University Press). (Chap. 21)

Arrianus Flavius (1807) *The Commerce and Navigation of the Ancients in the Indian Ocean*, Vol. I: The Voyage of Nearchus, Vol. II: The Periplus of the Erythraean Sea, tr. W. Vincent (1807) (London: Cadell & Davies).

Ascher, J. E. (1970) 'Graeco-Roman nautical technology and modern sailing information. A confrontation between Pliny's account of the voyage to India and that of the *Periplus Maris Erythraei* in the light of modern knowledge', *JTG*, 31, pp. 10–26. (Chap. 22)

Atherton, J. H. (1972) 'Excavations at Kambamai and Yagala rock shelters, Sierra Leone', *WAJA*, 2, pp. 39ff. (Chap. 24)

Auber, J. (1958) *Français, Malgaches, Bantous, Arabes, Turcs, Chinois, Canaques – Parlons-nous d'une même langue?* (Tananarive: Impr. off. Paris: Maisonneuve) (Chap. 28)

Aubreville, A. (1948) 'Étude sur les forêts de l'Afrique équatoriale française et du Cameroun', *BS*, 2, p. 131 (Chap. 24)

Aurigemma, S. (1940) 'L'elefante di Leptis Magna', *AI*, pp. 67–86. (Chap. 20)

Avery, G. (1974) 'Discussion on the age and use of tidal fish traps', *SAAB*, p. 30. (Chap. 26)

Aymard, J. (1951) *Essai sur les chasses romaines des origines à la fin du siècle des Antonins* (Paris: Bibliothèque des Ecoles Françaises d'Athènes et de Rome). (Chap. 20)

Ayoub, M. S. (1962) 'Excavations at Germa, the capital of the Garmantes', *Sheba*, I. (Chap. 20)

Ayoub, M. S. (1967a) 'Excavations at Germa, the capital of the Garamantes', *Sheba*, II. (Chap. 20)

Ayoub, M. S. (1967b) 'The royal cemetery of Germa', *Libya Antiqua* (Tripoli), pp. 213–19. (Chap. 20)


Badawy, A. (1965) 'Le grotesque, invention égyptienne', *Gazette des beaux arts*, pp. 189–98. (Chap. 6)

Badawy, A. (1968) *A History of Egyptian Architecture (The New Kingdom): From the Eighteenth Dynasty to the End of the Twentieth Dynasty 1580–1085 BC* (Berkeley/Los Angeles: University of California Press). (Chap. 11)

Bailloud, G. (1969) 'L'évolution des styles céramiques en Ennedi (République du Tchad)', *Actes 1er Coll. Intern. Archéol. Afr.*, Fort Lamy, 1966, pp. 31–45. (Chap. 24)

Bakry, H. S. K. (1967) 'Psammetichus II and his newly-found stela at Shellae', *Oriens Antiquus*, 6, pp. 225–44. (Chap. 10)

Ball, J. (1942) *Egypt in the classical geographers* (Cairo: Government Press, Bulâq). (Chap. 6)

Balout, L. (1955) *Préhistoire de l'Afrique du Nord* (Paris: AMG), pp. 435–57. (Chap. 17)

Balout, L. (1967) 'L'homme préhistorique et la Méditerranée occidentale', *ROMM*, Aix-en-Provence, 3. (Chap. 17)

Baradez, J. (1949) *Vue-aérienne de l'organisation romaine dans le Sud-Algérien. Fossatum Africae* (Paris: AMG). (Chaps 19, 20)

Barguet, P. (ed.) (1967) *Le Livre des Morts des anciens Egyptiens* (Paris: Editions du Cerf). (Chaps 2, 3)

Barraux, M. (1959) 'L'auge de Sima', *BAM*. n.s., XXXVII, pp. 93–9. (Chap. 28)

Barrow, J. (1801–4) *An Account of travels into the Interior of southern Africa in the Years 1797 and 1798*, 2 Vols (London). (Chap. 26)

Basham, A. L. (1954) *The Wonder That Was India. A survey of the Indian sub-continent before the coming of the Muslims* (London: Sidgwick & Jackson). (Chap. 22)

Basset, H. (1921) 'Les influences puniques chez les berbères', RA, 62, p. 340. (Chap. 17)

Bates, O. (1914) *The Eastern Libyans* (London: Macmillan). (Chaps 4, 17)

Bates, O. and Dunham, D. (1927) 'Excavations at Gammai', *HAS*, 8, pp. 1–122. (Chap. 11)

Baumann, H. and Westermann, D. (1962) *Les peuples et les civilisations de l'Afrique: suivi de: Les langues et l'éducation* (Paris: Payot). (Chap. 29)

Baxter, H. C. (1944) 'Pangani: the trade centre of ancient history', *TNR*, pp. 15–25. (Chap. 22)

Bayles des Hermens, R. de (1967) 'Premier aperçu du paléolothique inférieur en RCA', *Anthropologie*, 71, pp. 135–66. (Chap. 21)

748

**Bayle des Hermens, R. de** (1971) 'Quelques aspects de la préhistoire en RCA', *JAH*, XII, pp. 579–97. **(Chap. 21)**

**Bayle des Hermens, R. de** (1972a) 'Aspects de la recherche préhistorique en République Centrafricaine', *Africa-Tervuren*, XVIII, 3/4, pp. 90–103. **(Chap. 25)**

**Bayle des Hermens, R. de** (1972b) 'La civilisation mégalithique de Bouar. Prospection et fouille 1962–6 par P. Vidal. Recension', *Africa-Tervuren*, XLII, 1, pp. 78–9. **(Chap. 25)**

**Beauchêne, M. C. de** (1963) 'La préhistoire du Gabon', *Objets et Mondes*, III, 1, p. 16. **(Chap. 21)**

**Beauchêne, M. C. de** (1970) 'The Lantana mine near the Rapoa/Niger confluence of Niger', *WAAN*, 12, p. 63 **(Chap. 29)**

**Beaumont, P. B. and Boshier, A. K.** (1974) 'Report on test excavations in a prehistoric pigment mine near Postmasburg, Northern Cape', *SAAB*, 29, pp. 41–59. **(Chap. 29)**

**Beaumont, P. B. and Vogel, J. C.** (1972) 'On a new radiocarbon chronology for Africa south of the Equator', *AS*, 31, pp. 66–89. **(Chap. 26)**

**Beck, P. and Huard, P.** (1969) *Tibesti, carrefour de la préhistoire saharienne* (Paris: Arthaud). **(Chaps 17, 20)**

**Beckerath, J. von** (1965) *Untersuchungen zur politischen Geschichte der Zweiten Zwischenzeit in Ägypten* (University of Munich, Heft 23) (Glückstadt: Ägyptologische Forschungen). **(Chap. 2)**

**Beckerath, J. von** (1971) *Abriss der Geschichte des alten Ägypten* (Munich: Oldenbourg). **(Chap. 2)**

**Beek, G. W. Van** (1967) 'Monuments of Axum in the light of south Arabian archaeology', *JAOS*, 87, pp. 113–22. **(Chap. 14)**

**Beek, G. W. Van** (1969) 'The rise and fall of Arabia Felix', *SA*, 221, 6, pp. 36–46. **(Chap. 22)**

**Belkhodja, K.** (1970) L'Afrique byzantine à la fin du VIe siècle et au début du VIIe siècle', *Revue de l'Occident Musulman et de la Méditerranée*, (Aix-en-Provence), N.S., pp. 55–65. **(Chap. 19)**

**Bell, H. I.** (1948) *Egypt from Alexander the Great to the Arab Conquest. A Study in the Diffusion and Decay of Hellenism* (Oxford: Clarendon Press). **(Chap. 6)**

**Bell, H. I.** (1957) *Cults and Creeds in Graeco-Roman Egypt* (Liverpool: University Press), 2nd edn. **(Chap. 6)**

**Bénabou, M.** (1972) 'Proconsul et légat. Le tèmoignage de Tacite', *Ant. Afr.*, VI, pp. 61–75. **(Chap. 19)**

**Bénabou, M.** (1976) *La résistance africaine à la romanisation* (Paris: Maspero). **(Chaps 17, 19)**

**Bernand, A.** (1966) *Alexandrie la Grande* (Paris: Arthaud). **(Chap. 6)**

**Bernand, E.** (1969) *Inscriptions méroïtiques de l'Égypte gréco-romaine. Recherches sur la poésie epigrammatique des grecs en Égypte* (Paris: Les Belles Lettres). **(Chap. 6)**

**Bernhard, F. O.** (1961) 'The Ziwa ware of Inyanga', *NADA*, XXXVIII, pp. 84–92. **(Chap. 27)**

**Bernhard, F. O.** (1964) 'Notes on the pre-ruin Ziwa culture of Inyanga', *Rhodesiana*, XII. **(Chap. 27)**

**Berthelot, A.** (1931) *L'Afrique saharienne et soudanaise. Ce qu'en ont connu les Anciens* (Paris: Les Arts et le Livre). **(Chap. 20)**

**Berthier, A.** (1968) 'La sépulture du lecteur Georges à Sila', *BAA*, II, pp. 283–92. **Chap. 19)**

**Berthier, A. and Charlier, R.** (1955) *Le sanctuaire punique d'El-Hofra à Constantine* (Paris: Direction de l'Intérieur et des Beaux-Arts, Service des Antiquités, Missions Archéologiques). **(Chap. 18)**

**Bevan, E.** (1927) *A History of Egypt under the Ptolemaic Dynasty* (London: Methuen) 2nd edn. 1961. **(Chap. 6)**

**Bieber, M.** (1955) *Sculpture of the Hellenistic Age* (New York: Columbia University Press). **(Chap. 6)**

**Bierbrier, M.** (1975) *Late New Kingdom in Egypt* c. *1300–664 BC Genealogy and Chronology* (Warminster: Aris & Phillips). **(Chaps 2, 3)**

**Bietak, M.** (1965) 'Ausgrabungen in der Sayala District', *Nubien*, Vienna, pp. 1–82. **(Chap. 9)**

'Bion and Nicholas of Damascus', in C. Müller (ed) *Fragmenta Historicum Graeconum*, Vol. 3, p. 463; Vol. 4, p. 351. **(Chap. 11)**

**Birch, S. and Rhind, A. H.** (1863) *Facsimilies of two papyri found in a tomb at Thebes*, Rhind Mathematical Papyrus, British Museum nos 10057, 10058 (London; Oberlin, USA).

**Bisson, M. S.** (1975) 'Copper currency in central Africa: the archaeological evidence', *WA*, 6, pp. 276–92. **(Chap. 29)**

**Blankoff, B.** (1965) 'La préhistoire au Gabon', *BSPPG*, pp. 4–5 **(Chap. 25)**

**Bloch, M. and Verin, P.** (1966) 'Discovery of an apparently neolithic artefact in Madagascar', *Man*, I, pp. 240–1. **(Chap. 28)**

**Bobo, J. and Morel, J.** (1955) 'Les peintures rupestres de l'abri du Mouflon et la station préhistorique de Hamman Sidi Djeballa dans la cheffia (Est-Constantinois)', *Libyca*, 3, pp. 163–81. **(Chap. 17)**

**Bonsma, J. C.** (1970) 'Livestock production in the sub-tropical and tropical African countries', *SAJS*, 66, 5, pp. 169–72. **(Chap. 24)**

Borchardt, L. (1938) in *Annales du Service des Antiquités*, 38, pp. 209–15. (Chap. 2)

Borghouts, J. F. (1973) 'The evil eye of Apopis', *JEA*, 59, pp. 114–50. (Chap. 3)

Boshier, A. and Beaumont, P. (1972) 'Mining in southern Africa and the emergence of modern man', *Optima*, 22, pp. 2–12. (Chap. 29)

Boubbe, J. (1959–60) 'Découvertes récentes à Sala Colonia (Chellah)', *BSAC*, pp. 141–5. (Chap. 19)

Bourgeois, R. (1957) 'Banyarwanda et Barundi, Tombe I – ethnographie', *ARSC*, XV, pp. 536–49. (Chap. 25)

Bovill, E. W. (1968) *The Golden Trade of the Moors* (London: OUP), 2nd edn. (Chap. 21)

Bowdich, T. E. (1821) *An Essay on the Superstitions, Customs and Arts Common to the Ancient Egyptians, Abyssinians and Ashantees* (Paris: Smith). (Chap. 4)

Bowen, R. Le Baron (1957) 'The dhow sailor', *American Neptune* (Salem, Mass.), II. (Chap. 22)

Bowen, R. Le Baron and Albright, F. P. (eds) (1958) *Archaeological Discoveries in South Arabia* (Baltimore: John Hopkins Press).

Brabant, H. (1965) 'Contribution odontologique à l'étude des ossements trouvés dans la nécropole protohistorique de Sanga, République du Congo', *AMRAC*, 54. (Chap. 25)

Brahimi, C. (1970) L'Ibéromaurusien littoral de la région d'Alger, *Mém. CRAPE*, pp. 77. (Chap. 17)

Breasted, J. H. (1906) *Ancient Records of Egypt. Historical documents from the earliest times to the Persian Conquest*, 5 Vols (Chicago: University of Chicago Press). (Chaps 2, 4, 9, 10, 11)

Breasted, J. H. (1930) *The Edwin Smith Surgical Papyrus*, 2 Vols (Chicago: University of Chicago Press). (Chap. 5)

Breasted, J. H. (1951) *A History of Egypt from the Earliest Times to the Persian Conquest* (London: Hodder & Stoughton), 2nd edn fully revised. (Chap. 2)

Breccia, W. (1922) *Alexandria ad Aegyptum. A guide to the ancient and modern town and to its Graeco-Roman museum* (Bergamo for Alexandria Municipality). (Chap. 6)

Breton, R. (1892) *Dictionnaire Caraïbe-Français* (Leipzig: Platzmann). Reprint. (Chap. 28)

Briant, R. P. M. (1945) *L'Hébreu à Madagascar* (Tananarive: Pitot de la Beaujardière). (Chap. 28)

Briggs, L. C. (1957) 'Living tribes of the Sahara and the problem of their prehistoric origin', *Third Pan-African Congress on Prehistory, Livingstone, 1955* (London: Chatto), pp. 195–9. (Chap. 20)

Brinton, J. Y. (1942) Article in *BSRA*, 35, pp. 78–81, 163–5, and pl. XX, fig. 4. (Chap. 17)

Brothwell, D. and Shaw, T. (1971) 'A late Upper Pleistocene proto-west African negro from Nigeria', *Man*, 6, 2, pp. 221–7. (Chap. 21)

Broughton, T. R. S. (1968) *The Romanization of Africa Proconsularis* (New York: Greenwood Press). (Chap. 19)

Brown, B. R. (1957) *Ptolemaic Paintings and Mosaics and the Alexandrian Style* (Cambridge, Mass.: Archaeological Institute of America). (Chap. 6)

Brunner, H. (1957) *Altägyptische Erziehung* (Wiesbaden: Harrassowitz). (Chap. 3)

Brunner, H. (1964) 'Die Geburt des Gottkönigs. Studien zur Uberlieferungeines altägyptischen Mythos', *ÄA*, 10. (Chap. 3)

Brunner-Traut, E. (1974) *Die Alten Ägypter: Verborgenes Leben unter Pharaonen 2-durchgegehen Aufl.* (Stuttgart: Kohlhammer), p. 272. (Chap. 3)

Brunt, P. A. (1971) *Italian Manpower 225 BC–AD 14* (London: Oxford University Press), pp. 581–3. (Chap. 19)

Bücheler, F. and Riese, A. (eds) (1899) *Anthologia latina* (Leipzig), 183. (Chap. 17)

Buck, A. de (1952) *Grammaire élémentaire du moyen égyptien*, tr. B. van de Walle and J. Vergote (Leiden: Brill). (Chap. 1)

Buck, A. de (1935–61) 'The Egyptian coffin texts', *Oriental Institute of Chicago Publications*, 34, 49, 64, 67, 73, 81, 87. (Chaps 2, 3)

Budge, E. A. T. Wallis (1912) *Annals of Nubian Kings, with a Sketch of the Story of the Nubian Kingdom of Napata*, Vol. 2 of *Egyptian Literature* (London: Routledge & Kegan Paul). (Chap. 11)

Budge, E. A. T. Wallis (1928a) *The Book of the Saints of the Ethiopian Church: a translation of the Ethiopic synaxarium made from Oriental Manuscripts nos. 660 and 661 in the British Museum*, 4 Vols (Cambridge: CUP). (Chap. 16)

Budge, E. A. T. Wallis (1928b) *A History of Ethiopia, Nubia and Abyssinia, according to the Hieroglyphic Inscriptions of Egypt and Nubia and the Ethiopian Chronicles* 2 Vols (London: Methuen (Chap. 16)

Budge, E. A. T. Wallis (1966) *A History of Ethiopia*, Anthropological Publications (Netherlands: Cosferhout NB), Vol. I. (Chap. 16)

Bunbury, E. H. (1959) *A History of Ancient Geography among the Greeks and the Romans from the Earliest Ages to the Fall of the Roman Empire*, 2 Vols (New York: Dover Publications), 2nd edn. (Chap. 22)

Bushra, S. (1972) 'Urbanization in the Sudan', *Actes Conf. Ann. Soc. Phil. Soudan.* (Chap. 11)

Butzer, K. W. (1961) *Climatic Change in Arid Regions since the Pliocene* (Arid Zone Research: Unesco), 17, pp. 31–56. (**Chap. 17**)

Bynon, J. (1970) 'The contribution of linguistics to history in the field of Berber studies', in D. Dalby (ed.), *Language and History in Africa* (London: Cass), pp. 64–77. (**Chap. 20**)

Cabannes, R. (1964) *Les Types hémoglobiniques des populations de la partie occidentale du continent africain* (*Maghrib, Sahara, Afrique noire occidentale*) (Paris: CRNS). (**Chap. 20**)

Callet, F. (1908) *Tantaran ny Andriana nanjake teto Imeria* (Tananarive). (**Chap. 28**)

Callet, F. (1974) *Histoire des rois de Tantaran'ny Andriana*, trs G.-S. Chaput and E. Ratsimba (Tananarive: Librairie de Madagascar), Vols. 1–3. (**Chap. 28**)

Calza, G. (1916) 'Il Piazzale delle Corporazioni', *Boll. Comm.*, pp. 178ff. (**Chap. 19**)

Caminos, R. A. (1954) *Late-Egyptian Miscellanies* (London: OUP). (**Chap. 3**)

Caminos, R. A. (1964a) 'Surveying Semna Gharbi', *Kush*, 12, pp. 82–6. (**Chap. 9**)

Caminos, R. A. (1964b) 'The Nitocris adoption stela', *JEA*, 50, pp. 71–101. (**Chap. 10**)

Caminos, R. A. (1975) *New Kingdom Temples of Buhen*, 2 Vols (London: Egypt Exploration Society). (**Chaps, 2, 9**)

Camps, G. (1954) 'L'inscription de Béja et le problème des Dii Mauri', *RA*, 98, pp. 233–60. (**Chap. 17**)

Camps, G. (1960a) 'Les traces d'un âge du bronze en Afrique du Nord', *RA*, 104, pp. 31–55. (**Chap. 17**)

Camps, G. (1960b) 'Aux origines de la Berbérie: Massinissa ou les débuts de l'histoire', *Libyca*, 8, 1. (**Chaps 17, 19, 24**)

Camps, G. (1961) *Monuments et rites funéraires protohistoriques: aux origines de la Berbérie* (Paris: AMG). (**Chaps 17, 20**)

Camps, G. (1965) 'Le tombeau de Tin Hinan à Abalessa', *Trav. IRS*, 24, pp. 65–83. (**Chaps 17, 20**)

Camps, G. (1969a) 'Amekini, néolithique ancien du Hoggar', *Mém. CRAPE*, 10, pp. 186–8. (**Chap. 24**)

Camps, G. (1969b) 'Haratin-Ethiopiens, réflexions sur les origines des négroides sahariens', *Actes Coll. Intern. Biolog. Pop. Sahar.*, pp. 11–17. (**Chap. 20**)

Camps, G. (1970) 'Recherches sur les origines des cultivateurs noirs du Sahara', *ROMM*, 7, pp. 39–41. (**Chap. 17**)

Camps, G. (1974a) 'Le Gour, mausolée berbère du VIIe siècle', *AA*, VIII, pp. 191–208. (**Chap. 19**)

Camps, G. (1974b) 'Tableau chronologique de la préhistoire récente du Nord de l'Afrique', *BSPF*, 71, 1, p. 262. (**Chap. 17**)

Camps, G. (1974c) 'L'âge du tombeau de Tin Hinan, ancêtre des Touareg du Hoggar', *Zephyrus*, XXV, pp. 497–516. (**Chap. 20**)

Camps, G. (1974d) *Les civilisations préhistoriques de l'Afrique du Nord et du Sahara* (Paris: Doin. (**Chaps 17, 20**)

Camps, G. (1975) 'Recherches sur les plus anciennes inscriptions libyques de l'Afrique du Nord et du Sahara', *Encyclopédie berbère*, 24. (**Chap. 20**)

Camps, G. (1978) *Les Relations du monde méditerranéen et du monde sud-saharien durant la préhistoire et la protohistoire* (Aix-en-Provence: GERESM). (**Chap. 20**)

Camps, G., Delibrias, G. and Thommeret, J. (1968) 'Chronologie absolue et succession des civilisations préhistoriques dans le Nord de l'Afrique', *Libyca*, XVI, p. 16. (**Chap. 17**)

Camps-Fabrer, H. (1953) *L'Olivier et l'huile dans l'Afrique romaine* (Algiers: Imprimerie officielle). (**Chap. 19**)

Camps-Fabrer, H. (1966) *Matière et art mobilier dans la préhistoire nord-africaine et saharienne* (Paris: Mémoires du Centre de Recherches Anthropologiques, Préhistoriques et Ethnographiques). (**Chap. 17**)

Capot-Rey, R. (1953) *Le Sahara français* (Paris: PUF). (**Chap. 20**)

Caquot, A. (1965) 'L'inscription éthiopienne à Marib', *AE*, VI, pp. 223–5. (**Chaps 15, 16**)

Caquot, A. and Drewes, A. J. (1955) 'Les monuments recueillis à Magallé (Tigré)', *AE*, I, pp. 17–41. (**Chaps 13, 15**)

Caquot, A. and Leclant, J. (1956) 'Rapport sur les récents travaux de la section d'archéologie', *C-RAI*, pp. 226–34. (**Chap. 15**)

Caquot, A. and Leclant, J. (1959) 'Ethiopie et Cyrénaique? A propos d'un texte de Synesius', *AE*, III, pp. 173–7. (**Chap. 15**)

Caquot, A. and Nautin, P. (1970) 'Une nouvelle inscription grecque d'Ezana, roi d'Axoum. Description et étude de l'inscription grecque', *JS*, pp. 270–1. (**Chap. 15**)

Carcopino, J. (1948) *Le Maroc antique* (Paris: Gallimard). (Chaps 17, 19, 20)

Carcopino, J. (1956) 'Encore Masties, l'empéreur maure inconnu', *RA*, pp. 339–48. (Chap. 19)

Carcopino, J. (1958) *La mort de Ptolémée, roi de Maurétanie* (Paris), pp. 191ff. (Chap. 19)

Carneiro, R. L. (1970) 'A theory of the origin of the state', *American Association for the Advancement of Science*, 169, 3947, pp. 733–8. (Chap. 29)

Carpenter, R. (1958) 'The Phoenicians in the west', *AJA*, LXVII. (Chap. 15)

Carpenter, R. (1965) 'A trans-Saharan caravan route in Herodotus', *AJA*, pp. 231–42. (Chap. 20)

Carter, H. and Mace, A. C. (1963) *The Tomb of Tut-Ankh-Amon Discovered by the late Earl of Caernarvon and H. Carter*, 3 Vols (New York: Cooper Square Publishers). (Chap. 2)

Carter, P. L. (1969) 'Moshebi's shelter: excavation and exploitation in eastern Lesotho', *Lesotho*, 8, pp. 1–23. (Chap. 26)

Carter, P. L. (1970) 'Late stone age exploitation patterns in southern Natal', *SAAB*, 25, 98, pp. 55–8. (Chap. 26)

Carter, P. L. and Flight, C. (1972) 'A report on the fauna from two neolithic sites in northern Ghana with evidence for the practice of animal husbandry during the 2nd millennium BC', *Man*, 7, 2, pp. 277–82. (Chap. 24)

Carter, P. L. and Vogel, J. C. (1971) 'The dating of industrial assemblages from stratified sites in eastern Lesotho', *Man*, 9, pp. 557–70. (Chap. 26)

Castiglione, L. (1967) 'Abdalla Nirgi. En aval d'Abou Simbel, fouilles de sauvetage d'une ville de l'ancienne Nubic chrétienne', *Archeologia*, 18, Paris, pp. 14–19. (Chap. 12)

Castiglione, L. (1970) 'Diocletianus und die Blemmyes', *ZÄS*, 96, 2, pp. 90–103. (Chap. 10)

Caton-Thompson, G. (1929) 'The Southern Rhodesian ruins: recent archaeological investigations', *Nature*, 124, pp. 619–21. (Chap. 27)

Caton-Thompson, G. (1929–30) 'Recent excavations at Zimbabwe and other ruins in Rhodesia', *JRAS*, 29, pp. 132–8. (Chaps 20, 27)

Cenival, J. L. de (1973) *L'Égypte avant les pyramides, 4e millénaire*, Grand Palais, 29 May–3 September (Paris: Musées nationaux). (Chap. 2)

Černý, J. (1927) 'Le culte d'Amenophis I chez les ouvriers de la nécropole thébaine', *BIFAO*, 27, pp. 159–203. (Chap. 2)

Černý, J. (1942) 'Le caractère des oushebtis d'après les idées du Nouvel-Empire', *BIFAO*, 41, pp. 105–33 (Chap. 3)

Černý, J. (1973) *A Community of Workmen at Thebes in the Ramesside Period* (Cairo: Institut Français d'Archéologie Orientale). (Chap. 3)

Cerulli, E. (1943) *Etiopi in Palestina; storia della communità etiopica di Gerusalemme*, Vol. I (Rome: Libreria dello Stato). (Chap. 16)

Cerulli, E. (1956) *Storia della letteratura etiopica* (Milan: Nuova accademia editrice). (Chap. 16)

Chace, A. B. (1927–9) *The Rhind Mathematical Papyrus, British Museum, 10057 and 10058* (Oberlin). (Chap. 5)

Chaker, S. (1973) 'Libyque: épigraphie et linguistique', *Encyclopédie berbère*, 9. (Chap. 20)

Chamla, M. C. (1958) 'Recherches anthropologiques sur l'origine des malgaches', *Museum*, Paris. (Chap. 28)

Chamla, M. C. (1968) 'Les populations anciennes du Sahara et des régions limitrophes. Études des restes osseux humains néolithiques et protohistoriques', *Mém. CRAPE*, IX (Chaps 17, 20, 21)

Chamla, M. C. (1970) 'Les hommes épipaléolithiques de Columnata (Algérie occidentale)', *Mém. CRAPE*, XV, pp. 113–14. (Chap. 17)

Chamoux, F. (1953) *Cyrène sous la monarchie des Battiades* (Paris: de Boccard). (Chap. 17)

Champetier, P. (1951) 'Les conciles africains durant la période byzantine', *RA*, pp. 103–20. (Chap. 19)

Champollion-Figeac, J. J. (1839) *Egypte ancienne* (Paris: Firmin Didot). (Chap. 1)

Chaplin, J. H. (1974) 'The prehistoric rock art of the Lake Victoria region', *Azania*, IX, pp. 1–50. (Chap. 29)

Charles-Picard, G. (1954) *Les Religions de l'Afrique antique* (Paris: Plon). (Chap. 18)

Charles-Picard, G. (1956) *Le Monde de Carthage* (Paris: Corrêa).

Charles-Picard, G. (1957) 'Civitas Mactaritana', *Karthago*, 8, pp. 33–9. (Chap. 17)

Charles-Picard, G. (1958a) 'Images de chars romains sur les rochers du Sahara', *C-RAI*.

Charles-Picard, G. and C. (1958b) *La Vie quotidienne à Carthage au temps d'Hannibal, IIIᵉ siècle avant Jésus-Christ* (Paris: Hachette). (Chap. 18)

Charles-Picard, G. (1959) *La Civilisation de l'Afrique romaine* (Paris: Plon). (Chap. 19)

Charles-Picard, G. (1968) *Les Cahiers de Tunisie, Mélanges Saumagne*, pp. 27–31. (Chap. 20)

Charlesworth, M. P. (1926) *Trade Routes and Commerce of the Roman Empire* (Cambridge: CUP). (Chap. 22)

Charlesworth, M. P. (1951) 'Roman trade with India: a resurvey', in A. C. Johnson, *Studies in Roman Economic and Social History in Honour of Allen Chester Johnson*, ed. P. R. Coleman-Norton (Princeton: Princeton University Press). (Chap. 22)

Chassebœuf de Volney, Count C. F. (1825) *Voyages en Egypte et en Syrie pendant les années 1783, 1784 et 1785*, 2 Vols (Paris).

Chastagnol, A. (1967) 'Les gouverneurs de Byzacène et de Tripolitaine', *AA*, 1, pp. 130–4. (Chap. 19)

Chastagnol, A. and Duval, N. (1974) 'Les survivances du culte impérial dans l'Afrique du Nord à l'époque vandale. Mélanges d'histoire ancienne offerts à W. Seston', *Publications de la Sorbonne*, Étude IX, pp. 87–118. (Chap. 19)

Chevallier, R. and Caillemer, A. (1957) 'Les centuriätions romaines de Tunisie', *Annales*, 2, pp. 275–86. (Chap. 19)

Chevrier, H. (1964–70–1) 'Technique de la construction dans l'ancienne Égypte': I: 'Murs en briques crues', *RE*, 16, pp. 11–17; II: 'Problèmes posés par les obélisques', *RE*, 22, pp. 15–39; III: 'Gros œuvre, maconnerie', *RE*, 23, pp. 67–111. (Chap. 3)

Chittick, N. (1966) 'Six early coins from new Tanga', *Azania*, 1, pp. 156–7. (Chap. 22)

Chittick, N. (1969) 'An archaeological reconnaissance of the southern Somali coast', *Azania*, IV, pp. 115–30. (Chap. 22)

Cintas, P. (1950) *Céramique punique* (Paris: Librairie C. Klincksieck). (Chap. 18)

Cintas, P. (1954) 'Nouvelles recherches à Utique', *Karthago*, V. (Chap. 18)

Cintas, P. and Duval, N. (1958) 'L'église du prêtre Félix, région de Kélibia', *Karthago*, IX, pp. 155–265. (Chap. 19)

Clark, J. D. (1957) 'Pre-European copper working in south central Africa', *Roan Antelope*, pp. 2–6. (Chap. 25)

Clark, J. D. (1967) 'The problem of Neolithic culture in sub-Saharan Africa', in W. W. Bishop and J. D. Clark (eds), *Background to Evolution in Africa* (Chicago: University of Chicago Press), pp. 601–27. (Chap. 25)

Clark, J. D. (1968) 'Some early iron age pottery from Lunda', in J. D. Clark (ed.), *Further Palaeo-Anthropological Studies in Northern Lunda* (Lisbon), pp. 189–205. (Chap. 27)

Clark, J. D. (1970) *The Prehistory of Africa* (London: Thames & Hudson). (Chap. 23)

Clark, J. D. (1972) 'Prehistoric populations and pressures favouring plant domestication in Africa', *BWS 56*. (Chap. 24)

Clark, J. D (1974) 'Iron age occupation at the Kalambo Falls', in J. D. Clark (ed.), *Kalambo Falls Prehistoric Site*, Vol. II (Cambridge: CUP), pp. 57–70. (Chap. 25)

Clark, J. D. and Fagan, B. M. (1965) 'Charcoal, sands and channel-decorated pottery from northern Rhodesia', *AA*, LXVII, pp. 354–71. (Chap. 29)

Clark, J. D. and Walton, J. (1962) 'A late stone age site in the Erongo mountains, south west Africa', *Proc. PS*, 28, pp. 1–16. (Chap. 26)

Clarke, S. and Engelbach, R. (1930) *Ancient Egyptian Masonry, the Building Craft* (London: OUP). (Chap. 5)

Clavel, M. and Levêque, P. (1971) *Villes et structures urbaines dans l'Occident romain* (Paris: A. Colin), pp. 7–94. (Chap. 19)

Clemente, G. (1968) *La Notitia Dignitatum* (Cagliari: Editrice Sarda Fossataro), pp. 318–42. (Chap. 19)

Codex Theodosianus: *Theodosiani Libri XVI cum constitutionibus Sirmondianis et leges novellae ad Theodosianum pertinentes*, T. Mommsen and P. Meyer (eds) (1905) (Berlin: Societas Regia Scientarum). (Chap. 15)

Codine, J. (1868) *Mémoire géographique sur la Mer des Indes* (Paris: Challamel). (Chap. 28)

Cohen, D. and Maret, P. de (1974) 'Recherches archéologiques récentes en République du Zaïre', *Forum-Université Libre de Bruxelles*, 39, pp. 33–7. (Chap. 25)

Cohen, D. and Martin, P. (1972) 'Classification formelle automatique et industries lithiques; interprétation des hachereaux de la Kamoa', *AMRAC*, 76. (Chap. 21)

Cohen, D. and Mortelmans, G. (1973) 'Un site tschitolien sur le plateau des Bateké', *AMRAC*, 81. (Chap. 25)

Connah, G. (1967a) 'Excavations at Daima, N.E. Nigeria', *Actes VI Congr. PPEQ*, pp. 146–7. (Chap. 24)

Connah, G. (1967b) 'Radiocarbon dates for Daima', *JHSN*, 3 (Chap. 24)

Connah, G. (1969a) 'The coming of iron: Nok and Daima', in T. Shaw (ed.), *Lectures on Nigerian Prehistory and Archaeology* (Ibadan: Ibadan University Press), pp. 30–62. (Chap. 21)

Connah, G. (1969b) 'Settlement mounds of the Firki: the reconstruction of a lost society', *Ibadan*, 26. (Chap. 24)

Contenson, H. de (1960) 'Les premiers rois d'Axoum d'après les découvertes récentes', *JA*, 248, pp. 78–96. (Chap. 13)

Contenson, H. de (1961) 'Les principales étapes de l'Ethiopie antique', *CEA*, 2, 5, pp. 12–23. (Chap. 13)

Contenson, H. de (1962) 'Les monuments d'art sud-arabes découverts sur le site Haoulti (Ethiopie) en 1959', *Syria*, 39, pp. 68–83, (Chap. 13)

Contenson, H. de (1963a) 'Les subdivisions de l'archéologie éthiopienne. Etat de la question', *R. Arch.*, pp. 189–91. (Chap. 13)

Contenson, H. de (1963b) 'Les fouilles de Haoulti en 1959. Rapport préliminaire', *AE*, 5, pp. 41–86. (Chaps 13, 15)

Contenson, H. de (1963c) 'Les fouilles à Axoum en 1958. Rapport préliminaire', *AE*, 5, pp. 3–39. (Chap. 15)

Contenson, H. de (1965) 'Les fouilles à Haoulti en 1959; rapport préliminaire', *AE*, 5, pp. 45–6. (Chap. 15)

Contenson, H. de (1969) 'Compte-rendu bibliographique de "Annales d'Ethiopie" vol. 7', *Syria*, 46, pp. 161–7. (Chap. 13)

Conti-Rossini, C. (1903) 'Documenti per l'archeologia d'Eritrea nella bassa valle dei Barca', *RRAL*, 5, XII. (Chap. 15)

Conti-Rossini, C. (1928) *Storia di Etiopia* (Bergamo: Instituto Italiano d'Arti Grafiche). (Chaps 13, 16)

Conti-Rossini, C. (1947) 'Ieha, Tsehuf Enni e Dera', *RSE*, 6, pp. 12–22. (Chap. 13)

Conti-Rossini, C. (1947–8) 'Gad ed il dio luna in Etiopia', Studi e materali di storia delle religione (Rome). (Chap. 15)

Cooke, C. K. (1971) 'The rock art of Rhodesia', *SAJS*, Special Issue 2, pp. 7–10. (Chap. 27)

Coon, C. S. (1968) *Yengema Cave Report* (Philadelphia: University of Pennsylvania). (Chap. 24)

Coppens, Y. (1969) 'Les cultures protohistoriques et historiques du Djourab', *Actes 1er Coll. Intern. Archéol. Afr.*, pp. 129–46. (Chap. 24)

Cornevin, R. (1967) *Histoire de l'Afrique*, Vol. I: *Des origines au XVIe siècle* (Paris: Payot) 2nd edn (Chap. 20)

*Corpus inscriptionum semiticarum ab academia inscriptionum et Litterarum Humaniorum conditum atque digestum* (1881–1954) (Paris: Académie des Inscriptions et Belles Lettres). (Chap. 15)

Cosmas Indicopleustes, *The Christian Topography of Cosmas Indicopleustes*, tr. E. O. Winstedt (1909) (Cambridge: CUP). *Topographie chrétienne*, tr. W. Walsca (Paris: Cerf). (Chaps 15, 22)

Coulbeaux, J. B. (1928) *Histoire politique et religieuse d'Abyssinie depuis les temps plus reculés jusqu'à l'avènement de Menelik II*, Vol. I (Paris: Geuthner). (Chap. 16)

Courtin, J. (1969) 'Le Néolithique du Borkou, Nord Tchad', *Actes 1er Coll. Intern. Archéol. Afr.*, pp. 147–59. (Chap. 24)

Courtois, C. (1942) Article in *RA*, pp. 24–55. (Chap. 19)

Courtois, C. (1945) 'Grégoire VII et l'Afrique du Nord. Remarques sur les communautés chrétiennes d'Afrique du XIe siècle', *RH*, CXCV, pp. 97–122, 193–226. (Chap. 19)

Courtois, C. (1954) *Victor de Vita et son oeuvre* (Algiers: Impr. off.). (Chap. 19)

Courtois, C. (1955) *Les Vandales et l'Afrique* (Paris: AMG). (Chaps 19, 20)

Courtois, C., Leschi, L., Miniconi, J., Ferrat, C. and Saumagne, C. (1952) *Tablettes Albertini: Actes privés de l'époque vandale, fin du Ve siècle* (Paris: AMG). (Chap. 19)

Cracco-Ruggini, L. (1974) 'Leggenda e realtà Etiopi nella cultura tardoimperiale', *Attiiv Congr. Intern. Stud. Et.*, 191, pp. 141–93. (Chap. 20)

Crowfoot, J. W. (1911) 'The island of Meroe', *Archaeological Survey of Egypt*, Memoire no. 19, London, p. 37 (Chap. 11)

Crowfoot, J. W. (1927) 'Christian Nubia', *JEA*, XIII, pp. 141–50. (Chap. 12)

Culwick. A. I. and G. M. (1936) 'Indonesian echoes in central Tanganyika', *TNR*, 2, pp. 60–6. (Chap. 28)

Curto, S. (1965) *Nubia; storia di anu civittà favolosa* (Novara: Istituto geografico de Agostini). (Chap. 11)

Curto, S. (1966) *Nubien. Geschichte einer rätselhaften Kultur* (Munich: Goldmann). (Chap. 9)

Cuvillier, A. (1967) *Introduction à la sociologie* (Paris: Colin). (Chap. 1)


Dahl, O. Ch. (1951) 'Malgache et Maanjan, une comparaison linguistique', *AUEI*, 3, (Chap. 28)

Dahle, L. (1889) 'The Swahili element in the new Malagasy English dictionary', *Antananarivo*, III, pp. 99–115. (Chap. 28)

Dalby, D. (1970) 'Reflections on the classification of African languages', *ALS*, 11, pp. 147–71. (Chap. 21)

Dalby, D. (1975) 'The prehistorical implications of Guthrie's comparative Bantu. I. Problems of internal relationship', *JAH*, XVI, pp. 481–501. (Chap. 23)

Dalby, D. (1967) 'The prehistorical implications of Guthrie's comparative Bantu. II. Interpretation of cultural vocabulary', *JAH*, XVII, pp. 1–27. (Chap. 23)

Daniels, C. M. (1968a) *Garamantian Excavations: Zinchecra 1965–1967* (Tripoli: Department of Antiquities). (Chap. 20)

Daniels, C. M. (1968b) 'The Garamantes of Fezzan', in *Libya in History* (Beirut, Lebanon). (Chap. 4)

Daniels, C. M. (1970) *The Garamantes of Southern Libya* (Wisconsin: Cleander Press). (Chaps 17, 21)

Daniels, C. M. (1972–3) 'The Garamantes of Fezzan. An interim report of research, 1965–73', *SLS*, IV, pp. 35–40. (Chap. 20)

Daniels, S. G. H. and Phillipson, D. W. (1969) 'The early iron age site at Dambwa near Livingstone', in B. M. Fagan, D. W. Phillipson and S. G. H. Daniels (eds), *Iron Age Cultures in Zambia*, (London: Chatto & Windus), Vol. II, pp. 1–54. (Chap. 27)

Darby, W. J., Ghalioungui, P. and Grivetti, L. (1977) *Food: the Gift of Osiris*, 2 Vols (London/New York/San Francisco: Academic Press). (Chap. 3)

Daris, S. (1961) *Documenti per la storia dell'esercito romano in Egitto* (Milan: Università Cattolica del Sacro Cuore). (Chap. 7)

Dart, R. A. and Beaumont, P. (1969a) 'Evidence of ore mining in southern Africa in the middle stone age', *CA*, 10, pp. 127–8. (Chap. 29)

Dart, R. A. and Beaumont, P. (1969b) 'Rhodesian engravers, painters and pigment miners of the fifth millennium BC', *SAAB*, 8, pp. 91–6. (Chap. 29)

Datoo, B. A. (1970a) 'Misconception about the use of monsoons by dhows in East African waters', *EAGR*, 8, pp. 1–10. (Chap. 22)

Datoo, B. A. (1970b) 'Rhapta: the location and importance of East Africa's first port', *Azania*, V, pp. 65–75. (Chaps 22, 28)

Datoo, B. A. and Sheriff, A. M. H. (1971) 'Patterns of ports and trade routes in different periods', in L. Berry (ed.), *Tanzania in Maps* (London: University of London Press), pp. 102–5. (Chap. 22)

Daumas, F. (1967) 'Ce que l'on peut entrevoir de l'histoire de Ouadi Es Sebua, Nubie', *CHE*, X, pp. 40ff. (Chap. 12)

Daumas, F. (1976) *La Civilisation de l'Égypte pharaonique* (Paris: Arthaud) 2nd edn. (Chaps 2, 12)

Davico, A. (1946) 'Ritrovamenti sud-arabici nelle zona del cascase', *RSE*, 5, pp. 1–6. (Chap. 13)

Davidson, B. (1959) *Old Africa Rediscovered* (London: Gollancz). (Chaps 4, 20)

Davidson, C. C. and Clark, J. D. (1974) 'Trade wind beads: an interim report of chemical studies', *Azania*, IX, pp. 75–86. (Chap. 29)

Davies, N. M. (1936) *Ancient Egyptian Paintings*, 3 Vols (Chicago: University of Chicago Oriental Institute). (Chap. 5)

Davies, N. M. (1958) *Picture Writing in Ancient Egypt* (London: Oxford University Press for Griffith Institute). (Chap. 5)

Davies, N. M. and Gardiner, A. H. (1926) *The Tomb of Huy, Viceroy of Nubia in the Reign of Tutankhamun* (London: Egypt Exploration Society Theban Tombs Series). (Chap. 9)

Davies, O. (1962) 'Neolithic culture in Ghana', *Proceedings of the Fourth Panafrican Congress of Prehistory*, 2, Brussels, pp. 291–302. (Chap. 21)

Davies O. (1964) *The Quaternary in the Coast Lands of Guinea* (Glasgow: Jackson). (Chap. 24)

Davies, O. (1967a) *West Africa before the Europeans: archaeology and prehistory* (London: Methuen). (Chap. 24)

Davies, O. (1967b) 'Timber construction and wood carving in west Africa in the 2nd millennium BC', *Man*, 2, 1, pp. 115–18. (Chap. 24)

Davies, O. (1968) 'The origins of agriculture in west Africa', *CA*, 9, 5, pp. 479–82. (Chap. 24)

Davies, O. (1971) 'Excavations at Blackburn', *SAAB*, 26, pp. 165–78. (Chap. 26)

Dawson, W. R. (1938) 'Pygmies and dwarfs in ancient Egypt', *JEA*, 25, pp. 185–9. (Chap. 2)

Deacon, H. J. (1966) 'Note on the X-ray of two mounted implements from South Africa', *Man*, 1, pp. 87–90. (Chap. 26)

Deacon, H. J. (1969) 'Melkhoutboom cave, Alexandria district, Cape Province: a report on the 1967 investigation', *ACPM*, 6, pp. 141–69. (Chap. 26)

Deacon, H. J. and J. (1963) 'Scotts cave; a late stone age site in the Gamtoos valley', *ACPM*, 3, pp. 96–121. (Chap. 26)

Deacon, H. J. and J. (1972) 'Archaeological evidence for demographic changes in the eastern Cape during the last 2000 years', Report at AGM of the Archaeological Association, University of Witwatersrand, Johannesburg. (Chap. 26)

**Degrassi, N.** (1951), 'Il mercato Romano di Leptis Magna', *QAL*, 2, pp. 37–70. (**Chaps 11, 19**)

**Delibrias, G., Hugot, H. J. and Quézel, P.** (1957) 'Trois datations de sédiments sahariens récents par le radio-carbon', *Libyca*, 5, pp. 267–70. (**Chap. 17**)

**Demougeot, E.** (1960) 'Le chameau et l'Afrique du Nord romaine', *Annales*, pp. 209–47. (**Chaps 19, 20**)

**Derchain, P.** (1962) *Le sacrifice de l'oryx* (Brussels: Fondation égyptologique reine Elisabeth). (**Chap. 3**)

**Derricourt, R. M.** (1973a) 'Radiocarbon chronology of the late stone age and iron age in South Africa', *SAJS*, 69, pp. 280–4. (**Chap. 26**)

**Derricourt, R. M.** (1973b) 'Archaeological survey of the Transkei and Ciskei: interim report for 1972', *Fort Hare Papers*, 5, pp. 449–55. (**Chap. 26**)

**Desanges, J.** (1949) 'Le statut et les limites de la Nubie romaine', *Chronique d'Égypte*, 44, pp. 139–47. (**Chap. 10**)

**Desanges, J.** (1957) 'Le triomphe de Cornelius Balbus, 19 av. J.-C.', *RA*, pp. 5–43. (**Chap. 20**)

**Desanges, J.** (1962) *Catalogues des tribus africaines de l'antiquité classique à l'ouest du Nil* (Dakar: Université de Dakar, Section d'Histoire). (**Chaps 17, 20**)

**Desanges, J.** (1963) 'Un témoignage peu connu de Procope sur la Numidie vandale et byzantine', *Byzantion*, XXXIII, pp. 41–69. (**Chap. 19**)

**Desanges, J.** (1964) 'Note sur la datation de l'expédition de Julius Maternus au pays d'Agisymba', *Latomus*, pp. 713–25. (**Chap. 20**)

**Desanges, J.** (1967) 'Une mention alterée d'Axoum dans l'exposition totius mundi et gentium', *AE*, VII, pp. 141–58. (**Chap. 15**)

**Desanges, J.** (1968) 'Vues grecques sur quelques aspects de la monarchie méroïtique'. *BIFAO*, LXVI, pp. 89–104. (**Chaps 10, 11**)

**Desanges, J.** (1970) 'L'antiquité gréco-romaine et l'homme noir', *REL*, XLVIII, pp. 87–95. (**Chaps 17, 20**)

**Desanges, J.** (1971) 'Un point de repère chronologique dans la période tardive du royaume de Meroé', *MN*, 7, pp. 2–5. (**Chap. 10**)

**Desanges, J.** (1972) 'Le statut des municipes d'après les données africaines', *Revue Historique de Droit français et étranger* (Paris: Editions Sirey), pp. 253–73. (**Chap. 19**)

**Desanges, J.** (1975) 'L'Afrique noire et le monde méditerranéen dans l'antiquité. Ethiopiens et gréco-romains', *RFHOM*, 228, pp. 391–414. (**Chap. 20**)

**Desanges, J.** (1976) 'L'Iconographie du noir dans l'Afrique du nord antique', in J. Vercoutter, J. Leclant and F. Snowden (eds), *L'Image du noir dans l'art occidental*, Vol. I. *Des pharaons à la chute de l'empire romain* (Fribourg: Menil Foundation), pp. 246–68. (**Chap. 20**)

**Desanges, J.** (1977) 'Aethiops', *Encyclopédie berbère*. (**Chap. 20**)

**Desanges, J. and Lancel, S.** (1962–74) 'Bibliographie analytique de l'Afrique antique', *BAA*, 1–5. (**Chaps 19 and 20**)

**Descamps, C., Demoulin, D. and Abdallah, A.** (1967) 'Données nouvelles sur la préhistoire du cap Manuel (Dakar)', *Acts VI Congr. PPEQ* , pp. 130–2. (**Chap. 24**)

**Descamps, C. and Thilmans, G.** (1972) *Excavations at DeNdalane (Sine Saloum) 27 November–16 January 1972.* (**Chap. 24**)

**Deschamps, H.** (1960) *Histoire de Madagascar* (Paris: Berger-Levrault), 3rd edn., 1965 (**Chap. 28**)

**Deschamps, H.** (ed.) (1970) *Histoire générale de l'Afrique noire, de Madagascar et des archipels*, Vol. I: *Des origines à 1800* (Paris: PUF), pp. 203–10. (**Chap. 20**)

**Despois, J.** ( ) 'Rendements en grains du Byzacium', *Mélanges F. Gauthier*, p. 187ff. (**Chap. 19**)

**Desroches-Noblecourt, C.** (1963) *Life and Death of a Pharaoh: Tutankhamen*, tr. Claude (London: Michael Joseph/*The Connoisseur*). (**Chaps 2, 3**)

**Desroches-Noblecourt, C. and Du Bourguet, P.** (1962) *L'Art égyptien* (Paris: PUF). (**Chap. 3**)

**Desroches-Noblecourt, C. and Kuentz, C.** (1968) *Le petit Temple d'Abou-Simbel*, 2 Vols (Cairo: Ministry of Culture). (**Chap. 3**)

**Devic, L. M.** (1883) *Le pays des Zendj d'après les écrivains arabes* (Paris). (**Chap. 28**)

**Dez, J.** (1965) 'Quelques hypothèses formulées par la linguistique comparée à l'usage de l'archéologie', *Taloha*, Madagascar, 2, pp. 197–214. (**Chap. 28**)

**Dicke, B. H.** (1931) 'The lightning bird and other analogies and traditions connecting the Bantu with the Zimbabwe ruins', *SAJS*, 28, pp. 505–11. (**Chap. 27**)

**Diehl, C.** (1896) *L'Afrique byzantine. Histoire de la domination byzantine en Afrique, 533–709* (Paris: Leroux). (**Chap. 19**)

**Diesner, H. J.** (1965) 'Vandalen', **Pauly-Wissowa**, *Realencyclopedie*, Supp. X, pp. 957–92 (**Chap. 19**)

**Diesner, H.-J.** (1966) *Das Vandalenreich, Aufstieg und Untergang* (Stuttgart/Berlin/Cologne/Mainz: Kohlhammer). (**Chap. 19**)

Diesner, H.-J. (1969) 'Grenzen und Grenzverteidigung das Vandalenreiches', *Studi in onore di E. Volterra*, III, pp. 481–90. **(Chap. 19)**

Dillmann, A. (1878) 'Über die Anfange der Axumitischen reiches', *AAW*, 223. **(Chap. 14)**

Dillmann, A. (1880) *Zur geschichte des axumitischen reichs in vierten bis sechsten jahrhundert* (Berlin: K. Akademie der Wissenschaften). **(Chap. 14)**

Dindorf, L. A. (1831) *Joannis Malle Chronographia ex Recensione Ludovici Dindorgii* (Corpus scriptorum historiae byzantinae) (Bonn: Weber). **(Chap. 15)**

Dindorf, L. A. (1870–1) *Historici graeci minores* (Leipzig: Teubner) **(Chap. 15)**

Diodorus Siculus, *The Library of History of Diodorus of Sicily*, tr. C. H. Oldfather *et al.* (1933–67) 12 Vols (Cambridge, Mass.: Harvard University Press; London: Heinemann). **(Chaps 1, 6, 10, 11, 17, 22)**

Diogenes Laertius, *Lives of Eminent Philosophers*, 2 Vols, tr. R. D. Hicks (1925) (Cambridge, Mass.: Harvard University Press; London: Heinemann). **(Chap. 1)**

Diop, C. A. (1955) *Nations Nègres et Cultures. De l'Antiquité Nègro-Egyptienne aux Problèmes Culturels d'Afrique Noire d'Aujourd'hui* (Paris: Présence africaine). **(Chap. 1)**

Diop, C. A. (1967) *Anteironté des civilisations nègres; mythe du vènté historique* (Paris: Présence Africaine). **(Chap. 1)**

Diop, C. A. (1968) 'Metallurgie traditionelle et l'âge du fer en Afrique', *BIFAN*, B, XXX, 1, pp. 10–38. **(Chaps 21, 24)**

Diop, C. A. (1973) 'La métallurgie du fer sous l'ancien empire égyptien', *BIFAN*, B, XXXV, pp. 532–47. **(Chaps 21, 24)**

Diop, C. A. (1977) 'Parenté génétique de l'égyptien pharaonique et des langues africaines: processus de sémitisation'; 'La pigmentation des anciens Egyptiens, test par la mélanine', *BIFAN*. **(Chap. 1)**

Dittenberger, G. (1898–1905) *Sylloge inscriptionum graecarum*, 5 Vols (Leipzig). **(Chap. 6)**

Dixon, D. M. M. (1964) 'The origin of the kingdom of Kush (Napata-Meroe)', *JEA*, 50, pp. 121–32. **(Chap. 11)**

Dixon, D. M. M. (1969) 'The transplantation of Punt incense trees in Egypt', *JEA*, 55, pp. 55ff. **(Chap. 4)**

Dogget, H. (1965) 'The development of the cultivated sorghums', in J. B. Hutchinson (ed.), *Essays on Crop Plant Evolution* (Cambridge: CUP), pp. 50–69. **(Chap. 24)**

Donadoni, S. (ed.) (1967) *Tanit 1964, Missione Archeologica in Egitto Dell' Università di Roma* (Rome).

Donadoni, S. (1970) 'Les fouilles à l'église de Sonqi Tino', in E. Dinkler (ed.), *Kunst und Geschichte Nubiens in christlicher Zeit: Ergebnisse und Probleme auf Grund der jüngsten Ausgrabungen* (Recklinghausen: Verlag Aurel Bongers), pp. 209–18. **(Chap. 12)**

Donadoni, S. and Curto, S. (1965) 'Le pitture murali della chiesa di sonki nel Sudan', *La Nubia Cristiana*, Quaderno No. 2 del Museo eglizio di Torino (Turin: Fratelli Pozzo-Salvati), pp. 123ff. **(Chap. 12)**

Donadoni, S. and Vantini, G. (1967) 'Gli scavi nel diff di songi tino (Nubia Sudanese)', *RRAL*, 3, XL, pp. 247–73. **(Chap. 12)**

Doresse, J. (1957) 'Découvertes en Ethiopie et découverte de l'Ethiopie', *BO*, 14, pp. 64–5. **(Chap. 13)**

Doresse, J. (1960) 'La découverte d'Asbi-Dérà', *Atti del Convegno. Intern. Stud. Et.*, Rome 2–4 April 1959, pp. 229–48. **(Chap. 15)**

Dornan, S. S. (1915) 'Rhodesian ruins and native tradition', *SAJS*, 12, pp. 501–16. **(Chap. 27)**

Drewes, A. J. (1954) 'The inscription from Dibbib in Eritrea', *BO*, 11, pp. 185–6. **(Chap. 13)**

Drewes, A. J. (1956) 'Nouvelles inscriptions de l'Ethiopie', *BO*, 13, pp. 179–82. **(Chap. 13)**

Drewes, A. J. (1959) 'Les inscriptions de Mélazo', *AE*, 3, pp. 83–99. **(Chap. 13)**

Drewes, A. J. (1962) *Inscriptions de l'Ethiopie Antique* (Leiden: Brill). **(Chaps 13, 15)**

Drewes, A. J. and Schneider, R. (1967–70–2) 'Documents épigraphiques de l'Ethiopie I, II, III', *AE*, VII, pp. 89–106; VIII, pp. 57–72; IX, pp. 87–102. **(Chaps 13, 14)**

Drioton, E. and Vandier, J. (1962) *Les peuples de l'Orient méditerranéen*, 4th edn enlarged, 1: '"Clio", introduction aux études historiques'; 2: *L'Egypte* (Paris: PUF). **(Chaps 2, 17)**

Drouin, E. A. (1882) 'Les listes royales éthiopiennes et leur autorité historique', *RA*, August–October. **(Chap. 16)**

Drury, R. (1731) *Madagascar or, Robert Drury's journal during Fifteen Years of Captivity on that Island* (London). **(Chap. 28)**

Dubief, J. (1963) 'Le climat du Sahara', *Institut de Recherches Sahariennes*, Algiers. **(Chap. 20)**

Du Bourguet, P. (1964a) *L'Art copte*, Exhibition catalogue, 17th June–15 September (Paris: Palais des Beaux Arts). **(Chap. 12)**

Du Bourguet, P. (1964b) 'L'art copte pendant les cinq premiers siècles de l'Hégire', *Christentum am Nil* (Recklinghausen: Verlag Aurel Bongers), pp. 221ff. **(Chap. 12)**

757

Du Mesgnil, F. (1897) *Madagascar, Homère et la civilisation mycénienne* (Saint-Denis, Réunion: Dubourg). (Chap. 28)

Dunbabin, T. J. (1948) *The Western Greeks. The History of Sicily and South Italy from the Foundation of the Greek Colonies to 480 BC* (Oxford: Clarendon Press). (Chap. 18)

Duncan-Jones, R. P. 'City population in Roman Africa', *JRS*, 53, pp. 85ff. (Chap. 19)

Dunham, D. and Bates, O. (1950–7) *Royal Cemeteries of Kush*, I: 'El-Kurru'; II: 'Nuri'; III: 'Royal tombs at Meroe and Barkal' (Cambridge, Mass.: Harvard University Press). (Chaps 10, 11)

Dupire, M. (1962) 'Peuls nomades', *Etude descriptive des Woolabe du Sahel Nigérien* (Paris: Travaux et mémoires de L'Institut d'éthnologie). (Chap. 24)

Dupire, M. (1972) 'Les facteurs humains de l'économie pastorale', *Etudes nigériennes*, 5, (Chap. 24)

Dutton, T. P. (1970) 'Iron-smelting furnace date 630 ± 50 years AD in the Ndumu game reserve', *Lammergeyer*, XIII, pp. 37–40. (Chap. 27)

Duval, N. (1971– ) *Recherches archéologiques à Sbeitla* (Paris: de Boccard). (Chap. 19)

Duval, N. (1974) 'Le dossier de l'église d'el Monassat au sud–ouest de Sfax, Tunisie', *AA*, VIII, pp. 157–73. (Chap. 19)

Duval, N. and Baratte, F. (1973) *Sbeitla: Les ruines de Sufetula* (Tunis: STD). (Chap. 19)

Duval, N. and Baratte, F. (1974) *Haïdra: Les ruines d'Ammaedara* (Tunis: STD). (Chap. 19)

Duval, Y. and Fevrier, P. A. (1969) 'Procès verbal de disposition des reliques de la région de Telerma, VIIe siècle', *Mélanges école française de Rome* pp. 257–320 (Institut Français de Rome, Villa Farnese, Rome). (Chap. 19)

Duyvendak, J. J. L. (1949) *China's Discovery of Africa* (London: Probsthain). (Chap. 22)


Ebbell, B. (1937) The Papyrus Ebers, the greatest Egyptian medical document (London, Copenhagen). (Chap. 5)

Edkins, Rev. J. (1885) 'Ancient navigation in the Indian Ocean', *JRAS*, XVIII, pp. 1–27. (Chap. 22)

Edwards, I. E. S. (1970) *The Pyramids of Egypt* (London: Penguin). (Chap. 2)

Ehret, C. (1967) 'Cattle-keeping and milking in eastern and southern African history: the linguistic evidence', *JAH*, VIII, pp. 1–17. (Chaps 21, 27)

Ehret, C. (1971) *Southern Nilotic History: Linguistic Approaches to the Study of the Past* (Evanston: Northwestern University Press). (Chap. 23)

Ehret, C. (1972) 'Bantu origins and history: critique and interpretation', *TJH*, II, pp. 1–19. (Chap. 21)

Ehret, C. (1973) 'Patterns of Bantu and central Sudanic settlement in central and southern Africa (c. 1000 BC – 500 AD)', *TJH*, III, pp. 1–71. (Chaps 21, 23)

Ehret, C. (1974) *Ethiopians and East Africans: the problems of contacts* (Nairobi: East African Publishing House). (Chap. 23)

Ehret, C. et al. (1972) 'Outlining southern African history: a re-evaluation AD 100–1500', *Ufahamu*, III, pp. 9–27. (Chap. 27)

Elgood, P. G. (1951) *Later Dynasties of Egypt* (Oxford: Blackwell). (Chap. 2)

Elphick, R. H. (1972) 'The Cape Khoi and the first phase of South African race relations', thesis (Yale University). (Chap. 26)

Emery, W. B. (1960) 'Preliminary report on the excavations of the Egypt Exploration Society at Buhen, 1958–59', *Kush*, 8, pp. 7–8. (Chap. 9)

Emery, W. B. (1961) *Archaic Egypt* (London: Penguin). (Chap. 2)

Emery, W. B. (1963) 'Preliminary report on the excavations at Buhen, 1962', *Kush*, 11, pp. 116–20. (Chap. 9)

Emery, W. B. (1965) *Egypt in Nubia* (London: Hutchinson). (Chaps 4, 9, 12)

Emery, W. B. and Kirwan, L. P. (1935) *Mission archéologique en Nubie, 1929–34. The Excavations and Survey between Wadi es-Sebua and Adindan, 1929–31*, 2 Vols (Cairo: Government Press). (Chap. 9)

Emery, W. B. and Kirwan, L. P. (1938) *The Royal Tombs of Ballana and Qustul* (Cairo: Government Press). (Chaps 10, 12)

Emin-Bey, (n.d.) 'Studii-storico-dogmatici sulla chiesa giacobina Roma Tip Caluneta Tarique Neguest ...', ms. deposited at the Bibliothèque nationale no. P.90. (Chap. 16)

Emphoux, J. P. (1970) 'La grotte de Bitorri au Congo-Brazzaville', *Cahiers ORSTOM* (Office de Recherche Scientifique et Technique Outre-Mer), VII, 1, pp. 1–20. (Chap. 25)

*Encyclopaedia Britannica* (1974) 30 Vols (London/Chicago), 15th edn.

Epstein, H. (1971) *The Origin of the Domestic Animals in Africa*, 2 Vols (New York: Africana Publishing). (Chap. 21, Concl.)

Erman, A. (1927) *The Literature of the Ancient Egyptians*, tr. A. M. Blackman (London: Methuen). **(Chap. 5)**

Erman, A. (1966) *The Ancient Egyptians. A Sourcebook of Their Writings*, tr. A. M. Blackman (New York: Harper & Row). **(Chap. 3)**

Erroux, J. (1957) 'Essai d'une classification dichotomique des blès durs cultivés en Algérie', *Bulletin de la Société d'Histoire Naturelle de l'Afrique du nord*, 48, pp. 239–53. **(Chap. 17)**

Esperandieu, G. (1957) *De l'art animalier dans l'Afrique antique* (Algiers: Imprimerie Officielle). **(Chap. 17)**

Eusebius of Pamphylia (1675) transln. *Vie de l'Empereur Constantin* (Paris). **(Chap. 16)**

Euzennat, M. (1976) 'Les recherches sur la frontière romaine d'Afrique, 1974–76', *Akten XI Intern. Limeskong.*, pp. 533–43. **(Chap. 20)**

Evans-Pritchard, E. E. (1968) *The Nuer: Description of Modes of Livelihood and Political Institutions of a Nilotic People* (London: OUP). **(Chap. 24)**

Evetts, B. T. A. and Butler, A. J. (1895) *The Churches and Monasteries* (Oxford). **(Chap. 12)**

Eyo, E. (1964–5) 'Excavations at Rop rock shelter', *WAAN*, 3, pp. 5–13. **(Chap. 24)**

Eyo, E. (1972) 'Excavations at Rop rock shelter 1964', *WAJA*, 2, pp. 13–16. **(Chap. 24)**

Fagan, B. M. (1961) 'Pre-European iron working in central Africa with special reference to northern Rhodesia', *JAH*, II, 2, pp. 199–210. **(Chap. 25)**

Fagan, B. M. (1965) 'Radiocarbon dates for sub-Saharan Africa – III', *JAH*, VI, pp. 107–16. **(Chap. 27)**

Fagan, B. M. (1967) 'Radiocarbon dates for sub-Saharan Africa – V', *JAH*, VIII, pp. 513–27. **(Chaps 25, 27)**

Fagan, B. M. (1969a) 'Early trade and raw materials in south central Africa', *JAH*, X, 1, pp. 1–13. **(Chap. 29)**

Fagan, B. M. (1969b) 'Radiocarbon dates for sub-Saharan Africa – VI', *JAH*, X, pp. 149–69. **(Chap. 27)**

Fagan, B. M. and Noten, F. L. Van (1971) 'The hunter-gatherers of Gwisho', *AMRAC*, 74, XXII + 230pp. **(Chap. 25)**

Fagan, B. M., Phillipson, D. W. and Daniels, S. G. H. (eds) (1969) *Iron Age Cultures in Zambia* (London: Chatto & Windus) **(Chaps 25, 27)**

Fagg, A. (1972) 'Excavations of an occupation site in the Nok valley, Nigeria', *WAJA*, 2, pp. 75–9. **(Chap. 24)**

Fairman, H. W. (1938) 'Preliminary report on the excavations at Sesebi and Amarah West, Anglo-Egyptian Sudan, 1937–8', *JEA*, XXIV, pp. 151–6. **(Chap. 9)**

Fairman, H. W. (1939) 'Preliminary report on the excavations at Amarah West, Anglo-Egyptian Sudan, 1938–9', *JEA*, XXV, pp. 139–44. **(Chap. 9)**

Fairman, H. W. (1948) 'Preliminary report on the excavations at Amarah West, Anglo-Egyptian Sudan, 1947–8', *JEA*, XXXIV, pp. 1–11. **(Chap. 9)**

Fattovich, R. (1972) 'Sondaggi stratigrafici. Yeha', *AE*, 9, pp. 65–86. **(Chap. 13)**

Faublée, J. and M. (1964) 'Madagascar vu par les auteurs arabes avant le XIXe siècle', *communication at the 8e Congrès. Intern. Hist. Marit.* and *Studia*, 11. **(Chap. 28)**

Faulkner, R. O. (1962) *A Concise Dictionary of Middle Egyptian* (Oxford: Griffith Institute). **(Chap. 1)**

Faulkner, R. O. (tr.) (1969) *The Ancient Egyptian Pyramid texts* (Oxford: Clarendon Press). **(Chaps 2, 3)**

Faulkner, R. O. (tr.) (1974, 1978) *The Ancient Egyptian Coffin texts*, 3 Vols (Warminster: Aris & Phillips). **(Chaps 2, 3)**

Faulkner, R. O. (1975) 'Egypt from the inception of the nineteenth dynasty to the death of Rameses III', *Cambridge Ancient History* (Cambridge), Vol. II, pt. 2, ch. xxiii. **(Chap. 2)**

Fendri, M. (1961) *Basiliques chrétiennes de la Skhira* (Paris: PUF). **(Chap. 19)**

Ferguson, J. (1969) 'Classical contacts with West Africa', in L. A. Thompson and J. Ferguson (eds), *Africa in Classical Antiquity* (Ibadan: Ibadan University Press), pp. 1–25. **(Chap. 21)**

Ferguson, J. and Libby, W. F. (1963) 'Ugla radiocarbon dates, II', *Radiocarbon*, V, p. 17 **(Chap. 27)**

Ferrand, G. (1891–1902) *Les Musulmans à Madagascar et aux îles Comores*, 2 Vols (Paris: Leroux). **(Chap. 28)**

Ferrand, G. (1904) 'Madagascar et les îles Uaq-Uaq', *JA*, pp. 489–509. **(Chap. 28)**

Ferrand, G. (1908) 'L'origine africaine des Malgaches', *JA*, pp. 353–500. **(Chap. 28)**

Ferrand, G. (1913–14) *Relation des voyages et textes géographiques arabes, persans et turcs relatifs à l'Extrême-Orient du VIII^e au XVIII^e siècles*, 2 Vols (Paris: Leroux). **(Chap. 28)**

Fevrier, P. A. (1962–7) Inscriptions chrétiennes de Djemila-Cuicul', *BAA*, I, pp. 214–22; *BAA*, II, pp. 247–8. (**Chap. 19**)

Fevrier, P. A. (1965) *Fouilles de Sétif. Les basiliques chrétiennes du quartier nord-ouest* (Paris: Centre de Recherches Scientifiques sur l'Afrique Méditerranéenne). (**Chap. 19**)

Fevrier, P. A. and Bonnal, J. (1966–7) 'Ostraka de la région de Bir Trouch', *BAA*, II, pp. 239–50. (**Chap. 19**)

Firth, C. M. (1910–27) *The Archaeological Survey of Nubia. Report for 1907–8–1910–11* (Cairo: National Print Dept). (**Chap. 9**)

Flacourt, E. (1661) *Histoire de la grande île de Madagascar* (Paris: Clougier). (**Chap. 28**)

Fleischhacker, H. von (1969) 'Zur Rassen und Bevölkerungsgeschichte Nordafrikas unter besonderer Berüchsichtigung der Aethiopiden, der Libyer und der Garamanten', *Paideuma*, 15, pp. 12–53. (**Chaps 17, 20**)

Flight, C. (1972) 'Kintampo and West African Neolithic civilizations', *BWS 56*. (**Chap. 24**)

Fontane, M. E. (1882) *Les Égyptes, de 5000 a 715 av. J.C.* (Vol. 3 of his *Histoire universelle*) (Paris: Lemerre). (**Chap. 1**)

Forbes, R. J. (1950) *Metallurgy in Antiquity: a notebook for archaeologists and technologists* (Leiden: Brill). (**Chap. 21**)

Forbes, R. J. (1954) 'Extracting, smelting and alloying', in C. Singer, E. J. Holmyard and A. R. Hall (eds), *History of Technology*, 4 Vols (Oxford: Clarendon Press), pp. 572–99. (**Chap. 21**)

Franchini, V. (1954) 'Ritrovamenti archeologici in Eritrea', *RSE*, 12, pp. 5–28. (**Chap. 13**)

Frankfort, H. (ed.) (1929) *The Mural Paintings of El-'Amarneh* (London: Egypt Exploration Society). (**Chap. 5**)

Fraser, P. M. (1967) 'Current problems concerning the early history of the cult of Serapis', *OA*, VII, pp. 23–45. (**Chap. 6**)

Fraser, P. M. (1972) *Ptolemaic Alexandria*, 3 Vols (Oxford: Clarendon Press). (**Chap. 6**)

Frazer, J. G. (1941) *The Golden Bough: A Study of Magic and Religion*, 12 Vols (New York/London: Macmillan), 3rd edn. (**Chap. 29**)

Freeman-Grenville, G. S. P. (1960) 'East African coin finds and their historical significance', *JAH*, I, pp. 31–43. (**Chap. 22**)

Freeman-Grenville, G. S. P. (1962a) *The Medieval History of the Coast of Tanganyika: with special reference to recent archaeological discoveries* (London: OUP). (**Chap. 22**)

Freeman-Grenville, G. S. P. (1962b) *The East African Coast. Select documents from the first to the earlier nineteenth century* (Oxford: Clarendon Press). (**Chaps 22, 27**)

Freeman-Grenville, G. S. P. (1968) 'A Note on Zanj in the Greek authors', Seminar on language and history in Africa (London). (**Chap. 22**)

Frend, W. H. C. (1968) 'Nubia as an outpost of Byzantine cultural influence', *Byzantinoslavica*, 2, pp. 319–26. (**Chap. 12**)

Frend, W. H. C. (1972a) 'Coptic, Greek and Nubian at Qasr Ibrim', *Byzantinoslavica*, XXXIII, pp. 224–9. (**Chap. 12**)

Frend, W. H. C. (1972b) *The Rise of the Monophysite Movement: chapters in the history of the Church in the fifth and sixth centuries* (Cambridge: CUP). (**Chap. 12**)

Frobenius, L. (1931) *Erythräa: Länder und Zeiten des heiligen Königsmondes* (Berlin/Zurich: Atlantis). (**Chap. 11**)

Frontinus, Sextus Julius, *Strategemeton*, ed. G. Gundermann (1888); English edition (1950), *The Stratagems and the Aqueducts of Rome* (London: Heinemann), I, 11, 18. (**Chap. 17**)

Furon, R. (1972) *Eléments de paléoclimatologie* (Paris: Vuibert). (**Chap. 20**)


Gabel, C. (1965) *Stone Age Hunters of the Kafue. The Gwisho A site*, (Boston, Mass.: Boston University Press). (**Chap. 21**)

Gadallah, F. F. (1971) 'Problems of pre-Herodotan sources in Libyan history', *Libya in History* (Benghazi), pt. 2, pp. 43–75 (Arabic edition, résumé in English, pp. 78–81). (**Chap. 17**)

Gagé J. (1964) *Les classes sociales dans l'empire romain* (Paris: Payot). (**Chap. 19**)

Galand, L. (1965–70) 'Les études de linguistique berbère', *Ann. Afr.* (**Chap. 20**)

Galand, L. (1969) 'Les Berbères; la langue et les parlers', *Encyclopedia Universalis* (Paris), pp. 171–3. (**Chap. 20**)

Galand, L. (1974) 'Libyque et berbère', *AEPHE*, pp. 131–53. (**Chap. 20**)

Gardiner, A. H. (1909) *The Admonitions of an Egyptian Sage. From a hieratic papyrus in Leiden* (Leipzig: Hinrichs). (**Chap. 2**)

Gardiner, A. H. (1950) *Egyptian Grammar*, 2nd edn., p. 512. (**Chap. 4**)

Gardiner, A. H. (1961) *Egypt of the Pharaohs: an introduction* (Oxford: Clarendon Press). Reprint 1964. (**Chaps 2, 4**)

Gardner, T., Wells, L. H. and Schofield, J. F. (1940) 'The recent archaeology of Gokomere, Southern Rhodesia', *TRSSA*, XVIII, pp. 215–53. (Chap. 27)

Garlake, P. S. (1967) 'Excavations at Maxton Farm, near Shamwa Hill, Rhodesia', *Arnoldia*, (Rhodesia), III, 9. (Chap. 27)

Garlake, P. S. (1969) 'Chiltope: an early iron age village in northern Mashonaland', *Arnoldia*, (Rhodesia), IV, 19. (Chap. 27)

Garlake, P. S. (1970a) 'Iron age sites in the Urungwe district of Rhodesia', *SAAB*, XXV, pp. 25–44. (Chap. 27)

Garlake, P. S. (1970b) 'Rhodesian ruins. A preliminary assessment of their styles and chronology', *JAH*, XI, 4, pp. 495–513. (Chap. 27)

Garlake, P. S. (1973) *Great Zimbabwe* (London: Thames & Hudson). (Chap. 27)

Garstang, J., Sayce, A. H. and Griffith, F. L. (1911) *Meroë, the City of the Ethiopians; an Account of a First Season's Excavations on the Site 1909–10* (Liverpool: University of Liverpool Institute of Archaeology). (Chap. 11)

Gartkiewicz, P. (1970–2) 'The central plan in Nubian church architecture', *Nubian Recent Research*, pp. 49–64.

Gascou, J. (1972) *La Politique municipale de l'empire romain en Afrique proconsulaire de Trajan à Septime-Sévère* (Rome: Ecole Française de Rome). (Chaps 11, 19)

Gast, M. (1972) 'Témoignages nouveaux sur Tin Hinan, ancêtre légendaire des touareg Ahaggar', *Mélanges Le Tourneau*, Revue de l'Occident Musulman et de la Méditerranée (Aix-en-Provence), pp. 395–400. (Chap. 20)

Gauckler, P. (1925) *Nécropoles puniques de Carthage* (Paris). (Chap. 18)

Gaudio, A. (1953) 'Quattro ritrovamenti archeologici e paleografici in Eritrea', *Il Bolletino*, Asmara I, pp. 4–5. (Chap. 15)

Gautier, E. F. (1925–31) *Dictionnaire des noms géographiques contenus dans les textes hiéroglyphiques*, 7 Vols (Cairo). (Chap. 17)

Gautier, E. F. (1952) *Le passé de l'Afrique du Nord* (Paris: Payot). (Chap. 18)

Germain, G. (1948) 'Le culte du belier en Afrique du Nord', *Hesperis*, XXXV, pp. 93–124. (Chap. 17)

Germain, G. (1957) 'Qu'est-ce que le périple d'Hannon? Document, amplification littéraire ou faux intégral?', *Hesperis*, pp. 205–48. (Chaps 20, 21)

Ghalioungui, P. (1963) *Magic and Medical Science in Ancient Egypt* (London: Hodder & Stoughton). (Chap. 3)

Ghalioungui, P. (1973) *The house of life; Per ankh. Magic and medical science in ancient Egypt* (Amsterdam: Israël). (Chap. 5)

Gilot, E., Ancien, N. and Capron, P. C. (1965) 'Louvain natural radiocarbon measurements III', *Radiocarbon*, II, pp. 118–22. (Chap. 25)

Giorgini, M. S. (1965) 'Première campagne de fouilles à Sedeinga 1963–4', *Kush*, 13, pp. 112–30. (Chap. 10)

Girgis, M. (1963) 'The history of the shipwrecked sailor', *Bulletin de la Faculté des Lettres de l'Université du Caire*, XXI, I, pp. 1–10. (Chaps 4, 11)

Glanville, S. K. R. (ed.) (1942) *The Legacy of Egypt* (Oxford: Clarendon Press). (Chap. 2)

Glaser, E. (1895) *Die Abessiner in Arabien und Afrika auf Grund neuendeckter Inschriften* (Munich: Hermann Lukaschik). (Chap. 11)

Gobert, E. (1948) 'Essai sur la litholâtrie', *RA*, 89, pp. 24–110. (Chap. 17)

Golénicshev, V. S. (1912) *Le Conte du naufragé*, tr. W. Golénischeff (Cairo: Institut Français de l'Archéologie Orientale). (Chap. 4)

Golgowski, T. (1968) 'Problems of the iconography of the Holy Virgin murals from Faras', *Etudes et Travaux*, II, pp. 293–312. (Chap. 12)

Gomaa, F. (1973) 'Chaemwese, Sohn Rameses II und Hoher Priester von Memphis', *ÄA*, 27. (Chap. 3)

Goodchild, R. G. (1962) *Cyrene and Apollonia; an historical guide* (Libya: Antiquities Department of Cyrenaica). (Chap. 6)

Goodchild, R. G. (1966) 'Fortificazioni e palazzi bizantini in Tripolitania e Cirenaica', *CC*, XIII, pp. 225–50. (Chap. 19)

Goodwin, A. J. H. (1946) 'Prehistoric fishing methods in South Africa', *Antiquity*, 20, pp. 134–9. (Chap. 26)

Gostynski, T. (1975) 'La Libye antique et ses relations avec l'Egypte', *BIFAN*, 37, 3, pp. 473–588. (Chaps 10, 20)

Goyon, G. (1957) *Nouvelles inscriptions rupestres du Wadi-Hammamat* (Paris: Imprimerie Nationale). (Chap. 3)

Goyon, G. (1970) 'Les navires de transport de la chaussée monumentale d'Ounas', *BIFAO*, LXIX, pp. 11–41. (Chap. 3)

Goyon, J. C. (tr.) (1972) *Rituels funéraires de l'ancienne Egypte; le rituel de l'embaumement, le rituel de l'ouverture de la bouche, le livres des respirations.* (Paris: Editions du Cerf).

Grandidier, A. (1885) *Histoire de la Géographie de Madagascar* (Paris: Imprimerie Nationale). (Chap. 28)

Grapow, H. (1954–63) *Grundriss der Medizin der alten Ägypter*, 9 Vols (Berlin: Akademie-Verlag). (Chap. 5)

Greenberg, J. H. (1955) *Studies in African Linguistic Classification* (New Haven: Compass). (Chap. 25)

Greenberg, J. H. (1963) *Languages of Africa* (Bloomington, Ind.: University of Indiana Press), 3rd edn. 1970. (Chaps 21, 23)

Greenberg, J. H. (1972) 'Linguistic evidence regarding Bantu origins', *JAH*, XIII, 2, pp. 189–216. (Chap. 21)

Griffith, F. L. *Karanog. The Meroitic Inscriptions of Shablul and Karamog* (Philadelphia). (Chap. 11)

Griffith, F. L. (1911–12) *Meroitic Inscriptions*, 2 Vols (London: Archaeological Survey of Egypt). (Chap. 11)

Griffith, F. L. (1913) *The Nubian Texts of the Christian Period* (Berlin: Akademie der Wissenschaften). (Chap. 12)

Griffith, F. L. (1917) 'Meroitic studies III–IV', *JEA*, 4, p. 27. (Chap. 11)

Griffith, F. L. (1921–8) 'Oxford excavations in Nubia', *LAAA*, VIII, 1; IX, 3–4; X, 3–4; XI, 3–4; XII, 3–4; XIII, 1–4; XIV, 3–4; XV, 3–4. (Chaps 9, 12)

Griffith, F. L. (1925) 'Pakhoras-Bakharas–Faras in geography and history', *JEA*, XI, pp. 259–68. (Chap. 12)

Griffith, J. G. (1970) *Plutarch, De Iside et Osiride* (Cambridge). (Chap. 2)

Groag, E. (1929) *Hannibal als Politiker* (Vienna). (Chap. 18)

Grobbelaar, C. S. and Goodwin, A. J. H. (1952) 'Report on the skeletons and implements in association with them from a cave near Bredasdorp, Cape Province', *SAAB*, 7, pp. 95–101. (Chap. 26)

Grohmann A. (1914a) 'Eine Alabasterlampe mit einer Ge'ezschrift', *WZKM*, XXV, pp. 410–22. (Chap. 15)

Grohmann, A. (1914b) *Göttersymbole und Symboltiere auf südarabische Denkmäler* (Vienna: Akademie der Wissenschaften). (Chap. 13)

Grohmann, A. (1915) 'Über den Ursprung und die Entwicklung der äthiopischen Schrift', *Archiv für Schriftkunde*, I, 2–3, pp. 57–87. (Chap. 15)

Grohmann, A. (1927) in *Handbuch des attarabische Aetertumskunde*, ed. D. Nielson, Vol. 1 (Copenhagen). (Chap. 13)

Grossman, P. (1971) 'Zur Datierung der Frühen Kirchenlagen aus Faras', *Byzantinische Zeitschrift*, 64, pp. 330–50. (Chap. 12)

Gross-Mertz, B. (1952) 'Certain titles of the Egyptian queens and their bearing on the hereditary right to the throne', dissertation, University of Chicago. (Chap. 3)

Gsell, S. (1915) *Hérodote* (Algiers: Typographie A. Jourdan), pp. 133–4. (Chap. 17)

Gsell, S. (1913–28) *Histoire ancienne de l'Afrique du Nord*, 8 Vols (Paris: Hachette). (Chaps 17, 19, 20)

Gsell, S. (1926) 'La Tripolitaine et le Sahara au IIIe siècle de notre ère', *MAI*, XLIII, pp. 149–66. (Chap. 20)

Guéry, R. (1972) in *Bulletin de la Société nationale des Antiquaires de France*, pp. 318–9. (Chap. 19)

Guidi, I. (ed.) (1896) *Il Gradla 'Aragâwî: Memoria del Socio Ignazio Guidi* (Rome). (Chap. 16)

Guidi, I. (1906) *The Life and Miracles of Tekle Haymanot* (London), Vol II. (Chap. 16)

Gumplowicz, L. (1883) *Der Rassenkampz sociologische Untersuchungen* (Innsbruck). (Chap. 1)

Guthrie, M. (1962) 'Some developments in the pre-history of the Bantu languages', *JAH*, III, 2, pp. 273–82. (Chap. 25)

Guthrie, M. (1967–71) *Comparative Bantu: an introduction to the comparative linguistics and pre-history of the Bantu languages*, 4 Vols (Farnborough: Gregg International). (Chap. 25)

Guthrie M. (1970) 'Contributions from comparative Bantu studies to the prehistory of Africa', in D. Dalby (ed.), *Language and History in Africa* (London: Frank Cass), pp. 20–49. (Chap. 21)

Habachi, L. (1955) 'Preliminary report on the Kamose stela and other inscribed blocks found re-used in the foundations of two statues at Karnak', *ASAE*, 53, pp. 195–202. (Chap. 9)

Hailemarian, G. (1955) 'Objects found in the neighbourhood of Axum,' *AE*, 1, pp. 50–1. (Chap 13)

Halff, G. (1963) 'L'onomastique punique de Carthage', *Karthago*, XIII. (Chap. 18)

Hama, B. (1967) *Recherche sur l'histoire des touareg sahariens et soudanais* (Paris: Présence Africaine). (Chap. 20)

Hamy, E. T. (1969) in *African Mythology*, ed. G. Parrinder (London: Hamlyn) 2nd edn. (Chap. 4)

Hani, J. (1976) *La religion égyptienne dans la pensée de Plutarque* (Paris: Société d'Editions Les Belles Lettres). (Chap. 2)

Harden, D. B. (1963) *The Phoenicians* (London: Thames & Hudson), revised edn. (Chap. 18)

Hardy, E. R. (1931) *The Large Estates of Byzantine Egypt* (New York: Ams Press) revised edn 1968. (Chap. 7)

Harlan, J. R., Wet, J. M. J. de and Stemler, A. (eds) (1976) *Origins of African Plant Domestication* (The Hague/Paris; Mouton, World Anthropology Series). (Chap. 21)

Harris, J. R. (1966) *Egyptian Art* (London: Spring Books). (Chap. 5)

Harris J. R. (ed.) (1971) *The Legacy of Egypt* (Oxford: Clarendon Press), 2nd edn. (Chap. 3)

Hartle, D. (1966) 'Bronze objects from the Ifeka gardens site, Ezira', *WAAN*, 4, p. 26. (Chap. 24)

Hartle, D. (1968) 'Radiocarbon dates', *WAAN*, 13, p. 73. (Chap. 24)

Hasan, H. (1928) *A History of Persian Navigation* (London). (Chap. 22)

Havinden, M. A. (1970) 'The history of crop cultivation in West Africa: a bibliographical guide', *EHR*, 2nd ser., XXIII, 3, pp. 532–55. (Chap. 24)

Haycock, B. G. (1954) 'The kingship of Kush in the Sudan', *CSSH*, VII, 4, pp. 461–80. (Chaps 10, 11)

Hayes, W. C. (1953–9) *The Scepter of Egypt: A background for the study of Egyptian antiquities in the Metropolitan Museum of Art*, 2 Vols (Cambridge, Mass.: Harvard University Press). (Chaps 2, 3)

Hayes, W. C. (1965) *Most Ancient Egypt*, ed. K. C. Steele (Chicago/London: University of Chicago Press). (Chap. 2)

Hayes, W. C. (1971) 'The middle kingdom in Egypt's internal history', *Cambridge Ancient History* (Cambridge), Vol. I, pt. 2. (Chap. 2)

Hayes, W. C. (1973) 'Egypt; internal affairs from Thutmosis I to the death of Amenophis III', *Cambridge Ancient History* (Cambridge), Vol. II, pt. 1 (Chap. 2)

Haywood, R. M. (1938) *An Economic Survey of Ancient Rome*, Vol. IV: *Roman Africa*, ed. T. Frank (1933–40) (Baltimore: Johns Hopkins Press). (Chap. 19)

Hearst, P. A. (1905) 'Medical Papyrus', *Egyptian Archaeology*, Vol. 1 (Berkeley, California: University of California). (Chap. 5)

Hébert, J. C. (1968a) 'Calendriers provinciaux malgaches', *BM*, 172, pp. 809–20. (Chap. 28)

Hébert, J. C. (1968b) 'La rose des vents malgaches et les points cardinaux', *CM*, 2, pp. 159–205. (Chap. 28)

Hébert, J. C. (1971) 'Madagascar et Malagasy, histoire d'un double nom de baptème, *BM*, 302–3, pp. 583–613. (Chap. 28)

Heekeren, H. R. van (1958) *The Bronze-Iron Age of Indonesia* ('s-Gravenhage: Nijhoff). (Chap. 28)

Helck, W. (1939) *Der einfluss der militärführer in der 18. ägyptischen dynastie* (Leipzig: Hinrichs). (Chap. 5)

Helck, W. (1958) 'Zur Verwaltung der Mittleren und Neuen Reichs', *Probleme der Ägyptologie*, 3, Leiden/Köln. (Chap. 3)

Helck, W. and Otto, E. (1970) *Kleines Wörterbuch der Ägyptologie*, 2nd rev. edn (Wiesbaden: Harrassowitz). (Chap. 3)

Helck, W. and Otto, E. (1973) *Lexikon der Ägyptologie* (Wiesbaden: Harrassowitz. (Chap. 3)

Herbert, E. W. (1973) 'Aspects of the uses of copper in pre-colonial West Africa', *JAH*, XIV, 2, pp. 170–94. (Chap. 24)

Herin, A. (1973) 'Studie van een Verzameling Keramiek uit de Bushimaie Vallei "Kasai-Zaire" in Het Koninklijk Museum voor Midden Afrika te Tervuren', thesis, University of Ghent. (Chap. 25)

Herodotus, *Histoires*, text established and tr. P.-E. Legrand (1932–54), 11 Vols (Paris: Collection des Universités de France). (Chaps 1, 10)

Herodotus, *Works*, tr. A. D. Godley (1920–4), 4 Vols (London: Heinemann; Cambridge, Mass.: Harvard University Press). (Chap. 4)

Herzog, R. (1957) *Die Nubier Untersuchungen und Beobachtungen zur Gruppengleiderung, Gesellschaftsform und Wirtschaftsweise* (Berlin: Akademie der Wissenschaften). (Chaps 1, 11)

Herzog, R. (1968) in *Punt*, Proceedings of the German Archaeological Institute of Cairo, 5 (Glückstadt). (Chap. 4)

Heurgon, J. (1958) *Le Trésor de Ténès* (Paris: Direction de l'Intérieur et des Beaux Arts). (Chap. 19)

Heurgon, J. (1966) 'The inscriptions of Pyrgi', *JRS*, LVI. (Chap. 18)

**Heuss, A.** (1949) 'Der erste punische Krieg und das Problem des römischen Imperialismus', *Historische Zeitschrift* CLXIX. **(Chap. 18)**

**Heyler, A. and Leclant, J.** (1966) in *Orientalistiche Literaturzeitung, 61, p. 552.* **(Chap. 10)**

**Hiernaux, J.** (1968a) *La Diversité humaine en Afrique subsaharienne* (Brussels: Université Libre de Bruxelles, L'Institut de sociologie). **(Chap. 21)**

**Hiernaux, J.** (1968b) 'Bantu expansion: the evidence from physical anthropology confronted with linguistic and archaeological evidence', *JAH*, IX, 4, pp. 505–15. **(Chap. 25)**

**Hiernaux, J., Longrée, E. De and Buyst, J. De** (1971) 'Fouilles archéologiques dans la vallée du Haut-Lualaba, I, Sanga, 1958', *AMRAC*, 73, p. 148. **(Chap. 25)**

**Hiernaux, J. and Maquet, E.** (1957) 'Cultures préhistoriques de l'âge des métaux au Rwanda-Urundi et au Kiva (Congo belge)', Ière partie, *ARSC*, pp. 1126–49. **(Chap. 25)**

**Hiernaux, J. and Maquet, E.** (1960) 'Cultures préhistoriques ...', 2e partie, *ARSC*, X, 2, pp. 5–88. **(Chap. 25)**

**Hiernaux, J. and Maquet, E.** (1968) 'L'âge du fer au Kibiro (Ouganda)', *AMRAC*, 63, p. 49. **(Chap. 29)**

**Hiernaux, J., Maquet, E. and Buyst, J. De** (1973) 'Le cimetière protohistorique de Katoto (vallée du Lualaba, Congo-Kinshasa)', *Actes VI Congr. PPQS*, pp. 148–58. **(Chap. 25)**

**Hintze, F.** (1959a) *Studien zur Meroitischen Chronologie und zu den Opfertafeln aus den Pyramiden von Meroe* (Berlin: Akademie-Verlag). **(Chaps 10, 11)**

**Hintze, F.** (1959b) 'Preliminary report of the Butana expedition 1958 made by the Institute for Egyptology of the Humboldt University, Berlin', *Kush*, 7, pp. 171–96. **(Chap. 11)**

**Hintze, F.** (1962) *Die Inschriften des Löwentempels von Musawwarat es Sufra*, Abhandlungen der Deutschen Akademie der Wissenschaften zu Berlin (Berlin: Akademie-Verlag). **(Chap. 11)**

**Hintze, F.** (1964) 'Das Kerma Problem', *ZÄS*, 91, pp. 79–86. **(Chap. 9)**

**Hintze, F.** (1965) 'Preliminary note on the epigraphic expedition to Sudanese Nubia, 1963', *Kush*, 13, pp. 13–16. **(Chap. 9)**

**Hintze, F.** (1968) *Civilizations of the Old Sudan* (Leipzig). **(Chap. 9)**

**Hintze, F.** (1971a) *Mussawwarat es Sufra*. Vol. I, pt. 2: *Der Löwentempel*. With the assistance of U. Hintze, K. H. Priese and K. Stark (Berlin: Akademie-Verlag). **(Chap. 11)**

**Hintze, F.** (1971b) 'Stand und Aufgaben der Chronologischen Forschung', Internationale Tagung für Meroitistiche Forschungen, September 1971, in Berlin; Humboldt University, Berlin, Bereich Aegyptologie und Sudanologie Meroitistik. **(Chap. 11)**

**Hintze, F.** (1976) *Die Grabungen von Mussawwarat es Sufra*, Vol. I, pt. 2: 'Tafelband Löwentempel' (Berlin: Akademie-Verlag). **(Chap. 10)**

**Hintze, F. and U.** (1967) *Alte Kulturen im Sudan* (Munich, Callwey). **(Chaps 9, 12)**

**Hintze, F. and U.** (1970) 'Einige neue Ergebnisse der Ausgrabungen des Instituts für Ägyptologie der Humboldt-Universität zu Berlin in Mussawwarat es Sufra', in E. Dinkler (ed.), *Kunst und Geschichte Nubiens in christlicher Zeit. Ergebnisse und Probleme auf Grund der jüngsten Ausgrabungen* (Recklinghausen: Verlag Aurel Bongers), pp. 49–70. **(Chap. 11)**

**Histoire et Tradition Orale** (1975) 'L'Empire du Mali', *Actes Coll. Bamako I*, Fondation SCOA pour la recherche fondamentale en Afrique noire. **(Chap. 21)**

**Hobler, P. M. and Hester, J. J.** (1969) 'Prehistory and environment in the Libyan desert', *South African Archaeological Journal*, 23, 92, pp. 120–30. **(Chap. 24)**

**Hofmann, I.** (1967) *Die Kulturen des Niltals von Aswan bis Sennar, vom Mesolithikum bis zum Ende der Christlichen Epoche* (Monographien zur Völkerkunde-Hamburgischen Museum für Völkerkunde, IV) (Hamburg). **(Chap. 12)**

**Hofmann, I.** (1971a) *Studien zum Meroitischen Königtum* (Brussels: FERE). **(Chap. 10)**

**Hofmann, I.** (1971b) 'Bemaehungen zum Ende des Meroitischen Reiches', in Afrikanische Sprachen und Kulturen, ein Querschnitt, Hamburg, Deutschen Institut für Afrika-Forschung, 1971, *HBZA-K*, 14, pp. 342–52. **(Chap. 10)**

**Hofmann, I.** (1975) *Wege und Möglichkeiten eines indischen Einflusses auf die meroitische Kultur* (St Augustin bei Bonn: Verlag des Anthropos-Instituts). **(Chap. 10)**

**Hölscher, W.** (1955) 'Libyer und Ägypter, Beiträge zur Ethnologie und Geschichte Libyscher Völkerschaften', *ÄFU*, 5. **(Chaps 2, 17)**

**Hornell, (1934)** 'Indonesian influences on East African culture', *JRAI*. **(Chap. 28)**

**Hornung, E.** (1965) *Grundzüge der Ägyptischen Geschichte* (Darmstadt: Wissenschaftliche Buchgesellschaft). **(Chap. 2)**

**Hornung, E.** (1971) *Der Eine und die Vielen. Ägyptische Göttesvorstellung* (Darmstadt: Wissenschaftliche Buchgesellschaft). **(Chap. 3)**

**Hornung, E.** (1972) *Ägyptische Unterweltsbücher* (Zurich/Munich: Artemis Verlag). **(Chap. 3)**

Hourani, G. F. (1963) *Arab Seafaring in the Indian Ocean* (Beirut), 2nd edn 1969. (Chap. 22)

Huard, P. (1966) 'Introduction et diffusion du fer au Tchad', *JAH*, VII, pp. 377–404. (Chaps 20, 21)

Huard, P. and Leclant, J. (1972) *Problèmes archéologiques entre le Nil et le Sahara* (Cairo). (Chap. 17)

Huard, P. and Massip, J. M. (1967) 'Monuments du Sahara nigéro-tchadien', *BIFAN*, B, pp. 1–27. (Chap. 20)

Huffman, T. N. (1970) 'The early iron age and the spread of the Bantu', *SAAB*, XXV, pp. 3–21. (Chaps 21, 27)

Huffman, T. N. (1971a) 'A guide to the iron age of Mashonaland', *OPNM*, pp. 20–44. (Chap. 27)

Huffman, T. N. (1971b) 'Excavations at Leopard's Kopje main kraal: a preliminary report', *SAAB*, XXVI, pp. 85–9. (Chap. 27)

Huffman, T. N. (1973) 'Test excavations at Makuru, Rhodesia', *Arnoldia*, (Rhodesia) V, 39. (Chap. 27)

Huffman, T. N. (1974) 'Ancient mining and Zimbabwe', *JSAIMM*, LXXIV, pp. 238–42. (Chap. 27)

Hugot, H.-J. (1963) 'Recherches préhistoriques dans l'Ahaggar Nord-Occidental 1950–7', *Mém. CRAPE*, I. (Chaps 17, 24)

Hugot, H.-J. (1968) 'The origins of agriculture: Sahara', *CA*, 9, 5, pp. 483–9. (Chap. 24)

Hugot, H.-J. and Bruggmann, M (1976) *Les gens du matin Sahara, dix mille ans d'art et d'histoire* (Paris: Bibliothèque des arts). (Chap. 4)

Huntingford, G. W. B. (1963) in *Oxford History of East Africa*, eds R. Oliver and G. Mathew, Vol. 1. (Chap. 4)

Inskeep, R. R. (1971) Letter to the Editor, *SAJS*, LXVII, pp. 492–3. (Chap. 27)

Inskeep, R. R. and Bezing, K. L. Von (1966) 'Modelled terracotta head from Lydenburg, South Africa', *Man*, 1, p. 102. (Chap. 27)

Irfann, S. (1971) *The Martyrs of Najran. New Documents* (Brussels: Société des Bollandistes) pp. 242–76. (Chaps 15, 16)

Isserlin, B. S. J. *et al.* (1962–3) 'Motya, a Phoenician-Punic site near Marsala', *ALOS*, IV, pp. 84–131. (Chap. 18)

Jaffey, A. J. E. (1966) 'A reappraisal of the Rhodesian iron age up to the fifteenth century', *JAH*, VII, 2, pp. 189–95.

Jakobielski, S. (1966) 'La liste des évêques de Pakhoras', *CAMAP*, III, pp. 151–70. (Chap. 12)

Jakobielski, S. 'Polish excavations at Old Dongola', *Nubische Kunst*, pp. 167ff. (Chap. 12)

Jakobielski, S. (1970) 'Polish excavations at Old Dongola, 1969', in E. Dinkler (ed.), *Kunst und Geschichte Nubiens in christlicher Zeit. Ergebnisse und Probleme auf Grund der jüngsten Ausgrabungen* (Recklinghausen: Verlag Aurel Bongers), pp. 171–80. (Chap. 12)

Jakobielski, S. (1972) *A History of the Bishopric of Pachoras on the Basis of Coptic Inscriptions* (Warsaw: PWN Editions Scientifiques de Pologne). (Chap. 12)

Jakobielski, S. (1975a) 'Polish excavations at Old Dongola 1970–72', *Actes Coll. Nubiol Interm.*, pp. 70–5. (Chap. 12)

Jakobielski, S. (1975b) 'Old Dongola 1972–3', *Etudes et Travaux*, VIII, pp. 349–60. (Chap. 12)

Jakobielski, S. and Krzysaniak, L. (1967–8) 'Polish excavations at Old Dongola, third season, December 1966 – February 1967', *Kush*, XV, pp. 143–64. (Chap. 12)

Jakobielski, S. and Ostrasz, A. (1967) 'Polish excavations at Old Dongola, second season, December 1965 – February 1966', *Kush*, XV, pp. 125–42. (Chap. 12)

James, T. G. H. (1973) Egypt from the Expulsion of the Hyksos to Amenophis I, in *Cambridge Ancient History*. (Chap. 2)

Jamme, A. (1956) 'Les antiquités sud-arabes du museo nazionale romano', *Antichita Publicati per Cura della Accademia Nazionale dei Lincei*, 43, pp. 1–120. (Chap. 13)

Jamme, A. (1957) 'Ethiopia. Annales d'Ethiopie', *BO*, 14, pp. 76–80. (Chap. 15)

Jamme, A. (1962) *Sabaean Inscriptions from Mahram Bilqîs, Mârib* (Baltimore: Johns Hopkins Press). (Chap. 15)

Jamme, A. (1963) 'Compte-rendu bibliographique des Annales d'Ethiopie, vol. 3', *BO*, 20, pp. 324–7. (Chap. 13)

Jansma, N. and Grooth, M. de (1971) 'Zwei Beiträge zur Iconographie der Nubisnen Kunst', *NKJ*, pp. 2–9. (Chap. 12)

Janssen, J. J. (1975) 'Prolegomena to the study of Egypt's economic history during the new kingdom', *SAK*, 3, pp. 127–85. (Chap. 3)

**Jenkins, G. K. and Lewis, R. B.** (1963) *Carthaginian Gold and Electrum Coins* (London: Royal Numismatic Society). **(Chap. 18)**

**Jennison, G.** (1937) *Animals for Show and Pleasure in Ancient Rome* (Manchester: University of Manchester). **(Chap. 20)**

**Jéquier, G.** (1930) *Histoire de la civilisation égyptienne des origines à la conquête d'Alexandre* (Paris: Payot). **(Chap. 2)**

**Jodin, A.** (1966) *Mogador; comptoir phénicien du Maroc atlantique* (Tangier: Editions marocaines et internationales). **(Chaps 19, 20)**

**Johnson, A. C.** (1936) *Roman Egypt to the reign of Diocletian. An Economic Survey of Ancient Rome*, ed. T. Frank (Baltimore: Johns Hopkins Press). **(Chap. 7)**

**Johnson, A. C.** (1951) *Egypt and the Roman Empire* (Ann Arbor: University of Michigan Press). **(Chap. 7)**

**Johnson, A. C. and West, L. C.** (1949) *Byzantine Egypt. Economic Studies* (Princeton: Princeton University Press). **(Chap. 7)**

**Joire, J.** (1947) 'Amas de coquillages du littoral sénégalais dans le banlieue de Saint-Louis', *BIFAN*, B, IX, 1–4, pp. 170–340. **(Chap. 24)**

**Joire, J.** (1955) 'Découvertes archéologiques dans la région de RAO', *BIFAN*, B, XVII, pp. 249–333. **(Chap. 24)**

**Jones, A. H. M.** (1937) *The Cities of the Eastern Roman Provinces* (Oxford: Clarendon Press). **(Chap. 6)**

**Jones, A. H. M.** (1964) *The Late Roman Empire* (Oxford: Blackwell). **(Chap. 7)**

**Jones, A. H. M.** (1968) 'Frontier defence in Byzantine Libya', *Libya in History* (Benghazi: University of Benghazi), pp. 289–97. **(Chap. 19)**

**Jones, A. H. M.** (1969) 'The influence of Indonesia: the musicological evidence reconsidered', *Azania*, IV, pp. 131–90. **(Chaps 22, 28)**

**Jones, N.** (1933) 'Excavations at Nswatugi and Madiliyangwa', *OPNM*, I, 2, pp. 1–44. **(Chap. 27)**

**Jouguet, P.** (1947) *La Domination romaine en Egypte aux deux premiers siècles après JC* (Alexandria: Publications de la Société Royale d'Archéologie). **(Chap. 7)**

**Julien, C. A.** (1966) *Histoire de l'Afrique du Nord. Tunisie, Algérie, Maroc, de la conquête arabe à 1830* (Paris: Payot), 2nd edn rev. **(Chap. 19)**

**Julien, G.** (1908–9) *Institutions Politiques et Sociales de Madagascar d'après des documents authentiques et inédits*, 2 Vols (Paris). **(Chap. 28)**

**Junker, H.** (1919–22) *Bericht über die Grabungen der Akademie der Wissenschaft in Wien auf den Friedhöfen von El-Kubanich* (Vienna: Holder). **(Chap. 9)**

**Junker, H.** (1921) *Der nubische Ursprung der sogenanten Tell el-Jahudíye-Vasen* (Vienna: Akademie der Wissenschaften). **(Chap. 9)**

**Junker, H.** (1933) *Dievölker des antiken Orients. Die Ägypter* (Freiburg, Germany: Herder). **(Chap. 2)**

**Juvenal,** *Satires*, text established and tr. P. de Labriolle and F. Villeneuve (1951), 5th edn rev. and corr. (Paris: Belles Lettres). **(Chap. 1)**

**Juvenal,** *Works of Juvenal and Persius*, tr. G. G. Ramsay (1918) (London: Heinemann; Cambridge, Mass.: Harvard University Press).

**Kadra, F.** (1978) *Les Djedars, monuments funéraires berbères de la région de Farenda* (Algiers). **(Chap. 19)**

**Kahrstedt, U. and Meltzer, O.** (1879–1913) *Geschichte der Karthager* (Berlin). **(Chap. 18)**

**Katznelson, I. S.** (1966) 'La Candace et les survivances matrilinéaires au pays de Kush', *Palestinskij Sbornik*, XV, 78, pp. 35–40. **(Chap. 10)**

**Katznelson, I. S.** (1970) *Napata i Meroe – drevnive tzarstva Sudana* (Moscow), pp. 289 ff. **(Chap. 11)**

**Kees, H.** (1926) *Totenglauben und Jensertsvolrstellung der alten Ägypter* (Leipzig; Berlin, 1956). **(Chap. 2)**

**Kees, H.** (1933) *Kulturgeschichte des Alten Orients*, Vol. I, Ägypten (Handbuch der Altertums III) (Munich). **(Chap. 3)**

**Kees, H.** (1941–56) *Gütterglaube im alten Ägypten* (Leipzig, 1941; Berlin, 1956). **(Chaps 2, 3)**

**Kees, H.** (1953) *Das Priestertum im ägyptischen Staat* (Probleme der ägyptologie 1) (Leiden). **(Chap. 3)**

**Kees, H.** (1956) *Totenglauben und Jenseitsvorstellungen der alten Ägypter*, 2. Auflage (Berlin). **(Chaps 2, 3)**

**Kees, H.** (1958) *Das alte Ägypten. Eine Kleine Landeskunde* (Berlin)

**Kees, H.** (1961) *Ancient Egypt, a cultural topography*, ed. T. G. H. James, (London). **(Chap. 2)**

**Kendall, R. L. and Livingstone, D. A.** (1972) 'Paleo-ecological studies on the East African Plateau, *Acts VI Congr. PPQS* **(Chap. 21)**

**Kent, R.** (1970) *Early kingdoms in Madagascar, 1500–1700* (New York: Holt, Reinhardt and Winston). **(Chap. 28)**

**Klapwijk, M.** (1973) 'An Early Iron Age site near Tzaneen, North-Eastern Transvaal, SAJS, LXIX. **(Chap. 27)**

Klapwijk, M. (1974) 'A preliminary report on pottery from the North-Eastern Transvaal, South Africa, SAAB, 29. (Chap. 26)

Kieran, J. A. and Ogot, B. A. (1968) *Zamani: a survey of the East African History* (Nairobi, London) revised edn 1974. (Chap. 23)

Kirk, W. (1962) 'The North-East Monsoon and some aspects of African history', JAH, III. (Chap. 22)

Kirwan, L. P. (1939) *Oxford University Excavations at Firka*, pp. 49–51. (Chap. 12)

Kirwan, L. P. (1957) 'Tanqasi and the Noba', *Kush*, V. (Chap. 10)

Kirwan, L. P. (1960) 'The decline and fall of Meroe', *Kush*, VIII. (Chaps 10, 13)

Kirwan, L. P. (1963) 'The X-group enigma. A little known people of the Nubian Nile', *Vanished Civilizations of the Ancient World* (New York pp. 55–78). (Chap. 12)

Kirwan, L. P. (1966) 'Prelude to Nubian Christianity (Prélude a la chrétienté nubienne)', *Melanges K. Michalowski* (Warsaw): abr. Nubian Christianity. (Chap. 12)

Kirwan, L. P. (1972) 'The Christian Topography and the Kingdom of Axum', *GJ*, 138, 2, pp. 166–77. (Chap. 14)

Kirwan, L. P. and Emery, W. B. (1935) *The Excavations and survey between Wadi-es-Sebua and Aindan* (Cairo: Governments Press). (Chap. 9)

Kitchen, K. A. (1971) Article in *Orientalia*. (Chap. 4)

Kitchen, K. A. (1973) *The Third Intermediate Period in Egypt* (Warminster). (Chaps 2, 5)

Ki-Zerbo, J. (1972) *Histoire de l'Afrique noire* (Paris: Hatier). (Chaps 20, 21)

Klasens, A. (1964) 'De Nederlandse opgravingen in Nubie; tweede seicoeh 1962–4', *Phoenix*, X, 2, pp. 147–56. (Chap. 12)

Klasens, A. (1967) 'Dutch archaeological mission to Nubia. The excavations at Abu Simbel North 1962–4', *Fouilles en Nubie* (1961–3) (Cairo: Service des antiquités de l'Egypte), pp. 79–86. (Chap. 12)

Klein, R. G. (1972) 'Preliminary report on the July through September 1970 excavations at Nelson Bay Cave, Plettonberg Bay, Cape Province, South Africa', in E. M. van Zinderen Bakker (ed.), *Palaeoecology of Africa and of the Surrounding Islands and Antarctica* (Cape Town: Balkema), Vol. VI, pp. 177–208. (Chap. 26)

Kobisachanov, Y. M. (1966) *Aksum* (Moscow: Nauka). (Chap. 14)

Koerte, A. (1929) *Hellenistic Poetry* tr. J. Hammer, M. Hadas *et al.* (New York: Columbia University Press). (Chap. 6)

Kolb, P. (1719) *The Present State of the Cape of Good Hope: or a particular account of the several nations of the Hottentots ... with a short account of the Dutch settlements at the Cape*, tr. Mr Medley (1731), 2 Vols. (London: Innys). (Chap. 26)

Kolendo, J. (1970) 'Epigraphie et archéologie: le praepositus camellorum dans une inscription d'Ostie'. *Klio*, pp. 287–98. (Chap. 20)

Kolendo, J. (1970) 'L'influence de Carthage sur la civilisation matérielle de Rome', *Archeologia*, XXI (Warsaw). (Chap. 17)

Kornemann, E. (1901) Article in *Philologus*, LX. (Chap. 19)

Korte, A. (1929) *Hellenistic poetry*, tr. J. Hammer and M. Hodas (New York). (Chap. 6)

Kotula, T. (1964) 'Encore sur la mort de Ptolémée, roi de Maurétanie', *Archeologia* (Paris), XV, pp. 76–92. (Chap. 6)

Krakling, C. H. (1960) *Ptolemais, city of the Libyan Pentapolis* (Chicago). (Chap. 6)

Kraus, J. (1930) 'Die Anfange des Christentums in Nubien', in J. Schmidlin (ed.), *Missionswissenschaftliche Studien*, 2. (Chap. 12)

Krencker, D. M. (1913) *Deutsche Aksum-Expedition II. Ältere Denkmäler Nordabessiniens*, Band II (Berlin: G. Reisner), pp. 107, 113 ff. (Chaps 13, 15)

Krencker, D. M. and Littman, E. (1913) *Deutsche Axum Expedition*, Band IV (Berlin), pp. 4–35 (Chap. 16)

Kuentz, C. and Desroches-Noblecourt, C. (1968) 'Le petit temple d'Abou Simbel, I', *Memoires du Centre d'études sur l'ancienne Egypte* (Cairo). (Chap. 3)

Kryzyaniak, K. L. and Jakobielski, S. (1967) 'Polish Excavation at Old Dongola, Third Season, 1966–67', *Kush*, XV. (Chap. 12)

Labīd ibn Rabī'ah, *Die Gedichte des Lebîd, Nach der Wiener Ausgabe übersetzt und mit Anmerkungen versehn aus dem Nachlasse des Dr. A. Huber*, ed. C. Brockelmann (1891–2) (Leiden). (Chap. 15)

Lambert, N. (1970) 'Medinet Sbat et la protohistoire de Mauritanie occidentale', *Ant. Afr.*, IV, pp. 43–62. (Chaps 20, 21)

Lambert, N. (1971) 'Les industries sur cuivre dans l'ouest saharien', *WAJA*, I, pp. 9–21. (Chap. 29)

Lambert, R. (1925) *Lexique hiéroglyphique* (Paris), (Chap. 1)

Lancel, S. and Pouthier, L. (1957) 'Première campagne de fouilles à Tigisis', *Mélanges de l'école française de Rome* (Rome: Institut Français), pp. 247–53. (**Chap. 19**)

Lapeyre, G. G. and Pellegrin, A. (1942) *Carthage punique (814–146 avant J.-C.)* (Paris: Payot). (**Chap. 18**)

Lassus, J. (1956) 'Fouilles à Mila. Une tour de l'ancienne byzantine', *Libyca*, IV, 2, pp. 232–9. (**Chap. 19**)

Lassus, J. (1975) 'La forteresse byzantine de Thamugadi', *Actes XIV Congr. Intern. Et. Byz.*, pp. 463–76. (**Chap. 19**)

Lauer, J. P. (1938) 'La pyramide a Degrés, *Fouilles á Saqqarah*, 5 Vols (Cairo: Imprimerie de l'Institut Français d'Archéologie Orientale). (**Chap. 5**)

Law, R. C. (1967) 'The Garamantes and trans-Saharan enterprise in classical times', *JCH*, pp. 181–200. (**Chap. 20**)

Lawal, B. (1973) 'Dating problems at Igbo Ukwu', *JAH*, XIV, pp. 1–8. (**Chap. 29**)

Leakey, M. D., Owen, W. E. and Leakey, L. S. B. (1948) 'Dimple-based pottery from central Kavirondo, Kenya', *Coryndon Mem. Mus. Occ. Papers*, 2, p. 43. (**Chap. 25**)

Lebeuf, J.-P. (1962) *Archéologie tchadienne; les Sao du Cameroun et du Tchad* (Paris: Hermann). (**Chaps 21, 24**)

Lebeuf, J.-P. (1970) *Carte archéologique des abords du lac Tchad au 1/300 000* (Paris: CNRS). (**Chap. 20**)

Lebeuf, J.-P. and Griaule, M (1948) 'Fouilles dans la région du Tchad', *JSA*, 18, pp. 1–116. (**Chap. 21**).

Leca, A. P. (1971) *La Médecine égyptienne au temps des pharaons* (Paris: Éditions Roger Da costa). (**Chap. 5**)

Leclant, J. (1950a) See Rowe, A. (**Chap. 17**)

Leclant, J. (1950b) 'Per Africae sitientia, temoignage des sources classiques sur les pistes menant à l'oasis d'Ammon', *BIFAO*, 49, pp. 193–253. (**Chaps 17, 20**)

Leclant, J. (1954) 'Fouilles et travaux en Égypte 1952–1953', *Orientalia*, 23, 1, pp. 64–79. (**Chaps 12, 17**)

Leclant, J. (1956a) 'Egypte-Afrique, quelques remarques sur la diffusion des monuments égyptiens en Afrique', *BSFE*, 21, pp. 29–41. (**Chap. 4**)

Leclant, J. (1956b) 'Le fer dans l'Egypte ancienne, le Soudan et l'Afrique', *Actes Coll. Intern. Fer.*, pp. 83–91. (**Chap. 20**)

Leclant, J. (1958–74) 'Fouilles et travaux en Égypte et au Soudan', *Orientalia*. (**Chap. 12**)

Leclant, J. (1959a) 'Les fouilles à Axoum en 1955–1956', rapport préliminaire', *AE*, 3, pp. 3–23. (**Chap. 14**)

Leclant, J. (1959b) 'Haoulti-Mélazo (1955–6)', *AE*, 3, pp. 43–82. (**Chap. 13**)

Leclant, J. (1961) 'Découverte de monuments égyptiens ou égyptisants hors de la vallée du Nil, 1955–60', *Orientalia*, 30, pp. 391–406. (**Chap. 13**)

Leclant, J. (1962) Article in *BSA Copte*, 16, pp. 295–8. (**Chap. 13**)

Leclant, J. (1964–7) 'Au sujet des objets égyptiens découverts en Ethiopie', *Orientalia*, 33, pp. 388–9; 34, p. 220; 35, p. 165; 36, p. 216. (**Chap. 14**)

Leclant, J. (1965a) 'Le musée des antiquitiés à Addis-Ababa', *BSAC*, 16, pp. 86–7. (**Chap. 13**)

Leclant, J. (1965b) *Recherches sur les monuments thébains de la XXVe dynastie, dite éthiopienne* (Cairo: Imprimerie de l'Institut Français d'Archéologie Orientale). (**Chaps 10, 11**)

Leclant, J. (1965c) 'Note sur l'amulette en cornaline: J.E. 2832', *AE*, VI, pp. 86–7. (**Chap. 15**)

Leclant, J. (1970a) 'L'art chrétien d'Ethiopie. Découvertes récentes et points de vue nouveaux', in E. Dinkler (ed.), *Kunst und Geschichte Nubiens in christlischer Zeit. Ergebnisse und Probleme auf Grund der jüngsten Ausgrabungen* (1970) (Recklinghausen: Verlag Aurel Bongers), pp. 291–302. (**Chap. 12**)

Leclant, J. (1970b) 'La religion méroïtique', *Histoire des Religions*, publ. under the direction of M. Brillant and R. Aigrain (Paris: Blond et Guy). (**Chap. 11**)

Leclant, J. (1973a) 'Glass from the meroitic necropolis of Sedeinga (Sudanese Nubia)', *JGS*, XV, pp. 52–68. (**Chap. 10**)

Leclant, J. (1973b) *Lexikon der Aegyptologie* (Wiesbaden), 1, 2, collection 196–9. (**Chap. 10**)

Leclant, J. (1974) 'Les textes des pyramides. Textes et languages de l'Égypte pharaonique II', *BIFAO*, 64, 2, pp. 37–52. (**Chap. 10**)

Leclant, J. (1976a) 'Koushites et méroïtes. L'iconographie des souverains africains du Haut Nil antique', *L'Image du noir dans l'art occidental*, Vol. I: *Des Pharaons à la chute de l'empire romain*, eds J. Vercoutter, J. Leclant and F. Snowden (Fribourg: Menil Foundation), pp. 89–132. (**Chap. 11**)

Leclant, J. (1976b) 'L'Egypte, terre d'Afrique dans le monde gréco-romain', *L'Image du noir dans l'art occidental*, Vol. I (see under Vercoutter, J.), pp. 269–85. (**Chap. 6**)

Leclant, J. and Leroy, J. (1968) 'Nubien', *Propyläen Kunstgeschichte, Byzanz und Christlischen Osten*, Vol. III (Berlin). (**Chap. 12**)

Leclant, J. and Miquel, A. (1959) 'Reconnaissances dans l'Agamé: Goulo-Makeda et Sabéa (Octobre 1955 et Avril 1956)', *AE*, III, pp. 107–30. (**Chap. 13**)

Lee, R. B. (1968) 'What hunters do for a living: or how to make out on scarce resources', in R. B. Lee and I. De Vore, *Man the Hunter* (Chicago: Aldine Press), pp. 30–48. (**Chap. 26**)

Lee, R. B. (1972) 'The !Kung bushmen of Botswana', in M. G. Bicchieri (ed.), *Hunters and Gatherers Today* (New York: Holt, Rinehart & Winston). (**Chap. 26**)

Lefebvre, G. (1949) *Romans et contes égyptiens de l'époque pharaonique* (Paris). (**Chap. 2**)

Lefebvre, G. (1956) *Essai sur la médecine égyptienne de l'époque pharaonique* (Paris). (**Chap. 5**)

Leglay, M. (1966) *Saturne africain, histoire* (Paris: de Boccard). (**Chaps 17, 19**)

Leglay, M (1967) *Saturne africain, monuments*, 2 Vols. (Paris: Arts et Métiers Graphiques). (**Chap. 19**)

Lepelley, C. (1967) 'L'agriculture africaine au Bas-Empire', *Ant. Afr.*, 1, pp. 135–44. (**Chap. 19**)

Lepelley, C. (1968) 'Saint Léon Le Grand et l'église mauritanienne. Primauté romaine et autonomie africaine au Ve siècle', *Mélanges Ch. Saumagne* (*Tunis*), pp. 189–204. (**Chap. 19**)

Leschi, L. (1945) 'Mission au Fezzan', *Trav. IRS*, pp. 183–6. (**Chap. 20**)

Lesquier, J. (1918) *L'Armée romaine en Egypte d'Auguste à Dioclétien* (Cairo: Imprimerie de l'Institut Français d'Archéologie Orientale). (**Chap. 7**)

Levaillant, F. (1970) *Voyage de Monsieur le Vaillant dans l'intérieur de l'Afrique par le Cap de Bonne Espérance, dans les années 1780, 81, 82, 83, 84, et 85*, 2 Vols (New York/London: Johnson Reprint Corp.) (English tr.). (**Chap. 26**)

Levtzion, N. (1973) *Ancient Ghana and Mali* (London: Methuen). (**Chap. 29**)

Lézine, A. (1959) *Architecture Punique: recueil de documents* (Paris: PUF). (**Chap. 18**)

Lézine, A. (1960) 'Sur la population des villes africaines', *Ant. Afr.*, 3, pp. 69–82. (**Chap. 19**)

Lhote, H. (1953) 'Le cheval et le chameau dans les peintures et gravures rupestres du Sahara', *BIFAN*, XV. (**Chaps 17, 21**)

Lhote, H. (1954) 'L'expédition de C. Balbus au Sahara en 19 av. J.-C. d'après le texte de Pline', *RA*, pp. 41–83. (**Chap. 20**)

Lhote, H. (1955) *Les Touareg du Hoggar* (*Ahaggar*) 2nd edn (Paris: Payot). (**Chap. 20**)

Lhote, H. (1958) *The Search for the Tassili Frescoes*, tr. A. H. Broderick (1959) (London: Hutchinson). (**Chap. 24.**)

Lhote, J. (1963) 'Chars rupestres du Sahara', *CRAI*, pp. 225–38. (**Chap. 17**)

Lhote, H. (1967) 'Problèmes sahariens: l'outre, la marmite, le chameau, le délou, l'agriculture, le negre, le palmier', *BAM*, Vii, pp. 57–89. (**Chaps 17, 20**)

Lhote, H. (1970) 'Découverte de chasse de guerre en Air', *NA*, pp. 83–5. (**Chap. 20**)

Lichtenstein, H. *Travels in Southern Africa in the Years 1803, 1804, 1805 and 1806*, tr. A. Plumptre (1928–30) (Cape Town: Van Riebeeck Society). (**Chap. 26**)

Lieblein, J. D. C. (1886a) 'Der Handel des Landes Pún', *ZÄS*, XXIV, pp. 7–15. (**Chap. 4**)

Lieblein, J. D. C. (1886b) *Handel und Schiffahrt auf dem roten Meere in alten Zeiten* (Christiania: Dybwad). (**Chap. 4**)

Linares de Sapir, O. (1971) 'Shell middens of Lower Casamance and problems of Diola protohistory', *WAJA*, 1, pp. 23–54. (**Chaps 24, 29**)

Littmann, E. (1910–15) *Publications of the Princeton Expedition to Abyssinia*, 4 Vols (Leiden). (**Chap. 15**)

Littmann, E. (1950) *Äthiopische Inschriften*. (Berlin: Akademie-Verlag). (**Chap. 11**)

Littmann, E. (1954) 'On the old Ethiopian inscription from the Berenice road', *JRAS*, pp. 120–1. (**Chap. 15**)

Littmann, E., Krencker, D. and Lupke, Th. von (1913) *Vorbericht der deutschen Aksum Expedition*, 5 Vols (Berlin). (**Chaps 13, 15, 16**)

Longpérier, A. de (1856–74) Article in *Revue numismatique*, I. (**Chap. 16**)

Lonis, R. (1974) 'A propos de l'expédition des Nasamons à travers le Sahara', *AFLSD*, 4, pp. 165–79. (**Chap. 20**)

Loundine, A. G. (1972) 'Sur les rapports entre l'Ethiopie et le Himyar du VI siècle', *Atti IV Congr. Intern. Stud. Et.* (**Chap. 15**)

Loundine, A. G. and Ryckmans, G. (1964) 'Nouvelles données sur la chronologie des rois de Saba et du Du-Raydan', *Le Muséon*, LXXVII, pp. 3–4. (**Chap. 15**)

Lucas, A. (1962) *Ancient Egyptian Building Materials and Industries* (London: Edward Arnold), 4th edn. (**Chap. 3**)

Lucian, *Works*, tr. A. M. Harman, K. Kilburn and M. D. McLeod (1913–67) 8 Vols (Cambridge, Mass.: Harvard University Press; London: Heinemann). (**Chap. 1**)

Macadam, M. F. L. (1949, 1955) *The Temples of Kawa*, Vol. I: *The Inscriptions;* Vol. II: *History and Archaeology of the Site* (London: Oxford University Press). **(Chap 9, 10, 11, 17)**

Macadam, M. F. L. (1950) 'Four meroitic inscriptions', *JEA*, 36, pp. 43–7. **(Chaps 11, 17)**

Macadam, M. F. L. (1966) 'Queen Nawidemak', *Allen Memorial Art Museum*, XXIII, 2, pp. 46–7. **(Chaps 10, 11)**

McCrindle, J. W. (ed) (1879) *The Commerce and Navigation of the Erythraean Sea* (Calcutta). **(Chap. 22)**

MacIver, D. R. (1906) 'The Rhodesian ruins, their probable origins and significance', *GJ*, 4, pp. 325–47. **(Chap. 27)**

MacIver, D. R. (1906) *Mediaeval Rhodesia* (London: Frank Cass). **(Chap. 27)**

MacIver, D. R. and Woolley, C. L. (1911) *Buhen* (Philadelphia: University Museum), 2 Vols. **(Chap. 9)**

McMaster, D. N. (1966) 'The ocean-going dhow trade to East Africa', *EAGR*, 4, pp. 13–24. **(Chap. 22)**

Maggs, T. M. O'C. (1971) 'Some observations on the size of human groups during the late stone age', *SAJS*, 2, pp. 49–53. **(Chap. 26)**

Maggs, T. M. O'C. (1973) 'The NC₃ Iron Age Tradition', *SASS*, LXIX, p. 326. **(Chap. 27)**

Mahy, F. de (1891) *Autour de l'île Bourbon et de Madagascar* (Paris). **(Chap. 28)**

Maier, J.-L. (1973) *L'Episcopat de l'Afrique romaine, vandale et byzantine* (Rome: Institute Suisse de Rome). **(Chap. 19)**

Maingnard, L. F. (1931) 'The lost tribes of the Cape', *SAJS*, 28, pp. 487–504. **(Chap. 26)**

Maître, J. P. (1966) 'État des recherches sur le Néolithique de l'Ahaggar', *Trav. IRS*, pp. 95–104. **(Chap. 24)**

Maître, J. P. (1971) *Contribution à la préhistoire de l'Ahaggar* (Paris: AMG). **(Chap. 17)**

Maître, J. P. (1976) 'Contribution à la prèhistoire récente de l'Ahaggar dans son contexte saharien', *BIFAN*, 38, pp. 759–83. **(Chap. 20)**

Mahjoubi, A. (n.d.) *Les Cîtés romaines de la Tunisie* (Tunis). **(Chap. 19)**

Mahjoubi, A. (1966) 'Nouveau témoignage épigraphique sur la communauté chrétienne de Kairouan au XIe siecle', *Africa* (Tunis), I, pp. 85–104. **(Chap. 19)**

Mahjoubi, A., Ennabli, A. and Salomonson, J. W. (1970) *La Nécropole de Raqqada* (Tunis). **(Chap. 19)**

Malala, J. (1831) *Ioannis Malalae chronographia. Ex recensione Ludovici Dindorfii* (Corpus Scriptorum historiae byzantinae. Ioannes Malala) (Bonn: Weber).

Malhomme, J. (1953) 'Les représentations anthropomorphes du Grand Atlas', *Libyca*, I, pp. 373–85. **(Chap. 17)**

Mallon, A. (1926) *Grammaire copte avec bibliographie, chrestomathie et vocabulaire* (Beirut: Imprimerie Catholique) 3rd edn. **(Chap. 1)**

Malzac, V. (1912) *Histoire du royaume Hova depuis ses origines jusqu'à sa fin* (Tananarive: Impr. catholique) 2nd edn 1930. **(Chap. 28)**

Manetho, *Aegyptiaca*, etc., tr. W. G. Waddell (1940) (London: Heinemann; Cambridge, Mass.: Harvard University Press).

Marcillet-Jaubert, J. (1968) *Les Inscriptions d'Altava* (Gap: Éditions Ophrys). **(Chap. 19)**

Maret, P. de (1972) *Étude d'une collection de céramiques protohistoriques du Bas-Zaïre*, Mémoire de Licence (Brussels: University Library of Brussels). **(Chap. 25)**

Maret, P. de (1975) 'A Carbon-14 date from Zaïre', *Antiquity*, XLIX, pp. 133–7. **(Chap. 25)**

Marks, S. (1972) 'Khoisan resistance to the Dutch in the seventeenth and eighteenth centuries', *JAH*, XIII, 1, pp. 55–80. **(Chap. 26)**

Marliac, A. (1973) 'État des connaissances sur le Paléolithique et le Néolithique du Cameroun-Yaoundé', *ORSTOM* (Office de la Recherche Scientifique et Technique Outre-Mer), roneo. **(Chap. 21)**

Martens, M. (1972) 'Observations sur la composition du visage dans les peintures de Faras (VIIIe–IXe siècles)'. *CAMAP*, VI, pp. 207–50. **(Chap. 12)**

Martens, M. (1973) 'Observations sur la composition du visage dans les peintures de Faras (IXe–XIIe siècles)', *CAMAP*, VII. **(Chap. 12)**

Mason, R. J. (1973) 'First early iron age settlement in South Africa: Broederstroom 24–73, Brits District, Transvaal', *SAJS*, LXIX, pp. 324–5. **(Chaps 26, 27)**

Mason, R. J. (1974) 'Background to the Transvaal iron age discoveries at Olifantspoort and Broederstroom', *JSAIMM*, LXXXIV, 6, pp. 211–16. **(Chaps 21, 27)**

Maspero, G. (1904) *Histoire ancienne des peuples de l'Orient classique* (Paris) 5th edn. **(Chaps 1, 11)**

Maspero, J. (1912) *L'Organisation militaire de l'Egypte byzantine* (Paris: Honoré Champion). **(Chap. 7)**

Maspero, J. (1923) *Histoire des patriarches d'Alexandrie depuis la mort de l'empereur Anastase jusqu'à la réconciliation des églises jacobites 516–616* (Paris: Bibliothèque de l'École des Hautes Études). (Chap. 7)

Massoulard, E. (1949) *Préhistoire et Protohistoire d'Egypte* (Paris: Université of Paris, Travaux et Mémoires de l'Institut d'ethnologie). (Chap. 1)

Mathew, G. (1963) 'The East African coast until the coming of the Portuguese', in R. A. Oliver and G. Mathew (eds), *History of East Africa* (Oxford: Clarendon Press), Vol. I. (Chap. 22)

Mathew, G. (1975) 'The dating and significance of the Periplus of the Erythraean Sea', in R. I. Rotberg and H. N. Chittick (eds), *East Africa and the Orient* (New York/London: Africana Publishing Co.). (Chap. 22)

Mauny, R. (1940) *Leptis Magna, capitale portuaire de la Tripolitaine, Africa Italiana* (Rome). (Chap. 20)

Mauny, R. (1947) 'L'ouest africain chez Ptolémée', *Actes 11e Conf. Intern. Afr. Ouest*, I, pp. 241–93. (Chap. 20)

Mauny, R. (1950) 'Villages néolithiques de la falaise (dhar) Tichitt-Oualata', *Na*, 50, pp. 35–43. (Chap. 24)

Mauny, R. (1951) 'Un âge du cuivre au Sahara occidental', *BIFAN*, XIII, pp. 165–80. (Chap. 24)

Mauny, R. (1952) 'Essai sur l'histoire des métaux en Afrique occidentale', *BIFAN*, XIV, pp. 545–95. (Chap. 21)

Mauny, R. (1954) 'Gravures, peintures et inscriptions de l'ouest Africain', *IFAN*, XI. (Chap. 20)

Mauny, R. (1956a) 'Monnaies antiques trouvées en Afrique au sud du Limes romain', *Libyca*, pp. 249–61. (Chap. 20)

Mauny, R. (1956b) 'Préhistoire et géologie: la grande faune éthiopienne du nord-ouest africain du Paléolithique à nos jours', *BIFAN*, A, pp. 246–79. (Chap. 20)

Mauny, R. (1960) *Les Navigations médiévales sur les côtes sahariennes antérieures à la découverte portugaises* (Lisbon). (Chap. 21)

Mauny, R. (1961) 'Tableau géographique de l'ouest africain au Moyen-Age d'après les sources ecritez, la tradition orale et l'archéologie', *IFAN*, 61 (Chaps 20, 29)

Mauny, R. (1968) 'Le périple de la Mer Erythrée et le problème du commerce romain en Afrique au sud du Limes', *JSA*, 38, 1, pp. 19–34. (Chap. 28)

Mauny, R. (1970) *Les Siècles obscures de L'Afrique noire* (Paris: Fayard). (Chap. 20)

Maurin, L. (1968) 'Thuburbo Majus et la paix vandale', *Mélanges Ch. Saumagne* (Tunis), pp. 225–54. (Chap. 19)

Medic, M. (1965) 'Vadi es Sebua', *ZZSK*, XVI, pp. 41–50. (Chap. 12)

Meillassoux, C. (1960) 'Essai d'interprétation du phénomène économique dans les sociétés traditionnelles d'autosubsistance', *CEA*, 4, pp. 38–67. (Chap. 21)

Mekouria, T. T. (1966–7) *Yeityopia Tarik Axum Zagoué*, Vol. II. *Brehanena Selam, Matemiva Bete* (D. Eth.), pp. 203–17; *Yeityopia Tarik Nubia* (*Napata–Meroe*), pp. 2–7. (Chap. 16)

Mekouria, T. T. (1967) *L'Eglise d'Ethiopie* (Paris). (Chap. 16)

Mellis, J. V. (1938) *Nord et nord-ouest de Madagascar.* '*Volamena et Volafotsy' suivi d'un vocabulaire du nord-ouest expliqué, commenté et comparé au Merina* (Tananarive: Pitot de la Beaujardière). (Chap. 28)

Meltzer, O. and Kahrstedt, U. (1879–1913) *Geschichte der Karthager* (Berlin), Vols I–III. (Chap. 18)

Mesgnil, F. de (    ) *Madayana, Homère et la tribu mycénienne* (Tananarive). (Chap. 28)

Meyer, E. (1913–31) *Geschichte des Altertums*, 5 Vols (Berlin Stuttgart: Cotta). (Chap. 11)

Meyerowitz, E. L.-R. (1960) *The Divine Kingship in Ghana and Ancient Egypt* (London: Faber & Faber). (Chap. 4)

Michalowski, K. (1962) *Faras: Fouilles Polonaises* (Warsaw: Polich Academy of Science). (Chap. 12)

Michalowski, K. (1964) 'Die wichtigsten Entwicklungsetappen der Wandmalerei in Faras', in *Christentum am Nil* (Recklinghausen: Verlag Aurel Bongers), pp. 79–94. (Chap. 12)

Michalowski, K. (1965a) 'La Nubie chrétienne', *AB*, 3, pp. 9–25. (Chap. 12)

Michalowski, K. (1965b) 'Polish excavations at Faras, fourth season, 1963–64', *Kush*, XIII, pp. 177–89. (Chap. 12)

Michalowski, K. (1966a) 'Polish excavations at Old Dongola: first season (November–December 1964)', *Kush*, XIV, pp. 289–99. (Chap. 12)

Michalowski, K. (1966b) *Faras, centre artistique de la Nubie chrétienne* (Leiden: Nederlands Instituut voor het Nabije Oosten). (Chap. 12)

Michalowski, K. (1967a) 'Pro-Preshnemu li ostayetya zagadkoy gruppa X?', *Vestnik drevney Istoryi*, 2, pp. 104–211. (Chap. 12)

Michalowski, K. (1967b) *Faras, die Kathedrale aus dem Wüstensand* (Einsiedeln/Zürich/Cologne: Benziger Verlag). (Chaps 8, 12)

Michalowski, K. (1969) *The Art of Ancient Egypt*, tr. and adapted by N. Gutermann (London: Thames & Hudson). (Chap. 12)

Michalowski, K. (1970) 'Open problems of Nubian art and culture in the light of the discoveries at Faras', in E. Dinkler (ed.) (Recklinghausen). (Chap. 12)

Michalowski, K. (1974) *Faras. Wall Paintings in the Collection of the National Museum in Warsaw* (Warsaw: Wydawnictwo Artystyczno–Graficzne). (Chap. 12)

Michalowski, K. (ed.) (1975) 'Nubia, récentes recherches', *Actes Coll. Nubiol. Intern.* (Chaps 10, 12)

Migne, J. P. (1884) *Patrologia graeca, xxv; Athanasuis Apologia ad Constantium* (Paris), p. 635. (Chap 15)

Miller, J. I. (1969) *The Spice Trade of the Roman Empire* (Oxford: Clarendon Press). (Chap. 22)

Miller, S. F. (1969) 'Contacts between the later stone age and the early iron age in southern central Africa', *Azania*, 4, pp. 81–90. (Chap. 27)

Miller, S. F. (1971) 'The age of Nachikufan industry in Zambia', *SAAB*, 26, pp. 143–6. (Chap. 25)

Mills, E. A. C. and Filmer, N. T. (1972) 'Chondwe iron age site, Ndola, Zambia', *Azania*, VII, pp. 129–47. (Chap. 27)

Milne, J. G. (1924) *A History of Egypt under Roman Rule*, 3rd ed. rev. (London: Methuen). (Chap. 7)

Møberg, A. (1924) *The Book of Himyarites. Fragments of a hitherto unknown Syrian work on the Himyarite Martyrs* (Lund: Gleerup). (Chap. 15)

Möller, G. (1924) 'Die Aegypten und ihre libyschen Nachbaren', *ZDMG*, 78, p. 38. (Chap. 17)

Mommsen, Th. (1908) *Eusebius: Historia ecclesiastica*, II, 2 (Leipzig) pp. 972–3. (Chap. 15)

Monneret de Villard, U. (1935–57) *La Nubia médiévale*, Vols 1–4 (Cairo: Service des Antiquités de l'Égypte). (Chap. 12)

Monneret de Villard, U. (1938) 'Storia della Nubia christiana', *OCA*, 118. (Chap. 12)

Monneret de Villard, U. (1941) *La Nubia romana* (Rome: Instituto per l'Oriente). (Chap. 11)

Monod, T. (1948) *Mission au Fezzan*, Vol. II: *Reconnaissance au Dohone*. (Chap. 20)

Monod, T. (1967) 'Notes sur le harnachement chamelier', *BIFAN*. (Chap. 20)

Monod, T. (1974) 'Le mythe de l'émeraude des Garamantes', *AA*, VIII, pp. 51–66. (Chap. 20)

Montagu, M. F. A. (1960) *An Introduction to Physical Anthropology* (Springfield, Ill.: Thomas), 3rd edn. (Chap. 1)

Montet, P. (1958) *Everyday Life in Egypt in the Days of Ramesses the Great*, tr. A. R. Maxwell-Hyslop and Margaret S. Drower (London: Edward Arnold). (Chaps 2, 3)

Montet, P. (1964) L'Égypte eternelle (Paris), tr. Doreen Weightman *Eternal Egypt* (London: Weidenfeld & Nicolson). (Chap. 3)

Montevecchi, O. (1937) *La papirologia* (Turin: Societa Editrice Internazionale). (Chap. 7)

Moorsel, P. Van (1966) 'Une téophanie nubienne', *RAC*, XLII, 1–4, pp. 297–316. (Chap. 12)

Moorsel, P. Van (1967) 'Abdallah Nirqi', *Spiegel Historiael*, II (Netherlands), pp. 388–92. (Chap. 12)

Moorsel, P. Van (1970) 'Die Wandmalerlien der Zentralen Kirche von Abdallah Nirqi', in E. von Dinkler (ed.) *Kunst und Geschichte Nubiens in Christlicher Zeit* (1970) (Recklinghausen: Verlag Aurel Bongers), pp. 103–111. (Chap. 12)

Moorsel, P. Van (1972) 'Gli scavi olanolesi in Nubia', *Actas VIII Congr. Intern. Arqueo. Christ.* pp. 349–95. (Chap. 12)

Moorsel, P. Van, Jacquet, J. and Schneider, H. (1975) *The Central Church of Abdallah Nirqi* (Leiden: Brill). (Chap. 12)

Mordini, A. (1960) 'Gli aurei Kushàna del convento di Dabra-Dàmmo', *Atti Convegno Intern. Stud. Et.*, 2–4 April 1959, Rome, p. 253. (Chap. 15)

Morel, J. P. (1968) 'Céramique à vernis noir du Maroc', *Ant. Afr.*, 2, and 'Céramique d'Hippone', *BAA*, 1, 1962–5. (Chap. 19)

Moret, A. (1926) *Le Nil et la civilisation égyptienne* (Paris: L'Évolution de l'Humanité), Vol. VII. (Chap. 2)

Mori, F. (1964) 'Some aspects of the rock art of the Acacus (Fezzan, Sahara) and dating regarding it', in L. Pericot García and E. Ripoll Parello (eds) (1964) *Wartenstein Symposium on Rock Art of the Western Mediterranean and the Sahara: Prehistoric art of the western Mediterranean and the Sahara.* (New York: subscribers edn distributed through *Current Anthropology* for the Wenner-Gren Foundation for Anthropological Research), pp. 247–59. (Chap. 17)

Mori, F. (1965) *Tadrart Acacus: Arte rupestre e culture del Sahara prehistorico* (Turin: Einaudi). (Chap. 24)

Mori, F. (1972) *Rock Art of the Tadrart Acacus* (Graz.) (Chap. 21)

Morrisson, C. (1970) *Catalogue des monnaies byzantines de la Bibliothèque nationale* (Paris). (Chap. 19)

Mortelmans, G. (1957) 'La préhistoire du Congo belge', *RUB*, 2–3. (Chap. 25)

Mortelmans, G. (1962) 'Archéologie des grottes Dimba et Ngoro (région de Thysville, Bas-Congo)', *Actes IV Congr. PPEQ*, pp. 407–25. (Chap. 25)

772

Moscati, S. (1968) *L'épopée des Phéniciens* (Paris: Fayard), 1971 edn, tr. A. Hamilton *The World of the Phoenicians* (London: Weidenfeld & Nicolson). (**Chap. 18**)

Müller, W. M. (1906–20) *Egyptological Researches*, Vol. II: 'Results of a journey in 1906' Washington, DC: Carnegie Institution). (**Chap. 17**)

Munier, H. (1943) *Recueil des listes épiscopales de l'Eglise copte* (Cairo: La Société de l'Archaéologie Copte). (**Chap. 12**)

Munson, P. J. (1967) 'A survey of the Neolithic villages of Dhar Tichitt (Mauretania) and some comments on the grain impressions found on the Tichitt pottery', *Actes VI Congr. PPQS*. (**Chap. 24**)

Munson, P. J. (1968) 'Recent archaeological research in the Dhar Tichitt region of south central Mauretania', *WAAN*, 10, pp. 6–13. (**Chap. 24**)

Munson, P. J. (1969) 'Engravings of ox-drawn chariots', *NA*, 122, pp. 62–3. (**Chap. 21**)

Munson, P. J. (1970) 'Corrections and additional comments concerning the Tichitt tradition', *WAAN*, 12, pp. 47–8. (**Chap. 24**)

Munson, P. J. (1972) 'Archaeological data on the origin of cultivation in the south-western Sahara and its implications for west Africa', *BWS 56*. (**Chap. 24**)

Murdock, G. P. (1959) *Africa: Its Peoples and Their Culture History* (New York: McGraw Hill). (**Chaps 21, 23**)

Naville, E. (1907–13) *The XIth Dynasty Temple at Der-el-Bahari*, 3 Vols (London: Office of the Egypt Exploration Fund). (**Chap. 2**)

Nenquin, J. (1959) 'Dimple-based pots from Kasai, Belgian Congo', *Man*, 59, 242, pp. 153–5. (**Chap. 25**)

Nenquin, J. (1961) 'Protohistorische Metaaltechniek in Katanga', *Africa-Tervuren*, VII, 4, pp. 97–101. (**Chap. 25**)

Nenquin, J. (1963) 'Excavations at Sanga, 1957. The protohistoric necropolis', *AMRAC*, 45. (**Chaps 25, 29**)

Nibbi, A. (1975) *The Sea Peoples and Egypt* (Park Ridge, NJ: Noyes Press). (**Chap. 2**)

Nicolaus, R. A. (1968) *Melanins* (Paris: Hermann). (**Chap. 1**)

Noshï, I. (1937) *The Arts in Ptolemaic Egypt: A Study of Greek and Egyptian Influences in Ptolemaic architecture and sculpture* (London: OUP). (**Chap. 6**)

Noten, F. Van (1968) 'The Uelian. A culture with a Neolithic aspect, Uele Basin (N.E. Congo Republic), *AMRAC*, 64. (**Chap. 25**)

Noten, F. Van (1972a) 'Les tombes du roi Cyirima Rujugira et de la reine-mère Nyirayuhi Kanjogera', *AMRAC*, 77. (**Chap. 25**)

Noten F. Van (1972b) 'La plus ancienne sculpture sur bois de l'Afrique centrale', *Africa-Tervuren*, XVIII, 3–4, pp. 133–5. (**Chap. 25**)

Noten, F. Van and Het, E. (1974) 'Ijzersmelten bij de Madi', *Africa-Tervuren*, XX, 3–4, pp. 57–66. (**Chap. 25**)

Noten, F. Van and Hiernaux, J. (1967) 'The late stone age industry of Mukinanira, Rwanda', *SAAB*, 22, IV, pp. 151–4. (**Chap. 25**)

Nunoo, R. (1969) 'Buruburo factory excavations', *Actes 1er Coll. Intern. Archéol. Afr.*, pp. 321–33. (**Chap. 29**)

Obenga, T. (1973) *L'Afrique dans l'antiquité – Egypte pharaonique – Afrique noire* (Paris: Présence Africaine). (**Chaps 4, 21**)

Odner, K. (1971a) 'Usangi hospital and other archaeological sites in the North Parc mountains, north-eastern Tanzania', *Azania*, VI, pp. 89–130. (**Chap. 22**)

Odner, K. (1971b) 'A preliminary report of an archaeological survey on the slopes of Kilimanjaro', *Azania*, VI, pp. 131–50. (**Chap. 22**)

Ogot, B. A. and Kieran, J. A. (eds) (1974) *Zamani: A Survey of the East African History* (Nairobi/London: East African Publishing House/Longmans). (**Chap. 23**)

Olderogge, D. A. (1972) 'L'Arménie et l'Ethiopie au IVᵉ siècle (a propos des sources de l'alphabet arménien)' *IVᵉ Congrès international des études ethiopiennes*, pp. 195–203. (**Chap. 15**)

Oliver, J. A. (1963) 'Discernible developments in the interior, c. 1500–1840', in R. A. Oliver and G. Mathew (eds), *Oxford History of East Africa* (London), Vol. I, pp. 169–211. (**Chap. 28**)

Oliver, R. A. (1966) 'The problem of the Bantu expansion', *JAH*, VI, 3, pp. 361–76. (**Chaps 21, 22, 23**)

Oliver, R. A. and Fagan, B. M. (1975) *Africa in the Iron Age, c. 500 BC to AD 1400* (Cambridge: Cambridge University Press). (**Chap. 29**)

Oliver, R. A. and Mathew, G. (eds) (1963) *Oxford History of East Africa* (London: Oxford University Press). (Chap. 4)

Orteil, F. (1952) 'The economic unification of the Mediterranean region: industry, trade and commerce', in S. A. Cook *et al.* (eds), *Cambridge Ancient History* (Cambridge: Cambridge University Press). (Chap. 22)

Orteil, F. (1956) 'The economic life of the Empire', in S. A. Cook *et al.* (eds), *Cambridge Ancient History* (Cambridge: Cambridge University Press). (Chap. 22)

Otto, E. (1969) 'Das Goldene Zeitalter in einem Ägyptischen Text', *Religions en Egypte héllenistique et romaine*, Colloque de Strasbourg, 16–18 May 1967 (Paris), pp. 93–100. (Chap. 3)


Pace-Caputo, S. (1951) *Scavi Sahariani. Monumenti antichi* (Rome: Accademia dei Lincei). (Chap. 20)

Painter, C. (1966) 'The Guang and West African historical reconstruction', *GNQ*, 9, pp. 58–66. (Chap. 21)

Palmer, J. A. B. (1947) 'Periplus Mari Erythraei; the Indian evidence as to its date', *CQ*, XLI, pp. 136–41. (Chap. 22)

Pankhurst, R. K. P. (1961) *An Introduction to the Economic History of Ethiopia from early times to 1800* (London: Lalibela House). (Chap. 22)

*Papyrus Ebers. The Greatest Egyptian Medical Document*, trs B. Ebbell (1937) (Copenhagen: Levin & Munksgaard; London: Oxford University Press).

*Papyrus Rhind. The Rhind mathematical papyrus, British Museum 10057 and 10053* (Oberlin). (Chap. 5)

Paribeni, E. (1959) *Catalogo delle sculture de Cirene. Statue e rilievi di carattere religioso* (Rome), Monografie di Archeologia libica No. 5. (Chap. 6)

Paribeni, R. (1908) 'Richerche nel luogo dell'antica Adulis', *Antichita Publicati per Curia della Accademia Nazionale dei Lincei*, 18, pp. 438–572. (Chaps 13, 15)

Parkington, J. E. (1972) 'Seasonal mobility in the later stone age', *AS*, 31, pp. 223–43. (Chap. 26)

Parkington, J. E. and Pöggenpoel, C. (1971) 'Excavations at De Hangen 1968', *SAAB*, 26, pp. 3–36. (Chap. 26)

Paterson, W. (1789) *A Narrative of Four Journeys into the Country of the Hottentots and Caffraria, in the Years 1777, 1778, 1779* (London). (Chap. 26)

Pedrals, D. P. de (1950) *Archéologie de l'Afrique noire; Nubie, Éthiopie, Niger sahélien, L'Aire tchadienne, Niger inférieur, Zimbabwé, Sénégambie, Congo belge* (Paris: Payot). (Chap. 1)

Perret, R. (1936) 'Recherches archéologiques et ethnographiques au Tassili des Ajjers', *JSA*, 6, pp. 50–1. (Chap. 17)

Perrot, J. *et al.* (1972) 'Une statue de Darius découverte à Suse', *JA*, pp. 235–66. (Chap. 10)

Perroy, L. (1969) *Gabon, cultures et techniques* (Libreville: Cah. ORSTOM, Office de la Recherche Scientifique et Technique Outre-Mer, Musée des Arts et Traditions), 275/195. (Chap. 21)

Pesce, G. (1961) *Sardegna Punica* (Cagliari). (Chap. 18)

Petrie, W. M. F. (1901) *Diospolis Parva, the cemeteries of Abadiyeh and Hu, 1898–9* (London/Boston, Mass.: Egypt Exploration Fund). (Chap. 9)

Petrie, W. M. F. (1939) *The Making of Egypt* (London: Sheldon Press; New York: Macmillan). (Chap. 1)

Pettigrew, T. J. (1834) *A History of Egyptian Mummies, and an Account of the Worship and Embalming of Sacred Animals by the Egyptians* (London: Longman). (Chap. 1)

Pflaum, H. G. (1957) 'A propos de la date de la création de la province de Numidie', *Libyca*, pp. 61–75. (Chap. 19)

Phillipson, D. W. (1968a) 'The early iron age in Zambia – regional variants and some tentative conclusions', *JAH*, IX, 2, pp. 191–214. (Chaps 21, 25, 26, 27)

Phillipson, D. W. (1968b) 'The early iron age site at Kapwirimbwe, Lusaka', *Azania*, III, pp. 87–105. (Chap. 27)

Phillipson, D. W. (1968c) 'Cewa, Leya, and Lala iron-smelting furnaces', *SAAB*, XXIII, pp. 102–13. (Chap. 27)

Phillipson, D. W. (1969) 'Early iron-using peoples of southern Africa', in L. Thompson (ed.), *African Societies in Southern Africa* (London: Heinemann), pp. 24–49. (Chap. 27)

Phillipson, D. W. (1970a) 'Excavations at Twickenham Road, Lusaka', *Azania*, V. pp. 77–118. (Chap. 27)

Phillipson, D. W. (1970b) 'Notes on the later prehistoric radiocarbon chronology of eastern and southern Africa', *JAH*, XI, pp. 1–15. (Chap. 27)

Phillipson, D. W. (1971) 'An early iron age site on the Lubusi river, Kaoma district, Zambia', *ZMJ*, II, pp. 51–7. (Chap. 27)

Phillipson, D. W. (1972a) *Prehistoric Rock Paintings and Engravings of Zambia* (Livingstone, Zambia: Exhibition catalogue of Livingstone Museum). (**Chap. 29**)

Phillipson, D. W. (1972b) 'Early iron age sites on the Zambian copperbelt', *Azania*, VII, pp. 93–128. (**Chap. 27**)

Phillipson, D. W. (1973) 'The prehistoric succession in eastern Zambia: a preliminary report', *Azania*, VIII, pp. 3–24. (**Chap. 27**)

Phillipson, D. W. (1974) 'Iron age history and archaeology in Zambia', *JAH*, XV, pp. 1–25. (**Chap. 27**)

Phillipson, D. W. (1975) 'The chronology of the iron age in Bantu Africa', *JAH*, XVI, pp. 321–42. (**Chaps 23, 27**)

Phillipson, D. W. (1977) *The Later Prehistory of Eastern and Southern Africa* (London: Heinemann). (**Chap. 27**)

Phillipson, D. W. and Fagan, B. M. (1969) 'The date of the Ingombe Ilede burials', *JAH*, X, pp. 199–204. (**Chap. 27**)

Pigache, J. P. (1970) 'Le Problème anthropobiologique à Madagascar', *Taloha* (Tananarive), 3, pp. 175–7. (**Chap. 28**)

Pigulevskaya, N. V. (1951) *Vizantiya na putyah v Indiyu* (Moscow: Izdatel'stvo Akademiya, Nauk). (**Chap. 15**)

Pigulevskaya, N. V. (1969) *Byzanz auf den Wegen nach Indien: aus der Geschichte des byzantinischen Handels mit dem Orient vom 4, bis 6. Jahrhundert* (Berlin: Akademie-Verlag; Amsterdam: Hakkert). (**Chap. 16**)

Pirenne, J. (1955) *La Grèce et Saba: Une nouvelle base pour la chronologie sud-arabe* (Paris: Imprimerie Nationale). (**Chap. 13**)

Pirenne, J. (1956) *Paléographie des inscriptions sud-arabes. Contribution à la chronologie et à l'histoire de l'Arabie du Sud antique* (Brussels: Paleis der Academiën), Vol. I. (**Chap. 13**)

Pirenne, J. (1961) 'Un problème clef pour la chronologie de l'Orient: la date du "Périple de la Mer Erythrée"', *JA*, 249, pp. 441–59. (**Chap. 13**)

Pirenne, J. (1961–3) *Histoire de la civilisation de l'Égypte ancienne*, 3 Vols (Paris: Neuchâtel). (**Chap. 2**)

Pirenne, J. (1965) 'Arte Sabeo d'Etiopia', *Encyclopedia dell'arte antica* (Rome), Vol. VI, pp. 1044–8. **Chap. 13**)

Pirenne, J. (1967) 'Haoulti et ses monuments. Nouvelle interprétation', *AE*, 7, pp. 125–33. (**Chap. 13**)

Pirenne, J. (1969) 'Notes d'archéologie sud-arabe, VI', *Syria*, 46, pp. 308–13. (**Chap. 13**)

Pirenne, J. (1970a) 'Haoulti, Gobochela (Mélazo) et le site antique', *AE*, 8, pp. 117–27. (**Chap. 13**)

Pirenne, J. (1970b) 'Le développement de la navigation Egypte-Inde dans l'antiquité, sociétés et compagnies de commerce en Orient et dans l'Océan Indien', *Actes 8e Coll. Intern. Hist. Marit.*, pp. 101–19. (**Chap. 22**)

Pliny, *Natural History*, tr. H. Rackham *et al.* (1938–62), 11 Vols (Cambridge, Mass.: Harvard University Press; London: Heinemann). (**Chaps 11, 13, 15, 17, 22**)

Plumley, J. M. (1970) 'Some examples of Christian Nubian art from the excavations at Qasr Ibrim', in E. Dinkler (ed.), *Kunst und Geschichte Nubiens in christlicher Zeit. Ergebnisse und Probleme auf Grund der jüngsten Ausgrabungen* (Recklinghausen: Verlag Aurel Bongers), pp. 129–40. (**Chap. 12**)

Plumley, J. M. (1971) 'Pre-Christian Nubian (23 BC – 535 AD) evidence from Qasr Ibrim', *Etudes et Travaux*, 5, pp. 7–24. (**Chaps 10, 12**)

Plumley, J. M. and Adams, W. A. (1974) 'Qasr Ibrim 1912', *JEA*, 60, pp. 237–8. (**Chap. 12**)

Poinsot, L. and Lantier, R. (1923) 'Un sanctuaire de Tamit à Carthage', *RHR*, LXXXVII. (**Chap. 18**)

Poinssot, C. (1962) 'Immunitas Perticae Carthaginiensium', *CRAI*, pp. 55–76. (**Chap. 19**)

Poirier, C. (1954) 'Terre d'Islam en mer malgache', *BAM*, Cinquantenaire, pp. 71–115. (**Chap. 28**)

Poirier, C. (1965) 'Données écologiques et démographiques de la mise en place des protomalgaches', *Taloha* (Tananarive), pp. 61–2. (**Chap. 28**)

Pommeret, Y. (1965) *Civilisations préhistoriques au Gabon. Vallée du Moyen Ogooné*, 2 Vols (Libreville: Centre culturel français St. Exupery), Vol. II, 'Notes préliminaires à propos du gisement lupembien et néolithique de Ndjole'. (**Chap. 25**)

Pons, A. and Quézel, P. (1957) 'Première étude palynologique de quelques paléosols sahariens', *Trav. IRS*, 16, 2, pp. 27–35. (**Chaps 17, 24**)

Porter, B. and Moss, R. L. B. (1951) *Topographical Bibliography of Ancient Egyptian Hieroglyphic Texts, Reliefs and Paintings* (Oxford: Clarendon Press), Vol. VII, pp. 264ff. (**Chap. 11**)

Portères, A. (1950) 'Vieilles agricultures de l'Afrique intertropicale: centre d'origine et de diversification variétale primaire et berceaux d'agriculture antérieure au XVIe siècle', *AT*, 5, 9–10, pp. 489–507. (**Chap. 24**)

Portères, A. (1951a) 'Géographie alimentaire, berceaux agricoles et migrations des plantes cultivées, en Afrique intértropicale', *C-RSB*, 239, pp. 16–21. (Chap. 24)

Portères, A. (1951b) 'Une céréale mineure cultivée dans l'Ouest africain (Brachiarta deflexa C. E. Hubbard *var* sativa nov. var)', *AT*, 6, 1–2, pp. 38–42. (Chap. 24)

Portères, A. (1962) 'Berceaux agricoles primaires sur le continent africain', *JAH*, 3, 2, pp. 195–210. (Chap. 24)

Posener, G. (1936) 'La première domination perse en Egypte. Recueil d'inscriptions hiéroglyphiques', *BIFAO*, XI. (Chap. 2)

Posener, G. (1956) *Littérature et politique dans l'Egypte de la XIIe dynastie* (Paris: Champion). (Chaps 2, 5)

Posener, G. (1958) 'Pour une localisation du pays Koush au Moyen-Empire', *Kush*, 6, pp. 39–65. (Chaps 4, 9)

Posener, G. (1960) 'De la divinité de pharaon', *CSA*, XV, (Chaps 2, 3)

Posener, G., Sauneron, S. and Yoyotte, J. (1959) *Dictionnaire de la civilisation égyptienne* (Paris), tr. A Macfarlane *A Dictionary of Egyptian Civilization* (London: Methuen) 1962. (Chaps 2, 3, 4)

Posnansky, M. (1966a) 'The origin of agriculture and iron-working in southern Africa', in M. Posnansky (ed.), *Prelude to East African History* (London: Oxford University Press), pp. 82–94. (Chap. 22)

Posnansky, M. (1966b) 'Kingship, archaeology and historical myth', *UJ*, 30, pp. 1–12. (Chap. 29)

Posnansky, M. (1967) 'The iron age in east Africa', in W. W. Bishop and J. D. Clark (eds), *Background to Evolution in Africa* (London/Chicago: University of Chicago Press), pp. 629–49. (Chap. 25)

Posnansky, M. (1968) 'Bantu genesis: archaeological reflexions', *JAH*, IX, 1, pp. 1–11. (Chap. 23)

Posnansky, M. (1969) 'Yams and the origins of west African agriculture', *Odù*, 1, pp. 101–7. (Chap. 21)

Posnansky, M. (1969–70) 'Discovering Ghana's past', *Annual Museum Lectures*, p. 20. (Chap. 29)

Posnansky, M. (1971) 'Ghana and the origins of west African trade', *AQ*, XI, pp. 110–25. (Chaps 24, 29)

Posnansky, M. (1972a) 'Archaeology, ritual and religion', in T. O. Ranger and I. Kimambo (eds), *The Historical Study of African Religion; with special reference to East and Central Africa* (London: Heinemann), pp. 29–44. (Chap. 29)

Posnansky, M. (1972b) 'Terminology in the early iron age of east Africa with particular reference to the dimple-based wares of Lolui island, Uganda', *Actes VI Congr. PPQS*, pp. 577–9. (Chap. 21)

Posnansky, M. (1973a) 'Aspects of early west African trade', *WA*, 5, pp. 149–62. (Chap. 21)

Posnansky, M. (1973b) 'Review of T. Shaw, "Igbo Ukwu"', *Archaeology*, 25, 4, pp. 309–11. (Chap. 29)

Préaux, C. (1939) *L'Économie royale des Lagides* (Brussels: Foundation Egyptologique Reine Elisabeth). (Chap. 6)

Préaux, C. (1943) 'Les Egyptiens dans la civilisation hellénistique d'Egypte', *Chronique d'Egypte*, XVIII, pp. 148–60. (Chap. 6)

Préaux, C. (1950) 'La singularité de l'Egypte dans le monde gréco-romain', *Chronique d'Egypte*, XXV, pp. 110–23. (Chaps 6, 26)

Préaux, C. (1952) 'Sur la communication de l'Ethiopie avec l'Egypte hellénistique', *Chronique d'Egypte*, XXVII, pp. 257–81. (Chap. 6)

Préaux, C. (1954) 'Sur les origines des monopoles lagides', *Chronique d'Egypte*, XXIX, pp. 312–27. (Chap. 6)

Préaux, C. (1957) 'Les grecs à la découverte de l'Afrique par l'Egypte', *Chronique d'Egypte*, XXXII, pp. 284–312. (Chaps 4, 6)

Priaulx, B. (1863) 'On the Indian embassies to Rome, from the reign of Claudius to the death of Justinian', *JRAS*, XX, pp. 277–8. (Chap. 15)

Priese, K. H. (1968) 'Nichtägyptische Namen und Wörter in den Ägyptischen Inschriften der Könige von Kush', *MIOD*, 14, pp. 165–91. (Chap. 10)

Priese, K. H. (1970), article in *ZÄS*, 98, 1, pp. 16–32. (Chap. 10)

Pritchard, J. B. (ed.) (1969) *The Ancient Near East: supplementary texts and pictures relating to the Old Testament* (Princeton: Princeton University Press). (Chap. 2)

Procopius, *De bello persico, Destunis, Spiridors et Gavriil*, ed. *Istoriya voyn rimlau spersami*, Kniga I, (St Petersburg: Nauk) 1876, pp. 274–7.

Procopius, *History of the Wars, Secret History*, tr. B. H. Dewing, *et al.* (1914–40), 7 Vols (Cambridge, Mass.: Harvard University Press; London: Heinemann) *The Vandal War, The Buildings*, ed. B. H. Dewing (1954) (London); *Iohannis*, ed. Partsch (1879) (Leipzig), Diggle-Goodyear (1970) (Cambridge). (Chaps 15, 19, 22)

**Ptolemaeus, Claudius** (Ptolemy, Claudius) *The Geography*, tr. E. L. Stevenson (1932) (New York). **(Chaps 13, 15, 22)**

**Ptolemaeus Claudius**, ed. K. Müller (1901) *Geographia* (Paris: A. Firmin Didot), IV, 6, 5, 6, pp. 743–5. **(Chap. 17)**

**Pullan, R. A.** (1965) 'The recent geomorphological evolution of the south central part of the Chad basin', *JASA*, 9, 2. **(Chap. 24)**

**Quézel, P. and Martinez, C.** (1958) 'Le dernier interpluvial au Sahara central', *Libyca*, 6–7, p. 224. **(Chap. 1)**

**Quiring, H.** (1946) *Geschichte des Goldes. Die Goldenen Zeitalter in ihren kulturellen und wirtschaftlichen Bedeutung* (Stuttgart). **(Chap. 11)**

**Rachet, M.** (1970) *Rome et les Berbères: un problème militaire d'Auguste à Dioclétien* (Brussels: Latomus Revue d'Études Latines). **(Chap. 19)**

**Rakoto-Ratsimamanga, A.** (1940) 'Tache pigmentaire et origine des malgaches', *R. Anth.*, pp. 6–130. **(Chap. 28)**

**Ramilisonina** (1951–2) *Histoire du Zafimamy* (Ny loharon'ny Andriamamilaza) (Tananarive: Impr. Volamahitsy). **(Chap. 28)**

**Ranke, H.** (1948) *Medizin und Chirurgie im alten Ägypten* (Heidelberg: Kerle). **(Chap. 5)**

**Rahtz, P. A. and Flight, C.** (1974) 'A quern factory near Kintampo, Ghana', *WAJA*, 4, pp. 1–31. **(Chap. 29)**

**Rauning, W.** (1964) *Die kulturellen Verhaltnisse Nord und Ost Afrika im ersten nach Christlichen Jahrhundert entworfen an Hand des Periplus des Erythraischen Meeres* (Vienna). **(Chap. 22)**

**Rauning, W.** (1965) 'Die Bedeutung des Periplus des Erythraischen Meeres für Africa', *MAGW*, XCV, pp. 55–60. **(Chap. 22)**

**Rawlinson, H. G.** (1916) *Intercourse between India and the Western World from the Earliest Times to the Fall of Rome* (Cambridge: Cambridge University Press). **(Chap. 22)**

**Rebuffat, R.** (1969–70) 'Zella et les routes d'Egypte', *Libya Antiqua* (Tripoli), VI–VII, pp. 181–7. **(Chaps 17, 20)**

**Rebuffat, R.** (1970) 'Route d'Egypte et de la Libye intérieure', *SM*, 3, pp. 1–20. **(Chaps 17, 20)**

**Rebuffat, R.** (1972) 'Nouvelles recherches dans le sud de la Tripolitaine', *C-RAI*, pp. 319–39. **(Chap. 20)**

**Rebuffat, R.** (1974) 'Vestiges antiques sur la côte occidentale de l'Egypte au sud de Rabat', *AA*, VIII, pp. 25–49. **(Chap. 20)**

**Rebuffat, R.** (1975) 'Trois nouvelles campagnes dans le sud de la Tripolitaine', *C-RAI*, pp. 495–505. **(Chap. 20)**

**Rebuffat, R.** (1977) 'Bu Ngem', *LAPPMO*, Cah. no. 20. **(Chap. 20)**

**Redford, D. W.** (1967) 'History and chronology of the eighteenth dynasty of Egypt', *NAS*. **(Chap. 2)**

**Reichold, W.** (1978) 'Les noirs dans le livre du prophète Isaïe', *Afrique noire et monde mediterranéen dans l'antiquité*, Colloque de Dakar, 19–24 January 1976, Dakar-Abidjan, *Nouvelles Editions Africaines*, pp. 276–85. **(Chap. 4)**

**Reinach, A.** (1913) *Egyptologie et histoire des religions* (Paris), p. 17. **(Chap. 1)**

**Reisner, G. A.** (1910) *The archaeological survey of Nubia. Report for 1907, 1908* (Cairo: National Printing Department), Vol. I. **(Chaps 9, 12)**

**Reisner, G. A.** (1918) 'The Barkal temples in 1916', *JEA*, V. **(Chap. 11)**

**Reisner, G. A.** (1918–19) 'Outline of the ancient history of the Sudan', *SNR*, I, pp. 3–15, 57–79, 217–37; II, pp. 35–67. **(Chap. 11)**

**Reisner, G. A.** (1923a) *Excavations at Kerma* (Cambridge, Mass.: HAS), Vols V and VI. **(Chaps 9, 11)**

**Reisner, G. A.** (1923b) 'The meroitic kingdom of Ethiopia: a chronological outline', *JEA*, 9, pp. 33–77. **(Chap. 11)**

**Reisner, G. A.** (1929) 'Excavations at Simna and Uronarti by the Harvard Boston expedition', *SNR*, XII, pp. 143–61. **(Chap. 11)**

**Reisner, G. A.** (1931) 'Inscribed monuments from Gebel Barkal', *ZÄS*, 66, p. 100. **(Chap. 10)**

**Reisner, G. A.** (1936) *The Development of the Egyptian Tomb down to the Accession of Cheops* (Cambridge, Mass.: Harvard University Press). **(Chap. 5)**

**Reisner, G. A.** (1942–55) *A History of the Giza Necropolis* (Cambridge, Mass.: Harvard University Press), Vol. II (completed and rev. by W. S. Smith) *The tomb of Hetep-herès, the mother of Cheops*. **(Chap. 2)**

**Reisner, G. A.** (1955) *A History of the Giza Necropolis*, Vol. II, The tomb of Hetep–Heres, the mother of Cheops (Cambridge, Mass.: Harvard University Press). **(Chap. 2)**

**Repiquet, J.** (1902) *Le Sultanat d'Anjouan, îles Comores* (Paris). **(Chap. 28)**

**Resch, W.** (1967) *Das Rind in den Felsbilddarstellungen Nordafrikas* (Wiesbaden: Franz Steiner Verlag). **(Chap. 17)**

**Reusch, R.** (1961) *History of East Africa* (New York: Ungar). **(Chap. 22)**

**Reygasse, M.** (1950) *Monuments funéraires préislamiques de l'Afrique du Nord* (Paris: Arts et métiers graphiques). **(Chap. 20)**

**Reynolds, V.** (1967) *The Apes: the gorilla, chimpanzee, orangutan and gibbon; their history and their world* (New York: Dutton). **(Chap. 21)**

**Riavi, S. A.** (1967) 'Zanj: its first known use in Arabic literature', *Azania*, II, pp. 200–1. **(Chap. 22)**

**Ricci, L.** (1955–8) 'Retrovamenti archeologici in Eritrea', *RSE*, 14, pp. 51–63. **(Chap. 13)**

**Ricci, L.** (1959–60) 'Iscrizioni rupestre dell'Eritrea', *RSE*, 15, pp. 55–95; 16, pp. 77–119. **(Chap. 13)**

**Ricci, L.** (1960a) 'Notizie archeologiche', *RSE*, 16, pp. 120–3. **(Chap. 13)**

**Ricci, L.** (1960b) 'Iscrizioni rupestre dell'Eritrea', *Atti Congr. Intern. Stud. Et.*, pp. 447–60. **(Chap. 13)**

**Ricci, L.** (1961) 'Antichità nello Agámè, *RSE*, 17, 116–18. **(Chap. 13)**

**Ricks, T. M.** (1970) 'Persian Gulf seafaring and East Africa: ninth–twelfth centuries', *AHS*, III, pp. 339–58. **(Chap. 22)**

**Riese, A.** (1894) *Anthologia Latina*, ed. F. Buecheler (Leipzig: Teubner), No. 183, pp. 155–6. **(Chap. 17)**

**Roberts, A. D.** (1974) 'Precolonial trade in Zambia', *ASR*, 10, p. 720. **(Chap. 29)**

**Robineau, C.** (1966) 'Une étude d'histoire culturelle de l'île d'Anjouan', *RH*, 35, pp. 17–34. **(Chap. 28)**

**Robinson, E. S. G.** (1956) 'The Libyan hoard', *Numismatic Chronicle*, LVI, p. 94. **(Chap. 18)**

**Robinson, K. R.** (1961a) *Archaeological Report in Rhodesian Schoolboys' Exploration Society Expedition to Buffalo Bend* (Salisbury). **(Chap. 27)**

**Robinson, K. R.** (1961b) 'An early iron age site from the Chibi district, Southern Rhodesia', *SAAB*, XVI, pp. 75–102. **(Chap. 27)**

**Robinson, K. R.** (1963) 'Further excavations in the iron age deposits at the tunnel site, Gokomere Hill, Southern Rhodesia', *SAAB*, XVIII, pp. 155–71. **(Chap. 27)**

**Robinson, K. R.** (1966a) 'The Sinoia caves, Lomagundi district, Rhodesia', *Proceedings of the Rhodesian Science Association*, LI, pp. 131–55. **(Chap. 27)**

**Robinson, K. R.** (1966b) 'The Leopard's Kopje culture: its position in the iron age in Southern Rhodesia', *SAAB*, 21, pp. 81–5. **(Chap. 27)**

**Robinson, K. R.** (1966c) 'A preliminary report on the recent archaeology of Ngonde, northern Malawi', *JAH*, VII, pp. 169–88. **(Chap. 27)**

**Robinson, K. R.** (1966d) 'The iron age in Southern Rhodesia', *SAAB*, XXI, pp. 5–51. **(Chap. 27)**

**Robinson, K. R.** (1970) 'The iron age in the southern lake area of Malawi', *MADP*, 8. **(Chap. 27)**

**Robinson, K. R.** (1973) 'The iron age of the upper and lower Shire Malawi', *MADP*, 13, **(Chap. 27)**

**Robinson, K. R. and Sandelowsky, B.** (1968) 'The iron age in northern Malawi: recent work', *Azania*, III, pp. 107–46. **(Chap. 27)**

**Roeder, G.** (1961) *Der Ausklang der ägyptischen Religion mit Reformation, Zauberei und Jenseitsglauben* (Zürich: Artemis Verlag). **(Chap. 3)**

**Roeder, K. G.** (1912) 'Die Christliche Zeit Nubiens und des Sudans', *ZK*, XXXIII, pp. 364–98. **(Chap. 12)**

**Roeder, K. G.** (1913) 'Die Geschichte Nubiens', *Klio*, XII, pp. 51–82. **(Chap. 12)**

**Romanelli, P.** (1959) *Storia delle province romane dell'Africa* (Rome). **(Chaps 17, 19)**

**Romanelli, P.** (1970) 'Mura e fortesse bizantine in topographia e archeologia dell'Africa romana', *Enciclopedia classica* (Rome), X, 7, pp. 398–407. **(Chap. 19)**

**Rosenbaum, E.** (1960) *A Catalogue of Cyrenaican Portrait Sculpture* (London: Oxford University Press). **(Chap. 6)**

**Rostovstev, M. I.** (1959) *The Social and Economic History of the Hellenistic World*, 3 Vols, 2nd edn. (Oxford: Clarendon Press). **(Chaps 6, 19)**

**Rotberg, R. T. and Chittick, H. N.** (eds) (1975) *East Africa and the Orient* (New York/London: Africana Publishing Co.) **(Chap. 22)**

**Rouillard, G.** (1853) *La Vie rurale dans l'Égypte byzantine* (Paris: Adrien-Maison Neuve). **(Chap. 7)**

**Rouillard, G.** (1928) *L'Administration civile de l'Égypte byzantine*, 2nd edn rev. (Paris: Geuthner). **(Chap. 7)**

**Rowe, A.** (1948) 'A history of ancient Cyrenaica. New light on Aegypto-Cyrenaean relations. Two Ptolemaic statues found in Tolmeita', *SASAE*, Cah. no. 12. Report by J. Leclant in *REA*, 52, 1–2, pp. 337–9. **(Chap. 17)**

**Rudner, J.** (1968) 'Strandloper pottery from south and south-west Africa', *ASAM*, 49, pp. 441–663. **(Chap. 26)**

**Rufinus, Tyrannus** (1908) *Historia ecclesiastica* (Leipzig). **(Chap. 15)**

**Rufinus, Tyrannus**, *Opera*, ed. A. Engelbrecht (1910) (Vienna; Leipzig). **(Chap. 15)**

Ryckmans, G. (1953, 1955, 1956) 'Inscriptions sud-arabes', *Le Muséon*, X, LXVI, 3–4, XII, LXVIII, 3–4; XIV, LXIX, 1–2, 3–4. (Chap. 15)
Ryckmans, G. (1964) 'Compte-rendu de A. Jamm: Sabaean inscriptions from Mahram Bilqis (Nârib)', *BO*, XXI, 5–6, p. 90. (Chap. 15)


Salama, P. (1951) *Les voies romaines de l'Afrique du Nord* (Algiers: Imprimerie officielle). (Chap. 19)
Salama, P. (1953–5) 'Nouveaux témoignages de l'œuvre des Sévères dans la Maurétanie césarienne', *Libyca B* (Algiers), pp. 231–51, 329–67. (Chap. 20)
Salama, P. (1954a) 'Hypothèse sur la situation de la Maurétanie occidentale au IVe siècle', *Libyca II*, pp. 224–9. (Chap. 19)
Salama, P. (1954b) 'L'occupation de la Maurétanie césarienne occidentale sous le Bas-Empire', *Mélanges Piganiol*, pp. 1292–311. (Chap. 19)
Salama, P. (1959) 'Deux trésors monétaires du Ve siècle en petite Kabylie', *BSNAF*, pp. 238–9. (Chap. 19)
Salama, P. (1973) *Un point d'eau du limes maurétanien* (*Maghrib et Sahara*), Etudes géographiques offertes à J. Despois (Paris: Société de Géographie). (Chap. 20)
Salama, P. (1976) 'Les diplacements successifs du Limes en Maurétanie césarienne. Essai de synthèse', *Akten XI Intern. Limeskong.*, pp. 577–95. (Chap. 20)
Sampson, C. G. (1974) *The Stone Age Archaeology of Southern Africa* (New York: Academic Press). (Chap. 26)
Sattin, F. and Gusmano, G. (1964) *La cosidetta 'Mummia' infantile dell'Acacus: nel quadro delle costumanze funebri prehistoriche mediterranee e sahariane* (Tripoli: Directorate-General of Antiquities, Museums and Archives). (Chap. 17)
Saumagne, C. (1965) *Le droit latin et les cités romaines sous l'Empire* (Paris: Sirey). (Chap. 19)
Sauneron, S. (1957) *Les prêtes de l'Ancienne Egypt* (Paris: Seuil) tr. A. Morrissett *The Priests of Ancient Egypt* (New York: Grove Press; London: Evergreen Books) 1960. (Chaps 3, 4)
Sauneron, S. and Stierlin, H. (1975) *Edfou et Philae: derniers temples d'Egypte* (Paris: Chêne). (Chap. 3)
Sauneron, S. and Yoyotte, J. (1952) 'La campagne nubienne de Psammetique II et sa signification historique', *BIFAO*, 50, pp. 57–207. (Chaps 2, 3, 10, 12)
Sauneron, S. and Yoyotte, J. (1959) *La Naissance du monde selon l'Egypte ancienne* (Paris: Seuil). (Chap. 3)
Savary, J. P. (1966) 'Monuments en pierres sèches du Fadnoun (Tassili N'Ajjer)', *Mém. CRAPE*, VI. (Chap. 20)
Säve-Söderbergh, T. (1941) *Ägypten und Nubien. Ein Beitrag zur Geschichte altägyptischer Aussenpolitik* (Lund: Ohlssons). (Chaps 4, 9)
Säve-Söderbergh, T. (1953) Article in *BIFAO*, 52, p. 177. (Chap. 4)
Säve-Söderbergh, T. (1956) 'The Nubian kingdom of the second intermediate period', *Kush*, 4, pp. 54–61. (Chap. 9)
Säve-Söderbergh, T. (1960) 'The paintings in the tomb of Djehuty-Hetep at Debeira', *Kush*, 8, pp. 25–44. (Chap. 9)
Säve-Söderbergh, T. (1963) 'Preliminary report of the Scandinavian joint expedition: archaeological investigations between Faras and Gemai, November 1962 – March 1963', *Kush*, 12, pp. 19–39. (Chaps 1, 12)
Säve-Söderbergh, T. (1965) *The C-Group, Nubia Abu Simbel* (Stockholm: Kungl; Boktreycheriet, P. A. Norstedt Soner). (Chap. 9)
Säve-Söderbergh, T. (1970) 'Christian Nubia, the excavations carried out by the Scandinavian joint expedition to Sudanese Nubia', in E. Dinkler (ed.), *Kunst und Geschichte Nubiens in christlicher Zeit. Ergebnisse und Probleme auf Grund der jüngsten Ausgrabungen* (Recklinghausen: Verlag Aurel Bongers), pp. 219–44. (Chap. 12)
Säve-Söderbergh, T. (ed. (1970–    ) *Scandinavian Joint Expedition to Sudanese Nubia* (Oslo: Universitetsforlaget). (Chap. 12)
Säve-Söderbergh, T. (1972) 'The Twilight of Nubian Christianity', Nubia, Récentes Recherches, *Actes Coll. Nubiol. Intern.*, pp. 11–17. (Chap. 12)
Sayce, A. H. (1909) 'A Greek inscription of a king of Axum found at Meroe', *Proceedings of the Society of Biblical Archaeology*, XXXI, London. (Chap. 15)
Sayce, A. H. (1911) 'Second interim report on the excavations at Meroe in Ethiopia II. The historical results', *LAAA*, IV, pp. 53–65. (Chaps 11, 12)
Schäfer, H. (1901) *Die aethiopische Königsinschrift des Berliner Museums: Regierungsbericht des Königs Nastesen des Gegneeß des Kambyses* (Leipzig: Hinrichs). (Chap. 11)

**Schäfer, H.** (1905–8) *Urkunden der älteren Äthiopenkönige*, (Leipzig: Hinrichs), nos 1–2 **(Chap. 11)**

**Schapera, I.** (1930) *The Khoisan Peoples of South Africa: bushmen and Hottentots* (London: Routledge & Kegan Paul) 2nd edn 1951. **(Chap. 26)**

**Schapera, I.** (1933) *The Early Cape Hottentots Described in the Writings of Olfert Dappe, 1668, Willem Ten Rhyne (1686) and Johannes Guliemus de Grevenbroek (1695)* (Cape Town: Van Riebeeck Society) 2nd edn 1951. **(Chap. 26)**

**Scharff, A. and Moortgat, A.** (1950) *Ägypten und Vorderasien im Altertum* (Munich: Bruckmann). **(Chap. 5)**

**Schauenburg, K.** (1955–6) 'Die Cameliden in Altertum', *Bonner Jahrbücher*, pp. 59–94. **(Chap. 20)**

**Schenkel, W. C.** (1973) *Lexicon der Ägyptologie* I, 5 (Wiesbaden), coll. 775–82. **(Chap. 3)**

**Schneider, R.** (1961) 'Inscriptions d'Enda Čerqos', *AE*, 4, pp. 61–5. **(Chap. 13)**

**Schneider, R.** (1965a) 'Notes épigraphiques sur les découvertes de Matarā', *AE*, 6, pp. 89–142. **(Chap. 13)**

**Schneider, R.** (1965b) 'Remarques sur les inscriptions d'Enda Čerqos', *AE*, 6, pp. 221–2. **(Chap. 13)**

**Schneider, R.** (1974) 'Trois nouvelles inscriptions royales d'Axoum', *Atti IV Congr. Intern. Stud. Et.*, I, pp. 87–102. **(Chap. 15)**

**Schoff, W. H.** tr. (1912) *The Periplus of the Erythraean Sea* (New York/London: Longmans, Green). **(Chaps 16, 22)**

**Schoff, W. H.** (1917) 'As to the date of the Periplus', *JRAS*, pp. 827–30. **(Chap. 22)**

**Schofield, J. F.** (1948) *Primitive Pottery: an introduction to South African ceramics, prehistoric and protohistoric* (Cape Town: Rustica Press). **(Chap. 27)**

**Schönbäck, B.** (1965) *The Late Stone Age and the A-Group, Nubia Abu Simbel* (Stockholm: Kungl; Boktryekeriet, P. A. Norstedt Soner). **(Chap. 9)**

**Schubart, W.** (1918) *Einführung in die Papyrunskunde* (Berlin: Weidmann). **(Chap. 7)**

**Schweitzer, F. R.** (1970) 'A preliminary report of excavation of a cave at Die Kelders', *SAAB*, 25, pp. 136–8. **(Chap. 26)**

**Schweitzer, F. R. and Scott, K.** (1973) 'Early appearance of domestic sheep in sub-Saharan Africa', *Nature*, 241, pp. 547–8. **(Chap. 26)**

**Seneca, Lucius Annaeus,** *Questions naturelles*, 2 Vols, text established and tr. P. Oltramare (1930) (Paris: Belles Lettres). **(Chaps 1, 11)**

**Seneca, Lucius Annaeus,** *Works of Petronius and Seneca*, tr. M. Heseltine and W. H. D. Rouse (1969 rev. ed.) (Cambridge, Mass.: Harvard University Press; London: Heinemann).

**Sergew Hable Selassie** (1972) *Ancient and Medieval Ethiopian History to 1270* (Addis Ababa: United Printers). **(Chap. 14)**

**Sergi, S.** (1951) 'Scavi Sahariani' (Sahara Excavations), *Monumenti Antichi*, 41, Accademia dei Lincei, XLI (Rome), coll. 443–504. **(Chap. 17)**

**Seters, J. van** (1964) 'A date for the admonitions in the Second Intermediate Period', *JEA*, 50, pp. 13–23. **(Chaps 3, 9)**

**Sethe, K.** (1930) Urgeschichte und älteste Religion der Ägypten, in *Abschaulungen für die Kunde des Morgensland*, XVIII, 4 (Leipzig: Deutsche morgenländische Gesellschaft). **(Chap. 2)**

**Shackleton, N. J.** (1973) 'Oxygen isotope analysis as a means of determining season of occupation of prehistoric midden sites', *Archaeometry*, 15, 1, pp. 133–41. **(Chap. 26)**

**Shahid, I.** (1971) 'The Martyrs of Naǧran, new documents', *Société des Bollandistes* (Brussels), pp. 242–76. **(Chap. 15)**

**Shaw, T.** (1969a) 'On radio chronology of the iron age in sub-Saharan Africa', *CA*, 10, pp. 226–8. **(Chap. 24)**

**Shaw, T.** (1969b) 'The late stone age in the Nigerian forest', *Actes 1er Coll. Intern. Archéol. Afr.*, pp. 364–73. **(Chap. 24)**

**Shaw, T.** (1970a) *Igbo-Ukwu: an account of archaeological discoveries in eastern Nigeria*, 2 Vols (London: Faber) for the Institute of African Studies, University of Ibadan. **(Chaps 24, 29)**

**Shaw, T.** (1970b) 'Those Igbo Ukwu radiocarbon dates: facts, fictions and probabilities', *JAH*, XVI, pp. 503–17. **(Chap. 29)**

**Shaw, T.** (1971) 'Africa in prehistory; leader or laggard?', *JAH*, XII, 1, pp. 143–53. **(Chap. 24)**

**Shaw, T.** (1972) 'Early crops in Africa: a review of evidence', *BWS 56*. **(Chap. 24)**

**Sherif, N. M.** (1971) *A Short Guide to the Antiquities Garden* (Khartoum: Sudan Antiquities Service). **(Chap. 9)**

**Shiferacu, A.** (1955), 'Rapport sur la découverte d'antiquités trouvées dans les locaux du gouvernement général de Magallé', *AE*, 1, pp. 13–15. **(Chap. 13)**

**Shinnie, P. L.** (1954a) *Medieval Nubia* (Khartoum: Sudan Antiquities Service). **(Chap. 12)**

**Shinnie, P. L.** (1954b) 'Excavations at Tanqasi, 1953', *Kush*, II, pp. 66–85. **(Chap. 10)**

**Shinnie, P. L.** (1965) 'New light on medieval Nubia', *JAH*, VI, 3, pp. 263–73. **(Chap. 12)**

Shinnie, P. L. (1967) *Meroe, A Civilization of the Sudan* (New York: Praeger; London: Thames & Hudson). (**Chaps 6, 9, 11**)

Shinnie, P. L. (1971a) *The Culture of Medieval Nubia and its Impact on Africa.* (Khartoum). (**Chap. 12**)

Shinnie, P. L. (1971b) 'The legacy to Africa', in J. R. Harris (ed.), *The Legacy of Egypt* (Oxford: Clarendon Press), pp. 434–55. (**Chap. 4**)

Silberbauer, G. B. (1972) 'The G/wi Bushmen', in M. G. Bicchieri (ed.), *Hunters and Gatherers Today* (New York: Holt, Rinehart & Winston). (**Chap. 26**)

Simpson, W. K. (1963) *Heka-nefer and the dynastic material from Tashka and Arminna* (New Haven: Peabody Museum of Natural History, Yale University). (**Chap. 4**)

Simpson, W. K. (ed.) (1972) *The Literature of Ancient Egypt. An Anthology of Stories, Instructions and Poetry*, tr. R. D. Faulkner, E. F. Wente and W. K. Simpson (New Haven/London: Yale University Press). (**Chaps 2, 3**)

Singer, R. and Weiner, J. A. (1963) 'Biological aspects of some indigenous African populations', *SJA*, 19, pp. 168–76. (**Chap. 21**)

Slim, H., Mahjoubi, A. and Belkodja, Kh. (n.d.) *Histoire de la Tunisie*, Vol. I: *L'Antiquité* (Tunis). (**Chap. 19**)

Smith, A. B. (1974) 'Preliminary report on excavations at Karkarichinkat north and south, Tilemsi valley, 1972', *WAJA*, 4, pp. 33–55. (**Chap. 24**)

Smith, Sir G. E. and Dawson, W. R. (1924) *Egyptian Mummies* (London: G. Allen & Unwin). (**Chap. 5**)

Smith, H. S. (1966) 'The Nubian B-group', *Kush*, 14, pp. 69–124. (**Chap. 9**)

Smith, H. S. (1976) *The Fortress of Buhen; the inscriptions* (London: Egypt Exploration Society). (**Chap. 9**)

Smith, W. S. (1949) *A History of Egyptian Sculpture and Painting in the Old Kingdom*, 2nd edn (Boston Museum of Fine Arts). (**Chap. 3**)

Smith, W. S. (1965a) *Interconnections in the ancient Near East. A study of the relationships between the arts of Egypt, the Aegean and Western Asia* (New Haven/London: Yale University Press). (**Chap. 5**)

Smith, W. S. (1965b) *The Art and Architecture of Ancient Egypt* (Harmondsworth: Penguin Books, Pelican History of Art). (**Chap. 3**)

Smith, W. S. (1971) 'The Old Kingdom in Egypt and the beginning of the First Intermediate Period', *Cambridge Ancient History*, I, part 2. (**Chap. 2**)

Smits, L. (1967) 'Fishing scenes from Botsabelo, Lesotho', *SAAB*, 22, pp. 60–7. (**Chap. 26**)

Snowden, F. M., Jnr (1970) *Blacks in Antiquity; Ethiopians in the Greco-Roman Experience* (Cambridge, Mass.: Harvard University Press). (**Chaps 6, 17, 20**)

Snowden, F. M., Jnr (1976) 'Témoignages iconographiques sur les populations noires dans l'antiquité gréco-romaine', in J. Vercoutter, J. Leclant and F. Snowden, *L'Image du noir dans l'art occidental*, Vol. I: *Des Pharaons à la chute de l'empire romain* (Fribourg: Menil Foundation), pp. 135–245. (**Chap. 6**)

Solheim, W. (1965) 'Indonesian culture and Malagasy origins', *Taloha* (Tananarive), I, pp. 33–42. (**Chap. 28**)

Soper, R. C. (1967a) 'Kwale: an early iron age site in south eastern Kenya', *Azania*, II, pp. 1–17. (**Chaps 22, 27**)

Soper, R. C. (1967b) 'Iron age sites in north eastern Tanzania', *Azania*, II, pp. 19–36. (**Chap. 22**)

Soper, R. C. (1971) 'A general review of the early iron age in the southern half of Africa', *Azania*, VI, pp. 5–37. (**Chaps 21, 27**)

Souville, G. (1958–9) 'La pêche et la vie maritime au Néolithique en Afrique de nord', *BAM*, II, pp. 315–44. (**Chap. 17**)

Sparrman, A. (1789) *A Voyage to the Cape of Good Hope, towards the Antarctic Polar Circle, Round the World, and the Country of the Hottentots and Caffres, from the year 1772 to 1776* ed. V. S. Forbes, rev. tr. J. and I. Rudner (Cape Town: Van Riebeeck Society) 1975–7. (**Chap. 26**)

Spencer, J. E. (1968) 'Comments on the origins of agriculture in Africa', *CA*, 9, 5, 501–2. (**Chap. 24**)

Spiegel, J. (1950) *Soziale und weltanschauliche Reformbewegungen im alten Ägypten* (Heidelberg: Kerle). (**Chap. 2**)

Spruytte, J. (1967) 'Un essai d'attelage protohistorique', *Plaisirs équestres*, 34, pp. 279–81. (**Chap. 17**)

Spruytte, J. (1968) 'Le cheval de l'Afrique ancienne', *Le Saharien*, 48, pp. 32–42. (**Chap. 17**)

Spruytte, J. (1977) *Etudes expérimentales sur l'attelage* (Paris: Crepin-Leblond). (**Chap. 20**)

Stein, A. (1915) *Untersuchengen zur Geschichte und Verwaltung Aegyptens unter römischer Herrschaft* (Stuttgart). (**Chap. 7**)

Stein, E. (1949) *Histoire du Bas Empire*: Vol. II *De la disparition de l'Empire de l'Occident à la mort de Justinien, 476–565* (Paris/Brussels/Amsterdam: de Brouwer). (**Chap. 7**)

781

Steindorff, G. (ed.) (1903) *Urkunden des Ägyptischen Altertums* (Leipzig: Hinrichs). (Chap. 11)

Stemler, A. B. L., Harlam, J. R. and Dewet, J. M. F. (1975) 'Caudatum sorghums and speakers of Shari-Nile languages in Africa', *JAH*, XVI, 2, pp. 161–83. (Chap. 24)

Stock, H. (1949) *Die Erste Zwischenzeit Ägyptens. Untergang der Pyramidenzeit, Zwischenreiche von Abydos und Herakleopolis, Aufstieg Thebens* (Rome: Pontificium Institutum Biblicum). (Chap. 2)

Strabo *Geography*, tr. H. L. Jones (1917–32), 8 Vols (Cambridge, Mass.: Harvard University Press; London: Heinemann). (Chaps 1, 6, 11, 22)

Summers, R. F. H. (1958) *Inyanga. Prehistoric settlements in Southern Rhodesia* (Cambridge: CUP). (Chap. 27)

Summers, R. F. H. (1969) 'Ancient mining in Rhodesia', *Mining Magazine*, 3 (Salisbury). (Chaps 27, 29)

Summers, R. F. H., Robinson, K. R. and Whitty, A. (1961) 'Zimbabwe excavations', *OPNM*; III, 23a. (Chap. 27)

Sutton, J. E. G. (1966) 'The archaeology and early peoples of the highlands of Kenya and northern Tanzania', *Azania*, I, pp. 37–57. (Chap. 22)

Sutton, J. E. G. (1971) 'The interior of east Africa', in P. L. Shinnie (ed.), *The African Iron Age* (Oxford: Clarendon Press). (Chap. 23)

Sutton, J. E. G. (1972) 'New radiocarbon dates for eastern and southern Africa', *JAH*, XIII, 1, pp. 1–24. (Chap. 27)

Sutton, J. E. G. (1973) *The Archaeology of the Western Highlands of Kenya* (Nairobi/London: British Institute of Eastern Africa). (Chap. 23)

Sutton, J. E. G. (1974) 'The aquatic civilisation of middle Africa', *JAH*, XV, pp. 527–46. (Chaps 21, 23)

Sutton, J. E. G. and Roberts, A. D. (1968) 'Uvinza and its salt industry', *Azania*, III, pp. 45–86. (Chap. 29)

Szumowski, G. (1957) 'Fouilles du nord du Macina et dans la région de Segou', *Bulletin de L'Institut d'Afrique noire*, B, 19, pp. 224–58. (Chap. 24)


Tamit (1967) 'Missione archeologia', *Egitto dell' Università di Roma* (Rome). (Chap. 12)

Tämrät, T. (1972) *Church and State in Ethiopia 1270–1527* (Oxford: Clarendon Press). (Chap. 16)

Tarn, W. W. (1930) *Hellenistic Civilization* (London). (Chap. 6)

Tarn, W. W. (1966) *The Greeks in Bactria and India* (Cambridge: CUP). (Chap. 22)

Tarn, W. W. and Griffith, G. T. (1966) *Hellenistic Civilization*, 3rd edn (London: Edward Arnold). (Chaps 6, 22)

Teutsch, L. (1962) *Das Stadtewesen in Nordafrika in der Zeit von C. Gracchus bis zum Tode des Kaisers Augustus* (Berlin: De Gruyter). (Chap. 19)

Thabit, H. T. (1957) 'Tomb of Djehuty-Hetep (Tehuti-Hetep), Prince of Semna', *Kush*, 5, pp. 81–6. (Chap. 9)

Thom, H. B. (ed.) (1952–8) *The Journal of Jan Van Riebeeck*, tr. W. P. L. Van Zyl, J. Smuts, C. K. Johnmann and A. Ravenscroft, 3 Vols (Cape Town: Balkema). (Chap. 26)

Thomas, E. M. (1959) *The Harmless People (On the Bushmen of the Kalahari Desert)* (London: Secker & Warburg). (Chap. 26)

Thomas, W. R. (1931) 'Moscow mathematical papyrus no 14', *JEA*, XVII, pp. 50–2. (Chap. 5)

Thompson, G. (1827) *Travels and Adventures in Southern Africa*, ed. V. S. Forbes (Cape Town: Van Riebeeck Society) 1967. (Chap. 26)

Thunberg, C. P. (1795) *Travels in Europe, Africa and Asia Performed between 1770 and 1779* (London). (Chap. 26)

Tixeront, J. (1960) 'Reflexions sur l'implantation ancienne de l'agriculture en Tunisie', *Karthago*, X, pp. 1–50. (Chap. 19)

Török, L. (1971) 'Fragment eines Spätantiken roten Tongefässe mit Stempelverzierung aus Nubien und Dessen Problemkreis', *MAI*, 2. (Chap. 12)

Touny, A. D. and Wenig, S. (1971) *Sport in Ancient Egypt*, tr. J. Becker (Leipzig: Ed. Leipzig: Amsterdam: Grüner). (Chap. 3)

Toynbee, J. M. C. (1973) *Animals in Roman Life and Art; Aspects of Greek and Roman Life* (London: Thames & Hudson). (Chap. 20)

Tozer, H. F. (1964) *History of Ancient Geography* (New York: Biblo & Tannen). (Chap. 22)

Trigger, B. G. (1965) *History and Settlement in Lower Nubia* (New Haven), Yale University Publications in Anthropology No. 69. (Chaps 9, 11, 12, 17)

Trigger, B. G. (1969) 'The myth of Meroe and the African iron age', *IJAHS*, II, 1, pp. 23–50. (Chaps 10, 11, 21, 24)

Trigger, B. G. (1970) 'The cultural ecology of Christian Nubia', in E. Dinkler (ed.), *Kunst und Geschichte Nubiens in christlicher Zeit. Ergebnisse und Probleme auf Grund der jüngsten Ausgrabungen* (Recklinghausen: Verlag Aurel Bongers), pp. 347–87. **(Chap. 12)**

Tufnell, O. (1959) 'Anklets in western Asia', *Bulletin of the Institute of Archaeology, London*, pp. 37–54. **(Chap. 13)**

Turcan, R. (1961) 'Trésors monétaires trouvés à Tipasa. La circulation du bronze en Afrique romaine et vandale au Ve et VIe siècles ap. J.-C.', *Libyca*, pp. 201–57. **(Chap. 19)**

Twisselmann, F. (1958) 'Les ossements humains du site mésolithique d'Ishango', *Exploration du Parc national Albert, Mission J. de Herzelin de Braucourt* (1950), Facsimile 5 (Brussels). **(Chap. 25)**

Tylecote, R. F. (1970) 'Iron working at Meroe, Sudan', *BHM*, 4, pp. 67–72. **(Chaps 11, 21)**

Unesco (1963–7) *Fouilles de Nubie* (Cairo). **(Chap. 20)**

Vaal, J. B. de (1943) 'In Soutpansbergse Zimbabwe', *SAJS*, XL, pp. 303–18. **(Chap. 27)**

Valbelle, D. (1974) *Lexikon der Ägyptologie I*, no. 7, cols 1028–34. **(Chap. 3)**

Van Seters, J. (1964) 'A date for the admonitions in the second intermediate period', *JEA*, 50, pp. 13–23. **(Chaps 2, 3)**

Van Seters, J. (1966) *The Hyksos, a New Investigation* (New Haven/London: Yale University Press). **(Chap. 2)**

Vansina, J. (1962) 'Long-distance trade routes in central Africa', *JAH*, III, 3, pp. 375–90. **(Chap. 25)**

Vansina, J. (1966) *Kingdoms of the Savanna* (Madison: University of Wisconsin Press). **(Chap. 27)**

Vantini, J. (1970) *The Excavations at Faras: a contribution to the history of Christian Nubia* (Bologna: Nigrizia). **(Chap. 12)**

Vasilyev, A. E. (ed.) (1907) 'Zhitiye grigentiya, yepiscopa Omiritskago (vita Saneti Gregenti)', *Vizantiyskiy Vremennik*, XIV, pp. 63–4. **(Chap. 15)**

Veh, O. (ed.) (1971) *Vandalenkriege von Prokopius Caesariensis* (Munich: Heimeran). **(Chap. 19)**

Velde, H. Te (1967) *Seth, God of Confusion. A Study of his Role in Egyptian Mythology and Religion* tr. G. E. van Baaren-Pape) (Leiden: Brill). **(Chap. 3)**

Vercoutter, J. (1945) *Les Objets égyptiens et égyptisants du mobilier funéraire carthaginois* (Paris), Bibliothèque archéologique et historique, Vol. 40. **(Chap. 9)**

Vercoutter, J. (1956) 'New Egyptian inscriptions from the Sudan', *Kush*, IV, pp. 66–82. **(Chap. 9)**

Vercoutter, J. (1957) Article in *Kush*, V, pp. 61–9. **(Chap. 4)**

Vercoutter, J. (1958) 'Excavations at Saï 1955–57', *Kush*, VI, pp. 144–69. **(Chap. 9)**

Vercoutter, J. (1959) 'The gold of Kush. Two gold-washing stations at Faras East', *Kush*, VII, pp. 120–53. **(Chaps 9, 11)**

Vercoutter, J. (1962) 'Un palais des Candaces contemporains d'Auguste, fouilles à Wad-ban-Naga, 1958–60', *Syria*, 39, pp. 263–99. **(Chaps 10, 11)**

Vercoutter, J. (1964) 'Excavations at Mirgissa I (October–December 1962)', *Kush*, XII, pp. 57–62. **(Chaps 2, 9)**

Vercoutter, J. (1970) 'Les trouvailles chrétiennes françaises à Aksha, Mirgissa et Saï', in E. Dinkler (ed.), *Kunst und Geschichte Nubiens in christlicher Zeit. Ergebnisse und Probleme auf Grund der jüngsten Ausgrabungen* (Recklinghausen: Verlag Aurel Bongers), pp. 155–62. **(Chap. 12)**

Vercoutter, J. (1976) *L'Egypte ancienne*, no. 247 (Paris: PUF). **(Chap. 2)**

Vercoutter, J., Leclant, J. and Snowden, F. (1976) *L'Image du dans l'art occidental*. Vol. I: *Des pharaons à la chute de l'empire romain* (Fribourg: Menil Foundation). **(Chap. 6)**

Vérin, P. (1967) 'Les antiquités de l'île d'Anjouan', *BAM*, XLV, 1, pp. 69–79. **(Chap. 28)**

Vérin, P. (1968) 'Several types of obsolete Madagascar pottery', *Asian Perspectives*, XI, pp. 111–18. **(Chap. 28)**

Vérin, P. (1970a) 'Un conte antalaote, Mojomby, la ville disparue', *BM*, 293–4, pp. 256–8. **(Chap. 28)**

Vérin, P., Kottak, C. and Gorlin, P. (1970b) 'The glottochronology of Malagasy dialects', *OL*, VIII, 2. **(Chap. 28)**

Vidal, P. (1969) *La civilisation mégalithique de Bouar; prospection et fouilles 1962–66* (Paris: Firmin-Didot). **(Chap. 25)**

Villiers, A. (1949) 'Some aspects of the dhow trade', *MEJ*, pp. 399–416. **(Chap. 22)**

Villiers, H. de (1970) 'Dieskettreste der Ziwa', *Homo*, XXI, pp. 17–28. **(Chap. 27)**

Vincent, W. (1807) *The Commerce and Navigation of the Ancients in the Indian Ocean* (London). **(Chap. 22)**

Vincent, W. (1809) *The Voyage of Nearchus and the periplus of the Erythraean Sea* (Oxford). **(Chap. 22)**

Vinicombe, P. (1960) 'A fishing scene from the Tsoelike, south-eastern Basutoland', *SAAB*, 15, pp. 15–19. **(Chap. 26)**

Vinicombe, P. (1965) 'Bushmen fishing as depicted in rock paintings', *Science South Africa*, 212, pp. 578–81. (**Chap. 26**)

Vila, A. (1970) 'L'armement de la forteresse de Mirgissa-Iken', *RE*, 22, pp. 171–99. (**Chap. 3**)

Vita, A di (1964) 'Il limes romano de Tripolitania nella sua concretezza archeologica e nella sua realta storica', *Libya antiqua* (Tripoli), pp. 65–98. (**Chaps 19, 20, 29**)

Vittmann, G. (1974) 'Zur lesung des königsnamens', *Orientalia*, 43, pp. 12–16. (**Chap. 10**)

Vogel, J. O. (1969), 'On early evidence of agriculture in southern Zambia', *CA*, X, p. 524. (**Chap. 27**)

Vogel, J. O. (1970) 'The Kalomo culture of southern Zambia: some notes towards a reassessment', *ZMJ*, I, pp. 77–88. (**Chap. 27**)

Vogel, J. O. (1971a) 'Kamangoza: an introduction to the iron age cultures of the Victoria Falls region', *ZMP*, II. (**Chap. 27**)

Vogel, J. O. (1971b) 'Kumandzulo, an early iron age village site in southern Zambia', *ZMP*, III. (**Chap. 27**)

Vogel, J. O. (1972) 'On early iron age funerary practice in southern Zambia', *CA*, XIII, pp. 583–8. (**Chap. 27**)

Vogel, J. O. (1973) 'The early iron age at Sioma mission, western Zambia', *ZMJ*, IV. (**Chap. 27**)

Volney, M. C. F. (1787) *Voyages en Syrie et en Egypte pendant les années 1783, 1784, 1785* (Paris). (**Chap. 1**)

Vuillemot, G. (1955) 'La nécropole punique du phare dans l'ile de Rachgoum', *Libyca*, III, pp. 7–76. (**Chap. 18**)

Vychichl, W. (1956) 'Atlanten, Isebeten, Ihaggaren', *RSO*, 31, pp. 211–20. (**Chap. 17**)

Vychichl, W. (1957) 'Ergzi'abehēr "Dieu"', *AE* II, pp. 249–50. (**Chap. 15**)

Vychichl, W. (1961) 'Berber words in Nubian', *Kush*, 9, pp. 289–90. (**Chap. 17**)

Vychichl, W. (1972) *Die Mythologie der Berber*, ed. H. W. Haussig (Stuttgart). (**Chap. 17**)


Wainwright, G. A. (1945) 'Iron in the Napatan and Meroitic ages', *SNR*, 26, pp. 5–36. (**Chap. 11**)

Wainwright, G. A. (1947) 'Early foreign trade in East Africa', *Man*, XLVII, pp. 143–8. (**Chap. 22**)

Wainwright, G. A. (1951) 'The Egyptian origin of a ram-headed breastplate from Lagos', *Man*, LI, pp. 133–5. (**Chap. 4**)

Wainwright, G. A. (1962) 'The Meshwesh', *JEA*, 48, pp. 89–99. (**Chap. 17**)

Wallace, L. (1938) *Taxation in Egypt from Augustus to Diocletian* (Princeton). (**Chap. 7**)

Walle, B. van de (1953) 'La cippe d'Horus découverte par J. Bruce à Axoum', *Chronique d'Egypte*, 56, pp. 238–47. (**Chap. 15**)

Wallert, I. (1962) *Die Palmen im Alten Ägypten. Eine Untersuchung ihrer praktischen, symbolischen und religiösen Bedeutung* (Berlin: Hessling). (**Chap. 17**)

Walsh, P. (1965) 'Masinissa', *JRS*, LV. (**Chap. 18**)

Warmington, B. H. (1954) *The North African Provinces from Diocletian to the Vandal Conquest* Cambridge: CUP). (**Chap. 19**)

Warmington, E. H. (1928) *The Commerce between the Roman Empire and India* (Cambridge) 2nd edn (London: Curzon Press) 1974. (**Chap. 22**)

Warmington, E. H. (1963) 'Africa in ancient and medieval times', in E. A. Walker (ed.), *Cambridge History of the British Empire* (Cambridge: Cambridge University Press), Vol. VIII. (**Chap. 22**)

Warmington, B. H. (1964) *Carthage*, rev. edn (London: Robert Hale) 1969. (**Chap. 21**)

Waterhouse, G. (ed.) (1932) *Simon van der Stel's Journal of His Expedition to Namaqualand, 1685–6* (Dublin: Dublin University Press). (**Chap. 26**)

Webster, T. B. L. (1964) *Hellenistic Poetry and Art* (London: Methuen). (**Chap. 6**)

Weitzmann, K. (1970) 'Some remarks on the sources of the fresco paintings of the cathedral of Faras', in E. Dinkler (ed.), *Kunst und Geschichte Nubiens in christlicher Zeit. Ergebnisse und Probleme auf Grund der jüngsten Ausgrabungen* (Recklinghausen: Verlag Aurel Bongers), pp. 325–46. (**Chap. 12**)

Welbourne, R. G. (1973) 'Identification of animal remains from the Broederstroom 24/73 early iron age site', *SAJS*, LXIX, p. 325. (**Chap. 27**)

Wendt, W. E. (1972) 'Preliminary report on an archaeological research programme in south-west Africa', *Cimbebasia B*, 2, 1, pp. 1–45. (**Chap. 26**)

Wenig, S. (1967) 'Bemerkungen zur meroitische chronologie', *MIOD*, 13, pp. 9–27. (**Chaps 10, 11**)

Wenig, S. (1969) *The Woman in Egyptian Art*, tr. B. Fischer (New York: McGraw-Hill). (**Chap. 3**)

Wenig, S. (1974) Article in *ZÄS*, 101, pp. 243–4. (**Chap. 10**)

Wessel, K. (1964) *Zur Ikonographie der Koptischen Kunst, Christentum am Nil* (Recklinghausen: Verlag Aurel Bongers). (**Chap. 12**)

Wessel, K. (1966) *Coptic Art*, tr. J. Carroll and S. Hatton (London: Thames & Hudson). (Chap 12)

Westendorf, W. (1968) *Das alte Ägypten* (Baden-Baden: Holle). (Chap. 2)

Wheeler, Sir R. E. M. (1954) *Rome beyond the Imperial Frontiers* (London: Bell). (Chap. 22)

Wheeler, Sir R. E. M. (1966) *Civilizations of the Indus Valley and Beyond* (London: Thames & Hudson). (Chap. 22)

Will, E. (1966) *Histoire politique du monde hellénistique 323–30 avant J.-C.*, 2 Vols (Nancy: Berger-Levrault). (Chap. 6)

Willett, F. (1967) *Ife in the History of West African Sculpture* (London: Thames & Hudson). (Chap. 24)

Williams, D. (1969) 'African iron and the classical world', in L. A. Thompson and J. Ferguson (eds), *Africa in Classical Antiquity* (Ibadan: Ibadan University Press), pp. 62–80. (Chap. 21)

Wilson, J. A. (1951) *The Burden of Egypt. An Interpretation of Ancient Egyptian Culture* (Chicago: University of Chicago Press). (Chap. 2)

Wilson, J. A. (1969) in J. B. Pritchard (ed.), *The Ancient Near East* (Princeton). (Chaps 2, 4)

Winlock, H. E. (1947) *The Rise and Fall of the Middle Kingdom in Thebes* (New York: Macmillan). (Chap. 2)

Winlock, H. E. (1955) *Models of Daily Life in Ancient Egypt, from the Tomb of Meket-Rē' at Thebes* (Cambridge, Mass.: Harvard University Press for the Metropolitan Museum of Art). (Chap. 5)

Winstedt, E. O. (tr.) (1909) *The Christian Topography of Cosmas Indicopleustes* (Cambridge: CUP). (Chap. 15)

Wissmann, H. von (1964) 'Ancient history', *Le Muséon*, LXXVII, pp. 3–4. (Chap. 15)

Wissmann, H. von and Rathjens, C. (1957) 'De Mari Erythraeo: Sonderdruck aus der Lauten Sich', *Festschrift Stuttgarter Geographische Studien*, 69. (Chap. 24)

Woldering, I. (1963) *Egypt, the Art of Pharaohs*, tr. A. E. Keep (London: Methuen). (Chap. 5)

Wolf, W. (1957) *Die Kunst Aegyptens; Gestalt und Geschichte* (Stuttgart: Kohlhammer). (Chap. 3)

Wolf, W. (1971) *Das alte Ägypten* (Munich: Deutscher Taschenbuch-Verlag). (Chap. 2)

Wolska-Conus, W. (ed.) (1968–73) *Cosmas Indicopleustes: Topographie chrétienne*, 3 Vols (Paris: Cerf). (Chaps 16, 22)

Word, W. (1965) *The Spirit of Ancient Egypt* (Beirut). (Chap. 3)

Wörterbuch (1971) *Der Aegyptischen Sprache Fünfter Band* (Berlin: Akademie Verlag). (Chap. 1)


York, R. N. *et al.* (1974) 'Excavations at Dutsen Kongba', *NAS*. (Chap. 24)

Yoyotte, J. (1958) 'Anthroponymes d'origine libyenne dans les documents egyptiens', *C-RGLCS*, 8, 4. (Chap. 17)

Yoyotte, J. (1958) in *Dictionnaire de la Bible*, Suppl. VI, I (Paris), p. 370. (Chap. 4)

Yoyotte, J. (1961) 'Les principautés du delta au temps de l'anarchie libyenne', *Mélanges Maspéro*, 1, 4, pp. 122–51. (Chaps 2, 17)

Yoyotte, J. (1965) 'Egypte ancienne', *Histoire Universelle* (Paris: Gallimand) Encyclopédie de la Pléiade, pp. 104–285. (Chap. 2)

Yoyotte, J. (1975) 'Les Sementious et l'exploitation des régions minières de l'Ancien Empire', *BSFE*, 73, pp. 44–55. (Chap. 3)


Zaba, Z. (1953) *L'Orientation astronomique dans l'Ancienne Egypte et la précession de l'axe du monde* (Prague). (Chap. 5)

Zabkar, L. V. (1975) *Apedemak, Lion God of Meroe* (Warminster). (Chaps 10, 11)

Zawadzki, T. (1967) 'Les fouilles de la mission archéologique polonaise à Faras, leur importance pour l'histoire de l'art byzantin', *RESEE*, V. (Chap. 12)

Zeissl, H. von (1944) *Anthiopen und Assyer in Ägypten* (Glückstadt, Hamburg: J. J. Augustin). (Chaps 2, 10)

Zibeuus, K. (1972) *Afrikanische Arts und Volkernamen in hieroglyphischen und hieratischen Texten* (Wiesbaden). (Chap. 4)

Zohrer, L. G. (1952–3) 'La population du Sahara antérieure à l'apparition du chameau', *BSNG*, 51, pp. 3–133. (Chap. 20)

# Subject Index

# Index of Persons

# Index of Places

# Index of Ethnonyms

# Index of Dynasties